Pacific Northwest

Oregon & Washington

Bill McRae
Judy Jewell
Jennifer Snarski

Pacific Northwest USA

2nd edition

Published by
   Lonely Planet Publications
   Head Office: PO Box 617, Hawthorn, Vic 3122, Australia
   Branches: 150 Linden St, Oakland, CA 94607, USA
                  10A Spring Place, London NW5 3BH, UK
                  1 rue du Dahomey, 75011 Paris, France

Printed by
   Colorcraft Ltd, Hong Kong

Photographs by
   Front cover: Stanley Park totem, Nik Wheeler (Hillstrom Stock Photo)

Dennis Frates	Bill McRae	Dave Skibinski
Rick Gerharter	Dave Peevers	Jennifer Snarski
Dave G Houser	Doug Plummer	Nik Wheeler
Carolyn Hubbard	Scott Price	Tony Wheeler
Judy Jewell	Kevin Schafer	

Published
   January 1999

National Library of Australia Cataloguing in Publication Data

McRae, W.C., 1956-
   Pacific Northwest USA

   2nd ed.
   Includes index.
   ISBN 0 86442 534 1.

   1. Northwest, Pacific – Guidebooks. I. Jewell, Judy, 1957-
   II. Snarski, Jennifer, 1971-   III. Title.

   917.950443

text & maps © Lonely Planet 1999
photos © photographers as indicated 1999
climate charts compiled from information supplied by Patrick J Tyson, © Patrick J Tyson 1999

Bill McRae

Bill McRae was born and raised in rural eastern Montana on a cattle and sheep ranch. After a year of university, a rather misguided, late-adolescent nostalgia for his grandparents' homeland in Scotland led him back to the Old Country. The trip brought a serious travel bug to the fore. For the next 10 years he manipulated his academic career to study at as many foreign universities as possible. Five university settings in seven years didn't make for a great scholastic career, but it did make for a great education.

Bill has also written travel guides about Montana, Utah and Canada, and has written for websites on Western Europe and the western US. In addition to travel writing, Bill has worked as a copywriter, a journalist and as a website content provider for Microsoft. When he's not at his computer, you can usually find him with a paintbrush or hammer in his hand, as his avocation is home remodeling and rehabilitation. Bill lives in Portland, Oregon.

Judy Jewell

Judy Jewell lives in Portland, Oregon, where she manages two Powell's bookstores. She has spent the past 20 years traveling around the Pacific Northwest, and the past 10 years writing about it. For research and for fun, she's climbed Mt Rainier, swum across the Columbia River and cycled the length of the Oregon coast.

Jennifer Snarski

A product of a small timber town on the southern Oregon coast, Jennifer Snarski set off for India, Sri Lanka and Thailand during her college years with no goals other than to blow her mind and to learn to like vegetables. She achieved both, and upon returning put her degree in religious studies to use by writing for a cultural guide to India. She soon became an editorial assistant for Bill McRae on the 1st edition of *Pacific Northwest*, which led to co-authoring this 2nd edition.

Jennifer loves the wilderness and has been busy hiking all over Oregon and Washington for Lonely Planet's upcoming *Hiking in the USA*. When not communing with nature, she's either out riding a bicycle or dancing at a ceilidh.

From the Author

Bill McRae Many people deserve thanks. Beth and Pierre were valuable authorities on Vancouver issues, and made great dining companions. Pam and Sarah provided the lowdown on Olympia. Kathy, Cindy, and Jim and Larry: thanks for guidance on all things Seattle. I'm especially grateful to Kerrie and Stewart for their West Seattle hospitality and friendship. Lydia Fisher proved to be a marvelous vintage photo collaborator; thank you. Closer to home, Steve and Maggie again put up with a travel writer's late nights and fretful schedule. To the many folks at Lonely Planet: thank you. It's great working with pros.

Judy Jewell Thanks to Sarah Butler, Mary Packenham-Walsh and Emily Roth, who took along copies of the 1st edition of *Pacific Northwest* and packs of sticky notes when they went out to inventory Oregon's forests and suss out its wetlands. Thanks also to Paul Levy for all his support, and to the many friendly folks who shared their knowledge and opinions about the state.

Jennifer Snarski A huge debt of gratitude goes out to my colleagues for their continued support, especially writers Mary Orr and Bill McRae: thanks for the years of opportunity, encouragement and gourmet meals. My parents, Carol and Eugene Snarski, deserve a heartfelt thanks. Laurie McLain helped hold down the fort, and was an invaluable companion to have on that trip to the hospital. Thanks also to the staff at Pittock Mansion and to Leo Sudnik for his enthusiasm for Klamath Falls.

This Book
Bill McRae and Judy Jewell researched and wrote the 1st edition. This 2nd edition was updated by Bill, Judy and Jennifer Snarski. Bill was the coordinating author and wrote the introductory chapters, Portland, Seattle, Tacoma & Olympia, Northwest Washington & the San Juan Islands, Olympic Peninsula, Southwestern Washington, South Cascades, Vancouver and Vancouver Island. Judy wrote Columbia River Gorge & Mt Hood, Central Oregon, Northeastern Oregon and Southeastern Oregon. Jennifer wrote Willamette Valley, Southern Oregon, North Cascades, Central Washington, Northeastern Washington and Southeastern Washington. Bill and Jennifer co-wrote Oregon Coast.

From the Publisher
This 2nd edition of *Pacific Northwest* is a product of Lonely Planet's US office.

Many people contributed their energy, time, patience and enthusiasm to this book. Susan Charles was the project editor. Maia Hansen, Adrienne Costanzo and Susan edited the text and maps. Julie Connery, Joslyn Leve and Maia proofread it, and indexing was done by Maia, Joslyn and Susan. Margaret Livingston drew the maps, researched illustrations, designed and laid out the book. Richard Wilson, Rini Keagy and Scott Summers assisted with design and layout. Bart Wright, Patrick Huerta, Deborah Rodgers and Amy Dennis also drew maps. Hayden Foell, Rini, Lara Sox-Harrison, Lisa Summers and Mark Butler drew the illustrations, and Hayden did the chapter ends. Rini designed the cover. Many thanks to Carolyn Hubbard and Brigitte Barta for providing editorial supervision throughout the project, Alex Guilbert for coordinating cartography and Scott Summers for overseeing production.

Warning & Request
Things change – prices go up, schedules change, good places go bad and bad places go bankrupt – nothing stays the same. So, if you find things better or worse, recently opened or long since closed, please tell us and help make the next edition even more accurate and useful.

We value all the feedback we receive from travelers. A small team reads and acknowledges every letter, postcard and email, and ensures that every morsel of information finds its way to the appropriate authors, editors and publishers. Everyone who writes to us will find his or her name in the next edition of the appropriate guide and will also receive a free subscription to our quarterly newsletter, *Planet Talk*. The very best contributions will be rewarded with a free Lonely Planet guide.

Excerpts from your correspondence may appear in new editions of this guide, in *Planet Talk* or in the Postcards section of our website – so please let us know if you don't want your letter published or your name acknowledged.

Contents

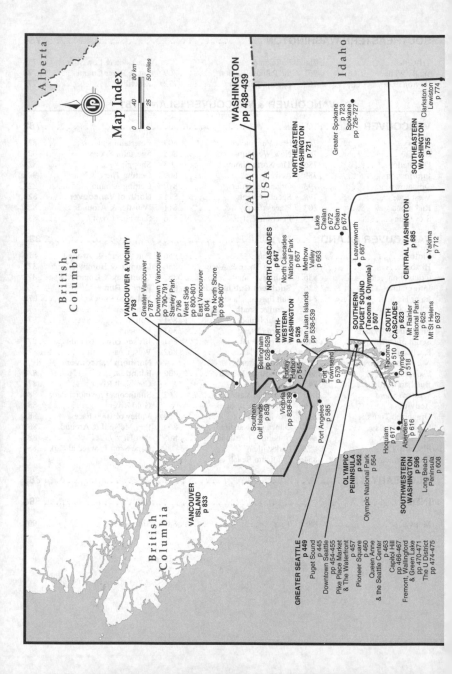

Map Index

0 40 80 km
0 25 50 miles

Alberta

British Columbia

CANADA
USA

WASHINGTON
pp 438-439

Idaho

British Columbia

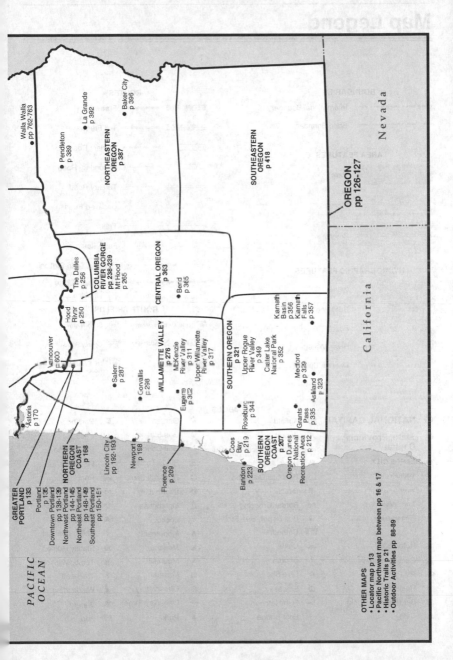

Map Legend

PACIFIC
OCEAN

GREATER
PORTLAND
p 133
Portland
p 135
Downtown Portland
pp 138-139
Northwest Portland
pp 144-145
Northeast Portland
pp 148-149
Southeast Portland
pp 150-151

NORTHERN
OREGON
COAST
p 168

Astoria
p 170

Vancouver
p 600

Lincoln City
pp 192-193

Newport
p 198

Florence
p 209

Coos
Bay
p 219

Bandon
p 223

SOUTHERN
OREGON
COAST
p 207

Oregon Dunes
National
Recreation Area
p 212

Salem
p 287

Corvallis
p 298

Eugene
p 302

WILLAMETTE
VALLEY
p 276

McKenzie
River Valley
p 311

Upper Willamette
River Valley
p 317

Roseburg
p 344

Grants
Pass
p 335

Medford
p 329

Ashland
p 323

SOUTHERN OREGON
p 321

Upper Rogue
River Valley
p 349

Crater Lake
National Park
p 352

Klamath
Basin
p 356
Klamath
Falls
p 357

California

Hood
River
p 250

The Dalles
p 256

COLUMBIA
RIVER GORGE
pp 238-239
Mt Hood
p 265

CENTRAL OREGON
p 363

Bend
p 365

Pendleton
p 389

Walla Walla
pp 762-763

La Grande
p 392

Baker City
p 396

NORTHEASTERN
OREGON
p 387

SOUTHEASTERN
OREGON
p 418

OREGON
pp 126-127

Nevada

OTHER MAPS
• Locator map p 13
• Pacific Northwest map between pp 16 & 17
• Historic Trails p 21
• Outdoor Activities pp 88-89

Map Legend

BOUNDARIES

International Boundary

State Boundary

AREA FEATURES

Park

Forest

Reservation

HYDROGRAPHIC FEATURES

Water

Coastline

Beach

River, Waterfall

Swamp, Spring

ROUTES

Freeway

Toll Freeway

Primary Road

Secondary Road

Tertiary Road

Unpaved Road

Trail

Ferry Route

Railway, Train Station

Mass Transit Line & Station

ROUTE SHIELDS

90 Interstate Freeway

1 Trans-Canada Hwy

84 US Highway

10 State Highway

229 County Road

USFS 604 US Forest Service Road

SYMBOLS

✪ **NATIONAL CAPITAL**

◉ **State, Provincial Capital**

● **LARGE CITY**

● **Medium City**

● Small City

● Town, Village

○ Point of Interest

■ Hotel, B&B

⚠ Campground

🚐 RV Park

▼ Restaurant

🍺 Bar (Place to Drink)

☕ Cafe

✚ Airfield

✈ Airport

∴ Archaeological Site, Ruins

$ Bank, ATM

🔲 Baseball Diamond

🏖 Beach

✦✦ Border Crossing

🚌 Bus Depot, Bus Stop

🚻 Cathedral

🕳 Cave

✝ Church

🐚 Dive Site

◯ Embassy

🐟 Fish Hatchery

✕ Foot Bridge

❄ Garden

⛽ Gas Station

🏌 Golf Course

卍 Hindu Temple

✛ Hospital, Clinic

❶ Information

☗ Lighthouse

☀ Lookout

🗿 Monument

☪ Mosque

▲ Mountain

🏛 Museum

⚜ Observatory

← One-Way Street

♦ Park

🅿 Parking

) (Pass

🎋 Picnic Area

★ Police Station

🏊 Pool

✉ Post Office

❖ Shopping Mall

⛷ Skiing (Alpine)

⛸ Skiing (Nordic)

🏛 Stately Home

◼ Tomb, Mausoleum

🚶 Trailhead

🏄 Windsurfing

🍷 Winery

🐘 Zoo

Note: Not all symbols displayed above appear in this book.

Introduction

The Pacific Northwest – Oregon, Washington and southwestern British Columbia (BC) – contains some of the most diverse and extravagantly scenic landscapes in North America. To the west, the turbulent Pacific Ocean pounds the cliff-hung Oregon coast and swirls among the islands and fjords of the Puget Sound, Vancouver Island and the Georgia Strait. Just inland, massive volcanic peaks, including Mt St Helens, Mt Rainier, Mt Hood and the imploded cone that now forms Crater Lake, rise above dense forests. Canyon-cut plateaus and arid mountain ranges stretch for hundreds of desert miles to the east before buckling up to form the foothills of the Rocky Mountains, the spine of the North American continent.

These pristine landscapes aren't just to look at: in the Northwest, you're expected to get outdoors and enjoy yourself. The forests and coastlines are webbed with hiking trails, rafts and kayaks plunge down white-water rivers, and every mountain peak is fair game for rock climbers and mountaineers. Some of the best skiing in North America is found here – BC's Whistler, Oregon's Mt Bachelor, Washington's Stevens Pass and dozens of other ski resorts. Hood River, in the imposing Columbia River Gorge, is one of the world's most popular and challenging windsurfing spots.

The cities of the Pacific Northwest are noted for their high standards of living and vibrant civic and cultural life. In the last decade, Seattle and Portland have each been named the most 'livable city' in the US. Vancouver is one of the most cosmopolitan and truly international cities on the

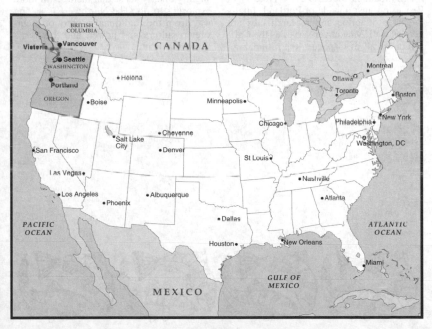

continent, with a cultural vitality that derives from its mosaic of ethnic heritages. Victoria – with its core of Victorian architecture and oh-so-English quaintness – seems a world away from other urban centers in the Pacific Northwest.

These cities are also among the fastest growing in the US and Canada, as the dynamic economies of the region attract a youthful generation that likes the Northwest's progressive politics, its easygoing sophistication and the vast tracts of wilderness right out the back door.

Seattle is the largest city in the Pacific Northwest. Long known as a slightly stodgy – if beautifully situated – city, it is now recognized around the world as one of the most vital, trendy hot spots of youth culture and high-tech industry, complete with Boeing and Microsoft headquarters. More reserved, Portland hides its fun-loving and sophisticated spirit behind an outwardly quiet, gracious facade. The international headquarters for Nike is in Beaverton, just outside of Portland; Intel's largest production and research labs are here as well. Vancouver serves as the California for all of Canada – the filmmaking

center, the arts center, the lifestyle center. As the largest city on the Canadian west coast, and the second largest English-speaking city in Canada, Vancouver combines worldly savoir-faire with a New Age inquiring spirit.

But there's more to the Pacific Northwest than just hip cosmopolitan cities and rugged landscapes: there's something quirky to life up in the left-hand corner of the USA and southwest Canada. Unified by the Cascade Range, it's a region (often referred to as Cascadia) defined less by its national borders than by its spiritual and environmental similarities. Today's Northwest was born of the Oregon Trail, whose pioneers were fueled by resilience and determination. Nowadays, life is a lot easier than 150 years ago, when this region was settled, and people are as likely to be fueled by espresso as by a higher purpose. However, this is a culture founded on restless idealism, and there is the strong, slightly uneasy sense that there's still more exploring to do. The Northwest is a long way from the traditional centers of mainstream culture and power, and the locals like it that way.

Facts about the Pacific Northwest

HISTORY

Nearly 20,000 years ago, when the accumulated ice of the great polar glaciers of the Pleistocene epoch (commonly referred to as the Ice Age) lowered sea levels throughout the world, the ancestors of North American Indians migrated from Siberia to Alaska via a land bridge across the Bering Strait. Over millennia, subsequent migrations distributed the population southward through North and Central America, and down to the southern tip of South America.

Native Peoples

The first inhabitants of North America some 20,000 years ago were nomadic hunter-gatherers who lived in small bands, a type of society that existed on this continent even into very recent times. In the West, along the Pacific Ocean, Puget Sound and major coastal river valleys, natives developed societies based on fishing and scavenging from the sea. While native tribes such as the Quinault, Quileute, Makah and Nootka went to sea in pursuit of whales, other tribal groups – notably the Coast Salish, Chinook, Coos and Tillamooks – depended on catching salmon, cod and shellfish. On land, deer and elk were hunted; it was the hides of the animals, not the flesh, that were treasured.

Summer and fall were dedicated to harvesting the bounty of the sea and forest. Food was stored in such quantities that the long winter months could be given over to activities other than those concerned with subsistence. Therefore, in terms of artistic, religious and cultural forms, the Northwest coastal Indians reached a pinnacle of sophistication unmatched in most Native American groups.

Ornately carved cedar canoes served as transport, which led to extensive trading networks between the permanent settlements stretched up and down the coast and along the river valleys. Extended family groups lived in cedar-sided longhouses, which were constructed over a central pit-like living area. The social structure in these self-sustaining villages was quite stratified, with wealth and power held by an aristocratic class of chiefs. Wealth was measured in goods such as blankets, salmon and fish oil. These items were consumed and, to some degree, redistributed in potlatches, or ceremonial feasts, in which great honor accrued to the person who gave away valued items.

The aristocrats of these tribes often practiced head flattening. Infants were strapped to a cradleboard, while another board at an angle pressed against the forehead. The result was a sloped forehead and a conical skull, a sign of high birth. Coastal tribes also kept slaves, which were generally received from trade with other tribes, not from warfare.

Inland, on the arid plateaus between the Cascades and the Rocky Mountains, a culture developed based on seasonal migration between rivers and temperate uplands. These tribes, which included the Nez Perce, Cayuse, Spokane, Yakama and Kootenai, displayed cultural features of both the coastal Indians and Plains Indians east of the Rockies. During salmon runs, the tribes gathered at rapids and waterfalls to net or harpoon fish, which they then dried or smoked. At other times, these tribes would move to upland hunting grounds, where they gathered fruit and pursued deer and elk. Tribal groups returned to traditional winter camps at the end of the year, where they maintained semipermanent pit-type dwellings. Most transportation was overland, with large dogs serving as pack animals before horses arrived on the scene in the 18th century. Authority in tribal units was loosely organized, with responsibility for leading the tribe divided among a number of chiefs, each of whom had specific duties. Great religious importance was attached to vision quests, in which young men sought to recognize the supernatural guardian that guided individual lives.

In the harsh landscapes of Oregon's southern desert, another culture evolved. Tribes like the Shoshone, Paiute and Bannock were nomadic peoples who hunted and scavenged in the northern reaches of the Great Basin desert. Berries, roots and small game such as gophers and rabbits constituted their meager diet. Easily transported shelters constructed of woven reeds made up migratory villages. Religious and cultural life focused on shamans, who could intercede with the spirit world to heal sickness or bring success in hunting. The Shoshone and Paiute became fearsome warriors and hunters after the 18th century, when horses – stolen from Spanish California – gave them easy mobility.

These desert tribes were remnants of a larger culture that once lived along the enormous freshwater lakes that formed in the Great Basin after the melting of the last ice age about 12,000 years ago. An isolated pocket of this culture survived along the shallow seasonal lakes and marshes of the Klamath River valley in southern Oregon, where Klamath and Modoc tribe members hunted birds and small game from cedar canoes and lived in domed structures woven from reeds.

The Pacific Northwest's one great center of trade and activity was Celilo Falls, a series of rapids and waterfalls on the Columbia River near today's The Dalles. Here, the river's enormous population of migrating salmon was forced to struggle through powerful eddies and chutes, making them prey for natives wielding nets and harpoons. During the summer salmon run, tribal rivalries were laid aside and individuals from all over the inland Northwest would journey here to harvest salmon and dry the fish for winter usage; beads, tools, skins and foodstuffs were traded, and a great deal of socializing and gambling took place. Coastal Indians would paddle upriver to the falls to trade precious dentalia (tooth shells) and other shells for animal hides and slaves. A variation of the Chinookan language, called Chinook Jargon (which included words from many native languages as well as English, French and Russian), evolved to serve as a common language of trade at areas like Celilo Falls.

Based on studies of oral histories and the wealth of rock carvings in the area, anthropologists consider the Celilo Falls site one of the greatest trade centers in prehistoric America. Another large trading area in the Pacific Northwest was Kettle Falls on the Columbia River in northeastern Washington. Both sites are now flooded by hydroelectric dams.

Early Exploration

This distant corner of the world map was one of the last to be explored by Europeans. In fact, exactly 300 years passed between Columbus' discovery of America and the discovery of the Columbia River – the continent's second-largest river. The Pacific Northwest was, therefore, one of the last areas up for grabs for European colonialism and economic exploitation.

The rocky and storm-wracked coast of the Pacific Northwest resisted many early seafaring explorers. Probably the first Europeans to see the Oregon country were those accompanying Spanish explorer Juan Rodriguez Cabrillo. In 1543 his ship reached the mouth of the Rogue River, but the coastline was too wild and stormy to attempt landing. By the 18th century, the Spanish had colonized the southern parts of California, and had begun to explore the northern Pacific Coast, in part seeking to discover the Strait of Anian (the Spanish term for the fabled Northwest Passage, a water route from the Pacific Ocean to the Atlantic Ocean around the north coast of North America). The Spanish also sought to explore the land that lay between them and their potential new neighbor to the north, Russia. (The Russians had begun to make claims along the Pacific coast of North America in the late 18th century, after the voyages of Danish explorer and navigator Vitus Bering.) By 1774 Spanish

DOUG PLUMMER

BILL MCRAE

RICK GERHARTER

Top Left: Fish seller, Pike Place Market, Seattle, WA
Bottom: British Columbia's counterculture is still alive at
Wreck Beach, Vancouver, BC

Top Right: Wading in the surf, Oregon Coast, OR

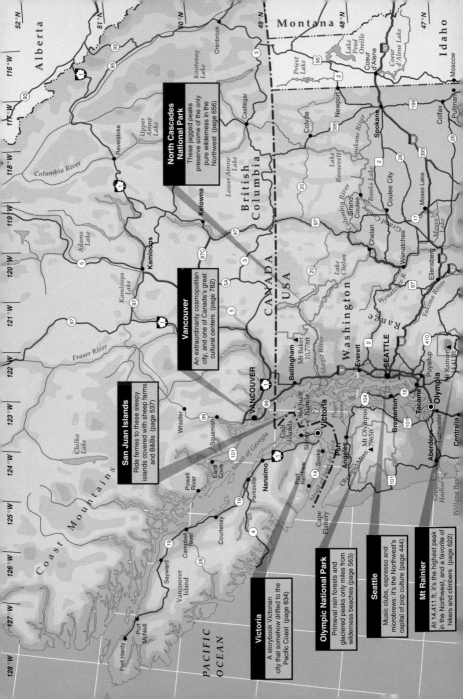

North Cascades National Park
These jagged peaks preserve some of the only pure wilderness in the Northwest (page 656)

Vancouver
An extraordinarily cosmopolitan city, and one of Canada's great cultural centers (page 782)

San Juan Islands
Ride ferries to these sleepy islands covered with sheep farms and B&Bs (page 537)

Victoria
A storybook Victorian city that somehow drifted to the Pacific Coast (page 834)

Olympic National Park
Primeval rain forests and glaciered peaks only miles from wilderness beaches (page 563)

Seattle
Music clubs, espresso and microbrews: it's the Northwest's capital of pop culture (page 444)

Mt Rainier
At 14,411 ft, it's the highest peak in the Northwest, and a favorite of hikers and climbers (page 622)

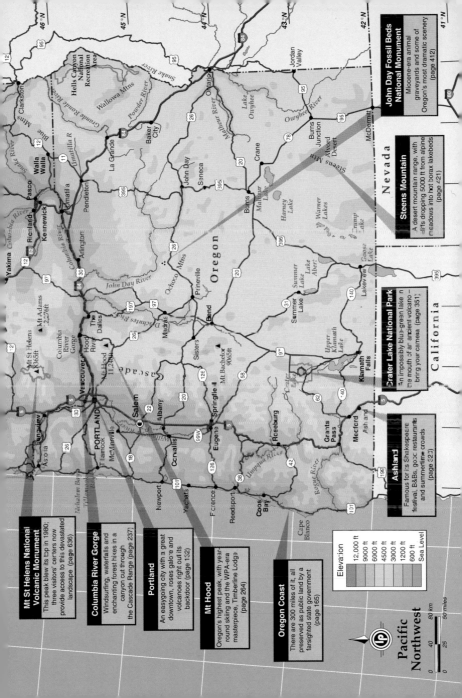

Mt St Helens National Volcanic Monument
This peak blew its top in 1980; three visitors' centers now provide access to this devastated landscape (page 636)

Columbia River Gorge
Windsurfing, waterfalls and enchanting forest hikes in a canyon cut through the Cascade Range (page 237)

Portland
An easygoing city with a great downtown, roses galore and volcanoes right out its backdoor (page 152)

Mt Hood
Oregon's highest peak, with year-round skiing and the WPA-era masterpiece, Timberline Lodge (page 264)

Oregon Coast
There are 300 miles of it, all preserved as public land by a farsighted state government (page 165)

John Day Fossil Beds National Monument
Miocene-era animal graveyards and some of Oregon's most dramatic scenery (page 412)

Steens Mountain
A desert mountain range, with cliffs dropping 5000ft from alpine meadows into hot borax lakebeds (page 421)

Crater Lake National Park
An impossibly blue-green lake in the mouth of an ancient volcano – bring your camera (page 351)

Ashland
Famous for its Shakespeare festival, B&Bs, good restaurants and summertime crowds (page 322)

Elevation
12,000 ft
9000 ft
6000 ft
4500 ft
3000 ft
1200 ft
600 ft
Sea Level

Pacific Northwest

SCOTT PRICE

SCOTT PRICE

SCOTT PRICE

SCOTT PRICE

SCOTT PRICE

SCOTT PRICE

SCOTT PRICE

BILL MCRAE

SCOTT PRICE

Top Row (l to r): Arrowleaf balsamroot; Indian paint-brush and lupine; forget-me-not wildflowers
Middle Row (l to r): Northern spotted owl; sea anemone, sea urchins and blood star; bighorn sheep

Bottom Row (l to r): Western larch trees in autumn; ponderosa pine; aspen trees

frigates reached as far north as the Queen Charlotte Islands, claiming the Northwest coast for the Spanish crown.

The British also sought to find a Northwest Passage. Fresh from their victory over the French in the French & Indian War (1756-63), the British were eager to explore the western shores of British Canada. In 1778 Captain James Cook explored the coast of present-day Oregon, Washington and British Columbia (BC). Cook landed and traded at Nootka Sound on Vancouver Island. Captain George Vancouver was, in 1792, the first explorer to sail the waters of Puget Sound; thereby, he asserted British sovereignty over the entire region. He was also responsible for the first accurate maps of the region. The British also sought to explore the region by land from its colonies in eastern Canada. The first white man to cross the continent, the fur-trader Alexander Mackenzie followed native trails across the Canadian Rockies to arrive at Bella Coola on the British Columbia coast in 1793.

The Spanish attempted to build colonies along the Northwest coast, first at Neah Bay on the Olympic Peninsula in 1790, and then at Nootka Sound. Cattle and horses were imported from Spanish California, and fields cleared for cultivation. However, for reasons that had more to with European politics than the success of these rain-drenched colonies, Spain gave over its claim to the Northwest coast to Britain in 1792.

The Americans also entered the region in 1792, when Captain Robert Gray discovered the mouth of the Columbia River, obscured by sandbars and hazardous currents. Gray sailed up the great river, traded with the natives, and named his discovery the Columbia, after his ship.

The Lewis and Clark Expedition (1803-1806) was promoted as an exploration of the USA's newly acquired Louisiana Purchase, which extended from the Mississippi River to the northern Continental Divide of the Rocky Mountains. Somewhat circumspectly, the US explorers also crossed over the Rockies into then-Spanish territory, and made their way down the Columbia River to the Pacific Ocean. By doing so, they established a further US claim on the territory.

The Corps of Discovery, as the Lewis and Clark party was officially known, spent a miserable winter on the Oregon coast near Astoria, battling fleas, suffering from venereal disease and eating dog meat. Come spring, they returned up the Columbia, Snake and Clearwater Rivers, eventually arriving in St Louis, where stories of the Northwest caught the fancy of American merchants and frontiersmen. See the Lewis and Clark Expedition sidebar for more details.

It is important to note that this exploration did not lead directly to a pioneer settlement or even a permanent trading post. However, what the British and Americans did discover was the Northwest's bounty of fur-bearing wildlife and the profits to be made in the peltry trade. While in the Northwest in 1778, Captain Cook's crew traded buttons, cloth and trinkets with the natives for sea otter skins. When Cook and his crew later called into Asian ports, they discovered that the Chinese were willing to pay a high price for such pelts.

Thus was born the Chinese trade triangle which would dominate British and US economic interests in the northern Pacific for the next 30 years. Ships entered the waters of the Pacific Northwest, traded cloth and trinkets with natives for pelts of sea otters, and then set sail for China, where the skins were traded for tea and luxury items. The ships then returned to their port of call – usually London or Boston – where the Asian goods were sold. Vast fortunes were made by profiteers before the sea otters died out and the War of 1812 between the US and Britain made such trade expeditions dangerous as ships were often threatened by buccaneers from the warring nations.

The Fur Trade

The first white settlements in the Pacific Northwest did not arrive from the coast (which had already seen dozens of exploratory voyages) but from inland. Trappers

The Lewis & Clark Expedition

Meriwether Lewis   William Clark

When President Thomas Jefferson made the decision in 1801 to explore the unchartered western part of North America to find a waterway to the Pacific, he enlisted his young protégé and personal secretary, Meriwether Lewis, to lead an expedition. Lewis, then 27, had no expertise in botany, cartography or Indian languages, and was known to have bouts of 'hypochondriac affections' – a euphemism for schizophrenia – but couldn't resist the opportunity. He in turn asked his good friend William Clark, already an experienced frontiersman and army veteran at the age of 33, to join him. In 1803 they left St Louis, MO, and headed west with an entourage of 40, including 27 bachelors, Clark's African American servant, York, and a dog.

They traveled some 8000 miles in about two years, documenting everything they came across in their journals with such bad spelling that it must have taken historians a few extra years just to sort out what they wrote. In an almost biblical fashion they named some 120 animals and 170 plants, including the grizzly bear and the prairie dog. While Clark's entries are the more scientific, Lewis was known to explore alone and write pensive, almost romantic, accounts of the journey.

Despite hostilities shown to them, the Corps of Discovery – their official name – faired quite well, in part because the party was accompanied by the legendary Sacagawea, a young Shoshone woman who had been sold to and became the wife of Toussaint Charbonneau, a French Canadian trapper who joined Lewis & Clark on their journey. The presence of Sacagawea and her baby boy eased many a potential conflict between the explorers and the Native Americans. York also softened tensions between the group and the locals – his color and stature both fascinated and intimidated the Indians.

Lewis and Clark returned to a heroes' welcome in St Louis in 1806, and were soon appointed to high offices. In 1808 Lewis was appointed governor of the just-purchased Louisiana Territory, but died a year later, purportedly during a 'fit' in which he either committed suicide or was murdered. Clark dealt with his new fame a bit better, and was appointed superintendent of Indian Affairs in the Louisiana Territory and governor of the Missouri Territory. He died at the age of 68. ■

from two competing British fur-trading companies – the Hudson's Bay Company (HBC) and the North West Company – began to expand from their base around Hudson's Bay and the Great Lakes. By 1809 both companies had edged over the Rocky Mountains into today's British Columbia, Montana, Idaho and eastern Washington to establish fur-trading forts. These trading posts were quite successful, even though each was linked to eastern markets by an 1800-mile overland trail. Each fort was given an assortment of trade goods to induce the local Indians to trap beaver, otter, fox, wolf or whatever fur-bearing animals were present. While blankets, beads and cloth were popular with the natives, nothing produced the goods as dependably as whiskey. (One historian estimates that 195,000 gallons of alcohol were traded with the natives for fur during the heyday of the Northwest fur trade.)

As the fur-trading forts edged closer to the Pacific Coast, it became clear that shipment of furs made more and more sense; however, there was no coastal port as of yet. Even though British fur interests controlled inland Pacific Northwest, American fur magnate John Jacob Astor was the first to establish a coastal fur-trading post in 1811, at the mouth of the Columbia River. However, the trading post, called Fort Astoria, was assailed by bad luck from its inception. When British soldiers arrived during the War of 1812 to take possession of the fort, the bedraggled Americans seemed only too glad to sell the operation to British fur-trading companies.

With the Americans out of the way, the British fur-trading company HBC moved quickly to establish a network of fur-trading forts and relationships with Indian tribes throughout this region, working its way into the drainages of the Columbia River, the Willamette and Umpqua Rivers in Oregon and the Fraser River in BC.

Fort Vancouver – located at the strategically important confluence of the Willamette and Columbia Rivers – was established in 1824 to serve as the headquarters for the entire Columbia region, and was placed under the leadership of the capable Dr John McLoughlin, often called the Father of Oregon. As chief factor of HBC, the largest commercial enterprise and administrative organization in the region, McLoughlin played an important role in the economic development of the Northwest. He also played both a conscious and an unwitting role in the founding of the Willamette Valley settlements that would become the state of Oregon.

By 1827 significant changes in European and American colonial aspirations in the Northwest had led to treaties and events that served to better define the territory. Spain had withdrawn its claim to the Northwest, establishing the northern border of New Spain at the 47th parallel (the current Oregon-California border); Russian ambitions were limited to the land north of the 54°40' parallel. The USA, through the Louisiana Purchase, owned all the land east of the Rocky Mountains and south of the 49th parallel. Britain controlled the land north of the border and east of the Rockies. This left a vast territory – which included all of present-day British Columbia, the states of Oregon, Washington and Idaho and parts of western Montana and Wyoming – open to claims by both Britain and the US.

The terms of an 1818 codicil to the Treaty of Ghent (which ended the War of 1812) sought to resolve the competing British and US territorial claims in the Northwest by declaring that the region was open to joint occupancy by both nations: Britain and the US could continue economic development in the area but neither could establish an official government.

The First White Settlements
Unlike most other early trading posts, which were basically repositories for goods, Fort Vancouver became, under the stewardship of the Canadian-born McLoughlin, a thriving, nearly self-sufficient agricultural community complete with mills, a dairy, gardens and fields. Civility and propriety were held in high regard. All evening meals were held in McLoughlin's formal dining room using fine china, and McLoughlin's generosity and consideration extended to all who chanced through this remote area.

McLoughlin also encouraged settlement beyond the precincts of the fort. Contrary to protocol, McLoughlin allowed older trappers who were retiring from the HBC to settle along the Willamette River, in an area still called French Prairie (just upriver from Champoeg State Park). By 1828 these French Canadians, with their Native American wives, began to clear the land and build cabins: these were the first true settlers in the Northwest. McLoughlin established a mill and incorporated the first town in the Northwest in 1829 at Oregon City.

American trapping and trading parties began to filter into the Northwest in the 1830s. McLoughlin graciously welcomed these groups to Fort Vancouver, traded with them for goods, and then urged the newcomers to move south along the

Willamette River. McLoughlin sensed that one day the US and Britain would probably divide the territory; if US settlement could be limited to the territory south of the Columbia, then Britain would have a stronger claim to the land north of the river.

Accompanying one of these groups in 1834 were Daniel and Jason Lee, Methodist missionaries from New England with an interest in converting the local Indians to Christianity. The Lees founded a mission in 1834 north of present-day Salem, but soon discovered that the local Native Americans weren't particularly susceptible to Christianity. The Methodists did, however, establish the first schools in Oregon, and they succeeded in infusing the young territory with rather doctrinal idealism. The Lees' failure, however, didn't deter an increasing number of missionaries from streaming into the Oregon country. Protestant missionaries Marcus and Narcissa Whitman and Henry and Eliza Spalding crossed the North American continent in 1836 (Narcissa and Eliza were the first women to cross what would later be known as the Oregon Trail), establishing missions near Walla Walla, Washington and Lapwai, Idaho. In 1838 a Catholic mission was established at St Paul on the Willamette River.

The ranks of the Methodists in the Willamette Valley were greatly bolstered in 1837 and 1840, when missionary 'enforcements' arrived from the eastern US. However, the interests of these Yankee missionaries rather quickly turned from Indian salvation to carving out farmsteads and fomenting anti-British sentiment. Although the Treaty of Ghent didn't allow either the US or Britain to establish a government in the territory, the HBC, with its strict code of procedures and conduct for employees, provided the effective legal background for the nascent settlement, particularly as long as the majority of the settlers were retired trappers. Yet even though the HBC's influence in matters was largely benign, the Methodists refused to tolerate any degree of British hegemony. To make matters worse, McLoughlin and most of the French Canadian settlers were Catholic. With tensions

mounting, the HBC established another center of operations, Fort Victoria on Vancouver Island, far from the Yankee rabble-rousers.

This was an era when belief in the USA's manifest destiny ran strong, and sentiment to annex the Northwest ran high. However, despite fulminations from Protestant pulpits and fiery oratory in the US Senate, federal troops were not ordered into a military occupation of the lower Columbia River in order to rid the region of the British and the natives. If the settlers in the Oregon country were to have an independent civil authority, they would have to take the steps themselves.

The Vote at Champoeg

By 1843 most settlers began to feel the need for organized laws and regulations, particularly regarding land ownership, inheritance and community protection. Roughly 700 people were living in the Willamette Valley then, a ragtag mixture of French Canadian trappers and their half-Indian families, Protestant missionaries, and a group of men – both American and British – who are best and most simply described as mountain men, and who were often married to native women.

The Methodists, who were the most anxious to link the young settlement with the US, held a series of meetings, and drew up a framework for a provisional government. The French and British settlers initially balked at the plan, which would replace the authority of the HBC with an independent – but largely American – code of laws. In the end, an up-or-down vote was called at Champoeg along the Willamette River about 30 miles south of Portland in 1843, with Americans, Canadians and Britons about equally represented. A bare majority voted to organize a provisional government independent of the HBC, thereby casting the settlement's lot with the USA. The land north of the Columbia remained in the control of the HBC. Had the vote gone differently, today's maps of the Pacific Northwest might look quite different.

The USA-Canada boundary dispute became increasingly antagonistic. The popular slogan of the 1844 presidential campaign was '54/40 or fight,' which urged the US to occupy all the Northwest up to the present Alaskan border, including all of Washington State and BC. Finally, in 1846, the British and the Americans agreed to the present border along the 49th parallel. The HBC headquarters withdrew from Fort Vancouver to Fort Victoria on Vancouver Island, and many British citizens moved north as well. In order to better protect its interests and citizens, Vancouver Island became a crown colony in 1849.

Fort Vancouver's longtime leader McLoughlin was forced to retire, in part because of his aid to US settlers (he would allow them to settle on HBC land, which was strictly forbidden). He and his wife moved to Oregon City where he built a home, and later they became US citizens.

The Oregon Trail

American settlers had been straggling into the Willamette Valley since the late 1830s. However, in 1843, an overland party of nearly 900 arrived in the Willamette Valley, more than doubling the region's population. Thus began the greatest migration in US history, across the 2000-mile-long Oregon Trail, which between 1843 and 1860 brought an estimated 53,000 settlers to the Northwest.

The trail began in Independence, Missouri, followed the North Platte River to South Pass in Wyoming, across the Snake River Plain in Idaho, up and over the Blue Mountains of eastern Oregon to the Columbia River at The Dalles. The six-month journey across the continent was a time of great adventure, hazard and hardship. Families embarked with their belongings in canvas-topped wagons, often trailing cattle and livestock. By the time the emigrants reached eastern Oregon, food stores were running low, people and livestock were exhausted and autumn had arrived in the high mountain passes.

When the parties arrived at the Columbia River in The Dalles, they faced one of the most treacherous parts of their journey: weary travelers had to choose between rafting themselves and all their belongings through the rapids in the Columbia River Gorge, or struggling up the flanks of

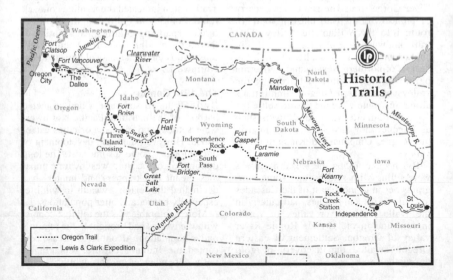

Mt Hood and descending into the Willamette Valley via the precipitous Barlow Trail.

Ultimately, the Oregon Trail ended at Oregon City in the Willamette Valley. Here settlers established farms, businesses and towns. The major towns of the new land tended to be along the Willamette River. Portland, near the Willamette's confluence with the Columbia River, took on an early importance as a trade center. Oregon City, at the falls of the Willamette River, was the early seat of government, while above the falls, in the river's broad agricultural basin, small farming communities sprang up.

Initially, the Oregon Trail pioneers avoided moving north of the Columbia River because it was under HBC control. However, the US gained control of Fort Vancouver in 1846, and settlers began to spread up the Cowlitz River (which flows into the Columbia River) to the Puget Sound area. One of the first American settlements in the Northwest was Tumwater, near Olympia on the Puget Sound. By 1851, the Denny party, a group of Oregon Trail pioneers led by brothers Arthur and David Denny, set sights on Elliott Bay and founded the port city of Seattle.

The difficult passage of the Columbia River Gorge from The Dalles led a party of pioneers in 1846 to blaze a southern route into the Willamette Valley. This trail, known as the Applegate Trail, cut south from Fort Hall, Idaho, through the deserts of northern Nevada and California before turning north and traversing the valleys of southern Oregon. Immigrants along this route were the first to settle the upper Willamette Valley and towns such as Eugene; they also scouted the land in the Rogue, Umpqua and Klamath River valleys.

By the late 1850s the western valleys were filling with settlers, and some emigrants began to move east of the Cascades to begin farms and ranches, particularly in the Walla Walla River valley in Washington, and in the Grande Ronde River valley of Oregon. Settlement of eastern Oregon awaited the discovery of gold during the 1860s.

Latter-day Oregonians have always made much of the assumedly stellar qualities of these early settlers. Indeed, there are some notable traits common to those who chose to settle the Northwest. The Oregon Trail was an arduous and costly adventure. Those who chose to travel it had to be able to afford a wagon or two, sufficient foodstuffs for a six-month journey and livestock or other means of sustaining a living. In other words, the Northwest was not settled by penniless wanderers: early pioneers were economically solid yet enterprising people from established backgrounds.

Also, the Oregon Trail had already been traversed by thousands before gold was discovered in the West (gold was discovered at Sutter's Mill in 1849, commencing the California gold rush). These early emigrants went West to start farms, businesses and communities, not in search of easy wealth. Also important is the fact that early emigrants were quite young: the Northwest's first settlers were mostly of one generation, and were remarkably homogeneous in their philosophy, goals and culture.

The pride that Northwesterners take in their early settlers is best illustrated by an apocryphal story. At a fork in the Oregon Trail, a sign indicated the terminus of each route. Pointing to California, the sign pictured a sparkling gold nugget. Pointing to the north the sign read: To Oregon. Only those who could read made their way to the Northwest.

The 19th Century

By 1860 the coastal valleys and protected harbors of the maritime Pacific Northwest were settled, and most major cities established. However, the rapid development of the region had come at some cost. The long domination of the Northwest by fur companies meant that trappers and hunters had decimated the region's wealth in wildlife, especially beaver and otter populations.

More deplorable was the toll that contact with the whites had brought to the region's native population. Alcohol and disease corrupted the Indian's culture, replacing it with dependence on the whites' trade goods. Indian hunters and gatherers, who once followed a seasonal pattern of fishing salmon and stalking deer, now trapped the streams of their homelands free of beaver in return for a steady flow of whiskey. The natives had no natural immunity to diseases brought by the whites, and the mortality rate, particularly along the coast, was devastating. Contemporary observers estimated that nine-tenths of the population of Chinook tribes along the Columbia River died of a mysterious fever during the summer of 1829.

However lamentable the impact of the fur traders on the natives, the traders made no conscious attempt to change the general culture of the Indians or to move them from their homelands. This awaited the arrival of the missionaries and agricultural settlers of the 1830s and 1840s. Methodist missionaries among the Calapooia Indians in Oregon had little luck converting adult Indians, so they turned their attention to native children, whom they took from their families and placed in Methodist religious schools.

The Whitman mission near Walla Walla also attempted to bring Christianity to the native Cayuse, Umatilla and Walla Walla tribes. Here, misunderstandings between the cultures reached a tragic conclusion. In 1847, after an epidemic of measles raged throughout the Cayuse villages, resentful natives began to believe that Whitman, a medical doctor, had introduced the disease in order to decimate the Indian population. In early winter, a group of Cayuse entered the mission, asking to speak to Whitman. After Whitman welcomed the Indians into his kitchen, they drew their weapons, killing the missionary and his wife. The attack spread throughout the mission grounds. Within minutes, 12 others were dead, and 53 women and children were taken captive.

The Whitman Massacre – as the attack became known – horrified and frightened white settlers throughout the Northwest. Until this event, the natives and the settlers had lived in an uneasy peace. Hereafter, the American settlers felt justified and com-pelled to remove the Indians from their land and incarcerate them on reservations. That this would also make the territory safer for farmers and miners could not be ignored.

In general, the coastal Indians had been so debilitated by disease that they could mount little resistance to white incursions. These tribes were marched or shipped to reservations in 1855 and 1856, where increased illness, starvation and dislocation led to the complete extinction of many tribal groups. Even on Vancouver Island, where British policies were generally more enlightened regarding Indian culture, most of the arable land was given over to white settlers; the natives retained only their village sites. Christian missionaries worked to make illegal the traditional potlatches that formed the nucleus of coastal Indian religion and social life.

The Native Americans east of the Cascades resisted manipulation by white settlers and the military more strenuously than the coastal tribes. A series of fierce battles was fought between the US Army and various Indian tribes from 1855 to 1877. Especially bloody were the Rogue River and the Modoc Wars in southern Oregon, and the Cayuse War near Walla Walla. However, in the end, these Native American groups also ended up on reservations, deracinated, alienated from their traditional cultural lives and utterly dependent on the federal government for subsistence.

The Northwest was now wide open for settlement and Oregon, Washington and British Columbia quickly grew into economic forces on the national and international stage.

See the introductory chapters to Oregon and Washington, and the Vancouver chapter for history from this point on.

GEOGRAPHY

The Pacific Northwest is a somewhat imprecisely defined geographical area. While the states of Oregon, Washington and the province of British Columbia certainly constitute the bulwark of the region (never mind that to a Canadian this would be the Pacific Southwest), many people also include the western third of Montana and most of Idaho in more expansive discussions of the area.

The Northwest comprises two major geographical regions: the islands, mountains and valleys of the Pacific coastline and the Cascade Range; and the plateaus east of the Cascades to the Rocky Mountain foothills. Linking these two regions is the mighty Columbia River, which drains a 259,000-sq-mile area, taking in nearly all of Oregon, Washington and Idaho, as well as much of British Columbia, Montana and parts of Utah, Wyoming and Nevada.

The Columbia River
The Columbia River is an intrinsic part of life throughout the Pacific Northwest. The river rises in British Columbia in Lake Columbia, on the western flanks of the Rockies, and flows for 465 miles through western Canada before crossing into the northeast corner of Washington State. A long series of dams harness this river – the strongest flowing in North America – with the hydroelectric potential to power one-third of the USA. Inexpensive Columbia River electricity was important for the early industrial development of the entire Northwest. Irrigation is another vital element of the river's many reservoirs: in the otherwise arid plateaus between the Grand Coulee Dam and The Dalles, thousands of acres of cropland now flourish beneath center pivot sprinklers.

Two of the Northwest's most significant geological features are due to the Columbia River. The Grand Coulee in central Washington is an abandoned ice-age channel of the ancient Columbia that cuts through spectacular lava flows. The Columbia River Gorge is the river's canyon incised through the mighty Cascade Range. The Gorge is famous for its many waterfalls, including Multnomah Falls, which at 642 feet is the second-highest year-round falls in North America.

West of the Cascades
Much of the northern Pacific Coast is quite rugged, lined with cliffs and rocky promon-

tories and arrayed with mountainous islands. Sandy beaches dominate only along the Long Beach Peninsula north of the Columbia River, along Oregon's central coast at the Oregon Dunes and at Vancouver Island's Long Beach. Rising from the Pacific shore are coastal mountains – in Oregon the Coast Range, in Washington the Olympic Mountains, in British Columbia the Coast Mountains – which are covered with dense forests of Douglas fir, cedar and hemlock. These mighty forests are some of the last remaining virgin woodlands in North America, and have recently witnessed a lot of logging, court battles and media attention.

Throughout much of the Northwest, the coastal ranges and the towering volcanic peaks of the Cascades are separated by a low-lying basin officially known as the Willamette-Puget Trough. In Oregon and southern Washington these basins are drained by the Willamette and Cowlitz Rivers, respectively, while in northern Washington and British Columbia, the ocean has partially invaded the lowlands to form the Puget Sound, Hood Canal and Georgia Strait. These lowlands – protected to some extent from the extremes of Pacific weather and rainfall – contain extremely fertile agricultural land. Farms, dairies, plant nurseries, orchards and vineyards thrive in the mild climate and rich soil; not coincidentally, these valleys also contain the vast majority of the region's population. The rugged western slopes of the Cascades are heavily forested, and often heavily logged.

In southern Oregon two major rivers, the Rogue and Umpqua, drain from the Cascades directly into the Pacific. In northern Washington several large rivers, most notably the Skagit, debouch into the Puget Sound, while the Fraser River drains a wide basin of central BC before fanning into a delta and emptying into the Georgia Strait at Vancouver.

East of the Cascades
The Cascade mountains run like a spine along the western third of Oregon and

Washington. The famous and eye-catching peaks of this range include Mt Baker, Mt Rainier, Mt St Helens, Mt Hood and Crater Lake's Mt Mazama, among many others. These geologically very recent peaks sit atop a much older and more massive volcanic province, and it is this wide barrier that serves to halt the moist easterly flow of Pacific air, creating the arid plateaus of central and eastern Oregon and Washington.

This entire region east of the Cascades is underlain by enormous flows of lava, some of the largest in the world. These vast steppe-like uplands are now devoted to dry-land farming and ranching. The meager rainfall in this region nonetheless produces some major rivers and has trenched majestic canyons: the Deschutes, John Day, Grande Ronde and Yakima Rivers – to say nothing of the massive Columbia – have each furrowed deeply into the underlying basalt.

Isolated mountain ranges also float above the lava prairies, especially in northeastern Washington and in eastern Oregon, where peaks in the Ochoco, Blue and Wallowa ranges reach as high as 10,000 feet. Ponderosa pine forests coat these rambling mountains, and valleys are filled with livestock ranches.

South of the Columbia Basin in southern Oregon are the arid fault-block mountain ranges of the Great Basin desert. Rainfall is so slight in these regions that no stream network exists to carry runoff to the ocean. Instead, what rainfall they do get accumulates in landlocked basins; these lakes are usually saline.

The mighty Snake River rises in the mountains of Yellowstone Park, only to drain through a desertlike volcanic basin in southern Idaho. As the Snake River drops out of this high basin on its way to meet the Columbia, it charges through the wild Hells Canyon, North America's deepest gorge.

GEOLOGY

The Pacific Northwest's geology is a textbook example of plate tectonics, a theory which holds in part that the continents drift around the earth's surface on crustal plates.

Nearly all the elements of the region's geology derive from the fact that the Pacific Northwest is at the leading edge of North America's westward movement.

About 200 million years ago the North American continent wrenched loose from Europe and Africa, beginning its inexorable westward journey. At that time the continent's western coastline stretched along a line just west of today's western borders of Idaho and Alberta.

As the continent drifted westward (an inch or two a year, over millions of years), the coastal plain was buckled by the collision with the Pacific sea floor, forming the mountainous ridges that would grow into the Rocky Mountains. As the impact continued, the heavier rocks of the sea floor dove under the lighter rocks of the continent. Eventually, the basaltic sea floor began to melt into the earth's mantle, then rose back up through the earth's crust as magma.

Islands Dock

As North America continued to move westward into the Pacific Ocean, the continental landmass would occasionally encounter offshore islands and small continents. Because these pieces of land were too light to be forced beneath the continent, they collided with the moving landmass.

Eventually, these independent provinces became embedded along the coast of North America, adding mountain ranges to British Columbia (the Selkirks), to eastern and southern Oregon (the Klamaths, Wallowas, Ochocos and Blues) and to northern Washington (the Okanogans and the North Cascades). Between these northern and southern highlands was a large shallow bay.

A snapshot of the Pacific Northwest 60 million years ago would show a vista of jumbled offshore islands, low coastal mountains and marine marshes, all invaded by the shallow Pacific. Slowly, sediment was filling the channels between the island chains that had accreted to the coast. Plant and animal life thrived in the warm tropical climate: fishlike swimming reptiles, flying pteranodons and tree ferns were abundant. As there was no extensive coastal mountain range, Pacific weather flowed inland unobstructed, resulting in a widespread moist environment.

Come the Volcanoes

At the beginning of the Cenozoic era, about 60 million years ago, a large chunk of continental crust again docked onto the westward-trending edge of the Northwest. The seacoast shifted from the huge bay that covered present-day central Oregon and Washington far to the west. The sea floor continued to descend beneath the Northwest, but now along a line parallel to the present coastline. As before, coastal sediments and offshore islands began to be wedged and jumbled together along the new shoreline to form today's Coast Range and Olympic Mountains. The San Juan and Gulf Islands as well as Vancouver Island also docked against the Pacific Coast during this time.

Three intense periods of volcanism soon followed, each of which would utterly change the face of the region. First, a line of volcanoes shot up through the newly arrived landmass about 40 million years ago. As the range – called the Old or Western Cascades – grew higher, it isolated the old ocean bay of the interior Northwest, creating an inland sea surrounded by temperate grasslands. Enormous volcanic explosions of ash and mud repeatedly buried the plant and animal life of this area, resulting in the John Day formations, whose fossil beds have become national monuments.

Then, about 20 million years ago, the volcanic scene shifted eastward. Extensive faulting of the southern and eastern Oregon and Idaho bedrock allowed vast amounts of lava to rise to the surface. Rather than create volcanic peaks, the lava simply oozed out of the earth in incredible amounts. From volcanic sources near the Wallowa Mountains, lava leaked out of the earth in sufficient quantities to repeatedly flood the sea of central Oregon and Washington with molten

rock. In fact, successive lava flows (there was a major eruption about every 10,000 years for a period of almost 10 million years) eventually left only the highest peaks of Oregon's eastern mountains above the basalt plain, known as the Columbia Plateau. Several eruptions of lava were so huge and so hot that lava from the Grande Ronde valley of eastern Oregon flowed down the Columbia River all the way to the Pacific, nearly 300 miles away. In some places in central Washington, the basalt formations are more than a mile deep.

At the end of this period, the Northwest had taken on much of its present shape. However, it would be many millions of years before the barren lava fields would erode into soil.

About 17 million years ago in southeastern Oregon, the lava plateau was fractured by massive faulting, producing the scarps and lakes of the Basin and Range provinces. After the bedrock had rifted, geologic pressure forced up one side of the fault, while the other sank. The rising fault block often rose to mountain heights, while the descending basin filled with water. As the climate became increasingly arid, these isolated bodies of water lost their outlet streams and became salt lakes. These mountain ridges and saline lakes became the northernmost extension of the continent's Great Basin desert.

The region's last great volcanic era began relatively recently. The present peaks of the Cascade Range began to rise about 4 million years ago, but the conical, uneroded peaks of the Northwest skyline indicate much more recent activity. Mt Mazama, better known as the caldera of Crater Lake, erupted 6900 years ago, devastating much of central Oregon with its massive explosion. Mt St Helens drew worldwide attention in 1980 when its eruption killed 55 people and spread ash through five states and three Canadian provinces. Mt Hood, Mt Rainier, Mt Baker and the region around the Three Sisters have each seen eruptions in the last 500 years, and are still considered volcanically active today.

Ice-Age Floods

The climatic chill of the ice ages produced extensive glaciation in the Northwest. Almost all of British Columbia and the northern third of Washington was overlain by continental ice fields, and the mountains throughout the region were clad in glaciers. Valley glaciers trenched out the fjords and inlets of Vancouver Island and the BC mainland. (Glaciers remain in most ranges in British Columbia, and in the Cascade, Olympic and Wallowa ranges in Oregon and Washington.)

The most amazing effect of the ice ages in the Northwest, however, was not the effect of the glaciers themselves, but of the floods they caused indirectly. Glacial Lake Missoula in western Montana was formed 15,000 years ago when part of a glacier blocked the drainage of the Clark Fork River, a major Columbia River tributary. This ice dam backed up a lake containing about 500 cubic miles of water, reaching depths of more than 2000 feet. In many ways, ice isn't a very good material for making dams, because after sufficient water mass forms behind an ice dam, the dam floats, releasing the backed up water. However, after the water escapes, the glacier again begins to dam the valley, renewing the flood cycle; geologists believe that as many as 40 different catastrophic floods barreled out of Montana, heading for the Columbia Basin and the Pacific Ocean.

Each time the dam broke, an enormous surge of water thundered across central Washington and down the Columbia drainage. The floods scoured the soil off the Columbia Plateau, furrowing deep channels into the underlying basalt; these still barren and rocky plains are known as the Channeled Scablands. The flood waters dammed behind the narrow defile where the Columbia cuts through the Cascade Range, and served to trench the deep and spectacular canyon that we now know as the Columbia Gorge. Geologists claim that the floods from Glacial Lake Missoula were probably the greatest floods in the world's geological record.

CLIMATE

Generally speaking, there are two distinct weather patterns in the Pacific Northwest: west of the Cascade mountains and east of the Cascades. West of the Cascades the weather is dominated by the marine air of the Pacific Ocean. Winter temperatures are moderate, with freezing temperatures uncommon except at higher elevations. In Portland, Seattle and Vancouver, winter temperatures range from 30°F to 50°F. Summer highs occasionally reach into the 90s, though pleasant 80°F days are more the rule, and summer evenings are usually cool enough for a jacket. Spring and fall are transitional, with warm but rainy days common in the spring. Beautiful Indian summers can last well into October.

Rainfall is seasonally abundant, particularly along the coastal areas and the Coast Range, Olympic Mountains and Vancouver Island, where precipitation in excess of 100 inches falls yearly. In the interior Willamette Valley and the inland waterways of Washington and British Columbia, rainfall is more moderate; Vancouver, Seattle and Portland each receive less than 40 inches of rain a year. However, marine clouds and fog are prevalent year-round, particularly in the winter and early spring, when gray and damp weather prevails. Snowfall is heavy in the coastal ranges and the Cascade mountains, yet infrequent in the Willamette Valley, in the areas along the Puget Sound and Georgia Strait or on Vancouver Island.

The Cascades halt the flow of moist and cloudy Pacific air, allowing a continental weather pattern to prevail east of the mountains. Precipitation is much less abundant, though rainfall patterns vary greatly throughout the region. Some areas of southeastern Oregon receive as little as 4 inches of rain a year, while mountainous areas receive as much as 20 inches, with much of it as snow.

Sunshine is the norm in both winter and summer. Summer temperatures can be extreme: highs above 100°F are common, particularly along the Columbia Plateau

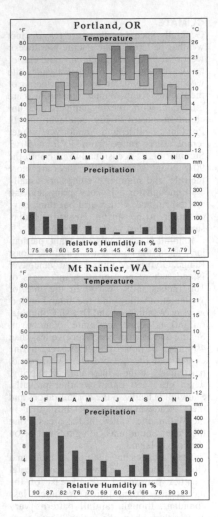

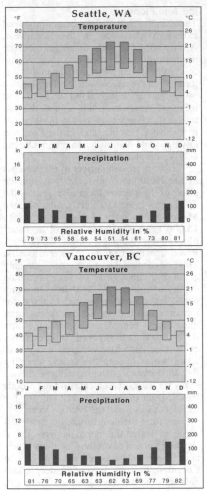

and the deserts of southern Oregon. Even in the mountains of eastern Oregon, expect summer highs in the 90s. Humidity is low, however, and evenings are cool. Snow is common throughout the area and can make for difficult driving conditions. Winter temperatures vary greatly, and can drop below 0° for short periods. Spring weather doesn't really arrive in the region until

May. Fall arrives in September, with unpredictable winter weather in tow.

ECOLOGY & ENVIRONMENT
Environmental issues dominate politics and civic life in the Northwest. The region's vast forests, mighty rivers, rocky islands and glaciered volcanic peaks are more than a touristic backdrop: the beauty of and access

to the natural world is what brought many residents to the Northwest, and preserving the environment is a deeply felt concern. However, the natural ecosystem for one person is another person's natural resource bonanza. Thus, the Northwest is home to incredibly contentious and difficult environmental issues. The traditional Northwest economy was largely based on logging and other resource-extractive industries, with the changeover to a more modern service-based economy has had tremendous impact, particularly in the rural areas and small towns. Another source of increasing concern is the endangered fish runs, especially for sea-going salmon. Just who is culpable for the species seemingly fast-approaching extinction is one of the region's most hotly contested political issues.

Logging the Old-Growth Forests

Low-cost timber sales, unsustainable harvest levels and devastating logging practices have made logging one of the region's most heated environmental issues. Much of the logging is done on national forest lands, which are administered by the government under the US Forest Service (USFS). Because the Cascades and coastal mountain ranges are densely covered with national forest lands, a traveler need not stray too far from the interstate before coming across a clear-cut – a series of hillsides logged flat and stripped of all vegetation. Clear-cutting, the most questionable logging practice, erodes hillsides and chokes streambeds (salmon habitat) with silt, and destroys wildlife habitat. And although the forests are regarded as an agricultural crop, which (in theory) can be planted and harvested indefinitely, they're being cut down much faster than they can grow back.

Due to successful lawsuits against the USFS by environmental groups seeking to protect wildlife habitat, the late 1980s and early 1990s saw federal forests closed to logging. The endangered spotted owl in particular became a political football in an emotional skirmish between environmentalists and timber interests. Once old trees

were proved to be the birds' primary nesting habitat, courts ordered millions of acres of federal forests ripe with old-growth timber to be removed from sale. Mills closed, leaving embittered loggers and mill workers to spend their days screen-printing T-shirts with anti-spotted owl slogans, such as 'I love spotted owl . . . fried.'

To ameliorate the economic loss to Northwest timber communities, the sale of national forest land is still permitted for 'salvage logging,' a practice at the center of the most recent forest battles. Muddied with environmentalist rhetoric, salvage logging asserts that forests which have been burned by fires or are diseased by wood-boring insects should be logged to protect the forest's overall health. Thrown in with the sale of charred and diseased logs, however, are stands of perfectly healthy trees, dubiously removed for 'thinning.' It wasn't long before the national forests were declared in a state of 'forest health emergency,' a concept more accurately described as a gigantic loophole through which the USFS ushered millions of dollars in money-losing timber sales.

The endangered spotted owl

Making matters worse, in 1995 President Clinton signed a congressional bill authorizing the USFS to also sell forests in the *vicinity* of any salvage area, in effect opening the doors to old-growth forests protected by previous legislation. 'Salvage' timber sales now account for 42% of all USFS timber sales.

Saving the Salmon

Logging – because it ruins mountain streams, which are the spawning habitat for salmon – is also considered a contributing factor to the decline in the Chinook salmon population. However, by far the biggest threat to salmon is hydroelectric power: on the Columbia and Snake Rivers the fish have been reduced nearly to extinction due to a series of eight massive hydroelectric dams. Every spring, salmon migrating from mountain streams in Idaho down the Snake and Columbia must face these imposing obstacles on their 800-mile journey to the ocean. Their odds are slim – two decades of menacing hydroelectric turbines have effectively reduced the adult salmon population from about 28,000 to a meager 4000.

To the dissatisfaction of Native American tribes and environmental groups, the Bonneville Power Administration (BPA) has responded to this crisis by sucking the fish out of the water, pumping them into special containerized boats and shipping the salmon downriver on barges. Activists, preferring that the fish make the trip on their own, have recently pressured the government to breach four of the dams so that the fish can safely swim around the dams. The plan is actually more cost-effective

Chinook salmon

than the BPA's current salmon enhancement efforts. However, since these rivers are also a major shipping corridor for grain and other crops coming from both Northwestern and Midwestern states (60% of the grain destined for export to Pacific Rim countries is barged down this waterway), the plan is stiffly opposed by shipping and irrigation interests.

Responsible Tourism

The landscapes and seascapes of the Pacific Northwest are incredibly beautiful. And for many travelers the whole reason to come to this part of North America is to get out into the open air and experience the deep forests, expansive deserts and ocean beaches. However, the natural environment of the Pacific Northwest is very fragile, and you should be very careful that your urge to experience these wonders doesn't end up damaging the environment you treasure.

Be sure to follow all laws regarding fishing and seafood collecting. While sport or charter fishing are almost certainly not the reasons that these fish are now threatened, restrictive catches are necessary (even though it might not seem so after looking at the piles of fish at Seattle's Pike Place Market). In fact some runs of wild salmon – particularly Chinook – and steelhead trout are very endangered and the survival of individual fish is important to the entire species continued existence. Certain shellfish, such as razor clams, are protected seasonally in order that they do not become endangered.

Soil erosion is another major problem in the rainy Pacific Northwest. Again, the original culprits here aren't hikers or recreationists, but logging companies and agriculturists who have clear-cut mountainsides and broken down stream banks. However, individual hikers need to stay on trails, as impromptu shortcuts can expose soil and form new water courses. Be sure not to remove vegetation from hillsides, and do your best not to muddy streams. Certain kinds of recreational activities are enormously erosive, and should be avoided. These include four-wheeling, dirt biking and ATVing. Even mountain biking can be destructive: be sure to obey trail signs where mountain biking is prohibited.

FLORA & FAUNA

The Cascade mountains effectively divide the Northwest into two ecosystems. West of the mountains are mossy, heavily forested valleys, while arid uplands and high deserts stretch east of the Cascades.

West of the Cascades

Flora Forests on the Pacific side of Washington, Oregon and maritime British Columbia are dense and fast growing. In established stands, you'll encounter a wide mix of trees. Dominant throughout the western valleys is the Douglas fir, a statuesque conifer that can grow to nearly 300 feet high. In coastal forests you'll also find Douglas fir, plus Sitka spruce, Western hemlock, maples, oaks and, especially along streams, red cedar.

Watch for madrone trees, with distinctive red, peeling bark and broad, though evergreen, leaves, and stands of white oak in forests on Vancouver Island and in southern Oregon. In isolated areas near the California border are several redwood groves; you can walk through old-growth redwoods along the Chetco River (near Brookings) at Loeb State Park.

In the understory of old forests grow a number of ferns, rhododendrons and the purple-fruited Oregon grape (Oregon's state flower). Fall brings bright red leaves to vine maple, salmonberries with orange fruit and omnipresent thorny blackberries that grab at clothing but provide welcome sweet snacks.

You'll discover the most recently commercialized of the Northwest's riches – wild mushrooms – on the forest floor. Chanterelle, morel, porcini and oyster mushrooms are a few of the mountains' fungal varieties. In many coastal centers, wild mushroom gathering has replaced logging as the forest's contribution to local economies. Northwest mushrooms are flown out daily from obscure rural airports to Tokyo and Paris.

Fauna Despite the area's logging history, much of the Northwest still seems wild and unpopulated. However, the lack of major wildlife reveals the fragility of its ecosystems.

Crested, blue-bodied Steller's jays are noisy and common in forests, as are enormous crows and ravens. Sharp eyes may spot rufous hummingbirds buzzing around flowers. Bird watchers may want to concentrate on the region's many varieties of woodpeckers, with the large, red-crested pileated woodpecker especially worthy of pursuit.

Notable streamside birds include blue herons, belted kingfishers and many kinds of ducks; watch for handsome, black-necked loons. Along the coast, gulls are ubiquitous, but to see other sea birds, such as puffins, cormorants or pelicans, usually requires more stealth and a pair of binoculars.

Almost all of Oregon's sea-flowing rivers and streams produce their own salmon runs; salmon must return to their own birthplace to spawn. This means that each river has essentially engendered its own native species of salmon. The salmon that run the Rogue River are not the same fish, say, that run the Skagit River. Northwestern waters are also trout-rich. Notable is the seagoing steelhead trout. Harder to spot along streams are river otters and mink; a patient stance near a logjam is usually necessary. Beavers, whose abundance was responsible for bringing white settlement to the Northwest in the first place, are still found along mountain streams.

Tide pools provide a window into the ocean. Look for sea anemones, starfish, mussels and hermit crabs. Sea mammals such as seals and sea lions are not uncommon along the coast, especially along quiet, rocky promontories. From these same outcroppings, travelers in the spring can watch for whales migrating up the coast. Those traveling by ferry between the San Juan, Vancouver and Gulf Islands are often treated to views of orcas, or killer whales.

Mule deer and elk are the most easily seen of the forests' large mammals. Black bears inhabit the deep woods and although not as dangerous as the grizzly (which isn't found here), deserve respect. If you see a bear, allow it ample time to vacate the area, which it almost certainly will do. The old saw about coming between a bear and its cubs contains a central truth: bears with young offspring are protective, which can translate into aggression. If you come upon a young bear, head back the way you came.

East of the Cascades

Flora The dry uplands east of the Cascades receive much less rain than the western valleys, and the shallow soils eroded from the region's vast lava flows don't allow for deep-rooted growth. Forests are dominated by ponderosa and lodgepole pines. The former are tall, handsome trees with long, bunched needles and characteristic cinnamon-stick colored trunks (when mature). Sporadic, low-growing western juniper trees dominate the region's extensive savannas, along with silver sage. Along prairie rivers and irrigation canals, cottonwood and poplar trees abound.

Eastern Oregon and Washington hillsides are covered in late spring with bunches of vibrantly colored yellow flowers with silvery swordlike leaves. The balsamroot was an important food source for early Native Americans, who dug this bitter, bulbous root and treated it like a potato. You will often find spectacular displays of lupine's deep-blue spikes sharing a hillside with golden balsamroot and fresh green grass shoots.

In the desert areas of southeastern Oregon, plant life is found along seasonal lakes and intermittent streams. Tule, a rush-like reed, grows in marshy lake bottoms; Native Americans used tule to weave house-building mats (large panels used as house walls). Where alkaline soils dominate, light green, spindly greasewood endures. In arid steppes, rabbit-brush, with its yellow flowers, brings the late-summer desert to bloom.

Fauna The open landscapes of central and eastern Oregon and Washington make bird life even more visible. Western meadowlark, Oregon's state bird, trills its lovely song across the region. Spot the male's telltale black 'V' on its yellow breast. Listen at dusk for the swooping whistle of the nighthawk, whose sudden dives to seize insects create a sound like a sharp, echoing intake of breath. Raptors are common: watch for falcons, hawks and, especially along the desert lakes, osprey and bald eagles.

The large rivers of central and eastern Oregon are home to salmon and various kinds of trout, though bass and sturgeon tempt anglers in the Columbia. Rainbow trout is the most common variety of sport fish, though the Deschutes River boasts its own sub-species of rainbow trout – called the red side – with ruby-red flanks.

Campers in any part of eastern Oregon and Washington are likely to be serenaded by coyotes. Large herds of elk are found in the Blue Mountains of Oregon. Mule deer are also abundant throughout the region and, with pronghorn antelope, make the area popular with hunters in the autumn. Bighorn sheep have been reintroduced into the high mountain peaks and river canyons.

The hot, dry conditions in central and eastern Oregon and Washington make for ideal snake territory. Rattlesnakes are common in rocky terrain. If you're hiking in the desert, or around boulders, watch where you put your feet. Even more importantly, if you are scrambling or climbing on rock faces, beware of the rattlers sunning themselves on the ledges.

Parks & Wildlife Refuges

The states of the Pacific Northwest have four national parks: Olympic, North Cascades and Mt Rainier National Parks in Washington; and Crater Lake National Park in Oregon. The National Park Service (NPS) also administers a number of other sites throughout the Northwest, notably the John Day Fossil Beds, Fort Clatsop and the Oregon Caves in Oregon; and the Whitman Mission and Fort Vancouver in Washington. British Columbia has six national parks, including Pacific Rim National Park on Vancouver Island.

The real riches in the Northwest, however, are the many state and provincial parks and wildlife refuges, which preserve historic and geologic curiosities, as well as valuable habitat for plants and animals. Often these less hyped sites provide more intimate contact with nature or history than the major nationally administered parks.

Oregon has, at 224, the greatest number of state parks in the nation. Washington isn't far behind, and between the two states there are over 400 state parks. Eighty of Oregon's state parks are along the coast; at times, it can seem as if the entire shoreline is one long state park. State parks throughout the region feature facilities as diverse as historic hotels, caverns, islands, museums, waterfalls, rock-climbing areas, botanical gardens and an observatory.

British Columbia counts a whopping 444 provincial parks, and over 200 'protected areas.' Practically the entire mountain skyline north of Vancouver is protected by provincial parks, and much of the inland passage between the mainland and Vancouver Island is preserved as marine parks.

Parks designed for picnicking, hiking or other daytime recreation – called day-use parks – are abundant in the Northwest. You can't camp at these (parks open for camping will have a sign stating 'camping' as well as a tent symbol).

The effect of tax revenue shortages is being felt at many state parks. Increasingly, even day-use parks demand the payment of a usage fee. Camping fees are also escalating to the point where there's not a lot of difference between camping and staying at a bottom-end motel. Expect these fees to increase even more, and for more and more facilities formerly paid for by tax dollars to become fee-based.

Wildlife refuges are increasingly a draw for travelers focused on the environment, as well as for bird watchers and plant and animal enthusiasts. Of special note are Malheur Wildlife Refuge (a wetlands marsh in the midst of a desert, and a major stopover for migrating waterfowl) and Hart Mountain National Antelope Refuge (with the largest herds of antelope in North America) in southeastern Oregon; Bear Valley National Wildlife Refuge near Klamath Falls, where the nation's greatest concentration of bald eagles winter; and the South Slough Estuarine Reserve near Coos Bay, which is an extensive and fragile preserve of coastal plant and animal life.

In Washington the Willapa Bay National Wildlife Refuge preserves a marine tide flat and bay famous for its oysters. Just north of the otherwise spooky Hanford Atomic Reservation, is the Saddle Mountain National Wildlife Refuge, which preserves the high desert plant and wildlife of the Columbia Plateau.

In British Columbia the Desolation Sound area along the Sunshine Coast is preserved as a marine park to protect these fragile ecosystems. This is an area very popular with scuba divers.

Many refuges and wilderness areas have informal campsites on or near the facility.

GOVERNMENT & POLITICS

The USA has a federal system with a president and a bicameral Congress, consisting of the 100-member Senate and the 435-member House of Representatives. Each of the 50 states has two senators and a number of representatives in proportion to its population; Oregon has five representatives, Washington nine.

The president, whose term is for four years, is chosen by the Electoral College, which consists of electors (chosen by voters) from each state equivalent to its number of senators and representatives, who vote in accordance with the popular vote within their state. To be elected, the president must obtain a majority (270 – half plus one) of the total 538 electoral votes (the District of Columbia, which has three nonvoting representatives in Congress, nevertheless has three electoral votes). The president is elected for no more than two four-year terms.

The federal government has three branches: the legislature branch makes the laws, the executive branch carries them out and the judiciary branch studies and interprets both the Constitution and the laws.

The two main political parties are the Democrats and the Republicans; smaller parties include the Green party. Currently, the presidency is held by Bill Clinton, a Democrat.

The head of the state government is the governor, who presides over a bicameral legislature consisting of a senate and a house delegation. Smaller administrative districts within the states are divided into counties and cities. Governors John Kitzhaber of Oregon and Gary Locke of Washington are Democrats.

Oregon and Washington both share a reputation for progressive, somewhat maverick politics. It's a long ways to the traditional centers of American politics on the East Coast, and people tend to look elsewhere for political leadership and innovation.

Recent important issues include preserving the wild runs of native salmon even as the Pacific Northwest is experiencing the greatest population and economic boom in its history. The salmon recovery issue is especially thorny as it pits individual states against each other (especially Oregon and Washington against Alaska), and involves cooperation with other sovereign governments such as Canada and individual Indian tribes.

In metropolitan areas in the Northwest, a major political issue is land-use planning. Oregon has had strict land-use laws on the books for years (these limit the size of cities to their pre-established urban growth boundaries in order to protect agricultural and recreational lands). However, as population density increases, cities like Portland are under pressure either to expand their urban growth boundaries into the countryside or to enforce even greater population density, a policy called urban infill.

Washington came late to land-use planning, and consequently policy makers are forced to try to put the genie back in the bottle when it comes to urban sprawl. In Seattle local politics pits developers against neighborhood activists in a battle of the city's future: Will Seattle remain a quaint city of charming neighborhoods with a dynamic livability, or will it become the cosmopolis that ate Puget Sound? Transportation infrastructure is a hot topic in Seattle as well, with everyone looking for a fix for the city's traffic nightmares – but one preferably that costs no tax dollars and one that, once built, complies with the old NIMBY rule: Not In My Back Yard.

Canada

Canada is a constitutional monarchy. That is, Canada is ruled by a parliamentary system with the head of state officially remaining the monarch of Britain. The national capital is Ottawa, Ontario.

The 10 provinces are largely self-governing and are presided over by premiers, elected provincially. Provinces are much more autonomous from the federal government than US states are of the US federal government.

Additionally, there are two Canadian territories, the Yukon and the Northwest Territories. The latter will further divide in 1999, when the eastern half will become the territory of Nunavut, effectively an Inuit homeland.

The head of the BC government is the premier, the leader of the party who seats the most representatives in the Legislative Assembly. Elections must be called every five years. The provincial capital is Victoria.

The national Canadian parties, the Liberals and the Progressive Conservatives, don't have much of a toehold in BC; instead, the pro-business, small government party – the Social Credit Party – and the party favoring a more activist government and more liberal social policies, called the New Democratic Party (NDP), do.

Most of the 1990s have seen the rise of the NDP, whom have taken over from the long run of premiers from the Social Credit Party that largely governed BC from 1952 to 1991.

Indian Reservation Self-Government

US Indian reservations are recognized by the federal government as independent political units. Legal jurisdiction on reservations, therefore, can be something of a puzzle. Canadian Indian reservations also share many of the same complexities.

Tribes have certain inherent sovereign rights. They can run their own schools, regulate transport and trade and have their own constitutions, legislative councils and tribal court and police systems. The state cannot tax reservation land or transactions that occur on reservations. While such legal considerations may not seem crucial to the traveler, the US Northwest has in effect 50 independent political entities within its borders. Visitors need to be aware that certain state laws do not apply on reservations.

State fuel and cigarette taxes aren't levied on those products sold by tribal members within reservations. State gambling restrictions likewise don't pertain to reservations, and some Northwest tribes are in the process of building casinos on their land. Some local roads on reservation land are maintained by the tribes. Do not automatically assume that there is public access; sometimes use is reserved for tribal members only. For instance, much of the Yakama Reservation in Washington is off-limits to non-Indians.

Also, not all areas are open for recreation. The state does not have authority to regulate hunting, fishing or recreation on reservations. Tribes can issue their own licenses for hunting and fishing, and may levy a user fee for hikers and campers. If you are not a tribal member, always check with tribal authorities before crossing reservation land.

ECONOMY

Even though the United States has the largest gross national product in the world of $6350 billion, the average Belgian, Norwegian or Kuwaiti has a higher per capita income. In addition, the USA's national debt, created by a truly breathtaking spate of overspending that began in the early 1980s, stands at a rough $4350 billion and keeps growing. A trade deficit of $254 billion has also been a point of concern.

Citizens of the US pay taxes on a sliding scale, with the poorest paying around 15% of personal earnings, while the richest fifth pay around 40%. The average American can expect to pay out 20% of their earnings in taxes.

While TV programs and Hollywood movies may show the flashy, wealthy side of the US, the country is as diverse in its economic circumstances as it is in its cultures. Whole areas of the USA are wealthier than others and within a city the standard of living can vary considerably from neighborhood to neighborhood. The lowest 20% of the population receives only 4.4% of the national income distribution, while the top 5% receive 17.6%.

Blessed with abundant natural resources, busy international waterways and a well-educated populace, the Pacific Northwest's economy has out-performed the US and Canadian average since the 1980s. The traditional engines of the Pacific Northwest economy have been resource-extractive industries. Logging especially has been and still is a very big business: Oregon leads the US in lumber production and British Columbia contains nearly 50% of the marketable timber in Canada. However, high-tech firms and computer hardware and software companies are fast making inroads into the economy.

Logging

The Northwest's economy has traditionally been tied to lumber and wood products. However, most of the easily cut, easily transportable trees were logged long ago. The US federal government's restrictions on logging public land has crippled much of what remained of the established forest-products industry. Also, US state laws have prohibited exportation of raw lumber from state-owned lands, leaving only private land available for old-fashioned, wide-open logging. Until very recently, logging in British Columbia has been less fettered by laws and court battles than in its sister states to the south. The BC government owns 94% of the harvestable forests in the province, and pro-business provincial governments have allowed multinational timber resource companies almost unrestricted access to the centuries-old forests.

In the highly contentious debate over logging, the spotted owl, a sensitive denizen of the old-growth forest, has become the symbol of the enormous changes taking place in the Northwest's lumber industry. In addition to the federal protection of ancient forests, many other factors have contributed to the decline of the lumber industry, including outmoded equipment, high labor costs, raw log exports to mills in East Asia and dwindling stands of adult trees. See the Ecology & Environment section for more information on the effect logging is having on the environment.

Agriculture

The moist valleys of the Rogue, Umpqua, Willamette, Skagit and Fraser Rivers combined with the temperate grasslands east of the Cascades make the Northwest an important producer of agricultural products.

Cattle and sheep graze the eastern uplands, and golden wheat fields stretch across volcanic plateaus. Federally funded irrigation projects have made the desert bloom along numerous rivers, notably the Columbia, Yakima and Deschutes. Crops as varied as marigolds, garlic, mint, potatoes, melons, grapes and onions are grown in irrigated fields east of the Cascades. Along the Columbia and Okanogan Rivers are vast orchards of apples, cherries, peaches and pears, which are produced for the international market.

West of the Cascades is a completely different picture. In the extraordinarily fertile Willamette Valley, crops are as varied as hops, sod, wheat, berries, Christmas trees and grass seed. Wine grapes planted in the northern end of the Willamette have achieved great success. Another Northwest specialty is nuts, especially walnuts and filberts. The region's mild climate makes it ideal for plant nurseries and tree farms, which comprise the Northwest's third-largest agricultural commodity.

Along the Pacific Coast, the rain-swept valleys are famous for their dairy farms, especially along the Tillamook estuary, the Rogue River and on Vancouver Island. Bulb farms are grown extensively along the Skagit River in northern Washington. Although not strictly agricultural, mushroom gathering is an increasingly fundamental part of coastal Oregon economies (see the Ecology & Environment section for more information).

Fishing

The Northwest has long been one of the world's great salmon fisheries, until hydroelectric dams – which serve to halt the migration of the seagoing fish – brought about the near extinction of the species in many rivers (see the Ecology & Environment section). Many small coastal towns have lost most of their sport-fishing industries. However, fishing for crab, cod, shark, tuna, shrimp, bottom fish and salmon continues. In contrast, oyster and mussel farming is a growth business along much of the coast.

International Trade

The ports of Seattle, Tacoma, Portland and Vancouver are among the largest on the West Coast; in fact, Vancouver is the second-busiest port in all of North America. Part of the reason for all this business is that these cities are the closest ports for imported products from Japan and Korea. Practically all of Canada's trade with the Pacific Rim passes through Vancouver. Consumer goods like TVs and electronic gadgets pour through the port of Seattle, while Japanese and Korean cars arrive in Tacoma and Portland. Portland, at the terminus of the Columbia River barge system, is also the principal grain shipment point for the West Coast. Even after all the legal restrictions, vast flotillas of logs leave the ports of Longview and Coos Bay for foreign mills.

High-Tech Industries

The Northwest is home to some of the largest high-tech firms in the world. Boeing, the largest aircraft manufacturer in the world, is the main economic engine of western Washington. Also in the Seattle area is the headquarters for Microsoft, the software giant. The suburbs west of Portland are home to software developers Techtronix and to Intel's largest 'campuses' and construction plants.

POPULATION & PEOPLE

The current population of Oregon and Washington is about 8.7 million, which amounts to about 3% of the total US population. By far the greatest concentration of people is in Washington's Puget Sound area and Oregon's Willamette Valley. Nearly three-quarters of each state's population live in these metropolitan areas. These areas are also among the fastest-growing in the USA: urban planners anticipate that Washington and Oregon will absorb another 2 million inhabitants in the next 15 years.

The population of British Columbia is 3.3 million; two-thirds of this number live in Vancouver and its suburbs. British Columbia is the fastest-growing Canadian province, due both to immigration (largely from China and southeast Asia) and from movement within Canada (BC's vibrant economy and mild climate attracts many people from eastern and maritime Canadian provinces).

The population of the Northwest states is overwhelmingly white. According to the 1990 census, Oregon is over 93% white, and Washington is 87% white. Hispanics make up the second-largest ethnic group in the Northwest, closely followed by Asians. African Americans comprise about 1.5% of the population, just slightly more than the number of Native Americans in the region. British Columbia, while largely founded by British settlers, has a much more racially mixed population than its southern neighbors. In fact, Vancouver has the largest Chinese population outside of Asia.

Native Americans

The US federal government recognizes 50 tribes in the Pacific Northwest. These federally recognized tribes have reservations or trust lands set aside for them. In addition, there are a number of Native American groups in the Northwest without federally recognized status – which is important to a tribe – or a land base. Federally recognized status is very important to a tribe. Not only is government assistance important to support tribal schools and cultural centers, but without recognition, it is difficult to maintain cultural identity. The total Native American population of Oregon and Washington is over 130,000 people.

EDUCATION

School attendance is usually obligatory to the age of 16, and almost everyone graduates from high school. However, local school districts are funded by property taxes, and consequently there are great disparities in the resources available to affluent suburbs versus the impoverished inner city neighborhoods or depressed rural areas.

The percentage of students who go to colleges or universities is much higher than in most European countries, as secondary instruction is much less rigid. There are several levels of higher education: junior or community colleges (two-year institutions with advanced career training or introductory university courses); colleges or universities with four-year baccalaureate programs; and research universities with advanced degree programs.

The largest university in the Pacific Northwest is the University of Washington in Seattle, with about 35,000 students. Other large public universities include Western Washington University in Bellingham and Washington State University in Pullman. A notable private university is Evergreen State College in Olympia, infamous for its unstructured curriculum and politically idealistic students. In Oregon the two main universities are the University of Oregon and Oregon State University, just miles apart in Eugene and Corvallis, respectively. The Oregon university system also includes Portland State University and Southern Oregon University in Ashland. Oregon's most notorious private university is undoubtedly Reed College in Portland, a haven of lefty politics, environmentalism and fairly unabashed hedonism.

Vancouver is home to a number of institutes of higher learning, including the University of British Columbia with 32,000 students, and Simon Fraser University. The University of Victoria is in the BC capital.

ARTS
Music
Portland, Vancouver and Seattle offer a full array of classical music venues, including well-respected professional symphony and opera companies, and smaller centers such as Spokane, Victoria and Eugene have community classical music companies.

Summer music festivals take music out of doors, to unlikely places like vineyards, remote islands and mountain lakes. Ask representatives of state tourist boards for a full listing of summer festivals. See Special Events in the Facts for the Visitor chapter and regional chapters for more information.

Thanks to the success of several Seattle bands – notably Nirvana and Pearl Jam – who gave birth to the post-punk rock phenomenon called grunge, the Northwest is well-known for its modern music scene. Seattle, Vancouver and Portland are filled with dark and smoky music clubs, each with youthful musicians hoping to make the leap to stardom.

The Northwest sound isn't as distinctive as it was during the grunge era, although the locals maintain a fierce loyalty to live music and clubbing. Although the alternative rock scene dominates nightlife in Northwestern cities, jazz and blues clubs – and some Celtic music bars – are also found. Check with local newspapers for listings. Country & western music is popular in smaller towns: many bars will have a local band playing familiar cowboy hits on weekend nights.

Literature
Portland and Seattle boast some of the largest independent bookstores in the nation, with author readings and signings among the cities' most popular events. Seattle claims to have the most bookstores per capita in the nation, while Portland boasts the busiest public library system per capita. Book clubs are in vogue and coffee shops bring readers out of their seclusion. Vancouver's literary scene is no less rich, with literary cafes and bookstores dotting the streets of residential neighborhoods. The standard joke is that it rains so much in the Northwest that there's little to do but read.

The Northwest isn't just a consumer of reading material, it is also a major producer. Small publishing houses abound in the Northwest, and small newspapers and tabloids are published to serve just about every interest group. The music scene is an especially rich vein for young journalists, with Seattle's *Stranger* maintaining both a high standard of writing and a truly gimlet eye. Portland's lesbian and gay community somehow manages to support three contending gay newspapers. You'll also find newspapers and magazines devoted to local wine, mushroom hunting and comic strips.

Writers also find the Northwest an accommodating place in which to live and write. Internationally recognized writers like Ken Kesey, Tom Robbins, Ursula Le Guin, Jean Auel, Anne McCaffrey, Barry Lopez, Sallie Tisdale, Robert Fulghum, Ivan Doig, Gary Snyder and JA Jance live in the Northwest states.

Vancouver and southwest BC is home to a number of noted international authors. *Generation X* chronicler Douglas Copeland lives here, as does Jane Rule *(Desert of the Heart)*. William Gibson is a science-fiction writer whose dark vision of the cyberfuture attracts a large young audience. WP Kinsella *(Shoeless Joe)* and mystery writer Lawrence Gough also make their home here.

See Literature in the Facts about Oregon and Facts about Washington chapters for additional information on writers living in Oregon and Washington. For information on some good literature about the Northwest see Books in the Facts for the Visitor chapter.

Theater & Film
Seattle and Vancouver have two of the most vibrant professional theater scenes on

the West Coast. There are apparently more equity theaters in Seattle than anywhere in the US except New York City. Portland is no slouch either: if you simply count theater companies (amateur and equity), Portland has even more venues than Seattle. Ashland, in southern Oregon, is famous for its Shakespeare Festival, with open-air and indoor productions of Elizabethan drama.

The film and TV industry are quite active in the Northwest, largely because production costs are lower here than in California and other major film centers. Portland and Seattle also have well-preserved old downtown areas that can be used to create a period mood. Seattle's skyline and quirky lifestyles are recognizable internationally thanks to such comedy films as *Sleepless in Seattle* and *Singles*. TV also mines the Northwest's reputation as a hip hotbed for Seattle-based *Frasier* and recently departed *Northern Exposure*, set in Alaska, shot in Roslyn. A far darker treatment of the Northwest's eccentric culture was *Twin Peaks*, David Lynch's odd and disturbing TV series shot in Washington in 1990. Portland also shows up as a menacing backdrop in the brooding films – like *Mala Noche* and *Drugstore Cowboy* – of Gus Van Sant, a Portland native.

Vancouver serves as the Canadian 'Hollywood'; much of the country's TV and film production takes place here, including, until recently, the filming of Fox Network's *The X-Files*.

For more about films set in the Pacific Northwest, see Films in the Facts for the Visitor chapter. Also look under Theater & Film in Facts about Oregon and Facts about Washington.

Visual Arts

The Northwest has a lively and sophisticated art scene, based largely in Portland, Seattle, Vancouver, the Oregon coast, Victoria and the San Juan Islands.

One of the most noted art forms in the Northwest is art glass from the Pilchuk School in the Puget Sound area, where artisans seek to create a sculptural yet fluid substantiality out of brightly colored blown glass. Dale Chihuly is the most prominent of many glass artists in the Seattle area.

A number of galleries also feature contemporary and historic Native American art from the Northwest.

SOCIETY & CONDUCT

Visitors from other parts of the world are often struck by the informality of Northwesterners: dressing up and putting on airs is not a part of life for very many people, even in situations where formal dressing is usually expected (ie, the opera or dining out). In general, this is good news for travelers, who don't have to worry much about dress codes at restaurants, concerts or social functions.

In a broad sense, the Northwest shares the general US and Canadian culture, but with a few important twists. Parts of eastern Oregon and Washington are very rural; the culture of the Old West and the cowboy is still very much alive here. Fishing towns along the coast and islands have a distinctive and often gritty sensibility that comes from making a living on the stormy and dangerous Pacific Ocean. Urban dwellers get out of town on weekends to ski, hike, climb or windsurf. It's fair to say that the natural environment is an overriding and cherished part of life for most people in this region.

The Northwest still puts a lot of emphasis on 'old family' legitimacy and connections. People who can boast ancestors who came across the Oregon Trail, or who were early Brits in Victoria, are inordinately proud of their birthright. Northwesterners will notice if you have a last name like Applegate, or share a surname with a frontier-era county. While not exactly clubby, there are certainly some longtime Northwesterners who differentiate between newcomers (ie, anyone who moved to the region after WWII) and members of old families.

While most urban Americans and Canadians are tolerant of individual eccentricities, rural Northwesterners in particular may be skeptical of outsiders and may resent what they perceive as an unfair criticism of their country or as interference in local matters. Visitors should try to be aware of local political issues – don't broadcast your animal rights convictions in a bar full of hunters or denounce clear-cutting in a mill town, for example, without having some idea of your audience.

RELIGION

The US Constitution mandates separation of church and state and tolerance is the norm. However, matters like prayer in public schools and abortion have brought theological issues onto the secular stage. Nominal allegiance is more widespread than church attendance, but many church-goers are extremely devout.

The oldest religions in North America are Native American religions, which have been greatly modified since contact with the Europeans. Some, like the Native American Church, which uses hallucinatory peyote buttons as a sacrament, are in part pan-Indian responses to encroachment by the politically dominant culture.

The dominant religion in the US and Canada is Christianity, with Catholicism and Protestant sects roughly equal in number of adherents. The Mormon church is prevalent throughout the Northwest.

Judaism, Islam and Buddhism are also represented in urban areas. Rural areas, especially in the Willamette Valley are home to Mennonites and Protestant communes (there's a Russian Old Believer community in the Willamette Valley, and a Dukhobor enclave in BC, not too far from the city of Vancouver).

The libertarian Northwest also attracts a number of religious sects of dubious derivation. The most famous of these was the cult of the Bhagwan Shree Rajneesh, who built a religious empire in central Oregon before federal marshals deported him and jailed some of his followers on a variety of charges, including attempted murder (see the Bhagwan Shree Rajneesh sidebar in the Northeastern Oregon chapter).

Nature religions also have a firm foothold in the Northwest, perhaps due to the Celtic gloom that presides here much of the year. Forms of Wicca (a pagan nature religion), and a myriad of other nature-based spiritual movements, are found in the woods of western Oregon, Washington and British Columbia.

Oregon has the distinction of having the lowest churchgoing rate in the USA. Evangelist Billy Graham cited this fact when he brought his crusade to Portland in 1992.

Facts for the Visitor

This chapter provides travel information primarily for the US. For additional information on traveling to British Columbia's Vancouver and Vancouver Island, including details on customs, border crossing and money, see the Traveling to Canada sidebar in the beginning of the Vancouver chapter.

PLANNING
When to Go
When to visit the Pacific Northwest depends largely on what you want to do when you get there.

Most travelers choose to visit the region in the summer and fall, when the weather is pleasant and rainfall infrequent. If your trip includes hiking and camping, then it's best to plan to be west of the Cascades after May, when the weather has settled down a bit (this part of the region receives 65% of its precipitation from November to March). September and October are often glorious months, as the Indian summer brings warm days and cool nights. In the bountiful Northwest, there is a palpable sense of harvest in the autumn, with

---

You know you're In the Pacific Northwest if...

- you make $30,000 a year, yet still can't find a place to live
- you know the vast differences among Coffee People, Torrefazione and Starbucks
- you can list more than five reasons why Starbucks is evil
- every July 1st it takes half a day to find your sunglasses and sunscreen
- anything not right you blame on ex-Californians
- you remember where you were and how long the power was out for every winter weather event over the last five years
- it's not unusual in a coffee bar to see two guys get into a fight over who makes the best IPA
- you own more than 10 articles of clothing with the names of microbreweries/brewpubs printed on them – bonus for embroidered stuff
- you have a bookstore, coffee bar and brewpub within walking distance of your house
- you think downtown is 'scary' because you were panhandled there once

- you can point in the direction of two or more volcanoes even though you can't see them because of the clouds
- when you drive out of town even the Hondas have gun racks
- you can name more than 10 kinds of berries and where to get them
- you can name more than 10 beer styles and their hop profiles
- when the weather gets above 50°F, you put on your shorts, but you still wear your hiking boots and parka
- when the weather gets above 60°F, you replace your hiking boots with sandals
- you think umbrellas are for wimps
- you're at a red light surrounded by Subaru Legacy Outbacks
- 'today's forecast – showers, followed by rain; tomorrow – rain, followed by showers' doesn't faze you
- you can't wait for a day with 'showers and sunbreaks'
- you go skiing after work
- you live equidistant to a symphony hall, a winery and a volcano ■

---

apples, pears, wine grapes, nuts and vegetables all ripe at once. The weather begins to deteriorate after October, when the gray Pacific pall moves in and the rains begin.

Spring comes to eastern Oregon and Washington in May; a trip to the high desert and the eastern mountain ranges in May and June will reward the traveler with beautiful weather and wildflower viewing.

If your itinerary brings you to the Northwest in winter, all is not lost. Many cultural events like the symphony, opera and theater are most active during winter months. The Northwest features some incredible skiing at Whistler in BC, Oregon's Mt Bachelor and Mt Hood, and Snoqualmie Pass and Stevens Pass in Washington.

Winter also brings storms to the Pacific Coast, and coastal towns are often busy at such times with 'storm watchers' – people who come to the coast to watch and be part of the spectacular weather changes, high winds and waves that batter the coast.

Maps

Highway Maps The American Automobile Association (AAA) issues the most comprehensive and dependable highway maps, which are free with an AAA membership (see Useful Organizations) or available for a price to nonmembers. These range from national, regional and state maps to very detailed maps of cities, counties and even relatively small towns. (The Canadian equivalent is the Canadian Automobile Association, or CAA, which offers parallel services and products. Membership privileges between the AAA and the CAA are reciprocal.)

State and provincial Depts of Transportation put out free maps that are widely available from tourist offices or by calling the appropriate tourism hotlines. Oregon also prints a specialized map of campsites for campers; ask at the visitors' center.

Topographic Maps The US Geological Survey (USGS), an agency of the federal Dept of the Interior, publishes very detailed topographic maps of the entire country, at different scales up to 1:250,000. Maps at 1:62,500, or approximately 1 inch:1 mile, are ideal for backcountry hiking and backpacking. Some private cartographers are producing updated versions of old USGS maps at 1:62,500. Many bookstores and outdoor equipment specialists carry a wide selection of topographic maps.

Atlases Visitors spending any significant amount of time in the USA should try to acquire the appropriate state volume of the DeLorme Mapping series of atlases and gazetteers, which contain detailed topographic and highway maps at a scale of 1:250,000. Available in some bookstores, these are especially useful off the main highways and cost about $20 each.

What to Bring

The Northwest is a very casual place, so pack the clothes that you are comfortable wearing. Even if your trip will include dining out or attending formal events, there's no special need to wear formal clothes: people in the Northwest do dress up, they just don't require it.

Summers are usually warm, but not too humid. Evenings are often cool, so bring a jacket. In all seasons but the height of summer, it's a good idea to bring a rain jacket, or at least an umbrella. Don't bring clothing that can't stand up to a little rain.

Unless you are planning a sustained mountain trip in winter, heavy winter gear isn't usually necessary. Winters in western Oregon, Washington and BC are usually chilly and wet, but not extremely cold. If you're planning to travel in the eastern parts of these areas, take along a windproof coat, gloves, hat and scarf.

If you're planning on camping, make sure that your tent is waterproof: Northwest dews are as heavy as rain showers elsewhere. Nights will be cool, so bring a reasonable weight sleeping bag. Hiking trails are often muddy; dedicating a pair of shoes (tennis shoes are usually OK unless you're planning strenuous outings) to trail walking and beachcombing is probably a good idea.

In all seasons, it's wise to bring along a pair of binoculars. You'll be glad to have them when you spot your first sea lion or bighorn sheep. Likewise, consider bringing along or buying a good wildlife or wild-flower guide. There is a rich diversity of plants and animals in the Northwest, and you'll end up wishing that you knew how to identify them.

HIGHLIGHTS

The Pacific Northwest is a large area, and it will take travelers at least a couple of weeks to truly capture the breadth and diversity of this region. However, shorter trips can serve to capture the flavor and spirit of the place.

Most travelers are drawn to the western edge of the region, to the coastal regions and the cities of Portland, Seattle and Vancouver; remember that while the region itself is large, these cities are each only six hours apart, south to north, by car. If visiting urban centers isn't what you had in mind for a Northwest adventure, the Oregon coast, the San Juan Islands and Vancouver Island are great destinations for adventurous travelers. Eastern Oregon is a region of great beauty and incredible landscapes; any traveler who likes off-the-beaten-path adventures should consider a detour.

The following highlights give an indication of what your itinerary might include.

Oregon

Although a sizable city, Portland has a small-town feel, with ample parks and gardens, a clean and accessible downtown and an easygoing pace. There's plenty of culture as well, with a noted symphony, a lively club scene and excellent restaurants.

The Oregon coast is one of the most beautiful parts of the region – spectacular cliffs drop off into the throbbing surf, small towns cling to rocky escarpments and wild, forested mountains rise into the Pacific mists.

Mt Hood rises like a white incisor above northern Oregon, and provides year-round skiing, plus great summer hiking and camping. The mile-wide Columbia River carves a majestically deep gorge through the Cascade mountains just north of Mt Hood. Spectacular waterfalls, such as the 640-foot-high Multnomah Falls, spill over the edge of the gorge and tumble into the Columbia River. Oregon's only national park, Crater Lake National Park, contains the continent's deepest lake at 1932 feet – a startlingly blue-green souvenir of an immense volcanic explosion.

East of the Cascades, the three units of the John Day Fossil Beds National Monument are among the most overlooked but fascinating side trips in the state. At Steens Mountain in southeastern Oregon, a scenic road winds up the back of an immense fault block to vistas where the mountain drops away in astonishing 5000-foot cliffs onto a barren desert.

Washington

The largest and most exciting city in the Northwest, Seattle is the natural center of exploration. Beautiful and cosmopolitan, Seattle is famous for its youthful music scene, good restaurants and lively street life. The San Juan Islands, northwest of Seattle toward Vancouver Island, are small rural islands with a sleepy pace and an abundance of cozy resorts and B&Bs. West of Seattle rises the Olympic Peninsula, whose rugged glacier-hung peaks are enclosed in the Olympic National Park.

Washington's wide band of Cascade peaks is a mecca for outdoor recreationists. Towering Mt Rainier, the region's highest peak at 14,411 feet, is the centerpiece of one of the oldest national parks. The jumbled and serrated peaks of the North Cascades are also protected as a national park. Mt St Helens, famous for its massive 1980 eruption, is laced by hiking trails today. A brand-new visitors' center looks into the volcano's crater and provides information about the rebirth of life in the charred blast zone.

Vancouver & Victoria

The largest city on the Canadian west coast, and the second-largest English-speaking city in the country, Vancouver is an international center of culture, business and the arts. Its beautiful setting – below snow-covered peaks on a series of peninsulas jutting into the sea – only increases the pleasure of visiting this vital and cosmopolitan city. Food, museums, and accommodations are world class.

Victoria, on Vancouver island, is a study in contrasts. Self-consciously quaint, Victoria is an open-air museum of English gentility. The old town center, facing onto a lovely bay, is a preserve of late Victorian architecture. It's not all tea and scones, however: up-to-date Northwest cuisine reigns in the dining rooms; there's hearty recreation to be had on land and sea; and clubs and pubs thunder until the wee hours.

TOURIST OFFICES

Oregon, Washington and British Columbia have state and provincial tourist bureaus that offer glossy guides, maps and scads of other pertinent travel information. If you have any special interest (ie, wineries, B&Bs, ranch vacations, fishing trips, etc), be sure to ask a tourist bureau representative for information. Individual cities and regions also have tourist offices; addresses and phone numbers for these are in the text.

Oregon

In Oregon contact the Oregon Tourism Commission (☎ 800-547-7842 out of state, 800-543-8838 in state), 775 Summer St, Salem, OR 97310 for tourist information.

When you call, write or visit a tourist information office in Oregon, there are a few publications that you should be sure to ask for: *Where To Stay In Oregon*, a listing of accommodations throughout the state, with prices and amenities noted; the official state road map; a state campground map; the *Oregon State Park Guide*; an Oregon events calendar; and, if you're planning on outdoor recreation, *Oregon Outdoors*, the official directory to outfitters and guides.

Oregon: The Official Travel Guide, a glossy magazine-size publication, is a good introduction to the state and its regions. It also contains addresses of local tourism bureaus and tourist facilities.

Washington

In Washington contact the Washington State Tourism Division (☎ 360-586-2088, 800-544-1800), 101 General Administration Bldg, AX-13, Olympia, WA 98504-1800. Washington also has several staffed point-of-entry visitors' centers stationed around the state, many at rest areas near the state's borders. Except for the Vancouver/Fourth Plain information center off I-5, which is open year-round, these centers are open from May to September only. The visitors' center at Sea-Tac International Airport (at baggage claim No 9) is open year-round.

Order the comprehensive *Washington State Field Guide* from the Washington State Tourism Division (☎ 800-544-1800 ext 001). Ask them to throw in a copy of the *Washington State Lodging & Travel Guide* and a map, and you should have all the information and special interest contacts you'll ever need. Just in case, the tourist division headquarters (☎ 360-586-2088) can be reached 9 am to 4 pm weekdays to answer your questions.

Vancouver & Vancouver Island

Tourism BC (☎ 604-663-6000, 800-663-6000 in North America, 250-387-1642 overseas), PO Box 9830, Stn Prov Govt, Victoria, BC V8W 9W5, is the name of the body which operates the province's comprehensive tourism infrastructure. It produces a mountain of literature covering just about everything the visitor needs to know.

Tourism BC also oversees a broad network of well-signposted tourist offices – called Travel InfoCentres – throughout BC, many of which operate as an arm of, or in conjunction with, the local chamber of commerce. To contact Vancouver's local tourist office, write or call the Vancouver InfoCentre (☎ 604-683-2000), Waterfront Centre, 200 Burrard St, Vancouver, BC V6C 3L6. For tourist information on Victoria and beyond, contact the Victoria Info-

Centre (☎ 250-953-2033), at 18 Wharf St, Victoria, BC V8W 1T3.

Some tourist offices (mainly those located in towns) are open year-round but the majority are seasonal, only opening their doors between April or May and the first weekend in September.

Tourism BC also offers a free accommodations reservation service; just call and the representative can discuss your itinerary and make the appropriate reservations. When requesting information, be sure to ask for a free map and a copy of the accommodations guide.

VISAS & DOCUMENTS

All important documents should be photocopied (passport data page and visa page, credit cards, travel insurance policy, air/bus/train ticket, driver's license etc) before you leave home. Leave one copy with someone at home and keep another one with you, separate from the originals. There's nothing worse than losing your identity on a trip.

Make sure you bring a picture ID with you (either a driver's license with a photo on it or some other form of ID). You'll need a picture ID to show that you are over 21 (or over 19 in Canada) to buy alcohol or gain admission to bars or clubs.

Passports & Visas

To enter the US, Canadians must have proper proof of Canadian citizenship, such as a citizenship card with photo ID or a passport. Visitors from other countries must have a valid passport and many visitors also require a US visa.

However, there is a reciprocal visa-waiver program in which citizens of certain countries may enter the USA for stays of 90 days or less with a passport but without first obtaining a US visa. Currently these countries are Andorra, Argentina, Australia, Austria, Belgium, Brunei, Denmark, Finland, France, Germany, Iceland, Ireland, Italy, Japan, Liechtenstein, Luxembourg, Monaco, The Netherlands, New Zealand, Norway, San Marino, Slovenia, Spain, Sweden, Switzerland and the United Kingdom. Under this program you must have a roundtrip ticket that is nonrefundable in the USA, and you will not be allowed to extend your stay beyond 90 days.

Other travelers will need to obtain a visa from a US consulate or embassy. In most countries the process can be done by mail.

Your passport should be valid for at least six months longer than your intended stay in the USA and you'll need to submit a 1½-inch-square (37mm x 37mm) recent photo with the application. Documents of financial stability and/or guarantees from a US resident are sometimes required, particularly for those from Third World countries.

Visa applicants may be required to 'demonstrate binding obligations' that will ensure their return to their countries. Because of this requirement, those planning to travel through other countries before arriving in the USA are generally better off applying for their US visa while they are still in their home country – rather than while on the road.

The most common visa is the Non-Immigrant Visitors Visa; B1 for business purposes, B2 for tourism or visiting friends and relatives. A visitor's visa is good for one or five years with multiple entries, and it specifically prohibits the visitor from taking paid employment in the USA. The validity period for US visitor visas depends on what country you're from. The length of time you'll be allowed to stay in the USA is ultimately determined by US immigration authorities at the port of entry. If you're coming to the USA to work or study, you will probably need a different type of visa, and the company or institution to which you're going should make the arrangements. You should allow six months in advance for processing the application. For information on work visas and employment in the US, see Work later in this chapter.

Visa Extensions & Re-Entry

If you want, need, or hope to stay in the USA longer than the date stamped on your passport, go to the local INS office (or call ☎ 800-755-0777, or look in the local white pages telephone directory under US Government) *before* the stamped date to apply for an extension. Anytime after that will usually lead to an unamusing conversation with an INS official who will assume you want to work illegally. If you find yourself in that situation, it's a good idea to bring a US citizen with you to vouch for your character. It's also a good idea to have some verification that you have enough money to support yourself.

Alternatively, cross the border into Mexico or Canada, and apply for another period of entry when you come back. US officials don't usually collect the Departure Record cards (which are handed out on planes) from your passport when you leave at a land border, so they may not notice if you've overstayed by a couple of days. Returning to the USA, you go through the same procedure as when you entered the USA for the first time, so be ready with your proposed itinerary and evidence of sufficient funds. If you try this border hopping more than once, to get a third six-month period of entry, you may find the INS very strict. Generally it seems that they are reluctant to let you stay more than a year. See Entering the USA in the Getting There & Away chapter for more information on Arrival/Departure Cards.

Travel Insurance
No matter how you're traveling, make sure you take out travel insurance. This should cover you not only for medical expenses and luggage theft or loss, but also for cancellations or delays in your travel arrangements, and everyone should be covered for the worst possible case, such as an accident that requires hospital treatment and a flight home.

Coverage depends on your insurance and type of ticket, so ask both your insurer and your ticket-issuing agency to explain the finer points. STA Travel and Council Travel offer travel insurance options at reasonable prices. Ticket loss is also covered by travel insurance. Make sure you have a separate record of all your ticket details – or better still, a photocopy of it. Also make a copy of your policy, in case the original is lost.

Buy travel insurance as early as possible. If you buy it the week before you fly, you may find, for instance, that you're not covered for delays to your flight caused by strikes or other industrial action that may have been in force before you took out the insurance.

Insurance may seem very expensive – but it's nowhere near the cost of a medical emergency in the USA.

Driver's License
A driver's license is a valid form of ID. An International Driving Permit is a useful accessory for foreign visitors in the USA. Local traffic police are more likely to accept it as valid identification than an unfamiliar document from another country. Your national automobile association can provide one for a small fee, and they're usually valid for one year.

Hostel Card
Most hostels in the USA are members of Hostelling International/American Youth Hostel (HI/AYH), which is affiliated with the International Youth Hostel Federation (IYHF). You can purchase membership on the spot when checking in, although it's probably advisable to purchase it before you leave home. Most hostels allow nonmembers to stay but charge them a few dollars more.

Student & Youth Cards
If you're a student, get an international student ID or bring along a school or university ID card to take advantage of the discounts available to students.

Seniors' Cards
All people over the age of 65 get discounts throughout the USA. All you need is ID with proof of age should you be carded. There are organizations such as AARP (see Senior Travelers) that offer membership

cards for further discounts and extend coverage to citizens of other countries.

Automobile Association Membership Cards

If you plan on doing a lot of driving in the USA, it would be beneficial to join your national automobile association. For information, see Useful Organizations, later in this chapter.

Lost or Stolen Documents

Carry a photocopy of your passport separately from your passport. Copy the pages with your photo and personal details, passport number and US visa. If it is lost or stolen, this will make replacing it easier. In this event, you should call your embassy. You can find your embassy's telephone number by dialing ☎ 202-555-1212 (directory inquiries for Washington, DC).

Similarly, carry copies of your traveler's check numbers and credit card numbers separately. If you lose your credit cards or they get stolen, contact the company immediately (see the Money section for company phone numbers). Contact your bank if you lose your ATM card.

EMBASSIES & CONSULATES

US diplomatic offices abroad include the following:

Australia
    21 Moonah Place, Yarralumla ACT 2600
    (☎ 2-6270-5900)
    Level 59 MLC Center 19-29 Martin Place,
    Sydney NSW 2000
    (☎ 2-9373-9200)
    553 St Kilda Rd, Melbourne, Victoria
    (☎ 3-9526-5900)
Canada
    100 Wellington St, Ottawa, Ontario K1P 5T1
    (☎ 613-238-5335)
    1095 W Pender St, Vancouver, BC V6E 2M6
    (☎ 604-685-1930)
    1155 rue St-Alexandre, Montreal, Quebec
    (☎ 514-398-9695)
France
    2 rue Saint Florentin, 75001 Paris
    (☎ 01 42 96 12 02)

Germany
    Deichmanns Aue 29, 53179 Bonn
    (☎ 228-33-91)
Ireland
    42 Elgin Rd, Ballsbridge, Dublin
    (☎ 1-687-122)
Japan
    1-10-5 Akasaka Chome, Minato-ku, Tokyo
    (☎ 3-224-5000)
Netherlands
    Lange Voorhout 102, 2514 EJ The Hague
    (☎ 70-310-9209)
    Museumplein 19, 1071 DJ Amsterdam
    (☎ 20-310-9209)
New Zealand
    29 Fitzherbert Terrace, Thorndon,
    Wellington
    (☎ 4-722-068)
UK
    5 Upper Grosvenor St, London W1
    (☎ 0171-499-9000)
    3 Regent Terrace, Edinburgh EH7 5BW
    (☎ 31-556-8315)
    Queens House, Belfast BT1 6EQ
    (☎ 232 328 239)

Consulates in the USA

Addresses and phone numbers of foreign diplomatic representatives can be found in the yellow pages under 'Consulates.' Most nations' principal diplomatic representation is in Washington, DC. To find out the telephone number of your embassy or consulate in DC, call ☎ 202-555-1212.

There are no embassies in the Northwest states or BC. However, 26 nations maintain consular offices in Seattle, 14 in Portland and 40 in Vancouver. Many of these are not regular offices, but rather individuals who represent their native countries in ceremonial functions. To find addresses and numbers of consular offices in Portland, Seattle and Vancouver, look under 'Consulates' in the appropriate yellow pages.

CUSTOMS

US Customs allows each person over the age of 21 to bring 1 liter of liquor and 200 cigarettes duty-free into the USA. US citizens are allowed to import, duty-free, $400 worth of gifts from abroad, and non-US citizens are allowed to bring in $100 worth.

Should you be carrying more than $10,000 in US and foreign cash, traveler's checks, money orders or the like, you need to declare the excess amount. There is no legal restriction on the amount that may be imported, but undeclared sums in excess of $10,000 may be subject to confiscation.

MONEY
Currency & Exchange Rates
The US dollar is divided into 100 cents (¢). Coins come in denominations of 1¢ (penny), 5¢ (nickel), 10¢ (dime), 25¢ (quarter) and the seldom seen 50¢ (half-dollar). There is also a $1 coin that the government has tried unsuccessfully to bring into mass circulation (called the Susan B Anthony Dollar); you may get it as change from ticket and stamp machines. Be aware that these coins look similar to quarters. Quarters are the most commonly used coins in vending machines and parking meters, so it's handy to have a stash of them. Notes, commonly called bills, come in $1, $2, $5, $10, $20, $50, and $100 denominations – $2 bills are rare, but perfectly legal.

Most banks will exchange cash or traveler's checks in major foreign currencies, though banks in outlying areas don't do so very often, and it may take them some time. It's probably less of a hassle to exchange foreign currency in larger cities. Additionally, Thomas Cook, American Express, and exchange windows in international airports offer exchange (although you'll get a better rate at a bank).

At press time, exchange rates were:

Australia	A$1	=	$0.62
Canada	C$1	=	$0.68
France	FF1	=	$0.16
Germany	DM1	=	$0.55
Hong Kong	HK$10	=	$0.13
Japan	¥100	=	$0.69
New Zealand	NZ$1	=	$0.52
United Kingdom	UK£1	=	$1.60

What to Carry
Cash & Traveler's Checks Though it is more risky to carry cash it's still a good idea to travel with some for the conve-nience; it's useful to help pay all those tips and some smaller, more remote places may not accept credit cards or traveler's checks. Traveler's checks offer greater protection from theft or loss and in many places can be used as cash. American Express and Thomas Cook are widely accepted and have efficient replacement policies.

Keeping a record of the check numbers and the checks you have used is vital when it comes to replacing lost checks. Keep this record separate from the checks themselves.

You'll save yourself trouble and expense if you buy traveler's checks in US dollars. The savings you *might* make on exchange rates by carrying traveler's checks in a foreign currency don't make up for the hassle of exchanging them at banks and other facilities. Restaurants, hotels and most stores accept US-dollar traveler's checks as if they were cash, so if you're carrying traveler's checks in US dollars, the odds are you'll rarely have to use a bank or pay an exchange fee.

Take most of the checks in large denominations. It's only toward the end of a stay that you may want to change a small check to make sure you aren't left with too much local currency.

Credit & Debit Cards Major credit cards are accepted at hotels, restaurants, gas stations, shops and car-rental agencies throughout the USA. In fact, you'll find it hard to perform certain transactions such as renting a car or purchasing tickets to performances without one.

Even if you loathe credit cards and prefer to rely on traveler's checks and Automatic Teller Machines (ATMs), it's a good idea to carry one for emergencies. If you're planning to rely primarily upon credit cards, it would be wise to have a Visa or MasterCard in your deck, since other cards aren't as widely accepted.

Places that accept Visa and MasterCard are also likely to accept debit cards. Unlike a credit card, a debit card deducts payment directly from the user's checking account. Instead of an interest rate, users are charged a minimal fee for the transaction. Be sure to check with your bank to confirm that your debit card will be accepted in other states – debit cards from large commercial banks can often be used worldwide. For information on what to do if you lose a credit card see Emergency below.

Carry copies of your credit card numbers separately from the cards. If you lose your credit cards or they get stolen, contact the company immediately. Following are toll-free numbers for the main credit card companies. Contact your bank if you lose your ATM card.

American Express	☎ 800-528-4800
Diners Club	☎ 800-234-6377
Discover	☎ 800-347-2683
MasterCard	☎ 800-826-2181
Visa	☎ 800-336-8472

Changing Money
ATMs ATMs are a convenient way of obtaining cash from a bank account back home (within the USA or from abroad). Even small-town banks in the middle of nowhere have ATMs. They are common in most shopping areas.

Most banks have these machines, which are available 24 hours a day. There are various ATM networks and most banks are affiliated with several. Exchange, Accel, Plus and Cirrus are the predominant networks in the Northwest. For a nominal service charge, you can withdraw cash from an ATM using a credit card or a charge card. Credit cards usually have a 2% fee with a $2 minimum, but using bank cards linked to your personal checking account is usually far cheaper. Check with your bank or credit card company for exact information.

International Transfers You can instruct your bank back home to send you a draft. Specify the city, bank and branch to which you want your money directed, or ask your home bank to tell you where a suitable one is, and make sure you get the details right. The procedure is easier if you've authorized someone back home to access your account.

Expect money sent by telegraphic transfer to reach you within a week; by mail allow at least two weeks. When it arrives it will most likely be converted into local currency – you can take it as cash or buy traveler's checks.

You can also transfer money by American Express, Thomas Cook or Western Union, though the latter has fewer international offices.

Security
You should be cautious – but not paranoid – about carrying money. If your hotel or hostel has a safe, keep your valuables and excess cash in it. It's best not to display large amounts of cash in public. A money belt worn under your clothes is a good place to carry excess currency when you're on the move or otherwise unable to stash it in a safe. Avoid carrying your wallet in a back pocket of your pants. This is a prime target for pickpockets, as are handbags and the outside pockets of day packs and fanny packs (bum bags). See Dangers & Annoyances, later in this chapter.

Costs
Cost for accommodations vary seasonally, between the cities and the countryside, and between resorts and everywhere else. Generally rates are higher in summer, between Memorial Day and Labor Day, but winter rates at ski resorts can be astronomical. The cheapest motel rates will usually be in the $25 to $35 range, and cities will have inexpensive hotels as well. Rustic camping can be inexpensive, only about $10 or so per night, but only costlier formal sites have amenities like hot showers. Additionally, many public campgrounds in state parks or national forests have increased their fees drastically due to cutbacks in government funds.

Food can be very reasonable. The occasional splurge at a first-rate restaurant will cost anywhere between $25 and $35 depending on where you are, but good restaurant meals can be found for $10 – or even half that for some lunch specials. If you purchase food at markets you can get by even more cheaply.

Intercity public transportation costs are relatively inexpensive; buses or subways will cost anywhere from 80¢ to $1.50 depending on distance and the system; some regional bus companies offer free transport.

Owning or renting a car is much less expensive than in other parts of the world. In many areas of the Pacific Northwest, a car is really the only way of getting around. Rental cars are fairly inexpensive in most large cities, and gasoline costs a fraction of what it does in Europe and most of the rest of the world.

See the Getting Around chapter for more information on purchasing a car.

Tipping

Tipping is expected in restaurants and better hotels, and by taxi drivers, hairdressers and baggage carriers. In restaurants, wait staff are paid minimal wages and rely upon tips for their livelihoods. Tip 15% unless the service is terrible (in which case a complaint to the manager is warranted) or up to 20% if the service is great. Never tip in fast-food, take-out or buffet-style restaurants where you serve yourself.

Taxi drivers expect 10% and hairdressers get 15% if their service is satisfactory. Baggage carriers (skycaps in airports, attendants in hotels) get $1 per bag and 50¢ for each additional bag. In budget hotels (where there aren't attendants anyway) tips are not expected.

Special Deals

The USA is probably the most promotion-oriented society on earth. Though the bargaining common in many other countries is not generally accepted in the US, you can work angles to cut costs.

For example, at hotels in the off-season, casually and respectfully mentioning a competitor's rate may prompt a manager to lower the quoted rate. Artisans may consider a negotiated price for large purchases. Discount coupons are widely available – check circulars in Sunday papers, at supermarkets, tourist offices, or chambers of commerce.

Taxes & Refunds

Almost everything you pay for in the USA is taxed. Occasionally, the tax is included in the advertised price (eg, plane tickets, gas, drinks in a bar and entrance tickets for museums or theaters). Restaurant meals and drinks, accommodations, and most other purchases are taxed, and this is added to the advertised cost. Unless otherwise stated, the prices given in this book don't reflect local taxes.

One exception to the above general rule is Oregon, which has no sales tax or value-added tax (VAT), only one of three states in the US that can claim that distinction. Washington's base state sales tax is 6.5%; counties and cities can assess an additional few percent on top of this, so the actual rate of tax varies from community to community. This tax is not levied on food in grocery stores; it does, however, apply to food in restaurants. BC assesses the national Canadian Goods and Services Tax (GST) of 7%, and also a provincial sales tax of 7%. If you're not Canadian you can request that your federal GST expenditures be rebated (see the Vancouver chapter for details).

When inquiring about hotel or motel rates, be sure to ask whether taxes are included or not. The so-called 'Bed Tax' is a percentage tax added to the cost of accommodations in motels, hotels, lodges and B&Bs in all US states in the Northwest (the tax is usually levied on all charges accrued at the accommodation, including everything from phone calls to parking fees to room service). These fees normally range from 4% to 7% (though they can be much higher), and vary from community to community. In parts of Seattle, the room tax is over 15%, which can be a significant additional cost.

POST & COMMUNICATIONS
Postal Rates

US postage rates increase every few years. At the time of writing, rates for 1st-class mail within the USA are 32¢ for letters up to 1oz (23¢ for each additional ounce) and 20¢ for postcards.

International airmail rates (except to Canada and Mexico) are 60¢ for a half-ounce letter, $1 for a 1oz letter and 40¢ for each additional half ounce. International postcard rates are 50¢. Letters to Canada are 46¢ for a half-ounce letter, 52¢ for a 1oz letter and 40¢ for a postcard. Letters to Mexico are 40¢ for a half-ounce letter, 46¢ for a 1oz letter and 35¢ for a postcard. Aerogrammes are 50¢.

The cost for parcels airmailed anywhere within the USA is $3 for 2lb or less, increasing by $1 per pound up to $6 for 5lb. For heavier items, rates differ according to the distance mailed. Books, periodicals and computer disks can be sent by a cheaper 4th-class rate.

For full details on Canada's postal system, go to a post office in BC; full-page pamphlets which explain all the various options, categories, requirements and prices are available.

Sending Mail

If you have the correct postage, you can drop your mail into any blue (or in Canada, red) mailbox. However, to send a package 16oz or larger, you must bring it to a post office. If you need to buy stamps or weigh your mail, go to the nearest post office. The address of each town's main post office is given in the text. In addition, larger towns have branch post offices and post office centers in some supermarkets and drugstores. For the address of the nearest, call the main post office listed under 'Postal Service' in the blue US Government section of the white pages telephone directory, or call the United States Postal Service at ☎ 800-275-8777.

Usually, post offices in main towns are open 8 am to 5 pm, Monday to Friday and 8 am to 3 pm Saturday, but it all depends on the branch; call first. If the branch has a local phone number, it is given in the text; otherwise, call USPS at the number listed above to obtain further information.

Receiving Mail

In the US and Canada, you can have mail sent to you care of General Delivery at any post office that has its own zip (postal) code. Mail should be addressed like this: your name, c/o General Delivery, town, state, zip code. Mail is usually held for 10 days before it's returned to the sender; you might request your correspondents to write 'hold for arrival' on the outside of their letters. Alternatively, you can have mail sent to the local representative of American Express or Thomas Cook – both provide mail service for their customers.

Telephone

All phone numbers within the USA and Canada consist of a three-digit area code followed by a seven-digit local number. If calling locally, just dial the seven-digit number. If you are calling long distance, dial ☎ 1 + the three-digit area code + the seven-digit number. If you're calling from abroad, the international country code for the USA and Canada is 1.

For local directory assistance dial ☎ 1 + the three-digit area code of the place you want to call + 555-1212. To obtain directory assistance for a toll-free number, dial ☎ 1-800-555-1212. Area codes for places outside the region are listed at the beginning of the white pages telephone directories. If you don't know the area code, dial ☎ 0 (free of charge) for operator assistance. Be aware that due to skyrocketing demand for phone numbers (for faxes, cellular phones, etc), some metropolitan areas are being divided into multiple new area codes, which are not reflected in older phone books. When in doubt, ask the operator.

The 800, 877 and 888 area codes are designated for toll-free numbers within the USA and sometimes from Canada as well. If you are dialing locally, the toll-free number is not available. Also, toll-free 800 numbers can be limited to specific regions (ie, the number may work in Oregon but not in Washington).

The 900 area code is designated for calls for which the caller pays at a premium rate – phone sex, horoscopes, jokes, etc.

Local calls usually cost 25¢ at pay phones, although occasional private phones may charge more. Long-distance rates vary depending on the destination and which telephone company you use – call the operator (☎ 0) for rate information. Don't ask the operator to put your call through, however, because operator-assisted calls are much more expensive than direct-dial calls. Generally, nights (11 pm to 8 am), all day Saturday and 8 am to 5 pm Sunday are the cheapest times to call (60% discount). Evenings (5 to 11 pm, Sunday to Friday) are mid-priced (35% discount). Day calls (8 am to 5 pm, Monday to Friday) are full-price calls within the USA.

Many US and Canadian businesses use letters instead of numbers for their telephone numbers in an attempt to make them snappy and memorable. Sometimes it works, but sometimes it is difficult to read the letters on the keyboard. If you can't read the letters, here they are: 1 is unassigned; 2 – ABC, 3 – DEF, 4 – GHI, 5 – JKL, 6 – MNO, 7 – PRS, 8 – TUV, 9 – WXY. Sorry, no Qs or Zs.

International Calls To make an international call direct, dial ☎ 011, then the country code, followed by the area code and the phone number. You may need to wait as long as 45 seconds for the ringing to start. International rates vary depending on the time of day and the destination. Call the operator (☎ 0) for rates. The first minute is always more expensive than extra minutes.

Hotel Phones Many hotels (especially the more expensive ones) add a service charge of 50¢ to $1 for each local call made from a room phone, and they also have hefty surcharges for long-distance calls. Public pay phones, which can be found in most lobbies, are always cheaper. You can pump in quarters, use a phone credit card or make collect calls from pay phones.

Phone Debit Cards A new long-distance alternative is phone debit cards, which allow purchasers to pay in advance, with access through a toll-free 800 number. In amounts of $5, $10, $20 and $50, these cards are available from Western Union, machines in some supermarkets and various other sources.

When using phone credit cards, be cautious of people watching you dial in the numbers – thieves will memorize numbers and use your card to make phone calls to all corners of the earth.

Fax & Email
Fax machines are easy to find in the Northwest, at shipping companies (such as Mail Boxes Etc in the US), photocopy stores and hotel business service centers, but be prepared to pay high prices (over $1 a page). Email is quickly becoming a preferred method of communication; however, unless you have a laptop and modem that can be plugged into a telephone socket, it's difficult to get online. Hotel business service centers may provide connections, and trendy restaurants and cafes sometimes offer Internet service as well.

WEBSITES
Following is a sampling of general websites that will help you plan your travels in the Pacific Northwest.

Great Outdoor Recreation Pages
www.gorp.com
   This is an overwhelming site packed with information for the outdoor enthusiast, with links to attractions and activities throughout the US, including the Pacific Northwest.

Guide to the Olympic Peninsula
www.olympus.net
   This helpful site contains information on the Olympic Peninsula, including lodging, dining, local events, arts and maps.

National Park Service
www.nps.gov
   This website, administered by the National Park Service, features information on, and links to, all US National Parks.

Oregon Tourism Commission
www.traveloregon.com
   This is the official Oregon Tourism website where you will pretty much find everything you need to plan a vacation. Plus there's a state map and calendar of events.

The Pink Pages
www.gayvictoria.com/pinkpages
  Has links to gay and lesbian companies and
  activities in Victoria, BC, as well as links to
  Portland and Vancouver sites.

Washington State Ferries
www.wsdot.wa.gov/ferries
  Contains ferry fares and schedules, route
  maps and tourist information, plus links to
  other ferry services.

Washington State Tourism Division
www.tourism.wa.gov
  Includes everything you need to know about
  accommodations, travel, sights and the community, and has links to other helpful travel
  sites.

Welcome to Oregon
www.el.com/to/oregon
  A good site about Oregon – its history, government and individual communities – and
  has numerous links to other Oregon sites.

BOOKS

There's a vast array of books written about
the Pacific Northwest. Following are titles
of general interest as well as titles specific
to Oregon, Washington and BC.

Lonely Planet

Lonely Planet's *Seattle City Guide*, *Rocky
Mountain States* and *Canada* are good sup-
plemental guides for travelers heading to
North America's western region.

History & Culture

Oddly, there isn't one single book currently in print that does a decent job of
detailing Northwest history. History buffs
are left to individual state histories. *The
Great Northwest* by OO Winteher (Knopf,
New York, 1955 and 1982) is about the
best book on the area, and very readable.
Look for it in a used-book store or library.

  The daily journals of Lewis and Clark,
equally full of wild adventures and mis-
spellings, are wonderful in their detail and
candor. Bernard DeVoto's carefully edited
Journals of Lewis and Clark makes for fascinating reading. For a narrative retelling of
the Corps of Discovery's journey, turn to

David Lavender's *The Way to the Western
Sea: Lewis and Clark Across the Continent*.
Bestselling author Stephen E Ambrose
recounts the expedition in splendid detail in
his book *Undaunted Courage: Meriwether
Lewis, Thomas Jefferson, and the Opening
of the American West*.

  In *Stepping Westward: The Long Search
for Home in the Pacific Northwest*, Sallie
Tisdale tells her story of growing up in the
Northwest, with insights into its culture;
look for a copy at Powell's Books in Portland or in the library. *The Good Rain:
Across Time and Terrain in the Pacific
Northwest* by Timothy Egan is an insightful
discussion of the Northwest and its people
by the local *New York Times* correspondent.

Oregon *That Balance So Rare: The Story
of Oregon* by Terrance O'Donnell is, in
an oddly limited field, the most recent cat-
echistic history of the state. Why is Murderer's Creek called Murderer's Creek?
Find out in *Oregon Geographic Names* by
Lewis A McArthur, an amazingly hefty
guide to place names; it's also a solid
guide to regional history.

  Oregon's written literary history begins
with journal keeping; journals and memoirs remain one of the state's major literary
forms. While Lewis and Clark set the standard, journal keeping was also part of the
long trek made by tens of thousands along
the Oregon Trail during the 1840s and
1850s. Diaries kept by women along the
trail provide an especially revealing look
into the day-to-day life of travelers in the
American West's greatest migration. *Wom-
en's Diaries of the Westward Journey*,
edited by Lillian Schlissel, is a good compilation of these writings.

  Memoirs of frontier childhood form an
important part of Oregon literature. *Cathlamet on the Columbia* by attorney Thomas
Nelson Strong (Metropolitan Press, New
York, 1936) is a vivid retelling of his pioneer upbringing, and also provides a picture
of early Portland. Contemporary mem-
oirists include Clyde Rice (*Heaven in the
Eye*) and William Kittredge (*Hole in the
Sky: A Memoir*).

Washington The single best traveler's guide to Washington history is *Exploring Washington's Past: A Road Guide to History* by Ruth Kirk and Carmela Alexander. *Washington State Place Names* by James W Phillips is a good resource on names and pronunciation, including derivations of Washington's many Native American place names.

Early writing in Washington tended to be chronicles of pioneer days. In 1888 Arthur A Denny, one of the founders of Seattle, wrote *Pioneer Days on Puget Sound* (Harriman, Seattle, 1908); James G Swan, a colorful character whose life was later documented by Ivan Doig, wrote *The Northwest Coast* (Harper & Row, New York, 1969) and *Indians of Cape Flattery* (Smithsonian, Philadelphia, 1870) during the 1850s. *Canoe and Saddle* by Theodore Winthrop (Ticknor & Fields, Boston, 1863) recounts a young man's trip across Washington in 1853.

British Columbia Pierre Berton is Canada's prime chronicler of the country's history. He has written on a wide range of subjects such as the gold rush, the railways and the Depression in an entertaining and informative way. Peter C Newman writes on Canadian business but has also produced an intriguing history of the Hudson's Bay Company, *Caesar's of the Wilderness*, beginning with the early fur-trading days.

For a specific history of BC, try *British Columbia: An Illustrated History* by Geoffrey Molyneux, or *The West Beyond the West: A History of British Columbia* by Jean Borman. Review Vancouver's past with *Vancouver: A History in Photographs* by Aynsley Wyse and Dana Wyse. For a history of Victoria and Vancouver Island, read *Seven Shillings a Year: The History of Vancouver Island* by Charles Lillard.

Natural History
In addition to the following books, Audubon Society guides and Peterson Field Guides are available to many specialized natural history areas, including guides on butterflies, birds of prey and mushrooms.

The Audubon Society's guide to *Western Forests* and *A Field Guide to the Cascades and Olympics* are both by Stephen R Whitney. The latter is a good one-volume guide to the region's plant and wildlife. *Cascade-Olympic Natural History: A Trailside Reference* by Daniel Matthews is the single best guide to plants and wildlife on the western slopes of Washington and Oregon. *Plants & Animals of the Pacific Northwest: An Illustrated Guide to the Natural History of Western Oregon, Washington, and British Columbia* by Eugene N Kozloff is another good general resource.

Bird watchers might want to pick up a copy of *Familiar Birds of the Northwest* by Harry B Nehls. Flower enthusiasts should check out *Wayside Wildflowers of the Pacific Northwest* by Dr Dee Strickler and *Sagebrush Country: A Wildflower Sanctuary* by Ronald J Taylor.

Also of interest are *A Waterfall Lover's Guide to the Pacific Northwest: Where to Find More Than 500 Spectacular Waterfalls in Washington, Oregon and Idaho* by Gregory A Plumb and *Garden Touring in the Pacific Northwest: A Guide to Gardens and Specialty Nurseries in Oregon, Washington, and British Columbia* by Jan Kowalczewski Whitner.

Oregon *Oregon Wildlife Viewing Guide* is a guide to designated wildlife-viewing areas throughout the state.

Geology of Oregon by Elizabeth L Orr, William N Orr and Ewart M Baldwin is the single best book on Oregon's curious geologic story. *Roadside Geology of Oregon* by David D Alt and Donald W Hyndman takes you road by road, rock by rock, across Oregon.

Washington *Washington Wildlife Viewing Guide* by Joe La Tourrette is a guide to the designated wildlife-viewing sites in Washington. *Roadside Geology of Washington* by David D Alt and Donald W Hyndman takes the geology of the state road by road.

Ferryboat Field Guide to Puget Sound by Robert U Steelquist is a naturalist's guide to the wildlife and ecology of the Puget Sound, written to accompany various ferry crossings.

British Columbia *Trees, Shrubs, and Flowers to Know in British Columbia* by TM Dent, says and does it all. *British Columbia: A Natural History* by Richard Cannings is an in-depth guide to the province's plants, animals and geography.

Native Peoples
A Guide to the Indian Tribes of the Pacific Northwest and *Indians of the Pacific Northwest: A History* by Robert H Ruby and John A Brown are both superlative. The first is a tribe-by-tribe encyclopedia of the region's Native Americans, the second an overview of Northwest Indian history and culture. Also of interest is the book *Indian Rock Art of the Columbia Plateau* by James D Keyser.

For information on Canada's native peoples, read *Native Peoples and Cultures of Canada* by Alan D McMillan which includes both history and current issues. The classic book on Canada's Indigenous peoples, *The Indians of Canada* was written in 1932 by Diamond Jenness. Originally from New Zealand, the author's life is an amazing story in its own right as he spent years living with various indigenous people across the country.

The Northwest's Native American oral literary tradition has largely been lost. For a flavor of indigenous myths and stories, read *Coyote Was Going There* by Jarold Ramsey.

Fiction
Astoria by Washington Irving, found in many editions in used-book stores and libraries, is a classic on frontier travel to the Northwest, written in 1836. Also in many editions, *Honey in the Horn* by HL Davis (Harper & Bros, New York, 1935), for which Davis won the 1936 Pulitzer Prize in fiction, tells the gritty story of Oregon pioneer farmers. One of the most prolific Washington writers of the early 20th century was Archie Binns. Of his

many novels, *The Land is Bright* (Scribner & Sons, New York, 1939) – the story of an Oregon Trail family – is still read today. Oregon history was a rich vein to mine for early novelists. *Bridge of the Gods* by Frederic Homer Balch (Binford & Mart, Portland, OR, 1965) was an early bestseller; although its style is dated, this novel of early Indian life along the Columbia was historically accurate.

Northwest Passage edited by Bruce Barcott and *Edge Walking on the Western Rim* edited by Mayumi Tsutakawa and Bob Peterson are both anthologies of modern Northwest writers.

Don Berry's *Trask* (Comstock Editions, Inc, Sausalito, CA, 1960) tells the story of an early Oregon trapper and his life on the land. *Jump Off Creek* by Molly Glass is the diary-cum-novel of a women homesteader in northeastern Oregon.

See the Literature sections in Facts about the Pacific Northwest, Facts about Oregon and Facts about Washington for literature written by authors living in the Northwest.

FILMS
Seattle has come a long way as a movie mecca since Elvis starred in 1963's *It Happened at the World's Fair*, a chestnut of civic boosterism. Nowadays, Seattle is where directors come to shoot droll and stylish comedies, which have helped create Seattle's current reputation as a hip and youthful place to slack off and be trendy. Seattle is practically a character in such films as *Sleepless in Seattle*, *Georgia* and *Singles*. *Twin Peaks*, the moody and disturbing TV series set in Alaska was shot in Washington, as was the survivalist paean, *First Blood*.

Portland is not so easily recognized in films (in fact in one film, *Body of Evidence*, street scenes meant to take place in Europe were filmed in downtown Portland). Films by acclaimed director Gus Van Sant, a Portland native, are shot largely in-state (see Theater & Films in the Facts about Oregon chapter). Other films shot in Oregon include *Free Willy*, *Animal House*,

One Flew Over the Cuckoo's Nest and *The Shining*.

British Columbia is one of the centers of film in Canada, and many Canadian features are set in Vancouver. Many Hollywood films are also shot in BC: *Legends of the Fall*, *Little Women*, *Jumanji* and *Rambo: First Blood* give an idea of the range of films shot here. One of the few films to feature Vancouver as Vancouver (not as somewhere else) was *Intersection*, with Sharon Stone and Richard Gere. The most noted recent production in the Vancouver area was TV's *The X-Files*, which was shot in and around the city; Vancouver doubled as many locals, notably Washington, DC.

NEWSPAPERS & MAGAZINES

National newspapers like the *New York Times*, *USA Today* and *Wall Street Journal* are widely available in the cities and larger towns of the Northwest. Seattle's two dailies, the *Post-Intelligencer* and the *Times*, Vancouver's *Province* and *Sun*, and Portland's *Oregonian* are the region's principle sources for print news. Friday editions have extended arts and events information. Travelers will discover that there are dozens of weekly newspapers throughout the Northwest which discuss music, the visual arts and local issues from a hipper, more youthful and political point of view. Usually available free of charge, look for these in coffeehouses, bars, bookstores and music stores.

The Pacific Northwest is the best broad-focused travel magazine, with glossy articles on festivals, weekend getaways and dining. Other magazines focus on specific interests, such as *Northwest Palate* and *Northwest Food and Wine*, which are food and travel publications.

RADIO & TV

All rental cars have car radios, and travelers can choose from hundreds of stations to listen to. Most radio stations have a range of less than 100 miles, with scores of stations in and near major cities crowding the airwaves with a wide variety of music and entertainment. In rural areas, be prepared for a predominance of country & western music, local news and 'talk radio.' Public radio stations carrying news-oriented National Public Radio (NPR) can usually be found in the lower numbers of the radio band. Many public stations also carry the BBC World Service, which is a good source for foreign news.

All the major TV networks have affiliated stations throughout the USA. These include ABC, CBS, NBC, FOX and PBS. Most hotels have cable.

Many Canadians can readily tune into radio and TV stations from the US and often do.

PHOTOGRAPHY & VIDEO
Film & Equipment

Print film is widely available at supermarkets and discount drugstores. Color print film has a greater latitude than color slide film; this means that print film can handle a wider range of light and shadow than slide film. However, slide film, particularly the slower speeds (under 100 ASA), has better resolution than print film. Like B&W film, slide film is rarely sold outside of major cities and when available it's expensive.

Film can be damaged by excessive heat, so don't leave your camera and film in the car on a hot summer's day, and avoid placing your camera on the dash while you are driving.

It's worth carrying a spare battery for your camera to avoid disappointment when your camera dies in the middle of nowhere. If you're buying a new camera for your trip do so several weeks before you leave and practice using it.

Drugstores are a good place to get your film cheaply processed. If you drop it off by noon, you can usually pick it up the next day. A roll of 100 ASA 35mm color film with 24 exposures will cost about $7 to get processed.

If you want your pictures right away, you can find one-hour processing services in the yellow pages under 'Photo Processing.' The prices tend to creep up to the $12 scale, so be prepared to pay. Many one-hour photo finishers operate in the larger cities and a few can be found near tourist attractions.

Overseas visitors who are thinking of purchasing videos should remember that the USA and Canada use the National Television System Committee (NTSC) color TV standard, which is not compatible with other standards (Phase Alternative Line or PAL; Système Electronique Couleur avec Mémoire or SECAM) used in Africa, Europe, Asia and Australasia unless converted. It's best to keep those seemingly cheap movie purchases on hold until you get home.

Airport Security All passengers on flights have to pass their luggage through x-ray machines. Technology as it is today doesn't jeopardize lower speed film, so you shouldn't have to worry about cameras going through the machine. If you are carrying high speed (1600 ASA and above) film, then you may want to carry film and cameras with you and ask the X-ray inspector to manually check your film.

TIME

All of Washington, most of Oregon and western British Columbia are on pacific standard time (PST), which is eight hours behind Greenwich mean time (GMT), three hours behind New York City on eastern standard time (EST) and 17 hours ahead of Tokyo. A small sliver of easternmost Oregon is on mountain standard time (MST).

The Northwest states and BC observe the switch to daylight-saving time, which goes into effect the first Sunday in April to the last Sunday in October.

ELECTRICITY

In Canada and the USA voltage is 110V and the plugs have two (flat) or three (two flat, one round) pins. Plugs with three pins don't fit into a two-hole socket, but adapters are easy to buy at hardware or drugstores.

WEIGHTS & MEASURES

In the USA, distances are in feet, yards and miles. Three feet equals one yard (.914 meters); 1760 yards or 5280 feet are one mile. Dry weights are in ounces (oz), pounds (lb) and tons (16 ounces are one pound; 2000 pounds are one ton), but liquid measures differ from dry measures. One pint equals 16 fluid ounces; two pints equals one quart, a common measure for liquids like milk, which is also sold in half gallons (two quarts) and gallons (four quarts). Gasoline is dispensed by the US gallon, which is about 20% less than the imperial gallon. Pints and quarts are also 20% less than imperial ones.

Measures in Canada are in metric, though many people persist in thinking of distance in miles.

There is a conversion chart on the inside back cover of this book.

LAUNDRY

You will find self-service, coin-operated laundry facilities in most towns of any size and in better campgrounds. Washing a load costs about $1 and drying it another $1. Some laundries have attendants who will wash, dry and fold your clothes for you for an additional charge. To find a laundry, look under 'Laundries' or 'Laundries – Self-Service' in the yellow pages of the telephone directory. Dry cleaners are also listed under 'Laundries' or 'Cleaners.'

RECYCLING

Traveling in a car seems to generate large numbers of cans and bottles. If you'd like to save these for recycling, you'll find recycling centers in the larger towns. Materials usually accepted are plastic and glass bottles, aluminum and tin cans and newspapers. Some campgrounds and a few roadside rest areas also have recycling bins next to the trash bins.

Many gas stations and convenience stores sell large plastic insulated cups with lids which are inexpensive and ideal for both hot and cold drinks; reusing the cups will usually get you a discount.

Oregon's Bottle Bill

In 1973 Oregon was the first state in the nation to pass a revolutionary law geared towards eliminating litter and promoting recycling. For every beer or soda purchased at a grocery store, an extra 5¢ deposit is charged at the register for the container. This 5¢ deposit is later returned when these plastic or glass bottles and aluminum cans are returned, or 'redeemed,' at the store. Beverage distributors pick up the cans and bottles from the stores, and take them to be recycled.

Stores will take back the cans and bottles of beverage brands they sell in their stores, and may refuse brands they don't carry or ones purchased in other states. Wine and liquor bottles are exempt from the bottle bill, as are certain juices and mineral waters. Check the labels to see if containers are redeemable.

Oregonians save and redeem their cans and bottles religiously, but to an out-of-state visitor, five cents may seem too petty to warrant an extra trip to the store. Whatever you do, don't throw redeemable cans and bottles away. Instead, leave empty cans and bottles near, but not in, a garbage can, where they will all but certainly be picked up by someone who needs a nickel. ■

When hiking and camping in the wilderness, take out everything you bring in – in some wilderness areas this includes *any* kind of garbage you may create.

HEALTH

For most foreign visitors no immunizations are required for entry, though cholera and yellow fever vaccinations may be required of travelers from areas with a history of those diseases. In the Pacific Northwest there are no unexpected health dangers, excellent medical attention is readily available and the only real health concern is that a collision with the medical system can cause severe injuries to your financial state.

Hospitals and medical centers, walk-in clinics and referral services are easily found throughout the region.

In a serious emergency, call ☎ 911 for an ambulance to take you to the nearest hospital's emergency room. But note that emergency room charges in the USA and Canada are incredibly expensive.

Predeparture Preparations

Make sure you're healthy before you start traveling. If you are embarking on a long trip, make sure your teeth are in good shape. If you wear glasses, take a spare pair and your prescription. You can get new spectacles made up quickly and competently for under $100, depending on the prescription and frame you choose. Most optometrists can fill prescriptions for soft contact lenses. Lenses can be very inexpensive; disposable lenses now cost just dollars a pair. If you require a particular medication, take an adequate supply and bring a prescription in case you lose your medication.

Health Insurance A travel insurance policy to cover theft, lost tickets and medical problems is a good idea, especially in the USA and Canada, where some hospitals will refuse care without evidence of insurance. There is a wide variety of policies and your travel agent will have recommendations. International student travel policies handled by STA Travel and other student travel organizations are usually a good value. Some policies offer lower and higher medical expenses options, with the higher option chiefly for countries like the USA with extremely high medical costs. Check the fine print.

Some policies specifically exclude 'dangerous activities' like scuba diving, motorcycling and even trekking. If these activities are on your agenda, avoid this sort of policy.

You may prefer a policy that pays doctors or hospitals directly, rather than your having to pay first and claim later. If you have to claim later, keep *all* documentation. Some policies ask you to call back (reverse charges) to a center in your home country for an immediate assessment of your problem.

Check whether the policy covers ambulance fees or an emergency flight home. If you have to stretch out, you will need two seats and somebody has to pay for it!

Medical Kit It's wise to carry a small, straightforward medical kit. The kit should include:

- aspirin, acetaminophen or Panadol, for pain or fever
- antihistamine (such as Benadryl), which is useful as a decongestant for colds; to ease the itch from allergies, insect bites or stings; or to help prevent motion sickness
- kaolin preparation (Pepto-Bismol), Immodium or Lomotil, for stomach upsets
- rehydration mixture, to treat severe diarrhea, which is particularly important if you're traveling with children
- antiseptic, mercurochrome and antibiotic powder or similar 'dry' spray, for cuts and grazes
- calamine lotion, to ease irritation from bites or stings
- bandages, for minor injuries
- scissors, tweezers and a thermometer (note that airlines prohibit mercury thermometers)
- insect repellent, sunscreen lotion, lip balm and water purification tablets

Basic Rules

Care in what you eat and drink is the most important health rule; stomach upsets are the most common travel health problem (between 30% and 50% of travelers in a two-week stay experience this), but the majority of these upsets will be relatively minor. Canadian and American standards of cleanliness in places serving food and drink are very high.

Bottled drinking water, both carbonated and noncarbonated, is widely available in the USA and BC. Tap water is usually OK to drink; ask locally.

Travel- & Climate-Related Problems
Motion Sickness Eating lightly before and during a trip will reduce the chances of motion sickness. If you are prone to motion sickness, try to find a place that minimizes disturbance, for example, near the wing on aircraft, near the center on buses or close to midships on ferries. Fresh air usually helps, reading or cigarette smoke don't. Commercial anti-motion sickness preparations, which can cause drowsiness, have to be taken before the trip commences; once you feel sick, it's too late. Ginger, available in capsule form from health-food stores and peppermint (including mint-flavored sweets) are natural preventatives.

Jet Lag Jet lag is experienced when a person travels by air across more than three time zones (each time zone usually represents a one-hour time difference). It occurs because many of the functions of the human body are regulated by internal 24-hour cycles called circadian rhythms. When we travel long distances rapidly, our bodies take time to adjust to the 'new time' of our destination, and we may experience fatigue, disorientation, insomnia, anxiety, impaired concentration and a loss of appetite. These effects will usually be gone within three days of arrival, but there are ways of minimizing the impact of jet lag:

- Rest for a couple of days prior to departure; try to avoid late nights and last-minute dashes for traveler's checks or your passport.
- Try to select flight schedules that minimize sleep deprivation; arriving in the early evening means you can go to sleep soon after you arrive. For very long flights, try to organize a stopover.
- Avoid excessive eating (which bloats the stomach) and alcohol (which causes dehydration) during the flight. Instead, drink plenty of noncarbonated, nonalcoholic drinks such as fruit juice or water.
- Make yourself comfortable by wearing loose-fitting clothes and perhaps bringing an eye mask and ear plugs to help you sleep.

Sunburn Most doctors recommend sunscreen with a high protection factor for easily burned areas like your shoulders and, especially if you will be on nude beaches, those areas not normally exposed to sun.

Heat Exhaustion Dehydration or salt deficiency can cause heat exhaustion. Take time to acclimatize to high temperatures and make sure that you get enough liquids. Salt deficiency is characterized by fatigue, lethargy, headaches, giddiness and muscle cramps. Salt tablets may help. Vomiting or diarrhea can also deplete your liquid and salt levels. Anhydrotic heat exhaustion, caused by the inability to sweat, is quite rare, but unlike the other forms of heat exhaustion it is likely to strike people who have been in a hot climate for some time, rather than newcomers. Again, always carry – and use – a water bottle on long trips.

Heat Stroke Long, continuous periods of exposure to high temperatures can leave you vulnerable to this serious, sometimes fatal, condition, which occurs when the body's heat-regulating mechanism breaks down and body temperature rises to dangerous levels. Avoid excessive alcohol intake or strenuous activity when you first arrive in a hot climate such as summertime in eastern Oregon and Washington.

Symptoms include feeling unwell, lack of perspiration and a high body temperature of 102° to 105°F (39° to 41°C). Hospitalization is essential for extreme cases, but meanwhile get out of the sun, remove clothing, cover yourself with a wet sheet or towel and fan continually.

Hypothermia Changeable weather at high altitudes can leave you vulnerable to exposure: after dark, temperatures in the mountains or desert can drop from balmy to below freezing, while a sudden rainfall or snowfall and high winds can lower your body temperature too rapidly. If possible, avoid traveling alone; partners are more likely to avoid hypothermia successfully. If you must travel alone, especially when hiking, be sure someone knows your route and when you expect to return.

Seek shelter when bad weather is unavoidable. Woolen clothing and synthetics, which

retain warmth even when wet, are superior to cottons. A quality sleeping bag is a worthwhile investment, although goose down loses much of its insulating qualities when wet. Carry high-energy, easily digestible snacks like chocolate or dried fruit.

Get hypothermia victims out of the wind or rain, remove their clothing if it's wet and replace it with dry, warm clothing. Give them hot liquids – not alcohol – and high-calorie, easily digestible food. In advanced stages it may be necessary to place victims in warm sleeping bags and get in with them. Do not rub victims but place them near a fire or, if possible, in a warm (not hot) bath.

Altitude Sickness Acute mountain sickness (AMS) occurs at high altitude and can be fatal. In the thinner atmosphere of the high mountains like the Cascade peaks, lack of oxygen causes many individuals to suffer headaches, nausea, nose bleeds, shortness of breath, physical weakness and other symptoms that can lead to very serious consequences, especially if combined with heat exhaustion, sunburn or hypothermia.

Most people recover within a few hours or days. If the symptoms persist, it is imperative to descend to lower elevations. For mild cases, everyday painkillers such as aspirin will relieve symptoms until the body adapts. You should avoid smoking, drinking alcohol, eating heavily or exercising strenuously.

There is no hard and fast rule as to how high is too high: AMS has been fatal at altitudes of 10,000 feet, although it is much more common above 11,500 feet. It is always wise to sleep at a lower altitude than the greatest height reached during the day. A number of other measures can prevent or minimize AMS:

• Ascend slowly – take frequent rest days, spending two to three nights for each climb of 3000 feet (900 meters). If you reach a high altitude by trekking, acclimatization takes place gradually and you are less likely to be affected than if you fly direct.

- Drink extra fluids. Mountain air is dry and cold and you lose moisture as you breathe.
- Eat light, high-carbohydrate meals for more energy.
- Avoid alcohol, which may increase the risk of dehydration.
- Avoid sedatives.

Infectious Diseases

Diarrhea A change of water, food or climate can all cause the runs; diarrhea caused by contaminated food or water is more serious, but it's unlikely in the USA. Despite all your precautions you may still have a mild bout of traveler's diarrhea from exotic food or drink. Dehydration is the main danger with any diarrhea, particularly for children, where dehydration can occur quite quickly. Fluid replacement remains the mainstay of management. Weak black tea with a little sugar, soda water or soft drinks diluted 50% with water are all good. With severe diarrhea a rehydrating solution is necessary to replace minerals and salts. Such solutions, like Pedialyte, are available at pharmacies throughout the region.

Giardiasis Commonly known as giardia, this microscopic parasite lives in mountain streams, and with bad luck, in your lower intestinal tract. Giardia enters streams through the fecal remains of animals – especially beaver (which gives the condition its common nickname, 'beaver fever'). Unfiltered or untreated water straight from streams, springs or lakes should never be drunk, as giardia is prevalent throughout the Northwest.

Symptoms are stomach cramps, nausea, a bloated stomach, watery, foul-smelling diarrhea and frequent gas. Giardia can appear several weeks after exposure to the parasite; symptoms may disappear for several days and then return, a pattern which may continue. Tinidazole, known as Fasigyn, or metronidazole (Flagyl) are the recommended drugs for treatment. Either can be used in a single treatment dose. Antibiotics are useless.

Giardia is a fairly common summer affliction in this region and has been known to enter the water supply of mountain towns.

Hepatitis Hepatitis is a general term for inflammation of the liver. There are many causes of this condition: poor sanitation, contact with infected blood products, drugs, alcohol and contact with an infected person are but a few. The symptoms are fever, chills, headache, fatigue, and feelings of weakness and aches and pains, followed by a loss of appetite, nausea, vomiting, abdominal pain, dark urine, light-colored feces and jaundiced skin. The whites of the eyes may also turn yellow. Viral hepatitis is an infection of the liver, which can have several unpleasant symptoms, or no symptoms at all, with the infected persons not knowing that they have the disease. The discovery of new strains has led to a virtual alphabet soup, with hepatitis A, B, C, D, E and a rumored G. Hepatitis C, D and E are fairly rare.

HIV/AIDS Any exposure to blood, blood products or bodily fluids may put an individual at risk for HIV/AIDS. Infection can come from practicing unprotected sex or sharing contaminated needles. Apart from abstinence, the most effective preventative is always to practice safe sex using condoms. It is impossible to detect a person's HIV status without a blood test.

HIV/AIDS can also be spread through infected blood transfusions; most developing countries cannot afford to screen blood for transfusions, though the blood supply in the USA is now well screened. It can also be spread if needles are reused for acupuncture, tattooing or body piercing.

A good resource for help and information is the US Center for Disease Control AIDS hotline (☎ 800-342-2437, 800-344-7432 in Spanish). AIDS support groups are listed in the front of phone books or under 'Aids' in the yellow pages.

Red Tide Before harvesting wild shellfish from the Pacific Ocean, check with local health officials. A bacterial condition called 'red tide' can affect shellfish, rendering them lethal to humans. When a red tide alert is in effect, most beach access sites are posted with warning signs. The Puget Sound area in Washington is often affected by red tide, and red tide areas have recently begun to spring up increasingly in small bays along the Oregon coast.

Tetanus Tetanus is difficult to treat but is preventable with immunization. Tetanus occurs when a wound becomes infected by a germ that lives in the feces of animals or people, so clean all cuts, punctures or animal bites.

Cuts, Bites & Stings
Treat any cut with an antiseptic such as Betadine. Where possible avoid bandages and Band-Aids, which can keep wounds wet.

Bee and wasp stings and nonpoisonous spider bites are usually painful rather than dangerous. Calamine lotion will give relief and ice packs will reduce the pain and swelling. Bites are best avoided by not using bare hands to turn over rocks or large pieces of wood.

Mosquitoes breed readily in the damp climate of the Northwest, and can be especially annoying in forest areas from spring to late summer. Although they don't spread any illnesses in the Northwest, they're voracious enough to irritate even the hardiest outdoor enthusiast. Pet owners should know that fleas also thrive in the northwest climate.

Black Widow Spiders This glossy black spider is relatively small, with a body averaging half an inch in diameter and a leg span of two inches, and sports a characteristic red hourglass mark on its abdomen. Classified as a ground-dwelling spider, black widows prefer dark, quiet nooks and crannies such as brush piles, sheds and under rocks as their choice habitat. A black widow bite may be barely noticeable, and at most feel like a subtle pin prick. However, a black widow sting can result in agonizing pain, muscle spasms and intestinal cramping; the sting

is rarely fatal for otherwise healthy people. If you are bitten by a black widow, wash the wound area well and seek medical attention.

Ticks Ticks are a parasitic arachnid that may be present in brush, forest and grasslands, where hikers often get them on their legs or in their boots. The adults suck blood from hosts by burying their head into skin, but they are often found unattached and can simply be brushed off. However, if one has attached itself to you, pulling it off and leaving the head in the skin increases the likelihood of infection or disease, such as Rocky Mountain spotted fever or Lyme disease.

Always check your body for ticks after walking through a high-grass or thickly forested area. If you do find a tick on you, induce it to let go by rubbing on oil, alcohol or petroleum jelly, or press it with a very hot object like a match or a cigarette. The tick should back out and can then be disposed of. If you get sick in the next couple of weeks, consult a doctor.

Rattlesnakes Rattlesnakes are pervasive in much of eastern Oregon, Washington and BC. There's no mistaking this snake for anything else, with its distinctive diamondback markings and rattle. Rattlesnakes are not naturally aggressive, and if given their druthers, will slink away after sounding a warning rattle. However, if riled, they will coil and strike. If hiking in rattlesnake

country, it's a good idea to wear heavy boots and long pants as added protection.

If you are bitten or stung by a rattlesnake, wash the wound with soap and water and apply a clean dressing. If in pain, take aspirin. If the area swells, apply ice; this will also slow the spread of the toxin. Immobilize the bitten area if possible, and keep below the level of the heart. Get to a hospital as quickly as you can. If the snake was killed, bring it along for identification, which can facilitate treatment.

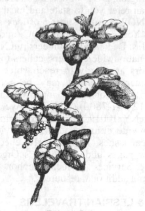

Poison Oak

Poison Oak Just brushing past this plant while on a hike can cause a blistery and extremely itchy rash on bare skin, which should be washed with a strong soap (Fels Naphtha is a recommended brand) immediately after exposure. Cortisone creams will lessen the itching in minor cases. Poison oak, related to poison ivy, is a tall, thin shrub with shiny three-part leaves that grows in shady, moist areas in the western USA, including the Pacific Northwest.

Allergies

Oregon is the largest grower of grass seed in the US. Combine this with a proliferation of other green growing things, and there's a good chance that, if you are susceptible to allergies at all, you will have problems in the Northwest. Pollens and molds can be really intense during the summer. If you know you have a potential problem, you may want to bring along your inhaler and prescription drugs. Over-the-counter antihistamine drugs help in less severe cases, but with sleepy side effects.

WOMEN TRAVELERS

Women often face different situations when traveling than men do. Women, especially those traveling alone, need a little extra awareness of their surroundings.

In the Pacific Northwest people are generally friendly and happy to help travelers, and women travelers usually have a wonderful time unmarred by dangerous encounters. To ensure that this is the case, consider the following suggestions.

Exercise more vigilance when in large towns and cities than in rural areas. Try to avoid unsafe or 'bad' neighborhoods or areas. If you are unsure whether an area is safe or unsafe, ask at your hotel or call the tourist office for advice. When you must go into or through these areas, it is safest to travel in a private vehicle (eg, car or taxi). Traveling is more dangerous at night, but in the worst areas daytime crimes occur. Carry the best available maps and familiarize yourself with them. Tourist maps can sometimes be deceiving, compressing areas that are not tourist attractions and making distances look shorter than they are. Always look confident and act like you know where you are going.

The risk of sexual assault exists in cities and, to a lesser degree, in rural areas. By avoiding vulnerable situations such as drinking, using drugs or traveling alone, you can reduce your chances of becoming a victim. While there may be less to watch out for in rural areas, men who are unaccustomed to seeing women traveling alone may still harass them. Try to avoid hiking or camping alone, especially in unfamiliar places.

To further reduce your risk of sexual assault, exercise common sense and communicate honestly, assertively and clearly. Look people in the eye instead of looking down, letting them know you are aware of their presence. Watch for people who invade your personal space or try to isolate you.

Men may interpret a woman drinking alone in a bar as a bid for male company, whether a woman intends it that way or not. If the company is unwelcome, most men respect a firm, but polite, 'No thank you'. Be aware of Rohypnol or 'roofies', a drug that can be slipped into drinks causing blackouts. Rohypnol has been used nationwide in sexual assault cases.

It might be a good idea to carry money (and only money you need for that day) inside your clothing (in a money belt, a bra or your socks) instead of in a backpack, purse or an outside pocket. Stash the money in several places, and always carry enough cash for a telephone call or a taxi. Hide or avoid wearing any valuable jewelry.

Do not hitchhike alone, and do not pick up hitchhikers when driving alone. If you get stuck on the road and need help, it is a good idea to have a premade sign to signal for help. Avoid getting out of your car to flag down help. Stay inside, lock the doors, turn on the hazard lights and wait for the police to arrive. Carry the phone number for AAA emergency road service if you are a member. When traveling in remote areas where help may not be readily available, you may want to carry a cellular telephone, if this option is available. If using public transportation, make sure to check the times of the last bus or train before you go out at night.

To deal with potential dangers, many women protect themselves with a whistle, mace, cayenne pepper spray or some self-defense training. Remember to have a 'getaway' plan in your head at all times. If you decide to carry a spray, contact the local police to find out about regulations and training classes. Laws regarding sprays vary from state to state, so know the laws for the region through which you are traveling. Airlines do not allow sprays onboard; carrying them is a federal felony because of their combustible design.

If despite all precautions you are assaulted, call the police or ☎ 911, which connects you with the emergency operator for police, fire and ambulance services. In some rural areas where ☎ 911 is inactive, call ☎ 0 for the operator. Larger towns and cities usually have rape crisis centers and women's shelters that can provide help and support. Check the telephone directory for listings or ask the police for referrals.

The headquarters for the National Organization for Women (NOW) (☎ 202-331-0066), at 1000 16th St NW, suite 700, Washington, DC 20036, is a good resource and can refer you to state and local chapters. NOW's fully staffed offices are in New York, Washington, DC and Los Angeles. Dedicated volunteers run NOW's other nationwide chapters; callers to these chapters are likely to reach voice mail. Nonemergency calls may be returned within a day or two. Planned Parenthood (☎ 212-541-7800), 810 7th Ave, New York, NY 10019, gives referrals to their nationwide clinics and offers advice on medical issues. Alternatively, check the yellow pages under 'Women's Organizations & Services' for local telephone numbers and additional resources.

GAY & LESBIAN TRAVELERS

There are gay people everywhere in the USA, but by far the most visible are in the major cities. In the cities and on both coasts it is easier for gay men and women to live their lives with a certain amount of openness. As you travel into the middle of the country it is much harder to be open. Gay travelers should be careful, *especially* in the rural areas where holding hands might get you bashed.

While San Francisco and New York have the nation's largest gay populations, larger cities throughout the country have a gay neighborhood or area. Whereas Seattle, Vancouver and Portland, and even some smaller towns like Eugene and Victoria, are liberal-minded and accepting of alternative lifestyles, much of the rural Northwest is far more conservative – the Oregon Citizens Alliance (OCA) is known for its attempts to limit gay civil rights.

Resources & Organizations

The Women's Traveller with listings for lesbians and *Damron Address Book* for men, are both published by Damron Company (☎ 415-255-0404, 800-462-6654), PO Box 422458, San Francisco, CA 94142-2458. Ferrari's *Places for Women* and *Places for Men* is also useful. These can be found at any good bookstore as can guides to specific cities.

In Search of Gay America: Women and Men in a Time of Change by Neil Miller is a good book about gay and lesbian life across America in the 1980s. It's a bit dated but gives a good view of life outside of the major cities. For a pre-plague view there is Edmund White's *States of Desire* about gay men in the 1970s.

Another good resource is the *Gay Yellow Pages* (☎ 212-674-0120), PO Box 533, Village Station, NY 10014-0533, which has both national and regional editions.

These national resource numbers may prove useful: National AIDS/HIV Hotline (☎ 800-342-2437), National Gay/Lesbian Task Force (☎ 202-332-6483 in Washington, DC) and Lambda Legal Defense Fund (☎ 212-995-8585 in New York City, 213-937-2728 in Los Angeles).

In Oregon, Phoenix Rising (☎ 503-223-8299), 620 SW 5th Ave, Suite 710, Portland, OR 97204, is a lesbian and gay advocacy group and community resource that specializes in mental health counseling. Other resources can be found by looking in *Just Out*, Portland's local gay newspaper.

In Seattle there's the Lesbian Resource Center (☎ 206-322-3953) at 1208 E Pine St, or stop by Beyond the Closet bookstore (☎ 206-322-4609), 1501 Belmont Ave, to pick up flyers and newspapers and check the bulletin board. Gay Community Social Services (☎ 206-322-2873) at PO Box 22228, Seattle, WA 98122 is another good contact.

Vancouver has a large and active gay and lesbian community. The best resource for news and information is the biweekly *Xtra! West*. Their Xtensions phone bulletin board (☎ 604-688-9378), connects callers to businesses, clubs, support groups and so on. It's a handy service, but it's best to have a copy of the paper and all the extensions at hand.

DISABLED TRAVELERS

Public buildings (including hotels, restaurants, theaters and museums) are required by law to be wheelchair accessible and to have restroom facilities available. Public transportation services (buses, trains and taxis) must be made accessible to all, including those in wheelchairs, and telephone companies are required to provide relay operators for the hearing impaired. Many banks now provide ATM instructions in Braille and you will find audible crossing signals as well as dropped curbs at busier roadway intersections.

Larger private and chain hotels (see Accommodations later in this chapter for listings) have suites for disabled guests. Main car-rental agencies offer hand-controlled models at no extra charge. All major airlines, Amtrak trains and Greyhound buses allow service animals to accompany passengers and frequently sell two-for-one packages when attendants of seriously disabled passengers are required. Airlines will also provide assistance for connecting, boarding and deplaning the flight – just ask for assistance when making your reservation. (Note: airlines must accept wheelchairs as checked baggage and have an onboard chair available, though some advance notice may be required on smaller aircraft.) Of course, the more populous the area, the greater the likelihood of facilities for the disabled, so it's important to call ahead to see what is available.

Resources & Organizations

A number of organizations and tour providers specialize in the needs of disabled travelers:

Access-Able Travel Source – Has an excellent website with many links. PO Box 1796, Wheat Ridge, CO 80034 (☎ 303-232-2979, fax 239-8486, www.access-able.com)

Mobility International USA – Advises disabled travelers on mobility issues. It primarily runs an educational exchange program. PO Box 10767, Eugene, OR 97440 (☎ 541-343-1284, fax 541-343-6812, info@miusa.org)

Moss Rehabilitation Hospital's Travel Information Service – 1200 W Tabor Rd, Philadelphia, PA 19141-3099 (☎ 215-456-9600, TTY 456-9602)

SATH – Society for the Advancement of Travel for the Handicapped, 347 Fifth Ave, No 610, New York, NY 10016 (☎ 212-447-7284, sathtravel@aol.com)

Travelin' Talk – An international network of people providing assistance to disabled travelers. PO Box 3534, Clarksville, TN 37047 (☎ 615-552-6670, fax 552-1182, trvlntlk @aol.com)

Twin Peaks Press – A quarterly newsletter; also publishes directories and access guides. PO Box 129, Vancouver, WA 98666 (☎ 360-694-2462, 800-637-2256)

SENIOR TRAVELERS

Though the age where the benefits begin varies with the attraction, travelers 50 years and up can expect to receive cut rates and benefits at many hotels, campgrounds, restaurants, parks and museums; be sure to inquire about such rates.

Visitors to national parks and campgrounds can cut costs greatly by using the Golden Age Passport, a card that allows US citizens aged 62 and over (and those traveling in the same car) free admission nationwide and a 50% reduction on camping fees. You can apply in person for any of these at any national park or regional office of the USFS or NPS.

Organizations

Some national advocacy groups that can help in planning your travels include the following:

American Association of Retired Persons (AARP) – An advocacy group for Americans 50 years and older and a good resource for travel bargains. US residents can get one-year/three-year memberships for $8/20. Citizens of other countries can get the same memberships for $10/24. 3200 E Carson St, Lakewood, CA 90712 (☎ 800-424-3410, www.aarp.org)

Elderhostel – A nonprofit organization that offers seniors the opportunity to attend academic college courses throughout the USA and Canada. The programs last one to three weeks and include meals and accommodations, and are open to people 55 years and older and their companions. 75 Federal St, Boston, MA 02110-1941 (☎ 617-426-8056)

Grand Circle Travel – This group offers escorted tours and travel information in a variety of formats and distributes a free useful booklet, *Going Abroad: 101 Tips for Mature Travelers*. 347 Congress St, Boston, MA 02210 (☎ 617-350-7500, 800-350-7500, www.gct/ gcc.com)

TRAVEL WITH CHILDREN

Children receive discounts on many things in the USA, ranging from motel stays to museum admissions. When making reservations, inquire if there are special family discounts. The definition of a child varies widely – some places count anyone under 18 eligible for children's discounts while other places only include children under the age of six.

Often hotels and motels let children under a certain age stay for free with parents, though B&Bs rarely do and some don't allow children at all. More expensive hotels can arrange baby-sitting services or have 'kids' clubs' for younger children. Restaurants offer inexpensive children's menus with a limited selection of kid-friendly foods at cheap prices only for patrons under 12 or 10 years of age.

Airlines do discount children's tickets, but these are often more expensive than the cheapest APEX adult tickets. Most buses and tours have discounted children's prices, though the discounts are not always very big. Car rental companies provide infant seats for their cars on request.

Child safety seats are required in all motor vehicles for children under two years of age. If you are renting a car and will be traveling with young children, be sure to indicate that you'll need a child's seat when you make a reservation; rental agencies will provide them free of charge.

Various children's activities are mentioned in appropriate places in the text. For information on enjoying travel with the young ones, read *Travel With Children* by Lonely Planet cofounder Maureen Wheeler.

USEFUL ORGANIZATIONS

See also the organizations listed above for seniors and disabled travelers, gay and lesbian travelers and women travelers. Also see the Outdoor Activities chapter for more useful organizations.

American Automobile Association

For its members AAA provides great travel information, distributes free road maps and guide books, and sells American Express traveler's checks without commission. The AAA membership card will often get you discounts for accommodations, car rental and admission charges. If you plan to do a lot of driving – even in a rental car – it is usually worth joining the AAA. It costs $56 for the first year and $39 for subsequent years.

Members of other auto clubs, including the Canadian Automobile Association (CAA) and Automobile Association in the UK, are entitled to the same services if they bring their membership cards.

AAA also provides emergency roadside service to members in the event of an accident, breakdown or if you lock your keys in the car. Service is free within a given radius of the nearest service center; service providers will tow your car to a mechanic if they can't fix it. The nationwide toll-free roadside assistance number is ☎ 800-222-4357 (800-AAA-HELP). All major cities and many smaller towns have an AAA office where you can become a member.

National Park Service & US Forest Service

The National Park Service (NPS), part of the Dept of the Interior, administrates the use of parks in the US. The US Forest Service (USFS) is under the Dept of Agriculture and administrates the use of forests. National forests are less protected than parks, allowing commercial development in some areas (usually logging or privately owned recreational facilities).

National parks most often surround spectacular natural features and cover hundreds of square miles. A full range of accommodations can be found in and around national parks. Contact individual parks for more specific information (see also the Outdoor Activities chapter for contact information). National park campground and reservations information can be obtained by calling ☎ 800-365-2267 or writing National Park Service Public Inquiry, Dept of the Interior, PO Box 37127, Washington, DC 20013-7127.

Current information about national forests can be obtained from ranger stations, which are also listed in the text. National forest campground and reservation information can be obtained by calling ☎ 800-280-2267. Contact the Pacific Northwest regional USFS office (☎ 503-326-2971) at PO Box 3623, Portland, OR 97208. General information about federal lands is also available from the Fish & Wildlife Service and the Bureau of Land Management (see below).

Golden Passports You can apply in person for any of the following at any US national park or regional office of the USFS or NPS.

Golden Eagle Passports cost $50 annually and offer one-year entry into national parks to the holder and accompanying guests.

Golden Age Passports are free and allow US residents 62 years and older unlimited entry to all sites in the national park system, with discounts on camping and other fees.

Golden Access Passports offer the same to US residents who are medically blind or permanently disabled.

Fish & Wildlife Service

Each state has a few regional Fish & Wildlife Service (FWS) offices that can provide information about viewing local wildlife. Their phone numbers appear in the blue section of the local white pages directory under US Government, Dept of the Interior or you can call the Federal

Information Center (☎ 800-688-9889). For specific fish and wildlife information you can also contact the following:

Oregon Dept of Fish & Wildlife
    2501 SW 1st Ave, Portland, OR 97201
    (☎ 503-229-5403)
Washington State Fish & Wildlife Dept
    PO Box 43135, 1111 Washington St SE,
    Olympia, WA 98504 (☎ 360-902-2200)

Bureau of Land Management

The BLM, as it is commonly called, manages public use of US federal grasslands. Facilities aren't as common as in the national forests, with occasional no-frills campgrounds and some hiking trails in rural areas of the West. Each state has a regional office located in the state capital. Look in the blue section of the local white pages directory under US Government, Dept of the Interior or call the Federal Information Center (☎ 800-688-9889). In Oregon you can contact BLM (☎ 503-952-6602) at 1515 SW 5th Ave, Portland, OR 97201.

Nature Conservancy

With a mission to protect the rarest living things for future generations, the Nature Conservancy organizes field tours for its members and can advise on interesting areas for the general public. The Oregon office (☎ 503-228-9561) is at 1205 NW 25th Ave, Portland, OR 97210. The Washington office (☎ 206-343-4344) is at 217 Pine St, Suite 1100, Seattle, WA 98101.

DANGERS & ANNOYANCES

For a largely sedate and seemingly sensible culture, the Northwest has a high rate of crime. As most crimes are 'property' crimes (that is, theft), travelers needn't inordinately fear random violence. However, there's no denying that North American urban culture can be menacing, and too frequently dangerous. As a rule of thumb, you'll be safer if you don't walk around central Vancouver, Portland or Seattle alone at night. In wilderness areas the consequences of an accident can be very serious, so inform someone of your route and expected return.

Personal Security & Theft

Although street crime is a serious issue in large urban areas, visitors need not be obsessed with security.

Always lock cars and put valuables out of sight, whether you are in a town or in the remote backcountry – even if you're leaving the car for just a few minutes. Rent a car with a lockable trunk. If your car is bumped from behind by another vehicle in a remote area, it's best to keep going to a well-lit area or service station.

Be aware of your surroundings and who may be watching you. Avoid walking on dimly lit streets at night, particularly when alone. Walk purposefully. Avoid unnecessary displays of money or jewelry. Divide money and credit cards to avoid losing everything. Aim to use ATM machines in well-trafficked areas.

In hotels don't leave valuables lying around your room. Use safe-deposit boxes or at least place valuables in a locked bag. Don't open your door to strangers – check the peephole or call the front desk if unexpected guests try to enter.

Street People The USA has a lamentable record in dealing with its most unfortunate citizens, who often roam the streets of large cities in the daytime and sleep by storefronts, under freeways or in alleyways and abandoned buildings at night.

This problem is less acute in the mostly rural states than in urban areas on both coasts, but it is certainly not absent. Street people and panhandlers may approach visitors in the larger cities and towns; nearly all of them are harmless. It's an individual judgment call whether it's appropriate to offer them money or anything else.

Guns The USA has a widespread reputation – partly true but also propagated and exaggerated by the media – as a dangerous place because of the availability of firearms. Residents of more rural states sometimes carry guns, but they most often target animals or isolated traffic signs, rather than humans. Do be careful in the woods during the fall hunting season, when unsuccessful or drunken hunters may be less selective in their targets than one might hope.

Wildlife

As more and more people spend time in the backcountry or impinge on wildlife habitat, attacks on humans and pets are becoming more common. Black bears, grizzly bears and pumas (mountain lions) are the most serious hazards, but seemingly placid and innocuous beasts like bison and mule deer are equally capable of inflicting serious injury or even fatal wounds on unsuspecting tourists. Some carry rabies. Keep your distance from all wild animals – even prairie dogs.

Bears Black bears are found in mountainous areas throughout the region, while grizzly bears are found only rarely in the regions covered in this guide. If you plan to continue your travels into BC's wilderness areas or to the Rocky Mountains, you should acquaint yourself with the grizzly and the threat it presents.

Black bears usually weigh about 200lb and stand about 3 feet tall. Color is not a reliable distinguishing trait – shades of brown are not at all unusual for a black bear.

Try not to surprise a bear. Stay alert and make some noise while hiking – many hikers will wear bells. Avoid strong odors by not wearing perfumes or cooking strong-smelling foods (freeze-dried foods are almost odor-free). At night keep food and smelly clothing inside a car or strung high in a tree. Sleep well away from the cooking area.

If you do see a bear, give it plenty of room. Try to stay upwind of the bear so it can get your scent. If the bear becomes aggressive, drop something that may absorb its attention and climb the nearest tall tree. If this isn't possible, the next best bet is probably to curl up into a ball, clasp your hands behind your neck and play dead, even if the bear begins to bat you around.

Bears (almost always grizzlies) can, and occasionally do, kill people, but most people who enter bear country never have any problem. Precautions and respect for bears will ensure not only your continued survival, but theirs as well.

Other Wildlife Mountain lions (also called cougars or pumas) are not as dangerous as bears, but as their territory in the mountains gets whittled away by development, there is more and more contact between humans and mountain lions. Also, mountain lions are increasing in population, which makes sighting one of these big cats more of a possibility than in the past. Adults aren't much at risk of mountain lion attack, but unattended children have been attacked and killed in recent years. If you come upon a moose (which live in parts of Northeastern Washington and on Vancouver Island) keep your distance. They aren't blood-thirsty, but they are given to anger: if surprised, they might charge. Fleeing an angry, 1800lb moose is to be avoided.

Marijuana Farms

In the US possession and use of marijuana is a federal felony. However, persistent demand for cannabis creates a lively, highly profitable market for the producer. Conditions for growing pot – which calls for both the right climate and near total seclusion – are perfect in remote southern Oregon and elsewhere in the Northwest. There, maverick pot growers often hide plots of marijuana in isolated pockets of national forests.

Travelers who accidentally stumble upon hidden marijuana fields are at risk: growers are especially protective of their plots, and have been known to rig the area with traps set to maim or kill trespassers. Hikers, especially those intent upon venturing off the beaten path, should be able to identify and keep an eye out for this plant, especially in Douglas County, OR, where marijuana is one of the biggest cash crops. If you do wander onto a marijuana field, it is important to leave the area as quickly and quietly as possible.

Mushroom Wars

Some of the same conditions, but not quite the same threat of harm, have come to surround the harvesting of wild mushrooms. For many unemployed timber workers, and others in rural communities, picking wild mushrooms has become a vital part of making a living, as prices for rare mushrooms right out of the forest can be as high as $40 a pound.

Understandably, knowledge of especially rich mushroom gathering areas has become highly guarded information. There have been instances where territorial disputes over mushroom beds have been settled with guns. The Forest Service is now trying to regulate mushroom hunting a bit more carefully, though casual mushroom picking by amateurs or hobbyists continues to be perfectly legal within guidelines. However, if while harvesting or hiking, you come upon an armed mushroom baron, simply retreat quietly. It is not worth fighting over mushrooms.

Ocean Safety

Coastal beaches are unsupervised, and those who venture into the water to wade or bodysurf should be wary of rip tides and drop-offs. Never turn your back on the ocean when beachcombing in or near the water. Large 'sneaker waves' may catch you unexpectedly during incoming tides. If caught in a rip tide or undertow, it's best to relax and go with the flow of the current until it dissipates (struggling will only exhaust you). Incoming tides also have the potential to strand visitors busily exploring tide pools or climbing coastal rocks.

EMERGENCY

Throughout most of the USA and Canada dial ☎ 911 for emergency service of any sort; in large cities or areas with substantial Hispanic populations, Spanish-speaking emergency operators may be available, but other languages are less likely. This is a free call from any phone. A few rural phones might not have this service, in which case dial ☎ 0 for the operator and ask for emergency assistance – it's still free. Each state also maintains toll-free numbers for traffic information and emergencies.

Oregon

State Police	☎ 503-378-3720
Road Conditions	☎ 541-889-3999
Weather Reports	☎ 541-779-5990

Washington

State Police	☎ 425-649-4370
Road Conditions	☎ 206-368-4499
	☎ 800-695-7623
Weather Reports	☎ 206-526-6087

Vancouver & Vancouver Island

Royal Canadian Mounted Police (RCMP)	☎ 604-264-3111
Road Conditions	☎ 604-299-9000 ext 7623
Weather Reports	☎ 604-299-9000 ext 3501

LEGAL MATTERS

If you are stopped by the police for any reason in the US, bear in mind that there is no system of paying fines on the spot. For traffic offenses, the police officer will explain your options to you. Attempting to pay the fine to the officer is frowned upon at best and may compound your troubles by resulting in a charge of bribery. Should the officer decide that you should pay up front, he or she can exercise the authority to take you directly to the magistrate instead of allowing you the usual 30-day period to pay the fine.

If you are arrested for more serious offenses, you are allowed to remain silent.

There is no legal reason to speak to a police officer if you don't wish, but never walk away from an officer until given permission. All persons who are arrested are legally allowed – and given – the right to make one phone call. If you don't have a lawyer or family member to help you, call your embassy. The police will give you the number upon request.

Drinking & Driving Laws

Each state and province has its own laws and what is legal in one jurisdiction may be illegal in others.

Some general rules are that you must be at least 16 years of age to drive (older in some states). Speed limits are 65 to 75 mph on interstates and freeways unless otherwise posted; in urban areas, the freeway speed limit is 55 mph. You can drive 5 mph over the limit without much likelihood of being pulled over, but if you are doing 10 mph over the limit, you'll probably be caught sooner or later. In small towns, driving over the posted speed by any amount may attract attention. Speed limits on other highways are 55 mph or less, and on city streets can vary from 25 to 45 mph. Watch for school zones, which can be as low as 15 mph during school hours – these limits are strictly enforced. Seat belts and motorcycle helmets must be worn in most states and in BC.

The drinking age is 21 in the US and 19 in Canada, and you need an ID (identification with your photograph on it) to prove your age. You could incur stiff fines, jail time and penalties if caught driving under the influence of alcohol. During festive holidays and special events, road blocks are sometimes set up to deter drunk drivers.

BUSINESS HOURS & PUBLIC HOLIDAYS

Most businesses stay open from 9 am to 5 pm, but there are certainly no hard and fast rules. In any large city, a few supermarkets and restaurants are open 24 hours. Shops are usually open from either 9 or 10 am to 5 or 6 pm (often until 9 pm in shopping malls), except Sundays when hours are noon to 5 pm (often later in malls). Post offices are open 8 am to 4 or 5:30 pm, Monday to Friday, and some are open 8 am to 3 pm on Saturday. Banks are usually open from either 9 or 10 am to 5 or 6 pm Monday to Friday. A few banks are open 9 am to 2 or 4 pm on Saturdays. Basically hours for post offices and banks are decided by individual branches, so if you need specifics give the branch you want a call.

Many art galleries are closed on Mondays, as are many fine restaurants.

National public holidays are celebrated throughout the USA and Canada. Banks, schools and government offices (including post offices) are closed and transportation, museums and other services are on a Sunday schedule. Holidays falling on a weekend are usually observed the following Monday.

Listed below are official US and Canadian national holidays.

New Year's Day
    January 1 (US & Canada)
Martin Luther King Jr Day
    third Monday in January (US only)
Presidents' Day
    third Monday in February (US only)
Easter
    a Sunday in late March or early April
    (US & Canada)
Victoria Day
    Monday preceding May 24 (Canada only)
Memorial Day
    last Monday in May (US only)
Canada Day
    July 1 (Canada only)
Independence Day (or the *Fourth of July*)
    July 4 (US only)
Labor Day
    first Monday in September (US & Canada)
Columbus Day
    second Monday in October (US only)
Thanksgiving Day
    second Monday in October (Canada only)
    fourth Thursday in November (US only)
Veterans' Day
    November 11 (US only)
Remembrance Day
    November 11 (US only)
Christmas Day
    December 25 (US & Canada)
Boxing Day
    December 26 (Canada only)

SPECIAL EVENTS
Each region of the Pacific Northwest celebrates unique local festivals, including the
following:

Oregon
May
All-Indian Rodeo
  Tygh Valley, mid-May

June
Portland Rose Festival
  Portland, early June
Pi Ume Sha Treaty Days Celebration
  Warm Springs, late June
Corvallis Folklife Festival
  Corvallis, late June

July
Albany Timber Carnival
  Albany, 4th of July weekend
Oregon Country Fair
  Veneta, first weekend after the 4th of July
Oregon Brewers Festival
  Portland, late July
Chief Joseph Days
  Joseph, late July
Sand Castle Building Contest
  Lincoln City, late July

August
Mt Hood Festival of Jazz
  Gresham, early August

September
Pendleton Round Up
  Pendleton, third weekend of September
Mt Angel Oktoberfest
  Mt Angel, mid-September
Eugene Celebration
  Eugene, third weekend of September

October
Cranberry Festival
  Bandon, mid-October

Washington
February
Upper Skagit Bald Eagle Festival
  Concrete, Rockport and Marblemount,
  first weekend of February

April
Skagit Valley Tulip Festival
  Mt Vernon, first two weeks of April

May
Bloomsday Run
  Spokane, first Sunday in May
Northwest Folklife Festival
  Seattle, Memorial Day weekend

July
Yakima Nation Cultural Powwow & Rodeo
  Toppenish, Fourth of July weekend
Seafair
  Seattle, third weekend in July
Jazz
  Port Townsend, last weekend in July

August
Washington State International Kite Festival
  Long Beach, third weekend in August
Fort Vancouver Founder's Day
  Vancouver, August 25

September
Bumbershoot
  Seattle, Labor Day weekend
Historic Homes Tour
  Port Townsend, mid-September (and first
  week of May)

Vancouver & Victoria
January/February
Chinese New Year
  Vancouver, end of January or beginning
  of February

May
Victoria Day Festival
  Victoria, fourth week of May

June
Canadian International Dragon Boat Festival
  Vancouver, late June
Victoria International Festival
  Victoria, June through August

July
Vancouver Folk Music Festival
  Vancouver, mid-July

August
Abbotsford International Air Show
  Abbotsford, early August
First Peoples' Festival
  Victoria, mid-August

September
Fringe Theatre Festival
  Vancouver, late August and early September

Let's Celebrate

The US is always ready to call a day an 'event.' Here are some of the most widely celebrated ones:

January

Chinese New Year – begins at the end of January or beginning of February and lasts two weeks. The first day is celebrated with parades, firecrackers, fireworks and tons of food.

February

Valentine's Day – the 14th. No one knows why St Valentine is associated with romance in the USA, but this is the day to celebrate.

March

St Patrick's Day – the 17th. The patron saint of Ireland is honored by all those who feel the Irish in their blood and by those who want to feel Irish beer in their blood. Everyone wears green (if you don't, you can get pinched).

April

Easter – those who observe the holiday may go to church, paint eggs, eat chocolate eggs or any mixture of the above. Travel during this weekend is usually expensive and crowded. Incidentally, Good Friday is not a public holiday and often goes unnoticed.

Passover – either in March or April, depending on the Jewish calendar. Families get together to remember the persecution of forebears, partake in the symbolic seder dinner and eat unleavened bread.

May

Cinco de Mayo – the 5th. The day the Mexicans wiped out the French Army in 1862. Now it's the day all Americans get to eat heaps of Mexican food and drink margaritas.

Mother's Day – the 2nd Sunday. Children send cards and flowers and call Mom. Restaurants are likely to be busy.

June

Father's Day – the 3rd Sunday. Same idea as Mother's Day, different parent.

October

Halloween – the 31st. Kids and adults dress in costumes. In safer neighborhoods children go 'trick-or-treating' for candy. Adults go to parties to act out their alter egos.

November

Day of the Dead – the 2nd. Observed in areas with Mexican communities, this is a day for families to remember dead relatives, and make breads and sweets resembling skeletons, skulls and such.

Thanksgiving – held on the last Thursday of the month. The most important family gathering is celebrated with a bounty of food and football games on TV. The following day is declared by retailers as the biggest shopping day of the year with everyone burning off pumpkin pie by running shopping relays through the malls.

December

Christmas – the night before the 25th is as much of an event as the day itself with church services, caroling in the streets, people cruising neighborhoods looking for the best light displays and stores full of last-minute shoppers.

Hanukkah – eight days in December, according to the Jewish calendar; also called 'The Feast of Lights.'

Kwanzaa – starts on December 26 and lasts to the 31st. This African American celebration is a time to give thanks for the harvest.

New Year's Eve – the 31st. People celebrate by dressing up and drinking champagne, or staying home and watching the festivities on TV. The following day people stay home to nurse their hangovers and watch college football. ■

WORK

It's possible to find seasonal work in national parks and other tourist sites in the US, especially ski areas; for information, contact park concessionaires or local chambers of commerce.

If you're not a US citizen, you'll need to apply for a work visa from the US embassy in your home country before you leave. The type of visa varies depending on how long you're staying and the kind of work you plan to do. Generally, you will need either a J-1 visa, which you can obtain by joining a visitor-exchange program, or an H-2B visa, which you get when being sponsored by a US employer. The latter is not easy to obtain (since the employer has to prove that no US citizen or permanent resident is available to do the job); the former is issued mostly to students for work in summer camps.

Casual labor can be found in the Northwest during the harvest seasons, when farmers hire hundreds of laborers to pick fruit and other crops. Cafes and coffee shops are also good bets for quick employment.

ACCOMMODATIONS
Camping

Camping is the cheapest – and in many ways the most enjoyable – approach to a vacation. Visitors with a car and a tent can take advantage of hundreds of public and private campgrounds and RV parks at prices of $10 per night or even less.

Public Campgrounds These are on public lands such as national forests, state, provincial and national parks, BLM lands, etc (see Useful Organizations, above).

Free dispersed camping (meaning you can camp almost anywhere) is permitted in many public backcountry areas. Sometimes you can camp right from your car along a dirt road, especially in BLM and national forest areas. Obviously, in this situation there are no facilities. In other places, backpack your gear in to a cleared campsite.

Information and detailed maps are available from many local ranger stations or BLM offices (addresses and telephone numbers are given in the text) and may be posted along the road. Sometimes, a free camping permit is required, particularly in national parks or wilderness areas, less frequently in forests and BLM areas.

When camping in an undeveloped area choose a camp site at least 200 yards (approximately 70 adult steps) from water and wash up at camp, not in the stream, using biodegradable soap. Dig a 6-inch deep hole to use as a latrine and cover and camouflage it well when leaving the site. Burn toilet paper, unless fires are prohibited. Carry out all trash. Use a portable charcoal grill or camping stove; don't build new fires. If there's already a fire ring, use only dead and downed wood or wood you have carried in yourself. Make sure to leave the campsite as you found it.

Developed areas usually have toilets, drinking water, fire pits (or charcoal grills) and picnic benches. Some do not have drinking water (this is mentioned in the text). At any rate, it is always a good idea to have a few gallons of water when venturing out to the boonies. These basic campgrounds usually cost about $8 to $11 a night.

More developed areas may have showers or RV hookups. On the whole, national forest and BLM campgrounds tend to be of

---

Camping Etiquette

Camping in an undeveloped area demands basic responsibility. Choose a campsite at least 100 yards from water and wash up at camp, not in the stream. Dig a 6-inch-deep hole to use as a latrine and burn your toilet paper (unless fires are prohibited because of high forest-fire danger). Carry out all trash. Use a portable charcoal grill or camping stove instead of building new fires. If there already is a fire ring, use only dead and down wood or wood you have carried in yourself. Make sure to leave the campsite as you found it. ■

the less-developed variety, while national park and state park campgrounds are more likely to have showers or RV hookups available. The less-developed sites are often on a 'first-come, first-served' basis, so plan on an early arrival, preferably during the week, as sites fill up fast on Fridays and weekends. More-developed areas may accept or require reservations; details are given in the text.

Costs given in the text for public camp grounds are per site. One site normally accommodates up to six people (or two vehicles). If there are more of you, you'll need two sites. Public campgrounds often have seven- or 14-night limits.

Due to budget cutbacks, the price of camping in state and provincial parks and other publicly owned areas has skyrocketed in recent years, and will continue to climb as funding decreases even further. When exact prices aren't mentioned in the text, assume that a tent site in a public campground will cost $10 to $15; sites with hookups for RVs will run between $15 to $25.

Reservations for campsites at state parks are both possible and advised during the summer. Oregon and Washington sponsor a toll-free number (☎ 800-452-5687) that you can use to make reservations for both states' parks. The reservations service costs $6, which is added to your first night's fee (ie, if you reserve three nights at the same campsite, you only pay the $6 once) To make a reservation, you must pay with a Visa or MasterCard. For sites in national forests call ☎ 800-280-2267.

In BC, provincial park campsites can be reserved by calling ☎ 800-689-9025 or 604-689-9025 in Vancouver. There's a C$6 *per night* reservation fee, with a maximum of C$18 for the same site (ie, reserving a site for two nights will cost C$12, five nights will be C$18).

Private Campgrounds These are on private property and are usually close to or in a town. Most are designed with RVs in mind; tenters can usually camp at some sites but fees are several dollars higher than in public campgrounds. Fees given in the text are for two people per site. There is usually an extra person charge of $1 to $3 each. In addition, state and city taxes apply. However, campgrounds may offer discounts for weekly or monthly stays.

Facilities can include hot showers, coin laundry, swimming pool, full RV hookups, games area, playground and a convenience store. Kampgrounds of America (KOA) is a national network of private campgrounds with sites usually ranging from $15 to $22, depending on hookups. You can get an annual directory of KOA sites by contacting KOA (☎ 406-248-7444), PO Box 30558, Billings, MT 59114-0558.

Hostels
The US hostel network is less widespread than in Canada, the UK, Europe and Australia and is predominately in the north and coastal parts of the country. Not all are directly affiliated with Hostelling International/American Youth Hostels (HI/AYH). Those that are offer discounts to HI/AYH members and usually allow nonmembers to stay for a few dollars more. Dormitory beds usually cost about $12 to $17 a night. Rooms are in the $20s for one or two people, sometimes more.

HI/AYH hostels expect you to rent or carry a sheet or sleeping bag to keep the beds clean. Dormitories are segregated by sex and curfews may exist. Kitchen and laundry privileges are usually available in return for light housekeeping duties. There are information and advertising boards, TV rooms and lounge areas. Alcohol may be banned.

Reservations Reservations are accepted and advised during the high season, when there may be a three-night limit. Get further information from HI/AYH (☎ 202-783-6161, fax 202-783-6171, hiayhserve @hiayh.org; www.hiayh.org), 733 15th St NW, Suite 840, Washington, DC 20005, or use their code-based reservation service at ☎ 800-909-4776 (you need the access code for the hostels to use this service, available from any HI/AYH office or listed in their handbook).

Independent hostels have comparable rates and conditions to HI/AYH hostels and may sometimes be better. They often have a few private single/double rooms available, sometimes with private bathrooms. Kitchen, laundry, notice board and TV facilities are available. *The Hostel Handbook* by Jim Williams is a 66-page listing of all hostels and is available for $5 payable to the author at 722 St Nicholas Ave, New York, NY 10031 (☎ 212-926-7030; infohostel@aol.com). The Internet Guide to Hostelling (www.hostels.com) lists hostels throughout the world.

For a complete description of all eight HI/AYH hostels throughout Washington, contact Hostelling International, Washington State Council (☎ 206-281-7306), No 102, 419 Queen Anne Ave N, Seattle, WA 98109. You will find hostels in Bellingham, Blaine, Chinook, Fort Flagler, Port Townsend, Seattle, Spokane and Vashon Island.

Oregon also has eight hostels, in Ashland, Bandon, Bend, Cave Junction, Corvallis, Dexter, Portland and Seaside. The HI/AYH office in Portland (☎ 503-223-1873, 235-9493) is at 1520 SE 37th Ave, Portland, OR 97214.

There are 16 HI hostels in BC, including Victoria, Salt Spring Island, Whistler and two in Vancouver. For information on all hostels in BC, contact the Jericho Beach hostel in Vancouver, at 1515 Discover St, Vancouver, BC V6R 4K5 (☎ 604-684-7181). In addition, a number of hotels in Vancouver and Victoria offer hostel-style lodging.

B&Bs

European visitors should be aware that North American B&Bs are often not the casual, inexpensive sort of accommodations found on the continent or in Britain. While they are usually family-run, many if not most B&Bs require advance reservations, though some will be happy to oblige the occasional drop-in.

A large majority of B&Bs prohibit smoking, many also restrict children (ie, no children under 12). All have substantial breakfasts included in their prices, but lighter continental breakfasts are not unheard of. The cheapest establishments, with rooms in the $30s and $40s, may have clean but unexciting rooms with a shared bathroom.

Pricier places have rooms with private baths and, perhaps, facilities like fireplaces, balconies, and dining rooms with enticingly grand breakfasts and other meals. They may be in historical buildings, quaint country houses or luxurious urban townhouses. Most B&Bs fall in the $50 to $100 price range, but some go over $100. The best are distinguished by a friendly attention to detail by owner/hosts who can provide you with local information and contacts and a host of other amenities. Particularly in rural areas, homes advertising 'bed and breakfast' are usually more modest, and you'll be dealing with a family whose main business is usually agriculture rather than serving as a professional innkeeper. You be the judge if that's something you'd prefer.

The B&Bs listed in this guide are usually well established and reputable. However, B&Bs come and go quickly (some are only seasonal), so be sure to call ahead to make sure the inn is still in operation. Also, check with the local chamber of commerce to find out what new B&Bs might have opened.

In Washington, the Washington State Bed & Breakfast Guild (☎ 800-647-2918), 2442 NW Market St, Seattle, WA 98107, publishes a yearly directory of member B&Bs. The islands of the Puget Sound, particularly the San Juans, are loaded with B&Bs.

There are a number of Oregon B&B associations. You can contact either Oregon B&B Directory, 230 Red Spur Drive, Grants Pass, OR 97527, or Oregon B&B Guild, PO Box 3187, Ashland, OR 97520, for brochures with B&B listings statewide. Ashland is Oregon's B&B hotbed with over 60 in this little theater-loving town. Portland offers some spectacular B&Bs in old mansions. Older towns along the coast, like Newport and Astoria, also offer quality B&B lodgings in classic old homes.

Though not a booking agency, contact the Western Canada B&B Innkeepers Association (☎ 604-255-9199), PO Box 74534, Vancouver, BC V6K 4P4, for a brochure with member listings in Vancouver and across the province.

Motels & Hotels

Motel and hotel prices vary tremendously in price from season to season. A hotel charging $40 for a double in the high season may drop to $25 in the low and may raise its rates to $55 for a special event when the town is overflowing with visitors. Prices in this guide can only be an approximate guideline at best. Also, be prepared to add room tax to prices. Children are often allowed to stay free with their parents, but rules for this vary. Some hotels allow children under 18 to stay free with parents, others allow children under 12 and others may charge a few dollars per child. You should call and inquire if traveling with a family.

The prices advertised by hotels are called 'rack rates' and are not written in stone. If you simply ask about any specials that might apply you can often save quite a bit of money. Booking through a travel agent also saves you money as well. Members of AARP, CAA, or AAA can qualify for a 'corporate' rate at several hotel chains.

Most hotels hike up the price of local calls by almost 200% and long-distance rates are gouged up from 100% to 200%! The best plan of action is to use a pay phone for all your calls.

Special events and conventions can fill up a town's hotels quickly, so call ahead to find out what will be going on. The visitors center is always a good resource.

Price Categories In this guide, prices for motels and hotels listed as 'budget' vary quite a lot in price. In the major cities, the lower end of accommodations can range from $25 to $60 per night, while in small rural towns $60 will buy you the best room in the area. In general, motels and hotels listed as budget will cost you between $25 and $40.

Gas, Food, Lodging

When coming into a city on the highway you will notice signs that say 'Gas Food Lodging' followed by something like 'Next Three Exits'. Don't assume these exits will lead you directly into the city center – they won't. You'll end up traveling along strips of chain motels, fast-food restaurants and gas stations with small grocery stores. If you have no intention of staying in town, but would rather catch a few hours' sleep and head out early on the road, these establishments do provide a cheap alternative to downtown and a bit of true Americana. ■

Motels with $25 rooms are found especially in small towns on major highways and the motel strips of larger towns. Rooms are usually small, and beds may be soft or saggy, but the sheets should be clean. A minimal level of cleanliness is maintained, but expect scuffed walls, atrocious decor, old furniture and strange noises from your shower. Even these places, however, normally have a private shower and toilet and a TV in each room. Most have air-con and heat.

Some of even the cheapest motels may advertise kitchenettes. These may cost a few dollars more but give you the chance to cook a simple meal for yourself if you are fed up with restaurants. Kitchenettes vary from a two-ring burner to a spiffy little mini-kitchen and may or may not have utensils. If you plan on doing a lot of kitchenette cooking, carry your own set of utensils.

Throughout this guide, motels and hotels listed as 'middle' generally have rooms ranging from $40 to $80, though in cities like Portland, Seattle and Vancouver, the cost of mid-range rooms can reach up to $100. With mid-range lodgings, you can usually expect a certain level of amenities, often including a swimming pool, TV with movie channels and a laundry. Most rooms will come standard with queen beds.

Full-service hotels, with bellhops and doormen, restaurants and bars, exercise rooms and saunas, and room service and concierge, are found in Portland, Seattle, Vancouver and Victoria, and in resort areas. In this guide, hotels with nightly rates of over $100 are considered 'top end', though often rates will top $200 a night for this class of hotel.

Chains There are many motel and hotel chains in the USA. The level of quality and style tends to be repeated throughout the chain. If you plan to stay at hotels of the same chain, investigate the chain's frequent-guest program – discounts and guaranteed reservations are offered to faithful guests.

The cheapest national chain is Motel 6. Rooms start in the $20s for a single in smaller towns, in the $30s in larger towns. They usually charge a flat $6 for each extra person.

Motel chains in the next price level start in the $30s in the smaller towns or in the $40s in larger or more popular places. The main difference is the size of the room and the quality: firmer beds, cable TV, free coffee. If these sorts of things are worth an extra $10 or $15 a night, then you'll be happy with the Super 8 Motels, Days Inn or Econo Lodge.

Stepping up to chains with rooms in the $45 to $80 range, depending on location, you'll find noticeably nicer rooms; cafes, restaurants or bars may be on the premises

or adjacent to them; the swimming pool may be indoor with a spa or exercise room also available. The Best Western chain offers good rooms in this price range. Less widespread but also good are the Comfort Inns, Quality Inns and Sleep Inns.

Reservations The cheapest bottom-end places may not accept reservations, but at least phone from the road to see what's available; even if they don't take reservations they'll often hold a room for an hour or two.

Chain hotels will all take reservations days or months ahead. Normally, you have to give a credit-card number to hold the room. If you don't show and don't call to cancel, you will be charged the first night's rental. Cancellation policies vary so find out when you book.

Also make sure to let the hotel know if you plan on a late arrival – many motels will give your room away if you haven't arrived or called by 6 pm. Chains have toll-free numbers but their central reservation system might not be aware of local special discounts. Booking ahead, however, gives you the peace of mind of a guaranteed room when you arrive.

The reservation numbers of some of the best known chains are:

Best Western	☎ 800-528-1234
Comfort Inn, Sleep Inn	☎ 800-221-2222
Days Inn	☎ 800-329-7466
Econo Lodge, Rodeway Inn	☎ 800-424-4777
Howard Johnson	☎ 800-446-4656
Motel 6	☎ 800-466-8356
Super 8 Motel	☎ 800-800-8000
Quality Inn	☎ 800-228-5151
Travelodge	☎ 800-578-7878

Lodges

The word 'lodge' is used with great latitude in the Northwest. Places like Timberline Lodge on Mt Hood and Paradise Lodge on Mt Rainier are magnificent old log structures with dozens of rooms infused with a sense of the woods and hand-crafted venerability. Most other lodges are more modest. Many lakes in the Cascades boast lodges which offer cabin accommodations, campsites, boat rentals and at least a small store if not a cafe. Some of these lodges are just fine; others are quite funky and unspectacular. If your standards are exacting, make careful inquiries before heading up long mountain roads to marginal accommodations best suited to hardened anglers.

In national parks, accommodations are usually limited to either camping or park lodges operating as a concession. These lodges are often rustic looking but usually quite comfortable inside. Restaurants are on the premises and tour services are often available. National park lodges are not cheap, with most rooms going for close to $100 for a double during the high season, but they are your only option if you want to stay inside the park without camping. If you are coming during the high season make a reservation months in advance.

Guest Ranches

The rural Pacific Northwest has a number of guest ranches, where guests stay in Old West surroundings (ie, log ranch buildings and cabins, horse corrals and a central lodge hung with mounted animal heads). These can range from family ranches that also take in guests during the summer, to upscale dude ranches with a number of recreational options. Most guests ranches ask for minimum stays and prices include all meals and lodging. Advance reservations are usually required. If you're contemplating staying at a guest ranch, be sure to ask specific questions about lodgings and work requirements. Expectations of the guest and host can vary widely.

Resorts

In central Oregon and Washington especially, the last 20 years have seen a proliferation of resorts. Most of these establishments are quite upscale and include many recreational facilities, including golf courses, tennis courts, swimming pools and guided outdoor activities. The price for resort accommodations can be steep, but if it includes golf fees and access to recreational facilities, then the price tag may not seem prohibitive. Lodging options usually include staying in condominiums, hotel-like lodge rooms, or in privately owned homes rented on a short-term basis.

Property Management Agents

In many coastal areas and in central Oregon and Washington, private homeowners keep weekend or vacation homes, but depend on occasional rentals to help pay the mortgage. Most of these homes have at least three bedrooms, and are decorated, well maintained and furnished like a regular home.

To rent a private home, contact a local property management company. Obviously some restrictions apply: the family has first dibs on the home, usually for major holiday and summer weekends. There's usually a minimum stay of two nights and there may be a housekeeping fee. However, for a family, or for a group of friends, these homes may represent one of the best lodging values in the area.

A good way to determine the real value of a rental home is to divide the cost of the house per night by the number of bedrooms, and then compare that price to the cost of a local motel. Usually, if you plan on filling at least three bedrooms, you will probably be more comfortable – and more cheaply – lodged in a private home.

Listings for property agents are included in the text for those communities where there is a sufficient number of rental homes. Contact the local chamber of commerce for property management firms in other communities.

FOOD

With a long seacoast, fertile valleys filled with farms and orchards, and miles and miles of grasslands devoted to livestock, the Northwest offers high-quality, locally grown food products to both enterprising home cooks and restaurant chefs. There's little that's unique to Northwest kitchens, but there are a number of items and dishes that are regional specialties, or that at least are symptomatic of the Northwest's taste in food.

Master chef and food writer James Beard was a native of Portland, and many Northwest chefs have personal stories to tell of him. Beard's legacy to Northwest regional food is an appreciation of local or indigenous ingredients, prepared with simple elegance, and an attitude that eating great food ought to be great fun.

Mealtimes

Usually served roughly between 6 am and 10 am, typical American breakfasts are large and filling, often including eggs or an omelet, bacon or ham, fried potatoes, toast with butter and jam and coffee or tea. Some diners offer a breakfast menu throughout the day. More and more, people opt for the easier alternative of cereal or coffee and a pastry or bagel.

Lunch is usually available between 11 am and 2 pm. One strategy for enjoying good restaurants on a budget is to frequent them for lunch, when fixed-price specials for as little as $5 or slightly more are common.

Dinners, served between about 5 pm and 10 pm, are more expensive but often very reasonably priced; portions are usually large. Specials may also be available, but they will usually be more expensive than lunch specials. Some of the better restaurants require reservations.

Restaurants in the Northwest are often closed on Mondays; phoning ahead is a good idea.

Price Categories

In this guide restaurants are sometimes broken down into budget, middle and top-end listings. In general, budget restaurants have main dishes that are under $10 for an evening meal. These are often ethnic restaurants, classic American diners or informal eateries with carryout options. Main dishes in middle-range restaurants will cost from $10 to $18. These restaurants are usually informal (you won't need to dress up), though the food is often of high quality. Even though entrées may not be expensive in mid-range restaurants, you can often rack up quite a bill by the time

you add an appetizer, a salad, dessert, or a bottle of wine.

Top-end restaurant menus have entrées or selections that top $20 per person. These restaurants will often serve Northwest cuisine or high-end French or Italian cooking. Some restaurants will have prix-fixe menus that offer a number of courses for a set price, usually from $40 to $60. Note that entrées at high-end restaurants are almost always served à la carte; that is, soup, salad, dessert and appetizers are all extra. A leisurely meal with several courses and a bottle of wine at top Northwest restaurants can easily top $50 per person. And don't forget the tip.

However, it is important to note that you can eat cheaply in almost any expensive restaurant; a salad and a meatless pasta dish, or a couple appetizers and a glass of wine, can be quite inexpensive and allow you entry into dining rooms you otherwise could not afford to grace.

Northwest Cuisine

From the Sea Seafood is a cornerstone of the Northwest table. Coastal restaurants vie to claim the best clam chowder, which is often thick and starchy. Crab, fresh from the boat, is available almost everywhere along the coast. It's usually served in salad, or else simply with drawn butter.

Oyster farms are springing up along the coast; the chill waters of the Pacific produce sweet-tasting, delicately tangy oysters of the highest quality. In good restaurants, discerning diners can choose which Northwest bay their oysters on the half shell hail from. Stop by an oyster farm and handpick a dozen tiny komomoto oysters for an impromptu hors d'oeuvre. Clams, usually steamed in broth or in seawater, are a common appetizer; if you have a chance to order razor clams, by all means do. These elongated, delicately flavored clams are the nobility of Northwest shellfish. Mussels, which cover practically every rock along the Pacific Coast, are only lately catching favor as a harvestable seafood.

Locally caught fish include red snapper, flounder and sole, tuna, halibut and cod.

Shrimp is another major catch. Salmon, still a menu staple, are as likely to be from Alaska as from the Northwest. Local trout are also found in fish markets and on menus: watch for vibrantly yellow golden trout.

From the Field & Orchard The Northwest offers an incredibly rich diversity in fruits and berries. Marionberries, unique to Oregon, are like a cross between raspberries and blackberries, but twice as big and more succulent. Try a slice of marionberry pie, or cobbler, with a scoop of local ice cream. Blueberries thrive in the acidic soil of the Northwest, and appear in pies, breads, muffins and scones. Mt Hood strawberries are renowned for their spicy, near-wild taste; they're completely unlike the hard red-and-white objects found in most grocery stores.

The thick forests also provide a bounty of fruit. Blackberry brambles snag clothing and grab at the legs of hikers. They're a great annoyance until they produce their heady abundance of purple-black fruit, which makes great jam and pies. More delicate salmonberries are a light orange, and make a good hiker's snack, or, if you can gather enough, a beautiful pastel jelly. Huckleberries, found high up in mountain meadows, are a favorite of black bears. These small wild blueberries are fun to pick and make great pies. Look for huckleberry ice cream in out-of-the-way mountain cafes. Another berry that's become an important component of the coastal economy and of cutting-edge cooking is the cranberry. This part of the country is a major producer of this tart, bright-red berry.

Wild forest mushrooms, which have garnered a great deal of interest over the last 15 years, are indigenous to Northwest forests, including the most noted and expensive varieties favored in French, Italian and Japanese cuisine; chanterelle, oyster, morel, porcini and shiitake mushrooms are shipped worldwide. Expect forest mushrooms to turn up on your plate indiscriminately as the pedigree of genuine Northwest cuisine.

Many of the vegetables produced by small specialty farmers in the lower Willamette Valley, Fraser Valley, Sauvies Island and along the Puget Sound are grown organically. Some eastern Oregon and Washington ranchers have taken to raising organic cattle and sheep.

Along the coast and western valleys, dairies produce abundant milk, which is made into noted cheeses. The center of Oregon's dairy industry is the Tillamook Valley, with its famous Tillamook Cheddar. Other dairies in the Rogue and Umpqua valleys also produce traditional orange cheeses; one Tillamook-area dairy has begun to fashion French-style brie cheeses. In BC, dairies in the Fraser Valley and on Vancouver Island produce excellent cheddar cheeses. Locally made ice creams are favored by many people.

No discussion of food from the Pacific Northwest would be complete without mentioning nuts; Oregon is one of the few states that has an official state nut, the filbert. The filbert (or hazelnut) grows profusely here. Look for hazelnut gift packs (some jazzed up in smokehouse or jalapeño style) or hazelnuts served in baked goods or with meat for that special, Northwest touch.

Fast Food
All the usual run-of-the-mill chains – McDonald's, Burger King, Kentucky Fried Chicken and so on – are widely dispersed throughout the Northwest, as well as pizza outlets like Pizza Hut. Since these fast-food chains are so abundant and conspicuous, they're only rarely mentioned in the text. It's worth noting, though, that in a small town vegetarians will often find that the local fast-food restaurant has the only meat-free options; Pizza Hut, for instance, always features a salad bar.

DRINKS
Nonalcoholic Drinks
Tap water in the Northwest is safe and perfectly acceptable to drink. In fact, its purity is legendary. Bottled water, including local brands from storied glaciers or lakes, are

readily available in supermarkets. Water from streams, however, should never be drunk without purifying, as giardia is a major problem (see Health earlier in this chapter).

Bottled fruit juices are widely available, even in gas stations. In larger centers, ask around for a juice bar, where you can buy freshly extracted elixirs. Soft drinks, also called 'pop,' are sold nearly everywhere.

Coffee

In case you haven't heard, the Pacific Northwest is the hub of a coffee craze that seems to be sweeping the USA and Canada. It started out with a few espresso bars serving up European-style coffee drinks like cappuccinos and caffe lattes. Soon, the entire region was buzzing with caffeine, and asking for more. Standards for coffee quality – and strength – keep elevating.

In centers like Vancouver, Victoria, Portland, Seattle, Bellingham and Eugene, you can expect to have at least one coffee shop on almost every downtown block, while every major building will have an espresso cart out front. Even out-of-the-way gas stations and fast-food restaurants offer espresso drinks. It's part of life in the Northwest.

Starbucks, the now-international chain of coffee bars from the Seattle area, is by no means the only coffee empire in the region. As standards for taste and strength of coffee increase, locals can be fickle about Starbucks, now that they have achieved such notoriety. There's competi-

tion too, including Seattle's Best Coffee (SBC) in Seattle, Torrefazione Italia in Portland and Seattle, Coffee People in Portland, Blenz in Vancouver and Allann Bros in Eugene and Corvallis.

In addition to simple dash-in dash-out coffee bars and on-the-fly espresso carts, there are drive-through espresso bars, coffee delivery services (they will bring coffee to your motel room) and coffeehouses (see Coffeehouses under Entertainment, later in this chapter).

Wines

Northwest wines have an excellent international reputation. Especially noted are wines from an area south and west of Portland called Yamhill County. Conditions are very similar to France's Burgundy region, and chardonnay and pinot noir grapes do very well. Further south, in the Rogue River drainage, hot-weather grapes like Cabernet sauvignon and merlot are more the norm. On the slopes of the Columbia River Gorge, Rieslings, pinot gris and Gewürtzraminer grapes produce soft, dry white wines.

In Washington, the principal wine-growing region is east of the Cascades, in the arid foothills of the Yakima and Walla Walla River valleys. The sturdy, hot-weather grapes of southern France do best out here; Cabernet sauvignon wines from these areas can rival California wines in strength, if not always in subtlety. Merlots and Semillons are also popular, often boasting an herbaceous intensity not found in these varieties elsewhere. BC has a burgeoning wine industry based in the Okanagan Valley. Conditions are similar to Washington, and the same varietals are cultivated.

Enologists can contact the Washington Wine Commission (☎ 206-728-2252) PO Box 61217, Seattle, WA 98121 and the Oregon Winegrowers Association (☎ 503-228-8403), 1200 NW Front Ave, suite 400, Portland, OR 97209 for more information.

Winery Visits Most wineries are owner-operated and welcome visitors to their vineyard tasting rooms for small sips of wines gratis or for a nominal fee. There is no obligation to buy wine after a tasting. The wineries recommended in this guide are among the best, though some are included as much for the view or gracious facility as much as for the quality of wine. *Northwest Wines & Wineries* by Chuck Hill (Speed Graphics, Seattle 1993) is a good resource for traveling wine lovers.

Microbrewed Beers & Ales
Perhaps it's due to all the rain, but the Pacific Northwest has become a bastion of locally microbrewed beers. Small breweries have sprung up across the region, providing fantastic beers and ales to appreciative audiences. While most regular bars will offer at least one local brew, go to the brewery itself to get the real microbrewery experience. Most brewpubs offer a taster's selection of the house brews. Almost all brewpubs also offer light dining. In this guide, microbreweries are usually listed under the Entertainment heading.

Alcohol & Drinking Age
Persons under the age of 21 (minors) are prohibited from consuming alcohol in the USA; the drinking age in Canada is 19. Carry a driver's license or passport as proof of age to enter a bar, order alcohol at a restaurant or buy alcohol. Servers have the right to ask to see your ID and may refuse service without it. Minors are not allowed in bars and pubs, even to order nonalcoholic beverages. Unfortunately, this means that most dance clubs are also off-limits to minors, although a few clubs have solved the underage problem with a segregated drinking area. Minors are, however, welcome in the dining areas of restaurants where alcohol may be served. Alternatively, in larger cities some coffee shops offer live entertainment for customers of all ages.

ENTERTAINMENT
Portland, Seattle and Vancouver are cosmopolitan cities and offer a wide variety of films, music, theater, sports and nightlife. Eugene, Bellingham and Victoria, are all home to large well-respected universities that draw speakers, concerts, foreign films, art shows and student-oriented happenings like dance clubs and demonstrations.

In Ashland, with its Shakespearean theaters, bars fill up with young actors

---

Microbreweries
The Pacific Northwest is a major center of the US boom in small, specialty beer-making operations called microbreweries. Beers from these independent businesses tend to echo either British or German brewing styles, but generally conform to the sorts of standards and styles known as British 'real ale' beers. While microbrewed beer is available throughout the region either in bottles or on tap at many bars and restaurants, for the real microbrew experience, head to the brewery itself, which often features a pub within sight of the brewing tanks. In addition to standard brews, there are often seasonal or specialty beers and ales available at the brewpub, often cask-conditioned. You can usually arrange a tour of the brewery, if sufficient notice is given.

Portland is a real center for microbrewing; its summer Oregon Brewers Festival brings in microbrewed beers from all over the nation. In the tradition of the frontier era, when every town had its own brewery, many out-of-the-way places now have their own, sometimes *very micro* brewery. Look for the local beer in places as diverse as Hood River, Cave Junction, Newport, Roslyn, Government Camp, Yakima and Bend.

Most brewpubs exist to sell only their own beers and ales, though others are like British 'free-houses' and offer a selection of regional brews. In this guide, brewpubs are found under Entertainment or Places to Eat. ∎

recently divested of roles like Hamlet, Juliet or Bottom. Boise, Bend, Spokane and Hood River also serve up diversions for the traveler, mostly live music in the back of energetic bars.

Coffeehouses

Portland and Seattle particularly abound with coffeehouses, which often offer unique and inexpensive entertainment, including literary readings, slam poetry contests, acoustic music and discussion groups. Coffeehouses are also just about the only venue where underage travelers can easily meet their peers. Throughout this guide, coffeehouses of note (whether for entertainment, food, the scene or just for the quality of their coffee) are noted under Entertainment or Places to Eat.

Bars, Taverns & Brewpubs

Oregon and Washington law makes a strict differentiation between bars and taverns. Bars can sell hard liquor as well as beer and wine; taverns can sell only beer and wine. Taverns, more often than not, are intensely local pubs with limited tolerance for strangers. Brewpubs sell locally made beers, ales and wine, and are quite trendy. They often serve quite good food, too.

SPECTATOR SPORTS

There aren't a lot of professional teams in the Pacific Northwest. Universities offer the most events throughout the year and are very popular with both students and the general community.

Football draws enormous crowds in the fall. The Seattle Seahawks – the Northwest's only National Football League team – are very popular. The BC Lions are member of the Canadian Football League. Games with university teams, most notably the U of W Huskies, the WSU Cougars and the U of O Ducks are always big crowd pleasers. The season runs from the first week in September (when school starts) to the end of January.

Baseball is even less well represented. The Seattle Mariners are the region's only professional team. Other cities have farm teams.

The season starts the first week of April and ends in October with the World Series.

The basketball season starts in late October and lasts until mid-June. The National Basketball Association's Vancouver Grizzlies, Seattle SuperSonics and Portland Trail Blazers always draw a crowd of frenzied fans. Both Portland and Seattle have new women's professional basketball teams, Portland Power and Seattle Reign, respectively.

If you're in Vancouver during the ice-hockey season, October to April, try to see a home game of the Vancouver Canucks of the National Hockey League. Both Portland and Seattle have American Hockey League teams, the Portland Winter Hawks and the Seattle Thunderbirds.

Universities throughout the region offer a great wealth of sporting events. Around the Puget Sound, university crew teams and sailing teams compete in regattas in the spring.

Soccer, although not a standard sport in much of the US, is increasingly popular in the Northwest. Portland, Vancouver and Seattle each have professional teams. The Portland Pride, the Vancouver 86ers and the Seattle Sounders are professional teams belonging to the American Professional Soccer League (APSL). The University of Portland's women's soccer team recently won the national championship.

SHOPPING

Oregon is a good place to shop, because it doesn't have a sales tax or VAT. Seattle is a shoppers paradise, especially the area around Pike Place Market and the downtown core. Many towns along the Oregon coast, particularly Cannon Beach, are full of boutiques, as is Friday Harbor in the San Juan Islands. Vancouver's Robson Street and Pacific Centre are major downtown shopping areas, while Chinatown offers visitors a chance to experience Hong Kong without leaving the continent.

Probably the most common souvenir of Oregon is something made from myrtle wood. This rare tree grows only in southern Oregon and Lebanon; it's even mentioned in the Bible. If it weren't uncommon no one would be making a fuss about it. But here, it's turned into a dizzying array of carved items, from bowls to statuettes to golf clubs.

Pendleton Woolen Mills has its headquarters in the Northwest, and its trademark plaid shirts make a nice, although pricey, souvenir.

Northwest food and wine are good purchases. Oregon grows over 90% of the nation's filberts. Various kinds of hazelnut products are everywhere. Smoked salmon has a long pedigree here, beginning with the Northwest Indian tribes, who smoked the fish to preserve it over long periods. Local cheeses are popular throughout the region. Northwest's wine has been accorded inter-

national honors, and is worth a try. Most fish markets can pack fresh fish or seafood for air journeys or overnight delivery. Berry jams and syrups made from wild and locally grown berries are easily found; as are candies and food products made from cranberries. Seattle's Pike Place Market and Vancouver's Granville Island Market are good places to shop for food and wine gifts.

A number of Northwest cities have 'Saturday Markets' where local artisans and farmers bring products to sell. Portland's Saturday Market is reputed to be the largest open-air crafts fair in the nation. Eugene, Sisters and other cities have also picked up on the idea. More than half of Pike Place Market in Seattle is devoted to local crafts and gifts.

Outdoor Activities

This chapter explores the many options available to a recreationist in the Pacific Northwest, ranging from near universals like hiking, backpacking and skiing to more esoteric, specialized pursuits like clamming and crabbing.

USEFUL ORGANIZATIONS
Oregon
Oregon Guides & Packers Association – statewide listings for guided fishing, hunting and river-floating trips; PO Box 10841, Eugene, OR 97440 (☎ 503-683-9552)

Oregon State Parks & Recreation Dept – supervises the state park and campground system; 525 Trade St SE, Salem, OR 97310 (☎ 503-378-6305)

Oregon Natural Resources Council – clearinghouse for information on environmental issues and organizations; 3921 SE Salmon St, Portland, OR 97214 (☎ 503-236-9772)

Oregon Dept of Fish & Wildlife – responsible for wildlife issues, including hunting and fishing, and maintains wildlife refuges and habitat; 2501 SW 1st Ave, Portland, OR 97201 (☎ 503-229-5403)

Washington
Washington State Park Headquarters – detailed listings of campgrounds and facilities; 7150 Clearwater Lane, PO Box 42650, Olympia, WA 98504-2650 (☎ 360-902-8500)

Outdoor Recreation Information Center – a shared USFS headquarters and NPS information center; 915 2nd Ave, suite 422, Seattle, WA 98174 (☎ 206-220-7450)

Washington State Outfitters & Guides Association – statewide listings for guided fishing, hunting and river-floating trips; c/o High Country Outfitters, 22845 NE 8th, suite 331, Redmond, WA 98053 (☎ 425-753-5700)

Professional River Outfitters of Washington – contact for a member list of rafting and kayaking outfitters; c/o Cascade Adventures, 1202 E Pike St, No 1142, Seattle, WA 98122 (☎ 206-323-5485)

Washington Trails Association – advocacy group working to preserve and enhance Washington's trail system; 1305 4th Ave, No 512, Seattle, WA 98101 (☎ 206-625-1367)

Cascade Orienteering Club – private group that organizes orienteering events in the Northwest; PO Box 31375, Seattle, WA 98103 (☎ 206-783-3899)

Vancouver & Vancouver Island
Tourism BC – the general information hotline for British Columbia handles most inquiries, including those for outdoor recreation; (☎ 800-663-6000)

BC Parks – supervises and maintains provincial park system; 800 Johnson St, Victoria, BC V8V 1X4 (☎ 250-387-4550)

Extension & Information Branch – good source for maps and environmental information; Ministry of Environment and Parks, Parks and Outdoor Recreation Division, 400 Seymour Place, 3rd floor, Victoria, BC V8V 1X5 (☎ 250-387-1161)

Fish & Wildlife Branch – responsible for wildlife issues, including hunting and fishing, and maintains wildlife refuges and habitat; Ministry of Environment, Parliament Buildings, Victoria, BC V8V 1X5 (☎ 250-387-9717)

HIKING & BACKPACKING
Hiking is a major part of the recreational lifeblood of the Northwest. With so many mountain ranges, public forests, wilderness areas, wildlife refuges and coastal regions, the incentive to get out there and walk around is nearly overwhelming.

The Pacific Crest Trail is one of several National Scenic Trails, and is the perfect way for the outdoorsperson to see the Northwest (see The Pacific Crest Trail sidebar).

What to Bring
Equipment The following is meant to be a general guideline for backpackers, not an 'if I have everything here I'll be fine' checklist. Know yourself and what special things you may need on the trail, and consider the area and climatic conditions you

will be traveling in. This list is inadequate for the snow country or in winter.

Boots – light to medium boots are recommended for day hikes, while sturdy boots are necessary for extended trips with a heavy pack. Most importantly they should be well broken in and have a good heel.

Alternative footwear – thongs/sandals/mukluks/running shoes for wearing around camp (optional), and canvas sneakers or Tevas for crossing streams.

Socks – heavy polypropylene or wool will stay warm even if it gets wet. Frequent changes during the day reduce the chance of blisters.

Colors – subdued colors are recommended, but if hiking during hunting season, blaze orange is a necessity.

Shorts, light shirt – for everyday wear; remember that heavy cotton takes a long time to dry and is very cold when wet.

Long-sleeve shirt – light cotton, wool or polypropylene. A button-down front makes layering easy and can be left open when the weather is hot and your arms need protection from the sun.

Long pants – heavy denim jeans take forever to dry. Sturdy cotton or canvas pants are good for trekking through brush, and cotton or nylon sweats are comfortable to wear around camp. Long underwear with shorts on top is the perfect combination – warm but not cumbersome – for trail hiking where there is not much brush.

Wool/polypropylene/polar fleece sweater or pullover – essential in cold weather.

Rain gear – light, breathable and waterproof is the ideal combination. If nothing else is available, use heavy-duty trash bags to cover you and your packs.

Hat – wool or polypropylene is best for cold weather, while a cotton hat with a brim is good for sun protection. About 80% of body heat escapes through the top of the head. Keep your head (and neck) warm to reduce the chances of hypothermia.

Bandana/handkerchief – good for a runny nose, dirty face, unmanageable hair, picnic lunch and flag (especially a red one).

Small towel – one which is indestructible and will dry quickly.

First aid kit – should include self-adhesive bandages, disinfectant, antibiotic salve or cream, gauze, small scissors and tweezers.

Knife, fork, spoon & mug – a double-layer plastic mug with a lid is best. A mug acts as eating and drinking receptacle, mixing bowl and wash basin; the handle will protect you from getting burned. Bring an extra cup so that you can eat and drink simultaneously.

Pots & pans – aluminum cook sets are best, but any sturdy 1-quart pot is sufficient. True gourmands who want more than pasta, soup and freeze-dried food will need a skillet or frying pan. A pot scrubber is helpful for removing stubborn oatmeal, especially when using cold water and no soap.

Stove – lightweight and easy to operate is ideal. Most outdoor equipment stores rent propane or butane stoves; test the stove before you head out, even cook a meal on it, to familiarize yourself with any quirks it may have.

Water purifier – optional but really nice to have; water can also be purified by boiling for at least 10 minutes.

Matches/lighter – waterproof matches are good, and it's smart to have several lighters on hand.

Candle/lantern – candles are easy to use, but do not stay lit when they are wet or dropped and can be hazardous inside a tent. Outdoor equipment stores rent lanterns; as with a stove, test it before you hit the trail.

Flashlight – each person should have his/her own, and should be sure its batteries have plenty of life left in them.

Sleeping bag – goose-down bags are warm and lightweight, but worthless if they get wet; most outdoor equipment stores rent synthetic bags.

Sleeping pad – this is strictly a personal preference. Use a sweater or sleeping bag sack stuffed with clothes as a pillow.

Tent – make sure it is waterproof, or has a waterproof cover, and know how to put it up before you reach camp. Remember that your packs will be sharing the tent with you.

Camera/binoculars – don't forget extra film and waterproof film canisters (sealable plastic bags work well).

Compass and maps – each person should have his/her own.

Eyeglasses – contact lens wearers should always bring several backup sets.

Sundries – toilet paper, small sealable plastic bags, insect repellent, sun screen, lip balm, unscented moisturizing cream, moleskin for foot blisters, dental floss (burnable, and good when there is no water for brushing), sunglasses, deck of cards, pen/pencil and paper/notebook/journal, books and nature guides.

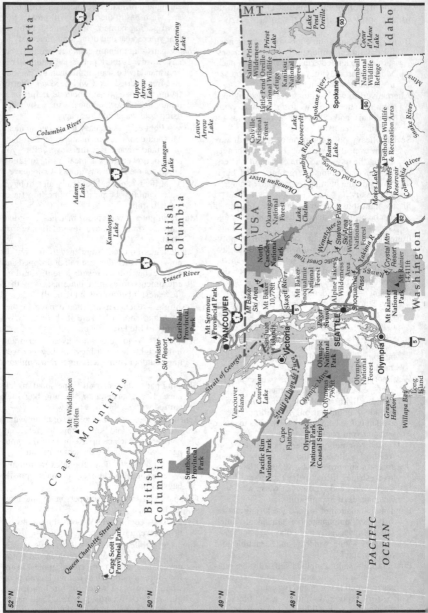

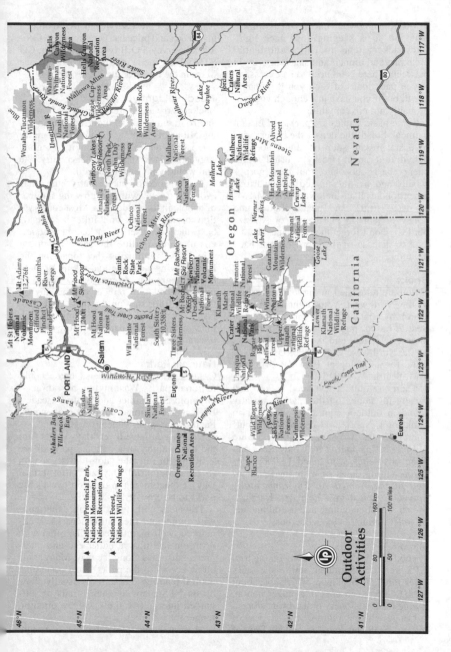

Outdoor Activities

Food Keeping your energy up is important, but so is keeping your pack light. Backpackers tend to eat a substantial breakfast and dinner, and snack heavily in between. There is no need to be excessive. If you pack loads of food you'll probably use it, but if you have just enough you will probably not miss anything.

Some basic staples are packaged instant oatmeal, bread (the denser the better), rice or pasta, instant soup or ramen noodles, dehydrated meat (jerky), dried fruit, energy bars, chocolate, trail mix (gorp – raisins and peanuts mixed with various other goodies like sunflower seeds, M&Ms or dried fruit), and peanut butter and honey or jam (in plastic jars or squeeze bottles). Don't forget the wet-wipes, but be sure to dispose of them properly or pack them out.

Books
If you are interested in outdoor recreation in the Northwest, you might begin your search by contacting The Mountaineers, a Seattle-based publisher that offers the largest selection, and most reliable books on the Northwest. Call ☎ 800-553-4453 or write for a catalog at 1011 SW Klickitat Way, Seattle, WA 98134.

There are quite a few good how-to and 'where-to' books on the market, usually found in outdoor equipment stores or in bookstores' sports and recreation or outdoors section. Two books to check out are *A Hiker's Companion* by Cindy Ross and Todd Gladfelter, who hiked 12,000 miles before sitting down to write, and *How to Shit in the Woods: An Environmentally Sound Approach to a Lost Art*, Kathleen Meyer's explicit, comic and useful manual on toilet training in the wilderness.

Maps
A good map is essential for any hiking trip. NPS and USFS ranger stations usually stock topographical maps which cost about $2 to $6. In the absence of a ranger station, try the local stationery or hardware store.

Longer hikes require two types of maps: USGS Quadrangles, and US Dept of Agriculture-Forest Service maps. To order a map index and price list, contact the US Geological Survey, PO Box 25286, Denver, CO 80225. For general information on maps, see Maps in the Facts for the Visitor chapter.

Treading Lightly
Backcountry areas are composed of fragile environments and cannot support an inundation of human activity, especially insensitive and careless activity. A good suggestion is to treat the backcountry like you would your own backyard.

A new code of backcountry ethics has evolved to deal with the growing number of people in the wilderness. Most conservation organizations and hiker's manuals have their own set of backcountry codes, all of which outline the same important principles: minimizing the impact on the land, leaving no trace and taking nothing but photographs and memories. The three important rules to remember are: stay on the main trail, stay on the main trail, and, lastly, even if it means walking through mud or crossing a patch of snow, *stay on the main trail*.

National Parks
Crater Lake National Park is Oregon's only national park. Washington has three – Olympic, Mt Rainier and North Cascades. BC has six national parks, one of which, Pacific Rim, is on Vancouver Island.

Unless you have a few days to get into the backcountry of a national park, or are visiting during the non-tourist season (before Memorial Day and after Labor Day), expect hiking in the Northwest's big parks to be crowded.

Travelers with little hiking experience will appreciate the national parks' well-marked, well-maintained trails, often with restroom facilities at either end and interpretive displays along the way. Many trails allow access to the parks' most accessible natural features. These trails usually show up on NPS maps as nature trails or self-guided interpretive trails and are often no longer than 2 miles.

Most national parks require overnight

hikers to follow a specific itinerary and carry backcountry permits, available from visitors' centers or ranger stations, which must be obtained 24 hours in advance. While this system reduces the chance of people getting lost in the backcountry, and limits the number of people using one area at any given time, it may detract from the sense of space and freedom hiking can give. Hikers seeking a true wilderness trip, away from heavy foot traffic, should avoid national parks and try instead the less-celebrated wilderness areas and mountain ranges.

Wilderness Areas

The 1964 Wilderness Act, the first major act of Congress to set aside large roadless areas as federally administered wilderness, defines wilderness as:

an area where the earth and its community of life are untrammeled by man, where man himself is a visitor who does not remain . . . It is a region which contains no permanent human inhabitants, no possibility for motorized travel, and is spacious enough so that a traveler crossing it by foot or horse must have the experience of sleeping out of doors.

The NPS, USFS and BLM all manage substantial roadless areas in the Pacific Northwest as wilderness, inaccessible to mechanized travel. Most of these designated areas are on USFS land; while the BLM is a relative latecomer to the concept, its wilderness areas can be among the best in terms of sheer solitude.

Wilderness Camping

Camping in undeveloped areas is rewarding for its peacefulness, but presents special concerns. Take care to insure that the area you choose can comfortably support your presence, and leave the surroundings in better condition than on arrival. The following list of guidelines should help:

- Camp below timberline, since alpine areas are generally more fragile. Good campsites are found, not made. Altering a site shouldn't be necessary.
- Camp at least 200 feet (70 adult steps) away from the nearest lake, river or stream.

- Bury human waste in holes dug 6 to 8 inches deep at least 200 feet from water, camp or trails. The salt and minerals in urine attract deer; use a tent-bottle (funnel attachments are available for women) if you are prone to middle-of-the-night calls by mother nature. Camouflage the hole when finished.
- Use soaps and detergents sparingly or not at all, and never allow these things to enter streams or lakes. Scatter dishwater after removing all food particles. When washing yourself (a backcountry luxury, not necessity), lather-up with biodegradable soap and rinse yourself with cans of water 200 feet away from your water source.
- Carry a lightweight stove for cooking, and use a lantern instead of a fire.
- If a fire is allowed and appropriate, dig out the native topsoil, and build a fire in the hole. Gather sticks no thicker than 3 inches. Do not snap branches off live, dead or downed trees. Pour wastewater from meals around the perimeter of the campfire to prevent it from spreading, and thoroughly douse it before leaving or going to bed.
- Establish a cooking area at least 100 yards away from your tent and designate cooking clothes to leave in the food bag, away from your tent.
- Burn cans to get rid of their odor, then remove the ashes and pack them out with you.
- Pack out what you pack in, including all trash – yours and others'.

Safety

The major forces to be reckoned with while hiking and camping are the weather, which is uncontrollable, and your own frame of mind. Be prepared for the Northwest's unpredictable weather – you may go to bed under a clear sky and wake up to two feet of snow. Carry a rain jacket and light pair of long underwear at all times, even on short afternoon hikes. Backpackers should have a pack-liner (or heavy-duty garbage bags work well), full set of rain gear and food which does not require cooking. A positive attitude is helpful in any situation. If a hot shower, comfortable mattress and clean clothes are essential to your wellbeing, don't head out into the wilderness for five days – stick to day hikes.

Highest safety measures suggest never hiking alone, but solo travelers should not be discouraged, especially if they value solitude. The important thing is to always let someone know where you are going and how long you plan to be gone. Use sign-in boards at trailheads or ranger stations. Travelers looking for hiking companions can inquire or post notices at ranger stations, outdoor equipment stores, campgrounds and youth hostels.

Forging rivers and streams is another potentially dangerous but often necessary part of being on the trail. In national parks and along maintained trails in national forests, bridges usually cross large bodies of water (this is not the case in designated wilderness areas, where bridges are taboo). Upon reaching a river, unclip all of your pack straps – your pack is expendable, you are not. Avoid crossing barefoot – river cobbles will suck body heat right out of your feet, numbing them and making it impossible to navigate. Bring a pair of Tevas or lightweight canvas sneakers to avoid sloshing around in wet boots for the rest of your hike. Although cold water will make you want to cross as quickly as possible, don't rush things: take small steps, watch where you are stepping and keep your balance. Using a staff for balance is helpful, but don't rely on it to support all your weight. Don't enter water higher than mid-thigh; any higher than that and your body gives the current a large mass to work against.

If you happen to get wet, you should wring your clothes out immediately, wipe off all the excess water on your body that you can and put on any dry clothes you might have. Synthetic fabrics and wool retain heat when they get wet, but cotton does not.

People with little hiking or backpacking experience should not attempt to do too much, too soon or they might end up being non-hikers for the wrong reasons. Know your limitations, know the route you are going to take and pace yourself accordingly. Remember, there is absolutely nothing wrong with turning back or not going as far as you originally planned.

Long-Distance Backpacking

Careful preparations for a long-distance backpack hike (that is, long enough that you will need to resupply along the way) are of the utmost importance. Don't think you can jump from weekend trips into a multiple-week trek without preparation; you've got to train and you've got to lay out a resupply plan in advance. Many established hiking trails have organizations which can supply you with a list of area post offices, stores and ranger stations who can receive your re-supply packages in the mail and hold them until you arrive to claim them. If you can't dig up such a list, try calling post offices. Some establishments may charge a holding fee. Preparations for a long-distance trip should include the following:

- Buy the proper equipment; learn first aid suitable to mountaineering situations, backcountry protocol and how to care for the outdoors.
- Practice on weekend trips; be able to cover between 10 and 20 miles per day.
- Study guides and maps to the trail or region you plan to cover; plan a daily itinerary taking into account resupply points.
- Buy supplies; pack resupply packages for mailing to resupply points.

Trails

Oregon From coast to river gorge, mountain scape to desert, Oregon offers some of the USA's most diverse hiking. Below is a sampler of the state's spectacular trails.

A good way to see the country in and around Portland is by following the 40-Mile Loop, which originates in Portland's Washington Park and circles the city, linking 35 state and city parks.

The Oregon Coast Trail is a not-yet-complete trail system that will link the entire 362-mile Oregon coast. Significant portions of the trail are complete, and can be utilized as either a long-distance hike or as a day-hiking trail. A brochure is available from the Oregon State Parks Dept (see Useful Organizations, at the beginning of this chapter, for contact information).

The Timberline Trail, which encircles

Mt Hood, is a 40-mile long trail that passes waterfalls and glaciers, wildflower meadows and alpine forests. It is coincident, in segments, with the Pacific Crest Trail. Also in the Mt Hood National Forest, the Eagle Creek Trail is a 13-mile route that follows the cliffs of the Columbia River Gorge past many spectacular waterfalls.

Southwestern Oregon's two primary rivers, the Rogue and the Umpqua, are accompanied by hiking trails. The 40-mile Rogue River Trail and the 77-mile North Umpqua Trail both offer terrific wildlife viewing and recreational opportunities.

The Nee-Me-Poo Trail, which follows the path of Chief Joseph and the Nez Perce through three states, begins just north of the Imnaha Bridge near Hells Canyon, and in 3½ miles climbs to a viewpoint over the Snake River.

Washington It is said that Washington is where hikers go when they die. There are gorgeous trails in virtually every corner of the state. Olympic National Park is a par-ticularly rich area, as most of its interior is accessible only by foot. The Hoh River Trail is one of the longest and most popular hikes, passing through the Hoh Rain Forest on the way to Mt Olympus (7965 feet), the park's highest peak.

The Wonderland Trail in Mt Rainier National Park is a 93-mile loop trail that circles the heavily glaciated mountain; it takes about 1½ weeks to complete in its entirety. At nearby Mt St Helens Naional Volcanic Monument, the short Ape Cave Trail passes through the longest lava tube in the 48 contiguous states.

The North Cascades area is a wonderfully rich region for hikers. Many trails around nearby Mt Baker require fairly strenuous climbs up glacier-carved valleys to viewpoints and wildflower meadows.

On Lake Chelan, the village of Stehekin is approachable only by ferry, seaplane or foot, and makes for a good long-distance hike over Cascade Pass from Marblemount. The Alpine Lakes Wilderness Area, near Leavenworth, is another region of

---

The Pacific Crest Trail

A truly amazing thing about the West Coast of the USA is that you can walk from Mexico to Canada, across the entire expanse of California, Oregon and Washington, almost without ever leaving national park or national forest lands. Simply follow the Pacific Crest Trail (PCT). This 2638-mile trail passes through 24 national forests, seven national parks, 33 designated wilderness areas and six state parks, always following as closely as possible the crest of the Sierra Mountains in California and the Cascade Range in Oregon and Washington, at an average elevation of 5000 feet.

To hike the trail in its entirety, at a good clip of 15 miles a day, would take nearly half a year; the Oregon and Washington portions can each feasibly be hiked in one month. But you don't have to undertake such a dramatic, cross-state trek to take advantage of the PCT. Day or weekend hikers can plan short trips along any stretch of the trail.

Many of the West Coast's most spectacular wilderness sites are traversed by the PCT, including Yosemite and Sequoia National Parks in California, Crater Lake National Park, Three Sisters Wilderness and Mt Hood in Oregon, and Mt Rainier and North Cascades National Parks in Washington.

The Pacific Crest Trail Association, headquartered in California, can provide detailed information on the trail, as well as addresses for regional USFS and Wilderness Area offices, tips on long- and short-distance backpacking trips, weather conditions and which areas require wilderness permits. Contact the association at ☎ 888-728-7245 or ☎ 916-349-2109, or write to 5325 Elkhorn Blvd, suite 256, Sacramento, CA 95842. You can also visit their website (www.gorp.com/pcta) to obtain information. ■

countless hikes, encompassing the aptly named Enchantment Lakes.

In the northeastern corner of the state, the Shedroof Divide National Recreation Trail is a 22-mile trail through the Salmo-Priest Wilderness Area, where a few grizzly bears and caribou still dwell.

And don't forget the San Juan Islands. Orcas Island's Moran State Park is well-equipped for hikers and campers.

Vancouver & Vancouver Island From Vancouver, hiking trails that go into the mountain valleys start practically at the city's northern borders. Capilano, Mt Seymour and Cypress parks are filled with good day hikes, famous suspension bridges and lovely forests and streams. A more wilderness experience can be had at Garibaldi Provincial Park, near Whistler.

On Vancouver Island, the main focus of long-distance hiking is the West Coast Trail, part of the Pacific Rim National Park. This 48-mile trails edges a wilderness beach between Port Renfrew and Bamfield on the island's west coast. Also popular with hikers is Strathcona Park, which contains the highest waterfall in North America

BIKING
Oregon
The Oregon Coast Bike Route follows US 101 between Astoria and Brookings (which is on the California border). A few side loop routes make passes of scenic areas not accessible from the highway. The Cascade Lakes Hwy, in central Oregon, is also popular with bicyclists. It passes many small lakes in the mountainous region south of Mt Bachelor and the Three Sisters Wilderness. Not far away, the Newberry Crater Rim Loop, 14 miles long, winds around one of the state's most fascinating volcanic features.

Contact the Bikeway Program Manager (☎ 503-378-3432), Oregon Dept of Transportation, Room 200, Transportation Building, Salem, OR 97310, for the free *Oregon Bicycling Guide*, and a map of the Oregon Coast Bike Route.

Washington
A favorite destination for cyclists, the San Juan Islands are mostly flat, with gently rolling hills and inland lakes and forests just minutes from stunning coastal paths. Bikes can be transported by ferry to the islands for a fee, or rented on the islands.

Other popular cycling areas include the Methow Valley, where cross-country skiing trails are taken over by mountain bikers in the summer.

Vancouver & Vancouver Island
The Gulf Islands are the favorite destination of leisure cyclists due to the quiet roads, gentle terrain and lovely marine landscapes. Smaller roads on the eastern side of Vancouver Island are also popular with more ambitious cyclists. Put your bicycle on a ferry and head to Salt Spring, Saturna and Galiano Islands, which are specially suited for exploring on two wheels due to their easygoing topography and tranquil back roads. On Vancouver Island cycle the byroads around Sooke Harbour, or explore the Cowichan Valley vineyard country west of Duncan. Smaller, coast-hugging roads on the eastern side of Vancouver Island are also popular with more ambitious cyclists. In Vancouver heavy vehicular traffic makes bicycling less than pleasant on the streets, but Stanley Park, with its miles-long paved cycling and walking path – much of it along a sea wall – makes a great destination for the casual cyclist.

SKIING
During the winter, skiing takes over the slopes of the volcanic peaks of the Cascade Range, as well as the snow-glazed backcountry byways, riverside trails and non-mountainous wilderness areas.

Downhill
Noted downhill ski areas in Oregon include the five resorts at Mt Hood – the most famous of which, Timberline Lodge, offers nearly year-round conditions – and Mt Bachelor and Anthony Lakes, both famous for their powder skiing. In Washington,

Organized Bicycling Tours

Bicycle Adventures, the bike gurus of Washington State, offers numerous bicycle tours of the Pacific Northwest. Tours in Washington include the Cascades, Olympic Peninsula, Puget Sound and the San Juan Islands. In Oregon you can choose from a tour of the Columbia Gorge, the Oregon Cascades or the Oregon coast. And, in BC, they will take you on a cycling tour of the Gulf Islands. Depending on the trip, you'll cycle 15-70 miles a day. Call ☎ 800-443-6060, or write to Bicycle Adventures, PO Box 11219, Olympia, WA 98508.

A kind of week-long party on wheels, the Cycle Oregon ride traverses 60 to 80 miles a day of Oregon landscape, covering a different route each year. Cyclists from all over the USA vie for one of 2000 spaces in the limited registration, and then take to the road in September in a huge caravan of bikes, supply trucks, portable toilets, mobile snack stands and the like. The $579 fee covers camping (bring your own tent), food, gear transport and emergency bike repair and medical care. Cycle Oregon also organizes the one-day Summer Century Ride in July. This all-day ride includes meals, and is a great diversion for in-shape travelers looking for some serious exercise. Call ☎ 800-292-5367, or write to Cycle Oregon, 8700 SW Nimbus Ave, suite B, Beaverton, OR 97008.

Riders who really want to see America can go all out on the Cycle America ride, which crosses the country from coast to coast for the duration of the summer. The ride is broken down into 12 week-long segments; you can do any or all of them, and the cost depends on how long you're on the road. For information, call ☎ 800-245-3263, or write to Cycle America, PO Box 485, Cannon Falls, MN 55009. ∎

Crystal Mountain, Stevens Pass, Mt Baker and Snoqualmie Pass are the popular resorts. Recognized as the premier ski resort in North America by most major ski magazines, Whistler in BC is by far the region's most sophisticated destination in the Northwest. Grouse Mountain, perched above Vancouver, is just minutes from the city center and has night skiing.

Cross-Country

Cross-country skiing is also very popular in the Northwest. A number of downhill ski resorts also offer groomed cross-country trails; private ski groups (groups of skiers who maintain trails, usually on national forest lands) sometimes offer groomed trails for a small fee. However, cross-country skiing need not be so regimented. The heavy snowfall in the Northwest converts the vast wilderness areas of Washington, Oregon and BC into winter playgrounds. When there's enough snow, any USFS road is a make-shift ski trail; better yet, you'll probably have the road, and the mountainside, to yourself.

The Rim Drive that circles Oregon's Crater Lake is popular with Nordic skiers in the winter. All Mt Hood downhill resorts also offer trails, but a better bet may be the Tea Cup Lake trails maintained by the Oregon Nordic Club, with 18.6 miles of skiing. Mt Hood National Forest offices can provide a list of other trails in the area.

Some spectacular regions for off-the-beaten-path skiing in Washington are Mt St Helens, Mt Rainier, the Lake Chelan area and Olympic National Park (Hurricane Ridge, near the park's northern entrance, accesses high mountain meadows). In the Methow Valley, a series of ski huts are spaced along the trails for multi-day expeditions; you can even hire outfitters to transport your gear.

Garibaldi Park, in BC, is a popular cross-country destination for skiers in Vancouver, as are the provincial parks – Mt Seymour and Cypress – that flank the mountains directly north of the city. Whistler Mountain offers 16 miles of groomed nordic trails.

SNOWBOARDING
Snowboarding has recently swept the nation's ski culture and taken on a following of its own. Baggy pants, psychedelic jackets and funky hats have replaced more traditional ski garb. Snowboarders stand sideways, strapped to a board 4 or 5 feet long, to cruise down the mountains. The motion is comparable to surfing or skateboarding, rather than skiing, which may explain why many snowboarders look like skate rats. As a rule, snowboarders

love powder snow, hate moguls and ice and need an older sibling's ID to get into bars at night.

CLIMBING & MOUNTAINEERING
If you're interested in climbing in the Cascades, the local USFS office is a good place to inquire for information about guided hikes. You'll also want to procure the book *Selected Climbs in the Cascades* by Jim Nelson and Peter Potterfield. This book also covers rock climbing, particularly in the North Cascades area.

Recently, rock climbers have subordinated the idea of reaching summits to testing their skills on varied routes on difficult terrain, with the achievement of a summit either secondary or unimportant; the technique is the important matter.

Climbing and mountaineering are demanding activities requiring top physical condition, an understanding of the composition of various rock types and their hazards, other hazards of the high country and familiarity with a variety of equipment, including ropes, chocks, bolts, carabiners and harnesses. Many climbers prefer granite, because of its strength and frequent handholds, but some climbers prefer limestone for a challenge. Some sedimentary rock is suitable for climbing, but crumbling volcanic rock can be very difficult.

Mountaineers and climbers categorize routes on a scale of one to five; Class I is hiking, while Class II involves climbing on unstable materials like talus and may require use of the hands for keeping balance, especially with a heavy pack. Class III places the climber in dangerous situations, involving exposed terrain (the Sierra Club uses the example of a staircase on a high building without handholds – scary but not difficult), with the likely consequences of a fall being a broken limb.

Class IV involves steep rock, smaller holds and great exposure, with obligatory use of ropes and knowledge of knots and techniques like belaying and rappelling; the consequences of falling are death rather than injury. Class V divides into a dozen or more subcategories based on degree of difficulty and requires advanced techniques, including proficiency with rope.

The Access Fund, PO Box 67A25, Los Angeles, CA 90067, is a nonprofit organization working to keep climbing areas open to the public by purchasing or negotiating access to key sites.

Safety

Climbing is potentially a hazardous activity, though serious accidents are more spectacular than frequent; driving to the climbing site can be more dangerous than the climb itself. Nevertheless, climbers should be aware of hazards which can contribute to falls and very serious injury or death.

Weather is an important factor, as rain makes rocks slippery and lightning can strike an exposed climber; hypothermia is an additional concern. In dry weather, lack of water can lead to dehydration.

Minimum Impact

Many climbers are now following guidelines similar to those established for hikers to preserve the resource on which their sport relies. These include concentrating impact in high-use areas by using established roads, trails and routes for access; dispersing use in pristine areas and avoiding the creation of new trails; refraining from creating or enhancing handholds; and eschewing the placement of bolts wherever possible. Climbers should also take special caution to respect archaeological and cultural resources, such as rock art, and refrain from climbing in such areas.

Sites

Oregon Mt Hood (11,245 feet) claims the distinction of being the world's second most-climbed peak over 10,000 feet (after Japan's Mt Fuji). The climb is a sort of an Oregonian pilgrimage – a trek that many feel must be made at least once during a lifetime.

Smith Rock is a world-renowned rock-climbing venue – towering above central Oregon's Crooked River and the Cascades'

South Sister – and, at 10,358 feet, can be conquered without technical equipment.

Washington The highest peak in the Cascades is Mt Rainier at 14,411 feet; it is also the most heavily glaciated peak in the lower 48 states. Emmons Glacier, on the mountain's east side, is a popular and challenging ascent. Mt Adams at 12,276 feet, also in the South Cascades, is one of Washington's easiest peak climbs, and the all-too-recently-active volcano, Mt St Helens, is a unique challenge.

The craggy peaks of the North Cascades offer extremely challenging ascents for experienced climbers. Mt Baker, at 10,778 feet, is another heavily glaciated peak with a number of glacier climbs; Easton Glacier is the easiest ascent, while Coleman and Roosevelt are more technically demanding.

To complete the trio of Washington's national parks, Olympic National Park also contains glaciated mountain peaks for climbers. Mt Olympus, at 7965 feet, is the most popular, but is reached only by a 17-mile trail from the nearest road, at the Hoh Rain Forest Visitors Center.

Vancouver & Vancouver Island BC's most noted rock-climbing destination is the massive granite faces near Squamish, midway between Vancouver and Whistler. The second-largest freestanding granite outcropping in the world (the largest is the Rock of Gibraltar), Stawamus Chief has 280 climbing routes on its various faces, walls and slabs. The University Wall, one of the climbs, is rated the most difficult in Canada. The pullout off Hwy 99 for Shannon Falls is a good place to watch climbers scale these massive cliffs. For information on climbing Stawamus Chief or information on other climbs in BC, contact the Federation of Mountain Clubs of British Columbia (☎ 640-737-3053).

RAFTING & KAYAKING

The mighty rivers of the Northwest make this one of the top rafting and kayaking areas in the US. A large number of outfitters guide trips down the many rivers, ranging from half-day floats to three- and four-day expeditions through untracked wilderness.

Kayak and raft rentals are also available for those who feel confident enough to take on a river, although be aware that many of these rivers are not for novices. Note that some rivers are closely regulated and have rafting seasons; permits, which are limited in number and issued by a random draw, are necessary on some rivers. Another type of thrill offered on the river is a jet boat tour, particularly popular on the Rogue in Oregon and the Snake, which cuts across Idaho to Hells Canyon on the Idaho/Oregon border. These flat-bottomed boats skim at great speeds over the surface of the water, making for loud, bumpy, exciting entertainment. Grants Pass, OR, is the place to go for excursions on the Rogue; Lewiston, ID, is a center for jet boat outfitters for trips up Hells Canyon.

River trips are classified on a scale of one to six according to difficulty (see rankings, below). On any given river, classifications can vary over the course of the year, depending on the water level. Higher water levels, usually associated with spring runoff, can make a river trip either easier or more difficult by covering up hazards or increasing the velocity of the river, while lower water levels can expose hazards like rocks and whirlpools, making the river more exciting. Some, if not most, rivers depend on water releases from upstream dams.

White-water trips take place in either large rafts seating a dozen or more people, or smaller rafts seating half a dozen; the latter are more interesting and exciting because the ride over the rapids can be rougher, and because everyone participates in rowing. While white-water trips are not without danger, and it's not unusual for participants to fall out of the raft in rough water, serious injuries are rare and a huge majority of trips are without incident.

All participants must wear US Coast Guard-approved life jackets, and even nonswimmers are welcome. All trips have at least one river guide trained in lifesaving techniques.

River Rankings

Class I (easy) – the river ranges from flat-water to occasional series of mild rapids.

Class II (medium) – the river has frequent stretches of rapids with waves up to 3 feet high and easy chutes, ledges and falls. The best route is easy to identify and the entire river can be run in open canoes.

Class III (difficult) – the rivers feature numerous rapids with high, irregular waves and difficult chutes and falls that often require scouting. They are for experienced paddlers who either use kayaks and rafts or have a spray cover for their canoe.

Class IV (very difficult) – rivers with long stretches of irregular waves, powerful back eddies and even constricted canyons. Scouting is mandatory and rescues can be difficult in many places. Suitable in rafts or white-water kayaks with paddlers equipped with helmets.

Class V (extremely difficult) – rivers with continuous violent rapids, powerful rollers and high, unavoidable waves and haystacks. These rivers are only for white-water kayaks and paddlers who are proficient in the Eskimo roll.

Class VI (highest level of difficulty) – these rivers are rarely run except by highly experienced kayakers under ideal conditions.

Wild & Scenic Rivers

Congressional legislation establishes certain criteria for the preservation of rivers with outstanding natural qualities; these are called Wild & Scenic Rivers. Wild rivers

are, simply speaking, free-flowing and remote, while scenic rivers enjoy relatively natural surroundings and are free of impoundments, but have better access by road. Recreational rivers are more developed and usually have roads close by.

Sites

Oregon Favorite rafting rivers in Oregon are the Deschutes River and the Rogue River. On the Deschutes, the trip between Sherar's Falls and the Columbia River is a multi-day trip with Class IV rapids and no road access for miles and miles. The 84-mile stretch of the Rogue River within the Wild Rogue Wilderness Area is definitely one of the most legendary white-water runs in the country, with abundant Class IV rapids and waterfalls and rustic lodges along the way where you can sleep and eat. The Upper Rogue, where runoff from Crater Lake and the Cascades gives birth to the river, is popular for gentler, more leisurely float trips.

The Snake River through Hells Canyon, on the Oregon-Idaho border, also offers some mean rapids and some of the most striking scenery in the state.

Washington The Skagit, Yakima and Wenatchee Rivers in Washington are the principle kayaking and rafting rivers. Some outfitters on the Skagit River offer eagle-watching trips in winter; these are float trips. In the Olympic National Park, outfitters run white-water trips down the Hoh, Elwha and Queets Rivers, through some of North America's only rain forests. Along the park's Olympic Coastal Strip, the same outfitters run sea-kayaking trips.

Sea kayaking in the Puget Sound can be an extraordinary adventure. Whether you're just puttering in the shadow of Seattle's skyline or paddling from island to island in the San Juans, kayaks make for a unique Northwest experience. Outfitters offer rentals or guided tours. This is an exciting way to see the killer whales, or orcas.

Around Vancouver BC's most popular white-water rafting rivers include the Fraser, Thompson, Chilliwack and the Lillooet Rivers; these are all handy to Vancouver, and many outfitters run day trips.

WINDSURFING

While activities like fishing and sailing have always been popular on the mighty Columbia River, it's windsurfing that has elevated the town of Hood River from a sleepy orchard town to a sports capital. Reckoned to be one of the world's best windsurfing locales, the Columbia River Gorge is the gathering place of 'boardheads' from around the world. Certainly nowhere else in Oregon can boast more colorful, polyglot and youthful crowds than Hood River.

Lakes throughout the Northwest are havens for windsurfing, and rentals are easy to find in most towns. Summer is obviously the best time to be in the water anywhere in the Northwest; beside, that's when the big afternoon winds blow up the Gorge, against the current, creating the kinds of waves that bring boardheads in from around the world.

BIRD & WILDLIFE WATCHING

The vast number of wildlife refuges and public lands in the Pacific Northwest – ranging from the rocky shores of the Pacific to the high desert of the Columbia Basin – make this a great place to watch for wildlife. Bird watching is particularly well rewarded. Local Audubon Society organizations often sponsor hikes and trips to birding areas.

Oregon

The Malheur Wildlife Refuge, located in southeastern Oregon, covers 289 sq miles of protected lands, teeming with coyote, deer and over 200 species of birds. It is the perfect place to study a high-desert eco-system; seminars are offered at its facilities.

Southern Oregon's Klamath Basin Wildlife Refuges support over 400 species of wildlife. The Lower Klamath Refuge was established in 1908 as the nation's first wildlife refuge. Bird watchers may be interested in the Klamath Basin Eagle Conference held in February, open to the public.

The Heart Mountain National Antelope Refuge in southeastern Oregon is home to herds of antelope that number in the thousands. This is also a great place to watch for raptors.

Along the length of the Oregon Coast, all offshore sea stacks and promontories are preserved as wildlife refuges, and are home to seals, sea lions and a wide variety of sea birds. A trip to the Sea Lion Caves, south of Yachats, is mandatory; an elevator drops you into a giant natural sea cave filled with brawling sea lions.

Washington

The Upper Skagit Bald Eagle Area, in Washington's North Cascades, is best visited in the winter, when eagles come to feast on the salmon spawning in the Skagit River. The Turnbull National Wildlife Area near Spokane and the Little Pend Oreille Wildlife Area north, near Colville, are stopovers for migratory waterfowl; you may see some black bear, too.

Potholes Wildlife & Recreation Area in central Washington, an irrigated wetlands surrounded by sand dunes, is a haven for a variety of waterfowl. Near Ellensburg, to the west, the Dept of Wildlife's elk-feeding program brings in hundreds of breakfasting elk each day when there's snow on the ground.

The Willapa National Wildlife Refuge, composed of five different areas in and around Willapa Bay on Washington's southern coast, is an excellent spot for watching shore birds. On Long Island – part of the refuge accessible only by canoe or kayak – black bear, coyote and elk roam undisturbed by man.

Wolves aren't exactly prolific in Washington, but Wolf Haven America, a wolf-rehabilitation center south of Olympia, offers visitors an educational look at these beautiful animals.

Vancouver & Vancouver Island

Considering that Vancouver is a huge metropolitan area, it's relatively easy to get out of the city and into the natural world. The region's primary bird-watching area is the George C Reifel Migratory Bird Sanctuary, at the mouth of the Fraser River, just south of Vancouver and west of Ladner. More than 250 species of birds can be sighted in this wetlands environment. Occasionally, migratory birds from Asia lose their way and end up here, causing immense excitement with 'life-list' birders.

Just north of Vancouver, near Brackendale, is found one of the largest winter populations of bald eagles in North America. Hundreds of eagles come here in December and January to feast on the carcasses of late-fall run salmon that have spawned in the Squamish River.

Victoria is one of the best centers for joining boat trips to spot killer whales, or orcas. Outfitters along Victoria harbor often combine whale-watching trips with excursions to islands and rocky promontories covered with sea lions, seals and seabird colonies. To watch migrating gray whales, which travel between Mexico and Alaska from November to April, it's best to head out to the west coast of Vancouver Island. Charter boats set sail from Tofino, Bamfield and Ucluelet to view the vast sea mammals close up. For distant viewings, watch from Wickaninnish Beach with a pair of binoculars.

COASTAL ACTIVITIES

While the coast is too cold much of the year for sunbathing and swimming, its brisk climate is perfect for other activities. The Oregon Coast Trail runs nearly the length of the entire Oregon coast, although state parks often have shorter hiking trails to hidden beaches or tide pools. The Coast Range and the Olympic Mountains, damp and heavily wooded (where not lumbered off), also make for good summer hikes. Biking coastal roads is also popular, but heavy traffic and narrow roads can make it unpleasant. Kite flying approaches near mania on sandy beaches. Exploring rocky tide pools for colorful marine life is a more introspective coastal pursuit.

While not the surf capital of the world, the Pacific Northwest does nonetheless feature surfing and boogie-boarding along the Pacific Coast. Most coastal destinations offer equipment rentals and sales, as well as advice.

Whale Watching

The high capes and headlands of the Oregon coast are excellent vantage points to watch for gray whales. There are both spring and fall migrations; the spring migration – which peaks in March – brings the whales closer to the shore. Favorite whale-watching spots include Cape Sebastian, Cape Blanco, Cape Perpetua, Neahkahnie Mountain and Cape Arago. On weekends, at most of these sites, volunteers from local wildlife groups will answer questions and help locate whales. Although whales can occasionally be seen with the naked eye, it's best to have a good pair of binoculars.

The Washington coastline also offers glimpses of the migrating mammals. Whale lovers, however, should not stick to the ocean: the Puget Sound waters around the San Juan Islands are home to the sleek and powerful orca, or killer whale, and expeditions can be organized out of Bellingham or the islands themselves. Guided wildlife-seeking kayaking tours are an adventurous way to cruise the coves and channels of this archipelago. There's even a state park – Lime Kiln State Park on San Juan Island – devoted to whale watching.

Vancouver Island is also an excellent place for whale watching. Dozens of outfitters offer whale-watching cruises from Victoria Harbor.

Many charter fishing boat companies throughout the region also offer whale-watching trips.

Clamming & Crabbing

Clamming and crabbing are fun alternatives to fishing: rent a boat and crab rings and catch yourself some dinner, or dig a big bucket of clams and have yourself a bake.

A state fishing license is not needed, though you must abide by the bag limits stated in the most recent Fish & Wildlife guidelines (available from most public offices on the coast). Otherwise all you need is a shovel and a bucket. Clams require a bit of excavation along riverbeds and sandy beaches. Razor clams quickly burrow into the sand and demand a fair amount of spading to unearth. You can also find mussels in abundant numbers along intertidal rocks. Be sure that the shellfish is free of red tide (see information on red tide under Health in the Facts for the Visitor chapter).

Dungeness crab live in quiet bays along the coast and are easily caught. Rowing out into the bay and waiting for the crab rings to fill is a relaxing way to snare a fine meal. Many marinas will rent a boat and crab rings, and will clean and boil the crabs for around $35 for a two-hour rental. The namesake of the scrumptious Dungeness crab is in Washington: Dungeness Spit is a long arm of land north of Sequim, on the Olympic Peninsula.

Most Oregon beaches are open for gathering shellfish; Netarts, Wheeler and the Reedsport are known for great crabbing.

FISHING

The fishing mainstay of the Northwest for thousands of years has been the salmon;

The gray whales' migration takes them up the Pacific Coast.

today, populations of the seagoing fish are so threatened that sport-fishing seasons on many rivers are offered only sporadically. If you want to go salmon fishing, it is still possible, but be sure to link up with a reputable outfitter, and keep in contact with the local Fish & Wildlife Departments. Regulations and seasons change quickly.

Fish with a less ambitious life cycle than salmon are still abundant in the Northwest, and make for great fishing. Various kinds of trout, sturgeon and bass are found in most streams and rivers. The great fishing rivers of Oregon include the Deschutes River in central Oregon and the Rogue and Umpqua Rivers in the southern part of the state.

The Yakima and Wenatchee Rivers in central Washington, the many rivers and lakes in Olympic National Park, the North Cascades' Methow and Stehekin Rivers, Lake Chelan (the USA's third-deepest lake) and Lake Roosevelt are Washington hot spots.

Many coastal towns offer charter fishing trips into the Pacific. For decades, charter fishing for salmon was one of the Northwest coast's biggest industries. However, in recent years declining salmon numbers have led federal agencies to severely limit sport fishing for salmon. Fishing for halibut and other fish is still legal, however.

Charter boats out of Port Townsend, WA, prowl the Strait of Juan de Fuca in search of salmon and bottom fish; excursions also depart from West Port in Gray's Harbor.

The Columbia's convergence with the Pacific Ocean is a noted fishing area; a number of companies in Astoria and Warrenton offer charter trips. Fishing is excellent off Garibaldi, whether in Tillamook Bay or the Pacific. Charter boats fish for whatever is in season or available at the time, including salmon, cod, red snapper or rockfish. Depoe Bay, Newport and Winchester Bay are some of the coast's busiest charter fishing harbors, offering good ocean fishing and whale watching during the spring whale migration.

Anglers are required in all situations to have the appropriate state licenses and to abide by whatever seasonal or territorial restrictions are in place. For instance, the same stream may have several sections that have quite different restrictions on types of hooks, bait, seasons and what size and type of fish can be kept. It can be complicated, so be sure to ask for current regulations at bait or sporting-good stores or fish and wildlife offices.

Fishing licenses are issued to in-state and out-of-state anglers; the latter are more expensive. Both licenses can be bought (at bait shops or hardware stores) for a year, or for shorter intervals.

Getting There & Away

AIR
Airports & Airlines
Most air travelers to the Pacific Northwest will arrive either at Seattle-Tacoma International (Sea-Tac) – the region's largest airport – or Vancouver International Airport (YVR). Both are served by most national and international airlines, and each has regularly scheduled flights to many points worldwide. Portland International Airport, called PDX, has connections to most US domestic destinations, as well as direct flights to Asia.

Major international airlines serving the US include:

Air Canada	☎ 800-776-3000
Air France	☎ 800-237-2747
Air New Zealand	☎ 800-262-1234
American Airlines	☎ 800-433-7300
British Airways	☎ 800-247-9297
Canadian Airlines	☎ 800-426-7000
Continental Airlines	☎ 800-231-0856
Japan Airlines (JAL)	☎ 800-525-3663
KLM	☎ 800-374-7747
Lufthansa Airlines	☎ 800-563-5954
Northwest Airlines	☎ 800-447-4747
Qantas Airways	☎ 800 227 4500
Scandinavian Airlines (SAS)	☎ 800 221 2350
TWA	☎ 800-221-2000
United Airlines	☎ 800-538-2929
US Airways	☎ 800-428-4322
Virgin Atlantic	☎ 800-862-8621

Major domestic airlines in the US include:

Alaska Airlines	☎ 800-426-0333
America West Airlines	☎ 800-235-9292
American Airlines	☎ 800-433-7300
Continental Airlines	☎ 800-523-3273
Delta Air Lines	☎ 800-221-1212
Hawaiian Airlines	☎ 800-367-5320
Horizon Air	☎ 800-547-9308
Northwest Airlines	☎ 800-225-2525
Reno Air	☎ 800-736-6247
Southwest Airlines	☎ 800-435-9792
TWA	☎ 800-221-2000
United Airlines/ United Express	☎ 800-241-6522

Buying Tickets
The plane ticket will probably be the single most expensive item in your budget, and buying it can be intimidating. Rather than just walking into the nearest travel agency or airline office, it is always worth putting aside a few hours to research the current state of the market and to shop around. Start shopping for a ticket early – some of the cheapest tickets must be bought months in advance, and some popular flights sell out early.

Talk to other recent travelers – they may be able to stop you from making some of the same mistakes they did. Look at ads in the travel sections of magazines and newspapers. They often offer cheap fares, but don't be surprised if they happen to be sold-out when you contact the agency: they're often low-season fares on obscure airlines with conditions attached. Consult reference books and watch for special offers.

You can also use the Internet to hunt for low fares. Two services that have been recommended by some travelers are Cheap Tickets (www.cheaptickets.com) and Travelocity (www.travelocity.com). To buy a ticket via the Web you'll need a credit card. Also, while some find this a convenient way to purchase budget tickets, other travelers have reported long wait times and disconnections, or have found that the online services can't always match travel agencies or the airlines themselves.

United Airlines recently introduced e-fares, a program in which tickets for selected routes and dates are released every Wednesday at substantial discounts. These tickets are snapped up almost as soon as they are released, so you'll need to log-on to United's website (www.ual.com) early Wednesday. To purchase these tickets you'll need to register with United and also be a member of United's Mileage Plus

Air Travel Glossary

Apex Apex, or 'advance purchase excursion,' is a discounted ticket that must be paid for in advance. There are penalties if you wish to change it.

Bucket Shop An unbonded travel agency specializing in discounted airline tickets.

Cancellation Penalties If you must cancel or change an Apex ticket there are often heavy penalties involved, but insurance can sometimes be taken out against these penalties. Some airlines impose penalties on regular tickets as well, particularly against 'no show' passengers.

Check In Airlines ask you to check in a certain amount of time before the flight departure (usually two hours on international flights). If you fail to check in on time and the flight is overbooked the airline can cancel your booking and give your seat to somebody else.

Confirmation Having a ticket written out with the flight and date you want doesn't mean you have a seat until the agent has checked with the airline that your status is 'OK' or confirmed. Meanwhile you could just be 'on request.'

Discounted Tickets There are two types of discounted fares – officially discounted (see Promotional Fares) and unofficially discounted. The lowest prices often impose drawbacks such as flying with unpopular airlines, inconvenient schedules or unpleasant routes and connections. A discounted ticket can save you other things than money – you may be able to pay Apex prices without the associated Apex advance booking and other requirements. Discounted tickets only exist when there is fierce competition.

Full Fares Airlines traditionally offer 1st class (coded F), business class (coded J) and economy class (coded Y) tickets. These days there are so many promotional and discounted fares available from the regular economy class that few passengers pay full economy fare.

Lost Tickets If you lose your airline ticket an airline will usually treat it like a traveler's check and, after inquiries, issue you another one. Legally, however, an airline is entitled to treat it like cash and if you lose it then it's gone forever. Take good care of your tickets.

No Shows No shows are passengers who fail to show up for their flight. Full-fare passengers who fail to turn up are sometimes entitled to travel on a later flight. The rest of us are penalized (see Cancellation Penalties).

On Request An unconfirmed booking for a flight; see Confirmation.

Open Jaws A return ticket for when you fly to one place but return from another. If available this can save you backtracking to your arrival point.

frequent flyer program (call ☎ 605-399-2400 to sign up). Ticket conditions are highly inflexible, so read the directions and requirements carefully before making any purchases.

Note that high season in the USA is from mid-June to mid-September and the week before and after Christmas. The best rates for travel to and within the USA are generally found November to March.

Call travel agencies for bargains (airlines can supply information on routes and timetables; however, except at times of fare wars, they do not supply the cheapest tickets). Airlines often have competitive low-season, student and senior citizens' fares. Find out the fare, the route, the duration of the journey and any restrictions on the ticket.

Cheap tickets are available in two dis-

Overbooking Airlines hate to fly empty seats and since every flight has some passengers who fail to show up they often book more passengers than they have seats. Usually the excess passengers balance those who fail to show up but occasionally somebody gets bumped. If this happens guess who it's most likely to be? The passengers who check in late.

Promotional Fares Officially discounted fares like Apex fares which are available from travel agents or direct from the airline.

Reconfirmation At least 72 hours prior to departure time of an onward or return flight you must contact the airline and 'reconfirm' that you intend to be on the flight. If you don't do this the airline can delete your name from the passenger list and you could lose your seat. You don't have to reconfirm the first flight on your itinerary or if your stopover is less than 72 hours. It doesn't hurt to reconfirm more than once.

Restrictions Discounted tickets often have various restrictions on them – advance purchase is the most usual one (see Apex). Others are restrictions on the minimum and maximum period you must be away, such as a minimum of 14 days or a maximum of one year. See Cancellation Penalties.

Standby A discounted ticket allowing you to fly only if there is a seat free at the last moment. Standby fares are usually only available on domestic routes.

Transferred Tickets Airline tickets cannot be transferred from one person to another. Travelers sometimes try to sell the return half of their ticket, but officials can ask you to prove that you are the person named on the ticket.

Travel Agencies Travel agencies vary widely – ensure you use one that suits your needs. Some simply handle tours, while full-service agencies handle everything from tours and tickets to car rental and hotel bookings. A good one will do all these things and can save you money but if all you want is a ticket at the lowest possible price, then you really need an agency specializing in discounted tickets. A discounted ticket agency, however, may not be useful for things like hotel bookings.

Travel Periods Some officially discounted fares, Apex fares in particular, vary with the time of year. There is often a low (off-peak) season and a high (peak) season. Sometimes there's an intermediate or shoulder season as well. At peak times, when everyone wants to fly, not only will the officially discounted fares be higher but so will unofficially discounted fares or there may simply be no discounted tickets available. Usually the fare depends on your outward flight – if you depart in the high season and return in the low season, you pay the high-season fare. ∎

tinct categories: official and unofficial. Official ones have a variety of names including advance-purchase fares, budget fares, Apex and super-Apex (see the Air Travel Glossary sidebar). Unofficial tickets are simply discounted tickets that the airlines release through selected travel agencies (not through airline offices). The cheapest tickets are often nonrefundable and require an extra fee for changing your flight. Many insurance policies will cover this loss if you have to change your flight for emergency reasons. Return (roundtrip) tickets usually work out cheaper than two one-way fares – often *much* cheaper.

You may decide to pay more than the rock-bottom fare by opting for the safety of a better known travel agency. Established firms like STA Travel (☎ 800-777-0112) and Council Travel (☎ 800-226-8624), which have offices worldwide, and Travel CUTS (☎ 800-663-6000) in Canada are valid alternatives, and they offer good prices to most destinations.

Once you have your ticket, write down its number, together with the flight number and other details, and keep the information somewhere separate. If the ticket is lost or stolen, this will help you get a replacement.

Remember to buy travel insurance as early as possible (see Travel Insurance in the Visas & Documents section in the Facts for the Visitor chapter).

Use the fares quoted in this book as a guide only. They are approximate and based on the rates advertised by travel agencies and airlines at press time. Quoted airfares do not necessarily constitute a recommendation for the carrier.

Special Fares for Foreign Visitors Almost all domestic carriers offer Visit USA passes to non-US citizens. The passes are actually a book of coupons – each coupon equals a single flight. Typically, the minimum number of coupons is three or four and the maximum is eight or 10, and they must be purchased in conjunction with an international airline ticket to the USA from a foreign country other than Canada or Mexico. Coupons cost from $100 to $160, depending on how many you buy. Most airlines require you to plan your itinerary in advance and to complete your flights within 60 days of arrival, but rules can vary between individual airlines. A few airlines may allow you to use coupons on standby, in which case call the airline a day or two before the flight and make a 'standby reservation.' Such a reservation gives you priority over all other travelers who just appear at the airport, hoping to get on the flight the same day.

Round-the-World Tickets Round-the-World (RTW) tickets have become very popular in the last few years. Airline RTW tickets are often real bargains and can work out to be no more expensive – or even cheaper than – an ordinary return ticket. Prices start at about $1300. These are for 'short' routes such as Los Angeles, New York, London, Bangkok, Honolulu. As soon as you start adding stops south of the equator, fares can go up to the $2000 to $3000 range.

The official airline RTW tickets are usually put together by a combination of two airlines, and they permit you to fly anywhere you want on their route systems as long as you do not backtrack. Other restrictions are that you must usually book the first sector in advance and cancellation penalties apply. There may be restrictions on the number of stops permitted, and tickets are usually valid from 90 days up to a year. An alternative type of RTW ticket is one put together by a travel agency using a combination of discounted tickets.

Although most airlines restrict the number of sectors that can be flown within the USA and Canada to four, and some airlines black out a few heavily traveled routes (like Honolulu to Tokyo), stopovers are otherwise generally unlimited. In most cases a 14-day advance purchase is required. After the ticket is purchased, dates can be changed without penalty and tickets can be rewritten to add or delete stops for $50 each.

Most RTW tickets restrict you to just two airlines. For example, Qantas Airways flies in conjunction with either American Airlines, British Airways, Delta Air Lines, Northwest Airlines, Canadian Airlines, Air France or KLM. Canadian Airlines links up with Philippine Airlines, KLM or South African Airways, among others. Continental Airlines flies with either Malaysia Airlines, Singapore Airlines or Thai Airways International. The possibilities go on and on. Your best bet is to find a travel agency that advertises or specializes in RTW tickets.

Circle Pacific Tickets Circle Pacific tickets use a combination of airlines to circle the Pacific – combining Australia, New Zealand, North America and Asia. Rather than simply flying from point A to point B, these tickets allow you to swing through much of the Pacific Rim and eastern Asia taking in a variety of destinations – as long as you keep traveling in the same circular direction. As with RTW tickets, there are advance-purchase restrictions and limits on how many stopovers you can take. These fares are likely to be around 15% cheaper than RTW tickets.

Circle Pacific routes essentially have the same fares: $2449 when purchased in the USA, C$3309 when purchased in Canada and A$2999 when purchased in Australia. Circle Pacific fares include four stopovers with the option of adding additional stops at $50 each. There's a 14-day advance-purchase requirement, a 25% cancellation penalty and a maximum stay of six months. There are also higher business class and first-class fares. Departure and airport-use taxes, which will vary with the itinerary, are additional.

Qantas Airways offers Circle Pacific routes in partnership with Delta Air Lines, JAL, Northwest Airlines or Continental Airlines. In the off-season (the Australian winter), Qantas occasionally offers hefty discounts on tickets that use Qantas as the primary carrier.

United Airlines flies in conjunction with Cathay Pacific Airways, Qantas, Ansett, Malaysia Airlines or British Airways. Canadian Airlines has Circle Pacific fares from Vancouver that include, in one combination or another, virtually all Pacific Rim destinations. Canadian's partners include Qantas, Air New Zealand, Singapore Airlines, Garuda Indonesia, Cathay Pacific or Malaysia Airlines.

Getting 'Bumped'
Airlines routinely overbook and count on some passengers canceling or not showing up. Occasionally, almost everybody does show up for a flight, and then some passengers must be 'bumped' onto another flight. Getting bumped can be a nuisance because you have to wait around for the next flight, but if you have a day's leeway, you can turn this to your advantage.

On oversold flights, the gate agent will first ask for volunteers to be bumped in return for a later flight plus compensation

of the airline's choosing. (If there aren't enough volunteers, some passengers will be forced onto a later flight. Each airline has its own method of choosing which customers will be bumped.) When you check in at the airline counter, ask if the flight is full and if there may be a need for volunteers. Get your name on the list if you don't mind volunteering. Depending on how oversold the flight is, compensation can range from a discount voucher toward your next flight to a fully paid roundtrip ticket or even cash. Be sure to try and confirm a later flight so you don't get stuck in the airport on standby. If you have to spend the night, airlines frequently foot the hotel bill for their bumpees. You don't have to accept the airline's first offer: you can haggle for a better deal.

However, be aware that, due to this same system, being just a little late for boarding could get you bumped with none of these benefits.

Travelers with Special Needs
If you have special needs of any sort – dietary restrictions, dependence on a wheelchair, responsibility for a baby, fear of flying – you should let the airline know as soon as possible so that they can make arrangements accordingly. You should remind them when you reconfirm your booking (at least 72 hours before departure) and again when you check in at the airport. It may also be worth calling various airlines before you make your booking to find out how they can handle your particular needs.

Airports and airlines can be surprisingly helpful, but they do need advance warning. Most international airports can provide escorts from the check-in desk to the plane where needed, and there should also be reachable phones, ramps, lifts and accessible toilets in the airport. Aircraft toilets, on the other hand, are likely to present a problem; travelers should discuss this with the airline at an early stage and, if necessary, with their doctor.

Guide dogs for the blind will often have to travel in a specially pressurized baggage compartment with other animals, away from their owner, though smaller guide dogs might be allowed in the cabin. As long as they have proof of being vaccinated against rabies, guide dogs are not subject to quarantine.

Deaf travelers can ask for airport and in-flight announcements to be written down for them.

Children under two travel for 10% of the standard fare (or free on some airlines), as long as they don't occupy a seat, in which case they don't get baggage allowance. Children between two and 12 can usually occupy a seat for half to two-thirds of the full fare, and do get a baggage allowance. Strollers can often be taken on as hand luggage. 'Skycots' should be provided by the airline if requested in advance; these can hold a child weighing up to about 22lb.

Baggage & Other Restrictions
On most domestic and international flights you are limited to two checked bags, or three if you don't have a carry-on. There could be a charge if you bring more or if the size of the bag exceeds the airline's limits. It's best to check with the individual airline if you are worried about this. On some international flights the luggage allowance is based on weight; again, check with the airline.

If your luggage is delayed upon arrival (which is rare), some airlines will give you a cash advance to purchase necessities. If sporting equipment is misplaced, the airline may pay for rental equipment. Should the luggage be lost, it is important to submit a claim. The airline doesn't have to pay the full amount of the claim, rather they can estimate the value of your lost items. It may take them anywhere from six weeks to three months to process the claim and pay you.

Smoking is prohibited on all domestic flights within the USA. Many international flights are following suit, so be sure to call and find out. Many airports in the USA also restrict smoking.

Items that are illegal to take on a plane,

either checked or as carry-on, include aerosols of polishes, waxes, etc; tear gas and pepper spray; camp stoves with fuel; and divers' tanks that are full.

Within the USA
Seattle's Sea-Tac and Portland's PDX are the principal hubs for air travel to the US Pacific Northwest. Flights to the West Coast from the East Coast usually take about five hours. (If you're planning on flying from the East Coast to the Northwest, you're better off flying to Seattle or Portland rather than Vancouver since flights to Canada are generally more expensive.)

Horizon Air and United Express (a subsidiary of United Airlines) – the primary carriers for small Northwest cities – sometimes offer direct flights from San Francisco or Los Angeles, depending on your destination.

US domestic airfares vary tremendously depending on the season you travel, the day of the week you fly, the length of your stay and the flexibility the ticket allows for flight changes and refunds. Still, nothing determines fares more than demand, and when things are slow, regardless of the season, airlines will lower their fares to fill empty seats. There's a lot of competition, and at any given time any one of the airlines could have the cheapest fare.

If you are buying tickets within the US, the *New York Times*, *Los Angeles Times*, *Chicago Tribune*, *San Francisco Examiner* and other major newspapers all produce weekly travel sections that have numerous travel agencies' advertisements. Council Travel (☎ 800-226-8624) and STA Travel (☎ 800-777-0112) have offices in major cities nationwide. The magazine *Travel Unlimited*, PO Box 1058, Allston, MA 02134, publishes details of the cheapest airfares and courier possibilities.

The following roundtrip fares are based on high-season rates, with a 14-day advance purchase and a Saturday-night stay over. Remember, fares change dramatically according to season, promotions and other factors.

To Portland from:	Fare
Chicago	$358
Los Angeles	$196
Miami	$341
New York City	$394
San Francisco	$124

To Seattle from:	Fare
Chicago	$431
Los Angeles	$201
Miami	$373
New York City	$536
San Francisco	$137

Canada

Canada 3000 (☎ 604-273-0930), one of the first discount airlines to operate in Canada, offers flights to Vancouver from other major Canadian cities. A US discounter, Reno Air, flies to Vancouver from California and the US Southwest.

If you want to connect to the rest of Canada from the US Pacific Northwest, you'll most likely need to go through Vancouver. Many people traveling across the continent find it cheaper to fly to the Northwest from New York rather than from a Canadian point. Bus connections can be made between Canadian and US airports at either end.

Canada's Travel CUTS (☎ 800-663-6000), a student-oriented travel agency, has offices in all major cities. The Toronto *Globe & Mail* and the *Vancouver Sun* carry travel agencies' ads.

The following roundtrip fares are based on high-season rates, with a 14-day advance purchase and a Saturday-night stay over.

To Vancouver from:	Fare
Chicago	$509
Los Angeles	$240
Miami	$412
New York City	$564
San Francisco	$194

The UK & Ireland

The primary airlines serving Seattle are British Air, SAS and United. Air Canada and Canadian Airlines both have flights to Vancouver from London; fares fluctuate

Sample Fares

The following roundtrip fares are examples of what you can expect to pay for flights to the Pacific Northwest and other cities in the US.

City	low season/high season
Auckland to:	
Denver	NZ$1619/2572
Los Angeles	NZ$1519/2027
New York City	NZ$1619/2569
Seattle	NZ$1619/2398
Vancouver, BC	NZ$1999/2165
Frankfurt to:	
Denver	DM750/1858
Los Angeles	DM499/1543
New York City	DM799/1795
Seattle	DM799/1908
Vancouver, BC	DM799/1863
London to:	
Denver	UK£334/552
Los Angeles	UK£311/488
New York City	UK£236/426
Seattle	UK£322/575
Vancouver, BC	UK£426/667
Paris to:	
Denver	FF3000/5000
Los Angeles	FF1400/2600
New York City	FF1250-1800/
	FF1950-2500
Seattle	FF3700/4500
Vancouver, BC	FF3700/4750
Sydney to:	
Denver	A$1000/2055
Los Angeles	A$1609/1955
New York City	A$1699/2055
Seattle	A$1699/2055
Vancouver, BC	A$1609/1955
Tokyo to:	
Denver	¥105,000/152,000
Los Angeles	¥92,000/124,000
New York City	¥113,000/150,000
Seattle	¥92,000/139,000
Vancouver, BC	¥114,000/134,000
Toronto to:	
Denver	C$371/628
Los Angeles	C$330/646
New York City	C$138/603
Seattle	C$316/646
Vancouver, BC	C$355/542

wildly. If you're planning to remain on the Pacific Coast, you can save hours of flight time and airport dawdling if you fly directly from London to Seattle or Vancouver.

Most British travel agents are registered with the ABTA (Association of British Travel Agents). If you paid an ABTA-registered agent for your flight who then goes out of business, ABTA will guarantee a refund or an alternative. Unregistered 'bucket shops' are riskier (tickets are highly restricted and may not leave you with many rights if your flight is canceled) but sometimes cheaper.

London is arguably the world's head-quarters for bucket shops, which are well advertised and can usually beat published airline fares. Called bucket shops in the trade, they are given seats to sell by the airlines that otherwise would be empty. You will probably find that the cheapest flights are being advertised by obscure bucket shops whose names haven't yet reached the telephone directory. Many such firms are honest and solvent, but there are a few rogues who will take your money and disappear, to reopen elsewhere a month or two later under a new name. If you feel suspicious about a firm, don't pay for the ticket all at once – leave a deposit of 20% or so and pay the balance on receiving the ticket. If they insist on cash in advance, go elsewhere. And once you have the ticket, call the airline to confirm that you are booked on the flight.

Good, reliable agents for cheap tickets in the UK are Trailfinders (☎ 0171-937-5400), 194 Kensington High St, London, W8 7RG; Council Travel (☎ 0171-437-7767), 28a Poland St, London, W1; and STA Travel (☎ 0171-581-4132), 86 Old Brompton Rd, London, SW7 3LQ.

The Globetrotters Club (BCM Roving, London, WC1N 3XX) publishes a news-letter called *Globe* that covers obscure destinations and can help you find trav-eling companions.

Look for travel agencies' ads in maga-zines like *Time Out*, the *Evening Stan-dard* and *TNT*. Also check out the free magazines widely available in London – start by looking outside the main railway stations.

Continental Europe

There are nonstop flights to Seattle from Copenhagen and Amsterdam. Vancouver, which is also convenient, has direct air links to Frankfurt, Zurich and Ams-terdam. You can also fly directly from Paris to San Francisco, where you can easily catch a flight to Portland, Seattle or Vancouver.

In Amsterdam, NBBS is a popular travel agency. Council Travel has offices in Paris (☎ 01 44 41 89 80), 1 place de l'Odeon, 75006 Paris; in Düsseldorf (☎ 211-36-30-30), Graf Adolph Strasse 18, 42112 Düs-seldorf; and in Münich (☎ 089-39-50-22), Adalbert Strasse 32, 80799 Münich 40.

In Frankfurt, STA Travel (☎ 4969-43-01-91) is at Berger Strasse 118, 60316 Frankfurt 1. For great student fares, contact USIT Voyages (☎ 01 42 34 56 90) at 6, rue de Vaugirard, 75006 Paris.

Australia & New Zealand

There are no direct flights to the Pacific Northwest from Australia or New Zealand: travelers must connect through Honolulu or LA.

The cheapest tickets have a 21-day advance-purchase requirement, a minimum stay of seven days and a maximum stay of 60 days. Flying with Air New Zealand is slightly cheaper, and both Qantas and Air New Zealand offer tickets with longer stays or stopovers, but you pay more.

STA Travel has many offices in the major cities of Australia and New Zealand. They sell tickets to everyone but have spe-cial deals for students and travelers under the age of 30. Head offices are at STA Travel (☎ 1300-360-960, 3-9347-6911), 224 Faraday St, PO Box 75, Carlton South, Melbourne, VIC 3053, Australia, and STA Travel (☎ 0800-100-677, 309-0458), 10 High St, Auckland, New Zealand.

In Australia, STA Travel and Flight Centres International are major dealers in cheap airfares; check the travel agencies' ads in the yellow pages and call around. Qantas flies to Los Angeles from Sydney, Melbourne (via Sydney or Auckland) and Cairns. United Airlines flies to San Francisco from Sydney and Melbourne (via Sydney) and also flies to Los Angeles. In New Zealand, STA Travel and Flight Centres International are also popular travel agencies.

Look for travel agencies' ads in newspapers like the *Sydney Morning Herald* and *The Age* in Australia for cheap flights.

Asia

Delta Air Lines has daily nonstop flights to Portland from Tokyo, Nagoya and Seoul, Korea. Northwest Airlines has service to Seattle from the Pacific Rim, including Japan and Korea. JAL has flights to Vancouver.

United has three flights daily to Honolulu from Tokyo with connections to US West Coast cities like Seattle, Los Angeles and San Francisco. JAL also flies to Honolulu from Osaka, Nagoya, Fukuoka and Sapporo, with links to the US West Coast.

Northwest Airlines flies to Honolulu from Hong Kong, Bangkok, Manila, Seoul and Singapore, with connections to the US West Coast. Korean Air and Philippine Airlines also have flights from a number of Southeast Asian cities to Honolulu, with onward connections to the Northwest. Tickets to the US West Coast often allow a free stopover in Honolulu.

Hong Kong was once the discount plane ticket capital of the region. But now Bangkok and Singapore, which have a number of bucket shops, are better places for getting the cheapest fares. Ask the advice of other travelers before buying a ticket. STA Travel (which is dependable) has branches in Hong Kong, Tokyo, Singapore, Bangkok and Kuala Lumpur.

Central & South America

Most flights to the US from Central America and South America go via Miami, Houston or Los Angeles, though some fly via New York. Most countries' international carriers, such as Aerolíneas Argentinas and LanChile, as well as US airlines like United and American, serve these US destinations, with onward connections to the Pacific Northwest. Continental has flights to the US from Central America, including San Jose, Guatemala City, Cancún and Mérida.

Arriving in the USA

The first US airport that you land in is where you must carry out immigration and customs formalities – even if you are continuing immediately to another city in the US. For instance, if your luggage is checked from, say, London to Seattle, you will still have to take it through customs if you first land in New York.

If you have a non-US passport, with a visa, you must complete an Arrival/Departure Record (form I 94) before you go to the immigration desk. It's usually handed out on the plane, along with the customs declaration. It's a rather badly designed form, and lots of people take more than one attempt to get it right. Some airlines suggest you start with the last question and work upwards. Answers should be written *below* the questions. For question 12, 'Address While in the United States,' give the address of the location where you will spend the first night. Complete the Departure Record (the lower part of the form), giving exactly the same answers for questions 14 to 17 as for questions 1 to 4.

The staff of the Immigration & Naturalization Service (INS) can be less than welcoming. Since their main concern is to exclude those who are likely to work illegally or overstay, visitors will be asked about their plans, and perhaps about whether they have sufficient funds for their stay in the US. If the INS official thinks you're OK, a six-month entry is usually approved.

It's a good idea to be able to list an itinerary that will account for the period for which you ask to be admitted, and to be able to show you have $300 or $400 for every week of your intended stay. These

HIV & Entering the USA

Everyone entering the USA who isn't a US citizen is subject to the authority of the Immigration & Naturalization Service (INS). The INS can keep someone from entering or staying in the USA by excluding or deporting them. This is especially relevant for travelers with HIV (human immunodeficiency virus). Though being HIV-positive is not grounds for deportation, it is a 'ground of exclusion' and the INS can invoke it to refuse admission.

Although the INS doesn't test people for HIV at customs, it may try to exclude anyone who answers yes to this question on the nonimmigrant visa application form: 'Have you ever been afflicted with a communicable disease of public health significance?' INS officials may also stop people if they seem sick, are carrying AIDS/HIV medicine or, sadly, if the officer happens to think the person 'looks gay,' though sexual orientation is not legally a ground of exclusion.

It's imperative that visitors know and assert their rights. Immigrants and visitors who may face exclusion should discuss their rights and options with a trained immigration advocate before applying for a visa. For legal immigration information and referrals to immigration advocates, contact the National Immigration Project of the National Lawyers Guild (☎ 617-227-9727), 14 Beacon St, suite 506, Boston, MA 02108; or Immigrant HIV Assistance Project, Bar Association of San Francisco (☎ 415-782-8995), 465 California St, suite 1100, San Francisco, CA 94104. ∎

---

days, a couple of major credit cards will go a long way toward establishing 'sufficient funds.' Don't make too much of having friends, relatives or business contacts in the USA – the INS official may decide that this will make you more likely to overstay.

See the Traveling to Canada sidebar at the beginning of the Vancouver chapter for information on arriving in Canada.

Departure Tax

Airport departure taxes are normally included in the cost of tickets purchased in the USA. Tickets purchased abroad, however, may not include this tax. There's a $6.50 North American Free Trade Agreement (NAFTA) tax charged to passengers entering the USA from a foreign country. However, this tax, as well as a $6 airport departure tax charged to all passengers bound for a foreign destination, are hidden taxes added to the cost of your airline ticket.

LAND
Bus

Because buses are so few, schedules are often inconvenient and fares are relatively high; bargain airfares can often undercut bus fares on long-distance routes. In some cases it can be cheaper to rent a car than to ride the bus, especially on shorter routes. However, very long-distance bus trips are often available at bargain prices if you purchase or reserve tickets three days in advance. For more details on fares, see Bus in the Getting Around chapter.

Greyhound The only nationwide bus company in the US and Canada, Greyhound (☎ 800-231-2222), runs cross-country buses between New York and Seattle ($140 one-way, $226 roundtrip). Along the US West Coast, you can travel to Vancouver from Los Angeles ($125 one-way, $248 roundtrip) via Seattle, Portland and San Francisco. The shortest Greyhound routing up and down the West Coast follows I-5, though if you have time, the route from Portland to San Francisco following US 101 along the coast is much more scenic

Tickets can be bought over the phone with a major credit card (MasterCard, Visa or Discover), and mailed to you if purchased 10 days in advance or picked up at the terminal with proper ID. Greyhound terminals also accept American Express, travelers' checks and cash. Note all buses are nonsmoking, and that only by purchasing a ticket can you reserve a space.

Special Fares Greyhound's $59 one-way unlimited mileage ticket can be a bargain if you're looking for cheap way to cover a long distance (Portland to Chicago, for instance). Certain restrictions apply, and it's a good idea to check the regular fare anyway. The ticket must be booked at least three weeks in advance and no stopovers are allowed. As with regular fares, these promotional fares are subject to change.

Ameripass Greyhound's Ameripass is potentially useful, depending on how much you plan to travel, but the relatively high price may impel you to travel more than you normally would simply to get your money's worth. There are no restrictions on who can buy an Ameripass; it costs $199 for seven days of unlimited travel year-round, $299 for 15 days and $409 for 30 days. Children under 12 travel for half-price. With the pass, you can get on and off at any Greyhound stop or terminal, and the Ameripass can be purchased at every terminal.

International Ameripass Greyhound's International Ameripass can be purchased only by foreign tourists and foreign students and lecturers (with their families) staying less than one year. Prices are $119 for a five-day pass for unlimited travel Monday to Thursday; $159 for a seven-day pass; $219 for a 15-day pass and $299 for a 30-day pass. The International Ameripass is usually bought at overseas travel agencies or can be bought in the US at the Greyhound International Office in New York City (☎ 212-971-0492) at 625 8th Ave at the subway level of the Port Authority Bus Terminal. It's open 8 am to 4 pm Monday to Thursday and Friday until 7 pm. The office accepts MasterCard, Visa, traveler's checks and cash, and allows purchases to be made by phone.

Green Tortoise The near mythic Green Tortoise (☎ 415-956-7500, 800-867-8647), 494 Broadway, San Francisco, CA 94133, offers alternative bus transportation to Portland and Seattle from San Francisco via intervening hot springs, national parks and sporadic stops for skinny-dipping and cookouts. Green Tortoise buses are cheaper than Greyhound and *a lot* more interesting. Meals are cooperatively cooked, you sleep on bunks on the bus or camp, easy chairs replace bus seats, and music, drink and a carnival atmosphere prevail. Two buses a week make the trip back and forth between Seattle and San Francisco. A one-way fare from San Francisco to Portland is $49; just add $10 to continue onto Seattle. A 10 to 14 day cross-country tour including food costs around $450.

Train
The Pacific Northwest is well served by trains. Amtrak's *Coast Starlight* links Oakland, CA, to Portland and Seattle, and other major US West Coast cities. Portland and Seattle are both western termini of the *Empire Builder* line, with links to Spokane, WA, Minneapolis, MN, and Chicago, IL. Note that schedules can be very fluid: arrival and departure times are often very tenuous the farther you are from the starting point.

Amtrak tickets may be purchased aboard the train without penalty if the train station is closed 30 minutes prior to boarding; otherwise there is a $7 penalty. You can beat the rather stiff full-price fares by purchasing special fares in advance. Roundtrips are the best bargain, but even these are usually as expensive as airfares.

The best value overall is Amtrak's All Aboard America fare, which enables you to travel anywhere you want for $318 (adults). There are limitations, however. Travel must be completed in 30 days, and you are allowed up to three stopovers. Additional stopovers can be arranged for an extra cost. Your entire trip must be reserved in advance and seats are limited, so book as far ahead as possible. Travel between mid-June and late August will cost slightly more. These tickets are for reclining seats; sleeping cars cost extra.

If you want to travel in just the western, eastern or central parts of the US, All Aboard America fares are available for $168.

For non-US citizens, Amtrak offers three types of USA Rail Passes – national, regional and coastal – which must be purchased outside the US (check with your travel agent). A 15-day national pass costs $355/$245 (high/low season) and a 30-day national pass costs $440/$350. Regional passes vary: a 15-day pass ranges from $175 to $265/$155 to $215; a 30-day pass is $205 to $330/$195 to $290. Coastal passes for either the East or West Coast cost $235/$205. Sleeping accommodations cost extra. Advanced booking is highly recommended, especially during the peak season.

For further assistance, contact Amtrak (☎ 800-872-7245, www.amtrak.com) or call your travel agent. Note that most small train stations don't sell tickets; you have to book tickets with Amtrak over the phone. Some small stations have no porters or other facilities; trains may only stop if someone has bought a ticket in advance.

Car & Motorcycle

Drivers of cars and riders of motorcycles will need the vehicle's registration papers, liability insurance and an international driver's permit in addition to their domestic license. Canadian and Mexican driver's licenses are accepted.

Note that customs officials along the entry points between Canada and Montana can be strict and wary of anyone that doesn't look straight-laced. To avoid unnecessary conflicts dress well and be cordial during the time it takes to cross the border.

For information on buying or renting a car, see the Getting Around chapter.

SEA

Chances that you will arrive on a boat and still have time to enjoy being in the USA

are few. There are cruises, such as the QE2 from England, that make transatlantic voyages, but the cruise itself is usually the vacation. Cities in the Puget Sound and Georgia Strait region of the Pacific Northwest are linked by ferry, and while – strictly speaking – they're international journeys, they are best thought of as commuter ferries. Probably the granddaddy of all Northwest ferry rides is the Inland Passage trip between Bellingham, WA, and Skagway, Alaska.

Those few cruise ships that do serve the US West Coast are usually in transition from summer sailings in Alaska and winter sailings in the Caribbean. Vancouver is the main port of departure for cruises to Alaska.

ORGANIZED TOURS

Tours of the USA are so numerous that it would be impossible to attempt any kind of comprehensive listing. Probably those of most interest to the general traveler are coach tours that visit the national parks and guest ranch excursions. For those with limited time, package tours can be an efficient and relatively inexpensive way to go. For overseas visitors, the most reliable sources of information on the constantly changing offerings are major international travel agents like Thomas Cook and American Express.

Trek America (☎ 201-983-1144, 800-221-0596, fax 983-8551), PO Box 189, Rockaway, NJ 07866, offers roundtrip camping tours to different areas of the US. In England (☎ 01295-256777, fax 257399) they're at 4 Water Perry Court, Banbury, Oxon OX16 8QG, and in Australia contact Adventure World (☎ 9956 7766, 800-221-931, fax 4956 7707, www.trekamerica.com), 75 Walker St, North Sydney, NSW 2060. These tours last from one to nine weeks and are designed for small, international groups (13 people maximum) of 18- to 38-year-olds. Tour prices vary with season, with July to September being the highest. Tours including food and occasional hotel nights cost about $1000 for a 10-day tour, up to $3500 for a nine-week tour of the entire country. Some side trips and cultural events are included in the price, and participants help with cooking and camp chores.

Similar deals are available from Suntrek (☎ 707-523-1800, 800-786-8735, fax 523-1911), Sun Plaza, 77 West Third St, Santa Rosa, CA 95401. Suntrek also has offices in Germany (☎ 089 480 2831, fax 089 480 2411), Sedanstrasse 21, D-81667, München; and Switzerland (☎ 1 462 6161, fax 462 6545), Birmensdorferstr 107, PO Box 8371, CH-8036, Zurich. Their tours are for the 'young at heart' and attract mostly young international travelers, although there is no age limit. Prices range from about $847 for the three-week trek to about $3194 for the 13-week around America trek.

Road Runner USA/Canada (☎ 800-873-5872), 1050 Hancock, Quincy, MA 02169, organizes one- and two-week treks in conjunction with Hostelling International to different parts of the USA and Canada. They also have offices in England (☎ 892-512700), 64 Mt Pleasant Ave, Tunbridge Wells, Kent TN1 1QY. Prices run $449 for one week to $849 for two weeks. AmeriCan Adventures (☎ 800-864-0335) offers seven- to 21-day trips to different parts of the USA, usually following a theme like Route 66 or the Wild West. Prices range from $450 for seven days to $1200 for 21 days.

WARNING

The information in this chapter is particularly vulnerable to change: prices for international travel are volatile, routes are introduced and cancelled, schedules will change, special deals come and go and rules and visa requirements are amended. Airlines and governments seem to take a perverse pleasure in making price structures and regulations as complicated as possible. You should check directly with the airline or a travel agent to make sure you understand how a fare (and ticket you may buy) works. In addition, the travel industry is highly competitive and there are many lurks and perks.

The upshot of this is that you should get opinions, quotes and advice from as many airlines and travel agencies as possible before you part with your hard-earned cash. The details given in this chapter should be regarded as pointers and are not a substitute for your own careful, up-to-date research.

Getting Around

This chapter deals with the intricacies of getting around *within* the Pacific Northwest; see the Getting There & Away chapter for details on getting *to* the Northwest. Don't automatically assume that, once arriving in the Northwest, ground travel is going to be the cheapest method of transport. The US West Coast and the Canadian west coast are home to a number of inexpensive, no-frills airlines, whose rates rival bus and train fares. Ask a travel agent for information about discount airlines.

AIR

Portland, Seattle and Vancouver are linked by frequent flights; between Portland and Seattle, for instance, there is usually a flight every half-hour (and the flight lasts just 20 minutes). Both Portland and Seattle have frequent and inexpensive flights to Vancouver, which is serviced by both Air Canada and Canadian Airlines. A roundtrip flight between Seattle and Vancouver is usually less than $100.

Portland and Seattle are the principal hubs for flights to outlying Northwest communities. United Express, a subsidiary of United Airlines, and Horizon Air are the most common carriers on these commuter flights. From Portland, flights are available to Pendleton, Klamath Falls, Coos Bay, Salem, Astoria, Bend, Eugene, Corvallis and Medford. Flights leave from Seattle for Port Angeles, Olympia, Yakima, the Tri-Cities, Walla Walla, Spokane, Bellingham and Wenatchee, as well as to destinations in the San Juan Islands. Vancouver serves as a hub for flights to Victoria and Whistler.

These short flights are usually moderately priced if bought with sufficient advance notice, especially when considering the distance covered and the rather grim overland alternatives. Generally, fares can drop by about half if you are able to fly very early in the morning, late at night or on specific flights. Ask airlines and travel agents about special fare flights.

If you are arriving in the Northwest from overseas or another major US airport, it is usually much cheaper to buy a through ticket to small airports as part of your fare rather than separately, unless your travel plans are so spontaneous as to preclude doing so.

Another alternative for traveling within the Northwest is the air pass, available from major airlines that fly between the USA and Europe, Asia and Australia. Air passes are particularly valuable if you're flying between destinations that are widely separated. For more information on air passes, see the Special Fares for Foreign Visitors section in the Getting There & Away chapter.

Regional Carriers

The following list includes both major airlines and smaller commuter carriers, some of which also serve US states such as Arizona, California, Idaho, Kansas, Nebraska, Nevada, Oklahoma, North Dakota, South Dakota and Utah. Phone numbers for international airlines and other US domestic airlines are listed at the beginning of the Getting There & Away chapter.

Air Canada	☎ 800-776-3000
American Airlines	☎ 800-433-7300
Canadian Airlines	☎ 800-426-7000
Delta Air Lines	☎ 800-221-1212
Horizon Air	☎ 800-547-9308
Reno Air	☎ 800-736-6247
Southwest Airlines	☎ 800-435-9792
United Express	☎ 800-241-6522

Within the maritime Northwest, commuter flights are sometimes on floatplanes. Small floatplanes serve the San Juan Islands from Seattle, and Victoria from Vancouver. See appropriate chapters for details.

BUS
Greyhound
Since Americans rely so much on their cars and usually fly longer distances, bus transport is less frequent than is desirable in the US, but some good deals are available. Greyhound (☎ 800-231-2222), the main bus line for the region (and the US), has extensive fixed routes and its own terminal in most central cities, often in undesirable parts of town. However, the company has an exceptional safety record, the buses are comfortable and they usually run on time.

In the Northwest, Greyhound service largely sticks to the interstate freeway system. Regional carriers link with Greyhound to provide service to outlying areas. In almost all cases, these smaller bus lines share depots and information services with Greyhound.

Greyhound has reduced or eliminated services to smaller rural communities it once served efficiently. In many small towns Greyhound no longer maintains terminals, but merely stops at a given location, such as a grocery store parking lot or cafe. In these unlikely terminals, boarding passengers usually pay the driver with exact change.

Tickets can be bought over the phone with a major credit card, and mailed to you if purchased 10 days in advance or picked up at the terminal with proper identification. Greyhound terminals also accept American Express, travelers' checks and cash. Note all buses are nonsmoking, and that only by purchasing a ticket can you reserve a space.

Green Tortoise
Green Tortoise (☎ 415-956-7500, 800-867-8647), 494 Broadway, San Francisco, CA 94133, is a fun alternative to Greyhound, if you're traveling between Seattle and San Francisco or points along I-5. Fares are lower than Greyhound, and the trip may take a little longer because of sporadic stops for cookouts or skinny-dipping. See Green Tortoise under Bus in the Getting There & Away chapter for more information.

TRAIN
Amtrak (☎ 800-872-7245, www.amtrak.com) fares vary greatly, depending on different promotions and destinations. Reservations (the sooner made, the better the fare) can be held under your surname only. Tickets can be purchased by credit card over the phone, from a travel agent or at an Amtrak depot.

A branch of Amtrak's *Empire Builder* leaves Portland, crosses to Vancouver, WA, before running up the north side of the Columbia Gorge to meet the other eastbound half of the train in Spokane. It is one of the most spectacular train rides you'll find in the USA. The Seattle branch of the *Empire Builder* heads north to Everett before winding east to Wenatchee and Spokane. If you're coming in from the east on this train, note that the westbound *Empire Builder* divides in Spokane for Portland and Seattle: make sure you're sitting in the correct portion of the train! The *Empire Builder* runs four times weekly.

The daily *Coast Starlight* connects Seattle to Tacoma, Olympia, Portland, Salem, Albany and Eugene; it then sets off for Klamath Falls in southern Oregon.

Amtrak's two commuter trains, *Mt Adams* and *Cascadia*, provide daily service between Portland and Seattle; the fare is about $31 return. The daily *Mt Baker International* links Seattle to Vancouver, BC, with stops in Bellingham; in Vancouver the train links to VIA Rail.

In addition to daily train service, Amtrak also runs three buses a day between Vancouver, BC, and Seattle, and Portland and Eugene.

CAR & MOTORCYCLE
The US highway system is very extensive, and, since distances are great and buses can be infrequent, auto transport is worth considering despite the expense. Officially, you must have an International or Inter-American Driving Permit to supplement your national or state driver's license, but US police are more likely to want to see your national, provincial or state driver's license. See the Traveling to Canada

Driving Distances

Portland to	Distance	Hours
Bend	160 miles	3
Eugene	110 miles	2
Lincoln City	88 miles	1½
Medford	273 miles	5
Pendleton	208 miles	4
Salem	47 miles	1
Vancouver, BC	313 miles	6

Seattle to		
Bellingham	89 miles	1½
Portland	172 miles	3
Spokane	280 miles	5
Tri-Cities	216 miles	4
Yakima	142 miles	2½
Vancouver, BC	141 miles	3

Vancouver to		
Portland	313 miles	6
Seattle	141 miles	3
Victoria	70 miles	3½
Whistler	75 miles	1½

(Note: driving time to Victoria is approximate due to ferry schedules.)

sidebar in the Vancouver chapter for details on driving across the border.

Safety

Drivers should be aware that much of the Pacific Northwest region is open-range country in which cattle and, less frequently, sheep forage along the highway. A collision with a large animal (including game animals like deer or elk) can wreck a car and severely injure or kill the driver and passengers, not to mention the animal, so pay attention to the roadside – especially at night. In the Northwest, seat belts are obligatory for the driver and all passengers.

During winter months – especially at the higher elevations – there will be times when tire chains are required on snowy or icy roads. Sometimes such roads will be closed to cars without chains or 4WD. So it's a good idea to keep a set of chains in the trunk. (Note many car-rental companies specifically prohibit the use of chains on their vehicles. You are responsible for any damage due to chains.) Roadside services might be available to attach chains to

your tires for a fee (around $20). Other cold-weather precautions include keeping a wool blanket, a windshield ice scraper, a spade or snow shovel, flares and an extra set of gloves and boots in the trunk for emergencies.

Some but not all US states have motorcycle helmet laws. Oregon and Washington both require that anyone (including passengers) riding a motorcycle wear a helmet. BC has a similar helmet law.

Weather is a serious factor throughout the Pacific Northwest, especially in the wintertime. Both Oregon, Washington and BC provide road and travel information as well as state and provincial highway patrol information by telephone. For these numbers, see the Emergency section in the Facts for the Visitor chapter.

To avert theft, do not leave expensive items, such as purses, CDs, cameras, leather bags or even sunglasses, visibly lying about in the car. Tuck items under the seat, or even better, put items in the trunk and make sure your car does not have trunk entry through the back seat; if it does, make sure this is locked. Don't leave valuables in the car overnight.

Rental

Major international rental agencies like Hertz, Avis, Budget and A-1 have offices throughout the region. To rent a car, you must have a valid driver's license, be at least 21 years of age (sometimes 25) and present a major credit card or else a large cash deposit.

Many rental agencies have bargain rates for weekend or weeklong rentals, especially outside the peak summer season or in conjunction with airline tickets. Prices vary greatly in relation to region, season and type or size of the car you'd like to rent.

Basic liability insurance, which covers damage you may cause to another vehicle, is required by law and comes with the price of renting the car. Liability insurance is also called third-party coverage.

Collision insurance, also called the Liability Damage Waiver, is optional. It covers the full value of the vehicle in case

Accidents Do Happen

Accidents do happen – especially in such an auto-dependent country as the USA. It's important that a visitor knows the appropriate protocol when involved in a 'fender-bender.'

- DON'T TRY TO DRIVE AWAY! Remain at the scene of the accident; otherwise you may spend some time in the local jail.
- Call the police (and an ambulance, if needed) immediately, and give the operator as much specific information as possible (your location, if anyone is injured, etc). The emergency phone number is ☎ 911.
- Get the other driver's name, address, driver's license number, license plate and insurance information. Be prepared to provide any documentation you have, such as your passport, international driver's license and insurance documents.
- Tell your story to the police carefully. Refrain from answering any questions until you feel comfortable doing so (with a lawyer present, if need be). That's your right under the law. The only insurance information you need to reveal is the name of your insurance carrier and your policy number.
- Always comply if asked to take an alcohol breathalyzer test. If you choose not to, you'll almost certainly find yourself with an automatic suspension of your driving privileges.
- If you're driving a rental car, call the rental company promptly. ■

of an accident, except when caused by acts of nature or fire. For a midsize car the cost for this extra coverage is around $15 per day. You don't need to buy this waiver to rent the car. Rental agencies also tack on a daily fee per each additional driver in the car.

Some credit cards, such as the Master Card Gold Card, will cover collision insurance if you rent for 15 days or less and charge the full cost of rental to your card. If you opt to do that, you'll need to sign the waiver, declining the coverage. If you already have collision insurance on your personal policy, the credit card will cover the large deductible. To find out if your credit card offers such a service, and the extent of the coverage, contact the credit card company.

Be aware that some major rental agencies no longer offer unlimited mileage in noncompetitive markets (which is most of the Pacific Northwest); this greatly increases the cost of renting a car.

Purchase

If you're spending several months in the USA and Canada, purchasing a car is worth considering; a car is more flexible than public transport and likely to be cheaper than a rental. But buying one can be very complicated and requires plenty of research.

It is possible to purchase a viable car in the USA for about $1500, but don't expect to get too far before you'll need some repair work that could cost several hundred dollars or more. It doesn't hurt to spend more to get a quality vehicle. It's also worth spending $50 or so to have a mechanic check the vehicle for defects (some AAA offices have diagnostic centers where they can do this on the spot for its members and those of foreign affiliates).

You can check out the official valuation of a used car by looking it up in the *Kelley Blue Book* (www.kbb.com), a listing of cars by make, model and year and the average resale price. Local public libraries have copies of the *Blue Book*, as well as back issues of *Consumer Reports*, a magazine that annually tallies the repair records of common makes of cars.

If you want to purchase a car, the first thing to do is contact AAA (☎ 800-222-4357) for some general information. Then contact the Department of Motor Vehicles (DMV) to find out about registration fees and insurance, which can be very confusing and expensive. As an example, say you are a 30-year-old non-US citizen and you want to buy a 1989 Honda. If this is the first time you have registered a car in the USA, you'll have to fork over about $300 first and then about $100 to $200 more for general registration.

Inspect the title carefully before purchasing the car; the owner's name on the title must match the identification of the person selling you the car. If you're a foreigner, you may find it very useful to obtain a notarized document authorizing your use of the car, since it may take the DMV in the state where you buy the car several weeks or more to process the change in title.

Insurance

While insurance is not obligatory in every state, all states have financial responsibility laws and insurance is highly desirable; otherwise, a serious accident could leave you a pauper. In order to get insurance some states request that you have a US driver's license and that you have been licensed in the US for at least 18 months. If you meet those qualifications, you may still have to pay anywhere from $300 to $1200 a year for insurance, depending where the car is registered. Rates are generally lower if you register it at an address in the suburbs or in a rural area, rather than in a central city. Collision coverage has become very expensive, with high deductibles, and is generally not worthwhile unless the car is somewhat valuable. Regulations vary from state to state but are generally becoming stringent throughout the USA.

Obtaining insurance, however, is not as simple as walking into an agency, filling out a form and paying for it. Many agencies refuse to insure drivers who have no car insurance – a classic Catch-22! Those agencies who will do so often charge much higher rates because they presume a higher risk. Male drivers under the age of 25 will pay astronomical rates. The minimum term for a policy is usually six months, but some insurance companies will refund the difference on a prorated basis if the car is sold and the policy voluntarily terminated. It is advisable to shop around.

BICYCLE

Cycling is an interesting, inexpensive and increasingly popular way to travel in the USA, especially in the Pacific Northwest. Roads are good, shoulders are usually wide and there are many decent routes for road bikes as well as mountain bikes. The changeable weather can be a drawback, especially at high altitudes where thunderstorms are frequent. In some areas the wind can slow your progress to a crawl (traveling west to east is generally easier than east to west), and water sources are far apart. Cyclists should carry at least two full bottles and refill them at every opportunity. Spare parts are widely available and repair shops are numerous, but it's still important to be able to do basic mechanical work, like fixing a flat, yourself.

Bicycles can be transported by air. You *can* disassemble them and put them in a bike bag or box, but it's much easier to simply wheel your bike to the check-in desk, where it should be treated as a piece of baggage, although airlines often charge an additional fee. You may have to remove the pedals and front tire so that it takes up less space in the aircraft's hold; check all this with the airline well in advance, preferably before you pay for your ticket. Be aware that some airlines welcome bicycles, while others treat them as an undesirable nuisance and do everything possible to discourage them.

Though motorists often drive too fast, they are generally courteous to cyclists. However, cyclists may encounter the occasional arrested-development imbecile or perpetual adolescent who harasses cyclists to show off. Some cities require helmets, others don't, but they should always be worn. Bicycle riders in BC are required to wear a helmet.

For more details on cycling in the Pacific Northwest, see Biking in the Outdoor Activities chapter.

HITCHHIKING

Hitchhiking is never entirely safe in any country in the world, and has a reputation for being much more dangerous in the USA than in Europe. We don't recommend it, and travelers who decide to hitch should understand that they are taking a small but serious risk. You may not be able to identify the local rapist/murderer, thief, or even a driver who's had too much to drink, before you get into the vehicle. People who do choose to hitch a ride will be safer if they travel in pairs and if they let someone know where they are planning to go.

Because public transport is so limited in parts of the Pacific Northwest, some visitors may be tempted to hitchhike to areas where access is difficult. Should you hitch, keep a close watch on your possessions; there have been recent instances of 'friendly' drivers absconding with an innocent hitchhiker's possessions while the latter visited the toilet during a gasoline stop.

WALKING

Because of the great distances only a handful of people care to use their feet as a primary means of transportation. However, it is possible to walk all the way from Canada to Mexico via the Pacific Crest Trail, and to cover other interesting areas on foot. For more information, see the Hiking & Backpacking section in the Outdoor Activities chapter.

FERRY

Washington and BC have two of the largest state-owned ferry systems in the world, and you cannot travel very extensively in the Pacific Northwest without hopping a ferry. Note that there are both passenger-only, and car and passenger ferries to popular destinations.

Washington State Ferries (☎ 206-464-6400, 800-843-3779 in WA) operates most of the ferries that run in the Puget Sound area. Popular routes include trips to Bremerton and to Bainbridge and Vashon Islands from Seattle. Washington State Ferries also operates the ferry system through the San Juan Islands, and to Sydney (on Vancouver Island) from Anacortes. In all, 14 different ferry lines link islands, peninsulas and the mainland via Washington State Ferries.

BC Ferries (☎ 604-277-0277) operates most of the ferries in that province. Primary links are between Tsawwassen and Swartz Bay on Vancouver Island, and to Nanaimo from Tsawwassen and Horseshoe Bay. The Gulf Islands are also linked to Tsawwassen and Swartz Bay by ferries.

Privately operated ferries are also important transportation links in this area. Black Ball's Coho Ferry (☎ 360-457-4491) links Victoria and Port Angeles year-round. Clipper Navigation (☎ 206-448-5000 in WA, 250-382-8100 in BC) operates the *Victoria Clipper*, a year-round passenger ferry, and a summer-only car ferry from Seattle to Victoria. In summer this company also offers passenger service from Seattle to Victoria with stops in the San Juan Islands.

TAXI

Taxis are expensive for long distances, but aren't so outrageous if shared among two or three people. Check with the service before setting out regarding fares per person, return-trip fees and taxes. Check the yellow pages under 'Taxi' for phone numbers and services. Drivers often expect a tip of about 10% of the fare.

ORGANIZED TOURS

A number of cruise lines offer trips up the Columbia River from Portland to Lewiston, ID. The weeklong trip passes through the spectacular Columbia Gorge and through the lock systems of eight major dams. Fares are seasonal and range from $925 to $1700. For information on trips, call Specialized Expeditions at ☎ 800-606-6363.

Maupintours (☎ 800-255-4266) offers full-service tours to the Pacific Northwest with a number of slightly varying itineraries that include many of the highlights, such as Seattle, the San Juans, Olympic Peninsula, Portland, the Oregon coast and Crater Lake. Their 11-day Pacific Wonder Tour, which includes all meals, lodging and fees, costs $2140 per person based on double occupancy.

Tauck Tours (☎ 800-468-2825), the nation's largest full-service tour operator, offers frequent tours of Oregon, Washington and Canada during the spring and summer. Travel is done mostly on buses, but may also include trips on company-owned trains, cruise ships and helicopters. All expenses are paid, including lodging in upscale hotels and resorts and fees for activities and attractions. Most, but not all, meals are paid for, giving travelers the opportunity to occasionally try a restaurant on their own. An eight-day tour of Oregon, which takes in the Oregon coast, Crater Lake, Mt Hood and the Columbia Gorge, and includes theater tickets to Ashland's Shakespeare Festival, costs $1830 for one

person. Their 15-day tour of the entire Pacific Northwest, from San Francisco to Calgary, costs around $3900 for one-person. Prices are approximately 75% less for couples sharing a hotel room. Tour bookings are made through local travel agents.

Local day tours are available from Seattle to Mt Rainier and the islands of the Puget Sound, and from Portland to the Columbia Gorge, Mt Hood, Oregon's wine country and the northern Oregon coast. Gray Line (☎ 800-426-7532), a national tour franchise, has operations in Portland, Seattle and Vancouver.

In Vancouver, numerous tour companies, including Gray Line (☎ 604-879-3363), make day runs to Victoria and Butchart Gardens (see the Organized Tours section in the Vancouver chapter for complete details).

The major long distance tour operator in western Canada is Brewster Tours (☎ 800-661-1152), which runs a great many trips from Vancouver, including circle tours of Vancouver Island and multi-day tours to the Canadian Rockies.

Oregon

DENNIS FRATES

Facts about Oregon

Few states can boast such a varied landscape as Oregon. Beginning with the distinctively rugged Pacific Coast, passing over rich valleys to glaciered volcanic peaks and on to rolling expanses of high-desert plains cut by deep river canyons and spiked with errant mountain ranges, the land is epic in its breadth and drama.

But what makes Oregon more than a scenic abstraction is the attitude of its citizens. Oregonians are fiercely proud of and involved with their state, its cities, culture and wild areas. Whether it's grand opera in Portland, rock climbing at Smith Rock, biking along the Oregon coast or shooting Widowmaker Rapids on the Owyhee River, you're expected to get out there and enjoy yourself.

Oregon's unique character as a state can be traced to its history. While the growth of West Coast neighbors Washington and California derived from the outbreaks of gold fever, Oregon was settled by the greatest human migration in US history. During the 1840s and 1950s, over the 2000-mile-long Oregon Trail came 53,000 young, sturdy and idealistic farmers,

traders and their families, looking not for gold but to create enduring settlements. This pioneer purposefulness is still felt in the attitudes that Oregonians bring to land-use legislation, cultural institutions, civic planning and environmental concerns.

And the movement to Oregon is scarcely over. The same vague agrarian ideals still lure people to this state, currently one of the fastest-growing in the country.

HISTORY

After the pivotal vote at Champoeg in 1843, where the citizens of Oregon – then an ad hoc collection of New England missionaries and French and British trappers – voted to organize a local government on the US model, the path to territorial status and statehood should have been assured. However, partisan rankling in Washington, DC, delayed the action until 1848, when Oregon officially became a US territory.

The years leading up to Oregon's statehood were also the years in which the issues of the Civil War began to play out across the USA. The admission of Oregon to the Union became a political football between advocates and opponents of slavery, with southern senators in the capitol blocking consideration of statehood unless Oregon was admitted as a slave state. However, in 1859 when Oregon became the 33rd state to enter the Union, it voted overwhelmingly to do so as a free state. Salem and Oregon City contended for the capital; Salem – with its ties to early Methodist missions – eventually prevailed.

The Oregon Trail, a six-month journey across the continent filled with hardship and danger, ultimately ended at Oregon City, in the Willamette Valley. Remarkably few travelers along the Oregon Trail chose to stay in the valleys of eastern Oregon. However, in the 1850s and 1860s, when the Willamette Valley was experiencing near population saturation, settlement began to spread.

OREGON
Statehood: February 14, 1859
Area: 98,386 sq miles,
    9th largest in the USA
Population: 3,243,000
Capital: Salem
Nickname: The Beaver State
Animal: beaver
Bird: Western meadowlark
Fish: Chinook salmon
Flower: Oregon grape
Nut: filbert
Stone: thunderegg
Tree: Douglas fir

In 1852, gold was discovered near Jacksonville in southern Oregon. After the gold ran out, settlers filled the steep valleys with orchards and logging camps. In 1861, gold was discovered in the Blue Mountains of eastern Oregon and the gold rush was on. However, gold wasn't discovered in a vacuum. The Native Americans and white settlers clashed when traditional homelands were invaded by new Oregonians. Rogue River Indians fought against white settlement in southern Oregon, Modocs waged a war against the US Army, the Nez Perce under Chief Joseph fled the army up into Canada, and the Bannock Indians led an uprising of several eastern Oregon tribes. The result was incarceration on reservations for most Native Americans, in some cases on reservations as far from their tribal lands as Oklahoma.

From the 1880s onward, the grasslands of eastern Oregon were open to settlement. Huge ranches held sway until homesteaders arrived – the early 1900s brought many thousands – breaking the land into 1-sq-mile lots. The high lava plains of central Oregon were tilled and blossomed with wheat.

End of the Frontier

By the end of the century, Portland was a boomtown, acting as the trade conduit for agricultural products of the fertile inland valleys. Portland was also the terminus of the Northern Pacific Railroad, which in 1883 linked the Pacific Northwest to the eastern USA. Three years later, Portland and San Francisco were linked by rail. Grain poured into Portland from the Columbia River basin and as far away as Montana. By 1890, Portland was one of the world's largest wheat-shipment points.

The world wars brought further economic expansion to Oregon, much of it related to resource exploitation. In the early years of the 20th century, logging of the great forests of the Pacific Northwest began in earnest; by WWII, Oregon had become the nation's largest lumber producer. (The nation's need for lumber products seems to increase exponentially; in the 1980s nearly all of the state's ancient forests were slated for logging. A series of court battles, mostly involving the bashful spotted owl, has turned the Pacific Northwest's forests into a war between traditional industry and environmentalism.)

During WWII, the shipyards and light manufacturing of Portland brought the state another flood of immigrants. A large part of this new migration was made up of African Americans, the first influx of nonwhite settlers in the state's history (it was only in 1926 that the state legislature repealed an 1844 law excluding blacks from the state).

From the 1960s onward, Portland – and western Oregon in general – has seen a new migration of settlers. Educated, idealistic and politically progressive, these newcomers from the eastern USA and California served to tilt the state's political balance toward a liberal and environmental stance during the 1970s and early 1980s. Oregon passed a number of conservation minded bills (a strict land-use planning law, a bottle-recycling bill) which gained it the reputation of a bellwether state.

However, the 1990s have seen Oregon retrenching in the face of economic and social change. A number of heated controversies – from logging to gay rights – between liberal and conservative factions have created a political rift in this close-knit state. Oregon faces the 21st century wearily divided.

GEOGRAPHY

Given Oregon's extremely diverse geology, it is surprising that most people, including Oregonians, accept the generalization that Oregon is best divided into two geographic regions: the western coast and valleys, and the eastern and central high deserts. In fact, the state, especially its eastern section, is much more subtle.

West of the Cascade Range, there are three major land types. Oregon coast is the most striking, with densely forested (though heavily *de*forested) mountains abutting the Pacific with rocky cliffs and sandy beaches. Inland, between the coast mountains and the Cascades, the Willamette

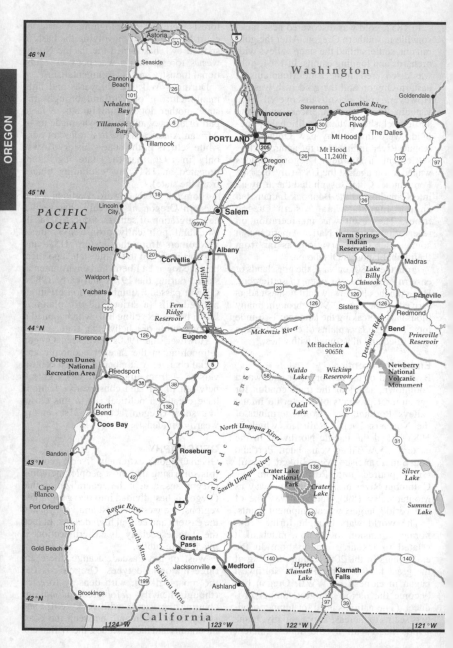

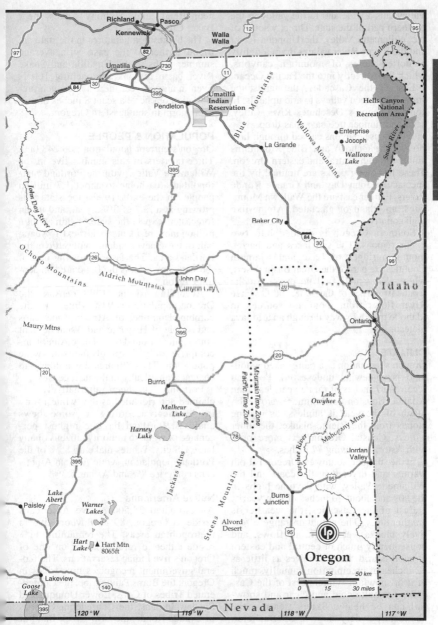

Valley cuts a wide and fertile valley in the northern part of the state. Directly south of the Willamette Valley, the Umpqua River and the Rogue River valleys drain a tightly contorted series of mountain canyons, which flow directly into the Pacific Ocean.

East of the Cascades, the landscape shifts from green valleys to arid uplands. In central Oregon's Deschutes River valley, sage and juniper-tree savannas drop away into immense canyons carved through lava flows. The Ochoco and Blue Mountains amble through central and eastern Oregon. These low-slung peaks are drained by the spectacular John Day and Grande Ronde Rivers. Farther east are the Wallowa Mountains, an island of glaciated, Alpine-like high country.

Southern Oregon is divided into two major regions. The salt lakes and barren mountain ridges of Lake and Klamath Counties are part of the Great Basin desert, whose watersheds find no outlet. In the southeast corner of the state, the Owyhee River flows from mountain sources in Idaho to trench its way through an arid lava plateau.

CLIMATE

Oregon's reputation as a rain-soaked woodland is somewhat undeserved. Portland receives 37 inches of rain a year, less than Atlanta, Houston or Baltimore. However, much of the year is sunless, as marine clouds from the Pacific blanket the inner valleys. Coastal Oregon gets more rain, with Astoria receiving 77 inches.

In the summer, southwest Oregon is both warmer and drier than the coast and the Willamette Valley, with daytime highs in the 90s and about 20 inches of rain yearly.

East of the Cascades, the weather is another story. The mountain range effectively blocks wet Pacific air flows, and consequently much of central and eastern Oregon is arid. Bend receives as little as 12 inches of precipitation annually, much of it in snowfall. Winters east of the Cascades are quite cold and clear and snowfall can be heavy. Skiers treasure the abundant powdery snow of Mt Bachelor,

near Bend, and Anthony Lakes, near Baker City.

The highest temperatures in the state are found farther to the east, with average summer highs in the Umatilla and Snake River basin regions approaching 100°F. Even in a good year there's not much precipitation out here: a scant 8 inches of rain is the norm in southeastern Oregon.

POPULATION & PEOPLE

Oregon's current population is 3,243,000. Three-quarters of this number live in the Willamette Valley, with the Portland metropolitan area home to about 1.7 million people. In the early 1990s, the state was growing at a rate of 3% a year, and urban forecasters expect the state to gain about a million more residents in the next 15 years; half of these new residents will settle in the Portland area. The fastest-growing part of the state, however, is the Bend area, in central Oregon.

According to the 1990 census, the Oregon population is 93% white, with the combined number of African Americans and people of Hispanic and Asian descent coming in at around 6%. Native Americans comprise only 1.4% of the state-wide population. These figures are unlikely to change dramatically in the next census.

Portland has been alternatively acclaimed and ridiculed as the 'whitest' city in America: according to some news analyses, Portland has the highest percentage of white to minority citizens of any large US city. Whites make up 85% of the Portland population, while African Americans comprise 8% and Asians 5.3%.

Native Americans

An estimated 38,500 Native Americans reside in Oregon, 89% of whom live in metropolitan areas. The remaining 11% reside either in rural areas or on one of Oregon's five Indian reservations. The federal government recognizes nine tribes in Oregon: the Burns Paiute tribe, the Confederated Tribes of Coos, Lower Umpqua and Siuslaw Indians, the Confederated Tribes of Grande Ronde, the Cow Creek Band of the Umpqua Indians, the Confederated Tribes of Siletz, the Confederated Tribes of Warm Springs, the Klamath tribe, the Confederated Tribes of Umatilla Indian Reservation and the Coquille tribe. Many other Indian tribes reside in Oregon without federally recognized status or a land base. Federally recognized status is very much a political tool, which tends to give the mes-sage to unrecognized tribes that they simply don't exist.

ARTS
In keeping with a seeming Oregon paradigm, even the arts scene in the state is informal and participatory. Summer brings a bounty of music festivals, outdoor theater productions and art shows. Even normally

OREGON

Is Oregon Conservative or Liberal?
Most people would characterize Oregon's culture in terms of its politics: words like politically progressive, liberal, environmentally aware and ex-hippie capture the image that many hold of the state. However, anyone who has followed the politics in recent years knows that there's another side to Oregon that is very socially conservative, reactionary and hostile to environmentalism. Both of these archetypes are true of the state's culture at the same time. What makes Oregon such a unique state is that the same idealism informs both liberal and conservative elements in the Oregon cultural mix. In some senses, this contradiction is at the heart of what it is to be an Oregonian.

Elements that give the state its progressive reputation are in evidence everywhere. Land-use laws strictly limit urban growth; all Oregon beaches are public property; and bike paths, parks and public art are scattered across the state. A live-and-let-live attitude toward minorities and alternative lifestyles typifies the larger cities, and out-of-the-way towns have thriving artistic and countercultural communities.

However, the same urban centers that are models of tolerance also harbor some of the fastest-growing cells of neo-Nazi youth in the USA. Communities vote to limit the civil rights of their citizens, and conservative tax revolts have resulted in the evisceration of public institutions and educational facilities. A narrow hatred of spotted owls and environmentalists is a pervasive passion for many individuals in rural communities, and the Oregon Citizens Alliance's campaign against gays and lesbians has succeeded in dividing families and communities on highly emotional social issues.

Which of these is the real Oregon? The truth is that both urges – to change Oregon in order to save it, and to save Oregon by halting change – derive from the same impulse. Most Oregonians believe in the intrinsic worth and value of the state, its institutions and its land. Both sides are ready and willing to fight in the public forum to preserve the state that they see threatened. The desire to save Oregon from itself is the one value that unites both sides in this ideological battle. ■

The Hanis Coos Indians

The bay of the Coos River was the traditional home of the Hanis Coos, one of the tribes moved to the Alsea Reservation in the late 1850s. However, when that reservation was dissolved, the remaining Hanis Coos drifted back to the Coos Bay area without any land holdings. Attempts to receive compensation for the taking of their reservation lands, or to gain acknowledgment as a tribe from the US government, have met with failure. The Hanis Coos, Siuslaw and the Lower Umpqua tribes are currently confederated and number about 500 members. ■

solitary literary pursuits become group events, as Portland bookstores and coffeehouses vie with each other for the number and prestige of author readings.

If you're wondering about the plethora of outdoor sculpture in Portland, it's due to the city's '1% for art' program, established in 1980, which allocates 1.33% of funding for public buildings to the purchase and siting of public art.

Music

The Oregon Symphony and the Portland Opera are both popular Portland institutions. One of few African American conductors of a major US orchestra, James dePriest, conductor of the Oregon Symphony, has led the 100-year-old institution into the 20th century by introducing more contemporary, avant-garde music into the repertoire.

Summertime brings a number of noted classical-music festivals to the state. Chamber Music Northwest, a series of concerts by a superior ensemble of young musicians, plays a large and varied program of chamber music in Portland during July and August. The Britt Festival in Jacksonville provides a series of informal concerts from June through Labor Day; these outdoor, evening concerts blend music and picnics. Eugene's Oregon Bach Festival is another noted concert series, held during the last week in June and the first week in July.

Portland has the state's most vital music club scene. Jazz, Celtic, punk, blues and country music can be found throughout the city in clubs that range from upscale to real dives.

The popular music scene really opens up during the summer. Throughout the state, weekend festivals bring all types of music to the concert stage. Sometimes it seems as if Portland's Waterfront Park is nothing more than a summertime concert stage with the Cinco de Mayo celebration, June's Rose Festival, July's Blues Festival, and the Brewer's Festival and The Bite in August. The Mt Hood Jazz Festival is one of the state's largest concert series, held in August in Gresham, a suburb of Portland.

The Siuslaw Indians

The estuary along the Siuslaw River was home to the Siuslaw, a small tribe related to the Umpqua and Coos Indians farther south. The Siuslaw lived in underground shelters roofed with wooden frames and accessed by ladders. For their diet, they fished in the river and hunted the dense forests for game. Because the Siuslaw were not a very large tribe, they were frequently the target of forays by more hostile tribes to the north, who raided Siuslaw villages for slaves and wives.

Generally peaceable, the Siuslaw were removed from their homelands in 1859 and marched northward to the Alsea Reservation near Yachats. When that reservation closed in 1875, most of the Siuslaw were bereft of land and drifted back to the Florence area. The Siuslaw were among the coastal tribes that unsuccessfully sued the federal government in 1917 for remuneration for the loss of their reservation lands. ■

Literature

Quite a number of noted contemporary writers live in Oregon. Ken Kesey, whose *One Flew Over the Cuckoo's Nest* became a textbook of 1960s nonconformity, is a native Oregonian. His earlier novel, *Sometimes a Great Notion* captures the brio of rural life in a small logging community. Craig Lesley's *Winterkill* is the story of an eastern Oregon Native American rodeo rider down on his luck and looking to get out. David Duncan *(The River Why* and *The Brothers K)*, Katherine Dunn *(Geek Love)* and Tom Spanbauer *(The Man Who Fell in Love With the Moon)* are highly acclaimed contemporary novelists.

Oregon seems to attract novelists whose bent is toward science fiction and fantasy. Ursula K Le Guin *(The Left Hand of Darkness)*, Jean Auel *(Clan of the Cave Bear)* and Anne McCaffrey *(Dragonquest)* all live in the state.

Theater & Film

Ashland's Oregon Shakespeare Festival is one of the state's crown jewels. During high season, performances are held on one outdoor and two indoor stages. While Shakespeare is the principal draw, contemporary drama and comedies are also produced. About 350,000 people a year attend performances in Ashland.

Portland Center Stage, formerly an affiliate of the Oregon Shakespeare Festival, also mounts productions at the Portland Center for the Performing Arts. This beautiful facility is also home to other dramatic companies, whose specialties range from musical comedy to Greek tragedy. Not all theater in Portland is so grand; a number of small troupes provide productions in more intimate settings.

In recent years, Oregon has become increasingly popular as a locale for films, due to its handsome landscapes and cheap labor. Portland's Old Town is especially popular for directors seeking late-19th-century authenticity. Films shot in Oregon include *Animal House*, *One Flew Over the Cuckoo's Nest*, *The Shining* and *Body of Evidence*.

Acclaimed director Gus Van Sant, whose films include *Drugstore Cowboy*, *My Own Private Idaho*, *Mala Noche*, *Even Cowgirls Get the Blues* and *Good Will Hunting* lives in Portland. His films are shot largely in-state.

Visual Arts

Portland – Oregon's center for painting and sculpture – has a large number of galleries. The Portland Art Museum's collection includes Asian porcelains and a representative overview of European Art; regional art shows are also held.

The visual art scene in Portland is quite dynamic and sophisticated, considering the size of the city. A number of factors account for this, including the existence of the museum art school (the Pacific Northwest College of Art) and cheaper rents than most urban centers on the West Coast.

INFORMATION

Area Codes

Oregon has just two area codes. Portland, Salem, the northern Willamette Valley and the northern coast are served by 503. The rest of the state is served by 541.

Taxes

Oregon has no sales tax or value added tax (VAT), one of only three states in the USA that can claim that distinction. However, accommodations in hotels, motels, lodges and B&Bs are subject to local bed taxes that can range from 4% to 9%; the price quoted or advertised by hoteliers for rooms may or may not include the tax. Ask to be certain.

Gasoline

If you're driving, keep in mind that Oregon law prohibits you from pumping your own gasoline – all gas stations are full service, so just sit back and enjoy it.

OREGON

Portland

Oregon's largest city, Portland is at the junction of two great rivers; it is ringed by vast forests and dominated by ancient volcanoes. This vernal setting belies a cosmopolitan city with an easygoing, can-do spirit. Although nearly 1.7 million people live in the Portland metropolitan area, the city has the feeling of a friendly, smaller town.

One hundred miles from the Pacific Ocean, Portland is one of the West Coast's busiest ports. But nowadays, Portland is known less for its role on the front line of international trade than for its 'lifestyle.' Perennially near the top of the list of the USA's 'most livable cities,' Portland is known nationally for its progressive politics, its relaxed pace of life and its love of the outdoors and the environment. An hour's drive from the city center finds year-round skiing on a volcanic peak, rolling hills covered with vineyards and the rugged Pacific Coast. But Portlanders don't live in their city just because of access to the countryside. Citizens are proud of their vibrant downtown, its beautiful parks and architecture and its worldly but unfussy comforts.

Settled initially by New England traders and Midwest farmers, Portland has always been practical, purposeful, and foresighted. It lacks the brash energy of Seattle or San Francisco and their high prices. Its beautiful setting and friendly sophistication make Portland a great city to explore.

HISTORY

Portland sits near the confluence of two of the West's mightiest rivers, the Columbia and the Willamette. Unsurprisingly, Portland's early growth was fueled by shipping and trade. The terminus of continental railroads and port city to the Pacific Rim, Portland was ideally situated to export the agricultural riches of the western USA.

The settlement of Portland is inextricably linked to nearby Fort Vancouver, the Hudson's Bay Company fur-trading post established in 1825 on the northern bank of the Columbia River. Retiring trappers moved south, up the Willamette River, to establish settlements. The first building in what would become Portland was erected in 1829 by Étienne Lucier, a former trapper who was looking to establish a farm along the Willamette River. Although Lucier abandoned his homestead a year later and moved farther up the river to Champoeg, activity continued at the site of future Portland.

In 1844 two New Englanders filed a claim for 640 acres of land on the west bank of the Willamette River. They built a store, platted streets, and decided to name the new settlement after one of their hometowns. A coin-toss resulted in Portland winning over Boston and the new town was up and running.

Trade, not industry or natural-resource exploitation, was the engine that drove the growth of the city. The California gold rush of 1849 and the building of San Francisco demanded lumber, which was routed through the fledgling port city on the Willamette. At the same time, Oregon Trail settlers brought agriculture to the Willamette Valley and mining and ranching developed throughout the inland West. Each demanded a coastal city of trade, and Portland became that mercantile and shipping center for much of the Northwest.

Portland's primacy in the Northwest was solidified when the Northern Pacific Railroad arrived in 1883, linking Portland and the Pacific Northwest to the rest of the country. The first bridges were built across the Willamette in the late 1880s and the city spread eastward. Portland's population increased five-fold between 1880 and 1900.

During the 20th century Portland has enjoyed steady growth. The influx of

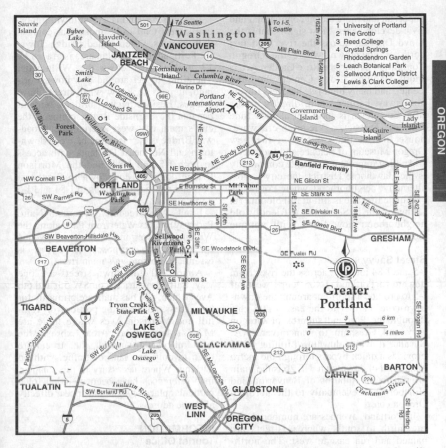

1 University of Portland
2 The Grotto
3 Reed College
4 Crystal Springs
   Rhododendron Garden
5 Leach Botanical Park
6 Sellwood Antique District
7 Lewis & Clark College

OREGON

Greater
Portland

workers to the ship-building factories during WWII was so great that an entire new city, called Vanport, was created in 1944 to house them. Unwisely built on a Columbia River flood plain, Vanport was destroyed by a wall of water that burst through a dike in 1948, killing 18 people and leaving almost 20,000 homeless.

ORIENTATION
Neighborhoods
Portland straddles the Willamette River just below its confluence with the Columbia River. Although downtown is built on a narrow flood plain, much of the rest of the

city sits high above the river on heavily forested volcanic ridges and bluffs.

The Willamette River also divides the city into its two major districts, logically and informally known as the East Side and West Side. The West Side contains the main city center area, Portland's frontier-era Old Town, rapidly gentrifying warehouse districts, and many exclusive residential areas, particularly those in the West Hills. Also in the West Hills are some of Portland's most magnificent parks and the 7-sq-mile wilderness area, Forest Park.

The East Side is a mix of late-19th-century residential neighborhoods and important and more recent commercial and civic developments. Most significant is the Lloyd District, across the river and just north of downtown, where the Oregon Convention Center, the Rose Garden Arena sports stadium, Lloyd Center Shopping Center, and many high-rise business towers hold sway. Farther south, directly across from downtown is the Central East Side Business District, a Victorian-era warehouse district that's home to the new Oregon Museum of Science and Industry.

Another important East Side community is the Hawthorne District, the city's most alternative neighborhood, where Portland's ex-hippie lifestyle is still in full bloom. Yet farther south is Sellwood, a friendly old neighborhood now filled with antique stores.

Street Savvy

I-5 and I-84 intersect across the river from downtown Portland. I-405 loops west off I-5 to provide a short-cut around the downtown core. Farther to the east, I-205 cuts through the Portland suburbs of Oregon City and Gresham to Vancouver, WA. Because it avoids downtown traffic, I-205 provides a quick bypass through the metro area. West of downtown, US 26 is the main arterial to the suburbs of Beaverton and Hillsboro and eventually to the northern Oregon coast.

In Portland, avenues are numbered and run north to south, whereas streets are named and run east to west. The north-flowing Willamette River and the east-west trending Burnside St quarter the city into Northwest, Southwest, Northeast and Southeast quadrants. Be attentive of address prefixes: for instance, NE Davis St and NW Davis St are on opposite sides of the Willamette River; NW 6th Ave and SW 6th Ave are on opposite sides of Burnside.

If you're trying to find your way around Northwest Portland, there's an easy way to keep the streets straight. Named for early settlers, the streets proceed northward in alphabetical order. Thus, one block north of Burnside is Couch, followed by Davis, Everett, and so on.

Because Portland is a river town, important streets tend to be those that connect with bridges. Often called Bridge Town, the Portland metropolitan area is graced by 12 bridges that cross the Willamette. Therefore, to get around downtown Portland, it pays to know what streets have bridges. Besides freeway bridges, remember that the Burnside Bridge connects the city's main east-west arterial; the Broadway Bridge is the main link between downtown and Northeast Portland, with access to both I-5 and I-84; and the Morrison Bridge connects downtown to Southeast Portland and has on-ramps to I-84 and I-5 north.

Front Ave (recently renamed Naito Parkway) flanks Waterfront Park along the Willamette River and is the 'zero' avenue for numbering purposes. Broadway is essentially downtown's main street.

Almost all downtown streets are one way; traffic is restricted on SW 5th and 6th Aves which, as a bus mall, are primarily for bus access. Also, on the portions of Yamhill and Morrison Aves where there are MAX (Metropolitan Area Express, the light rail system) tracks, the streets are open to only one lane of traffic, with no parking. Where necessary in this chapter, map references have been included for a particular place or sight and appear directly after the address.

INFORMATION
Tourist Office

The main office of the Portland/Oregon Visitors Association (☎ 503-222-2223, 800-345-3214), is at 26 SW Salmon St, though the actual visitors' center is across the street at 25 SW Salmon St. In addition to information on Portland and all of Oregon, there's a ticketing kiosk for local entertainment and events.

Money

Opportunities to exchange foreign currency in Oregon are, for the most part, limited to Portland. If you think you are going to need to change money and the next major US city on your itinerary is a few

OREGON

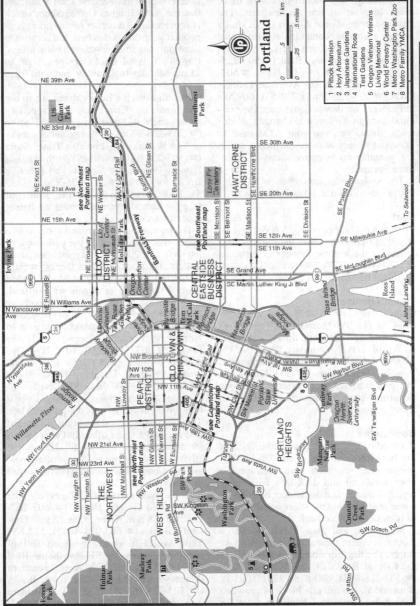

Portland

0   .5   1 km
0   .25   .5 miles

1 Pittock Mansion
2 Hoyt Arboretum
3 Japanese Gardens
4 International Rose
  Test Gardens
5 Oregon Vietnam Veterans
  Living Memorial
6 World Forestry Center
7 Metro Washington Park Zoo
8 Metro Family YMCA

weeks away, you should probably make plans to wait in line somewhere. The Portland International Airport (PDX) has a foreign-exchange counter in the main lobby, open 5:30 am to 5 pm daily. The main branches of Wells Fargo Bank (☎ 503-225-2022), 1300 SW 5th Ave, US Bank (☎ 503-275-7344), 321 SW 6th Ave, and Thomas Cook (☎ 503-222-2665), 701 SW 6th Ave in Pioneer Courthouse Square, are the principal foreign-currency exchanges downtown. Better yet, use your ATM card to draw out money at cash machines, which are as numerous as coffee shops in downtown Portland.

The American Express office (☎ 503-226-2961) is downtown at 1100 SW 6th Ave.

Post
The main post office is at 715 NW Hoyt St. If you're right downtown, the Pioneer Post Office, in the historic Pioneer Courthouse at the corner of SW 6th Ave and Yamhill St, might be handier.

Travel Agencies
Council Travel (☎ 503-228-1900, 800-228-2854) at 715 SW Morrison St, specializes in student and discount travel. Journeys: A World Travel Company (☎ 503-226-7200), 1536 NW 23rd Ave, and Journeys at Powell's Travel Store (☎ 503-226-4849), 701 SW 6th Ave, both offer full-service ticketing, plus adventure and discount travel options.

Bookstores
Portland is, by anyone's evaluation, one of the bookstore capitals of the USA. That people read so much here because it's always raining and dark is a frequently repeated canard. But no amount of flooding could really explain the success and quality of bookstores in Portland.

Megalithic and many-faced, Powell's Books is one of the nation's largest bookstores. The flagship store, known simply as the City of Books or the Burnside Store (☎ 503-228-4651, 800-878-7323), 1005 W Burnside St, is a full city block of crowded bookshelves with over 1 million titles for

sale. Powell's has become such a hangout that the Anne Hughes Coffee Shop, which is squeezed into a corner of the store, is as popular as most singles bars and serves the same purpose for love-starved book lovers. Powell's City of Books is open 9 am to 11 pm Monday to Saturday, and until 9 pm on Sunday.

Not all Powell's Books stores are so big and imposing. Check out their specialty stores such as Powell's Technical Store (☎ 503-228-3906), only two blocks away at 33 NW Park Ave, Powell's Travel Store (☎ 503-228-1108), 701 SW 6th Ave, in Pioneer Courthouse Square, and Powell's Books for Cooks (☎ 503-235-3802), 3739 SE Hawthorne Blvd (see the Southeast map), which shares space with an Italian specialty food shop.

By no means do Portland's bookstore riches end with Powell's; the yellow pages list well over 200 new and used bookstores in Portland. Looking Glass Books (☎ 503-227-4760), 318 SW Taylor St, is a good general bookstore in downtown Portland. In Northeast Portland, go to Broadway Books (☎ 503-284-1726), 1714 NE Broadway, for a good independent bookstore. In Northwest Portland, Twenty-third Ave Books (☎ 503-224-5097), 1015 NW 23rd Ave, is another good source for general reading material. Laughing Horse Books (☎ 503-236-2893), 3652 SE Division St (see the Southeast map), is Portland's best bookstore for readers on the political left. They also have a good selection of feminist and gay and lesbian titles. In Other Words (☎ 503-232-6003), 3734 SE Hawthorne Blvd (see the Southeast map), offers new and used books by women writers, as well as video rentals.

Downtown used-book stores of note include Old Oregon Books (☎ 503-227-2742), 1128 SW Alder St, and Steve Holland's Books (☎ 503-224-4242), 527 SW 12th Ave. For a neighborhood full of used-book stores, try SE Hawthorne Blvd between 33rd and 38th Aves. South of downtown you'll find Water Tower Books (☎ 503-228-0290), 5331 SW Macadam Ave, and Compass Books (☎ 503-292-

5065), 4907 SW 76th St, the latter of which focuses on travel. To the east is Tower Books (☎ 503-253-3116), 1307 NE 102nd St, where the I-205 crosses I-84. Ask at any of these bookstores for a map of the neighborhood and its bookstores.

Media
Portland's only daily newspaper is the *Oregonian*; there's both a morning and evening edition. The Friday *Oregonian* contains a weekly arts and entertainment section, called the *A&E*. *Willamette Week*, an alternative newsweekly, also contains full entertainment coverage; it's free and appears on Wednesdays. The principal gay and lesbian newspaper is a biweekly called *Just Out*.

Oregon Public Radio can be heard on 91.5 FM.

Photography
Downtown's most comprehensive camera and film supply store is Camera World (☎ 503-299-4010), 500 SW 5th Ave. For one-hour print development, check for the closest Flashback or Sandy's Camera Shops. Both have several locations in central Portland.

Childcare
If you need a baby sitter while visiting Portland, call Child Care To Go (☎ 503-256-1985). They can provide child-care professionals to watch your child at your hotel. There are drop-in day-care facilities at the Metro Family YMCA (☎ 503-294-3366), 2831 SW Barbur Blvd (see the Portland map).

Laundry
In Southeast Portland, go to the Washboard (☎ 503-236-4947), 2525 SE 20th Ave, where there are not only washers and dryers, but also an espresso bar and tanning salon. In Northeast Portland, go to The Cleanery (☎ 503-282-4505), 1925-A NE 42nd Ave, in the Hollywood District.

The only laundry convenient to downtown and Northwest Portland is City Laundry (☎ 503-224-4204), 1414 NW Glisan St (see the Northwest map).

Medical Services
On the East Side, go to Providence Medical Center (☎ 503-215-1111), 4805 NE Glisan St. On the West Side, Good Samaritan Hospital and Health Center (☎ 503-229-7711), 1015 NW 22nd Ave, is the medical facility most convenient to downtown. Go to Good Samaritan Convenience Care Center (☎ 503-229-8090), at the same location, for minor illness and injuries. It's a lot cheaper and quicker than the emergency room and is open 9 am to 9 pm on weekdays, 10 am to 9 pm on weekends.

Emergency
The Portland Police Station is at 1111 SW 2nd Ave. Call ☎ 911 for medical, fire or crime emergencies.

DOWNTOWN
City Center
Downtown Portland – filled with notable architecture, tree- and cafe-lined streets, and bustling crowds – is an urban success story. An activist city government began work in the 1970s to insure that Portland's business and nightlife did not flee the city center. The effort was largely successful and downtown Portland is still vital and bustling. A cap on building height and a 1%-for-art program keep even the most modern areas human-sized and comfortable.

Any visitor to downtown should be armed with Powell's *Walking Map of Downtown Portland*. Free from any Powell's Books stores and available from most hotels and information bureaus, the map charts a historical and architectural route through the city's center, and provides hints for shoppers and travelers. Also available from information desks are more specialized map guides of local art galleries, public art and brewpubs.

If you don't have the walking tour map, the following sights are listed in an order that takes the visitor from the center of the city, at Pioneer Courthouse Square, through a beautiful park flanked by historic civic buildings, down through the new commercial center and to the Willamette's waterfront park and marina. If you have

OREGON

PLACES TO STAY
22 Mark Spencer Hotel
23 Ben Stark
   International Hostel
25 The Benson Hotel
28 Embassy Suites
36 Mallory Hotel
38 Governor Hotel
44 Hotel Vintage Plaza
45 Imperial Hotel
46 Fifth Avenue Suites Hotel
58 Riverside Inn
67 Heathman Hotel
69 Portland Hilton
81 Days Inn City Center
85 Portland Marriott
86 RiverPlace Hotel
89 Saharan Motel
91 Caravan Motor Hotel

PLACES TO EAT
3 Fong Chong
10 Phu Ho
11 Hung Far Low
13 Alexis
14 Opus Too, Jazz de Opus
15 Uogashi
21 Jake's Famous Crawfish
26 Saucebox
27 Atwater's
29 Bijou Café
31 Toulouse
42 Good Dog/Bad Dog
44 Pazzo
50 Al-Amir
51 McCormick & Schmick's
54 Bush Garden
59 Chef's Corner
63 Higgins
67 Heathman Restaurant
68 Macheezmo Mouse
72 Cascades
78 Fernando's Hideaway

OTHER
1 Main Post Office
2 Greyhound Bus Depot
4 Powell's City of Books
5 Powell's Technical Store
6 Dollar Rent-A-Car
7 Embers
8 Satyricon
9 Chinatown Gates
12 Hobo's
16 Oregon Mountain Community
17 Saturday Market
18 Japanese-American
   Historical Plaza
19 Cassidy's
20 Crystal Ballroom
24 Panorama
30 Berbati's Pan
32 Elizabeth Leach Gallery
33 Kell's
34 Skidmore Fountain
35 Oregon Maritime Center
   & Museum
37 Old Oregon Books
39 Galleria Shopping Center
40 Brasserie Montmartre
41 Council Travel
43 Quintana Native American Art
47 Camera World
48 Avis
49 Huber's
52 Cascade Sternwheelers
53 Bike Gallery
55 Real Mother Goose
56 Powell's Travel Store
57 Pioneer Place
60 Heathman Brewpub
61 Northwest Film Center
62 Portland Art Museum
64 Oregon History Center
65 Portland Center
   for the Performing Arts
66 Arlene Schnitzer Concert Hall
70 Broadway Cinema
71 Hertz
73 American Express
74 Portland Building, *Portlandia*
75 Looking Glass Books
76 Lotus Card Room
77 Police Station
79 Portland/Oregon
   Visitors Association
80 Salmon Springs Fountain
82 Ira Keller Memorial Fountain
83 KOIN Center Cinema
84 Civic Auditorium
87 Green Tortoise Pick-Up
88 Budget Rent A Car
90 Pilsner Room

Downtown Portland

0   150   300 m
0   150   300 yards

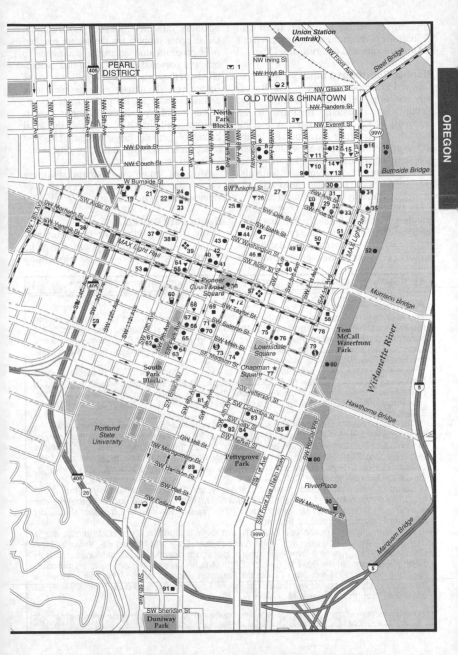

OREGON

time, an excursion into Old Town and Chinatown is recommended for mavens of old architecture and colorful street life.

Pioneer Courthouse Square
This red-brick plaza between SW Broadway and 6th Ave, and SW Morrison and Yamhill Sts, is usually regarded as the center of downtown Portland. A roaring fountain, a 'weather machine' sculpture and many levels of open-air seating bring people to the square to lounge, play music, eat lunch and gawk. Concerts, festivals, exhibits and rallies occur almost daily in summer, especially over the lunch hour.

On this block stood one of Portland's grandest Victorian hotels; it fell into disrepair and was torn down and replaced by a parking structure. When the city decided to build Pioneer Courthouse Square, downtown business interests blocked park funding. Grass-roots support for the square resulted in a program that encouraged citizens to buy and personalize the bricks that eventually built the square. As you walk across the square, read the names of the people whose contributions made the park possible.

Across 6th Ave is the **Pioneer Courthouse**. Built in 1875, this was the legal center of 19th-century Portland. The post office in its lobby is handy for city center visitors.

Most of downtown's main shopping venues are within a two-block radius of Pioneer Courthouse Square.

South Park Blocks
Many of Portland's most important museums and civic buildings are along the South Park Blocks, the 12-block-long

Portland's Public Art
The abundance of public art in Portland derives from city, county and state programs that require a certain percentage (usually 1%) of any major construction be set aside for public art. Pick up the brochure *Public Art Walking Tour*; it costs $1 at area bookstores and information centers. Most public art is found along the 5th and 6th Ave Transit Mall, the South Park Blocks and near the Convention Center.

Many traditional commemorative statues are found in the South Park Blocks, though a number of more conceptual projects have slipped in since the park was refurbished in the 1980s. The South Park Blocks also flank the Portland Art Museum complex. Note the amazing trompe l'oeil mural on the back of the Oregon History Center at Park Ave and Jefferson St.

The transit mall is lined with statues and fountains. Not to be missed is *Portlandia*, the enormous statue of the city's supposed protectress, which crouches above the entry of the Portland Building, at SE 5th Ave and Main St. On the building's 2nd floor atrium is a display about Portland's public art and an information center. The mounted boulders, called *Soaring Stones*, outside Pioneer Place at Taylor St and 5th Ave, are known to locals as Stonehenge on a Stick.

Some of the most popular statues in the city are the bronze animals playing in the fountains surrounding the Pioneer Courthouse. The bronze female nude on 5th Ave near Washington St was made famous in the 1980s *Expose Yourself to Art* poster (featuring a former Portland mayor as a flasher).

As a river city, it's appropriate that Portland loves a fountain. The most notable is the Ira Keller Memorial Fountain at SW 4th Ave between Clay and Market Sts, in front of the Civic Auditorium, where a river's worth of water roars down a series of ledges. Salmon Springs Fountain, at the base of Salmon St, pulses and sprays according to an intricate, day-long schedule. Handsome Skidmore Fountain, located on SW 1st Ave under the Burnside Bridge, is one of Portland's oldest public art works, and was originally built as a watering trough for horses. ∎

greenway between SW Park and 9th Aves that runs through much of the downtown. Just as tempting to a traveler are the enormous old elms, beseeching flocks of pigeons and old, slumbering statues. This is a beautiful and leafy refuge from the bustle of downtown.

Facing Broadway, but backed up to the vernal South Park Blocks, are the **Arlene Schnitzer Concert Hall** (☎ 503-228-1353, 800-228-7343), home of the Oregon Symphony and the **Portland Center for the Performing Arts**. The 'Schnitz,' as the symphony hall is known, is open only for performances, but the Center for Performing Arts is open during regular business hours. Stop by to check on performance schedules and to admire the beautiful cherry-wood lobby. Both facilities face onto SW Main St at Broadway; call ☎ 503-796-9293 for theater information.

The **Oregon History Center** (☎ 503-222-1741) at 1200 SW Park Ave, maintains the state's primary history museum, research library, press and bookstore in its complex along the South Park Blocks. The bookstore has a good collection of history books and regional travel guides. The complex is open 10 am to 5 pm Tuesday to Saturday, and noon to 5 pm on Sunday. Admission is $6/3/1.50 adults/students/children (six to 12). Seniors enter free on Thursdays.

Across the park is the **Portland Art Museum** (☎ 503 226 2811), 1219 SW Park Ave. Its permanent exhibit of Northwest Native American carvings is especially good. The upper galleries contain a small but representative international collection. Changing exhibits usually feature regional artists. The museum is open 10 am to 5 pm Tuesday to Sunday. Admission is $6/4.50/2.50 adults/seniors/children (five to 16). Pick up a schedule for the **Northwest Film Center**, which shows foreign and art films in a museum annex.

At the southern end of the Park Blocks is **Portland State University**. The park bustles with students between classes and at lunch hour, when there's cheap and satisfying ethnic food sold from carts.

Portland Building & Portlandia

Downtown Portland went through a building spurt during the 1980s that left the city with a vastly changed skyline and an international reputation for architectural innovation. No building has drawn more notoriety than the Portland Building at SW 5th Ave and Main St, designed by postmodern architect Michael Graves to house city government bureaus. No one seems indifferent about this blocky, pastel-colored edifice decorated like a wedding cake. The Portland Building is considered the world's first major structure in the postmodern style.

Towering above the main doors of the Portland Building is *Portlandia*, an immense statue meant to represent the Goddess of Commerce (Portland's supposed

Portlandia, patroness of Portland

patroness). This crouching female figure with one hand extended and the other grasping a trident is, at 36 feet, the second-largest hammered copper statue in the world (the largest is the Statue of Liberty).

Tom McCall Waterfront Park & RiverPlace

Two-mile-long Waterfront Park, which flanks the west bank of the Willamette River, was once a freeway. It was torn up and replaced with a grassy park, complete with fountains and an esplanade. Popular with joggers, in-line skaters, strollers, sun-bathers and anglers, the park also hosts a number of summer festivals and concerts. RiverPlace, at the southern end of Water-front Park, is a hotel, restaurant, condo-minium, and boutique development offering drinks and dining overlooking a marina. Salmon Springs Fountain, at the base of Salmon St, is programmed to change its play of water with the pace of the city; wild displays at rush hour are meant to calm the jangled commuter. Toward the north end of the park is the Japanese-American Historical Plaza, a memorial to Japanese Americans who were interned by the US government during WWII.

Old Town & Chinatown

The core of 1890s Portland, the tattered-on-the-edges Old Town has become popular in recent years as a set for period movies. Despite the best plans of the city elders and the district's architectural gems, Old Town resists gentrification. Missions for the homeless coexist with galleries, fine restaurants and specialty shops. The boundaries of Old Town vary depending upon whom you ask, but the essence of old Portland is captured between SW Pine St and NW Glisan St, east of NW Broadway to the Willamette River.

Contiguous with Old Town is Portland's Chinatown. The **Chinatown Gates**, at the corner of NW 4th Ave and Burnside St, announce the old Asian businesses that have thrived in this neighborhood since the 1880s. Everyone in Portland has a favorite

Chinatown restaurant; there are also many gift shops and Asian groceries.

Rail travelers should not be the only ones to enjoy the beautiful, Italianate **Union Station**. Built in 1890, the spacious marble-walled train station near the corner of NW 6th Ave and Irving St is one of the city's landmarks.

The Old Town area becomes less savory by night. Although there is no great danger, you might feel uncomfortable walking around alone. Taxiing in and out is prob-ably a good idea.

Saturday Market & Skidmore Fountain

A preserve of Victorian-era architecture, the district that surrounds the lovely Skid-more Fountain at SW 1st Ave and Ankeny St bustles on weekends when the Saturday Market (also open Sundays) sets up beneath the Burnside Bridge. Saturday Market is reputed to be the nation's largest outdoor craft fair. Street entertainers and ethnic food carts round out the carnival atmosphere. This seasonal market is in operation from the first weekend in March to Christmas Eve. The hours are 10 am to 5 pm Saturday, and 11 am to 4:30 pm Sunday.

Beside the fountain is the **New Market Theater**, built in 1871 as Portland's first theater for stage productions. Some of the city's oldest seafood restaurants and best art galleries share the neighborhood.

Oregon Maritime Center & Museum

At 113 SW Front Ave (between SW Ash and SW Ankeny Sts), this museum (☎ 503-224-7724) charts Portland's long history as a seaport and ship-building center. The museum is open 11 am to 4 pm Wednesday to Sunday. Admission is $4/3/2 adults/seniors/students. Children under eight are free.

INNER WEST SIDE
Northwest

When Portlanders talk about the North-west, they are referring to the neighbor-hood bisected by NW 21st and 23rd Aves, north of Burnside. The residential heart of late-19th-century Portland, this attractive neighborhood fairly hums with street life. This is the city's high-end mecca for shopping, eating and drinking. Much in favor with Portland's student, gay and upwardly mobile population, this is the city's Trend Central.

For shopping, NW 23rd Ave is lined with clothing boutiques, interior design shops, and other trendy venues. Serious restaurants – including some of Portland's finest – stretch along NW 21st Ave. The Northwest also offers a number of good art galleries, brewpubs and friendly sidewalk cafes. This is a great neighborhood for people watching, browsing and consuming. Northwest Portland also has the highest population density in the city, so parking can be very vexing.

Pearl District
Just east of trendy Northwest Portland, the Pearl District is an old warehouse and light industrial precinct that has gone the way of loft development. Once an eyesore, the area between NW 14th and 10th Aves and NW Hoyt and Everett Sts is now one of Portland's most chic neighborhoods. The Pearl District has Portland's highest concentration of art galleries, and there's an increasing number of shops devoted to home design, furniture and antiques. The cafes and restaurants here are some of the city's most aggressively stylish.

Southwest
Downtown Portland constitutes much of inner Southwest Portland, though areas of interest to travelers continue up the west bank of the Willamette. Just south of downtown along Macadam Ave is John's Landing, a sprawling development of shopping boutiques, riverfront restaurants and upscale condominiums.

WEST HILLS & WASHINGTON PARK
Behind downtown Portland are the West Hills, a ridge of ancient volcanic peaks that divide Portland from her westerly suburbs. Some of the city's most beautiful homes

are perched on the forested West Hills, overlooking downtown and distant Mt Hood. Here also is the enormous Washington Park complex that includes the city's zoo and rose gardens, with hiking access to larger wilderness parks and historic buildings. On a clear day, this is one of Portland's greatest glories.

To reach Washington Park and associated sites, take Tri-Met bus No 63 from downtown's SW Washington St or catch MAX. To reach the park by car, take the zoo exit off US 26, or follow signs for the Rose Gardens off W Burnside St at Tichner Drive. See the Portland map for the following sights.

International Rose Test Gardens
Here is one of the reasons that Portland is called the Rose City. One of the nation's oldest rose gardens, and certainly one of the most stunningly situated, the International Rose Test Gardens sprawl across 4.5 acres of manicured lawns, fountains and flower beds.

More than just a beautiful public park, the rose gardens are also the testing grounds for the American Rose Society and All-American Rose selections. Over 400 rose varieties are contained in the permanent gardens, including many old and rare varieties. From June to September, the scent and colors are almost overpowering.

Japanese Gardens
Farther uphill, past the tennis courts, this tranquil and intimate formal garden (☎ 503-223-4070) encompasses 5 acres of tumbling water, pools of koi, flowers, a teahouse, a sand garden and views east onto Mt Hood. Admission to the Japanese Garden is $5 for adults and $2.50 for seniors/students (including college students with valid ID). Children ages five and under are free. The garden is open 10 am to 6 pm daily, April to May and the full month of September; 9 am to 8 pm, June to August; and 10 am to 4 pm, October to March. Tours are available at 10:45 am and 2:30 pm, April to October.

OREGON

OREGON

Metro Washington Park Zoo

In summer, ride the Zoo Train from the rose gardens to Metro Washington Park Zoo (or follow Kingston Rd up the hill). The zoo (☎ 503-226-1561), 4001 SW Canyon Rd, is one of Portland's premier attractions. Exhibits focus on ecosystems and the inter-relationships of animal life and the environment. Of special note are the zoo's Asian elephants; the Portland zoo maintains one of the world's most successful elephant breeding programs. Inquire about summer concerts on the zoo's terraced lawns. To reach the zoo from downtown, follow US 26 west 1 mile and take the zoo exit.

Admission to the zoo is $5.50/4/3.50 adults/seniors/children (three to 11). Zoo hours are 9:30 am to 5 pm daily, April 3 to May 27; 9:30 am to 6 pm, May 28 to September 5; and 9:30 am to 4 pm, September 6 to April 2.

World Forestry Center

Sharing the parking lot with the zoo is the World Forestry Center (☎ 503-228-1367), an educational facility that promotes understanding of the world's forests, their ecosystems and forestry industries. Opening hours in summer are 9 am to 5 pm daily, and 10 am to 5 pm in winter. Admission is $3 for adults, $2 for youth ages six to 18 and seniors 62 and up.

Oregon Vietnam Veterans Living Memorial

Next to the World Forestry Center are these spiraling black granite slabs, inscribed with details of events and circumstances in both Vietnam and Oregon, conjuring up the memories of the tumultuous Vietnam War years.

Hoyt Arboretum

Nine miles of trails wind through Hoyt Arboretum, a ridge-top tree garden above the zoo that features the world's largest collection of conifers and many other labeled plants and trees. Pick up a map at the Tree House Visitor Center (☎ 503-228-8733), 4000 Fairview Blvd, open 9 am to

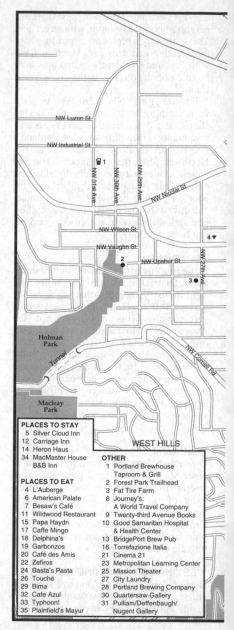

PLACES TO STAY
5 Silver Cloud Inn
12 Carriage Inn
14 Heron Haus
34 MacMaster House B&B Inn

PLACES TO EAT
4 L'Auberge
6 American Palate
7 Besaw's Café
11 Wildwood Restaurant
15 Papa Haydn
17 Caffe Mingo
18 Delphina's
19 Garbonzos
20 Café des Amis
22 Zefiros
24 Basta's Pasta
26 Touché
29 Bima
32 Cafe Azul
33 Typhoon!
35 Plainfield's Mayur

WEST HILLS

OTHER
1 Portland Brewhouse Taproom & Grill
2 Forest Park Trailhead
3 Fat Tire Farm
8 Journey's: A World Travel Company
9 Twenty-third Avenue Books
10 Good Samaritan Hospital & Health Center
13 BridgePort Brew Pub
16 Torrefazione Italia
21 Cinema 21
23 Metropolitan Learning Center
25 Mission Theater
27 City Laundry
28 Portland Brewing Company
30 Quartersaw Gallery
31 Pulliam/Deffenbaugh/ Nugent Gallery

OREGON

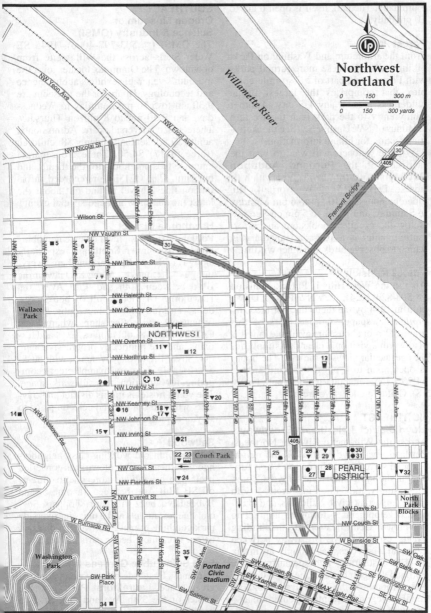

Northwest Portland

NW Yeon Ave

Willamette River

NW Front Ave

30

405

NW Nicolai St

Fremont Bridge

Wilson St

NW 26th Ave
NW 25th Ave
NW 24th Ave
NW 23rd Ave
NW 22nd Ave
NW 21st Place

NW Vaughn St

■ 5   ▼ 6

30

NW Thurman St

NW Savier St

NW Raleigh St

● 8

NW Quimby St

Wallace
Park

NW Pettygrove St

THE
NORTHWEST

NW Overton St

11 ▼

■ 12

NW Northrup St

12

NW Marshall St

9 ●   ✚ 10

NW Lovejoy St

▼ 19

▼ 20

NW Kearney St

NW 28th Ave
NW 9th Ave

● 16   18 ▼
17 ▼

NW Johnson St

NW 21st Ave
NW 20th Ave
NW 19th Ave
NW 18th Ave
NW 17th Ave
NW 16th Ave
NW 15th Ave
NW 14th Ave
NW 13th Ave
NW 12th Ave
NW 11th Ave
NW 10th Ave
NW 9th Ave

14 ■

NW Wilson Rd

15 ▼

NW Irving St

● 21

NW Hoyt St

22 23   Couch Park
▼ ▼

25 ●

26 ▼   ▼
29

●●30
■ 31

NW Glisan St

27 ●   28 ●

PEARL
DISTRICT

▼ 32

NW Flanders St

▼ 24

North
Park
Blocks

33 ▼

NW Everett St

W Burnside Rd

NW Davis St

NW Couch St

W Burnside St

Washington
Park

35 ▼

Portland
Civic
Stadium

SW Vista Ave
SW St Clair St
SW King St
SW 21st Ave
SW 20th Ave
SW 18th Ave

SW Morrison St

SW 13th Ave
SW 12th Ave
SW 11th Ave

SW Oak
St

SW Stark St

SW Washington St

SW Yamhill St

MAX Light Rail

SE Washington St

SW Park
Place

SW Salmon St

SE Alder St

34 ■

3 pm daily. The park itself is open 6 am to 10 pm daily.

Forest Park

From the arboretum and Washington Park, hiking trails join these more formal parks with Forest Park, part of a 7-sq-mile complex that comprises the largest urban wilderness area in any US city. Another handy entry to the park is at the western terminus of NW Upshur St. (See the Activities section for hiking information.)

Wildlife watchers will want to visit the facilities of the **Portland Audubon Society** (☎ 503-292-6855), in a gulch of Forest Park, 5151 NW Cornell Rd. Opening hours are 10 am to 6 pm Monday to Saturday, and 10 am to 5 pm on Sunday. Below the excellent bookstore and information center is a 100-acre sanctuary in which to observe birds and other wildlife.

Pittock Mansion

Also in the West Hills is Pittock Mansion (☎ 503-823-3624), 3229 NW Pittock Drive, built in 1914 by the then editor of the *Oregonian* newspaper. Guided tours of this grand, 22-room house are available, but it is also worth a visit on a clear day simply for the spectacular views to the east. The house is open noon to 4 pm daily; admission is $4.25/3.75/2 for adults/seniors/youth (six to 18). Children under five are free.

NORTHEAST
Lloyd District & Northeast Broadway

Across the Willamette River in Northeast Portland, the Lloyd District is the neighborhood surrounding the nation's first full-blown shopping mall, the Lloyd Center. Increasingly, this booming area – with many important civic buildings and business developments – forms an adjunct to downtown. Gentrification of surrounding streets, especially NE Broadway between 12th and 21st Aves, has brought an influx of good restaurants and specialty shops. Portland's largest cinema, the Rose Garden Arena (home of the NBA Trail Blazers), and the Oregon Convention Center are also here (see the Portland map).

SOUTHEAST
Oregon Museum of Science & Industry (OMSI)

The OMSI (☎ 503-797-4000), 1945 SE Water St, is across the Willamette from downtown. The Omnimax theater joins the museum's venerable exhibits about science and technology. Hours for the museum are 9:30 am to 5:30 pm Saturday to Wednesday, and 9:30 am to 8 pm on Thursday. There's also a riverside cafe. Admission is adults $9.50; seniors/students $8; children (three to 17) $4.50. There are separate entrance fees and hours for the theater and museum. Call OMSI's prerecorded information line (above) to find out about the latest theater showings and special events.

Hawthorne District

Portland's funkiest, most diverse neighborhood is the inner Southeast, especially along Hawthorne Blvd; around here, everything is 'alternative.' Along SE Hawthorne Blvd between 30th and 45th Aves, the Hawthorne District is full of bookstores, delis, antique stores, brewpubs, ethnic restaurants and coffee shops where Reed College students, old hippies, gays and lesbians, and the politically progressive hang out. Street life is very dynamic, with buskers, friendly dogs and pamphleteers competing for attention and sidewalk space. The youth hostel is in this district and travelers will find it a fun and eclectic place to stay or explore.

Sellwood

Sellwood, an old working-class neighborhood southeast of downtown, has converted itself into an antique-store ghetto. Streets off SE 13th Ave, between Tacoma St and Bybee Blvd, buzz with curio shoppers. Several fine restaurants and a pleasant riverside park combine to make Sellwood a pleasant detour from more hectic parts of Portland.

East Side Public Gardens & Parks

Portland's East Side offers a rich variety of green space. **Laurelhurst Park**, near the corner of SE 39th Ave and Oak St, is a beautiful urban park with a small lake, towering conifers, flocks of ducks and geese, playgrounds and picnic areas. **Mt Tabor Park**, near the corner of SE 69th Ave and Yamhill St, boasts of being the only city park in the country that's also an extinct volcano. Heavily forested, it's a great place to picnic, or to unleash pets and kids. **Crystal Springs Lake**, near lovely Reed College at SE 28th Ave and SE Woodstock St, is popular in early spring for the amazing display of flowering shrubs at its Rhododendron Garden. There are more than 2000 full-grown rhododendrons and azaleas here. The park winds past duck-filled ponds and streams.

The Grotto (☎ 503-254-7371), NE 85th Ave at Sandy Blvd, is a religious retreat also known as the Sanctuary of Our Sorrowful Mother; it's open 9 am to 5:30 pm daily. In addition to an outdoor shrine, the beautiful grounds of the Servite Monastery are maintained as a public sanctuary. The **Streamside Leach Botanical Park** (☎ 503-761-9503), 6704 SE 122nd Ave near Foster Rd, is a lovely 5-acre estate now maintained by the city for its collection of rare plants. It's open to the public 9 am to 4 pm Tuesday to Saturday.

ACTIVITIES
Hiking
In Portland's West Hills, **Forest Park** offers hikers 30 miles of trails in one of the largest urban parks in the country. Several trails begin near the World Forestry Center and include the **Wildwood Trail**, which winds through miles of deep forest, and the **40-Mile Loop**, a series of trails that link 35 state and city parks circling Portland. A map of the trail system is available from the City Parks Department (☎ 503-823-2223), on the 4th floor of the Portland Building, 1120 SW 5th Ave. Another trailhead begins at the western end of NW Upshur St.

Out past Lewis & Clark College in Southwest Portland is **Tryon Creek State Park** (☎ 503-653-3166), 11321 SW Terwilliger Blvd, with 8 miles of trails. Streamside wildlife includes beavers and songbirds. In late March there are won-

drous displays of trillium, a wild marsh lily.

Biking
Portland was recently honored by *Bicycle Magazine* as the most bike-friendly city in the nation. A map of metro-area bike routes is available from bike shops or Powell's Travel Store. Mountain bikers need go no farther than Leif Ericson Drive in Forest Park for an exhilarating backwoods workout.

For bicycle rentals, see the Getting Around section at the end of this chapter. You can repair bikes at the Bicycle Repair Collective (☎ 503-233-0564), 4438 SE Belmont St.

Swimming
The following public indoor pools are open year-round and are convenient to downtown: Dishman Center (☎ 503-823-3673), 77 NE Knott St; Buckman Pool (☎ 503-823-3668), 320 SE 16th Ave; and the Metropolitan Learning Center (☎ 503-823-3671), 2033 NW Glisan St. In summer, the outdoor pool at US Grant Park (☎ 503-823-3674), near the corner of NE 33rd Ave and US Grant St, is a great place for hot kids.

Public beaches and swimming along the Willamette and Columbia Rivers are popular in summer. Sellwood Riverfront Park, on the east end of the Sellwood Bridge, is a good place for a picnic and a wade in the Willamette (there's also an outdoor pool). Ten miles north of Portland, the beaches along the east side of Sauvie Island are also popular and are reached from US 30. Nude sunbathing becomes the norm the farther north you go.

Golf
The Portland Metro area has dozens of golf courses and driving ranges. Contact the chamber of commerce for a complete listing.

One of the city's best and most central is the Eastmoreland Golf Course (☎ 503-775-2900) 2425 SE Bybee Blvd. This 18-hole municipal course and driving range is nationally recognized. As it was founded in 1918, the grounds feature mature and

OREGON

OREGON

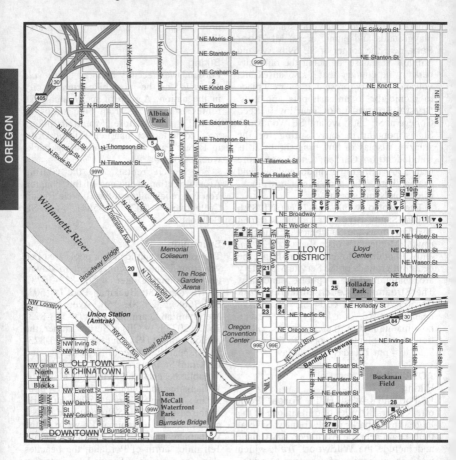

beautiful landscaping. Another well-respected, city-owned course is Heron Lakes Golf Course (☎ 503-289-1818), 3500 N Victory Rd. At Heron Lakes, there are 27 holes, with fairways and traps to challenge the most complacent golfer.

ORGANIZED TOURS
A number of individuals offer walking tours of downtown Portland; however, it's a changing cast of characters and it's best to ask at the visitors' center to find out what's current.

Other small tour companies offer both standard and customized tour packages of Portland and northwest Oregon. Popular excursions include winery or brewpub tours, or trips to the Oregon coast or the Columbia River Gorge. Van Go (☎ 503-292-2085) or Far West Tours (☎ 503-640-3223) both offer a full range of options; see tour operators in the yellow pages for a full listing. Ecotours of Oregon (☎ 503-245-1428) specializes in naturalist tours in northwest Oregon, such as day hikes and whale-watching trips.

Gray Line Buses (☎ 503-285-9845) conducts guided bus tours of Portland during

OREGON

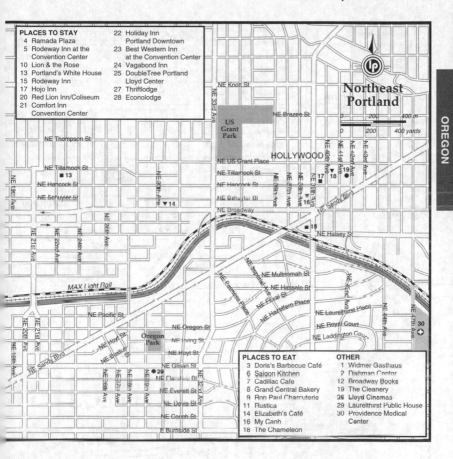

PLACES TO STAY
4 Ramada Plaza
5 Rodeway Inn at the
   Convention Center
10 Lion & the Rose
13 Portland's White House
15 Rodeway Inn
17 Hojo Inn
20 Red Lion Inn/Coliseum
21 Comfort Inn
   Convention Center
22 Holiday Inn
   Portland Downtown
23 Best Western Inn
   at the Convention Center
24 Vagabond Inn
25 DoubleTree Portland
   Lloyd Center
27 Thriftlodge
28 Econolodge

Northeast
Portland

HOLLYWOOD

PLACES TO EAT
3 Doris's Barbecue Café
6 Saigon Kitchen
7 Cadillac Cafe
8 Grand Central Bakery
9 Ron Paul Charcuterie
11 Rustica
14 Elizabeth's Café
16 My Canh
18 The Chameleon

OTHER
1 Widmer Gasthaus
2 Dishman Center
12 Broadway Books
19 The Cleanery
26 Lloyd Cinemas
29 Laurelthirst Public House
30 Providence Medical
   Center

summer and also hosts tours to other north-west Oregon sites.

Cruise & Excursion Boats

Explore Portland's maritime past and present on a riverboat or yacht cruise. Cascade Sternwheelers (☎ 503-223-3928), 1200 SW Front Ave, offers weekend tours of Portland's waterfront ($8.95 to $10.95); call for times and special seasonal cruises. Rose City Riverboat Cruises (☎ 503-234-6665), RiverPlace Marina, runs daily tours of Portland's harborfront ($10.50) and a city lights tour in the evening ($22). The

Crystal Dolphin (☎ 503-226-2517), is a luxury yacht that features tours of the waterfront and Willamette River. Portland Spirit (☎ 503-224-3900, 800-224-3901), offers both sightseeing tours ($14) and full-service dining cruises with notably good food ($24 to $46).

SPECIAL EVENTS

At some point during the year, nearly every nationality and interest group in Portland claims a public park to celebrate their heritage with food, drink and music. Contact the visitors' center for current information

OREGON

PLACES TO STAY
14 Hostelling International-
   Portland

PLACES TO EAT
2 Old Wives' Tale
4 Esparza's
5 Montage
6 Caswell's
8 Zell's
9 Bangkok Kitchen
10 Genoa
12 Jarra's
15 Hawthorne Café
16 Bread & Ink Café
21 Tabor Hill Café
27 Indigine

OTHER
1 LaLuna
3 Buckman Pool
7 Rimsky-Korsakoffee House
11 Lucky Labrador
   Brewing Company
13 Café Lena
17 Hawthorne Ale House
18 Bagdad Theater
19 Powell's Books for Cooks
20 In Other Words
22 Oregon Museum of Science
   & Industry (OMSI)
23 Aladdin Theater
24 Washboard
25 Third World Coffee Co
26 Laughing Horse Books

Southeast
Portland

0   200   400 m
0   200   400 yards

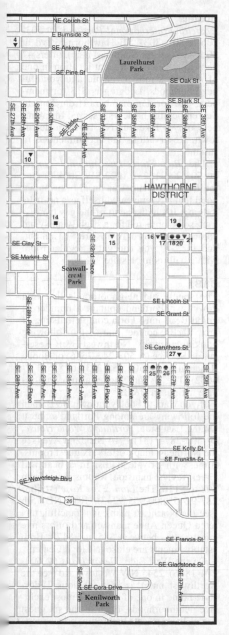

OREGON

and a complete listings of events. Below are some of the many parties and gatherings that the city throws for itself.

Portland Rose Festival

The city's doyen of festivals and its oldest civic event is the Portland Rose Festival, held in early June. The beautiful floral display at the International Rose Test Gardens is the nominal excuse for nearly two weeks of festivities, but the real focus of events are the parades (the Grand Floral is the second-largest floral parade in the nation), the riverfront carnival, immense naval ships docked right downtown and the crowning of the Rose Queen. Contact the Rose Festival (☎ 503-227-2681) for a schedule of events.

Music Festivals

Portland's most important and noted musical festival is the Chamber Music Northwest series (☎ 503-223-3202), a season of chamber music concerts held at both Reed College campus and at Catlin-Gable School. In early July the Waterfront Blues Festival (☎ 503-282-0555) brings life to downtown's riverside park.

In early August, the Mt Hood Jazz Festival (☎ 503-666-3810) attracts nationally recognized artists to Mt Hood Community College in Gresham, 12 miles east of Portland – call for details.

The hottest alternative and rock bands hit Portland in mid-September for the new North by Northwest (NXNW) festival (☎ 503-243-2122 ext 380). Over 200 bands from across the nation and Canada converge for a wild weekend featuring the latest sounds in clubland.

Other Summer Celebrations

Portland's Gay Pride Parade & Celebration takes place in late June and attracts 10,000 participants; contact Stonewall Northwest (☎ 503-223-1656) for more information on this celebration.

In late July, the region's brewers take over the waterfront festival grounds for the Oregon Brewers Festival. Stay late for live music. Call ☎ 503-241-7179 for details.

OREGON

A celebration of Portland's restaurants called The Bite (☎ 503-248-0600) takes place in August on the Waterfront. Eat your fill and then rock out to local bands.

PLACES TO STAY

The accommodations listed here have been selected with convenience to downtown as a guiding criterion. Outside of the central city, chain motels can be easily found clustered at freeway exits. In particular, on NE Airport Way, at I-205 exit 24, there are dozens of moderately priced hotels, most national chains.

The majority of central Portland's hotels are right downtown, or on the East Side, near the Lloyd District and convention center. Make summer reservations well ahead of time, as hotels and motels are often booked up months in advance. Prices noted are for the high summer season; a 9% bed tax is added to all lodging prices.

Camping

Portland is not very amenable to campers. If you are planning to visit downtown Portland, be prepared for a long commute from your campsite. For RV campsites in the Portland Metro area, check out *Fairview RV Park* (☎ 503-661-1047), 21401 NE Sandy Blvd, along the Columbia River near the suburb of Gresham; it's 15 miles to downtown. Sites here are $25 per day. *Jantzen Beach RV Park* (☎ 503-289-7626), off I-5 exit 308, a half-mile west on Hayden Island Rd, is across the Columbia River from Vancouver, WA; it's 8 miles to downtown. Hookups are $22 to $25.

Tent campers will certainly be more comfortable at attractive campgrounds in slightly more distant state parks. About 25 miles south of Portland, *Champoeg State Park* (☎ 503-678-1251) is a cradle of early Northwest history and offers campsites in a beautiful riverside setting. Hiking, museums and bike trails complete the package; Champoeg is west of I-5 exit 282. *Milo McIver State Park* (☎ 503-630-7150) stretches along the Clackamas River in a quiet sylvan setting. Exit I-205 at Hwy 224 and head east about 12 miles towards Estacada.

Hostels

Hostelling International-Portland (☎ 503-236-3380), 3031 SE Hawthorne Blvd at 30th Ave (see the Southeast map), offers 47 beds to travelers in a great location in one of the city's most dynamic and youthful neighborhoods. Lodging is $13 for members, $16 for non-members (from June to September, the hostel is reserved for members only). Take bus No 14 from downtown. Reservations are recommended in summer.

The *Ben Stark International Hostel* (☎ 503-274-1223), 1022 SW Stark St (see the Downtown map), is an old downtown hotel that has reinvented itself as a no-frills lodging. It's in the heart of the gay bar district, so be prepared for a slightly noisy but colorful stay. Dorm rooms are $12 a night, and for $40 you can get a regular room with a bathroom en suite.

B&Bs

The stately old neighborhoods that ring downtown Portland contain a number of grand B&B inns. For a complete listing of area B&Bs, contact one of the following booking agencies: Northwest B&B Reservation Service (☎ 503-243-7616) or Booka Reservation (☎ 503-452-2334 or 888-272-6652). The visitors' center also has up-to-date listings of B&Bs.

If you want to book your own B&B, then the following are among Portland's finest. On the East Side, *Portland's White House*, (☎ 503-287-7131) 1914 NE 22nd Ave (see the Northeast map), offers six guest rooms, some with private baths, in a beautiful Greek-revival mansion. Rooms range from $98 to $116. The *Lion & the Rose* (☎ 503-287-9245, 800-955-9247), 1810 NE 15th (see the Northeast map), is a fanciful, turreted Queen Anne mansion and offers five guest rooms between $85 and $120. Both establishments are close to Lloyd Center.

On the West Side, *Heron Haus* (☎ 503-274-1846), 2545 NW Westover Rd (see the Northwest map), is in a fabulous Tudor-style home in one of the city's most exclusive neighborhoods. Each of the six guest rooms has a private bathroom; prices range from $125 to $155. Within walking distance of the rose gardens is *MacMaster House B&B Inn* (☎ 503-223-7362, 800-774-9523), 1041 SW Vista Ave (see the Northwest map). It has six rooms, two with private bathroom; prices range from $75 to $120.

The area's most unusual B&B is at the *Edgefield* (☎ 503-669-8610), 2126 SW Halsey St, 18 miles east of Portland in Troutdale, a complex of buildings and fields that was once the county poor farm. The handsome brick edifices include the historic lodging (with delightful 1930s-era furnishings), a vineyard, two restaurants, a brewery, and a pub. Rooms range from $75 to $100.

Hotels – downtown & Northwest
Budget Some older motels offer a good value and clean rooms near the city center. *Saharan Motel* (☎ 503-226-7646), 1889 SW 4th Ave, is near Portland State University, just south of the city center. Singles/doubles are $42/50. Also convenient, the *Caravan Motor Hotel* (☎ 503-226-1121, 800-636-2401), 2401 SW 4th Ave, has rooms at $55/60.

Quieter, and in dynamic Northwest Portland, is the *Carriage Inn* (☎ 503-224-0543), 2025 NW Northrup St, with rooms at $48/65.

Middle Right downtown, the face-lifted *Imperial Hotel* (☎ 503-228-7221, 800-452-2323), 400 SW Broadway, has singles/doubles for $75/80 and is convenient to downtown restaurants, shopping and entertainment. Likewise, the *Mallory Hotel* (☎ 503-223-6311, 800-228-8657), 729 SW 15th Ave, is only blocks away from the city center and offers free parking; rooms cost $65/70.

Another good deal downtown is the *Mark Spencer Hotel* (☎ 503-224-3293, 800-548-3934), 409 SW 11th Ave, at $72/99; all rooms have full kitchens. Ask for river-view rooms at the *Riverside Inn* (☎ 503-221-0711, 800-899-0247), 50 SW Morrison St, at the base of the Morrison Bridge. Rooms are $99/109.

Right downtown, *Days Inn City Center* (☎ 503-221-1611, 800-899-0248), 1414 SW 6th Ave, has rooms for $85/100, a pool and its own coffee shop. New and upscale, the *Silver Cloud Inn* (☎ 503-242-2400, 800-551-7207 ext 8), at 2426 NW Vaughn St, is a good base for exploring Northwest Portland. Rooms are $85/88.

Top End If it's time for a splurge, Portland offers a few classic old hotels with first-class service and amenities – and some of the best restaurants in the city. Prices for lodgings in these hotels are affected by room availability or the particular day of the week you stay; packages and promotions can greatly lower the cost.

The *Heathman Hotel* (☎ 503-241-4100, 800-551-0011), 1001 SW Broadway, is one of the city's finest. The Heathman's service is legendary: when Pavarotti stayed here, the Heathman prevailed on the city to stop daytime construction nearby so that the tenor could rest before his performance. Room rates are $140/165. The *Benson Hotel* (☎ 503-228-2000), 309 SW Broadway, with a lobby filled with chandeliers and lined with walnut, is another old showcase Portland hotel. This is where the president stays when in town. Rooms start at $215. Topped by penthouse suites, the *Hotel Vintage Plaza* (☎ 503-228-1212, 800-243-0555), 422 SW Broadway, has rooms for anything from $165 to $400, and the art deco *Governor Hotel* (☎ 503-224-3400, 800-554-3456), at the corner of 611 SW 10th Ave at Alder St, charges $165 to $195. Both are examples of old neglected hotel buildings that have undergone complete renovation to emerge as beautiful, luxury accommodations, without losing their period charm.

Modern and right on the waterfront is the *RiverPlace Hotel* (☎ 503-228-3233, 800-227-1333), 1510 SW Harbor Way, $195/215. Ask for a room overlooking the marina.

Portland's newest hotels – both of which are, in fact, extensively refurbished downtown landmarks – are all-suites hotels. After a complete makeover, the massive building that was once one of Portland's fanciest 1920s hotels is now back in the lodging business as the *Embassy Suites* (☎ 503-279-9000, 800-362-2779), 319 SW Pine St. Right in the heart of downtown, *Fifth Avenue Suites Hotel,* (☎ 503-222-0001, 800-711-2971), 506 SW Washington St, offers luxurious two-room suites.

The *Portland Marriott* (☎ 503-226-7600, 800-228-9290), 1401 SW Front St, at $165/180, and the *Portland Hilton* (☎ 503-226-1611, 800-445-8667), 921 SW 6th Ave, at $145/175, offer the facilities you'd expect from major international hotels.

Hotels – Northeast
Budget The *Econolodge* (☎ 503-234-0316), 1415 NE Sandy Blvd, charging $45/55, is across the Burnside Bridge from downtown. Even closer to downtown across the Willamette River is the *Thriftlodge* (☎ 503-234-8411, 800-525-9055), 949 E Burnside St, where rooms are $49/54 ($4 higher on weekends).

Hojo Inn (☎ 503-288-6891), 3939 NE Hancock St, with rooms for $40/42, and the *Rodeway Inn* (☎ 503-460-9000), 3800 NE Sandy Blvd, at $59 for a single or double, are a quick five-minute commute east of downtown off I-84's Hollywood exit.

Middle A cluster of moderately priced hotels is found just across the Willamette River, between downtown and Lloyd Center, within easy walking distance of the Oregon Convention Center. The *Red Lion Inn/Coliseum* (☎ 503-235-8311, 800-547-8010) is right on the Willamette River, 1225 N Thunderbird Way. Rooms are $75/95. *Rodeway Inn – Convention Center* (☎ 503-231-7665, 800-421-7665), 1506 NE 2nd Ave charges $65/75. The *Ramada Plaza* (☎ 503-233-2401), 1441 NE 2nd Ave, has rooms with views for $89/99.

The following hotels are right on, or very close to, the MAX lines, seconds away from the Convention Center: the *Comfort Inn Convention Center* (☎ 503-233-7933, 800-221-2222), 431 NE Multnomah St ($69/79); the *Holiday Inn Portland Down-town* (☎ 503-235-2100, 800-343-1822), 1021 NE Grand Ave ($87); the *Vagabond Inn* (☎ 503-234-4391, 800-424-4777), 518 NE Holladay St ($59/69); and the *Best Western Inn at the Convention Center* (☎ 503-233-6331), 420 NE Holladay St ($58/63).

Top End Near both Lloyd Center and the Convention Center, the *DoubleTree Portland Lloyd Center* (☎ 503-281-6111, 800-222-8733), 1000 NE Multnomah St, is the East Side's nicest hotel. Rooms go for $175/195.

PLACES TO EAT
Portland offers a wide variety of dining options, ranging from ethnic restaurants and trendy Northwest cuisine to classic American steak houses. The city's best food, whatever its origins, features fresh, local ingredients and an often eclectic mingling of food traditions.

Light meals are often served at coffeehouses and brewpubs (see the Entertainment section for listings).

Downtown & Old Town
Budget There are food carts on nearly every corner downtown, most offering cheap carry-out ethnic food. Downstairs at Pioneer Place, at SW 6th Ave and Taylor St, is *Cascades*, a subterranean food court with dozens of food vendors with inexpensive fast food.

Bijou Café (☎ 503-222-3187), 132 SW 3rd Ave, is Portland's favorite downtown place to eat breakfast. At lunch, they serve sandwiches and luncheon specials. *Macheezmo Mouse* (☎ 503-228-3491), 723 SW Salmon St and other metro locations, offers cheap and healthy Mexican food in a wildly decorated storefront. Most entrées are under $5.

Sausage lovers need go no farther than *Good Dog/Bad Dog* (☎ 503-222-3410), 708 SW Alder St. Extremely meaty and spicy dogs of all descriptions make a quick and hearty meal for less than $5. Along SW Alder St, between 10th and 12th Aves, is a strip of cheap, quite good ethnic restaurants, including Mexican, Thai and Indian. You will be hard-pressed to spend more than $8 a plate for dinner at any of these small, family-owned restaurants.

Middle *Bush Garden* (☎ 503-226-7181), 900 SW Morrison St, features a sushi bar and tatami table service. In Old Town, *Uogashi* (☎ 503-242-1848), 107 NW Couch St, features sushi and traditional Japanese specialties. Salmon sashimi goes for $10 and vegetable tempura is $12.

Old-fashioned Chinese restaurants line the blocks between Burnside and Everett Sts, and between NW 2nd and 4th Aves in Old Town/Chinatown. Explore on your own, or try *Fong Chong* (☎ 503 220-0235), 301 NW 4th Ave, for dim sum; *Phu Ho* (☎ 503-229-1888), 28 NW 4th Ave, for seafood; and *Hung Far Low* (☎ 503-223-8686), 112 NW 4th Ave, which is open all night and hums with night owls – come here for the scene as much as the food.

Al-Amir (☎ 503-274-0010), 223 SW Stark St, serves delicious Lebanese food in a delightful old building that was once the residence of Portland's Catholic archbishop. A generous dinner portion of succulent lamb kebabs costs $12. *Alexis* (☎ 503-224-8577), 215 W Burnside St, is a fixture of Old Town, serving up well prepared and generously portioned Greek food in a lively ambiance.

Spanish food is making big inroads in Portland, and for great tapas and a Sunday-only paella fest, head to *Fernando's Hideaway* (☎ 503 248-4709), 824 SW 1st Ave. Asian fusion cooking dominates the menu at super-trendy *Saucebox* (☎ 503-241-3393), 214 SW Broadway; stay late for cocktails and DJ-spun hits. Things are a little more laid-back at stylish *Toulouse* (☎ 503-241-4343), 71 SW 2nd Ave, where a wood-fired rotisserie meets up with country French cooking. There's a good wine list, too.

For a unique experience, go to the *Chef's Corner* at the Western Culinary Institute (☎ 503-223-2245), 1316 SW 13th Ave, where chefs-in-training cook and serve meals for their willing, and sometimes

understanding, customers. A five-course lunch goes for $7.95; reservations are required. *Higgins* (☎ 503-222-9070), 1239 SW Broadway, close to the Performing Arts Center, offers stylish ingredients and innovative preparations without high prices. With numerous vegetarian options, this is probably the least expensive of Portland's top-notch restaurants, with most entrées under $15.

Top End Portland's most famous restaurant may not be its greatest, but *Jake's Famous Crawfish* (☎ 503-226-1419), 401 SW 12th Ave, captures more of the city's charm and esprit than fussier locales. Fresh seafood, steak, and a vibrant bar scene make this vintage landmark perennially popular. The same menu and atmosphere pervade Jake's sister restaurant, *McCormick & Schmick's* (☎ 503-224-7522), at the corner of SW 1st Ave and Oak St. Prices at these two bastions of traditional Portland cooking vary (there's usually a choice of nearly 25 fresh fish and seafood varieties), but $15 to $18 will buy a great meal and lots of atmosphere at either location. McCormick & Schmick's offers an early-bird menu, available between 5 and 6:30 pm only, with daily fish specials in the $9 range.

Opus Too (☎ 503-222-6077), 33 NW 2nd Ave, is another seafood institution and one of Portland's best-loved restaurants, offering plenty of Old Portland atmosphere, live jazz and a wide selection of mesquite-grilled fresh fish; prices range from $15 to $20.

Don't always mistrust hotel restaurants. The *Heathman Restaurant* (☎ 503-241-4100), 1001 SW Broadway, serves the city's most refined and provocative dishes and is probably the exemplar of oft-cited Pacific Northwest cuisine. Dishes like seared salmon with wasabi béarnaise sauce fetch $20. (The Heathman also serves a wonderful afternoon tea.) *Pazzo* (☎ 503-228-1515), 627 SW Washington St in the Hotel Vintage Plaza, offers downtown Portland's best Italian cooking. The designer pizzas are a real knockout at lunch

($7 to $9). Their dinner specials like cod cheeks and spring vegetable risotto cost around $17.

Atwater's (☎ 503-275-3600), 111 SW 5th Ave, offers fine dining 30 floors above the city in the Bankcorp Tower. Local rack of lamb, served with wild mushroom polenta, costs $24.

Northwest
One of the most frenzied shopping areas of Portland by day, the Northwest shifts gears by evening and opens for dinner. Coffeehouses, brewpubs, bakeries and wine bars are abundant and offer cheap snacks and refreshments. Be warned: Northwest Portland is often a nightmare for parking.

Budget For the neighborhood's best breakfast, head to *Besaw's Cafe* (☎ 503-228-2619), 2301 NW Savier St. For a quick and easy meal, the Lebanese-style entrées at *Garbonzos* (☎ 503-227-4196), at the corner of NW 21st Ave and Lovejoy St, are a good value; a falafel sandwich is $4.

Middle Though the architecture reveals the restaurant's former existence as a drive-in, *Basta's Pasta* (☎ 503-274-1572), 410 NW 21st Ave, serves up good, inexpensive pasta. Basta's country-style bread is among the best in town. Busy and dependable *Delphina's* (☎ 503-221-1195), 2112 NW Kearney St, serves Italian entrées and pizza. A second location, called *Caffe Mingo* (☎ 503-226-4646), 807 NW 21st Ave, offers designer Italian fare in a trattoria setting. Nationally recognized for its innovative Thai cuisine, *Typhoon!* (☎ 503-243-7557), 2310 NW Everett St, is one of the hottest spots in the Northwest.

Though most come to *Papa Haydn* (☎ 503-228-7317), 701 NW 23rd Ave, for the incredible desserts, the light meals and salads are very good and inexpensive.

In the Pearl District, *Bima* (☎ 503-241-3465), 1338 NW Hoyt St, offers Gulf Coast cooking in an aggressively high-design setting. This is also a great place for stylish cocktails. If you're a night owl,

Touché (☎ 503-221-1150), 1425 NE Glisan St, open till 4 am, is the place to head for good pasta, pizza and pool. *Cafe Azul* (☎ 503-525-4422), 112 NW 9th Ave, specializes in saucy cuisine from central and southern Mexico. It'll take every bit of willpower to resist intriguing dishes such as toasted green pumpkin-seed mole with chicken breast and seared vegetables. Entrées range from $15 to $22. Those who want to indulge in other Mexican traditions can have margaritas and tequilas at the bar. Cafe Azul is open for dinner only.

Top End Usually considered the city's best restaurant, trendy *Zefiros* (☎ 503-226-3394), 500 NW 21st Ave, features eclectic, Continental-influenced cuisine in a see/be-seen atmosphere. Entrées are in the $20 range.

Equally cosmopolitan and well regarded is the dining room at *Wildwood Restaurant* (☎ 503-248-9663), 1221 NW 21st Ave, where noisy crowds of Northwest style-setters graze on ingredient-du-jour cuisine. Friendlier and less of a scene, *American Palate* (☎ 503-223-6994), 1937 NW 23rd Place, is one of the city's best places for New American cuisine.

For French cooking in a homey, country atmosphere, go to *Café des Amis* (☎ 503-295-6487), 1987 NW Kearney St. There's a bistro menu set at the $10 range and pricier full dinners (such as filet mignon with garlic and port sauce) for $18 and thereabouts. *L'Auberge* (☎ 503-223-3302), 2601 NW Vaughn St, hearkens back to the French provinces for its inspiration. Its four-course feast, starring such favorites as filet mignon with onion marmalade, costs $39. You can also order à la carte dinners for about half the fun and money. On Sunday nights, you can sit in the quaint L'Auberge bar, watch old movies on TV, and enjoy one of the Auberge's signature burgers. Pure bliss.

For the city's best Indian cuisine, you'll need to venture a bit out of downtown to *Plainfield's Mayur* (☎ 503-223-2995), 852 SW 21st Ave, housed in a refurbished grand Victorian home. For a full, multicourse Indian meal it is easy to spend $25 a head.

Northeast
Northeast Broadway near Lloyd Center is filling up with trendy eateries; stand at the corner of NE 15th Ave and Broadway and survey your choices.

Budget For breakfast and tasty sandwiches for lunch, go to the *Cadillac Cafe* (☎ 503-287-4750), 914 NE Broadway. People in Portland argue over the best inexpensive Vietnamese and Thai restaurant, and several contenders are found along NE Broadway. A perennial favorite, *Saigon Kitchen* (☎ 503-281-3669), 835 NE Broadway, features both Vietnamese and Thai dishes. Main dishes cost around $9. In addition to the great breads and pastries at *Grand Central Bakery* (☎ 503-288-1614) at NE 15th Ave and Weidler St, soup, pizza and light entrées are available in the cafe.

For really good, inexpensive Chinese and Vietnamese food, head up to Hollywood where *My Canh* (☎ 503-281-0594), 1801 NE 39th Ave, serves up some of the best Asian food on the East Side. Prices are right: vegetarian lunch specials are just under $4.

Middle *Ron Paul Charcuterie* (☎ 503-284-5347), 1441 NE Broadway, offers light meals and desserts in a bistro-like atmosphere. By the time you assemble a meal out of various salads and entrée specials, it's easy to spend $10 to $12. Bustling *Rustica* (☎ 503-288-0990, 1700 NE Broadway, offers moderately priced pasta and Italian-style grilled meats.

Doris's Barbecue Café (☎ 503-287-9249), 352 NE Russell St, offers Southern specialties and some of the city's best ribs: they're so messy that bibs are mandatory.

Farther up on Broadway, and higher up on the food chain, is *Elizabeth's Café* (☎ 503-281-8337), 3135 NE Broadway, where the cuisine is innovative and the atmosphere homey. Duck with walnuts, peas and blood-orange sauce goes for $17.

There's outdoor seating during the summer months.

In Hollywood, *The Chameleon* (☎ 503-460-2682), 2000 NE 40th Ave, serves eclectic international preparations of fresh fish and seafood.

Southeast
Budget The funky, eclectic neighborhoods of Southeast Portland are where you would legitimately expect to find lots of comfortable, cheap cafes, bakeries, brewpubs, and coffeehouses. You will have no problem finding a good and inexpensive place to eat, especially along Hawthorne Blvd. *Hawthorne Café* (☎ 503-232-4982), 3354 SE Hawthorne Blvd, in a refurbished old mansion, is popular for breakfast. It is located very near the Hawthorne HI hostel. Another neighborhood breakfast joint of choice is *Zell's* (☎ 503-239-0196), 1300 SE Morrison St.

One of the most popular scenes in this part of town is *Montage* (☎ 503-234-1324), 301 SE Morrison St. Open 6 pm to 4 am, Montage is a creole nightspot with delicious, inexpensive dishes that you can assemble into a snack or a full meal, all while watching the arty creatures of the night. Vegetarian jambalaya goes for $7.

If you don't want to wait in line at Montage, go to *Caswell's* (☎ 503-232-6512), 533 SE Grand Ave, another hipster favorite and a sure hit with plenty of vegetarian options, pasta, pizza and a full bar.

Middle *Tabor Hill Café* (☎ 503-230-1231), 3766 SE Hawthorne Blvd, and the *Bread & Ink Café* (☎ 503-239-4756), 3610 SE Hawthorne Blvd, are both fixtures and popular for lunches and light dinners. Pasta, chicken and seafood dishes are the norm at both venues; prices for a full dinner range between $10 and $12. Known mostly for its desserts, *Papa Haydn* (☎ 503-232-9400), 5829 SE Milwaukie Ave in Sellwood, is also a great place for lunch or light dinners.

Authentic where others are trendy, the Tex-Mex food at *Esparza's* (☎ 503-234-7909), 2715 SE Ankeny St, has people

OREGON

lined up out the door. Home-smoked brisket ($9) is a specialty. *Old Wives' Tales* (☎ 503-238-0470), 1300 E Burnside St, welcomes vegetarians, gays, lesbians and children, and has yummy international comfort food.

In Portland, Thai food doesn't get much better than at the *Bangkok Kitchen* (☎ 503-236-7349), 2534 SE Belmont St. If Ethiopian food suits your palate, then *Jarra's* (☎ 503-230-8990), 1435 SE Hawthorne Blvd, is ready to serve you up searingly hot, authentically potent dishes.

Top End Nouveau-Indian cooking and Continental favorites mix and mingle at *Indigine* (☎ 503-238-1470), 3723 SE Division St. On Saturday nights, Indigine only serves its $26 Indian feast, an entire evening's worth of pungent scents and wondrous flavors. The meal includes seasonally selected raitas, breads, dahls, chutneys and entrées. Reservations are usually mandatory for this popular Portland tradition. On Friday nights there's a three-course menu of both Continental and Indian food; entrées like rabbit in mustard sauce go for $19. From Tuesday to Thursday, the same menu is available à la carte.

Tiny and informal, *Caprial's Bistro* (☎ 503-236-6457), 7015 SE Milwaukie Ave, in Sellwood, offers noteworthy Continental-influenced food in a cafe that by day doubles as a wine shop (chef Caprial Pense also hosts a PBS TV cooking program). There's no menu, just the daily-changing chalkboard. Select your wine yourself and add just $3 to its shelf price. Specials like sweetbreads with a port wine sauce go for $17.

Also in Sellwood is one of Portland's more unusual restaurants. *Fiddleheads* (☎ 503-233-1547), 6716 SE Milwaukie Ave, brings together New American and Native American ingredients and techniques to produce stylish and usually excellent cuisine.

Arguably Portland's favorite special-occasion restaurant, *Genoa* (☎ 503-238-1464), 2832 SE Belmont St, is a prix-fixe bastion of cucina Italiana. If you want to splurge Italian style, then $50 for seven courses may not put you off.

ENTERTAINMENT

The best guide to local entertainment is *Willamette Week (WW)*, a newsweekly that comes out on Wednesdays and contains complete listings of all theater, music, clubs, cinema and events in the metro area. The Friday edition of the *Oregonian* contains the *A&E*, an insert with arts and entertainment information. Or you can call the 24-hour Events & Information Hotline (☎ 503-225-5555) for a synopsis of area happenings.

Coffeehouses

Starbucks, the Seattle-based coffee company, has branches everywhere, as does locally owned *Coffee People*. At *Torrefazione Italia* (☎ 503-228-2528), 838 NW 23rd Ave (see the Northwest map), there's great Italian coffee as well as stylish surroundings.

However, for the coffeehouse experience, don't miss the following venues. *Anne Hughes Coffee Shop*, at Powell's City of Books (☎ 503-228-4651) at 1005 W Burnside St, serves caffeine to book-lovers. According to surveys, it's also one of the best singles scenes in the city.

In Southeast Portland, coffeehouses burgeon. *Café Lena* (☎ 503-238-7087), 2239 SE Hawthorne Blvd, near the Hawthorne HI hostel, features acoustic guitar and open-mike poetry. The stacks of current periodicals available for reading in cozy, overstuffed living-room furniture make *Common Grounds Coffee House* (☎ 503-236-4835), 4321 SE Hawthorne Blvd, a comfortable place for introverts to become quietly politicized. Portland's most unusual nightspot is the rather eccentric *Rimsky-Korsakoffee House* (☎ 503-232-2640), 707 SE 12th Ave, next door to the Plaid Pantry (there's no sign, so act like a regular and barge right in). A tribute to Rimsky-Korsakov himself, this charming old house-turned-cafe frequently features live classical music. Also, be sure to check out the bathroom upstairs. Musicians of an alternative kind can be found on weekends at *Third World Coffee Co* (☎ 503-233-8968), 3588 SE Division St, the only coffeehouse in Portland serving coffee purchased directly from coffee farmers in developing countries.

Brewpubs

Small breweries have sprung up everywhere in Portland, providing fantastic beers and ales to appreciative audiences. Oregon law requires that alcohol be served with food, so at the least all of the following brewpubs also feature snacks and light meals; many offer full lunch and dinner service. Most brewpubs offer a taster's selection of the house brews.

BridgePort Brew Pub (☎ 503-241-7179), 1313 NW Marshall St (see the Northwest map), is housed in an old, red-brick warehouse. Earthy and informal, it has outdoor seating on a former loading dock. Pizza by the slice and British-style brews make this pub very popular with the locals. Bridge-Port's East Side location, called the *Hawthorne Ale House* (☎ 503-233-6540), 3632 SE Hawthorne Blvd, is notably upscale and features an outstanding food menu and a friendly welcome.

Heathman Brewpub (☎ 503-227-5700), 901 SW Salmon St, is a bit more upscale and convenient to downtown, combining a bakery, deli, salad bar and pizza oven with Widmer's German-style beers. Widmer's has also opened its own brewpub called the *Widmer Gasthaus* (☎ 503-281-3333), 929 North Russell St (see the Northeast map), below the arches of the Fremont Bridge. It's worth the trip just to quaff the wonderful hefeweizen (unfiltered wheat beer), but don't ignore the schnitzel at this bustling and friendly pub.

The *Pilsner Room* (☎ 503-220-1865), overlooking the Willamette River at River-Place esplanade, 0309 SW Montgomery St, manages to combine local brews (from the Hood River Brewery) with a singles bar atmosphere. *Portland Brewing Company* (☎ 503-222-7150), 1339 NW Flanders St (see the Northwest map), serves a dynamite Scottish ale, with live music on

the weekends. Portland Brewing's newest location is in industrial Northwest Portland and is called *Portland Brewhouse Taproom & Grill* (☎ 503-228-5269), 2730 NW 31st Ave (see the Northwest map). The Taproom has better food than most brewpubs and features summer outdoor seating. *Lucky Labrador Brewing Company* (☎ 503-236-3555), 915 SE Hawthorne Blvd (see the Southeast map), is a friendly, student-oriented pub with a great mascot.

Ubiquitous *McMenimans* brewpubs are found all over the city. They offer their own locally brewed ales and a wide selection of ales, stouts and brews from other regional producers. Check the phone book for the McMenimans nearest you. Also, McMenimans has bought two historic movie houses and turned them into cinema-pubs. (See the Bagdad and Mission Theaters under Cinemas.) Even more unique is McMenimans establishment at the *Edgefield* (☎ 503-669-8610), 2126 SW Halsey St, about 18 miles east of Portland in Troutdale. This complex of historic buildings serves as a B&B, pub, restaurant, vineyard and brewery.

Cinemas

Lloyd Cinemas (☎ 503-248-6938), on the corner of NE 15th Ave and Multnomah St (see the Northeast map), is the city's largest venue for new films. It's right off the MAX line's Lloyd Center stop. *Cinema 21* (☎ 503-223-4515), 616 NW 21st Ave (see the Northwest map), is Portland's art and foreign film theater. Even more unusual films make it to the *Northwest Film Center* (☎ 503-221-1156), 1219 SW Park Ave (see the Downtown map), part of the Oregon Art Institute. The *KOIN Center Cinema* (☎ 503-243-3515) at 222 SW Columbia St, and the *Broadway Cinema* (☎ 503-248-6960), 1000 SW Broadway, are downtown's first-run movie complexes.

The *Mission Theater* (☎ 503-223-4031), 1624 NW Glisan St (see the Northwest map), and the *Bagdad Theater* (☎ 503-230-0895), 3702 SE Hawthorne Blvd (see the Southeast map), are both picturesque old movie theaters now owned by brewpubs.

OREGON

Order beer and snacks and watch a film. Call for current schedules.

Performing Arts

The oldest symphony orchestra west of St Louis, the century-old Oregon Symphony has grown in stature with conductor James dePriest at its helm. Concerts are held in the beautiful, if not acoustically brilliant, *Arlene Schnitzer Concert Hall* (☎ 503-228-1353, 800-228-7343), on the corner of Broadway and SW Main St; call for performance information.

The *Portland Opera* (☎ 503-241-1802) stages five performances a year at the Civic Auditorium, 222 SW Clay St. The *Oregon Ballet Theatre* (☎ 503-222-5538), 1120 SW 10th Ave, is Portland's resident dance troupe and stages a number of classical and contemporary dance programs each year.

The *Portland Baroque Orchestra* (☎ 503-222-6000) and the *Oregon Repertory Singers* (☎ 503-230-0652) are other notable classical music fixtures.

Theater Portland's showcase theatrical stages are at the *Portland Center for the Performing Arts* (☎ 503-796-9293), 1111 SW Broadway. Call for information on current shows; the recording gives phone numbers for ticket ordering. Portland Center Stage, a spin-off of Ashland's Oregon Shakespeare Festival troupe, and several other local theater groups perform here. Portland has a very active non-equity and student theater scene – check local papers for schedules.

The *Artist's Repertory Theatre* (☎ 503-241-1278), 1516 SW Alder St, specializes in revivals, dramas and ensemble pieces. *Echo Theatre/Do Jump Dance Theatre Co* (☎ 503-231-1232), 1515 SE 37th Ave, offers experimental dance and theater. *Firehouse Theatre* (☎ 503-289-5450), 5340 N Interstate Ave, puts on interracial and socially relevant productions, and *Portland Women's Theatre* (☎ 503-287-7707), 1728 NE 40th Ave, gives all-women performances. Try *Tygres Heart Shakespeare Co* (☎ 503-222-9220), 309 SW 6th Ave, for Shakespearean and Elizabethan drama. *Triangle Productions* (☎ 503-230-9404), 3430 SE Belmont St, specializes in gay theater.

Nightlife

Like Seattle, Portland is flush with live music and late-night clubs. For the most recent developments, check the Head Out section of *Willamette Week*. *Satyricon* (☎ 503-243-2380), 125 NW 6th Ave (see the Downtown map), serves up rough-and-ready punk and alternative rock in authentic grunge surroundings. Find more of Portland's club scene at *LaLuna* (☎ 503-224-4400), 221 SE 9th Ave (see the Southeast map), where Monday night is Queer Night, and at *Berbati's Pan* (☎ 503-226-2122), 19 SW Ankeny St (see the Downtown map). The *Lotus Card Room* (☎ 503-227-6185), 932 SW 3rd Ave (see the Downtown map), is ragged on the edges, but offers great local bands and hip-hop discos. If you missed Portland's hippie glory days, you can still catch the flavor at the *Laurelthirst Public House* (☎ 503-232-1504), 2958 NE Glisan St (see the Northeast map), with some of the city's best folk and bluegrass bands. Early in the week, this is where local musicians come to jam.

Jubitz (☎ 503-283-1111), 10310 N Vancouver Way, is a Portland institution: live, boot-stomping country music at an all-night truck stop. *Kell's* (☎ 503-227-4057), 112 SW 2nd Ave (see the Downtown map), offers Celtic music and Guinness on tap. Catch the downtown jazz scene at *Brasserie Montmartre* (☎ 503-224-5552), 626 SW Park Ave, or at *Jazz de Opus* (☎ 503-222-6077), 33 NW 2nd Ave.

The McMeniman Brothers, of local brewpub fame, have bought and refurbished the *Crystal Ballroom* (☎ 503-778-5625), 1332 W Burnside St (see the Downtown map), one of Portland's historic ballrooms, complete with floating dance floor. It's a great place to see touring regional national bands. Once a week, free ballroom dance lessons are offered, followed by waltz or swing bands. Another major venue for touring bands is the intimate *Alladin Theater* (☎ 503-223-1994) 3017 SE Milwaukie Blvd (see the Southeast map).

For a quiet drink downtown, go to *Cassidy's* (☎ 503-223-0054), 1331 SW Washington St, a bar right out of the 1890s, with a late-night influx of thespians. *Huber's* (☎ 503-228-5686), 411 SW 3rd Ave, is one of Portland's oldest bars, famous for its lethal Spanish coffees; expect lines late at night.

The hub of Portland's gay bar nightlife is found in the downtown neighborhood flanking Stark St and SW 11th Ave. Find a wild and mixed gay/straight disco scene at the *Panorama* (☎ 503-221-7262), part of a three-bar complex at the corner of SW 10th Ave and Stark St. It's open till 4 am on weekends. The '70s have never died at *Embers* (☎ 503-222-3082), 110 NW Broadway, a club with drag shows in the front and disco in the back. *Hobo's*, 120 NW 3rd Ave, offers a pleasant piano bar in a historic old storefront.

SPECTATOR SPORTS

The National Basketball Association's Portland Trail Blazers are an obsession in Portland. Home-court tickets are nearly impossible to find. The Blazers play at the new Rose Garden Arena, at N Williams Ave at Hassalo St; call ☎ 503-231-8000 for tickets.

It's a little easier to get to see the Portland Winter Hawks (☎ 503-238-6366), Portland's Western Hockey League franchise, and the Portland Power women's professional basketball team (☎ 503-249-1130). They also play in the Rose Garden Arena. The Portland Rockies (☎ 503-223-2837), a farm team for the Denver Rockies, play at Civic Stadium, SW 20th Ave and Morrison St.

SHOPPING

Portland's main shopping district extends in a two-block radius from Pioneer Courthouse Square. Department stores Nordstrom, Meier & Frank and Sak's Fifth Avenue are all found here. Pioneer Place, a boutique mall, is found between SW Morrison and Yamhill Sts on 5th Ave. Lloyd Center, just across the Willamette River in Northeast Portland, is a full-service shopping mall just 10 minutes from downtown on MAX.

Art Galleries

Portland has a thriving gallery scene. For a full listing of downtown art galleries, ask for the gallery walking-tour map at the visitors' center, or check out the gallery listings in the *Willamette Week* newspaper.

On the first Thursday of every month, the First Thursday Art Walk brings out Portland's art lovers. Galleries remain open till 8 pm and many serve complimentary hors d'oeuvres. It's a great way to see both art and the arty set.

For a good representation of Northwest artists don't miss the following galleries: Elizabeth Leach Gallery (☎ 503-224-0521), 207 SW Pine St; Quintana Native American Art (☎ 503-223-1729), 501 SW Broadway; Quartersaw Gallery (☎ 503-223-2264), 528 NW 12th; and Pulliam/Deffenbaugh/Nugent Gallery (☎ 503-228-6665), 522 NW 12th Ave, the latter two at the heart of Pearl District's gallery row (see the Northwest map).

Local Products

A good place to check out local crafts is Saturday Market, held on Saturday and Sunday beneath the Burnside Bridge (see the Saturday Market entry in the Downtown section of this chapter). You'll find higher quality and prices at Real Mother Goose (☎ 503-223-9510), 901 SW Yamhill St, a showcase of local artisans.

Made in Oregon stores offer locally made gifts and food products; they feature an excellent selection of Oregon wines as well. Locations near Saturday Market (☎ 503-273-8354), 10 NW 1st, and in the Galleria shopping center (☎ 503-241-3630), SW 10th Ave and Alder St, are convenient to downtown. There's also one in the airport's main terminal, perfect for last-minute gifts.

Camping & Outdoor Gear

Downtown's best outdoor store is Oregon Mountain Community (☎ 503-227-1038), 60 NW Davis St; they also rent equipment, including skis. The warehouse-like REI (☎ 503-283-1300), 1798 Jantzen Beach Center, is north on I-5, just shy of the Columbia River.

GETTING THERE & AWAY
Air

Portland International Airport (PDX) is served by over a dozen airlines, with connections to major US cities. Commuter flights on Horizon Air link Seattle and Portland every half-hour during the day. In addition, United Airlines and Alaska Airlines have frequent jet service linking San Francisco, Portland and Seattle. There's a nonstop flight to Vancouver, BC, every two hours on Air BC. Bargain fares up and down the West Coast are available from Southwest Airlines.

Regular flights from PDX on Horizon Air and United Express serve many smaller Oregon and Washington communities, such as Bend/Redmond, Pendleton, Eugene and Yakima.

Portland is the West Coast hub of Delta Air Lines, with daily flights to Japan, Korea and Hong Kong.

Following are the addresses of major airlines with downtown offices:

Alaska Airlines, 530 SW Madison St
    (☎ 503-224-2547)
American Airlines, 1216 SW 6th Ave
    (☎ 800-433-7300)
Delta Air Lines, 1211 SW 5th Ave
    (☎ 503-242-1919)
Northwest Airlines, 910 SW 2nd Ave
    (☎ 800-225-2525)
United Airlines, 502 SW Madison St
    (☎ 800-241-6522)

Bus

Greyhound buses, with a depot at 550 NW 6th Ave, connect Portland with cities along I-5, the major freeway that traverses the West Coast. There are nine buses a day to Seattle (less than $20 one way) and four to San Francisco. Greyhound serves Vancouver, BC, via Seattle as well as outlying communities of Portland such as Bend and Newport.

Portland is the western terminus of buses traveling along I-84. Twice-daily service links Portland to both Chicago (through Spokane, WA, and Montana) and Denver, CO (through Boise, ID, and Salt Lake City, UT).

For more colorful bus service, try Green Tortoise buses. On Sunday and Thursday, the bus leaves from 616 SW College, near Portland State University, for Eugene and San Francisco. The converted buses are meant to be lounged around in: there are tables, mattresses, music and good conversation. The Green Tortoise to San Francisco takes a break in southern Oregon at an outdoor camp, where riders can sit around a campfire, take a sauna, or swim (in bathing or birthday suits) and eat a meal cooked by staff and volunteers. The one-way fare to or from San Francisco is $49. On Tuesday and Saturday, the bus leaves for Seattle ($19 one way). It's wise to make reservations a few weeks in advance, especially during spring and summer.

Train

Amtrak (☎ 503-241-4290) at Union Station, NW 6th Ave at Irving St, offers service up and down the West Coast, with four trains daily to Seattle and two south to Eugene (both fares are usually around $25 one way) and on to California. East-west trains travel the Columbia River Gorge on their way to and from Chicago via the *Empire Builder*. The Pioneer line to Salt Lake City and Denver no longer operates.

Car

Portland is at the junction of I-84 and I-5, part of the national freeway system. Travelers from the east on I-84 will pass through the magnificent Columbia River Gorge. Travelers arriving from the north or south on I-5 pass through verdant forests and farmland, within sight of the looming volcanic peaks of the Cascades. US 26 stretches from the Oregon coast through Portland, past Mt Hood, and on to central Oregon.

Most major car-rental agencies have outlets both downtown and at the Portland International Airport (PDX):

Avis, 330 SW Washington St, (☎ 503-227-0220)
    PDX (☎ 503-249-4950, 800-831-2847)
Budget Rent-A-Car, 2033 SW 4th Ave,
    (☎ 503-249-6500)
    PDX (☎ 503-249-6500, 800-527-0700)
Dollar Rent-A-Car, 132 NW Davis St,
    (☎ 503-228-3540)
    PDX (☎ 503-249-4792, 800-800-4000)
Hertz, 1009 SW 6th Ave, (☎ 503-249-5727)
    PDX (☎ 503-249-8216, 800-654-3131)

Frequently cheaper are local companies with older-model rentals. Close to Lloyd Center is Bee Rent-A-Car (☎ 503-233-7368), 84 NE Weidler St, and Practical Rent-A-Car (☎ 503-230-1103), 1315 NE Sandy Blvd.

GETTING AROUND
To/From the Airport
PDX is about 15 minutes northeast of downtown, along the Columbia River. Tri-Met's bus No 12 runs between PDX and downtown's 5th Ave bus mall (see the next section); allow 45 minutes for the journey. If you're taking bus No 12 from downtown to PDX, catch it outbound along 6th Ave. Buses depart about every 15 to 20 minutes.

Raz Transport (☎ 503-249-1837), offers bus service between PDX and most major downtown hotels. Depending on the number of hotel stops, the $7 trip can take a half-hour.

The taxi fare and tip to or from the airport and downtown will cost between $20 to $25.

If you're driving, the airport is east of Portland. From downtown, take I-84 east, follow signs to I-205 north and get off at exit 24A.

Bus & Light Rail
Portland's public transport company is called Tri-Met (☎ 503-238-7433). It operates the local commuter bus service as well as a light-rail train system called Metropolitan Area Express (MAX).

Within the downtown core, roughly bounded by I-405, the Willamette River and Hoyt St, all public transportation is free. Fareless Square, as this area is known, was instigated in hopes of inducing downtown patrons to park their cars and use public transport. Outside this area there are three zones in the Tri-Met fare system; tickets for travel within zones 1 and 2, which cover most close destinations (including the zoo, the hostel and Lloyd Center), cost $1.05. Your ticket is your transfer, good for two hours on all Tri-Met transport. Buy your ticket from the driver no change is given.

Most downtown buses travel along 5th and 6th Aves, the 'bus mall.' Lined with outdoor art, these streets are largely off-limits to private vehicles.

The MAX is Portland's successful experiment in mass transit. Linking east Portland suburbs and the Lloyd Center/Convention Center area to downtown, these commuter trains have become a prototype of the city's public transit future. MAX lines to the zoo and on to the West Side suburbs of Beaverton and Hillsboro were due to open in September 1998. Plans call for more MAX lines to be built along the Willamette River between Lake Oswego and Vancouver, WA.

Tickets for MAX are figured according to the same zone map as Tri-Met buses. Bus and light-rail tickets are completely transferable (within the two-hour time constraints). However, tickets for MAX must be bought from ticket machines at MAX stations; there is no conductor or ticket-seller.

To purchase tickets in advance, or for more information, visit the Tri-Met Information Bureau (☎ 503-231-3198) at Pioneer Courthouse Square.

Taxi
There are taxi stands near most major downtown hotels. Contact the following companies for radio-dispatched cabs: Broadway Cab (☎ 503-227-1234), Radio Cab (☎ 503-227-1212) and New Rose City Cab (☎ 503-282-7707).

Bicycle
Buy a *Getting There by Bike* map, available from bike shops and Powell's Travel Store, and see Portland over the handlebars. Rent a bike from Bike Gallery (☎ 503-222-3821), 821 SW 11th Ave or Fat Tire Farm (☎ 503-222-3276), 2714 NW Thurman St.

Around Portland

The Pacific Coast, the Columbia River Gorge and Mt Hood all make good day trips from Portland. A popular loop tour combines a trip up the Gorge as far as Hood River, turning south on Hwy 35 to Mt Hood and returning to Portland via US 26. See the relevant chapters for information about these areas.

SAUVIE ISLAND
The largest island in the Columbia River, Sauvie Island is only 10 miles north of Portland, but in ambiance, it seems much more distant. Here, vegetable gardens, berry fields and orchards stretch for miles. Shop for the Pacific Northwest's bounty at farmers' markets or pick your own produce from the orchards and fields. Much of the north end of the island is contained in the Sauvie Island Wildlife Area, a 20-sq-mile refuge for waterfowl. Ask at the refuge headquarters (2 miles north on Sauvie Island Rd) for a map and bird-watching advice. During summer, the sandy beaches along the east side of the island are popular

with picnickers and sunbathers, and the island's flat, bucolic landscape is immensely popular with cyclists. Parking permits ($5 for a year, available at island businesses) are required if you plan to park at the beaches or wildlife refuge.

WINE COUNTRY
Although grapes are grown in many parts of western Oregon, the focus of Oregon's wine trade is hilly Yamhill County, just south and west of Portland. Here, about 20 minutes from downtown, are prime plantings of pinot noir and chardonnay grapes, the famous Burgundy grape varieties which thrive in cool Oregon. Many vineyards are small, especially by Californian standards, but most are open daily for tasting and on-site sales. The area between Newberg and McMinnville is nominally the center of the wine country, easily reached from Portland on Hwy 99W. See Yamhill County Wine Country in the Willamette Valley chapter for details.

MT ST HELENS (WA)
This Cascade volcano gained worldwide notoriety when it blew its top in 1980. Today, Mt St Helens National Volcanic Monument preserves 171 sq miles of volcano-wracked wilderness. From Portland, a trip to the new visitors' center at Coldwater Ridge (off I-5 at Castle Rock, WA) takes just two hours and affords a glimpse into the mouth of the crater. Entry to the area is $8 per person. See Mt St Helens in Washington's South Cascades chapter.

Oregon Coast

Forest, mountain, beach, ocean and river all meet through a prism of mist and green translucence along the Oregon coast. Rocky headlands rise hundreds of feet above the ocean, dropping away to the pounding waves below. Spires and columns of rock march far out into the surging sea and arch up out of sandy beaches. The remains of ancient lava flows, many of these crags of basalt are now home to vast colonies of sea birds, sea lions and seals.

Rising just to the east of the shoreline is the Coast Range, a young mountain range deeply etched by great rivers and shrouded by a patchwork of deep forests and recent clear-cuts: these are the forests of the spotted owl controversy (see Ecology & Environment in the Facts about the Pacific Northwest chapter). Along the bays of mighty rivers such as the Columbia, the Yaquina, the Rogue and the Umpqua, civilization grew first in Native American villages, whose members fished the bays, traded with inland tribes and hunted the mountain valleys.

The Oregon Dunes, among the largest ocean-fronting sand dunes in the world, drift along the edge of the coast for over 50 miles. From Charleston south to the California border, the beaches are increasingly flanked by high, rocky cliffs and craggy teeth of rock, home to rookeries of puffins, penguin-like murres and wheeling gulls. Sea lions and seals bask on offshore rocks and whales arch out of the water to spout as they migrate to and from Arctic waters.

For generations, families have returned to the same sleepy coastal town for long

Conde McCullough

The strikingly beautiful and massive bridges along US 101 are the work of Conde McCullough, an engineer and lawyer who brought dramatic style to the utilitarian business of bridge building. McCullough worked for the Oregon State Highway Department from 1920 till 1946, a period of unrivaled road and bridge construction.

Although McCullough designed bridges across the state, his most famous and remarkable bridges are along the Oregon coast. Until the 1930s, the coast was ill-served by highways, in part because the coast's many wide estuaries presented problems to contemporary bridge engineering, and partly because steel – the bridge-making ingredient of choice – didn't last very long on the stormy Pacific Coast. In 1936, McCullough was given teams of WPA workers to span the final links of US 101.

In order to span wide rivers and bays, McCullough turned to new engineering and design techniques. From France he borrowed the Freyssinet method, which pioneered the use of pre-stressed concrete arches in bridge building. From the Arts and Crafts movement, he developed a sensitivity for harmony of structures and their natural surroundings. From the art deco movement, he borrowed a severe, neo-Gothic formality. The result was bridges that were able to span the wide gulfs of the Oregon coast in a high-flying, immediately identifiable style; bridges that have almost become metaphors for the coast itself.

McCullough's most famous bridges are across Coos Bay at North Bend, Alsea Bay at Waldport, Yaquina Bay at Newport and Cape Creek Bridge at Devil's Elbow State Park, near Yachats. Once you've seen one, you'll recognize McCullough bridges at many other places throughout the state. The gasp-producing bridge that spans the Crooked River Gorge in central Oregon was also built by McCullough. ∎

holidays. The last decade, however, has brought great changes to the Oregon coast. More than ever before, the coast is a destination for travelers from across the US, with an estimated 3 million travelers visiting the 300-mile coastline annually. Both the quality and quantity of facilities are growing quickly.

Thanks to a farsighted state government in the 1910s, the entire length of the Pacific Coast in Oregon was set aside as public land. This has left most of the coast, especially in the central and southern regions, almost untrammeled by development.

History

Although Lewis and Clark visited the northern coast in 1805-06, and Astoria was founded as a fur-trading fort in 1811, settlement didn't really start until the 1860s, after Native American tribes had been restricted to reservations.

Fishing, logging and agriculture formed the nucleus of the early coast economy, while dairy took hold along the northern coast. In the 1850s gold was discovered in beach sand along the mouths of the large rivers to the south. However, the lodes were never very great and the boom fizzled, but not before little settlements like Port Orford – in 1851 – took hold. The California gold rush and the boomtown of San Francisco demanded a ready supply of lumber and agricultural products, which the young coastal communities of southern Oregon were happy to ship out. The little port town of Bandon became a summer resort for wealthy San Franciscans who made the two-day journey from California by ship.

Transport remained the biggest stumbling block of economic development along the Oregon coast. While steamers and trains provided some transportation, the rugged coast was just too wild a place for a highway, given engineering technology and budgets of the day. US 101, which traverses the Pacific Coast north to south, wasn't completed through Oregon until the 1930s; some isolated sections weren't entirely finished until the 1960s.

In this century, logging has been by far the mainstay of the southern Oregon economy, as trees grow relatively quickly to enormous size in the coastal mountain range that flanks the Pacific. The port city of Coos Bay became the major shipping point for Port Orford cedar, a versatile wood that once grew abundantly in the southern part of Oregon (it's now quite rare, due to overcutting and disease). Coos Bay boomed during WWI and WWII, when the war machine demanded lumber. In the 1940s, Oregon became the largest timber producer in the USA, and Coos Bay became the world's largest timber-shipping port.

The depletion of old-growth forests, federal protection of the forests that remain and the shipping of raw logs overseas for milling has spelled the end of the boom for many lumber-dependent workers and their families. Niche industries, such as lily bulb production, goat and cow dairy farms, wild mushroom hunting and tourism, seek to fill the gulf in local economies left by the decline in logging.

Getting There & Away

The Oregon coast is not well served by public transport. However, it's not just the paucity of public buses (there are no trains and only Astoria and Coos Bay have scheduled air service) that makes travel difficult: it's almost impossible to find out what service there is. Only Newport and Coos Bay have staffed bus stations that answer queries. Other towns simply have stops in grocery store parking lots and at gas stations.

Air Harbor Air has several flights daily from Portland and Seattle to the Astoria Airport on the northern coast. Horizon Air flies five times daily to Coos Bay's North Bend Airport on the southern coast.

Bus Bus travelers will find that bus service is sketchy to nonexistent along the northern Oregon coast. In particular, there is currently no public transport between Cannon Beach and Lincoln City along US 101.

OREGON

The Great Outdoors
While wandering along the pounding surf, beachcombing and gazing out to sea are principal diversions of the coast, there are numerous outdoor activities as well.

Biking The Oregon Coast Bike Route follows busy US 101 along the Oregon coast between Astoria and Brookings. There are some side trips along less congested roads. Most cyclists travel north to south, in the direction of the wind, then take public transportation back to their original destination. Be warned that the cardboard cartons in which buses and airlines require you to pack your bicycle are hard to find toward the end of the tourist season. For a free brochure about the route, contact the Dept of Transportation in Salem (☎ 503-986-4000). A good book describing this and other biking routes along the coast is *Bicycling the Pacific Coast* by Tom Kirkendall.

Charter Fishing Vastly reduced numbers of salmon have changed the charter fishing industry. Charter boats still leave from most ports, but bottom fish (like flounder and ray), tuna, shark, halibut, rockfish and red snapper are now the common catches. Call the Oregon Dept of Fish & Wildlife (☎ 503-229-5403) for information on the season, or contact a charter operation for local details and restrictions.

Most charters will offer several options that range in price from $45 to $60 a trip. An Oregon fishing license is required, which is generally available from most charter operations.

Whale Watching The high capes and headlands of the Oregon coast are good vantage points to watch for gray whales. There are both spring and fall migrations; the spring migration – peaking in March – brings the whales closer to the shore. Favorite whale-watching spots include Cape Sebastian, Cape Blanco, Cape Perpetua, Neahkahnie Mountain and Cape Arago. On weekends at most of these sites, volunteers from local wildlife groups will answer questions and help locate whales. Although whales can occasionally be seen with the naked eye, it's a good idea to have a good pair of binoculars.

Many charter fishing boats also offer whale-watching trips. Excursions last two to three hours and cost around $25.

Clamming & Crabbing Most Oregon beaches are open for gathering shellfish. A state fishing license is not needed, though you must abide by the bag limits stated in the most recent Fish & Wildlife guidelines (available from most public offices on the coast). Otherwise all you need is a shovel and a bucket. Mussels are found in abundant numbers along intertidal rocks. Clams require a bit of excavation along riverbeds and sandy beaches. Razor clams quickly burrow into the sand and demand a fair amount of spading to unearth. Be sure that the shellfish is free of red tide (see the Red Tide section under Health in the Facts for the Visitor chapter).

Dungeness crab live in quiet bays along the coast and are easily caught. Rowing out into the bay and waiting for the crab rings to fill is a relaxing way to snare a fine meal. Many marinas will rent a boat and crab rings, and will clean and boil the crabs for around $35 for a two-hour rental.

Surfing Surfers appear all along the beach, but the best waves are in coves along headlands and capes. Popular spots are near Otter Cove, Sunset Beach and Smugglers Cove. Surf gear can be rented in larger cities along the coast. A board, wetsuit and booties rent for about $35 a day. ■

Greyhound buses traveling between Portland and San Francisco, via Hwys 18 and 101, make stops in Lincoln City, Newport and points south twice daily in each direction. You can purchase tickets either upon boarding, or upon arrival at the next bus depot. Call the bus depot in Newport (☎ 541-265-2253) for the latest schedule information. From Newport there's also bus service to Corvallis in the Willamette Valley.

Northern Oregon Coast

Oregon's northern coast begins at the Columbia River and stretches south to Florence. Oregon's most famous beach resorts – Seaside, Cannon Beach and Lincoln City – are here on long strips of sandy beach. Affable Newport, known since the 1860s for its oysters, is now famed for its aquarium, the largest in the Northwest, and home to Keiko, the orca of *Free Willy*. Astoria is the oldest US settlement west of the Mississippi.

Increasingly, the coast between Newport and Seaside is the domain of tourism. Proximity to Portland and the Willamette Valley means that most coastal towns are now dominated by weekenders. Some coastal restaurants don't even bother opening until the weekend, and prices double at upscale lodgings on Friday night. Galleries and boutiques now grace buildings that once served the needs of sailors and loggers. It's easy to feel appalled – and then a little guilty – that all this development was built for tourists.

US 101 stretches the length of the northern Oregon coast and crosses to Washington State on the Astoria Bridge. Several two-lane highways connect the Willamette Valley to major coastal towns.

Traffic on US 101 can be very heavy in the summer. Intense traffic is also the norm along the arteries that feed Portland crowds to their weekend homes on the coast.

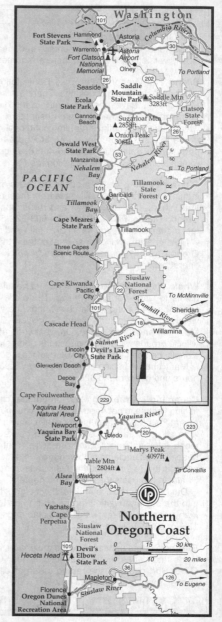

Northern Oregon Coast

ASTORIA
Population 10,100

Astoria sits at the mouth of the 5-mile-wide Columbia River. The 4.1-mile-long **Astoria Bridge** on US 101 is the world's longest continuous truss bridge, crossing the Columbia River to Washington State. The city contains a great deal of history and scruffy charm.

Lewis and Clark and the Corps of Discovery tolerated the winter of 1805-06 at a crude fort along an inlet of Youngs Bay, just south of present-day Astoria. When they returned to St Louis they told all who would listen about the great wealth in pelts in the Pacific Northwest, and within months the first fur-trapping expeditions began to thread their way into the West. John Jacob Astor and his Pacific Fur Trading Company established a small fur-trading fort in the spring of 1811 at the mouth of the Columbia, making this the first US settlement in the West.

Trade and fishing made Astoria a very powerful and wealthy city in the late 19th century. A salmon cannery opened here in 1866, the first of many businesses that would capitalize on the immense runs of salmon in the Columbia River. Other industries, such as sawmills, flour mills, shipping and deep-sea fishing, took hold, and by the turn of the century Astoria was Oregon's second-largest city. In 1900, a full quarter of the population was comprised of Finnish-born settlers, as they – as well as the Swedes and Norwegians – found ample work in the area's forests, sawmills and fishing boats. The city's reputation for affluence and gentility was rivaled only by its reputation for bawdy excess in the bar and brothel district near the harbor.

Magnificent Victorian homes built on the cliffs overlook downtown and the Columbia River. While the local economy has bottomed out over the last 20 years, and the once booming harbor has largely gone derelict, Astoria is beginning to revitalize. Low rents and a sense of history attract a number of artists, writers and restaurateurs.

Orientation
The main downtown district is perched on a relatively narrow slip of land between the river and the steep slopes of the residential area. US 101 enters the city from the southwest along Youngs Bay Bridge, almost instantly to corkscrew up and cross the towering Astoria Bridge.

While the residential area behind downtown contains many lovely homes, the streets can be *very* steep and some are closed to trailers and RVs. It's a good idea to park and walk if you plan to explore this area.

Information
The Astoria Visitors Center (☎ 503-325-6311) is at 111 W Marine Drive, Astoria, OR 97103. The post office is at 748 Commercial St.

Godfather's Books & Espresso Bar (☎ 503-325-8143), 1108 Commercial St, is a nice bookstore, with a selection of books on local travel and history. *North Coast Times Eagle*, a monthly journal of 'art and opinion' has quite a lot to say about coastal issues and also gives a good idea of what's going on in the galleries. Coast Community Radio is heard at 91.9 FM.

Clean Services Coin Laundry (☎ 503-325-2027), 823 W Marine Drive, offers both self-service and drop-off laundry facilities. The Astoria-area hospital is the Columbia Memorial Hospital (☎ 503-325-4321), 2111 Exchange St.

Historic Astoria Homes
Astoria contains some of the most lovingly restored and precipitously poised homes outside of San Francisco. In the 1880s sea captains and other captains of industry built magnificent homes overlooking the Columbia River. Many fell into disrepair after WWII (some distinguished houses still need attention), but the last decade's renewed interest in historic homes has brought these beauties back to life.

The Flavel House (see Other Museums) is the only historic home regularly open for touring; however, many others are now operated as B&Bs. Most historic homes

OREGON

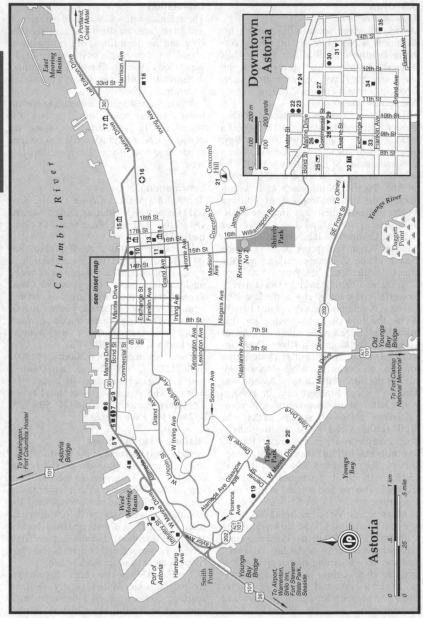

Columbia River

To Portland,
Crest Motel

East
Mooring
Basin

33rd St

Harrison Ave

18

17

16

15

18th St
17th St
16th St

14th St
13
10
11

Marine Drive

Jerome Ave

Irving Ave

Marine Drive

Bond St

Commercial St

6th St

Grand Ave

Astoria
Bridge

To Washington,
Fort Columbia Hostel

8
7
9
6
5

4

3

2

West
Mooring
Basin

Port of
Astoria

Industry St

W Marine Drive

Taylor Ave

Hamburg Ave

Smith Point

Youngs Bay
Bridge

101

26

To Airport,
Warrenton,
Shilo Inn,
Fort Stevens
State Park,
Seaside

ALT
101

202

Florence
Ave

19

20

Tapila Park

Alameda Ave Glasgow
Ave

Denver St

W Marine Drive

Vista Drive

Youngs
Bay

W Irving Ave

W Lincoln St

Grand Ave

Skyline Ave

Kensington Ave
Lexington Ave

Sonora Ave

8th St

Irving Ave

Franklin Ave

Exchange St

14th St

15th St

Madison Ave

Niagara Ave

Klaskanine Ave

5th St
7th St

Olney Ave

W Marine Drive

Coxcomb Dr

James St

16th

Williamsport Rd

Reservoir
No 2

Shively
Park

Coxcomb
Hill
21

SE Front St

SE Front St

To Olney

202

Old
Youngs
Bay
Bridge

ALT
101

To Fort Clatsop
National Memorial

Youngs River

Daggett
Point

see inset map

Astoria

0   .5   1 km
0   .25   .5 mile

see inset map

Downtown Astoria

35

14th St

30

31

24

27

12th St

34

Grand Ave

22
23

Marine Drive

Commercial St

26

28   29

11th St

10th St

9th St

Franklin Ave
Exchange St

33

Duane St

8th St

32

Astor St

Bond St

25

0   100   200 m
0   100   200 yards

have an informational plaque outside, giving basic information about the structure.

A quick walk through the blocks around 8th to 17th Sts and Grand to Exchange Sts will lead you to the Grace Episcopal Church, Astoria's oldest (1885); the Heritage Museum; Foard House, a magnificently ornate Queen Anne home built in 1892, now wildly painted and carefully restored; and the Rosebriar Hotel, built in 1902, and for many years a convent.

A walking tour map and brochure about historic homes is available from the Heritage Museum (see Other Museums, below) for $3.

Columbia River Maritime Museum

Astoria's 150-year-old seafaring heritage is well interpreted and nicely displayed at the Columbia River Maritime Museum (☎ 503-325-2323), 1792 Marine Drive, a modern, 25,000-sq-foot facility.

In the main hall of the museum there are a number of small boats and a periscope from a US Navy submarine from which to watch river traffic on the Columbia. The galleries explore Astoria's maritime past, including the salmon-packing industry, local lighthouses, the evolution of boat design, delicate ivory scrimshaw work and a creepy display on harpoons. Also part of the museum is the Columbia Lightship No 604, a floating lighthouse that was moored for years outside the mouth of the Columbia; the boat is open to visitors. The small bookshop and gift store is quite good and has a number of titles specific to Astoria and its seafaring history.

The museum is open 9:30 am to 5 pm daily. Admission is $5/4/2 adults/seniors/students; children under six are free.

Other Museums

Housed in the former city hall building, the **Heritage Museum**, 1618 Exchange St, contains a commemoration of Astoria's fishing past, as well as an exhibit dedicated to the various ethnic communities that came together to form the city – note the Tong shrine. Another room is dedicated to the Clatsop Indians and the early days of exploration.

Captain George Flavel was one of Astoria's leading citizens during the 1870s and 1880s. He built a highly ornamented mansion, **Flavel House**, 441 8th St, with great views over the harbor (especially from the three-story corner tower) in order to keep an eye on his ships. The house has been restored throughout and has been repainted with its original colors; the grounds have been returned to Victorian-era landscaping.

The interesting **Upper Town Fire Fighters Museum**, 2986 Marine Drive, is a fire hall turned-museum housing a collection of vintage fire-fighting equipment. The museum also displays photos of Astoria's big fire in 1922.

PLACES TO STAY		
1	Bayshore Motor Inn	
2	Red Lion Inn	
4	Dunes Motel of Astoria	
6	Lamplighter Motel	
11	Grandview B&B	
13	Columbia River Inn B&B	
18	Astoria Inn B&B	
33	Clementine's B&B	
34	Franklin St Station B&B	
35	Rosebriar Hotel	

PLACES TO EAT	
5	Cafe Uniontown
24	Columbian Cafe-Fresca Deli

28	Ira's
29	Someplace Else
31	Community Store

OTHER	
3	Tiki Charters
7	Astoria Visitors Center
8	Josephson's Smoke House
9	Bus Depot
10	Hertz
12	Heritage Museum
14	Foard House
15	Columbia River Maritime Museum
16	Columbia Memorial Hospital

17	Upper Town Fire Fighters Museum
19	Clean Services Coin Laundry
20	Senior High School
21	Astoria Column
22	Persona Vintage Clothing
23	Ricciardi Gallery
25	Post Office
26	Eagle's Lodge
27	Godfather's Books & Espresso Bar
30	Liberty Theater
32	Flavel House

Sacagawea, the only woman to accompany
the Lewis and Clark Expedition.

Hours for the museums are 10 am to
5 pm daily, May to September, and 11 am
to 4 pm, October to April. Admission is
$5/2.50 adults/children, which gets you
into all three museums. Contact the Clatsop County Historical Society Museums
(☎ 503-325-2203) for more details.

Astoria Column

Built in 1926, this 125-foot tower rises high
on Coxcomb Hill. The column's exterior was
painted with figures and scenes of the westward sweep of US exploration and settlement. A series of 166 spiraling steps leads
to the top of the column, from which there are
good views over Astoria, the Clatsop Spit
and Youngs Bay. From downtown follow
14th St south (uphill) to Jerome Ave. Turn
east one block and continue up 15th St to the
park entrance on Coxcomb Drive.

Fort Clatsop National Memorial

Reconstructed Fort Clatsop (☎ 503-861-
2471), just 8 miles south of Astoria off US
101, is well worth a stop, especially for
families with children, or anyone with an
interest in the history of the West and the
Lewis and Clark Expedition.

Lewis and Clark, and Charbonneau,
Sacagawea and their son Jean Baptiste
stayed here in the winter of 1805-06 with
the rest of the Corps of Discovery. The
expedition named their small fortification
Fort Clatsop, after the local Native American tribe that had befriended them.
(Throughout the journey, Sacagawea acted
as a liaison between the tribes and the
corps. Many potential conflicts were
averted thanks to the presence of this
young legendary Shoshone woman.) Life
at the fort was pretty rudimentary: food,
salt and high spirits were in short supply,
especially as the camp was infested with
vermin and the winter was excessively wet
(even for Astoria).

The site is now administered by the NPS.
The modest log structure was built according to sketches left by Lewis and Clark.
During summer, costumed docents demonstrate the various pastimes and tasks of the
corps, including candle making and leather
tanning. They also give demonstrations of
frontier skills like flintlock marksmanship
and cedar canoe building.

The visitors' center, 100 yards from the
fort, contains a very good interpretation of
the events and personalities that came
together at Fort Clatsop, including artifacts
from the Clatsop Indians, diary selections
from the corps and a number of slide and
video presentations.

Fort Clatsop is open every day except
Christmas. The visitors' center is open
8 am to 5 pm (to 6 pm June 10 to Labor
Day). Admission is $2 for adults or a maxi-
mum of $4 for the whole family.

Charter Fishing

The Columbia's convergence with the
Pacific is a noted fishing area. Tiki Charters
(☎ 503-325-7818), 352 Industry St, offers
charter trips for bottom fish, sturgeon and

salmon fishing when the seasons open. Tiki also offers river cruises. A 1½-hour tour of the Astoria waterfront costs $15, while an eight-hour cruise of the Columbia River estuary costs $60. All trips depart from the West Mooring Basin, just west of the Astoria Bridge. In nearby Warrenton, contact Charlton Deep Sea Charters (☎ 503-861-2429), 795 Cedar Ave, for sturgeon and bottom-fish trips.

For season information, licenses and tackle, contact the Tackle Time Bait Shop (☎ 503-861-3693), 222 E Galena St.

Special Events
Astoria's biggest celebration is the Scandinavian Festival (☎ 503-325-6311), held the third weekend of June to honor the area's Swedish, Finnish and Norwegian heritage. The festival includes ethnic food booths, dance contests, the crowning of Miss Scandinavia and a parade through downtown. Events take place at the high school, 1001 W Marine Drive.

Places to Stay
Camping The most pleasant campgrounds in the area are out on the Clatsop Spit near Warrenton, just southwest of Astoria. *Kampers West Kampground* (☎ 503-861-1814, 800-880-5267), 1140 NW Warrenton Drive, has tent sites for $16 and RV hookups for $18.50. *KOA Astoria Warrenton Seaside* (☎ 503-861-2606, 800-562-8506), 1100 NW Ridge Rd, is in Hammond, just north of Warrenton. A tent site is $22 per night, hookups are $24, and cabins start at $35.

Hostels The closest hostel is the *Fort Columbia Hostel* (☎ 360-777-8755) across the Astoria Bridge in Chinook, WA (see Chinook in the Southwest Washington chapter for more information).

B&Bs If you've been considering a night in a B&B, Astoria is a good place to do it, as there are some gorgeous homes here.
Astoria Inn B&B (☎ 503-325-8153, 800-718-8153), 3391 Irving Ave, is an 1890s farmhouse in the eastern limits of town. Rooms range from $70 to $85. *Clementine's*

B&B (☎ 503-325-2005, 800-521-6801), 847 Exchange St, is an 1888 Italianate mansion with five guest rooms with prices from $55 to $90.

Franklin St Station B&B (☎ 503-325-4314, 800-448-1098), 1140 Franklin Ave, has seven rooms, each with private bath and some with river views; decks hang off the hill overlooking the town. Rooms range from $63 to $110. *Columbia River Inn B&B* (☎ 503-325-5044, 800-847-2475), 1681 Franklin Ave, is an ornate 1870 home decorated with period furnishings; there's a garden in the back. The four guest rooms each have a private bathroom and cost $75 to $125.

Grandview B&B (☎ 503-325-5555, 800-488-3250), 1574 Grand Ave, sits on a double lot, with stunning views of the river. The six rooms and suites range from $39 to $92. *Rosebriar Hotel* (☎ 503-325-7427, 800-487-0224), 636 14th St, was originally built as a lodging in 1902 and later became a convent. This lovely B&B sits high above the street, with wide porches, a brick patio and nicely landscaped grounds; rooms are $49 to $119.

Hotels Most hotels are right along US 30 and can be noisy. Hotels with rates ranging from $45 to $75 include *Lamplighter Motel* (☎ 503-325-4051), 131 W Marine Drive; *Dunes Motel of Astoria* (☎ 503-325-7111, 800-441-3319), 288 W Marine Drive; and the *Bayshore Motor Inn* (☎ 503-325-2205, 800-621-0641), 555 Hamburg Ave.

The *Crest Motel* (☎ 503-325-3141, 800-421-3141), 5366 Leif Ericson Drive, is on the eastern edge of Astoria, on a small, wooded and grassy hill overlooking the river. Rates begin at $52/62; add $20 for view rooms.

Red Lion Inn (☎ 503-325-7373, 800-547-8010), 400 Industry St, has rooms with balconies and views over the river and marina. Prices range from $99 to $109. The *Shilo Inn* (☎ 503-861-2181, 800-222-2244), across the Youngs Bay Bridge at 1609 E Harbor Drive in Warrenton, has a pool and fitness center and offers suite-style rooms with microwaves and refrigerators. Rooms begin at $89/95.

OREGON

Places to Eat
Downtown has its share of pleasant, old-fashioned diners and cafes, so you can luxuriate in food nostalgia. Astoria also has a number of more up-to-date eateries with great food and an informal atmosphere.

Ira's (☎ 503-338-6192), 915 Commercial St, is an intimate restaurant with excellent international fare, with an emphasis on fresh local fish and meats. Lamb osso buco, jerked chicken and fresh oysters are some of the entrées ($13 to $18).

Someplace Else (☎ 503-325-3500), 965 Commercial St, is a tiny Italian-style cafe with red checkerboard tablecloths and a busy, informal atmosphere. Pasta dishes (most under $8) are the specialty; meat and chicken entrées are under $10.

Columbian Cafe-Fresca Deli (☎ 503-325-2233), 1114 Marine Drive, offers a selection of fish each night, chosen daily from local fishing boats, and served with fresh local vegetables. Prices range from $10 to $15. Don't let the down-on-its-luck facade of this family-owned cafe put you off: the food is great.

Cafe Uniontown (☎ 503-325-8708), 218 W Marine Drive, was established in 1934 in the old fish-processing district and was frequented by Scandinavian fishers and longshoremen. The bar and restaurant is now a local favorite for its bountiful fish and meat entrées. Full dinners range from $11 to $17.

The *Community Store* (☎ 503-325-0027), 1389 Duane St, is a good natural-foods store and organic grocery. It's also one of the hippie gathering places of Astoria.

Entertainment
Theater & Cinema *Shanghaied in Astoria*, a spoofy musical comedy about the bad old days of Astoria is a production put on by the *Astor Street Opry Company Theatre* (☎ 503-325-6104) and performed Thursday to Saturday at the Eagles Lodge, 894 Commercial St. Tickets range from $5 to $12. It's actually kind of fun.

The old *Liberty Theater* (☎ 503-325-4191), 1203 Commercial St, shows first-run movies.

Live Music For a bit of nightlife, head to the bar at *Cafe Uniontown* (☎ 503-325-8708), 218 W Marine Drive, where there's live acoustic music Thursday, Friday and Saturday nights.

Shopping
The last of many canneries and smokehouses that once thrived here, Josephson's Smoke House (☎ 503-325-2190), at 106 Marine Drive, produces a wide range of smoked fish and shellfish. Gift packs and clam chowder are also available.

Astoria has been attracting artists for a number of years and, now that storefront rent in the downtown area is cheap, suddenly Astoria is filled with quite a number of interesting galleries and antique stores. A complete list of local galleries appears in the *Daily Astorian Vacation Guide*, available from the visitors' center. Otherwise start looking at Ricciardi Gallery (☎ 503-325-5450), 108 10th St, a combination coffee shop and gallery. Another interesting shop is Persona Vintage Clothing (☎ 503-325-3837), 100 10th St, a great second-hand clothing store.

Getting There & Around
The Astoria Airport is on Flightline Drive, off US 101 near Fort Clatsop, west of Astoria. Harbor Air provides flights to/from Portland and Seattle.

The Astoria bus depot (☎ 503-325-1870) is at 95 W Marine Drive. The fare on Pierce Pacific Stages between Portland and Astoria is $20. Sunset Empire Transit (☎ 503-325-0563) buses provide service to Warrenton (as close to Fort Stevens as public transport gets), Seaside and Cannon Beach.

Pacific Transit (☎ 360-642-9418) out of Long Beach, WA, offers bus service across the Astoria Bridge to communities on the Long Beach Peninsula.

There is a Hertz car-rental agency (☎ 503-325-7700) at 1492 Duane St. If you need a cab, call Roadrunner Transportation (☎ 503-325-3131).

OREGON

FORT STEVENS STATE PARK

Located on the Clatsop Spit, the long neck of sand that stretches along the Columbia River out to its final debouchment into the Pacific Ocean, Fort Stevens State Park (☎ 503-861-1671) commemorates the historic military and strategic garrisons here and offers near-endless beach access and camping facilities. A number of roads wind through the 6-sq-mile park – stop at the campground office or the museum and ask for a map.

There is a $3 day-use fee from mid-May to the end of September. To reach Fort Stevens State Park from Astoria, cross the Youngs Bay Bridge on US 101 and turn toward Warrenton and Hammond on Fort Stevens Hwy. The park is 10 miles west of Astoria.

Fort Stevens Military Museum Area

The Military Museum (☎ 503-861-2000) explains the history and lore of the fort; the displays capture especially well the mood of the nation and the Astoria area during WWII. A free trail guide available from the museum points out the areas of historic interest, including reconstructed Civil War earthworks, complete with moat. Over Labor Day weekend, re-enactments of Civil War battles take place using period weapons.

Hardly anything except concrete foundations remain of the extensive barracks, command stations, hospital and other military buildings, but by far the most interesting remnants are the concrete batteries, which are grim, warren-like garrisons dug into sand dunes.

Between Memorial Day and Labor Day, volunteers give tours of the garrison; the schedule changes often so call for tour times and charges (☎ 503-861-1671). All tours leave from the Military Museum.

The museum's hours are slowly cut back as winter approaches. Summer hours are 10 am to 6 pm daily, June to September; winter hours are 10 am to 4 pm Wednesday to Sunday, November to April. Call for other times. Admission is by donation.

Peter Iredale Shipwreck

Crossing the Columbia bar was once a very dangerous enterprise and over 2000 ships have sunk or wrecked while attempting to enter the Columbia River, earning the area the name 'Graveyard of the Pacific.' On the sands of Fort Stevens is the rotting hull of one such ship, the *Peter Iredale*.

In 1906, the British four-masted freight ship sailed from Australia to Astoria to pick up a load of wheat. As the ship approached the Columbia bar, it encountered a dense fog and the crew lost their bearings. A strong wind kicked up and the ship ran aground on the Clatsop Spit. No lives were lost in the accident, but the ship was so battered it was declared a total loss.

To reach the shipwreck, follow signs for the Fort Stevens Campground area; drive past the campground entrance about 1 mile, to the beach access. The ship is just there, like the skeleton of a whale on the beach.

Biking

Bicycles are a popular way of getting around the park, and the park's network of trails features a 2-mile bike path along the beach. Maps are available at the entrance booths or the Military Museum.

Places to Stay

With 400 campsites, *Fort Stevens State Park* (☎ 503-861-1671) is the largest campground in the state parks' system. Facilities include showers, hiking and biking trails and wheelchair-accessible restrooms. Near the campground is a small freshwater lake with a boat launch and swimming area. Access to ocean beaches is less than a mile away. Fees are $16 for tent campers and $18 for full hookups.

Just outside the boundaries of the state park is the lovely *Officer's Inn B&B* (☎ 503-861-0884, 800-377-2524), 540 Russell Place, with eight guest rooms, each with private bath, for $75 to $95. This 8000-sq-foot building is truly spectacular – officers had it pretty nice in 1906. From the B&B, it is an easy walk to the Military Museum and tours.

OREGON

Mines & Submarines

Fort Stevens was established at the height of the Civil War in 1863 by orders of President Abraham Lincoln. US military leaders feared a widening of the conflict to the western states and territories that were officially Unionist. Fort Stevens, however, did not see action during the Civil War.

The Columbia River's increasing strategic importance as a trade and transportation route led to a substantial upgrading of Fort Stevens' armaments in the early 1900s. At the height of WWII, 2500 soldiers were stationed here. Guns were ready for assault from the Japanese Navy and much of the Columbia's mouth was planted with mines.

On the night of June 21, 1942, a Japanese submarine approached the mouth of the Columbia, following local fishing vessels up the channel in order to elude mines. The submarine fired 17 shells around Fort Stevens but did no damage, and no firepower was returned, as the submarine was out of range of the fort's guns. Fort Stevens is the only military installation in the continental USA to be fired on by a foreign power since the War of 1812.

After WWII the fort was demilitarized, and the facility was used by the Coast Guard and military reserves. In 1976 the fort was acquired by the state and turned into a state park. ∎

SEASIDE
Population 5860

Subtlety is not among the allures of Seaside, one of the largest of Oregon's oceanfront resort towns. On summer weekends, the town's central precinct – dominated by bumper-car tracks, fish-and-chip shops, video-game arcades and gift stores – is completely thronged with tourists. Bicycles, so-called 'fun-cycles' and 'surreys' largely have the run of Seaside's boardwalk, called 'the prom.' Pedestrians simply serve as the obstacles along the course. The miles of sandy beach are quite pleasant, largely because most visitors are off buying things.

Summer holidays in Seaside are a family tradition. At its best, Seaside seems old-fashioned and venerable, but it can also seem garish and crowded. Generally, kids will like it here, while adults may want to seek out more calming surroundings. Quiet Gearhart (population 1045) across the Necanicum River is an alternative (see Getting There & Around).

Orientation & Information

Seaside is 76 miles northwest of Portland on US 26.

The old town center is several blocks from the beach along Holladay Drive. Broadway, the main tourist strip, intersects Holladay Drive and leads out to the beach and the Turnaround (the equivalent of ground zero in Seaside), where a statue of Lewis and Clark overlooks the Pacific. The Prom is a 2-mile-long cement boardwalk stretching along the beach.

The Seaside Visitors Bureau (☎ 503-738-6391, 800-444-6740) is located at 7 N Roosevelt Drive, Seaside, OR 97138.

Golf

Gearhart Golf Links (☎ 503-738-5248), just north of Gearhart on N Marion St, was established in 1892, making it the second-oldest in western North America. The 18-hole course is built in the British 'links' fashion. A newer course in Gearhart is The Highlands (☎ 503-738-0959), off Del Rey Beach Rd. This nine-hole course was originally designed as an 18-hole field until the second nine holes were discovered to be prime habitat for an endangered butterfly.

The Seaside Golf Course (☎ 503-738-5261), 451 Ave U, in Seaside, is a nine-hole course that's popular with tourists and novice players.

Surfing

To rent surfing gear and to get advice on where to hit the waves, go to Cleanline Surf Company (☎ 503-738-7888), at 710 1st St. They also rent in-line skates and boogie boards.

Special Events

Avoid Seaside when it's convulsed with one of its festivals. Rooms are impossible to find and you'll spend hours just looking for a place to park. The Miss Oregon Contest is held here every July, usually the weekend after the Fourth of July. The Hood to Coast Relay Marathon, a team endurance race that begins on Mt Hood and follows US 26 all the way to Seaside, not only jams the main road between Portland and Seaside with runners on a busy summer weekend, it also packs out Seaside, where a huge beach party is thrown for the runners. The relay is usually held the third weekend in August. The Seaside Beach Volleyball Tournament is held on the beach the weekend before Labor Day. Call the visitors' center for more information.

Places to Stay

Here's one of those places where room prices fluctuate wildly. The rates below are meant as a median price. If you plan to be in Seaside on a summer weekend, reserve a room well in advance, especially if you want rooms with a view or rooms close to the beachfront.

Camping Most campgrounds at Seaside are near US 101. *Circle Creek Campground* (☎ 503-738-6070), 1 mile south of town, offers both tent and RV sites in a grassy meadow alongside a river. Tent sites are $16 a night, $21 for full hookups. Facilities include showers and a laundry. *Bud's Campground & Grocery* (☎ 503-738-6855), 4410 US 101, is across from the turnoff for Gearhart and offers showers, laundry, a store and gas station. Tent sites at Bud's will cost you $12 per night, full hookups will cost $17.

For less noisy campsites, head north to the *Fort Stevens State Park*, or drive inland to *Saddle Mountain State Park*.

Hostels The *Seaside International Hostel* (☎ 503-738-7911, 800-909-4776), 930N Holladay Drive, offers both private rooms and dorms ($13/16 for members/non-members).

B&Bs *Gilbert House B&B* (☎ 503-738-9770, 800-410-9770), 341 Beach Drive, is a large, classic beach house just one block from the beach and downtown. The 10 guest rooms all have private baths and range from $89 to $105. *Beachwood B&B* (☎ 503-738-9585), 671 Beach Drive, is a lovely, 1900 Cape Cod-style home on a double lot with a beautifully landscaped yard complete with hammock. The three guest rooms each have a private bathroom, and one has a fireplace and Jacuzzi. Rates are $65 to $115.

Hotels – budget The *Mariner Motel* (☎ 503-738-3690), 429 S Holladay Drive, is an older motel near the old downtown center; it's a 10-minute walk from the beach. Singles/doubles begin at $45/56. The *Coast River Inn* (☎ 503-738-8474, 800 479-5191), 800 S Holladay Drive, is five blocks from the beach and has well maintained rooms with kitchenettes for $64 to $82. Only a block from the beach, the aging *City Center Motel* (☎ 503-738-6377), 250 1st Ave, is nothing fancy, but it has location. Rooms are $63/74 (add $10 if it is the weekend).

Hotels – middle The *Tides Condominiums* (☎ 503-738-6317, 800-548-2846), 2316 Beach Drive, away from the frenzy of downtown, is one of the best deals in Seaside. Ocean-view studio rooms can start as low as $63, though prices between $80 and $90 are more common.

The *Sundowner Motor Inn* (☎ 503-738-8301, 800-645-8678), 125 Oceanway, one block off the beach, has rooms for $59 to $69. The *Comfort Inn Boardwalk* (☎ 503-738-3011, 800-228-5150), 545 Broadway, sits downtown by the river and has rooms for $99/109.

Hotels – top end The *Edgewater Inn* (☎ 503-738-4142, 800-822-3170), 341 S Prom, offers two different lodging options close to the beach. Newer rooms fronting the Pacific begin at $129 while rooms in an older wing begin at $99. At the six-floor *Seaside Beach Club* (☎ 503-738-7113, 888-

733-7113), 561 S Prom, condo-style rooms start at $160.

The attractive *Hi-Tide Motel* (☎ 503-738-8414, 800-621-9876), 30 Ave G, is right on the beach with lots of views and amenities. Rooms range from $85 to $115. *Inn at the Shore* (☎ 503-738-3113, 800-713-9914), 40 Ave U, has spacious suites with fireplaces, balconies and great views. Rooms range from $109 to $169 and two-bedroom suites start at $239. The *Shilo Inn* (☎ 503-738-9571, 800-222-2244), 30 N Prom, sits right at the Turnaround and offers a great restaurant, room service, an indoor pool, fireplaces, a spa, exercise facilities and meeting rooms. It is one of the nicest lodgings on the northern coast. Rooms range from $109 to $185.

Resorts The *Gearhart-by-the-Sea Resort* (☎ 503-738-8331, 800-547-0115), 1157 N Marin Ave, offers condominium rooms overlooking the ocean and easy access to a great restaurant and Gearhart Golf Links. One-bedroom apartments start at $119, two-bedroom units start at $150.

Vacation Home Rentals Pacific Northwest Properties (☎ 503-738-2600, 800-203-1681), 1905B Spruce St, rents private homes.

Places to Eat
There are few hidden secrets to dining in Seaside. The following are a step above the usual chowder emporiums.

The old-fashioned *Harrison Bakery* (☎ 503-738-5331), 608 Broadway, offers coffee and fresh baked goods. At *Little New Yorker on Broadway* (☎ 503-738-5992), 604 Broadway, start the day with a bagel, or try the house specialty, panuzzi (a beef sausage sandwich), for $4.25. The whole-grain bread here is the best in Seaside.

At *Pudgy's* (☎ 503-738-8330), 227 Broadway, there's a good selection of fresh fish and steak dishes in the $13 range; the atmosphere is quiet and pleasant. *Vista Sea Cafe* (☎ 503-738-8108), 150 Broadway, is a lively restaurant with sandwiches, gourmet pizzas and microbrewed beers.

For cuisine, the *Shilo Inn Restaurant* (☎ 503-738-8481), 30 N Prom, offers up both innovative and traditional seafood and meat dishes, from $15 to $20. There's also an extensive regional wine list.

The *Pacific Way Bakery & Cafe* (☎ 503-738-0245), 601 Pacific Way in Gearhart, is in a charming old storefront with a cozy back garden. Omelets, waffles and fresh baked breads have people lined up out the door.

Getting There & Around
Pierce Pacific Stages (☎ 503-717-1651) runs one bus daily ($20 one way) between Portland and Seaside, and Sunset Transit (☎ 503-325-0563) provides service with Astoria and Cannon Beach; there are eight buses daily, and the fare is $2.25 from Seaside to Astoria.

To reach Gearhart from Seaside take US 101 (its called Roosevelt Drive in town) north and cross the Necanicum River. In half a mile, turn west on Pacific Way (it's the first blinking light).

Holladay Car Rental (☎ 503-738-6596), is at 601 S Roosevelt Drive. Roadrunner Transportation (☎ 503-738-3131) is Seaside's cab company.

SADDLE MOUNTAIN STATE PARK
Thirteen miles east of Seaside on US 26, this woodsy state park centers around Saddle Mountain (3283 feet), the highest peak in northwest Oregon.

The barren monolith of stone that juts up out of the dense forest was formed underwater when molten rock rose up through soft sedimentary deposits and hit seawater. The magma cooled rapidly, creating the curious formations, called pillow basalt, that hikers encounter at the top of the mountain. Later, as North America rammed into the old Pacific sea floor, the formation containing Saddle Mountain was hoisted high above sea level, and erosion eventually wore away the softer sedimentary rock, leaving this gray volcanic plug exposed.

During the last Ice Age, Saddle Mountain remained unglaciered and became a refuge for alpine plants. Today, these plants still survive on the flanks of the mountain.

There's a hiking trail that leads from the campground area up through wildflower meadows to the top of Saddle Mountain. Views from the top are pretty spectacular, but the trail is steep and grueling. Once on top, the trail is quite exposed as it crosses the mountain's rocky face. Storms can blow in quickly from the ocean, so be prepared for changeable weather. If you want to hike to the botanical area, follow the trail up about a mile. From the campground, it's about 3 miles to the top of Saddle Mountain. Saddle Mountain State Park offers 10 campsites for $14 each for tent campers only. There are flush toilets and drinking water.

To reach Saddle Mountain State Park, follow US 26 to Necanicum Junction, 13 miles east of Seaside. Half a mile toward Portland, a sign indicates the 7-mile paved road that winds through clear-cuts and young forests on its way to the park.

CANNON BEACH
Population 1270

Miles of sandy beaches, broken by immense basalt promontories and rocky tide pools, front Cannon Beach. Directly behind, the Coast Range rises in steep parapets.

Cannon Beach is without a doubt one of the most popular beach towns of northern Oregon and, at the right time, it can be very charming. Unlike Seaside's Coney Island-like atmosphere, Cannon Beach is artsy and a little smug. It wasn't until the 1970s that Cannon Beach became a real focus for vacationers, a fact that partially explains why it isn't marred by unsightly developments.

However, this high-toned attitude has its downside. The city is so accustomed to upscale visitors that the city council, in a case that went to the Oregon Court of Appeals, attempted to block the building of a federally funded low-cost housing development (many of the day workers are currently shipped in on special buses from Hillsboro, which is near Portland). Apparently, Cannon Beach is meant to be reserved for the wealthy.

Some of the coast's premier hotels and restaurants are here, along with interesting

shops and galleries. The small downtown area is especially delightful. The area around Hemlock and 2nd Sts is filled with little alleys winding around a maze of boutiques and cafes. In summer the streets are ablaze with flowers.

Prices of accommodations shoot through the roof in summer. And without long-standing reservations, you can forget about getting into the trendy restaurant that may well have been the reason for a spontaneous trip to Cannon Beach in the first place. Just getting around the streets can be problematic. On a sunny Saturday, you will spend the better part of an hour just finding a place to park. Thankfully, most people who visit Cannon Beach come to poke around the shops, leaving lots of space down by the truly lovely beaches.

Orientation & Information
Cannon Beach, 78 miles northwest of Portland, is on a short loop road off US 101, 9 miles south of Seaside.

The Cannon Beach Chamber of Commerce & Information Center (☎ 503-436-2623), 2nd St, Cannon Beach, OR 97110, has a lodging map that gives prices of all accommodations in the area. The *Cannon Beach Magazine*, a list of local businesses and activities, is also helpful.

Beaches
The beaches at Cannon Beach are some of the most beautiful in Oregon, with **Haystack Rock** and other outcroppings rising out of the surf. Tide pools around the base of Haystack Rock are great for observing intertidal creatures as well as for watching sea birds. There's easy access to the beach at the end of Harrison St downtown, or at the end of Gower St, a mile south.

A third beach access is at Tolovana Beach Wayside, about 3 miles south of Cannon Beach along Hemlock Ave. Other beach points are accessible at Hug Point State Park, 5 miles south on US 101.

Galleries
White Bird Gallery (☎ 503-436-2681), 251 N Hemlock St, did a lot to establish the

town's reputation as a serious artists' community. In this warren-like building, two or three artists are featured at one time. The gallery also has interesting pottery and crafts.

Another noteworthy gallery is North by Northwest (☎ 503-436-0741), 239 N Hemlock St, which specializes in glass art and ceramics. Valley Bronze (☎ 503-436-2118), 186 N Hemlock St, is a showroom for the noted foundry in Joseph (see Joseph in the Northeastern Oregon chapter), where Western bronze sculptures are cast.

Ecola State Park
Just north of Cannon Beach is Ecola State Park, with picnic areas, short walks to dramatic beach vistas and longer hikes to a remote headland overlooking a lighthouse island.

From the parking lot a short, paved trail leads along a brush-lined path to views of Cannon Beach's 7-mile long sandy shore, sharply punctuated with stone monoliths, all hunkered beneath the Coast Range, which edges close to the coast. This is one of the most photographed vistas in the state.

Beneath the headland are picnic tables; trails lead from the paved path both down to the beach and to **Indian Beach**, 1½ miles north of the viewpoint. At Indian Beach, rocky cliffs hedge round a secluded

sandy cove, a favorite with surfers and anyone else wanting to escape the hordes at Cannon Beach. In summer, there is a road from the main Ecola State Park parking lot to the Indian Beach Picnic Area.

Longer hiking trails lead to **Tillamook Head**, looming 1200 feet above the crashing Pacific. This trail, which is the same as the one traversed by the Corps of Discovery, affords tremendous vistas of a series of offshore islands, which are now protected as wildlife refuges. **Tillamook Lighthouse** sits out to sea on a 100-foot-high sea stack. Now inactive, the lighthouse is used as a columbarium, or resting place for cremation ashes. The 7-mile trail ends at the end of Sunset Blvd in Seaside.

In summer, a $3 day-use fee per vehicle is collected.

Haystack Program
in the Arts & Sciences
Portland State University (PSU) sponsors a six-week series of seminars each summer at Cannon Beach. Most of the courses offered are either writers' workshops or seminars devoted to music or the visual arts. In recent years, however, classes that explore the ecology of the Oregon coast have been added. The quality of the classes is usually quite high; nationally recognized artists and writers serve as faculty.

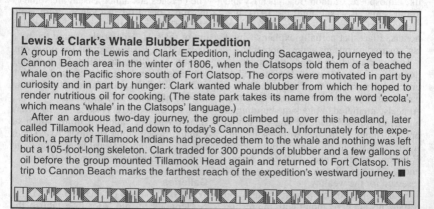

Lewis & Clark's Whale Blubber Expedition
A group from the Lewis and Clark Expedition, including Sacagawea, journeyed to the Cannon Beach area in the winter of 1806, when the Clatsops told them of a beached whale on the Pacific shore south of Fort Clatsop. The corps were motivated in part by curiosity and in part by hunger: Clark wanted whale blubber from which he hoped to render nutritious oil for cooking. (The state park takes its name from the word 'ecola', which means 'whale' in the Clatsops' language.)

After an arduous two-day journey, the group climbed up over this headland, later called Tillamook Head, and down to today's Cannon Beach. Unfortunately for the expedition, a party of Tillamook Indians had preceded them to the whale and nothing was left but a 105-foot-long skeleton. Clark traded for 300 pounds of blubber and a few gallons of oil before the group mounted Tillamook Head again and returned to Fort Clatsop. This trip to Cannon Beach marks the farthest reach of the expedition's westward journey. ■

The seminars may be taken for college credit through PSU. Courses vary in length from a weekend to a five-day week and cost between $155 and $375. Although PSU does not provide housing, it does have a list of both public and private lodgings available to students. Contact Portland State University, Extended Studies (☎ 503-725-4027, 800-547-8887 ext 4027), PO Box 1491, Portland, OR 97207.

Sandcastle Day

Cannon Beach's largest festival – among the most famous on the entire coast – is Sandcastle Day, held on a Saturday in June. The date changes due to the tides; call the visitors' center (☎ 503-436-2623) for exact dates. It's great fun and the resulting sculptures are usually very impressive. Teams compete for the most original and well-executed sand sculpture, many of which go far beyond standard castles. Each team is limited to eight members and has a 21-sq-foot patch of sand as raw material; four hours is the time limit for construction.

Be warned that Cannon Beach is usually booked up on this weekend, so call well in advance. Parking and general mobility in the town is also much worse than usual.

Places to Stay

Cannon Beach is not a cheap place to stay. The older motels that anywhere else would be rundown and cheap are instead quaint and expensive here. As elsewhere along the northern coast, midweek, off-season rates are lower. Some of the mid-range accommodations also have rooms without a view at a much cheaper rate.

Camping The *RV Resort at Cannon Beach* (☎ 503-436-2231, 800-847-2231), 345 Elk Creek Rd at US 101, has an indoor pool and laundry facilities. Sites range between $29 and $35; there are no tent facilities. *Sea Ranch RV Park* (☎ 503-436-2815) across from the entrance to Ecola State Park, has full hookups for $20, and tent sites for $18.

Hotels – bottom end The older *McBee Motel* (☎ 503-436-2569), 888 S Hemlock St, is kind of charming; some rooms have kitchens and fireplaces; rooms are $69. *Hidden Villa* (☎ 503-436-2237), 188 E Van Buren St, a few blocks from the beach, charges $85 for a single or double.

Hotels – middle The original *Cannon Beach Hotel* (☎ 503-436-1392), 1116 S Hemlock St, was once a boarding house for loggers. Now thoroughly updated, rooms are $89. Rates are good at *Major Motel* (☎ 503-436-2241), 2863 Pacific St, considering that many rooms face the ocean. Most rooms have kitchens and cost $85 to $119.

Blue Gull Inn Motel (☎ 503-436-2714, 800-507-2714), 487 S Hemlock St, has cabins, studios and houses, most a block away from the beach, for $45 to $105. Likewise, the *Sand Trap Inn* (☎ 503-436-0247, 800-400-4106), 539 S Hemlock St, controls a number of houses and cabins, ranging from $55 to $120. *Quiet Cannon Lodgings* (☎ 503-436-2415), 732 N Spruce St, rents a number of homey cabins close to the beach at the north end of Cannon Beach, off bustling Hemlock St. Rooms range from $85 to $95. *Haystack Resort Inn* (☎ 503-436-1577, 800-499-2220), 3339 S Hemlock St, offers ocean-view rooms with fireplaces and kitchens for $89 to $129. There's also an indoor pool.

Close to downtown, *The Waves Oceanfront Motel* (☎ 503-436-2205, 800-822-2468), 188 W 2nd St, has rooms in several nearby homes in addition to the motel. Rates in the motel begin at $79; many rooms have kitchens, some have fireplaces. *Webb's Scenic Surf* (☎ 503-436-2706, 800-374-9322), on N Larch St between 2nd and 3rd Sts, also close to downtown, offers oceanfront rooms with kitchens from $109 to $145.

The *Tolovana Inn* (☎ 503-436-2211, 800-333-8890), 3400 S Hemlock St, near Tolovana Beach State Wayside, is a large condo complex. The accommodations in the back (no ocean view) are usually reasonably priced, considering that all rooms have kitchens and access to an indoor pool and recreation room; there's also great beach access. Prices for rooms range from $68 to $239.

Hotels – top end One of the newest and certainly one of the nicest lodgings at Cannon Beach is the *Stephanie Inn* (☎ 503-436-2221, 800-633-3466), 2740 Pacific St, an exclusively adult resort operated as a very upscale B&B. Gabled and turreted in a kind of Queen Anne-revival style, this 'country inn' sparkles with leaded glass and chandeliers. Rooms have terraces and fireplaces. Mountain-view rooms start at $119, ocean-view rooms at $229. Breakfast and an afternoon wine gathering are included in the price.

Both the following large oceanfront motel complexes offer the usual luxuries of fireplaces, kitchens, pools, etc. The *Best Western Surfsand Resort* (☎ 503-436-2274, 800-547-6100), at Oceanfront and Gower Sts, has rooms from $159 to $259. *Hallmark Resort* (☎ 503-436-1566, 800-345-5676), 1400 S Hemlock St, fronts onto Haystack Rock; rates are $119 to $165.

Vacation Home Rentals Cannon Beach Property Management (☎ 503-436-2021), PO Box 231, Cannon Beach, OR 97110, has rental homes in Cannon Beach.

Places to Eat
Bear in mind that Cannon Beach is a week-enders' kind of place. While hotels may be cheaper on weekdays, almost all of Cannon Beach's better places to eat are closed Monday and Tuesday.

Budget *Midtown Cafe* (☎ 503-436-1016), 1235 S Hemlock St, has pastries fresh from the oven, as well as omelets and frittatas, all made from organic ingredients. The Midtown is also one of the few places along the coast where you can find bagels and lox. Another great breakfast and lunch place is *Lazy Susan Cafe* (☎ 503-436-2816), 126 N Hemlock St. At *Pizza a Fetta* (☎ 503-436-0333), 231 N Hemlock

St, in the courtyards, pizza is served by the slice.

Middle *Doogers* (☎ 503-436-2225), 1371 S Hemlock St, has good food and is one of the few establishments that's open on Monday and Tuesday. *Pullucci's Italian Restaurant* (☎ 503-436-1279), 988 S Hemlock St, serves well-prepared pasta dishes that don't cost a bundle. *JP's Restaurant* (☎ 503-436-0908), 1116 S Hemlock St, in the Cannon Beach Hotel, serves a good selection of dishes at fair prices in a bistro atmosphere.

Top End For fine dining, two restaurants stand out. *The Bistro Restaurant & Bar* (☎ 503-436-2661) is a tiny establishment in the courtyard that serves very good seafood dishes prepared from locally caught fish and shellfish, as well as imaginative chicken and beef dishes. Entrées are in the $14 to $19 range. *Cafe de la Mer* (☎ 503-436-1179), 1287 S Hemlock St, is one of the best-loved restaurants on the Oregon coast and serves some splendid seafood dishes. Quality doesn't come cheap – dinners are mostly in the $20 to $25 range.

Entertainment
The community *Coaster Theater* (☎ 503-436-1242), 108 N Hemlock St, puts on drama and musical comedies, chamber music concerts and events associated with the Haystack Program in the Arts.

Getting There & Around
Cannon Beach, for all its popularity, is not well serviced by public transportation. There are two buses a day from Seaside on Sunset Transit (☎ 503-325-0563); they pick up passengers across from the information center on 2nd St and at the RV Resort at Cannon Beach (345 Elk Creek Rd at US 101). You can also flag them down along the route.

A wheelchair-accessible shuttle runs the length of Cannon Beach, from Les Shirley Park in the north to Maher and Hemlock Sts in the south. The bus runs every half-hour from 10 am to 6 pm; a donation is requested.

OSWALD WEST STATE PARK

Nine miles south of Cannon Beach on US 101, this beautiful preserve of beach, mountain, rocky headland and coastal rain forest is named after Governor Oswald West, who championed the state's milestone beach-access bill, putting all oceanfront land into public ownership. A tent-only campground, a lovely beach popular with surfers and miles of hiking trails in lush old-growth forests make this state park a real treasure.

Short Sands Beach is an isolated little beach where dense forests press down to the edge of the beach and two creeks run together in the tide line. Two major headlands, Neahkahnie Mountain and Cape Falcon, reach far out into the Pacific, protecting a small bay, called **Smugglers Cove**. Fishing and leisure boats frequently anchor offshore, and the rocky prominences along Cape Falcon are good places to watch for sea birds. Smugglers Cove is one of the north coast's most popular places to surf.

To reach the beach requires about a quarter-mile hike. Be sure to follow the signs pointing to the beach trail, as the trail from the old picnic area has largely washed away.

Hiking

Two excellent hikes begin from the campground. The easiest leads 2 miles out to **Cape Falcon**, a sheer headland rising 750 feet out of the Pacific. Expansive views from here stretch past Neahkahnie Mountain to distant Cape Lookout far to the south. The trail passes through a magical old-growth coastal rain forest, with ancient Sitka spruce and fir trees towering high above. When the trail passes through a clearing, all manner of plant life springs forward, including vibrant ferns, salmonberries and dense stands of salal. At the viewpoint, thickets of salal are so dense and high that you'll need to blindly trust that the trail leads out of the maze.

For a more strenuous hike, a 4-mile path leads from the campground to the top of **Neahkahnie Mountain**, the 1661-foot coastal mountain that rises between Cape Falcon and Manzanita. The trail crosses a small stream and, after passing through forests, opens out onto a wide meadow, edged by sheer cliffs that drop away to the raging Pacific. After crossing US 101, the trail climbs to the summit, where views are amazing – on a clear day, you can see 50 miles out to sea.

Camping

Oswald West (☎ 800-551-6949) is one of the few campgrounds in the state parks system devoted to tent camping. It's a short quarter-mile hike on a paved trail to the 36 campsites. The campsites are available from March to mid-autumn on a first-come, first-served basis and cost $14 a night. Wheelbarrows are provided to get your gear from the roadside parking lot to your tent space. The campsites are in dense mature forest; flush toilets and drinking water are available. While this is undeniably a lovely place to camp, Oswald West is popular with young campers (particularly surfers) and can get rowdy.

NEHALEM BAY

The Nehalem River rises high in the Coast Range and courses through some of the range's wildest country. This bright, rushing river slows down considerably as it approaches the Pacific, creating both a wide estuarial valley that is prized by farmers, and narrow Nehalem Bay, protected from the lashings of the Pacific by a 7-mile-long sand spit.

A developing fishing industry in the bay led to the establishment of the towns Wheeler (population 335) and Nehalem (population 235) in the 1870s. Along with Manzanita (population 590) – on the ocean side of the spit – these communities nestle in one of the coast's most spectacular settings. Jagged peaks reach heights of 3000 feet, while just north of Manzanita, magical Neahkahnie Mountain rises above the Pacific, dropping away in 700-foot-high cliffs to the pounding waves. Wide, white-sand beaches stretch 7 miles from Neahkahnie Mountain to the end of the Nehalem Spit.

Given the beauty of the area, these communities are relatively ignored, lacking the near-carnival atmosphere of the more famous beach destinations like Cannon Beach and Lincoln City. Manzanita, with a lovely sandy beach, dramatic rocky cliffs and good restaurants downtown, is the center of tourism. There is beach access along the entire length of Ocean Rd, west of downtown. Right on the river, historic and colorful Nehalem and Wheeler are becoming centers for antique boutiques and recreation.

Wineries
One the oldest wineries in Oregon and one of the few on the coast, Nehalem Bay Winery (☎ 503-368-5300), 34965 Hwy 53, north of Wheeler, originally made fruit wines like cranberry and loganberry, but now also makes pinot noirs and Rieslings. The winery is one of the stops on the Fun Run Express Train (see the Garibaldi section) and is open from 10 am to 5 pm daily.

Fishing & Crabbing
The towns of Wheeler and Nehalem used to offer charter fishing, but the declining number of salmon has all but ruined that business. The bay, however, is exceptional for crabbing. Contact Wheeler Marina (☎ 503-368-5780), 278 Marine Drive, Wheeler, to rent a boat and crab rings. Two miles south of Wheeler, there's Brighton Marina (☎ 503-368-5745), with more boat rentals. If you aren't having any luck fishing, you can buy fish from the marina's fish shop.

The Nehalem River is famous for its steelhead and trout fishing. Contact SMS Guide Service (☎ 503-368-7409) if you'd like a guide.

Other Activities
The quiet waters of Nehalem Bay are good for contemplative paddling and bird

watching, as the estuaries are rich in bird life. Rent a **kayak** from Wheeler on the Bay Lodge (see below).

On weekends, a trailer full of horses appears at the end of Nehalem Beach Rd. Show up to join a **horseback riding** group, or contact Sundown Beach Rides (☎ 503-368-7170), 320 Laneda Ave, for mounts at other times.

Plain old **bicycles** are available for rent from Manzanita Fun Merchants (☎ 503-368-6606), 186 Laneda Ave, Manzanita.

Places to Stay
Camping *Nehalem Bay State Park* (☎ 503-368-5154), on the extensive dunes of the Nehalem Spit, has nearly 300 campsites with showers, horse paths and stables, wheelchair-accessible bathrooms, firewood and a boat ramp. Fees are around $19. The turnoff for the park is between Manzanita and Nehalem on US 101. *Paradise Cove Resort & Marina* (☎ 503-368-6333, 800-345-3029), half a mile south of Wheeler on US 101 is an RV campground with tremendous views over the Nehalem Bay and rugged mountains rearing up immediately behind.

B&Bs The *Arbors at Manzanita* (☎ 503-368-7566), 78 Idaho Ave, Manzanita, has two ocean-view rooms with private baths for $99 to $110. *View of the West Country Inn* (☎ 503-368-5766), at 294 Hall St, Wheeler, is an old inn high above town, with rooms from $60 to $85.

Hotels In Manzanita, the *Sunset Surf Motel* (☎ 503-368-5224, 800-243-8035), at 248 Ocean Rd, has some ocean views and an outdoor swimming pool. Prices vary widely depending on whether you are staying in the old or new building, so expect to pay anywhere between $55 and $119 for a basic room. *Manzanita Beach Fireside Inn* (☎ 503-368-1001, 800-368-1001), 114 Laneda Ave, is only a block from the beach and near restaurants and shops. Basic rooms are $55 to $90.

Inn at Manzanita (☎ 503-368-6754), 67 Laneda Ave, between the beach and downtown, has Manzanita's most sought-after lodgings. Rooms have hot tubs and fireplaces and range from $100 to $145.

Wheeler on the Bay Lodge (☎ 503-368-5858, 800-469-3204), 580 Marine Drive, off US 101, is an old motel once dedicated to anglers. The small rooms have been totally renovated, and the courtyard leads to a marina with great views of Nehalem Bay and the Coast Range. This is a fun and friendly place to stay. Rooms are $75 to

$105 and you can rent kayaks from the management.

Places to Eat

For a coffeehouse atmosphere, go to *Manzanita News and Espresso* (☎ 503-368-7450), 500 Laneda Ave, which combines a newsstand and espresso bar. For a full morning meal, Wheeler's *Treasure Cafe* (☎ 503-368-7740), 92 Rorvik St, serves breakfast from 6 am till noon-ish. You can

The Mystery of Neahkahnie Mountain

According to stories told by Nehalem Bay's Tillamook and Clatsop tribes, a Spanish ship landed long ago at the base of Neahkahnie Mountain. The crew disembarked, dug a deep hole in the side of the mountain and lowered a chest into the cavity. Crew members placed heavy bags inside the chest and sealed it. The captain of the ship then shot a black sailor, whose body was thrown on top of the chest before it was buried. The Native Americans who had witnessed the scene abandoned the site, fearing the spirits of the murdered man.

This tale might have simply been considered Native American folklore, if it weren't for a series of uncanny incidents.

By the time explorers reached the Nehalem Bay area, the tribes along northern Oregon had gathered a great deal of beeswax along the shore. Beeswax, used in candle making, was a common article of trade aboard 17th-century Pacific-going Spanish vessels. Old shipping records document that a number of Spanish ships bearing beeswax were lost in the northern Pacific.

Large amounts of beeswax have been discovered along the northern coast of Oregon, especially along the Nehalem Spit. Some of the large chunks of beeswax found on the coast were carved with cryptic letters and patterns. One piece was engraved with the date 1679, others with crosses and designs. In total, about 10 tons of beeswax have been uncovered along the Oregon coast.

Around 1890, a farmer found a curiously carved rock in a meadow on the southern face of the mountain. Etched in the rock were Christian crosses; the letters D, E and W; arrows; and a series of dots. Later, other rocks were discovered nearby that repeated the letters and designs. The immediate assumption was that the stones contained information that would, if properly decoded, lead to the buried treasure.

Early in the century, there was a lot of digging in the side of the mountain, and many people claim to have solved the mystery of the buried treasure. However, no one has come forward with the treasure, nor has anyone produced a theory that adequately accounts for all the elements of the story.

The State Parks Department now tries to limit wildcat excavation on the mountain. The curiously carved rocks, usually called the Neahkahnie Stones, are on display at the Tillamook Pioneer Museum, as are several pieces of etched beeswax. ■

sit outside at picnic tables, take in the view and savor oyster hash for $7.

Manzanita also offers some of the northern coast's best, and most expensive, dining. *Jarboe's* (☎ 503-368-5113), 137 Laneda Ave, is housed in an old, very small cottage. The menu changes daily and meals are available á la carte, with most main dishes in the $17 range, or on a prix-fixe menu, at $27 to $30. Entrées feature local fresh fish and seafood, often mesquite-grilled. Call for reservations; there are only eight tables at Jarboe's and the restaurant is only open Thursday to Monday evenings.

Manzanita's other restaurant of note is the *Blue Sky Cafe* (☎ 503-368-5712), 154 Laneda Ave. A less formal and less precious dining experience than Jarboe's, the menu features pan-Pacific touches, such as soy-tamarind salmon and sushi served with goat cheese. Entrées range from $15 to $21; the regional wine list is extensive.

TILLAMOOK & TILLAMOOK BAY

The Tillamook Indians who controlled the land around Tillamook Bay were renowned hunters. They lived in framed, woven-reed houses in villages and the aristocracy practiced head flattening and decorative tattooing. They refused to enter the Indian Wars of the 1850s and were essentially disbanded by white settlement in the area, never to be granted a reservation.

Today, the first thing you'll notice when you arrive in Tillamook is the smell: it's fairly obvious that *a lot* of cows live in the area. Five coastal rivers flow from the mountains into flat Tillamook Valley, making it perfect for raising dairy cattle. Cheese making and other dairy-related industries are the focus of the local economy. The Tillamook Cheese Factory ships out 40 million pounds of cheese – mostly cheddar – each year.

Tillamook (population 4145) is one of the few working towns left on the coast. Coffee shops haven't yet evolved into espresso bars, and the local feed store – not the metaphysical bookstore – is where the locals converge.

At the mouth of Tillamook Bay sits Garibaldi, a sleepy village that's home to one of Oregon's largest charter-fishing fleets.

Orientation & Information
The only way to get to Tillamook is by car. Going south, US 101 follows the Nestucca River through pastureland and heavily lumbered mountains. Alternatively, the slower but prettier 30-mile Three Capes Scenic Route follows the coast.

The visitors' center (☎ 503-842-7525) is in the parking lot of the Tillamook Cheese Factory at 3705 N US 101, Tillamook, OR 97141. The post office, bookstores, laundry, etc, are all within the area between 1st and 3rd Sts.

Cheese Factories
Cheese production began in Tillamook in the 1890s, when an English cheese maker brought his cheddar-making techniques to the fledgling dairies along Tillamook Bay.

Two cheese factories in Tillamook are open for tours. Opening hours are 8 am to 8 pm daily; admission is free. The Tillamook Cheese Factory (☎ 503-815-1300), about 2 miles north of town at 4175 N US 101, is the largest and most famous, visited by over 750,000 people a year. There are self-guided tours, videos explaining the cheese-making process, and samples of cheese and ice cream available. In the large sales and delicatessen area, many regional foods, wines and gifts are for sale. There's also a small cafe for light meals.

At the Blue Heron French Cheese Company (☎ 503-842-8281), 2001 Blue Heron Drive off N US 101, 1 mile south of Tillamook, cheese makers serve samples and sell locally produced Brie and Camembert along with other European-style cheeses. A winetasting bar in this converted barn offers wine samples for a small fee; you get to choose from a selection of 12 to 15 regional wines. Kids can spend their time at the petting zoo.

Tillamook Pioneer Museum
Housed in the old courthouse, this county museum (☎ 503-842-4553) at 2106 2nd St,

is worth a stop. There's a natural science display of shore birds and waterfowl, or more exactly, a paean to the art of taxidermy. Other items of note include a display of artifacts and photographs of the Tillamook tribe; carved beeswax from a 17th-century Spanish ship that wrecked somewhere in the Pacific; and the Neahkahnie Stones, whose curiously carved surfaces were meant to point to a legendary buried treasure near Manzanita.

The bookstore has a good selection of regional history and travel books. The museum is open 8:30 am to 5 pm weekdays, and noon to 5 pm on weekends. Entry is $2/1.50/50¢ adult/seniors/students.

Tillamook Naval Air Museum
Opened in 1943, Tillamook Naval Air Station is one of 10 air bases built by the US Navy during WWII for a fleet of blimps that patrolled the northern Pacific looking for enemy warships. The one remaining hangar is open to the public as the Tillamook Naval Air Museum (☎ 503-842-1130), about 3 miles south of Tillamook off US 101.

The enormous wooden building covers 7 acres. Only half the hangar is currently used by the museum, but there's enough room for two dirigibles, a hot-air balloon and a large collection of old fighter planes including a Spitfire, a Messerschmidt and an Avenger – the same type of aircraft George Bush was shot down in.

Opening hours are 9 am to dark daily, May to September, and 9 am to 5 pm daily the rest of the year. Admission is $6/5/4 adults/seniors/students, and $2.50 children (seven to 12).

Air tours over Tillamook Bay and the Three Capes are available from the airfield adjacent to the museum.

Munson Creek Falls
The highest waterfall in the Coast Range, Munson Creek Falls drops 266 feet down a succession of mossy, stair-stepped ledges. The easy half-mile hike to the falls passes through a dense forest. To reach the trailhead, drive 7 miles south of Tillamook on US 101 to a gravel road with signs indicating Munson Creek County Park. The trailhead is 1.6 miles east.

Garibaldi
Ten miles north of Tillamook on Tillamook Bay, Garibaldi began its life as a lumber town. Today, this scrappy little village ekes out a living from fishing: this is the north coast's largest **charter-fishing** port. While it won't win any awards for quaintness, this hard-working community, which has 915 residents, is a nice antidote to the forced cuteness of many of Oregon's coastal towns. Stop and walk around the harbor area and watch salmon, crab, halibut and shrimp come off fishing boats, or rent a boat and some crab rings and go get yourself a crab dinner.

Troller Deep Sea Fishing (☎ 332-3666, 800-546-3666) and Siamez Charters (☎ 503-842-2200), both in the mooring basin, specialize in **deep-sea fishing**. At Garibaldi Marina (☎ 503-322-3312), 302 Mooring Basin Rd, you can rent boats, crab rings, tackle, and whatever else you need to outfit your own fishing trip. Most charter-fishing boats also run **whale-watching trips** during the spring migration.

The other activity in Garibaldi is the **Fun Run Excursion Train** (☎ 503-355-8667), which cruises the old Southern Pacific rails on a 28-mile run between Garibaldi's Lumberman Park and the Nehalem Bay Winery with stops at Rockaway Beach and Wheeler. The train runs weekends only; $10/5 adults/children. Call for schedule information.

Special Events
The Dairy Parade & Festival (☎ 503-842-7525), is held the last weekend of June – the Dairy Month. Celebrations include a parade, street dance and the crowning of the Dairy Queen. The Tillamook County Fair (☎ 503-842-2272) is held Thursday to Saturday the second week in August. Events include horseracing, livestock, home and garden shows, a carnival and musical performances. Both events are held at the county fairgrounds, 4603 3rd St.

OREGON

Places to Stay

Camping The *Pleasant Valley RV Park* (☎ 503-842-4779) just 6 miles south of Tillamook on US 101 has tent sites for $14 and RV sites for $17.50 to $19.50. Garibaldi's lumbering past is still alive at the *Old Mill Marina Resort* (☎ 503-322-0324), at 3rd St and American Ave, a large and pleasant campground on the grounds of a late-19th-century lumber mill. There are lots of grassy expanses in the campground, plus a marina, restaurant, swimming pool and a separate tent area. Rates are $15 for tent sites and $18 for RVs.

Hotels The *Mar-Clair Inn* (☎ 503-842-7571, 800-331-6857), 11 Main Ave, is right downtown along the Trask River. Rooms range from $56 to $64. The *El Ray Sands Motel* (☎ 503-842-7511, 800-257-1185), 815 Main Ave, is on the south end of Tillamook and charges $50 to $60.

Western Royal Inn (☎ 503-842-8844, 800-624-2912), 1125 N Main Ave is an older,

well-kept motel on the US 101 strip. Rooms are $70 to $75. The *Shilo Inn* (☎ 503-842-7971, 800-222-2244), 2515 N US 101, is one of Tillamook's newest accommodations, with rooms from $65 to $110.

If you are looking for no-frills lodging at budget prices, check along Garibaldi's piers, where modest motels provide shelter for charter fishers.

Places to Eat

Muddy Waters Coffee & Tea Co (☎ 503-842-1400), 1904 3rd St, is a small espresso shop with a good selection of newspapers. It's a good place to unwind from driving harrowing US 101.

Some of the best food in Tillamook is served in its Mexican restaurants. *Casa Medello* (☎ 503-842-5768), out on the US 101 strip, offers good deals in well-prepared Mexican food. *La Mexicana Restaurant* (☎ 503-842-2101), 2203 3rd St, has an extensive menu including prawns mole and lobster meunière for $18, and oysters sautéed in hot sauce for $8. There are also standard Mexican dishes for under $8.

McClaskey's (☎ 503-842-5674), 2102 1st St at Pacific Ave, offers sandwiches and soups for lunch. A house specialty, the oyster burger, goes for $7. For dinner, steak, pasta and fresh seafood are in the $10 range.

In Garibaldi, *Pirates Cove Restaurant* (☎ 503-322-2092), 14170 US 101 N, is the locals' favorite for fine dining and cocktails, all with a view over the bay.

THREE CAPES SCENIC ROUTE

This highway is an alternative route to US 101, between Tillamook and the Pacific City junction. The 30-mile route passes through three state parks with some of the coast's most stunning headlands and some charming towns that are among the few beach towns not bisected by busy US 101.

The pace of traffic is slow. Unless you plan on stopping at the state parks, you may want to stay on US 101. If you tire of the winding road, two side roads – at Netarts and Sand Lake – will return you to US 101.

The Bayocean Folly

The 4-mile-long Bayocean Sandspit that reaches across the mouth of Tillamook Bay was the site of one of Oregon coast's most ambitious, and ultimately foolish, resort developments. In 1906 a land developer from Kansas City decided that the narrow spit would be turned into a vast entertainment, recreation and housing complex called Bayocean. Six years later a grand hotel, natatorium, docks, rail access and 4 miles of paved streets were completed.

However, winter storms began to eat away at the spit. By 1932 the natatorium collapsed into the sea, and in 1952 a storm so lashed the area that the Bayocean Spit was breached in three places, reducing its tip to an island. Erosion continued to work away at the spit, and the last house of the Bayocean resort community tumbled into the sea in 1960. ∎

Cape Meares State Park

Ten miles west of Tillamook, this 233-acre state park is a welcome relief from the relentless clear-cutting that edges much of the Three Capes Drive. Of interest is the **Cape Meares Lighthouse**, built in 1890. During summer, a small gift shop is open at its base and the curious can hike up to the top of the building. Also, the **Octopus Tree** is a massive Sitka spruce whose low-slung branches reach far out from the base of the tree before spreading upward. Native American legends hold that the tree was shaped to cradle funeral canoes.

There are hiking trails to both sites from the parking lot.

Oceanside

Once an unheralded beach resort, Oceanside has been 'discovered.' Now a massive condominium resort clings to the headland above the town. Rising immediately out to sea are the towering 400-foot-high Three Arch Rocks, preserved as a sea-bird refuge. Seals and sea lions also take their place on the flanks of these dramatic protrusions.

Places to Stay & Eat The nicest place to stay in Oceanside is *House on the Hill Motel* (☎ 503-842-6030), on Maxwell Point on the bluff above Oceanside; rooms are $75 to $115.

Widely noted for its good food, *Roseanna's Cafe* (☎ 503-842-7351), 1490 NW Pacific St, has a casual maritime atmosphere. The service, however, is excruciatingly slow. People from the city often note that people on the coast live at a slower pace, but after waiting 20 minutes for your table to be cleared and set, it's hard not to jump in and help out. Bring your patience, if not a snack, for you may need it.

Netarts

Netarts offers few facilities for the traveler and the locals prefer it that way. The area is known for its excellent clamming and fishing. Rent a boat at Bay Shore RV Park & Marina (☎ 503-842-7774), about a mile south of Netarts on Three Capes Drive and try your luck at crabbing. Or take a boat

across the narrow bay and sunbathe on the spit with the sea lions.

You can camp at *Bayshore RV Park & Marina* (☎ 503-842-7774), a mile south of Netarts on Three Capes Drive. Sites start at $18. The *Terimore Motel* (☎ 503-842-4623), 5105 Crab Ave, sits high on a cliff; rates range from $45 to $87.

Cape Lookout State Park

This 2000-acre state park (☎ 503-842-4981) includes the entire length of sandy Netarts Spit, as well as Cape Lookout, which juts out nearly a mile from the mainland like a finger pointing out to sea. The cliffs along the south side of the cape rise 800 feet from the Pacific Ocean's pounding waves. The rock exposed at Cape Lookout, as at the other capes along this route, is formed of Columbia Basin basalts, the lava flows that traveled here 15 million years ago from a spot near present-day Idaho.

Hiking The most popular hiking trail in the park is to the end of Cape Lookout. The trail begins either at the campground, where it climbs 2½ miles up to a ridge-top parking lot, or you can drive to here and hike 2½ miles to the cape's cliff edge, with views of Cape Kiwanda to the south.

Informal hiking trails lead out onto Netarts Spit, a grassy dune that stretches nearly 4 miles across Netarts Bay. Clamming is popular at low tides along the wide sandy beach.

Camping The *Cape Lookout Campground* has nearly 250 campsites at the park, 197 intended for tents. Facilities include showers, evening ranger programs in the summer, meeting rooms and wheelchair-accessible toilets. Sites can be reserved in summer. Fees for camping begin at $16 a night for tents and go to $20 for full hookups.

Cape Kiwanda

The third in this route's trilogy of capes is Cape Kiwanda, a sandstone bluff that rises just north of the little town of Pacific City. To reach Cape Kiwanda you'll have to hike

OREGON

OREGON

up the spine of the dunes that drape around the cape. The top of the dunes is a popular place to hang-glide.

Just over the dune is the Pacific Ocean and miles and miles of sandy beach. The beaches south along the Nestucca Spit are part of **Robert Straub State Park**, which provides restrooms, a parking lot and easy beach access.

Pacific City is noted for two things: its Haystack Rock and the dory fleet. Watching dory crews struggle from the beach, into the surf and out to sea, is usually quite amusing.

Places to Stay & Eat *Cape Kiwanda RV Park* (☎ 503-965-6230), 33005 Kiwanda Rd, has 130 RV sites with hookups and a separate tent-camping area. *Inn at Pacific City* (☎ 503-965-6366, 800-722-2489), 35215 Brooten Rd, is a nice lodging with moderately priced rooms at $49 to $64. The *Three Capes Motel* (☎ 503-965-6464), 35280 Brooten Rd, has rooms ranging from $40 to $63.

Pacific City has a number of burger and fish-and-chip restaurants. Instead, *Grateful Bread Bakery* (☎ 503-965-7337), 34805 Brooten Rd, serves breakfast and lunch – sandwiches, soups and pizzas – either indoors, or, in good weather, on the deck. The French loaf is excellent. Go to *White Moon Cow Cafe* (☎ 503-965-5101), 35490 Brooten Rd, for espresso and pastries.

Cozy and unpretentious, *The Riverhouse* (☎ 503-965-6722), 34450 Brooten Rd, on the Nestucca River, is one of the favorite restaurants along this stretch of the coast. Dinners range between $11 and $19.

LINCOLN CITY
Population 6090
A 7-mile-long series of commercial strips, motels, snack bars and gift shops that fronts onto a fairly wide – if lackluster – stretch of sandy beach, Lincoln City is also the principal trade center for a large area of the coast; lumber yards, supermarkets and car dealerships crowd along US 101. Additionally, Lincoln City is known for its complex of outlet stores off East

Devil's Lake Rd at US 101, where dozens of national chain stores dump their seconds and last year's models at reduced prices. The newest attraction in town is Chinook Winds Casino, in the convention center north of town, which is operated by the Siletz Indians.

Lincoln City isn't a very attractive town and it sprawls uncontrollably across too much of the Oregon coast. But before passing too harsh a judgment on the area, realize that this is just about the only affordable beach town left on the Oregon coast and there are a lot of places to stay: in Oregon, only Portland has more hotel rooms. And if you like lying on the beach, there's a lot of it here. This is a major family vacation destination, with all that that connotes.

Orientation
Lincoln City is divided into quadrants by the D River and US 101. Hwy 18 from the Willamette Valley joins US 101 in town.

To the north is one of the coast's major capes, Cascade Head, and to the south is Gleneden Beach, the site of the Salishan Lodge, Oregon coast's most upscale retirement and golfing resort.

Information
The visitors' center (☎ 541-994-3070, 800-452-2151) is at 801 SW US 101, Lincoln City, OR 97367.

The post office is at 1501 SE Devil's Lake Rd. The daily newspaper is the Lincoln City *News Times*. North Lincoln Hospital (☎ 541-994-3661) is at 3043 NE 28th St.

Beaches
Lincoln City's 7-mile stretch of wide sandy beaches endears the town to holidaymakers, particularly family groups. The main public access points are at the D River State Wayside, in the center of town where the river meets the Pacific; at the north end of Lincoln City, at Road's End State Wayside off Logan Rd; and along Siletz Bay south of town at the end of SW 51st St at Taft City Park.

Cascade Head & Harts Cove
A favorite hiking destination, Cascade Head was slated to become a resort development in the 1960s, but the Nature Conservancy bought up the land and worked with the USFS to have the area declared a Scenic Research Area.

Note that the Nature Conservancy trails are not always open, due to habitat restoration or other reasons. Call the local Nature Conservancy office (☎ 541-994-5564) before heading out.

However, the Forest Service's trail should always be open. Drive north on US 101 toward Tillamook, 4 miles from the Hwy 18 junction. Turn west off US 101 onto USFS Rd 1861, called Cascade Head Rd. The trailhead is 3.3 miles along this road.

A mile farther down USFS Rd 1861 is the trailhead to the 2.6-mile hike to Harts Cove, a remote meadow along a bay lined with cliffs; the area is frequented by sea lions.

Sitka Center for Art & Ecology
A series of summer workshops on nature, art and Native American culture is held at this private educational facility at Cascade Head Ranch along Three Rocks Rd. For information on the courses, contact the Sitka Center (☎ 541-994-5485) at PO Box 65, Otis, OR 97368.

Activities
For bike rentals, go to David's Bicycle Rental (☎ 541-996-6001), 960 SE US 101. **Canoeing** on Devil's Lake, east of town, and on Siletz Bay, is popular for recreation and **wildlife viewing**. Blue Heron Landing (☎ 541-994-4708), 4006 W Devil's Lake Rd, rents both canoes and motorboats.

Surfing is an increasingly popular pastime along the coast. Rent equipment at Oregon Surf Shop (☎ 541-996-3957), 4933 SW US 101, or Safari Town Surf Shop (☎ 541-996-6335), 3026 NE US 101.

Special Events
The self-proclaimed 'Kite Capital of the World,' Lincoln City hosts two kite festivals annually. Enormous kites – some over 100 feet in length – take off to twist and dive in the ocean breezes. It's a colorful event by day and by night, when kites are illuminated.

The spring festival is usually held the second weekend in May and the fall festival is usually held the last weekend of September. Both festivals take place at the D River State Wayside in the center of Lincoln City. Call the visitors' center for more details.

In late July, Lincoln City hosts a sand castle building contest.

Places to Stay
Lincoln City offers some of the coast's most reasonably priced lodging, especially if you're willing to listen to the roar of traffic rather than the sea. And in Lincoln City, you're rarely more than a five-minute walk from the beach no matter where you stay. Call the visitors' center (☎ 541-994-8378, 800-452-2151) if you're having trouble finding rooms; although they don't offer a reservation service, they do track which hotels have available rooms.

Camping *Devil's Lake State Park* (☎ 541-994-2002), at NE 6th Drive and US 101, is a five-minute walk to the action on the D River Beach and downtown Lincoln City. There are showers and flush toilets. You can also go swimming and boating in freshwater Devil's Lake. Camping fees are $17 for tents, $19 for full hookups. The *Lincoln City KOA Kampground* (☎ 541-994-2961), 5298 NE Park Lane, is near the northern edge of Devil's Lake, but isn't so convenient to the beaches. Campground facilities include showers, laundry and a playground. Tent sites are $17, full hookups cost $23 and cabins cost $30.

B&Bs The *Brey House B&B* (☎ 541-994-7123), 3725 NW Keel Ave, offers four rooms with private baths; some have decks, fireplaces and ocean views. Rates are $70 to $135. The *Inlet Garden B&B* (☎ 541-994-7932), 646 NW Inlet Ave, has rooms with private baths and fireplaces

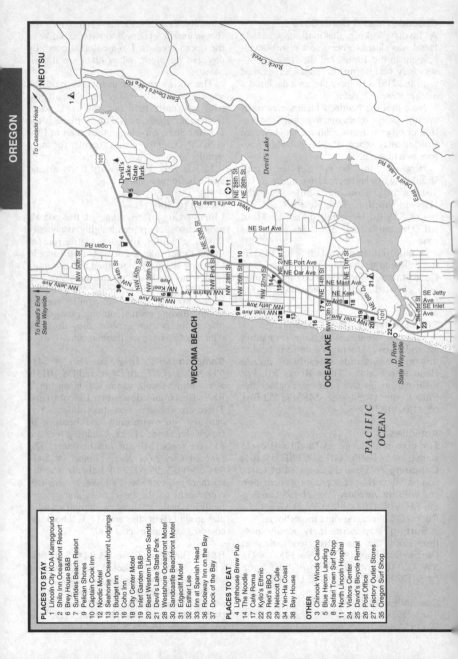

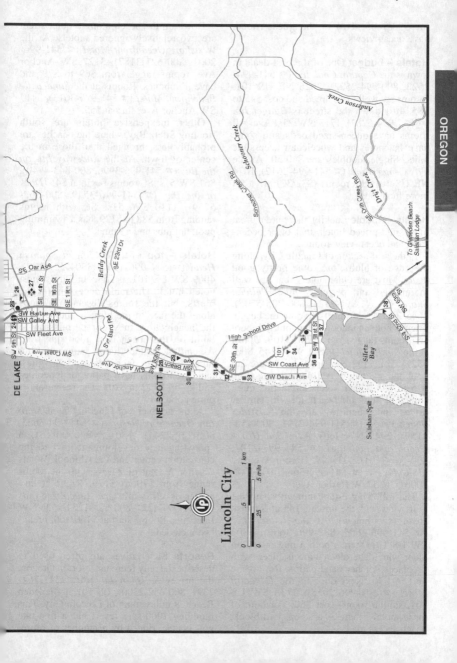

Lincoln City

for $98/$105. Two of the guest rooms have ocean views.

Hotels – budget One of the best deals in town is the *Captain Cook Inn* (☎ 541-994-2522, 800-994-2522), 2626 NE US 101. Rooms are well maintained and cost $45 to $85. Just down the street is *Budget Inn* (☎ 541-994-5281), 1713 NW 21st Ave. All rooms have queen-sized beds and some have balconies and wheelchair-accessible units. Singles/doubles are $40/50. At the *City Center Motel* (☎ 541-994-2612), 1014 NE US 101, the rooms ($32/37) are a bit more functional.

Hotels – middle Luckily, there are a great many mid-priced hotels that offer ocean-front and ocean-view rooms.

In the mid-section of Lincoln City, along the edge of bluffs, are some pretty good deals. Most are older hotels that are well maintained and perfectly nice. *Pelican Shores* (☎ 541-994-2134, 800-705-5505), 2645 Inlet Ave, fronts right onto the beach. There's both an indoor and an outdoor pool and rooms range from $79 to $109. Uphill at the *Nordic Motel* (☎ 541-994-8145, 800-452-3558), 2133 NW Inlet Ave, there are pool and spa facilities. Rooms range from $75 to $95. Other hotels along this quiet stretch of bluff and beach, all with similar prices and amenities, are the *Surftides Beach Resort* (☎ 541-994-2191, 800-452-2159), 2945 NW Jetty Ave; *Sea Horse Oceanfront Lodgings* (☎ 541-994-2101, 800-662-2101), 2039 NW Harbor Ave; and the *Coho Inn* (☎ 541-994-3684, 800-848-7006), 1635 NW Harbor Ave.

The following establishments share the bluff view with the upscale Inn at Spanish Head (see below). At the *Esther Lee* (☎ 541-996-3606, 888-996-3606), 3803 SW US 101, there's both a newer and an older wing. The older wing is nicer, with fireplaces, kitchens and patios. Rooms are $60 to $76. Next door at the *Edgecliff Motel* (☎ 541-996-2055), 3733 SW US 101, similar rooms cost $50. For both of these motels, there is a steep, two-block beach access road.

Down on the beach along a quiet street are two relatively ignored motels. At the *Westshore Oceanfront Motel* (☎ 541-996-2001, 800-621-3187), 3127 SW Anchor Ave, rooms range from $69 to $79 and have no phones. Rooms at the *Sandcastle Beachfront Motel* (☎ 541-996-3613), 3417 SW Anchor Ave, start at $55.

Other inexpensive hotels are south fronting Siletz Bay, where the beaches are probably less thronged than those in the center of town. At the *Rodeway Inn on the Bay* (☎ 541-996-3996, 800-843-4940), 861 SW 51st St, rooms begin at $45. *Dock of the Bay* (☎ 541-996-3549, 800-362-5229), 1116 SW 51st St, with rooms ranging from $88 to $129, has a swimming pool, hot tubs and a sauna.

Hotels – top end The *Inn at Spanish Head* (☎ 541-996-2161, 800-452-8127), 4009 SW US 101, is Lincoln City's most noted hotel. The main access is on the bluffs, but the rooms descend in steps along the face of the bluff to the level of the beach; how they got permission to build on the beach is a good question. Amenities include a pool, saunas and hot tubs, exercise facilities and a guest laundry. Rooms have patios or balconies and go for $112 to $205. The restaurant is quite good.

At the north end of Lincoln City is *Shilo Inn Oceanfront Resort* (☎ 541-994-3655, 800-222-2244), 1501 NW 40th St, a sprawling new development next to the convention center and the Chinook Winds Casino. A total of 247 beachfront rooms range from $79 to $179. Right at city center is *Best Western Lincoln Sands* (☎ 541-994-4227, 800-528-1234), 535 NW Inlet Ave. Rooms start at $140/160, breakfast included.

Resorts Superlatives are often used to describe the only four-star resort in Oregon, the pricey *Salishan Lodge* (☎ 541-764-2371, 800-452-2300), US 101 at Gleneden Beach, 9 miles south of Lincoln City. This rambling 1000-acre resort has a first-rate golf course, ringed by a number of retirement homes and condominiums. Rooms in the condos range from $189 to $249.

Vacation Home Rentals To rent a private home contact Oregon Coast Vacation Rentals (☎ 541-994-5674), at 1734 NW Harbor Ave, Lincoln City, OR 97367.

Places to Eat
Budget *Nelscott Café* (☎ 541-996-2900), 3243 SW US 101, has the best breakfasts in Lincoln City and it's also open for light meals at lunch and dinner. *Cafe Roma* (☎ 541-994-6616), 1437 NW US 101, serves pastries, sandwiches and espresso drinks, and sells new and used books. This is about as close to an alternative hangout as you'll find in Lincoln City.

Yen-Ha Coast (☎ 541-994-7557), 4649 SW US 101, is an Asian seafood restaurant. Head to *Red's BBQ* (☎ 541-994-2626), 220 SE US 101, for a meal of beef brisket, or barbecued chicken or ham.

Middle *Kyllo's Ethnic* (☎ 541-994-3179), 1110 NW 1st Court, overlooks the D River and the Pacific. The modern, echoey decor is quite a contrast to the rest of '60s-era Lincoln City, but the food is good, focusing on zesty seafood dishes, pasta and steaks. A nice addition to the prevalent chowder houses of Lincoln City is *The Noodle* (☎ 541-994-8800), 2145 NW US 101, a good pasta house with meals averaging $10.

Otis Cafe (☎ 541-994-2813), 3 miles northeast of Lincoln City on Hwy 18, is an unpretentious but highly touted little diner in the woods that serves up great home baked bread and pies. The German hash browns with melted cheese and the ample burgers are popular. On weekends anticipate a wait.

Top End The *Bay House* (☎ 541-996-3222), 5911 SW US 101, about 2 miles south, is an elegant restaurant overlooking Siletz Bay. The menu is seasonal but always features standards like local seafood and fish, rack of lamb and duck ($19 to $26). The new bistro offers lighter, less expensive dining.

The Dining Room at Salishan Lodge (☎ 541-764-2371), 7760 N US 101, Gleneden Beach, 9 miles south of Lincoln City, is credited with preparing the best menu in the state. Dinners, however, usually total about $50 to $60 per person, before exploring the extensive wine list. The restaurant offers tours of the wine cellar, which contains over 20,000 bottles. The food can be excellent and the service slightly ostentatious. Meals in the *Sun Room*, the casual dining room, are much more reasonable; sandwiches at lunch hover around the $8 mark.

Directly across from the Salishan is another excellent restaurant. *Chez Jeannette* (☎ 541-764-3434), 7150 Gleneden Beach Loop, has classic French cuisine and a charming rustic, European-style dining room; entrées average $20.

Entertainment
Brewpubs The *Lighthouse Brew Pub* (☎ 541-994-7238), 4157 N US 101, is in a shopping mall just north of Lincoln City. This brewpub is an offshoot of the McMenimans chain out of Portland and serves light meals.

Getting There & Around
Greyhound and Central Coast Connections buses both stop in Lincoln City. The depot for Greyhound is at SE 14th St and US 101; there are two buses daily in each direction between Portland and Lincoln City ($13 one way). Central Coast Connections runs four buses daily to Newport ($2 one way).

Call Lincoln Cab Company (☎ 541-996-2003) for a taxi.

DEPOE BAY
This small fishing community is 11 miles south of Lincoln City. South of the town, US 101 climbs up to Cape Foulweather, 500 feet above the Pacific.

The tiny 6-acre boat basin was formed when the pounding waves battered a narrow channel through the basalt cliffs. The 50-foot-wide passage out to the ocean can be a challenge. Today, whale-watching

OREGON

Whale Watching

Each year, the longest migration known for any mammal takes place in the Pacific Ocean, when approximately 20,000 gray whales make their annual 10,000-mile roundtrip journey between the Arctic Sea and the warm lagoons of Baja California. Along the Oregon Coast, gray whale migration peaks in late December, when southbound whales can be spotted at the rate of about 30 an hour. Whales can also be spotted from March to May as they gradually meander back north, although sightings are less frequent during this leg of the migration. Most gray whales pass within 5 miles of the shore and can be easily viewed from any coastal headland or ocean viewpoint.

Whales are air-breathing mammals and must frequently come to the surface for oxygen. When they do, they exhale with great force through a blowhole on the top of their head, creating a warm, vaporous cloud of mist (not water) 6 to 12 feet high called a blow or spout. To see a blow, cast your gaze about halfway between the shore and the horizon and wait to see a burst of white mist. Blows can be seen with the naked eye, but a pair of binoculars will make it much easier to see them. Mornings and cloudy skies present the best conditions for whale watching.

Once a blow is sighted, watch for glimpses of the whale's head, knuckled back and flukes (tail). A whale's rhythmic breathing and diving usually follows a pattern of three to five short, shallow dives spread a minute or two apart, followed by one deep dive (sounding) lasting five minutes or more. A tail that breaks the surface usually indicates a sounding – watch for the whale to reappear approximately 300 to 400 yards from where it was last sighted.

The uninitiated might find the sight of a blow unimpressive, even with a pair of binoculars. Whale watching takes patience, and enjoyment is derived mainly from observing

---

trips and charter fishing are popular, as is watching the boats maneuver through the passage. Parts of the film *One Flew Over the Cuckoo's Nest* were filmed here. Both the chamber of commerce and a post office are along US 101.

Charter Fishing & Whale Watching

This is one of the coast's busiest charter-fishing harbors, offering good ocean fishing and whale watching during the spring migration. Call Dockside Charter (☎ 541-765-2545), or Tradewinds Sportfishing (☎ 541-765-2345) for prices and information. Fishing trips begin at $45. Whale-watching trips are usually $10 for an hourlong excursion.

Places to Stay & Eat

At *Holiday RV Park*, (☎ 541-765-2302), north on US 101, sites range between $13 and $17; facilities include a swimming pool and laundry.

The nicest place to stay in Depoe Bay is the *Channel House Inn* (☎ 541-765-2140, 800-447-2140), 35 Ellingson St, an old inn right on the mouth of the harbor with 11 rooms, decorated with a nautical theme. Prices range from $75 to $225. For something cheaper, try the *Whale Inn* (☎ 541-765-2789), 416 N US 101, an older but attractive motel on the wrong side of US 101, or *Trollers Lodge* (☎ 541-765-2287, 800-472-9335), 355 SW US 101, a snug older motel with some ocean-view rooms.

The *Sea Hag* (☎ 541-765-2734) 58 E US 101, has fried fish and seafood, a salad bar and good clam chowder. The area's best dining is at the *Whale Cove Inn* (☎ 541-765-2255), 2 miles south on US 101, with great shoreline views and seafood dishes. Try smoked scallops or salmon at the *Siletz Tribal Smokehouse* (☎ 541-765-2286), 272 SE US 101, a business owned by the tribe that also sells gift items from the Siletz reservation.

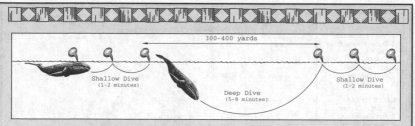

300–400 yards

Shallow Dive
(1-2 minutes)

Deep Dive
(5-8 minutes)

Shallow Dive
(1-2 minutes)

OREGON

and learning about animal behavior and relaxing amid the spectacular coastal scenery (winter temperatures also tend to be warmer on the coast than they are inland). Vigilant whale watching pays off the first time a 30- to 40-ton whale is spotted breaching, which is when a whale propels about half of its body straight out of the water, turns, and then splashes onto its side or back.

For a close-up view of whales, take a short boat trip out onto the ocean. Almost every coastal port has at least one charter-boat operator who offers whale-watching trips as a side venture to charter fishing. These excursions are an especially good activity for children and cost around $10 to $15 for a 90-minute trip. Longer trips of two to three hours cost around $25.

Roadside signs that say 'Whale Watching Spoken Here' indicate viewpoints staffed with volunteers who can help identify and interpret gray whale behavior. These viewpoints are typically staffed on weekends and extended holiday periods (such as Christmas and spring breaks) during the migration seasons. Call Oregon State Parks (☎ 800-551-6949) for specific times and locations. ■

Getting There & Around

Both Greyhound and the local Central Coast Connection buses pass through Depoe Bay. Call their Newport numbers for information.

NEWPORT
Population 9100

Oregon's second-largest commercial port, Newport was first explored by fishing crews in the 1860s, who found high-quality oyster beds at the upper end of Yaquina Bay. In 1866 a road was built from Corvallis to the coast, and Newport's first hotel, the Ocean House, was built (on the site of the present Coast Guard Station). During the 1870s, steamboats brought holidaymakers up from San Francisco.

Summer cottages and hotels began to appear on the north side of the sheltered harbor, along Nye Creek. Newport continues to expand north along the headland and US 101 as tourism dominates the local economy. Old downtown Newport, centered on Bay Blvd, is still a very lively seafront, complete with seafood markets, the smells of a working port and the bark of seals. The gray and rather ramshackle buildings along the water's edge are fish-processing plants. On the other side of Bay Blvd are chandlers, 24-hour restaurants, art galleries and brewpubs. About halfway down Bay Blvd there's a wax museum, a so-called undersea garden on a floating barge and a Ripley's Believe It or Not! museum.

A better use of time may be a boat excursion around Yaquina Bay, a trip out into the Pacific to view whales, or even popping into a bayfront restaurant for a beer and a bowl of clam chowder.

Information

There's a visitors' center (☎ 541-265-8801, 800-262-7844) at 555 SW Coast Hwy, Newport, OR 97365. The post office is located at 310 SW 2nd St. Canyon Way

OREGON

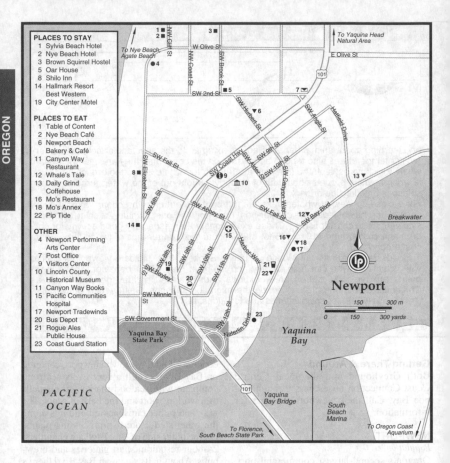

PLACES TO STAY
1 Sylvia Beach Hotel
2 Nye Beach Hotel
3 Brown Squirrel Hostel
5 Oar House
8 Shilo Inn
14 Hallmark Resort
    Best Western
19 City Center Motel

PLACES TO EAT
1 Table of Content
2 Nye Beach Café
6 Newport Beach
    Bakery & Café
11 Canyon Way
    Restaurant
12 Whale's Tale
13 Daily Grind
    Coffeehouse
16 Mo's Restaurant
18 Mo's Annex
22 Pip Tide

OTHER
4 Newport Performing
    Arts Center
7 Post Office
9 Visitors Center
10 Lincoln County
    Historical Museum
11 Canyon Way Books
15 Pacific Communities
    Hospital
17 Newport Tradewinds
20 Bus Depot
21 Rogue Ales
    Public House
23 Coast Guard Station

Newport

Books (☎ 541-265-8319), at 1216 SW Canyon Way, is one of the coast's best bookstores; pick up a book-on-tape for the road.

Eileen's Coin Laundry (☎ 541-265-5474), 1078 N Coast Hwy, has drop-off and self-service facilities. Pacific Communities Hospital (☎ 541-265-2244) is at 930 SW Abbey St.

Oregon Coast Aquarium
Opened in 1992, the Oregon Coast Aquarium (☎ 541-867-3474, 541-867-3123), 2820 SE Ferry Slip Rd, has become one of the biggest attractions in Oregon. Room-sized exhibits are grouped by ecosystem with interactive displays to explain the dynamics of the various forms of life found there. At a supervised 'petting area,' visitors can touch the denizens of a tide pool and ask marine specialists questions. Especially arresting are the luminous jellyfish in cylindrical floor-to-ceiling aquariums.

Outside, trails lead around natural-looking enclosures for seals, sea lions and sea otters; the sea-bird aviary includes puffins and murres. A great favorite with kids is the giant octopus that lives in a glass-walled sea grotto. Other trails lead from the aquarium along Yaquina Bay estuarial wetlands.

In terms of draw, though, undoubtedly the star of the aquarium is Keiko, the orca made famous by the film *Free Willy*. After the film, Keiko festered in a tiny aquarium in Mexico City, where he became ill. He was moved to Newport, where he is now thriving, much to the delight of children.

The aquarium is open 9 am to 6 pm daily May 15 to October 14, and 10 am to 5 pm the rest of the year. Admission is \$8.50/7.50/4.25 adults/seniors/children (four to 13). There's also a cafe and a gift shop with books on the premises. To reach the aquarium, cross onto the south end of the Yaquina Bay Bridge, turn east onto SE 32nd St and follow the signs a half mile.

Mark O Hatfield Marine Science Center

This older science center (☎ 541-867-0100), 2030 Marine Science Drive, run by Oregon State University, has some aspects in common with the new aquarium (a glowering octopus and a hands-on tide pool), but exhibits here also focus on the deterioration of the marine environment and the impact of political policies on our oceans. Hours are the same as the Oregon Coast Aquarium; admission is free.

Yaquina Bay State Park

The Yaquina Bay Lighthouse was originally meant to be the partner of a lighthouse on Cape Foulweather 10 miles north. However, the engineers couldn't get the building materials up the steep headland. Apparently two lighthouses for Newport was one too many, and in 1874 the Yaquina Bay Lighthouse was extinguished and the building left derelict – or so it seemed. Visit the lighthouse to hear the ghost story of a young woman's mysterious disappearance – there's even a short film. The lighthouse is open as a museum (☎ 541-867-7451) noon to 4 pm daily. You can tour the living quarters and climb the steps to the lookout; admission is by donation.

The state park occupies a green and brushy bluff above the point where Yaquina Bay and the Pacific Ocean meet, immediately west of the Yaquina Bay Bridge's north embankment. Picnic tables and grassy meadows make this a good place to bring a lunch.

Lincoln County Historical Museum & Burrows House

What sets this small community museum (☎ 541-265-7509), 545 SW 9th St, apart from the others is an excellent collection of Siletz artifacts, including beaded robes, headdresses, baskets and tools, donated by a woman who ran a trading post on the nearby Siletz reservation.

Behind the museum is the Burrows House, an old boarding house that preserves household goods, furnishings and kitchen tools from the turn of the century.

Both museums are open 10 am to 5 pm Tuesday to Sunday, June to September, and 11 am to 4 pm the rest of the year. Admission is free, though donations are encouraged.

Beaches

There's beach access down a trail from Yaquina Bay State Park and at several points along Elizabeth St. Nye Beach, at the west end of 3rd St, was one of the first of Newport's beach developments; there's still access along Coast St. At Agate Beach State Wayside, 3 miles north of the Yaquina Bay Bridge, there's ample parking and restrooms, as well as beach access.

Yaquina Head Natural Area

This 100-acre preserve is 3 miles north of Newport on an exposed headland. The coast's tallest, still-functioning, lighthouse here is open to visitors. The real treat though, is the extensive tide pool area below the bluffs. The BLM, which administers the site, is planning the development of a wheelchair-accessible marine garden along the tide pools.

Charter Fishing & Whale Watching

With its deep and sheltered harbor, Newport is a noted base for charter-fishing trips out into the Pacific. Contact the following for information on fishing trips, or for

OREGON

The Confederated Siletz Tribes

The Native Americans that lived around the Siletz, the Yaquina and the Alsea Rivers hunted seals and sea lions, netted salmon and gathered shellfish. Their cultural and religious life centered around the invocation of animal spirits through shamans. These rituals assured them of bountiful hunting and fishing.

In 1855 they were restricted to the Coast Reservation, a 2160-sq-mile block of land, including all territory west of the Coast Range between Tillamook and Reedsport. Two years later, many of the Takilma and Latgawa Indians who had been sent to the Grand Ronde Reservation walked to the Coast Reservation, near Siletz. The tribes became known as the Confederated Siletz Tribes.

In 1865 the US Government removed a 25-mile-wide parcel of land around Yaquina Bay in order to make way for oyster harvesting and tourism.

By the 1950s less than 8½ sq miles of the original reservation remained in Siletz hands. Under President Dwight Eisenhower, the Siletz and 43 other groups of western Oregon Native Americans lost their tribal status in 1954. With no reservation lands, no government assistance for education or community facilities and no further official recognition of the tribe's cultural or ethnic status, the cohesion of the tribe frayed.

In 1973 a group of Siletz Indians petitioned the government to reinstate legal recognition of the tribe, and in 1977 President Jimmy Carter signed a law restoring the Siletz as a federally acknowledged tribe. The law did not restore any land to the tribe, although some forested BLM land has subsequently been transferred to the tribe's ownership. ■

whale-watching trips during the migration season: South Beach Charters (☎ 541-867-7200) at South Beach Marina; Newport Tradewinds (☎ 541-265-2101), 653 SW Bay Blvd; and Newport Sportfishing (☎ 541-265-7558), 1000 SE Bay Blvd.

To rent a boat and crab rings, contact Embarcadero Dock (☎ 541-265-5435), 1000 SE Bay Blvd.

Special Events

One of the coast's premier events, the Newport Wine & Seafood Festival (☎ 541-265-8801) takes place at South Beach Marina in late February, when people hereabouts can usually use something to cheer them up. Besides wine and seafood tasting, there's also a crafts fair. This festival is popular, so make sure to reserve rooms in advance.

The Nesika Illahe Powwow (☎ 541-444-2532), held the second weekend of August, celebrates the restored federal recognition of the Siletz tribe. Dancing, crafts and food fill the little town of Siletz, 14 miles northeast of Newport. Admission is free.

Places to Stay

Camping *South Beach State Park* (☎ 541-867-4715), 2 miles south of Newport on US 101, has 254 campsites with showers, flush toilets and a playground. Access to the beach is good and there are a number of hiking trails within the park. Make reservations for the summer months. Sites cost $19.

Seven miles north is *Beverly Beach State Park* (☎ 541-265-9278), with over 300 campsites and a $19 camping fee. There's easy access to the beach, showers and wheelchair-accessible restrooms, summer programs and firewood.

Hostels The *Brown Squirrel Hostel* (☎ 541-265-3729, 888-265-3729), 44 SW Brook St, is in a former church. Dorm-style beds cost $15; kitchen and laundry facilities are available. It's open year-round.

B&Bs The *Oar House* (☎ 541-265-9571, 800-265-9571), 520 SW 2nd St, a grand old home built in 1900, has four guest rooms with private bathrooms ranging from $90 to $120. For a less formal stay, the *Sea Cliff B&B* (☎ 541-265-6664), 749 NW 3rd St, offers three guest rooms ($75) with shared bathroom in a rambling old building that also houses an artsy coffeehouse.

Hotels – budget Hotels in Newport are divided into those that face the Pacific and those that face US 101. There's obviously quite a difference in price.

There are plenty of older, well-kept motels along US 101 north of Newport, most of which allow pets and have kitchens in the rooms. Rooms start below $40 at the following: the truth-in-advertising honor goes to *Penny Saver Motel* (☎ 541-265-6631), 710 N Coast Hwy. It has scads of rooms, not all of which face right onto the highway. Another good deal is *Newport Motor Inn* (☎ 541-265-8516), 1311 N Coast Hwy, and the *City Center Motel* (☎ 541-265-7381, 800-628-9665), 538 SW Coast Hwy.

Hotels – middle Near Nye Beach there are a couple of moderately priced beachfront motels. For starters, try the *Viking Condominiums* (☎ 541-265-2477, 800-480-2477), at 729 NW Coast St, which has cottages above the beach (prices start at $55) and rooms in oceanfront condominiums (prices start at $85). There is a private stairway leading down to the beach. Just behind the Viking Condominiums is the *Waves Motel* (☎ 541-265-4661, 800-282-6993), at 820 NW Coast St, with rooms starting at $58.

The most charming lodging options in Newport are two converted old hotels which face the ocean. The *Sylvia Beach Hotel* (☎ 541-265-5428), at 267 NW Cliff St, is a hotel for book lovers with each room decorated in the style of a famous author. The 3rd-floor library that towers over the Pacific Ocean would be a waste of ocean view if the guests weren't all bibliophiles. The Sylvia Beach Hotel is very popular, so reservations are necessary. All rooms come with private baths; prices begin at $68 and go to $145, breakfast included.

A few yards away, the *Nye Beach Hotel* (☎ 541-265-3334), at 219 NW Cliff St, is also a restored 1910s hotel with spacious and comfortable rooms ranging from $60 to $125. Some include fireplaces, balconies and hot tubs. A cafe on the main floor is open for breakfast, lunch and dinner.

Hotels – top end Each of the following offer many options, including fireplaces and hot tubs. Prices are for the basic room package.

Newport's grandest hotel is the *Embarcadero Resort* (☎ 541-265-8521, 800-547-4779), behind the marina in Yaquina Bay at 1000 SE Bay Blvd. Rooms are in condolike suites and cost $110 to $220.

Out on the headland is the enormous *Shilo Inn* (☎ 541-265-7701, 800-222-2244), 536 SW Elizabeth St. This lodging complex offers almost 200 rooms with ocean views, numerous restaurants and convention facilities. Singles/doubles begin at $129/135. The *Hallmark Resort Best Western* (☎ 541-265-8853, 800-982-8668), 744 SW Elizabeth St, also sits above the beachfront; rooms begin at $99.

Agate Beach, the most northerly of Newport's beaches, is where you'll find the upscale *Holiday Inn at Agate Beach* (☎ 541-265-9411, 800-547-3310), 3019 N Coast Hwy, with amazing views over Yaquina Head and the Pacific. Rooms range from $104 to $155. One of the nicest and most secluded places to stay in Newport is *Little Creek Cove* (☎ 541-265-8587, 800-294-8025), 3641 NW Oceanview Drive, a condominium complex right on the beach. Both one- and two-bedroom units are available; rates begin at $99.

Resorts Nine miles north of Newport is the *Inn at Otter Crest* (☎ 541-765-2111, 800-452-2101), a destination resort with 100 suites overlooking the ocean, a swimming pool, tennis courts, spa and exercise facilities, and an on-premises restaurant and lounge. The location, just under the headland at Cape Foulweather, is outstanding, with miles of beach and tide pools just outside your door. Rooms begin at $89 to $169, depending on the view.

Vacation Home Rentals If you're interested in renting a home, contact Yaquina Bay Property Management (☎ 541-265-3537), 1164 SW Coast Hwy, suite C, Newport, OR 97365.

Places to Eat
Like most beach towns, there's no end to family-style eateries offering fast food. What's unusual is that Newport also offers a number of good, and sometimes innovative, restaurants that make the most of the harbor's fresh seafood.

Budget A standby for early-morning fishing crews and late-night revelers is the 24-hour *Pip Tide* (☎ 541-265-7797), 836 SW Bay Blvd. For coffee and pastries, go to the *Daily Grind Coffeehouse* (☎ 541-265-6263), 156 SW Bay Blvd or *Newport Beach Bakery & Café* (☎ 541-265-7231), 715A SW Hurbert St, for cinnamon rolls, croissants and breads right from the oven. *Hungry Crocodile* (☎ 541-265-4585), 2005 N Coast Hwy, offers vegetarian dishes in addition to espresso drinks.

Middle *Nye Beach Cafe* (☎ 541-265-3334), 219 NW Cliff St, in the hotel, offers good omelets, sandwiches and great views. In good weather, there's seating on the verandah above the beach. For burgers, go to the *Big Guy's Diner* (☎ 541-265-5114), 1801 N Coast Hwy.

Mo's Restaurant (☎ 541-265-2979), 622 SW Bay Blvd, is a kind of tradition. Mo's seafood restaurants were started decades ago by Mohava Niemi, a local Siletz whose clam chowder and fried fish became the standard of coastal fare; seafood dinner specials are $10. The first Mo's is still here among the crusty bayfront chandlers and bars. Directly across the street, on the edge of the wharf, is *Mo's Annex* (☎ 541-265-7512), 657 SW Bay Blvd. Both offer buckets of steamed clams, baskets of fried fish and bowls of creamy clam chowder.

The *Whale's Tale* (☎ 541-265-8660), 452 SW Bay Blvd, is yet another Newport tradition, considered a kind of shrine to 1960s hippie restaurants. You can't beat its location on the waterfront or its cozily exaggerated maritime motif. This is Newport's most convivial restaurant for favorite seafood dishes. A dinner of Yaquina Bay oysters goes for $13, and for the real

seafood enthusiast there's the Captain's Plate with five kinds of fresh fish for $17.

Top End Upscale *Canyon Way Restaurant* (☎ 541-265-8319), 1216 SW Canyon Way, is in an old storefront complex with a bookstore, gift shop and deli. Although innovative fresh seafood preparations make up much of the menu, there are also good steaks, prime rib and delicious barbecued lamb ribs; entrées are $14 to $21. Save room, if possible, for the wondrous desserts.

At Sylvia Beach Hotel's dining room, the *Table of Content* (☎ 541-265-5428), 267 NW Cliff St, dinners for non-guests are by reservation only. The prix-fixe menu is $17.50 a person.

Entertainment
The *Rogue Ales Public House* (☎ 541-265-3188), 748 SW Bay Blvd, is the brewpub for local Rogue Ales and offers sandwiches, pizza and other light entrées in the $6 range.

Newport Cinemas (☎ 541-265-2111) is at 5837 N Coast Hwy. The *Newport Performing Arts Center* (☎ 541-265-2787), 777 W Olive St, is Newport's venue for touring regional and national entertainment.

Getting There & Around
Newport is one of the only coastal towns with a bona fide bus depot (☎ 541-265-2253), 956 SW 10th St. Greyhound buses pass through running between Portland and San Francisco. Daily Valley Retriever buses to Corvallis and Bend also depart from here, and Central Coast Connections buses (☎ 541-265-4900) link Newport to other coastal towns. Four buses daily make runs from Lincoln City via Newport down to Yachats. One-way fare to Lincoln City from Newport is $2; Newport to Yachats is $3.

Call Yaquina Cab Company (☎ 541-265-9552) to hire a cab.

WALDPORT
Population 1665
Waldport, at the mouth of the Alsea River, revels in its 'relative obscurity.' The area boasts long stretches of sandy beach, with a number of day-use state park access

points and inexpensive lodging. Seal Rock, where a massive hump of rock protects a beach and tide pools, is a good place for young children to explore the coast.

Hwy 34, following the Alsea River from the Willamette Valley, is one of the most scenic routes between the valley and the coast.

The Waldport Visitors Center (☎ 541-563-6086) is at 620 NW Spring St, Waldport, OR 97394. The Waldport Ranger Station for the Siuslaw National Forest (☎ 541-563-3211) is at 1049 SW Pacific Coast Hwy. The post office is at the corner of Hemlock and Johns Sts.

Alsea Bay Bridge
Historical Interpretive Center
Travel along Oregon's rugged coast was not always simple, as this interesting museum of transport (☎ 541-563-2002) makes evident. The facility traces the history of transportation routes along the coast, beginning with trails used by Native Americans and moving on to the sea, rail, and finally, road routes now in use.

The center is at the southern end of the Alsea Bay Bridge and is open 9 am to 4 pm daily, Memorial Day to Labor Day, and 9 am to 4 pm Wednesday to Sunday the rest of the year; admission is free.

Fishing
A number of moorages and friendly fishing outfitters flank the lower reaches of the river and bay, providing rental boats, tackle and refreshments for anglers. Contact Oakland's Fish Camp (☎ 541-563-5865), by milestone 4 on Hwy 34, for a sample of rates and services. The Alsea Bay is also one of the very best **crabbing** areas in the state. To rent a boat and crab rings, contact Dock of the Bay Marina (☎ 541-563-2003), along the Old Town Wharf. The upper river is widely noted for its fall steelhead fishing. For a professional outfitting service, call Gene O's Guide Service (☎ 541-563-3171) or write PO Box 43, Waldport, OR 97394.

Places to Stay
Beachside State Park (☎ 541-563-3023), 4 miles south of Waldport on US 101, has over 80 sites for $17 to $19, with showers and wheelchair-accessible restrooms. Just down the road is *Tillicum Beach*, a USFS campground with 60 campsites at $10, flush toilets and drinking water.

The best of the in-town motels is the *Alsea Manor Motel* (☎ 541-563-3249), 190 SW Arrow St, with rooms for $48 to $58.

Charming *Cape Cod Cottages* (☎ 541-563-2106), 4150 SW US 101, just south of town along the beach, are small whitewashed cabins with ocean views. All units have kitchens and fireplaces and range in price from $67 to $79.

Places to Eat
Family-style restaurants with fish and chips and sandwiches pretty much begin and end the selection here. However, for espresso and muffins, head to *Bumps & Grinds Coffeehouse* (☎ 541-563-5769), 225 Waldport St. The *Seafood Grotto* (☎ 541-563-5104), at Spring Court and US 101, is as good a place as any for steak, fish and seafood.

Kozy Kove Kafe (☎ 541-528-3251), 9 miles east of Waldport on Hwy 34 in Tidewater is on a kind of log barge and claims to be the coast's only floating restaurant. It's charming in a whimsical way, with nice views over the river and attendant bird life. The food is pretty good, too: steak and prime rib ($14), honey-fried chicken ($11), seafood entrées like scallops with garlic and mushrooms ($16) and even a selection of Mexican food.

Getting There & Around
Two Greyhound buses pass each way daily through Waldport on the run between Portland and San Francisco. Four daily Central Coast Connections buses from Newport pass through Waldport ($2.50). Bus stops are at the Waldport Ranger Station, 1049 SW Pacific Coast Hwy, and the Waldport Senior Center, 265 Elsie Hwy.

YACHATS & AROUND
The Alsea word 'Yachats' (pronounced Ya-HOTS), means 'at the foot of the mountain.' It's an apt description for this wonderful little community at the base of

OREGON

massive Cape Perpetua. Yachats (population 580) is homey and welcoming, yet rugged and wind-whipped, preserving the illusion that this is a village that the tourist industry hasn't yet discovered.

Beginning at Cape Perpetua and continuing south about 20 miles is some of Oregon's most spectacular shoreline. This entire area was once a series of volcanic intrusions, which resisted the pummeling of the Pacific long enough to rise as oceanside peaks and promontories. Tiny beaches lined by cliffs seem almost serendipitous. Acres of tide pools appear and disappear according to the fancy of the tides and are home to starfish, sea anemones and sea lions. Picturesque lighthouses rise above the surf. It's a beautiful area; if it weren't so far from centers of population, it would certainly be more highly developed than it is.

Seven miles south of Yachats is a small community sometimes called Searose Beach or Tenmile Creek, with a number of B&Bs and a motel above the beach.

The Yachats Chamber of Commerce (☎ 541-547-3530) is located at 441 US 101, Yachats, OR 97498.

Beaches
Beaches around here are small, secluded affairs that have to share space with expanses of tide pools and rocky spires. The closest beach to Yachats is about a mile to the north, often called **Smelt Sands Beach** for the run of smelt (sardine-sized fish) that ground themselves here during spawning season. At the mouth of Yachats River is Yachats State Park, with a wheelchair-accessible trail along the surf.

South of Yachats, **Strawberry Hill Wayside** and **Neptune State Park** offer enjoyable prowling among intertidal rocks and sandy inlets. Sea lions are common along this part of the beach.

One of the most enchanting of all beaches in Oregon is the little sandy cove at **Devil's Elbow State Park**, about 10 miles south of Yachats, with the Heceta Head Lighthouse keeping guard, a dense forest bounding the beach and a Conde

McCullough bridge arching across placid Cape Creek.

Cape Perpetua
Cape Perpetua, 2 miles south of Yachats, was first sighted and named by England's Captain James Cook in 1778. This remnant of a volcano is one of the highest points on the Oregon coast. Views from the cape are incredible, taking in coastal promontories from Cape Foulweather to Cape Arago. The USFS has designated the 2700-acre area a Federal Scenic Area, and it has a visitors' center, camping, hikes and trails to ancient shell middens, tide pools and unique natural formations.

From US 101, turn on USFS Rd 55 and follow the signs to Cape Perpetua Viewpoint.

The Cape Perpetua Visitors Center provides good background material on the human and natural history of Cape Perpetua with displays on the culture of the Alsea tribe who journeyed here to feast on the abundant shellfish near the tide pools. Middens, centuries-old mounds of shells, attest to their banqueting.

Other exhibits discuss the ecology of the seashore (focusing on intertidal life) and the natural life of the dense spruce, cedar and hemlock forests. From the viewing platforms, watch for migrating whales. A small gift shop provides one of the best selections of books in the area on local travel and natural history. Slide and video shows about Cape Perpetua are screened according to demand.

The Cape Perpetua Visitors Center (☎ 541-547-3289) is open from 9 am to 6 pm daily, May through September, and 10 am to 4 pm on weekends the rest of the year.

The Devil's Churn Deep fractures in the old volcano allow waves to erode narrow channels into the headland, creating the compelling Devil's Churn. Waves race up a deep but very narrow channel between basalt ledges, then shoot up the 30-foot inlet only to explode against the narrowing sides of the channel.

Trails from the visitors' center, or from the Devil's Churn parking lot one mile north, follow steep stairs that are frequently slick and muddy. Only the sure of foot should go all the way to the bottom, and even then care is demanded near the edge of the channel. Children must be supervised.

From the base of the Devil's Churn Trail, turn south to explore acres of tide pools.

Hiking Most of the sites at Cape Perpetua require only a short stroll, but there are longer day hikes along the ocean and into forested wilderness areas.

The most popular hike is the 1.3 mile climb from the visitors' center up to the lookout on Cape Perpetua. This area was first developed by the CCC during the 1930s. The rock shelter at the top of the cape was used as a lookout for enemy vessels during WWII.

An easier trail down to the tide pools is the **Captain Cook Trail**. This paved 1.2-mile roundtrip trail leaves from the visitors' center and passes through dense stands of salal before reaching ancient shell middens. Watch for the spouting horn, a geyser-like blast of water that shoots out of a sea cave.

The **Giant Spruce Trail** leads up Cape Creek from the visitors' center to the so-called Giant Spruce, a 500-year-old tree with a nine-foot circumference. The 7-mile **Cook's Ridge-Gwynn Creek Loop Trail** leads back into the deep forests along Gwynn Creek. Follow the Oregon Coast Trail south from the visitors' center and turn up Gwynn Creek. The trail returns along the ridge between Gwynn and Cape Creeks.

Heceta Head Lighthouse
At **Devil's Elbow State Park**, 14 miles south of Yachats, turn west to the beachside parking lot. On a bluff to the north is **Heceta House**, an 1893 lighthouse keeper's house, now used as a facility of Lane County Community College. From the parking lot a trail leads to this lovely whitewashed structure and on to the Heceta Head Lighthouse, built in 1894. The cape and the buildings were named for Bruno Heceta (pronounced he-SEE-ta), a Spanish navigator who explored the area in 1775.

The lighthouse is still functioning and is not open to the public, but the trail continues to the end of the cape. The lighthouse is one of the most photographed features in Oregon, particularly from the viewpoint on US 101 a mile south of the park.

Sea Lion Caves
This enormous sea grotto (☎ 541-547-3111), 91560 US 101, filled with smelly, shrieking sea lions, is a highlight of the central Oregon coast. A 208-foot elevator deposits you in a small natural shaft that opens onto the larger grotto. From this observation point 50 feet above the cave, you can watch almost 200 Steller's sea lions clambering onto rocks, jockeying for position at the top of ledges and letting loose with mighty roars.

While Sea Lion Caves is heavily promoted and may seem like a tourist trap, it is definitely worth a stop. If you don't like crowds, plan to go early or off-season.

Opening hours are 9 am to 7 pm, May to September, and 9 am to 4 pm October to April. Admission is $6.50/4.50 for adults/children (six to 15).

OREGON

Places to Stay

Camping At the *Cape Perpetua Campground*, which is administered by the Siuslaw National Forest, there are 37 campsites for $11.

Seven miles south of Yachats is the *Sea Perch Campground* (☎ 541-547-3505), with 75 sites near Tenmile Creek. Facilities include showers, flush toilets and hookups, plus a small grocery store. Ocean-view sites are $20, others are $18. *Carl G Washburne State Park*, 13 miles south, has nearly 70 campsites, with showers and flush toilets; rates are $17 to $19. Although the campground is on the opposite side of the road from the ocean, trails lead to beaches and to a 4-mile hiking trail system within the park.

B&Bs The following B&Bs are 7 miles south of Yachats, in the little community that slumbers at the mouth of Tenmile Creek. All have ocean-view rooms and access to a small beach. The most eye-catching is the *Ziggurat B&B* (☎ 541-547-3925), 95330 US 101, which is more like some fanciful temple (hence the name) than a private home. The three rooms are filled with commissioned furniture and art. Prices range from $125 to $140. The *Sea Quest B&B* (☎ 541-547-3782, 800-341-3782), 95354 US 101, has five guest rooms. Each room comes with private bath, entrance, spa and deck. Prices start at $125.

Hotels At the northern end of Yachats, the *Dublin House* (☎ 541-547-3200), at 7th St and US 101, offers an indoor swimming pool, kitchens and ocean-view rooms. The staff can also arrange fly-fishing trips and lessons. Rooms range from $55 to $75. The *Fireside Motel* (☎ 541-547-3636, 800-336-3573), 1881 N US 101, has rooms with wood-burning stoves for $60 to $88. Pets are OK.

The *Adobe Resort Inn* (☎ 541-547-3141, 800-522-3623), 1555 US 101, includes a restaurant and lounge on its premises. Most rooms have ocean views and some have fireplaces and balconies. There's also an exercise room, hot tub and sauna. Rooms range from $61 to $120.

The *Shamrock Lodgettes* (☎ 541-547-3312, 800-845-5028), at 105 S US 101, seems to sit in a large park by the ocean. There's lodging either in a modern motel unit, or charming older cabins, all with kitchenettes and stone fireplaces. Some rooms have kitchens, the modern units have ocean views. Rates range from $70 to $100.

The newest and nicest lodging option in Yachats is *Overleaf Lodge* (☎ 541-547-4880, 800-338-0507), 2055 N US 101, with luxury-level rooms complete with fireplaces, Jacuzzis, balconies, and more. Rooms begin at $105.

There are more options in out-of-the-way pockets south of Cape Perpetua. One of the real deals along this part of the coast is *The See Vue* (☎ 541-547-3227), 95590 US 101, in Tenmile Creek. Rooms are theme decorated: there is the Sante Fe Room, the Northwest Room, the Princess & the Pea Room and so on. All have ocean views and some have kitchens and fireplaces. Prices for rooms range from $42 to $65.

Even more remote is the *Oregon House* (☎ 541-547-3329), 94288 S US 101, set on a cliff 9 miles south of Yachats. A private estate built in the 1930s and '50s, the various buildings – the gardener's cottage, the orchid greenhouse, the main lodge and an art studio – have been renovated and converted into one-of-a-kind accommodations. Most units have ocean views and kitchens, some have fireplaces, and all have private baths. Several of the units have two bedrooms and can sleep from four to six guests. No pets are allowed and some units have restrictions on children. For those who like their seclusion and value a break from chain motel rooms, this is a favorite. Room rates fall between $50 and $110.

Vacation Home Rentals If you are interested in renting a home, contact Yachats Village Rentals (☎ 541-547-3501) at PO Box 44, Yachats, OR 97498.

Places to Eat
Yachats' choices are limited, but very
pleasant. The *New Morning Coffeehouse*
(☎ 541-547-3848), at 4th St and US 101,
will get you into the laid-back pace of
beach life. Espresso, pastries and conversation are the pastimes here. For breads and
even more pastries, go to *On the Rise
Bakery* (☎ 541-547-3440), 281 US 101, a
homespun affair with good scones and
slices of pizza.

For many, dinner at *La Serre* (☎ 541-
547-3420), at 2nd and Beach Sts, is a highlight of a trip to Yachats. The waitstaff
dresses in rather silly pioneer outfits but
the food is as good as any on the coast. The
cioppino is great ($17), as is the steak and
fresh fish.

Getting There & Away
Two northbound and two southbound
Greyhound buses pass daily through Yachats on their way up and down the coast;
one-way fare to/from Portland is $20. Four
daily Central Coast Connections buses
bound for Newport depart from Clark's
IGA grocery store, on the corner of W 2nd
St and US 101 ($3 one way).

Southern
Oregon Coast

While the northern Oregon coast surely
boasts beautiful locations, the southern
coast is a near continuous succession of
dramatic seascapes. Far from any major
population center and serviced by few and
slow roads, none of the towns along the
southern coast is experiencing the kind of
boom evident at Cannon Beach or Lincoln
City to the north. Repeated years of short-
ened or suspended salmon fishing seasons
and a dried-up wood-products industry
have created somewhat of a recession
along this part of the coast. There's still
deep-sea fishing for bottom fish, halibut,
shark and other brawny specimens, though
by now most charter operators have been

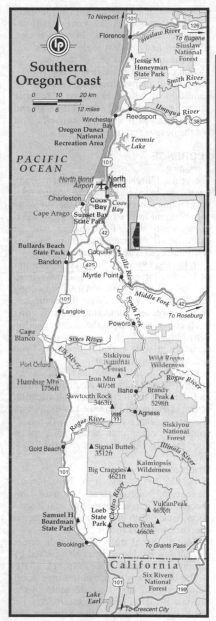

starved out of business. Don't go looking for exquisite sauces for your mesquite-grilled calamari or for a four-star resort. Chowder and modest older motels are more the norm in this part of the state.

Much of the coastline here is nearly pristine and in many places approaches the condition of wilderness. Find a favorite sandy beach at the end of a hiking trail and chances are you'll have it to yourself on all but the busiest summer weekends.

FLORENCE
Population 5475

For years, Florence was one of the beach towns you loved to hate: strip commercial development stretched along the highway for miles, the whine of dune buggies navigating sandy bluffs filled the air, and the extensive, if characterless, sandy beaches were thronged with idle family groups.

In the last few years, however, the center of life in Florence has shifted away from the malls along US 101 to Old Town along the Siuslaw River, with good restaurants, coffeehouses and interesting shops. Fishing boats come and go from the harbor, bearing their burden of freshly caught flounder or shrimp and seals bark for handouts from spectators along the wharf.

Florence is at the northern end of the Oregon Dunes National Recreation Area, and much of the increasing sophistication of the amenities in Florence has to do with the growing appreciation of the dunes as something other than sandy hills to be dominated by dune buggies and dirt bikes.

Orientation

Hwy 126 heads east from here toward Eugene, 63 miles distant. South of Florence is the Oregon Dunes National Recreation Area. North of town, the coast again becomes wild and rocky.

Roughly speaking, Old Town is under the Siuslaw Bridge and can be reached by turning south down Maple St from US 101.

The best access to ocean beaches is off South Jetty Rd, about a mile south of the Siuslaw Bridge. From the South Jetty Rd north to the mouth of the Siuslaw, the beach is closed in the summer to vehicles. Another beach access is at Heceta Beach, about 3 miles north of Florence. Turn west on Heceta Beach Rd.

Information

The Florence Chamber of Commerce (☎ 541-997-3128) is at 270 US 101, Florence, OR 97439, just north of the bridge.

The post office is at 770 Maple St. Old Town Books (☎ 541-997-6205), 1340 Bay St, is a small bookstore that offers a little bit of everything, even gifts and coffee.

Do laundry and take a shower while you wait at 37th St Coin Laundry & Showers (☎ 541-997-5111), N US 101 and 37th St. Peace Harbor Hospital (☎ 541-997-8412) is at 400 9th St.

Siuslaw Pioneer Museum

Housed in an unusual old church (built from a barn kit), this regional museum (☎ 541-997-7884), 85294 S US 101, contains the usual mementos of lumbering and items from old kitchens, but also has a good selection of Siuslaw Indian artifacts. Opening hours are 10 am to 4 pm, Tuesday to Sunday, with a requested $1 donation for adults.

American Museum of Fly Fishing

This Old Town museum (☎ 541-997-6102), 280 Nopal St, features a large private collection of hand-tied flies displayed in frames. Some flies date back to the 1800s, and the 15,000 flies in the collection represent the work of fly-tiers from more than 20 countries. There's also a number of fishing-related sculptures and paintings. Call ahead, as the museum is only open by appointment. Admission is $2.50.

Darlingtonia Botanical Wayside

At this small park 5 miles north of Florence on US 101, boardwalks lead out into dense wetlands to a patch of *Darlingtonia californica*, the unusual flesh-eating plant also called pitcher plant or cobra-lily. Placards explain the life cycle of these oddities. Apparently, their meat-eating ways evolved because the soils available to them are generally very low in nutrients. The process of luring insects in and digesting them is quite slow and unspectacular, but it's pretty interesting to visit the Darlingtonia bog to see these rare plants in their native habitat.

Fishing

The Siuslaw River has a major salmon and steelhead run in the fall. Additionally, you'll find that there's good cutthroat and rainbow trout fishing. There are a number of fishing access points east of town toward Mapleton. Contact Bing Nelson (☎ 541-997-6508) if you want to hire a fishing guide on the Siuslaw River.

Golf

Sixty-foot sand dunes surround the 18-hole Ocean Dunes Golf Links (☎ 541-997-3232, 800-468-4833), 3345 Munsel Lake Rd, threatening golfers with the world's worst sand trap.

Horseback Riding

Rent a horse for beach riding 8 miles north of Florence at C&M Stables (☎ 541-997-7540), 90241 N US 101.

Flower Nursery

Woodsman Native Nursery (☎ 541-997-2252), 4385 N US 101, offers lots of local bloomers and climbers for sale. Even if you are not in the market, it's a really pleasant stop.

Rhododendron Festival

Held the third weekend of May, the Rhododendron Festival (☎ 541-997-3128) has been celebrated for over 80 years to honor the ubiquitous shrubs that erupt into bloom in May. A floral parade, flower show, the Rhodie Run, a crafts fair and a slug race are some of the events.

Places to Stay

Camping The most pleasant campgrounds in the Florence area are north of town where streams are trapped by the dunes and form freshwater lakes. *Alder Dune*, 7

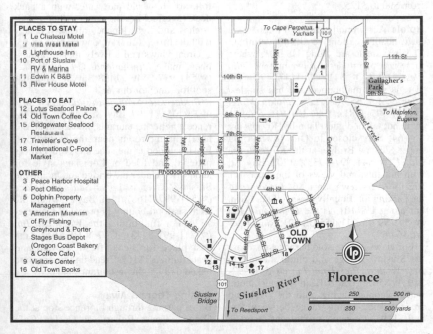

PLACES TO STAY
1 Le Chateau Motel
3 Villa West Motel
8 Lighthouse Inn
10 Port of Siuslaw
   RV & Marina
11 Edwin K B&B
13 River House Motel

PLACES TO EAT
12 Lotus Seafood Palace
14 Old Town Coffee Co
15 Bridgewater Seafood
   Restaurant
17 Traveler's Cove
18 International C-Food
   Market

OTHER
3 Peace Harbor Hospital
4 Post Office
5 Dolphin Property
   Management
6 American Museum
   of Fly Fishing
7 Greyhound & Porter
   Stages Bus Depot
   (Oregon Coast Bakery
   & Coffee Cafe)
9 Visitors Center
16 Old Town Books

Florence

miles north on US 101, and *Sutton*, 6 miles north, are USFS campgrounds with flush toilets and access to lakes and the beach. Sites at both campgrounds cost $10. Happily, there is no dune buggy access at this part of the dunes.

For RVers who want to camp right on the Pacific, go to *Heceta Beach RV Park* (☎ 541-997-7664), on Heceta Beach Rd. It has showers and a laundry, and sites start at $19. There are both tent and RV sites right on Florence Harbor in Old Town at *Port of Siuslaw RV & Marina* (☎ 541-997-3040), at 1st and Harbor Sts. It has showers, a boat launch and easy access to shops and restaurants; sites are $16.

B&Bs The *Edwin K B&B* (☎ 541-997-8360, 800-833-9465), 1155 Bay St, is an attractive Arts and Crafts home down along the Siuslaw River near Old Town. The four nicely furnished units each have private bathrooms. One room has a balcony and even boasts its own waterfall! Rooms range from $90 to $125.

Hotels Accommodations in Florence are inexplicably expensive during summer. The best deals are along US 101, where there is a plenitude of older motels. *Villa West Motel* (☎ 541-997-3457), 901 US 101, is well maintained and has singles/doubles for $55/68. *Le Chateau Motel* (☎ 541-997-3481), 1084 US 101, offers a pool, hot tub and guest laundry. Rooms are $54/64. Stay closer to Old Town, right under Siuslaw Bridge, at the *River House Motel* (☎ 541-997-3933), 1202 Bay St, with hot tubs and views of the river. It's $78 for river-view rooms, $64 for views of the parking lot. Equally close to Old Town, but along US 101, is the *Lighthouse Inn* (☎ 541-997-3221), 155 US 101; room rates are $64/69.

For views over the old harbor area, cross the Siuslaw Bridge and climb the hill to *Best Western Pier Point Inn* (☎ 541-997-7191), 85625 US 101, an upscale motel with balconies facing onto the river and spa facilities; rooms range between $99 and $119. Florence's beachfront resort is

Driftwood Shores (☎ 541-997-8263, 800-422-5091), 88416 First Ave, which offers condo-style suites, all with ocean views. Most rooms have kitchens and fireplaces, and there's an indoor pool; rates begin at $79.

Vacation Home Rentals To rent a private home for extended stays in Florence, contact the Dolphin Property Management (☎ 541-997-7368), 396 US 101, Florence, OR 97439.

Places to Eat
Start the day at *Old Town Coffee Co* (☎ 541-902-9336), 1269 Bay St, where you can get espresso and pastries. For an incredible omelet, head out to *Blue Hen Cafe* (☎ 541-997-3907), 1675 US 101.

Along the harbor in Old Town are quite a few good cafes and fish markets that serve up inexpensive fish and chips and clam chowder. *Traveler's Cove* (☎ 541-997-6845), 1362 Bay St, is part international folk art shop and part cafe, with a back deck (overlooking the water) where sandwiches and light lunches are served. Try the hot shrimp (or crab) on toast for $8.95.

Great views and a lively market atmosphere make *International C-Food Market* (☎ 541-997-9646), 1498 Bay St, a popular spot for lunch or dinner.

Bridgewater Seafood Restaurant (☎ 541-997-9405), 1297 Bay St, is one of Florence's better restaurants, housed in an old hotel dining room near the waterfront. Fresh seafood is the specialty; order yours battered and fried or Louisiana style for about $15. Under the bridge and facing the Siuslaw River is *Lotus Seafood Palace* (☎ 541-997-7168), 1150 Bay St, where the local seafood bounty is prepared Chinese-style. For fine-dining the *Windward Inn* (☎ 541-997-8243), 3757 N US 101, is the best place for steak, fresh seafood and pasta dinners ($16). Bread and pastries are baked daily at the restaurant's bakery.

Getting There & Away
Buses passing through Florence stop at the Oregon Coast Bakery & Coffee Cafe

(☎ 541-902-9076), 327 Laurel St (an old sign incorrectly points down Nopal St). The Greyhound bus comes down from Portland once daily via Lincoln City on the way to San Francisco along US 101 ($26 one way). Porter Stages (☎ 800-540-7100) has two buses on weekdays and one on weekends to Eugene and south to Coos Bay; a ticket from Eugene to Florence is $14.

OREGON DUNES NATIONAL RECREATION AREA

The Oregon Dunes stretch for 50 miles between Florence and Coos Bay, forming the largest expanse of coastal sand dunes in the USA. The National Recreation Area was created in 1972 and takes in 50 sq miles. Adjacent to the area are Honeyman and Tugman State Parks.

The dunes front the Pacific Ocean but undulate east as much as 3 miles to meet coastal forests, with a succession of curious ecosystems and formations between. Streams running down from the Coast Range form lakes surrounded by Sahara-like banks of sand. A number of hiking trails, bridle paths and boating and swimming areas have been established throughout this unique place, and the entire region is noted for its abundant wildlife, especially birds.

That's the good news. Ownership of the areas adjacent to the Oregon Dunes is mixed: some of the land is controlled by the state park system, but a lot of it is privately owned. Many of the lakes are flanked by resort homes and are churned by motorboats. And, however democratic it may seem, the National Recreation Area is open to 'mixed use,' meaning that about half of the area is dominated by off-road vehicles (ORVs) or all-terrain vehicles (ATVs), which means dune buggies and dirt bikes tearing up and down the dunes and the tell-tale smell and demonic whine of two-stroke engines in the air.

The USFS has decided to cut back on the areas open to vehicular use, in order to increase hiking access and wildlife territory. Be sure to get a detailed map of the area in order to determine where the restrictions are in place. The lower half of the dunes, south of Reedsport, sees the most ORV traffic, while the upper half has the most hiking trails.

Information

The headquarters for Oregon Dunes National Recreation Area (☎ 541-271-3611) is at 855 Highway Ave, Reedsport, OR 97467. In addition to hiking information and maps, there's a 20-minute film that explains the formation of the dunes and the different ecosystems found here. The hours are 8 am to 4:30 pm daily.

Be prepared to pay a $3 per vehicle user fee at most trailheads, picnic areas, boat launches, ORV staging areas and beach parking lots serviced by the Siuslaw National Forest.

Hiking

Short hikes from roadside trailheads lead through the dunes, lakes and scrub forests out to the beach. Once on the beach, long hikes along the shore can lead to other trails. Be sure to pick up a trail map and the brochure *Hiking Trails in the Oregon Dunes National Recreation Area* from the headquarters.

From the **Stagecoach Trailhead**, three easy, short trails lead along a river and wetlands, affording good wildlife viewing. One of these, the **Waxmyrtle Trail**, winds along the Siltcoos River, where herons, deer and waterfowl can be seen. Part of this trail passes an area protected for nesting snowy plovers, a threatened species of shore bird that has only six known nesting sites in Oregon. In 1½ miles, hikers reach the beach. The other trails from the Stagecoach Trailhead lead to a freshwater lagoon or up to a forested vista point. To reach this trailhead, turn onto Siltcoos Beach Rd at the sign for Siltcoos Dunes and Beach Access, 7 miles south of Florence on US 101. There are a number of campgrounds here.

Another trailhead is found at the **Oregon Dunes Overlook**, 10 miles south of Florence. This wheelchair-accessible vista also

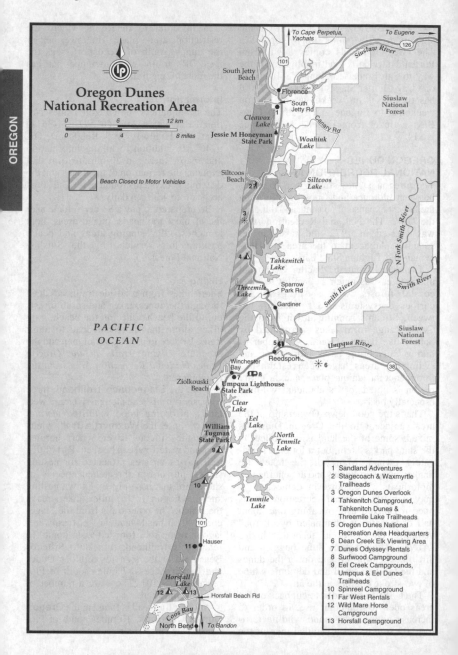

**Oregon Dunes
National Recreation Area**

0   6   12 km
0   4   8 miles

Beach Closed to Motor Vehicles

To Cape Perpetua,
Yachats

To Eugene →

126

Siuslaw River

101

South Jetty
Beach

Florence

South
Jetty Rd

Siuslaw
National
Forest

Canary Rd

Cleawox
Lake

Jessie M Honeyman
State Park

Woahink
Lake

Siltcoos Beach

Siltcoos
Lake

N Fork Smith River

2

3

4

Tahkenitch
Lake

Sparrow
Park Rd

Smith River

Smith River

Threemile
Lake

Gardiner

PACIFIC
OCEAN

Siuslaw
National
Forest

Umpqua River

5

Reedsport

6

38

Winchester
Bay

7

8

Ziolkouski
Beach

Umpqua Lighthouse
State Park

Clear
Lake

Eel
Lake

North
Tenmile
Lake

William
Tugman
State Park

9

10

Tenmile
Lake

101

11   Hauser

Horsfall
Lake

12   13

Horsfall Beach Rd

Coos Bay

North Bend   To Bandon

1 Sandland Adventures
2 Stagecoach & Waxmyrtle
   Trailheads
3 Oregon Dunes Overlook
4 Tahkenitch Campground,
   Tahkenitch Dunes &
   Threemile Lake Trailheads
5 Oregon Dunes National
   Recreation Area Headquarters
6 Dean Creek Elk Viewing Area
7 Dunes Odyssey Rentals
8 Surfwood Campground
9 Eel Creek Campgrounds,
   Umpqua & Eel Dunes
   Trailheads
10 Spinreel Campground
11 Far West Rentals
12 Wild Mare Horse
   Campground
13 Horsfall Campground

serves as a trailhead for a 1-mile hike to the beach. There's a $1 parking fee.

For a longer loop trail through dunes, forest and marsh, take trails west from Tahkenitch Campground Trailhead, 8 miles north of Reedsport on US 101. The **Tahkenitch Dunes Trail** leads to the beach in less than 2 miles. Walk south along the beach until directional posts point to the **Threemile Lake Trail**, which passes a freshwater lake and goes through deep forests before reaching the campground. The entire loop trail is roughly 6 miles long.

To check out some of the biggest dunes in the area, take hikes from the **Eel Creek Campgrounds Trailhead**, 8 miles south of Reedsport. The 2½-mile **Umpqua Dunes Trail** leads out from the campground into a wilderness of massive sand peaks before reaching the beach. This trail involves some dune climbing and probably isn't for the casual hiker. It can also be unpleasant in windy weather. To find out whether you're up for the 5-mile hike to the beach and back, pick up the **Eel Dunes Trail** from campsite No 50, which winds along a forested dune for three-quarters of a mile before feeding into the Umpqua Dunes Trail.

Fishing
While primarily regarded as a 50-mile ribbon of sand, the Oregon dunes also comprise a 50-mile strip of small, freshwater lakes. Largemouth bass lurk in most of these lakes and many are stocked with rainbow trout. Coho salmon, steelhead and cutthroat trout can be caught in larger lakes like Siltcoos, Tahkenitch and Tenmile. A free fishing guide is available from the Oregon Dunes National Recreation Area headquarters.

Swimming & Boating
Jessie M Honeyman State Park (☎ 541-997-3641) has two lakes. **Cleawox Lake** is the smaller of the two and, although motorized boats are allowed here, most speedboat drivers prefer **Woahink Lake**, which is deeper and doesn't fill with weeds.

> ## Mountains of Sand
> The wild and rocky coasts of southern Oregon are the western flanks of the Klamath geologic province, once an island that stood offshore from the West Coast. The coast along this section of Oregon is so steep and rocky, and the continental shelf so narrow, that there is little place for beaches or sand deposits. However, the major rivers of the area – the Chetco, the Smith, the Rogue and the Coquille – are constantly flushing sand into the ocean. The waves battering the headlands are also constantly reducing the coastline to sand. Since there is no place for it to accumulate along the coast, this bounty of sand shifts northward along ocean currents. Between Cape Arago and the volcanic seaside mountains south of Cape Perpetua – a 50-mile-long area – no cliffs or rock formations resist the flows of sand, and it washes ashore and forms into massive dunes. The Oregon Dunes, now protected by the government, contain some of the largest oceanfront dunes in the world. Some are 500 feet high and form banks sometimes 3 miles deep. ■

Canoes and pedal boats are available for rent at the park concession along Cleawox Lake. A $3 day-use fee is charged unless you're staying the night.

Both lakes have designated swimming areas. Cleawox Lake is especially popular with children as the west bank of the lake is a high sand dune and they love skittering down the sand into the water.

Likewise, in William Tugman State Park, you can go boating and swimming in **Eel Lake**. Although motorized boats are allowed, a 10-mph speed limit keeps the water-skiers away.

Off-Road Vehicles
About one-third of the visitors to the Oregon Dunes come to race around on ORVs (called OHVs, or Off-Highway Vehicles, in these

parts), which include dune buggies, all-terrain vehicles, motorcycles, souped-up pick-ups and jeeps.

Some restrictions apply: drivers of ORVs must have a driver's license, or else be supervised by an adult who has one; children under 18 must wear helmets; vehicles (except motorcycles) must have roll bars and seat belts; and vehicles have to sport a red flag at least 9 feet high in order to increase their visibility. Oregon's regular speeding and drinking-while-driving laws apply to ORV operators. Operators must also respect quiet hours (from either 10 pm or midnight to 6 am) and mufflers must meet decibel requirements.

Any number of concessions in the Oregon Dunes area rent ORVs and most also offer dune tours on large ORVs. Near Florence, Sandland Adventures (☎ 541-997-8087), 85366 S US 101, about a mile south of the Siuslaw Bridge, rents a full line of ORVs and runs dune buggy tours. Near Reedsport, go to Dunes Odyssey Rentals (☎ 541-271-3863), 75303 US 101, Winchester Bay. Down south by North Bend, try Far West Rentals (☎ 541-756-2322), 2580 Broadway, in the little community of Hauser.

One-hour rental of an ORV usually ranges between $30 and $35; prices go down for subsequent hours rented. There's a hefty deposit, which can be left as a check or credit card imprint. Tours of the sand dunes are generally $15 for a half-hour jaunt and $25 for an hour's outing.

Camping
Jessie M Honeyman State Park (☎ 541-997-3641), 3 miles south of Florence on US 101, is one of Oregon's most popular state parks. There are nearly 400 camp-

Dune Buggy Danger
Designated ORV and non-ORV areas are set up to restrict ORVs, not hikers, who have full freedom to explore any public areas of the dunes. However, since the pleats and folds of the dunes often make it difficult to see or be seen, hikers venturing into ORV territory need to remain aware of the direction of ORV traffic. Climbing the crest of a high dune is an especially bad place to be when some kid comes flying over the top in a dune buggy. Be careful on routes that wind through short, sandy hummocks – these serve as key ORV trails. Red (sometimes orange) flags waving above the dunes indicate oncoming ORVs. If one is moving fast in your direction, get out of the way! ■

sites, swimming and boating in Cleawox and Woahink Lakes and lots of hiking and recreation in the dunes. Facilities include showers, flush toilets, a camp shop, boat and bike rentals and ranger-led tours and activities. Campsites cost $16 to $20 and it's a good idea to make reservations in summer.

William Tugman State Park is along Eel Lake, 8 miles south of Reedsport, and offers 115 sites with hookups. You can go swimming and boating in the lake, and there are showers, a wheelchair-accessible fishing pier and a playground. Camping fees are $15.

USFS campgrounds have the best dune access and feature flush toilets and water but no hookups; sites cost $10. Specific facilities for each campground vary, since they've been conscientiously designed to keep hot rodders and naturalists amicably divided into separate camps. Distinctive, smoothly paved ORV camps are more like giant parking lots and feature ORV staging areas and lots of pull-through spaces and turnarounds for RVs and trailers. A cluster of four separate campgrounds off Siltcoos Dunes and Beach Access Rd, 7½ miles south of Florence, obligingly provides for either type of camper.

In the southern section of the Oregon Dunes, *Horsfall Campground*, just north of North Bend, represents the ultimate party for ORV-enthusiasts. It's also the only USFS campground to boast a shower. *Wild Mare Horse Campground* is nearby, but far enough away to keep dune buggies from spooking the horses. It features equestrian facilities and access to horse trails in the southernmost (and ORV-free) section of dunes. *Spinreel Campground*, 12 miles south of Reedsport near Tenmile Creek is another rowdy ORV camp. You can take refuge from ORVs in one of the shrubby sites at *North*, *Mid* or *South Eel Creek Campgrounds*, just a mile from lake recreation at Tugman State Park.

If you're looking for adventure, you can camp informally anywhere in the National Recreation Area. For information on campgrounds near Reedsport, see the next section.

REEDSPORT & WINCHESTER BAY

Five miles from where the mighty Umpqua River joins the Pacific Ocean, Reedsport (population 5030) is the historic port that ushered out the immense bounty of logs cut in the wide Umpqua River drainage. Reedsport wasn't established until the early years of this century, when the forests along the Umpqua River began to fall. Winchester Bay, out by the bar on the Umpqua River, has long been a stopping point for fishing boats. It was, until very recently, the state's largest sport-fishing port.

With today's limits on logging, and uncertain fishing seasons, plain seaside communities like these have been struggling to find a tourist draw to suit the realities of the present. For travelers, these towns offer inexpensive lodging and access to the Oregon Dunes National Recreation Area.

Information

Contact the Lower Umpqua Chamber of Commerce (☎ 541-271-3495, 800-247-2155) at PO Box 11, Reedsport, OR 97467. There's a rack of tourist brochures in the lobby of the Oregon Dunes National Recreation Area Headquarters (☎ 541-271-3611), 855 Highway Ave, Reedsport, at the junction of US 101 and Hwy 38.

The post office is at 301 Fir Ave. Lower Umpqua Hospital (☎ 541-271-2171), 600 Ranch Rd, keeps busy with dune buggy crashes all summer long.

Umpqua Discovery Center Museum

This museum (☎ 541-271-4816), at 409 Riverfront Way, combines exhibits on Umpqua Indian culture and the early steamboat era with a special center devoted to the exploration of Antarctica. It's open 9 am to 5 pm daily during the summer, and 10 am to 4 pm during the off-season; $3/1.50 adults/students.

Beaches

Ziolkouski Beach in Winchester Bay is a peaceful, though somewhat windswept, expanse of sand bordering the Oregon Dunes. There are three parking areas – the

OREGON

The Kuitsh Indians
The Kuitsh Indians, often referred to as the Lower Umpquas, lived along the estuarial plains at the mouth of the Umpqua River. The Kuitsh were linguistically related to the Coos Indians farther south and shared much of their culture and lifestyle.

Contact between the Kuitsh Indians and traders was initially friendly. However, relations quickly worsened when Iroquois scouts, in the employ of white trappers, ambushed and killed 14 Kuitsh. When Jedediah Smith, who was a trapper, chanced into the Umpqua Bay in 1821, his party was attacked by the Kuitsh, leaving 13 dead.

Smallpox and fever brought in by traders weakened the Kuitshs' resistance to the influx of settlers to the region in the 1850s. They were incarcerated on the Alsea Reservation in 1859. But the reservation was dissolved in 1875, leaving them landless. ■

first is free and provides access to the jetty, the last is extremely popular for its ORV staging area, dune access trail and pit toilets. The gate to this day-use area is locked at 9 pm each night.

A lesser-known and less-developed beach access road can be found 3 miles north of Reedsport. Continue north on US 101 about a mile past the stinky International Paper mill and turn left onto Sparrow Park Rd. This gravel road continues another 3 miles before ending at the beach. After a short hike towards the river, you'll find great **clam digging**, not to mention a large sea lion hangout. Park vehicles with respect to the incoming tide.

Umpqua Lighthouse State Park
The Umpqua Lighthouse was built in 1894, replacing the original that toppled off a nearby sandy headland during a winter storm in 1861. The lighthouse is still in operation and is open for tours from 10 am to 4 pm Wednesday through Saturday, and 1 to 4 pm on Sunday. Directly opposite the lighthouse is a **whale-watching** platform, with displays that explain various whale species and their habits. Also at the lighthouse, in an old barracks, is a small, free museum (☎ 541-271-4631) with memorabilia from the early days of the Coast Guard. Sign-up for the tour at the museum – space is limited to six people.

The other draw in the park is **Lake Marie**, a small freshwater lake with swimming, nonmotorized boating and picnicking. From the parking area, there's also a hiking trail around the lake and access to the Oregon Dunes, which gets pretty heavy ORV usage.

Dean Creek Elk Viewing Area
East of Reedsport on Hwy 38, in a grassy meadow alongside the road, live a herd of about 100 Roosevelt elk. The elk, one of the largest members of the deer family in North America, live in the refuge, along with herons, nutria, black-tailed deer and Canadian geese. The elk are almost always in sight from the road. However, it's probably safest to turn in to one of the viewing areas (which feature interpretive information), so as not to get run over by logging trucks.

Fishing
Before charter fishing went bad, local anglers had the Umpqua River and its bounty of sturgeon, coho salmon and steelhead all to themselves. For advice, licenses and tackle, go to the Reedsport Outdoor Store (☎ 541-271-2311), 2049 Winchester Ave.

Rent traps for **crabbing** from Stockade Market & Tackle (☎ 541-271-3800), 1310 4th St, in Winchester Bay.

Golf
Forest Hills Country Club (☎ 541-271-2626), 1 Country Club Drive, is a nine-hole course, buried within a quiet residential area.

Places to Stay
Camping RV campgrounds are abundant around Winchester Bay, though most of

these front onto the harbor and are too exposed for tent campers. There are quieter and more sheltered campsites south of Winchester Bay. Just north of Winchester Bay is *Surfwood Campground* (☎ 541-271-4020), 75381 US 101, with both tent and RV sites. Showers and a swimming pool are among the facilities; sites cost $13 to $14 a night.

At *Umpqua Lighthouse State Park*, 1 mile south of Winchester Bay, there are pleasant, wooded campsites adjacent to tiny Lake Marie, which warms up quite nicely for swimming. Amenities include showers, flush toilets, drinking water, and full hookups. Sites cost $13 to $17 a night and can be reserved in advance (☎ 800-452-5687).

Hotels Most hotels in Reedsport are right on US 101, tend to be clean and simple and have kitchenettes. The *Salty Seagull* (☎ 541-271-3729), 1806 US 101, is a great deal with three-room units with full kitchens for $40. There's a pool and rooms for the same price at the *Tropicana Motel* (☎ 541-271 3671), 1593 US 101. The *Best Budget Inn* (☎ 541-271-3686), 1894 Winchester Ave, offers kitchenettes for $45. The *Best Western Salbasgeon Inn* (☎ 541-271-4831, 800-528-1234), 1400 US 101, is Reedsport's best motel, with an indoor pool, spa and hot tub and meeting rooms for $74/79.

Off busy US 101, *Winchester Bay Rodeway Inn* (☎ 541-271-4871, 800-228-2000), 390 Broadway, in Winchester Bay is a large motel with views over Umpqua Harbor. Singles/doubles begin at $56/70; spa rooms are also available. Seven miles east of Reedsport, the *Salbasgeon Inn of the Umpqua* (☎ 541-271-2025), 45209 Hwy 38, has rooms right on the Umpqua River. The inn was once popular as an anglers' resort, but now is more of a romantic hideaway. Rooms begin at $70. (The name 'Salbasgeon' is the invention of a local hotelier, who merged the words 'salmon,' 'bass' and 'sturgeon' to reflect the fishing possibilities of the area.)

Places to Eat
Unsurprisingly for a fishing community, big breakfasts and fresh fish are the specialties of Reedsport and Winchester Bay. The longtime local favorite for family dining is *Don's Diner* (☎ 541-271-2032), 2115 Winchester Ave, which has good burgers and homemade soup. Finish up with Umpqua Dairy ice cream. Seafood and prime rib is the hallmark of fine dining in Reedsport at *Unger's Landing* (☎ 541-271-3328), 345 Riverfront Way, on the river near the Umpqua Discovery Center. For Italian food, go to *Red Shoes Cafe* (☎ 541-271-3650), 454 Fir Ave, where the chef makes his own sausages; a spaghetti dinner goes for $6.25.

In Winchester Bay, the *Crabby Gourmet* (☎ 541-271-9294), 225 8th St, is the successful venture of a chef and cookbook author known for her excellent soups and freshly baked sandwich breads. Their reputation has spread faster than the tiny five-table dining room has been able to keep up with, so you may have to wait for lunch. Reservations are required for dinner. Another really good choice is the *Bayfront Bar & Bistro* (☎ 541-271-9463), 208 Bayfront Loop, which offers enticing pasta and seafood preparations.

Seafood Grotto (☎ 541-271-4250), 115 8th St, offers fresh seafood and standard American meals in a old-fashioned maritime atmosphere.

Getting There & Away
Greyhound and Porter Stages both run buses south to Coos Bay and north to Eugene (via Florence) through Reedsport. The Greyhound bus comes once daily, and Porter Stages (☎ 800-540-7100) has two buses on weekdays and one on weekends. The bus stop moves around town quite a bit and was last spotted at the Moo Mall Cafe (☎ 541-271-2159), 379 Fir Ave (Hwy 38). A one-way ticket to either Coos Bay or Florence costs $6.

COOS BAY & NORTH BEND
The largest natural harbor between San Francisco and Seattle, Coos Bay has long

been a major shipping and manufacturing center, driving the engines of commerce and industry of most of southern Oregon. The port facilities here are thronged with foreign vessels waiting to take on board immense mountain-high stacks of timber. Smokestacks and warehouses line the bay and the smell of freshly cut wood fills the air.

Coos Bay had its beginnings in the 1870s as a ship-building center called Marshfield, but it wasn't until WWI created a vast market for local spruce trees – used to construct airplanes – that the area really boomed. For many years, Coos Bay was the largest timber port in the world.

The bloom went off the rose in the late 1980s, as the coastal forests were cleaned of easily harvested timber and the remaining forests fell under the protection of federal laws. Lumber mills closed, due to the lack of suitable timber and also due to the fact that large forest-product conglomerates found it cheaper to mill remaining timber either in other countries or offshore, using foreign labor. Recent commercial fishing restrictions, due to salmon scarcity, have also dealt an economic blow to Coos Bay.

Orientation

The city of Coos Bay (population 15,520), along with its twin, North Bend (population 9885), combine to make up the largest urban area on the Oregon coast. Coos Bay has the larger downtown area, roughly flanked by Johnson and Park Aves, 6th St and the bay. West of the city, the Cape Arago Hwy leads 9 miles to Charleston, a fishing village on an inlet at the end of the Coos Bay, and then on to a clutch of beautiful state parks.

North Bend is at the end of the peninsula that juts into the bay and begins north of Thompson Rd, with its western border along Fir St. From North Bend, US 101 sails across the Coos Bay on high-flying McCullough Bridge into the southern edges of the Oregon Dunes National Recreation Area.

Information

Contact the Bay Area Chamber of Commerce (☎ 541-269-0215, 800-824-8486), at 50 E Central Ave, Coos Bay, OR 97420. The post office is at Golden Ave at 4th St. Harvest Book Shoppe (☎ 541-267-5824), 307 Central Ave, is buried in Coos Bay's downtown district.

Allen's Wash Tub (☎ 541-267-2814), 255 Golden Ave, is open 24 hours a day and offers a drop-off service. Bay Area Hospital (☎ 541-269-8111) is at 1775 Thompson Rd.

Coos County Historical Museum

This museum (☎ 541-756-6320), in Simpson Park at 1220 Sherman Ave, North Bend, offers artifacts and photos from the area's history. The collection of Coos beadwork and basketry is good, as are the mementos from the days when Coos Bay was a world-class shipping center. Also note the myrtle-wood coins, which were issued as legal tender during the Depression. It's open 10 am to 4 pm, Tuesday to Saturday; $1/25¢ adults/children.

Coos Art Museum

The Coos Art Museum (☎ 541-267-3901), 235 Anderson Ave, is the only civic art gallery on the Oregon coast. It hosts touring shows and exhibits and has a permanent collection of prints by modern artists. Museum hours are 10 am to 4 pm, Tuesday to Friday, and from 1 to 4 pm on Saturday; $2.50/1 adults/students and seniors.

Activities

You can rent **scuba** gear at Sunset Sports (☎ 541-756-3483) in the Pony Village Mall on Virginia Ave in North Bend.

Access to the 18-hole **golf** course, the Kentuck Golf Course (☎ 541-756-4464), 675 Golf Course Rd, North Bend, is via East Bay Drive at the northern end of the McCullough Bridge. The North Bend Swimming Pool (☎ 541-756-4915), 1500 Pacific Ave, is the bay area's only indoor **swimming** pool, just off the Cape Arago Hwy behind Pony Village Mall.

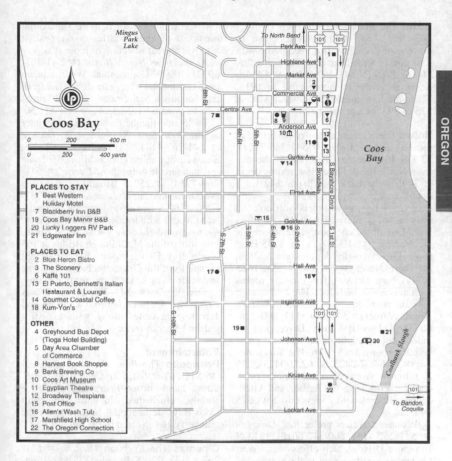

OREGON

Coos Bay

0   200   400 m

0   200   400 yards

PLACES TO STAY
1   Best Western
    Holiday Motel
7   Blackberry Inn B&B
19 Coos Bay Manor B&B
20 Lucky Loggers RV Park
21 Edgewater Inn

PLACES TO EAT
2   Blue Heron Bistro
3   The Scenery
6   Kaffe 101
13 El Puerto, Bennetti's Italian
    Restaurant & Lounge
14 Gourmet Coastal Coffee
18 Kum-Yon's

OTHER
4   Greyhound Bus Depot
    (Tioga Hotel Building)
5   Bay Area Chamber
    of Commerce
8   Harvest Book Shoppe
9   Bank Brewing Co
10 Coos Art Museum
11 Egyptian Theatre
12 Broadway Thespians
15 Post Office
16 Allen's Wash Tub
17 Marshfield High School
22 The Oregon Connection

Special Events

The Oregon Coast Music Festival (☎ 541-267-0938), is one of southern Oregon's largest festivals, with three weeks of musical acts in July between Bandon and Florence, although the concerts center in Marshfield High School Auditorium at Hall Ave and 7th St in Coos Bay. For tickets, contact The Box Office (☎ 800-676-7563).

The Blackberry Arts Festival is held in downtown Coos Bay the fourth Saturday in August. Booths selling blackberry food items are the most apparent reason for this late summer shindig, but local arts and crafts people are also on hand.

Places to Stay

Camping There are oceanside campgrounds near Charleston, only 11 miles west, or north in the Oregon Dunes National Recreation Area. See those sections for more information. For an urban setting, go to *Lucky Loggers RV Park* (☎ 541-267-6003, 800-267-6426), 250 E Johnson Ave; sites begin at $21.

B&Bs The *Blackberry Inn B&B* (☎ 541-267-6951), 843 Central Ave, close to downtown Coos Bay, is a 1903 home with four guest rooms from $55. The *Coos Bay Manor B&B* (☎ 541-269-1224), 955 S 5th St, is an imposing home built in 1911. There are five guest rooms, which start at $75 or $93 for a private bathroom.

Hotels There's quite a view of the bridge at the *Bay Bridge Motel* (☎ 541-756-3151), 33 US 101, on the other side of the bay from North Bend. For a view, rooms begin at $49; in the back, you'll pay $42 for a double room.

In Coos Bay, most hotels overlook the busy harbor or sit by busy US 101, or often both. One of the cheapest places to stay is the *Motel 6* (☎ 541-267-7171), 1445 Bayshore Drive; singles/doubles are $32/38. *Bayshore Motel* (☎ 541-267-4138), 1685 N Bayshore Drive, offers cut-rate rooms with queen-size beds for $34/37.

A bit more upscale, the *Best Western Holiday Motel* (☎ 541-269-5111, 800-228-8655), 411 N Bayshore Drive, has an indoor pool, weight room, spa and guest laundry; rooms are $71/76. The *Edgewater Inn* (☎ 541-267-0423, 800-233-0423), 275 E Johnson Ave, offers an indoor pool, decks overlooking the harbor and kitchenettes. Rooms with a view cost $80, $75 without.

Business travelers prefer *Red Lion Inn* (☎ 541-267-4141, 800-547-8010), 1313 N Bayshore Drive, which offers views over the harbor, courtesy vans to the airport and an outdoor pool. Rates are $79/89. The restaurant here is pretty good, too.

Places to Eat
While Coos Bay may not have Oregon's best food, you won't need to look hard for reasonably priced, easy-to-devour meals. *Kaffe 101* (☎ 541-267-4894), 134 S Broadway, offers espresso drinks and muffins. Likewise, at *Gourmet Coastal Coffee* (☎ 541-267-5004), 273 Curtis Ave, there are bagels and pastries to go with cafe lattes. Try *The Scenery* (☎ 541-267-5600),

190 Central Ave, for a more substantial breakfast of eggs, waffles or oatmeal. It also has a great selection of loose teas.

At the *Blue Heron Bistro* (☎ 541-267-3933), 100 W Commercial Ave, the menu goes continental with pasta dishes and fresh fish for lunch and dinner. Seafood fettuccine in tomato basil sauce goes for $12.50.

Table-side flambé dishes are a specialty at the *Red Lion Restaurant & Lounge* (☎ 541-267-4141), 1313 N Bayshore Drive. Sante Fe filet mignon and chili-stuffed sole are standard features at *El Puerto* (☎ 541-269-7754) at 252 S Broadway. *Benetti's Italian Restaurant & Lounge* (☎ 541-267-6066), 260 S Broadway, remains a consistent favorite with locals. The *Hilltop House Restaurant & Lounge* (☎ 541-756-4160), just north of the McCullough Bridge at 166 North Bay Drive, makes for a pleasant escape from the downtown bay area. Steak and seafood make the menu for fine dining.

Kum-Yon's (☎ 541-269-2662), 835 S Broadway, features familiar Chinese and Japanese favorites along with a distinguished Korean menu.

Entertainment
Brewpubs The *Bank Brewing Company* (☎ 541-267-0963), 201 Central Ave, produces hand-crafted beers and ales in a stately, refurbished old bank. The light Coos Bay Ale is good – be sure to try the cranberry Hefeweizen in the fall.

Cinemas The *Egyptian Theatre* (☎ 541-267-6115), 229 S Broadway, shows first-run films in an old-style movie house with a fun Egyptian motif. The lap of a giant concrete-molded, gold-painted mummy provides a place to sit while you wait for friends to buy popcorn.

In contrast, *Pony 4 Theatres* (☎ 541-756-3447), adjacent to the Pony Village Mall on Virginia Ave, is a boringly modern theater in North Bend.

Theater The Coos Bay Area has a surprising number of local theater groups. *On Broadway Thespians* (☎ 541-269-2501),

226 S Broadway, Coos Bay, and *Little Theater on the Bay* (☎ 541-756-4336), 2100 Sherman Ave, in North Bend, are the most active and put on several plays a year. Contact The Box Office (☎ 800-676-7563) to get information and tickets for upcoming performances.

Shopping

Myrtle Wood Across southern Oregon, wherever tourists have been known to tread, there are myrtle-wood gift shops. While you may or may not want to buy milled bowls, Christmas tree ornaments, golf clubs and ornamental clocks made out of this rare wood, do go into one of the gift shops to find out what the fuss is about. At The Oregon Connection (☎ 541-267-7804), 1125 S 1st St, you'll find a large gift shop filled with carved-wood products, as well as kiosks selling other local products like fudge and jelly. Take the free factory tour (offered on the hour when there's demand) to find out all you need to know about myrtle-wood production.

Chocolate Although the south coast is more renowned for its cranberry confections than for its chocolate, the International Deli & Restaurant (☎ 541-756-0621), known locally as the German Deli, 1802 Virginia Ave, near the Pony Village Mall in North Bend, sells chocolate bars molded into a bas-relief of Leonardo da Vinci's *The Last Supper*. Available in milk, white or dark chocolate, these inexpensive bars are made especially for the Easter season. The deli also sells candy crosses.

Getting There & Around

Daily Greyhound buses from Portland and Lincoln City come to Coos Bay along the coast; tickets cost around $27 one-way. There are two Porter buses a day between Eugene and Coos Bay ($20 one way). The bus depot (☎ 541-267-4436) is at 275 Broadway Ave, in the old Tioga Hotel building.

Call Yellow Cab (☎ 541-267-3111) if you need a taxi.

CHARLESTON

West of Coos Bay on Cape Arago Hwy, Charleston is the state's busiest commercial fishing port and one of Oregon's premier sport-fishing harbors. There's a kind of maritime hustle and bustle to the town that makes it a nice stopover on the way to the trio of splendid state parks on the headlands fronting Coos Bay.

South of Charleston is Seven Devils Rd. Winding through miles of clear cut forest, this road serves both as a shortcut between Charleston and Bandon and as access to a number of popular beaches south of Cape Arago, such as Whisky Run and Agate.

The Charleston Information Center (☎ 541-888-2311), PO Box 5735, Charleston, OR 97420, is at the corner of Cape Arago Hwy and Boat Basin Drive. It's staffed from May to September.

Sunset Bay State Park

This beautiful state park (☎ 541-888-4902) takes in a small, protected bay walled by extremely dramatic cliffs which were once topped by a popular hotel in the 1910s. It is popular with swimmers, divers and surfers, as well as hikers and vista lovers. The year-round campground here is one of the most popular on the coast.

Cape Arago Lighthouse sits right offshore on a rocky crag, linked to shore by a footbridge (no public entry). Waves over 75 feet in height regularly overwhelm the headlands here, spraying unwary tourists.

To reach Sunset Bay State Park from Charleston, take Cape Arago Hwy 3 miles west of Charleston. A 3-mile, cliff-edged stretch of the **Oregon Coast Trail** continues south from Sunset Bay and links the three state parks.

Shore Acres State Park

Louis Simpson, an important shipping and lumber magnate, was exploring for new stands of lumber in 1905, when he discovered this wildly eroded headland and decided that the location would make a good site for a country home. After buying up the 320 acres, Simpson built a three-story mansion here, complete with formal gardens and tennis courts. He called his estate Shore Acres. The timber industry went into decline shortly after the original home burned down in 1921. By the 1930s, Simpson found it too expensive to maintain the estate and the rebuilt home (bigger than the first) was eventually bulldozed.

In 1971, the State Parks Department began its historically accurate reconstruction of the neglected gardens, including the sunken water garden and rose garden. A trail leads out from the gardens to the cliffs. Here, in a glass-protected vista point (near where the original mansion stood), the wild surf hammers against the headlands. The trail also continues on to the beach.

The old garden house, which sits to the left of the main gate, serves as a free museum of the old estate. There are picnic facilities; a $3 day-use fee helps support the gardens. The park (☎ 541-888-3732) is 1 mile south of Sunset Bay Park along the Cape Arago Hwy, or along the Oregon Coast Trail.

Cape Arago State Park

Another wild vista point above a pounding sea is Cape Arago State Park, at the termination of Cape Arago Hwy. A washout has closed the last half mile of road to automobiles from the **sea lion lookout** at Simpson's Reef. The cape is a good place to look for migrating whales in the springtime. Trails lead down to the beach where there are great tide pools off the rocks at South Cove.

Picnic tables are scattered along the green and grassy headland near the parking area. The 3-mile hiking trail takes off north from here and leads back to Shore Acres and then to Sunset Bay.

South Slough National Estuarine Reserve

Charleston sits on a body of water evocatively called South Slough, which, south of the town, widens from a tidal river basin into a vast, muddy estuary. South Slough National Estuarine Reserve, 5 miles south of Charleston on Seven Devils Rd, was the

nation's first estuary preserve. The interpretive center (☎ 541-888-5558), PO Box 5417, Charleston, OR 97420, provides a good multimedia introduction to the rich abundance of life that inhabits these estuaries and runs guided walks with naturalists. Call beforehand, as the schedule changes, or take your own tour by hiking along several interpretive trails. **Wildlife viewing** is great here, especially for shore birds. Canoeists can explore the life of the estuary by coordinating with the tides; ask at the interpretive center for tide information.

The interpretive center is open 8:30 am to 4:30 pm daily during summer and the same hours on weekdays the rest of the year; admission is free. The trails remain open dawn to dusk. Rent **kayaks** ($35 a day) for exploring the estuary from Sunset Sports (☎ 541-756-3483), in the Pony Village Mall on Virginia Ave in North Bend.

Charter Fishing & Whale Watching

Charleston remains an important fishing center, and there are still a few charter companies offering sport-fishing packages for around $55 for a five- to six-hour trip. Contact Betty Kay Charters (☎ 541-888-9021, 800-752-6303), on the Charleston Boat Basin, or Bob's Sport Fishing (☎ 541-888-4241, 800-628-9633), 8013 Albacore Ave, for more information. Betty Kay also offers whale-watching trips during the spring migratory season at around $25 for two to three hours.

Places to Stay & Eat

Sunset Bay State Park, (☎ 541-888-4902), 3 miles southwest of Charleston on Cape Arago Hwy, has tent sites for $16, electrical hookups for $18, full hookups for $19 and yurts for $25. Showers, drinking water and a playground are available. Call ☎ 800-452-5687 for reservations. *Bastendorff Beach County Park* (☎ 541-888-5353), just west of Charleston on Cape Arago Hwy, has convenient campsites from $11 near a stretch of beach and offers showers, fire pits and playgrounds.

The *Talavar Inn & Retreat* (☎ 541-888-5280), 4367 Cape Arago Hwy, is a rustic home built in 1945 across the bay from Charleston. There are two guest rooms, one with a private bathroom and balcony, starting in high season at $105 for two people.

A popular place with anglers, *Captain John's Motel* (☎ 541-888-4041), 8061 Kingfisher Drive, has a great location right on the boat basin. Rooms, some equipped with kitchenettes, start at $48.

The *Portside Restaurant* (☎ 541-888-5544), Charleston Boat Basin, serves an extensive menu including fresh fish, beef, lobster, salmon, razor clams and a fine bouillabaisse. Full dinners range from $13 to $17.

BANDON
Population 2770

The little town of Bandon is one of the real jewels on the Oregon coast. Bandon-by-the-Sea, as its promoters have renamed it, sits at the bay of the Coquille River. South of town are miles of sandy beaches, rhythmically broken by outcroppings of towering rock,

home to a large number of chattering sea birds. Ledges of stone rise out of the surf to provide shelter for seals, sea lions and myriad forms of life in tide pools.

Jetties reach out into the bay to protect the old port area, still active with fishing boats and Coast Guard vessels. For the traveler, the center of Bandon is Old Town, which houses most of the town's cafes, gift shops and taverns. A small concentration of art galleries lend Bandon a focus and vigor lacking in most other south coast communities. Even the logging and farming locals seem proud to think that their little town has developed into an 'artists' colony.' Bandon also has the reputation of being a center of alternative spirituality.

As in most coastal towns, fishing, logging and lumber mills propel the local economy. Today, Bandon's most noteworthy industry is cranberry farming. In autumn, watch for fields filled with low-growing, bright-red berries: these bogs yield a considerable percentage of the cranberry harvest in the US.

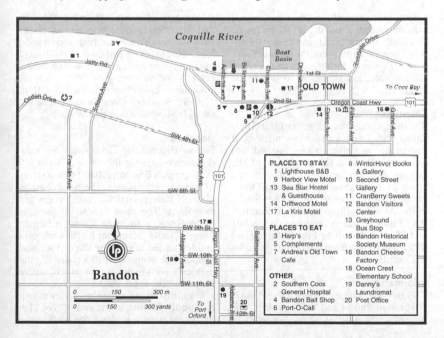

OREGON

Native American Rivalries
Near present-day Bandon, the Miluk Coos, a branch of the Coos Indians from farther north, were dominant, while inland along the Coquille River, the forests were controlled by the Coquille Indians, culturally and linguistically part of the Rogue Indian nation to the south. Relations between these two tribes were largely hostile, and each regularly raided the other for slaves.

In 1851 the Miluk Coos were sent to Yachats to live on the Alsea Reservation along the coast with other Coos Indians, while the Coquilles, along with many of the other southern Oregon tribes were freighted north on steamships to the Grande Ronde Reservation on the Yamhill River in 1856.

This century each of the tribes sued the federal government to settle land claims. The Coos lost their claim, but the Coquilles, along with other Rogue tribes, received a sum of more than $3 million in compensation. A number of the Miluk Coos were able to prove some Coquille ancestry and successfully petitioned to receive part of the Coquilles' settlement. However, this move caused great disharmony within the remaining body of the Miluk Coos, as it weakened that group's claim for federal acknowledgment as a tribe.

Today, the Coquille Indian Tribe contains both Miluk Coos and Coquilles and was acknowledged as an official tribe in 1989. Neither tribe has any reservation lands, though the Coquilles own a small parcel of land where a sacred rock once stood (the rock was blown up for riprap for the Bandon harbor jetties). The Coquilles plan to build a ceremonial longhouse and museum on their holding. ■

One local company makes much-touted cranberry candies, and the tart fruit turns up frequently in local breads and desserts. Bandon's largest annual event, the autumn Cranberry Festival, brings together cooks, craftspeople and gardeners to honor the berry.

Orientation
The main commercial district of Bandon is called Old Town, a five-block nucleus of restaurants and shops along 1st and 2nd Sts at the Bandon Harbor. Many of the famous Bandon beaches are found just south of town along Beach Loop Drive. North of town, dunes, rather than rocky cliffs, dominate the coast. From Bandon, it's 21 miles north to Coos Bay on US 101 and 27 miles south to Port Orford. Hwy 42S leads inland from Bandon to the town of Coquille.

Information
The Bandon Visitors Center (☎ 541-347-9616) is at 2nd St and Chicago Ave. The post office is at 105 12th St. WinterRiver

Books & Gallery (☎ 541-347-4111), 170 2nd St, offers a wide selection of books with an alternative focus. It also has a good local travel section and an odd assortment of country-themed crafts, New Age music, crystals and whatnot.

Danny's Laundromat is on US 101 at 11th St. Southern Coos General Hospital (☎ 541-347-2426) is at 640 W 4th St.

Beaches
Follow Beach Loop Drive south from the downtown area (or follow signs from US 101) to reach **Bandon State Park**, a series of beach access points. The beach here is liberally interspersed with rocky crags and monoliths. The most famous of these is **Face Rock**, a huge rock with a human visage. Native American legends tell of a maiden turned to stone by the evil sea god Seatka. The vengeful Seatka also flung the maiden's pet kittens far out to sea, where they now rise as sea stacks.

Within walking distance of downtown is **Coquille Point**, at the end of SW 11th St, where steps lead down the bluff to the

DENNIS FRATES

DENNIS FRATES

BILL MCRAE

Top Left: Base of Three Fingered Jack Mountain, OR
Bottom: Downtown Portland and Mt Hood, OR

Top Right: Mt Bachelor and fall huckleberry, OR

BILL MCRAE

BILL MCRAE

Top: Rock columns near Ione, OR   **Bottom:** Crater Lake and Wizard Island, OR

rocky beach. The offshore crags are protected as wildlife preserves.

Bandon Historical Society Museum

Bandon's event-filled past is captured in this museum (☎ 541-347-2164) at 270 Fillmore St and US 101. There's a good display of artifacts from the Coquille Indians, the history of the cranberry industry is documented, and photographs show the town before and after its two disastrous fires. During summer it's open 10 am to 4 pm, Monday to Saturday, and noon to 3 pm on Sunday; call for winter hours. Admission is by donation.

Bandon Cheese Factory

Oregon's second-largest cheese producer, this factory (☎ 541-347-2456, 800-548-8961), at 680 2nd St, offers samples of cheddar and many varieties of flavored cheeses. You can watch the cheese-making process through glass windows and shop for Oregon-made gifts and food products in the sales area. It's open from 8:30 am to 5:30 pm, Monday to Saturday, and 9 am to 5 pm on Sunday.

Bullards Beach State Park

Opposite Bandon on the north shores of the Coquille River, this state park (☎ 541-347-2209) offers beach access to the dune country 2 miles to the north. Hiking and biking trails wind through the woods or to the beach, and there's also an equestrian camp and bridle paths. The **Coquille River Lighthouse**, built in 1896, hasn't functioned as such since 1939, but it has been restored as a fairly basic museum commemorating boat travel. Informal tours can be arranged by request; ask at the Bullards Beach State Park office.

A boat ramp and viewing platforms provide access to the **Bandon Marsh National Wildlife Refuge**, a protected stretch of the Coquille River which extends south to Bandon Harbor. Rent kayaks for $12 an hour or $40 a day at Adventure Kayak (☎ 541-347-3480), 315 1st St, for close up views of blue herons, egrets and other estuarine bird life.

There are also flush toilets, picnic areas and a popular campground here.

Whale Watching

The bluffs south of Bandon are popular places to spot migrating whales in winter and spring. A good place to watch in the morning is Coquille Point, off the end of SW 11th St.

Fishing

The Bandon area offers good fishing both on the Coquille River and the Pacific Ocean. Steelhead, red snapper, rainbow trout and ling cod are good in the Coquille, as is Chinook salmon, but the season can be pretty crowded for the quantity of fish remaining in the river. Crabs are numerous in the bay as well. For fishing information, licenses, crab rings and tackle, go to the Bandon Bait Shop (☎ 541-347-3905), along the harbor.

Port O' Call (☎ 541-347-2875), 155 1st St, offers **charter fishing** for bottom fish and halibut. A half-day trip will cost you around $50.

Other Activities

Bandon Beach Riding Stables (☎ 541-347-3423), 3 miles south of town on Beach Loop Drive, has **horseback riding**; it costs $20 for an hourlong beach ride.

Coquille River Lighthouse

The nine-hole Bandon Face Rock Golf Course (☎ 541-347-3818), 3225 Beach Loop Rd, allows players to pit themselves against the tempests of the Pacific on this pretty, beach-facing **golf** course.

Special Events
Over Memorial Day weekend, regional wine producers match their vintages with fresh seafood at the Storm Watchers Wine & Seafood Festival (☎ 541-347-4721). Other activities include the annual blessing of the fleet. In mid-June teams compete to build the most imaginative structures along the beachfront at the annual Bullard's Beach State Park Sandcastle Contest.

The largest civic event is the Cranberry Festival (☎ 541-347-9616), usually held mid- to late-September. There's a parade, the crowning of the Cranberry Queen, a craft show, music, a beef barbecue and the food fair, where cranberries find their way into dozens of dishes prepared by local cooks.

Places to Stay
Camping Just two miles north of Bandon on US 101, *Bullards Beach State Park* (☎ 541-347-2209) offers almost 200 campsites with easy access to ocean beaches. A thin forest shelters these campsites from the worst of the wind, which can be quite fierce around here. Facilities include flush toilets, showers, an equestrian area, an RV dumping area and six yurts. Tent sites are $13, full hookups are $19 and yurts are $25.

Hostels The *Sea Star Guesthouse* (☎ 541-347-9632), 375 2nd St, is the only HI hostel on the Oregon coast. At this very pleasant inn, dorms are $13 to $16 and private rooms for couples start at $24 a night. The facility includes common areas, a kitchen and a laundry room. There are also spacious guesthouse rooms ($40 to $85) which have better views, more privacy and kitchenettes.

B&Bs The *Lighthouse B&B* (☎ 541-347-9316), 650 Jetty Rd, has great views of the lighthouse from the four guest rooms with

private bathrooms. Some rooms have fireplaces; rates range between $80 and $100.

Hotels Bandon hotels are divided into those in town and those along the Beach Loop Rd south of town, which afford more or less direct beach access and ocean views.

Out along the loop road, the *Table Rock Motel* (☎ 541-347-2700), 840 Beach Loop Rd, has two family cottages for rent with singles/doubles starting at $35/40. Another good deal is *Bandon Beach Motel* (☎ 541-347-4430, 800-822-8765), 1110 SW 11th St, which has a pool and rooms from $65/75. *Windermere Motel* (☎ 541-347-3710), 3250 Beach Loop Rd, offers older but refurbished chalet-like cottages on the beach south of Bandon for $70.

On the main highway, try the following older motels. *La Kris Motel* (☎ 541-347-3610), on US 101 at 9th St, is well maintained and has the cheapest rooms at $45. *The Driftwood Motel* (☎ 541-347-9022), 460 US 101, is right downtown and has rooms for $50/60.

On the bluff above Old Town is the *Harbor View Motel* (☎ 541-347-4417, 800-526-0209), 355 2nd St, a newer facility affording great views of the bay and ocean. The complimentary breakfast, wheelchair-accessible rooms and spa are among the draws; rates are $70/75.

Resorts At *The Inn at Face Rock* (☎ 541-347-9441, 800-638-3092), 3225 Beach Loop Rd, you have the Pacific Ocean on one side and a golf course on the other. The condo-style suites have great ocean views and fireplaces starting at $109. There's also a lounge and restaurant in the main lodge.

Vacation Home Rentals To rent a home in Bandon, contact Coastal Vacation Rentals (☎ 541-347-3009, 800-336-5693), PO Box 702, Bandon, OR 97411.

Places to Eat
There are pastries, espresso drinks and sandwiches at *Complements* (☎ 541-347-9440), 160 2nd St.

Andrea's Old Town Cafe (☎ 541-347-3022), 160 Baltimore Ave, is a bright and airy storefront overgrown with house plants and comfortable booths. The real treat here is the lamb raised on Andrea's farm. The dinner menu changes daily, with most entrées (like Russian braised lamb shanks) for $10 to $15. It's also the best place for lunch, with fresh salads, homemade soups and sandwiches going for $5 to $7. Andrea's is open for breakfast and lunch daily; evening service is daily in summer, but only on Friday and Saturday in the dead of winter.

Another Old Town favorite is *Harps* (☎ 541-347-9057), 130 Chicago Ave, a small bistro that specializes in fresh local ingredients and careful preparations such as cream of shrimp soup with shallots and tarragon, or the famed halibut with spicy pistachio sauce ($17). Pasta dishes and steak range between $12 and $17. It is open for dinner only.

Bandon Boatworks (☎ 541-347-2111), at the end of South Jetty Rd, has wonderful views of the Coquille Lighthouse and the Pacific Ocean. Though carefully prepared, dishes on the extensive menu are not very adventurous.

Entertainment
Bandon Playhouse (☎ 541-347-2506) is an ambitious community theater that stages musicals, classical drama and contemporary plays at the auditorium of Ocean Crest Elementary School on Allegany Ave at 9th St.

Shopping
CranBerry Sweets (☎ 541-347-9475), at 1st St and Chicago Ave, makes cranberry-based candies. At their factory outlet, there are free samples, plus a video showing the cranberry harvest. Other homemade candies, cranberry products and food gifts are available.

Old Town Bandon also offers a startlingly wide selection of craft shops, art galleries and artists' studios. You'll find the largest and most eclectic selection of art at the Second St Gallery (☎ 541-347-4133), 210 2nd St.

Getting There & Away
Greyhound buses stop and pick up in front of the Sea Star Guesthouse at 375 2nd St. A one-way fare from Eugene costs $17. There's one bus during the day, and another that passes through in the middle of the night.

LANGLOIS
Unassuming Langlois, 14 miles south of Bandon, is the closest town to Floras Lake, a covert **windsurfing** hot spot. Only a thin sand spit separates this spring-water lake from the ocean, which gets enough exposure to make even spectators feel like they're right on the Pacific. Calm morning winds and warm, shallow water keep the lake suitable for windsurfers of all skill levels. Summer is the peak season, when the lake is blasted by a steady supply of fierce, Cape Blanco winds, though sporadic winter storm winds attract windsurfers year-round. Put in at Boice-Cope County Park, which charges a $3 day-use fee. To reach it, head 2 miles south of Langlois on US 101 and turn right onto Floras Lake Rd, following the signs to the lake.

Equipment rental and lessons are available on-site at the Floras Lake Windsurfing School (☎ 541-348-9912), which is operated by the owners of Floras Lake House B&B. Big Air Windsurfing (☎ 541-348-2213), 48435 US 101 in Langlois, sells new and used equipment (open weekends only from October to April). Langlois' big blowout is the Floras Lake Speedcheck, a three-day windsurfing event held in late June.

Places to Stay & Eat
Facilities are limited in these remote parts, so count on trading comfort and convenience for miles of deserted beach and rugged landscape. Boice-Cope County Park has a sparsely sheltered campground with flush toilets and showers for RVs and tent campers (bring lots of stakes). The *Floras Lake House B&B* (☎ 541-348-2573), 92870 Boice Cope Rd, is right outside the park entrance and popular with windsurfers. For food you'll have to either bring groceries or rely upon *The Greasy Spoon*

OREGON

(☎ 541-348-2514), on US 101 in Langlois, a cafe and hangout that taunts hungry windsurfers with a brazen name and un-promising exterior. Other motels and restaurants can be found in Bandon and Port Orford (12 miles south).

PORT ORFORD
Population 1050
Sleepy Port Orford is so far from most centers of population that it hasn't yet been developed as a tourist trap, but it's not for lack of beauty. Port Orford is magically situated on a grassy headland overlooking a natural harbor. In fact, Port Orford is one of Oregon's only true ocean harbors (others are situated along the mouths of rivers) and has a long history as a fishing and lumber port. Port Orford cedar was an especially important export.

During WWII the southern Oregon coast was repeatedly hit by the Japanese with incendiary balloons aiming to ignite the forests of the Pacific Coast, which they believed were important to the building of US military ships and airplanes.

Port Orford is on US 101, 27 miles south of Bandon and 20 miles north of Gold Beach. Just north of town is Cape Blanco, one of the westernmost points of the continental USA. South of the town rises Humbug Mountain, one of the highest seaside peaks along the coast.

If a beautiful ocean view, a great beach and a few businesses are all you require, you may fall under the spell of Port Orford. There's beach access and picnicking at windy **Battle Rock City Park**, on a natural promontory overlooking the harbor. For information, you can stop at the friendly Battle Rock Information Center (☎ 541-332-8055), or write PO Box 637, Port Orford, OR 97465.

Humbug Mountain State Park
At Humbug Mountain State Park (☎ 541-332-6774), 6 miles south of Port Orford on US 101, mountains edge down to the ocean and heavily wooded Humbug Mountain rises 1756 feet from the surf. A 3-mile trail leads from the campground (or from the trailhead parking lot just to the south) through beautiful virgin forests – the groves of now-rare Port Orford cedar here are the largest remaining along the Oregon coast – to the top of the mountain for a great view of Cape Sebastian and the dramatic Pacific Ocean.

When white settlers first came to the area in 1851, the Tututnis lived in a large village along the beach just north of Humbug Mountain. Facilities at the park include wheelchair-accessible flush toilets and a large campground.

Cape Blanco State Park
First sighted in 1603 by Spanish explorer Martin d'Anguilar, Cape Blanco's thin neck of land juts far out into the Pacific withstanding the lashing winds and fierce winter storms – more than 100 inches of rain fall here a year and the wind frequently passes the 100-mph mark. These conditions, and the treacherous, rocky coastline hereabouts, make Cape Blanco a real danger to ships. The state park is 4 miles north of Port Orford and 5 miles west on an access road.

The current **Cape Blanco Lighthouse** was built in 1870 and is the highest and oldest operational lighthouse in the state. You can take a tour (limited to five people) and explore the grounds 10 am to 3:30 pm, Thursday to Monday. The tour schedule runs on demand and admission is by donation. For $50 per person you can opt to tour the lighthouse at night, when it's at its most spectacular. The three-hour tour is led by guides who pose as early lighthouse keepers and lament the hardships of keeping the Fresnel lens clean of soot. For reservations call Siskiyou Coast Escapes (☎ 541-332-2750) .

A mile east of the lighthouse is **Hughes House** (☎ 541-332-0248), 91814 Cape Blanco Rd, a two-story Victorian home built in 1898 by Patrick Hughes, an Irish dairy rancher and sometime gold miner. Tours are available 10 am to 4 pm, Thursday to Monday, and noon to 4 pm on Sunday, May to September; admission is by donation.

Both sites operate seasonally in coordination with the campground and are generally closed from early October to the end of April.

Places to Stay & Eat

Six miles south of Port Orford on US 101, *Humbug State Park* (☎ 541-332-6774), has a great campground that's right on the beach yet protected by the coastal forest. It has over 100 campsites ($16 for a standard

site, $18 for hookups). Showers and flush toilets are available. Call ☎ 800-452-5687 for reservations. *Cape Blanco State Park* (☎ 541-332-6774) has 58 campsites on a rocky headland with beach access and great views of the lighthouse. There are flush toilets, showers, a boat ramp and an RV dump station. All sites have electric hookups and are $18, except primitive hiker-biker sites which cost $13.

The *Home by the Sea B&B* (☎ 541-332-2855), 444 Jackson St, is a newer home with four guest rooms. Views are wonderful and rooms cost $85 and $95. The *Castaway-by-the-Sea Motel* (☎ 541-332-4502), 545 W 5th St, has ocean-view rooms above the harbor, some with fireplaces from $45. The *Shoreline Motel* (☎ 541-332-2903), 206 6th St, is an easy walk to the beach and to shops; singles/doubles are $36/38. The *Sea Crest Motel* (☎ 541-332-3040), 44 S US 101, offers ocean-view rooms for $49/54.

Food and service at *Spaghetti West* (☎ 541-332-9378), 236 US 101, is about as capricious as the clashing Italian menu and Southwest-meets-coastal-trailer-park decor. Still, it's the most interesting place to eat around here, with pasta dishes like mushrooms and greens flamed in vodka and cream ($10.50). There's also a list of good regional wines and an adjacent pool hall and bar.

The *Port & Starboard* (☎ 541-332-4515), on US 101 at 436 Madrona Ave, is less of a gamble and features fresh fish, steaks, pizza and other family fare. It's open daily for breakfast, lunch and dinner.

Getting There & Away

Greyhound stops at 1025 N Oregon St, near the Circle K. Two buses a day go north and south along the coast.

GOLD BEACH
Population 1640
While Gold Beach faces out onto the Pacific Ocean, its soul looks inland to the Rogue River, which meets the ocean here. The recreation-minded resort facilities in the area make Gold Beach a favorite with

---

Battle Rock

In the 1850s, Port Orford was the scene of some of the state's bloodiest encounters between Native Americans and the whites trying to establish a settlement. Tututni Indians, or Coastal Rogues, were especially resistant to white incursions and had a fearsome reputation with early fur traders and miners.

In June 1851, a group of men took up positions on a natural promontory (now known as Battle Rock) that was surrounded by water on three sides and connected to land only at low tide. When a group of Tututnis approached the rock, the white men opened fire at point-blank range with a small cannon, killing 13. Later, the settlers killed several Tututni chiefs and went on to establish Port Orford without further conflict.

In early spring 1856, following gold discoveries along the southern Oregon coast, the Tututnis attacked Port Orford, killing 26 settlers, and then continued their campaign all along the coast, burning most settlements between Port Orford and California. But, by mid-spring most Tututnis had been driven away from the coast by US Army troops and moved inland to join the Takilmas and other southern Oregon tribes who were also fighting the army and miners in conflicts that came to be called the Rogue River War.

In total, almost 1500 Native Americans were incarcerated and shipped out of Port Orford in just one year. ∎

well-heeled travelers who like a little bit of the outdoors with their leisure.

Gold Beach is named for the oceanfront mines that yielded gold in the 1850s. Apparently, the Rogue River brings gold dust downstream when in flood. Over the centuries, gold accumulated into bands in the dark sand dunes along the river's mouth. The little settlement here didn't amount to much until the early years of this century when the salmon-rich waters of the Rogue caught the fancy of gentleman anglers like Jack London and Zane Grey (well known for his Western adventure novels) and captured the entrepreneurial zeal of Thomas Hume, who established a salmon cannery here.

If you're not an angler, Gold Beach's main allure is jet boats that zip up the Rogue River to remote upstream outposts and beauty spots in the Rogue River Wilderness Area. Most of these trips include a stop for lunch at rustic lodges in the little community of Agness.

Leading inland from Gold Beach is USFS Rd 33, also called Agness Rd, which follows the Rogue upriver to Agness and Illahe (in town, the road is called Jerry's Flat Rd). This road, wrapped in old-growth forests, is paved as far as Illahe and is an alternative for Rogue River explorers who can't abide jet boats. For off-road enthusiasts, USFS Rd 33 continues on to Powers and down the South Fork Coquille River to Myrtle Point.

Orientation & Information
Despite its centrality for recreation on the Rogue River, the joylessly utilitarian town of Gold Beach doesn't offer the charm or esprit evident in many other coastal towns. Ellensburg Ave (US 101), is the main drag through town.

The Gold Beach Chamber of Commerce (☎ 541-247-7526, 800-525-2334) and the Siskiyou National Forest offices (☎ 541-247-3600) are at 29279 S Ellensburg Ave, Gold Beach, OR 97444. The post office is on 150 W Moore St.

From Gold Beach it is 44 miles south to the California border and 78 miles north to Coos Bay.

Curry County Museum
This small museum (☎ 541-247-6113), 29410 Ellensburg Ave, preserves Native American and early settlement history. Of particular interest are the displays relating to the beachfront gold rush in the late 1880s. The museum is open noon to 4 pm, Tuesday to Saturday, June to October, noon to 4 pm Saturday only the rest of the year. Donations are accepted.

Cape Sebastian State Park
About seven miles south of Gold Beach, this small park is mostly a vista point on a rocky cliff-hung headland, but what a vista! On clear days, the seascapes stretch for miles, from California to Cape Blanco. A short trail leads from the parking lot out to the cliff's edge. Hardy hikers can continue down a steep trail to the beach at the base of the cape.

Hiking
The 40-mile **Rogue River Trail** ends (or begins) at Illahe. Day hikers who want to explore the Rogue River canyon can hike 4.3 miles one way up to Flora Dell Creek, where a waterfall drops into the Rogue. For information on long-distance hikes along the Rogue River Trail, see the Wild Rogue Wilderness Area in the Southwestern Oregon chapter.

Fishing
Spring Chinook salmon (April to June) and fall and winter steelhead runs keep anglers fishing the Rogue River year-round. Guided fishing excursions are especially popular – a five-hour trip costs around $100 and includes all tackle and bait. Gold Beach offers plenty of experienced guides, and it's worthwhile to call around if you're particular about equipment or locale. For starters, you can try Don Pedro (☎ 541-247-7946), Steve Beyerlin Guide Service (☎ 541-247-4138), Terry Kennedy Guide Service (☎ 541-247-9219), or End of the Rogue Guide Service (☎ 541-247-2049).

Anglers wanting to fish the Rogue on their own can find tackle and fishing information at the Rogue Outdoor Store (☎ 541-247-7142), 29865 Ellensburg Ave.

Jet Boat Tours

The Rogue River is one of Oregon's wildest and most remote rivers, with access largely limited to hikers and white-water rafters. However, you can explore the lower reaches of the Rogue on jet boat tours, which use hydrofoils that can skim over the surface of shallow streams and river rapids. Jet boats were originally used to deliver mail to far-reaching outposts. The tours travel to the rugged and barren canyon whose walls tower 1500 feet above the river in the Rogue River Wilderness Area. Wildlife viewing is good, with deer, elk, otters, beavers, eagles and osprey seemingly unaffected by the deafening growls of the jet boat engines.

Two companies offer similar trips: a six-hour excursion to the little resort community of Agness, 30 miles inland, or a slightly longer run that goes past Agness to shoot white-water rapids. Both these trips include a layover for lunch in one of three lodges at Agness. A longer eight-hour trip features lighter and smaller jet boats that are able to climb shallow rapids up to Blossom Bar Rapids. This trip includes a lunch break at *Paradise Bar Lodge*, 50 miles up the river.

Contact Jerry's Rogue Jets (☎ 541-247-4571, 800-451-3645), or Rogue River Mail Boats (☎ 541-247-7033, 800-458-3511) for tour information.

Despite what all the brochures say, the times and frequency of trips vary, so call ahead and reserve a space. Costs range from $30 for the trips between Gold Beach and Agness to $75 for the trip between Gold Beach and Paradise Bar; lunches are not included.

Places to Stay

Camping Closest to Gold Beach, and on the Rogue River's south bank, is *Indian Creek Recreation Park* (☎ 541-247-7704), 94680 Jerry's Flat Rd. There's a separate tent area, showers and a shop for provisions. Campsites are $15 for tents, $20 for

hookups. *Four Seasons RV Resort* (☎ 541-247-4503), 96526 N Bank Rogue Rd, is right on the river; tents are $16, RV hookups $22.50. Fishing is the thing here, with a boat ramp, guide service and tackle shop on the grounds.

If tent campers want to avoid the comforts of RV campgrounds, head up USFS Rd 33 toward Agness for 9 miles to *Lobster Creek Campground*, a USFS campground on the banks of the Rogue River. Farther up USFS Rd 33 there's a nice riverside facility at Illahe called *Illahe Campground*. Sites cost $6 at both places. More formal RV sites are available at *Agness RV Park* (☎ 541-247-2813), 04215 Agness Rd. Sites are $15 for electric hookups.

B&Bs *Inn at Nesika Beach* (☎ 541-247-6434), 33026 Nesika Rd, is a Victorian-style inn with four guest rooms, private baths and ocean views; three have fireplaces. Rates range from $100 to $130.

Hotels For a town its size, Gold Beach has a surprising number of hotels. Most are modest but nice, though there are also several resorts and lodges to cater to anglers and such.

The *City Center Motel* (☎ 541-247-6675), 94200 Harlow St, is a clean, older motel with rooms at $45. The *Drift In Motel* (☎ 541-247-4547, 800-424-3833), 94250 Port Drive, is on the river near the bridge; rates are $50. At the *Inn at Gold Beach* (☎ 541-247-6606, 800-503-0833), rooms have views and cost $55.

Lodges Take USFS Rd 33 about 32 miles east of Gold Beach to reach the three rustic lodges at Agness that serve the needs of groups of anglers, jet boat passengers and the occasional stray traveler. *Lucas Lodge* (☎ 541-247-7443), 03904 Cougar Lane, offers rooms in the 1910s-era lodge ($45) or in cabins ($60 to $65). At the *Singing Springs Resort* (☎ 541-247-6162), on USFS Rd 33, rooms in cabins, some with kitchenettes cost $40 to $65. The newest of the lodges is the *Cougar Lane Lodge* (☎ 541-247-7233), 04219 Agness Rd, which offers rooms ($40 to $60) in motel-like units. Each of the above lodges offers buffet-style lunch and dinner.

Tu Tu Tun Lodge (☎ 541-247-6664, 800-864-6357), 96550 N Bank Rogue River Rd, 7 miles east of Gold Beach, is a rustic hideaway on the north banks of the Rogue River. Large rooms with decks, a pool and access to boats and fishing off the dock make this one of the few destination resorts on southern Oregon coast's. Prices start at $135. The dining room is private and serves wonderful meals to lodge guests.

Resorts Overlooking the ocean from downtown, the *Gold Beach Resort & Condominiums* (☎ 541-247-7066, 800-541-0947), 29232 Ellensburg Ave, is a relatively new resort offering condo-style rooms, some with fireplaces, from $89, with access to an indoor pool and spa.

Jot's Resort (☎ 541-247-6676, 800-367-5687), 94360 Weddurburn Loop, just north of the bridge, is one of the original resorts on this part of the coast. It has nearly 150 guest rooms and condo suites overlooking the harbor, two pools and a marina with boat rentals and fishing guide service; rooms start at $85.

Vacation Home Rentals Gold Beach Vacation Homes (☎ 541-247-6670, 800-816-4676), PO Box 147, Ophir, OR 97464, has a wide selection of beach homes, condos, ranches and fishing lodges for all budgets. Contact the chamber of commerce for other suggestions.

Places to Eat
There's nothing very memorable about the selection of restaurants in Gold Beach. Chowder and fish and chips seem to be the basic menu selections whether you eat high or low. You might as well go for views and atmosphere.

The *Nor'Wester Seafood Restaurant* (☎ 541-247-2333), Port of Gold Beach, serves grilled salmon, halibut or whatever's in season, as well as good steaks. Full dinners are in the $15 to $20 range. *Rod 'n Reel* (☎ 541-247-6823), 94321 Wedder-

burn Loop Rd, part of Jot's Resort (see above), offers a large variety of seafood and beef dishes. A shrimp-stuffed fillet of sole is $15. The Rod 'n Reel is also a good place for an old-fashioned breakfast.

Getting There & Away
The Greyhound station (☎ 541-247-7710) is at 310 Colvin St. Two buses run each direction daily; the fare between Gold Beach and Florence is $20 and to Brookings it's $6.

BROOKINGS
Population 4465
Just 6 miles north of the California-Oregon border on US 101, on the bay of the Chetco River, Brookings is a bustling town with lots of traffic crossing the state line to avoid sales taxes. The harbor is one of Oregon's busiest, with both commercial and sport fishing adding to the activity on the bayfront. Like so many other coastal towns, the awe-rendering beaches and magnificent state parks are very successful at seducing travelers to spend their vacations here. But after the romp, you're likely to look back on Brookings and wonder what you ever saw in this charmless commercial town.

Logging has long held the economy here, but, as elsewhere along the coast, recent restrictions have largely halted further clear-cutting. Many loggers, savvy in the ways of the forest, have turned their hands to wild-mushroom collecting for a living. Chanterelles, black trumpets, morels and porcini are among the forest's bounty.

Brookings leads the nation in Easter lily bulb production. In July, fields south of town are filled with bright color and heavy scent. Roads lead inland from Brookings up the Chetco River to the western edge of the Kalmiopsis Wilderness, the state's largest and one of its most remote. Oregon's only redwood forests are also found up the Chetco River. Some groves are preserved in Loeb State Park, also known for its myrtle trees.

Oregonians throughout the rest of the state refer to Brookings as being in 'the banana belt' of the state. During winter, temperatures hover around 60°F, which is indeed balmy compared to the stormy climes in the north.

Orientation

To get from inland southern Oregon to Brookings requires a trip down US 199 (called the Redwood Hwy), from Grants Pass to Crescent City, CA, and then north 15 miles. From Grants Pass to Brookings along this route is 105 miles. From Brookings, the next town north on US 101 is Gold Beach, 39 miles away along the spectacular cliff-lined coast.

What is referred to as Brookings is in fact two towns: Brookings proper, north of the Chetco River, and Harbor on the south shore, where the boat basin is. In the following addresses, note that the innocent-sounding Chetco Ave is actually US 101.

Information

The Brookings Harbor Chamber of Commerce (☎ 541-469-3181, 800-535-9469), is at 16330 Lower Harbor Rd, Brookings, OR 97415. For regional information drop by the Oregon State Welcome Center (☎ 541-469-4117), 1650 US 101, at Harris Beach State Park north of town. The Chetco Ranger Station (☎ 541-469-2196) is at 555 5th St.

The post office is at 711 Spruce St. You can wash your dirty clothes at Economy Laundry, next to the Westward Motel at 1026 Chetco Ave.

Beaches

There are beaches all along the Brookings seafront north of the mouth of the Chetco River. One nice in-town beach access is at the end of Wharf St, where **Mill Beach** and Agnew Park offer sandy beaches and views of promontories off Chetco Point.

There are miles of beaches, rocky cliffs and outcroppings and shoreline hiking trails at **Harris Beach State Park** (☎ 541-469-2021), just north of Brookings off US 101. From the picnic area, you can enjoy views of Goat Island, Oregon's largest offshore island and a bird sanctuary. Harris Beach State Park also has campsites.

Brookings Bomb Site

Brookings was the site of one of only two mainland US air attacks during WWII. A seaplane launched from a Japanese submarine in early September 1942 succeeded in bombing Mt Emily, behind the city. The main goal of the attack was to burn the forests, but they failed to ignite. There were no casualties. To see the bomb site, a source of peculiar fascination to the locals, follow South Side Chetco River Rd, and look for signs to the 'Bomb Site' (or ask for a map at the visitors' center). ∎

Chetco Valley Historical Society Museum

This community museum (☎ 541-469-6651), 15461 Museum Rd, is housed in an 1857 stagecoach station, Brookings' oldest building. Among the museum's items of special interest are an odd iron cast of a woman's face whose resemblance to Queen Elizabeth I is speculative and a cedar canoe used by Native American coastal fishers. Adjacent to the museum is the world's largest Monterey cypress tree, with a trunk girth of 27 feet.

The museum is open noon to 5 pm, Wednesday to Sunday, from the end of May to Labor Day; and noon to 4 pm, Thursday to Sunday, mid-March through October; $1/50¢ adults/children.

Azalea State Park

At this 26-acre park, hundreds of wild azaleas (some over 200 years old) hold forth in fragrant bloom in late May and early June. The rest of the year, Azalea Park is a pleasant place for a picnic or a stroll. The park is east of downtown near the corner of Pacific Ave and Park Rd.

The annual Azalea Festival (☎ 541-469-3181) on Memorial Day weekend (the last weekend in May), focuses on Azalea State Park. The festivities include a floral parade, crafts fair and food booths.

OREGON

Alfred A Loeb State Park

This state park was established to protect two of Oregon's rarest and most cherished trees: the redwood and the myrtle. There's fishing and swimming in the Chetco River, and the park has one of the most pleasant public campgrounds on the entire southern coast.

Two hiking trails lead through the dense forest from the trailhead at the park's picnic area. Three-quarter-mile **Riverview Nature Trail** follows the river through old-growth myrtle, ending at the highway. The trail then continues as the 1¼-mile **Redwood Nature Trail**, which climbs up the hillsides above the river to loop through a grove of ancient redwoods. One tree with a girth of 33 feet is reckoned to be over 800 years old. A brochure available at the trailhead identifies plant varieties along both trails.

Loeb State Park is 10 miles east of Brookings along North Bank Chetco River Rd.

Samuel H Boardman State Park

This 11-mile-long oceanfront state park begins 4 miles north of Brookings and contains some of Oregon's most beautiful coastline. Cliffs drop hundreds of feet into the surf and steep hiking trails lead down to tiny, beautiful beaches huddled at the base of a rocky canyon. Marching far out to sea are tiny island chains, home to shore birds and braying sea lions. There's no development along this stretch of the beach; this is how wild and ominous the Oregon coast must have seemed to both Native Americans and white settlers.

US 101 winds through Boardman State Park, often creeping along cliffs high above the raging Pacific. The grading and spans necessary for building a road along these cliffs was so difficult and expensive that several portions cost more than a million dollars a mile to construct in the 1930s.

Along the road you'll find a number of turnouts, picnic areas and viewpoints . At most, hiking trails lead from the parking lots to either a secluded beach or a more dramatic panorama.

The **Lone Ranch Picnic Area**, the southernmost turnout, is a secluded beach with swimming and tide pool exploring in a sandy cove studded with sea stacks. Just 1 mile to the north is **Cape Ferrelo**. A short path leads out to the tip of the cape, a popular spot for spring whale watching. At **Whalehead Cove**, a patchy but paved road drops steeply down to a fine little beach, sheltered on all sides by rocky headlands. This is a great place for picnicking or sunbathing. **Indian Sands Beach** is so named because for hundreds of years Native Americans harvested shellfish here, leaving high mounds of shells along the foredunes. From the turnout on US 101, a steep trail leads down to the ocean, where the beach is flanked by sandstone cliffs colored light-red by iron deposits.

After US 101 crosses the Thomas Creek Bridge, Oregon's highest at 345 feet, take the turn for **Natural Bridge Viewpoint**, where a short trail leads to views of rock arches just off the coast. The arches are the remains of sea caves that have been collapsed by the pounding of waves. Likewise, at **Arch Rock Point**, the volcanic headlands have been eroded to leave the arch of a lava tube. Follow the paths down to Whiskey Creek, where there are great tidal pools.

Most of the above sites have picnic tables and toilets, but there are no campgrounds in the park.

Hiking

For many hikers Boardman State Park is notable as the southern entry point of the **Oregon Coast Trail**, a long-distance trail that traverses the entire length of Oregon's Pacific Coast. While not all sections of the trail are currently complete (hikers have to walk along US 101 for short stretches), in Boardman Park two complete stretches of the trail offer good hikes.

The southern access to the Oregon Coast Trail begins at the Cape Ferrelo parking lot and leads north along headland cliffs, tide pools, rocky escarpments and beaches until it joins US 101, 7 miles later at the Thomas Creek Bridge. The second, 2-mile section of the Oregon Coast Trail begins at the Natural Bridge Viewpoint and ends at Miner Creek. The trail passes through some precipitous parts along the cliffs – parents should watch children carefully – and then leads to open, grassy headlands and deep rain forests. Watch along the rocky sea stacks for coastal fauna such as puffins, gulls, murres, cormorants and curious seals and sea lions.

Hikers with a high-clearance vehicle can take an hourlong drive to a short hike in the Kalmiopsis Wilderness. Oregon's largest wilderness area, the Kalmiopsis is a range of mountains noted for its rare botanical specimens. (See the Kalmiopsis Wilderness in the Southwestern Oregon chapter.)

Drive up North Bank Chetco River Rd and then onto USFS Rd 1909 for about 13 miles to the **Vulcan Lake Trailhead**. The trail into this remote rock cairn lake is 1.4 miles. A number of long-distance trails also lead out from the Vulcan Lake Trailhead. The road faces future closures to protect cedars in this area from a disease spread by road dust, so be sure to check with either the Chetco Ranger Station in Brookings (☎ 541-469-2196) or the Siskiyou National Forest Headquarters (☎ 541-471-6500) before setting out.

Fishing
The Chetco River is famous for its winter steelhead and fall Chinook salmon runs. Some of the best fishing areas are on the North Bank Chetco River Rd above Loeb State Park. For guided fishing trips, contact Gary Klein's Salmon & Steelhead Guide Service (☎ 541-469-6627), 613 Hassett St.

Brookings is one of the state's last hold-outs for **charter fishing**. Salmon fishing still occasionally opens up down here, and when it's closed ocean sport-fishing trips turn to bottom fish like flounder, rock fish and halibut. Expect to pay around $60 for a half-day of fishing, plus an additional $8.50 for a daily fishing license. Contact Tidewind Sportfishing (☎ 541-469-0337, 800-799-0337), 16368 Lower Harbor Rd, which also has whale-watching trips for $25; Star Charters (☎ 541-469-5151); or

Sporthaven Marina (☎ 541-469-3301), 16372 Lower Harbor Rd.

Places to Stay
Camping Brookings is blessed with two fine state park campgrounds in close proximity. *Loeb State Park*, 10 miles east of Brookings on North Bank Chetco River Rd, has 53 campsites with full hookups in a fragrant grove of rare myrtle trees; all campsites are $16 a night. *Harris Beach State Park*, 2 miles north of Brookings on US 101, has over 130 campsites, including a separate tent-camping area right on the ocean. Showers, flush toilets and coin laundry are among the amenities here, and campsites cost $16 to 19. The contact phone number for both state parks is ☎ 541-469-2021.

For RV campers who want to be closer to Brookings, there's *Beachfront RV Park* (☎ 541-469-5867, 800-441-0856), 16035 Boat Basin Rd, with 173 sites right on busy Brookings Harbor. Fees range from $12 to $14.

B&Bs The *Holmes Sea Cove B&B* (☎ 541-469-3025), 17350 Holmes Drive, is a modern seafront home with great views over the Pacific. Each of the three rooms has a private bath and entrance; rates range from $80 to $95. The *South Coast Inn B&B* (☎ 541-469-5557, 800-525-9273), at 516 Redwood St, is an Arts and Crafts-style home with four guest rooms with private bath, a hot tub, sauna and ocean views. Rooms cost $79 to $89.

Hotels *Pacific Sunset Inn* (☎ 541-469-2141, 800-469-2141), 1144 Chetco Ave, has singles/doubles for $45. The *Spindrift Motor Inn* (☎ 541-469-5345, 800-292-1171), 1215 Chetco Ave, is on the ocean side of US 101, with good views, a little less noise than others on the strip and rooms for $49/55. The *Westward Motel* (☎ 541-469-7471), 1026 Chetco Ave, is a well-maintained older motel with kitchenettes and nonsmoking rooms for $55/59. *Best Western Beachfront Inn* (☎ 541-469-7779, 800-468-4081), 16008 Boat

Basin Rd, faces right onto the ocean with its back to the active boat harbor. It is Brookings' finest lodging, with a swimming pool and some suites, private decks and kitchenettes. Rooms begin at $79.

Vacation Home Rentals If you are looking for short-term home rentals, contact the Practical & Professional Property Management (☎ 541-469-6456), at 611 Spruce St, Brookings, OR 97415.

Places to Eat

Just south of the bridge in Harbor is the *Hog Wild Cafe* (☎ 541-469-8869), 16158 S US 101, a favorite for good breakfasts, Cajun and Mexican-influenced lunches, and decent vegetarian offerings. A hearty bowl of chili with cornbread goes for $5. *Rubio's* (☎ 541-469-4919), 1136 Chetco Ave, is another unprepossessing little restaurant that turns out formidable Mexican food. Favorites include chili rellenos and the fresh seafood sautés; the salsa is locally noted and sold both at the restaurant and around town. Dinners are in the $7 to $11 range.

Wharfside Restaurant (☎ 541-469-7316), 16362 Lower Harbor Rd, doesn't look like much from the outside, but the fish come right off the boats and it's where the locals go for fish and chips. You'll have trouble spending more than $10 here for dinner. *O'Holleran's Restaurant & Lounge* (☎ 541-469-9907), 1210 Chetco Ave, is the place to go for good steak ($15) and traditional seafood dishes ($14 and up).

One of the better places to eat, *Bistro Gardens* (☎ 541-469-9750), 1130 Chetco Ave, features an ambitious list of seafood and Italian specialties like grilled salmon with chili lime butter ($15), and grilled polenta with ratatouille ($11). Meals start with a supply of crayons, though the wait isn't very long.

Over in the next strip mall, *Chives* (☎ 541-469-4121), 1025 Chetco Ave, is an upmarket restaurant that, in Brookings, comes across as just plain fussy. A dinner of salmon angel hair pasta in caper chive beurre blanc goes for $14. It's open for lunch and dinner Wednesday to Sunday only.

Getting There & Around

Bus Brookings is served by two Greyhound buses a day, which run between Portland and San Francisco along US 101. The one-way fare between Portland and Brookings is $32. The bus station (☎ 541-469-3326) is at Fiji Island Tan, 601 Railroad St, just north of the post office.

Bicycle For cyclists who choose to ride with the wind and cycle south, Brookings marks the end of the Oregon Coast Bike Route. In order to take a bus back to your original point of departure you'll need to pack your bicycle in a special cardboard box. Escape Hatch Sports & Cycles (☎ 541-469-2914), 624 Railroad Ave, gives away bicycle boxes as they are available and can suggest alternative sources if they happen to be out.

Car Coast Rent-A-Car (☎ 541-469-5321) is at 530 Chetco Ave. Bob's Taxi (☎ 541-469-7007) provides local taxi service.

Columbia River Gorge & Mt Hood

The Columbia River's enormous canyon, carved through the Cascade mountains, is one of the Pacific Northwest's most dramatic and scenic destinations. The river, over a mile wide, winds through a 3000-foot-deep gorge flanked by volcanic peaks and austere bands of basalt. Waterfalls tumble from the mountain's edge and fall hundreds of feet to the river. Clinging to the cliff walls are deep-green forests, filled with ferns and moss.

Immediately south of the Columbia River Gorge rises 11,240-foot Mt Hood, the highest peak in Oregon. Mt Hood is an all-season, outdoor playground for all of northern Oregon. Apart from its five ski areas, the mountain is popular with hikers, mountain climbers and those who come to marvel at the extravagant WPA-era Timberline Lodge.

The Columbia River divides Washington and Oregon, and both states share the wonders of the Gorge. Rather than arbitrarily divide the following sites according to state boundaries, Gorge sites and activities for both Oregon and Washington are included in this chapter. Pay attention to telephone area codes: this part of Washington is 509, while Oregon uses 503 at the western end of the Gorge and 541 from Hood River east. Also, there's no reciprocity between the two states regarding fishing or hunting licenses.

The Gorge

This awe-inspiring chasm has long served as more than a scenic wonder. As the only sea-level passage through the Cascade and Sierra Mountains between California and the Canadian border, the Columbia River Gorge has been a transportation corridor for centuries.

Ice-Age Floods

During the most recent Ice Age, which lasted until 15,000 years ago, 2500-foot-high glaciers filled the valleys that drained western Montana. An enormous lake covering 3000 sq miles – called Glacial Lake Missoula – formed behind the ice dam. However, when the water level of the lake grew high enough, it floated the plug of ice, and the entire lake of glacial melt water and icebergs rushed through the Columbia Basin in a flood of catastrophic dimensions.

At full flood, swiftly flowing waters lashed 1000 feet above the present site of The Dalles. The intense currents of the flood scoured out the constrictive Columbia watercourse and cut away the canyon walls. The waterfalls along the Gorge were formed when the floods flushed away the stream paths that entered the Columbia River, causing streams to tumble over towering cliffs.

As astonishing as the magnitude of these floods is the fact that over the course of about 2000 years they recurred at least 40 times. The ice dam would re-form after each flood and fill with melt water until the dam lifted with the pressure of the water. Each time the flood coursed through the Gorge, the chasm was cut deeper and the canyon walls scoured cleaner.

About 700 years ago, an enormous landslide fell into the Gorge, briefly damming the Columbia and forming the mighty rapids that were later called the Cascades. The Native American myth of the 'Bridge of the Gods' – a rock arch that once spanned the Columbia – apparently derived from this jumble of rock strewn across the river. ■

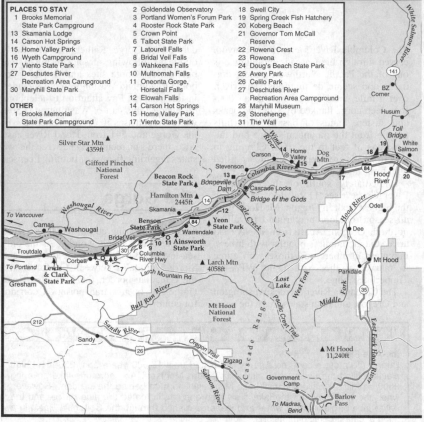

PLACES TO STAY
1 Brooks Memorial
   State Park Campground
13 Skamania Lodge
14 Carson Hot Springs
15 Home Valley Park
16 Wyeth Campground
17 Viento State Park
27 Deschutes River
   Recreation Area Campground
30 Maryhill State Park

OTHER
1 Brooks Memorial
   State Park Campground

2 Goldendale Observatory
3 Portland Women's Forum Park
4 Rooster Rock State Park
5 Crown Point
6 Talbot State Park
7 Latourell Falls
8 Bridal Veil Falls
9 Wahkeena Falls
10 Multnomah Falls
11 Oneonta Gorge,
   Horsetail Falls
12 Elowah Falls
14 Carson Hot Springs
15 Home Valley Park
17 Viento State Park

18 Swell City
19 Spring Creek Fish Hatchery
20 Koberg Beach
21 Governor Tom McCall
   Reserve
22 Rowena Crest
23 Rowena
24 Doug's Beach State Park
25 Avery Park
26 Celilo Park
27 Deschutes River
   Recreation Area Campground
28 Maryhill Museum
29 Stonehenge
31 The Wall

Five hundred years ago, nowhere in the Northwest boasted such a cosmopolitan mix of peoples as the area around The Dalles. During the great fall and spring migrations of salmon, the shores were lined with many Native American tribes trading, fishing, performing ceremonies, gambling and socializing. The migratory hunting-and-gathering tribes of the Columbia Plateau converged with the river- and ocean-going tribes of the coast. The tribes would swap stories in a pidgin language derived from Chinookan and Sahaptian, later incorporating words from English, French and Russian.

Over many generations, thousands of pictographs and petroglyphs were drawn into the rocky bluffs and outcroppings along this busy area, for ceremonial, informational and decorative purposes.

Lewis and Clark floated down the Gorge in the autumn of 1805, and later, the overland route of the Oregon Trail terminated at The Dalles. Here pioneers were forced to negotiate the rapids at the Cascade Locks or choose to attempt the Barlow Trail over Mt Hood, a dangerous end to a wearying 2000-mile journey.

As the West opened up, there was a great demand for better transportation through

OREGON

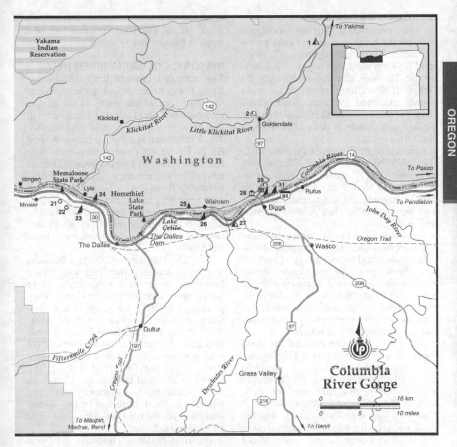

the Gorge. The Northern Pacific's transcontinental rail line – only the second in North America – pushed through the Gorge in 1883, and orchards of apple, cherry and pear began to develop along Gorge-side valleys once the railroad provided a market for agriculture.

The Columbia River Hwy of the 1910s, a marvel of modern engineering and a beautiful scenic route, opened the Gorge to automobile traffic. A series of dams transformed the Columbia River into a major waterway and hydroelectric source. Beginning with Bonneville Dam in 1938, the Columbia became a series of slack-water reservoirs enabling boats to range far inland

In 1986 the Gorge was declared a National Scenic Area, a move that has regulated further development of the area.

A freeway now zips through the Gorge, but it takes only a little effort to get out of the fast lane and partake of the spectacular recreational opportunities available. Hikes to waterfalls and wildflower habitats, backcountry camping, as well as swimming, fishing, sailing and – most notably – windsurfing on the Columbia River make the Gorge a favorite outdoor getaway for many Northwest residents and visitors.

OREGON

Orientation & Information

Two highways pass through the Gorge, one each on the north and south banks of the Columbia River. Heavily traveled, river-level I-84 traverses the Oregon side, and is by far the quickest route through the Gorge. It also offers access to the most popular sites and activities. Washington's Hwy 14 follows the north bank of the river; while much slower, it does offer spectacular vistas.

Remains of the Historic Columbia River Hwy (US 30) exist in two different sections, between Troutdale and Warrendale, and between Mosier and The Dalles. This narrow, winding and spectacular road links together waterfalls, vista points and forest trailheads.

Hood River and The Dalles are the major commercial centers in the Gorge, and provide ample lodging and dining opportunities. Washington-side towns are smaller and less tourist-oriented. Campers will find a number of state parks on both sides of the river, though on summer weekends campsites can be scarce, especially if the winds suit the purposes of windsurfers.

It's 63 miles between Portland and Hood River; 21 miles farther east is The Dalles.

Several good books and maps describe hikes and other recreation in the Gorge. For a good introduction to Gorge activities, look at *The Columbia River Gorge: A Complete Guide*, by Philip Jones. Another good resource for hikers and explorers in the western Gorge is the *Trails of the Columbia Gorge* map, published by the USFS. A good resource for Gorge hikers and photographers wishing to see more is *A Waterfall Lover's Guide to the Pacific Northwest* by Gregory A Plumb, which gives directions to a total of 49 falls along the Gorge.

Getting There & Away

The closest airport to the Gorge is Portland's PDX. Five Greyhound buses a day travel along the Oregon side of the Columbia River, on I-84. See individual towns for information.

Amtrak's *Empire Builder* runs along the Washington side of the Gorge four times a week on its Portland-Spokane leg, and stops at Bingen and Wishram.

HISTORIC COLUMBIA RIVER HWY

The western section of the old Columbia River Hwy, which links together some of the most spectacular sights in the Gorge, runs between Troutdale and Warrendale. It can be a very slow road in high season. Think twice before taking a trailer or large RV on US 30 – it's a precarious route built for Model Ts, not mobile homes. Despite admonitions, the narrow and shoulderless Columbia River Hwy is frequently jammed with huge RVs in summer.

Even if there's not much traffic, you'll be tempted to stop and picnic in wildflower meadows and hike in to more remote waterfalls.

Two late-19th-century Oregon business and civic leaders, Sam Hill and Simon Lancaster, are credited with the idea for an automobile route through the Gorge. They journeyed to Italy, Switzerland and Germany to view European mountain roads. With strong backing from Portland businessmen, Hill and Lancaster convinced the state government to finance the Columbia River Hwy, the first road linking The Dalles to Portland through the Gorge. To these idealists, the highway was not intended to be an intrusion on the wilderness; instead, the road was designed to be a part of the landscape.

The road between Troutdale and Hood River opened in 1915; the section between Hood River and The Dalles was finished in 1922. The opening of the road – the first large-scale paved road in the Northwest – was greeted with excitement across the USA.

Orientation

There are several options for getting onto US 30 from Portland. If you're in no particular hurry, head east on I-84 and take exit 17, turning right at the outlet mall, left at the blinking light up the hill from the outlets onto the Historic Columbia River Hwy. (Follow the signs to Corbett.) This

Outdoors in the Gorge

Hiking the Waterfalls After winding down the cliffs from Crown Point, Hwy 30 enters the Gorge's most bountiful waterfall area. Gorge Trail No 400 winds for 35½ miles along the face of the Gorge, passing many of the major falls along the way. You can hike portions of the trail or the whole thing.

Wildflowers & Butterflies Near Rowena, the McCall Wildflower Preserve has paths that lead through cliff-top meadows that explode with blossoms in April and May. Yellow-flowered balsamroot and cobalt-blue lupines are among the many wildflowers found at this beautiful vista point. It's also a great place to watch for butterflies.

Sternwheeler Cruise Take a tour of the Columbia River's Cascade Locks in the *Columbia Gorge*, a historic paddle-propelled steamboat. Enjoy the beautiful scenery and learn about local history and lore.

Mt Hood Scenic Railroad Tour Wind through blossom- and fruit-laden orchards on this historic rail line beneath the snowy peak of Mt Hood. Bring a bottle of local wine along for the ride.

Stonehenge Sam Hill's curious full-scale replica of the ancient British monument is a good place to spend an equinox or an Earth Day. Pretend you're in a faraway land. Zip up to the Goldendale Observatory when the sun sets, and stargaze for free through one of the nation's largest public telescopes. ■

route snakes up the Sandy River and through the pleasant small towns of Troutdale and Corbett before reaching the gorge's big attractions.

For quicker access to waterfalls and hikes, take exit 28 at Bridal Veil. To reach this section of US 30 from the east, take exit 35 at Ainsworth State Park.

Information

Most of the following sites are waterfalls and viewpoints contained within the Columbia Gorge National Scenic Area, a complex bureau made up of state and federal agencies. Their USFS office (☎ 541-386-2333) is at 902 Wasco Ave, suite 200, Hood River. The Forest Service information center in the Multnomah Falls Lodge (☎ 503-695-2376) is also a good source of information about the Gorge.

Crown Point

Famous as the western entry to the Gorge, this viewpoint and interpretive center sits atop a craggy point of basalt. Views from the park look down on Beacon Rock on the Washington side, and on Rooster Rock 800 feet directly below on the Oregon side. To the east, as far as the eye can see, the Columbia River unfurls between green cliffs.

Coiling down from the cliffs below Crown Point are a series of switchbacks and curves that were considered marvels of design and execution when the Columbia River Hwy was constructed. Even in such precipitous territory, the grade of the road is never more than 5%, with a minimum curve radius of 100 feet.

The centerpiece of Crown Point is **Vista House**, a Gorge observatory and a commemoration of Oregon pioneers, with an information center and gift shop. Built in 1916, the art nouveau-style rotunda is constructed from native basalt and marble.

Larch Mountain

At 4058 feet, Larch Mountain is one of the highest peaks rising out of the Gorge; from its flanks flow Multnomah and Oneonta Creeks.

A paved USFS road winds up the side of the mountain to a picnic area and trailhead. From here, a short trail leads to **Sherrard Point**, a rocky promontory over the Gorge with views across dense forests onto five volcanic peaks. On a clear day, the vistas are spectacular – it's one of the few places where the sheer magnitude of the Gorge and the Cascade Range can be seen.

OREGON

OREGON

To reach Larch Mountain, leave the Columbia River Hwy between the Portland Women's Forum Park and Crown Point at a Y-junction: follow signs for 'Larch Mountain Rd,' which trends south from the main highway. It is a slow 14 miles from the junction to the picnic area. Take the trail on the far right side of the parking lot (not the steps); it's a quarter mile to the viewpoint, and another 6½ downhill miles to Multnomah Falls. This road is closed in winter.

Latourell Falls
The first major waterfall you encounter coming east on US 30, Latourell Falls drops 249 feet into a rocky pool. A 10-minute hike leads to the base of the falls and back along Latourell Creek to a picnic area in Talbot State Park. It's about 2 miles roundtrip to Upper Latourell Falls, a 100-foot-high chute. Both trails begin at the bridge over Latourell Creek.

Bridal Veil Falls
It's a 1-mile roundtrip hike in to Bridal Veil Falls, a substantial, two-tiered cascade that first plunges 100 feet in one direction, and immediately turns a right angle to drop another 60 feet. The moderately steep trail to the falls also passes the spectral remains of an old mill and lumber flumes.

At Bridal Veil State Park there's also a wheelchair-accessible interpretive nature trail. The paths lead onto a meadow where spring wildflowers abound. In April look for the blue-flowering camas, an onion-like bulb that was a staple of the Native American diet. The trail also leads to cliff-edge viewpoints over the Columbia.

Wahkeena Falls
Indians named this 242-foot waterfall Wahkeena, meaning 'the most beautiful.' While modern taste may favor more spectacular chutes, Wahkeena Falls also serves as a trailhead for some of the most popular hiking trails in the Gorge. Hike up the Wahkeena Trail to the side of the falls, then follow the creek and trace the canyon wall to join the Larch Mountain Trail No 441. Follow this trail down Multnomah Creek to

Myths & Legends of the Columbia Gorge

Latourell Falls According to Native American tale, these falls represent the spirit of the Coyote God's wife, who was transformed into this beautiful waterfall to prevent her from ever leaving her husband.

Multnomah Falls Native American legends tell of a maiden princess who leaped to her death from these cliffs in order to save her people from pestilence. The Great Spirit created the Multnomah Falls in her memory. Her face appears in the shifting rainbows of mist floating from the upper falls.

The Bridge of the Gods The Native Americans who lived along the Gorge believed that a bridge of rock, called the Bridge of the Gods, once spanned the Columbia River. It was tended by Loo-Wit, a venerable but old and homely woman. The spirit of Mt Adams, called Klickitat, and the spirit of Mt Hood, called Wy'east, fell to feuding, as they both loved the female spirit of Squaw Mountain (a lesser Cascade peak). The two volcanic peaks exploded in anger, hurling rock and fire. Finally so many rocks were thrown between the two peaks that the Bridge of the Gods collapsed. Loo-Wit, the bridge guardian, fell with the bridge. However, the Great Spirit felt sorry for her and granted her wish to be made young and beautiful once more. She moved west from the warring peaks where she came to rest as Mt St Helens.

Beacon Rock In mythology, this rock was the final resting place of the Native American princess Wahatpolitan and her young son. She sought refuge on the rock when her father became angry about her marriage to an unsuitable warrior. Mother and son died atop the rock, and legends have it that you can hear the mother's grief in the howling of the winds. ■

the top of the awe-producing falls of the same name; from here the trail descends to Multnomah Falls Lodge (a 5-mile hike).

Multnomah Falls

At 642 feet, Multnomah Falls is the second-highest nonseasonal waterfall in the nation, and one of the most spectacular sites in the Northwest. The falls drop twice: once over 560 feet from a notch in an amphitheater of vertical rock, and then another 70 feet over a ledge of basalt. A short trail leads to an arch bridge directly over the second falls.

Multnomah Falls was one of the major sites along the old Columbia River Hwy. Multnomah Falls Lodge, constructed in 1925, was built as a restaurant and stopover for travelers. Today it offers meals that only a starving hiker could love in the rustic 2nd-story restaurant, and snacks and gift items on the main floor (see Places to Eat).

Continue past the viewing bridge up a steep trail (Larch Mountain Trail No 441) to the top of the falls. The Larch Mountain Trail continues up Multnomah Creek, leading – arduously – to the top of Larch Mountain, the highest peak along this end of the Gorge; or hikers can make a loop by catching Gorge Trail 400 (also known as Wahkeena Trail in this area) to Wahkeena Falls.

The waters of Multnomah Creek form a popular, though not always that pleasant, freeway-side swimming lake with many shaded picnic spots in **Benson State Park**, which is accessible from the Wahkeena Falls parking lot.

Drivers on I-84 should note that the exits for Multnomah Falls are from the freeway's left hand lanes. More importantly, the on-ramps back onto the freeway also join the left lanes, normally the freeway's fast lanes. This means that slow-moving vehicles are forced to merge into heavy, fast-moving traffic. Exercise caution.

Oneonta Gorge & Horsetail Falls

These two closely spaced sites are easily accessible from US 30. However, a highly recommended hike leads behind these curiosities to a more remote waterfall and views over a deep, stream-filled fissure.

Oneonta Gorge is a narrow chasm cut into a thick basalt flow by Oneonta Creek. Walls over 100 feet high arch over the stream. This peculiar ecosystem, preserved as Oneonta Gorge Botanical Area, is home to a number of rare, cliff-dwelling plants which thrive in this moist, shadowy chasm. There's no room along the sheer walls of Oneonta Gorge for a trail. However, for those unperturbed by the thought of wet sneakers, the shallow stream can be waded for about a half mile to **Oneonta Falls**, where Oneonta Creek drops 75 feet into its gorge.

Only a few hundred feet east of Oneonta Gorge is **Horsetail Falls**, which drops out of a notch in the rock to fall 176 feet. While it is easily visible from the turnout along US 30, hikers should consider the 3-mile **Horsetail-Oneonta Loop Trail**. Beginning at Horsetail Falls, the trail quickly climbs up the side of the gorge wall and along the edge of a lava flow. The trail continues behind **Ponytail Falls** (also called Upper Horsetail Falls) which pours out of a tiny crack into a mossy cirque. The trail then drops onto Oneonta Creek, with great views over its narrow gorge and waterfalls. The trail returns to US 30 about a half mile west of the Horsetail Falls Trailhead.

Elowah Falls

One of the most stunning Gorge waterfalls, 289-foot Elowah Falls is much less visited than its brethren along the Columbia River because it's not easily linked to the scenic Columbia River Hwy, and you need to hike nearly a mile to see it.

Like Multnomah Falls, Elowah Falls plunges into an enormous rock-walled bowl. Mosses, ferns, and wildflowers thrive in the mists and breezes. From a short wooden bridge across McCord Creek, hikers too will be cooled by the falls' wafting mists.

To reach Elowah Falls requires just enough diligence to guarantee the falls relative obscurity. If you are on US 30

OREGON

Hiking & Biking the Historic Highway

You can still drive along much of the Historic Columbia River Highway, but some stretches were closed when I-84 was built. Now, the abandoned roadbed is being restored, not for auto use, but as a biker-hiker trail. The first 1½-mile section runs from Tanner Creek, near Bonneville Dam, to Eagle Creek.

The paved trail parallels the noisy interstate, but quickly climbs above the auto traffic. There are some great views of the Columbia River and the Bonneville Dam, and the renovated sections of road are as architecturally graceful as the original.

Catch the Historic Highway Trail at the I-84 Bonneville Dam exit. Park at the Wahclella Falls Trailhead, immediately south of the freeway exit, or head about a quarter mile east up the gravel road to find a larger parking lot. As more of the old roadway is reclaimed, the trail will extend farther to the east. ■

---

already, then at Ainsworth State Park, where all signs invite the driver to rejoin I-84, continue east instead on Frontage Rd toward Dodson. If you're traveling on I-84, take the Ainsworth State Park exit 35, and follow the eastbound Frontage Rd. From this point, continue 2½ miles until, at signs for Yeon State Park, you see a parking area on the right side of the road. It's a 2-mile roundtrip hike to Elowah Falls, with some steep switchbacks. From the same trailhead, the **McCord Creek Falls Trail** leads to the top of the Elowah Falls, with views into the falls' enormous rock bowl and then to **McCord Falls**, higher up on the same stream. The roundtrip to McCord Creek Falls is 2½ miles.

Places to Stay

Camping Campers are in luck with *Ainsworth State Park* (☎ 503-731-3411), 3 miles east of Multnomah Falls. Besides campsites ($18 for full hookups) and picnic areas in a pretty wooded grove, Ainsworth Park provides easy access to trails leading to Horsetail and Elowah Falls.

Hotels None of the above sights is more than 35 miles from Portland or 25 miles from Hood River, both of which offer lots of lodging and eating options. The *Bridal Veil Lodge* (☎ 503-695-2333), in Bridal Veil State Park, is the only hostelry along this stretch of the Gorge. Guest rooms are available in this 1920s-era lodge and in an adjacent cottage ($75 a night, by reservation only), both in a mossy, well-shaded dell near Bridal Veil Falls.

Places to Eat

At the beginning of the scenic highway, along the Sandy River is *Tad's Chicken N Dumplings* (☎ 503-666-5337). Open for dinner only, the food is agreeably old-fashioned – Tad's is famous for its fried chicken. Having drinks on the deck over the Sandy River is also popular.

In this area, the architecturally noteworthy place to eat is *Multnomah Falls Lodge* (☎ 503-695-2376). The main reason to frequent this historic lodge is the stone-vaulted dining room, a preserve of rustic, Craftsman-era architecture. Lunches go for $6 to $9, and dinners for $15 to $20. The food is unexceptional.

CASCADE LOCKS
Population 970

An early Gorge transport center and summer home to the sternwheeler *Columbia Gorge*, Cascade Locks derives its name from the navigational locks, completed in 1896, that cut through the series of treacherous rapids here.

Steamboat traffic once plied the Gorge, but ended when Bonneville Lake flooded the old rapids in 1938. The town flourished throughout the 1930s, when the area was home to thousands of construction workers drawn to the WPA project's promise of employment.

The Bridge of the Gods, a steel cantilever bridge spanning the Columbia at Cascade Locks, was built in 1926, thus replacing the legendary one (see Myths & Legends of the Columbia River Gorge sidebar).

Orientation & Information
Cascade Locks is 44 miles east of Portland on I-84, exit 44. Stevenson, WA, is 3 miles east of the Bridge of the Gods. There's a 75¢ toll to cross the bridge. From Cascade Locks it's 19 miles east to Hood River. The main street in town is Wa-Na-Pa St.

Cascade Locks Visitor Center (☎ 541-374-8619), PO Box 355, Cascade Locks, OR 97014, is in the Marine Park complex, about a half mile down Wa-Na-Pa St from exit 44.

Cascade Locks Historical Museum
This museum (☎ 541-374-8535), in the Marine Park complex on Wa-Na-Pa St, is in an old lockmaster's residence, built in 1905. Besides a good display of Native American artifacts, the museum commemorates the early transportation history of the Gorge. Also on exhibit is a fish wheel, a water-wheel-like machine designed to harvest vast amounts of migrating salmon. Fish wheels proved so successful in trapping fish in the early years of this century that they were outlawed in order to protect salmon from extinction.

Columbia Gorge Sternwheeler
Cruises along the Columbia River are run on the diesel-powered *Columbia Gorge* (☎ 503-223-3928, 541-374-8427). Embark from the eastern end of the old lock system within Marine Park. There are three cruises daily at 10 am, 12:30 and 3 pm, from the third weekend in June to the last week in September. No reservations are necessary. Besides providing an unusual vantage point from which to see Bonneville Dam and the beautiful scenery of the Gorge, the cruise includes historical commentary on the Oregon Trail, Native American lore and the

Lewis and Clark Expedition. Call to inquire about special musical or brunch cruises.

There is an on-board snack bar, with both indoor and outdoor seating. Tickets are $9.95/5 for adults/children (four to 12).

Windsurfing
Rig and launch from the east end of the Marina Park on days when the east winds are blowing. It's also possible to catch some good westerly winds here, but Cascade Locks lights up with sails on hot summer mornings when the wind blows down the river.

Places to Stay
Camping Campers can stay alongside the old lock canal at *Cascade Locks Marine Park* for $10 (☎ 541-374-8619), on Wa-Na-Pa St or at the *Cascade Locks KOA* (☎ 541-374-8668), at the east end of town.

East of Cascade Locks are more forest parks with campgrounds. Take I-84 exit 51 to reach the USFS *Wyeth Campground*, just off the freeway. At exit 56, *Viento State Park* offers camping in a nice wooded area. Windsurfers frequently set sail from the picnic area near the river.

Hotels The *Best Western Columbia River Inn* (☎ 541-374-8777, 800-595-7108), on Wa-Na-Pa St just east of the Bridge of the Gods, is Cascade Locks' best lodging option, with singles/doubles at $74/79. Cross the Bridge of the Gods to Stevenson, WA (see that section), for other options.

Places to Eat
Basic food predominates in Cascade Locks. The *Char Burger* (☎ 541-374-8477), 714 SW Wa-Na-Pa St, serves good burgers and onion rings. Local Native Americans sometimes sell smoked salmon in the parking lot. Stop by the *East Wind Drive-In* (☎ 541-374-8380), 395 SW Wa-Na-Pa, for a bargain-priced milkshake and an ear in on the local gossip. After a long, thirsty hike, go to *Salmon Row Pub* (☎ 541-374-9310), at the corner of Wa-Na-Pa and Regulator Sts. It's a pleasant pub offering pizza, sandwiches and microbrewed beers.

OREGON

AROUND CASCADE LOCKS
Bonneville Dam
Bonneville Dam was one of the largest and most ambitious of the Depression-era New Deal projects. Completed in 1937, it was the first major dam on the Columbia River. The building of the dam brought Oregon thousands of jobs on construction crews, and the cheap electricity that it produced promised future industrial employment. President Franklin D Roosevelt officiated at the dam's opening in 1938, attended by cheering throngs of thousands.

The two hydroelectric powerhouses together produce over 1 million kilowatts of power, and back up the Columbia River for 15 miles.

The Bradford Island Visitor Center is accessed from the Oregon side by crossing one of the two powerhouse dams. Fish ladders, which allow migrating fish to negotiate around the dams, circle around the visitors' center. In season, salmon and steelhead trout leap up the ladder, and a fish counter is on duty, tabulating the numbers of migrating fish; both can be seen from a glass-walled underwater viewing area.

On the main floor of the visitors' center are displays of local Native American culture and the history of the dam; there is also a slide and video theater.

From the Washington side of the dam, follow signs to the Visitor Orientation Building near the second powerhouse. From here there's access to self-guided tours of the hydroelectric generation facilities and to views of another fish ladder.

All facilities at Bonneville Dam (☎ 541-374-8427) are free; it's open 9 am to 5 pm daily, and till 8 pm, May to October.

Bonneville Fish Hatchery
At this fish hatchery (☎ 541-374-8393) – Oregon's oldest – are reared many of the salmon that are returned to the Columbia River, helping to augment natural salmon runs. Here too is the nation's only hatchery for white sturgeon. At viewing ponds, visitors can watch and feed enormous mature trout and sturgeon.

The hatchery is directly west of the dam, and is accessed from the same road and keeps the same hours.

Eagle Creek Recreation Area
Hikes up a spectacular side canyon of the Gorge are the highlight of this popular recreational area, formed of a narrow swath along Eagle Creek. The **Eagle Creek Trail No 440**, constructed in 1915, was a kind of engineering feat. Volunteers blasted ledges for trails along vertical cliffs, spanned a deep chasm with a suspension bridge, and burrowed a 120-foot tunnel behind a waterfall. If you have time for only one day hike in the Gorge, this should be it.

The classic day hike into Eagle Creek leads up along the face of a cliff to a viewpoint over Metlano Falls. Part of the trail then drops back to a streamside near Punchbowl Falls, a good spot to break for lunch and splash in pools of cool water. Casual day hikers can return at this point; the hike is an easy 4½-mile roundtrip stroll.

More ambitious hikers can continue along to High Bridge, a suspension bridge spanning a crevasse, and Tunnel Falls, so named because of the 120-foot tunnel blasted into the rock behind it. Work your way through the tunnel for great views up and down Eagle Creek's canyon. The roundtrip hike from the trailhead to High Bridge is 6½ miles. To Tunnel Falls and back, it's a strenuous 12 miles.

Be warned that the Eagle Creek Trail is very popular. Try to avoid summer weekends when the trail teems with hikers. Some sections of the trail inch along sheer cliffs, with cable handrails drilled into the cliff side for safety. This isn't a good trail for unsupervised children or unleashed pets.

Just east of the Eagle Creek Trailhead is the *Eagle Creek Campground*, with WPA-era stone shelters. Backpackers will be more interested in campsites farther up Eagle Creek. Just past High Bridge is *Tenas Campground*, and nearer to Tunnel Falls is *Blue Grouse Campground*.

To reach the trailhead from eastbound I-84, take exit 41. Westbound travelers need to take the Bonneville Dam exit 40, and double back 1 mile.

STEVENSON (WA)
Population 1100

The little town of Stevenson was just a slumbering mill town along the Columbia River with nice riverside parks until the views from the hills above the village caught the fancy of Oregon-based resort developers. Stevenson still maintains its small town feel, though the quality of the restaurants and the coffee (espresso has arrived) has improved. For travelers who aren't prone to luxury hotels or first-class museums, Stevenson's riverfront parks, with swimming, windsurfing, picnicking and playgrounds will be a draw.

Orientation & Information
Stevenson is 38 miles east of Vancouver, WA, on Hwy 14, and 3 miles north of the Bridge of the Gods, with access to Oregon and I-84.

Contact the Skamania County Chamber of Commerce (☎ 509-427-8911) at PO Box 1037, Stevenson, WA 98648. For local hiking and recreational information in the Gifford Pinchot National Forest, contact the Wind River Ranger Station (☎ 509-427-5645) 8 miles north of Carson, WA.

Columbia Gorge Interpretive Center
Established by the Skamania County Historical Society and Washington State, the interpretive center (☎ 509-427-8211), which is below the Skamania Lodge on 2nd Ave near Rock Creek Cove, attempts to weave together the many threads – Native American, early explorer, pioneer settlers, logging, fishing, shipping, power generation and recreation – that form the complex history of this area. The center's 15,000-sq-foot facility opened in early 1995.

The center is open 10 am to 5 pm daily. Admission is $6/5/4 for adults/seniors/children.

Places to Stay
Campers will want to stay at *Home Valley Park*, a lovely park right on the river with a swimming beach, picnic area and campsites ($7). The park is near the community

of Home Valley, on Hwy 14, 4 miles east of Stevenson.

Econo Lodge (☎ 509-427-5628, 800-424-7777), just east of Stevenson on Hwy 14, is a good, cheap motel, with rooms at $45/55.

The *Skamania Lodge* (☎ 509-427-7700, 800-221-7117), 1131 SW Skamania Lodge Way, overlooking Stevenson, is the Gorge's biggest resort. Opened in 1993 by the same company that developed the Snoqualmie Falls Lodge in Washington and Portland's ornate gem, the Governor Hotel, the Skamania Lodge is easily the most comfortable and beautiful lodging in the Gorge. The facilities include swimming pools, exercise rooms, horseback riding, hiking trails, tennis courts, and an 18-hole golf course. Rooms start at $135 and go up to $210 a night for suites with views of the river.

Places to Eat
Windsurfers and the spillover from the Skamania Lodge have created a market for tasty, informal food in Stevenson. The *Big River Grill* (☎ 509-427-4888), 192 SW 2nd Ave, is a comfortable little cafe with nice salads and light entrées. A grilled salmon salad is $8, a steak dinner only $12. At *El Rio* (☎ 509-427-4479), right across the street from the Big River Grill, the motto is 'Big Strong Mexican Food' and home-smoked meats are featured. The food is good and meals are generally less than $10.

For fine dining overlooking the Gorge, go to *Skamania Lodge* (see Places to Stay, above). The emphasis here is on high-quality local ingredients prepared with determined eclecticism. Fresh Chinook salmon is roasted on an alder plank, a local Native American method, while lamb T-bone is grilled with red pepper juice and served with roasted onions (both dishes cost $21).

AROUND STEVENSON
Carson Hot Springs
Feeling stiff and sore after days of traveling? Then this old-fashioned restorative spa (☎ 509-427-8292) might be just what

you need. After soaking in 126°F mineral water, you're swaddled in towels to bake a while, then unrolled and massaged vigorously. The whole experience is redolent of the past – including the tiled bathing chambers and wordlessly efficient masseurs. A soak-and-wrap session lasts an hour and costs $10; an hourlong massage is $40.

In addition to the hot-springs therapy, there's a golf course right up the hill. RV and tent sites are available, as are rooms and food in the venerable St Martins Hotel (see below). The hot springs are busy – in the winter with skiers, in the summer with hikers – so it pays to call ahead and make a reservation for treatment. The hot-springs complex is about half a mile north of Hwy 14, just east of Carson (3 miles east of Stevenson, WA) on the Wind River.

Soakers can stay at the historic *St Martins Hotel* (☎ 509-427-8292), which features therapeutic soaks in the mineral hot springs and sessions with massage therapists. Rooms start at $40. Cabins are available for $50, and the Hot Tub Suite for $100. Campers get a pretty good deal with tent spaces at $4.82, and RVs at $11 to $13.

Dog Mountain
Hikes up this imposing 2900-foot sentinel over the Gorge are popular, especially in May, when wildflowers are abundant along the trail. The grade is frequently steep, and it gains almost 3000 feet in elevation, so this isn't a casual stroll. But once on top, the views up and down the Columbia River, and over the nearby Cascade volcanoes, are spectacular. Allow approximately six hours roundtrip.

To reach the trailhead for Dog Mountain Trail No 147, drive 9 miles east of Stevenson, near Hwy 14 milepost 54.

Beacon Rock State Park
One of the Gorge's most conspicuous landmarks, 848-foot Beacon Rock rises like an enormous thumb from the north bank of the Columbia River. The state park (☎ 509-427-8265) on Hwy 14, 3 miles northeast of Skamania, WA, or about 7 miles west of the Bridge of the Gods, is one of the most

An Oregon State Park . . . in Washington?
Reckoned to be the second-largest monolith in the world (after the Rock of Gibraltar), Beacon Rock was very nearly an Oregon state park, even though it is in Washington.

Early this century, the Army Corps of Engineers decided that they needed riprap for a jetty in the Columbia River, and they made plans to blow up Beacon Rock in order to access its cache of rock. The owners of Beacon Rock at the time, the Biddle family, offered to donate the property to the state of Washington in order to preserve the landmark as a state park. However, the governor refused the offer. Not to be thwarted, the Biddle family then offered the land to the state of Oregon, to be turned into an Oregon state park in Washington. Finally, the Washington governor was embarrassed into accepting the gift, and a Washington state park was formed. ■

pleasant on the north side of the Columbia River, and offers hiking, mountain bike trails, picnicking, camping and river access.

There's hiking for just about everyone in Beacon Rock State Park. Most famous is the ascent up the face of Beacon Rock itself, a three-quarter-mile trail with 53 switchbacks that clambers up the south face of the rock. The views from the top are amazing.

If you're looking for a short hike that is fairly easygoing, there's a nature trail through a wetlands meadow to tiny Riddell Lake. For a more strenuous hike to the top of the Columbia River Gorge, consider a climb up Hamilton Mountain. At 2445 feet, Hamilton Mountain is the most westerly of the peaks that rise out of the Gorge. If you're not up to the roundtrip hike to the top, which will take approximately five hours, then consider hiking a mile up the trail to Hardy and Rodney Falls. To reach the trailhead, park in the picnic area lot. A branch of the trail also leads out from the campground.

Beacon Rock offers one of the few rock-climbing opportunities in the Gorge, as the rock comprising this sheer volcanic plug is much more stable than other cliffs in the area. The majority of climbs are on the south face of Beacon Rock, where 60 routes have been documented. The routes are for experienced climbers only.

Old logging and fire roads wind through the state park's 4500 acres. These mostly deserted roads are available for mountain biking and offer access to the upper reaches of Hardy Creek, as well as to the back side of Hamilton Mountain. Horseback riders also use the roads, so be courteous. Access to the road system begins at a locked gate about half a mile up the Group Camp road.

Beacon Rock State Park offers camping with no hookups. The 33 sites are across the road from Beacon Rock and the Columbia River, but are in a forested area near a small stream. Overnight fees are $10.

HOOD RIVER & AROUND
Population 5000

Set at the mouth of a broad valley along the Columbia River, Hood River is the Gorge's most dynamic city. It's the center for recreation on the Columbia River, along the Gorge, and for nearby Mt Hood. A combination of strong river currents, prevailing westerly winds and a vast body of water make the Columbia River around Hood River a windsurfing hot spot. When the conditions are right – and they frequently are in the Gorge – thousands of windsurfers will be zipping across the wide Columbia River at any given moment.

Because of this, Hood River is one of the most international towns in the Northwest: stroll along the steep streets in the old part of town, and hear French, Japanese or German. A sense of fun and youthfulness pervades the town, making it a great base from which to explore the Gorge.

South of town, the river of the same name drains a wide valley filled with orchards. During spring, nearly the entire

region is filled with the scent and color of pink and white blossoms. Later on, fruit stands spring up along roadsides, selling apples, pears, cherries, berries and vegetables. Watch for wineries: wine grapes are the most recent crop to find a home in this fabulously fertile valley. Hwy 35, which traverses the valley, leads up the south and east flanks of Mt Hood, only 25 miles south.

Orientation
Hood River is 63 miles east of Portland on I-84 and 21 miles west of The Dalles. On Hwy 35, it's 45 miles from Hood River to Government Camp on Mt Hood.

The old part of Hood River faces onto the Columbia River, along steeply terraced streets cut into the walls of the Gorge. The I-84 exit 63 puts you onto 2nd St, which crosses the rail lines to intersect with Oak St, the town's old main street. This attractive area is filled with boutiques devoted to recreation, coffeehouses and upbeat street life.

Information
The Hood River County Chamber of Commerce (☎ 541-386-2000, 800-366-3530), is in the Port Marina Park, Hood River, OR 97031. Besides the usual volunteers and brochure racks, there's a large relief map/display of the surrounding area that helps make sense of local geography.

The headquarters for the Columbia River Gorge National Scenic Area (☎ 541 386 2333) are in the Wacoma Center, 902 Wasco Ave.

The Hood River post office is on 4th St at Cascade Ave. The Wacoma Bookstore (☎ 541-386-5353), 212 Oak St, is a good bookstore with a strong regional travel section. It also sells local Green Trail maps. You can get USGS maps at Cascade Whitewater (☎ 541-386-4286), 6 Oak St. The local newspaper is the *Hood River News*. Oregon Public Radio is heard on 94.3 FM.

You can wash those dirty clothes at Westside Laundry (☎ 541-386-5029), 1911 W Cascade Ave. Hood River Memorial Hospital (☎ 541-386-3911) is at the corner of 13th and May Sts.

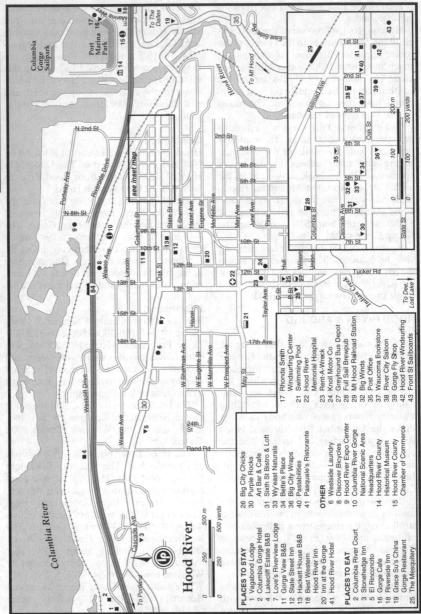

Hood River County Historical Museum

This regional museum (☎ 541-386-6722), in Port Marina Park along the Columbia River, retells the history of the Hood River area. Native American artifacts, pioneer quilts and early logging equipment are some of the displays at this generally well-thought-out museum. It is open 10 am to 4 pm, Wednesday to Saturday, April to October; admission is free.

Mt Hood Scenic Railroad

This rail line (☎ 541-386-3556, 800-872-4661), built in 1906, once transported fruit, berries and lumber from the upper Hood River valley to the main railhead in Hood River. The railroad was revived in the 1980s when train enthusiasts brought vintage diesel-electric engines and rolling stock back to the line. The train now operates between the Blossom Festival (late April) and Harvest Fest (autumn) as a scenic excursion through the valley, beneath the snowy peak of Mt Hood and past fragrant orchards.

Trains depart from the station at 110 Railroad Ave, right under the viaduct between I-84 exit 63 (2nd St) and downtown Hood River. Four hour excursions depart daily at 10 am, with an extra run at 3 pm on weekends. The train stops for approximately an hour in Parkdale, an old farm and orchard town south of Hood River with antique stores and a couple of cafes. The fare is $22/19/14 for adults/seniors/children. Saturday evening dinner ($68) and Sunday morning brunch ($55) are served on special train runs. Call ahead for reservations as the train is frequently sold out.

Wineries

The Hood River area now features quite a few wineries. Hood River Vineyards (☎ 541-386-3772), 4693 Westwood Drive; Flerchinger Vineyards (☎ 541-386-2882), 4200 Post Canyon; and Three Rivers Winery (☎ 541-386-5453), 275 Country Club Rd, offer winetasting. All are found off Country Club Rd, west of Hood River.

Distillers are also springing up around Hood River. At the Eve Atkins Distilling Company (☎ 541-354-2550), Marichelle brand *eau de vie* (brandy) is made from local fruits. The tasting room at 4420 Summit Drive, out toward Odell off Hwy 35, is open from 11 am to 5 pm Monday to Saturday.

Lost Lake

The postcard photo of Mt Hood from 240-acre Lost Lake – the white mountain peak rising from a deep-blue lake amid a thick green forest – is probably the most famous image of Oregon's most famous volcano. This side trip onto the northern flanks of Mt Hood is popular when the Gorge gets hot.

To reach Lost Lake, take Hwy 281 south from Hood River to Dee. Signs will point to Lost Lake Rd; the lake is 25 miles south of Hood River. Canoe rentals are available at the resort here.

Fishing

The Hood River is noted for a good steelhead trout run throughout the year, with an especially good summer run. Fishing is best in the lower 3 miles, near town. The river is also fine for rainbow trout.

Steelhead and sturgeon are found in the Columbia River near Hood River, while bass thrive in the small roadside ponds beside the river. Fishing for salmon in the Columbia River is now restricted. Visit the Gorge Fly Shop (☎ 541-386-6977), 201 Oak St, for up-to-date information, tackle and licenses.

Mountain Biking

Head south of town toward Mt Hood to enjoy some great mountain biking. Most of the area's trails are off Hwy 35 and Forest Rd 44 (which comes off Hwy 35 about 20 miles south of Hood River). The 5-mile East Fork Trail connects Sherwood and Robinhood Campgrounds, and is a fairly easy ride. For more of a challenge, ride the Tilly Jane loop; follow the signs from Hwy 35 to Cloud Cap, about 25 miles southwest of town.

Windsurfing

Twenty years ago, the wind was just a nuisance. West winds in the summer, east winds in the winter meant messy hair year-round. Now, in the windsurfing era, folks read the river and sky for wind, and listen for wind reports on the local radio stations.

No matter what the wind reports say, the cardinal rule of windsurfing is 'Never leave wind to find wind.' A fairly reliable way to find wind is to look at the sky and find the place where clouds end and the sun begins – this is usually the windiest spot. Or, get on the computer and check out the excellent Wind Cam reports at www.windance.com.

In summer, winds tend to shoot up the Gorge from the cool coastal west to the hot, dry east. These westerlies, which directly oppose the river's flow, are generally strongest at the eastern end of the Gorge. Viento State Park, with its campground and recently improved river access, is a good place to stop and check the wind. Swell City, the Spring Creek Fish Hatchery and Doug's Beach are Washington-side sites with reliably strong west winds. Experienced windsurfers head upriver, where there are a couple of heavy-duty sites near Maryhill. Maryhill State Park has camping, free parking and a spacious beach to complement the strong river current and strong west winds. Just upriver, The Wall is a small launch spot that attracts expert windsurfers who can handle huge swells.

Wintertime east winds shift the focus to the western end of the Gorge, where Rooster Rock State Park and the Cascade Locks marina both provide good river access and strong easterlies.

If you're new to big winds, try setting out from the Hood River marina or Rhonda's, just to the east. The wind's not quite so gusty in these somewhat sheltered spots. Another fairly protected beach is across the river at Home Valley, where the west winds are relatively gentle. A very popular spot for beginners is The Dalles' Riverfront Park, with a long, sandy shoreline, light west winds and a fairly smooth stretch of river.

Many of these sites, especially on the Oregon side, have a $3 parking fee.

If you've never windsurfed, it really helps to take a lesson. Rhonda Smith Windsurfing Center, at the Port Marina Park in Hood River (☎ 541-386-9463, 800-241-2430), has a two-day beginners' class for $125, including equipment. Gorge Wind Guide Service (☎ 541-490-4401) in Hood River offers advanced windsurfing instruction and transportation to the day's windiest launch sites.

Rent equipment in Hood River from Rhonda Smith's or Windance (☎ 541-386-2131), 108 Hwy 35; Front Street Sailboards (☎ 541-386-4044), 207 Front St; Big Winds (☎ 541-386-6086), 505 Cascade Ave; or Hood River Windsurfing (☎ 386-5787), 101 Oak St. A full rig for a day costs about $35 to $40. ∎

Discover Bicycles (☎ 541-386-4820), 1020 Wasco Ave, rents full suspension mountain bikes and can sell you a good trail map. They also run guided mountain bike tours ($50 for a half-day, $80 full day, with group discounts). Check out their web site for more trail information: www.gorge.net/business/discover/.

Other Activities

For white-water **kayaking**, head to the White Salmon, Hood, or Klickitat Rivers. Cascade Whitewater (see Information) rents kayaks, runs classes and leads trips on local rivers. It costs $50 for a trip on Klickitat River, $65 on Hood River, and $80 on Deschutes River.

If you're looking to **golf**, the nine-hole Hood River Golf & Country Club (☎ 541-386-3009), on Country Club Rd west of Hood River, has beautiful mountain views, rentals, a club house and wineries nearby. The city **pool** is on the corner of May St at 17th Ave. Swim in the Columbia River at Koberg Beach, 2 miles east of Hood River off I-84 exit 67 (westbound only).

Special Events

Hood River valley springs to life with the Blossom Festival (☎ 386-2000), which is held the third weekend of April. Tours through the orchards, fragrant and colorful with bloom, are the main event. Complete the weekend with visits to an antique fair, musical events and special food and craft booths in Hood River and smaller orchard communities.

Mid-July brings to Hood River the Gorge Games (☎ 541-386-7774), a week-long extravaganza of windsurfing, mountain biking, kayaking and a host of other outdoor sports. Competitions are wide-open, age-group events. There are also instructional clinics, kids' events and concerts.

The annual Columbia River Cross Channel Swim (☎ 541-386-2000) is held on Labor Day. More than 300 swimmers brave the cold water and unpredictable currents of the Columbia to cross from Bingen to Hood River.

Held the second weekend of October, the Hood River Harvest Fest (☎ 541-386-2000) celebrates the agricultural bounty of the valley with local crafts, food and musical entertainment at the Hood River Expo Center along the riverfront.

Places to Stay

Camping The closest public campgrounds are at *Viento State Park*, 8 miles west of Hood River, where there are 63 campsites along the river; it costs $14 to camp. *Memaloose State Park* is accessible from westbound I-84 only. It's about 11 miles east of Hood River, and offers over 100 campsites; there is a $15 fee (no reservations). Call ☎ 541-374-8811 for information on either park. A lot of windsurfers opt to camp out at these local state parks, which means that many of them are packed and kind of rowdy on weekends.

B&Bs Have the Hood River B&B Association book you a room by calling ☎ 541-386-6767.

Otherwise you can choose between

bunkroom and privacy at the *Gorge View B&B* (☎ 541-386-5770), 1009 Columbia St. Meet up with other windsurfers, mountain bikers, and snowboarders in the $35 bunkroom, or go for a single/double private room for $65/75. Everybody mingles at breakfast or in the hot tub.

The Dutch Colonial *Hackett House B&B* (☎ 541-386-1014), 922 State St, was built in 1903, and offers four guest rooms with shared bath; rates range from $45 to $75. The *Inn at the Gorge* (☎ 541-386-4429), 1113 Eugene St, is an attractive 1908 home with wide porches. The three rooms ($42 to $78) have private bathrooms and separate guest entrances. The *State Street Inn* (☎ 541-386-1899), 1005 State St, is a 1930s home with rooms from $60 to $80. It's open April to October.

Hood River's most exclusive B&B is *Lakecliff Estate B&B* (☎ 541-386-7000), 3020 Westcliff Drive. Designed by Albert Doyle, the architect responsible for the Multnomah Falls Lodge, this historic, 1908 summer home sits on 3 wooded acres on the cliffs above the Columbia River. There are four guest rooms, with rates from $85 to $100.

Motels It can be extremely hard to find rooms in Hood River during summer (especially if the wind is blowing), so plan well ahead. If Hood River is all booked up, try The Dalles, 21 miles east, where there are usually plenty of rooms. Gorge Central Reservations (☎ 541-386-6109) can help you find lodging in hotels or vacation homes.

Cross the Columbia River to Bingen, WA, for the area's best lodging value and quirkiest atmosphere. The *Bingen School Inn* (☎ 509-493-3363) is sort of a cross between a hostel and an inn, with private rooms going for $29 a double, and hostel bunks running $11 a night. There's a large common area with kitchen access, a gym, a weight room, and rock-climbing walls. The inn is housed in an old elementary school built by the Civilian Conservation Corps (CCC) in 1938 (thus the gym); lodgings are in the old classrooms. Find the Bingen School Inn a block north of Hwy 14 at Cedar and Humbolt Sts.

Just upriver from Bingen, in Lyle, WA, the newly renovated but still decidedly old-fashioned *Lyle Hotel* (☎ 509-365-5953) has rooms for $35 at the foot of 7th St. There's a restaurant downstairs.

Vagabond Lodge (☎ 541-386-2992), at 4070 Westcliff Drive, is between the freeway and the river, next to the swanky Columbia Gorge Hotel. Rates range from $40 to $90; pleasant rooms overlooking the Columbia River go for $59 in the high summer season. A little farther west on the same road, at *Meredith Gorge Motel* (☎ 541-386-1515), 4300 Westcliff Drive, the rooms are a few dollars cheaper ($33 to $46), but they're not quite as nice. Closer to the city center, there are condo-like rooms at *Love's Riverview Lodge* (☎ 541-386-8719), 1505 Oak St, for $50/55.

Right on the river, the *Best Western Hood River Inn* (☎ 541-386-2200, 800-828-7873), 1108 E Marina Way, has a swimming pool, restaurant and meeting rooms. Rooms with a river view run $90/95; it's $10 less to look out onto the parking lot. The *Hood River Hotel* (☎ 386-1900), 102 Oak St, is a 1913 hotel that's been tastefully refurbished; rooms are $50 to $145.

If you're looking for a classy and romantic place to stay in Hood River, and you don't mind dropping big bucks, stay at *The Columbia Gorge Hotel* (☎ 541-386-5566, 800-345-1921) at 4000 Westcliff Drive. Built in 1921 by Simon Benson, one of the early backers of the Columbia River Hwy, this beautiful, Spanish-influenced hotel sits in a 5-acre garden directly above 207-foot Wah Gwin Gwin Falls. The hotel is listed in the National Register of Historic Places. Rooms range from $170 to $270.

Lodges *Lost Lake Resort* (☎ 541-386-6366), PO Box 90, Hood River, OR 97031, on Mt Hood's northern flank, rents small, basic cabins ($40 to $95) and campsites ($15). It also rents canoes and small boats (no motorized boats allowed), and the fishing is good for trout. There's a small store but no restaurant.

Places to Eat
Budget If you are hungry for a full breakfast, go to *Bette's Place* (☎ 541-386-1880), 416 Oak St. Let 'eggs Benedict' ($4.95) be your mantra. *Holstein's Coffee Co* (☎ 541-386-4115), 12 Oak St, is a great place for coffee, pastries and panini sandwiches. Plan a picnic at *Pastabilities* (☎ 541-386-1903), 106 Oak St, where Italian deli dishes are available to go. *Wy'east Naturals* (☎ 541-386-6181), 110 5th St, is the local organic and natural-foods store and also has a juice bar.

The Gorge's best tacos are at *El Rinconcito* (no phone), a small trailer across from the Subway on the way out of town on W Cascade Ave. A well-seasoned beef taco on a delicate homemade corn tortilla costs $1.40.

Purple Rocks Art Bar & Cafe (☎ 541-386-6061), 606 Oak St, offers vegetarian breakfasts and other light meals, but the funked-out indolence of this cafe makes it a good place to catch up with a newspaper or write letters. Sometimes there's acoustic entertainment in the evenings.

Middle *Big City Chicks* (☎ 541-387-3811), 1303 13th St, has healthy food from all sorts of cultures for very inexpensive prices. Moroccan apricot chicken with vegetable couscous is a real hit, as is raspberry salmon with wild mushrooms; both cost less than $10. Downtown, *Big City Wraps* (☎ 541-387-5511) serves untraditional burritos for $4.25 at 212 4th St.

The Gorge Cafe (☎ 541-386-8700), Port Marina Park, is right on the waterfront and offers light meals and sandwiches. It's open in summer only. *Grace Su's China Gorge Restaurant* (☎ 541-386-5331), 2680 Old Columbia River Drive, offers spicy Sichuan-style food. *Sixth Street Bistro & Loft* (☎ 541-386-5737), on the corner of 6th St and Cascade Ave, has good burgers, pasta dishes ($8 to $10) and full dinners (chicken Marsala for $12), as well as local microbrews. There's outdoor seating in a garden area. *The Mesquitery* (☎ 541-386-2002), 1219 12th St, is Hood River's best barbecue joint, with just-right spicy sauces. Prices are in the $8 range for ribs or chicken.

Top End As the name indicates, *Pasquale's Ristorante* (☎ 541-386-1900), 102 Oak St, specializes in Italian cuisine. The charming dining room is in the historic Hood River Hotel. Pasta dishes go for $10 to $12, lamb chops with green peppercorn sauce are $15. Another hotel restaurant, *Riverside Inn* (☎ 541-386-2200) in the Best Western Hood River Inn, offers great views and surprisingly good cooking. Favorites are the Northwest bouillabaisse ($15) and spicy salmon ($17).

The only views at the *Stonehedge Inn* (☎ 541-386-3940), 3405 Cascade Ave, are of antiques. This well-loved restaurant is in a graciously dilapidated old home in a wooded grove. There's a light entrée menu, with á la carte dishes (around $10), or full dinners such as veal chanterelle ($17.50) or duck á l'orange ($16.50).

Double the prices and your expectations at the *Columbia River Court* in the Columbia Gorge Hotel (☎ 541-386-5566), 4000 Westcliff Drive. By far the most famous meal served in this beautiful river-view dining room is the 'Farm Breakfast' brunch, served on weekends. The five-course extravaganza will leave you wondering what farmer could have conceived of such bounty (or, at $23 a head, what farmer could afford it). Reservations are a must. Dinner features local salmon, lamb and game prepared á la Northwest.

Entertainment

At any given moment, there are hundreds of vigorous recreationists in Hood River. After a day on the slopes or on the river, it's time to head out for nightlife. Catch a movie at *Trail Twin Theater* (☎ 541-386-1666), on Tucker Rd, or go for a drink at one of Hood River's rowdier spots.

At the *River City Saloon* (☎ 541-386-4005), on the corner of 2nd St and Cascade Ave, there's live music and dancing three to four nights a week. If you like it loud and rowdy, then across the bridge in Bingen, WA, the *Northshore Bar & Grill* (☎ 509-493-4440), 216 W Steuben St, is the place, with live music on weekends.

Full Sail Brewpub (☎ 541-386-2281), 506 Columbia St, Hood River's own brewery, has developed a loyal following across the West Coast with such offerings as its rich golden ale. The hours are short: daily from noon to 8 pm only.

Getting There & Around

Greyhound (☎ 541-386-1212), 1205 B St, runs five buses a day from Hood River to Portland and points east. Fares are $10.50 one way to/from Portland.

For car rentals in Hood River, contact Rent-A-Wreck (☎ 541-386-8776), 1040 12th St, or Knoll Motor Co (☎ 541-386-3011), 1111 12th St. Call Hood River Taxi (☎ 541-386-2255) for a cab.

THE DALLES
Population 11,370

As an important transport hub on the Oregon Trail, The Dalles played a preeminent role in the history of white settlement in Oregon. French Canadian trappers used the area as the head of navigation for transporting furs to Fort Vancouver. The trappers named the rocky bench of land below

OREGON

the river rapids *Les Dalles*, meaning 'flagstones,' apparently referring to the shards of rock strewn everywhere.

The first white settlement at this transport spot was a Methodist mission, established in 1838. Within three years a Catholic mission was established here as well, and the representatives of the two faiths spent more time bickering with each other than saving souls. In 1854 the town of The Dalles was platted, and a town charter granted in 1857.

The discovery of gold and the establishment of open-range agriculture in eastern Oregon made The Dalles an important

trade town and transport point. Then, as now, the Gorge was the principal corridor between eastern and western Oregon, and almost all freight bound in either direction passed through The Dalles. Steamboats docked at the riverfront, stagecoaches rattled off to far-flung desert communities, and the streets were crowded with miners, ranchers and traders.

The completion of first the railroad and then barge lines through Columbia River reservoirs served to increase freight transport through The Dalles. Today, The Dalles continues its legacy as a thriving transport hub. The area is also the nation's largest

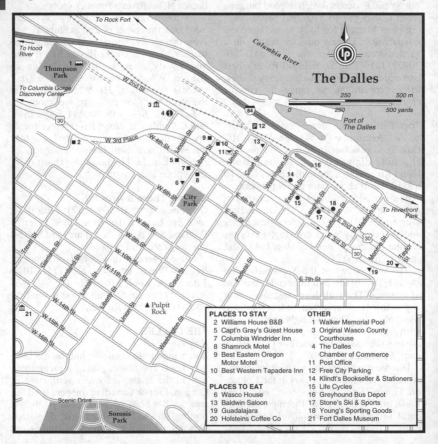

The Dalles

PLACES TO STAY	OTHER
2 Williams House B&B	1 Walker Memorial Pool
5 Capt'n Gray's Guest House	3 Original Wasco County
7 Columbia Windrider Inn	Courthouse
8 Shamrock Motel	4 The Dalles
9 Best Eastern Oregon	Chamber of Commerce
Motor Motel	11 Post Office
10 Best Western Tapadera Inn	12 Free City Parking
	14 Klindt's Bookseller & Stationers
PLACES TO EAT	15 Life Cycles
6 Wasco House	16 Greyhound Bus Depot
13 Baldwin Saloon	17 Stone's Ski & Sports
19 Guadalajara	18 Young's Sporting Goods
20 Holsteins Coffee Co	21 Fort Dalles Museum

Top Left: Yurt camping, Honeyman State Park, OR
Bottom Left: Ramona Falls, Mt Hood Wilderness, OR

Top Right: Multnomah Falls, OR
Bottom Right: Screen door, Joseph, OR

Top Left: Sunrise on the Powder River, OR
Bottom Left: Sand dunes in Malheur National Wildlife
Refuge, OR

Top Right: Crater Lake and Phantom Ship seen through
twisted tree, OR
Bottom Right: Wind-carved snow and Mt Hood, OR

producer of sweet cherries, and orchard workers from Latin America lend the community a distinct Hispanic character. Despite the recreational boom of the last decade, The Dalles remains largely hard working and down-to-earth.

Orientation

The Dalles is 84 miles east of Portland along I-84. US 197 cuts south from The Dalles to Bend, about 131 miles away. The Dalles Bridge crosses the Columbia River to link up with Hwy 14 in Washington.

The Dalles is built on a series of steep terraces, with rocky outcroppings jutting up unexpectedly in the middle of streets and people's backyards. Ask for a walking tour map at the visitors' center; it's worth the walk to see the fins and ledges of rock incorporated into streets and gardens.

The main business district lies along 2nd and 3rd Sts, both of which are one-way streets. Above this level of town is the principal residential area, linked to downtown by 10th St.

Information

The Dalles Chamber of Commerce (☎ 541-296-6616, 800-255-3385) is at 404 W 2nd St. The post office is at 100 W 2nd St. Klindt's Bookseller & Stationers (☎ 541-296-3355), 315 E 2nd St, has been in operation since 1883. Check out its excellent selection of local history books. The Dalles Chronicle is the local daily paper. Tune in to Oregon Public Radio on 91.5 FM.

You can do laundry at the Washin' Shop (☎ 541-296-9722), 1256 W 6th St. The Mid-Columbia Medical Center (☎ 541-296-1111) is at 1700 E 19th St.

Columbia Gorge Discovery Center

Since its opening in 1997, this museum (☎ 541-296-8600), with its striking riverbank setting and dramatic architecture, has become *the* reason to visit The Dalles. Exhibits, both indoors and out, focus on the land and what people have made of it.

In the main foyer, the Columbia River is mapped in granite inlaid in the tile floor. A large, three-dimensional model of the un-dammed river is filled with rushing water; push a button and The Dalles Dam rises up, stilling and pooling the water.

Films spotlight the geology and formation of the gorge, and the construction of the historic highway. Outdoor exhibits focus on Native American and pioneer life.

The Discovery Center is open 10 am to 6 pm daily. It's at 5000 Discovery Drive, on the western edge of The Dalles. From the west, take exit 82 off Hwy 84, turn right onto the Historic Columbia River Hwy (US 30) for 1½ miles, then turn right at the orange sign onto Discovery Drive. From the east, take exit 84 onto W 2nd St, turn left at the first light onto W 6th St, continue for 3 miles, then turn right at the sign onto Discovery Drive. Admission is $6.50/5.50/3 adults/seniors/children (six to 16).

The Dalles Dam & Lock

The Dalles Dam, built in 1957, produces enough electricity to power a city the size of Seattle. Access to this power came at a price, however. The dam's reservoir, Lake Celilo, flooded the culturally rich area around Celilo Falls, for thousands of years a meeting place and fishery for Native Americans.

The falls had hampered commercial navigation on the Columbia River since the days of the fur traders, and all the old transportation routes, as well as the troublesome falls themselves, were inundated when The Dalles Dam impounded the river, creating 24-mile-long Lake Celilo.

Tours of the facilities are offered from two points. In Seufert Park, east on the frontage road from I-84 exit 87, is The Dalles Dam Visitor Center (☎ 541-296-9778). This small museum and information center contains the usual homage to hydroelectricity, along with exhibits on local history. From here, a small train (no charge) leaves every half-hour to visit the dam itself. The visitors' center and tour train operate 9 am to 5 pm daily, June to Labor Day weekend.

To skip the train ride, take I-84 exit 88 directly to The Dalles Dam. The self-guided tour of the turbines and the powerhouse is open from 9 am to 5 pm weekdays, year-round.

Horsethief Lake State Park

At this Washington state park (☎ 509-767-1159), just across from The Dalles, are preserved some of the most famous remaining **pictographs** along the Columbia River. *Tsagaglalal*, or 'She Who Watches,' is probably the most widely known image: an owl-like female presence presiding over what was once a thriving Native American crossroads.

The pictograph area, once open to the public, can now be visited only on a guided tour, due to vandalism. The park is open April to October, and free tours are offered at 10 am Friday and Saturday only. Reservations are recommended, as tours are limited to 30 people.

The central aspect of this park is **Horsethief Lake**, a small inlet of Lake Celilo. Rising from the eastern edge of the lake are the imposing basalt walls of **Horsethief Butte**, popular with beginning rock climbers. There's no parking area for Horsethief Butte, but at milepost 86 on Hwy 14 there's a trailhead to the cliffs.

Green, well-watered Horsethief Lake State Park also offers fishing and swimming in the lake, as well as camping and picnicking.

Other Attractions

Established in 1850, **Fort Dalles** was meant to protect the incoming settlers along the Oregon Trail from the large Native American presence in the area, the 1847 Whitman Massacre having galvanized a general fear of Indians. At the time it was built, Fort Dalles was the only US Army garrison between the Pacific Coast and Wyoming.

Of the original 10-sq-mile encampment, only a grassy park with the surgeon's quarters remains. The Fort Dalles Museum (☎ 541-296-4547), at the corner of W 15th and Garrison Sts, is open 10:30 am to 5 pm weekdays, and 10 am to 5 pm on weekends, March to October. In winter it's open noon to 4 pm Wednesday to Friday, and 10 am to

4 pm on weekends. Admission is $2 for adults; children and students are free.

When the **Wasco County Courthouse** (☎ 541-296-4798), at 406 W 2nd St, was built in 1859, it served as county seat for the largest county in US history. Wasco County comprised 130,000 sq miles at that time, and included parts of Idaho and Wyoming. The courthouse has been moved to a site beside the chamber of commerce, where it now serves as a museum, welcome center and gift shop.

Pulpit Rock, a curious thumb of rock near the corner of 12th and Court Sts, combines geology and theology. From this natural pulpit, early Methodist missionaries preached to the Native Americans. The rock still serves as a pulpit for local Easter services.

High on the cliffs above The Dalles, pleasantly wooded **Sorosis Park** affords wonderful views over the town, the river and surrounding mountains. There are picnic tables, tennis courts and a playground, and the civic rose garden is here, too. To reach Sorosis Park from downtown, take Trevitt St south and follow the signs.

Rock Fort, a naturally fortified indentation in the rocky riverbank, was Lewis and Clark's favored local campsite both to and from the Pacific. The corps must have presented a curious spectacle to the Native Americans who gathered around them: at Celilo Falls, the explorers had become infested with fleas. Lewis wrote in his journal:

[The fleas] are very troublesom and dificuelt to get rid of, perticularly as the men have not a Change of Clothes to put on, they strip off their Clothes and kill the flees, dureing which time they remain nakid.

To reach Rock Fort from downtown, follow US 30 west (it becomes W 6th St). Turn right on Webber St and drive toward the river into an industrial area. Turn right on 1st St and continue half a mile to a sign pointing to a parking area. There's not much interpretive information at Rock Fort, but kids and Lewis-and-Clark buffs will enjoy the site.

Windsurfing

Hood River may wear the crown when it comes to the windsurfing lifestyle, but the wind blows at The Dalles too. Right in town, Riverfront Park (exit 85) is a good spot for beginners. A favorite entry point, with strong west winds, is Celilo Park, 9 miles east of The Dalles. Avery Park, 4 miles upriver from Horsethief Lake State Park, offers good access to the river from the Washington side.

Fishing

While the locals fish for sturgeon, walleye and pan fish in the Columbia River above The Dalles Dam, for many the real angling scene is the Deschutes River, which joins the Columbia just upriver from The Dalles. For information and tackle, go to Young's Sporting Goods (☎ 541-296-2544), 515 E 2nd St. Young's Fishing Service (☎ 541-296-5371, 800-270-7962), 720 E 14th St, organizes guided fishing trips on the John Day, Columbia and Deschutes Rivers.

Other Activities

Rent a bicycle at Life Cycles (☎ 541-296-9588), 418 E 2nd St. Skis, snowboards and in-line skates are available at Stone's Ski & Sports (☎ 541-298-5886), 500 E 2nd St. Walker Memorial Pool (☎ 541-298-2020), 602 W 2nd St, is in Thompson Park, just west of downtown.

Special Events

The Dalles' biggest summer event is Fort Dalles Day (☎ 541-296-6616, 800-255-3385), held the second weekend of July. There's a parade and chili cook-off, but the big event is the PRCA Rodeo. Call for details and rodeo tickets.

Places to Stay

Camping The closest public campground to The Dalles is in Washington, across The Dalles Bridge at *Horsethief Lake State Park* (☎ 509-767-1159), 2 miles east on Hwy 14 from the junction with US 197.

On the Oregon side, *Memaloose State Park*, 11 miles west of The Dalles on I-84 (westbound access only), offers riverside camping at a spot overlooking a Native American burial island. Fourteen miles east of The Dalles, there's a nice campground at *Deschutes State Park* (☎ 541-739-2322).

B&Bs Not all B&Bs are fussy, frilly places. Take the *Columbia Windrider Inn* (☎ 541-296-2607, 800-635-0051), 200 W 4th St, a casual but tidy place catering to windsurfers and other sports enthusiasts. Rates start at $45 and include use of the swimming pool, hot tub and pool table.

Capt'n Gray's Guest House (☎ 541-298-8222), 210 W 4th St, is a well-preserved Queen Anne confection with rooms from $50 to $65. *The Williams House B&B* (☎ 541-296-2889), 608 W 6th St, is one of the most elaborate homes in a town full of historic buildings; rates are $65 to $75.

Motels The Dalles has many affordable motels. The *Shamrock Motel* (☎ 541-296-5464), 118 W 4th St, is right downtown with singles/doubles for $30/34. *Best Eastern Oregon Motor Motel* (☎ 541-296-9111), 200 W 2nd St, also downtown, has a pool and rooms for $40/46. The nicest lodging downtown is the *Best Western Tapadera Inn* (☎ 541-296-9107), 112 W 2nd St, with a pool, room service and restaurant; rooms are $50/55.

If you want a view, head over to the *Inn at the Dalles* (☎ 541-296-1167), 3550 SE Frontage Rd. Above the eastern edge of town, the hotel has an outdoor pool and some kitchenettes; rooms start at $35.

On the west end of town is another hotel strip. The *Quality Inn* (☎ 541-298-5161), 2114 W 6th St, offers a pool, hot tub, guest laundry and some kitchenettes. Rooms cost $65/69. *Days Inn* (☎ 541-296-1191), 2500 W 6th St, offers kitchenettes and indoor pool for $58/60.

Places to Eat

Espresso and cinnamon rolls from a drive-through window makes *Holsteins Coffee Co* (☎ 541-298-2326), at the corner of E 3rd and Taylor Sts, the place to stop when you're in a hurry (there's pleasant seating inside, too).

For authentic Mexican food, try the selection at *Guadalajara* (☎ 541-296-4996), 728 E 3rd St. A tamale and taco for lunch costs $4.

In its 120-year history, *Baldwin Saloon* (☎ 541-296-5666), 205 Court St, has been a bar, brothel, saddlery and warehouse. Now it's back to its original purpose, serving up good food and strong drinks. Fresh oysters are a specialty (pan-fried for dinner at $12), though it's hard to beat the burgers and tasty barbecued ribs.

Wasco House (☎ 541-296-5158), 515 Liberty St, is another historic building (built in 1865) put to good use. Grilled fresh salmon and halibut are $15, but filet mignon and baby back ribs at the same price are the house favorites. There's a lounge upstairs. At an entirely different level of sophistication, *Ole's Supper Club* (☎ 541-296-6708), 2620 W 2nd St, is totally unprepossessing on the exterior, but this is where the locals come when they want a really good steak or prime rib dinner ($15). The wine selection is probably the best in town.

Getting There & Around
Greyhound's depot (☎ 541-296-2421) is at 201 1st St. Five Greyhound buses a day travel between The Dalles and Portland ($13 one way). Two buses a day link The Dalles to Spokane and Montana.

For car rentals in The Dalles, contact Brace Bros Rent-a-Car (☎ 541-296-3761), 1119 W 2nd St. Call West Way Taxi (☎ 541-296-5621).

AROUND THE DALLES
Rowena Crest
The Columbia River Hwy reached Hood River in 1915; it took another seven years for the highway to reach The Dalles. One of the engineering challenges involved in constructing this second part of the Gorge highway was dealing with the Rowena Crest, which is a plateau hundreds of feet above the Columbia River. With characteristic aplomb, the road builders corkscrewed the highway down the cliff face to the river's edge.

The views of the Gorge along this section of old US 30 are spectacular: between Hood River and The Dalles, the heavy vegetation of the western Gorge diminishes, and suddenly the barren, basaltic architecture of the Gorge appears. The black walls of rock rear back from the river's edge, notched here and there with deeply incised canyons.

On top of Rowena Crest is a roadside viewpoint, and access to hundreds of acres of meadowlands now preserved as a wildflower sanctuary. Established by the Nature Conservancy, the **Governor Tom McCall Reserve** on Rowena Plateau is one of the best places to see native plants, watch raptors hovering on updrafts, and enjoy great views. From the viewpoint parking area, cross the road and a stile, and follow trails through grassy meadows. In April and May, the wildflower display is amazing, with balsamroot, wild parsley, penstemons and wild lilies leading out. On spring weekends, volunteers often lead informal wildflower-identification hikes. Be very careful of poison oak.

To reach this section of the Historic Columbia River Hwy from The Dalles, follow W 6th St westward out of town until it becomes US 30 or take I-84 exit 69 at Mosier, and travel east on US 30.

DESCHUTES RIVER RECREATION AREA
The mighty Deschutes River, Oregon's second-largest, rises far to the south in the Three Sisters Wilderness. By the time it reaches the Columbia River, it has cut a massive canyon through much of central Oregon. At this state park, the Deschutes and the Columbia Rivers meet.

For recreationists, it's a busy place. The fishing is great, and rafting parties take out after their four-day ride down the Deschutes from Sherar's Bridge while anglers put in to fish Lake Celilo. Hiking trails explore the east side of the river's desert canyon: the park is a good place to watch for raptors and migrating songbirds, and view seasonal wildflowers. In spring, especially, when western Oregon is dank and wet, this is a great place to find sage-scented warmth and sun.

Hiking & Mountain Biking

From the south end of the park, there are trails for both hikers and mountain bikers. The Atiyeh River Trail follows the Deschutes closely, through old homesteads, springs, and groves of willow and locust trees. The Upper River Loop follows a path along the side of the canyon, through sagebrush and rocky outcroppings. After about a mile on this trail, the steeper Ferry Springs Trail divides off and leads to a rock-strewn spring high on the canyon's wall, with good views over the river and desert hills. All three of these trails meet up at the end of the park, making for different combinations of loop trails. Watch for snakes in this area.

The mountain biking trail leads off from Deschutes State Park, at the northern end of the recreation area, and continues some 25 miles upriver, though after the 11-mile point there may be some big washouts. Those first 11 miles are fairly easy, and an out-and-back ride makes a relaxed two-day trip – there are several places to camp along the way. This path was once the railbed for the Deschutes Railroad Company, which attempted but failed to build a line to Bend in the early 20th century.

Fishing

Trails follow the Deschutes for 12 miles from its mouth on the Columbia River, allowing anglers to hike into remote fishing holes (no motorized vehicles are allowed between the park and Mack's Canyon Campground, 25 miles south). Summer steelhead fishing is very good along this stretch.

At the mouth of the river, where it meets Lake Celilo, there's good fishing for walleye, steelhead and sturgeon.

Camping

Camp riverside at *Deschutes State Park* (☎ 541-739-2322). This can be a popular spot during summer weekends; $13 is the overnight fee (no hookups available).

MARYHILL MUSEUM

Eccentric Sam Hill is responsible for some of the most famous building projects in the Gorge, not the least of which is the Maryhill Museum (☎ 509-773-3733), at 35 Maryhill Museum Drive, WA, on a bluff overlooking the Gorge. Known for its quirky collections, the museum is the perfect focus for a day trip up the Gorge from Portland, or a great stop for anyone needing a break from I-84 heat and traffic.

As the story of Maryhill is odd, so is the collection of artifacts it houses. Queen Marie of Romania (ruled 1914-27) donated a great many unusual items to the museum, including the dress she wore to the coronation of Czar Nicholas II and several pieces of enormous furniture she supposedly made herself.

Downstairs is a very good collection of Native American baskets, carvings, tools and other cultural items. There is also another curiosity: one of the world's largest collections of chess sets.

One of Hill's jet-set friends was Loie Fuller, an American dancer with ties to artistic circles in Paris. After the First World War, she helped Hill obtain a collection of French drawings and sculpture by a then-unheralded artist named Auguste Rodin. A cast of his *The Thinker* now greets visitors on the 3rd floor.

Among the curiosities is a collection of French fashion mannequins. In 1945 some of the top houses of the Parisian fashion trade, seeking to revitalize the industry, sewed haute-couture clothing for a traveling display. Artists of the time, including Jean Cocteau, painted backdrops for the mannequins, and special music was composed to accompany the viewing. The show toured Britain and the USA, and orders for fashions came pouring into Paris. The mannequins, the clothing and the painted screens languished in San Francisco until arts maven Alma de Bretteville Spreckels, another long-time friend of Sam Hill, arranged for them to be donated to Maryhill.

Almost neglected in all these odd displays is a small, but quite fine collection

What in the Sam Hill…?

Sam Hill was an impertinent young lawyer in Minneapolis in the 1880s whose reputation was made in part by his success in bringing legal suits against the Great Northern Railroad. Great Northern mogul James Hill (no relation at the time) decided to co-opt the young attorney. He brought Sam into the company, and soon into his family: Sam wooed and married James' daughter Mary.

With the Great Northern's financial security behind him, Sam Hill turned toward a life of good works. His great contribution to the Northwest was the Columbia River Hwy, the region's first paved road and a wonder of engineering and scenic value. Hill worked closely with Oregon businessmen and state officials to promote the road, which began construction in 1913.

At the same time that the highway was being built, Hill began construction of a vast country home at the top of an 800-foot cliff along the Columbia River. Ever an idealist, Hill hoped that the estate would be home to him and his wife (who refused to live in this god-forsaken country), and the center of a utopian Quaker farm community.

The Maryhill Castle, as it was then called, was constructed to resemble a French country chateau; it encompasses 20,000 sq feet. However, Hill's plans began to fall apart when his wife returned to her beloved Philadelphia and the imported Belgian Quakers found the desiccated cliff sides unsuitable for agriculture. Hill's enthusiasm for the project flagged and the building was not completed until 1926, when Hill's friend, Queen Marie of Romania, came to the USA to dedicate Maryhill as a museum. However, the museum did not open to the public until 1940. ■

of late-19th- and early-20th-century landscape and portrait paintings. Also, there are changing exhibits of works by regional artists in a basement display area.

Maryhill Museum is 10 miles south of Goldendale, WA, on US 97, and 22 miles east of The Dalles, along I-84. Cross the US 97 bridge and look up: you can't miss it. The museum is open 9 am to 5 pm daily, March to November. Admission for adults/children is $5/1.50.

The area around Maryhill is locally acclaimed for the quality of its fruit, especially peaches and apricots. A number of fruit stands spring up along Hwy 14 in July.

Stonehenge

Not one for small gestures, Sam Hill built a full-scale replica of Salisbury Plain's Stonehenge a few miles from Maryhill on the cliffs above the Columbia River. Dedicated as a memorial to Klickitat County's WWI dead, his Stonehenge was built of poured concrete, and was constructed to represent Stonehenge as it was when it stood intact (unlike its knocked-over and cluttered English cousin).

Hill planned that his Stonehenge would line up for celestial events like equinoxes and such, but there's a difference of opinion between adherents as to whether the key stone is in the right place. You can imagine that this is a popular place for odd, usually harmless rites and ceremonies.

To reach Sam Hill's Stonehenge from Maryhill, continue east on Hwy 14 past the US 97 junction. One mile later, follow signs to the right for Stonehenge. You can't miss it.

Places to Stay & Eat

The place to camp is *Maryhill State Park* (☎ 509-773-5007). At the base of the US 97 bridge on the Washington side, this large, riverside campground offers swimming, boating and windsurfing access, as well as covered picnic shelters. There are 50 campsites with showers and hot water.

Across the Columbia River from Maryhill is the little town of Biggs. This is a busy crossroads for trucks and travelers along both US 97 and I-84, so there are a number of nondescript motels. The best bet is the *Best Western Riviera Inn* (☎ 541-739-2501), with rooms for $56/60. It also has a pool, which is a real plus in this hot canyon.

There's a small cafeteria in the basement at Maryhill Museum. The lines can be long, and food (though nothing special) sometimes runs out. At such times, drive across the Columbia River to Biggs and eat at *Biggs Cafe* (☎ 541-739-2395). Formerly a drive-in with car hops, the old service area is still covered with a protective metal roof that provides much-needed shade in summer.

GOLDENDALE (WA)
Population 3375

Up over the escarpment of the Gorge, on a fertile plateau beneath forested hills and distant Mt Adams, lies Goldendale, a small agricultural community that serves as one of Washington's gateways to the Gorge. Settled in 1872, by the beginning of the 20th century there was sufficient wealth in Goldendale to build an impressive collection of late-Victorian homes. One of the old homes is now open as a museum. For fans of turn-of-the-century design, this ought to be a certain stop.

Nearby is the Goldendale Observatory, maintained by the State Parks Department as a free public observatory (see below).

Orientation & Information
Goldendale is 31 miles northeast of The Dalles and about 10 miles north of the Columbia River on US 97. Drivers towing large loads need to be aware that the climb up out of the Gorge on US 97 is very protracted: the steep uphill pull is nearly 8 miles long. Vehicles prone to overheating will surely do so, especially on sweltering summer days.

You can write the Goldendale Chamber of Commerce (☎ 509-773-3400), PO Box 524, Goldendale, WA 98620. During the summer, there's an informational kiosk near the entrance to Maryhill State Park.

Goldendale Observatory State Park
Located on an old volcanic cone just north of town, this observatory (☎ 509-773-3141), 1602 Observatory Drive, houses a 24.5-inch reflecting telescope built by the volunteer labor of four Vancouver, WA-area retirees. The telescope is one of the largest available to the public in the USA.

The best time to go is in the evening, when there are programs that include videos, slide presentations and talks. Depending on what's going on astronomically, there are also views through the telescope to planets, galaxies, stars and comets. Admission is free.

The observatory is open 2 to 5 pm, and 8 pm to midnight, Wednesday to Sunday, May to September. October to April it's open 2 to 5 pm and 7 to 9 pm. Call in advance to confirm times and ask about special programs.

Presby House Museum
Winthrop Presby came to Goldendale in 1888 and eventually became an attorney and state senator. He built his 20-room mansion in 1902. In the 1970s the Klickitat County Historical Society took possession of this splendid Queen Anne home and turned it into a community museum.

Thankfully, much of the old structure is still intact, and rooms have been outfitted sparely – for a museum – preserving the feel of a late-19th-century home. Especially noteworthy are the beautiful fireplaces and fine leaded glass.

The Presby House Museum is open 9 am to 5 pm daily, May to October. Admission is $2/1 adults/students; children under 12 are free.

Places to Stay
Campers in the Goldendale area will want to stay at either *Maryhill State Park* down on the Columbia River (see above), or, if it's too hot in the Gorge, at *Brooks Memorial State Park* (☎ 509-773-4611), 13 miles north of Goldendale on US 97. This cool and wooded park is near the Little Klickitat River; hiking trails explore the pine forests and beaver dams along the stream. There

are 45 campsites, some with hookups. In the day-use area are picnic tables and playing fields.

The *Ponderosa Motel* (☎ 509-773-5842), 775 E Broadway Ave, is a well-kept motor hotel off the main highway, not far from downtown Goldendale. Singles/doubles are $36/47. The newest place to stay in town is the *Far Vue Inn* (☎ 509-773-5881) at the windy, dusty Simcoe St exit off US 97; rooms are $49/67.

Places to Eat
Don't go to Goldendale looking for a culinary experience. In fact, it's worth knowing that the little store near Brooks Memorial State Park makes good deli sandwiches. Breakfast is served all day at the *Homestead* (☎ 509-773-5559), at the Simcoe St exit off US 97. *Roadhouse 97* (☎ 509-773-3553) is a diner 3 miles north of town on US 97.

Mt Hood

The state's highest peak at 11,240 feet, Mt Hood looms above all of northern and central Oregon. As a child you drew mountains like this: a snow-capped triangle of rock that incises the skyline, solitary and commanding. Mt Hood, rising above the deep forests, is the closest thing there is to a single, iconic image of Oregon – a metaphor for the state.

It's also a wildly popular destination for sightseers and recreationists. On its flanks are five downhill ski areas and Timberline Lodge, a well-crafted gem from the 1930s. Cross-country skiing is as easy as renting skis and gliding away from the shop toward the mountain, and in summer hikers traverse the flanks of the mountains to find hidden lakes and wildflower meadows.

Mt Hood rises on the shoulders of the Western Cascades, a long ridge of older volcanoes stretching between Mt Rainier and Mt Shasta. These volcanoes erupted between 40 and 20 million years ago, so long ago that their peaks have long since eroded. Although Mt Hood began to erupt toward the end of the last Ice Age, it's clear that there have been many more recent eruptions. The peak's near-perfect conical shape is evidence that new lava flows have repaired whatever damage Pleistocene-era glaciers – which retreated about 10,000 years ago – had done. Geologists reckon that Mt Hood's last major eruption was about 1000 years ago, although Native American lore and early settlers both report small eruptions in the last 200 years.

Mt Hood was known to local Native Americans as Wy'east, who in mythology was a brash young warrior fond of fiery outbursts and cantankerous behavior, such as hurling fire and rock into the air. In 1792 English Captain William Broughton, under the command of Captain George Vancouver, sailed up the Columbia River as far as Crown Point and first sighted Mt Hood. He named the peak after a famed British admiral, Lord Samuel Hood.

Orientation
Mt Hood remains accessible year-round on US 26 from Portland, and from Hood River on Hwy 35. Together with the Columbia River Hwy, these routes comprise the Mt Hood Loop, one of the most popular scenic road excursions in the USA. Government Camp is at the pass over Mt Hood, and – such as it is – constitutes the center of business on the mountain. From Portland, it's 56 miles east to Government Camp; from Hood River, it's 44 miles south. US 26 continues on to Madras and Bend. From Madras to Government Camp is 40 miles.

Most facilities for travelers are located on the western side of Mt Hood, and serve Portlanders as they zip back and forth to the mountain. At the little villages of Sandy, Welches, Zigzag, Wemme and Rhododendron, all on US 26, are a number of restaurants and motels that cater to passers-through.

Information
The Mt Hood Area Chamber of Commerce and the USFS tourist information office are at the Mt Hood Information Center (☎ 503-

622-4822 or 888-622-4822 serves both agencies), 68260 E Welches Rd, Welches.

Maps, special-use permits and other related information can be obtained from the information center or from the Zigzag Ranger Station (☎ 503-622-3191, 503-666-0704 in Portland), which serves the Mt Hood National Forest. This USFS office is at the Mt Hood Information Center and is open from 7:45 am to 4:30 pm daily except holidays.

The most convenient post office on Mt Hood is at Government Camp (☎ 503-272-3238), 88331 E Government Camp Loop. Hoodland Family Medical Clinic (☎ 503-622-3126), 24461 Welches Rd in Welches, is the nearest medical facility. Hours are 8:30 am to 5 pm weekdays.

Weather & Road Conditions The pass at Mt Hood receives a lot of snow, and in all but the best of winter weather, travelers should check on road conditions before starting up the mountain.

For up-to-date conditions, call the ski areas directly to hear prerecorded information: Mt Hood Meadows & Hood River Meadows (☎ 503-227-7669), Timberline (☎ 503-222-2211), Mt Hood SkiBowl (☎ 503-222-2695) and Summit Ski Area

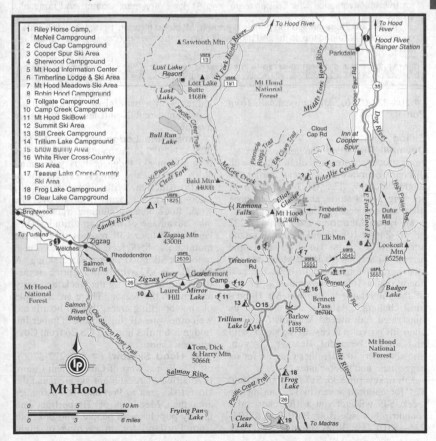

1   Riley Horse Camp,
    McNeil Campground
2   Cloud Cap Campground
3   Cooper Spur Ski Area
4   Sherwood Campground
5   Mt Hood Information Center
6   Timberline Lodge & Ski Area
7   Mt Hood Meadows Ski Area
8   Robin Hood Campground
9   Tollgate Campground
10 Camp Creek Campground
11 Mt Hood SkiBowl
12 Summit Ski Area
13 Still Creek Campground
14 Trillium Lake Campground
15 Snow Bunny Area
16 White River Cross-Country
    Ski Area
17 Teacup Lake Cross-Country
    Ski Area
18 Frog Lake Campground
19 Clear Lake Campground

Mt Hood

0   5   10 km
0   3   6 miles

The Barlow Pass

Some of the first explorations of the area around Mt Hood were carried out by trailblazers seeking an alternative route for the Oregon Trail pioneers. The original emigrant trail brought travelers overland to The Dalles, from which point began a treacherous journey on raft through the Columbia River Gorge. Samuel Barlow decided to find an all-land route to the Willamette Valley and, in 1845, began to scout the passes over Mt Hood for a suitable trail. The route he blazed left The Dalles, passed Dufur, crossed the White River near Tygh Valley and then climbed on to Barlow Pass near Government Camp. Up to this point, the pioneers who followed Barlow's trail (no philanthropist, Barlow was charging a hefty toll for travelers to take what became known as the Barlow Rd) agreed that this route was better than the white-water raft trip down the Columbia River. However, the near-vertical descent of Laurel Hill, just west of Government Camp, changed many minds. The road here was so steep that wheels had to be taken off wagons and the wagon bodies lowered down the hill on winches strapped to trees. The toll charged for this inconvenience was $5 per team, and $1 for every man, woman and head of cattle.

The Barlow Rd remained the principal route to Mt Hood through 1919, when the state government obtained the route and proceeded to construct a new paved road to join the Columbia River Hwy. ■

(☎ 503-272-0256). All are local calls from Portland.

Skiing

Downhill Throughout Oregon, paper bags from grocery stores are often laden with discount coupons to ski areas during the winter months. The GI Joe's chain of sporting goods stores also offers advance discounts and package deals.

Mt Hood Meadows (☎ 503-337-2222 or 503-246-1810), 76 miles from Portland and 36 miles from Hood River, is the largest ski area on Mt Hood Meadows and is generally considered to have the best conditions, as it is on the sunnier, drier side of the mountain. It also has Mt Hood's most challenging slopes, with 20% of its runs rated 'advanced.' Meadows' newest chair lift provides access to the steep, wild and utterly beautiful Heather Canyon. Snowboarders like Heather Canyon for its ruggedness and steep chutes.

Lift tickets run $35, $17 for night skiing, $21 for children seven to 12. During the week, $49 will get you a lift ticket and a roundtrip bus ride from Portland (☎ 503-246-1810). Facilities include two day lodges with a handful of snack bars and restaurants; rentals and lessons are easily available.

Timberline Lodge (☎ 503-272-3311, 503-231-7979 in Portland) is famed for its magnificent ski lodge and its year-round skiing (it has the longest ski season in North America, with lifts running till Labor Day). Ski teams from all over the world flock here for summer training, and take advantage of the high altitude. Timberline's Palmer Lift reaches way up the mountain, to 8500 feet. The ski area is also noted for its good intermediate skiing. A lift ticket is $32, with reduced prices sometimes available during the week, and early and late in the season. There are a couple of snowboarding areas, though boards are welcome on all the trails. Timberline Lodge is 6 miles north of US 26 from Government Camp.

Mt Hood SkiBowl (☎ 503-272-3206), off US 26 just west of Government Camp, is America's largest night-ski area, and the closest ski area to Portland. It's a smaller area than Meadows or Timberline, and mostly popular with people who buzz out from Portland for an evening of night skiing. Lift tickets cost $25, or $14 after 3:30 pm.

Summit Ski Area (☎ 503-272-0256, 503-294-2104 in Portland) is a family- and beginners-oriented ski area with gentle terrain. There's a mere 320-foot drop, and lift tickets range between $10 and $15. This is a good place for lessons in both alpine and cross-country, and there's also a separate sledding area. Summit Ski Area is right in Government Camp, at the east end of the loop road.

Cooper Spur Ski Area (☎ 503-352-7803), is on the northeast slopes of Mt Hood, on Cloud Cap Rd off Hwy 35, 26 miles south of Hood River. This ski area caters to beginning skiers and families. It also offers the cheapest lift tickets on Mt Hood at $12. (Don't get excited, it's a T-bar lift.) There's a 500-foot drop, 10 runs, and night skiing Thursday to Saturday.

Cross-Country Just down the road from the Mt Hood Meadows ski area is **Hood River Meadows** (☎ 503-337-2222, ext 262), also known as the Nordic Center. Mt Hood Meadows maintains about 9 miles of groomed cross country trails and a small lodge here. Ski rentals and instruction are available. Trail-use fees are $7/10 for a half/full day. Hood River Meadows is open 9 am to 4 pm daily. In addition to the groomed fee-for-use trails, there are several other free trails starting from the same parking area. An easy mile-long trail leads to Sahalie Falls; warm up on this, then make the slightly longer and more challenging ski to Elk Meadows.

Tea Cup Lake, with about 20 miles of groomed trails, is operated by the Oregon Nordic Club. A donation is asked for use of the trails. It's on Hwy 35, opposite Hood River Meadows. A few miles from the US 26 junction on Hwy 35, **White River** is another popular public ski area with a big bowl popular with telemark skiers, and nice trails up through the trees.

A list of other trails in the area is available from any Mt Hood National Forest office; there are trails leading off from all Sno-Park locations.

Rentals It's easiest to rent downhill skis at ski areas, although several rental shops supply both alpine ski packages and cross-country equipment. In Government Camp, rent cross-country skis at the Race Base (☎ 503-272-3519), 88220 E Government Camp Loop, or the Winter Fox Shop (☎ 503-272-3380), in the Huckleberry Inn at 88611 Government Camp Loop. If you're driving up from Portland, you can also stop in Sandy to rent ski equipment at Otto's Cross-Country Ski Shop (☎ 503-668-5947), 38716 Pioneer Blvd, or the Winter Fox Shop (☎ 503-668-6500), 38454 Pioneer Ave. It usually costs between $12 and $15 a day to rent cross-country skis, boots and poles.

Sledding

At Snow Bunny, 1½ miles east of Government Camp on US 26, are three supervised inner-tubing and saucer sled areas. This is great fun for kids and families. However, you can't bring your own equipment – you have to rent.

Hiking

Ask around for advice on people's favorite hiking trail, and you'll get a lot of different, opinionated answers. The USFS has an excellent free pamphlet called *Day Hikes around Mt Hood* which lists 30 hikes that range greatly in difficulty and popularity. Hikers should also have the 1:100,000 series map of Mt Hood from Geo Graphics or the *Mt Hood National Forest* map, both available from ranger stations and most outdoor stores.

Following are a few deservedly popular day hikes on trails that are easy to moderate in grade: on a sunny weekend these trails won't provide an experience of wilderness solitude, but they are well loved for good reasons.

Ramona Falls A lower and an upper trailhead lead to beautiful Ramona Falls, which tumbles 120 feet down a face of mossy, columnar basalt. To reach the trail, turn north at Zigzag onto Lolo Pass Rd for 5 miles; turn right on USFS Rd 1825 for

3 miles. The first trailhead is here. A very rocky road leads to an upper trailhead, 1.4 miles distant. From the lower trailhead, it's a 7½-mile roundtrip hike to the falls.

Mirror Lake Another very popular trail climbs up to Mirror Lake, which serves as a reflecting pond for the mass of Mt Hood rearing up in the near distance. Follow US 26 west 1½ miles west from Government Camp. The trailhead begins at the gravel parking area between mileposts 51 and 52. This easy 4-mile roundtrip hike through thick forest gains only 700 feet, and is perfect for casual hikers.

Salmon River Trail The Salmon River Trail follows the Salmon River through lush old-growth forests. The grade is very gentle and the trail parallels a USFS road much of the way, so it's easy to arrange a shuttle. To find the trailhead, at Zigzag turn south on Salmon River Rd and drive 3 miles to a sign for the Old Salmon River Trail. Most day hikers continue on the trail to the Salmon River Bridge for a 2.6-mile hike. The trail continues along the Salmon River for those who want a longer hike.

Laurel Hill Trail On this trail you can hike a piece of history. The Laurel Hill Trail follows a section of the Barlow Trail that was roundly cursed by the Oregon Trail pioneers who were forced to winch their wagons down the precipitous slopes. Thanks to the CCC, who constructed the present trail in the 1930s, modern hikers have it somewhat easier than the pioneers. The trail also follows a portion of the original Mt Hood Loop, constructed in 1921 as the first paved road over Mt Hood. The upper trailhead is near milepost 52, 2½ miles west of Government Camp on US 26, just off USFS Rd 552. The lower trailhead is just off US 26 on USFS Rd 2639, called the Kiwanis Camp Rd. The trail is 3.7 miles long, all up or downhill, depending on which trailhead you choose.

Timberline Trail The most noted long-distance trail on Mt Hood is the Timberline Trail, which circumscribes the mountain at the timberline level. The entire hike around the mountain takes three to five days of backpacking, and is advisable only after the snow melts (in mid-July) until snowfall (usually in mid-October). Portions of the trail make good day hikes, especially from two car-accessible trailheads.

A very popular day hike along the Timberline Trail leads from the back of the Timberline Lodge to the **Zigzag Canyon Overlook**. This 4½-mile roundtrip hike leads through wildflower meadows to a vista across a 700-foot-deep canyon cut in the flank of Mt Hood by glacial streams. This easy hike has an elevation change of only 500 feet, and is perfect for moderately keen walkers.

A more remote departure point on the Timberline Trail is from **Cloud Cap Trailhead** on the eastern side of Mt Hood. To reach the trailhead, turn on Cooper Spur Rd from Hwy 35, following signs for the so-named ski area; and from there, continue another 11 miles up a fairly good graveled road toward Cloud Cap and Tilly Jane campgrounds. The road ends at Cloud Cap, a historic lodge turned mountain-rescue station.

From the trailhead, hikers have two choices. One trail follows the Timberline Trail west towards **Elk Cove**, winding through forests and meadows with great views over the Gorge and the Cascade peaks in Washington. There is no loop trail, so simply hike to a convenient ending point and retrace your steps.

Otherwise follow the Timberline Trail east towards 'Gnarl Ridge,' up barren rock fields for 1.2 miles. At this point, views open up over **Eliot Glacier** and onto the summit of Mt Hood. Follow **Cooper Spur Trail** uphill for a couple of hundred yards to a CCC-built stone shelter for even more expansive views to the north and east. To complete the loop, return to the Timberline Trail and continue straight downhill on the trail to Tilly Jane Campground, 1 mile away. From there, it's an easy half-mile hike back to the Cloud Cap Campground and Trailhead.

Lookout Mountain For a charming and easy hike that affords views onto Mt Hood, consider a hike up Lookout Mountain, on the high escarpments east of Mt Hood. To reach the trailhead, turn off Hwy 35 onto the USFS Rd 44 (Dufur Mill Rd), for 4 miles; turn south onto USFS Rd 4410 (High Prairie Rd) and go uphill for 5 miles. From this trailhead, the path to Lookout Mountain passes through lovely wildflower meadows and marshes, all the more enchanting for being so close to the top of a mountain. From the trailhead, it's an easy 1.2-mile stroll to the 6525-foot summit of Lookout Mountain, where you seem to gaze at Mt Hood eye-to-eye across a deep valley.

Climbing

The second most-climbed peak over 10,000 feet in the world, after Japan's Mt Fuji, Mt Hood is very accessible, and many Oregonians feel that their lives cannot be complete without climbing it at least once. Debate still rages as to whether the first known ascent was made in 1845 or 1857. In 1867 the first women made the climb in full-length skirts, and photographs of Victorian ladies roped together on the slopes adorn the walls of the Mazama Lodge. About 10,000 people climb Mt Hood every year. It's been climbed both by a woman wearing high heels, and by a man without any legs!

This isn't to say Mt Hood does not require technical climbing skills: nearly every year a few people die making the ascent. Climbing is best between May and mid-July, and a typical climb from Timberline Lodge on the south side takes 10 to 12 hours. Experienced climbers who wish to organize their own climb can get information from the Mt Hood Information Center (☎ 503-622-4822 or 888-622-4822), 68260 E Welches Rd, Welches.

Climbing Instruction & Trips Timberline Mountain Guides (☎ 503-272-3699, 800-464-7704) is a well-established guide service and climbing school. Their basic Mt Hood summit climb starts off with a day of climbing instruction, followed early on the second day by a summit attempt. The basic package costs $245 and is offered daily from December through July. They also offer more advanced classes and climbs.

Northwest School of Survival (☎ 503-668-8264) has an eight-hour climbing program for beginners. Successful completion of the program entitles students to sign up for a trip to the summit, which may or may not be consecutive with their class. There are 15 to 20 climbs between early April and early August, and it's best to book at least two months in advance. Climbers must rent or buy their own gear, and make their own arrangements for transportation and accommodations. The cost is $245 for lessons and a climb.

The Mazamas (☎ 503-227-2345), 909 NW 19th Ave, Portland, a climbing and mountaineering club founded in the late 1800s, has some climbs for beginners. Membership isn't necessary, although you should realize that this a club, not a guide service. There are usually about 12 to 15 climbs each summer. Trip leaders volunteer, and not all take beginners. Climbs for nonmembers cost $14, and climbers are expected to come prepared with their own gear and knowledge of how to use it. The Mazamas' multi-session climbing school in January includes a trip to the summit, and is the best deal at $125.

Rentals In the Portland area, climbing equipment can be rented from REI at one of two locations: 1798 Jantzen Beach Center (☎ 503-283-1300), or 7410 Bridgeport Rd (☎ 503-624-8600) in Tigard. Their $18 climbing package includes plastic boots, crampons and an ice ax. Helmets cost an extra $7. You can rent the same list of equipment at Oregon Mountain Community (☎ 503-227-1038), in downtown Portland at 60 NW Davis St, for about $30 (helmet included).

Mountain Biking

During the summer months, Mt Hood Ski Bowl (☎ 503-272-3206) is transformed into a mountain bike arena. You can rent bikes from the on-site Hurricane Racing

(☎ 503-272-0240) for $10 per hour, $25 for four hours (helmet and trail pass included with rental). A chair lift up the mountain costs $4 to $7 per trip, or $15 for a day-long lift ticket. Trail passes alone cost $4. This special area is open 11 am to 6 pm daily.

Of course, mountain biking at a downhill ski area is a little bit like skiing there, and if you're more the cross-country type, cross US 26 to the free Government Camp recreational trail network. You'll find trail maps posted at Glacier View (just opposite the west entrance to SkiBowl), at the base of the Skiway Trail in Government Camp, and at the Summit ski area. The Crosstown Trail is a fairly easy 3-mile single track between Glacier View and the Summit ski area. Several more challenging trails sprout from it.

Most of the cross-country ski trails in the area are good for summertime mountain biking. The area around Trillium Lake has good trails shooting uphill from several points around the easy lake loop.

Fishing

There is good lake fishing for families at the popular and heavily stocked Trillium Lake, which is near Government Camp. Clear Lake offers good rainbow and brook trout fishing, and Lost Lake has a marina and good trout fishing.

For stream fishing, the best opportunities are on the Salmon River, a southerly tributary of the Sandy River. The summer steelhead run here is the real excitement. The Salmon River is accessed from the community of Brightwood on US 26, by good USFS roads and trails leading to isolated pools and rapids in deep old-growth forest. On the east side of Mt Hood, Hwy 35 follows the East Fork Hood River, which can be good fishing for rainbow trout.

The Fly Fishing Shop (☎ 503-622-4607), at the Hoodland Park Plaza in Welches, specializes in guided fly fishing adventures both on the upper Sandy River and in other areas of the state. Walk-in trips start at $80, float trips at $295 (for two people); fishing licenses are available here as well.

Places to Stay

Camping Camping on Mt Hood makes a convenient getaway from Portland, so competition for sites can be fierce. Reservations for some campgrounds can be made by calling the Mt Hood National Forest's reservation system (☎ 800-280-2267) between 5 am and 6 pm. Get an early start – it may take a while to get through. Reservations can also be made by mail, 10 to 14 days in advance; obtain a reservation form from the nearest ranger district office. There is an $8.25 charge on top of the daily camping fee for making a reservation.

Fees for camping at the following campgrounds range between $10 and $12. Each of them has drinking water and vault toilets, but no hookups.

West Side On the west side of Mt Hood, a number of USFS campgrounds are convenient to US 26. At the base of Mt Hood is *Tollgate Campground*, 1 mile southeast of Rhododendron, a CCC-constructed campground with 15 campsites. *Camp Creek Campground*, 3 miles southeast of Rhododendron, has 24 campsites, some of them streamside.

Riley Horse Camp caters to equestrians, but it's a great place for anyone to stay if the lingering odor of horse manure doesn't bother you. There's nearby access to several trails on Zigzag Mountain, including Ramona Falls. From US 26 at Zigzag go north on Lolo Pass Rd for 5 miles, turn east on USFS Rd 1825, and then make a right onto USFS Rd 380. Camping is free at *McNeil Campground*, adjacent to Riley Horse Camp, although there's no potable water.

Up on Mt Hood, the popular *Still Creek Campground*, is just half a mile east of Government Camp, and has 27 campsites. From here, all the recreation on Mt Hood is in your backyard. Even more popular is *Trillium Lake Campground*, on the shores of beautiful Trillium Lake. Fifty-five campsites with running water, a fishing pier and a boat ramp, are located in a post-card setting with Mt Hood rising above a placid lake.

East Side East of Mt Hood, Hwy 35 cuts off and heads toward Hood River, while US 26 continues to Madras. On Hwy 35, the *Robin Hood Campground* is 12 miles northeast of Government Camp on the East Fork of Hood River. *Sherwood Campground* is 4 miles farther north along the river.

Eight miles south of Government Camp on US 26, *Frog Lake Campground* offers 33 campsites along the shores of a tiny lake. At *Clear Lake Campground*, 10 miles south of Government Camp on US 26, there are 28 campsites and good fishing.

RV Campgrounds At 65000 E US 26 near Brightwood, *Mt Hood RV Village* (☎ 503-622-4011, 800-255-3069, 503-253-9445 in Portland), is a huge resort complex with over 420 sites, and the only RV campground on Mt Hood with hookups. Facilities include showers, flush toilets, indoor swimming pool, playground, electronic game arcade and laundry. Rates are $18 a night for full hookups.

Hostels *Silcox Hut* is a rustic, European-style alpine hut on Timberline's ski slopes, about a mile above the lodge. It sleeps 24 in dormitory-style accommodations. Check in at Timberline Lodge, and then hike or take a Sno-Cat to the hut. For $75 you get lodging in a bunkroom, roundtrip Sno Cat transportation, plus dinner and breakfast. Lodgers should bring their own sleeping bag. Call the Timberline Sales Office (☎ 503-295-1827) for reservations.

Down at Government Camp, two lodges operated by outdoor clubs offer bunk space to nonmembers. Call the *Cascade Ski Club* (☎ 503-272-9204) to reserve a $12 bed in their lodge at the foot of Blossom Trail, right in Government Camp. The *Mazama Lodge* (☎ 503-272-9214) is off Westlake Rd in Government Camp, and charges $16 for nonmembers.

The *Huckleberry Inn* (☎ 503-272-3325) runs a simple $16-a-bed bunkroom in their 'downtown' Government Camp hotel.

B&Bs In Welches, the *Old Welches Inn B&B* (☎ 503-622-3754), 26401 E Welches Rd, makes use of the original Welches Hotel, built in 1890. Rooms in the main lodge range from $65 to $75 a night; a separate one-bedroom cottage is $100.

The secluded *Brightwood Guest House* (☎ 503-622-5783) is a private guest cottage with a full kitchen well off busy US 26 at 64725 E Barlow Trail. Rates run $95 a night.

Hotels The tidy *Shamrock Motel* (☎ 503-622-4911), 12 miles east of Sandy at 59550 E US 26, is one of the best deals in the area, with basic room packages starting at $38, and a room with fireplace, kitchen and cable TV going for $59. *Snowline Motel* (☎ 503-622-3137), 73260 SE US 26, in Rhododendron, offers basic motel rooms at $40/50; some units have fireplaces.

Motel lodging in Government Camp is pretty expensive and often hard to find at short notice. If you're coming to ski, and don't mind commuting from Hood River, many Hood River motels offer good deals on Mt Hood lift tickets. In Government Camp, the *Huckleberry Inn* (☎ 503-272-3325), 88611 E Government Camp Loop, has several lodging options, from dormitory-style rooms ($16) to deluxe rooms that sleep up to 10 people ($90). Standard rooms run $50.

Mt Hood Inn (☎ 503 272 3205, 800 443-7777), 87450 E Government Camp Loop, is fancier, with suites and spa facilities. Rooms start at $105. *Thunderhead Lodge Condominiums* (☎ 503-272-3368), 87451 E Government Camp Loop, has an outdoor heated swimming pool and full kitchens. Rooms range from $90 studios to a $290 suite that will sleep 10.

On the northeast side of Mt Hood is the handsome *Inn at Cooper Spur* (☎ 541-352-6692), 10755 Cooper Spur Rd, south of the community of Mt Hood. Rooms are available in two-bedroom cabins or in the lodge. Singles/doubles start at $65/75, and cabins cost $119 to $129. Facilities include hot tubs, tennis courts and an adjoining restaurant. The Inn at Cooper Spur is 19 miles north of Government Camp on Hwy 35, and 25 miles south of Hood River.

OREGON

OREGON

Timberline Lodge
One of the unquestioned masterpieces of the WPA-era building boom, Timberline Lodge (☎ 503-272-3311, 503-231-7979 in Portland) is the culmination of a kind of rustic Craftsman design that came to be known as Cascadian, the influence of which is still being felt in contemporary building. The building of Timberline in 1936 and 1937 was the largest of the federal work creation projects directed by the WPA in Oregon, employing up to 500 workers to construct the four-story, 43,700-sq-foot log and stone lodge. For many employed on the project, Timberline was more than just a job, it was an expression of a cultural ideal. As stated in a 1937 publication that accompanied the dedication:

In Mt Hood's Timberline Lodge the mystic strength that lives in the hills has been captured in wood and stone and, in the hands of laborer and craftsman, has been presented as man's effort at approximating an ideal in which society, through concern for the individual, surpasses the standard it has unconsciously set for itself.

There is hardly an element of the building that was not handcrafted, from the selection of stones in the massive lobby fireplaces to the hand-loomed coverlets on the beds. In an effort to emphasize the natural beauty of the area, architects not only quarried local stone and utilized local timber, they also designed the six-sided central tower to echo the faceted peak of Mt Hood. The steeply slanted wings leading away from the common rooms are meant both to shed the heavy snowfalls and resemble mountain ridges. Even the exterior paint was specially mixed to match the color of mountain frost.

The interior of the lodge is where the careful workmanship is most evident. The central fireplace rises 92 feet through three floors of open lobby. All the furniture in the hotel was made by hand in WPA carpentry halls, and murals and paintings of stocky, stylized workers, in the best Socialist-Realist tradition, adorn the walls.

The Rachael Griffin Historic Exhibition Center, on the main floor, displays some of the history of the lodge in tools, drawings, weavings and photographs. In the Coyote Den room nearby, a free 30-minute video discusses the building of the lodge. The USFS offers 30- to 45-minute free interpretive tours of the lodge during the day.

Of course, Timberline Lodge is not a museum: it is a hotel, ski resort and restaurant. Don't feel so reverential about this magnificent old building that you don't at least enjoy a hot chocolate on the mezzanine, or strap on some skis and get out onto the mountain. And don't forget about its quirkier side: the horror movies *The Shining* and *Hear No Evil* were both filmed here – pass by room 217 ('redrum redrum') for a quick chill. ∎

Resorts Five miles north of Government Camp, the *Timberline Lodge* (☎ 503-272-3311, 503-231-7979 in Portland), Timberline, OR 97028, offers so many options in the way of accommodation packages with ski facilities, instruction and meals, that it's best to call or write to obtain their latest price leaflet. Basic room rates run $65 for a room with two bunk beds to $170 for a large room with a fireplace. Different package deals are available throughout the year, including a 'stay the night and ski free' deal, in which a complimentary lift ticket is thrown in on certain nights.

The Resort at the Mountain (☎ 503-622-3101), 68010 E Fairway Ave, in Welches, is a large resort that focuses on its 27-hole golf course in the summer, and ski and winter recreation packages in the wintertime. Facilities include a swimming pool, tennis courts and two restaurants. Room rates begin at $99 for a standard room or $155 with a fireplace; suites start at $175.

A little less la-dee-dah are the *Summit Meadow Cabins* (☎ 503-272-3494), just south of Government Camp in the Trillium Lake basin. During winter, it's a 1½-mile cross-country ski in to the A-frame cabins.

In summer it's possible to drive in. Ski and mountain bike trails surround the cabins, which rent for $90 to $175 a night.

For details on *Lost Lake Resort* (☎ 541-386-6366), on the north side of Mt Hood, see the Hood River section.

Places to Eat

US 26 up to Mt Hood from Portland offers a number of restaurants known mostly for their hearty breakfasts and afternoon cocktail bars, both favorites with the skiing crowd. At the *Barlow Trail Inn* (☎ 503-622-3122), in Rhododendron, breakfast is served all day, and is a favorite before hitting the slopes. *Alpine Hut Restaurant & Lounge* (☎ 503-622-4618), 73665 E US 26, serves breakfast, lunch and dinner, and is well established as a skiers' pit stop.

At Welches, stop at *Michael's Bread & Breakfast* (☎ 503-622-5333), one block south of US 26 on E Welches Rd, for fresh-baked cinnamon rolls, cookies and bread. *Mountain High Espresso* operates out of a trailer next door to the grocery store in Rhododendron. They have a better mastery of the espresso machine than anyone else on this stretch of US 26, and they have decent muffins, too.

On the way back down the hill, find good Northwest cuisine at *Rendezvous Grill & Tap Room* (☎ 503-622-6837) on US 26 in Welches, or wait until Sandy, where *Elusive Trout* (☎ 503-668-7884), 39333 Proctor Blvd (US 26), serves tasty sandwiches and microbrews.

Food in Government Camp is pretty basic. The *Huckleberry Inn* (☎ 503-272-3325), 88611 Government Camp Loop, is a family restaurant featuring home-style cooking and a steak house in the evenings; huckleberry pies are a specialty. *Mt Hood Brewing Company & Brew Pub* (☎ 503-272-3724), 87304 E Government Camp Loop, is Mt Hood's only brewery, and a very pleasant place it is. Their English-style beers go well with the very tasty gourmet pizzas; the goat's cheese and pesto pizza costs $9. Various sandwiches and other light meals are also available at the brewpub.

Five different restaurants operate at Timberline Lodge (☎ 503-272-3311). In the day lodge, *Wy'east Kitchen* has snacks for skiers; the *Country Store* serves espresso drinks, desserts and pastries. In the old lodge, the *Blue Ox Deli* is graced by a tiled mosaic of the legendary lumberjack Paul Bunyan and his ox Babe, and serves soups, sandwiches and light meals. At the *Ram's Head Bar* light snacks are available along with drinks; this is a great place to stake out a table and watch the sun set. Mt Hood's best food is served in the lodge's beautiful log-beamed *Cascade Dining Room*. Prices range from $15 to $23 for entrées such as bouillabaisse and nightly salmon specials.

If you're on the slopes, it is worth remembering that *Silcox Hut*, a mile above Timberline Lodge, serves food and beverages to passers-by between 11 am and 3 pm.

Getting There & Away

Bus Although Greyhound offers bus services to Mt Hood, the timing of the buses isn't really convenient for day-trippers. There's only one bus a day and it leaves Portland late in the afternoon. The return bus comes down the mountain just after noon. The fare is $15 one way.

Ski Buses During the peak ski season, which is from mid-December onwards, there are two buses daily to Mt Hood Meadows (☎ 503-287-5438), one coming from Beaverton, the other from Salem. You will find various pick-up points in the Portland area; it's best to call to determine the one nearest you. The cost is $49 for combination roundtrip transportation and lift ticket.

Timberline Lodge (☎ 503-231-7979 in Portland) operates buses from the Portland area to the lodge from December to March. Departure points are the GI Joe's stores in Gresham, 700 NW Eastman Parkway; Beaverton, 3485 SW Cedar Hills Blvd; and Portland, 3900 SE 82nd Ave. A combination roundtrip transportation and lift ticket can be purchased at any GI Joe's store through their TicketMaster (☎ 503-224-4440) outlets.

Car For statewide road conditions, dial the 24-hour information line (☎ 503-976-7277, 503-889-3999). State law requires traction devices to be carried in vehicles during most of winter, and trailers are often banned. For details on weather conditions, see the preceding Information entry.

In the wintertime, if you park a vehicle at most places on Mt Hood, you will need a Sno-Park permit; $2 daily, $3 for a three-day pass or $9.50 for a season pass. Permits are available at sports rental stores along US 26, from various businesses in Government Camp and also at the Timberline Lodge. During the summer months, similar parking passes are required at trailheads.

Willamette Valley

Between Portland and Eugene stretches the Willamette Valley, the incredibly fertile agricultural basin that was the destination of the Oregon Trail pioneers. A hundred and fifty years after the migration, the Willamette Valley is still the center of Oregon, with three-quarters of the state's population living here. While the upper valley near Portland is filling with suburbs, much of the rest of the valley is still quiet and rural, with slumbering old villages tucked into green landscapes and vineyard-covered countryside.

The historic sites in the northern valley and the Yamhill County vineyards are in easy reach of Portland for day trips, though B&B inns may entice travelers for country weekends. In the mid-valley is Salem, the state capital, bustling with politicians and issues, and center to a sprawling network of suburbs. Corvallis and Eugene, in the southern valley, are dominated by the state's two universities. Both are dynamic and engaging small cities with good, inexpensive food and lodging.

Most travelers zoom up and down the Willamette Valley on I-5. It's a pity, because side roads lead through beautiful farmland to sites as varied as vineyards, monasteries, historic settlements and charming old towns whose pedigrees extend back to the 1840s. Because the valley is largely flat and crisscrossed with slow-moving roads, the Willamette is a great place to explore on bicycle.

History

The Willamette Valley was home to a large number of Native Americans before the arrival of settlers. The Chinook and Calapooian tribes were the most numerous until their numbers were decimated by diseases like small pox, inadvertently introduced by white settlers. By the time the Calapooians were gathered onto Grande Ronde Reservation, they numbered only 42 members

and were gradually amalgamated into the tribal mix on the reservation; there are no Calapooian speakers today.

The first white settlement in the valley was in an area called French Prairie. In the triangle between St Louis, St Paul and Champoeg, this was where French Canadian trappers, retiring from the Hudson's Bay Company, established a small farming community in the 1820s. As US pioneers began to arrive and vie for land, the area soon became the scene of British and US rivalries.

Under a treaty signed in 1818, Oregon was part of an area held in joint occupancy by Britain and the USA. At a historic meeting in Champoeg in May of 1843, a report was read which proposed the establishment of a US-style self-government. It was defeated, as most of the settlers were loyal to the Hudson's Bay Company, and many of the French Canadians withdrew from the meeting in disgust at the US settlers' audacity.

The remaining settlers regrouped. Joe Meek, the legendary trapper and mountain man, brought the issue to a head by exclaiming, 'Who's for a divide? All in favor of the report and an organization follow me.' He drew a line in the sand, and the 'divide' commenced: those for the USA stood on one side; those favoring the British status quo stood on the other. When the active participants were counted, 50 men stood on each side of the divide. Two French Canadians, Étienne Lucier and FX Matthieu, after a heated conversation, decided to join the US side of the divide. The jubilant winners formed a committee to organize a program of government. Thereafter, the British claim to lands in the Pacific Northwest was increasingly insecure. Had the vote gone differently, Oregon and Washington might now be part of Canada.

By 1855, over 50,000 people made the

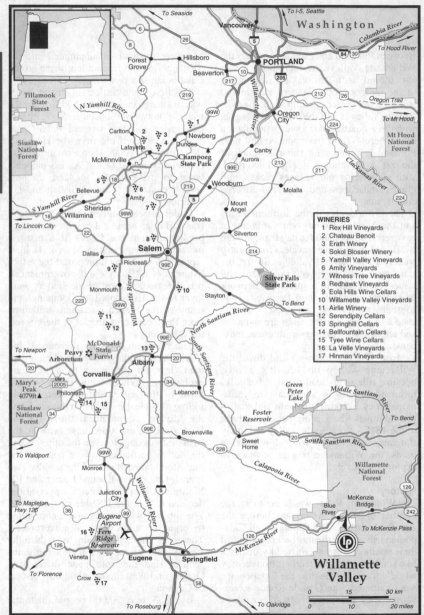

OREGON

WINERIES
1 Rex Hill Vineyards
2 Chateau Benoit
3 Erath Winery
4 Sokol Blosser Winery
5 Yamhill Valley Vineyards
6 Amity Vineyards
7 Witness Tree Vineyards
8 Redhawk Vineyards
9 Eola Hills Wine Cellars
10 Willamette Valley Vineyards
11 Airlie Winery
12 Serendipity Cellars
13 Springhill Cellars
14 Bellfountain Cellars
15 Tyee Wine Cellars
16 La Velle Vineyards
17 Hinman Vineyards

Willamette
Valley

| 0 | 15 | 30 km |
| 0 | 10 | 20 miles |

trek to the Northwest along the Oregon Trail, almost all with the goal of settling in the Willamette Valley. Many of the pioneers hailed from New England and quickly set about re-creating social and civic entities in the wilderness. Schools, universities, churches, debating societies, Masonic lodges and newspapers all sprang up in remarkably short order. By the 1860s, the Willamette Valley was largely settled and little land was available for latecomers.

Religious doctrine played a large role in the growth of Willamette Valley communities. The trappers from the Hudson's Bay Company were largely Catholic, while the majority of the earliest US settlers were Methodist. Missionary efforts on the part of both religious groups led to the establishment of various educational and cultural facilities in the valley, which have had a long-term impact on the cultural life of the state. Additionally, the Willamette Valley has provided a haven for other small, sometimes persecuted sects. Quaker Friends, Russian Old Believers, utopian German communists and Mennonites are among the groups that emigrated to the area. Currently, the area around Woodburn is filling with Russian Pentecostals.

With more and more land in production, transportation of agricultural products became increasingly important to the growth of communities in the valley. Steamboats were the first major means of transport and trade, and riverside towns like Albany, Corvallis and Eugene thrived as hubs of commerce and light industry. When railroads connected the Willamette Valley to California in the 1860s, industries like wool, saw and paper mills joined agriculture as the dominant economic foundations of the valley.

Orientation & Information
The Willamette Valley is the 60-mile-wide, fertile basin that lies between the Cascade and Coast mountain ranges.

The main transportation corridor in the valley is I-5. Hwys 99E and 99W, on either side of the Willamette River, are more scenic alternatives to I-5. Connected to them are a lacework of smaller roads. Train and bus service also runs up and down the valley.

The Willamette Valley Visitors Association (☎ 800-526-2256), at 420 NW 2nd St, No 200, Corvallis, OR 97330, has general information on the valley.

OREGON CITY
Population 16,810
One of the oldest incorporated towns west of the Mississippi, and Oregon's first territorial capital, Oregon City was founded in 1829 when Fort Vancouver factor John McLoughlin established a lumber mill at Willamette Falls. As the official end point of the Oregon Trail, Oregon City was the goal of almost all the pioneers who ventured across the continent during the 1840s and '50s. In the early days of Oregon, when trade and transportation depended largely on riverboats, Oregon City grew to be the territory's dominant city. When the settlers at Champoeg voted in 1843 to organize self-government, it was named the provisional capital. The first Oregon legislature met here the following year.

Oregon City boomed as the first industrial center in the Northwest. After the railroad and highways eliminated the portage around Willamette Falls, Oregon City fell into a slumber. Today, this once-vital frontier town has been swallowed up by Portland's suburbs, and its famous waterfall is a snaggle of electric generators. Parts of Oregon City have been preserved, with the old downtown designated a National Historic District, but much has been bulldozed in the name of enhanced traffic flow and questionable urban development. It's best to visit Oregon City as a day trip from Portland or as a stopover on the way to other Willamette Valley towns.

Orientation & Information
Thirteen miles south of Portland on I-205, Oregon City sits at a natural division point between the upper and lower portions of the Willamette River – the 42-foot Willamette Falls. Because the city is developed on

OREGON

The Father of Oregon

Most of the early pioneers who crossed the Oregon Trail arrived in Oregon without any provisions left from their long journey. The thriving British fur-trading post at Fort Vancouver, on the north bank of the Columbia, was self-sufficient as far as grain and livestock production was concerned, and Hudson's Bay Company (HBC) chief factor John McLoughlin was generous with the US settlers for credit on food and seed stock. This was in direct contradiction with HBC policy, and in 1845 McLoughlin was relieved of his duties.

He chose to move to his land holdings in Oregon City, where he planned to retire among the settlers he had generously aided.

However, distrust of the former British agent and general narrow-mindedness led the US citizens to treat their former benefactor poorly. Although many of the settlers still owed McLoughlin money for goods and services they had received at Fort Vancouver, the provisional government took away McLoughlin's land holdings in Oregon City after he moved there. McLoughlin, now often referred to as the Father of Oregon, eventually became a US citizen. His land claim, however, was not returned to his heirs until five years after his death in 1857. ■

several strata of lava flows, the town government has built a municipal elevator between Railroad and 7th Sts that gives free rides between the upper residential areas and the river level commercial district below.

Oregon City's visitors' center was washed away in the 1996 flood, though signs for it are still posted around town. In the meantime, you can either write or call the Oregon City Chamber of Commerce (☎ 503-656-1619, 800-424-3002), PO Box 226, Oregon City, OR 97045. The post office is at 606 15th St.

McLoughlin House

When John McLoughlin moved to Oregon City in 1845, he built this home for his family. Now a museum (☎ 503-656-5146), 713 Center St, the house originally stood in downtown. In 1909 it was slated for demolition, but concerned citizens raised money to move the house up onto the bluff where it now stands.

At the time the house was built, most settlers lived in shanties and log cabins, and this two-story clapboard home with three bedrooms was often referred to as McLoughlin's Mansion. Over the years, McLoughlin had accumulated considerable wealth, and his solid simple good taste is evident throughout. The museum is definitely worth a side trip if you are interested in period furnishings or life in early Oregon.

Immediately next door is the **Barclay House**, built in 1849 by Dr Forbes Barclay, one of McLoughlin's closest friends. It now serves as a gift shop and ticket office for the McLoughlin House museum. Between the two houses, in an ivy-covered plot, are the graves of McLoughlin and his wife, Marguerite.

Hours are 10 am to 4 pm Tuesday to Saturday, and 1 to 4 pm Sunday. The museum is closed on holidays and in the month of January; $3/2.50/1.50 adults/seniors/children. A guide will escort you to the house, though you can explore on your own if you want.

Clackamas County History Museum

Housed in an imposing modern structure, this museum (☎ 503-655-5574), 211 Tumwater Drive, contains several entertaining regional history displays. Highlights inlude interpretive exhibits on the local moonshine trade and the Willamette Meteor, and a collection of intricately etched military mess kits. There's a good exhibit on Native American basketry and interesting photos of what Willamette Falls once looked like. The display on domestic architectural styles is a good starting point for those planning to visit historic homes.

The museum is open 10 am to 4 pm weekdays, 1 to 4 pm weekends; adults/seniors/children $3/2/1.50. Admission price includes a tour through the **Stevens-Crawford House** (☎ 503-655-2866), 603 6th St, a 1907 home owned by a pioneer Oregon family. The house now preserves everyday items from the homes of early settlers.

End of the Oregon Trail Interpretive Center

Located at the end of the Oregon Trail, this museum and interpretive center (☎ 503-657-9339), at 1726 Washington St, commemorates the struggle of the Oregon pioneers on their overland journey, the challenges they faced when they arrived in Oregon and the plight of the Native Americans they displaced. The 75-minute tour is a combination living history/multimedia presentation and leaves at fixed times from 9:15 am to 4:45 pm Monday to Saturday, and 10 am to 4 pm Sunday, May 1 to September 30; the rest of the year, tours leave from 9:30 am to 3:30 pm Monday to Saturday, and 11:30 am to 4 pm on Sunday. Admission is $4.50/$2.50 adults/seniors and children, though there's no charge to visit the third building, which houses a gift shop and an exhibit of pioneer artifacts.

Willamette Falls

The Willamette Falls was a center of fishing and trade for many Indians of the northern Willamette Valley. When the salmon migrated up the Willamette River, the falls was a very active place, as many journeyed to the area to net and harpoon fish, which were dried for later use.

Today, you can see the city's most prominent natural landmark from Willamette Falls Vista, along Hwy 99E, immediately west of downtown. The water just below the falls is still popular with salmon anglers; it's also spectacular in spring when thousands of migrating lamprey eels climb up the rocks.

The impoundment on top of the falls was built to divert water to mills and hydroelectric generators, which now utterly dominate the river and the waterfall.

Special Events

The **Oregon Trail Pageant** (☎ 503-657-0988) returned in 1998 after taking a year off to write a new script. On evenings in July through the first week of August, actors, dancers and musicians gather on the lawn of the Oregon Trail Interpretive Center to perform an outdoor show about pioneers on the Oregon Trail. The revised play promises to give a more sympathetic depiction of the Cayuse Indians' role in the Whitman massacre (see History in the Facts about Pacific Northwest chapter). Expect to see lots of fiddlers and dancers performing period tunes. Tickets cost $12/5 adults/children.

Places to Stay & Eat

Directly across from the McLoughlin House is the *Hydrangea B&B* (☎ 503-650-4421, 800-649-5726), 716 Center St, a 1908 home with two guest rooms for $60.

South of town near the Willamette, the *Inn of the Oregon Trail* (☎ 503-656-2089, 888-650-9322), 416 S 99E, is an ornate 1867 farmhouse with a nicely landscaped garden. Rooms at this B&B range from $48 to $85. On the main floor is *Fellows House Restaurant*, open for lunch only.

The *Val-U Inn Motel* (☎ 503-655-7141, 800-443-7777), 1900 Clackamette Drive, has rooms for $56/60 and is central to the I-205 freeway exit.

Portland-based *McMenimans* (☎ 503-655-8032), 102 9th St, is a tranquil brew-pub with burgers, sandwiches and a host of locally brewed ales. It's family-friendly, and the glowing stained-glass windows are sure to soothe even the crankiest kids. Near McLoughlin House, the *Deli Planet* (☎ 503-655-1130), 710 Washington St, is a pleasant place for coffee or lunch.

Entertainment
Folk musicians gather at the handsome *Carnegie Center* (☎ 503-557-9199), 606 John Adams St, every Saturday night to perform in the free Saturday Nite Java concert series. The cozy sofas, colorful local artwork, and coffeehouse fare will warm up any spirit dampened by the dark, rainy evenings. During summer the series is called Concerts in the Park and is held outside on the grounds.

Getting There & Around
Portland's Tri-Met bus system (☎ 503-238-7433) offers service to Oregon City. Bus No 35 leaves Portland every half-hour throughout the day (hourly on weekends) and stops at the Oregon City Transit Center on 11th St between McLoughlin and Main Sts. The one-way fare is $1.35.

County office workers gobble up Oregon City's downtown parking on weekdays. If you're planning a full day of museum-hopping you're best off riding the free Oregon City Trolley, which stops at museums and historic homes between the Oregon Trail Interpretive Center and the Clackamas County Museum.

AROUND OREGON CITY
Champoeg State Park
One of the very first settlements in Oregon, Champoeg (apparently derived from the French *champ* for 'field') was on a flood plain along a bend in the Willamette River. After the historic 1843 vote, the town continued to grow as the era of riverboat travel brought increasing trade to the Willamette Valley. Unfortunately, the French Canadians who established the town, mill and fur warehouses at Champoeg did not antic-ipate the fury of the Willamette River. In December 1861 an enormous flood swept through the Willamette drainage. By the time the flood waters reached Champoeg, 27 feet of water rushed over the flood plain on which the town was built. After the flood had subsided, only three buildings of the old town remained.

Champoeg was never rebuilt. In 1901, the area was designated a state park. Today, the sites of many long-gone buildings are noted with plaques. With 107 acres of old-growth woodland and grassy meadows, campsites and nature trails, beautiful Champoeg State Park is deservedly well loved.

Ten miles of hiking and biking trails wind through the park. The hiking-only trail hugs the banks of the Willamette River, while the paved biking trail curves through the woods. Both offer excellent access to old-growth hardwood forests.

Grassy **Champoeg State Park Amphitheater** hosts a number of big-name performers throughout the summer, with a penchant for folk and acoustic-type groups like The Indigo Girls.

Orientation & Information Champoeg State Park is 19 miles southwest of Oregon City and 25 miles southwest of Portland, off I-5 exit 278. There's a $3 day-use fee per vehicle.

Near the entrance to the park, the Champoeg Visitors Center (☎ 503-678-1251), 8239 Champoeg Rd NE, serves as an interpretive center. Besides explaining events that led up to the famous vote at Champoeg with displays and films, the center also provides information about the Calapooians and the flood patterns of the Willamette River. The visitors' center and gift shop are open noon to 4:30 pm weekdays, and 9 am to 5 pm on weekends.

Pioneer Mothers Memorial Cabin Museum Closer to the Willamette, near the location of the old village of Champoeg, the local Daughters of the American Revolution have built a reconstruction of a pioneer-era log cabin. The cabin/museum

OREGON

The Aurora Colony

Dr William Keil, born in Prussia in 1811 (where he trained as a tailor before emigrating to the USA in 1831), had many near-fanatical interests, including the search for mystical cures for diseases (his title of 'Doctor' was self-conferred), Protestant communal religion, botany, magnetism and the theater. After developing a religious following in Pittsburgh, PA, and Bethel, MO, he decided to relocate his colony to the West Coast.

In 1855 Keil and his followers migrated over the Oregon Trail. A wagon containing the embalmed body of Keil's son Willie led the wagon train. Keil had promised the young boy that he would lead the westward migration, but the 19-year-old died of fever before the journey commenced. Keil embalmed the body with home-distilled alcohol, and set his casket at the front of the convoy. The migrants had no trouble with Native American hostility along the route, apparently due to the quality of the food and alcohol that the commune members doled out – or perhaps because the Indians were wary of the bizarre funeral procession. (See also The Grave of Willie Keil sidebar in the Southwest Washington chapter.)

The Aurora Colony, as the commune was called, was for many years very prosperous and successful. At its peak, the colony owned 15,000 acres of land. The town of Aurora contained a number of shops, flour mills, a tannery, bakery, a school and a hotel, as well as homes laid out according to an exacting streetless grid (only two houses per block, and only footpaths leading between homes).

The only radical social belief in his fundamentalist brand of Christianity was the communal sharing of property. The members of the colony were admonished to live somewhat apart from noncommunists, but the community relied on selling its products to the general public for income. Furniture, foodstuffs, leather goods and cloth from Aurora artisans found a ready market in the Willamette Valley (Aurora sausages were especially prized). The large Aurora Colony Hotel was on the stage line between Portland and California, and was a great favorite with travelers because of the food and beverages served there. Another somewhat quirky feature of the commune was the emphasis placed on music. Adherents were encouraged to sing and play instruments; the colony's brass band was a popular institution at public gatherings both in Aurora and around the state.

However, the Aurora Colony was unable to operate closely with regular Oregon society while maintaining the kinds of ideals and adherence that demanded isolation. Particularly nettlesome to the commune members was Keil's reluctance to allow young followers to marry and start families. After Keil's death in 1877, the colony assimilated into the larger rural culture of the Willamette Valley. ■

(☎ 503-633-2237) is filled with artifacts that were brought across the Oregon Trail, and other articles of frontier life. It's open 1 to 5 pm every day except Tuesday and Thursday, from March to October.

Places to Stay Campsites at Champoeg State Park are much sought after due to the park's verdant setting and proximity to Portland. There are 48 sites with hookups; an additional 46 walk-in tent sites accommodate overflow, and 12 sites are set aside for hikers/bikers. Shower facilities are also available. Tent sites cost $16 and hookups, $18. Call the visitors' center for more information, or ☎ 800-452-5687 to make a reservation.

Aurora
Population 620
Established in 1856 by Dr William Keil and his followers, the remains of this utopian colony of a small German Protestant sect are a reminder of the many and varied motives of people who came across the Oregon Trail to settle. Nowadays, Aurora is famous for its many antique stores. If you have an eye for collectibles and antiques, then you could easily while away several hours here.

To reach Aurora from the south, take I-5 exit 278 and go east for 3 miles. For a more scenic route Hwy 99E also runs through Aurora; it's 13 miles southwest of Oregon City.

Old Aurora Colony Museum This five-building museum complex (☎ 503-678-5754), at 2nd and Liberty Sts, tells the story of the utopian community in artifacts and exhibits. The museum contains a number of the old musical instruments, historic quilts, old tools and conveyances, a log cabin and a pioneer garden; it's open 10 am to 4 pm, Tuesday to Saturday, and noon to 4 pm Sunday. Guided tours are offered on weekends at 1 and 3 pm; the extended Saturday morning tour at 11 am also includes a tour of the whole town. Admission is $3.50/1.50 adults/children.

YAMHILL COUNTY WINE COUNTRY
The valleys between the rolling oak-forested hills of Yamhill County have been prime agricultural real estate since the days of the Oregon Trail pioneers. But the valley waited until 1965, passing through various agricultural stages, for the event that may have revealed the region's true calling: the planting of wine grapes near Dundee.

In 30 years, the wine industry in Oregon has grown from the crazy notion of a few zealous students of enology to a multi-million dollar industry. The wine country is convenient to Portland – an hour's drive leads to dozens of vineyards in a landscape of rolling hills, oak forests and lazy streams. The beauty and tranquillity of the valley, as well as a number of high-quality B&Bs and restaurants, make this a favorite weekend destination.

Orientation
Yamhill County is just southwest of the Portland metro area. Hwys 99W and 18 are the main roads through the wine country; watch for the blue roadside signs pointing to wineries. Newberg is 15 miles southwest of Portland on Hwy 99W. McMinnville, on Hwy 18, is another 25 miles southwest.

For an alternative to the unpleasantly clogged stretch of Hwy 99W from Portland heading to McMinnville, take I-5 south for 35 miles to exit 263 (Brooks) and follow signs west to the Wheatland Ferry, which crosses the Willamette River south of McMinnville. You won't gain much time by this route, but it's vastly more scenic and the short ferry ride beats waiting in a traffic jam.

Information
The Yamhill County Wineries Association (☎ 503-434-5814), PO Box 871, McMinnville, OR 97218, can brief you on the wines and vineyards of the area. Their free map of Yamhill County wineries is an excellent resource, with a brief discussion of individual wineries and local restaurants and lodging.

Contact the Newberg Area Chamber of Commerce (☎ 503-538-2014), at 115 N Washington St, Newberg, OR 97132, or the McMinnville Chamber of Commerce (☎ 503-472-6196) at 417 N Adams St, McMinnville, OR 97128, for more information on the area.

For medical emergencies, contact the Columbia Willamette Valley Medical Center (☎ 503-472-6131), 2700 Three Mile

The Wine Country

The state's first grapevine was planted by the Jesuits at St Paul in the 1830s, but it took 150 years for savvy viticulturists to realize Oregon's winemaking potential. Oregon's mild climate and long, but not terribly hot, summers allow some of the world's noblest but fussiest grapes to thrive.

Chardonnay and pinot noir grapes – the grapes of France's Burgundy region – flourish here. Oregon's chardonnays are generally light-textured and lemony white wines in the French style, lacking the thick oakiness of Californian and Australian chardonnays. Also much praised are Oregon pinot noir wines, delicate red wines that develop a refined fruitiness from mellow Oregon summers.

Pinot gris, another European grape suited to a cool climate, also produces white wines of distinction. Riesling grapes are among the most widely planted grapes in the area, reflecting the sweeter wine tastes of the 1970s, when many of the vineyards were planted. In Oregon, these grapes produce a pleasantly fruity, off-dry wine. Less successful are wines made from Cabernet sauvignon and merlot grape varieties, which need more sun and heat to ripen their complex flavors than northern Oregon usually affords.

Most vineyards are family-owned and operated. Nearly all vineyards welcome visitors to their tasting rooms, which are sometimes grand edifices but just as often homey affairs tucked into the corner of fermentation rooms. Oregon's so-called 'wine country' is convenient to Portland: an hour's drive into Yamhill County leads to dozens of vineyards in a landscape of rolling hills, oak forests and lazy streams. For those who would like to spend more time in the countryside, break off from the main highways and follow the blue signs to vineyards and wineries around Newberg, Dundee, Lafayette, Carlton and McMinnville. ■

Lane (Hwy 18), across from the factory outlet stores in McMinnville.

Getting There & Away

Two Greyhound (☎ 503-538-1225) buses a day link Newberg and McMinnville to Portland and the Oregon coast. In Newberg, catch the bus in the alley behind Book Stop Used Books at 211 E 1st St. In McMinnville, the bus stops at the Baker Street Market, 523 S Baker St. The one-way fare from Portland to McMinnville is $7.

Wineries

There are presently over 30 established wineries in Yamhill County, so unless you have a lot of time on your hands – and a designated driver – you will need to pick and choose to make up your own touring itinerary.

You won't want to miss the following wineries because of their quality wines and appealing locations. However, by all means do stop at other wineries; you'll get a friendly welcome from proud winemakers no matter where you visit. If you have time for only one stop, it ought to be at the **Oregon Wine Tasting Room** (☎ 503-843-3787), 9 miles southwest of McMinnville on Hwy 18 at Bellevue, where at least 30 Oregon wines are available for tasting and hundreds are for sale. It's open 11 am to 5:30 pm daily.

Sokol Blosser Winery (☎ 503-582-2282, 800-582-6668), 5000 Sokol Blosser Lane, Dundee, has some of Oregon's very best wines and a small gift shop. It's open from 11 am to 5 pm daily. **Erath Winery** (☎ 503-539-9463), also in Dundee on Worden Hill Rd, is a topnotch winery with a great pinot noir; it's open 10:30 am to 5:30 pm daily, May 15 to October 15, and 11 am to 5 pm the rest of the year.

Loved by tourists for its 'vineyard lifestyle,' **Rex Hill Vineyards** (☎ 503-538-

0666), at 30835 N Hwy 99W, Newberg, is an upscale winery with a tasting room. It's open 11 am to 5 pm daily, February to December; during January it's open for sales only. **Yamhill Valley Vineyards** (☎ 800-825-4845), 16250 NW Oldsville Rd, McMinnville, is open 11 am to 5 pm daily, June to November, and on weekends only from March to May. Try the pinot gris.

Farther south near the Eola Hills area is **Witness Tree Vineyards** (☎ 503-585-7874), 7111 Spring Valley Rd NW, Salem, just south of Lafayette on Hwy 221. The facilities are open noon to 5 pm, Tuesday to Sunday, June to September, and on weekends only the rest of the year. The low-key and informal **Amity Vineyards** (☎ 503-835-2362), at 18150 Amity Vineyards Rd SE in Amity, quietly pioneers sulfite-free wine made with organic grapes. Sample their novel 'Eco-Wine' and other hearty wines noon to 5 pm daily, February to December 23. **Chateau Benoit** (☎ 503-864-2991), 6580 NE Mineral Springs Rd, Carlton, offers a good sauvignon blanc, great views and a lovely tasting room. The hours are 10 am to 5 pm daily.

Organized Tours A number of tour companies in Portland offer personalized tours of the vineyards. Grape Escape (☎ 503-282-4262), 4304 NE 22nd Ave, specializes in wine-country tours. Try also EcoTours (☎ 503-245-1428), 1906 SW Iowa St, and Van Go Tours (☎ 503-292-2085), 8150 SW Barnes Rd.

Newberg
Population 14,707
Newberg is a fast-growing commercial hub at the edge of Portland suburbs and the beginnings of the wine country. Founded originally as a Quaker settlement, little of the town's original quiet ways remain. Instead, strip malls and shopping centers now lend the town its allure. The slightly make-believe world of winemaking has yet to transform Newberg from a scruffy mill town to the cultural center it would like to be. Dundee, officially 2 miles west on Hwy

99W, is pretty much just an adjunct to Newberg's sprawl.

George Fox College, founded in 1885 as a Quaker institute of higher education, is a private college with an enrollment of 1200 students. Herbert Hoover, the 31st president of the USA, spent his youth in Newberg.

In addition to wine grapes, the locale is famous for its plums and nut production. Local produce is often available from roadside stands and markets.

Hoover-Minthorn House This restored 1881 home (☎ 503-538-6629), 115 S River St, is the boyhood home of Herbert Hoover. His uncle, Dr Henry Minthorn, helped to raise young Hoover between 1884 and 1889, and the family home – the oldest remaining in Newberg – is now a museum of period furnishings and early Oregon history. It's open from 1 to 4 pm, Wednesday to Sunday; admission is $2/1.50 adults/seniors and students, 50¢ children.

Places to Stay Probably the cheapest place to stay in the wine country, the *Town & Country Motel* (☎ 503-538-2800), 1864 Portland Rd (Hwy 99W), is a no-frills hotel on the east side of town; singles/doubles are $44/48. The *Shilo Inn* (☎ 503-537-0303, 800-222-2244), 501 Sitka Ave, is Newberg's upscale lodging choice, with rooms ranging from $59 to $79. It also has a pool, hot tub and guest laundry.

Partridge Farm B&B (☎ 503-538-2050), 4300 E Portland Rd, offers four guest rooms in a Victorian farmhouse, with rates ranging from $60 to $90. Outside are landscaped gardens and pastures filled with llamas and game birds. *Springbrook Hazelnut Farm* (☎ 503-538-4606, 800-793-8528), 30295 N Hwy 99W, is a 60-acre estate with rooms in either an old carriage house or in the guest wing of the large, historic farmhouse. Guests have access to the swimming pool and tennis court. Rooms range from $74 to $125.

Places to Eat Start the day with espresso and fresh pastries at the *Coffee Cottage*

(☎ 503-538-5126), 808 E Hancock St. At *The Noodle* (☎ 503-537-0507), 2320 Portland Rd, just about every form of pasta is served. Prices range from $7 to $11 for a full dinner.

The best places to eat in the area are in Dundee, just down the road from Newberg. The *Red Hills Cafe* (☎ 503-538-8224), 976 Hwy 99W, is a real find. Unassuming and informal, the restaurant serves a changing menu featuring local products. Prices for dishes like pork tenderloin stuffed with prunes and fennel, or beef with wild mushrooms, average around $17. *Tina's* (☎ 503-538-8880), 760 Hwy 99W, considers itself a 'French country' restaurant, featuring local lamb, rabbit, vegetables and seafood. Dishes like roast duck with truffles go for $19.50. Both these restaurants offer vegetarian entrées and have extensive wine lists featuring local vintages.

McMinnville
Population 22,800

In many ways, McMinnville is a gratuitous suburb without the accompanying city to justify the sprawl. However, there's no denying that McMinnville is the center of the local wine industry. Unlike Newberg, the gentrifying effects of the lucrative, upmarket wine trade have finally caught on here, and art galleries, boutiques and fine restaurants now lure sophisticated wine-connoisseurs to McMinnville's quaint, red-brick downtown.

The *Spruce Goose*, built by Howard Hughes out of Oregon lumber and reckoned to be the world's largest airplane, is housed here. Grounded at a CIA-linked air base, it is currently not available for tours. A new aviation museum is being built to display the *Spruce Goose* and other military airplanes and should be completed in 2000.

That, along with pleasant hotels and plenty of B&Bs, pretty much encapsulates the attraction of the town.

Activities A favorite weekend **cycling** tour is to ride the back roads of the wine country. Pick up maps at the Newberg or McMinnville visitors' centers. However, as

neither Newberg nor McMinnville has rental bicycles, you'll need to bring your own bicycle or rent one in Portland.

Get a bird's-eye view of the wine country from Vista Balloon Adventures (☎ 503-625-7385, 800-622-2309), 575 SE Mansfield St, Sherwood. From April to November, **hot-air balloons** lift off from Newberg and drift across the vineyards of Yamhill County. The flight, which includes a champagne breakfast, lifts off at dawn seven days a week, and costs $350 per couple, or $600 for a group of four. Advance reservations are required.

Special Events Held at Linfield College in McMinnville the last weekend of July, the International Pinot Noir Celebration (☎ 503-472-8964) is one of the largest wine fairs in the Northwest, and an important testing ground for pinot noir wines from all over the world. In fact, the three-day festival of tastings, discussions and winery tours has become so popular that tickets are distributed in a lottery-sale held in March. Lucky winners shell out $595 per ticket. Tickets to the public tasting ($90) on the last Sunday are distributed the same way. Write to the International Pinot Noir Celebration, PO Box 1310, McMinnville, OR 97128, for registration details.

Anyone can attend the McMinnville Wine and Food Classic (☎ 503-472-4033), a worthwhile (and affordable) tasting fair and craft show held at the Armory in mid March. The Newberg version, called the Vintage Festival, is held early September at Sportsman Airpark in conjunction with a vintage car and airplane show.

Places to Stay Inexpensive and perfectly satisfactory, the *Safari Motor Inn* (☎ 503-472-5187, 800-321-5543), 345 N Hwy 99W, offers a spa and exercise facility, with singles/doubles at $44/48. At the *Paragon Motel* (☎ 503-472-9493, 800-525-5469), 2065 Hwy 99W, there's a pool and rooms are $42/45. McMinnville's nicest lodging is the *Best Western Vineyard Inn* (☎ 503-472-4900, 800-285-6242), 2035 S Hwy 99W, with an indoor pool, spa, guest

OREGON

laundry and mini-suites. Rooms begin at $70/78.

The chamber of commerce has a complete listing of B&Bs. Here are three of the nicest. Downtown, *Steiger Haus B&B* (☎ 503-472-0821), 360 Wilson St, is a new home offering five bedrooms with private bathrooms; rates range from $70 to $100. Out in the country, *Mattey House* (☎ 503-434-5058), 10221 NE Mattey Lane, is nestled in a vineyard. The 1869 farmhouse has four rooms ranging from $85 to $95. *Youngberg Hill B&B* (☎ 503-472-2727), at 10660 Youngberg Hill Rd, is a working farm. This immense home sits on a 700-acre estate filled with sheep, deer and grapevines. Rooms are available April to November, and cost $130 to $150.

Places to Eat Get wired for a day out in the wine country at *Cornerstone Coffee* (☎ 503-472-6622), 216 E 3rd St.

McMinnville offers plenty of savvy new restaurants waiting to round out a full afternoon of wine touring with an exceptional dinner. *Nick's Italian Cafe* (☎ 503-434-4471), 521 E 3rd St, is justifiably renowned as the wine country's long-standing favorite. While this old diner hasn't changed much in decor since the 1930s, the food is the thing – the five-course set menu at $29 a person (call ahead for vegetarian meals) includes a bowl of incredible minestrone, and features a comprehensive wine menu featuring over 100 local wines. On evenings other than Saturday, you can order á la carte. All-in-all you're looking at a great gastronomic evening. Call ahead for reservations.

The *Third Street Grill* (☎ 503-435-1745), 729 E 3rd St, in a 1907 house is one of the most intimate places to dine. Northwest and eclectic variations like grilled salmon on wild rice with lime beurre blanc go for $15.50. There's patio seating in good weather.

The only question in McMinnville is where to eat lunch. Your best bet is to fix a picnic and head for the vineyards. Stop by *Piontek's Bakery & Cafe* (☎ 503-434-6256), 411 E 3rd St, to load up a picnic basket with tasty sandwiches, pasta salads

and freshly baked bread. Immune to any wine country pretentiousness, the commodious *Golden Valley Brewery & Pub* (☎ 503-472-2739), 980 E 4th St, is a favorite gathering place where burgers, pizza and sausages are all washed down with plenty of the pub's own ales.

Shopping Most wineries have pre-boxed bottles for sale, which make good gifts for wine-drinking friends. If you're buying wine for yourself, wineries will also arrange the shipping for case lots of wine. Many wineries also feature a small gift shop with other food-related items from Oregon.

At Bellevue, 6 miles south of McMinnville on Hwy 18, is Lawrence Gallery (☎ 503-843-3633), part of a winetasting room and cafe complex. This famed gallery features local and regional artists and craftspeople. Paintings of the wine country and art glass seem to be the dominant products, although there's also jewelry and photography. Check out the outdoor sculpture garden.

Lafayette, between Dundee and McMinnville on Hwy 99W, has turned its three-story, 1910 school into Oregon's largest antique market. At the Schoolhouse Antique Mall (☎ 503-864-2720), 748 3rd Ave, over 100 different dealers share space, dividing up the school's eight original classrooms into wild collections of old collectibles, furniture and whatnot.

SALEM
Population 111,375

The Oregon state capital, Salem is a sprawling and slightly soulless city filled with gray marble buildings and bureaucrats: it's the sort of place that residents brag about being a good place to raise a family. In spite of such smug parents, downtown Salem is haunted by teenagers with shaved heads and spikes through their noses.

For the traveler, there are relics to visit, like the oldest university west of the Rocky Mountains, and the box-like state capitol. A couple of mammoth private estates from

OREGON

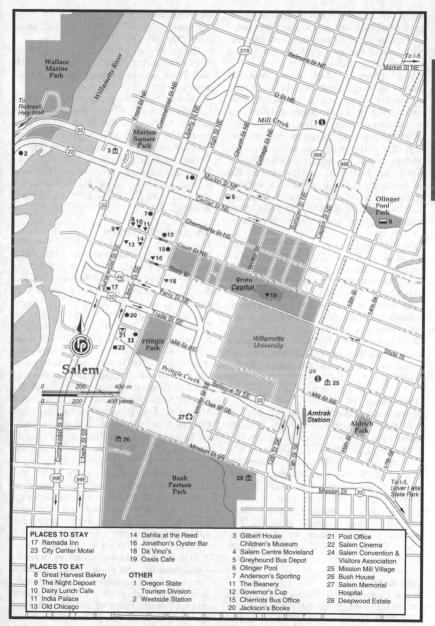

Salem

| 0 | 200 | 400 m |
| 0 | 200 | 400 yards |

PLACES TO STAY	14 Dahlia at the Reed	3 Gilbert House	21 Post Office
17 Ramada Inn	16 Jonathon's Oyster Bar	Children's Museum	22 Salem Cinema
23 City Center Motel	18 Da Vinci's	4 Salem Centre Movieland	24 Salem Convention &
	19 Oasis Cafe	5 Greyhound Bus Depot	Visitors Association
PLACES TO EAT		6 Olinger Pool	25 Mission Mill Village
8 Great Harvest Bakery	OTHER	7 Anderson's Sporting	26 Bush House
9 The Night Deposit	1 Oregon State	11 The Beanery	27 Salem Memorial
10 Dairy Lunch Cafe	Tourism Division	12 Governor's Cup	Hospital
11 India Palace	2 Westside Station	15 Cherriots Bus Office	28 Deepwood Estate
13 Old Chicago		20 Jackson's Books	

the 1880s are preserved as public parks, gardens and museums. Downtown is pleasant enough, but its unquestioned earnestness makes the city center seem like a museum of the 1950s.

Established in 1840, Salem was the second mission founded by the Methodist missionary Jason Lee in the middle Willamette Valley. As the Methodists' efforts at converting the Calapooian Indians hadn't been very successful at the first mission (the entire tribe was killed off with smallpox), the missionaries in Salem decided to establish an institution for schooling the children of the white settlers. The school, known as the Oregon Institute, held its first class in 1842, and by 1853 the school had been chartered as Willamette University.

In 1851 the legislature voted to move the capital from Oregon City to Salem. However, when the disgruntled members of the legislature convened in Salem in 1853, they found only half a dozen families living there, with very little in the way of accommodations or facilities. They voted to move the capital to Corvallis, which they did in 1855. Legislators were even less charmed with Corvallis than with Salem, and the capital moved back and remained in Salem thereafter.

Orientation

Salem is a very confusing place to drive in, with roads coming into the city at many angles, and with a numbering system that defies easy understanding. Most of the city lies on the east side of the Willamette River. State St, which cuts through the city, divides Salem into north and south halves. Therefore, an address with an SE tag is south of State St and east of the Willamette. The Marion St Bridge spans the Willamette to link west Salem with downtown. Hwys 22, 213, 219, 99E and I-5 all access the city.

Information

Salem Convention & Visitors Association (☎ 503-581-4325, 800-874-7012) is at 1313 Mill St SE, Salem, OR 97310. The Oregon State Tourism Division (☎ 503-986-0000, 800-547-7842) is at 775 Summer St, Salem, OR 97310.

The main post office is at 1050 25th St SE; however, the Pringle Park office, 410 Mill St SE, is more convenient for downtown visitors.

Salem's best independent bookstore is Jackson's Books (☎ 503-399-8694) at 320 Liberty St SE and the Salem *Statesman Journal* is the city's daily paper. Oregon Public Radio can be heard on 91.5 FM.

The State St Laundromat (☎ 503-371-6130), 2515 State St, offers drop-off service as well as dry cleaning. Salem Memorial Hospital (☎ 503-370-5200) is at 665 Winter St SE.

Oregon State Capitol

The state's first capitol building was burned down by incendiaries in 1856, and a domed neo-Greek edifice was built to replace it. However, that building burned down in 1935, and the current capitol was completed in 1939. Designed by Francis Keally, the capitol (☎ 503-986-1388), at Court and Capitol Sts, is very much a product of the 1930s. Bauhaus and art deco influences are apparent, especially in the strident bas-relief in the front statuary and the hat-box-like cupola. The building is faced with gray Vermont marble and the interior lined with brown travertine from Montana. The legislative chambers are paneled with Oregon oak and walnut.

The most notable features of the Oregon capitol are four WPA-era murals lining the interior of the rotunda, each depicting a turning point in Oregon history. Surmounting the dome is the gleaming *Oregon Pioneer*, a 23-foot-high gilded statue depicting a stylized, early male settler. The capitol grounds are landscaped with native trees and plants of Oregon.

The building is open to the public from 7:30 am to 5:30 pm on weekdays, 9 am to 4 pm Saturday, and noon to 4 pm Sunday. Free tours of the capitol are offered daily June 10 to Labor Day and run hourly (except noon). Tours of the tower for an up-close look at the gilded pioneer are offered Memorial Day to Labor Day and run every half-hour. Call ahead to check the schedule or to arrange a tour during other times of the year.

Willamette University
Just south of the capitol, Willamette University (☎ 503-370-6300), 900 State St, is apparently the oldest collegiate institution in North America west of the Missouri. The oldest remaining building on the campus is **Waller Hall**, built between 1864 and 1867. Willamette University, currently with 2500 students, is well respected for its liberal arts undergraduate program and its law school.

Bush Pasture Park
One of Oregon's leading citizens of the late 19th century was Asahel Bush, who established a newspaper in Oregon City in 1851, but moved his presses to Salem in 1853 along with the state capital. Bush was a true firebrand, advocating the rights of workers and farmers against the merchant classes, and calling the Republican politicians 'lick-spittles and toadies of official whiggery.'

He began to build his Salem mansion in 1877, by which time he was a highly successful banker. Surrounded by acres of gardens and a greenhouse, the Bush House was designed to be a self-sufficient farm. The estate and mansion are now preserved as the Bush Pasture Park (☎ 503-363-4714), 600 Mission St SE. The extensive grounds, now public gardens, include a large rose garden, picnic areas and hiking trails.

The rambling Italianate **Bush House** is open as a museum and showplace of Victorian design. Note the marble fireplaces, 10 in all. Most of the wallpaper is from the original 1887 construction and was made in France. The mansion is open 2 to 5 pm, Tuesday to Sunday, October to April, and noon to 5 pm the rest of the year. The house is open for guided tours only, which leave on the half-hour; $2.50/2 adults/seniors and students.

The reconstructed livery stable is the **Bush Barn Art Center** (☎ 503-581-2228), its main floor given over to the work

of local artists and craftspeople. It's a good place to look for handcrafted gifts and moderately priced art. The upstairs gallery displays touring art shows. It's open 10 am to 5 pm Tuesday to Friday, and 1 to 5 pm on weekends.

Deepwood Estate
Adjacent to the Bush Estate, this Queen Anne mansion (☎ 503-363-1825), 1116 Mission St SE, was built in 1894 on 6 acres of grounds. Topped by turrets and bejeweled with decorative moldings, the house manages to be fanciful and imposing at the same time. Especially beautiful are the stained-glass windows. The estate grounds contain a nature trail and a formal English tea garden, complete with gazebo. It's open for tours noon to 4:30 pm daily, May to September, except Saturday, when the grounds are reserved for weddings. During winter the estate is open 1 to 4 pm on Sunday, Monday, Wednesday and Friday. Admission is $3/2.50 adults/seniors and students; there's free access to the grounds during daylight hours, except on holidays.

Gilbert House Children's Museum
Built to honor Salem native AJ Gilbert, who invented the Erector Set, this hands-on children's center (☎ 503-371-3631), 116 Marion St NE, is half technology and science museum, and half playroom. There's a wide selection of things to do here, including the Wet & Wild Room, where there's bubble-making and a mock hydroelectric dam; the Mask Room, where kids can fashion their own masks; and a puppet theater, where children can put on shows.

The museum is open 10 am to 5 pm, Tuesday to Saturday, and noon to 4 pm Sunday; it's also open on Monday from March to June. Admission is $4 per person ($3 for seniors or anyone visiting after 3:30 pm).

Mission Mill Village
This 5-acre village complex (☎ 503-585-7012), 1313 Mill St SE, houses the visitors' center, a regional museum, a number of restored pioneer homes and a massive,

water-powered wool mill preserved as a museum.

A clutch of old pioneer buildings facing onto a grassy plaza includes the **Jason Lee Home & Methodist Parsonage**, built in 1841, an old church and the JD Boon home, built in 1847. Each of these buildings is maintained pretty much as it was in the 1840s.

The **Thomas Kay Woolen Mill** was built in 1889 and was powered by Mill Creek, which still runs through the grounds and still turns water wheels in the power house. Guided tours of the mill follow the process of washing, carding, dying and weaving the wool. Tours of the above two sites depart on the hour; tickets are $5/4.50/2 adults/seniors/students. The tours of the mill and the pioneer homes are each one hour long and are held consecutively; the ticket is good for both.

The **Marion County Historical Society Museum** (☎ 503-364-2128), 260 12th St SE, has a good exhibit on the local Calapooian culture and society, as well as pioneer artifacts. One display tells the story of Salem's long-gone Chinatown, while another examines the history of the region's hop industry. It's open 9:30 am to 4:30 pm, Tuesday to Saturday; $1/50¢ adults/seniors and children.

Activities

You can rent cross-country and downhill skis, as well as snowboards, at Anderson's Sporting Goods (☎ 503-364-4400), 241 Liberty St NE, before heading off to Santiam Pass, 85 miles east on US 20. Rent rafts, kayaks and canoes from Santiam Outfitters (☎ 503-361-7824), 1595 Cottage St NE.

Olinger Pool (☎ 503-588-6332), 1310 A St NE, right by Mill Creek, is the city's indoor pool. Salem Golf Club (☎ 503-363-6652), 2025 Golf Course Rd S, is semiprivate, and Salem's oldest. Call ahead to find out public playing hours.

Special Events

The biggest party of the year in Salem is the Oregon State Fair (☎ 503-378-3247),

held the 12 days prior to Labor Day. There's lots going on: livestock shows, wine judging and tasting, amusement rides, flower shows, a petting zoo, concerts and horse races. Take 17th St north to access the fairgrounds and Expo Center; admission is $6/3 adults/children.

Over 200 artists from around the country bring their work to the Salem Art Fair & Festival (☎ 503-581-2228), the state's largest juried art show. The free art fair is held the third weekend of July, at the Bush Pasture Park and Bush Barn Art Center. During this event, the estate grounds are turned into a kaleidoscope of art demonstrations, performance art, children's activities, craft goods and food carts.

Places to Stay

Camping The closest campground to Salem is the *Salem Campground & RV* (☎ 503-581-6736, 800-825-9605), 3700 Hagers Grove Rd SE, with 202 campsites, showers, a market, and a separate tenting area. Fees range from $13.50 for tents to $18 for full hookups.

B&Bs The *State House B&B* (☎ 503-588-1340, 800-800-6712), 2146 State St, offers six guest rooms (two in a back cottage) ranging from $50 to $70. There's also a penthouse room in the main house.

Hotels To stay close to the capitol, try *City Center Motel* (☎ 503-364-0121, 800-289-0121), 510 Liberty St SE, which has guest laundry and rooms for $38/40. Business travelers will feel right at home at the *Ramada Inn* (☎ 503-363-4123, 800-452-7879), 200 Commercial St SE, which is also right downtown; rooms are $60/65. There are meeting rooms and an outdoor pool.

There's a large concentration of chain hotels at the I-5 Market St exit 256. Least expensive is the tidy *Motel 6* (☎ 503-371-8024), 1401 Hawthorne Ave NE, with rooms for $32/38. At the top end, the *Quality Inn* (☎ 503-370-7888), 3301 Market St NE, has a restaurant and convention facilities, an indoor pool, guest laundry and suites; rooms range from $70 to $115.

Places to Eat

Budget Straight out of the 1930s, *Dairy Lunch Cafe* (☎ 503-363-6433), 347 Court St, is the place to go for an old-fashioned breakfast, or for a lunch featuring fresh cheeses. At *Great Harvest Bakery* (☎ 503-363-4697), 339 Court St NE, you can get a cup of coffee and fresh-baked muffins and breads. *Off Center Cafe* (☎ 503-363-9245), 1741 Center St NE, offers sandwiches and healthy, often vegetarian, meals. The diner in the basement of the capitol building, *Oasis Cafe* (☎ 503-371-6483), at Court and Capitol Sts, is operated by the same owners and offers unexpectedly tasty food. The buffet at *India Palace* (☎ 503-371-4808), 377 Court St NE, offers a good lunch value at $5.95 for all you can eat. They also have tandoori-baked meats. *Old Chicago* (☎ 503-391-0252), 120 Commercial St NE, has pizza and over 100 different kinds of beer and ale to placate crowds of beer-drinking university students.

Middle *Jonathon's Oyster Bar* (☎ 503-362-7219), 445 State St, is a popular watering hole. Fill up on jambalaya for $13 or local oysters at $1 each followed by a bottle from their good selection of wines. At the *Night Deposit* (☎ 503-585-5588), 195 Commercial St NE, the menu is a pan-Pacific blending of grilled steak ($13), seafood, raspberry pistachio chicken ($11) and Asian preparations. After dinner, head into the lounge, which has the air of a coy singles bar.

Casual *Da Vinci's* (☎ 503-399-1413), 180 High St SE, is a popular place for Italian and wood-fired pizza; pasta dishes cost $13 to $14.

Top End If you're in the area on Sunday, then the brunch at *Eola Hills Wine Cellars* (☎ 503-623-2405), 501 S Pacific Hwy (99W) in Rickreall, 11 miles west of Salem on Hwy 22, is an amazing feast. This all-you-can-eat brunch ($17.95) includes ome-

lets, Belgian waffles, fruit, desserts and wondrous fried potatoes, accompanied by local wines and champagne. The food is miles better than the tired fare offered at most brunches. Brunch is served from 9:30 am to 1 pm on Sunday only, and reservations are required.

Dahlia at the Reed (☎ 503-363-5414), 189 Liberty St NE, is in Salem's old opera house, which has gone through a questionable refurbishing. The Dahlia offers one of Salem's most enterprising, eclectic menus. Mediterranean snapper goes for $13.50, while beef medallions Madagascar is $15.50.

Along the Willamette's west bank, *Morton's Bistro Northwest* (☎ 503-585-1113), 1128 Edgewater St NW, offers a Northwest fare and formal dining in a quiet, garden-like setting; entrées start at $16.50. It's across the Marion St Bridge and south from downtown.

Entertainment

Coffeehouses A real hangout is *The Beanery* (☎ 503-399-7220), 220 Liberty St NE. Young staffers buzz with political intrigue, speculation and caffeine. In summer, tables spill into the street. Just down the street is the *Governor's Cup* (☎ 503-581-9675), 471 Court St NE, with a slightly more hushed coffeehouse scene.

Cinema *Salem Cinema* (☎ 503-378-7676), 445 High St SE, is as close to an arts cinema as Salem gets. Foreign and offbeat films are usually featured. The theaters at *Salem Centre Movieland* (☎ 503-588-3456), at the corner of Marion and High Sts, are central and offer first-run films.

Theater *Pentacle Theatre* (☎ 503-364-7200), 324 52nd Ave NW, is Salem's semi-professional theater company. Their 10-play season is a highlight of the city's cultural life.

Live Music *LB Day Amphitheater* (☎ 503-378-3247), in the state fairgrounds, about a mile north of downtown near Lana Ave and

Silverton Rd, is the local concert facility for touring music groups. Call to see what's upcoming.

Hear local groups on the weekends at the *Westside Station* (☎ 503-363-8012), 610 Edgewater St NW.

Getting There & Away

Air Horizon Airlines (☎ 800-547-9308) operates flights between Portland and Salem Airport (☎ 503-588-6314). The airport is just east of I-5 exit 253 on Hwy 22. The Hut Airport Shuttle (☎ 503-363-8059) provides frequent service between Salem and Portland International Airport.

Bus Five Greyhound buses a day run between Portland and Salem ($8 one way). There's one bus a day (except Sunday) between Salem and Bend, and two to four buses a day between Salem and Newport. The depot (☎ 503-362-2407) is at 450 Church St NE.

Train Amtrak offers two trains a day both north and south out of Salem; the *Coast Starlight* runs between Seattle and Oakland, CA, and the *Cascadia* runs between Eugene and Vancouver, BC. Three Amtrak Thruway Buses make daily trips to Portland for connections to other trains. The station (☎ 503-588-1551) is at 13th and Oak Sts.

Car For a rental, contact Budget (☎ 503-362-0041), 3065 Ryan Drive; Enterprise Rent-A-Car (☎ 503-364-1991), 808 SE 12th St; or Key Car Rental (☎ 503-378-0849), 1095 Commercial SE.

Getting Around

Cherriots (☎ 503-588-2877) buses serve the Salem metropolitan area. Standard fare is 75¢, though buses are free in the downtown area. Maps, free permits and instructions for carrying bikes on buses can be obtained by stopping at the main office, 183 High St NE. The transit mall is right across the street at High and Court Sts. There is no bus service on Sunday.

Call Salem-Keizer Yellow Cab Co at ☎ 503-362-2411 for a lift.

AROUND SALEM
Iris Gardens

Willamette Valley's most beautiful crops are undoubtedly grown by the many flower and bulb nurseries in the area. Two iris farms near Salem are among the largest in the world and are open in season to visitors free of charge.

Cooley's Gardens (☎ 503-873-5463), 11553 Silverton Rd NE, Silverton, opens its nursery to the public daily from 8 am to 7 pm in May, when iris blossoms cover the 250-acre farm. To reach Cooley's Gardens, take Hwy 213 from Salem toward Silverton; the farm is 2 miles west of Silverton, or 11 miles east of Salem. **Schreiner's Iris Gardens** (☎ 503-393-3232), about 2 miles north of Salem at 3625 Quinaby Rd, Salem, opens 10 acres of its grounds for free iris-viewing daily from 8 am to dusk, mid-May to early June.

Mount Angel
Population 2930

The little town of Mount Angel, with its Bavarian-style storefronts and its lovely Benedictine abbey, is like an Old World holdover in the Oregon countryside. Visit during Oktoberfest for maximum effect. Another interesting sideline, the town's old 1910 Catholic church, with mural-covered walls, was badly damaged in the 1993 Willamette Valley earthquake, which was centered near here. Mount Angel is 18 miles northeast of Salem on Hwy 214.

Contact the Mount Angel Chamber of Commerce (☎ 503-845-9440), 5 N Garfield St, for information.

Mount Angel Abbey Founded in 1882, this Benedictine monastery (☎ 503-845-3030), off College St, sits on a 300-foot butte in the middle of the Willamette Valley. The lovely setting alone justifies a side trip to the abbey. Cascade volcanic peaks rise above the mottled cropland, and paths wind through old forests, past red-brick buildings and manicured lawns. Tours of the abbey are available by prior arrangement, or you can pick up a walking tour map at the gift shop. Besides the church buildings, there's an interesting collection of ancient manuscripts on display in the library. Lodging is available at the abbey for those seeking a spiritual retreat.

Mount Angel Oktoberfest One of the state's largest harvest festivals is held in Mount Angel. It was the founding Swiss Catholic settlers who helped launch the hop-growing industry in the Willamette Valley. What better place to celebrate beer, sausage and sauerkraut?

The Oktoberfest has grown substantially in the years since Oregon has developed a viable wine and microbrewery industry to legitimize the festival's Old World pretensions. Lots of German food stands, brass bands and dancers, craft displays and beer and wine make this a fun day trip. A bus from the downtown takes visitors up the hill to the abbey for free tours of the grounds and facilities.

When you go, watch out for traffic – thousands of people turn up for Oktoberfest, slowing traffic on local narrow roads to a standstill. Try to avoid the weekend, or at least go early to find a parking spot.

Mount Angel Oktoberfest is held Thursday to Sunday on the third weekend of September. No admission charged.

Wineries
Some of Oregon's finest wines are grown across the Willamette River from Salem in the Eola Hills. Just as to the north, there are many wineries throughout this area to explore. **Redhawk Vineyard** (☎ 503-362-1596), 2995 Michigan City Ave NW, Salem, is noted for its great pinot noir. The tasting room is open noon to 5 pm Friday to Sunday, May to September.

Eola Hills Wine Cellars (☎ 503-623-2405), 501 S Pacific Hwy (99W), Rickreall, has one of the least-glamorous tasting rooms, but some of the best wines in the

state, especially a marvelous chardonnay. It's open noon to 5 pm daily.

On an imposing hilltop on the east side of the river, **Willamette Valley Vineyards** (☎ 503-588-9463), 8800 Enchanted Way, Turner, is Oregon's only publicly traded winery. Visit from 11 am to 6 pm daily.

Silver Falls State Park
Oregon's largest state park, 8700-acre Silver Falls (☎ 503-873-8681), 26 miles east of Salem on Hwy 214, is an easy day trip from Portland, Salem and Eugene. After a rainy spring morning, when the sun comes out, it's hard to resist the temptation to drive to Silver Falls State Park to see the falls in torrent and walk among wildflowers in moist, shady forests.

In the 19th century, the tremendous volume of falling water surrounded by virgin forest caught the attention of logging interests, and a sawmill was built near South Falls. The area was lumbered, and by the time the NPS surveyed the area in the 1920s and '30s, the judgment was that Silver Falls had simply been too altered by humans to qualify as a national park. The land was subsequently handed over to Oregon, which designated the area a state park in the 1940s. Thankfully, the forest has largely healed and this magnificent park is a busy place year-round.

The vast day-use area near **South Falls** is a deservedly popular place, almost too much so on summer weekends. Silver Creek is impounded here to form a small lake, a favorite with young waders and swimmers. Mature trees tower overhead, and picnic tables are scattered throughout the forest. The WPA built a number of stone shelters and the **South Falls Nature Lodge** during the Depression, which are now on the National Register of Historic Places.

There's a $3 day-use fee per vehicle. If you plan only to hike the loop trail, you can avoid paying the fee by commencing your hike at the **North Falls Trailhead**. There's no fee to use that parking lot, but there aren't any facilities either.

OREGON

Hiking & Mountain Biking The most famous hike in the park is the **Trail of Ten Falls Loop**, a 7-mile, roundtrip trail that joins all of the major falls in the park. Unfortunately, heavy rains in recent years have wiped out two bridges and a section of trail along North Fork Silver Creek, in effect closing the loop. It now takes some planning, backtracking and even some driving to see the majority of the falls in one day. The trail isn't particularly difficult, though the spray from the waterfalls can make parts of the trail slippery and muddy. Repairs are underway, but be sure to call ahead for the latest trail conditions.

The principal point of access to the trail system is off Hwy 214, either at South Falls, near the picnic and camping areas on the South Fork Silver Creek, or at North Falls, near the northern boundary of the park on the North Fork Silver Creek.

What makes the waterfalls in the park so magical is the fact that you can walk behind several of them. North Falls plunges 136 feet over a lava flow, and South Falls drops 177 feet. Over the millennia the spray from the falling water has eroded away the softer subsoils beneath the lava flows, creating hollow caverns behind the rocky edge of the waterfall.

Between falls, the trail passes through thick forests filled with a variety of ferns, moss and wildflowers. Watch for mule deer and beaver, and grand displays of colorful butterflies.

Mountain bikers have their own 4-mile trail along the canyon walls. Begin the trail at the South Falls day-use area.

Places to Stay The main campground (☎ 503-873-8681) is just upstream from the South Falls day-use area. There are over 100 campsites, half of which are reserved for tent campers ($16); hookup sites cost $18. Showers, wheelchair-accessible restrooms and a playground make this one of the most sought-after campgrounds in the Willamette Valley. Note that no reservations are taken.

ALBANY
Population 37,095

Probably no town in Oregon presents such an ugly face to the freeway as Albany. As signs on I-5 announce the town, the freeway passes an enormous pulp mill surrounded by mountains of wood chips belching out clouds of foul, sulfurous-smelling air. Nearby is a chemical plant, infamous in the 1980s for its toxic-waste pools.

But if you are willing to avert your eyes and nose and turn into downtown Albany, the intrusions of the 20th-century industrial landscape fall away. Once a thriving river port and rail center, Albany reveals its affluence and pride through its civic and residential architecture. Many grand homes still line the streets of the old town center – even modest homes were constructed with panache and flourish. The old downtown area was bypassed when modern highways were built through the Willamette Valley, leaving the old residential and commercial districts largely intact.

If your penchant is for antiques, then Albany is your town; so many businesses downtown are antique stores that the entire district seems like one antique mall.

Orientation

Albany is 24 miles south of Salem on I-5 and is connected to Corvallis, 13 miles southwest, by US 20. The city center is about 2 miles west of the freeway exits. About 350 homes and buildings in downtown Albany are registered as National Historic Sites. On a nice day, a walk through the old homes district is a pleasant way to spend an hour or two.

The visitors' center offers maps and resources for self-guided tours of the historic residential and commercial districts, as well as maps of the area's many covered bridges. Ask for their free map of 10 covered bridges. A suggested 2½-hour driving tour from Albany leads to five of them.

Information

The Albany Visitors Association (☎ 541-928-0911, 800-526-2256) is at 300 2nd

Ave SW, PO Box 965, Albany, OR 97321, in the Two Rivers Market.

The post office is at 525 2nd Ave SW.

The Rainbow's End Book Company (☎ 541-926-3867), 250 Broadalbin St SW in the Two Rivers Market, is a very good general bookstore with an outstanding selection of regional guides and histories. The Albany *Democrat-Herald* is one of the state's oldest papers, and public radio can be heard on 103.1 FM or 550 AM.

Dirty clothes go to the Cleanery (☎ 541-928-2405), 2504 Santiam Rd SE. Albany's General Hospital (☎ 541-812-4000) is at 1046 6th Ave SW.

Historic Districts

The citizens of Albany have taken great care in the restoration of these old buildings. In general, period house colors, landscaping and ornamentation have been reproduced with an eye toward historical authenticity.

The **Downtown District** is the old commercial and industrial area. The **Monteith District**, southwest of downtown, was developed by the town's founders – Walter and Thomas Monteith – in 1848. (The different spelling of the surname and the district is likely due to poor record-keeping of early settlers.) These Scottish brothers, along with other prosperous merchants, comprised the 'Republican' side of town. Democratic settler Abram Hackleman laid out an adjoining neighborhood in 1853 for the working class settlers. Rivalries between the **Hackleman District**, just east of downtown, and the Monteith District continued throughout the 19th century.

Monteith House Built by Albany's founders in 1849, Monteith House (☎ 541-967-8699), 518 2nd Ave SW, was Albany's first home. In fact, this box-like, Federal-style building is one of Oregon's oldest structures and is now a museum containing displays of pioneer artifacts. Among other historic events, the house saw the founding of the Oregon Republican Party under its roof. It's open noon to 4 pm, Wednesday to Sunday, Memorial Day to Labor Day, and at other times by appointment; admission is free.

Wineries

If you tire of Albany's old architecture or covered bridges, slip out of the city for a sip of the area's other vintage product. **Springhill Cellars** (☎ 541-928-1009), 2920 NW Scenic Drive, has a good pinot noir you can try between 1 and 5 pm on weekends, Memorial Day to December 24.

Heading north toward Monmouth on Hwy 99W, **Airlie Winery** (☎ 503-838-6013), 15305 Dunn Forest Rd, Monmouth, is known for its German-style wines, and affords some nice views of the region. It's open noon to 5 pm on weekends only, March to December. Close by, **Serendipity Cellars** (☎ 503-838-4284), 15275 Dunn Forest Rd, Monmouth, is open noon to 6 pm, Wednesday to Monday, May to October, and on weekends only the rest of the year. As the name suggests, they serve some unusual varietal wines.

Golf

The Golf Club of Oregon (☎ 541-928-8338), 905 NW Spring Hill Drive, is an 18-hole course across the Willamette River.

Organized Tours

Tours of the historic districts can be arranged by contacting Flinn's Heritage Tours (☎ 541-928-5008, 800-636-5008), 222 1st Ave W. Flinn's offers tours of Albany's historic districts in a vintage trolley from 2 to 3 pm on Saturday, from April to September. Tickets cost $6 and sell out far in advance. Less frequent tours provide a peek inside Albany's best historic homes or explore the area's covered bridges.

Special Events

The Albany Timber Carnival (☎ 541-928-2391), held at Timber-Linn Memorial Park just east of I-5 on US 20, is billed as the world's largest logging event. Contests include log-rolling, speed-cutting and tree-scaling. There's also a parade. The three-

OREGON

day event is held on the Fourth of July weekend.

During the Victorian Days, held the last weekend in July, many of the historic homes in Albany are open for guided tours. The visitors' center has details.

In July and August, free Thursday-night concerts are held at Monteith Park, downtown at 489 Water St NW. Call River Rhythms at ☎ 541-917-7777 for the concert line-up.

Places to Stay

Camping The closest campground to Albany is the *Corvallis/Albany KOA* (☎ 541-967-8521), 33775 Oakville Rd, 4½ miles west of I-5 exit 228 on Hwy 34, with 105 RV sites ($21) and a separate tent area ($16).

B&Bs A magnificent, 1880s Queen Anne extravaganza, the *Brier Rose Inn* (☎ 541-926-0345), 206 7th Ave SW, offers four rooms (from $59 to $90) and is well positioned for exploring the historic districts of Albany.

Hotels Along old Hwy 99E (Pacific Blvd) are a number of older, inexpensive hotels. The *Star Dust Motel* (☎ 541-926-4233), 2735 Pacific Blvd SE, is just across from a park. Some rooms have kitchenettes; singles/doubles are $32/39. The *Comfort Inn* (☎ 541-928-0921, 800-221-2222), 251 Airport Rd SE, has a covered swimming pool and spa facilities; rooms are $65/69.

The *Best Western Pony Soldier Motor Inn* (☎ 541-928-6322, 800-634-7669), 315 Airport Rd SE, has a pool, meeting rooms and guest laundry; rates are $73/75.

Places to Eat

A good place to fuel up in the morning is *Boccherini's Coffee & Tea House* (☎ 541-926-6703), 208 1st Ave SW. The Two Rivers Market houses a few good and inexpensive lunch and dinner spots. *Pastabilities* (☎ 541-924-9235), 250 Broadalbin SW, serves up a wide range of pasta dishes in the $7 range. *Albany Brew*

Company (☎ 541-928-1560), 300 2nd Ave, is more of a real restaurant. The broad, inspired menu includes vegetarian entrées and stands a cut above typical pub food.

One of Albany's best-loved and most-noted restaurants is *Novak's Hungarian Paprikas* (☎ 541-967-9488), 2835 Santiam Rd SE (US 20). Specializing in central European dishes, Novak's is known for its good sausages, sweet-and-sour cabbage and great desserts. For lunch, you'll spend around $7; at dinner there's both a light menu and full Hungarian-style dinners from $8 to $15.

For Italian cuisine in a historic storefront, head to *Capriccio Ristorante* (☎ 541-924-9932), 442 1st Ave SW, and dine on dishes like herbed rabbit in wine over penne ($13.50).

Getting There & Away

Four Greyhound buses run between Portland, Albany and Eugene. There is also a once-daily service to both Bend and Klamath Falls. The bus stop at Mike's Day-N-Nite Market (☎ 541-926-0243), 1757 Pacific Ave SE, is filthy and offensive.

Amtrak's *Coast Starlight*, running between Seattle and Oakland, CA, stops once a day in Albany, the northbound train at 12:45 pm, the southbound at 4:17 pm. The station (☎ 541-928-0885) is at 110 10th Ave SW. From this station Amtrak operates bus service to Eugene (four times daily) and Portland (three times daily) to help passengers catch eastbound buses.

Getting Around

Albany Transit System (☎ 514-917-7667), 333 Broadalbin St SW, in city hall, operates city buses for 50¢ on weekdays. Bicycles are welcome on the Linn-Benton Loop, which has special service between Albany and Corvallis. Loop stops include Oregon State University in Corvallis and Linn-Benton Community College, 6 miles south of Albany on Hwy 99E. Fare is 85¢. Catch buses downtown from the shelter at 2nd Ave and Broadalbin St.

For a cab call Timber Town Taxi (☎ 541-926-5588).

CORVALLIS
Population 49,275

Home to Oregon State University (OSU), Corvallis is a pleasant town at the base of the Coast Range, coursed by the Willamette River and surrounded by miles of farms, orchards and vineyards. The shops and vintage storefronts in the old, tree-lined downtown are busy, filled with bakeries, bookstores and cafes. If this sounds kind of idyllic, well, it *is* kind of idyllic in Corvallis – publications have rated the small city as one of the most livable 'micropolitan' cities, based on safety, environment, housing and education.

It's certainly hard to imagine a more prototypic university town. Over half of the city's population studies or works at the university, and another substantial percentage works at the Hewlett-Packard plant north of town. What's left of the citizenry is seemingly busy making espressos, selling bikes and keeping all the lawns and trees tended.

For the traveler, Corvallis is an easy place to spend a day drinking coffee, browsing in bookstores, watching students and waiting for dinner in one of the many diverse restaurants. It's also a good base from which to explore this part of Oregon. As implied in its name, Corvallis is at the 'heart (core) of the valley.'

Orientation

Corvallis is at the junction of Hwys 20, 34 and 99W, along the west bank of the Willamette River. It's 43 miles between Corvallis and Eugene on Hwy 99W; it's 13 miles from Corvallis to Albany on US 20.

From the east, Hwy 34 feeds straight into Harrison Blvd and leads to OSU on the west side of town. Corvallis' downtown district sits near the west bank of the Willamette along 3rd and 4th Sts (Hwy 99W). Monroe Ave (called Monroe Way on campus) splits the city into north and south halves. North Corvallis sprawls with modern, strip-like development along 9th St and Kings Blvd.

Information

The Corvallis Convention & Visitors Bureau (☎ 541-757-1544, 800-334-8118), at 420 NW 2nd St, has the details on the city and the annual festivities. The post office is at 311 SW 2nd St.

You'll find the largest selection of books at the Oregon State University Bookstore (☎ 541-737-4323), at 2301 SW Jefferson Way in the Memorial Union. For a good selection of alternative books, magazines and music, go to Grass Roots Bookstore (☎ 541-754-7668), 227 SW 2nd St. The Book Bin (☎ 541-752-0040), 351 NW Jackson Ave, is the town's best used-book store.

Oregon Public Broadcasting has one of its studios in Corvallis. Tune in on 103.1 FM or 550 AM. The OSU student newspaper, the *Barometer*, is published every weekday during the university term, and weekly during summer session.

An Allann Bros espresso bar makes Campbell's Cleaners (☎ 541-752-3794), 1120 NW 9th St, a popular place to do laundry.

Good Samaritan Hospital (☎ 541 757 5111) is at 3600 NW Samaritan Drive, about 3 miles north of town.

Oregon State University

Just west of downtown, this green and leafy campus filled with red-brick buildings was founded in 1852 as Corvallis College, but didn't take off until 1868, when the college received the federal government's land grant to establish an agricultural college. Today, OSU offers a broad range of degrees in the arts and sciences, specializing in computer and technical fields, engineering and pharmacy, as well as agricultural sciences and veterinarian medicine. Contact the OSU Administrative Services (☎ 541-737-0123) if you're interested in more details.

The campus, conforming to a vague quad and courtyard design, is bounded on

OREGON

OREGON

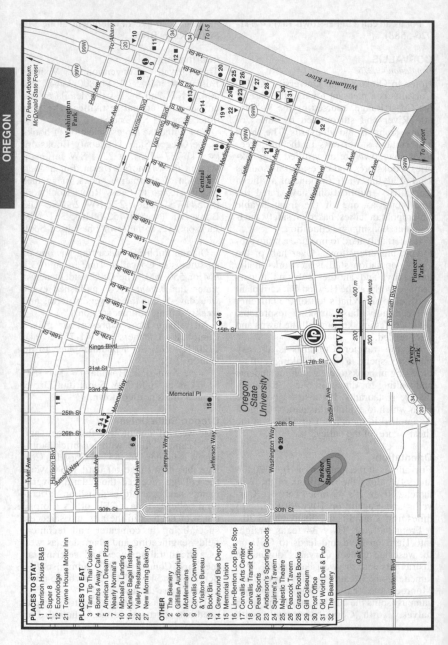

PLACES TO STAY
1   Harrison House B&B
11 Super 8
12 Econolodge
21 Towne House Motor Inn

PLACES TO EAT
3   Tarn Tip Thai Cuisine
4   Bombs Away Cafe
5   American Dream Pizza
7   Nearly Normal's
10 Michael's Landing
19 Kinetic Bagel Institute
22 Valley Restaurant
27 New Morning Bakery

OTHER
2   The Beanery
6   Gilfillan Auditorium
8   McMenimans
9   Corvallis Convention
    & Visitors Bureau
13 Book Bin
14 Greyhound Bus Depot
15 Memorial Union
16 Linn-Benton Loop Bus Stop
17 Corvallis Arts Center
18 Corvallis Transit Office
20 Peak Sports
23 Anderson's Sporting Goods
24 Squirrel's Tavern
25 Majestic Theatre
26 Peacock Tavern
28 Grass Roots Books
29 Gill Coliseum
30 Post Office
31 Old World Deli & Pub
32 The Beanery

the north by Monroe Way, which is home to a number of student-oriented businesses. Washington Way flanks the campus on the south; the university merges with downtown around 11th St. Jefferson Way winds up into the campus past parking lots and speed bumps.

The most notable building on campus is the **Memorial Union**, the student-union building. Flights of marble stairs lead past a flag draped vestibule to a beautiful commons room which has 18-foot ceilings, is filled with overstuffed furniture and lined with books. The university bookstore is here, along with several coffee shops and cafes open to students and visitors.

Wineries

Never forget that above all else this is wine country, and luckily there are two cellars that offer tasting. **Bellfountain Cellars** (☎ 541-929-3162), 25041 Llewellyn Rd, is open from noon to 5 pm Friday to Sunday. Take Hwy 99W 5 miles south and turn west on Llewellyn Rd. **Tyee Wine Cellars** (☎ 541-753-8754), 7 miles south off Hwy 99W at 26335 Greenberry Rd, is open noon to 5 pm on weekends, May to December; it's also open Friday from July to September.

Activities

You can rent cross-country and downhill **ski** equipment for Cascade ski areas at Anderson's Sporting Goods (☎ 541-757-1666), 137 SW 3rd St, and bikes from Peak Sports (☎ 541-754-6444), 129 NW 2nd St.

White Water Warehouse (☎ 541-758-3150), 625 NW Starker Ave, rents rafts and kayaks and also runs **white-water trips** to the Santiam River as well as the Deschutes, Rogue and Umpqua Rivers.

You can **golf** at the university-owned Trysting Tree Golf Club (☎ 541-752-3332), east on Hwy 34 at 34028 Electric Rd, one of the state's toughest. This 18-hole course features 25 sand traps and a number of physics-defying greens, and is purposely free of large trees in order to let the capricious weather have its way with your ball.

Special Events

Held in late June, the Corvallis Folklife Festival is one of Oregon's largest folk-music festivals. There are also workshops on folklore and arts and crafts. The festival is held in Starker Park, across from the Corvallis Country Club on Country Club Drive.

Held on the second weekend of July in Central Park at Monroe Ave and 7th St, Da Vinci Days (☎ 541-757-6363) is a celebration of the arts, sciences and technology, seeking to bridge the gap between high art and big science. Interactive displays include exhibits of computer-generated art, animation, virtual reality machines and other cutting-edge technical facilities. There's also music, food and wine booths and children's events.

The area's largest event, the Fall Festival, is held the last weekend of September in Central Park. The focus of the festival is local arts and crafts, with a juried art show featuring the work of nearly 150 artists. Local wineries, breweries and restaurants are also on hand to sell their wares, and live music fills the streets (there's a street dance on the Saturday night).

Places to Stay

Camping Just south of town, *Willamette Park* (☎ 541 757 6918) is a large grassy field that serves as a campground. There are also nature trails through the woods and access to the river for boating and angling. To reach the park, turn east on Goodnight Ave, 1 mile south of downtown; overnight fees are $7. Call ☎ 541-753-3119 for reservations.

The *Corvallis/Albany KOA* (☎ 541-967-8521), just a few miles east of town at 33775 Oakville Rd, offers full services for RVs.

B&Bs Set on a peaceful 5-acre estate, *The Hanson Country Inn* (☎ 541-752-2912), 795 SW Hanson St, has three comfortable guest rooms and a two-bedroom cottage within walking distance of the university. Rooms cost $65 to $75; the cottage goes for $145. On the other side of the campus, *Harrison House B&B* (☎ 541-752-6248), 2310 NW Harrison Blvd, offers four guest rooms in a Dutch Colonial residence, from $50 to $80.

Hotels Sitting right on the Willamette River just north of downtown, the *Econolodge* (☎ 541-752-9601), 101 NW Van Buren Blvd, offers suites and has singles/doubles from $38/42. At the *Towne House Motor Inn* (☎ 541-753-4496), 350 SW 4th St, between the university and downtown, rooms are $38/44 and some have kitchenettes. *Travel Inn* (☎ 541-752-5917), 1562 SW 3rd St, is also close and offers an outdoor pool, kitchenettes, a play area and rooms from $32.

Up a few notches in price and distance, the *Best Western Grand Manor Inn* (☎ 541-758-8571), 925 NW Garfield Ave, north of downtown, has a pool and spa facilities; rooms cost $69/75. Right downtown on the Willamette is the *Super 8* (☎ 541-758-8088), 407 NW 2nd St, a large conference-style motel with a pool and rooms for $57/64.

Places to Eat
Budget to Middle Downtown, the *New Morning Bakery* (☎ 541-754-0181), 219 SW 2nd St, is a good place for coffee and fresh baked rolls and muffins. Light lunch and dinners are served as well, and there's live music on Friday and Saturday. The *Kinetic Bagel Institute* (☎ 541-752-3044), 114 SW 3rd St, has hearty bagel sandwiches. Soup, salads and sandwiches are the order of the day at the *Valley Restaurant* (☎ 541-752-0933), 136 SW 3rd St, a bustling little cafe that's a favorite with the locals.

Near the university on Monroe Way there's a bunch of lively and inexpensive restaurants with some really good food. At many of the following, you can get in and out for less than $6 if you try. *Nearly Normal's* (☎ 541-753-0791), 109 NW 15th St, is a vegetarian cafe with organic falafel sandwiches, burritos, juice drinks and an exceedingly casual wait staff. *Tarn Tip Thai Cuisine* (☎ 541-757-8906), 2535 NW Monroe Way, offers the best Thai cooking in town.

Mexican dinners at the amusing *Bombs Away Cafe* (☎ 541-757-8380), 2527 NW Monroe Way, are innovative and tasty; there's a good selection of local beers and live music on weekends. Super funky *American Dream Pizza* (☎ 541-757-1713), 2525 NW Monroe Way, is right next door.

Top End For fine dining, *Gables Restaurant* (☎ 541-752-3364), 1121 NW 9th St, leads the list. At this converted old home, prime rib, chicken and seafood are served (around $12 to $20), though the chef gets more adventurous with the specials. Housed in Corvallis' old train depot, *Michael's Landing* (☎ 541-754-6141), 603 NW 2nd St, has the air of a steak house. It's right on the river, with drinks on the patio. Prime rib is the specialty here (starting at $14), and there's also pasta and seafood.

Entertainment
OSU offers a broad spectrum of entertainment, lectures, readings, films and theater. Call the recorded weekly calendar (☎ 541-737-6445) for a listing of events. Corvallis' main performing arts venue, the *Majestic Theatre* (☎ 541-757-6977), 115 SW 2nd St, hosts everything from community theater to the region's top dance troupes.

Coffeehouses There's no escaping the Beanery – an infectious strand of coffeehouses featuring locally roasted Allann Bros coffee. The campus *Beanery* (☎ 541-757-0858), 2541 NW Monroe Way, is a favorite student hangout. Closer to downtown (in a refurbished old storefront) the *Beanery* (☎ 541-735-7442), at 500 SW 2nd St, is a quieter place for a cup of coffee. Watch for events on weekends.

Brewpubs For a swig of the local brew, head to *Old World Deli & Pub* (☎ 541-752-8549), 341 SW 2nd St, for a glass of Oregon Trail Ale. The sandwiches and salads here make good picnic fixings. Portland-based *McMenimans* (☎ 541-758-6044), 420 NW 3rd St, has one of its few out-of-town locations in Corvallis. As usual, these pubs pour their own excellent brews and a large selection of ales and stouts from other local brewers.

Cinemas OSU's International Film Series (☎ 541-737-2450) puts on art and foreign films in *Gilfillan Auditorium* near the corner of Orchard Ave and 26th St. For first-run releases, try *Ninth St Cinema World* (☎ 541-758-7469), 1750 NW 9th.

Live Music The main venue for live music in Corvallis is the *Peacock Tavern* (☎ 541-754-8522), 125 SW 2nd St, with local blues and rock. Across the street, there's an older crowd at *Squirrel's Tavern* (☎ 541-753-8057), 100 SW 2nd St, where jazz and acoustic music is featured on weekends.

Spectator Sports
OSU's Beavers are frequent contenders in both college football and basketball. The football team plays at Parker Stadium, at 26th St and Stadium Ave, and the basketball team plays at Gill Coliseum, 26th St and Washington Way. Call ☎ 541-737-4455 for information on upcoming games and tickets.

Getting There & Away
Four Greyhound buses a day link Portland, Corvallis and Eugene. The one way fare between Corvallis and Eugene is $7; between Portland and Corvallis it's $13. There's also a daily bus to Bend and two to three buses to Newport (except Sunday) on the Valley Retriever. The bus depot (☎ 541-757-1797) is at 153 NW 4th St.

Enterprise Rent-A-Car (☎ 541-758-0000), is on the western outskirts of town at 400 NW Walnut Blvd.

Getting Around
Corvallis Transit (☎ 541-757-6998), 501 Madison Ave, operates city buses on weekdays; the fare is 50¢. Downtown buses rendezvous at 5th St and Jefferson Ave. A convenient route map is printed in the phone book. Corvallis is also served by Linn-Benton Loop buses, which run between Corvallis and Albany. Pick up the bus at the university, at the corner of 15th St and Jefferson Way.

Call A-1 Taxi (☎ 541-754-1111) to hire a cab.

AROUND CORVALLIS
Peavy Arboretum
& McDonald State Forest
Both these areas are administered by OSU. At the Peavy Arboretum, two interpretive walks wind through 40 acres of forest. From the arboretum, trails continue into McDonald State Forest, a research forest with 8 miles of hiking and mountain bike trails. Take Hwy 99W north for 8 miles, then turn west at the signs to get to the forests.

Mary's Peak
Mary's Peak, at 4097 feet, is the highest peak in the Coast Range. Just 16 miles from Corvallis in the Siuslaw National Forest, Mary's Peak is a favorite with student hikers, especially when clear weather allows views across the Willamette Valley to the glaciered central Oregon Cascades.

To reach the hiking trail to the peak, follow US 20 to Philomath, 6 miles west. Continue on US 20 for 1½ miles past the junction with Hwy 34, and turn onto USFS Rd 2005, called Woods Creek Rd. Follow this good graveled road for 7½ miles, until you reach the trailhead. The 4.2 mile hike climbs quickly through a dense hemlock forest before finally breaking out into the Mary's Peak Scenic Botanical Area, full of ferns, salal, firs and wildflowers.

An alternative route for the less ambitious (or for those picking up hikers on the top), involves driving most of the way up Mary's Peak from the other side. Take Hwy 34 about 10 miles southwest of Philomath to USFS Rd 3010, called Mary's Peak Rd. This winding road loops around the mountain, arriving at a parking area and primitive campground less than a mile from the top. A $3 fee is charged at either trailhead.

EUGENE
Population 126,325
In many ways, Eugene is the prototypic Oregon town, drawing its energy from equal measures of pragmatism and idealism. At the southern end of the wide Willamette Valley, the city maintains its solid, working-class base in the timber industry.

OREGON

OREGON

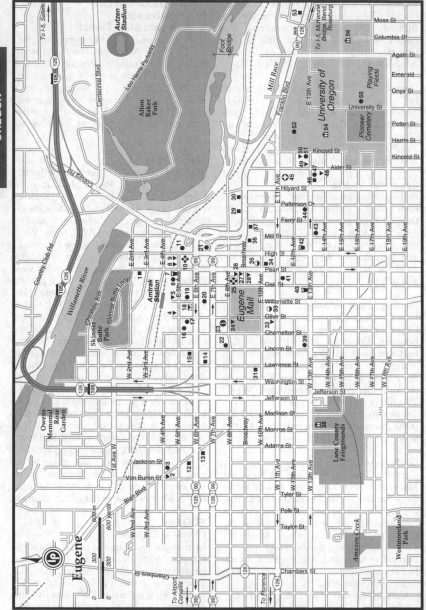

Eugene

PLACES TO STAY		24	West Brothers Bar-B-Que	22	WOW Hall
1	The Campbell House	26	Full City Coffee, Palace Bakery	23	Visitors Bureau
12	Red Carpet Motel			24	Eugene City Brewery
13	Executive House Motel	27	Zenon Cafe	25	Saturday Market
14	Downtown Motel	28	Ambrosia	33	LTD Transit Station
15	Courtesy Inn	32	The Kiva	35	Greyhound Bus Depot
20	Eugene Hilton	46	Excelsior Inn	38	Lane County Historical Museum
29	Manor Motel	48	Glenwood Inn		
30	66 Motel	49	China Blue	39	Berg's Ski Shop
31	The Oval Door B&B	50	Rennie's Landing	40	Fields Restaurant & Brewpub
34	Timbers Motel				
36	Campus Inn	**OTHER**		41	John Henry's
37	Eugene Motor Lodge	3	Sam Bond's Garage	42	High St Brewery & Cafe
46	Excelsior Inn	6	Euphoria Chocolate Co	43	The Bijou
53	Best Western New Oregon Motel	7	Steelhead Brewing Co	44	Club Wash
		10	Fifth Street Public Market	45	Sacred Heart Medical Center
PLACES TO EAT		11	Pedal Power Bicycles		
2	Hilda's	16	The Beanery	47	Smith Family Bookstore
4	Oregon Electric Station	17	Down to Earth	51	U of O Bookstore
5	Cafe Navarro	18	Main Post Office	52	Deady Hall
8	Chantrelle Restaurant	19	Smith Family Bookstore	54	U of O Museum of Art
9	Jo Federigo's Bar & Cafe	20	Hult Center, Convention Center	55	MacArthur Court
		21	Good Times	56	U of O Museum of Natural History

Yet the state's largest college campus and some of its most unconventional citizens also call Eugene home.

Established in 1846 by a Californian settler, Eugene Skinner, Eugene developed as a railroad hub and trading center for wheat, fruit, dairy and ever-present timber products. During the 1960s, Eugene became synonymous with the back-to-the-earth social movement. The city was rightly famous for its alternative communes, leftist politics and drug culture – in short, its 'hippie lifestyle.' Unrest built over US involvement in the Vietnam War, and the university became a hotbed of civil disobedience and counterculture.

In some ways, life in Eugene seems to be a denial that the '60s have passed. Many of the city's successful businesses are owned by former 'radicals.' Although more prosaic than during the heyday of the '60s, activism is still de rigueur in Eugene. Environmental issues especially motivate students, placing them again at odds with the community whose long-time economic base was in the forest products industry.

Parks flank the Willamette River along much of the length of Eugene, and some of the state's most beautiful public gardens grace its hillsides.

Travelers will find sophisticated yet inexpensive dining, lively shopping districts, and a youthful, relaxing and fun-seeking atmosphere that almost succeeds in making Eugene seem good for you. The revolution may have failed, but at least the food is better.

Orientation

Eugene is cradled in hills at the southern end of the Willamette Valley where two major tributaries, the Coast Fork and the McKenzie River, join the Willamette River. Directly east of Eugene is the city's blue-collar suburb of Springfield (population 50,140).

I-5 runs north-south through Eugene, and I-105/Hwy 126 cuts through east-west, depositing the traveler on 6th Ave, just south of the market district. Willamette St divides Eugene's numbered avenues into east and west.

The University of Oregon has extensive wooded grounds, roughly girded by Franklin Blvd and 18th Ave, and Alder and Agate Sts; the I-5 University exit (192) feeds into Franklin Blvd, which becomes Broadway through downtown, and Hwys 99 and 126 to the east.

Information
Tourist Office The Convention & Visitors Association of Lane County (☎ 541-484-5307, 800-547-5445) is at 115 W 8th Ave, Suite 190, Eugene, OR 97401.

The Willamette National Forest office (☎ 541-465-6521) is at 211 E 7th Ave. The BLM District Office (☎ 541-683-6600) is at 2890 Chad Drive.

Money The US Bank (☎ 541-836-4001), 811 Willamette St, will exchange foreign currency for account holders only. Foreigners should make use of the exchange counter at Eugene's Mahlon Sweet Airport.

Post The main post office is at 520 Willamette St.

Bookstores The University of Oregon Bookstore (☎ 541-346-4331), 895 E 13th Ave, is at the corner of E 13th Ave and Kincaid St. Eugene's premier used-book store is the Smith Family Bookstore, with two locations: near the university (☎ 541-345-1651) at 768 E 13th Ave, and downtown (☎ 541-343-4717) at 525 Willamette St. The Book Mark (☎ 541-484-0512), 856 Olive St, has Eugene's best selection of maps, as well as books on outdoor activities. Marketplace Books (☎ 541-343-5614), 296 E 5th Ave (in the Fifth Street Public Market), has a good selection of new books including a good travel and recreation section. Mother Kali's Books (☎ 541-343-4864), 720 E 13th Ave, is a good feminist bookstore.

Media Eugene's daily newspaper is the *Register-Guard*. The Friday paper contains an arts and events section. *Eugene Weekly* is the city's alternative newsweekly, with the focus on hip arts coverage. The *Daily Emerald* is the university newspaper. The biweekly *Comic News* is a local product that brings together political cartoons from around the world.

Laundry Club Wash (☎ 541-342-1727), 595 E 13th Ave, is open 24 hours.

Medical Services If you need medical attention, go to Sacred Heart Medical Center (☎ 541-686-7300), 1255 Hilyard St, between 11th and 13th Aves.

Fifth Street Public Market
At E 5th Ave between Pearl and High Sts, this is the anchor of a small but lively shopping and cafe district. The 'Market,' once an old mill, is in fact a boutique mall. Besides the lures of shopping, there's a good bakery and several inexpensive and ethnic places to eat in the building's central atrium. In neighboring blocks there's a good antique store, a brewpub and a chocolatier.

Eugene Mall
In a thoroughgoing fit of urban renewal, most of Eugene's old downtown core was torn down, the buildings replaced with 1960s-era structures, and much of the area turned into a pedestrian mall. The project has been less than successful.

The mall, in the blocks between 8th and 10th Aves from Charnelton to Oak Sts, is now filled with small specialty shops and cafes. You'll certainly have no trouble finding great food. After closing off all vehicular traffic in a 12-block area during the 1960s, the city has been slowly opening the streets back up to cars, trying to lure people back to the city center.

Saturday Market
The outdoor market in the park near E 8th Ave and Oak St brings in a grand mix of Eugene characters: buskers, vegetable hawkers, tie-dye artisans, mimes, ethnic food sellers and craftspeople. It's great fun, and a good introduction to Eugene's peculiar vitality. Saturday Market is open 10 am to 5 pm every Saturday. It moves indoors to the Lane County Fairgrounds roughly from November to April 1.

University of Oregon
Established in 1872, although classes didn't begin until 1876, the University of

Oregon (☎ 541-346-3014) is the state's foremost institution of higher learning, with a focus on the arts, sciences and law. The forest-like campus sits just south and east of downtown; the streets near the university – especially 13th Ave – are strewn with student-oriented bars, bookstores and coffeehouses. Tours of the campus are offered twice daily during the summer break.

The campus is filled with historic, ivy-covered buildings. The oldest is **Deady Hall**, which, for the first 10 years of the university, *was* the university.

The university's **Museum of Art** (☎ 541-346-3027), 1430 Johnson St, is renowned for its extensive collection of Asian and regional contemporary art. The **Museum of Natural History** (☎ 541-346-3024), 1680 E 15th Ave, is housed in a replica of a Native American longhouse. Its collection is the state's best display of fossils, Native American artifacts and geologic curiosities. A $1 donation is requested. Both museums are open noon to 5 pm, Wednesday to Sunday.

Pioneer Cemetery was once in a field but is now surrounded by the campus. Reading tombstones at one of Eugene's oldest cemeteries gives a vivid insight into life and death in the early settlement. Note especially the graves of Civil War veterans.

Lane County Historical Museum
This local museum (☎ 541-687-4239) sits in the county fairgrounds at 740 W 13th Ave. A collection of historical artifacts documents the growth of communities in the area. A popular exhibit details the experiences of Oregon Trail pioneers who made their way across the continent to settle in Lane County. Old logging tools and technology are also prominent in the collection. The museum is open 10 am to 4 pm, Wednesday to Friday, and noon to 4 pm Saturday; $2/1/75¢ adults/seniors/children.

Skinner Butte
Directly north of downtown is Skinner Butte. A hike to the top provides a good orientation and a little exercise (there's also a road to the top; follow the signs from Skinner Butte Loop). On the narrow strip of land between the wooded butte and the Willamette River, Eugene Skinner established the first business in Eugene. The grassy waterfront is now a park, popular with joggers and picnickers. There is also rock climbing along the landmark's western face. A number of beautiful Victorian homes ring the butte.

Alton Baker Park
Extending for 5 miles along the Willamette River, Alton Baker Park is a series of parks, bike and jogging paths and picnic areas. Paths lead through oak groves – watch for songbirds and waterfowl.

From downtown, the easiest access to the park network is on the north side of Skinner Butte (follow High St north). Follow the paths hugging the river's edge beneath the Hwy 126 bridge to the **Owens Memorial Rose Garden**. This lovely park features carefully trained climbing roses, as well as ornamental trees. Dominating all is an old cherry tree planted in the 1860s. From the university area, cross the footbridge to the park on the northern banks of the river. In-line skates can be rented from Anderson's Sporting Goods (☎ 541-484-7344), 199 W 8th Ave, for $4 to $10.

Hendricks Park
Rhododendron Garden
In May, this garden puts on a spectacular floral display. On a hill above the city, the garden is part of a larger park featuring native trees and shrubs. Over 5000 varieties of rhododendron and azalea erupt into bloom in the spring, along with dogwood and daffodils. During the rest of the year, the park is a quiet, vernal retreat with lovely views, worthy of a picnic. To reach Hendricks Park, turn south off Franklin Blvd onto Agate St and then turn east onto Heights Blvd.

Mt Pisgah Arboretum
This 120-acre plant sanctuary features trails that wind through a number of Northwest plant habitats, including a marsh, a conifer forest and wildflower meadows. At

OREGON

the gate to the arboretum there are brochures that help identify plant and animal species. To reach the arboretum, take I-5 south to the 30th Ave exit and turn east, following the signs. It's 7 miles outside of Eugene.

Wineries
Nestled in the hills at the southern end of the Willamette Valley are a number of good wineries. Take a picnic to **Hinman Vineyards** (☎ 541-345-1945), 10 miles southwest of Eugene at 27012 Briggs Hill Rd, to enjoy their nice facility and grounds; they're open noon to 5 pm daily. To get there from Eugene, go west on W 11th Ave, left on Bailey Hill Rd, right on Spencer Creek Rd and left on Briggs Hill Rd.

Noted for their red wines, **La Velle Vineyards** (☎ 541-935-9406), 89697 Sheffler Rd, Elmira, is open noon to 6 pm daily, May to September, and weekends only from March to April and October to November.

Biking
Rent a mountain bike or tandem from Pedal Power Bicycles (☎ 541-687-1775), 545 High St, then take off for the park.

Skiing
To rent cross-country or downhill skis, or snowboards, go to Berg's Ski Shop (☎ 541-683-1300), 367 W 13th Ave. The closest skiing is either near Willamette Pass, 65 miles southeast of Eugene on Hwy 58, or up the McKenzie River on Hwy 126 near Santiam Pass.

Swimming
There's an outdoor pool at Amazon Park (☎ 541-682-5350), near Hilyard St and E 26th Ave, and a year-round indoor pool at Sheldon Pool (☎ 541-687-5314), 2445 Willakenzie Rd. At Armitage State Park, north of Eugene on Coburg Rd, there's swimming in the McKenzie River when the weather allows.

Golf
There are several golf courses in the Eugene area. Try Oakway Golf Course (☎ 541-484-

1927), 2000 Cal Young Rd, for a beautiful 18-hole course with lots of mature trees. The nine-hole Laurelwood Golf Course (☎ 541-687-5321), 2700 Columbia St, is just south of the university.

Special Events
There's no doubt about it – Eugene knows how to throw a party.

Oregon Bach Festival While the music of Bach – especially the concertos and cantatas – takes center stage at the Hult Center for the Performing Arts (see Entertainment), the festival also includes concerts of contemporary music and jazz. Held for two weeks in late June and early July, the festival features about 25 separate concerts. Ticket prices begin at $10. Contact the Bach Festival Office (☎ 541-346-5666, 800-457-1468), for ticket information.

Oregon Country Fair A week after the Bach Festival (the weekend after the Fourth of July) and just about as far as you can get from highbrow pretensions, the Oregon Country Fair is a riotous three-day celebration of Eugene's folksy, hippie past and present. Booths are crammed with health food, tie-dyed garments, candles, herbs and crafts. Wandering minstrels, jugglers and mimes entertain. On the festival's many stages watch a variety of vaudeville acts, musicians and theater groups. Mostly gone are the old days when clothing was optional and drugs passed freely in the crowd. But it's still full of infectious high spirits and a kind of otherworldly goodwill.

The fair is held 15 miles west of Eugene on Hwy 126, near Veneta. If you are driving to the fair, note that parking anywhere close can be difficult. Avoid the parking nightmare and hop on one of the free, LTD express buses running between Autzen Stadium and the fair.

Tickets must be purchased in advance and are available through Fastixx (☎ 800-992-8499) or by calling ☎ 541-343-6554. For more information contact the festival headquarters (☎ 541-343-4298) at PO Box 2972, Eugene, OR 97402.

Lane County Fair This fun agricultural fair is held the third week of August at the Lane County Fairgrounds (☎ 541-687-4294). Events include livestock shows, live music, a carnival, and fruit and vegetable displays.

Eugene Celebration On the third weekend of September, this celebration takes over downtown Eugene. Concerts, juried fine-art shows and author appearances are some of the events, but by far the most vital part is the street fair. In time-tested Eugene fashion, food vendors mix with political activists, organic farmers with jewelry makers and all with students fresh from summer break. Call ☎ 541-682-5215 for details.

Places to Stay

Camping While most campgrounds in the area are primarily for RV campers, they all have tent areas; most charge around $20 for full hookups. *KOA Kamping World* (☎ 541-343-4832), a quarter mile west of I-5 exit 199, is 6 miles north of Eugene. Nine miles south of Eugene at Creswell (I-5 exit 182) is the *KOA Sherwood Forest* (☎ 541-895-4110), 298 E Oregon Ave. West of Eugene, along Fern Ridge Reservoir, is the *Fern Ridge Shores Campground* (☎ 541-935-2335), a pleasant spot with lakeside sites, when they're available (lately the campground has been heavily booked by homeless employees of Eugene's new Hyundai factory).

Hostels The pleasant *Eugene International Hostel* (☎ 541-349-0589), 2352 Willamette St, south of the university, is clean and quiet and has secure bicycle parking and locked storage. Dormitory beds cost $13 to $16, and private rooms start at $34. It's closed from 11 am to 4 pm daily.

B&Bs There's about a dozen B&Bs in the Eugene area. Contact the Eugene Area B&B Association (☎ 541-343-3553, 800-507-1354), for a complete directory. *The Oval Door B&B* (☎ 541-683-3160, 800-882-3160), 988 Lawrence St, is a newer home in an old neighborhood, with four guest rooms ranging from $70 to $93.

Historic homes refurbished as European-style hotels offer Eugene's most elegant lodgings. *The Campbell House* (☎ 541-343-1119, 800-264-2519), 252 Pearl St, is within walking distance of parks and downtown shopping and has 14 guest rooms from $75 to $275. Near campus, another 14 guest suites (two with whirlpool tubs) from $69 to $160 at the stately *Excelsior Inn* (☎ 541-342-6963), 754 E 13th Ave, share space with one of Eugene's finest restaurants.

Hotels – downtown If you're planning to spend some time in Eugene, call ahead for a room in one of several older hotels on the edge of the downtown area – it's an easy stroll to shopping, restaurants and parks. The *Courtesy Inn* (☎ 541-345-3391), 345 W 6th Ave, with singles/doubles at $45/50, and the *Downtown Motel* (☎ 541-345-8739, 800-648-4366), 361 W 7th Ave, with rooms for $33/42, are both attractive hotels convenient to downtown businesses. Continue west on 6th Ave for a strip of inexpensive motels, like the *Red Carpet Motel* (☎ 541-345-0579), 1055 W 6th Ave, and the *Executive House Motel* (☎ 541-683-4000), 1040 W 6th Ave, with rooms for around $30/35.

Immediately south of downtown is the *Timbers Motel* (☎ 541-343-3345, 800-643-4167), 1015 Pearl St. The sparsely decorated rooms make up in convenience for what they lack in style. The cheapest rooms are in the basement, for about $10 cheaper than the regular rates of $35/38.

The *Eugene Hilton* (☎ 541-342-2000, 800-937-6660), 66 E 6th Ave, is right in the center of downtown and is part of the convention center complex. It's also just next door to the artsy goings-on at the Hult Center. Be prepared to pay for the convenience, however: rooms start at $110 and go up to $150.

Hotels – university area Right along Broadway, which turns into Franklin Blvd (Hwys 99 and 126), you'll find a strip of inexpensive motels and restaurants, all handy to the university and riverside parks. Unless there's a special event going on, you can count on finding a room. The following motels offer rooms for around $32/38: the *66 Motel* (☎ 541-342-5041), 755 E Broadway; the *Manor Motel* (☎ 541-345-2331), 599 E Broadway; and the *Eugene Motor Lodge* (☎ 541-344-5233), 476 E Broadway, which has some kitchenettes. The latter two have pools. The *Campus Inn* (☎ 541-343-3376), 390 E Broadway, is slightly more expensive with rooms for $46/54.

The *Best Western New Oregon Motel* (☎ 541-683-3669), 1655 Franklin Blvd, across the street from campus, is the first choice for people attending university events and conferences. There's an indoor pool, sauna and exercise room, and rooms for $58/70.

Places to Eat
You won't have any trouble finding something good to eat in Eugene. The quality and variety of food here often surpass much of what gets flogged as cuisine in cities like Seattle and Portland. And what's better, even the best restaurants will offer items to fit on a student's budget.

Downtown Start out the day at *Full City Coffee* (☎ 541-344-0475), 842 Pearl St, for espresso drinks. There are baked goods at the *Palace Bakery* next door.

For the budget traveler, there are food carts with ethnic food on the pedestrian mall. In the atrium of the Fifth Street Market building (on 5th Ave between Pearl and High Sts), there's a great bakery and a number of small ethnic restaurants to choose from. Try *Mekala's* (☎ 541-342-4872), 296 E 5th Ave, for good Thai food. Eugene's other ethnic favorite, *Tres Hermanas* (☎ 541-342-4058), 99 W Broadway at Olive St, serves Mexican dinners under $10; the food is ordinary but strangely popular. If you've been looking for a good health-food store, head to *The Kiva* (☎ 541-342-8666), 125 W 11th Ave, which

has organic produce, bulk foods and deli items.

A short distance north from downtown is the city's spiciest restaurant, *Hilda's* (☎ 541-343-4322), 400 Blair Blvd, featuring Central and South American cuisine. If you're on a budget, the tapas are a good value. At the *West Brother's Bar-B-Que* (☎ 541-345-8489), 844 Olive St, home-brewed ales are teamed with superior barbecued ribs ($11.95) from the 'usual' menu; on the 'unusual' menu find vegetarian and eclectic ethnic specials.

Well-seasoned travelers will enjoy the Caribbean, Latin and African tanginess of *Cafe Navarro* (☎ 541-344-0943), 454 Willamette St. Their weekend breakfast menu draws quite a crowd. Intimate *Chantrelle* (☎ 541-484-4065), 207 E 5th Ave, prepares French classics and submits robust local standards like game to continental treatments.

For steak and seafood, go to the *Oregon Electric Station* (☎ 541-485-4444), 27 E 5th Ave. The restaurant is housed in an old railroad station, with wood and brass fixtures everywhere. In the waiting room, settle into an easy chair for a pre-dinner drink.

Two of Eugene's best restaurants face each other across East Broadway at the edge of the pedestrian mall. *Ambrosia* (☎ 541-342-4141), 174 E Broadway, features regional Italian cuisine and wood-fired specialty pizzas in a wonderfully preserved late-19th-century bar. *Zenon Cafe* (☎ 541-343-3005), 898 Pearl St, has a statewide reputation for excellent cuisine. Its extensive international menu, ranging from beef vindaloo to grilled quail and a great Caesar salad, makes imaginative use of local meats, mushrooms, fish and vegetables. Vegetarian dishes have their own section of the menu, and desserts are equally compelling. A number of 'small plates' are available as appetizers or light meals. An entrée and salad total about $22.

University Area For a full breakfast, with bleary-eyed students, try the *Glenwood Inn* (☎ 541-687-0355), 1340 Alder St.

University-area haunts provide inexpensive food. Besides the brewpubs in the area, check out *China Blue* (☎ 541-343-2832), 879 E 13th Ave, for northern Chinese food, and *Rennie's Landing* (☎ 541-687-0600), 1214 Kincaid St, for burgers and beer.

The *Excelsior Inn* (☎ 541-342-6963), 754 E 13th Ave, in a beautiful old home, is one of Eugene's finest restaurants. The menu changes seasonally, and ranges from pasta dishes to leg of lamb. Prices are modest considering the quality (grilled chicken breast with porcini mushrooms is $14.75). The menu also offers 'light suppers' for around $9.

Entertainment

The University of Oregon is host to a great many touring and local performing-arts groups. There are also a number of public lectures, films and activities. Call the Cultural Forum (☎ 541-346-4373) or pick up a copy of the *Daily Emerald* for information about campus activities.

The *Hult Center for the Performing Arts*, at 6th Ave and Willamette St, adjacent to the convention center and the Hilton, is the main civic performance space; the Eugene Opera, Symphony and Ballet each perform here, as do numerous festival acts and touring groups. Call the concert line at ☎ 541-682-5746; for tickets call ☎ 541-687-5000.

The *Actors Cabaret of Eugene* (☎ 541-683-4368), 996 Willamette St, is popular for its stand-up comedy, musicals and dinner theater.

Coffeehouses *The Beanery* (☎ 541-342-3378), 152 W 5th Ave, offering desserts and light meals, has folk and live jazz music. At any given time you're likely to find *Café Paradiso* (☎ 541-484-9933), 115 W Broadway at Olive St, packed with chess players. The only real exception is on weekend evenings, when there's folk and jazz music instead. *Sip n' Surf Cybercafe* (☎ 541-302-1581), 43 W Broadway (in the Eugene Mall), serves espresso and web pages to Internet junkies until midnight.

Brewpubs Eugene has several brewpubs, although most bars and taverns serve locally brewed beers. Kitty-corner to the Fifth Street Market, the *Steelhead Brewing Co* (☎ 541-485-4444), 199 E 5th Ave, serves German-style beers and light meals in an airy old storefront; you can usually find an empty table and enough quiet to talk. *Eugene City Brewery* (☎ 541-345-8489), 844 Olive St, connected to West Brother's Bar-B-Que, is a more student-oriented brewpub. Strong, dark ales are good here, well matched to the fiery entrées on the restaurant side of the business.

A local newspaper recently dubbed the handsome *Fields Restaurant & Brewpub* (☎ 541-341-6599), 1290 Oak St at 13th Ave, the 'people's choice' for Eugene's best beer, though it's really more of a restaurant than a brewpub; it's not far from campus, and minors are allowed until 9 pm. McMenimans' *High Street Brewery & Cafe* (☎ 541-345-4905), 1243 High St, also near campus, is a popular meeting place that is half pub, half coffee shop.

Cinemas *The Bijou* (☎ 541-686-2458), 492 E 13th Ave, is Eugene's art and foreign movie house. At *Movies 12* (☎ 541-741-1231), 2850 Gateway St, in the Gateway Mall in Springfield, a dozen first-run movies will be playing at any given time.

Live Music *WOW Hall* (☎ 541-687-2746), at 8th Ave and Lincoln St, is an old union hall and the main venue for touring bands. Call for a listing of upcoming events. At *Good Times* (☎ 541-484-7181), 375 E 7th Ave, there's a lively bar scene with straightforward rock music and dancing. Clubs like *Sam Bond's Garage* (☎ 541-343-2635), 407 Blair Blvd, and *John Henry's* (☎ 541-342-3358), 136 E 11th Ave, play more alternative music. For jazz, go to *Jo Federigo's Bar & Cafe* (☎ 541-343-8488), 259 E 5th Ave. Check the *Eugene Weekly* or the *Daily Emerald* for other venues and current listings.

Spectator Sports The Eugene Emeralds are a Class A baseball team who play during the summer at *Civic Stadium* (☎ 541-342-5367) at 20th Ave and Willamette St. The University of Oregon Ducks are the much-loved, though not always successful, sports teams of the university. The basketball team plays at *MacArthur Court*, at the university; the football team plays at *Autzen Stadium*, just east of downtown. Call ☎ 541-346-4461, 800-932-3668 for a current schedule of University of Oregon sports events.

Shopping
There's nothing more symbolic of Eugene than the business called Down to Earth (☎ 541-342-6820), 532 Olive St. This shop, full of garden and farm supplies, kitchen gear and food-preservation equipment, contains everything you need to establish a modern, wholly organic homestead. Add to it a cafe and a plant nursery, and you've got a great place to play out your farming fantasies. Where else could you buy a bagel, a vegetable juicer, and a self-composting toilet?

Euphoria Chocolate Co (☎ 541-343-9223), 199 E 5th Ave, are locally famed candy makers – try the truffles.

If the shops in downtown's Market District and the Eugene Mall don't have what you need, the 140 stores in Valley River Mall, just north of the city center off Delta Hwy, surely will.

Getting There & Away
Air Three airlines serve Eugene's Mahlon Sweet Airport (☎ 541-682-5544), 20 miles northwest of town on Hwy 99. Horizon Air, Skywest Airlines (☎ 800-453-9417) and United Airlines each link Eugene to Portland and other West Coast cities.

Lane Transit District (☎ 541-687-5555) buses make five trips between downtown Eugene and the airport – trips are timed to meet morning and evening flights.

Bus Ten Greyhound buses a day link Portland to Eugene ($13 one way) and San Francisco. Porter Stage Lines links Eugene to Bend with twice-daily minivan service ($20 one way). The bus depot (☎ 541-344-6265) is at 987 Pearl St.

The Green Tortoise (☎ 800-867-8647) also passes through Eugene on its twice-weekly run up and down the West Coast. The one-way fare to Portland is $10, to San Francisco, $39. Be sure to call for reservations and pick-up times.

Train Amtrak offers once daily service north to Portland and south to Sacramento on the *Coast Starlight*. The *Cascadia* provides daily express service north to Portland and Seattle. In addition, three daily Amtrak Thruway buses travel between Eugene and Portland to help make other rail connections. The one-way fare from Eugene to Portland is $24; between Eugene and San Francisco it's $104. The Amtrak station (☎ 541-687-1383) is at E 4th Ave and Willamette St.

Car Avis (☎ 541-688-9053), Budget (☎ 541-688-1229) and National Car Rental (☎ 541-688-8161) each have an office at Eugene airport. Enterprise (☎ 541-344-2020), 810 W 6th, has an office downtown.

Getting Around
Although not large, downtown Eugene can be an infuriating place to drive around. An extensive one-way grid was imposed on the city during the city's urban-renewal heyday; little subsequent growth has justified the tangled mess that it created.

Bike riders should rejoice. Not only are they generally free of the maddening one-way street system, but many Eugene streets also have room for bike lanes.

The Lane Transit District (LTD) (☎ 541-687-5555) is the local bus company; fares are $1. For maps and information go to their office at 10th Ave and Willamette St. The main downtown transit station is located between 10th and 11th Aves at Olive St.

Call Emerald Taxi (☎ 541-686-2010) for a cab.

OREGON

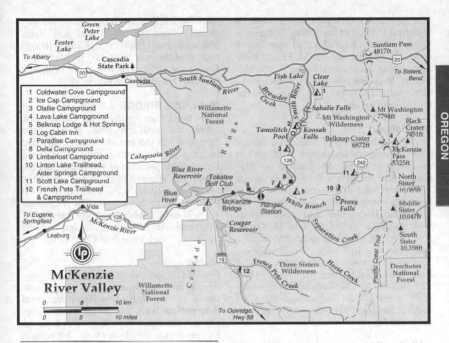

1 Coldwater Cove Campground
2 Ice Cap Campground
3 Olallie Campground
4 Lava Lake Campground
5 Belknap Lodge & Hot Springs
6 Log Cabin Inn
7 Paradise Campground
8 Delta Campground
9 Limberlost Campground
10 Linton Lake Trailhead,
   Alder Springs Campground
11 Scott Lake Campground
12 French Pete Trailhead
   & Campground

McKenzie
River Valley

McKenzie River Valley

The single name 'McKenzie' identifies a river, a mountain pass, a historic and spectacular highway, and one of Oregon's most unique and wondrous natural areas. Great fishing, easy hikes and rafting trips make this one of the state's premier recreation areas.

The McKenzie River is one of Oregon's most beautiful and mysterious rivers. A creature of the area's relatively recent volcanic history, the river plays hide and seek with the lava flows that cross its path. Over the course of millennia, waves of molten rock rolled down the flanks of the Cascades, damming the McKenzie to form the lakes and marvelous waterfalls that characterize its upper reaches. In other areas, however, the river seeps through the porous

lava, only to reappear as bubbling springs farther downstream. A national recreation trail opens the richly forested upper reaches of the McKenzie River to hikers.

One of the state's most astonishing drives follows a tributary of the McKenzie River through a heavily glaciated valley, up a hair-raising escarpment to McKenzie Pass, where the central Oregon volcanic peaks loom across barren lava flows – some only several hundred years old.

While the McKenzie River area is an easy day trip from either Eugene or the Bend area, riverside campgrounds and charming cabin accommodations at McKenzie Bridge will tempt the traveler to make the McKenzie River the focus of a longer visit.

The region is named for Donald McKenzie, an early fur trapper with JJ Astor's Pacific Fur Company. McKenzie explored the upper Willamette Valley in 1812, in the process noting the river that would come to bear his name. After gold was discovered in central Oregon in the 1860s, Willamette Valley residents hacked a trail over barren lava flows near the present McKenzie Pass. Astonishing as it seems today – the Mc-Kenzie Pass Hwy is hardly a thorough-fare – sufficient traffic once frequented the trail to justify a toll station.

Orientation

The little community of McKenzie Bridge offers accommodations and food, and is usually considered the gateway to Mc-Kenzie area recreation. McKenzie Bridge is 50 miles east of Eugene on Hwy 126. Four miles east of McKenzie Bridge, the McKenzie Hwy splits and continues as Hwy 242 (also called the Old McKenzie Hwy) over the Cascades toward McKenzie Pass on its way to Sisters, 34 miles distant. This road is closed in the winter, usually from November to June. The rest of Hwy 126 follows the McKenzie River valley north, joins US 20 and crosses the Cascades at Santiam Pass (which remains open year-round).

Information

For information on the McKenzie River area, contact the McKenzie River Chamber of Commerce (☎ 541-896-3330) at PO Box 1117, Leaburg, OR 97489. There's a rack of brochures and a post office at Myers General Store & Liquor Shop, 51748 Cascade St, in Blue River.

For information on recreation in the area contact the McKenzie River Ranger Station (☎ 541-822-3381), 57600 McKenzie Hwy, McKenzie Bridge. The ranger station has good information on mountain biking and hiking trails. They also issue overnight permits for camping in the Three Sisters Wilderness and sell trailhead permits.

Getting There & Away

The Eugene bus system, Lane Transit District (☎ 541-687-5555), provides service to McKenzie Bridge via bus No 91. On weekdays there are two early-morning buses, one afternoon and one late-afternoon bus departing from Eugene's downtown bus mall for McKenzie Bridge. On Saturday there is one morning and one late-afternoon bus. Trips to McKenzie Bridge take slightly over an hour. In McKenzie Bridge the bus can be met at the bridge or the ranger station. The fare is $1.

McKENZIE BRIDGE & HWY 126

Little more than a general store and a few cabins, the small crossroads of McKenzie Bridge offers the traveler food, drink and lodging in a stunning physical setting. Between the junction of Hwys 242 and 20, Hwy 126 follows the main branch of the McKenzie River north through a steep valley to the river's source. The McKenzie River National Recreation Trail skirts the river between McKenzie Bridge and the trailhead, 2 miles north of Clear Lake.

Hiking

One of Oregon's showcase Wild & Scenic Rivers, the McKenzie River is graced with the 26½-mile **McKenzie River National Recreation Trail**, which follows the here-again, gone-again cascading river from its inception to the hamlet of McKenzie Bridge. Access points appear at several places along Hwy 126, so hikers can select whatever portion of the trail suits their schedule or fancy.

Starting at the trailhead near **Fish Lake**, there are nice day hikes downstream to **Clear Lake**. Here the trail divides. To the east, the trail passes the large spring of an underground river, several groves of old-growth forest and an extensive lava flow to arrive at Coldwater Cove Campground. To the west, the path follows the lake past Clear Water Resort, where food, boat rentals and lodging are available.

For day hikers, access to another easy series of trails begins at the **Sahalie Falls**, where a footbridge crosses the upper falls viewpoint to join the McKenzie River Trail for a 2-mile stroll to Carmen Reservoir past **Koosah Falls**. On the highway side of the river is the more developed and shorter **Waterfall Trail**, which links Sahalie with Koosah Falls. Parts of this trail are wheelchair accessible.

For nearly 4 miles, the McKenzie disappears between Carmen Reservoir and Tamolitch Pool. Long-distance hikers are treated to a lush growth of cedar and fir trees along the dry river bed.

Day hikes can also reach stunning **Tamolitch Pool** from the south. Turn off Hwy 126 at Trail Bridge Reservoir, but follow the gravel road to the right, past the maintenance buildings to the McKenzie River Trailhead. The 2-mile trail passes through a mossy lava flow before coming upon the mighty McKenzie River surging up in a cliff-lined bowl of rock (Tamolitch means 'bucket' in Chinookan). Eerily calm and emerald, **Tamolitch Pool** is an unforgettably magical site.

Although lower portions of the McKenzie River Trail are open to mountain bikes, the trail is narrow and steep (certainly across the most recent lava flows), and offers bikers a fairly joyless challenge.

Fishing

The McKenzie River is one of the most storied fishing streams in Oregon. The favorite quarry of anglers is the redside trout, a variant of the rainbow whose sides are flecked with orange spots. The best fishing water is west of Blue River, where, as the river slows down, there are more pools and deeper water. Access to the river along this stretch is fairly restricted, however, as it passes through private land. Various state and county parks provide the most dependable access. Fishing for summer steelhead is also good along this stretch.

A summer release of hatchery rainbows between Belknap Hot Springs and McKenzie Bridge means that fishing is good throughout the Willamette National Forest lands, where frequent campgrounds and streamside trails allow easy access.

A number of restrictions apply to fishing at various places along the McKenzie River, so check with local tackle shops or the Fish & Wildlife office (☎ 541-726-3515) in Springfield for current regulations. In general, no rainbow or redside longer than 15 inches may be kept, in order to maintain natural propagation.

Various outfitters in the Eugene area offer guided fishing trips on the McKenzie River. Contact Justus Outfitters (☎ 541-342-1755), 1090 Snell St, Eugene, for information on year-round fishing trips in drift boats, instruction, and equipment rental. Jim's Oregon Whitewater (see Rafting, below) also does fishing excursions.

Rafting

White-water trips are popular on the McKenzie River's Class I to III rapids from April to October. The following outfitters run half- and full-day excursions. Jim's Oregon Whitewater (☎ 541-822-6003, 800-254-5467), 56324 McKenzie Hwy, in McKenzie Bridge, offers both rafting and fishing packages. Full-day raft trips with The Oregon Paddler (☎ 541-741-8661, 800-267-6848) include lunch at the Log Cabin Inn.

Half-day trips are generally around $50, and full-day excursions range between $60 and $75.

Golf

You wouldn't expect to find a first-class golf course out in the woods along the McKenzie River, but Tokatee Golf Club (☎ 541-822-3220, 800-452-6376), 54947 McKenzie Hwy, 3 miles west of McKenzie Bridge on Hwy 126, is reckoned to be one of the toughest golf courses in Oregon and has been repeatedly ranked by *Golf Digest* as one of the top 25 public courses in the nation. It winds along foothills, through forests and past streams and lakes, and the capricious valley winds are as much a part of the challenge as the topography of the course itself.

Places to Stay

Camping Between Blue River and the junction of US 20, USFS campgrounds appear regularly along the McKenzie River; expect pit toilets. About 3 miles east of McKenzie Bridge, the *Paradise Campground* offers 64 campsites in a beautiful riverside grove. *Delta Campground*, 3 miles east of Blue River near Cougar Reservoir, has 39 campsites and a short nature trail through the woods that identifies trees and plants and discusses forest ecology. Summertime campfire programs are held here Saturday nights at 7 pm. Sites at either cost $10.

You can camp on the quiet side of Clear Lake at *Coldwater Cove Campground*, 18 miles northeast of McKenzie Bridge on Hwy 126. A mile downriver is *Ice Cap Campground* on the shores of Carmen Reservoir, where there's good trout fishing. Ice Cap is also close to hiking trails leading to spectacular waterfalls. *Olallie Campground* is another nice riverside campground, 11 miles northeast of McKenzie Bridge on Hwy 126. Fees at USFS campgrounds are $6 to $10 per night.

Motels *Sleepy Hollow Motel* (☎ 541-822-3805), 54791 McKenzie Hwy, presents a standard motor inn, with singles/doubles at $43/48. The Sleepy Hollow is just next to Tokatee Golf Club.

Lodges Most lodging in the mountain community of McKenzie Bridge is in freestanding cabins, most of which are charmingly furnished and completely modernized. Overlooking the McKenzie River, the historic *Log Cabin Inn* (☎ 541-822-3432, 800-355-3432), 56483 McKenzie Hwy, is a handsome old lodge built in 1906. Its old-fashioned woodsy charm is accentuated by the good food served in its wood-paneled restaurant. Nine cabins line the river behind the lodge, each with a porch and fireplace; rates begin at $75. Riverfront teepees start at $45.

The *Horse Creek Lodge* (☎ 541-822-3243), 56228 Delta Drive, offers lodging for groups in the four-bedroom Delta House ($218), or in individual cabins (starting at $58). The *Country Place* (☎ 541-822-6008), 56245 Delta Drive, offers three cabins on the river, ranging from $68 to $81 a night, each with a full kitchen and living area; a four-bedroom house is also available.

Just off Hwy 126 on Belknap Springs Rd is the *Belknap Lodge & Hot Springs* (☎ 541-822-3512). Rooms are available in

the lodge itself ($60 to $90) or in cabins ($35). Campsites are also available. Nonguests can relax in the mineral pool for $3.

Resorts Four miles south of the junction of Hwys 20 and 126 is *Clear Lake Resort*, on Hwy 126 (no phone), which offers rustic cabins on the shores of 200-foot-deep Clear Lake. It's a lovely spot except for the gasoline generators. A basic cabin (sans bathroom) starts at $24. Rowboat rentals and a cafe are pluses. Reservations are recommended and can only be made by mail – contact the Santiam Fish & Game Association, PO Box 500, Lebanon, OR 97355.

Places to Eat
Just north of Blue River is the *Blue Heron Bakery* (☎ 541-822-8021), 52970 McKenzie Hwy, a great place for homemade cinnamon rolls, bagels and hamburger buns. It's only open Wednesday to Saturday; watch the roadside carefully for their small sandwich board sign. About 3 miles west of McKenzie Bridge is the *Rustic Skillet* (☎ 541-822-3400), 54771 McKenzie Hwy, a family restaurant offering three meals a day; they maintain an understandable pride in their homemade pies. The dining room at the *Log Cabin Inn* (☎ 541-822-3432), 56483 McKenzie Hwy, is charming and old-fashioned. Steaks and prime rib lead the menu, though there are unusual and intriguing dishes involving venison and buffalo as well as local trout. Dinners range from $14 to $18, and it's also open for lunch.

**McKENZIE PASS
& THE OLD McKENZIE HWY**
From its departure off Hwy 126, the old, historic leg of the McKenzie Hwy (Hwy 242) up Lost Creek Valley to the lava fields of 5325-foot-high McKenzie Pass offers stunning views of the Cascade Range, intriguing hikes and access to one of the largest and most recent lava flows in the continental USA. Even with such scenic competition, you're still likely to

remember the McKenzie Hwy itself – one local observer mused that the road was 'seemingly engineered by a madman.' From the pass area, Hwy 242 suddenly drops 4000 feet down the glaciated face of Lost Creek Valley, along a series of astonishingly narrow hairpin curves. If you plan to travel Hwy 242, make sure your brakes are in good shape. Trailer travel is not suggested, and the pass is closed in the winter.

Dee Wright Observatory

Perched on a swell of frozen rock, this fortress of lava built by the CCC surveys a desolate volcanic landscape. Its arched windows frame 11 volcanic peaks. Built in the 1930s, the observatory was named for a USFS trail guide. At its base begins the half-mile **Lava River Trail**, an interpretive trail explaining the volcanic formations. It's near milepost 77, about 22 miles east of the Hwy 126 junction.

Hiking

The **Upper & Lower Proxy Falls** tumble over glacier-carved walls to disappear into lava flows. An easy 1.2-mile loop hike leads to these delicate but popular falls. The trail begins directly east of milepost 64, about 12 miles east of McKenzie Bridge.

Enjoy a close-up view of a lava dam from **Linton Lake Trail**. The easy 2.8-mile trail begins across from Alder Springs Campground and leads to lava-dammed Linton Lake. In the distance, Linton Falls roars over the valley edge (no trail leads to the falls) and tumbles to the lake.

The subterranean waters of Lost Valley collect and surge to the surface in the lower valley. Directly east of milepost 59, turn north into a large clearing. Walk 100 yards along an informal trail to a lovely spot where the creek surfaces at **Lost Valley Spring**.

The Pacific Crest Trail crosses McKenzie Pass a half mile west of the Dee Wright Observatory parking lot. It's 2½ miles across lava flows to **Little Belknap** and **Belknap Craters**. You'll follow a good trail north along an easy grade, but be aware that there's no water or shelter along the trail. On a hot day, the hike can be oppressive.

A popular half-day hike leaves from Scott Lake Campground, 6 miles west of the pass. The trail winds past several small lakes (which act as reflecting ponds for the Three Sisters peaks) and on to **Hand Lake**. It's an easy 3-mile stroll there and back.

Five miles west of McKenzie Pass is the beginning of the **Obsidian Trail**, at Frog Camp Campground. This is one of the gentlest and most popular entrances into the Three Sisters Wilderness. A special 'limited-use' permit from the forest service is now required to visit this area. Permits are available up to 30 days in advance from the McKenzie River Ranger Station (☎ 541-822-3381). Day hikers might consider a 2½-mile hike through thick forest to reach a 50-foot-high lava flow. From the top is a sudden and exhilarating view directly onto the **Three Sisters**. The trail continues past Obsidian Cliffs to join the Pacific Crest Trail in another 1½ miles.

McKenzie Pass

McKenzie Pass was first traversed by white settlers in 1862, when Felix Scott and a party of 250 men, on their way to the Central Oregon gold fields, blazed a trail up to and across the area now known as McKenzie Pass. By 1872 John Craig had scouted a slightly different trail across the lava fields and opened a toll road from McKenzie Bridge to Sisters ($2 per wagon, $1 per horseman, and only 5¢ per sheep). Craig worked to secure a US mail delivery route for the McKenzie Pass trail, linking Eugene and Prineville. He started across the pass with Christmas mail from McKenzie Bridge in December, 1877, but never appeared at Camp Polk (near Sisters). His frozen body was found early the next year. Near the pass, a historical monument commemorates his death. ∎

OREGON

Places to Stay
Facilities are fairly basic at nearby camp-grounds. *Scott Lake Campground* offers pretty lakeside sites for tent campers, but no running water. A mile east of McKenzie Pass is *Lava Camp Lake Campground*, with similarly informal amenities. Mosquitos are voracious here until August.

Down in Lost Creek Valley, *Limberlost Campground* is just 5 miles east of McKenzie Bridge, on Hwy 242. The campground sits in a nice wooded location, near the springs of Lost Creek.

THREE SISTERS WILDERNESS
This 580-sq-mile wilderness area spans the Cascade Range, with access both from the Bend area to the east and the McKenzie River area to the west.

The focal points of the wilderness area are the glaciered Three Sisters, three recent volcanic peaks, each topping 10,000 feet in height. The wilderness takes in widely varying types of environments, though most of the wilderness accessible from the west side is dense, old-growth forest coursed with strong rivers and streams. It's also a haven for wildlife – Oregon's small population of wolverines live here, as do cougars and black bears. The area is traversed by the Pacific Crest Trail, which is easily accessed at McKenzie Pass.

Other trails lead up stream valleys to lakes and views of the peaks, and are accessed by USFS Rd 19, also known as the Aufderheide National Scenic Byway. One popular trailhead on this route is at the French Pete Campground, where a trail leads up **French Pete Creek** to Wolverine Meadows through old-growth forests.

For more information, contact the McKenzie River Ranger Station (☎ 541-822-3381), 57600 McKenzie Hwy in McKenzie Bridge. The best map of the area is the *Three Sisters Wilderness Map* published by Geo-Graphics, available at most local outdoor stores or by writing to 18860 SW Alderwood Drive, Beaverton, OR 97006. For details on hiking trails from the Bend area, see Three Sisters Wilderness in the Central Oregon chapter.

Upper Willamette River Valley

Southeast from Eugene, the Willamette River leaves its wide valley and becomes a rushing mountain river. That is, when it isn't impounded by dams. The reservoirs at Dexter and Lowell dam the main stem of the Willamette River, and above Oakridge the Middle Fork of the Willamette is also dammed. Only the North Fork of the Willamette runs unimpeded from its headwaters at Waldo Lake. A 65-mile National Forest Scenic Byway follows USFS Rd 19 along the North Fork. Forests here are extremely thick and home to such rare species as the spotted owl and wolverine. The road eventually emerges north near McKenzie Bridge.

Traffic is heavy along steeply pitched Hwy 58. You'll be glad for the opportunity to turn off the road and take in the sight of something besides a hurtling log truck. The scenery along most of the route consists of dense Douglas fir forests and the now usual handmaiden of these groves, clear-cuts. At the crest of the Cascades, near Willamette Pass, are a number of beautiful lakes and Oregon's second-highest waterfall, Salt Creek Falls. A popular hot springs bubbles up just beside the road at another point.

The only town along Hwy 58 is Oakridge (population 3200), a scruffy logging town with basic services for travelers.

Orientation & Information
Hwy 58 follows the Willamette River from near Eugene to tie into US 97 south of Bend. The entire route is 85 miles long; Oakridge is 35 miles from Eugene, Willamette Pass is another 52 miles from Eugene.

The Oakridge-Westfir Chamber of Commerce (☎ 541-782-4146) can be reached at PO Box 217, Oakridge, OR 97463.

For information about the Willamette National Forest and the local wilderness areas, contact the Oakridge Ranger Station (☎ 541-782-2291), 46375 Hwy 58.

Places to Stay

Camping Sites at the following USFS campgrounds range from $8 to $12. Six miles northwest of Oakridge on Hwy 58, along the Willamette River is *Black Canyon Campground*, with 72 sites. Drinking water and vault toilets are provided. A mile closer to Oakridge is *Shady Dell Campground*, with nine sites and similar facilities.

Ten miles east of Oakridge, a favorite campground is *Blue Pool*. Good access to fishing on Salt Creek and to McCredie Hot Springs make this a popular place on weekends. Running water and vault toilets are provided. At *Waldo Lake* there are three lovely campgrounds with flush toilets (to protect the lake). Between Odell and Crescent Lakes, on the east slopes of the Cascades, there are 11 public campgrounds.

B&Bs A stone's throw from Oregon's longest covered bridge (the Office Bridge), the *Westfir Lodge* (☎ 541-782-3103), 47365 1st St, Westfir, was formerly the executive offices of a logging company. However, the Craftsman-style building was converted into a spacious B&B in the early 1990s. Four guest rooms share two bathrooms in this handsome, rambling building, and an English-style flower garden makes the side patio a charming place to relax. Rates are $55 a night.

Hotels Oakridge offers just about the only point of civilization along this route. Motels can be busy during the ski season, so you may want to call ahead. Rooms at the *Ridgeview Motel* (☎ 541-782-3430), 47465 Hwy 58, and the *Arbor Inn* (☎ 541-782-2611, 800-505-9047) are $30/34. The *Best Western Oakridge Inn* (☎ 541-782-2212), 47445 Hwy 58, is Oakridge's most pleasant lodging, and offers rooms at $58/67.

Willamette Pass Inn (☎ 541-433-2211), 7 miles east of the pass near Crescent Lake, is the closest motel to the ski area. Rooms have fireplaces and kitchenettes and cost $48/58. There's also a free shuttle to the pass.

OREGON

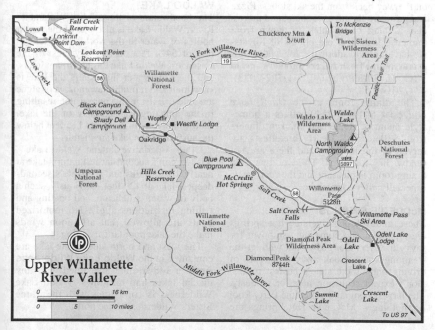

Upper Willamette River Valley

Lodges *Odell Lake Lodge* (☎ 541-443-2540), 6 miles east of Willamette Pass, offers a variety of lodging options. Rooms in the lodge range from $40 to $52; all have private bathrooms. There are also 13 cabins scattered along the lakefront, each with bathrooms, fully equipped kitchens and wood-burning stoves. Four-person cabins range from $65 to $85; six- and eight-person cabins range between $90 and $140. One cabin sleeps 16 for $210.

The lodge is busy during ski season, so early reservations are a must. The mailing address of the lodge is PO Box 72, Crescent Lake, OR 97425.

The lodge also offers a full range of rental equipment, from cross-country skis, mountain bikes, canoes and motorboats to snowshoes.

Places to Eat
Sort of a logging museum-cum-restaurant *Timber Jim's Pizza* (☎ 541-782-4310), 47527 Hwy 58, is a popular place to stop on the way back from the ski slopes. Pizza and pasta are the favorites here, and there's also a salad bar. Tables are hewn from immense logs, and old photos of forests-we-have-known adorn the log walls. For espresso and fresh bakery products, go to *Miss McGillicuty's* (☎ 541-782-2033), 47772 Hwy 58.

The dining room at the *Odell Lake Lodge* (☎ 541-433-2540) offers a home-style menu of steaks and chicken dinners from $10 to $12. Hearty breakfasts are served in the morning and there are hot sandwiches for lunch. The wood-paneled dining room is pleasant and the food tasty, especially after a long hike.

McCREDIE SPRINGS
These undeveloped riverside hot springs are a popular and convenient stopover for savvy travelers along Hwy 58, who let the steaming waters soak away the rigors of driving one of the state's busiest routes. Don't expect seclusion here, or modesty. The largest pool isn't called the Party Pool for nothing – McCredie Hot Springs are

popular with U of O students from Eugene, especially on weekends.

McCredie Hot Springs are 45 miles east of Eugene on Hwy 58. Look for a large, unpaved parking area just past the turn off for the Blue Pool Campground. Informal trails lead to Salt Creek and the hot springs, 100 yards distant.

SALT CREEK FALLS
Twenty miles east of Oakridge, this roaring giant of a falls is, at 286 feet, Oregon's second highest. Easy access from Hwy 58 makes it a must-see. All-ability trails lead out to the top of the falls, where you can crane your neck over the edge to see the trails of mist strike the mossy rocks far below. Standing just feet from the edge of a major waterfall is an uncanny, rather disquieting experience. Another trail leads to more distant viewpoints and eventually to the base of the falls. A picnic area and flush toilets are also available.

WALDO LAKE
The headwaters of the mighty Willamette River, Waldo Lake is also one of the purest bodies of water in the world. At an elevation of 5414 feet on the very crest of the Cascades, Waldo Lake has no stream inlets, and the only water that enters the lake is snowmelt and rainfall. Few mosses or algae are able to exist in this pure water, resulting in the amazing transparency of the lake. Studies indicate that objects 115 feet below the surface of the lake are visible.

Other superlatives attend Waldo Lake – it is Oregon's second-largest natural lake at nearly 10 sq miles and the state's second-deepest lake at 420 feet. Obviously, such a body of water is delicate, and boating and fishing restrictions apply. No motorized boats are allowed, but afternoon winds make the lake popular for sailing.

The west and north side of the lake are contained in the **Waldo Lake Wilderness Area**, a 148-sq-mile area filled with tiny glacial lakes and meadows. Waldo Lake Wilderness is contiguous with the Three Sisters Wilderness to the north.

Three USFS campgrounds flank the eastern half of the lake and hiking trails lead off into the wilderness. The 20-mile **Waldo Lake Trail** circles the lake. A less ambitious hike leads from North Waldo Campground to the outlet of the Willamette River, a 3.4-mile one-way hike that edges the lake and sandy swimming beaches. Make a loop trail by returning via Rigdon Lakes, which lie at the base of a volcanic butte.

Because of the lake's elevation, trails aren't free of snow until June, and are closed in October. In the interim, the lake and the surrounding area become the province of **cross-country skiers** who leave from the plowed Gold Lake Sno-Park area on Hwy 58.

For more information on the Waldo Lake Wilderness Area, contact the Willamette National Forest office (☎ 541-465-6521), 211 E 7th Ave, Eugene, OR 97440, or stop at the ranger station in Oakridge (see Orientation & Information above).

WILLAMETTE PASS SKI AREA

Although the Willamette Pass Ski Area (☎ 541-484-5030, 541-345-7669 for snow conditions) gets a lot of snow during winter, much of it is pretty wet. The ski area makes up for it by offering some of the steepest slopes around – US Olympic speed skiers practice here. The majority of the slopes are rated intermediate to advanced, and there's a vertical drop of 1563 feet with 29 runs. Snowboarders have specific runs, and there's a groomed 12-mile, cross-country trail. Lift tickets are $25.

ODELL LAKE

Immediately on the eastern slope of Willamette Pass is beautiful Odell Lake, resting in a steep glacial basin. Odell Lake is but one of many lakes in the area. A rustic lodge and campgrounds ring nearby Crescent Lake, while more remote Summit Lake is preferred by purists. In winter Odell Lake becomes an especially popular place for cross-country skiing.

Odell, Crescent and Summit Lakes flank the **Diamond Peak Wilderness Area**, a 126-sq-mile preserve of lakes, craggy mountains and deep forests. Hiking trails lead into this relatively unexplored wilderness from lakeside campgrounds. A popular hike from the Odell Lake Lodge leads 3.8 miles to **Fawn Lake**, below two rugged peaks. From the Trapper Creek Campground, energetic hikers should consider the 4.3-mile one-way hike to **Yoran Lake** to reach a great view of 8744-foot Diamond Peak. The Pacific Crest Trail winds through the high country in the wilderness. Pick up the trail at Willamette Pass and wind through old forests to Midnight Lake, an easy 3.3-mile one-way hike.

OREGON

Southern Oregon

Some of the state's most magical sites are contained within the valleys of the Rogue and Umpqua Rivers and the Klamath Basin, including Crater Lake National Park. Magic of another sort takes place at Ashland, home of the Oregon Shakespeare Festival.

The Rogue River, known for its challenging white-water rafting, rises from the flanks of Crater Lake before plunging oceanward in a spectacular mountain-lined gorge, and the brooding and quixotic North fork of the Umpqua River draws in anglers from around the world to match wits with steelhead trout, the monarch of Oregon rivers.

The Siskiyou Mountains expose some of Oregon's oldest and most puzzling geology, rich in vivid peridotite and serpentinite rock that originally formed as ocean bedrock. Here, orange-barked madrona, scrub oak and brushy manzanita replace the thick fir forests of the north. Cougars are more common in the south than anywhere else in Oregon, and another rare species is occasionally sighted – the legendary Sasquatch, or Big Foot (see the Big Foot Territory sidebar in the North Cascades chapter).

The communities of southern Oregon differ sharply in their genesis from the communities along the Willamette River. The Oregon Trail pioneers who settled the Willamette Valley were usually well-off New Englanders, whereas the settlers of southern Oregon were largely displaced southerners and Confederate soldiers migrating westward at the vanguard of gold rushes.

This mountainous region remained much more socially conservative than the rest of Oregon and developed a highly autonomous sensibility. But the traditional insularity was broken in the 1960s when young people moved here, setting up farms and communes as part of the 'back to the land' movement.

Southern Oregon's social conservatism and homogeneity are today both challenged and triumphant. The Oregon Citizens Alliance (OCA), an arch-conservative religious movement, is a phenomenon of this region. However, the OCA is currently finding a statewide audience even as southern Oregon fills up with educated professionals, displaced Californians, actors and wine-growers.

Getting There & Away

Air The Rogue Valley International Airport is north of Medford, off Table Rock Rd. Flights link Medford to Portland and San Francisco; United Express and Horizon are the primary carriers.

Cascade Airport Shuttle (☎ 541-488-1998) services Ashland and costs $10 per person, with a $16 minimum. Reservations are required.

Car The major car-rental companies, Hertz (☎ 541-773-4293), Avis (☎ 541-773-3003) and Budget (☎ 541-773-7023), are represented at the airport.

Road & Weather Conditions Siskiyou Pass on I-5 between Oregon and California is known for its treacherous winter driving conditions. Call the state road report (☎ 541-976-7277) if there's any question about road conditions.

ASHLAND

Population 16,775

Home to the internationally renowned Oregon Shakespeare Festival (OSF), Ashland is the cultural center of southern Oregon, and one of the most pleasant towns in the state.

Theater, B&Bs and food dominate life here – 350,000 people come to Ashland annually to attend the productions at the OSF's three venues, which include a large outdoor theater dedicated to Elizabethan

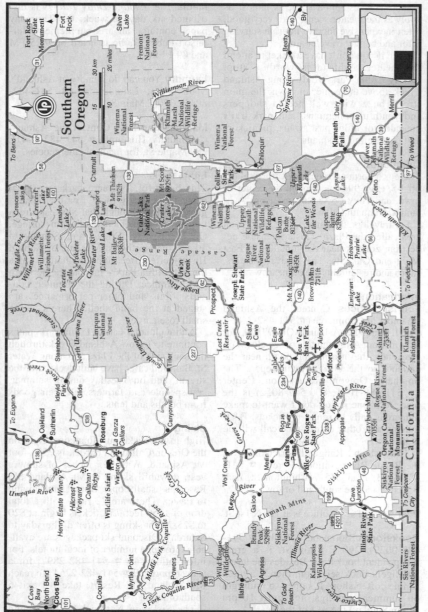

OREGON

drama. The restaurant scene is almost as lively as the theater scene, with very good, often inexpensive food to nourish starving actor and budget traveler alike.

Even if you don't have a ticket to attend the theater, Ashland is worth a stop. Lovely Lithia Park winds along Ashland Creek above the center of town, the main streets buzz with well-heeled shoppers and youthful bohemians, and park trails meander for miles past swans, picnickers and declaiming thespians.

Orientation

There is a north and south exit for Ashland off I-5. Hwy 99 runs through the center of town, and Hwy 66 winds east from Ashland to Klamath Falls.

For travelers, the center of Ashland is an area called the Plaza. This streamside pedestrian zone is near the junction of East Main and Oak Sts. The festival theaters, shops and restaurants are all nearby.

Information

Tourist Offices Contact the Ashland Chamber of Commerce (☎ 541-482-3486), 110 E Main St, Ashland, OR 97520, for information. Although this office closes on weekends, the information booth near the entrance to the Plaza remains open. The Southern Oregon Reservation Center (☎ 541-488-1011, 800-547-8052) is the place to phone if you don't want to make numerous calls to round up tickets, B&B lodging and other extras. One call will do it all.

The Ashland Ranger District office of the Rogue River National Forest (☎ 541-482-3333) is at 645 Washington St, near I-5 exit 14 at the south end of town.

Post Ashland's post office is at 120 N 1st St.

Bookstores Bloomsbury Books (☎ 541-488-0029), 290 E Main St, is a great independent bookstore. Besides the large, intelligent book selection, there's a mezzanine coffee shop. It's open to midnight on summer evenings, and until 10 pm (9 pm Sunday) the rest of the year.

Media The *Ashland Daily Tidings* is distributed six days a week; the Thursday paper contains an arts supplement. Jefferson Public Radio is heard on 91.5 FM and 89.1 FM.

Laundry You can do laundry at Ashland's Main Street Laundromat (☎ 541-482-8042), 370 E Main St.

Medical Services Contact the Ashland Community Hospital (☎ 541-482-2441), 280 Maple St, for medical emergencies.

Lithia Park

This beautiful, 100-acre park is a great place for a shady picnic, or for theatergoers to plow through that Shakespearean tragedy they avoided reading in college. On Wednesday, Friday and Sunday at 10 am, the Northwest Museum of Natural History offers free, hourlong nature walks through Lithia Park – meet at the northern park entrance. During the summer, concerts, films and other performances are staged at the band shell. There's also a small rose garden.

Although not a part of Lithia Park, paths continue to follow Ashland Creek through the back side of the Plaza and along Water St. Bars and cafes have built decks over the stream, and on Tuesday during summer, craftspeople and farmers sell their goods from booths and tents.

Skiing

High in the Siskiyou Mountains, right on the Oregon/California border, is 7533-foot Mt Ashland. With 325 inches of snow a year, downhill skiing at Mt Ashland Ski Resort is usually open from Thanksgiving to Easter. There are 22 runs, with a total drop of 1150 feet. Lift tickets begin at $20 to $25. Night skiing is offered Thursday to Saturday. Discount ski packages are available through a number of local motels. For information call ☎ 541-482-2897; for a snow report call ☎ 541-482-2754. To reach Mt Ashland Ski Resort, take I-5 exit 6 south of town.

The Siskiyou National Forest around

OREGON

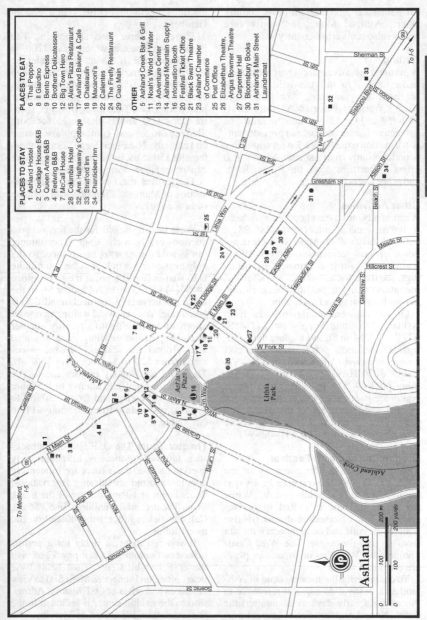

PLACES TO STAY
1 Ashland Hostel
2 Coolidge House B&B
3 Queen Anne B&B
4 Redwing B&B
7 McCall House
28 Columbia Hotel
32 Ann Hathaway's Cottage
33 Stratford Inn
34 Chanticleer Inn

PLACES TO EAT
6 Thai Pepper
8 Il Giardino
9 Bento Express
10 Brothers' Delicatessen
12 Big Town Hero
15 Alex's Plaza Restaraunt
17 Ashland Bakery & Cafe
18 Chateaulin
19 Macaroni's
22 Calientes
24 The Firefly Restaraunt
29 Ciao Main

OTHER
5 Ashland Creek Bar & Grill
11 Noah's World of Water
13 Adventure Center
14 Ashland Mountain Supply
16 Information Booth
20 Festival Ticket Office
21 Black Swan Theatre
23 Ashland Chamber
  of Commerce
25 Post Office
26 Elizabethan Theatre,
  Angus Bowmer Theatre
27 Carpenter Hall
30 Bloomsbury Books
31 Ashland's Main Street
  Laundromat

Ashland

Mt Ashland is a favorite for cross-country skiers. Ashland Mountain Supply (see below) also rents cross-country skis.

Rafting

A number of adventure sport outfitters make it easy to raft the wild rivers of southern Oregon from Ashland. Both Noah's World of Water (☎ 541-488-2811, 800-858-2811), 53 N Main St, and the Adventure Center (see below) provide half-day trips down the Rogue River, with three departures daily from Ashland. Noah's also offers longer trips down the Rogue River and other rivers in the area.

Other Activities

A raft of adventure travel options is offered by the Adventure Center (☎ 541-488-2819, 800-444-2819), 40 N Main St, a clearing-house of local recreation outfitters. While white-water rafting dominates the offerings, see them for adventures as various as mountain-biking trips, horseback riding, hot-air ballooning and spelunking.

Or you can rent mountain bikes from Ashland Mountain Supply (☎ 541-488-2749), 31 N Main St, and explore the countryside. Ashland's public, nine-hole golf course is called Oak Knoll (☎ 541-482-4311), 3070 Hwy 66. The public swimming pool (☎ 541-488-0313) and tennis courts are in Hunter Park, at the corner of Holmes and Hunter Sts. In the winter you can go ice-skating in Lithia Park at the Darex Family Ice Rink (☎ 541-488-9189).

Oregon Shakespeare Festival

The fifth-largest theater company in the USA, the Oregon Shakespeare Festival is highly respected and wildly popular. While the repertoire here is rooted in Shakespearean and Elizabethan drama, it also features revivals and contemporary theater from around the world. The West Coast premieres of West End or Broadway plays are often in Ashland.

To characterize the theater scene in Ashland as a 'festival' is a quaint reference to the troupe's early days as a summertime event. Nowadays, the official festival pro-

ductions begin in February and end in October.

There are three festival theaters. The Elizabethan Theatre, which seats 1200, is an outdoor stage; it can get chilly under the stars, so dress prudently. Open from June to October only, this theater shows almost exclusively Shakespearean productions or period tragedies. The Angus Bowmer Theatre seats 600 and is the stage for both Shakespearean and contemporary drama and comedy. The Black Swan, a small theater with 150 seats, is the playhouse for more experimental and intimate works.

The festival theaters are near the intersection of Main and Pioneer Sts, at the base of Lithia Park.

Tickets Getting tickets for the festival productions can be a challenge. The summer run is sold out months in advance, so the only chance to get tickets at the last minute is to wait in line at 6 pm at the ticket office (☎ 541-482-4331), 15 S Pioneer St, in the theater courtyard, when unclaimed tickets go on sale. You can avoid waiting in line all afternoon by picking up a priority number first thing in the morning. You can also wait around for scalpers. Ticket prices range from $20 to $33; kids get 25% off. There are no Monday performances. The box office is open 9:30 am to 8 or 8:30 pm, Tuesday to Sunday, and from 9:30 am to 5 pm on Monday, from February 17 to November 2.

Theater Tours The OSF also offers backstage tours of the theaters. Like seemingly everything else, these tours are immensely popular, and require advance reservations. Tours begin at 10 am in front of the Black Swan Theatre; adults/children $8.50/$6.30. Call the ticket office for availability and reservations.

If you fail to get a ticket for a performance or the tour, you can pay $2 to visit the OSF Exhibit Center (just behind the ticket office on Pioneer & Main Sts) to view costumes and relics of OSF history. Admission to the exhibit center is included in the backstage tour. It's closed on Monday.

The Festival's Beginnings

The Methodist Church is responsible for an important fixture of life in Ashland. The young town was included in the church's community adult-education program called the Chautauqua Series, an annual event that brought lectures, concerts and theater to far-flung communities. Ashland's Chautauqua Hall was built early in the 20th century, but had deteriorated to a dilapidated wooden shell by the 1930s. Angus Bowmer, a professor of drama at the local college, noted the resemblance of the roofless structure to drawings of Shakespeare's Globe Theatre. He convinced the people of Ashland to sponsor two performances of Shakespeare's plays (and a boxing match – the Bard would have approved) as part of the town's 1935 Fourth of July celebration. The plays proved a great success, and the Oregon Shakespeare Festival was off and running. ∎

OSF Courses & Lectures The Oregon Shakespeare Festival Institute (☎ 541-488-5406) sponsors a number of classes and lectures in conjunction with its productions. The courses range from two-week seminars for high school drama students to symposiums for school and community theater directors, to ticket/lecture packages for five or nine plays. Advance reservations are required.

The institute also sponsors a series of public lectures during summer. Formal lectures on scholarly and dramatic subjects take place on most Fridays and Wednesdays at noon and are delivered by visiting academics, actors and directors. August lectures are augmented by a series of medieval music concerts, held Wednesday and Saturday. Advance tickets are required and are available from the festival box office. Lectures and concerts are held at

Carpenter Hall, at the corner of Pioneer and Hargadine Sts. Admission is $5 to $6 for adults.

A second series of noontime discussions is called Talks in the Park and features festival actors, directors, designers and technical staff. The talks are actually informal question-and-answer sessions and are held, free of charge, on the grounds just outside the Elizabethan Theatre on Sunday, Tuesday and Thursday. Ask at the visitors' center for a 'Festival Noons' schedule.

Southern Oregon State College runs various courses through Elderhostel (☎ 541-552-6378), available to seniors ages 55 and older. The most popular weeklong session is called 'From Script to Stage,' which involves working with actors and directors from the Shakespeare Festival. To register for a course, contact the national Elderhostel office (☎ 617-426-8056) at 75 Federal St, Boston, MA 02110-1941.

Other Special Events

Ashland's biggest festival outside of the summer theater season is the wintertime Festival of Light. Beginning the day after Thanksgiving and continuing through New Year's Day, the festival includes candlelight tours of historic homes, special theater performances and displays of art and holiday lights. Contact the visitors' center for more information.

The opening of the Elizabethan Theatre is the impetus for the Feast of Will. This momentous event, usually held the third Friday of June, is celebrated with bagpipe music and a lively dinner party in Lithia Park. Call the box office (☎ 541-482-4331) to reserve a seat at the table; tickets cost $16.

Places to Stay

On any given summer evening, thousands of people converge on Ashland to see the plays. Don't expect to pull into town and easily find a room. Reservations are absolutely necessary, especially at B&Bs (some won't even take walk-ins).

The easy way around the hassle of finding a room is to contact one of the reservation services and let them do the work. Call the Southern Oregon Reservation Center (☎ 541-488-1011, 800-547-8052) for room reservations, as well as ticket, ski and recreation packages. The Ashland B&B Clearinghouse (☎ 541-488-0338, 800-588-0338) can help you find a room in a B&B and offer suggestions for other lodging options.

The following prices are for the high season; rates can drop by half in the off-season.

Camping The *KOA Glenyan* (☎ 541-482-4138), 5310 Hwy 66, is primarily a shady RV campground with some tent sites, 4 miles out of Ashland near Emigrant Lake. Prices are stiff ($20), facilities pleasant and reservations suggested. The *Emigrant Lake Recreation Area* is a county park and campground alongside the lake. It's a bit more rustic (no hookups), has showers and flush toilets and costs $14 a night. If you're camping out of season, then the *Jackson Hot Springs Resort* (☎ 541-482-3776), just 2 miles north of Ashland on Hwy 99, might be the place for you. Besides grassy camp-sites, the resort offers naturally heated swimming pools and mineral baths. Rates are $10 to 15 a night, and it's $2 to use the hot pools.

Hostels The *Ashland Hostel* (☎ 541-482-9217), 150 N Main St, is a great hostel in a great location. In one of the town's B&B neighborhoods, the hostel is only blocks from downtown, theaters and nightlife. Rates are $13/14 for members/non-members.

B&Bs For many people, staying in Ashland is inseparable from staying in so-called 'English-style' at a B&B inn. At last count, Ashland had about 60 B&Bs, which are similar in name only to their more humble British cousins. Most are magnificent old Victorian homes with two to three luxury bedroom suites. Expect to pay top dollar to stay at these small, exclusive inns, but if sleeping in an antique-filled room followed by a fancy breakfast appeals to you, here's your chance. It's an Ashland tradition.

Use one of the reservation services to shop the options. If you want to make your own reservations, check on the following, as they are convenient to the theaters. The *Queen Anne B&B* (☎ 541-482-0220, 800-460-6818), 125 N Main St, is an 1880 Victorian with rooms starting at $105. The *Redwing B&B* (☎ 541-482-1807, 800-461-6743), 115 N Main St, is an old Craftsman-style home; rooms are $97. *Coolidge House B&B* (☎ 541-482-4721, 800-655-5522), 137 N Main St, is a Victorian with an upper balcony overlooking the town and rooms from $85. The *McCall House* (☎ 541-482-9296), 153 Oak St, is a mansard-roofed Victorian with eight guest rooms, starting at $115. *Ann Hathaway's Cottage* (☎ 541-488-1050, 800-643-4434), 586 E Main St, is a fancifully-named old boarding house with six rooms at $105 to $160. The *Chanticleer Inn* (☎ 541-482-1919, 800-898-1950), 120 Gresham St, is another Craftsman-style home with six bedrooms. Rooms range from $125 to $160 and most have private bathrooms.

Hotels There's a number of middle-range ($55 to $60) hotels on Siskiyou Blvd (Hwy 99), most with swimming pools. Try the *Ashland Motel* (☎ 541-482-2561, 800-460-8858), 1145 Siskiyou Blvd, and neighboring *Timbers Motel* (☎ 541-482-4242), 1450 Ashland St, about a half mile from the theaters. The *Palm Motel & Houses* (☎ 541-482-2636), 1065 Siskiyou Blvd, rents out small houses in addition to motel rooms.

Two of Ashland's old hotels have been stylishly refurbished and updated. Downtown, the *Columbia Hotel* (☎ 541-482-3726, 800-718-2530), 262½ E Main St, is a modest-looking but charming establishment. Rooms begin at $49 with shared bath, $79 with private bath. If claw-foot bathtubs or Jacuzzis appeal to you, head for the historic *Peerless Hotel* (☎ 541-488-1082), 243 4th St, a handsomely refurbished European-style hotel with five fancifully decorated guestrooms ($98 to $175); breakfast for two is included.

Probably the most comfortable motel in Ashland is *Windmill's Ashland Hills Inn* (☎ 541-482-8310, 800-547-4747), 2525

Ashland St, with spa facilities and a shuttle service to theaters. Rooms are $88. The *Stratford Inn* (☎ 541-488-2151, 800-547-4741), 555 Siskiyou Blvd, is within walking distance of the theaters. Rooms are $94.

Save some money and escape the theater crowds by staying in Phoenix, a small town 7 miles north of Ashland. The clean and welcoming *Phoenix Motel* (☎ 541-535-1555), 510 N Main St, has singles/doubles for $40/42 and also has a pool.

If these prices, or the absence of rooms, give you grief, then consider staying in Medford, only 10 miles away.

Places to Eat

There's no difficulty in finding places to eat in Ashland. The three-block area around the festival stages must have more restaurants than anywhere else in the Pacific Northwest.

Ashland has the distinction of levying the only restaurant tax in the state. The 5% tax is added to prepared meals eaten in restaurants; 1% of the tax goes toward the purchase of green space in the city, and 4% goes toward the cost of a sewage-treatment facility. There is no tax on unprepared food in grocery stores.

Budget Breakfasts are the order of the day at the *Ashland Bakery & Cafe* (☎ 541-482-2117), 38 E Main St, and at the *Breadboard* (☎ 541-488-0295), 744 N Main St. Eat breakfast all day at *Brothers' Delicatessen* (☎ 541-482-9671), 95 N Main St, a New York-style kosher deli.

Eat cheap at *Big Town Hero* (☎ 541-488-1523), 75 N Main St, and *Bento Express* (☎ 541-488-3582), 3 Granite St, where meals are less than $4. Go a bit upmarket next door on the deck at *Il Giardino* (☎ 541-488-0816), 5 Granite St, where pasta dishes start at $9.

Middle For fiery Asian cooking, go to the *Thai Pepper* (☎ 541-482-8058), 84 N Main St, where red pork curry costs $12 and tables overlook Ashland Creek. In the same price range is *Macaroni's* (☎ 541-488-3359), 58 E Main St, with pizza and Italian fast food. Ashland's favorite Mexican

restaurant is *Calientes* (☎ 541-482-1107), 76 N Pioneer St.

At *Ciao Main* (☎ 541-482-8435), 272 E Main St, fresh ethnic inventions such as Malaysian curry chicken go for $13.95.

Top End For a splurge or special occasion, Ashland boasts some of southern Oregon's best restaurants. Call ahead for reservations. The *Chateaulin* (☎ 541-482-2264), 50 E Main St, serves topflight French cuisine in an attractive wood-lined dining room. *Escalopes de veau* go for $23. A lighter bistro menu features herb crepes with goat cheese for $12.95. Browse next door in the restaurant's gourmet shop for fancy picnic fare.

Bold new twists on old ethnic faves give the eclectic *Firefly Restaurant* (☎ 541-488-3212), 15 N 1st St, one of Ashland's most adventurous and flavorful menus, with a particular bent toward exotic seafood. Lunch with Thai fish cakes costs $9, and the mahi-mahi tamale dinner is $24. For steak and seafood, go to *Omar's* (☎ 541-482-1281), 1380 Siskiyou Blvd. *Alex's Plaza Restaurant* (☎ 541-482-8818), 35 N Main St, turns American standards into cuisine – pork ribs go for $19. In summer there's seating above the creek.

Entertainment
Brewpubs & Bars Obviously, theater's the thing in Ashland, but after a day with the Bard, who can blame an actor or spectator for being thirsty? Head to *Ashland Creek Bar & Grill* (☎ 541-482-4131), 92½ N Main St, for local microbrews and a pleasant deck overlooking the creek. For a quiet drink and snack, the back bar at the *Chateaulin* (☎ 541-482-2264), 50 E Main St, is popular with the after-theater crowd.

Off-'Bardway' Theater There's no question that the Shakespeare Festival is the big gun in town, but with all these actors and audience members flocking to the Ashland area, there's also a bevy of small, independent theater troupes and cabarets springing up. Contact the visitors' center for details or call the following for theater schedules and current locations: the *Lyric Theatre* (☎ 541-772-1555), the *Cygnet Theatre* for children's productions (☎ 541-488-2945), *Actors' Theatre* (☎ 541-482-9659) and the *Oregon Cabaret Theatre* (☎ 541-488-2902) for musical comedy.

Getting There & Around

If you're looking to fly into the region, see Getting There & Away at the beginning of this chapter for information on Medford's Rogue Valley International Airport.

Three Greyhound buses travel daily between Ashland and Portland ($41 one way); however, there is no bus depot. Greyhound discharges and picks up passengers at Mr C's Market (☎ 541-482-8803), near the I-5 freeway exit at 2073 N Hwy 99. It's a few miles north of town so you'll have to either take the local Rogue Valley Transit District bus (no weekend service) or call a cab. The nearest depot is in Medford (see below). Green Tortoise (☎ 800-867-8647) stops in Ashland on both north- and south-bound routes. Schedules are a bit tricky, so call for details and reservations.

Ashland is served locally by two RVTD buses (☎ 541-779-2877), which operate daytime hours on weekdays. The No 10 bus cruises Hwy 99 (Siskiyou Blvd) through Ashland and continues to Medford. Buses run every half-hour; the fare is $1. For a taxi, call Yellow Cab (☎ 541-482-3065).

MEDFORD & AROUND

What Medford lacks in charm, it makes up for in location. Southern Oregon's largest city, Medford (population 47,100) is at the center of the region's fruit and lumber industry, and is also central to southern Oregon's scenic and recreational glories. Ashland, Crater Lake, Oregon Caves National Monument and the Rogue River valley are all convenient to the city and its inexpensive motels.

Fruit trees, especially pears, are what made Medford famous. During the early years of this century, thousands of acres of fruit trees were planted, the newly built railroad providing a national market. In April the valley is bathed in pink and white blossoms.

No one would claim that Medford is a tourist town, but its downtown offers a pleasant, streamside park and better food than the freeway stops.

Orientation

I-5 passes through the center of Medford; Hwy 62, often called the Crater Lake Hwy, heads northeast from Medford to Crater Lake National Park. Hwy 99 is the main commercial strip in Medford; in town it divides into two one-way streets: Riverside Ave flows north and Central Ave flows south. Along these are most of Medford's cheaper motels and restaurants.

Information

The Visitors Information Center (☎ 541-776-4021) south of town at Harry & David's Country Store, 1314 Center Drive, is convenient to I-5 exit 27. The Medford Visitors & Convention Bureau (☎ 541-779-4847, 800-469-6307) is downtown at 101 E 8th St. The Rogue River National Forest District office (☎ 541-858-2200) is at 333 W 8th St, as is the post office.

The Medford daily newspaper is the *Medford Mail Tribune*. Jefferson Public Broadcasting is heard on 91.5 and 89.1 FM. West Main Laundromat (☎ 541-773-4803), 1712 W Main St, offers TV, snacks and games in addition to washers and dryers. For medical emergencies, contact the Providence Medford Medical Center (☎ 541-732-5000), 1111 Crater Lake Ave.

Southern Oregon History Center

This regional museum (☎ 541-773-6536), 106 N Central Ave, tells the story of the valley's farming, logging and mining past, and is noted for its large collection of period photographs. The Southern Oregon Historical Society offices and research library are also here. The museum is open 9 am to 5 pm weekdays, and noon to 5 pm on Saturday; $3/2 adults/seniors.

Harry & David's Country Store

Medford's most famous fruit growers are brothers Harry and David Holmes. In the early 1900s, their family orchard exported

OREGON

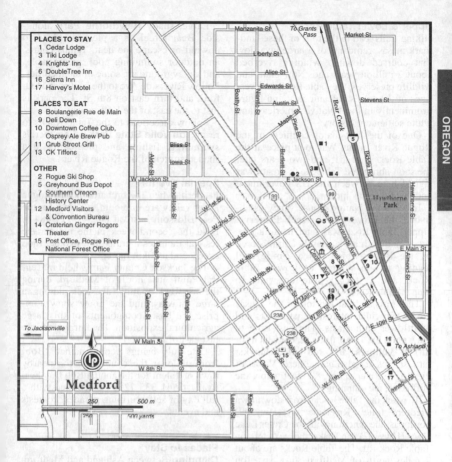

PLACES TO STAY
1 Cedar Lodge
3 Tiki Lodge
4 Knights' Inn
6 DoubleTree Inn
16 Sierra Inn
17 Harvey's Motel

PLACES TO EAT
8 Boulangerie Rue de Main
9 Deli Down
10 Downtown Coffee Club,
    Osprey Ale Brew Pub
11 Grub Street Grill
13 CK Tiffens

OTHER
2 Rogue Ski Shop
5 Greyhound Bus Depot
7 Southern Oregon
    History Center
12 Medford Visitors
    & Convention Bureau
14 Craterian Ginger Rogers
    Theater
15 Post Office, Rogue River
    National Forest Office

Medford

pears to grand European hotels. But when the 1930s Depression years put an end to that market, the two brothers decided to start a fruit-by-mail venture. The result was the wildly successful Harry & David's fruit mail-order business, led by the Fruit-of-the-Month Club.

The 'outlet store' for the mail-order fruit growers, this large produce-and-gift store (☎ 541-776-2277), immediately off I-5 exit 27 at 1314 Center Drive, is a great place to stock up on Oregon-made food products and fresh fruit. The prices and selection of fruit and vegetables are pretty good, and

you'll have no trouble putting together a healthy, inexpensive picnic. There's also an espresso bar and candy shop.

Half a mile south of the country store is the **Jackson & Perkins Test & Display Gardens**, one of the nation's largest commercial rose growers, also owned by Harry & David's. Although the location – along a busy highway – isn't idyllic, the roses don't seem to mind. A few shadeless picnic tables are provided.

Free tours of the food and rose-packing operations are available – just ask at the country store.

OREGON

Upper & Lower Table Rocks

Hiking trails lead to the tops of these landmark mesas, remnants of a large lava flow that coursed down a winding riverbed about 2 million years ago. Now plant and wildlife preserves, the Table Rocks are vestiges of the area's volcanic past and figure prominently in local Native American and white settlement history.

One of the first major conflicts of the Rogue River Indian War took place at the Table Rocks in 1851, and two years later the soon-abrogated Table Rock Treaty was signed here between the US government and the Takelmas Indians.

In 1979 the Nature Conservancy established the Lower Table Rock Preserve. Upper Table Rock was later made a preserve, and both are presently administered by the BLM, which has a 2-mile trail leading to the summit of Lower Table Rock, and a steeper mile-long path to Upper Table Rock.

The grasslands at the top of the mesas are of particular interest to naturalists and wildflower enthusiasts. The best time to view plant life is April. Be on the watch for turkey vultures and red-tailed hawks; rattlesnakes are also native here. Vistas of the Rogue River valley, 800 feet below the cliff edge, are stunning.

To reach the Table Rocks from downtown Medford, follow Riverside Ave (Hwy 99) north past the junction with the Crater Lake Hwy (Hwy 62), and take the next left on Table Rock Rd. The Table Rocks are about 7 miles north of Medford. Just past Tou Velle State Park, the road forks and you will need to decide which Table Rock to climb.

The Medford BLM office (☎ 541-770-2200), 3040 Biddle Rd, near the airport at I-5 exit 30, has more information on the Table Rocks.

Activities

Rent cross-country skis at Rogue Ski Shop (☎ 541-772-8047), 309 E Jackson St.

Cedar Links Golf Course (☎ 541-773-4373), 3155 Cedar Links Drive, is an 18-hole course northeast of Medford toward White City.

Large, shady **Hawthorne Park** alongside Bear Creek is a pleasant place to unwind or escape the heat. Tennis courts, an outdoor swimming pool, picnic tables and a playground are some of the facilities. Follow Riverside Ave to the center of Medford, and turn east on 8th St. The park is just to the east of the I-5 freeway.

Follow directions to the Table Rocks to reach **Tou Velle State Park**, where there's swimming, fishing and picnicking at a shaded stretch of the Rogue River.

Special Events

In April, when the orchards in the Rogue River valley are in bloom, it's time for the Pear Blossom Festival (☎ 541-779-4847). Held the second week in the month, the festival includes a crafts fair, parade, food events and a 20km run.

The Jackson County Fair is held in Central Point, just north of Medford, during the last week of July. Livestock judging, a large midway, and the home show comprise the basic components of this large agricultural exposition. The fairgrounds are just east of I-5 exit 33.

Late July brings people named 'Bob' from all over the country to the nearby town of Talent for the annual Bob Day Festival (☎ 541-535-7251), celebrated with a full day of self-affirming parades, contests and events.

Places to Stay

Camping Between Ashland and Medford, at I-5 exit 24, there are two large RV parks (no tent camping). The *Holiday RV Park* (☎ 541-535-2183, 800-452-7970) is on the west side of the freeway and the *Pear Tree RV Park* (☎ 541-535-4445, 800-645-7332) is on the east. They both offer full facilities for around $22.

Tent campers will want to continue past Medford to the little town of Rogue River. *Valley of the Rogue State Park* (☎ 541-582-1118) is set right along the river and has showers, a laundry and group sites. The park is at 3792 N River Rd; follow signs from I-5 exit 45A. Fees begin at $15.

Rogue River War

The Rogue River Indians, technically the Takelmas, received their popular name from French beaver trappers early in the 19th century who termed them *coquins*, or 'rogues,' because of their open hostility toward whites. This fierce tribe truly earned its nickname when the expedition seeking an all-land route to the Willamette Valley opened up southern Oregon to the settlers.

In 1846 a group of adventurous pioneers led by Jesse and Lindsay Applegate developed the South Road, or Scott-Applegate Trail, into Oregon. Although most settlers who chose this route continued over the mountains into the Willamette Valley, others who liked the wide Rogue and Umpqua Valleys settled there.

The Takelmas attacked immigrant parties, and refused to negotiate with the army to allow passage through their land. The discovery of gold near Jacksonville in 1852 – the first gold strike in southern Oregon – exacerbated tensions. Disenchanted gold panners from California streamed into the region. A series of conflicts developed among the Takelmas, the army and the settlers, with plenty of tit-for-tat butchery. The Table Rock Treaty, signed in 1853, kept the peace until 1855, when miners raided a Takelma village and killed a large number of women and children. In retaliation the Takelmas attacked a mining camp and killed 16 people.

The so-called Rogue River War was on. The army pursued the Takelmas into wild canyons of the western Rogue Valley in late fall 1855, but the Takelmas eluded them. However, the remote canyons provided scant winter shelter or food for the fleeing Indians, so after several months of skirmishes many of the Takelmas gave themselves up to the army. They were sent north to the Grand Ronde Reservation on the Yamhill River. ■

B&Bs *Under the Greenwood Tree* (☎ 541-776-0000), 3045 Bellinger Lane, is a beautiful, old home set on a 10-acre orchard southwest of town. The house was built in 1862, and has four guest rooms with private bath for $95 to $125 a night. The breakfasts are especially good, and afternoon tea is served to guests at 4:30 pm.

Hotels Hwy 99 (Riverside and Central Aves) is lined with lots of perfectly good and inexpensive motels.

The following are south of downtown, close to I-5 exit 27: the *Sierra Inn* (☎ 541-773-7727), 345 S Central Ave, *Harvey's Motel* (☎ 541-779-6561), 510 S Central Ave, and the *Sis-Q* (☎ 541-773-8411), 722 S Riverside. North of downtown is another strip of motels: the *Knights' Inn* (☎ 541-773-3676), 500 N Riverside Ave, the *Tiki Lodge* (☎ 541-773-4579), 509 N Riverside Ave, and the *Cedar Lodge* (☎ 541-773-7361, 800-282-3419), 518 N Riverside Ave. All offer rooms in the $30 to $40 range.

If you're looking for something upscale in Medford, then the *DoubleTree Hotel* (☎ 541-779-5811), 200 N Riverside Ave, is a good choice. It has a swimming pool and suite-style rooms beginning at $74.

Places to Eat

There are plenty of fast-food operations clustered around the freeway exits, but downtown offers more options and character. Muffins and bagels are the order of the day at *Downtown Coffee Club* (☎ 541-473-6831), 410 E Main St. For breakfast pastries or lunchtime baguette sandwiches, head to *Boulangerie Rue de Main* (☎ 541-772-5532), 237 E Main St. They also serve espresso drinks. *CK Tiffens* (☎ 541-779-0480), 226 E Main St, offers home-baked breads and meals that stress natural ingredients, often with an ethnic slant. Vegetarian dishes are available. Lunch specials, like vegetarian tostadas, are under $5.

Mexican laborers are the muscle behind the region's farm economy, and they also provide some of the area's best food. *Octavio's La Burrita Mexican Restaurant* (☎ 541-770-5770) is west of town at 2716 Jacksonville Hwy.

Grab a sandwich from the *Deli Down* (☎ 541-772-4520), 406 E Main St, and head to Hawthorne Park. The *Grub Street Grill* (☎ 541-773-4805), 35 N Central Ave St, is Medford's brewpub, and serves sandwiches for under $6.

The *Hungry Woodsman* (☎ 541-772-2050), 2001 N Pacific Hwy (Hwy 99), is a Medford tradition, with Bunyan-esque servings and decor, and an all-American kind of menu, with steak, chicken and seafood dinners starting at $12.

Forgo steaks for cuisine at *Streams* (☎ 541-776-9090), 1841 Barnett Rd, specializing in Oregon-grown products prepared with zesty sauces and herbs. Fish and pasta dominate the menu; linguini with smoked trout, walnuts and pesto costs $11.

Entertainment
Though Shakespeare and Britt Festival performances (see Jacksonville, below) are the main draw to this part of the state, Medford's new performing arts center, the *Craterian Ginger Rogers Theater* (☎ 541-779-3000), 23 S Central Ave, is southern Oregon's principal venue for dance, music and traveling theater productions.

If southern Oregon's high-brow performing arts scene has you hankering for a low-key hangout, head for the sports-oriented *Osprey Ale Brew Pub* (☎ 541-734-4808), 404 E Main St, for a night of pool and brew.

Getting There & Around
See Getting There & Away at the start of the chapter for information on Medford's Rogue Valley International Airport.

The Greyhound Bus Depot (☎ 541-779-2103) is at 212 Bartlett St. Six buses link Medford daily with Portland ($32 one way) and San Francisco.

Local Rogue Valley Transit District (☎ 541-779-2877) buses link communities in this part of the Rogue River valley. The

main transfer point in the system is in downtown Medford at the corner of Front and 8th Sts. For the traveler, the buses that run between Medford and Ashland (on the half-hour), and Medford and Jacksonville (at 8 am, 10 am, 3 pm and 5 pm), are potentially useful, though there is no weekend or evening service. Fare is $1.

For taxi service, call Metro Taxi (☎ 541-773-6665).

JACKSONVILLE
Population 1930
The oldest settlement in southern Oregon, Jacksonville is a well-preserved and beautifully renovated community little changed since the 1880s.

A gold-prospecting town on the main stage route between California and the Willamette Valley, Jacksonville was a trade center from the start. It was important enough to be named the seat of Jackson County, but lost that title in the 1920s when the railroad built Medford nearby, luring away local commerce.

For the next 40 years, the town slumbered, unvital but unaltered. By the 1960s, renewed interest in the region's history and early attempts to preserve Jacksonville's architectural heritage were rewarded when the US government named the entire downtown area a National Historic Landmark District, one of only eight such designations in the country. Over 100 individual buildings are listed on the National Register of Historic Places.

In addition to its reputation as an open-air museum, Jacksonville is also home to the Britt Festival, a summer-long musical celebration that presents a wide assortment of internationally acclaimed musicians.

Orientation & Information
Jacksonville is 6 miles west of Medford on Hwy 238. The center of the old downtown is at the corner of California and Oregon Sts. From there the town spreads out in a four-block radius.

The Jacksonville Chamber of Commerce (☎ 541-899-8118) is at 185 N Oregon St.

National Historic District

The former county courthouse has been converted into southern Oregon's showcase museum, the **Jacksonville Museum of Southern Oregon History** (☎ 541-773-6536), 206 N 5th St, and is a good place to start a tour of the town. The two-story, Italianate courthouse was built in 1883 and remained the Jackson County seat until it was moved to Medford in 1927.

The museum contains a tribute to photographer Peter Britt, who was the first to

The States of Jackson & Jefferson

The southern counties of Oregon and the northern counties of California, isolated from the major power centers of their respective states, have long been home to strong secessionist movements. While legislation to create a 'State of Shasta' was introduced twice in the California legislature during the early 1850s, the most serious attempt at secession occurred in 1854, when a public meeting was held in Jacksonville to gauge support for a separate 'Jackson Territory.' Response was very positive, and the group planned a convention the next year to be attended by delegates representing all southern Oregon and Northern Californian counties. At the convention, held in January in Jacksonville, HG Ferris of Siskiyou County was elected president of the new state, and individual secession resolutions were drafted to be presented to legislatures in Oregon and California. The outbreak of the Rogue River War, between the Oregon settlers and Rogue River natives forced the breakup of the convention, and the initiative lost steam for a few years. Plans for a new state, this time called Siskiyou, emerged again in 1857 and 1909.

The most memorable secessionist movement occurred in 1941, when residents aimed to attract nationwide attention to Oregon's and California's neglect of this rural area. A state judge in Crescent City spearheaded the action, and the insurrection began at Gold Beach. The State of Jefferson officially seceded from California and Oregon on Thursday, November 27, and it was planned that the territory would secede every Thursday thereafter. In Yreka, residents set up roadblocks on Hwy 99 to interrogate travelers crossing the new state line. These border patrols circulated copies of the state's declaration of independence. A newly appointed governor was officially inaugurated at the Yreka Courthouse on December 3. The occasion was celebrated by a torchlight parade, and border patrol stations passed out windshield stickers to motorists which read, 'I have visited Jefferson, the 49th State.'

The hoopla in the State of Jefferson captured national attention. Stanton Delaplane of the *San Francisco Chronicle* even received the 1941 Pulitzer Prize for regional reporting of the secessionist movement. Unfortunately for the State of Jefferson, the nation soon had more pressing news to attend to: the bombing of Pearl Harbor. Once again, the State of Jefferson took a back seat to more serious considerations.

Motivations behind the region's secession have varied. The most common argument has been that the Jefferson territory was of uniform character, unique and distinct from either Oregon or California. Furthermore, the area is far from the states' centers of population and power. The people of Jefferson felt that their under-represented interests could only be protected by the creation of a separate state.

It's also wise to remember that many of the original settlers in this mining region were Confederate soldiers displaced by the Civil War, and they knew a thing or two about secession. During the Civil War, the Jefferson territory was host to a number of secret Confederate organizations. 'Knights of the Golden Circle' and 'Friends of the Union' met openly in Jacksonville and were joined by disgruntled proponents of the 'State of Jackson.' Secession was a strong possibility throughout the war and a frequent topic of discussion at such meetings. This time the new nation was to be known as the 'Pacific Republic.' When a Confederate plot to capture Alcatraz and Fort Point in California was uncovered, the ringleaders were discovered to be Pacific Republic proponents. ■

take pictures of Crater Lake. There are also displays on local history. The old county jail, adjacent, is now a children's museum. Ask at the museum for a walking tour map of Jacksonville history. During summer the museum is open 10 am to 5 pm daily; $3/2 adults/seniors and children.

Peter Britt's mansion once sat in the lovely **gardens** at S 1st and W Pine Sts. Though the house burned down in 1960, the grounds remain as a public park. Note the redwood tree, planted by Britt to commemorate the birth of his son Emil.

The restored **Beekman House** at 470 E California St was built in 1873 by Cornelius Beekman, who founded Oregon's second bank (still standing at the corner of California and 3rd Sts). Tours are conducted by actors in period dress from 1 to 5 pm daily, Memorial Day to Labor Day weekend; admission is $2.

Another admirable Victorian residence is the ornate **Jeremiah Nunan House** at 635 N Oregon St, built in 1892 by Jeremiah Nunan, a local merchant. The house was bought from a catalog and shipped here unassembled from Tennessee, hence its sobriquet 'the Catalog House.' The home is still a private residence and not open for touring.

A more detailed history of Jacksonville's historic buildings is offered on hourlong narrated **tours** conducted on motorized trolley cars (from San Francisco), which leave from the corner of California and 3rd Sts on the hour from 10 am to 4 pm. The tour costs $4. Call ☎ 541-535-5617 for more information.

Peter Britt Music Festival

These summertime outdoor concerts, held mid-June to Labor Day weekend, are justly renowned throughout the Pacific Northwest as a showcase for a wide variety of musical performers and entertainment. Concerts are held in the Britt Pavilion at the corner of 1st and Fir Sts. There is limited reserved seating – patrons are instead encouraged to bring picnics and spread out on the grassy hillside. The picnic aspect of the festival is not to be overlooked. Most

restaurants in the vicinity are happy to prepare a hamper with a couple of hours notice. The festival was originally dedicated to classical music, but it now encompasses a bit of everything, from standard jazz to taiko drummers, folk singers to country crooners. In recent years, performers have included the likes of Art Garfunkel, Wynonna Judd and The Indigo Girls.

Tickets for the Britt Festival go quickly. Contact the festival office (☎ 541-773-6077, 800-882-7488) at PO Box 1124, Medford, OR 97501, for information and reservations.

Places to Stay

Camping There's a lovely Jackson County campground on the Applegate River, just over the hill from Jacksonville. Follow Hwy 238 west from Jacksonville about 8 miles to the little community of Ruch. The *Cantrall-Buckley Campground* (☎ 541-776-7001) is just beyond the town on the banks of the river and has sites for $10.

B&Bs Unsurprisingly, most lodgings in Jacksonville stress their authentic furnishings and are rather expensive. Contact the Jacksonville B&B Association, PO Box 787, Jacksonville, OR 97530, for a complete listing of area B&Bs. The following establishments are representative. *Colonial House B&B* (☎ 541-770-2783, 800-770-7301), 1845 Old Stage Rd, is a 1916 Georgian mansion sitting on a 5-acre holding. The two suites have private bathrooms; prices start at $110 to $125. The *McCully House Inn* (☎ 541-899-1942, 800-367-1942), 240 E California St, is one of Jacksonville's earliest homes, built for the town's first doctor. Upstairs are three guest rooms with private bath for $100. Downstairs is an intimate restaurant and lounge.

Hotels The *Jacksonville Inn* (☎ 541-899-1900, 800-321-9344), 175 E California St, is a refurbished hotel built in 1863, filled with antiques and modern comforts. There are only eight rooms, so reservations are suggested; breakfast is included. The inn's dining room is one of the best in southern Oregon. Singles/doubles begin at $90/100.

Less expensive is the *Stage Lodge* (☎ 541-899-3953, 800-253-8254), 830 N 5th St, with rooms for $69.

Places to Eat
Resist the ubiquitous fudge and frozen yogurt shops and eat in the historic dining rooms. (Call ahead to order picnic hampers for the festival.) The *Jacksonville Inn Dinner House* (☎ 541-899-1900), 175 E California St, is in the lobby of the hotel and is one of southern Oregon's best restaurants. A full seven-course dinner with a stuffed hazelnut chicken main dish is $23. *Bella Union Restaurant* (☎ 541-899-1770), 170 W California St, offers a wide range of prices and preparations, from sandwiches to pasta to full dinners in the $13 range. Try the antique-filled dining room at *McCully House Inn* (☎ 541-899-1942, 800-367-1942), 240 E California St, for classy and inventive dishes featuring local ingredients.

Getting There & Away
Medford's Rogue Valley Transit District bus No 30 leaves for Jacksonville at 8 am, 10 am, 3 pm and 5 pm from Front and 8th Sts, the Jacksonville stop is in front of the Jacksonville Museum at 206 N 5th St. Return buses depart at 18 minutes past these hours.

GRANTS PASS
Population 20,255

From the freeway, Grants Pass looks like just another down-on-its-luck mill town, and a homely one at that. Upon closer inspection, however, Grants Pass reveals itself to be a pleasant town filled with historic homes, attractive parks and an old downtown fronting the rushing Rogue River.

Grants Pass is the hub for recreation on the lower portion of the Rogue River. From here outfitters lead fishing expeditions and jet-boat cruises up and down the river.

The traveler may wonder about the prevalent caveman motif everywhere in

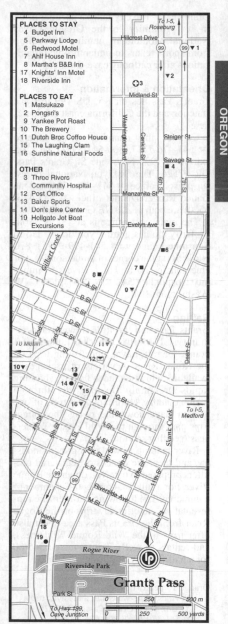

PLACES TO STAY
4 Budget Inn
5 Parkway Lodge
6 Redwood Motel
7 Ahlf House Inn
8 Martha's B&B Inn
17 Knights' Inn Motel
18 Riverside Inn

PLACES TO EAT
1 Matsukaze
2 Pongsri's
9 Yankee Pot Roast
10 The Brewery
11 Dutch Bros Coffee House
15 The Laughing Clam
16 Sunshine Natural Foods

OTHER
3 Three Rivers
    Community Hospital
12 Post Office
13 Baker Sports
14 Don's Bike Center
19 Hellgate Jet Boat
    Excursions

OREGON

Grants Pass

Grants Pass. The city takes a peculiar pride in its proximity to the Oregon Caves National Monument, naming everything from sports teams to philanthropic organizations after cartoony cave-dwellers.

Orientation & Information

Grant's Pass lies on I-5. US 199 to Cave Junction and the California coast originates here.

Contact the chamber of commerce (☎ 541-476-7717, 800-547-5927), near I-5 exit 58 at 1995 NW Vine St, Grants Pass, OR 97526. The Siskiyou National Forest supervisor's office (☎ 541-471-6724) and the Galice Ranger District office (☎ 541-476-6500) are both at 200 NE Greenfield Rd.

The main post office is at 132 NW 6th St. Dirty clothes getting you down? Go to Sunshine Laundry (☎ 541-479-9975), 870 NE D St (at the corner of Anderson St). For emergencies go to Three Rivers Community Hospital (☎ 541-479-7531), 1505 NW Washington Blvd.

Rafting

Grants Pass and the little downriver community of Merlin are the jumping-off points for raft, kayak and fishing trips on the Rogue River. A variety of packages is available, which includes fishing, shooting rapids or simply floating idly through scenic country. Outfitters offer trips of one to four days down the river. The longer trips pass through the Wild Rogue Wilderness (see that section).

River guiding is kind of a growth industry, and there are dozens of registered outfitters prepared to take you down the Rogue River. For a full list, contact the chamber of commerce. The following outfitters are representative and offer day trips on the Rogue River from the Grants Pass area (most also offer trips in the Wild Rogue Wilderness, and rentals as well). Trips average $45/60 for a half/full day of rafting.

Orange Torpedo Trips
Provides white-water raft and kayak trips;
PO Box 1111, Grants Pass, OR 97526
(☎ 541-479-5061, 800-635-2925)

Rogue Wilderness, Inc
Provides day trips and raft rentals;
PO Box 1647, Grants Pass, OR 97526
(☎ 541-479-9554, 800-336-1647)
Sundance Expeditions
Provides kayaking classes and guided tours;
14894 Galice Rd, Merlin, OR 97532
(☎ 541-479-8508)
River Trips Unlimited
Offers scenic or fishing excursions;
4140 Dry Creek Rd, Medford, OR 97504
(☎ 541-779-3798, 800-460-3865)
Ferron's Fun Trips
Provides white-water raft and fishing trips;
PO Box 585, Merlin, OR 97532
(☎ 541-474-2201, 800-404-2201)

Jet Boat Tours

Guided jet boat tours leave from downtown and explore the downstream Rogue River canyon. A number of tour options are available, including lunch trips and dinner excursions. The guides are usually knowledgeable about local history, lore and wildlife.

Tours run from May to September and prices vary, with most starting at $25. Be sure to call ahead. Boats leave from a dock between the downtown bridges. Contact Hellgate Jet Boat Excursions (☎ 541-479-7204, 800-648-4874), 953 SE 7th St, for reservations and information.

Jet boat tours also leave from the small town of Rogue River, between Medford and Grants Pass, and explore a section of the river upstream from Savage Rapids Dam. Contact Jet Boat River Excursions (☎ 541-582-0800), PO Box 658, Rogue River, OR 97537. The business is just off I-5 exit 48 – watch for signs.

Fishing

A number of Grants Pass-area outfitters provide fly-fishing instruction and guide service. Contact the chamber of commerce for a complete list of outfitters, or get in touch with the following for representative prices and services: Briggs Rogue River Guide Service (☎ 541-476-2941, 800-845-5091), 2750 Cloverlawn Drive, Grants Pass, OR 97527, or Geoff's Guide Service, (☎ 541-474-0602), at 2578 Midway St, Grants Pass, OR 97527.

Other Activities

Bicycle rentals are available from Bike-kraft (☎ 541-479-3912), 1515 Redwood Ave (near the fairgrounds). Be warned that citizens of both Grants Pass and Medford are known for their intolerance toward cyclists. You can rent cross-country skis from Baker Sports (☎ 541-476-0388), 226 SW G St.

The Grants Pass Golf Club (☎ 541-476-0849), 230 Espey Rd, is an 18-hole golf course with nice views over the Rogue Valley. Call ahead to find out daily hours for public play.

Special Events

The Josephine County Fair (☎ 541-479-3215) is held the third weekend of August in Grants Pass at 1451 Fairgrounds Rd.

The Jedediah Smith Mountain Man Rendezvous brings hatchet throwing and musket firing to Grants Pass. The festival goes on for six days, starting the Tuesday before Labor Day and lasting through the weekend. This he-man festival ends with a buffalo barbecue and is held at Sportsmans Park in Merlin, 5 miles north of Grants Pass, off I-5 exit 61.

Places to Stay

Camping The Grants Pass area is rich in camping options. There are a number of RV-oriented campgrounds clustered along the Rogue River near town. One of the best is *Riverpark RV Resort* (☎ 541-479-0046, 800-677-8857), 2956 Rogue River Hwy (Hwy 99), at a pretty spot along the river. Tent sites go for $16, RV sites for $20.

Josephine County maintains a number of attractive county parks. From downtown Grants Pass, head west on G St for 8 miles to reach *Whitehorse Park*, on Lower River Rd. *Indian Mary Park* is farther afield, about 8 miles west of Merlin on the Galice Rd, but it's right on the river, has showers and flush toilets, and is popular with rafting groups. Sites cost $12 to $17. Contact the Josephine County Parks Dept (☎ 541-474-5285), 101 NW A St, Grants Pass, OR 97526, to make reservations.

B&Bs Grants Pass has a number of very nice historic B&B inns. The *Ahlf House Inn* (☎ 541-479-4754, 800-863-1374), 746 NW 6th St, is a 1908 neo-Georgian home with four guest rooms at $65 to $110. *Martha's B&B Inn* (☎ 541-476-4330, 800-261-0167), 764 NW 4th St, is an old Victorian farmhouse with a wraparound porch and rooms from $75. All have private bathrooms.

Hotels There are a number of older, inexpensive ($30 to $45) motels along 6th St: the *Budget Inn* (☎ 541-479-2952), 1253 NE 6th St; the *Parkway Lodge* (☎ 541-476-4260), 1001 NE 6th St; and the *Knights' Inn Motel* (☎ 541-479-5595, 800-826-6835), 104 SE 7th St. The pleasant *Redwood Motel* (☎ 541-476-0878), 815 NE 6th St, is the nicest place on this strip, with rooms around $60.

Riverside Inn (☎ 541-476-6873, 800-334-4567), 971 SE 6th St, is the largest and best-located lodging in Grants Pass. Right downtown, with rooms and decks that front the Rogue River, the Riverside is also the departure point for jet boat tours. Rooms range from $60 to $110.

Opened in 1873 and in continuous operation ever since, the *Wolf Creek Tavern* (☎ 541-866-2474) is a stage coach-era hostelry that has survived as a charming small hotel and restaurant. Twenty miles north of Grants Pass on the old California-Oregon stage line (and, incidentally, I-5, which follows much of the old stage route), the inn has housed celebrities such as Jack London, Clark Gable and Mary Pickford. There are eight guest rooms, beginning at $69. The restaurant is open for lunch and dinner; dinner prices for hearty meals based on steak and local trout are fixed at $10.

Resorts Anglers and rafters may want to consider staying at a Rogue River lodge, where float trips to fishing holes can be part of the housing package. The *Galice Resort* (☎ 541-476-3818), 11744 Galice Rd, Merlin, OR 97532, offers rentals and guided trips, as well as lodging and food.

Lodging in cabins begins at $45 and rooms in the lodge begin at $80. The upscale *Morrison's Rogue River Lodge* (☎ 541-476-3825, 800-826-1963), 8500 Galice Rd, Merlin, OR 97532, likewise rents gear and guides trips. Lodging in deluxe cabins runs $90 per person and includes breakfast and a four-course dinner.

Fishing lodges don't come any more deluxe than the historic *Weasku Inn Resort* (☎ 541-471-8000, 800-493-2758), 5560 Rogue River Hwy (west of Grants Pass), an elegantly restored, log-cabin lodge right on the Rogue. Pine-walled lodge rooms start at $125 and riverfront cabins at $275.

Places to Eat

Della's (☎ 541-476-8513), 1802 NW 6th St, is a breakfast favorite, open 24 hours. For espresso, muffins, bagels and a jolt of youthful energy stop by *Dutch Bros Coffee House* (☎ 541-747-3321), 332 NW 6th St. Stock up on healthy foodstuffs and organic deli sandwiches and salads at *Sunshine Natural Foods* (☎ 541-474-5044), 128 SW H St.

As elsewhere in the agricultural valleys of southern Oregon, Mexican food is both inexpensive and authentic. Try *Mexx's* (☎ 541-474-6399), 820 NE E St. *Pongsri's* (☎ 541-479-1345), at 1571 NE 6th St, is southern Oregon's best Thai restaurant. *Matsukaze* (☎ 541-479-2961), 1675 NE 7th St, at the corner of Hillcrest Drive, features Japanese favorites. For hearty meat and potatoes, and waiters in period get-ups, go to *Yankee Pot Roast* (☎ 541-476-0551), 720 NW 6th St.

Food is fresh and flavorful at *The Laughing Clam* (☎ 541-479-1110), 121 SW G St, a casual brewpub with a rather sophisticated menu. Hearty vegetarian offerings feature the likes of grilled eggplant sandwiches ($6) and a tasty ginger vinaigrette coleslaw. For dinner there's lime cilantro salmon ($13) and, of course, plenty of clams.

Grants Pass' most favored steak house and bar is *The Brewery* (☎ 541-479-9850), 509 SW G St, housed in an old, red-brick brewery that used to make beer in the rowdy days of old Grants Pass. At the *Hamilton House* (☎ 541-479-3938), 344

NE Terry Lane, there's fine dining in a historic old home.

Getting Around

For transportation between Grants Pass and Medford Airport, contact Airport Transit Service (☎ 541-479-3217, 800-995-0588). The fare runs $12 to $15; call ahead for reservations.

Four Greyhound buses a day run between Portland and Grants Pass. Contact the station (☎ 541-476-4513), 460 NE Agness Ave, for more information.

For rental vehicles, contact Budget Rent-A-Car (☎ 541-471-6311), 825 NE F St. For a cab, call Grants Pass Cab Co (☎ 541-476-6444).

WILD ROGUE WILDERNESS

After the confluence of Grave Creek, the Rogue River enters a canyonland of deep forest, wild, jagged mountains and river chasms. Much of this 40-mile stretch of river is contained in the Wild Rogue Wilderness, a rugged, 56-sq-mile preserve of plants, wildlife and untamed river.

It is this section of the Rogue that has made it one of the most legendary whitewater rivers in the USA. Definitely not for amateurs, this trip takes at least three days. Abundant Class IV rapids and waterfalls make this a rafting trip to plan very carefully; hiring a guide service is a good idea for all but the most experienced.

Often neglected, the **Rogue River Trail** is a 40-mile hiking trail that links the edges of the wilderness, from Grave Creek to Illahe. In summer, the trail can be very hot, black bears have learned to raid camps for food and portions of the path are so precipitous that pack horses are not allowed. This is a trail for the hearty and adventurous. Day hikers can sample this rugged landscape by hiking along the Rogue River from the Grave Creek launch site to Whiskey Creek, a 7-mile roundtrip past waterfalls and rapids.

Orientation & Information

To reach the Wild Rogue Wilderness, take the I-5 Merlin exit. The Galice Rd runs through Merlin and Galice, and on to the head of the Rogue River Trail.

If you plan to float the Rogue independent of outfitters, you will need a permit from the USFS. From almost 100,000 applications, 9,000 permits are issued after a lottery process held in December and January. About 45% of those permits go unused and are returned to the 'open pool,' meaning they're available on a first-come, first-served basis by telephone. The only drawback is that you'll need to be ready to go on short notice – permits don't hit open pool until 10 days before their scheduled float date. For raft permits and additional information, contact the Rand Visitors Center (☎ 541-479-3735), 14335 Galice Rd, Merlin, OR 97532.

Rafting

The following outfitters provide guided white-water trips down the wild portion of the Rogue River. You do not need a permit if you accompany an outfitter registered with the USFS. Contact the agency at the above address for the most current listing of licensed outfitters.

A three-day trip down the Rogue River costs upwards of $500. The following are long-established outfitters:

River Trips Unlimited
  4140 Dry Creek Rd, Medford, OR 97504
  (☎ 541-779-3798, 800-460-3865)
River Adventure Float Trips
  PO Box 841, Grants Pass, OR 97526
  (☎ 541-476-6493, 800-790-7238)
Rogue Wilderness Inc
  325 Galice Rd, Merlin, OR 97532
  (☎ 541-479-9554, 800-336-1647)
Sundance Expeditions
  14894 Galice Rd, Merlin, OR 97532
  (☎ 541-479-8508)

Places to Stay & Eat

Although much of this region is roadless and has now been designated a wilderness area, several old-fashioned lodges still operate along the river. Facilities are usually rustic, typically a central lodge with bedroom cabins scattered among the trees. Plan well ahead, and make sure to call for reservations; lodging averages $75 a night

(this includes the next day's packed lunch). The lodges, starting upstream and going downstream, are: *Black Bar Lodge* (☎ 541-479-6507); *Mariel Lodge* (☎ 541-479-4923); *Paradise Lodge* (☎ 541-247-6504); and *Half Moon Lodge* (☎ 541-247-6968).

Primitive campgrounds exist along the Rogue River Trail; call the Rand Visitors Center (☎ 541-479-3735) for information.

Illinois River Valley

Rising in the Siskiyou Mountains and draining a wide, forested valley before plunging into a wilderness gorge on its way to meet the Rogue River, the Illinois River valley remains one of Oregon's most remote and neglected corners. While the Oregon Caves National Monument ought to keep the Illinois River valley in the forefront of tourism, the isolation of the area suits various kinds of back-to-the-earth idealists. Among the ghostly remnants of gold-mining towns like Kerby, utopian communes nestle against the fortress-like settlements of survivalists.

Remoteness also suits the wilderness areas. The Kalmiopsis Wilderness, coursed by the Illinois River, is a preserve of rare plants and rugged mountains. The Illinois River, whose roily waters are colored an uncanny green from the outcrops of serpentinite through which it flows, is one of the west's most challenging white-water rivers. Only the most experienced kayakers should attempt to navigate the river.

Orientation & Information

Cave Junction is 28 miles south of Grants Pass along US 199, frequently referred to as the Redwood Hwy. The Oregon Caves National Monument is 20 miles east of Cave Junction on Hwy 46. The final 8 miles of the road are quite steep and narrow. Leave trailers or any other towed vehicle at the visitors' center parking lot.

The Illinois Valley Visitor Information Center (☎ 541-592-2631) at 201 Caves Hwy, Cave Junction, OR 97523, is your

OREGON

Loners & Idealists

There's something about the mountains and valleys of the Illinois River drainage that attracts loners and idealists. Gold prospectors were the first whites to settle in the region, but the thousands of hopefuls who flooded in left just as quickly when the gold ran out early in the 20th century.

Today, the Illinois River valley is known for two seemingly opposing social phenomena. In the 1960s, 'back-to-the-earth' utopians founded Takilma, a then-notorious 'hippie' commune. The community still exists, although today it attracts less public indignation. Only the weathered sign stating 'Nuclear Free Zone' on the outskirts of the community gives an indication that Takilma is anything more than an outpost of rural poverty. The other recent emigrants to the Illinois River valley are backwood survivalists, whose compounds are meant to provide safety from Big Brother's many manifestations.

In some sort of fusion of these two social movements, the most recent development in the Illinois River valley is the rise of marijuana farming. The right climatic conditions, inaccessible tracts of public forest and underpopulation make this corner of Oregon one of the most noted marijuana-growing areas in the western USA. ∎

headquarters for local, national forest and cave information. The Siskiyou National Forest's Illinois Valley Ranger Station (☎ 541-592-2166), 26568 Redwood Hwy, also has information on outdoor recreation.

CAVE JUNCTION
Population 1165

The little community of Cave Junction exists to serve the needs of tourists bound for the Oregon Caves. It's also the main trade town for the farming communities of the upper Illinois River.

Oregon Caves National Monument

These caverns are a popular family destination. In addition to the caves themselves, the monument features hiking trails and accommodations in a beautiful old lodge, the Oregon Caves Chateau.

The Oregon Caves began as limestone deposits laid down in a shallow sea about 200 million years ago. Movements of the continental crust eventually hoisted the limestone up into the Siskiyou Mountains, and molten rock forced its way up into rock faults, baking the rock that it came into contact with and forming marble. Continued movement of the Siskiyou Mountains exposed the marble formations and water began to carve tunnels and caves in the soft rock.

The cave (there is only one cave) contains about 3 miles of chambers, the largest of which is about 240 feet long. A fast-moving stream, called the River Styx, runs the length of the cave.

In addition to the underground tours, the monument grounds contain several hiking trails. The **Cliff Nature Trail** is a three-quarter-mile loop trail with signs identifying the plants and geology of the Siskiyou Mountains. For a longer hike, take the **Big Tree Trail**, a 3½-mile loop through old-growth forest. The highlight of the hike is a huge Douglas fir that's reckoned to be at least 1200 years old.

Tours Guided tours of the Oregon Caves run year-round, leave from the chateau (see below) at least once an hour and last about 75 minutes. Tour groups are limited to 16 people, and tickets cost $7/4.50 for adults/children (who must be a minimum height of 42 inches to enter). Call the chateau (☎ 541-592-3400) for tour information.

The tour passes through a half mile of passages, with a total vertical climb of 218 feet. Make sure to bring warm clothing, as the cave preserves a year-round temperature of 41°F, and be prepared to get a little wet. If you visit the cave in the rainy season, you will get a vivid sense of how erosion carves through rock, and how the slow drip and flow of water builds formations. Some of the small, almost insignificant formations, such as cave popcorn, pearls and moonmilk, are as interesting as the classic pipe organs, columns and stalactites.

Oregon Caves Chateau Even if spelunking is not your interest, consider a side trip to the caves to see this truly wonderful log lodge. Built in 1934, the chateau is a six-story hotel (see Places to Stay) and dining room straddling the River Styx as it issues forth from the cave. The common rooms, with a huge central fireplace and windows overlooking the forest and a plunging ravine, look as if they are from another, perhaps mythical, era.

Wineries
A pair of wineries lie off Hwy 46 en route to the caves. **Foris Vineyards** (☎ 800-843-6747), 654 Kendall Rd, and **Bridgeview Winery** (☎ 541-592-4688), 4210 Holland Loop Rd, both provide daily winetastings 11 am to 5 pm year-round, and have attractive picnic grounds.

Places to Stay & Eat
DeWitt's Town & Country RV Park (☎ 541-592-2656), at 28288 Redwood Hwy (a few miles south of Cave Junction on US 199), is a pleasant campground along the Illinois River; rates begin at $15. The *Junction Inn* (☎ 541-592-3106), 406 S Redwood Hwy, is the largest and most comfortable lodging in Cave Junction; singles/doubles are $45/50. *Holiday Motel* (☎ 541-592-3003), 24810 Redwood Hwy, 2 miles north of town, is also a good choice; rates are $45/52.

There are several fast-food restaurants along the highway, so there's no problem finding something quick to eat. The *Wild River Brewing & Pizza Co* (☎ 541-592-3556), at 249 N Redwood Hwy, is the unlikely name of Cave Junction's brewpub. The beers are German-style, while the food ranges from sandwiches to pizzas.

The *Oregon Caves Chateau* (☎ 541-592-3400) is open for lodging and dining from Memorial Day to mid-October, with formal meals in the lodge dining room and sandwiches at an old-fashioned soda fountain. Rates begin at $74 to $89.

There are a number of USFS campgrounds just outside the monument, before Hwy 46 begins to climb the mountainside. Closest to the monument is *Cave Creek Campground*. However, at *Grayback Campground* you can reserve a site by calling ☎ 541-592-3400.

KERBY
Three miles north of Cave Junction, Kerby was founded as Kerbyville in 1858, when it was the center of gold prospecting in the area. Today what's left of the town is preserved as an open-air museum. The **Kerbyville Museum** (☎ 541-592-2076) contains remnants of the area's mining and logging history, as well as arrowheads and old pianos. The $2 admission includes a tour of the adjacent **Stith-Naucke House**, built in 1871.

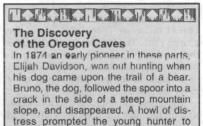

The Discovery of the Oregon Caves
In 1874 an early pioneer in these parts, Elijah Davidson, was out hunting when his dog came upon the trail of a bear. Bruno, the dog, followed the spoor into a crack in the side of a steep mountain slope, and disappeared. A howl of distress prompted the young hunter to follow his hound inside the cave entrance. Davidson was quickly lost in the dark labyrinth, and only escaped by following the cold stream back to the cave entrance (Bruno made it out alive as well).

Thus was discovered the Oregon Caves. Locals began exploring the cave in following years, and its fame as a tourist attraction grew during the early 20th century. The cave was made a national monument in 1909 in order to protect and regulate the site. ■

KALMIOPSIS WILDERNESS

One of the largest and most unique wilderness areas in the state, the Kalmiopsis is famous for its rare plant life and curious geology. This segment of the Klamath geologic province was formed when the North American continent collided with the Pacific Ocean floor about 200 million years ago. Offshore sedimentary beds buckled up and formed mountain-high ridges that didn't initially adhere to North America. So, as the continent inched westward, the proto-Siskiyous pivoted and rolled along the continental edge.

At one point, between 50 and 100 million years ago, a 60-mile gulf opened between the Siskiyou formation and the continent. The vegetation continued to evolve, and when the Siskiyous eventually docked against the North American continent and were fused to it by volcanic intrusions, the plant life in the Siskiyous was quite different from that of the mainland.

Today the mountains of the Kalmiopsis Wilderness are still home to unusual and unique plant species. The pink-flowered *Kalmiopsis leachiana* and the rare Port Orford cedar are found almost nowhere else on earth. The *Darlingtonia* (also called the pitcher plant) does not look to the impoverished soil for nutrition; this carnivorous plant instead traps and digests insects in its long throat.

If you have the time and don't mind getting off the main road, one easy hike leads into this curious region through dense forests and meadows – a designated botanical area – to **Babyfoot Lake**. This short hike is a good place for viewing the unique plant life of the Kalmiopsis. The deep-green Babyfoot Lake is surrounded by a thick growth of Brewer's weeping spruce, Port Orford cedars and madrona trees. Watch for pitcher plants in the meadows.

There is a *primitive campground* at Babyfoot Lake. To reach it, head 5 miles north of Cave Junction, turn west off US 199 onto Eight Dollar Mountain Rd (USFS Rd 4201), and follow signs for Babyfoot Lake Trailhead. It's a winding 20-mile drive to the trailhead. In addition to the entrance listed above, the wilderness area is also accessible from the coastal town of Brookings on USFS Rd 1909 up the Chetco River. For information, contact the Siskiyou National Forest Headquarters (☎ 541-471-6724), 200 NE Greenfield Rd, Grants Pass, OR 97526.

Umpqua Valley

The Native American word 'Umpqua' means 'thunder water,' an apt description of this mighty river, renowned for its beauty and recreational opportunities. The North Umpqua River is especially treasured for summer steelhead fishing. Hwy 138, which follows the North Umpqua through deep forests and past waterfalls and lakes to Crater Lake National Park, is one of the most scenic drives in the state.

Roseburg, the hub of the Umpqua Valley, is known mostly for its logging, but nowadays the locals are as apt to be discussing the harvest of pinot noir grapes as Douglas firs. Roseburg is an inexpensive base of operations for trips to the Oregon coast and the Cascade peaks.

The North Umpqua River was the homeland of the Southern Molala tribe, closely related to the Klamath Indians who lived along the lakes of south central Oregon. The South Umpqua was the homeland of the Upper Umpqua tribe, related to the Rogue Indians.

The two tribes resisted early trading relations with white trappers and traders. In the 1840s, as white pioneers began to settle the river valleys, the Molalas and Umpquas were forced farther into the mountains. Their plight worsened after the Applegate Trail brought emigrants into southern Oregon, and the California gold rush drew fortune hunters across their lands. In 1855 both tribes signed a treaty removing them from the Umpqua Valley and consigning them to the Grande Ronde Reservation on the Yamhill River.

One band of the Upper Umpquas under Chief Napesa refused to leave their lands, and eventually took to the forests. Despite many attempts to round them up, they eluded capture and lived in seclusion. These refugees became known as the Cow Creek tribe; their descendants now live in the Canyonville area.

Orientation & Information

The Umpqua River rises in Maidu Lake, high in the Cascades, and drains over 5500 sq miles of the Cascade and Coast mountains before debouching into the Pacific at Reedsport. Hwys 38 and 138 parallel the main stem Umpqua River and the North fork along most of its length. Hwy 227 and USFS roads follow the South fork from Canyonville.

I-5 shoots through the Umpqua Valley north to south. Just about the only town of consequence in the entire drainage is Roseburg.

ROSEBURG

Population 19,720

Roseburg has a real lived-in, worked-in feel. It has been hard hit by changes in the logging industry, and there's a general down on its luck feeling in the air. Nonetheless, enormous lumber mills ring the town, and entire forests lie supine at the mill south of town.

Roseburg was born when town-founder Aaron Rose arrived at the South fork in 1851 and built a tavern to service passing pioneers. The Oregon & California Railroad arrived from Portland in 1872 and discontinued construction for over a decade due to lack of funds, leaving Roseburg as its southern terminus. Large-scale logging didn't start until WWII, but when it did, Roseburg – Oregon's single greatest source of virgin trees – quickly became one of the greatest lumber mill towns in the world.

Slight of a motel room, Roseburg does not offer much for travelers aside from a good regional history museum. The hills south of Roseburg shelter vineyards and a drive-through zoo.

Orientation & Information

Sprawling, centerless Roseburg lies in a bowl-like valley, near where the South and North forks of the Umpqua River meet. The old downtown area is on the eastern side of the South Umpqua River, while I-5 and new businesses are on the western side. Pine and Stephens Sts are the primary thoroughfares through the downtown area; Harvard Ave leads west from the freeway to parks and the new commercial district. From the downtown area, Hwy 138 follows the North Umpqua River east to Diamond Lake.

For information, contact the City of Roseburg Visitors & Convention Bureau (☎ 672-9731, 800-444-9584), 410 SE Spruce St, PO Box 1262, Roseburg, OR 97470. The headquarters for the Umpqua National Forest (☎ 541-672-6601) is at 2900 Stewart Parkway, and the Fish & Wildlife office (☎ 541-440-3353) is at 4192 North Umpqua Hwy (Hwy 138).

The post office is at 519 SE Kane St. You can do laundry at Clothes Hamper Laundromat (☎ 541-672-0240), 2428 W Harvard Ave. For medical emergencies, go to Mercy Medical Center (☎ 541 673 6641), 738 W Harvard Ave.

Douglas County Museum of History & Natural History

The Douglas County Museum (☎ 541-440-4507, 800-452-0991), just east of I-5 exit 123, near the fairgrounds, is definitely worth the stop. Part of the museum serves as an interpretive center of local Cow Creek Indian culture and history. There are also photographs and relics of the region's early white settlers. The museum is open 10 am to 4 pm Tuesday to Saturday, and noon to 4 pm Sunday; a $2 donation is requested.

Activities

While most anglers head up the North Umpqua River to fish the waters around Steamboat, there is also good **fishing** where the North and South forks converge. To reach this area, travel 7 miles west on

OREGON

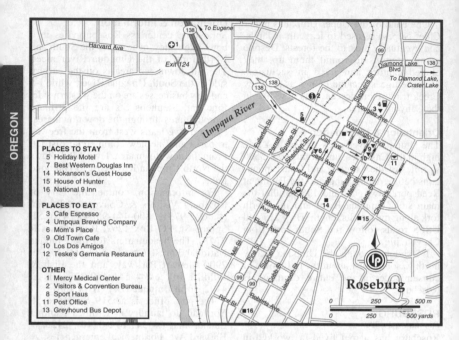

PLACES TO STAY
5 Holiday Motel
7 Best Western Douglas Inn
14 Hokanson's Guest House
15 House of Hunter
16 National 9 Inn

PLACES TO EAT
3 Cafe Espresso
4 Umpqua Brewing Company
6 Mom's Place
9 Old Town Cafe
10 Los Dos Amigos
12 Teske's Germania Restaraunt

OTHER
1 Mercy Medical Center
2 Visitors & Convention Bureau
8 Sport Haus
11 Post Office
13 Greyhound Bus Depot

Roseburg

Garden Valley Rd, and follow signs to River Forks Park.

Before setting out on a self-guided **rafting** trip, check first with the Umpqua National Forest (see Orientation & Information) for guidelines. Rent a raft from North Umpqua Equipment Rental (☎ 541-673-5391) at 14168 N Umpqua Hwy. Guided river trips are available from North Umpqua Outfitters (☎ 541-673-4599), PO Box 1574, Roseburg, OR 97470.

Rent **bicycles** and car racks from J&L's Bicycle Center (☎ 541-672-8139), 1217 NE Walnut St. Cross-country ski rentals are available from the Sport Haus (☎ 541-672-3018), 506 SE Jackson St. The area around Diamond Lake, 76 miles east on Hwy 138, is a favorite for **cross-country skiing**.

Special Events
The Summer Arts Festival, (☎ 541-672-2532) which brings together the works of over 100 regional artists, is held the last weekend of June at the Umpqua Valley Arts Association building, near Stewart Park.

The Douglas County Fair (☎ 541-440-4505), complete with carnival, entertainment, livestock and garden shows, is held the second week in August at the fairgrounds, just east of I-5 exit 123.

Places to Stay
Camping The county runs *Fairgrounds RV Park* (☎ 541-440-4505) at 2100 Frear St, at the fairgrounds off I-5 exit 123 near the South Umpqua. Sites cost $15 and tent campers aren't allowed to stay more than two days.

Amacher County Park (☎ 541-672-4901) at Winchester, 5 miles north of Roseburg at I-5 exit 123, is right on the North Umpqua, but it's also right underneath the freeway bridge. Tent sites are $11, RV sites are $14.

There's more rural camping at *Whistler's Bend County Park* (☎ 541-673-4863), 2828 Whistler's Rd, a beautiful wooded spot on a horseshoe bend of the North Umpqua River. In addition to camping ($8), there are picnic facilities and fishing access. Go 12 miles west of Roseburg on Hwy 138, and west 3 more miles on Whistler's Rd.

Fishing is also featured 6 miles west of town at *Twin Rivers Vacation Park* (☎ 541-673-3811), 433 River Forks Park Rd, where the North and South Umpqua Rivers come together. Tent sites are $15, full RV hookup sites are $21.

B&Bs *Hokanson's Guest House* (☎ 541-672-2632), at 848 SE Jackson St, right downtown, was built in 1882 and is listed in the National Register of Historic Places; rates are $65/75. Just above downtown is the *House of Hunter* (☎ 541-672-2335, 800-540-7704), at 813 SE Kane St, in a nice neighborhood of beautiful old homes. There are five guest rooms, with doubles starting at $65.

Hotels The best lodging deals in Roseburg are along old Hwy 99, now Stephens St. Spacious singles/doubles for $32/38 and a swimming pool put *Budget 16 Motel* (☎ 541-673-5556, 800-414-1648), 1067 NE Stephens St, at the top of the budget heap. You'll get less for the same price at the *Rose City Motel* (☎ 541-673-8209), 1142 NE Stephens St, across the street. To the south is the *National 9 Inn* (☎ 672-3354, 800-524-9999), 1627 SE Stephens St. The slightly more inviting *Holiday Motel* (☎ 541-672-4457) is near the railroad at 444 SE Oak Ave.

The nicest motels are two Best Westerns. Downtown is the *Best Western Douglas Inn* (☎ 541-673-6625, 800-528-1234), 511 SE Stephens St, with rooms for $60. Out at I-5 exit 125 is the *Best Western Garden Villa Motel* (☎ 541-672-1601, 800-547-3446), 760 NW Garden Way, for $68/78. Both places have a pool, exercise room and hot tub.

Places to Eat
Breakfast is an important meal in Roseburg. *Mom's Place* (☎ 541-672-8459), 634 SE Cass Ave, opens at 5 am for the mill

workers; meals are large and tasty. If you won't be working green chain today there's lighter fare at *Cafe Espresso* (☎ 541-672-1859), 368 SE Jackson St, which features breakfast croissants, good soups and fresh salads. Another traditional breakfast and lunch spot, the *Old Town Cafe* (☎ 541-440-4901), 527 SE Jackson St, often stays open on holidays.

The best purveyor of prime rib and steak in Roseburg is *Brutke's Wagon Wheel* (☎ 541-672-7555), 227 NW Garden Valley Blvd. If you're looking for more variety, try Roseburg's ethnic restaurants: *Teske's Germania Restaurant* (☎ 541-672-5401), 647 SE Main St, for German food, *Los Dos Amigos* (☎ 541-673-1351), 537 SE Jackson St, for Mexican.

Professionals, hippies and mill workers all peacefully coexist at the *Umpqua Brewing Company* (☎ 541-672-0452), 328 SE Jackson St, which brews English-style beers and ales, and serves them in a restored and pleasant old bar. The brewpub also offers pizza, burgers and great salads.

Getting There & Away
Greyhound runs four buses a day along I-5; the one-way fare between Roseburg and Eugene is $12. The depot (☎ 541-673-3348) is at 835 SE Stephens St.

AROUND ROSEBURG
Umpqua Valley Wineries
The Umpqua Valley is home to some of Oregon's oldest wineries. Most are in the rolling hills west of Roseburg and specialize in pungent pinot noirs and German-style Rieslings and Gewürztraminers.

For a complete listing of Umpqua Valley wineries, contact the visitors' center. The following are representative and easy to find: **Henry Estate Winery** (☎ 541-459-5120), 687 Hubbard Creek Rd; **Hillcrest Vineyard** (☎ 800-736-3709), 240 Vineyard Lane; **Callahan Ridge** (☎ 541-673-7901, 800-695-4946), 340 Busenbark Lane; and **La Garza Cellars** (☎ 541-679-9654), 491 Winery Lane, off I-5 exit 119. La Garza also has a deli and restaurant.

Wildlife Safari

Ten miles southwest of Roseburg near Winston is a 600-acre Wildlife Safari (☎ 541-679-6761), one of the largest drive-through zoos in the USA. A 3-mile loop takes vehicles through a series of enclosures featuring (successively) animals from Africa, Asia and North America. Lions, elephants, giraffes, hippos – they're all here, lolling around the Oregon countryside.

To find Wildlife Safari, take I-5 exit 119, drive 4 miles to Lookingglass Rd and follow the signs. It's open 9 am to 7 pm daily during the summer; in winter the park closes somewhere between 4 and 6 pm; $11.95/9.95/6.95 adults/seniors/children.

Oakland

Population 850

Tiny Oakland, 16 miles north of Roseburg, was originally a stop-over on the Portland-Sacramento stage line in the 1850s, and it's one of the best-preserved frontier towns in Oregon. Several of Oakland's original businesses still operate in the old storefronts; others have become antique and craft stores. This is a good place to get off the freeway and stop for a break. For information contact the Oakland City Hall (☎ 541-459-4531) at 117 3rd St.

The weekend after Labor Day, Oakland sponsors the Umpqua Valley Wine, Arts & Jazz Festival. For more information, call ☎ 541-672-2648.

Beckley House B&B (☎ 541-459-9320), 338 SE 2nd St, is an 1890s Queen Anne home with two guest suites for $65 to $80. *Tolly's* (☎ 541-459-3796), 115 Locust St, is also a beautifully preserved restaurant. It's the sort of place where couples from Roseburg come for a romantic evening. Dishes such as grilled salmon with fresh fruit chutney cost around $18, pasta dishes cost around $14.

NORTH UMPQUA RIVER

The North Umpqua River alternates between dark pools of quiet, swirling waters and surging cascades that send the river frothing over steep escarpments. Deep forests crowd down to the river's boulder-strewn edge, and enormous volcanic crags rise above the trees and twist down to flank the river.

Hwy 138 follows the North Umpqua River from Roseburg to Crater Lake. The North Umpqua is also known as one of the state's premier fishing streams.

In Glide, the Colliding Rivers Information Center (☎ 541-496-0157), right on the highway at 121 Glide Loop Rd, has recreation information and friendly volunteers, and is open daily, including most holidays. The Diamond Lake Information Center (☎ 541-793-3310) is open during summer. You can contact the Umpqua National Forest's North Umpqua District Ranger Station year-round at ☎ 541-496-3532.

Waterfalls

The North Umpqua River contains one of Oregon's greatest concentrations of waterfalls, with short hikes leading to most of them.

Steamboat Creek is prime spawning grounds for salmon and steelhead (fishing is prohibited the length of the stream). At **Little Falls** and **Steamboat Falls** the fish struggle up this fast-moving stream, offering a glimpse into the life cycle of anadromous (ocean-going) fish. Turn at Steamboat onto USFS Rd 38. Little Falls is just 1 mile upstream. Travel 6 miles along USFS Rd 38 to Steamboat Falls Campground, where a short trail leads to the viewing area.

Toketee Falls drops 120 feet in two stages, first into a mist-filled bowl flanked by columns of basalt, and then a final 80-foot plunge into a deep gorge. The waterfall viewpoint is at the end of an easy half-mile stroll through deep forests. To find the trailhead, turn at Toketee Junction onto USFS Rd 34, and take an immediate left to a parking area.

Awe-provoking **Watson Falls** is, at 272 feet, one of the highest waterfalls in Oregon. To reach it, turn onto USFS Rd 37, which is 2 miles east of Toketee Junction. Park at the picnic area and follow the half-mile trail. It climbs steeply through mossy old-growth forest to end at a footbridge with great views onto the falls.

To reach **Lemolo Falls** requires a bit more of a hike and some off-road driving, but seeing this wild 100-foot waterfall is worth it. Turn off Hwy 138 at USFS Rd 2610 (Lemolo Lake Rd) and continue 4.3 miles to Lemolo Lake, where you'll need to choose between two trails. The first proceeds left onto USFS Rd 3401, Thorn Prairie Rd, for a quarter mile and then right onto USFS Rd 800 for 2 miles to reach the trailhead. The trail is a steep 1-mile descent to the base of the falls. Or continue on USFS Rd 2610 over the reservoir's spillway and turn left on USFS Rd 600. Continue half a mile to the point where the North Umpqua Trail crosses the road. Follow this trail 1½ miles downstream to the falls.

Diamond Lake

Glaciers from the last Ice Age gouged out the basin of 3200-acre Diamond Lake, a beautiful deep-blue lake directly north of Crater Lake. It's an extremely popular lake for anglers and boaters, and winter brings lots of cross-country skiers.

The headquarters for recreation is the attractive Diamond Lake Lodge (☎ 800-733-7593), Diamond Lake Resort, Diamond Lake, OR 97731. Located right on the lake, the lodge offers accommodations (see Places to Stay), restaurants and rentals of cross-country skis, mountain bikes, boats, ice skates and even horses and snowmobiles. Also available are guided Sno-Cat and cross-country ski tours to Crater Lake.

Sno-Cat skiing is also offered at the lodge where a limited number of truly adventurous downhill skiers are taken to the top of 8363-foot Mt Bailey; the trails down the mountain are some of the steepest in the Northwest. Only 12 skiers a day can go. The equally steep $200-a-day price tag includes lunch at a shelter at the top of the mountain.

To reach Diamond Lake, take the North Umpqua Hwy (Hwy 138) east from Roseburg for 76 miles.

Hiking

The principal trail is the 79-mile **North Umpqua Trail**, which follows the river from near Idleyld Park to Lemolo Lake. One good access point is the **Wright Creek Trailhead**, on the south side of the North Umpqua River, just after the bridge on USFS Rd 4711. Follow the trail 5½ miles upstream through old-growth forest to Mott Bridge, near Steamboat.

Several shorter hikes lead to natural curiosities and Native American sites. From Susan Creek Campground, 33 miles east of Roseburg on Hwy 138, the 2-mile roundtrip **Indian Mounds Trail** passes Susan Creek Falls before climbing up to a vision quest site. Another short hike, the 1½-mile **Fall Creek Falls National Recreation Trail** begins at a footbridge 4 miles east of Susan Creek Campground and leads up a narrow fissure in columnar basalt formations to Jobs Garden, a natural shade garden of ferns and mosses, and on to Fall Creek Falls, a double-tiered cascade.

Another hiking trail leads to the popular **Umpqua Hot Springs**, a series of natural hot springs that flow down a bare hillside to join the North Umpqua. Turn at Toketee Junction onto USFS Rd 34 and turn right on Thorn Prairie Rd (USFS Rd 3401). For a 1.8-mile hike, stop just short of the bridge over the river, and follow the North Umpqua Trail upriver to the hot springs. If you're in a hurry to get to the hot springs, continue driving on Thorn Prairie Rd for another 1½ miles; from the parking lot, hike the last quarter mile.

Rising to the east of Diamond Lake is **Mt Thielsen**, one of the most distinctive of the Cascade peaks. At 9182 feet, Mt Thielsen is not the highest peak in the region, but it is undoubtedly the thinnest. Glaciers ate away the conical slopes of the 100,000-year-old volcano, leaving only a narrow plug of basalt to rise like a spire. Referred to as the Lightning Rod of the Cascades, it is so often struck that the rocks at the summit have been recrystalized into fulgurites by electrical fusion. The final 80-foot finger of rock is just as precipitous as it looks and requires technical climbing skills. The Mt Thielsen Trailhead is found 1 mile north of the junction of Hwys 138 and 62.

Fishing

The North Umpqua River is one of the best-loved fishing streams in Oregon, but special regulations limit the season and fishing methods along much of the river. For up-to-date information, contact the Fish & Wildlife office (☎ 541-440-3353) in Roseburg.

The summer steelhead run on the river partially accounts for the fame of the North Umpqua. There are fly-fishing-only restrictions in place between Rock Creek and Soda Springs Dam. Spring Chinook, coho salmon, rainbow trout and German brown trout are also found.

One of the reasons for the North Umpqua's popularity is not just the relative abundance of fish, but also the river itself. This is classic fly-fishing water, especially in the area around Steamboat, where a great inn (see Resorts below) and fly shop cater to the needs of anglers.

Places to Stay

Camping Between Idleyld Park and Diamond Lake there are dozens of campgrounds, many right on the river. For a complete list of public campgrounds, stop at the Umpqua National Forest office (☎ 541-672-6601), 2900 Stewart Parkway in Roseburg, or en route at the Colliding Rivers Information Center (☎ 541-496-0157) in Glide. Fees for the following BLM and USFS sites cost $5 to $10 unless otherwise noted; none offer hookups for RVs.

At the lower end of the North Umpqua River are *Susan Creek Campground*, 33 miles east of Roseburg in a mature Douglas fir forest and *Bogus Creek Campground*, 18 miles east of Glide.

Near Steamboat, *Canton Creek Campground* sits on the banks of Steamboat Creek a quarter of a mile up USFS Rd 38 from Steamboat. Six miles farther along is *Steamboat Falls Campground*, near the famous falls and fish ladder.

In the middle section of the river, the nicest campground is *Horseshoe Bend*, 30 miles east of Glide. The North Umpqua River flows on three sides of this forested campground, making it popular for angling and rafting. *Boulder Flat*, 6 miles farther east, is a primitive campground with good fly-fishing access and great views of lava formations along the river.

For the most part, in the upper reaches of the river, campgrounds tend to cluster around lakes. There are five public campgrounds around Lemolo Lake and three around Diamond Lake.

Hotels The *Dogwood Motel* (☎ 541-496-3403), 5 miles east of Idleyld Park, is a favorite with anglers. Some rooms have kitchens; singles/doubles begin at $25/45.

Lodges *Lemolo Lake Resort* (☎ 541-793-3300), HOC-60 Box 79B, Idleyld Park, OR 97447, is on Lemolo Lake, 75 miles east of Roseburg, with magical views across the lake to the precipitous face of Mt Thielsen. Facilities include indifferently maintained A-frame cabins ($55), RV campsites, a boat ramp, small store and cafe.

Diamond Lake Resort (☎ 800-733-7593) offers standard motel rooms from $70, and two-bedroom cabins with kitchens (for up to six people) from $100 to $155.

Resorts The *Steamboat Inn* (☎ 541-496-3495), 42705 Hwy 138, is an unlikely institution. This upscale fishing lodge, 38 miles east of Roseburg on the banks of the North Umpqua River, offers first-class accommodations and food right in the middle of the wilderness. Stay in rustic streamside cottages ($125 to $160) or in suites beside the lodge ($235).

Places to Eat

For food there's either a few resort-run restaurants or your own camp cooking. The famed lodge restaurant at the *Steamboat Inn* (☎ 541-496-3495), 42705 Hwy 138 in Steamboat, is open for breakfast and lunch, but the real treat is the nightly Fisherman's Dinner served family-style to overnight guests (and non-guests with reservations). The fixed menu changes nightly; it's $35 per person. It's open weekends only from November to March, except in January and February when it's completely closed.

Light meals are available all day at the *Diamond Lake Cafe* in the Diamond Lake Lodge; for fine dining go to the *Mt Thielsen Dining Room*. The *Lemolo Lake Resort* has a small cafe.

Upper Rogue River Valley

From Medford, Hwy 62 (Crater Lake Hwy) heads north and east following the Rogue River to its headwaters. Past Shady Cove, about 17 miles north, the valley walls close in and the silvery river quickens. Dense forests robe the steep mountainsides, with sheer volcanic formations thrusting through the blanket of green.

The Rogue River is noted for some of the best steelhead and trout fishing in Oregon, and modern-day adventurers put the river to good use as well. In summer, the Rogue River between Lost Creek Reservoir and Shady Cove is clotted with rafts and kayaks; on peak summer weekends, three or four boats float by each minute. Above Lost Creek Reservoir, the river abandons any semblance of gentleness, and channels a gorge through thick lava flows. Tributary streams tumble hundreds of feet over sheer walls to join the frenzied Rogue.

Upriver from Medford about 25 miles on Hwy 62, **McGregor Park** is a good place for a picnic or a stretch right by the base of Lost Creek Dam. If you brought your own raft, then this is the place to put in on the Rogue River. There's also an interpretive center focusing on the history, wildlife and geology of the Rogue. Next door is one of the largest fish hatcheries in the West, the **Cole M Rivers Fish Hatchery**, which produces a preponderance of the salmon, trout and steelhead fry that restocks rivers throughout the region.

OREGON

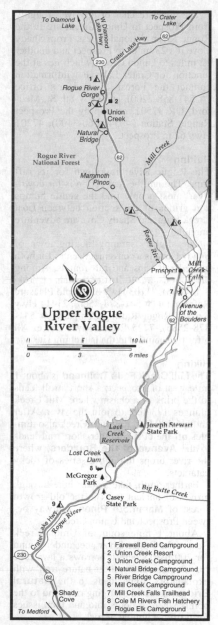

Upper Rogue River Valley

1 Farewell Bend Campground
2 Union Creek Resort
3 Union Creek Campground
4 Natural Bridge Campground
5 River Bridge Campground
6 Mill Creek Campground
7 Mill Creek Falls Trailhead
8 Cole M Rivers Fish Hatchery
9 Rogue Elk Campground

The upper reaches of the river, roughly from Prospect to Union Creek, are in the Rogue River National Forest. From Shady Cove it's 23 miles to Prospect and another 12 miles to Union Creek, which lies at the junction for Crater Lake. For information contact the Forest Supervisor's office (☎ 541-858-2200), at 333 W 8th St, Medford, OR 97501, or stop by the Prospect Ranger Station (☎ 541-560-3400), 47201 Hwy 62 in Prospect.

Rafting

The Rogue River is known for its raft trips. Though the real action is far downriver, most people find the gentle bumps and grinds of the section between Lost Creek Dam and Shady Cove are adventure enough.

The slightly scrappy-looking town of Shady Cove is a convenient center for both guided raft trips and raft rentals. Among the options are: Raft Rite Rentals (☎ 541-878-4005), 21103 Hwy 62; Rapid Pleasure Raft Rental (☎ 541-878-2500), 21411 Hwy 62; and Rogue Rafting Company (☎ 541-878-2585), 7725 Rogue River Drive. All offer free shuttles to the launching site.

Hiking

The **Mill Creek Falls Trailhead** is about 1 mile west of Prospect; a short stroll leads to the brink of a chasm where Mill Creek plunges 173 feet to join the river. After another 100 feet, tiny Barr Creek also tumbles off the cliff. Another short trail leads to the **Avenue of the Boulders**, where the river drops through a series of rocky cataracts.

Farther north, take a short hike through groves of ancient trees in the old-growth forest of **Mammoth Pines**, midway between Prospect and Union Creek.

About 1 mile south of Union Creek Resort, the Rogue River goes underground for 200 feet, where it borrows a lava tube for its channel. A short nature trail with explanatory signs leads to the **Natural Bridge**, across the surging river and to the points where it pours into and then issues forth from a jumble of rock.

Just a little farther upriver is the **Rogue River Gorge**, cutting a sheer-walled cleft into lava flows where a number of tributary creeks come together. While the word 'gorge' is a bit misleading, especially if you've been to the Columbia River recently, the quarter-mile trail along this narrow, turbulent section of the Rogue River is magical. At one point the trail drops down into the chasm, where the spray and mist sustain a shadowy moss garden.

For long-distance hikes, try the **Upper Rogue River Trail.** It follows the river for 47 miles between Prospect and Crater Lake National Park. Trails on both the east and west sides of the river between the Natural Bridge and the Rogue River Gorge are great for day hikers. Consult the Rogue River National Forest map or ask at ranger stations for other hiking options.

Fishing

Fishing is legendary on the Rogue River – Zane Grey, Herbert Hoover, Jack London and Teddy Roosevelt were early champions of the river.

In the stretch of river above Tou Velle State Park to Lost Creek Dam, salmon and steelhead fishing is especially good. Between Shady Cove and the dam the road hugs the river, and there are frequent parks and easy access to the riverbank. Many outfitters offer fishing trips on the Rogue River. The Rogue River Guides Association, PO Box 792, Medford, OR 97501, is a group representing river outfitters; contact them for a listing of fishing and floating options.

Places to Stay

Camping There are a number of campgrounds near Shady Cove. One of the best for RV campers is *Fly Casters RV Park* (☎ 541-878-2749), 211655 Hwy 62, with riverside sites from $15. *Rogue Elk Campground* (☎ 541-776-7001), halfway between Shady Cove and Lost Creek Reservoir, is a county park with showers, raft-launching areas, good fishing and hookup sites starting at $14.

On Lost Creek Reservoir, about 8 miles from both Prospect and Shady Cove, the nicest place to camp is *Joseph Stewart State Park* (☎ 541-560-3334), 35251 Hwy 62, with several hundred campsites alongside the reservoir. Showers, boat launches and bicycle paths are some of the offerings. Tent sites begin at $14.

There are various USFS campgrounds farther up on the Rogue River with sites from $8 to $10. *Mill Creek Campground* and *River Bridge Campground* are both close to food and drink at Prospect. *Union Creek* and *Farewell Bend* are close to Union Creek. For a $3 donation you can camp without water at the pleasant *Natural Bridge Campground*, about a mile south of Union Creek Campground. Hike down the river a short distance from here and you'll end up right on the Natural Bridge lava tube, from where you can look up at envious visitors stuck behind the fenced-off viewing platform

Hotels In Shady Cove the *Royal Coachman Motel* (☎ 541-878-2481), at 21906 Hwy 62, with rooms at $41, and the *Maple Leaf Lodge* (☎ 541-878-2169), 20717 Hwy 62, with singles/doubles for $35/39, are perfunctory riverside motels with some kitchenettes.

The Rogue River's real treasure is the *Prospect Hotel* (☎ 541-560-3664, 800-944-6490), 391 Mill Creek Drive, a grand old hotel built in 1889. The setting is beautiful, amid deep forests with the distant roar of the Rogue River. The hotel has a wraparound porch with a porch swing, and a notably good dining room. Although the rooms are charming, they are authentically small; no children or dogs are allowed. Smoking is also prohibited. Behind the hotel are a few modern motel units where these vices are allowed; prices of rooms and units range between $60 and $80.

At Union Creek, there is an old 1930s lodge called the *Union Creek Resort* (☎ 541-560-3565). Rooms are available in the old lodge and in free-standing cabins, beginning at $50.

Places to Eat

In Shady Cove, eat at *Mac's Diner* (☎ 541-878-6227), 22225 Hwy 62, for sandwiches and light meals. Just upriver from Shady Cove is the *Rogue River Lodge* (☎ 541-878-2555), 24904 Hwy 62, a more upscale bar and supper club right on the river. The best restaurant in the area is *Bel Di's* (☎ 541-878-2010), 21900 Hwy 62, where you can sit at a table laid with linen and crystal and look over the Rogue River. The menu mixes continental preparations and local ingredients; average price of an entrée is $16.

The century old dining room at the *Prospect Hotel* (☎ 541-560-3664) in Prospect has been lovingly maintained, with brass, oak and chandeliers from another era. The food's quite good too, with trout, steak and seafood dinners starting at $12. The Sunday brunch here is popular, and continues to 1 pm.

In Union Creek, *Beckie's Cafe* (☎ 541-560-3563), is the place to eat, with logger-style breakfasts and hearty food throughout the day. On a hot day, Beckie's ice-cream parlor next door to the cafe is a mandatory stop.

Crater Lake National Park

The deepest lake in the USA, and Oregon's only national park, Crater Lake is a stunning landmark to the violent geologic forces that formed the Northwest. Known mostly as a beauty spot – yes, you too will exclaim when you first glimpse this perfectly symmetrical, uncannily blue body of water – Crater Lake also offers hiking and cross-country skiing trails, a boat ride to a rugged island and scenic drives around the lip of the crater.

About 500,000 people visit the 286-sq-mile park annually. But after spending a considerable amount of time getting to the park, few people do more than take some photos from the vista points and then hurry

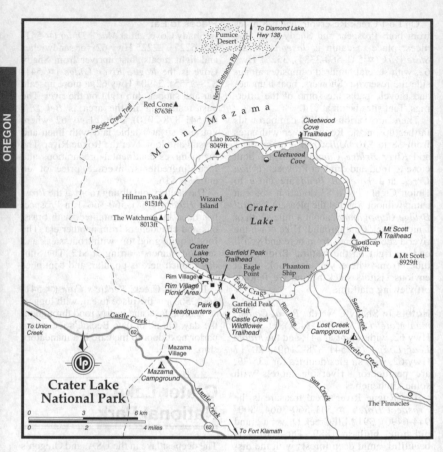

Crater Lake
National Park

on. It's true Crater Lake is no Yellowstone or Yosemite, but exploring the park's side roads will lead to interesting areas and recreational opportunities, and the historic Crater Lake Lodge, built between 1909 and 1915, is open again after years of extensive renovation.

Orientation & Information

Crater Lake National Park can be reached from Medford or Klamath Falls on Hwy 62. From Medford, it's 72 miles to Crater Lake; from Klamath Falls, it's 73 miles. Crater Lake is also reached from Roseburg along Hwy 138, a distance of 87 miles. If

you are driving south along US 97, it's 90 miles from Bend to the park.

The south entrance to the park is open year-round. The north entrance is not usually open until June and remains open until snow closes it, usually in October. Rim Drive opens and closes about the same time. Caldera viewpoints are cold and windy even during summer, so bring warm clothing. There is a $10 fee per vehicle to visit the park. Food concessions, an information center and a gift shop make up Rim Village, on the southern edge of the caldera. The park headquarters is at the Steel Visitors Center, just south of Rim Village.

For information on Crater Lake National Park, contact the park headquarters (☎ 541-594-2211), at PO Box 7, Crater Lake, OR 97604.

Rim Drive

A 33-mile loop road winds around the rim of Crater Lake, giving access to assorted viewpoints, trailheads and side roads. The paved, one-way-only route begins on the northwest edge of Crater Lake and follows the lip of the crater clockwise until the road ducks behind **Cloudcap**, a point rising 2000 feet above the lake. A paved side road leads to the crest of Cloudcap, affording some of the best views of the lake and distant peaks like Mt Shasta and Mt McLoughlin.

A few miles later, another side road off Rim Drive leads 10 miles southeast to **The Pinnacles**. This is an area where water erosion has carved extensive pumice and ash formations into 100-foot spires and minarets called hoodoos. Rim Drive continues in a full loop all the way around the lake.

Cleetwood Cove Trail

The mile-long Cleetwood Cove Trail is the only access to the lake itself and is very popular, since the end of the trail also serves as the departure point for the **Crater Lake Boat Tour**. About 500 people a day struggle down the 700-foot descent to the water, making this footpath more of an expressway than an escape.

Boats leave from the dock on the hour between 10 am and 4:30 pm for two-hour cruises around Crater Lake's 25-mile perimeter. Park rangers provide geologic and historic information. The boat stops at Wizard Island, a 760-foot cinder cone, for a brief layover. Hikers can elect to climb the short mile hike to the island's summit, or follow other trails to small icy bays, and return on later boats.

Boat excursions leave from Cleetwood Cove, on the north side of the lake, between late June and mid-September. The trip costs $12/6.50 adults/children, and children under two are free.

Hiking

Higher elevation trails aren't completely clear of snow until late July. From the eastern end of the parking lot at Rim Village, a 1.7-mile trail leads up **Garfield Peak** to an expansive view over the lake; in July the slopes are covered with wildflowers. Even better vistas are seen from the eastern edge of Rim Drive, where **Mt Scott** – the highest peak on the perimeter of Crater Lake – rises 8929 feet. The trailhead to

Explosions at Mt Mazama

The ancient mountain whose remains now form Crater Lake was Mt Mazama. It was a roughly 12,000-foot volcanic peak, heavily glaciered, that had been inactive for many thousands of years until for some reason, the volcano came to life again. Rhiolite, a kind of molten rock that, unlike basalt, contains a high concentration of water, created a very violent eruption. Geologists know that the lava that caused the eruption at Mt Mazama was rhiolite because it came to the surface as pumice, a type of rock infused with so many air chambers (due to the expanding water in the lava) that it floats on water.

The catastrophic explosion at Mt Mazama occurred only 7700 years ago, scattering pumice and ash for hundreds of miles across the Northwest. This first eruption was followed by flows of super-heated pumice that surged down Mt Mazama's slopes before solidifying into banks hundreds of feet in depth. The sparse forests north of Crater Lake grow in the pumice and ash of Mt Mazama. The best place to see this barren land is in the Pumice Desert, immediately north of Crater Lake along North Entrance Rd.

After the eruption, the magma chambers at the heart of the volcano were empty, and the summit cone collapsed into itself, forming a caldera.

Only snowfall and rain contribute to the lake water. It is this purity and the lake's great depth that give it its famous blue color. ■

OREGON

The New Crater Lake Lodge

When the NPS began construction of the old Crater Lake Lodge in 1909, they had in mind a grand timber and stone lodge in rustic Cascadian style, featuring huge fireplaces, tree trunks as columns and rafters, and a sense of being part of the landscape. However, after the frame of the building was completed, federal funding dried up. The lodge was completed hastily in a slap-dash manner, and opened to the public.

Eighty years later, time, the park's formidable weather and innumerable earthquakes had taken their toll on the lodge: foundations were crumbling, the roof was giving in and walls were sagging. In 1988 the foundation closed due to safety concerns, and plans were announced to raze the building, as engineers judged that it was no longer structurally sound enough to justify a remodel. After a strong public outcry, Congress came up with the money to preserve the lodge by essentially rebuilding the entire structure. A new foundation, roof frame, and steel and concrete structure replaced the old, while maintaining the historic appearance and much of the layout. Many elements of the old lodge were recycled by disassembling old fixtures, cleaning them and then replacing them in the new structure.

Some things did change. The lodge's original 150 cramped guest rooms were reduced to 71, each more sizable and with private bathrooms. The food in the lodge restaurant – which has one of the most astonishing views in the world – has been updated to represent the dishes of Northwest cuisine. Still, there are no telephones or TVs in the room: this is supposed to be a getaway, after all. ■

Mt Scott is on Rim Drive across from the Cloudcap viewpoint turnoff.

A less ambitious climb to another Crater Lake viewpoint follows a 1-mile trail from the northwest stretch of Rim Drive to **The Watchman**, an old lookout tower. From the park headquarters, another 1-mile nature trail leads through the **Castle Crest** wildflower gardens.

Cross-Country Skiing

In winter, only the southern entrance and the road to Rim Village are kept plowed, and the park is closed to all but cross-country skiers and snow-shoe enthusiasts. Skiing Rim Drive, and exploring the park under its massive snowfall (an average of 44 feet!), is a popular weekend excursion. A full circumnavigation of Crater Lake along Rim Drive takes at least two days and involves snow camping. You'll also need a permit and registration from park headquarters and lots of experience.

The weather is very changeable and avalanches are common on the caldera's dangerous steep outer slopes. Rentals are not available from the visitors' center, so bring your own skis.

Places to Stay & Eat

Facilities in the park are pretty limited. Many travelers just make a day trip to Crater Lake from Medford, Roseburg, Bend, or Klamath Falls. However, if you want to stay in the vicinity, and campsites and lodging in the park are booked up, then try the small community of **Fort Klamath**, just 15 miles southeast of Crater Lake on Hwy 62. Keep in mind that everything closes up at the end of October, when the snow takes over, and opens again around April. The season varies, so it's best to call ahead if you're on the fringe of those months.

Crater Lake *Mazama Campground*, near the park's south entrance, offers nearly 200 pleasant, wooded sites on a first-come, first-served basis. There are 12 more remote campsites at the slightly scruffy *Lost Creek Campground*, on the road to The Pinnacles. A $10 fee is charged at either campground.

In the park you can choose between *Mazama Village Motor Inn* (☎ 541-830-8700), at $78 a night in high season, and the grand old *Crater Lake Lodge* (☎ 541-830-8700). Rooms at the lodge cost $99 to $129, with two-bed loft rooms topping out at $188. It's typically booked out six months to a year in advance, though it's worthwhile to check for cancellations if you've arrived without a reservation.

In the lobby, the *Crater Lake Lodge Dining Room* showcases Northwest cuisine in its formal, lake-view restaurant. Entrees like poached salmon weigh in at around $20, with pasta dishes costing slightly less. In Rim Village there's family dining at the *Watchman Restaurant*, and cafeteria meals at the *Llao Rock Cafe*.

Fort Klamath If camping is out of the question, try Fort Klamath for a cheap motel room or cabins. *Fort Klamath Lodge* (☎ 541-381-2234) offers both motel rooms ($30/35) and RV sites ($12). The *Crater Lake Resort* (☎ 541-381-2349), PO Box 457, Hwy 62, also has RV sites ($14) and offers lodging in one- and two-bedroom cabins ($40 to $45). South of town is the *Aspen Inn Motel* (☎ 541-381-2321), 52250 Hwy 62, one of the nicer places with neat A-frame cabins for $55/60.

There's home-style cooking at the *Cattle Crossing Cafe* (☎ 541-381-9801) on Hwy 62, open for three square meals daily.

Klamath Basin

Oregon's most slighted region, the Klamath Basin is a broad, marshy floodplain extending from the southern base of Mt Mazama into the northernmost part of California. Once one of the world's largest lakes, the Klamath Basin was historically covered with nearly 290 sq miles of shallow water, reeds and rushes, which made it a great place to live – for birds. Roughly 6 million birds and waterfowl once made their homes here. Pioneers, on the other hand, turned up their noses at this swampy territory and continued west for friendlier prairies. People were only persuaded into settling Klamath Falls after the government began converting the lakes to farmland in 1905, an action which reduced the wetlands to an alarming quarter of their original size and led to the creation of the nation's first wildlife refuge.

Recently, Klamath Falls has done its best to promote itself as a retirement destination, and has been particularly successful in luring military retirees to the area. With some of the best bird watching in the West, great fishing in the beautiful Williamson and Klamath Rivers, and easy access to all-season recreation in the Cascades, in the local national forests and on Oregon's largest lake (the Upper Klamath), Klamath Falls has a lot to offer – especially if you're bankrolled by a retirement pension. Sadly, sagging economies in timber and ranching continue to offer little for the residents who have spent most of their lives here.

Klamath Falls is 79 miles east of Medford on Hwy 140, and 63 miles east of Ashland on Hwy 66. Klamath Falls is often used as a jumping-off point to visit Crater Lake, 73 miles to the north on US 97 and Hwy 62.

KLAMATH FALLS
Population 18,400

Klamath Falls is one of the state's most economically challenged cities. The end of logging-as we knew-it has left K Falls (as most people refer to the town) with one of the worst unemployment rates in the state. Klamath Falls is also known throughout the state as one of the most conservative communities in Oregon. Evangelical Christian churches seem to flourish here and keep close watch on the social and political fabric of the community; Klamath Falls was the birthplace of the Oregon Citizens Alliance.

Nearby recreation and the Klamath Basin National Wildlife Refuges are the main draws to Klamath Falls. The town itself lacks any attraction for travelers aside from an excellent Indian artifact museum. Motels and restaurants are mostly clustered in the old downtown area along Main St

OREGON

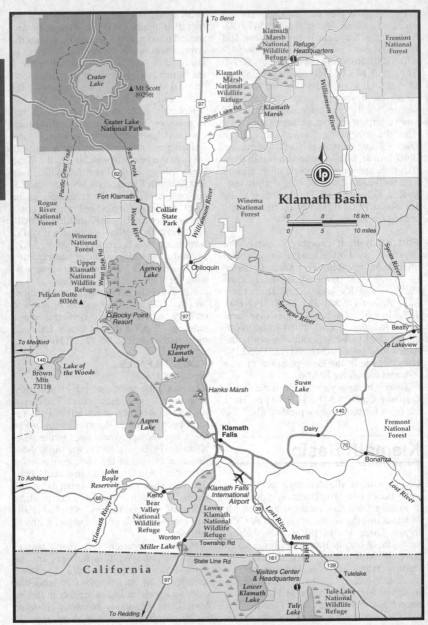

OREGON

and Klamath Ave. More recent commercial growth has occurred south of town, along S 6th St and Hwy 39.

Information

For tourist information, contact the Klamath County Chamber of Commerce (☎ 541-884-5193), 701 Plum Ave, Klamath Falls, OR 97601, or drop by the visitors' center at the Klamath County Museum (☎ 541-884-0666, 800 445-6728), at 1451 Main St. For information on recreation on public lands, contact the Klamath Ranger Station (☎ 541-883-3400), 1936 California Ave.

The post office is at 317 S 7th St. The *Herald & News* comes out daily except Saturday. Tune in to Jefferson Public Radio on KSKF 90.0 FM. Oregon Institute of Technology's KTEC at 89.5 FM is an alternative public radio station.

Robert's Wash & Dry (☎ 541-882-5417), is at 5708 Hart Court, and the local hospital is the Merle West Medical Center (☎ 541-882-6311) at 2865 Daggett St.

Favell Museum of Western Art & Indian Artifacts

Undoubtedly the best collection of Native American artifacts in Oregon, this impressive museum (☎ 541-882-9996), 125 W Main St, provides a fascinating interpretation of western Native American culture. The collection is the life work – or obsession – of Gene Favell, a Lakeview native. Opened in 1972, the Favell Museum houses an eclectic smorgasbord of Western American tools, weapons, basketry and beadwork. The museum is open 9:30 am to 5:50 pm, from Monday to Saturday; $4/3/2 adults/seniors/youth.

Klamath County Museum

Housed in the old art deco National Guard Armory, this community museum (☎ 541-883-4208), 1451 Main St, features displays on the natural history of the Klamath Lakes area, as well as exhibits that discuss the local Native American culture and the events of the Modoc War (1869-73). It is

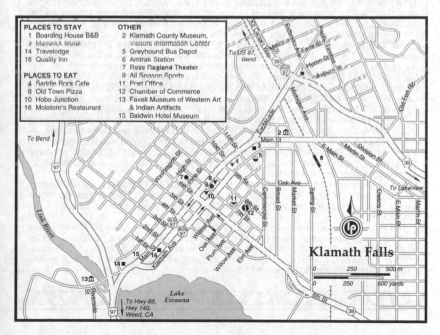

OREGON

The Modoc War

The Klamath Lakes were the traditional homelands of the Klamath and Modoc tribes. Although the tribes were linguistically related and lived close geographically, they were fierce rivals and were among the last of Oregon's Native Americans to have contact with white settlers and explorers. Relations were initially friendly, until the development of the Applegate (or Southern Oregon) Trail. White settlers crossing the trail onto Modoc land soon began demanding that the Modocs be moved onto the Klamath Reservation, which infuriated the Modocs and led to a raid which left 15 white settlers dead near Tule Lake, CA. Pioneer vigilante groups and the Modocs then began a series of fierce clashes. The US Army intervened in 1863 and built Fort Klamath to protect settlers from Indian hostilities.

Chief Keintpoos ('Captain Jack')

By 1864 the Modoc and the Klamath were forced to sign a treaty consigning them to the same reservation, north of Upper Klamath Lake. After Chief Keintpoos, better known as Captain Jack, killed a Klamath shaman, he led a group of Modoc off the reservation in 1865 to return to the Lost River area north of Tule Lake, where white farmers were beginning to settle. Further conflict ensued as the settlers tried to remove the Modoc. By the 1870s the remaining Modocs on the Klamath Reservation moved to the far eastern edge of the tribal land in order to protect themselves from the hostility of the Klamath.

The US Army's attempt to convince the Modoc to return to the reservation proved unsuccessful. Captain Jack demanded a separate Modoc reservation but was refused. He and his people began to raid emigrant wagon trains for livestock and food. In November 1872 the army moved in to arrest Captain Jack and two other Modoc leaders. Fighting broke out and Captain Jack and his group fled to the Lava Beds, south of Tule Lake. Hidden by the labyrinth of fissures and caverns, which the Modoc knew well, a group of 170 Modoc warriors successfully withstood 1000 army soldiers.

In April 1873 government officials approached the Modoc stonghold under a flag of truce. The Modoc opened fire, killing Brigadier General Canby and the federal Superintendent of Indian Affairs, Rev E Thomas. The Oregon Indian superintendent, AB Meacham, was shot five times, knifed and left for dead. A young Modoc princess, Winema, hurried to Meacham's rescue, and acted as interpreter and intermediary between the army and the Modoc.

Captain Jack and his chiefs were captured in June 1873, the Modoc chief and three of his men were hanged at Fort Klamath, and other leaders were sent to Alcatraz for life sentences. The remainder of Captain Jack's followers were sent to Oklahoma for resettlement.

The Klamath Reservation had totaled 1560 sq miles in 1864, but by 1986 had been whittled away by the government and Klamath landowners to nothing. Today, many Klamaths, Modocs and some Northern Paiutes live near the town of Chiloquin, 30 miles north of Klamath Falls. For more information about the Klamath tribes and local events, call ☎ 541-783-2219 or 800-524-9787. ■

open 9 am to 5:30 pm daily, June to September 30, and 8 am to 4:30 pm the rest of the year; admission is by donation.

Baldwin Hotel Museum

Built in 1904, the Baldwin Hotel (☎ 541-883-4208), 31 Main St, first served as a hardware store before being turned into a showcase hotel in 1911. In its day, Presidents Teddy Roosevelt, Taft and Wilson stayed here. The hotel has retained its glory, with many of its original fixtures and furnishings intact. The museum is open 10 am to 4 pm, Tuesday to Saturday, June to September 30, and the last tour departs at 3 pm; admission is $3.

Activities

To go **cross-country skiing** at Lake of the Woods or Crater Lake, rent equipment at All Season Sports (☎ 541-884-3863), 714 Main St.

The Upper Klamath River provides some of the best **white-water rafting** in the state. Adventure Center Raft Trips (☎ 541-883-6340), at 40 N Main St, Ashland, OR 97520, offers one- and two-day trips ($110 and $295) down the river, with enough thrills (several Class IV rapids) for even jaded rafters. The season lasts from April to October.

Fish for trophy-sized rainbow trout at the Williamson River north of Upper Klamath Lake. Dependable access is sometimes a problem; the best access is in Winema National Forest lands or from Collier State Park, north of Chiloquin. For licenses, information and fish stories, contact the Williamson River Anglers (☎ 541-783-2677) at the junction of Hwy 62 and US 97, near Chiloquin.

Special Events

Every February, the Klamath Basin Eagle Conference is held at the Oregon Institute of Technology and is open to the public. This meeting of conservationists, ecologists and bird watchers includes lectures, workshops and field trips, plus a wildlife art show and film festival. Call the Oregon Dept of Fish & Game (☎ 541-883-5732) or the chamber of commerce for information.

The Klamath Memorial Rodeo & Indian Dancing Festival (☎ 541-882-2095, 885-3911) is held at the Klamath County Fairgrounds, 3531 S 6th St, over Memorial Day weekend. The Klamath County Fair & Jefferson State Rodeo (☎ 541-883-3796), is held the first weekend of August at the fairgrounds.

Tribal Treaty Days, Powwow & Rodeo (☎ 541-783-2218), held in August at the Chiloquin Rodeo Grounds, offers an all-Indian Rodeo, marathon run, parade and salmon barbecue to celebrate the Klamath Indians' return to federally recognized tribal status in 1986.

Places to Stay

Camping At KOA's *Kampgrounds of Klamath Falls* (☎ 541-884-4644), 3435 Shasta Way, full hookups run around $20 and tent sites are $17. *Oregon 8 RV Park* (☎ 541-882-0482) is 3 miles north of Klamath Falls at 5225 N US 97, and sites are $15.

Directly west of Klamath Falls rise the Cascade mountains, where there's cooler and shadier camping. *Lake of the Woods Resort* (☎ 541-949-8300), 950 Harriman Route on Lake of the Woods, has tent sites ($8), RV sites ($12) and cabins for four ($40 to $65). There's also a room that sleeps four in the lodge for $32. The lodge is open year-round, though it's closed Monday and Tuesday in winter. Boat, cross-country ski, snowmobile and ice-skate rentals are available.

B&Bs *The Boarding House Inn B&B* (☎ 541-883-8584), 1800 Esplanade Ave, was once a lodging for rail workers in the early 1900s. All four guest rooms have private bathrooms and full kitchens. Rates range from $45 to $65.

Thompson's B&B by the Lake (☎ 541-882-7938), 1420 Wild Plum Court, offers views over Upper Klamath Lake and the Cascades. There are four guest rooms, two with private bath, and all have private entrances. Rooms begin at $70.

Hotels A few miles north of Klamath Falls are a couple of good deals in lodging: *High Chaparral Motel* (☎ 541-882-4675), 5440 N US 97, and the *Oregon 8 Motel* (☎ 541-883-3431), 3 miles north of Klamath Falls at 5225 US 97 N, are in the $30 to $40 range.

In town, rooms at the *Maverick Motel* (☎ 541-882-6688, 800-404-6690), 1220 Main St, the *Travelodge* (☎ 541-882-4494, 800-578-7878), 11 Main St, and the *Cimarron Motel* (☎ 541-882-4601, 800-742-2648), 3060 S 6th St, are $35 to $50.

The following hotels are a bit pricier at $55 to $80: The *Quality Inn* (☎ 541-882-4666, 800-732-2025), 100 Main St, the *Best Western Klamath Inn* (☎ 541-882-1200, 800-528-1234), 4061 S 6th St, and the *DoubleTree Hotel* (☎ 541-882-8864) at 3612 S 6th St. These last two hotels have pools.

Lodges *Rocky Point Resort* (☎ 541-356-2287), 28121 Rocky Point Rd, is on the northwest end of Upper Klamath Lake, near the wildlife refuge. From Hwy 140, turn at Harriman Lodge and follow the signs. Tent sites are $14, RV sites run $16 to $18, motel rooms start at $53 and cabins in the woods next to the lake start at $69. There's a full-service marina, tackle shop, restaurant and cocktail lounge.

Places to Eat
For espresso, bagels and pastries, go to *Renaldo's Cafe Espresso* (☎ 541-884-3846) at the Oregon Institute of Technology in Campus Square Plaza, north of the city center on Kit Carson Way.

Hobo Junction (☎ 541-882-8013), 636 Main St, has sandwiches and light meals. *Old Town Pizza* (☎ 541-884-8858), 722 Main St, serves Klamath Falls' best pizza. *Molatore's Restaurant* (☎ 541-884-6298), 100 Main St, part of the large Quality Inn motel complex, is open for three meals a day. *Saddle Rock Cafe* (☎ 541-883-3970), 1012 Main St, was one of the first fine restaurants in Klamath Falls, with pasta and carefully seasoned sauces and rotisserie chicken. At lunch, the salads are a welcome relief after traveling through red meat country.

Chez Nous (☎ 541-883-8719), 3927 S 6th St, sounds like a French restaurant, but most people go there for the steak and seafood. *Fiorella's* (☎ 541-882-1878), 6139 Simmers Ave, offers 11 different pastas, including gnocchi ($11.50), and four veal preparations (veal piccata is $16) as well as chicken and filet mignon.

Entertainment
The art deco *Ross Ragland Theater* (☎ 541-884-5483), 218 N 7th St, serves as the stage for the community symphony and chorus, as well as country & western celebrities and Broadway troupes. *Pelican Cinemas* (☎ 541-884-5000), 2626 Biehn St, offers six screens worth of first-run movies.

Getting There & Away
Air Klamath Falls International Airport (☎ 541-883-5372) is off Hwy 140 south of town. Horizon Airlines (☎ 541-884-3331) offers six flights a day to/from Portland. United Express has two flights every day between San Francisco and Klamath Falls, with a stopover in Chico, CA.

Bus Greyhound (☎ 541-882-4616) offers direct bus service to Eugene, Portland, Bend, and Redding, CA, from their depot at 1200 Klamath Ave. Surprisingly, there's no direct bus to Medford. One-way fare from Klamath Falls to Portland is $36.

Train Amtrak's *Coast Starlight* passes through twice daily between San Francisco and Portland. The station (☎ 541-884-2822) is at S Spring St and Oak Ave.

Getting Around
Contact Hertz (☎ 541-882-0220) at 6815 Rand Way, near the airport, to rent a car. Call AB Taxi (☎ 541-885-5607) for a cab.

KLAMATH BASIN NATIONAL WILDLIFE REFUGES
Six wildlife refuges totaling more than 263 sq miles string along the old basin of Ice-Age Modoc Lake (also known as Lower Klamath Lake), from Upper Klamath Lake in Oregon to Tule Lake in California. The

refuges support over 400 species of wildlife. These lakes are important stopovers on the Pacific flyway – 45,000 ducks and 26,000 Canadian geese are hatched here annually. Concentrations of up to 2 million birds are possible in spring and fall peak seasons. The basin is also prime winter territory for bald eagles.

For more information about the Klamath Basin National Wildlife Refuges (☎ 530-667-2231), contact the headquarters at Route 1 Box 74, Tulelake, CA 96134, or the Oregon Dept of Fish & Wildlife (☎ 541-883-5732), 1400 Miller Island Rd W, Klamath Falls, OR 97603.

There are no organized tours to the refuges, but all are open to visitors. Check with local officials for seasonal closures due to nesting or other circumstances. Following is basic information about the principal Klamath Basin refuges in Oregon.

The **Upper Klamath Refuge** is on the northwestern shore of shallow, marshy Upper Klamath Lake. Tule rushes fill the lake, lending shelter to colonies of cormorants, egrets, herons, cranes, pelicans and many varieties of ducks and geese. Access to the preserve is by canoe only, which can be rented at Rocky Point Resort (see Lodges above). To reach the refuge, follow Hwy 140 north from Klamath Falls to Harriman Lodge, and follow the signs to the Rocky Point Resort and the refuge.

The **Bear Valley Refuge**, west of Worden, is known mostly as a wintering area for bald eagles; 500 to 1000 gather here

The USA's national bird, the bald eagle, has a wing span of up to 8 feet.

between December and February. To reach the refuge, follow US 97 south to Worden, and turn west on the Keno-Worden Rd.

The **Lower Klamath Refuge** probably offers the best year-round wildlife viewing and the easiest access of the Klamath refuges. Established in 1908 as the nation's first wildlife refuge, this 83-sq-mile preserve begins in Oregon and stretches south into California. This mix of open water, shallow marsh, cropland and grassy upland is home to many species of wildlife. For a quick overview of the area, take the self-guided loop drive, 5 miles east of the western entrance to the refuge on Hwy 161, also called State Line Rd.

Central Oregon

For many people, central Oregon *is* recreation. Fishing, white-water rafting, rock climbing, skiing, hiking and wildlife viewing begin the list of outdoor activities that make Oregon's fair-weather region a favorite destination. The Deschutes and the Metolius Rivers are famous throughout the USA for trout fishing, and the thousands of acres of golf courses are considered by many the region's real treasure.

It's impossible to ignore the geography of central Oregon. Volcanoes and erosion have each indelibly marked the landscape with spectacular formations. Ten million years of prodigious volcanic activity in northeastern Oregon covered the land in successions of massive lava flows, creating a magma base that is reckoned to be, in some places, up to a half mile deep. The rivers and streams of central Oregon managed to carve extraordinary canyons through the deep lava beds, the Deschutes and Crooked Rivers in particular incising amazing gorges into the tortured volcanic landscape.

The Deschutes River, which descends from the Cascades to the Columbia River, cutting through central Oregon from south to north, is the region's main river and home to brown and rainbow trout (locally known as 'redsides' for their coppery flanks). Steelhead trout make their dramatic seasonal runs up it – watch them hurl themselves up the torrent at Sherars Falls.

Central Oregon's dry, sunny climate and high elevation – between 3000 and 4000 feet – give rise to an ecosystem called the high desert, characterized by ponderosa pines, sagebrush and scrub juniper. An array of animals find a home in this landscape. Raptors, including golden eagles and red-tailed hawks, are commonly seen hunting the open forests. Mule deer are pervasive throughout the region, and coyotes have adapted hastily to the inexorable suburbanization of central Oregon and are as happy to eat domestic cats as more traditional rodent fare.

Once the domain of the Wasco Indians, the Oregon Trail – and later, the promise of gold – brought settlers to the area; the native tribes were relegated to the Warm Springs Indian Reservation in 1855. Cycles of drought finished off all but the most persistent of the early homesteaders, until the 1940s when the US government built irrigation dams along the Deschutes. With a little water the fertile volcanic soil blossomed with traditional farm crops like alfalfa.

This part of the state has long been the provenance of cattle ranchers and irrigation farmers, but the region's beautiful setting and exceptional recreational opportunities have begun to lure a new breed of settler. Businesses began to relocate to central Oregon in the 1980s as 'lifestyle' considerations came to figure into corporate decisions. Retirees moved here to escape the clouds and gloom of coastal climates. As a result, real-estate developers have subdivided much of this high-savanna land into semirural suburbs and resort communities.

Getting There & Away

Air The Redmond/Bend Airport, the region's only airport served by commercial airlines, is just southeast of Redmond on US 97, 18 miles north of Bend. United Express and Horizon Air fly into the airport from Portland, Eugene, Seattle and San Francisco. The one-way airfare to/from Portland is about $70.

CAC Transportation's Redmond Airport Shuttle (☎ 541-389-7469, 800-955-8267) links Bend to the airport. Fares to Bend are $17 for door-to-door service; make reservations at least 24 hours in advance. The same company offers twice-daily bus service between Portland and Bend for $30.

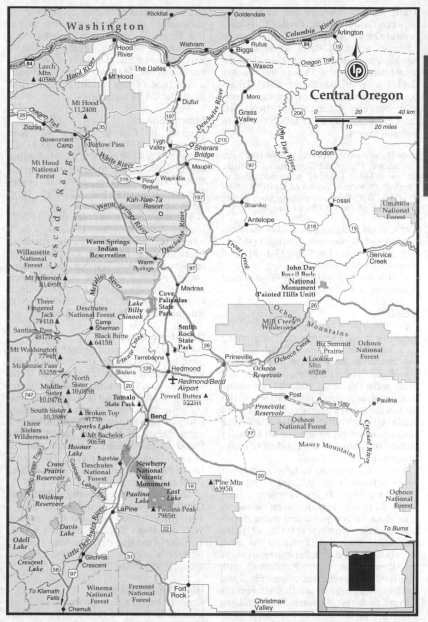

Train Amtrak operates one train a day between California and Portland. Its only central Oregon stop is in Chemult, about 65 miles south of Bend. Presently, the northbound train arrives at 9 am, and the southbound train at 8:55 pm. You can buy tickets from the conductor. CAC Transportation (see above) provides shuttle service between Chemult and Bend; by reservation only. The fare is $75 for one to five passengers.

Note If you do end up having to spend the night in Chemult, *Digit Point Campground* is on the shores of Miller Lake, 12 miles northwest of Chemult. Or try the *Chemult Motel* (☎ 541-365-2228) on US 97. For home cooking, go to the *Big Mountain Cafe* (☎ 541-365-4475) along US 97.

Car Car-rental agencies found at the Redmond/Bend Airport include Budget (☎ 541-923-0699), Hertz (☎ 541-923-1411) and National (☎ 541-548-0650).

Call ☎ 541-389-4815 for up-to-date road conditions and weather forecasts.

BEND
Population 32,715
Bend, the focus of Oregon's fastest-growing area, started out as Farewell Bend, a ford in the Deschutes River where pioneer roads converged. It later became a ranch site, and then, in the 1910s, the trailhead for intense logging of the region's vast pine forests. But the town was just a trading center, albeit in a stunningly beautiful location, until the development of skiing areas on Mt Bachelor in the 1960s brought more and more recreationists to central Oregon.

Today, it's possible to have ambivalent feelings about Bend and hard to get over first impressions. Is it a swaggering little city with tons of superb recreation out its back door, or is it just a real-estate developer's dream come true? US 97 (here called 3rd St) traverses one of the most relentless and god-awful commercial strips you'll encounter in the Northwest, with fast-food restaurants, real-estate offices and car lots stretching on for miles. However, a second look reveals downtown Bend, an older, prosperous area with beautiful river-side parks, great restaurants, coffeehouses, reasonable lodging, and browseable shops. But the real reasons to come here lie south of town: Mt Bachelor, arguably the state's best ski mountain, and the Newberry National Volcanic Monument, which includes a collection of lava-formed geologic sites along the US 97 corridor.

Information
Contact the Central Oregon Welcome Center (☎ 541-389-8799, 800-800-8334), 63085 N US 97, Bend, OR 97701, for free tourist information and lodging reservations. The Deschutes National Forest Ranger Station (☎ 541-388-2715) is at 1230 NE 3rd St.

The downtown post office is at 47 NW Oregon Ave. The *Bulletin* is the city's daily newspaper, and Oregon Public Radio is heard on 91.3 FM. You can wash your clothes at Nelson Self-Service Laundry (☎ 541-388-2140), 407 SE 3rd St, and seek medical attention at St Charles Medical Center (☎ 541-382-4321), 2500 NE Neff Rd, just north of Pilot Butte State Park.

Downtown Bend
Bend's old commercial center has in recent years been revivified by smart shops, galleries and fine restaurants. It's easy to spend several hours drinking coffee, nosing through bookstores and looking at antiques.

Public parks stretch along the Deschutes River throughout town. **Drake Park** and a calm stretch of the river called **Mirror Pond** lie just behind downtown and are beautiful spots for a picnic. Paths link Drake Park to Columbia Park upstream and Pioneer Park downstream.

The **Deschutes County Historical Center** is a community museum in Bend's 1914 grade school, on Idaho Ave between Wall and Bond Sts. The museum houses artifacts of the area's Native American and pioneer history. It's open 1 to 4:30 pm, Wednesday to Saturday.

High Desert Museum
One of Oregon's best museums, the High Desert Museum (☎ 541-382-4754), 6 miles

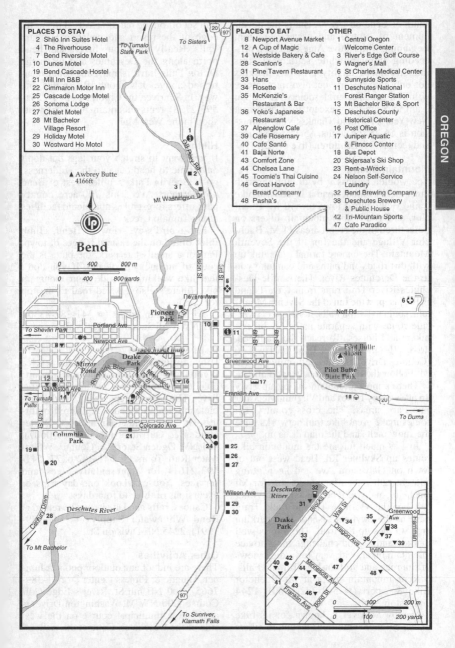

PLACES TO STAY
2 Shilo Inn Suites Hotel
4 The Riverhouse
7 Bend Riverside Motel
10 Dunes Motel
19 Bend Cascade Hostel
21 Mill Inn B&B
22 Cimmaron Motor Inn
25 Cascade Lodge Motel
26 Sonoma Lodge
27 Chalet Motel
28 Mt Bachelor
    Village Resort
29 Holiday Motel
30 Westward Ho Motel

PLACES TO EAT
8 Newport Avenue Market
12 A Cup of Magic
14 Westside Bakery & Cafe
28 Scanlon's
31 Pine Tavern Restaurant
33 Hans
34 Rosette
35 McKenzie's
    Restaurant & Bar
36 Yoko's Japanese
    Restaurant
37 Alpenglow Cafe
39 Cafe Rosemary
40 Cafe Santó
41 Baja Norte
43 Comfort Zone
44 Chelsea Lane
45 Toomie's Thai Cuisine
46 Groat Harvest
    Bread Company
48 Pasha's

OTHER
1 Central Oregon
   Welcome Center
3 River's Edge Golf Course
5 Wagner's Mall
6 St Charles Medical Center
9 Sunnyside Sports
11 Deschutes National
    Forest Ranger Station
13 Mt Bachelor Bike & Sport
15 Deschutes County
    Historical Center
16 Post Office
17 Juniper Aquatic
    & Fitness Center
18 Bus Depot
20 Skjersaa's Ski Shop
23 Rent-a-Wreck
24 Nelson Self-Service
    Laundry
32 Bend Brewing Company
38 Deschutes Brewery
    & Public House
42 Tri-Mountain Sports
47 Cafe Paradiso

Bend

▲ Awbrey Butte
   4166ft

OREGON

south of Bend on US 97, charts the development of central and eastern Oregon. Beginning with Native Americans and proceeding through white settlement, this indoor/outdoor facility provides insights not only into history, but also into nature, wildlife, art and rural society. It's open 9 am to 5 pm daily except for Christmas, New Year's Day and Thanksgiving; admission is $6.25 for adults, $5.75 for seniors and teens, $3 for children (five to 12).

Mountain Biking

You wouldn't guess it by driving through town on US 97, but Bend is laced with bike trails. Head out of town toward Mt Bachelor, and you'll spot mountain bikers on trails through the resort areas of Mt Bachelor Village and the Inn of the Seventh Mountain. These more formal trails link up with dirt roads and paths and can take you to the Deschutes River. The 6-mile Deschutes River Trail runs from Lava Island Falls, just past the Inn of the Seventh Mountain, south to Dillon Falls. It's a lovely riverside route with separate paths for bikers, hikers and horses. To reach the trailhead, drive 7½ miles west of Bend on Hwy 46 (Century Drive) and turn left on Forest Rd 41. Follow the signs to Lava Island Falls.

There's more mountain biking up Hwy 46 at Swampy Lakes and Virginia Meissner Sno-Park areas. The cross-country ski routes make great bike trail networks once the snow melts and the mud dries up.

Just as much fun are the mountain bike routes up Skyliner Rd. Head west out of town on Galveston Ave and keep going straight rather than hanging a left for Mt Bachelor, and you'll be headed up Skyliner Rd. For the 4½-mile Tumalo Falls Trail, park at the Skyliner's snow-play parking area 9 miles up the road. The trail is well marked and a good challenge for a novice mountain biker, with very rewarding views of rim rock and 90-foot-high Tumalo Falls.

Rent mountain bikes at Mt Bachelor Bike & Sport (☎ 541-382-4000), 1244 Galveston Ave.

Nearby Sunriver is known for its bike paths, but more ambitious mountain bikers

will set off on the red dirt roads at the north edge of the resort and pedal to Benham Falls. Really ambitious bikers can head north along the Deschutes and reach the Dillon Falls-Lava Island Falls route mentioned above. It's about 10½ miles one way. In Sunriver, the Chrome Pony (☎ 541-593-2728) rents mountain bikes from its shop in the West Mall.

Hiking

If you want to stretch your legs but don't have time to head out into the wilderness, go to Shevlin Park, 5 miles west of Bend on Newport Ave. This 700-acre county park offers forest hikes and picnic facilities along Tumalo Creek.

For a bird's-eye view of Bend, climb Pilot Butte, on the eastern fringes of town. Part of a small state park, the butte is the cone of an ancient volcano. If you don't feel like walking up, ride your mountain bike (there's also a paved road to the top for cars).

Tri Mountain Sports (☎ 541-382-8330), 815 NW Wall St, rents and sells hiking gear.

Rafting & Fishing

Hire a fishing or white-water guide service if you feel unknowledgeable or uncomfortable about recreation on the Deschutes River. The visitors' center can provide complete information about registered outfitters, or contact either High Desert Drifter Guides & Outfitters (☎ 541-389-0607), 721 NW Ogden St, or Sun Country Whitewater Raft Tours (☎ 541-382-6277, 541-593-2161) for representative fees and services. You can book one-day trips or excursions of three to four days.

Canoes, rafts and kayaks can be rented at Bend Whitewater Supply (☎ 541-389-7191), 2245 NE Division St.

Other Activities

There are indoor and outdoor pools at Juniper Aquatic & Fitness Center (☎ 541-389-7665), 800 NE 6th St. River's Edge Golf Course, 200 NW Mt Washington Drive, is an 18-hole municipal course on the west side of the Deschutes. Contact the visitors' center for a complete listing of the golf resorts in the area.

Places to Stay

For a centralized lodging and recreation reservation service, contact the Central Oregon Recreation Association (☎ 541-382-8334, 800-800 8334), PO Box 230, Bend, OR 97709.

Camping There are dozens of USFS campgrounds in the Deschutes National Forest. Contact the Bend & Fort Rock Ranger Station (☎ 541 388 5664), 1230 NE 3rd St, for complete information. Close to town, the *Bend KOA* (☎ 541-382-7728), 63615 N US 97, is open year-round, with a pool and store. *Tumalo State Park*, streamside amid pine forests, is 5 miles north of Bend off US 20; tent sites are $10, full hookups $13.

Hostels *The Bend Cascade Hostel* (☎ 541-389-3813), 19 SW Century Drive, is 1 mile southwest of downtown, on the road to Mt Bachelor. In addition to same-sex dormitories, there are rooms for couples and families; it is also wheelchair accessible. The simple, per head rate is $14. Call ahead for reservations.

B&Bs The *Mill Inn B&B* (☎ 541-389-9198) is near downtown Bend at 642 NW Colorado Ave. This erstwhile hotel and boardinghouse is now a very affordable B&B, known for its $15 per person bunk room. More private rooms are available, too, from $35/40 to $55/60 for a single/double.

Lara House B&B (☎ 541-388-4064), 640 NW Congress St, is across from lovely Drake Park. This National Register historic home, built in 1910, has five guest rooms with private bath from $60 to $95.

Motels – budget & middle There are dozens of inexpensive, perfectly adequate motels along the US 97 strip. During high season you should call ahead for reservations. *Sonoma Lodge* (☎ 541-382-4891), a particularly pleasant motel at 450 SE 3rd St, allows pets and has kitchens in non-smoking rooms; singles/doubles go for $35/39. *Dunes Motel* (☎ 541-382-6811), 1515 NE 3rd St, has rooms for $48/51 and a hot tub. At the *Cimmaron Motor Inn* (☎ 541-382-8282), 201 SE 3rd St, prices are $42/47. *Cascade Lodge Motel* (☎ 541-382-2612, 800-852-6031), 420 SE 3rd St, has an outdoor pool and rooms for $42/45. *Chalet Motel* (☎ 541-382-6124) at 510 SE 3rd St, allows pets; rates are $35/39. *Holiday Motel* (☎ 541-382-4620, 800-252-0121), 880 SE 3rd St, offers continental breakfast and rooms for $34/38. *Westward Ho Motel* (☎ 541-382-2111, 800-999-8143), 904 SE 3rd St, has a pool; rates are $35/39. And finally, *Super 8* (☎ 541-388-6888), 1275 SE US 97, has a laundry and an indoor pool and charges $52/58.

Motels – top end The *Riverhouse* (☎ 541-389-3111, 800-547-3928), 3075 N US 97, sits at a beautiful location with views onto the 18-hole golf course and the Deschutes River. There are full health spa facilities and two pools. Rooms begin at $65/74, and go to $89 for more deluxe rooms with views. *Bend Riverside Motel* (☎ 541-389-2363, 800-228-4019), 1565 Hill St, offers condominium-style accommodations ($69), riverside cabins ($75), and regular rooms ($52). It's in a pleasant location near the river and Pioneer Park and has an indoor pool.

The turreted *Shilo Inn Suites Hotel* (☎ 541-389-9600), 3105 OB Riley Rd, is on the north end of Bend along the Deschutes River. Facilities include an indoor pool, sauna and fitness center. Basic rooms begin at $89/99.

On the road to Mt Bachelor, *Best Western Entrada Lodge* (☎ 541-382-4080, 800-528-1234), 19221 Century Drive, is a large, comfortable motel with a pool and hot tub. Singles/doubles are $64/69 and pets are OK.

Ten miles north of Bend is the *Deschutes River Ranch* (☎ 541-382-7240), 20210 Swalley Rd, Bend, OR 97701, a resort and guest ranch with fishing, horseback riding and tennis courts on a 410-acre working ranch. Lodging is in completely furnished,

OREGON

three-bedroom homes; rates start at $150. Take US 20 to Redmond-Bend Hwy near Tumalo State Park, turn on Tumalo-Deschutes Hwy, and then turn right on Swalley Rd.

Places to Eat

Most of the restaurants listed here are within a two-block radius in the small city center. Wall and Bond Sts run parallel to each other, with Franklin, Minnesota and Oregon Aves crossing them. US 97 also has a high density of restaurants, particularly fast-food chains.

Outside of Portland, Bend probably offers the best selection of gourmet foodstuffs and wine in the state. If the rigors of traveling have you longing for good cheese or a healthy snack, try one of the following: *Chelsea Lane* (☎ 541-385-5648), 135 NW Minnesota Ave, has a great wine selection, some deli items and fancy tobacco products. For healthier options, try *Nature's General Store* (☎ 541-382-6732), 1950 NW 3rd St (in Wagner's Mall). Here you'll find organic produce, a juice bar, diet supplements and a deli. A good grocery store, *Newport Avenue Market* (☎ 541-382-3940), is at 1121 NW Newport Ave.

Budget For that morning jolt, skip the Starbucks and go local at the *Comfort Zone* (☎ 541-317-5717), 824 NW Wall St. Head around the block to *Great Harvest Bread Company* (☎ 541-389-2888) 835 NW Bond St for a whole-grain muffin or cinnamon roll. For a full breakfast or lunch, *Alpenglow Cafe* (☎ 541-383-7676), 1040 NW Bond St, puts the focus on fresh local ingredients.

Another good breakfast and lunch spot is *Cafe Santé* (☎ 541-383-3530), 718 NW Franklin Ave, a classy vegetarian restaurant; vegetarian lasagna goes for $5.75. Right around the corner, *Baja Norte* (☎ 541-385-0611), 801 Wall St, is a lively Mexican grill and a tasty and inexpensive place to see and be seen. Fill up on seafood tacos for less than $6. (There's also a Baja Norte in Sunriver's mall – prices run about a dollar higher there.)

Westside Bakery & Cafe (☎ 541-382-3426), 1005 NW Galveston Ave, is across the Deschutes River from downtown. Very large breakfasts are the main attraction – load up on pancakes, sweet rolls and pastries before hitting the slopes. A lighter and way hipper place to stop on the way out of town is *A Cup of Magic* (☎ 541-330-5539), a sunny, laid-back coffee and tea house at 1304 NW Galveston.

Middle *Yoko's Japanese Restaurant* (☎ 541-382-2999), 1028 NW Bond St, features Bend's only sushi bar. A dinner portion of vegetable tempura costs $9. *Toomie's Thai Cuisine* (☎ 541-388-5590), 119 NW Minnesota Ave, is a Thai restaurant with lunch specials for $4.50. *Pasha's* (☎ 541-382-5859), 61 NW Oregon Ave, offers superlative Lebanese cuisine. For $14, snack out on *masa*, a selection of spreadable and dippable delicacies from the appetizer menu. *Hans* (☎ 541-389-9700), 915 NW Wall St, serves upscale pizzas and pasta dishes for $9 to $13.

McKenzie's Restaurant & Bar (☎ 541-388-3891),1033 NW Bond St, is a nonsmoking restaurant in a historic storefront. Steak, pasta and seafood dominate the menu, though there's also a number of meat specialties, such as steak McKenzie topped with Dungeness crab for $16.95.

Top End *Pine Tavern Restaurant* (☎ 541-382-5581), 967 NW Brooks St, is probably Bend's best-loved restaurant. Steak, trout and lamb don't get much better than this; dinner prices are in the $11 to $19 range.

Menu eclecticism is the order of the day at starkly decorated *Rosette* (☎ 541-383-2780), 150 NW Oregon Ave. Asian and continental cooking traditions meld here. Salmon with pink peppercorn sauce goes for $17.

Simple decor and intense flavors make *Cafe Rosemary* (☎ 541-317-0276), 222 NW Irving, a good pick for lunch ($9 to $12) or dinner ($20 to $22).

Scanlon's (☎ 541-382-8769), in the Athletic Club of Bend at 61615 Mt Bachelor Drive (in the Mt Bachelor Village Resort), serves surprisingly good pasta and seafood

($9 to $18 entrées) for a swanky gym-side restaurant. The real plus here is free child-care for diners!

Entertainment
Deschutes Brewery & Public House (☎ 541-382-9242), 1044 NW Bond St, serves up Bend's microbrewed bitter, ale and porter in a gregarious pub atmosphere. The food is equally festive. The other brewpub in town, *Bend Brewing Company* (☎ 541-383-1599), is much smaller and right by the Deschutes. It's downtown at 1019 Brooks St.

Cafe Paradiso (☎ 541-385-5931), 945 NW Bond St, is a great place to hang out after dinner. Settle into the easy chairs and couches and enjoy pastries and live evening entertainment.

Getting There & Around
For information on air and train travel, see Getting There & Around at the beginning of this chapter.

Greyhound provides two buses a day between Portland and Bend via Madras and Redmond. A daily bus links Eugene and Bend via Sisters. There's one bus a day along US 97 between Bend, Klamath Falls and destinations in California. The bus depot (☎ 541-382-2151) is at 2045 E US 20.

Contact Rent-a-Wreck (☎ 541-385-7711, 800-562-0242), 315 SE 3rd St or Cheap Wheels (☎ 541-389-8893, 800-392-5440), 63360 N US 97, for rental vehicles. Call Owl Taxi (☎ 541-382-3311) for a cab.

AROUND BEND
Mt Bachelor
At 9065 feet, Mt Bachelor is scarcely the highest mountain in the Cascade Range, but its position grants it another title: that of the best skiing mountain in the region. Slightly east of the main line of Cascade peaks (22 miles southwest of Bend), Mt Bachelor is where the colder, continental air of central Oregon meets up with the warm, wet Pacific air of western Oregon. The result is tons of fine, dry snow, with ample sunshine.

Mt Bachelor is almost perfectly conical in shape, except for a small, distinct crater at its top. Lifts go right to the peak, and runs go down through the trees. Bachelor's newest lift, the Northwest Express, has opened up lots of steep, rugged territory on what was once considered a pretty easy mountain to ski or snowboard. With almost 300 inches of snow a year, the season begins in November and can last until June. To check on ski conditions, call ☎ 541-382-7888.

Ski and snowboard rentals are available at Mt Bachelor Ski and Sport Center (☎ 541-382-2442) at the base of the lifts. A one-day lift ticket is $39, or you can purchase a 200-point ticket for the same price, which is transferable, good for three years, and allows a certain number of lift rides. The sport center offers day-care, food, lessons and shopping.

A shuttle bus runs three times a day between Mt Bachelor and the ski area's corporate offices (☎ 541-383-2442), 335 SW Century Drive, in Bend.

Mt Bachelor also offers 34 miles of groomed cross-country trails, though the $9.75 day pass may prompt skiers to check out the many free cross-country trails at adjacent Dutchman Flat, on public land. To reach the Dutchman Flat area go past the turnoff for Mt Bachelor on Hwy 46; almost immediately there is a large parking area. This is as far as the snow plows maintain the highway during winter. From here on, you'll need skis or snowmobiles.

If there's adequate snow at lower elevations, forget Dutchman Flat and cross-country ski from the Virginia Meissner or Swampy Lakes Sno-Parks, between Bend and Mt Bachelor on Hwy 46.

If you park at any Sno-Park, you'll need a Sno-Park permit, which costs $3 from area businesses.

If you want to rent skis in town, stop by Skjersaa's Ski Shop (☎ 541-382-2154), 130 SW Century Drive, or any one of the multitude of ski shops on Century Drive. For cross-country rentals, try Tri Mountain Sports (☎ 541-382-8330), 815 NW Wall St or Sunnyside Sports (☎ 541-382-8018), 930 Newport Ave.

OREGON

OREGON

Places to Stay *Sunriver Lodge* (☎ 541-593-1000, 800-547-3922), PO Box 3609, Sunriver, OR 97707, just downhill from Mt Bachelor, has had a lot to do with establishing central Oregon's reputation as an enclave of upscale outdoor recreation. Rooms, condominiums and some private homes are available for rent at prices ranging from $139 to $350 a night. Many more private houses are available through Sunriver Realty Vacation Rentals (☎ 800-541-1756). While not cheap, if the cost of a large house (with access to the extensive recreational facilities included) is divided among a number of people, it's not an unreasonable splurge. During the winter, ski packages offer a deal on lift tickets at Mt Bachelor.

The Sunriver resort amenities include three 18-hole golf courses, tennis courts, riding stables and 25 miles of paved bike paths. It's also a good base for exploring the volcanic area south of Bend.

The closest accommodations to Mt Bachelor are at the *Inn of the Seventh Mountain* (☎ 541-382-8711, 800-452-6810), 18575 SW Century Drive. In addition to accommodations in condominium lodges (beginning at $60), dozens of recreational activities are offered to guests: swimming pools with a water slide, tennis courts, an 18-hole golf course, an ice-skating rink, horseback riding, bike paths and a kids' day camp, to name a few. There are also three restaurants to choose from.

Mt Bachelor Village Resort (☎ 541-389-5900, 800-547-5204), is a little closer to downtown Bend at 19717 Mt Bachelor Drive (just off Century Drive), and has very nice condos, with an outdoor pool, tennis courts and hiking trails. Prices start at $75 a night and run up to $285 for a well-appointed, three-bedroom condo overlooking the Deschutes.

Newberry National Volcanic Monument
The Lava Lands Visitor Center (☎ 541-593-2421), 58201 S US 97, about 11 miles south of Bend, provides information and exhibits on the geology, wildlife and archeology of the Newberry National Volcanic

Monument, a volcanic area south of Bend. A short trail leads to a lava flow. The ranger at the center has information about off-road exploration and remote destinations. Ask about campgrounds and road conditions at the information desk/bookstore.

Adjacent to the visitors' center is **Lava Butte**, a perfect cone rising 500 feet above the surrounding lava flows. A road spirals up the side of the butte to an observation deck, with spectacular views of the Cascades and nearby volcanic formations. Between Memorial Day and Labor Day shuttle buses run from the visitors' center to the butte summit every half-hour from 9 am to 5 pm.

Follow signs from the visitors' center to **Benham Falls** on the Deschutes River. More a series of rapids than a waterfall, Benham Falls was formed when lava from Lava Butte flowed down and blocked the river. Watch for otters during the half-mile hike.

Lava River Cave Lava tubes are formed when the surface of a lava flow solidifies, allowing the still-molten rock below it to flow out. The resulting cave, which often follows the course of a buried streambed, is clean and dry compared to caves caused by water erosion. Lava River Cave, one of many in the monument but the only one that's developed for visitors, is the longest lava tube in Oregon. Bring a flashlight and explore the cave on your own or rent a lantern at the gate, about 1 mile south of the visitors' center.

Lava Cast Forest About 6000 years ago, a wall of molten lava 20 feet deep flowed down from Newberry Crater and engulfed a forest of mature trees. The trees incinerated, but not before cooling and solidifying the lava. The resulting casts or molds of the forest are seen on a mile-long interpretive trail. The Lava Cast Forest is 9 miles east of US 97 on Lava Cast Forest Rd.

Newberry Crater While much of central Oregon is dominated by high mountains, the area south of Bend is dramatically influenced by a mountain that's largely absent. Newberry Crater was once one of the largest and most active volcanoes in North America, and its impact is seen in much of central Oregon.

The Newberry volcano began erupting about 500,000 years ago, and successive flows gradually built a steep-sided mountain almost a mile above the surrounding plateau. Lava flows were immense and flowed along the Deschutes drainage to reach as far north as Madras. As with Crater Lake, the summit of the volcano collapsed after a large eruption, creating a caldera. Obsidian flows partially served to divide the caldera into East and Paulina Lakes.

Native Americans frequented Newberry Crater in order to collect obsidian, from which they fashioned arrowheads. Such obsidian was a valuable item of trade, and Oregon obsidian has been found in archeological sites throughout the West.

During the 1980s, energy companies became interested in the Newberry Crater's geothermal potential. By tapping into the old volcano, these companies proposed to generate 1500 megawatts of energy annually. In response, a group of recreationists, environmentalists and politicians pushed through legislation (which was signed into law in 1990) to preserve the 78-sq-mile area as a national monument.

Newberry Crater is a favorite spot for camping and exploring truly remarkable volcanic geology. Looming above everything is 7985-foot Paulina Peak, a remnant of the much higher mountain that collapsed during the eruption that formed the present 5-mile wide crater.

Initially one large lake, **Paulina Lake** and **East Lake** are now separated by a lava flow and a pumice cone. The larger of the two bodies of water, Paulina Lake is over 250 feet deep. A 7-mile trail circles the lake. Ice Age glaciers carved a niche in the side of the crater, allowing Paulina Creek to drain the lake via a 100-foot-high waterfall. With no visible inflow or outflow, East Lake seems hermetic. However, snowmelt and springs feed the lake, and it

drains through subterranean passages into Paulina Lake.

Reckoned to offer some of the best fishing in Oregon, these lakes weren't even stocked with fish until a late-19th-century sportsman carted some rainbow trout up into the crater and planted them in East Lake. Due to the lakes' great depths and the constant flow of fresh mineral spring water, fish thrive here.

A short trail halfway between the two lakes leads to the **Big Obsidian Flow**. An enormous flow of obsidian – formed when silica-rich lava cools quickly into translucent, glass-like formations – covers the south flank of Newberry Crater.

The **Newberry Crater Rim Loop Trail** encircles Paulina Lake and is a good place for hiking and mountain biking, with a number of campgrounds within reach.

From US 97 take Paulina East Lake Rd to Newberry Crater.

Places to Stay Newberry Crater campgrounds usually open in late May and remain open until October. A total of eight campgrounds crowd around East and Paulina Lakes, with campsites starting at $12. *LaPine State Recreation Area*, on the banks of the Deschutes River north of LaPine (4 miles from US 97) has campgrounds and access to fishing on the Deschutes River. The recreation area provides a short hike to the Big Tree, Oregon's largest ponderosa pine.

Paulina Lake Lodge (☎ 541-536-2240), PO Box 7, LaPine, OR 97739, is a small fishing resort with cabins from $60 to $125, a restaurant, general store and boat rentals. It's open year-round and is popular with both cross-country skiers and snowmobilers. *East Lake Fishing Resort* (☎ 541-536-2230), PO Box 95, LaPine, OR 97739, is also an unassuming lodge for anglers, with cabins ($58 to $86), a restaurant open for breakfast and lunch only, and a fishing supply store.

CASCADE LAKES

Long ago, lava from the nearby volcanoes choked this broad basin beneath the rim of the Cascade Range. Lava flows dammed streams, forming lakes. In other areas, streams flowed underground through the porous lava fields to well up as lake-sized springs. Still other lakes formed in the mouths of small, extinct craters.

Hwy 46 is a designated National Forest Scenic Byway. Usually called the Cascade Lakes Hwy, or Century Drive (the loop road is roughly 100 miles long), it leaves Bend to travel west and south between high mountain peaks, and to link together alpine lakes. Bicyclists speed along the road in summer, while snowmobilers take over during the long winter months. Beyond Mt Bachelor the road is closed from November to mid-May.

Tiny **Todd Lake** offers views of Broken Top and relative seclusion, as getting there requires a quarter-mile hike. **Sparks Lake**, in a grassy meadow, is in the process of transforming itself from a body of water to a reedy marsh. It's a good place for bird-watching. **Hosmer Lake** is stocked with catch-and-release Atlantic salmon, making it popular with anglers. It's less commercial than nearby lakes and has beautiful views of Mt Bachelor. At **Little Lava Lake** the waters from the subterranean seeping of lakes farther up the basin finally pool and send forth a stream – the beginnings of the mighty Deschutes River.

The Deschutes is dammed at **Crane Prairie Reservoir**. The forest wasn't cleared before it was flooded, resulting in a lake of ugly dead snags. But an eyesore for some is a habitat for others – ospreys make use of the dead trees for nesting, and fish in the shallow lake water. Once considered a threatened species, ospreys have thrived here, with over 100 nesting pairs of osprey now returning annually to this protected wildlife preserve. Park at the Osprey Observation Point just east of the highway to watch these birds dive-bomb fish from their craggy perches.

The **Twin Lakes** were formed when molten rock came in contact with ground water. The resulting explosion created deep, perfectly symmetrical craters, which later filled with water. Both North and South Twin Lakes are noted for their good fishing.

The Bend & Fort Rock Ranger District Office (☎ 541-388-5664) can answer questions and send brochures.

Places to Stay & Eat

There are public campgrounds at each of the lakes along the route. Camping fees run $10 and up. The resorts listed below usually provide hookups for RVs.

A number of the Cascade Lakes have woodsy rustic cabin 'resorts' on their shores, which are usually homey, family-oriented facilities with a pleasant, live-in atmosphere. They also offer meals, boat rentals and groceries, making them popular with anglers, boaters and wildlife watchers. All but Elk Lake Resort are open from late spring to early fall; Elk Lake is also open mid-November through April for those who can get there on skis or snowmobiles. Rates run from about $60 to $100 for a cabin. Among those available are: *Elk Lake Resort* (☎ 541-317-2994), PO Box 789, Bend, OR 97709; *Cultus Lake Resort* (☎ 541-389-3230), PO Box 262, Bend, OR 97709; *Twin Lakes Resort* (☎ 541-593-6526), PO Box 3550, Sunriver, OR 97707; and *Crane Prairie Resort* (☎ 541-383-3939), PO Box 1171, Bend, OR 97709.

THREE SISTERS WILDERNESS

Hiking trails depart from the Cascade Lakes Hwy (Hwy 46) into the 580-sq-mile Three Sisters Wilderness. This preserve is dominated by four volcanic peaks and is popular for hikes to remote lakes surrounded by wildflower meadows. One caution – don't count on doing any early-season hiking here, as the trails are often snowed in until late June.

One of the most popular hikes in the area is to Green Lake Basin, high on a plateau between 9173-foot Broken Top and 10,358-foot South Sister. These celadon-green lakes are the centerpiece of a tremendous wildflower display in July and August, at which time the area throngs with crowds. Try to avoid the weekends. There are two trailheads to the Green Lakes. If you don't mind a rough road, turn north from Hwy 46 at Todd Lake, and continue 3 miles to Crater Creek Ditch. Turn left and continue to the trailhead. It's about 4½ miles to the lakes.

If you don't have an off-road vehicle, then park at the Green Lakes Trailhead along Hwy 46 above Sparks Lake and hike north. The 4.4-mile trail is fairly steep but passes some great waterfalls.

Ambitious hikers might consider climbing South Sister. It's Oregon's third-highest peak, but the southern approach doesn't demand any technical equipment. The steep 5.6-mile trail begins near Devils Lake (near Sparks Lake just off the Cascade Lakes Hwy), and is passable only in late summer.

Three Sisters Wilderness contains 111 lakes. An easy hike into an area densely packed with small lakes begins at the Six Lake Trailhead, a half mile south of Elk Lake on Hwy 46. You'll hit the first lake after about a mile of hiking. To reach a basin full of lakes (and in summer, mosquitos), continue another 4 miles.

For maps and more information, contact the Deschutes National Forest office (☎ 541-388-5564), 1230 NE 3rd St, Bend, OR 97701. For details on hiking trails from the McKenzie River area, see Three Sisters Wilderness in the Willamette Valley chapter.

SISTERS
Population 760

Near a large meadow with stunning views of snowy Cascade peaks, Sisters straddles the line where the mountain pine forests mingle with the desert sage and juniper.

Surely just about the most congested small town in Oregon, Sisters is a victim of its own success. Once a stagecoach stop and trade town for loggers and ranchers, Sisters was revitalized as a town when the city fathers decided to 'Westernize' the main shopping area. The false storefronts and hitching posts worked: Sisters is now packed full of people shopping the oh-so-Western galleries and gift shops.

Sisters gives proof of its *real* Western character during the second weekend of June, when the **Sisters Rodeo** comes to town; it's reckoned to be one of the best in the state. The rodeo grounds are about 4 miles south of town on US 20. For tickets call ☎ 800-827-7522.

Even the agricultural land surrounding Sisters has taken on a curious, unreal quality. The purebred horses may not seem out of place, but the llamas and ostriches definitely do (Sisters is the nation's largest llama-breeding area, and ostrich ranching is up and coming). And if you thought you passed a reindeer ranch on the way from Redmond, you were right.

Despite the town's commercial bent, there's no getting around the beauty of the Sisters area and the appeal of its clear, dry climate.

Orientation & Information
US 20 forms Sisters' principal and quite congested main street, though it's generally referred to as Cascade St. One block south is Hood St and one block north is Main St. Cross streets are Ash, Elm, Fir and Spruce Sts, from west to east respectively.

Contact the Sisters Area Chamber of Commerce (☎ 541-549-0251), PO Box 476, Sisters, OR 97759, and the local Forest Service office (☎ 541-549-2111) for information. The post office is at 160 Fir St.

Places to Stay
Camping Campers are welcome in the city park, at the southern end of Sisters. There's a USFS campground about 5 miles west of town at *Indian Ford*. The *Sisters KOA* (☎ 541-549-3021) is about 4 miles south of Sisters on US 20.

The savvy camper will continue on to the Metolius River, with its abundance of campsites in a beautiful valley filled with old-growth ponderosa pines.

Motels The nicest place to stay in Sisters is the *Best Western Ponderosa Lodge* (☎ 541-549-1234), 505 US 20 W, a spacious two-story motel built in a park-like meadow (complete with gamboling llamas) just north of the town; singles/doubles are $69/74.

OREGON

Sisters Motor Lodge (☎ 541-549-2551), 600 W Cascade St, is a comfortable older motel from before the resort era with rooms for $59/65.

Resorts *Black Butte Ranch* (☎ 541-595-6211), PO Box 8000, Black Butte Ranch, OR 97759, is the crown jewel of central Oregon resorts. Eight miles north of Sisters on US 20, the development fringes a vast meadow and lake, with Mt Washington and the Three Sisters towering over all.

Lodging is either in condominium lodges or in one of the large private homes available for rent. Prices begin at $50 for a very plain room, and move up quickly. With golf courses, pools, horseback riding and tennis, Black Butte delivers all the amenities you'd expect from this class of resort, but its greatest asset is that it seems integrated into, and not imposed on, the landscape. And what a landscape. If you're looking for a central Oregon splurge, this is it.

Places to Eat

The Sisters Bakery (☎ 541-549-0361), 120 E Cascade St, is the place for fresh pastries and coffee. If you just need coffee to refuel, try the *Sisters Coffee Company* (☎ 541-549-0527), 342 W Hood St.

Locals swear by *Papandrea's Pizza* (☎ 541-549-6081), 325 E Hood St, a thick-crusted pie designed for hearty central Oregon appetites. A large pepperoni will set you back $16.50.

The Hotel Sisters Restaurant (☎ 541-549-7427), 105 W Cascade St, is housed in a refurbished hotel, though no rooms are rented. Burgers, Mexican food and steak are the best bets here. Their self-mythologized Bronco Billy barbecued chicken and ribs average $15. At night, there's live music in the hotel's old-fashioned bar. At its most infectious, the music can be a jam session of local musicians, emboldened by a couple of drinks.

If you're in the mood for a fancy dinner, head on down to *Black Butte Ranch* (☎ 541-595-1260), where the lodge restaurant puts out very nice, though pricey, dinners.

Shopping

It's a sign of economic prosperity that Sisters now has its own Christmas shop. The town was invented for shoppers, so it seems foolish not to take advantage of what it does well.

Galleries and gift shops epitomize Sisters and some of them are quite good. Christmas Mountain Magic (☎ 541-549-1155), 516 W Cascade St, sells ornaments and trimmings year-round. Soda Creek Gallery (☎ 541-549-0600), 178 S Elm St, is a major Western art gallery with both blue-chip and regional artists. Ponderosa Woodworks (☎ 541-549-8153), at 160 E Hood St, is a showroom for handmade pine furniture.

For both ski and bicycle sales and rentals, go to friendly Eurosports (☎ 541-549-2471), 115 W Hood St. For hiking gear, try Mountain Supply (☎ 541-549-3251), 148 W Hood St.

Paulina Springs Book Company (☎ 541-549-0866), 367 W Hood St, is central Oregon's best bookstore.

Getting There & Away

Greyhound passes through Sisters twice daily. Buses stop at the corner of Elm St and US 20. There's no station here, so call the Bend station (☎ 541-382-2151) for information.

HOODOO SKI AREA

Hoodoo (☎ 541-822-3799), Box 20, US 20, Sisters, OR 97759, Oregon's oldest downhill ski area, is 25 miles west of Sisters at Santiam Pass, the crest of the Cascades. A total of 22 runs drop from a summit elevation of 5700 feet. Though it's pretty small, Hoodoo has a lot of variety in its terrain, with some surprisingly challenging skiing.

Snow conditions here are often better than at other Cascade divide ski areas, due to the north-facing slopes. Call ☎ 541-822-3337 for snow conditions. There's night skiing Thursday to Saturday. Facilities include two day lodges and complete rental and instruction packages. Lift tickets are $23 a day, with free skiing from 9 to 10 am every day (8 to 9 am on Saturday, January through March), so skiers can test the conditions. Ski packages are offered by several Sisters motels, Black Butte Ranch and the Metolius River Lodges.

Hoodoo also has groomed cross-country ski trails starting at many of the Sno-Parks along Santiam Pass.

METOLIUS RIVER

As if by enchantment, the Metolius River bursts out of a ferny cleft in Black Butte, a fully formed river at birth. As it flows north through its beautiful pine-filled valley, the Metolius passes beneath rugged Mt Jefferson (10,495 feet), Oregon's second-highest peak.

It's astonishing that such a magical valley has not been turned into an expensive, golf-course-ridden resort. Instead, the valley remains the province of campers, as the USFS maintains a dozen campgrounds along the river.

The spring-fed river maintains a constant temperature, a fact much appreciated by local trout. Fly-fishing on the Metolius is world renowned, and special restrictions are in place to keep it that way. Consult the posted fishing regulations before casting your line.

Orientation & Information

To reach the following destinations along the Metolius River, turn off US 20, 10 miles north of Sisters, and follow USFS Rd 14.

The Metolius Recreation Association (☎ 541-595-6117) can be contacted at PO Box 64, Camp Sherman, OR 97730.

Camp Sherman

This sleepy little settlement, about 5 miles north of US 20 on USFS Rd 14, seems to hail from another era, with its general store and streamside cabins beneath towering pines. Primarily a supply venue and post office for campers and anglers, Camp Sherman offers a few rustic accommodations and a spiffy restaurant (see Places to Eat, below).

Metolius Springs

A short path leads through a forest of ponderosa pines to these remarkable springs, where the Metolius flows out of a hillside. From the area above the springs, there's a wonderful view of the already-wide river winding through a grassy meadow, with Mt Jefferson directly above.

Oddly, there is no sign for the Metolius Springs as you come in from US 20. To find the head of the Metolius, turn east at the sign for 'Campgrounds,' which appears about 2 miles after joining USFS Rd 14. The springs are about a mile down this road.

Wizard Falls Fish Hatchery

You may or may not find visiting fish hatcheries compulsively fascinating, but you'll find few in such beautiful surroundings. Enormous old pines tower above the tanks, and lawns stretch between log outbuildings, all with the Metolius River splashing beside. The buildings date to President Franklin Roosevelt's WPA program that created jobs for unemployed Americans during the Great Depression. All in all, it seems more like a park than a fish-production area.

Signs describe the various fish produced at the hatchery – be sure to check out the tank with rare and unusual fish.

To reach the fish hatchery, continue on USFS Rd 14 past Camp Sherman for 5 miles.

Hiking

Trails lead from the Metolius Valley up into the **Mt Jefferson Wilderness Area**. While many hikes into these alpine areas are more than day trips, a few shorter hikes access the area's high country. From the USFS's Jack Lake Campground, a 4½-mile roundtrip hike climbs up to Canyon Creek Meadows, where summer produces a vibrant wildflower display and great views onto rugged **Three Fingered Jack**, a peak on the Cascade summit. To reach the trailhead from Sisters, drive 13 miles northwest on US 20. Just south of Suttle Lake, turn north on the 'Jack Lake Rd,' or USFS Rd 12. It's about 8 miles to the trailhead.

OREGON

From the same access road, a shorter hike leads to a high mountain lake. As above, turn onto USFS Rd 12, and after 1 mile leave the main road and take a west-turning fork (USFS Rd 1210) toward **Round Lake**. From the Round Lake Campground, a 2-mile trail leads past tiny Long Lake to **Square Lake**, nestled in thick forest.

For a less strenuous hike, follow the hiking trails on either side of the Metolius River between Wizard Falls Fish Hatchery and Pioneer Ford Campground. It's about a 2½-mile hike with lots of opportunity to see raptors and streamside mammals such as mink.

Places to Stay
Camping With over a dozen campgrounds facing the Metolius River and more in the forests near Mt Jefferson, there should be no problem finding campsites except on busy holiday weekends. The farther down-river you go from Camp Sherman, the better the chances are for relative solitude. The *Pioneer Ford Campground*, about 9 miles north of Camp Sherman, is a good choice, with campsites for $10.

Campers should take note that the two campgrounds above Camp Sherman, *Pine Rest* and *Riverside*, are reserved for tent campers only. Campsites cost $10 per night at Pine Rest and $6 at Riverside. For complete camping information, contact the Deschutes National Forest office (☎ 541-549-2111) in Sisters.

Lodges Camp Sherman offers a few rustic accommodations, largely designed with fly-fishers in mind. Be sure to call ahead, as serious anglers often have rooms booked well in advance. The *Metolius River Lodges* (☎ 541-595-6290), PO Box 110, Camp Sherman, OR 97730, has a number of lodging options in free-standing cabins overlooking the river, starting at $55. A bit more upscale is the *Metolius River Resort* (☎ 541-595-6281), PO Box 1210, Camp Sherman, OR 97730, with lodging in three-bedroom condominium units beginning at $120 a night.

Places to Eat
Kokanee Cafe (☎ 541-595-6420) is open for three meals a day, and even if it weren't the only restaurant in Camp Sherman, this would be a hard act to beat. Located near the Metolius River, this attractive log-cabin restaurant manages to be happily busy yet secluded. Dinner choices range from burgers to seafood fettuccine for $12.95; go Western and have a buffalo steak for $18.95.

REDMOND & AROUND
Population 8365

In the trio of towns that make up central Oregon's resort triangle, Redmond is the most neglected. On a treeless plain between the Cascade Range and Ochoco Mountains, it lacks the refinement and make-believe of more full-blown resort towns, and doesn't offer much in the way of charm. But it is close to Smith Rock, and thus a good base for climbers.

Redmond was established in 1905, when government programs brought first irrigation canals, and then settlers, to the high desert. However, here as elsewhere in trendy central Oregon, agriculture is giving way to golf courses and real-estate developments.

The **Deschutes County Fair & Rodeo** (☎ 541-548-2711), filled with the scents and sounds of an old country fair, is held on the first weekend of August at the fairgrounds at the junction of Hwys 97 and 126.

Orientation & Information
Redmond lies at the junction of two major routes. Hwy 126 acts as a shortcut to roads linking eastern Oregon to Eugene and Salem, while US 97 joins I-84 to California. It's a busy town with a lot of traffic flowing through it, as befits a town that calls itself the Hub of Central Oregon.

Contact the Redmond Chamber of Commerce (☎ 541-923-6442) at 106 SW 7th St, Redmond, OR 97756, for visitor information. The post office is at 507 SW 8th St, and the Central Oregon District Hospital (☎ 541-548-8131) is at 1253 N Canal Blvd.

Peter Skene Ogden Scenic Wayside

While driving along the prairie-like lava plateau on US 97 north of Redmond, there is no indication you're in the neighborhood of a river, much less one at the bottom of a 400-foot-deep chasm. Crossing the bridge that vaults the Crooked River Canyon is guaranteed to elicit a gasp. Stop at this small park area and have a longer look over the edge and at the two bridges.

Building the Crooked River Rail Bridge was no mean feat in 1911. Workers scaled rope ladders from the canyon floor to the bridge girders, and, as elsewhere in central Oregon's highly competitive early railroad history, there was sabotage and mischief from rival rail crews. The highway bridge was designed by Conde McCullough, famed architect of Oregon coast bridges. The canyon is 9 miles north of Redmond.

The Fantastic Museum

A good-natured collection of memorabilia and outright junk, this museum (☎ 541-923-0000), 1 mile south of Redmond on US 97, also has more than its share of real oddities, such as an early sedan of President John F Kennedy and the contents of Elizabeth Taylor's *Cleopatra* dressing room. It's open 10 am to 5 pm daily; $5/2 adults/children.

Places to Stay

Hotels For an inexpensive stay in downtown Redmond, go to the *City Center Motel* (☎ 541-548-3447), 350 NW 6th St; singles/doubles are $27/30. The *Redmond Inn* (☎ 541-548-1091, 800-833-3259), 1545 S US 97, has an outdoor pool and rooms for $48/52.

For a step up in comfort and a step back in time, there's the *Quality New Redmond Hotel* (☎ 541-923-7378), downtown at 521 S 6th St, a renovated historic hotel. The rooms ($49/56) are well appointed, and there's a spa and exercise room. On the south edge of town, the *Best Western Rama Inn* (☎ 541-548-8080, 800-821-0543), 2630 SW 17th Place, has a pool, conference facilities and exercise room. Rooms go for $65/70.

Resorts The Redmond-area resort is called *Eagle Crest* (☎ 541-923-2453, 800-682-4786), 1522 Cline Falls Rd, about 6 miles southwest of Redmond off Hwy 126. As elsewhere in central Oregon, the emphasis is on recreation, with an 18-hole golf course, tennis, swimming, horseback riding, weight room and so on. Lodging is in either the lodge hotel where rooms begin at $82, or in condos which sleep up to eight people, starting at $120.

Places to Eat

Redmond's brewpub, the *Seventh Street Brew House* (☎ 541-923-1795), 855 SW 7th St, is a good place to hang out, sip Scottish ale, and wolf down burgers. The *Paradise Grille* (☎ 541-548-0844), 404 SW 6th St, serves up reasonably priced mesquite-grilled meats, and Sante Fe-inspired dishes like tequila prawns. *Sully's of Redmond* (☎ 541-548-5483), in the Quality New Redmond Hotel at 521 SW 6th St, is Redmond's

Crooked River Dinner Train

The Prineville Municipal Railroad is the only city-owned railroad in the country. Prineville citizens raised the money to build the line in 1919 in order to link the town to the mainline rail lines at Redmond.

Today you can ride this historic line through canyon and ranchland while enjoying a fine dinner, by taking the Crooked River Dinner Train (☎ 541-388-1966), 115 NW Oregon St, suite 24, Bend. The journey begins 2 miles north of Redmond (off Hwy 97 at O'Neil Hwy), and takes about 2½ hours. The $69 ticket includes a four-course meal with three choices of entrées and entertainment by a theater group. There are seasonal excursion trains with other themes, such as winetasting, and holiday events. The train runs year-round and departs at 6:30 pm on Friday and Saturday only; on Sunday, there is a brunch run. Reservations are required. ■

other restaurant of note. Classic Italian cooking shares the kitchen with steak; dinners range from $10 to $16.

Six miles north of Redmond in Terrebonne is *La Siesta* (☎ 541-548-4848), 8320 N US 97, one of those little restaurants in an out-of-the-way place that somehow manages to command an enormous reputation. Here it's home-style Mexican food that brings people in from miles around.

Getting There & Around
For information on air travel to central Oregon, see Getting There & Around at the beginning of this chapter. Greyhound buses link Redmond to Portland and Bend. The depot (☎ 541-923-1923) is at 2456 S US 97. There are also several car-rental agencies at the airport. Call City Cab at ☎ 541-548-0919.

SMITH ROCK STATE PARK
A world-renowned venue for rock climbers, Smith Rock is an amazingly jagged and precipitous series of cliffs, carved by the misleadingly passive-looking Crooked River. The formation is related to the colorful tuff deposits of the John Day Fossil Beds. Ancient volcanoes spewed out vast amounts of hot ash that settled into 1000-foot-deep drifts and, as the ash cooled, fused into stone.

Today, Smith Rock's rust-colored palisades and 800-foot-high cliffs loom over the pools of the Crooked River. Good weather, especially in the spring and fall, brings out scores of climbers to scale Smith Rock, which is known primarily for its sport-climbing routes, well bolted with anchors. There are lots of great routes in the 5.6 to 5.10 range. On sunny weekends climbers line up to get at the most popular ones, such as Monkey Face. Many climbers aim for an early start, climb in the cool of the morning, sit out the blazing hot mid-afternoon, then return when the sun goes down a bit.

For full, technical route descriptions, pick up a copy of Alan Watts' comprehensive *Climber's Guide to Smith Rock*. It's available in Portland-area outdoor stores

and at the Smith Rock climbing shops. Rock-climbing classes are available at Vertical Ventures (☎ 541-389-7937).

If you're not a climber, the 7 miles of hiking trails in the state park afford great views of both landscape and climbers, and can involve a little simple rock scrambling.

A climber's bivouac provides basic campsites in a flat, dusty area a walk away from climbing sites. During climbing season, the parkside Rock Hard Climbing & Clothing Gear peddles gear to climbers and huckleberry ice cream to everyone else. They also have free maps of the local hiking trails. Another good climbing shop is Redpoint Climbers' Supply (☎ 800-923-6207), in Terrebonne at the Smith Rock turnoff from US 97.

To visit Smith Rock State Park, drive 6 miles north of Redmond on US 97, turn east at Terrebonne onto Smith Rock Way and continue for another 3 miles.

PRINEVILLE & THE OCHOCO MOUNTAINS
The old ranch town of Prineville (population 5626) backs up to the gently sloping Ochoco Mountains and sits in about the only wide spot in the otherwise precipitous Crooked River valley. The town's first structure was a saloon built in 1868, which established a tone for the early history of the settlement, a time of commerce from lumber and ranching. Vicious range wars between partisans of cattle and sheep ranching divided the young community in the 1900s, when cattlemen slaughtered upwards of 10,000 head of sheep and several sheepherders. More peaceable now, Prineville continues to be a ranch supply center.

After the immense lava flows of eastern Oregon began to spill down the Columbia Basin about 17 million years ago, only the highest elevations of central Oregon remained above the tremendous floods of lava, including the ridges of the Ochoco Mountains.

A series of meadows and streams ringed by gentle peaks, the Ochocos are now a beautiful, if undramatic, range undulating across much of Oregon's vast central province. The region is known mostly for its population of deer and elk. Majestic stands of mature ponderosa pine and juniper, spring wildflower meadows and wilderness areas offer the visitor a serene and largely unvisited outdoor destination. The region's gentle topography and many USFS roads make it great for mountain bikers (except during the fall hunting season).

Orientation & Information
Prineville is at the junction of Hwys 26 and 126; US 26 is the town's main street, and is called 3rd St in local addresses.

The Prineville Chamber of Commerce (☎ 541-447-6304) is at 390 N Fairview St. For information on hiking and camping in the area, contact the Prineville Ranger District (☎ 541-447-9641), 2321 E 3rd St. The Ochoco National Forest Headquarters (☎ 541-447-6247), 3000 E 3rd St, and the State Forestry Department (☎ 541-447-5658), 220710 Ochoco Hwy, are also in Prineville.

The Prineville post office is at 155 N Court St, and the local laundry is Ochoco Plaza Coin Laundry (☎ 541-447-2120), 1595 E 3rd St.

Prineville Reservoir
This long, narrow lake backs up through an arid juniper and sage savanna, a vivid band of green water in an otherwise desert landscape. Formed when Bowman Dam impounded the Crooked River, Prineville Reservoir is famous for bass fishing. It's also a favorite spot for boating, swimming and just plain summertime cooling off. In late summer, the green water is due to algae blossoms, not sparkling freshwater. The Prineville Reservoir State Park has campsites and picnic areas as well as a boat launch.

To reach Prineville Reservoir, turn south from US 26 onto Juniper Canyon Rd. It's 17 miles to the state park. Or, for great views of the river's rim-rocked valley, take scenic Hwy 27 to Bowman Dam; it turns to gravel after the dam and eventually meets US 20 between Bend and Burns.

Mill Creek Wilderness
Of the three wilderness areas in the Ochoco Mountains, the most accessible is Mill Creek, north of the Ochoco Creek. Hikes through old-growth pine forests and curious volcanic formations make for satisfying day outings.

To reach the Mill Creek Wilderness, follow US 26 east from Prineville for 9 miles, and turn north on USFS Rd 33 for 9 miles. Wildcat Campground is just off the road.

From the Wildcat Campground Trailhead, a gentle trail winds along the East Fork of Mill Creek through a lovely pine forest. For a long day hike, continue along the trail to **Twin Pillars**, two spire-like volcanic crags.

An even more impressive rock tower is **Stein's Pillar**, reached by a short hike from USFS Rd 3350. This 400-foot-high thumb of rock is popular with experienced climbers; it wasn't successfully scaled until 1950.

Big Summit Prairie
Another little-visited destination in the heart of the Ochocos is Big Summit Prairie, reached by well-maintained and scenic USFS roads. East of Prineville, roads climb up to a high central plateau. Surrounded by old forest, this large meadow encompasses about 35 sq miles of rolling pasture land. During late spring, the wildflowers are marvelous. Although much of Big Summit Prairie is privately owned and used as grazing land, roads ring the meadow.

From Prineville, head east for 12 miles on US 26, turn onto Ochoco Creek Rd, then turn onto USFS Rd 42 at the Ochoco Campground.

Places to Stay
Camping While the best camping is in the Ochoco Mountains, closer to Prineville campers can stay at *Ochoco Lake State Park* along US 26, just east of town. There's also camping at *Prineville Reservoir State Park*, 17 miles south of town.

The USFS has a number of campgrounds in the Ochoco Mountains. Convenient for

380 Central Oregon – Madras & Around

hikers in the Mill Creek Wilderness is the *Wildcat Campground*, right along Mill Creek at the base of the wilderness area.

More utilitarian for travelers along the highway is *Ochoco Divide Campground*, 30 miles east of Prineville on US 26 at the summit of Ochoco Pass. Near Big Summit Prairie is *Ochoco Campground*, about 6 miles east of US 26 on USFS Rd 22.

Motels Kids will like staying at Prineville's *Rustler's Roost* (☎ 541-447-4185), 960 W 3rd St, as the 2nd-floor balconies give the place a Wild West atmosphere. Singles/doubles are $39/42. Right downtown, the *Ochoco Inn & Motel* (☎ 541-447-6231), 123 3rd St, has good prices and an adjacent restaurant; rooms are $30/33.

Carolina Motel (☎ 541-447-4152), 1050 E 3rd St, is an attractive, older motel out on the road to Mitchell; rates are $34/40. For predictability and a pool, try the *Best Western of Prineville* (☎ 541-447-8080), 1475 E 3rd St, on the eastern outskirts of Prineville, near the Ochoco Plaza shopping mall; rooms start at $65.

Places to Eat
Gee's (☎ 541-447-6115), 987 W 2nd St, offers Sichuan and Mandarin Chinese food; Kung-pao beef goes for $9. *Morgan's Restaurant* (☎ 541-447-3880), 123 E 3rd St, is the place for steak and American-style food. Even if you go for a New York steak, it's hard to spend more than $10 here.

Getting There & Away
Greyhound (☎ 541-447-3646), 152 W 4th St, offers Prineville one-bus-a-day service between The Dalles and Bend. The *People Mover* offers Monday, Wednesday and Friday service between Bend, Prineville and John Day.

MADRAS & AROUND
The seat of Jefferson County and a major agricultural trade town, Madras (population 3820) is at the junction of US 26 and 97. On a broad and arid upland, the town is surrounded by fields of curious crops, such as garlic and mint. In fact, the Madras area is one of the principal producers of mint in the USA. Along the eastern and southern skyline are craggy volcanic buttes, and to the west, the towering Cascades.

For the traveler, Madras is hardly a major destination in itself, but the town is a useful jumping-off point for recreation on Lake Billy Chinook, 10 miles west, and for visits to nearby Warm Springs Indian Reservation.

Information
Contact the chamber of commerce (☎ 541-475-2350), 197 SE 5th St, PO Box 770, Madras, OR 97411. The post office is at 230 6th St.

Lake Billy Chinook
West of Madras the irrigated fields come to an abrupt end. Here, the three prodigious rivers of central Oregon – the Deschutes, Crooked and Metolius – join at Lake Billy Chinook. This large and spectacular canyon reservoir is a major playground for local residents. Its swallow-your-gum precipitousness and popular **Cove Palisades State Park**, with a marina, campground, boat launches and picnic areas, make the lake a great stopover for the traveler as well.

From Madras, follow signs to Cove Palisades State Park. The road (here called Jordan Rd) drops to lake level and climbs through first the Crooked and then the Deschutes River canyons. Separating these two gorges is a flat-topped, razor-thin isthmus called the Island, with cliffs towering 450 feet above the lake water.

The marina (with boat rentals), a cafe and the boat launch are at the base of the Crooked River canyon. Most other tourist facilities are on the Island. Nearly 100 campsites are available here, along with a swimming beach and hiking trails. Be sure to stop at the **Crooked River Petroglyph**, an elaborately carved boulder near the gulch on the Island. The boulder was moved to this location when the dam was built; the flooding waters covered many similar stone carvings by early Native

OREGON

Rock Collecting

The dusky volcanic mesas of central and eastern Oregon and Washington yield treasures for the rock hound. Sunstones, a pale yellow gemstone, are found north of Plush; to find thundereggs, round agatized geodes, go to commercial locations near Prineville, or Succor Creek State Park in far eastern Oregon. The Priday Agate Beds, north of Madras in central Oregon, is a fun thunderegg-hunting site, with campground and showers on the premises. Agates are also found along the southern Oregon coast, and famous blue agates are found near Ellensburg, in central Washington. Concessionaires in old gold mining areas of eastern Oregon and Idaho offer opportunities to pan for gold.

If you're interested in collecting rocks, check with the local BLM or USFS offices, who can usually direct you to likely areas. In some cases, you may need a permit to collect specimens. Remember that it is a federal felony to remove Native American artifacts from public land. ■

Americans. From the park office, a nature trail winds its way to viewpoints and picnic areas along the Deschutes canyon.

Jordan Rd continues to the Metolius branch of the lake. However, much of the lower portions of the canyon are privately owned and accessible only by boat. Fifteen miles from Cove Palisades State Park the road passes into USFS land, and there are two lakeside campgrounds. (Alternatively, after 9 miles head south at the Sisters junction and follow a good gravel road to US 20 near Sisters.)

Lake Billy Chinook and Cove Palisades State Park (☎ 541-546-3412) are both very popular. During summer weekends, the water is thick with jet boats, speedboats and water-skiers. Avoid weekends or the high season if you value quiet or solitude. Also, the west shore of the reservoir (accessible only by boat) belongs to the Warm Springs Reservation; it's forbidden to trespass, or even to land a boat, on reservation land.

Crooked River National Grassland

Administered by the USFS, this preserve of grass and scrub forest southeast of Madras offers an interesting introduction to the high-desert ecosystem which covers much of this part of Oregon.

From a trailhead 9 miles south of Madras on US 26 the **Rim Rock Springs Trail** winds through juniper savanna to a small marsh. The 1½-mile route overlooks volcanic buttes and scrambles up lichen-covered formations. The springs are home to raptors, pronghorn and mule deer, and are a stopover for migrating birds.

The Crooked River National Grassland headquarters (☎ 541-475-9272) at 813 S Hwy 97 in Madras, has more information about the grassland.

Priday Agate Beds

The Priday Agate Beds, a prime rock-hounding area, are owned and operated by Richardson's Recreational Ranch (☎ 541-475-2680), Gateway Route, Box 440, Madras, OR 97741, 11 miles north of Madras along US 97. In addition to plume agates, amateur geologists can dig for thundereggs, the agate and crystal-filled geode that is Oregon's state rock. Admission is free, but you must pay for the stones you take home.

Although the Richardsons loan out picks, it's a good idea to bring your own shovels, hammers and chisels. There's a gift shop with cut and polished rocks at the ranch, as well as a shower for dusty rock hounds. Free camping is available for customers, but there are no RV hookups.

Places to Stay

For campers, the first choice should be *Cove Palisades State Park* (☎ 541-546-3412) at Lake Billy Chinook. Otherwise, the *KOA Madras* (☎ 541-546-3046) is 9 miles south of Madras on US 97.

Both the *Juniper Motel* (☎ 541-475-6186), 414 N US 26, with rooms for $28/32, and *Hoffy's Motel* (☎ 541-475-4633), 600 N US 26, with rooms for $38/42, are at the north end of town, and are well kept and reasonably priced. Right downtown is the *Best Western Rama Inn* (☎ 541-475-6141), 12 SW 4th St, a motor inn with a pool; rooms are $47/52. On the south end of town is *Sonny's Motel* (☎ 541-475-7217, 800-624-6137), 1539 SW US 97. There's a pool and a restaurant and rooms are $46/53.

Places to Eat
For Mexican baked goods and a selection of great food to go, try *Pepi's Mexican Bakery* (☎ 541-475-3286), 221 5th St – it's the mainstay of seasoned Madras visitors. There's also pretty good Mexican food at *Martina's* (☎ 541-475-4469), 839 SW US 97, which is the Greyhound bus stop.

The *Original Burger Works* (☎ 541-475-3390), 84 SW 4th St, serves large, tasty burgers and sandwiches. You can eat here, albeit rather basically, for $5.

Getting There & Away
The Greyhound bus depot (☎ 541-475-4469), 839 SW US 97, is serviced by the Bend-Portland line; there is one bus a day in each direction. It's $18 one way from Madras to Portland.

LOWER DESCHUTES VALLEY
North of Madras, the rushing Deschutes River digs its deep and awe-inspiring canyon through the lava flows of the Columbia River. Rising above the arid, rim-rocked gorge to the west is Mt Hood, solitary and white. This is the most remote and magical portion of the Deschutes canyon, long the homeland of Chinook Indians. Scented by sage and juniper, here the Deschutes seems mystical and other-worldly.

Fishing and rafting are popular pastimes on this section of the powerful Deschutes. The river also passes the Warm Springs Reservation, whose residents have devel-

oped an excellent cultural museum of traditional Native American society and history, and a golf and hot-springs resort.

Warm Springs Indian Reservation
Home to three groups, the Wasco, the Tenino and the Northern Paiute (the Confederated Tribes), Warm Springs Reservation is a beautiful homeland that stretches from the peaks of the Cascades in the west to the banks of the Deschutes River to the east.

The Wasco, whose culture combined fishing elements of coastal tribes with the hunting and gathering heritage of plateau Indians, are native to this region. The Tenino, originally from the northern bank of the Columbia River, share with the Wasco their reliance on the Columbia salmon runs for sustenance and cultural focus. In 1855 a treaty between the Tenino, the Wasco and the US government was signed, confining the tribes to a reservation of 725 sq miles to the west of the Deschutes River and east of the Cascades.

After the Bannock Indian War of 1878 in southeastern Oregon, a part of the Northern Paiute Indian Federation was moved to the reservation. The Paiute are a desert group from eastern Oregon; their removal from that area was largely part of a strategy to divide the tribe into small, indefensible units.

The Pi Ume Sha Treaty Days Celebration is held on the third weekend of June at Warm Springs. Competitive dancing, horse races and a rodeo make this one of the reservation's biggest powwows.

Information Contact the Confederated Tribes of the Warm Springs Reservation (☎ 541-553-1161), 1233 Veteran St, PO Box C, Warm Springs, OR 97761, for information about the residents and events on the reservation.

Warm Springs Museum Opened in 1993, the Warm Springs Museum (☎ 541-553-3331), just west of the town of Warm Springs, is a wonderful evocation of traditional Native American life and culture,

The Railroad Race

As the area east of the Cascades became better explored, it quickly filled up with farmers and ranchers. The Homestead Acts especially lured in thousands of hopeful, but largely inexperienced, settlers. However, for these agricultural producers, there was no ready market for their goods; with only the most rudimentary overland trails for freight roads, and the wild, impassable Deschutes River as the only waterway, there was no transportation corridor into or out of central Oregon.

Two railroad companies – the Oregon Trunk Line and the Deschutes Railroad Company – sized up the opportunities and began to build lines up opposite sides of the Deschutes canyon in 1909. Competition flared between the two crews as they hewed a railbed out of the rock walls. Railroad owners spurred workers into longer and harder shifts, each seeking to be the first to arrive in the fast-growing agricultural basin of central Oregon. Sabotage and bloody fights erupted, and gunfire frequently disrupted the laying of track.

Finally, the Deschutes Railroad Line, on the east side of the canyon, called it quits, after spending millions of dollars to prepare the railbed. The Oregon Trunk Line, affiliated with Great Northern Railroad's James J Hill, completed its line to Bend in 1911. The grain, cattle and logs of central Oregon suddenly had a market.

The west-side line is still in operation and is run these days by Burlington Northern. The east-side grade of the Deschutes Railroad is used for roads and hiking paths. ∎

---

comprised of artifacts, audio-visual presentations, educational displays, exhibits of cultural art and re-creations of villages.

There's a gift shop and a fine art gallery in the facility. It's open 10 am to 5 pm daily. Admission is $6/5/3 adults/seniors/children.

Kah-Nee-Ta Resort In the early 1970s the Confederated Tribes built this hot-springs spa. It's popular with families and sun-starved Portlanders and is a great stopover for travelers. Facilities include a tribal casino, an 18-hole golf course, horseback riding, tennis, fishing and, of course, swimming in pools fed by hot springs. Day passes at the huge resort pool cost $5. It's a great place to stop for an hour or two on the way between Portland and central Oregon.

Lodging options include rooms in a handsome lodge overlooking the Warm Springs River beginning at $115, or down near the hot springs themselves in condo-like cottages at $169 a night. You can also stay in traditional teepees for $55. The two restaurants feature Native American specialties (like game hen baked in clay). Kah-Nee-Ta Resort (☎ 541-553-1112, 800-554-4786) is 11 miles north of the town of Warm Springs on well-marked reservation roads.

Lower Deschutes Canyon

Downstream from the little town of Maupin (population 470), the Deschutes River burrows an ever-deeper gorge before joining the Columbia River. This 70-mile stretch of the Deschutes is extremely popular for its white-water rafting and fishing. If you don't mind rough graveled roads or getting some dust in your car, follow fishing access roads along the river to explore this dramatic canyon.

Maupin, nestled along a bend in the Deschutes, is nominally the hub of the lower Deschutes River. Boat rentals, fly-fishing lessons, organized float trips and rudimentary food and lodging options are available in town.

Just west of the Deschutes River at the little community of Tygh Valley, 8 miles north of Maupin on US 197, the All-Indian Rodeo (☎ 541-255-3385), a wild evocation of Native America and the Old West, is held on the second weekend of May.

Orientation & Information From Maupin, river-access roads diverge from US 197 and wind up- and downriver. Below Sherars Bridge the roads are gravel and very washboarded. The road ends at Mack's Canyon, 17 miles below Sherars Bridge. From there the river is accessible only by raft until it reaches the Columbia River, 25 miles later.

Contact the Greater Maupin Chamber of Commerce (☎ 541-395-2599), PO Box 220, Maupin, OR 97037, for information on the area.

Tygh Valley State Wayside
A series of waterfalls on the White River and a ghostly 1930s electric power station make this little park an oddly compelling place to stop for a hike or picnic. The first spectacular waterfall is seen from the manicured park grounds. Scramble down the rough path to the river's edge to see the river drop over two other rock ledges in quick succession.

Tygh Valley State Wayside is about 4 miles east of the little town of Tygh Valley on Hwy 216.

Sherars Bridge
In 1979 the Warm Springs Reservation bought 888 acres around Sherars Bridge on the Deschutes River. Here, the mighty river, rushing down its deep desert canyon,

cuts into a flow of lava, and rages through a gorge only 20 feet across. This extraordinarily turbulent series of rapids, called **Sherars Falls**, is a traditional fish-netting location for Warm Springs Indians. The surrounding area is now de facto reservation; non-tribe members can fish from the rock cliffs, but only tribe members are allowed to use the netting platforms.

Plan to visit the Sherars Bridge area during the heavy runs of salmon from March to October, when you can watch Native Americans dip nets on long poles into the furious waters to catch salmon.

Hwy 216 winds down the steep Deschutes canyon to cross over this wild stretch of the river. The most spectacular approach is from the east, as the highway corkscrews down an escarpment before reaching the river.

Fishing
Fly-fishing on the Deschutes River is renowned throughout the USA. The challenge of the river, the abundance of fish and the beautiful remoteness of the desert canyon combine to make this an anglers' paradise.

Its reputation is enhanced by the presence of three types of fish: rainbow and steelhead trout and Chinook salmon. Steelhead and Chinook are both anadromous, or sea-going, spending their lives in the Pacific Ocean and returning to the streams of their birth to spawn.

To preserve the Deschutes fishery, certain restrictions are enforced. Angling from a boat of any sort is prohibited. Native steelhead trout must be released unharmed when caught. Native fish can be recognized by the unclipped adipose fin (the back, top fin); hatchery fish have notched adipose fins. No live bait or barbed hooks are allowed on this stretch of the river.

Fishing for Chinook and steelhead is best below Sherars Falls, while rainbow trout fishing is best above. Call the Fish & Wildlife Bureau (☎ 541-475-2183) for information.

The Deschutes Canyon Fly Shop (☎ 541-395-2565), 7 N US 197 in Maupin, is a great place to buy tackle and specialized flies and to find out what the fish are thinking.

Mike McLucas (☎ 541-395-2611) is the grand old man of the Deschutes River; what he doesn't know about the secret lairs and habits of Deschutes steelhead isn't worth spit.

Rafting

The Deschutes River near Maupin provides one of the Northwest's great white-water trips with a number of Class IV rapids.

The unnavigable Sherars Falls is an obstacle in the river between Maupin and the Columbia River. The Maupin-Sherars trip can be done in a day; if you're headed for the Columbia River be prepared to camp overnight. Most trips leave from Harpen Flats, about 5 miles upstream from Maupin, and end about 15 miles down the river at Sandy Beach, right before Sherars Falls. All floaters on the Deschutes River are required to carry a boater pass, available from area businesses for $2 per person.

For raft rentals, river gear, shuttle service and guided trips, contact Deschutes U-Boat (☎ 541-395-2503), PO Box 144, Maupin, OR 97037. The storefront is near the Oasis Cafe along south US 197. Other local outfitters offering raft rentals ($30 to $100, depending on the size of the raft and the day of the week) and guided trips (about $60 to $70 per person) include: Ewing Whitewater (☎ 800-538-7238), PO Box 427, Maupin, OR 97037; All Star (☎ 800-909-7238), above the local ice cream store; Deschutes River Adventures (☎ 800-723-8464), 602 Deschutes Ave; and Deschutes Whitewater Service (☎ 541-395-2232), on the north side of the Deschutes Bridge on US 197. Contact the chamber of commerce for a full listing of local outfitters.

Places to Stay

Camping There are a great number of informal campgrounds along the Deschutes River. Call the Deschutes National Forest Ranger Station (☎ 541-388-5664) for more information.

For RV hookups, go to *Maupin City Park*, just north of the US 197 bridge. Head upriver from Maupin on the dirt riverside road for a string of campgrounds conveniently located for raft launching. Below Sherars Bridge, there are a number of BLM campgrounds with minimal facilities. The nicest are at *Beavertail*, 8 miles south of Sherars Bridge, and at *Mack's Canyon*, where, after 17 miles, the bouncy east-side Deschutes River road terminates.

Motels Lodging in Maupin isn't fancy, but there are a couple of pleasant spots. The *Oasis* (☎ 541-395-2611), just south of the US 197 bridge, offers the best deal in Maupin lodging. The tiny-looking, free-standing cabins are quite well equipped and a marvel of efficient design; prices start at $45. *CJ Lodge* (☎ 541-395-2404, 800-395-3903), right on the river at 304 Bakeoven Rd, is an old motel transformed into a sort of B&B with rooms from $60.

Places to Eat

The *Oasis Cafe* (☎ 541-395-2611), south on US 197, is the best of Maupin's marginal restaurant offerings. Stop in after rafting for a milk shake, or make it your meal base for a weekend. You'll have a hard time spending more than $10 per person for dinner and a slice of homemade pie.

Northeastern Oregon

The Oregon Trail traversed this corner of the state, giving pioneers glimpses of the high mountains, imposing canyons and lava plateaus. Today, this part of the state offers the traveler a full-strength dose of history and remarkable scenery.

Rambunctious old cow towns like Baker City and Pendleton are centers of historic ranch lands, and relive their early days with wild rodeos and Baker City's wonderful pioneer museum. The Wallowa Mountains rise, seemingly spontaneously, from wide agricultural valleys. Often referred to as the Alps of Oregon, the Wallowas contain 19 of Oregon's 25 highest peaks. High mountain lakes and wilderness hikes make this range a favorite recreational destination.

Oregon's wild volcanic genesis began here. The most amazing of the prodigious lava flows was the Grande Ronde eruption, which occurred about 17 million years ago. The molten basalt flowed from a crack in the earth that was sometimes over 100 miles long. The lava was so fluid that it flowed as far as the Pacific Ocean before cooling, a distance of 460 miles.

East of the Wallowas, along the Oregon/Idaho border, the earth suddenly gives way to the Hells Canyon of the Snake River, the deepest gorge in North America, which cuts a chasm more than a mile deep. This is astonishingly wild and remote country, scarcely accessible except by boat or on foot. Back-road explorers can inch along cliff-edged roads and climb to high viewpoints in order to glimpse this spectacular wilderness canyon.

History

Oregon's northeast corner is home to several Native American tribes, the Cayuse, Umatilla, Walla Walla and the Nez Perce. Lewis and Clark's Corps of Discovery engaged in friendly trading with them in 1805-06, and were especially impressed with the civility of the Nez Perce.

Tantalized by the persistent legend of the Blue Bucket mine – a kind of lost El Dorado somewhere in the Blue Mountains – fortune hunters began to focus on eastern Oregon. As they encroached on the Wallowa Mountains, the ancestral homeland of the Nez Perce, relations quickly deteriorated between the Native Americans and whites. A series of tit-for-tat murders began the Nez Perce War in 1877. Chief Joseph and 800 Nez Perce fled Oregon, hoping to reach Canada and freedom from army retribution. Instead, they were defeated in Montana, just shy of the Canadian border, and sent to reservations in Oklahoma.

The Union Pacific Railroad opened a transcontinental rail line linking Omaha, NE, with Portland in 1884 via Baker City and La Grande, and, with the Native Americans incarcerated on reservations, the region quickly filled with farmers and ranchers.

Orientation

Northeastern Oregon is cut diagonally by I-84, which links Boise, ID, and Salt Lake City, UT, to Portland, and basically follows the route of the Oregon Trail throughout the region. Travelling on the freeway, it's 208 miles from Portland to Pendleton, and another 21 miles from Pendleton to Boise.

US 395 cuts south from the Tri-Cities in Washington to Pendleton and continues southward to John Day and Burns. The other major road in the area is Hwy 82, which links La Grande to the Wallowa Mountain resort towns of Enterprise and Joseph. From here, smaller roads explore the remote and precipitous canyons of the Snake and the Grande Ronde Rivers.

Getting There & Around

Air Pendleton is northeastern Oregon's air hub, receiving regularly scheduled flights from Portland and the Tri-Cities on

OREGON

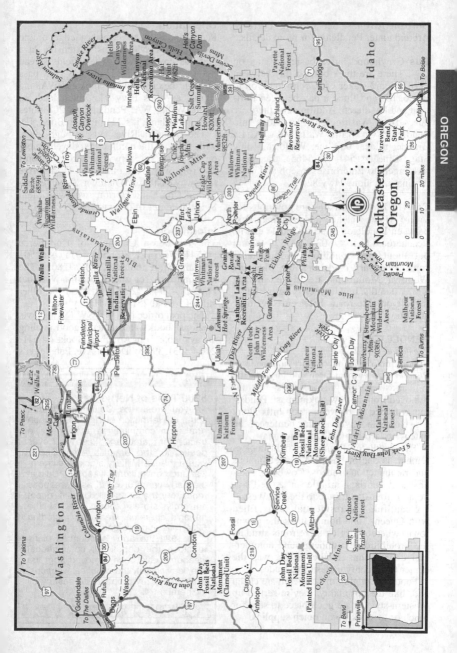

Horizon Airlines. See Getting There & Around under Pendleton for more details.

Bus Greyhound buses basically stay on I-84. There are three buses a day between Portland and Baker City, continuing on to Boise, ID, and three a day between Portland and Pendleton. Additionally, there are buses from Washington's Tri-Cities into Pendleton via Walla Walla, WA. At La Grande, a local bus line, Wallowa Valley Stage Line (☎ 541-963-5465), transports passengers to Enterprise, Joseph and other destinations along Hwy 82.

Car The Blue Mountains are notorious for severe winter weather, and Deadman Pass between Pendleton and La Grande can be treacherous. Call ☎ 503-976-7277 to find out about road conditions. Additionally, some secondary roads over the Blue and Wallowa Mountains are closed during winter months. Inquire locally before heading off on side roads between November and May.

PENDLETON
Population 15,930

Synonymous with wool shirts and rodeos, Pendleton is eastern Oregon's largest city. A handsome old town that's not far removed from its cow-poking past, Pendleton is folded in between steep hills along the Umatilla River at the center of an extensive farming and ranching area.

The Pendleton Round-Up, held in September, is one of the USA's most famous and rambunctious rodeos. Cowboys, Indians and tourists mingle in a hell's-a-poppin' four-day tribute to the Old West.

Beautiful, old residential areas filled with Queen Anne homes flank the downtown, where red-brick storefronts straddle the Prohibition-era underground commercial district that, in the 1910s, was the center for socially undesirable trades.

Food and lodging in Pendleton are cheap and, like the hospitality, they're served up Western-style. It's a good place to stop for lunch or to stock up on ranch supplies.

Orientation

Pendleton is at the western edge of the arching Blue Mountains. Extensive lava plateaus covered with wheat fields spread out to the west. I-84 and US 395 pass through the city, linking Spokane, WA, and Burns, as does Hwy 11, which leads to Walla Walla, WA. Pendleton is 208 miles east of Portland; it's 221 miles to Boise, ID.

The Umatilla River cuts through town, with most of the commercial development on the south side. Hwy 30 becomes Court Ave (one way westbound) and Dorion Ave (one way eastbound) in town. The intersection of Court and Dorion Aves with Main St is the center of downtown.

Information

The Pendleton Chamber of Commerce (☎ 541-276-7411, 800-547-8911) is at 501 S Main St, Pendleton, OR 97801. The headquarters for the Umatilla National Forest (☎ 541-278-3716) is on the other side of I-84 at 2517 SW Hailey Ave.

The post office is at 104 SW Dorion Ave. Regional books and general good reading are available from Armchair Books (☎ 541-276-7323), 39 SW Dorion Ave. Pendleton's

---

5200 Tons of Nerve Gas

As you cross the Columbia Plateau south of Hermiston along I-84, through rural farm communities and extensive tracts of irrigated land, keep your eyes peeled for the Umatilla Army Depot, where the US Military stockpiles chemical and conventional weapons. Built in the early years of WWII as a weapons repository, the 30-sq-mile Umatilla depot currently stores about 12% of the nation's chemical weapons, including 5200 tons of nerve gas.

In 1994 the army announced plans to close the depot. All conventional weapons have been removed from the site, leaving only the chemical weapons, which the army proposes to destroy by incineration. ■

OREGON

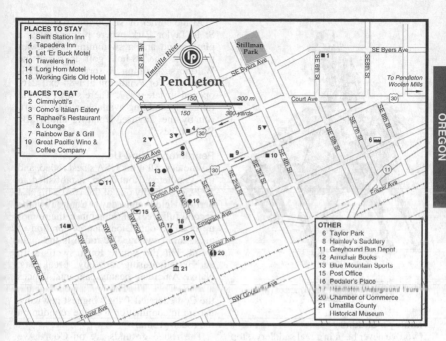

PLACES TO STAY
1 Swift Station Inn
4 Tapadera Inn
9 Let 'Er Buck Motel
10 Travelers Inn
14 Long Horn Motel
18 Working Girls Old Hotel

PLACES TO EAT
2 Cimmiyotti's
3 Como's Italian Eatery
5 Raphael's Restaurant
   & Lounge
7 Rainbow Bar & Grill
19 Groat Pacific Wino &
   Coffee Company

OTHER
6 Taylor Park
8 Hamley's Saddlery
11 Greyhound Bus Depot
12 Armchair Books
13 Blue Mountain Sports
15 Post Office
16 Pedaler's Place
17 Pendleton Underground Tours
20 Chamber of Commerce
21 Umatilla County
   Historical Museum

daily newspaper is the *Eastern Oregonian*. Oregon Public Radio is heard on 90.9 FM.

Do something about those dirty clothes at the Laundry Room (☎ 541-276-7782), 121 SW 18th St, and go to Saint Anthony Hospital (☎ 541-276-5121), 1601 SE Court Ave, for health needs.

Pendleton Woolen Mills

The Pendleton Woolen Mills (☎ 541-276-6911), 1307 SE Court Place, was founded here in 1909 by members of a family that had been weaving wool in Oregon since 1863. Built principally to scour local wool, it also produced blankets to sell on the nearby Umatilla Reservation. Today, its woolen products are known worldwide, and are produced nationally at 14 different locations. The red-brick mill is a Pendleton landmark.

The factory's salesroom is open from 8 am to 4:45 pm weekdays and 8 am to 2 pm Saturday from May to September. From October to April, the Saturday hours are 9 am to 1 pm.

Free, short tours of the factory, showing the old weaving process, are given at 9 and 11 am and 1:30 and 3 pm on weekdays, year-round. Tour groups are limited to 15, so call ahead.

Pendleton Underground Tours

At the end of the 19th century, a network of businesses and establishments boomed beneath Pendleton's old storefronts. Literally driven underground by prohibition and social tensions, saloons, Chinese laundries, card rooms and other businesses found cozy tunnels in which to operate. Pendleton Underground Tours (☎ 541-276-0730), 37 SW Emigrant Ave, tours the town's old, subterranean business district, opium dens and an above-ground 1890s brothel. Tours cost $10/5 adults/children and last 1½ hours. Call ahead for reservations and tour times.

Hamley's Saddlery
If you've never been in a real saddlery, stop by Hamley's (☎ 541-276-2321), 30 SE Court Ave, which is world-famous for its handmade saddles. If you ask nicely, they will show you the saddle-making process. Upstairs is a maze-like gallery of Western art.

Umatilla County Historical Museum
This museum (☎ 541-276-0012), 108 SW Frazer Ave, is housed in Pendleton's handsome old railroad station. Displays include an Oregon Trail commemoration, local Native American artifacts and memorabilia of the region's sheep industry and wool mills. The museum is open 10 am to 4 pm Tuesday to Saturday; admission is by donation.

Activities
Blue Mountain Sports (☎ 541-276-2269), 221 S Main St, rents downhill and cross-country skis and other outdoor gear. Rent mountain bikes at Pedaler's Place (☎ 541-276-3337), 318 S Main St.

At the corner of SE Dorion Ave and 7th St is Taylor Park, where picnic tables, a playground and a swimming pool await travelers. The 18-hole golf course at the Wildhorse Gaming Resort (☎ 541-278-2274), east of Pendleton at I-84 exit 216, opened in late 1997. There's also a wide range of gambling available at this resort, run by the Cayuse, Umatilla and Walla Walla tribes.

Pendleton Round-Up
Promoters call it the USA's best rodeo, and the Pendleton Round-Up, established in 1909, is certainly one of the West's biggest parties. Held Wednesday to Saturday in the second full week of September, the round-up is an all-out, Dionysian celebration of horse and cowboy. The rodeo is the main event, but the whole town swells with activity, featuring cowboy breakfasts, Native American beauty pageants, dances and art shows. The Happy Canyon Pageant, the Confederated Tribe's biggest powwow, is held in conjunction with the roundup on the rodeo grounds.

The rodeo grounds are on Court Ave (Hwy 30), west of downtown. Lodging is scarce at roundup time, so plan well in advance. For ticket information and a schedule of events, contact the Pendleton Round-Up (☎ 800-457-6336), 1205 SW Court Ave.

If you can't make it here during roundup week, you can still duck under the south grandstand and browse the Round-Up Hall of Fame (☎ 541-278-0815), chock full of great old photos of cowboys and cowgirls.

Places to Stay
Camping Tent campers will want to stay at *Emigrant Springs State Park*, 26 miles southeast on I-84, a historic Oregon Trail site. Quieter, but even more distant, is *Umatilla Forks*, a USFS campground 32 miles east of Pendleton. To reach the remote Umatilla Forks, take the road out of Pendleton east to Mission, continue to Gibbon and follow the Umatilla River to the Umatilla National Forest boundary. RV campers should try *Brooke RV & MH*

Court (☎ 541-276-5353), 5 NE 8th St, or *Stotlar's Mobile Home Court* (☎ 541-276-0734), 15 SE 11th St; both are on the Umatilla River.

B&Bs *The Swift Station Inn* (☎ 541-276-3739), 602 SE Byers Ave, offers four rooms in a historic home, starting at $55. *Working Girls Old Hotel* (☎ 541-276-0730), 21 SW Emigrant Ave, offers rooms in an old downtown hotel with a shady past. The five guest rooms, now run by Pendleton Underground Tours, are decorated with period furnishings and range from $55 to $65.

Motels Downtown there is *Travelers Inn* (☎ 541-276-6231), 310 SE Dorion Ave, with a hot tub and pool. Singles/doubles cost $38/42. Less expensive is the *Let 'Er Buck Motel* (☎ 541-276-3293), 205 SE Dorion Ave, where rooms are $28/34. The *Tapadera Inn* (☎ 541-276-3231), 105 SE Court Ave, has its own bar and restaurant; rooms are $39/44. *The Long Horn Motel* (☎ 541-276-7531), 411 SW Dorion Ave, is central and welcomes pets; rooms run $28/33.

Out by I-84 exit 210 there is the usual assortment of lodging choices. *Motel 6* (☎ 541-276-3160), 325 SE Nye Ave, is a good deal at $30/36. More upscale is the *Pendleton DoubleTree* (☎ 541-276-6111), 304 SE Nye Ave, where rooms begin at $65.

Places to Eat
For lighter fare and espresso, try the *Great Pacific Wine & Coffee Company* (☎ 541-276-1350), 403 S Main St; they can also provide the makings for a good picnic with wine and deli products.

Como's Italian Eatery (☎ 541-278-9142), 39 SE Court Ave, is a good place for lunch or an early dinner of pizza or pasta. Check out the *Rainbow Bar & Grill* (☎ 541-276-4120), 209 S Main St, for late-night burgers and beer, and for its cool neon.

Another local favorite is *Cimmiyotti's* (☎ 541-276-4314), 137 S Main St, featuring steak and Italian food in a bar/dining room that recalls an Old West speakeasy.

Raphael's Restaurant & Lounge (☎ 541-276-8500), 233 SE 4th St, began as the diner at the Pendleton Municipal Airport. The food was so good that locals would make the trip to the airport just to eat dinner. Success brought the business downtown to a beautifully refurbished old home, where the food is more popular than ever. Fresh seafood and smoked prime rib ($16) are favorites. Reservations are recommended.

Getting There & Around
Air Horizon Air (☎ 541-276-9777, 800-547-9308) connects Pendleton's Municipal Airport to Portland with five flights daily; one-way fares run $100 and up. Two flights daily link Pendleton with Washington's Tri-Cities, $46 one way. The airport is about 5 miles west of town on Hwy 30.

Bus Three Greyhound buses pass daily between Pendleton and Portland ($34 one way), and from Pendleton to Boise ($38 one way) and points east. There's also service to Walla Walla ($10 one way) and Washington's Tri-Cities ($18 one way to Pasco). The depot (☎ 541-276-1551) is at 320 SW Court Ave.

Car & Taxi Hertz (☎ 541-276-3783) does its business at the airport. For a local weather forecast and road reports, call ☎ 541-276-0103. For a cab, call Elite Taxis at ☎ 541-276-8294.

LA GRANDE & AROUND
Population 12,200
At the head of a vast valley ringed by snowy peaks, La Grande is a college town and trade center for the area's farms and ranches. (Eastern Oregon State College is the only four-year institution east of the Cascades.)

Early French traders, upon seeing the broad, seemingly circular valley, declared it to be the *Grande Ronde*, or big circle. Indeed, from the historical marker on Hwy 30 above town, it seems as if the valley forms a giant ring between mountain peaks.

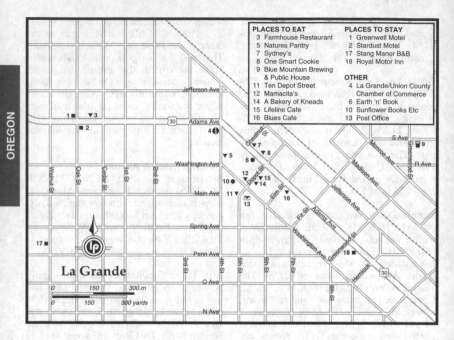

PLACES TO EAT
3 Farmhouse Restaurant
5 Natures Pantry
7 Sydney's
8 One Smart Cookie
9 Blue Mountain Brewing
   & Public House
11 Ten Depot Street
12 Mamacita's
14 A Bakery of Kneads
15 Lifeline Cafe
16 Blues Cafe

PLACES TO STAY
1 Greenwell Motel
2 Stardust Motel
17 Stang Manor B&B
18 Royal Motor Inn

OTHER
4 La Grande/Union County
   Chamber of Commerce
6 Earth 'n' Book
10 Sunflower Books Etc
13 Post Office

La Grande

The Oregon Trail crossed this valley, and at La Grande the pioneers rested and prepared to traverse the Blue Mountains. Some immigrants understood the agricultural potential of the wide, well-watered valley and settled. La Grande was established in 1864. A tavern on the south bank of the Grande Ronde River was the catalyst for the town's early growth. Today, a wealth of inexpensive eating and lodging options, and plenty of recreational opportunities in the surrounding mountains and canyons, make La Grande a great place to spend a night or two.

Orientation
Located on the Grande Ronde River, a confluent of the Snake River, La Grande is at the juncture of I-84 and Hwy 82, the road to the Wallowa Mountains.

The town is 44 miles north of Baker City, 52 miles southeast of Pendleton and 259 miles east of Portland.

Information
Contact La Grande/Union County Chamber of Commerce (☎ 541-963-8588, 800-848-9969) at 1912 4th St, suite 200, La Grande, OR 97850. La Grande Ranger Station of the Wallowa-Whitman USFS (☎ 541-963-7186), is at 3502 Hwy 30. Current fishing regulations and information about wildlife preserves can be obtained from the Fish & Wildlife office (☎ 541-963-2138), 107 20th St.

The post office is at 1202 Washington Ave. Sunflower Books (☎ 541-963-5242), 1114 Washington Ave, features an adjacent coffee shop. Earth 'n' Book (☎ 541-963-8057), 1104 Adams Ave, offers both new and used books. The La Grande *Daily Observer* is the region's local paper. Oregon Public Broadcasting is found on 89.9 FM.

La Grande's laundry is Bubbles Laundry (☎ 541-962-7578), 2001 Adams Ave, and the Grande Ronde Hospital (☎ 541-963-8421) is at 900 Sunset Drive.

Grande Ronde River

The upper reaches of the Grande Ronde River, one of Oregon's most dramatic and beautiful rivers, can be explored by taking Hwy 244, 8 miles west of La Grande from I-84 exit 252.

At the site of today's Hilgard State Park, just off the freeway exit, Oregon Trail pioneers gathered their strength before climbing up over the Blue Mountains. Information kiosks explain how the pioneers winched their wagons down the steep slopes of the Grande Ronde Valley.

Hwy 244 follows the Grande Ronde Valley, then climbs up to a low pass. Cross-country skiing is popular here in winter. Skiers and other explorers like to end their day with a soak at Lehman Hot Springs, (☎ 541-427-3015), 40 miles southwest of La Grande. The huge pool has three separate areas, with water ranging from warm to sizzling hot. Stop by for an afternoon of swimming ($5) or spend the night in the adjacent campground ($9) or a cabin ($85).

Hot Lake & Union

Some of eastern Oregon's first settlements were in the Grande Ronde Valley, southeast of La Grande. This lovely rural area combines Victorian farmhouses with spooky hot springs.

At Hot Lake, 9 miles south of La Grande on Hwy 203, 2½ gallons per minute of nearly-boiling water reach the surface and pour into a large pond. The Nez Perce, Cayuse, Umatilla and Walla Walla considered the extensive geothermals – reportedly the world's largest hot spring – a sacred area and treated the entire valley, which was known as the 'Valley of Peace,' as a cease-fire zone.

From Hot Lake, continue south on Hwy 203 to Union, the first settlement in the area, established in 1862. Union has a number of well-maintained Victorian buildings, as well as the **Union County Museum** (☎ 541-562-6003), 311 S Main Ave, which houses a great cowboy exhibit. Head north to Cove on Hwy 237, which, when first settled, was at the edge of a shallow lake. Return via Island City to La Grande.

The Haunted Sanatorium

As early as 1864, white settlers recognized Hot Lake's economic viability and proceeded to build a series of lakeside health resorts at the edge of the 8-acre lake. The grandest of all was built in 1906, a huge sanatorium/hotel with hundreds of rooms. In the 1930s a fire destroyed the grand ballroom and library, leaving just the brick hospital/hotel intact.

The Hot Lake Resort closed in the 1980s, and is widely considered to be haunted. Listen closely, late on a winter's day, when plumes of sulturous vapor dance across the lake, and hear the screams. Attempts in recent years to revive Hot Lake as a resort have met with failure. ■

OREGON

Blue Mountain Interpretive Center

Hiking paths and interpretive displays flank a portion of the Oregon Trail – still quite visible after 150 years – at this park. The Blue Mountains were an incredible concern to the pioneers. Not only were the grades quite steep, but early snowstorms could make crossing the Blues at the end of the journey (usually in early September) miserable, if not impossible.

Along the footpaths, there are interpretive panels documenting the challenges, dangers and choices that the Oregon Trail travelers faced.

The center is 13 miles west of La Grande off I-84 exit 248. From the exit, follow well-marked gravel roads about 3 miles toward the little community of Kamela. The center is open year-round, during daylight hours only.

Fishing

The Grande Ronde is one of Oregon's most unsung rivers, probably because it is so far from population centers. But just one glimpse of this beautiful river in its rugged canyon will stir anglers.

Around La Grande, fishing is good for rainbow trout – try your luck at Red Bridge State Park, west of La Grande on Hwy 244. Below Elgin, the river begins to furrow its canyon, on the way to its appointment with wild Snake River. Fly-fishing for steelhead is popular in winter near the little community of Troy. Special restrictions apply to fishing the Grande Ronde for steelhead and salmon, whose populations have been devastated by Columbia River and Snake River hydroelectric dams (you can fish for trout or smallmouth bass, however). Contact the Fish & Wildlife office (see Information, above) for current regulations and information.

Rafting

Floating the Grande Ronde's enormous canyon north of Elgin is one of Oregon's most unheralded and beautiful recreational opportunities. Float trips and raft rentals are available from Tilden's River Tours (☎ 541-437-9270). Wapiti River Guides (☎ 800-488-9872), based in Idaho, also offers float trips; some are held in conjunction with primitive survival and nature-lore workshops.

Skiing

Spout Springs Resort (☎ 541-556-2164), between Weston and Elgin on Hwy 204, is northeastern Oregon's low-key ski area. The vertical drop is only 550 feet, and the summit is at 5500 feet. However, it's the quality and quantity of the snow that make skiing here interesting, and with lift tickets at only $19 it's a good place to take a family or group.

For downhill skiers, there are 11 runs, two double chair lifts and one T-bar. There are also 13 miles of groomed cross-country ski trails. You can rent downhill and cross-country skis at the ski area or from Blue Mountain Sports (☎ 541-963-5115) in the Grande Ronde Mall.

Places to Stay

Camping Convenient but right beside the freeway is *Hilgard Junction State Park*, 8 miles west of La Grande at I-84 exit 252.

Catherine Creek State Park(☎ 541-963-0430) is 8 miles southeast of Union on Hwy 203. Both offer primitive sites with no hookups.

The Broken Arrow Lodge (see below) offers a few spaces to RVers near the motel.

B&Bs A 1920s Georgian mansion once owned by a lumber baron, the *Stang Manor B&B* (☎ 541-963-2400), 1612 Walnut St, offers guest rooms with private baths starting at $75.

Motels La Grande has an abundance of inexpensive accommodations along the old 'main drag,' Hwy 30, which is called Adams Ave in town. Take I-84 exit 259 for the *Stardust Motel* (☎ 541-963-4166), 402 Adams Ave, where singles/doubles go for $28/30. Rates are the same at the *Greenwell Motel* (☎ 541-963-4134), 305 Adams Ave.

Downtown, stay at the comfortable *Royal Motor Inn* (☎ 541-963-4154), 1510 Adams Ave; rates are $35/40. Farther east along old Hwy 30 are other older, well-kept motels. The *Orchard Motel* (☎ 541-963-6160), 2206 Adams Ave, takes pets and has no-smoking rooms and kitchenettes for $30/35. The *Moon Motel* (☎ 541-963-2724), at 2116 Adams Ave, charges $26/30, and the *Broken Arrow Lodge* (☎ 541-963-7116), 2215 Adams Ave, has rooms for $26/28.

If you want to stay out near the freeway ramps, you can do so at exit 261. Awaiting you are the *Super 8* (☎ 541-963-8080), 2407 East R Ave, with a pool, spa and rooms for $48/50. At the similarly appointed *Best Western Pony Soldier* (☎ 541-963-7195, 800-528-1234), 2612 Island Ave, rooms are $66/73.

Places to Eat

La Grande offers a surprisingly diverse and affordable selection of dining options. Really delicious baked goods are served by very nice folks at *A Bakery of Kneads* (☎ 541-963-5413), 109 Depot St. Next door, at 111 Depot St, the *Lifeline Cafe* (☎ 541-962-2568) serves healthy main courses and arguably unhealthy but very delicious desserts.

For espresso and freshly baked muffins, go to *One Smart Cookie* (☎ 541-963-3172), 1119 Adams Ave. For a traditional breakfast, go to *Sydney's* (☎ 541-963-6500), 1115 Adams Ave. Enjoy breakfast or burgers in the sunny *Blues Cafe* (☎ 541-963-0819), 1302 Adams Ave.

For a vegetarian deli and other natural foods, go to *Nature's Pantry* (☎ 541-963-7955), 1907 4th St. Across the street from the Stardust Motel is handy *Farmhouse Restaurant* (☎ 541-963-9318), 401 Adams Ave.

Mamacita's (☎ 541-963-6223), 110 Depot St, provides a good, bustling value in Mexican food; most full dinners are in the $6 range. *Ten Depot Street* (☎ 541-963-8766), at, of course, 10 Depot St, offers full-blown steak and fresh seafood meals in an old Mason's lodge; local loin of lamb with herbs goes for $18.

Blue Mountain Brewing & Public House (☎ 541-963-5426), 1502 S Ave, pours hearty beer, including Sneaky Wheat and Interstout 84, and serves locally made beer-simmered sausage sandwiches and other light meals.

Getting There & Around
The Greyhound bus depot (☎ 541-963-5165) is at 2108 Cove Ave; buses pass through four times daily. The Wallowa Valley Stage Line (☎ 541-963-5465) offers once-daily service to Joseph and Enterprise; the fare is $8 for the two-hour trip.

Rental cars are available from Tamarack Ford (☎ 541-963-2161), 2906 Island Ave (toward Island City, just east of La Grande). Call Designated Driver Cab Co (☎ 541-963-6960) for a lift.

BAKER CITY
Population 9300
Baker City, at the head of a wide valley beneath the snowcapped Elkhorn mountains, is Oregon's richest geologic region with 75% of the state's mineral wealth, and one of eastern Oregon's oldest commercial centers. Nearly all phases of Oregon's

development have been played out in Baker City's rich history.

Once the largest and most boisterous city between Salt Lake City and Portland, Baker City was a colorful, two-fisted party town during the latter years of the 1800s, with miners, cowboys, sheepherders, shopkeepers and loggers keeping each other company in the city's many saloons, brothels and gaming halls. Still an authentic Western town, Baker City's wide streets and gracious architecture recall both the swagger and courtliness of a not-too distant past.

Orientation
Located at the point where the Powder River leaves the Blue Mountains and enters its wide agricultural valley, Baker City is on I-84 at the junction of Hwy 7 to John Day, and of Hwy 86 to Hells Canyon. Baker City is 44 miles south of La Grande on I-84. Hwy 30 becomes 10th St in town.

Information
The Baker County Visitors & Convention Bureau (☎ 541-523-3356, 800-523-1235) is at 490 Campbell St, Baker City, OR 97814. The headquarters for the Wallowa-Whitman National Forest (☎ 541-523-6391) and BLM's regional office (☎ 541-523-6391) are located at 1550 Dewey Ave. The Wallowa-Whitman National Forest Ranger District office (☎ 541-523-4476) is at 3165 10th St.

The post office is at 1550 Dewey Ave. Betty's Books (☎ 541-523-7551), 1813 Main St, is the local independent bookstore, with a selection of regional history and touring books. The Baker City daily newspaper is the *Baker City Herald* and Oregon Public Radio is heard on 91.5 FM.

The Baker City Laundry (☎ 541-523-9817) is at 815 Campbell St. Baker City's medical center is St Elizabeth Hospital (☎ 541-523-6461), 3325 Pocahontas Rd.

Downtown
The old downtown retains much of its late-19th-century Victorian Italianate architecture and charm, and quite a bit of the city

OREGON

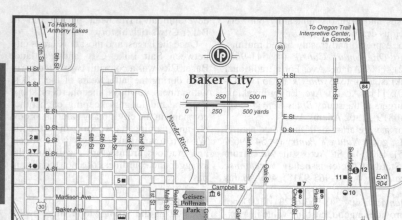

PLACES TO STAY
1 Western Motel
2 Trail Motel
5 Grant House B&B
9 Quality Inn
9 Eldorado Inn
11 Best Western Sunridge Inn
13 Super 8 Inn
17 Royal Motor Inn
22 Geiser Grand Hotel
27 A Demain B&B
30 Friendship Inn
31 Oregon Trail Motel

PLACES TO EAT
3 Inland Cafe
16 Brass Parrot
20 Phone Company Restaurant
21 Baker City Cafe-Pizza a'Fetta
23 Main Event
25 Front St Cafe
31 Oregon Trail Restaurant

OTHER
4 Ellison Motors
6 Oregon Trail
   Regional Museum
8 Baker City Laundry
10 Greyhound Bus Depot
12 Visitors & Convention
   Bureau
14 YMCA Pool
15 Flagstaff Sports
18 US Bank
19 Bella Fine Spirits
24 Crossroads Center for
   Creative & Performing Arts
26 Betty's Books
28 Hotel Baker
29 Wallowa-Whitman
   National Forest HQ,
   BLM (Federal Offices),
   Post Office
32 Baker Golf Club

center is listed in the National Register of Historic Places.

Several blocks of downtown, near Valley Ave and 1st St, are built of locally quarried basalt. **Hotel Baker**, still the tallest building in Oregon east of the Cascades, was built in 1929 (this nine-story landmark is now converted to apartments). Oregon's largest display of gold in its mineral state is found in the US Bank lobby at 2000 Main St, and includes a nugget weighing over 80 ounces. It's open to the public during regular banking hours.

Stop by the Crossroads Center for Creative & Performing Arts (☎ 541-523-5369), 1901 Main St, where there's a pretty good little gallery of local arts and crafts, and a performance space (the schedule's posted).

A brochure describing a walking tour of historic buildings in the city center is available from the visitors' center or the Oregon Trail Regional Museum.

Oregon Trail Regional Museum

Housed in a showcase natatorium built in 1920, this museum of local history contains a jumble of exhibits. The large space that once contained the pool (which was fed by hot springs) now contains furniture, vehicles and machinery from Baker City's frontier days. An extensive mineral collection, including a display of fluorescent rocks, will be of interest to more than avid rock collectors. The museum (☎ 541-523-9308) is at 2480 Grove St at Campbell St, and is open from 9 am to 5 pm daily, mid-April to October. An entrance donation is requested.

National Historic Oregon Trail Interpretive Center

An important historic and educational facility, the Oregon Trail Interpretive Center (☎ 541-523-1843) is the nation's foremost memorial to the pioneers who crossed the West along the Oregon Trail. Built on windswept Flagstaff Hill, 4 miles east of Baker City along Hwy 86, it overlooks well-preserved wagon ruts from the 1840s and '50s. The center opened in 1992 and is a must-see for anyone with an interest in the history of the West.

It was from this pass that emigrants along the Oregon Trail first saw the fertile and inviting uplands of Oregon, reminding the dispirited travelers of Oregon's promise. After traveling across deserts and canyon lands for weeks, the pioneers emerged from the aptly named Burnt Water Valley and onto Flagstaff Hill, where the Powder River valley blossomed beneath the forested Blue Mountains.

The 23,000-sq-foot center contains a maze of interactive displays, artifacts, films and exhibits that stress the day-to-day realities, choices and predicaments of the pioneers as they struggled across the West. A trail system explores an old mining claim, the arid sagebrush ecosystem and the ruts of the original Oregon Trail.

The center is open 9 am to 6 pm, May to September, and 9 am to 4 pm, October to April. Admission is $5/3.50 for adults/seniors and youth, or $10 per carload. Take I-84 to exit 302 (onto Hwy 86) just north of Baker City.

Activities

Baker City is the jumping-off point for both downhill and cross-country skiing at Anthony Lakes Mountain Resort (☎ 541-963-4599 or 541-856-3277) in the Blue Mountains. Rent cross-country skis at Flagstaff Sports (☎ 541-523-5702), 2101 Main St.

The YMCA pool (☎ 541-523-3189) is at 2020 Church Ave. The Baker Golf Club (☎ 541-523-2358), 2801 Indiana Ave, is a nine-hole golf course with views over the mountains and valleys. A highlight is the clubhouse, built in 1936 by the WPA.

Places to Stay

Camping The *Mountain View Holiday Trav-L-Park & Mobile Manor* (☎ 541-523-4824, 800-323-8899), 2845 Hughes Lane, accommodates both tent and RV campers; there's a heated pool. Take exit 304 off I-84, follow Campbell St and head right on 10th St for 1 mile. *Oregon Trails West RV Park* (☎ 541-523-3236), just off exit 302, has a separate tent area.

B&Bs A *Demain B&B* (☎ 541-523-2509), 1790 4th St, is a splendid old Victorian home, with rooms starting at $55. At the Arts and Crafts-style *Grant House B&B* (☎ 541-523-6685), 2525 3rd St, singles/doubles start at $49/59.

Hotels After years of work, Baker City's landmark downtown hotel, the *Geiser Grand Hotel* (☎ 541-523-1889), at 1996 Main St, has been completely restored. It's a stunning Italian Renaissance Revival building, with a corner cupola and a great stained-glass ceiling in the dining area. Locals, including hotel workers, swear the place is haunted. Rooms here run $85 and up, including breakfast.

A less imposing downtown motel is the *Royal Motor Inn* (☎ 541-532-6324), 2205 Broadway Ave, which charges $36/40. Also near downtown is the rather nice *Oregon Trail Motel & Restaurant* (☎ 541-523-5844), 211 Bridge St, where rooms are $32/38, and the *Friendship Inn* (☎ 541-523-6571), 134 Bridge St, which has rooms for $26/33.

Along 10th St are a number of comfortable, equally inexpensive lodgings. At the

Trail Motel (☎ 541-523-4646), 2815 10th St, rooms go for $26/30. The *Western Motel* (☎ 541-523-3700), 3055 10th St, offers lodging for $28/36.

At exit 304 there is a cluster of chain motels. At the *Super 8* (☎ 541-523-8282), 250 Campbell St, rooms cost $45/55. At the *Eldorado Inn* (☎ 541-523-6494), 695 Campbell St, rooms cost $39/46. At the *Quality Inn* (☎ 541-523-2242, 800-228-5151), 810 Campbell St, rooms are $44/49, and at *Best Western Sunridge Inn* (☎ 541-523-6444, 800-233-2368), 1 Sunridge Lane, they run from $63 to $73. Close by is all manner of fast food.

Places to Eat
Although there is the usual clumping of fast-food restaurants at the freeway exits, drive downtown to find more interesting options. *Front Street Cafe* (☎ 541-523-0223), 1840 Main St, is the place for breakfast (try their many fried-potato options), lunch, light dinner and good coffee. Another good spot for a light meal in the $6 to $8 range is *Pizza a'Fetta-Baker Cafe* (☎ 541-523-6099), 1915 Washington Ave, where gourmet pizza is the specialty.

The *Brass Parrot* (☎ 541-523-4266), 2190 Main St, is a little fancier, featuring Mexican specialties and steak in the $10 to $12 range. Another fairly upscale place for dinner is the *Phone Company* (☎ 541-523-7997), 1926 1st St. And dinner at the *Geiser Grand Hotel* (see Places to Stay) is particularly elegant, with dinners running in the $15 range.

For microbrews and hamburgers in a sports bar atmosphere, stop at *The Main Event* (☎ 541-523-6988), 1929 Main St. If you are staying on 10th St, head over to the *Inland Cafe* (☎ 541-523-9041), 2715 10th St, for home-style cooking popular with the locals.

For steak, drive 10 miles north on Hwy 30 to Haines, where the *Haines Steak House* (☎ 541-856-3639) has the well-deserved reputation of serving Oregon's best steak as well as having a great salad bar. It's open for dinner only.

If you'd like some good wine to drink in your hotel room, visit *Bella Fine Spirits* (☎ 541-523-4299) at 2040 Resort St. They also have a small deli case stocked with cheese.

Getting There & Around
The Greyhound bus depot (☎ 541-523-5011), 515 Campbell St, is served by four buses a day each way along its Portland-Boise route. The fare from Portland to Baker City is $42, one way.

Contact Ellison Motors (☎ 541-523-4488), 2615 10th St, for short-term car rentals. For local road conditions, call ☎ 541-523-6417. For a taxi, call Baker City Cab (☎ 541-523-6070).

BLUE MOUNTAINS
Rising to the west from ranch land near Baker City, the Blue Mountains were responsible for the magnificently rich gold strikes that established towns like Sumpter, Granite and Baker City itself. These and other boom towns that have passed out of existence thrived here in the 1860s (ask at the Baker City visitors' center for a brochure on the area's old mining towns). Now more famous for their excellent skiing and stands of pine forests, the Blue Mountains offer back roads to ghost towns, high mountain lakes, river canyons and hiking trails. Elkhorn Drive, a National Forest Scenic Byway, circles the gold-rich Elkhorn Ridge.

Orientation & Information
Hwy 7 connects I-84 with US 26 to the south, traversing the Blue Mountains. From Sumpter, USFS Rd 24 leads to Granite, and USFS Rd 73 goes to Anthony Lakes.

The Wallowa-Whitman National Forest Headquarters (☎ 541-523-6391) at 1550 Dewey Ave, Baker City, OR 97814, has information on the scenic byway and the Blue Mountains.

Elkhorn Drive Scenic Byway
Designated by the USFS, this 106-mile loop drive between Baker City and Granite (along Hwys 7 and 30, and USFS Rd 73) leads to many of the area's historic and

The Blue Gold Mountains

The Blue Mountains were Pacific reefs and islands before the North American continent collided with them about 200 million years ago, wedging them up to mountain heights. Between 160 and 120 million years ago, molten intrusions shot through the new mountains, forming batholiths, or sub-surface lakes of lava that hardened into igneous rock.

This unerupted lava was mostly made up of granite, but it also contained a number of other minerals. As the molten rock cooled, the various component minerals hardened differentially, as each have distinct melting points. Liquid gold, having a very low melting point, squeezed into veins as surrounding rock began to solidify.

The discovery in the 1860s of gold nuggets in streams in the Blue Mountains led to the unearthing of significant gold veins, or lodes, at several locations in the region. The richest lodes have been found in an arc between John Day, Baker City and Ukiah.

Ghost-town enthusiasts will find the Blue Mountains dotted with ruined mining camps. Easily reached from Sumpter is Bourne, 7 miles up Cracker Creek; gold mines are still producing in the area. Granite, 15 miles up Hwy 24, is a ghost town in aspect, but its population is actually growing – it recently reached 10 residents. ■

recreational sites in the Elkhorn Ridge, and to a multitude of pleasant public campsites along Phillips Lake. The eastern Oregon gold rush began in these mountains in 1861, when prospectors discovered colors at Griffin Creek south of Baker City.

By the way, those patches of dead pines between Granite and Gunsight Pass along USFS Rd 73 aren't all due to clear-cutting and forest fires. The byway passes through regions heavily afflicted with mountain-pine beetles.

Phillips Lake

Formed by the dammed Powder River, Phillips Lake offers good summer trout fishing. Ice-fishing is also very popular in winter. Public campgrounds ring the lake, making it a good stopover for families. The largest, *Union Creek*, is just off Hwy 7. On the south side of the lake are two smaller, less-developed campgrounds.

Sumpter
Population 125

A relic of the early gold and lumber boom days, Sumpter, 28 miles west of Baker City, now makes a living as a 'ghost town.' In 1862 five Confederate soldiers discovered gold in the area, but it wasn't until the

Sumpter Valley Railroad reached the town site in 1896 that it really began to boom. The town quickly grew to include 4000 residents, an opera house, three newspapers and a hospital.

The arrival of the railroad allowed the development of 'hard-rock' mining, which entailed underground mining of veins and processing of the ore by stamp mills. Much of the city burned down in a 1917 fire. Between the wars, the area was dredged for gold, leaving the valley's rocky soil in orderly piles. Today, Sumpter preserves its few remaining original buildings as tourist shops and antique stores; stop in the mercantile and visit the local **museum** – it's a good one. An abandoned, evil looking gold dredge is the focal point of a new state park.

The narrow-gauge **Sumpter Valley Railroad** was the economic lifeline of this area from the 1890s to the 1930s. Linking Prairie City on the John Day River to Baker City, the line served the mining, logging and livestock interests in the Blue Mountains. A portion of the wood-fired steam service remains open during summer weekends, linking Sumpter and Phillips Lake. Excursions leave Sumpter Depot at 10 am, noon, 2 and 4 pm, Memorial Day to

OREGON

the last weekend of September. Roundtrip passage is $9/6.50 adults/children, or $22 per family.

Anthony Lakes Recreation Area
Right below the impressive crags of Gunsight Mountain and Angell Peak is a lake basin offering campgrounds, fishing and hikes to alpine meadows. In summer, it's a popular getaway for families. In winter, downhill and cross-country skiers take over, as these remote mountains offer Oregon's best powder skiing.

Take USFS Rd 73, which climbs 19 miles to the Anthony Lakes area from the small town of North Powder (population 460, elevation 3256 feet) on I-84; it's open year-round only as far as the ski area. In summer, the road continues over Elkhorn Summit Pass (at 7392 feet, the highest paved road in Oregon) to join the Elkhorn Drive byway.

Hiking
Along the shores of Grande Ronde, Mud and Anthony Lakes are USFS campgrounds, which make the lakes popular for trout fishing and hiking. Trails lead out from Anthony Lake to several other small lakes.

For a short hike, follow the **Elkhorn Crest Trail** east from the lake, and hike up to Black Lake, immediately below impressive 8342-foot Gunsight Mountain. A steeper climb leads up Parker Creek to tiny Hoffer Lakes.

Skiing
The Elkhorn Mountains' height and location virtually guarantees tons of powdery snow each winter. Anthony Lakes Mountain Resort (☎ 541-963-4599) has the highest base elevation in Oregon (7100 feet) and 21 runs. The resort offers rentals, a day lodge with a restaurant and lounge and ski instruction. Lift tickets are $24.

Cross-country skiing is also popular. The lodge maintains 6 miles of groomed trails (and charges $7 to ski them), and nearby are miles of snowy USFS roads to explore.

Places to Stay & Eat
Besides the basic campgrounds at Anthony Lakes, the closest lodgings are in North Powder. The *Powder River Motel* (☎ 541-898-2829), 850 2nd St, has singles/doubles at $32/34.

In Sumpter, the comfortable log-built *Depot Inn Motel* (☎ 541-894-2522, 800-390-2522) shows that there's still some life left; rooms are $40/45. Other lodging options are available in Baker City or La Grande (see those sections).

A cafe at the *Anthony Lakes Resort Lodge* (☎ 541-963-4599, 541-856-3277) serves skiers' basic food needs during the ski season. There's basic truck-stop food at the *North Powder Cafe* (☎ 541-898-2332), 975 2nd St, down the hill in North Powder. The *Elkhorn Saloon* (☎ 541-894-2244) in Sumpter serves pizzas and burgers in a bar/restaurant combination; it's closed on Monday.

Wallowa Mountains

A spectacular mountain range tucked into Oregon's far northeastern corner, the Wallowas are one of the state's premier scenic and recreational destinations. Rising precipitously from park-like farm and ranch land, the Wallowas loom to 10,000 feet, with 17 individual peaks over 9000 feet. Ice Age glaciers carved sharp crags and deep canyons into the Wallowas, and the moraines of one such glacier now impound Wallowa Lake. Eastern Oregon's highest peak – the 9832-foot Matterhorn – and only remaining glacier are found in the Wallowas.

Much of the high country is part of Eagle Cap Wilderness Area, a 715-sq-mile natural area studded with high mountain meadows and lakes. It is no coincidence that the Wallowas are known as the 'Alps of Oregon.'

Pressed up against the Wallowas' north face, which rises up 4000 feet above the valley, are two Old West burgs, Enterprise and Joseph, in one of the Northwest's most dramatic settings. Beauty and just enough isolation draw artists to the area, in particular to Joseph, which now has a national reputation as a center for Western and wildlife art. In fact, it's become Oregon's version of Santa Fe, all glitzy shops with just enough boots-and-jeans street life to keep it from seeming totally fake.

Directly behind Joseph is Wallowa Lake, a glacial lake flanked by towering peaks. The lake is large enough to support an incredibly popular state park and deep enough for Wally, the Wallowa Lake Monster, sightings of which are the stuff of Native American legend and recent scientific debate.

The USFS has designated the Wallowa Mountain Loop Rd (which links Joseph and Halfway) and the Imnaha River Rd as scenic byways. The road to Hat Point (6982 feet), with views into Hells Canyon, is the area's most famous and most intimidating. Back roads such as these abound. Mountain bikers, cross-country skiers, anglers and other lovers of nature and dramatic landscape will cherish this part of northeast Oregon.

Because of the overwhelming beauty and scenic variety, visitors should not be surprised to find that trails, campgrounds and fishing holes get crowded in the high season. In particular, the lovely state park at Wallowa Lake can be oppressively overutilized during summer weekends.

Ringing the Wallowa Mountains to the south is the Powder River valley. Just as beautiful and isolated as Enterprise and Joseph, the little towns of Richland and Halfway are much less hyped and overrun. Additionally, Hwy 86, which follows the Powder River from near Baker City, leads to Oregon's only riverside access to Hells Canyon.

ENTERPRISE
Population 2020
The Wallowa county seat, and trade center for the area's vast farming and ranching operations, Enterprise both looks and feels the part of a handsome, red-blooded Western town. Much of the original downtown,

built in the 1890s, is still here and functions as the mercantile center.

Enterprise is a friendly kind of town that makes you want to spend a day or two, and you probably should: it's a perfect center for exploring the sights of northeastern Oregon.

Orientation & Information
Enterprise is 65 miles east of La Grande on Hwy 82; from here it's only 6 miles to Joseph on Hwy 82 and 12 miles to Wallowa Lake.

The Wallowa County Chamber of Commerce (☎ 541-426-4622, 800 585-4121), 107 SW First St, Enterprise, OR 97282, is open 10 am to 3 pm on weekdays. The Wallowa-Whitman National Forest office and the Hells Canyon National Recreation Area office share space (☎ 541-426-5546) at 88401 Hwy 82, Enterprise, OR 97282.

The post office is at 201 W North St. The Bookloft (☎ 541-426-3551), 107 E Main St, is one of eastern Oregon's best bookstores, complete with a friendly coffee bar, regional guides and the latest bestsellers.

Wallowa Memorial Hospital (☎ 541-426-3111), 401 E First St, serves the entire Wallowa Valley.

Activities
You can rent cross-country skis at Wallowa Outdoors (☎ 541-426-3493), 110 S River St, and bikes from Cycle Life Bike Shop (☎ 541-426-6134), 212 W North St; ask here for advice on local mountain-bike trails.

Places to Stay
The *Wilderness Inn* (☎ 541-426-4535), 301 W North St, is a good bet here; there's a sauna and singles/doubles are $48/50. The *Country Inn* (☎ 541-426-4986), 402 W North St, offers motel rooms or cabins for $40/46. Right on the edge of town, the *Best Western Rama Inn* (☎ 541-426-2000) has an indoor pool, sauna and fitness room, with rates starting at $63.

Places to Eat
Cloud 9 Bakery (☎ 541-426-3790), 105 SE 1st St, offers espresso, fresh baked goods

OREGON

and fresh-cut sandwiches. *Common Good* (☎ 541-426-4125), 100 Main St, has a small health-food store in the front and a restaurant behind. They serve huge, tasty sandwiches, and aren't purists (there are plenty of meaty options). Dinner is also a good bet here, with a cook who seems to like trying new recipes.

Toma's Restaurant (☎ 541-426-4873), 309 S River St, is a casual place serving up burgers and steak. If you'd rather steer clear of beef, try the *Blue Willow Sausage Eatery* (☎ 541-426-4663), 803 School St.

Getting There & Away
Catch the Wallowa Valley Stage Line (☎ 541-963-5465) at the Mountain Mart Station, 302 W North St. There's one bus a day between La Grande and Enterprise. The fare is under $10 one way; call for times.

JOSEPH
Population 1095
Like Enterprise, Joseph is little changed physically from its 1880s boom days – until you look closely. About half the old storefronts are now world-renowned art galleries. Valley Bronze, one of the largest and most respected foundries in the nation, relocated to Joseph in the 1970s, bringing an intense artistic focus to this old frontier town. Today artists, gallery owners and mavens of bronze sculpture flock here. Combine this with the Wallowa recreational elite, and it means that this is small-town Oregon in appearance only.

Orientation & Information
Joseph is 6 miles south of Enterprise and 6 miles north of Wallowa Lake State Park. Hwy 350 leaves from Joseph for Imnaha (28 miles northeast) where the Hat Point road climbs up to Hells Canyon vistas. Seasonal USFS Rd 39, part of the Wallowa Mountain Loop Rd, divides off Hwy 350, 7 miles east of Joseph, to wind over the east flank of the Wallowas to Hwy 86 near Halfway, 65 miles to the south. USFS Rd 39 is closed in winter because of snow. Call ☎ 541-742-7511 for information on the road's condition.

The Joseph Chamber of Commerce (☎ 541-432-1015) is located at 102 E First St, Joseph, OR 97846. The post office is at 101 N Main St.

Galleries
If Western art is your thing, then you'll find plenty to occupy a day in Joseph. Surely no other town in Oregon can boast more galleries than bars, but Joseph is no ordinary Western town.

The town is most noted for its cast bronze sculpture, due to the existence of the **Valley Bronze Foundry**, which now employs 65 people and is noted throughout the world for its ability to cast large statuary. Tours of the foundry are offered daily and can be scheduled at the Valley Bronze Showroom (☎ 541-432-7551), 18 S Main St.

Other Western art galleries line Main St. The **Manuel Museum** (☎ 541-432-7235), at Main and East Sts, is bronze artist David Manuel's studio; there's also a sculpture garden. The **Wildhorse Gallery** (☎ 541-432-4242), 508 N Main St, offers more bronzes and Western-themed original art and prints.

The **Wallowa Lake Gallery** (☎ 541-432-9555), 19 S Main St, features wildlife art and blue-chip Western prints.

Wallowa County Museum
This community museum (☎ 541-426-6095), at the corner of 2nd and Main Sts, housed in an old 1888 bank, is notable for its display on Nez Perce history. The 1896 robbery of the bank is another item of particular fascination to the locals.

Mountain Biking
Although you can't bike into the Eagle Cap Wilderness Area, the Wallowa-Whitman National Forest and the Hells Canyon National Recreation Area are full of dirt roads and single-tracks. The Wallowa-Whitman National Forest office in Enterprise (☎ 541-426-5546) has a good amount of information on bike trails. For starters, try the Wagon Loop Rd, a 10-mile loop starting on USFS Rd 39 at the Salt Creek

Summit. It's a challenging ride with great scenery. Head east out of town toward Imnaha on Hwy 350, after 8 miles turn right onto USFS Rd 39, and continue another 8 miles to Salt Creek Summit. After the snow falls, this becomes a great cross-country ski area.

Hells Canyon Bicycle Tours (☎ 541-432-2453) operates out of Joseph and offers both day trips and overnighters, running about $75 a day.

Special Events

Chief Joseph Days, held the last weekend of July, features four rodeos, Native American dancing, and a 10km (6.2 miles) run, among other activities. Plan ahead if you are going to need lodging during Chief Joseph Days – it gets pretty tight in both Joseph and Enterprise, and at Wallowa Lake. Contact the chamber of commerce for more information.

Taking its title as the 'Switzerland of America' seriously, Joseph hosts an Alpenfest (☎ 541-432-4704) in late September. Alpenfest features folk music and dancers, German food and local crafts. Be there for the yodeling contest.

Twice weekly, local actors re-enact the daring 1896 Joseph bank robbery along Main St, and stage period melodramas at the Main Street Theatre on Wednesday to Saturday evenings during summer. Call ☎ 541-519-5720 for reservations.

Places to Stay

In season, the real action is a few miles south at Wallowa Lake, but campers who want to avoid the bustle of the state park should try *Hurricane Creek Campground*, 7 miles south of Joseph on USFS Rd 8205, also called Hurricane Creek Rd.

The *Indian Lodge Motel* (☎ 541-432-2651), at the corner of Main and 3rd Sts, is clean and comfortable; singles/doubles go for $32/40. *Chandler's Bed, Bread & Trail Inn* (☎ 541-432-9765), 700 S Main St, is cozy and has rooms starting at $60. At *Wallowa River Camp* (☎ 541-432-9043), 501 Park Dr, you get to choose from rustic B&B cabin rooms ($65), a

bunkhouse that'll sleep five ($95) and teepees.

Places to Eat

The best place in town for breakfast or lunch is the *Old Town Cafe* (☎ 541-432-9892), 8 S Main St. Get coffee or pizza at the *Brew House* (☎ 541-432-2739), 206 N Main St. *Cactus Jack's* (☎ 541-432-6220), 100 N Main St, housed in a historic storefront, is a bar on one side and restaurant on the other.

Getting There & Away

Wallowa Valley Stage Line (☎ 541-963-5465) has bus service between La Grande and Joseph; the fare is $10 for the two-hour, one-way trip.

WALLOWA LAKE & AROUND

Wallowa Lake was formed when glaciers plowed down out of the Wallowas. As these glaciers flowed out of high mountain valleys, they pushed a bulwark of displaced rock. These rock moraines eventually stopped the progress of the glacier, which melted, creating a lake basin. Today, the morainal walls of Wallowa Lake rise 900 feet above the plateau at nearby Joseph. Rising precipitously on three sides of the lake are Wallowa peaks; Chief Joseph Mountain rises vertically a mile above the lake.

Old Chief Joseph, the father of Chief Joseph, is buried at a beautiful site at the north end of the lake.

Now a resort community, Wallowa Lake has a sizable huddle of motels, B&Bs, guest lodges and restaurants. Write to the Wallowa Lake Tourist Committee, PO Box 853, Joseph, OR 97846, for information.

Wallowa Lake State Park

Reckoned to be one of the most beautiful state parks in the western USA, Wallowa Lake State Park (☎ 541-432-4185) is the center of activities at the south end of Wallowa Lake. A swimming beach and boat launch generate much activity. The best hiking is from the end of Wallowa Lake Rd.

Chief Joseph & the Nez Perce

The Wallowa Mountains are at the center of the Nez Perce traditional homeland, which once encompassed adjacent areas of Washington and Idaho. Early treaties effectively divided the Nez Perce into a band that lived in the Wallowa Valley, and another that lived along the Clearwater River in Idaho. In 1863, in a move that demonstrated US diplomatic scheming as well as intertribal rivalries, the Idaho Nez Perce signed a treaty that turned the Oregon reservation lands over to white settlement, while maintaining the Idaho homelands. The Oregon Nez Perce, under Chief Joseph, refused to recognize the treaty and remained in the Wallowas.

Conflicts between settlers and Chief Joseph's Nez Perce left several white men dead, and the 1876 Battle of Little Bighorn in Montana – Custer's defeat at the hands of Sioux and Cheyenne Indians – was fanning distrust of Indians everywhere. Judging that flight to Canada was a wiser choice than awaiting punishment from the army, Chief Joseph and 800 Nez Perce fled eastward. They crossed Idaho and Montana, alternately eluding and fighting the army (most notably the 1877 Battle of the Big Hole in western Montana) before being apprehended within miles of the Canadian border. The Wallowa Nez Perce were removed to Indian Territory, now Oklahoma, before being allowed to move to the Colville Reservation in Washington. The Idaho Nez Perce remain on the Lapwai Reservation in Idaho. ∎

Mt Howard Gondola

The gondola (☎ 541-432-5331) leaves from Wallowa Lake and climbs 3200 feet to the top of 8200-foot Mt Howard. The ride is thrilling enough, and there's a cafe up top, but the real rewards are the easy alpine hikes around Mt Howard's summit, with views onto Hells Canyon, the Wallowas and Idaho's Seven Devils. The tramway operates from 10 am to 4 pm daily, June to Labor Day, and weekends only in May and September; tickets are $13.50/12/10 adults/seniors/children (10 and under).

Eagle Cap Wilderness Area

At 715 sq miles, this is Oregon's largest wilderness area. Glacier-ripped valleys, high mountain lakes and marble peaks are some of the rewards that long-distance hikers find on overnight treks. Few hiking destinations readily suit the schedules of day hikers.

A number of trailheads lead into Eagle Cap Wilderness Area from the south end of Wallowa Lake Rd. One of the most popular **hiking** routes from here is the 6-mile one-way hike to Aneroid Lake, where the remains of a cabin settlement add to the alpine lake's mystique. Other day hikes from this trailhead simply require hiking up trails until lunch, and then returning. One such option involves taking the West Fork Trail to the Chief Joseph Mountain Trail, which has good views down to Wallowa Lake. The peak is 7 miles from the trailhead.

The other main entry point into the Eagle Cap is from the Hurricane Creek Trailhead. Head south from Enterprise on Hurricane Creek Rd to find the campground and trailhead.

From the upper Lostine Valley or from USFS Rd 39's Sheep Creek Summit there is easier day-hike access to the Eagle Cap's high country. The Wallowa-Whitman National Forest office (☎ 541-426-5546) in Enterprise has lots of information.

Another option is **horse** or **llama pack trips**. Eagle Cap Wilderness Pack Station, (☎ 541-432-4145, 800-681-6222), 59761 Wallowa Lake Hwy, offers a variety of horseback trips, from hourlong $17 rides to extended pack trips. For llama excursions contact Wallowa Llamas (☎ 541-742-2961) in Halfway. They run three- to five-day trips into the Eagle Cap, with prices starting at $350. Hurricane Creek Llama Treks (☎ 541-432-4455) has five- to seven-day trips, including a five-day women's trip for $625 (including B&B accommodations on the first and last nights).

Go **skiing** in the backcountry with Wing Ridge Ski Tours (☎ 541-426-4322, 800-646-9050). Their six-day tours feature nights at a wilderness cabin and a tent camp, and days of challenging skiing in incredible country (you'll need metal edges and strong thighs). Trips run $300 to $450, depending on how much you're willing to pitch in doing camp work. Wing Ridge also rents solid, well-equipped tent shelters for about $60 a night. Call them for details.

Jazz at the Lake

The Jazz at the Lake festival (☎ 541-962-3593), held the middle weekend of July, features regional acts in a picnic setting.

Places to Stay

Camping *Wallowa Lake State Park* (☎ 541-432-8855) offers multitudes of campsites complete with flush toilets and showers. Set in a grove of ponderosa pines and cottonwoods, sites can fill up on weekends in good weather. Reservations are a good idea in summer; it's open April to October.

B&Bs *Tamarack Pines Inn B&B* (☎ 541-432-2920), 60073 Wallowa Lake Hwy, is somewhat set apart from the amusement-park aspect of Wallowa Lake; rooms for two people cost $65 to $75.

Motels *Wallowa Lake Lodge* (☎ 541-432-9821), Route 1 Box 320, is a fine-looking old hotel on the shores of the lake, with a beautiful fireplace-dominated lobby but tiny rooms. Also available are lakeside cabins. Lodging ranges from $75 to $115.

Matterhorn Swiss Village (☎ 541-432-4071), 59950 Wallowa Lake Hwy, offers chalet-like cabins starting at $50. Rates increase in the summer, during which time lodgers may be expected to stay a minimum of five nights. *Eagle Cap Chalets* (☎ 541-432-4704), 59879 Wallowa Lake Hwy, offers accommodations ranging from cabins and condos to a honeymoon suite; room rates run from $48 to $102. *Flying Arrow Resort* (☎ 541-432-2951), 59782 Wallowa Lake Hwy, features cabins and a pool. Like the Matterhorn, rates are seasonal and you may be required to stay a minimum number of nights. Double-occupancy cabins start at $65.

Places to Eat

Most food options at Wallowa Lake would be more properly designated as concessions than dining, with the following exceptions. The dining room at the *Wallowa Lake Lodge* (☎ 541-432-9821), 60060 Wallowa Lake Hwy, retains the charm of another era, and the food aspires to cuisine, with steak, salmon and chicken leading the menu. Most dishes are in the $15 range. For very good German and Hungarian specialties, go to *Vali's Alpine Deli & Restaurant* (☎ 541-432-5691), 59811 Wallowa Lake Hwy. There's only one meal (in the $10 range) on the menu per day: what the chef cooks up is what you get. Call ahead to find out what's cooking, and for reservations: this is a very popular restaurant.

WALLOWA MOUNTAIN LOOP RD

From Joseph, paved USFS Rd 39, part of the Wallowa Mountain Loop Rd, climbs to Sheep Creek Summit, east of the Wallowas' main peaks. Here, mountain bikers and skiers, each in their own season, share dominion. The road then winds along the Imnaha River, and pushes over another ridge to arrive at Hwy 86, midway between Halfway and Copperfield, on the southern side of the Wallowas.

OREGON

While landscapes along the road are pleasing enough, the real benefit of USFS Rd 39 is that it links the northern and southern halves of the Wallowas, travel between which would otherwise require hours of driving.

From Ollokot Campground, USFS Rd 3960 follows the Imnaha River west up to trailheads into the Eagle Cap Wilderness Area. Follow this road to find a number of remote riverside campgrounds.

This loop also gives access to the only paved viewpoint onto Hells Canyon. At Hells Canyon Overlook, about 2 miles off USFS Rd 39 on USFS Rd 3965, a vista point looks into the canyon.

USFS Rd 39 is closed in winter due to snow and, depending on the severity of the winter, it can stay closed into early summer. Call ahead to the USFS office (☎ 541-426-5546) in Enterprise to find out if the road is open. It's 65 miles between Joseph and Halfway along this route. There are no gas stations on these routes and no services. Plan your trip accordingly.

GRANDE RONDE CANYON COUNTRY

While the eye is drawn naturally upwards to the Wallowas, around here mountains are only half the story. Rivers rushing to meet the Snake River in its mile-deep Hells Canyon are themselves obliged to carve massive canyons. The following day trip from Enterprise or Joseph explores remote and beautiful river canyons.

North of Enterprise, Hwy 3 (which becomes Hwy 129 in Washington) heads off toward Lewiston, ID, across high plateaus covered with forests and meadows. At the Joseph Canyon Overlook, there's a vista over Joseph Creek.

Barely across the Washington state line the road plunges down into the 3000-foot-deep Grande Ronde Canyon. Nothing leading up to this chasm from either side prepares the traveler for the immensity of the scene. Cross the Grande Ronde and climb up switchback after switchback to the north side of the gorge. **Fields Spring State Park & Campground**, on the northern rim of the canyon, offers picnicking

and short hiking trails to more canyon vistas from Puffer Butte.

For a loop trip, return to the Grande Ronde bridge and turn west (near the roadhouse at Boggan's Oasis) toward Troy and follow the Grande Ronde River back into Oregon. Troy lies at a curve in the river, a tiny community dominated by a small fishing lodge. The log-built *Shilo Wilderness Resort* (☎ 541-828-7741) welcomes anglers and campers with food and lodging in a captivatingly remote setting. Gravel roads from Troy give access to trails leading into the canyons of the Wenaha-Tucannon Wilderness Area.

Roads lead back to Hwy 3 via Flora, or south to the town of Wallowa via Maxville. Both routes include steep climbs on good gravel roads.

RICHLAND
Population 170
Richland is an idyllic little town surrounded by old dairy farms at the base of the Wallowas. It's also near water recreation at Hewitt Park on the Snake River's Brownlee Reservoir. Richland is 40 miles east of Baker City; it's an additional 30 miles to north Copperfield on Hwy 86, on the Snake River.

Hewitt Park (☎ 541-893-6147) is on the Powder River, which here is backed up by the Snake's Brownlee Reservoir. It is a pleasant park that offers camping, swimming and fishing. Hewitt Park is 2 miles east of Richland off Hwy 86.

The clean and new *Hitching Post Motel* (☎ 541-893-6176), on Main St, is Richland's only motel; singles/doubles are $38/40.

The *Longbranch Restaurant & Saloon* (☎ 541-893-6169) serves big meals, with delicious fried bread. For breakfast, head to the *Shorthorn Heifer Restaurant & Bar* (☎ 541-893-6122), at the corner of 2nd and Main Sts.

HALFWAY
Population 320
Halfway is as close to a tourist town as there is in the southern Wallowas. The beautiful green valley is filled with old

barns and hayfields, but, as in the northern Wallowas, the meadows suddenly turn perpendicular and rise to mountain peaks.

Follow USFS Rd 413 for 8 miles up to ghostly Cornucopia for access to recreation in the Eagle Cap Wilderness Area.

The Hells Canyon Chamber of Commerce (☎ 541-742-5772), 160 S Main St, Halfway, OR 97834, has information on the southern Wallowa region. The Pine Ranger Station (☎ 541-742-7511) is 1 mile south of Halfway at Pine. Address queries to General Delivery, Halfway, OR 97834.

Places to Stay & Eat

The *Pine Valley Lodge* (☎ 541-742-2027) is a quirky collection of restored buildings with lodge rooms and guest houses. Rates run $65 to $95. The lodge's restaurant, the Halfway Supper Club, and a good bakery are housed in an old church.

The *Halfway Motel* (☎ 541-742-5722), 170 S Main St, consists of a traditional motel and a complex of trailer houses. Rooms range from $40 to $50.

Birch Leaf Farm B&B (☎ 541-742-2990), is a rural Victorian farmhouse turned country inn; rooms begin at $55. Take USFS Rd 413 north, and at Jimtown Store take the east fork in the road. The *Clear Creek Farm B&B* (☎ 541-742-2238), 4 miles north of Halfway on E Pine Rd, offers seclusion, a pond for swimming and rooms for $60 to $65.

Hells Canyon

The Snake River has been flowing through Hells Canyon for only about 13 million years. In fact, because the Snake River has cut so much rock from the Wallowa and Seven Devils ranges, the mountains and valleys in the region are rising. Such action makes the landmass much lighter than it once was. Consequently, the land buoys upward, which forces the Snake to dig its canyon ever deeper.

On the plateaus edging Hells Canyon, wildflower displays peak in June. Up here,

Hells Canyon & the Seven Devils
Nez Perce legend has it that Coyote, the trickster figure of Native American lore, dug Hells Canyon with a stick to protect the tribe from the Seven Devils. The strategy would seem to have worked, for the Seven Devils Mountains remain firmly rooted on the Idaho side of the Snake River. ■

there's about 25 inches of rainfall a year. However, 5500 feet down in the canyon, only 10 inches fall. Prickly-pear cactus and short-seasoned grasses eke out an existence on the thin soils along the canyon floors.

Cliff-dwelling bighorn sheep and mountain goats live along the canyon walls. Elk and mule deer are common, and black bears and mountain lions also haunt side valleys. Along the river's edge are found blue herons, various ducks and geese, and – on grassy embankments – sage grouse. Floating on updrafts are hawks and bald and golden eagles. Rattlesnakes are also common.

For such a severe landscape, there's a long and rich human history in Hells Canyon. Prehistoric Indians lived along the Snake River throughout the canyon, as evinced by abundant pictographs, petroglyphs and pit-dwellings. The Nez Perce and Shoshone battled for dominance along this stretch of the Snake, with the Nez Perce defeating their rivals at Battle Creek.

Relics of the mining era, from the 1860s to the 1920s, are found throughout the canyon, and tumbledown shacks remain from the unlikely settlement attempts of turn-of-the-century homesteaders.

The Hells Canyon National Recreation Area (☎ 541-426-5546) can be contacted at PO Box 490, Enterprise, OR 97828. There's also an information center at the Hells Canyon Dam (☎ 541-785-3395).

Hiking

There are long-distance, riverside trails on both the Oregon and Idaho shores of the Snake River, but reaching them is a

OREGON

OREGON

Massacre at Hells Canyon

One of Oregon's worst massacres took place in Hells Canyon. Throughout the West, immigrant Chinese sought work and fortune in restless gold camps, frequently reworking spent mine tailings for the traces of gold they might still hold. In 1887 a group of Chinese were working a sandbar just south of the mouth of the Imnaha. A group of lawless cowboys – there were many in the Hells Canyon area at the time – who had just crossed the Snake River from Idaho, came across the Chinese encampment. They robbed the miners of their gold and, in the process, shot and killed all the Chinese in the camp. For their trouble, the killers made off with less than $5000 in gold dust.

The estimated number of Chinese killed in the robbery ranges from 10 to 34. The six men were eventually indicted and tried in Enterprise in 1887, but were acquitted by the jury. ■

challenge. The rugged cliffs along the Hells Canyon Dam are too steep for hiking trails, although a short, mile-long trail from the jet boat launch area does pick its way down the Oregon side before ending precipitously. For longer hikes, you will need to start from trailheads along the ridges, and hike down to the river. Hat Point is a good place to drop onto the Oregon Snake River Trail, on the river's western edge. On the Idaho side, there's road access to the river at Pittsburgh Landing, near White Bird, ID. From here, hikers can walk back up into the wilderness area along the Idaho Snake River Trail. It's a good idea to talk to rangers before setting out, as this is extremely remote and challenging wilderness.

Rafting & Jet Boat Tours

By far the easiest way to see Hells Canyon is on a jet boat tour. These turbine-powered, flat-bottomed boats are able to maneuver shallow water and rapids, though they are also very noisy and annoying if you aren't among the passengers.

Boat trips begin below the Hells Canyon Dam. Roads to the boat landing cross onto and follow the Idaho side of the Snake River 28 miles before crossing over the dam's spillway back into Oregon.

From the landing just below Hells Canyon Dam, Hells Canyon Adventures, Inc (☎ 541-785-3352, 800-422-3568) offers jet boat tours daily from Memorial Day weekend to the end of September. They offer several different tour options: two-hour afternoon excursions, starting at 2 pm and costing $25; the 10 am three-hour excursion (which includes lunch) for $30 a person; and an all-day, $50 tour leaving at 9 am which runs all the principal rapids of the canyon and includes lunch and a stop at the Kirkwood Ranch Museum. For all tours, children under 12 are half-price. Hells Canyon Adventures also offers other tours, including float trips and fishing charters. Reservations are required.

Another local outfitter specializes in fishing and white-water raft trips. Canyon Outfitters (☎ 541-510-742-7238), runs three- or four-day rafting and fishing trips from April to October. Included in the excursion price ($650 and up) is a night's lodging and breakfast in Halfway, and all meals for the trip. At the end of the trip, jet boats pick up floaters and anglers and return them to Hells Canyon Dam, eliminating the need for lengthy shuttle trips on dodgy roads.

Both outfitters are licensed by the USFS. If you plan to shoot the Class III to IV Snake River rapids on your own, you'll need a permit from the Hells Canyon National Recreation office in Enterprise. Hells Canyon Shuttle (☎ 800-785-3358) can help you get back to your car.

Places to Stay & Eat

Just below Oxbow Dam, where Pine Creek joins the Snake River at the beginning of Hells Canyon, is the *Copperfield Campground* (☎ 541-785-3323), which provides riverside tent and RV sites. The *Hells Can-*

yon Inn (☎ 541-785-3393), also in Copperfield, provides light meals.

Five miles downriver on the road to Hells Canyon Dam is *Hells Canyon Campground*. It's right on the river and less crowded than Copperfield. Kleinschmidt Grade, a 5-mile long, steep and narrow gravel road climbs up a precipitous grade to Cuprum, ID, from the campground. Take note that while some road maps show the grade leaving from Copperfield it actually begins at Hells Canyon Campground.

HELLS CANYON WILDERNESS AREA

This roadless wilderness flanks the river from above Hells Canyon Dam to Dug Bar, near the mouth of the Imnaha River. This is where Hells Canyon cuts a trench in the earth nearly 8000 feet deep, making it both the deepest canyon in North America and the deepest river gorge in the world.

The little campground community of Copperfield is a crossroads of activity for recreation on the Snake. Hwy 71 from Cambridge, ID, drops into the Snake River valley here, forming this small oasis of accessibility in Hells Canyon. Just about anyone who fishes, boats or hikes in Hells Canyon comes through here.

The real action is below Hells Canyon Dam, 28 miles north (downriver) from Copperfield. The canyon becomes more and more precipitous, until only towering rock walls channel the river's surging current. The dam briefly pools the Snake in a slackwater reservoir, before releasing the river to boil down the mile-deep canyon. Between here and Lewiston, ID, 70 miles away, the Snake drops 1300 feet in elevation, creating wild scenery and river rapids that attract jet boat tourists, rafters and backpackers.

Hat Point

Not surprisingly, Hells Canyon is a difficult place to visit. South of the Wallowas there is river access from below Copperfield. But there is a classic view of the river from a lookout tower near Hat Point, high above the canyon on the Oregon side.

To reach Hat Point, follow Hwy 350 to the little community of Imnaha. From here,

a steep and very narrow graveled road climbs up the Imnaha River canyon. There are no guardrails along the first 5 miles of this single-lane road, and very few turnouts. Recent roadwork has improved the quality of the roadbed, but not its pitch or its width. Don't even think about taking a trailer up.

At the top, meadows covered in wildflowers give way to steep canyon walls. On each side of the canyon, mountains soar toward 10,000 feet. Across the canyon are the Seven Devils, a cluster of rugged peaks in Idaho. Behind are the towering, glacierbit pinnacles of the Wallowas.

From the Hat Point viewpoint, a hiking trail edges off the side of the canyon. It's a steep 4 miles to another vista from the top of the river cliffs. From this viewpoint, it's another 4 miles down to the river itself.

At the clifftop viewpoint, long-distance hikers can join the High Trail, which angles along the canyon walls north to Dug Bar.

There are a few primitive campsites at Hat Point. The closest facilities are found in Joseph.

It's 23 miles south from Imnaha to Hat Point along USFS Rd 4240; allow at least two hours each way for the journey. The road is closed during winter, but it's generally open from late May till snowfall (usually sometime in October). Call the Hells Canyon National Recreation office in Enterprise (☎ 541-426-5546) if you have questions about road conditions or navigability.

Imnaha River Valley

The Imnaha River digs a parallel canyon just to the west of Hells Canyon. The Imnaha Valley offers good roads, fishing access and beautiful pastoral scenery in addition to the region's mandatory vertical cliff faces.

The Imnaha River Rd (USFS Rd 3955) follows this lovely narrow valley between the tiny hamlet of Imnaha and the junction of USFS Rd 39. The lower valley (the northern end) is very dramatic, as the river cuts more and more deeply through stairstepped lava formations. The upper valley (going south) is bucolic, with meadows and old farmhouses flanking the rushing river.

North of Imnaha gravel roads continue for 20 miles to Imnaha Bridge. Past the bridge the road is suitable only for off-road vehicles.

From Imnaha Bridge, several hiking trails begin. The Imnaha River Trail follows the churning Imnaha River to its confluence with the Snake. The Nee-Me-Poo Trail, which follows the path of Chief Joseph and the Nez Perce through three states, begins just north of the bridge, and in 3½ miles climbs to a viewpoint over the Snake.

There are public fishing access points along the length of the river. The USFS maintains two campgrounds at the southern end of the canyon. Ollokot and Blackhorse Campgrounds are right on the river, near the junction of USFS Rd 39.

John Day Country

Oregon rivers take erosion seriously. And none more so than the John Day River, a canyon-cutter almost from its inception. This river gives its name to the enormous swath of land it drains in the center of Oregon, as well as to the John Day Fossil Beds, three national monuments where erosion has exposed spectacular formations rich in the remains of prehistoric life.

This remote region is, undeservedly, one of the least-visited parts of the state. The colorful fossil beds, the dramatic canyons and the river itself make the John Day area a worthwhile trip. The town of John Day, at the eastern edge of the region, provides the most complete tourist amenities. Outside of John Day, most small towns usually have a single motel.

Orientation
The town of John Day is at the eastern edge of the river basin that bears the same name; however, many of the sights associated with the John Day River are found farther

west, between Dayville and Service Creek. The Sheep Rock Unit, the closest, is 41 miles east on US 26 and Hwy 19; the most distant, the Clarno Unit, is over 120 miles northwest. Information on the area is available in John Day.

Rafting
From Clarno Bridge to Cottonwood Bridge, a distance of 70 miles, the John Day River cuts a deep canyon through basaltic lava flows on its way to the Columbia River. No roads reach the canyon here; along the river are the remains of homesteads, Native American petroglyphs and pristine wildlife habitat.

Plan to float the John Day in spring or early summer, when the toughest rapids are class III or IV, depending on the water levels.

Several outfitters offer guided trips down the John Day River. Most float trips take four days through this roadless area. For representative prices contact the CJ Lodge (☎ 541-395-2404) in Maupin. If you plan a trip down the John Day, be sure to contact the BLM office (☎ 541-447-4115), PO Box 550, Prineville, OR 97754, for maps and

Who was John Day?
Named for an early frontiersman, John Day is so common a label in this part of the state as to be all-purpose: a river, two towns, a dam and a series of parks were all named for a man who never visited the area.

As a trapper for the Pacific Fur Company, John Day was floating down the Columbia River with a companion when the pair was ambushed, robbed and stripped by hostile Cayuse Indians at the mouth of what was then known as the Mau Hau River. The two survived the ordeal and returned to safety in Astoria. Thereafter, the river was renamed for the ill-starred John Day. ∎

further information; they can also provide you with a list of outfitters.

JOHN DAY
Population 1900

The town of John Day strings along a narrow passage of the John Day River valley, at the confluence of gold-rich Canyon Creek. For a community with a long history and a rich heritage drawing on mining, ranching and logging, John Day is an oddly colorless and hermetic place to visit. Aside from the rather interesting Kam Wah Chung Museum and a more standard county historical museum, there's little left from the glory days, and what has replaced it is grimly utilitarian.

Orientation & Information

John Day is 264 miles east of Portland on US 26 and 81 miles southwest of Baker City. It's the only town of consequence in this part of Oregon. Luckily, there are decent amenities for travelers.

The Grant County Chamber of Commerce (☎ 541-575-0547) is at 281 W Main St, John Day, OR 97845. The administrative headquarters of the John Day Fossil Beds (☎ 541-575-0721) is also here, at 431 Patterson Bridge Rd, as is the Long Creek & Bear Valley Ranger Station (☎ 541-575-3300).

Kam Wah Chung Museum

This tiny stone building (☎ 541-575-0028), built in 1866, first served as an apothecary for Ing Hay, a Chinese herbalist and doctor. During the 1880s, the structure served as community center, temple, pharmacy, general store and opium den for the Chinese population that came to John Day to rework mine tailings. Ing Hay's reputation as a healer was widespread and many white miners also availed themselves of his lore.

The museum gives a look into the day-to-day life of the Chinese in the mining West, and commemorates an otherwise ignored facet of frontier history. Have a look into the old bunkroom-cum-opium den with its beams blackened from opium smoke.

The museum is just off US 26 at the city park, and is open 9 am to noon and 1 to 5 pm, Monday to Thursday, and 1 to 5 pm on weekends. Admission is $2.

Places to Stay & Eat

The best place to camp is at *Clyde Holliday State Park* (☎ 541-575-2773), a streamside park 6 miles west of town.

Miles from anywhere, the town has a captive audience, and lodgings tend to be eagerly sought. On any given night, all rooms in John Day may be rented. Call ahead for reservations. For a relatively inexpensive motel, try the *Budget 8 Motel* (☎ 541-575-2155), 711 W Main St; singles/doubles go for $39/42. The *Sunset Inn* (☎ 541-575-1462), 390 W Main St, has an indoor pool and restaurant in the complex and its rooms are $45/48. The *Dreamers Lodge* (☎ 541-575-0526), 144 N Canyon Blvd, is a pleasant and popular motel with kitchenettes; rates are $44/48. At the *Best Western Inn* (☎ 541-575-1700), 315 W Main St, rooms go for $49/53.

Put on your cowboy boots and stay at the *Ponderosa Cattle Company Guest Ranch* (☎ 541-542-2403, 800-331-1012), 32 miles south of John Day on US 395. This Sylvies Valley spread dates back to the 1860s, though the guest-ranch lodge and eight cabins are only a few years old. Room, board and unlimited riding for three days is $700 per person; a six-day package costs $1200. In winter, rates are $80 a day. Contact the ranch at HC 30 Box 190, Seneca, OR 97873.

Steak is the specialty at the *Grubsteak Mining Co* (☎ 541-575-1970), 149 E Main, and it's the best place in town to eat. If you're heading east from John Day, stop in Prairie City for microbrews and pizza at *Ferdinand's* (☎ 541-820-9359), 128 Front St. This old storefront used to be a meat market – note the carved-stone bull's head above the door.

Getting There & Away

The People Mover bus (☎ 541-575-2370) between Prineville and Prairie City stops

OREGON

daily in John Day. The fare from Bend to John Day is $18 one way.

STRAWBERRY MOUNTAIN WILDERNESS AREA

This 107-sq-mile wilderness contains a range of 15-million-year-old volcanoes. After smothering nearby valleys in thick basalt flows, the peaks of the Strawberry Mountains were incised by glaciers during the ice ages, leaving them razor-edged. Eventually, retreating glaciers created lake basins beneath these craggy ridges.

Named for the wild strawberries that thrive on the mountain slopes, the Strawberry Range is covered with ponderosa and lodgepole pines. On the southern slopes of the wilderness, there are isolated stands of mature forest. In the wildflower meadows at Wildcat Basin, look for Indian paintbrush and wild iris. Bighorn sheep, reintroduced here after they were hunted out by early miners, are often seen along the ridges at Sheep Rock. Black bears and mountain lions have also made a comeback in the wilderness.

The Strawberry Mountains contain deceptively high country for eastern Oregon: much of the wilderness is above 6000 feet, and the highest peak – Strawberry Mountain – rises to 9038 feet.

Hiking

A popular, 2½-mile roundtrip day hike winds up a steep valley to **Strawberry Lake**, which is nestled beneath 9000-foothigh peaks. A mile past the lake is **Strawberry Falls**. To reach the trailhead, head 2 miles south from John Day to Canyon City and follow signs; it's 11 miles from Canyon City to the trailhead.

Circle around to the south side of the wilderness area on Hwy 14 and paved USFS Rds 65 and 16, past old ponderosa pines and wide meadows, to find more trails. Hike into **High Lake Basin**, 2.6 miles roundtrip, from a trailhead high up the mountainside. From USFS Rd 16, turn on USFS Rd 1640 toward Indian Springs Campground. The trailhead is 11 miles up a steep graveled road.

Places to Stay

Strawberry Mountain Wilderness Area has a number of good campgrounds. The most convenient for travelers will be *McNaughton Springs*, 8 miles south of Prairie City on the Strawberry Lake Road, or *Trout Farm*, in a lovely streamside spot on USFS Rd 14 south of Prairie City.

JOHN DAY FOSSIL BEDS NATIONAL MONUMENT

Interesting geology and spectacular scenery don't always occur together. But in the John Day fossil country, the two form an amazing team. At Picture Gorge, the John Day River rips through an immense lava flow and begins digging its trench to the Columbia River. The countryside becomes drier, with sagebrush soon replacing pine forests. Along the canyon walls, bluffs of startling color appear, eroded into bizarre spires and crenelations.

Orientation & Information

The national monument includes 22 sq miles at three different sites: the Sheep Rock, Clarno and Painted Hills Units. Each site has hiking trails and interpretive displays. To visit all the units in one day requires quite a bit of driving, as over 100 miles separate the fossil beds.

The John Day Fossil Beds National Monument Headquarters (☎ 541-575-0721) is at 431 Patterson Bridge Rd, John Day. There is also a staffed visitors' center at the Sheep Rock Unit.

Sheep Rock Unit

The Sheep Rock Unit on the John Day River consists of two different fossil beds, a river canyon and the Cant Ranch House Visitors Center (☎ 541-987-2333).

Some of the monument's important fossil findings are on display at the visitors' center, including parts of a saber-toothed tiger and a three-toed horse. Exhibits explain the complex series of geologic events that conspired to form the John Day Formation. In the center's laboratory, you can watch as paleontologists and students clean more recent finds. Part of the large

A Plant & Animal Pompeii

Within the soft rocks and crumbly soils of John Day country lies one of the greatest collections of fossils in the world. Discovered in the 1860s by clergyman and geologist Thomas Condon, these fossil beds were laid down between 40 and 25 million years ago, when this area was a coastal plain with a tropical climate. Roaming the forests were saber-toothed tigers, pint-sized horses, bear-dogs and other early mammals.

Then, the climate and geology of the region began to change. A period of extensive volcanism of an almost unbelievable scale commenced, producing clouds of ash and mudflows that buried entire ecosystems in a matter of hours, like a plant and animal Pompeii, trapping unfortunate Eocene- and Miocene-era denizens. The cycle recurred over millennia: life would return to the area and again be buried beneath the residue of distant eruptions. Finally, the soft, easily eroded ash and mud that formed these beds – thousands of feet deep in some areas – was covered with several layers of molten ash and lava, which formed a resistant coating over the old mudflows. Only the Ochoco, Blue and Wallowa Mountains bobbed above the lava.

Sealed beneath layers of rock were the old marsh and meadow lands – now known as the John Day Fossil Beds National Monument – awaiting the mightily erosive John Day River to unlock their story. Fossils of over 100 different animal species have been found in the monument. ■

ranch house, built by a Scottish family early in the 20th century, is preserved to display period furnishings and everyday items. There's a ranger on duty to answer questions. The shaded grounds of the visitors' center are a good place for a picnic beside the river. The visitors' center is open 9 am to 5 pm daily. It's 10 miles northwest of Dayville. Take Hwy 19 north from US 26.

In the immediate vicinity of the visitors' center are a number of startling-looking formations. **Sheep Rock** rises immediately behind the center. This steep-sided mesa rises up hundreds of feet to a small cap of rock.

Picture Gorge Between the Old West town of Dayville (population 145) on US 26 and Sheep Rock, the John Day River incises its way through 1500 feet of lava flow to begin its vocation as a canyon-cutter. The transition is especially startling from the east approach: the heretofore placid-seeming river passes through a meadow-like valley before turning abruptly northward, slicing through the hillside. The gorge, just wide enough for the river and the road, is named for the pictographs

drawn there by early Indians. Look for the pictographs near milestone 125, on the west side of the road; ponder the mentality of those who see fit to spray paint over these dim drawings which are hundreds of years old.

Blue Basin From this trailhead, 2 miles north of the visitors' center off Hwy 19, several hikes lead out into the John Day fossil formations. The **Island in Time Trail** is a well-maintained, mile-long path that climbs up a narrow waterway to a badlands-basin of highly eroded, uncannily green sediments. Along the trail are displays that reveal fossils protruding from the soil.

For a longer hike, the **Overlook Trail** climbs up the side of the formation to the rim of Blue Basin. The views onto the fossil beds and the layer-cake topography of the John Day Valley are well worth the struggle up the 3-mile-loop trail.

At **Cathedral Rock**, a mile north on Hwy 19, erosion has stripped away a hillside to reveal the highly colored, banded sediments of the John Day Formation beneath a thick cap of basalt. No plant life grows in this poor and quickly eroded soil,

Bhagwan Shree Rajneesh

Out here, in a barren desert canyon, occurred one of Oregon's most interesting and peculiar episodes.

The religion of Bhagwan Shree Rajneesh has most commonly been described as a mix of Eastern religion and pop psychology. Taoism, Hinduism, Trantism, Buddhism, Zen, Sufism and even Christian theologies have contributed to the Bhagwan's practices and preachings. Since the beginning of his career as a religious figure in his native India in the early 1970s, Rajneesh's following has been comprised mostly of disillusioned Westerners. Middle-aged divorced women and doctors, lawyers and movie producers were especially drawn to the guru's worldwide ashrams. Followers referred to themselves by the Hindu title *sanyassin*. Upon initiation, these devotees renounced the rest of the world for a new Sanskrit name and a string of wooden beads with a picture of the Bhagwan on it called a *mela*. They dressed only in clothes the color of the sunset (red, orange and purple).

Rajneeshis attracted national media attention in the early 1980s when Bhagwan Shree Rajneesh transformed a ranch near Antelope into a multimillion dollar commune called Rajneeshpuram. Fleeing tax evasion, the Indian guru purchased the 1000-sq-mile Big Muddy Ranch (one of Oregon's largest) for $6 million, and beat it out of Pune, India, with the intention of building an isolationist 'oasis in the desert' – a self-sufficient city with its own fertile valley created by a private lake and dam. Since these plans violated state land-use laws and threatened the water rights of long-time residents, Rajneesh's first move was to take over nearby Antelope, a town with property already zoned for city use. Residents of Antelope watched in disbelief as the Bhagwan flooded the town with followers, and renamed the Antelope Cafe (the town's only general store-cum-cafe) 'Zorba the Buddha.' The predominantly Rajneeshi population then voted the local city council out of office and changed the town's name to Rajneesh, leaving the new council to legalize nudity in the public park, approve an increase in the water rates and make plans to raise local taxes. Property left behind by fleeing locals was promptly snatched up by the Rajneeshis.

The commune at Rajneeshpuram itself became unpopular as stories of the Bhagwan's posh lifestyle and the rampant hedonism of his followers circulated in journalistic accounts. The complex included $35 million of modular homes and the state's largest greenhouse and reservoir. Complete transportation facilities were provided to the commune via Buddhafield Transport Co, which even catered to air travelers by operating an airport and Air Rajneesh airline. The 'work is worship' 12-hour-workday philosophy was misinterpreted as justification for running a slave labor camp. Endless murmurs of drug use, sexual orgies and a blossoming arsenal of private weapons and arms created a leery public, as did reports of a scheme to increase Rajneesh votership and political

giving the outcropping the look of a fanciful, greatly deteriorated building.

Foree Picnic Area At this day-use area, a couple of miles farther north on Hwy 19, trails lead off into more fossil-rich formations. The Foree Loop Trail winds half a mile around a green mudstone badlands. The Flood of Fire Trail winds up to a ridge-top viewpoint over the John Day River.

Places to Stay & Eat Campers should head north from the Sheep Rock Unit to Kimberly, and turn east onto Hwy 402, where there are two shady, riverside BLM campgrounds, *Lone Pine* and *Big Bend*, right on the North Fork John Day River.

In Dayville, the *Fish House Inn* (☎ 541-987-2124), 110 E Franklin St, has B&B rooms, including two in a freestanding cottage, and a small RV or tent area.

power by busing in homeless people from San Francisco to register to vote as residents of Rajneeshpuram. At the height of it all, Rajneesh's commander-in-chief, Ma Anad Sheela, announced to the public that she would 'paint the bulldozers with blood,' before she would witness the collapse of the Bhagwan's empire. (The Bhagwan was apparently under a vow of silence shortly before his appearance in the USA, so it was really Ma Anad Sheela who was running the show. Serving as his commanding officer, it was Sheela who in fact arranged for the purchase of the ranch, oversaw its operation and served as the Bhagwan's spokesperson.)

Suspicious marriages between US citizens and foreigners turned heads at the INS, while the IRS raised its eyebrows at the fleet of 90 Rolls Royces given as 'gifts' to the Bhagwan. Mudslinging between leaders of the commune forced the Bhagwan to give the FBI a formal invitation to investigate criminal activity at Rajneeshpuram, eventually resulting in its closure.

When in September of 1985 Ma Anad Sheela suddenly left the commune, Rajneesh broke his vow of silence to declare her a fascist dictator. He poured forth a long chain of crimes she had committed while in her leadership of the commune: the murder attempt she had plotted on the life of his personal physician; her involvement in a mass salmonella poisoning of The Dalles residents (individual Rajneeshis went from salad bar to salad bar in all of the city's restaurants, tainting them with salmonella carried in glass vials – causing more than 750 people to get sick); her plot to murder Oregon's attorney general, Dave Frohnmeyer, and another attorney; and her mass spying and eavesdropping through a sophisticated wiretapping and bugging system.

It wasn't long before Sheela was apprehended in West Germany and indicted for eavesdropping and attempted murder. The Bhagwan, guilty of immigration violations, was apprehended in flight at an airport in North Carolina in October 1985. Having pleaded guilty to the charges, he was deported to India in November, and members at the commune dispersed soon thereafter. The Bhagwan returned to Pune, where, after taking the new name of Osho, he died in 1990. The ashram at Pune survived his death and currently functions as the worldwide headquarters for Osho's disenfranchised flock. ∎

Rooms range from $40 to $65. Nearby is the *Dayville Diggins Cafe* (☎ 541-987-2132).

Some of the most beautiful sunsets you'll ever see can be viewed from Spray, 30 miles northwest of the Fossil Beds visitors' center on Hwy 19. That's reason enough to stay at *Spray Asher Motel* (☎ 541-468-3569), where singles/doubles go for $30/32. Spray's local eatery is the *Rim Rock Cafe* (☎ 541-468-2861).

Painted Hills Unit

This formation near the town of Mitchell (population 160), consists of low-slung, colorfully banded hills. Red, yellow and ochre-hued ash from a series of volcanic eruptions drifted into beds hundreds of feet deep about 30 million years ago. Because there is no cap rock to protect them from erosion, the Painted Hills have slumped into soft mounds, rather like evil-colored, melting ice cream.

The Painted Hills are easily dismissed as a cliché: as one of central Oregon's most visited natural sites, people troop in, line up at the viewpoints and take requisite photos. Take one of the following hiking trails to get away from the crowds and the overly familiar, postcard vistas.

The easy **Fossil Leaf Trail** winds over the top of one of the banded hills, with interpretive signs pointing out plant life and geologic history. The **Caroll Rim Trail** winds to the top of a high bluff for great views over the Painted Hills. For a longer hike out into a badlands plant and wildlife preserve, take the 3-mile **High Desert Trail** loop.

At the unit headquarters (☎ 541-462-3961), there are picnic tables above a sheep-filled meadow. The Painted Hills are 3 miles west of Mitchell on US 26, then 6 miles north on a good gravel road.

Places to Stay & Eat The closest campgrounds are in the Ochoco National Forest. *Ochoco Pass Campground* is 15 miles west of Mitchell on US 26. Mitchell is a one-street town squeezed into a steep ravine. The *Sky Hook Motel* (☎ 541-462-3569), above the town, has rooms starting at $35.

A couple of local cafes include the *Blueberry Muffin Cafe* (☎ 541-462-3434) and the *Sidewalk Cafe* (☎ 541-462-3459).

Clarno Unit

The Clarno Unit is the most remote of the fossil beds and requires some patient driving along winding, but paved, roads. The formation is at the base of the John Day River's canyon, which is about as rugged and wild-looking country as you'll see in Oregon. From the divide on Hwy 218

between Clarno and Antelope, the view over the canyon opening up below is guaranteed to elicit a gasp of astonishment.

The oldest of the three fossil bed monuments, the 40-million-year-old Clarno Unit exposes mud flows that washed over an Eocene-era forest. The Clarno Formation eroded into distinctive, sheer-white cliffs topped with spires and turrets of stone. A series of short interpretive trails pass through boulder-sized fossils containing logs, seeds and other remains of an ancient forest.

Places to Stay & Eat The closest facilities to Clarno are in Fossil (population 465), a charming little town with plank sidewalks and old stone storefronts, 18 miles east on Hwy 218.

Five miles east of Fossil on Hwy 19 is *Bear Hollow County Park*, a pleasant, shady campground along a stream. Five miles farther south, Hwy 218 climbs over a pass and begins dropping into the John Day River canyon. Here, campers and picnickers should stop at *Shelton Wayside*, a state park with campsites and hiking trails.

The *Fossil Motel* (☎ 541-763-4075), 105 First St, has singles/doubles for $30/32 and RV pads. When in Fossil, have a bite to eat at the *Shamrock* (☎ 541-763-4896), where steak, chicken and a salad bar are the order of the day.

Up the hill from Antelope, on US 97, is the working ghost town of Shaniko. The *Shaniko Hotel* (☎ 541-489-3441) was an imposing landmark when it was built in 1909. It's now noteworthy as a comfortable, completely refurbished B&B. Rates range from $66 to $96; there's a restaurant on the main floor of the hotel.

Southeastern Oregon

This vast, underpopulated region of desert, mountain, canyon and marsh contains some of Oregon's most unusual and unvisited scenery. Towering fault-block peaks rise above powder-white dry lakebeds; lava flats cleave to reveal a tiny thread of river, burrowed hundreds of feet below the prairie surface; clouds of migratory birds bank to land in a wetland refuge.

Historically, southeastern Oregon was the home to huge open-range cattle and sheep outfits; today, almost two-thirds of this region is still managed by the BLM as rangeland. Some of the names that appear on maps are not towns, but ranch headquarters; boots and hats are part of the dress code and pickup trucks are the conveyance of choice.

Given the arid climate, southeastern Oregon is also home to a surprisingly varied and plentiful wildlife population. Malheur National Wildlife Refuge is one of the nation's major nesting and migratory stopovers along the Pacific Flyway. At the Hart Mountain National Antelope Refuge, watch for glimpses of speeding pronghorns, listen for coyotes and keep a sharp eye peeled for bighorn sheep along high, rocky escarpments.

Distances are great out here, and you can't count on paved roads, luxurious accommodations or many towns with more than a gas station. Plan your trip to end up near a town if you need a place to stay; Burns and Ontario have the most lodging. The traveler who's willing to turn off the main roads will find southeastern Oregon one of the state's most spectacular and uncrowded destinations.

Geography
This corner of Oregon represents the continent's northernmost extension of the Great Basin desert. Basin and range formations developed in the last 10 million years when a series of roughly parallel faults shattered bedrock beneath thick pre-existing lava deposits. One side of the fault was hoisted upwards, while the side facing it slumped downwards. Some of the rising fault blocks rose to the height of mountains. Meanwhile, lakes formed in the basins below the rising escarpments. During ice ages, the lakes were very large, isolating the fault blocks as long, ridge-like islands. Because the climate has turned much drier in recent centuries, few of the remaining lakes have external drainage, and are consequently highly alkaline. Other old lakes are now playas, or dry lakebeds.

Unlike the basin and range area, where scant rainfall finds no outlet, the neighboring and equally arid Owyhee region is deeply incised with canyons. The Owyhee River collects its deep-dug tributaries at Three Forks, and flows northward, flanked by lava cliffs 1000 feet high.

Northern Lake County is a continuation of the high volcanic plains of central Oregon, which were formed by floods of molten basalt. The region owes its most remarkable volcanic landmarks to enormous explosions caused when hot lava shot up through shallow ice-age lake water and mud flats. The resulting explosions caused such uncanny phenomena as Fort Rock (see Fort Rock under North Lake County, later in this chapter).

Getting There & Away
Public transport only shoots by on the periphery of this fairly remote country. Amtrak and Greyhound provide service to Ontario, along the Idaho border. There are two buses a day between Klamath Falls and Lakeview and one bus a day between Bend, Burns and Ontario. You'll need an automobile to get to almost all sites of interest in southeastern Oregon.

OREGON

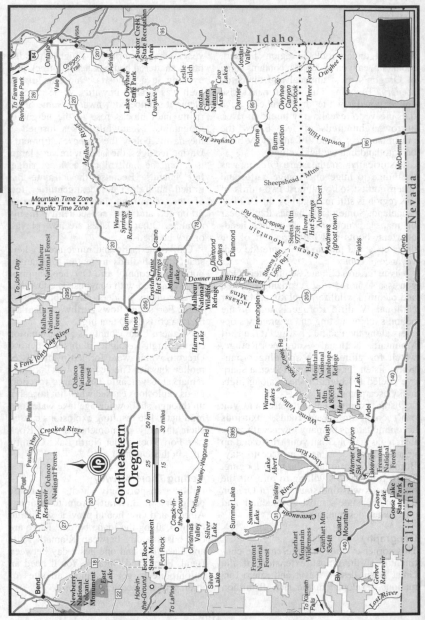

BURNS & AROUND

Named by a wistful early settler for the Scottish poet Robert Burns, this town (population 2913) was established in 1883 as the watering hole and social center for incoming settlers and roving cowhands. By the late 1880s it served as the capital of a vast cattle empire. With the arrival of the railroad in 1924, the timber resources of the Blue Mountains north of Burns attracted developers. Lots of historical memorabilia and some good early photographs are at the Harney County Historical Museum (☎ 541-573-5618), at 18 West D St, next to the chamber of commerce.

Today, this isolated town is the county seat and center of trade for the enormous agricultural district of Harney County. Burns, and immediate neighbor Hines, are useful jumping-off points for expeditions into more remote environs.

Orientation & Information

US 20 links Burns to Bend, and US 395 heads north to John Day.

The Harney County Chamber of Commerce (☎ 541-573-2636) is at 18 West D St, Burns, OR 97720. You can stop by and pick up the detailed Harney County recreation map here. The Burns District BLM office (☎ 541-573-4400) is at 12533 US 20W, Hines. You'll find information on Malheur or Ochoco National Forest (☎ 541-573-4300) in the same building.

The post office (☎ 800-275-8777) is located at 100 S Broadway.

Crystal Crane Hot Springs

This out-of-the-way hot-springs spa (☎ 541-493-2312), is 25 miles southeast of Burns on Hwy 78. It might be just what you need if you've been bumping around the back roads of southeastern Oregon. The springs flow into a large pond, and are also piped into cattle-trough hot tubs in small private bathhouses.

It costs $4 to use either the pond or a hot tub (go for the pond), and another $2 for a shower. There are a few tiny guest cabins ($25), and facilities for campers are also available.

Special Events

The High Desert Fiddlers Jamboree (☎ 541-573-1323), in late June, brings together regional talent for a two-day jam session. The Harney County Fair, held the weekend after Labor Day, also includes a rodeo. The fairgrounds are on Egan St, south of Burns.

Places to Stay

The closest public campground to Burns is *Idlewild Campground*, 17 miles north along US 395, in the Malheur National Forest. RVers should stop at *Village RV & Mobile Park* (☎ 541-573-7640), a quarter mile north of Burns on US 20, or *The*

The Bannock Indian War

The Oregon Trail crossed the Snake River near present-day Nyssa. As pioneers began to settle the valleys of this corner of Oregon, and after the discovery of gold in the Owyhee Mountains of Idaho, the whites came into conflict with the Native Americans.

Cattle drives began arriving from Texas in the late 1860s, but for the land to be used for cattle, it had to be cleared of Native Americans. Heavy-handed policies, corruption by US Government Indian agents and incarceration on inadequate reservations led to an uprising of the Paiute, Bannock and Snake tribes in 1878, known as the Bannock Indian War. Members of these tribes left their reservations, effectively declaring war against many of the settlers who had divided up their traditional hunting grounds and homelands into ranches and mining claims. The Indians attempted to revitalize old tribal alliances and to mobilize braves across the West (they hoped to lure Sitting Bull, the victor of Little Bighorn, down from Canada to join them) in order to throw out settlers. The Native American groups were pursued by the army, and did battle at Camp Curry west of Burns, and at Willow Creek, but factional and tribal infighting ultimately undid their efforts to force the whites from their old homelands. ∎

Sands (☎ 541-573-7010), 2 miles west of Burns on US 20.

The *Bontemps Motel* (☎ 541-573-2037, 800-229-1394) is a nicely renovated older motel at 74 W Monroe St; rooms start at $28. *The Silver Spur Motel* (☎ 541-573-2077), 789 N Broadway Ave, is comfortable and close to downtown; single/double rooms are $39/44. The *Orbit Motel* (☎ 541-573-2034), a half mile north of Burns, has a heated pool and rooms for $33/36. The *Royal Inn* (☎ 541-573-1700), 999 Oregon Ave, offers a sauna, hot tub and pool for $44/50. *Best Western Ponderosa Motel* (☎ 541-573-2047), 577 W Monroe St, features a heated pool and cable TV for $52/63.

Places to Eat

The *Pine Room Cafe* (☎ 541-573-6631), 543 W Monroe St, offers some of the region's best food, with homemade baked goods and hand-cut steaks. A specialty of the house is chicken livers in brandy sauce; fresh salmon goes for $15. It's open evenings only. Locals like *Ye Olde Castle* (☎ 541-573-6601), 186 W Monroe St, for a casual breakfast, lunch or dinner among antiques. The *Powerhouse* (☎ 541-573-9060), 305 E Monroe St, in an old power station, offers steak dinners for less than $15.

MALHEUR NATIONAL WILDLIFE REFUGE & AROUND

South of Burns, covering 289 sq miles of lake, wetland and prairie, the Malheur National Wildlife Refuge is an important breeding and resting area for birds traveling along the Pacific Flyway. It is also home to high-desert mammals such as pronghorn, mule deer and coyote, and to upland game birds such as sage grouse and quail.

In 1908 President Theodore Roosevelt created the refuge in response to the annihilation of certain species of birds used to adorn hats. Pete French's P Ranch (see Home on the Range sidebar), comprising much of the lower drainage of the Blitzen River, was added to the refuge in 1936.

While the refuge's two big, shallow

lakes are clearly a draw to waterfowl, the best wildlife viewing is found south along the Blitzen River, where wide, grassy marshes and ponds provide shelter to an abundance of animal life.

Over 200 species of birds have been sighted at the wildlife refuge. Waterfowl migration peaks in March, shore birds arrive in April and songbirds wing in during May. During summer, waterfowl broods skim across the ponds and lakes. By fall, the refuge is a staging ground for southward bird migrations.

Between the refuge headquarters and Frenchglen are 35 miles of intersecting gravel roads and paths, all of which offer great wildlife-viewing opportunities. The **George M Benson Memorial Museum**, in the refuge headquarters, contains 200 mounted specimens of animals found in the area.

Orientation & Information

At the Malheur National Wildlife Refuge headquarters, 32 miles south of Burns along Hwy 205, you'll find interpretive exhibits and information about exploring the area. Also available is a map guide to the refuge that shows the road system, and highlights 'hot spots' where wildlife viewing is most rewarding.

For more information, contact the Malheur National Wildlife Refuge (☎ 541-493-2612).

Diamond Craters

Adjacent to the wildlife refuge, 55 miles south of Burns along Hwy 205, is Diamond Craters. A series of volcanic craters, cinder cones and other lava formations, Diamond Craters were formed about 2500 years ago. Pick up an interpretive brochure from the BLM office in Burns to learn more about volcanics, and to find a map of the area's rather confusing road system.

Round Barn

Twenty miles north of the community of Diamond off Happy Valley Rd, is Pete French's Round Barn, the 100-foot-wide structure used to buck out broncos in the glory days of the open range. It's on what was once French's land, though quite a distance from his ranch house. Built in the 1880s, the barn has been donated to the Oregon Historical Society and can be visited informally. Look for birds in the rafters; you might even see a great horned owl perched up high inside.

Places to Stay & Eat
Hostels *Malheur Field Station* (☎ 541-493-2629), near the refuge headquarters, offers accommodations in dormitories or trailers. In addition to reasonably priced meals in the dining hall, cooking facilities are available in some housing units. The accommodations are heated, and laundry facilities are provided. During peak seasons, classes and lectures are offered. Bring your own bedding and a towel. Lodging starts at $18 a night for a dorm room; trailers are $27/36 single/double.

Home on the Range
Harney Basin and the Blitzen River valley in particular were two of the first and greatest venues in the days of eastern Oregon's cattle barons. Certainly the most notorious of these was Pete French, who in the 1880s owned the 156-sq-mile P Ranch that stretched from Harney Lake to Frenchglen. At once enterprising and unscrupulous, French resisted the rising tide of settlers who came to homestead this part of the state. His patrician sense of land ownership extended beyond his own land title, and he evicted settlers who dared to claim land in areas where he considered he had grazing privileges. In 1897 French was shot by Ed Oliver, a settler with whom French feuded over land ownership. His death, and the acquittal of Oliver, effectively ended the rootin'-tootin' days of the open range in Oregon. ∎

This is a popular place to stay, and can fill up with school groups; call ahead for a reservation.

Hotels Although Burns has the most rooms to offer travelers, those more interested in Western heritage will want to stay at small, historic hotels outside of Burns. In the tiny community of Diamond, just about the only surviving business is the *Hotel Diamond* (☎ 541-493-1898). This refurbished vintage hotel offers rooms starting at $50 for a double. The adjoining store makes deli sandwiches. Take the Diamond Grain Camp Rd east from Hwy 205.

Also in Diamond, the *McCoy Creek Inn* (☎ 541-493-2131) offers lodging in a self-contained guesthouse, or in the family ranch house, starting at $75 a night. The real pleasure here, especially after watching birds all day or bumping up the back of the Steens Mountain, is the food, with breakfast, lunch and dinner available by reservation.

Farther south, the *Frenchglen Hotel* (☎ 541-493-2825), Hwy 205 in Frenchglen, is a charming old hotel and state monument, pretty much unaltered in appearance since it was built in the 1910s. Make sure to call ahead, because the hotel is popular with people looking for real Western ambiance and hospitality. Dinners are family style, and are served promptly and abundantly at 6:30 pm; reservations are required. There are eight small, plain guest rooms, starting at $48. The hotel is open March 15 to November 15.

The *Buckaroo Room*, next to the Frenchglen Mercantile on Hwy 205, has microbrews and good dinners. They also have a couple of B&B rooms ($60) in the house next door.

STEENS MOUNTAIN
The highest peak in southeastern Oregon, Steens Mountain (9773 feet) is part of a massive, 30-mile-long fault-block range, formed about 15 million years ago.

On the western slope of the range, ice-age glaciers bulldozed massive U-shaped valleys into the flanks of the mountain; to the east, 'the Steens,' as the range is usually referred to, drop off dizzyingly to the Alvord Desert, 5000 feet below. While surrounded by desert, the Steens tower high enough above alkali basins to maintain delicate alpine meadows and lakes.

Although homesteaders attempted to settle the more hospitable valleys of the Steens, this landscape had traditionally been home to enormous flocks of sheep and Basque sheepherders. However, changes in public-land grazing laws in the 1930s ended sheep production on the Steens. The area is now managed by the BLM for recreational uses and wildlife habitat, as well as limited livestock grazing.

Steens Mountain Loop Rd

Beginning in Frenchglen, this gravel road negotiates the 4500-foot climb up the back side of the Steens onto the mountain's crest, and back down along the side of a glacier-ripped gorge, providing access to the BLM's 304-sq-mile **Steens Mountain Recreation Area**. The first 4 miles of the road pass through the Malheur National Wildlife Refuge, and by the old P Ranch buildings, once owned by cattle baron Pete French.

Climbing up the west face of the Steens, the traveler passes through a quick succession of eco-zones. Beginning in stark sagebrush desert, the mountain rises hastily through a band of junipers, into aspen forests, and finally into fragile, rocky tundra. Wild mustangs range along the southern reaches, elk, mule deer and pronghorn graze along the western flanks and bighorn sheep cling to the eastern precipices. The rocky faces are also home to many raptors, including golden eagles. **Wildhorse Lake** contains the rare Lahontan trout, found only in freshwater lakes in the Great Basin. The Steens' high alpine meadows produce a riot of wildflower color in mid-summer, including many rare and sensitive varieties.

Kiger Gorge, running north from the main body of the Steens, drops 1200 feet from the rim; look at the top of the can-

yon's eastern facade and see a notch carved in the rock wall by a smaller glacier.

The road climbs up onto the crest of the range, and continues along a narrow spit of land between the eastern flank of the range and a second glacier-carved valley, the **Little Blitzen**. Side roads branch off to various overlooks: The most tempting is the road to Wildhorse Lake and to the **summit of Steens Mountain**. Leading to the range's highest point is a steep, narrow road. Park and walk if you have doubts; it's about a mile roundtrip.

The road then drops sharply down the side of **Big Indian Gorge**. After crossing the Blitzen River, the road crosses sage and juniper savannas before reaching Hwy 205, 10 miles south of Frenchglen.

The 66-mile **Steens Mountain Byway**, which is another name for Steens Mountain Loop Rd, is also promoted as a mountain-bike trail. Remember that much of this trail is above 8000 feet; if you're not used to the altitude, even a gentle sashay around the parking lot will take your breath away. In the Steens, it's not always clear whether it's the views, vertigo or the altitude that leaves you breathless.

The road is open as weather allows, between June and November.

Places to Stay

Only 4 miles from Frenchglen along the Steens Mountain Loop Rd is *Page Springs Campground*, a pretty site along the Blitzen River. Practically next door, the *Steens Mountain Resort* (☎ 541-493-2415) has RV and tent sites, and showers. Farther up the mountain are two more isolated campsites: *Fish Lake*, 18 miles from Frenchglen, popular with trout anglers; and *Jackman Park*, 21 miles from Frenchglen. The more remote, primitive campsites are free; sites at Page Springs run $4, and $8 at Steens Mountain Resort, which is the only place that takes reservations.

ALVORD DESERT

Once a single, huge 400-foot-deep lake, the Alvord Basin is now a series of playas. Alternating with irrigated alfalfa fields, sagebrush prairies and old ranches, are startlingly white alkali beds, the residue of centuries of lake evaporation. Above everything looms Steens Mountain.

The 75-mile gravel road between the community of Fields and Hwy 78 is well maintained and open all year.

Alvord Hot Springs

Directly below the summit of the Steens, a few miles north of the near-ghost town of Andrews and about a hundred yards off the Fields-Denio Rd, is Alvord Hot Springs (look for the small metal shelter – it's hard to miss). Some travelers have reported unhappy altercations with locals about use of the hot springs; most folks use the facility with no problem. At the minimum, be respectful of other users and the site.

Places to Stay & Eat

In the isolated community of Fields, the *Fields General Store, Motel & Cafe* (☎ 541 495-2275) offers hotel rooms, gas, groceries, a post office and a cafe. Farther south, Denio straddles the Oregon-Nevada border. Once an Oregon town, the post office crossed the street into Nevada in 1950. Officially now located in Nevada, Denio's *Highway 140 Junction Motel & Restaurant* (☎ 702-941-0371) offers the usual border-town casino scene. Rooms range from $40 to $45.

Burns Junction, nearly 100 miles by dirt road from Fields, is a welcome sight to anyone needing gasoline, or a basic bite to eat. Even though there is a motel attached to the gas station, only car repairs or bad planning can justify spending a night.

ONTARIO
Population 11,000

Oregon's most easterly population center, Ontario and its surrounding communities are often considered to be an extension of Idaho's fertile Snake River valley. Ontario even shares the same time zone, mountain standard time (MST), with neighboring Idaho. Agriculture remains the backbone of the local economy. The Malheur, Payette and Owyhee Rivers join the Snake's wide valley here, with irrigated farms producing

varied crops; the region is the nation's largest producer of peppermint.

Orientation & Information

I-84, and US 20, 26 and 95 intersect near Ontario, putting the city at the hub of eastern Oregon's principal thoroughfares. The Snake River forms Ontario's eastern boundary and the Oregon-Idaho state line. Downtown streets are divided by Oregon St and by Idaho Ave into NE, NW, SE and SW quadrants. Avenues run east-west, while streets run north-south.

The Ontario Visitors & Convention Bureau (☎ 541-889-8012) is at 88 SW 3rd Ave, Ontario, OR 97914. The central post office (☎ 800-275-8777) is at 88 SW 2nd Ave. The *Ontario Argus Observer* is the local newspaper. Oregon Public Broadcasting is heard on 104.5 FM. Holy Rosary Hospital (☎ 541-889-5331) is at 351 SW 9th Ave.

Four Rivers Cultural Center

A far cry from the typical small-town museum, the Four Rivers Cultural Center (☎ 541-889-8191, 888-211-1222) celebrates the region's diversity, focusing on Paiute Indians, Basque sheepherders, and Japanese American and Mexican American (who came here as agricultural workers, largely in the past twenty to thirty years) farm workers. There are plans for a Japanese garden next to the cultural center,

---

Japanese Americans

During WWII, interned Japanese Americans from western Oregon were moved to the Ontario area, where they were forced to work in the fields. After the end of the war, several Japanese families remained and eventually became landowning farmers. Today, eastern Oregon's only Buddhist temple is in Ontario, and the Japanese American citizens celebrate their ancestry during the midsummer Obon Festival. ■

which is at 676 SW 5th Ave. The center is open 9 am to 5 pm daily (remember, Ontario is on Mountain Time). Admission is $4.

Special Events
Local cowboys and cowgirls come in off the range for Vale's Fourth of July Rodeo. It is one of eastern Oregon's largest and most authentic celebrations of the Old West. The rodeo grounds are south of town on Longfellow St.

Ontario's Obon Festival, a celebration of the area's Japanese American residents, takes place in mid-July. Japanese food, dancing and tours of the Buddhist temple, 286 SE 4th St, are among the activities.

Places to Stay
While there are no campsites right in Ontario, there is a large campground 25 miles north of Ontario on I-84 at historic *Farewell Bend State Park*. In Nyssa, 13 miles from Ontario, campers can find room at the *Kiwanis Park* near the school (Hwy 201 at Good Ave). In Ontario, RV campers can stay at *Curtis' Neat Retreat* (☎ 208-452-4324), on the Idaho side of the line. In Vale, 17 miles from Ontario, the *Prospector Travel Trailer Park* (☎ 541-473-3879) has sites for RVs and tent campers; it's a quarter-mile north of the junction of US 20 and 26.

Most of Ontario's lodgings are clustered around I-84 exits. The following lodgings are near exit 376. *The Holiday Motel* (☎ 541-889-9188), 615 E Idaho Ave, offers a swimming pool and nonsmoking single/double rooms at $35/39. At the *Super 8* (☎ 541-889-8282), 266 Goodfellow St, rooms start at $48. The *Colonial Inn Best Western* (☎ 541-889-2600, 800-828-0364), 251 Goodfellow St, has an indoor pool and rooms from $53/59. If you don't want to stay right on the main drag, try downtown's *Stockman's Motel* (☎ 541-889-4446), 81 SW 1st Ave; rates are $32/35.

Places to Eat
Start the day at *Moxie Java* (☎ 541-889-3574), 343 S Oregon St, for coffee and pastries. Another good coffee spot, with a big outdoor deck, is *Coyote Coffee* (☎ 541-889-4695), on busy SW 4th Ave at SW 1st St. For a traditional breakfast, try the *Fourth Avenue Diner* (☎ 541-889-4052), 1281 SW 4th Ave, or wait until lunch to try their great Mexican food.

Downtown offers a number of restaurants for a light lunch or supper. *Belly Buster Sandwich Shop* (☎ 541-889-9550), 31 SW 1st Ave, is where locals go to fill up. Some of the city's best food takes you south of the border, as befits a city with a large Mexican population. *Fiesta Guadalajara* (☎ 541-889-8064), 336 S Oregon St, is downtown's liveliest Mexican restaurant. Between the interstate and downtown is *Casa Jaramillo* (☎ 541-889-9258), 157 SE 2nd Ave, an Ontario institution for 25 years. A dinner of carne asada (roasted meat in a kind of green chili stew) costs about $10.

Cheyenne's Social Club Steakhouse (☎ 541-889-3777), 111 SW 1st Ave, serves the requisite steak and seafood dinners.

Getting There & Away
Greyhound Bus (☎ 541-889-5112), 510 NW Oregon St, offers two coaches east and west daily through Ontario, linking Portland, Boise, ID, and Salt Lake City, UT.

If you want to rent a car, inquire at Action Chrysler-Nissan (☎ 541-889-8989), 180 East Lane.

AROUND ONTARIO
Old Oregon Trail
Remnants of the Oregon Trail still cross this remote southeastern corner of Oregon. Museums, historic markers and wagon-rut memorials stud the area. Between Nyssa and Adrian along Hwy 201, a roadside monument commemorates the trail's **Snake River Crossing** into Oregon. Directly across the Snake from this point was Fort Boise, a Hudson's Bay Company fur-trading fort that doubled as a landmark and trade center for often desperate pioneers. The fort was swept away by floods years ago and the site is now part of a wildlife refuge.

Follow the Oregon Trail from Nyssa to Vale to find several other interpretive sites. Take Enterprise Ave just west of Nyssa and turn right on Lyttle Blvd. From here, the paved road closely follows the Oregon Trail until Vale. At Keeney Pass between the Owyhee and Malheur river drainages, there's an information kiosk and access to hikes along the trail. In many places, 150-year-old wagon ruts are still visible.

At **Malheur Crossing**, directly east of Vale, the Oregon Trail fords the Malheur River. On cool days, steam rises off the hot springs between the two highway bridges, which served as a laundry and bathing area for Oregon Trail travelers.

North of US 20, east of Vale rises **Malheur Butte**. This lone, mesa-like landmark is the remains of a volcanic plug; from its summit, the Paiutes watched the progress of the Oregon Trail pioneers.

Farewell Bend

Here, at Farewell Bend, travelers along the old Oregon Trail left the valley of the Snake River, which they had more or less followed since central Idaho, and climbed up into the desert uplands of eastern Oregon.

Before undertaking the strenuous journey through desert landscapes to the imposing Blue Mountains, Oregon Trail travelers usually rested at Farewell Bend, grazing livestock, gathering wood and otherwise preparing themselves for the arduous trip ahead. Today **Farewell Bend State Park**, which is 25 miles north of Ontario on I 84, commemorates this placid pioneer wayside with a picnic and play area, boat launch and large campground.

For a side trip, leave the freeway at the state park and follow a good graveled road north 60 miles to Richland, south of the Wallowa Mountains. The road never leaves the side of the Snake as it trenches deeper and deeper into the volcanic plateau. This is rugged land, and an enchanting detour into the Snake River canyon country for travelers who don't plan to spend time in Hells Canyon.

Leslie Gulch-Succor Creek National Back Country Byway

While easy access to the Owyhee River is limited, travelers can explore a sample of this wildly eroded country by driving (or mountain biking) the Leslie Gulch-Succor Creek National Back Country Byway, which runs between Adrian and a junction with US 95, 18 miles north of Jordan Valley. This 52-mile off-the-beaten-path gravel route passes landscapes of surpassing grandeur, as well as prime wildlife-viewing areas.

Follow the road south from near Adrian, through miles of sagebrush, thin grass and rolling hills until it drops steeply down onto Succor Creek. Here, 100-foot-high vertical walls of volcanic tuff divide to allow the stream and road to wind through. **Succor Creek State Recreation Area** sits at a narrow end of the canyon, with facilities for campers and picnickers (no water), take time to hunt for thundereggs, the agate and crystal-filled geode that is Oregon's state rock.

The eroded landscape is even more spectacular at **Leslie Gulch**, a 16-mile side road from the byway that drops over into the Owyhee River Canyon. This steep, though usually passable, gravel road careens down a narrow creek channel incised through vividly colored volcanic rock and eroded into amazing pinnacle and turreted formations. The narrow ribbon of Owyhee Reservoir awaits at the base of the narrow canyon, as well as rough campsites (bring water). Bighorn sheep haunt these rock cliffs; watch for them as they come down to drink at the creekside.

Owyhee Dam & Reservoir

At 417 feet in height, Owyhee Dam was once the highest dam in the world. Built in a spectacular desert canyon, this dam backs up the Owyhee River into Lake Owyhee, stretching 50 miles to the south. At Lake Owyhee State Park, on the east lakeside, there's a campground and picnic area; fishing and water sports are both popular activities for local residents.

OREGON

Hawaiian Namesakes

Although homeland to the Paiute and Snake Indians, this corner of Oregon is instead named for another, altogether unlikely, native people.

In 1819, the Hudson's Bay Company brought in two Hawaiian islanders as beaver trappers. They were killed by local Indians along the river, which now bears a name derived from the islands of their birth. *Owyhee* is one early phonetic spelling of 'Hawaii.' ∎

It's worth the drive to the reservoir and state park just to glimpse the Owyhee's dramatic canyon. Even here, where the gorge is less precipitous than at more remote sites upstream, sharp escarpments of colorful volcanic rock drop off hundreds of feet to the reservoir below.

JORDAN VALLEY
Population 364

The closest thing to a town in this enormous desert area is Jordan Valley. On US 95 only 5 miles from the Idaho border, Jordan Valley shares much of that state's early gold-mining history. The first large-scale cattle drive arrived here in 1869, establishing JV (as Jordan Valley is frequently abbreviated) as the center of a huge stock-raising country.

Basque sheepherders also flooded into this area in the 1890s, leaving an ongoing influence on JV. The Frontone, a stone ball court used for playing a traditional Basque game called *pelota*, still stands in JV.

Unfortunately, little else remains of the town's glory days. Truck stops now give the town its identity.

Jordan Craters

A sort of lava theme park, these formations have erupted since white settlement of North America. Craters, blowholes and lava tubes are among the volcanic outcroppings. The lava flow dammed Cow Creek to form Cow Lakes, where there's informal camping and fishing. The BLM now protects Jordan Craters as a natural area to preserve the ecosystem. Watch out for snakes.

To reach Jordan Craters Natural Area, travel 9 miles north along US 95 from JV; turn west and drive 26 miles along a gravel road to reach the volcanic site.

Rome

Here, along US 95, is the only bridge to cross the Owyhee River. Both the river and the landscape are misleadingly placid at this old-time ford. A gravel road south of Rome leads to rough country where the Owyhee River leaves its gorge. After a few miles, park your vehicle and hike over to the canyon for a view of the Owyhee far below. Three miles north of Rome, along a county road, are the outcroppings for which Rome was named. The fancifully named 'Pillars of Rome' are highly eroded cliffs of volcanic tuff several hundred feet high.

There's a tiny cafe (☎ 541-586-2294) in Rome that rents RV sites.

Three Forks

At Three Forks, the main body of the Owyhee River meets two tributaries, the North Fork and Middle Fork, in a small, enchanting oasis full of cottonwoods and prairie grasses. Two miles of steep switchbacks (high-clearance vehicles only) lead down the canyon wall to this site, where an early homestead and a primitive campground await. Here, the gorges cut by the rivers are hundreds of feet deep, but only 20 to 30 feet across. It's a magical point.

To reach Three Forks, turn south on the gravel road 1 mile east of the Danner junction on US 95. After 17 miles, Owyhee Canyon Overlook provides a glimpse of the river channeling its narrow gorge hundreds of feet beneath the prairie surface; another 18 miles will bring you to Three Forks. Alternatively, 7 miles east of JV, a county road turns south and leads 35 miles to Three Forks. Both roads are pretty well marked.

The Grave of Jean Baptiste Charbonneau

One of the early West's most colorful characters is buried at the old Inskip Ranch, near Danner between Rome and Jordan Valley. Jean Baptiste Charbonneau was the son of Toussaint Charbonneau and Sacagawea, who accompanied Lewis and Clark and the Corps of Discovery on their journey across the western USA between 1805 and 1806.

In all those pictures of Sacagawea, young Pomp, as he was known to the group, is the one in the papoose. Having been the youngest member of the expedition was just the beginning of his incredible life. William Clark was so taken with the young half-French Canadian, half-Indian infant that he sent the child to private schools in St Louis at his own expense.

At Fort Union in Montana, the adolescent Charbonneau met German nobleman-cum-scientist Prince Paul von Wurtemberg, who was impressed by the well-educated boy. He took Charbonneau back to Germany with him, where Charbonneau spent the next six years as a courtier. During this time, he learned five languages fluently and traveled across the Continent and to Africa with the prince. Charbonneau eventually returned to the western USA. He served as a guide through the Montana wilderness, trapped furs, served as alcalde at a California mission and prospected for gold in the 1850s California gold rush. In 1866 he hankered to return to Montana, where gold fever had broken out. He got no farther north than Danner, then a stage stop, where he died of pneumonia at the age of 61.

To visit the gravesite, follow signs to Danner and look for the ruins of an old ranch. ■

At the river's confluence is a nice swimming hole, and informal hikes are possible along the canyon floor. There are riverside hot springs after a 2 mile scramble up the main branch of the Owyhee. Ranch trails can serve as mountain-bike paths. Make sure to close the gates after you. Rafters can float the Owyhee River only in spring runoff; it's generally recognized as one of Oregon's wildest rivers, especially the stretch between Three Forks and Rome.

White-Water Rafting

The upper stretch of the Owyhee, below Three Forks, contains a number of Class IV rapids. Downstream from Rome the river is less turbulent, but the scenery – highly eroded desert cliffs – is still top-notch. The Owyhee River contains enough water to be safely rafted only in the early spring, usually from March through May. Call the BLM office in Burns (☎ 541-573-4400) to check on the river levels. There basically aren't any businesses of any sort out here, let alone a raft rental shop, so if you plan to shoot the river on your own, you need to bring gear from elsewhere.

Both Wapiti River Trips (☎ 208-628-3523, 800-488-9872), Box 1125, Riggins, ID 83459, and Steens Mountain Packers (☎ 541-495-2315, 800-977-3995) offer guided trips on the Owyhee.

Places to Stay & Eat

JV's two motels are found right along US 95. Quaint in name only, the *Basque Station Motel* (☎ 541-586-2244), with singles/doubles for $40/50, and the *Sahara Motel* (☎ 541-586-2810), at $38/41, are, like much of the rest of the town, offshoots of successful gas stations.

An old Basque hostelry has been converted into the *Old Basque Inn* (☎ 541-586-2298). The standard steak-dominated menu also features a few Basque dishes (roast lamb for $15). It's open for three meals a day. *JV Restaurant* along US 95 is where truckers stop.

Lake County

Wranglers, shifting deserts, fault-block mountains and alkaline lakes only begin to characterize this enormous county. Covering almost 8500 sq miles, but with less than one person to each of those miles, this is big, lonesome country.

For a county named for water, there's remarkably little of it here. When you pull into the towns of Christmas Valley or Silver Lake, don't be disappointed if you don't see any water. The locals haven't seen any for years either: the lakes in question are playas.

Hwy 31 cuts through this lonely country, passing a landscape characterized by its volcanic past to one dominated by enormous fault-block mountains. It's quite a distance between outposts, so have a good supply of water and a full tank of gas. Lakeview is the seat of the county and the best bet for lodging; to the east lie Hart Mountain and Warner Lakes. The region to north of Lakeview along Hwy 31 is chock full of geological curiosities.

Stands of sagebrush cover much of the desert-like plains, while to the west the Fremont National Forest offers recreation in cool, ponderosa pine forests.

LAKEVIEW
Population 2526
There's no longer any lake in view at Lakeview. Lakeview, at an elevation of 4800 feet, is the highest city in Oregon, the seat of Lake County, and a major trading center for farmers and ranchers.

Goose Lake, south of town at the California state line, used to be much closer to town. The increasingly arid climate, as well as the diversion of stream water into irrigation, have worked to diminish the size of the lake.

Orientation & Information
Lakeview is 96 miles east of Klamath Falls on Hwy 140, and 142 miles south of La-Pine on Hwy 31. It's 139 miles between Burns and Lakeview on US 395. It takes a kind of devotion, or else *extreme* carelessness, to end up out here.

The Lake County Chamber of Commerce (☎ 541-947-6040) is at 126 North E St, Lakeview, OR 97630. The Lakeview Ranger District of the Fremont National Forest (☎ 541-947-3334) is at 524 North G St. The BLM office (☎ 541-947-2177) is at 1000 9th St S. The US Department of Fish & Wildlife office (☎ 541-947-3315) is on the 3rd floor of the post office building, at G and Center Sts.

The post office is at 18 South G St. Lake District Hospital (☎ 541-947-2114) is at 700 South J St. Diane's Corner (☎ 541-947-3886), at 1103 N 4th St, is the place to do laundry.

Museums
The **Lake County Museum** (☎ 541-947-2220), 118 South E St, preserves the Western heritage of this old lumber and cow town. It also boasts some excellent artifacts of its earlier inhabitants such as bark sandals, dolls and pioneer potato mashers. The museum is open 9 am to 4:30 pm, Monday to Saturday, May to October. A $2 donation is requested.

Adjacent to the county museum, the **Schminck Memorial Museum** (☎ 541-947-3134), 128 South E St, maintains the home of one of the town's earliest and most successful residents. Family history is displayed side by side with collections of barbed wire and other oddities. It's open 1 to 5 pm, Tuesday to Saturday. Admission to the museum is $1.

Hiking
Old-growth ponderosa pine forests, cliffside hikes and solitude are the main attractions at **Gearhart Mountain Wilderness**, northwest of Lakeview in the Fremont National Forest. Erosion has rounded the landscape of these meadowy mountains, except for the resistant volcanic plugs that rise to steep summits. The Gearhart Mountain Trail transects the wilderness area, passing through meadows to reach the summit (8364 feet) of Gearhart Mountain.

To the north, the trail passes tiny Blue Lake.

To reach Gearhart Mountain from Lakeview, drive west on Hwy 140 and turn north at the little community of Quartz Mountain onto USFS Rd 3660. The trailhead is at Lookout Rock, close to the Corral Creek Campground, 11 miles from the highway.

Skiing
Seven miles east of Lakeview on Hwy 140, Warner Canyon Ski Area (☎ 541-947-5001) has 14 runs and about 3½ miles of cross-country trails. Though there's only a 730-foot vertical drop, the inexpensive lift ticket – just $15 a day – should get skiers' attention. There are no ski rentals at the ski area; rent them in town at M&D Ski (☎ 541-947-4862), 118 North L St.

Hang-Gliding
Towering, treeless fault-block rims and prevailing westerly winds make Lakeview one of Oregon's centers for hang-gliding. Favorite departure spots are **Black Cap Peak**, which rises over the town of Lakeview, and the southern end of **Abert Rim**, 20 miles north of Lakeview. Despite the sport's popularity here, hang-gliding rentals and lessons are not available from any businesses in the area.

Swimming
Take a dip in the hot-springs pool at Hunter's Hot Springs Resort (☎ 541-947-4800) on US 395 just north of town; it's $5 for a swim, and free to ogle Oregon's only geyser, which erupts every 90 seconds in a pond here. Hunter's is a quirky, not-quite-ramshackle place, with a motel, RV park and restaurant. During the summer, the large, geothermally heated Lakeview municipal pool, 300 Center St, charges $3 for admission.

Places to Stay
Camping *Junipers Reservoir RV Resort* (☎ 541-947-2050), 11 miles west on Hwy 140, has a ranch setting and is an official Oregon Wildlife Viewing Area, with deer, bald eagles and coyotes often seen. *Goose

Lake State Park (☎ 541-947-3111) is 14 miles south of Lakeview, situated right on the California border. Rates at these two campgrounds start at $14. *Willow Creek Campground* is a free USFS campground, 8 miles east on Hwy 140, then 6 miles south on USFS Rd 3915.

Motels *Budget Inn* (☎ 541-947-2201), 411 North F St, has kitchen units, a restaurant next door and single/double rooms for $34/40. *Lakeview Lodge* (☎ 541-947-2181), 301 North G St, is a nice place with rooms for $40/44. Another good bet with $34/38 rooms is the *Interstate 8 Motel* (☎ 541-947-3341), 354 North K St. At *Rim Rock Motel* (☎ 541-947-2185), 727 South F St, rooms start at $30/34. *Best Western Skyline Motor Lodge* (☎ 541-947-2194), 414 North G St, has a pool and hot tub; rooms start at about $60. At *Hunter's Hot Springs Resort* (☎ 541-947-4800), on US 395 just north of town, there's a geyser and a pool, and rooms start at $34.

Resorts *Aspen Ridge Resort* (☎ 541-884-8685, 800-393-3323), PO Box 2, Bly, OR 97622, is a guest ranch 45 miles west of Lakeview, and is probably the nicest place to stay in this corner of Oregon. Rooms range from $65 to $125. The 7000-sq-foot lodge has a good restaurant (open to the public) and there are also self-catering cabins available. As the resort is part of a large working ranch, there's lots of room for recreation: Wildlife viewing, horseback riding, mountain biking and fishing are some of the options. The resort is 18 miles southeast of Bly. Turn off Hwy 140 about a mile east of Bly, and continue on USFS Rd 3790 (Fishhole Creek Rd).

Places to Eat
Lakeview is the kind of hard-working town where you can expect big, meat-filled meals. *Eagle's Nest Food & Spirits* (☎ 541-947-4824), at 117 North E St, features fresh prime rib as their specialty. *Plush West* (☎ 541-947-2353), 9 North F St, offers good steak, lamb and seafood in a steakhouse atmosphere. The local Mexican

OREGON

OREGON

restaurant, *El Aguila Real* (☎ 541-947-5655), is at 406 North G St. For breakfast and more casual dining, *Mom's Corner Cafe* (☎ 541-947-5044), 930 South F St, is good and respectable, just like Mom. Get coffee and muffins at *Tall Town Burger Co & Bakery*, at North 4th and K Sts.

Getting There & Away
Greyhound operates two buses each day between Klamath Falls and Lakeview. The bus station (☎ 541-947-2255) is at 619 Center St.

HART MOUNTAIN & WARNER LAKES
Hart Mountain and Poker Jim Ridge form a near-vertical escarpment 3600 feet above Warner Lakes (which is actually a group of lakes, each with its own name). These wildlife areas contain magnificent scenery, stellar plant and wildlife viewing and expanses of open space. Both are near the tiny community of Plush, 43 miles northeast of Lakeview.

Rock Creek Rd, designated a BLM Scenic Byway, continues east through the Hart Mountain National Antelope Refuge, and on to Frenchglen. It's a slow, frequently rough road; allow several hours to travel the 50 miles between Plush and Frenchglen. Make sure you have plenty of fuel before embarking on this route.

Hart Mountain National Antelope Refuge
Created in 1936 as a refuge for pronghorn, the Hart Mountain National Antelope Refuge is home to roughly 1700 pronghorn on the 430 sq miles of sagebrush desert and steep mountain ravines. With so much room to roam, it's possible to visit the refuge and not see antelope: Keep an eye open for a cloud of dust, which the antelope kick up as they zip from place to place. Bighorn sheep were re-introduced to Hart Mountain in the 1970s, and have established a foundation herd. Coyotes, jack rabbits and kangaroo rats are also common denizens of this desert plateau.

From Plush, the road to the refuge crosses the Warner Lakes basin, before it begins to climb up a steep crevice in the face of the Hart Mountain fault block. Three thousand feet later, the road emerges onto the prairie-like expanses of the antelope refuge. From here, there are magically expansive views: Hart Mountain, 8065 feet in elevation, drops off precipitously to Hart Lake, while to the north, Poker Jim Ridge plunges off onto a series of dried lakebeds. It's easy to explore this amazing rim of rock on foot – in fact, it's hard to resist.

The US Department of Fish & Wildlife office (☎ 541-947-3315) in Lakeview has details on the refuge.

At the refuge field headquarters, 25 miles east of Plush on the road to Frenchglen (also known as Rock Creek Rd), pick up a brochure and information about recent wildlife sightings. The facility is often unstaffed, but this is the only place on the refuge with water and a toilet. It is a good idea to make the most of it.

Petroglyph Lake
Make a detour to this small watering hole flanked by a rocky cliff. Here, early Indians scratched symbols and animal likenesses. Follow the path to the cliff's end for the best display. The turnoff for Petroglyph Lake is about a mile west of the refuge headquarters, on the road to Plush; the lake

Bighorn sheep inhabit the mountainous regions of the Pacific Northwest.

Order of the Antelope

There aren't many fraternal organizations more peculiar than the Order of the Antelope, an exclusive all-male society that meets annually at the Hart Mountain National Antelope Refuge. The Order was established in 1932 to lobby the federal government for the establishment of the refuge; the original members were local businessmen and politicians from Lake County who got together each summer for a guys-only weekend at the reserve's so-called 'Blue Sky Hotel,' a hot-springs campground.

The refuge was indeed created in 1936 and, in celebration, the Order's weekend getaway devolved into a no-holds-barred party.

The Order's membership is limited to the sons, sons-in-law and grandsons of the original members, plus invited male guests who have traditionally included Oregon governors, US senators, congressmen and even a justice of the US Supreme Court. Whatever high-minded ideals may have motivated the first members, later gatherings of the Order began to be marked by extreme drunkenness, public lewdness and gambling.

The Order's annual party was considered simply a men-only, whiskey-driven gathering of about 500 men until an *Oregonian* newspaper reporter infiltrated the annual blowout in 1991. He reported back on contests involving massive amounts of drink, genital exposure, profanity, and reams of pornographic material and beer cans strewn about the camp, where butchered rear ends of cows and deer decorated trees and signposts. To make the situation even more seamy was the fact that the party was held on public wilderness land under a special-use permit from the US Fish & Wildlife Department. (Although the department had tried for years to revoke the permit, Oregon's senators and congressmen repeatedly used their clout to reinstate it.)

After the *Oregonian* article, other stories about the Order began to materialize, including incidents where members had menaced unwitting tourists who showed up at the refuge during the party. The outcry against the Order's event was swift. Because the gathering took place on federal land, where it is illegal to exclude women and minorities, strict controls on environmental degradation could therefore be enforced against the Order. Politicians who used to provide cover for the Order began to back away, and the Order's special-use permit was revoked in 1992. However, the permit was reinstated with restrictions in 1996. ■

is about a mile up a rutted jeep trail from the main road. Ask at refuge headquarters for other petroglyph sites as this area of Oregon is rich in petroglyphs and pictographs, remains from the region's long Native Indian inhabitancy.

Warner Lakes

This lake basin at the base of Hart Mountain attracts migrating waterfowl and desert wildlife. Bulrushes and cottonwoods grow at lakes' edge, while the dry lakebeds support alkali grass, greasewood and sagebrush.

Nesting white pelicans are so numerous at Pelican Lake that the lake's been named for them. Seasonally abundant waterfowl found in the lakes include Canadian geese, pied-billed grebes, snowy egrets, whistling swans and all manner of ducks (a checklist of bird species is available from the BLM office or from the antelope refuge). These shallow lakes are also the only habitat in the world for the Warner sucker, a bottom-feeding fish.

The entire Warner Valley was one enormous, 500-sq-mile lake at the end of the most recent ice age. Now, only three lakes – Pelican, Crump and Hart – hold water on a more than seasonal basis, and in drought periods these three can get pretty muddy. However, during wet springs, runoff can fill much of the basin (the lakes drain to the north), offering migrating

OREGON

waterfowl a resting and refueling stopover, and mule deer a watering hole. There's also a canoe trail through the lakes and wetlands, which is a great trip during a wet spring. Contact the Lakeview BLM office (☎ 541-947-2177), at 1000 9th St, for information about water levels.

A good information kiosk near the north end of Hart Lake has maps of lakeside hiking trails and a bird-viewing blind.

Mountain Biking

Hart Mountain has an extensive network of jeep trails and single-tracks, making for great mountain biking. After a long drive, test your lungs and legs by making the short hop from the refuge headquarters to Petroglyph Lake (see above). For more of a challenge, drive south from the headquarters toward Blue Sky, and park at Lookout Point. From there, pedal out to the **Skyline Trail**, which has some steep climbs before hitting a ridge, and great views. The refuge's ultimate ride is up **Hart Mountain** itself. Drive 15 miles south of the refuge headquarters to Blue Sky Hotel (the old Order of the Antelope base camp; see Order of the Antelope sidebar) and head uphill from there. Plan on spending a good bit of the day on this ride.

Places to Stay & Eat

The little community of Plush has very basic facilities. The *Hart Mountain Store* (☎ 541-947-2491) is a small store-cafe that also sells gasoline. Campers are welcome in the town's park.

Hot Springs Campground, in the refuge, offers informal campsites along a lovely wooded creek, about 4 miles south of the refuge headquarters on a graveled road. A plus is the open-air bathhouse which traps a hot spring – just the thing after a dusty day of hiking. Informal hiking trails lead up the side of Hart Mountain and its westfacing cliffs. Gentler trails from the campground lead up aspen-shaded creeksides.

Lakeview, 43 miles to the southwest of Plush, offers all services.

LAKE ABERT

Lake Abert, nearly 62 sq miles in size, is a remnant of the vast lakes that covered this landscape during the last ice age (look for old shoreline benchmarks on the hillsides). With only one active freshwater source and no outlet, this is Oregon's largest salt lake. Its mineral content is so high that it's dangerous to swim here. Brine shrimp abound, however, and migratory birds make Lake Abert a lunch stop.

The uneroded face of Abert Rim, the highest fault escarpment in the USA, rises 2000 feet above the eastern shores of the lake. It was formed when geologic forces boosted up the rim while the lake dropped.

PAISLEY

Population 350

Paisley, where the Chewaucan River leaves its mountain valley and flows into marshland, is an attractive old ranch town. Paisley was once headquarters for some of the largest open-range ranches in Oregon; ZX Ranch, which controls over a million acres of land, still operates in the area.

The Paisley Ranger Station of the Fremont National Forest was built in the 1930s by the CCC. The grounds and buildings are still in daily use, and typify the period's rustic architectural style. Within the compound visit the Paisley Ranger District (☎ 541-943-3114), 303 Hwy 31. Here they have a self-guiding brochure and recreational information for the area.

Roads lead westward into the Fremont National Forest, an overlooked but pleasant range of mountains filled with ponderosa pines and quiet streams.

Summer Lake Hot Springs

This tiny resort (☎ 541-943-3931), 6 miles north of Paisley, has a small hot-springs pool. In addition to the pool ($2 admission), there are campsites on a bluff overlooking Summer Lake.

Paisley Mosquito Festival

During the last weekend of July, the town celebrates the Mosquito Festival (☎ 541-

943-3303) with a parade, buffalo meat barbecue, street dance and the crowning of Miss Quito.

Places to Stay & Eat
Seven miles west of Paisley, in the Fremont National Forest, is a lovely free campsite at *Marster Spring*. To get there, turn west at Paisley's only traffic light. Back in town, at the *Miles Motel* (☎ 541-943-3148), you can get completely adequate rooms beginning at $25.

The Lodge at Summer Lake (☎ 541-943-3993) offers food and single/double rooms for $39/45. The *Summer Lake B&B* (☎ 541-943-3983, 800-261-2778) is south of town. Rooms here are $35/45, with condo units available for $60. Breakfast is an extra $5. The proprietor here is an expert on southeastern Oregon's petroglyphs; be sure to ask him for a map.

The *Pioneer Saloon & Restaurant* is, on one side, a great old bar filled with the drawls of ranchers thinking out loud. On the other side, the bar staff serves good, homemade Mexican food. Try the *Homestead Restaurant* (☎ 541-943-3187), for family dining. Both are very moderately priced.

NORTH LAKE COUNTY
This region is replete with geological curiosities. The following sites are easily reached by most cars and are near to main thoroughfares; others – equally interesting – require 4WD or a greater commitment to off-road travel time.

Ask locally for directions to oddities like Big Hole, The Devil's Garden, Fossil Lake and the Lost Forest. Christmas Valley-Wagontire Rd joins Fort Rock and Christmas Valley to US 395, linking many of the odd volcanic and desert features of the area.

The Silver Lake Ranger District (☎ 541-576-2107), on Hwy 31 at the west end of Silver Lake, has recreational and travel information. The Lakeview Chamber of Commerce, or the BLM office in Lakeview (☎ 541-947-2177), 1000 9th St S, Lakeview, OR 97630, has brochures on the volcanic formations.

Hole-in-the-Ground
This enormous blast hole was left when superheated steam and lava came in contact with a muddy, shallow sea bottom about 15,000 years ago. The resulting explosion created a perfectly circular crater a mile across and 300 feet deep. The rocks that ring the crater were thrown there by the force of the explosion (the crater was once credited to the impact of a meteorite). To get to Hole-in-the-Ground, drive 6 miles north of the Fort Rock junction on Hwy 31; the crater is another 6 miles along a graveled road. Follow the small roadside signs.

Fort Rock
A similar series of underwater blasts created Fort Rock, 35 miles southeast of LaPine on Hwy 31. This entire area was a huge ice-age lake stretching for hundreds of miles across central Oregon. Rising molten rock came into contact with mud and lake water, creating a series of massive explosions. As the ash and rock were thrown into the air, they came to rest in a ring. The tuff ring grew taller until the walls of the formation were hundreds of feet in height. Wave action from the lake eventually breached the southern wall, giving access to this otherwise impregnable formation.

Today, Fort Rock is a half mile across and rises 325 feet from a dry, perfectly flat lakebed. From a distance, the formation looks remarkably like a fortress or a sports stadium.

Early Indians lived in caves in and around Fort Rock. It is here that, in 1938, archeologists discovered remains of an early native culture dating from 9000 to 13,000 years ago.

Sagebrush-fiber sandals, tools, weapons and ceremonial items point to a relatively complex culture. Pictographs in the area also depict images of men harpooning fish – an odd sight in today's desert landscape. The ancestors of the Paiute tribe gradually moved into the area; their hunting and gathering culture suited the

Sagebrush

The otherwise arid landscape of central and eastern Oregon is dominated by a botanical abundance of the dusty gray sagebrush *(Artemesia tridentata)*. Although it shares a common name with culinary sage, the strong-smelling, pitchy sagebrush of the desert isn't welcome at the table: tales abound of frontier cooks who mistakenly added sagebrush leaves to poultry stuffing, with sad results.

Sagebrush was generally treated with scorn by the American settler of the high desert, as it occupied land that ought to be producing wheat. Others saw gold in the brushy, gray shrubs. During the homesteading era, highly optimistic boosters of the high desert claimed that sagebrush could be harvested and used for a base for perfume and for paper production. The distilled pitch of sagebrush was also touted as containing valuable amounts of tar, wood alcohol and acetic acid; the branches were thought a good source of charcoal. At least one factory plant opened east of Bend in 1910 to extract the untapped riches of the sagebrush that spread for hundreds of miles across the desert.

Native Americans had been at least as inventive in use of sagebrush. For the Indian peoples of this region, the shaggy, stringy bark of the plant was used in making rope, sandals and kindling.

More recently, sagebrush has been touted as a natural alternative to flea powders and collars used on household pets, due to its strong scent. Actually, the odor of sage is a natural defense mechanism to ensure the plant's survival. The decay of fallen leaves releases a toxic compound that actually limits the growth of would-be competitor species. (Although naturopathic pet owners may believe they are sparing themselves and their pets from the effects of harmful pesticides, they may not know that crushed leaves in kitty's eco-collar also possess volatile chemicals that may cause a mild allergenic effect.) ■

increasingly arid climate. The site is one of the earliest known human habitations in North America.

Fort Rock State Monument is 2 miles north of the town of Fort Rock. The park facility has a picnic area and bathrooms. There are a number of informal trails around and over the formation. The vertical faces are popular with novice rock climbers.

Crack-in-the-Ground

Like its volcanic cousins, Crack-in-the-Ground is self-descriptive. Formed about 1000 years ago when thick, cooling lava flows faulted and began to sink, this crack in the earth's surface is 2 miles long, an average of 7 to 10 feet across, and up to 70 feet deep. From the parking lot there are trails leading to the bottom of the crack.

Turn north on the gravel road that begins 1 mile east of the town of Christmas Valley. The next 8 miles are dusty; the last mile, after you climb up on the lava flow, is quite rough.

Places to Stay

Camping is informal, as most of the land is publicly owned. Though it's prohibited, people do camp inside the rim of Fort Rock. There's running water at the state monument parking lot. For something more legal, turn south 1 mile west of Silver Lake and drive 10 miles to *Silver Creek Marsh Campground* in the Fremont National Forest.

The *Christmas Valley Desert Inn Motel* (☎ 541-576-2262) is clean and dependable, with rooms starting at $25. *Lakeside Terrace Motel & Restaurant* (☎ 541-576-2309), also in Christmas Valley, sits beside the golf course, and has rooms for $30.

Places to Eat

Silver Lake Cafe & Bar (☎ 541-576-2221), is Silver Lake's lone eatery: Bypass it at your risk. *Christmas Valley Lodge* (☎ 541-576-2333), is that town's steak house; next to the golf course, it serves drinks to thirsty putters.

Washington

BILL MCRAE

Facts about Washington

People here like to joke about being in 'the upper left-hand corner.' That's because Washington State is squeezed into a corner between the Pacific Ocean, Canada and contiguous states. Apart from having a unique geographic position, Washingtonians take a great deal of pride in being at the northern and western extreme of continental USA. If there's a virtue to the country's long westering and northering instinct, then it is expressed in the qualities of this progress-oriented state.

Washington likes to keep its distance. Its residents have long known that by cloaking the state in tales of rain and gloom, they could keep the rest of the world away from what is undoubtedly one of the most beautiful corners of the country. However, by now there's scarcely a soul who doesn't acknowledge that Seattle is one of the major cultural and trend-setting centers of the USA, and that life in 'the Evergreen State' is as sweet as anywhere in this fallen world.

What's not to like? The western part of the state is about equally divided by glaciered peaks and wilderness, dynamic cities and a seascape of misty islands and harbors. To the east are more arid uplands with 300 days of sunshine, and all-season recreation. Does it rain? In the west, sure; but that's the price you pay to live in this well-washed, hospitable and sophisticated state.

HISTORY

Present-day Washington grew out of the old Oregon territory that consisted of today's Idaho, Washington, Oregon and western Montana, and lay under joint British and American rule. In the early days of settlement, the only towns and centers of population in the Northwest existed in Oregon's Willamette Valley, and Salem, OR, became the territorial capital for the entire region.

Although Hudson's Bay Company (HBC) factor Dr John McLoughlin had sought to restrict settlement of the greater Oregon Territory to the region south of the Columbia River, the easily settled land along the Willamette began to disappear as pioneers continued to roll into the Pacific Northwest. In the mid-1840s, settlers began streaming north, and the first American settlement in Washington was established in 1845 at Tumwater, on the southern edge of the Puget Sound. This group of 32 Missourians purposely chose to move to British territory (despite the disapproval of the HBC) because Oregon law – in order to sidestep the contentious issue of slavery – forbade the settlement of blacks. The settlers, some of whom were part African American, expected better treatment from the British. The village of Tumwater was soon thriving with mills and trading posts, and Olympia was founded as the mill town's port in 1846.

In 1851, both Seattle and Port Townsend were established and quickly became logging centers. The forests of the Pacific Northwest began to fall to the saw, and lumber was shipped at great profit to San Francisco, the boomtown of the California gold rush.

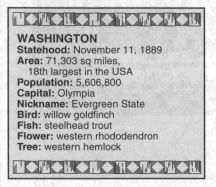

WASHINGTON
Statehood: November 11, 1889
Area: 71,303 sq miles,
   18th largest in the USA
Population: 5,606,800
Capital: Olympia
Nickname: Evergreen State
Bird: willow goldfinch
Fish: steelhead trout
Flower: western rhododendron
Tree: western hemlock

The Oregon-based territorial government tended to focus more on the well-established towns of the Willamette Valley and as communities in Washington grew, they found Salem – a couple hundred miles south through deep forest and across the Columbia River – too distant. In 1851 and 1852, representatives from western Washington met and called for the establishment of a separate territory north of the Columbia. The Oregon legislature concurred, and in 1853 the US Congress voted to create Washington Territory. Isaac Ingall Stevens was appointed governor and also Superintendent of Indian Affairs.

Cavalry vs Indians

One of the most immediate concerns facing the young territory was the quelling of Native American hostilities in the eastern part of the region. The seeds of unrest had been sown in 1847 when a group of Cayuse killed Marcus Whitman, his wife and 12 other white missionaries near Walla Walla. This act both horrified the white settlers of the Northwest and solidified opinion that the Native Americans had to be forced onto reservations. Although the Cayuse responsible for the killings were apprehended, tried and then hanged at Oregon City in 1850, tensions between the Native Americans and white settlers continued to grow. (See History in Facts about the Pacific Northwest for more details on the Whitman Massacre.)

Governor Stevens held a council at Walla Walla in 1855, with representatives of most eastern Indian tribes present. The tribes, which included the Cayuse, Walla-walla, Nez Perce, Yakama, and Umatilla were cajoled into signing various treaties that reduced the land shares open to native peoples for hunting and fishing. However, many of the tribes were not satisfied with their reservations, nor with Stevens' treatment of them. The US Congress was also dissatisfied with Stevens' methods, and refused to ratify the treaties. The situation rapidly deteriorated.

In 1856, a confederation of Plateau tribes led by the Yakama attacked steamboats on the Columbia River near The Dalles. Over the course of the year the army exchanged hostilities with the Yakamas and built Fort Simcoe (in central Washington) to protect the Columbia River from attack. The eastern half of Washington was proclaimed closed to settlement, and Stevens declared martial law in the region.

In the same year, the thrown-together town of Seattle was the scene of another Indian attack. Despite fierce fighting, the Nisqually, who led the attack, were defeated, in part due to the assistance of a US Navy sloop in Elliott Bay.

In 1858, trouble again broke out when a cavalry detachment led by Colonel EJ Steptoe departed from Fort Walla Walla to protect miners in the gold fields along the Okanogan River. Near Rosalia, the soldiers encountered a vastly larger confederated force of natives led by the Spokane tribe. The cavalry quickly ran through its ammunition and was forced into a humiliating retreat. Four months later a large army battalion returned for revenge. The Indian force was decisively defeated near Spokane, where the army rounded up and shot 800 of the tribe's horses. Deprived of their means of travel, the Indians were forced to surrender. By 1859, Congress finally ratified the eastern Washington treaties, and the tribes were resettled. With the Indians no longer a threat, the eastern part of the state was opened up to settlement.

Boom Times

Dairy farming, fishing and logging remained the chief economic underpinnings of settlements in western Washington. Port cities boomed because almost all the transportation to and from Washington was by ship; land transport to the rest of the nation was severely lacking.

Competition between fledgling cities became fierce when railroads began to contemplate lines into the Northwest. In 1883, Portland was the first Northwest city to be linked to the rest of the nation by rail, followed by Tacoma in 1887; Seattle didn't

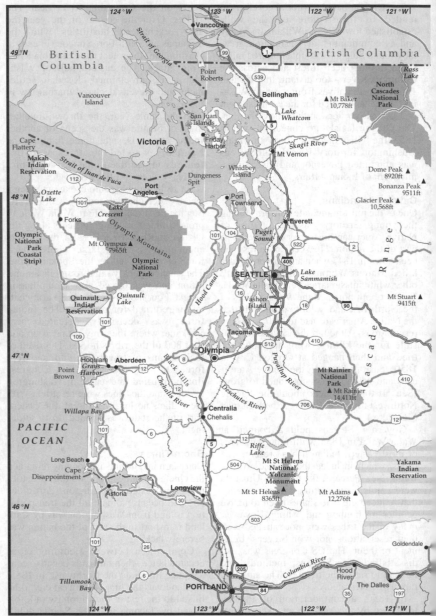

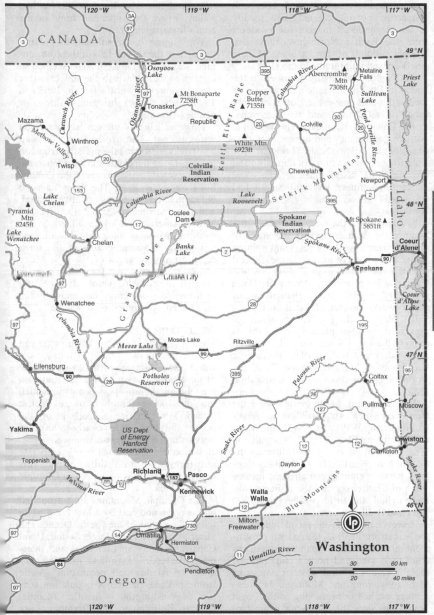

WASHINGTON

Washington

have railroad service until 1893. These rail connections not only created a new, readily accessible national market for products from the Pacific Northwest, they also brought in floods of settlers, many of them newly arrived immigrants to the USA.

Washington was finally admitted to the Union in 1889 and Seattle's supremacy as the Northwest's greatest seaport was established in 1897, when gold was discovered in the Canadian Klondike. The principal port for prospectors and adventurers destined for the Yukon, Seattle boomed. The waterfront became a flurry of departing and arriving ships, honky-tonks, brothels and mercantile outfitters. By 1900, Seattle had surpassed Portland as the largest city in the Northwest.

In many ways, the story of Washington State in the 20th century is the story of massive federal works projects and military spending. As early as 1902, the federal government was building dams on the Columbia River, and the Bonneville Dam, completed in 1937, was the single largest public works project of Franklin Roosevelt's New Deal. The cheap electrical power it provided proved an enormous boon to the Puget Sound's rapid industrial growth during WWII. In 1947, Bonneville was joined by Grand Coulee Dam, the world's largest hydroelectric and irrigation project.

The naval yards at Bremerton were the Northwest's major ship-building and repair facility during WWI and WWII, and home of the Northern Fleet. The city's population grew 235% in the two years following the bombing of Pearl Harbor. William Boeing's bustling commercial airplane factory south of Seattle received the military contracts to build the air force's fleet of 13,000 B-17 and B-29 bombers.

However, not everyone prospered during the war effort. In 1942, the federal government removed 18,000 Japanese Americans from their land and homes and interned them in camps in rural western states like Idaho, Wyoming and Montana. Japanese immigrants had been moving to the Puget Sound area since the 1880s, and a substan-tial population also lived in the Yakima Valley, where they operated some of the area's first irrigated farms.

Washington has continued to prosper throughout the second half of the 20th century. Seattle and, later, Spokane seemed so certain of their place in the universe that each city threw a world's fair (in 1962 and 1974, respectively), bringing millions of people to the state.

However, all this success has not come without cost. The production of cheap hydroelectricity and the massive irrigation projects along the Columbia have led to the near irreversible destruction of the Columbia River ecosystem. The dams have all but eliminated most runs of native salmon, and have further disrupted the lives of Native Americans who depended on the river for sustenance and cultural continuity.

The Puget Sound is one of the most rapidly growing areas of the US. Many people are finding that the region's much vaunted livability is rapidly disappearing as it becomes one enormous metropolitan area linked by jammed-up freeways.

GEOGRAPHY

The geography of coastal Washington can be described in two words: mountains and water. The mountains in this case are those of the highly glaciated Olympic range on the Olympic Peninsula, a peninsula which juts out like a thumb into the Pacific Ocean. Moist marine air rolls in off the ocean and hits these nearly 8000-foot peaks, dumping immense amounts of precipitation. North America's only temperate rain forests are the result; much of this unique ecosystem is preserved in Olympic National Park.

The Olympic Mountains are surrounded on the north and east by a low-lying basin fed by the waters of the Pacific Ocean. The Strait of Juan de Fuca, Puget Sound, Hood Canal and many smaller bays and inlets reach like tendrils far inland, isolating hundreds of islands and peninsulas. Aside from Spokane, the major population centers of Washington – Seattle, Tacoma, Everett, Bellingham and Olympia – are located along these inlets; all are dependent on deep-water harbors for much of their prosperity.

Marching north and south across the state are the massive volcanoes of the Cascade Range. The southern peaks, including Mt St Helens and Mt Rainier, rise up high from the horizon as isolated, snow-clad cones. The North Cascades are different; more recent volcanoes, like Mt Baker, have pushed up through an already rugged, mountainous landscape that formed when an offshore island rammed into the North American continent.

The Cascades effectively block the eastward flow of moist Pacific air. Heavy rains fall on the western slopes of the mountains, creating ideal conditions for thick Douglas fir forests. Eastern Washington receives much less rainfall.

Running across the northern boundary of Washington is a series of mountainous highlands (the Okanogans and the Selkirks) and, like the North Cascades, they are the buckled remnants of former Pacific islands that have been jammed onto the leading western edge of the continent. Vegetation is comparatively light on these uplands, with ponderosa pines dominant in the forests.

Encircled by the Columbia River, the desert basin of south-central Washington is given life through the river's many irrigation dams. The eastern edge of the basin, however, is an especially barren piece of real estate: it was denuded of much of its topsoil during massive ice-age floods. In the far east flank of the state the land begins to rise toward the foothills of the Rocky Mountains, alleviating the effects of the Cascade rain shadow.

CLIMATE

The Pacific Ocean and the towering Cascade peaks largely determine the climate of Washington. The coast receives the full brunt of moist, marine air, and coastal towns like Aberdeen get around 85 inches of rain a year. Temperatures are mild however, with only a 20°F variation between summer and winter averages. Throughout coastal Washington, temperatures rarely rise above 80°F, or fall below freezing. Seasonal change is gradual, as both spring and fall are periods of cloud and rain. However, heavy rainfall in the Olympic Mountains serves to insulate other parts of western Washington and the Puget Sound area. Sequim, in the rain shadow of the Olympic peaks, receives only 12 inches of rain a year. Seattle, while frequently wrapped in gray clouds and mist, actually has much less precipitation than many US cities.

Rain and snowfall are heavy in the western Cascades, with winter coming early, often in October. Trails may not be free of snow until July. Even in mid-winter, however, temperatures are also mild – around 20° or 30°F. In summer, highs remain in the 70°s.

East of the Cascades, the climate is very different. Summer temperatures on the Columbia Plateau reach highs of over 100°F, sometimes for days on end. Rainfall is scant; Yakima receives only 8 inches yearly. Winters can be harsh, with the average January temperature below 20°F.

POPULATION & PEOPLE

The current population of Washington is about 5,606,800, and growing fast. Urban forecasters predict that the population of the Puget Sound area alone will reach 5 million early in the 21st century. One of the fastest-growing states in the USA, Washington's dynamic economy and easygoing lifestyle have lured in young people from around the country.

Like the rest of the Pacific Northwest, Washington is overwhelmingly white (88% in the 1990 census). Only around 10% of the state's population is comprised of African, Asian and Hispanic Americans, and less than 2% of the population is Native American Indian.

Native Americans

The Puget Sound area was one of the most densely populated areas of prehistoric Native America, and a great many Indians still live here. On the 1990 census, 87,000 people identified themselves as Native

American; though still only 1.6% of the state's population, this is by far the largest number of Native Americans in the Northwest states. The federal government recognizes 26 different reservations in Washington, and many serve as home to more than one tribe. Some reservations, particularly along the coast, are very small, consisting basically of just a town and a harbor. The largest are east of the Cascades, where the Yakama and Colville Confederated Tribes each maintain million-plus-acre homelands.

ARTS

Seattle is without question the center of the performing art scene in Washington, with thriving theater, classical music and dance companies. However, high rents have served to drive many individual artists, painters and writers away from the city. You'll find skilled artisans living in many rural areas, especially on the Olympic Peninsula and the San Juan Islands. Don't hesitate to duck into art galleries in out-of-the-way places: you may be surprised by the sophisticated work done by lesser-known local artists.

Music

Seattle is probably best known for producing the early '90s rock music phenomenon called 'grunge,' a guitar- and angst-driven derivative of the punk rock scene. The band Nirvana was among the most popular of many Northwest bands that exemplified the sound. Soundgarden and Pearl Jam are other well-known bands that grew out of the grunge scene.

All the attention that Seattle has harvested from the success of grunge has led to an ongoing efflorescence of new rock bands. Seattle and other Puget Sound cities like Bellingham, Tacoma and Olympia are home to a great number of music clubs that feature local bands, each expressing the suburban teen anxiety that typifies the Northwest sound.

Of course, there was music in Seattle before grunge. A musical generation ago,

Seattle was known as the home of Jimi Hendrix, who is buried in the Renton cemetery. Quincy Jones also hails from Seattle, and Ray Charles had his first success in the 1950s as a musician on Seattle TV.

Seattle and other urban centers now offer a variety of live music. Hip-hop and world beat sounds are currently very popular, and Celtic music has a strong following with locals and Irish ex-pats alike. Blues, jazz and folk music are strongly represented in the cities and at popular summer festivals. Notable are the Friday Harbor Dixieland Jazz Festival and Jazz Port Townsend; both are in late July.

Seattle is also the state's center for classical music and the performing arts. Both the Seattle Symphony and Seattle Opera have national reputations, and the city boasts many other smaller classical music ensembles and festival performances. Tacoma, Spokane, the Tri-Cities and Walla Walla also have orchestras.

Theater & Film

Seattle has one of the most dynamic theater scenes in the USA. In addition to quality professional theater, the city offers a wide array of amateur and special-interest troupes. Western Washington State University has a noted drama program, and Bellingham is known as much for its theater students as its theaters.

Moviewise, Seattle has come a long way since the days Elvis starred in the 1963 *It Happened at the World's Fair*, a chestnut of civic boosterism. Nowadays, Seattle is where directors come to shoot droll and stylish comedies. *Say Anything*, *The Fabulous Baker Boys*, *Singles*, *Sleepless in Seattle* and TV's *Frasier* have each done a lot to create Seattle's current reputation as a hip and youthful place to slack off and be trendy.

The creepy, darker side of the Northwest is also displayed in films and TV. *Twin Peaks*, David Lynch's moody and disturbing TV series was shot in Washington, as was the survivalist paean, *First Blood*.

Visual Arts

Seattle is the center of the art and gallery scene in Washington. In addition to high-quality modern and Western art galleries, a number of galleries are devoted to contemporary Native American carvings and paintings. The Seattle Art Museum, housed in a stylish new building downtown, has an especially impressive collection of native artifacts and folk art. A sizable Asian art collection is located at the Seattle Asian Art Museum in Volunteer Park.

There is also an abundance of public art in the city, thanks to Seattle's 1% for Art program, which requires that 1% of the city's capital improvement funds go toward public artwork. The program, created in 1972 from a city ordinance, was the second of its kind in the country.

Another specialty of the Puget Sound area is glass blowing, led by a group of inventive and influential artisans from the Pilchuck School. The most famous of these artists is Dale Chihuly, whose work can be seen in a number of Seattle galleries and places in his hometown of Tacoma. The newly renovated Union Station Courthouse there contains massive works by Chihuly,

as does the Washington Historical Society Museum. The San Juan Islands are another hotbed of artistic activity; several of the islands have co-operative galleries that feature the arts and crafts of island artisans.

INFORMATION
Area Codes

Washington has five area codes. All of eastern Washington is 509, while western Washington is a confusing grid of new area codes. Seattle proper is 206, while Bellevue and the Eastside suburbs are 425. Tacoma's area code is 253, and the rest of western Washington is 360.

Taxes

Washington State sales tax is around 6.5%, and some areas add on their own small tax to the standard amount. The sales tax is not levied on food in grocery stores, but it does apply to food served in restaurants. Seattle's sales tax is 8.6%, and its tax on restaurant food is now 9.1%. When inquiring about hotel rates, be sure to ask whether taxes are included or not. The bed tax, applicable in lodgings across the state, can be as high as 15% (which includes the 6.5%).

Seattle

Population 534,700

More than any other city in the Pacific Northwest, Seattle epitomizes the area's trend from hick to hip. It wasn't long ago that many people hadn't the foggiest idea where this place was, nor where the state of Washington was, for that matter. Now it seems everyone knows someone who is living the good life in 'the Emerald City' (Seattle's alias), who is up on the music scene or who was there when the coffee craze first started.

Before the late '80s/early '90s – when grunge music, coffee, and microbrews came onto the scene – this city was conservative and tranquil, relatively provincial in comparison to larger cities. Today it seems larger than life, with more progress and fashions pouring out than ever before. Seattle city ordinances, adopted in 1973, also stipulate that one percent of all municipal capital-improvement project funds be set aside for public art. This '1% for art' clause has imbued Seattle with an extensive 'library' of artworks ranging from monumental sculpture to landscape design and personalized manhole covers.

The tallest building on the West Coast now shadows Seattle's downtown and over-exaggerated sports arenas draw rowdy crowds. But Seattle proper is really quite small; it's the surrounding neighborhoods that bolster its size and create the impression of a city where trees and azaleas outnumber houses.

Seattle's position on the protected waters of the Puget Sound has done more than ensure it a place at the table of international trade. The coastal mountains and the many islands and fingers of land and water that make up the complex geography of the Puget Sound give Seattle one of the most beautiful settings of any city in the USA. The snow-capped Olympic Mountains rise from the western horizon across the deep blue waters of the sound; ships and ferries wind through scattered, green-clad islands. South and east of the city appear the massive peaks of the Cascades, with Mt Rainier – known in Seattle simply as 'the mountain' – taking up half the skyline and rising to 14,410 feet.

Seattle's solid success as a trade and manufacturing center, mixed with its beautiful, big-as-all outdoors setting, has made the metropolitan area one of the fastest growing in the USA. Young people especially have found their way to this seaport in search of a city that offers economic opportunity, easy access to outdoor recreation and forward-looking politics and culture. In short, if you're looking for lifestyle (and who isn't?), Seattle has it in spades.

As a measure of its success, Seattle now finds itself a trend exporter. Musical and fashion tastes evolve and transform in the city's many clubs before leaking out to other pace-setting capitals. The city's homegrown 'grunge' music swept the nation in the early '90s; TV series and movies now base themselves here in order to partake of the city's hip but quirky cultural and social life, and the city has almost single-handedly made coffee a national obsession.

If Seattle has any one defining characteristic, it's that the city is open for business and ready for more – whether that's more talent, a better Italian restaurant, another military contract or software company, or just another caffe latte.

HISTORY
Seattle's Formative Years

The Elliott Bay and Lake Washington area was home to the Duwamish, a Salish tribe that fished the bays and rivers of the Puget Sound. Generally a peaceable tribe, the Duwamish befriended early white settlers.

David Denny was a New Yorker who in 1851 led a group of settlers across the Oregon Trail with the intention of settling

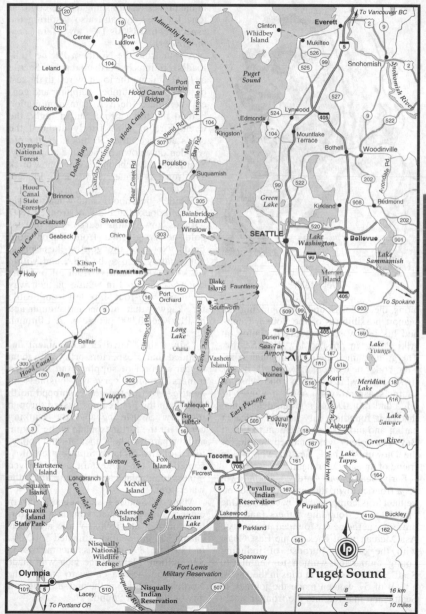

Puget Sound

Chief Sealth

along the Puget Sound. Recognizing the seaport possibilities of the Sound, Denny and his fellow settlers staked claims on Alki Point, in present-day West Seattle. The group named their encampment Alki-New York (the Chinookan word *alki* means 'by-and-by,' which gives a good sense of Denny's aspirations). After a winter of wind and rain, Denny's group determined that their foundling city needed a deeper harbor and moved the settlement to Elliott Bay. The colony was renamed Seattle for the Duwamish chief, Sealth, who was a friend of an early merchant.

Early Seattle was hardly a boomtown. As a frontier town, the majority of the settlement was comprised of bachelors. One of the town's founding fathers (and sole professor at the newly founded university), Asa Mercer, went back to the East Coast with the express purpose of inducing young unmarried women to venture to Seattle. On two different trips in the 1860s, a total of 57 women made the journey to Seattle and married into the frontier stock,

in the process establishing a more civilized tone for the city (and also inspiring the especially bad 1960s TV show, *Here Come the Brides*).

A spur from the Northern Pacific Railroad's terminus in Portland reached Seattle in 1893, linking the town by rail to the rest of the country. Lumber, shipping and general commerce derived from immigration helped the town grow. Surprisingly, the Great Fire of 1889 barely dimmed the city's advance; after 50 blocks of the old wooden downtown burned in a single day, Seattle quickly rebounded with a new brick and iron city centered in today's Pioneer Square.

Seattle's first boom came when the ship *Portland* docked at the waterfront in 1897 with its now-famous cargo: two tons of gold newly gleaned from Yukon gold fields. News of the gold strikes spread immediately across the USA and within weeks, fortune hunters from all over the country converged in Seattle on their way north. Seventy-four ships left from Seattle for Skagway that summer and autumn, and in all, over 40,000 people passed through the city.

Since the Canadian government demanded that prospectors bring with them a year's worth of supplies, outfitting the miners became very big business in Seattle. Most of the goods shipped north to sustain the gold camps passed through the city. Seattle became the banking center for the fortunes made in the Yukon, and the bars, brothels, theaters and honky-tonks of the Pioneer Square area blossomed as the entertainment-deprived miners took solace and pleasure along the waterfront.

Many of Seattle's shopkeepers, tavern owners and restaurateurs made quick fortunes in the late 1890s. While area merchants had grossed an estimated $300,000 in 1897, in 1898, the gross income rose to $25 million. Many of the men who made fortunes in Alaska chose to stay in the Northwest, settling in the now-thriving port city on the Puget Sound.

The War Years & Beyond

The boom continued through WWI, when Northwest lumber was greatly in demand; the opening of the Panama Canal in 1914 brought increased trade to Pacific ports, which were free of wartime threats. Shipyards opened along Puget Sound, bringing the ship-building industry close to the forests of the Northwest, a primary source of lumber.

The Boeing Empire

A seminal event in Seattle history occurred in 1916 when William Boeing, a pioneer aviator, began his air-transport empire by designing and producing a pontoon biplane. Boeing went on to establish an airline, Boeing Air Transport, which in 1927 flew the first commercial flight between Chicago and San Francisco. (The company later became United Airlines.) But it was WWII that really started the engines at Boeing, as the factory received contracts to produce the B-17 and B-29 bombers that led the fleet in the US air war against the Axis nations. Huge defense contracts began to flow into Boeing – and by extension into Seattle – fueling rapid growth and prosperity.

Because of Boeing and the shipyards at Bremerton, the Puget Sound became a highly defended area. Military bases brought in thousands of new residents, and at the same time, the boom in aircraft manufacturing and shipbuilding brought tens of thousands of new workers to the area. By the end of the war, Seattle had grown to nearly half a million people.

After the war, Boeing diversified its product line and began to develop civilian aircraft. In 1954, Boeing announced the 707, and led the revolution in air transportation. By 1960, the metropolitan population of Seattle topped one million people, and Boeing employed one in ten of these; moreover, one in four Seattleites was employed in a job directly affected by Boeing. Boeing was the biggest game in town.

However, the fortunes of Boeing weren't always to soar. A combination of over-stretched capital (due to cost overruns in the development of the 747) and a cut in defense spending led to a severe financial crisis in the early 1970s. Boeing was forced to cut its work force by two-thirds; in one year, nearly 60,000 Seattle workers lost their jobs, and the local economy went into a tail-spin for a number of years.

But recent history has been kind to Boeing, and hence to Seattle. Increased spending in the 1980s brought vigor back to aircraft production, and expanding trade relations with China and other Pacific Rim nations have also brought business to Boeing. Currently, one half of all commercial aircraft made by Boeing is sold into Asia.

Boeing was already the largest aircraft manufacturer in the world when in 1997 it merged with once rival McDonnell Douglas. The resulting company has 200,000 employees and operates with combined revenues estimated next year at $48 billion. ■

In 1916, William Boeing developed his first airplane and founded the Seattle-based aircraft manufacturing business that is still one of the largest employers in the city (see the Boeing Empire sidebar). During WWII, the Boeing company received government contracts to develop bomber planes. Because of Boeing and the shipyards at Bremerton, the Puget Sound became a highly defended area. Military bases brought in thousands of new residents, and the same time, the boom in aircraft manufacturing and shipbuilding brought tens of thousands of new workers to the area. By the end of the war, Seattle had grown to nearly half a million people.

However, WWII also brought less positive change to Seattle; about 6000 Japanese residents were removed from their jobs and homes and most were sent to internment camps in Idaho and eastern Oregon.

A High-Tech Capital

Thanks in part to Boeing, times were good in Seattle throughout the '50s; the city increasingly saw itself as the harbinger of all that was new and progressive. The self-assured, forward-ho swagger of Seattle was perfectly captured in the spirit of the 1962 World's Fair, also known as the 'Century 21 Exposition.' (The Space Needle and the Monorail now evoke a distinctly 1960s notion of tomorrow's world.)

Nonetheless, cuts in defense spending in the '70s brought a temporary lull to Seattle's forward momentum, as thousands of Boeing employees lost their jobs. The local economy suffered for several years before a reverse in defense spending in the '80s revived the aircraft industry, and helped bring it to its current position as a dominant force in the economics of Seattle.

In addition, the 1980s also brought other high-tech jobs to the Puget Sound. Microsoft, the software giant, is located in Redmond, across Lake Washington from Seattle. While Microsoft and other software developers in Seattle's 'Eastside' don't have quite the total control over Seattle economy that Boeing once had, it is increasingly hard to find someone who isn't a contractor, caterer, or car dealer for the Microsoft crowd.

CLIMATE

Seattle's reputation for rain is somewhat undeserved. With 38 inches of precipitation a year, Seattle ranks behind many midwestern and eastern cities. However, when it comes to damp and cold, there aren't many places in the USA that can top Seattle. The city receives an average of only 55 days of unalloyed sunshine a year; the remaining 310 days see some form of fog, mist or cloud. This pervasive grayness can make the city's otherwise moderate temperatures – winter highs range between 40° and 50°F, and summer highs are between 75° and 85°F – seem bone-chilling.

The majority of rain falls in the winter, between November and April. Snow is unusual, but when it comes, it really piles up; everyone in Seattle has a story about the last big snowfall. Because of moderate temperatures and quirky weather patterns, snow rarely lasts more than a few hours on the ground.

Summer is very pleasant, though cool, and often lingers into the fall (this is known as 'Indian summer'). Marine clouds often blanket the Seattle area in the morning but burn off completely by afternoon. A light jacket is often necessary even in the height of summer. Spring and fall are best described as transitional with rain and sun alternating several times a day.

ORIENTATION

Washington's largest city sits on a slim isthmus between two bodies of water, the Puget Sound and Lake Washington. North of Seattle's downtown is Lake Union, another fresh-water lake; all these bodies of water are now linked by locks and canals. Although Seattle is a major Pacific seaport, the ocean is 125 miles away; look at a map and trace the long route that ships must sail from Seattle to the open seas.

Seattle is a very hilly city. In fact, the pioneer settlers liked the fact that their fledgling community, like Rome, was founded on seven hills. While the distinctions

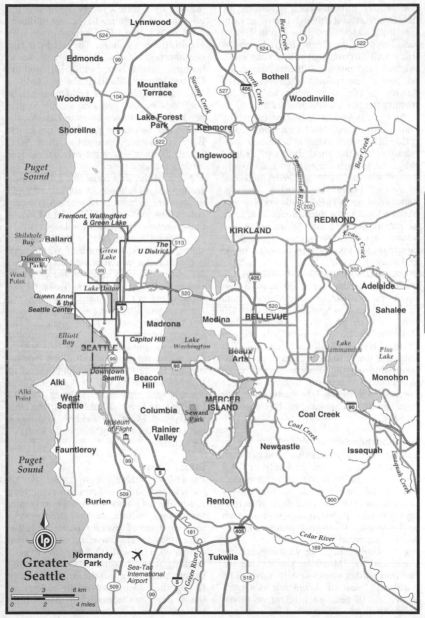

Greater
Seattle

0   3   6 km
0   2   4 miles

between the hills has been obfuscated by developments, and although one of the original hills was sluiced into Elliott Bay to make way for the Denny Regrade, pedestrians will discover that a lot of the city's original gradients are still here, especially on Queen Anne Hill and at the south end of downtown. (See if your Seattle hosts can identify the city's seven original hills.)

As the city proper is limited in size by water, most people and many businesses reside in the surrounding suburbs and communities. To the south is Kent, Federal Way, and Tacoma. East across Lake Washington are Bellevue and Kirkland and masses of brand new housing developments, and north is Edmonds and Everett. Many islands in the Puget Sound also serve as suburbs, particularly Bainbridge and Vashon Islands. Commuters from these communities take ferries between home and work in Seattle.

Interstate 5 runs north and south through the center of the city; I-90 joins it just south of downtown, crossing Mercer Island on its way east to Spokane. Highway 520 links downtown with Kirkland and Bellevue on the 2-mile-long Evergreen Point Floating Bridge. Interstate 405, known as the Eastside Freeway, cuts north-south through the suburbs east of Lake Washington. Vancouver, BC, is 141 miles north of Seattle on I-5; Portland is 172 miles south, and Spokane is 280 miles east on I-90.

Neighborhoods

Seattle is a very neighborhood-oriented city. Historically, this probably evolved because the hilly and difficult marine terrain around the city made it easier to stay close to home. Also, in the days when trolleys provided public transportation, each trolley stop tended to grow into a neighborhood commercial center.

Lake Union, the Lake Washington Ship Canal and the 'Montlake Cut' divide the city into northern and southern halves. Just north and west of downtown is Queen Anne, one of Seattle's original neighborhoods with two commercial hubs, one at

the top of Seattle's steepest hill and the other near the bottom. To the east of downtown rises Capitol Hill, synonymous with youthful urban culture. The old First Hill neighborhood is now largely given over to hospitals (and known as Pill Hill), and the Central District, Madison Valley, Madison Park, and Madrona are residential neighborhoods on the east side of the Seattle peninsula as it slopes down to Lake Washington. To the west of Seattle, across Elliott Bay, is another peninsula called West Seattle. This is where the original pioneer settlers founded the city.

North of the ship canal and Lake Union are the neighborhoods of Ballard (the old milltown), Fremont – now a hip counterculture hangout – and Wallingford. Each of these close-in neighborhoods has lively commercial centers filled with restaurants, shops, and bars. Just north of Wallingford is Green Lake, which is the hub of a large park area that also contains the city zoo. Just east of Wallingford, and flanking Lake Washington is the U District, home to the University of Washington.

There are four bridges (besides the freeway bridges) that cross the shipping canal, thus joining the city's two halves. The westernmost is the Ballard Bridge, linking Ballard and the neighborhood of Magnolia, west of Queen Anne; the Fremont Bridge crosses from Queen Anne to Fremont; and east of Lake Union, the University and Montlake Bridges both hook the U District to neighborhoods south of the canal.

Street Savvy

Because of Seattle's topographic stew of bays, islands, hills, and peninsulas, nothing as sensible as a standard street grid system fits the city. Instead, Seattle's street system is an amalgam of several separate grids that sometimes overlap, leading to maximum confusion. That said, it's fairly easy to get a working understanding of the numbering system and the way all the areas of the city fit together. Just don't try to understand the system intellectually; it makes little rational sense.

Jammed Up in the Emerald City

No discussion of getting around Seattle can avoid a mention of traffic; it can be heinous. According to an early 1990s study, Los Angeles was the only city in the US with worse traffic than Seattle. Unfortunately, unless you know the city intimately, there aren't many ways to avoid the congestion. With only two bridges across Lake Washington, you simply have to wait your turn. Also, because the Boeing shift changes begin at 2:30 pm, lunch is about the only time it's not rush hour somewhere in the city. If you have a choice, avoid traveling on freeways after 3 pm; chances are that traffic is at a standstill. Also, even when traffic is moving, heavy rains can make driving conditions nightmarish. Use caution and have patience. Seattle traffic will demand both. ■

Generally speaking, avenues run north and south, and streets run east and west. Yesler Way near Pioneer Square is the zero street for numbering addresses on streets; Western Way, near the Waterfront, is the zero street for addresses on downtown avenues. Generally, avenues have a directional suffix (6th Ave South), while streets have directional prefixes (South Charles St); however, downtown streets and avenues north of Yesler Way have no directional affixes.

Addresses with a West affix are in the Queen Anne and Magnolia neighborhoods, directly northwest of downtown. A swathe of streets cutting north from Lake Union, and taking in parts of the Fremont, Wallingford, and Green Lake neighborhoods take a simple North prefix (avenues with a North suffix, however, are north of downtown near the Seattle Center). Loosely speaking, streets and avenues with a North East affix are east of I-5 and north of Lake Union, an area that takes in the University of Washington. For maximum confusion, in much of this area both streets and avenues are

numbered. Remember, avenues run north and south, streets run east and west.

Streets and avenues with a North West affix are north of the shipping canal in and around Ballard. Addresses with a South West affix are in West Seattle, across Elliott Bay. Streets and avenues south of Yesler Way are labeled South. Up on Capitol Hill, watch for the East prefix on street names; these addresses suddenly begin numbering at Broadway, the 900 block.

Clearly, Seattle street addresses by themselves are confusing, and few people go to the trouble of figuring out how the system fits together. Instead, people use neighborhoods to indicate where things are found. For instance, '1st Ave on Queen Anne' distinguishes that 1st Ave from '1st Ave in Wallingford.'

Therefore, it's important to arrive at a working knowledge of Seattle's neighborhoods. With so many numbering systems at odds with each other, it's the only way to easily make sense of the city.

Downtown

Compared to the rest of the city, downtown orientation is pretty straightforward. The historic downtown area is called Pioneer Square and includes the area between Cherry and S King Sts, from 1st to 3rd Aves. The main shopping area of the city lies between 4th and 5th Aves, between Olive Way and University St. The Seattle Center, with many of Seattle's cultural and sport facilities as well as the Space Needle, is just northwest of downtown.

Unfortunately, city planners ran a freeway around the city (Hwy 99), dividing downtown from the Waterfront. Alaskan Way is the Waterfront's main drag; the Waterfront Streetcar runs the length of it.

INFORMATION
Tourist Office

The Visitor Information Center/Downtown Seattle (☎ 206-461-5840), 800 Convention Place, is at the Washington State Convention & Trade Center, built directly above I-5. You can enter this four-story structure either from Pike St or the Union St underpass.

Money

There are a number of options for exchanging money. Thomas Cook Foreign Exchange has an office downtown in the Westlake Center (☎ 206-623-6203, 800-877-9614) at 1601 5th Ave, suite 400, and in Bellevue (☎ 425-462-8225) at 10630 NE 8th Ave. The American Express office (☎ 206-441-8622) is at 600 Stewart St.

All branches of Seafirst, Wells Fargo and US banks can exchange foreign currency and traveler's checks; however, to buy foreign currency (except Canadian, which is usually available at most branches) and traveler's checks, you'll need to go to the main branches listed below. If you know someone with an account at one of the following branches, then exchanging the money through their account reduces the exchange fees slightly; also, Seafirst charges an additional $6 for exchanging money at its outlying branches; you can avoid paying it by going to the main branch (though your savings will probably be eaten up by parking charges).

In general, the main branches of the following banks offer international currency and business departments that can process transactions more quickly and efficiently than smaller branch offices. Also, if you plan on heading out into more rural areas in the Northwest, you may want to exchange your money in Seattle, for the same reasons.

Seafirst Bank, 701 5th Ave
   (☎ 206-358-7800)
Wells Fargo Bank, 999 3rd Ave
   (☎ 206-575-1200)
US Bank, 1420 5th Ave
   (☎ 206-344-3795)

At the Airport There are Thomas Cook booths throughout the airport where you can change money. The booth at the main terminal is open 6 am to 10 pm; in the north esplanade from 6 am to 8 pm; on the transit level from 8:45 am to 4:30 pm; and the booth on the concourse level is open11 am to 6 pm. Should your flight arrive after hours, you can get some cash from the credit card machines near the booths.

Post & Communications

Seattle's main post office is at 301 Union St, WA 98101. If you're staying near the university, go to University Station, 4244 NE University Way, WA 98105. On Capitol Hill, go to Broadway Station, 101 Broadway E, WA 98122.

Travel Agencies

Council Travel has two offices in Seattle. The one on Capitol Hill (☎ 206-329-4567) at 424 E Broadway is open 9 am to 5 pm weekdays, and 10 am to 2 pm Saturday for walk-ins only. The other office is in the University District (☎ 206-632-2448) at 4311 University Way NE, with the same hours.

Bookstores

Seattle is blessed with an abundance of bookstores. One of the best in the Northwest is the Elliott Bay Book Company (☎ 206-624-6600), 101 S Main St. This rambling bookstore has taken over most of the historic storefronts along a block of Pioneer Square. The interior, all exposed red brick and high ceilings, is absolutely stuffed full of new books and browsing customers. Downstairs is a popular cafe, and Elliott Bay is the local leader in author appearances, with writers appearing at readings or signings almost nightly. Check out the listings and ads in the *Seattle Weekly* or call for a current schedule.

Another vast all-purpose bookstore, the University Bookstore (☎ 206-634-3400), 4326 University Way NE, serves the university district. Just down the street is Bulldog News (☎ 206-634-3400), 4208 University Way NE, a great source for magazines, periodicals, and newspapers (including a good selection of foreign titles).

Travelers will want to make a pilgrimage to Wide World Books & Maps (☎ 206-634-3453) at 1911 N 45th Ave in Wallingford. In addition to a great selection of travel guides, this pleasant store offers travel gear. Downtown, the source for maps is Metsker Maps (☎ 206-623-8747), 702 1st Ave; they also carry a modest selection of travel guides.

On Capitol Hill, the best general bookstore is Bailey/Coy Books (☎ 206-323-8842), 414 Broadway E. Red & Black Books (☎ 206-322-7323), 432 15th Ave E, offers a great selection of books on gay, lesbian and feminist issues, and books with a multicultural focus. Beyond the Closet Bookstore (☎ 206-322-4609), 1501 Belmont Ave, is the city's gay-focused bookstore, and Marco Polo (☎ 206-860-3736) at 713 Broadway E is a new travel bookstore.

In the Queen Anne neighborhood, Tower Books (☎ 283-6333) at 20 Mercer St, is a solid general store with a focus on popular culture.

Check out the yellow pages to find a specialty store that focuses on your interests. Some of Seattle's great theme bookstores include The Seattle Mystery Bookstore (☎ 206-587-5737), 117 Cherry St, and Flora & Fauna Books (☎ 206-623-4727), 121 1st Ave S, both in Pioneer Square.

Media

Seattle's main newspapers are the morning *Seattle Post-Intelligence* (usually called the PI), and the afternoon *Seattle Times*. A good source for entertainment listings is 'The Ticket,' the *Seattle Times'* entertainment supplement distributed on Thursday.

Seattle also has a lively alternative publishing scene. The most interesting of the many papers that litter clubs and cafes is *The Stranger*, the closest thing there is to a weekly voice of Seattle's trendy counterculture. It's a valuable source for film and music information and is a great guide to the club scene; it also features weird local cartoons and the mandatory Savage Love column. The *Rocket* focuses on the music scene, and the *Seattle Gay News* covers the gay and lesbian beat.

The *Seattle Weekly* has full listings of arts and entertainment, and investigative pieces exposing city hall bad guys. Check their 'Cheap Thrills' section for free or inexpensive entertainment.

National Public Radio is heard on KUOW at 94.9 FM, and on KPLU at 88.5 FM. You can pick up the Canadian Broadcasting Corporation at 92.3 FM.

Childcare

If you need childcare while in Seattle, contact either Panda Dial-A-Sitter (☎ 206-325-2327) or Best Sitters (☎ 206-682-2556), both of whom can arrange for a licensed child-care professional to watch the kids at your hotel room. For the name of a licensed daycare facility with drop-in services in your area, contact Child Care Resources (☎ 206-461-3207), 2915 E Madison, suite 305, a city/private agency that does daycare referrals; there is sometimes a fee for their services.

Laundry

Sit & Spin (☎ 206-441-9484) at 2219 4th Ave in Belltown, is a cafe, art gallery, dance club *and laundry*, which leaves you no reason to do your laundry anywhere else. Check local club listings for current acts. On Capitol Hill, go to 12th Ave Laundry (☎ 206-328-4610), 1807 12th Ave. North of downtown is University Maytag Laundry (☎ 206-526-8992), 4733 University Way.

Medical Services

If your medical needs aren't grave, then one of the following walk-in clinics should be able to deal with most situations. The Downtown Clinic (☎ 206-682-3808) is at 509 Olive Way, suite 217, near the uptown (Seattle Center) end of the Monorail. The Virginia Mason Fourth Ave Clinic (☎ 206-223-6490) is at 1221 4th Ave. Both of these offices are open 8 am to 5 pm weekdays, and 9 am to noon Saturday.

For complete medical care, including an emergency room, go to Providence Medical Center (☎ 206-320-2111) at 500 17th Ave, or to Virginia Mason Hospital (☎ 206-624-1144), 925 Seneca St on First Hill.

DOWNTOWN

The area that most people associate with downtown Seattle encompasses the business district, Pike Place Market and Pioneer Square. Starting from the visitors' center in the Convention Center, the best way to see it all is to walk toward the water down either Pike or Pine Sts.

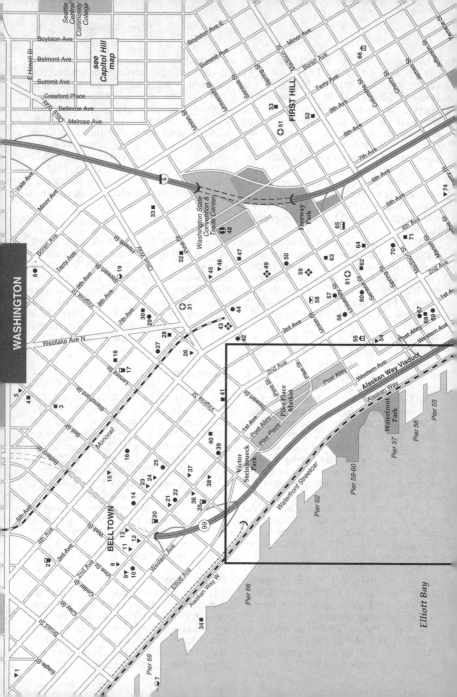

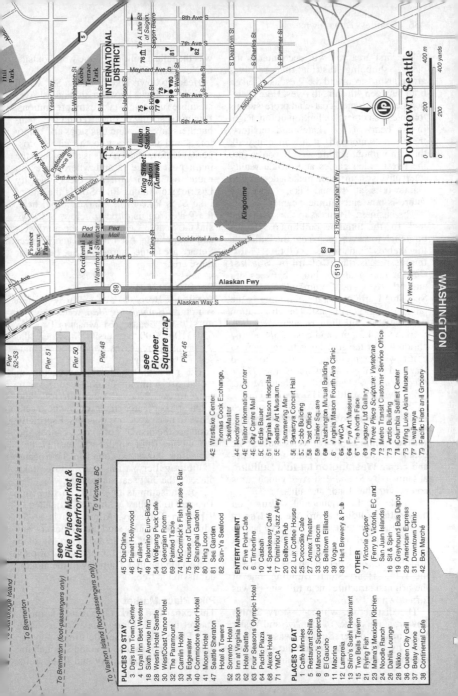

Downtown Seattle

WASHINGTON

INTERNATIONAL DISTRICT

To A Little Bit of Saigon, Saigon Bistro

Union Station

King Street Station (Amtrak)

Kingdome

see Pioneer Square map

see Pike Place Market & the Waterfront map

PLACES TO STAY
3 Days Inn Town Center
4 Loyal Inn Best Western
18 Sixth Avenue Inn
28 Westin Hotel Seattle
30 WestCoast Vance Hotel
32 The Paramount
33 Camlin Hotel
34 Edgewater
40 Commodore Motor Hotel
41 Moore Hotel
47 Seattle Sheraton Hotel & Towers
52 Sorrento Hotel
53 Inn at Virginia Mason
62 Hotel Seattle
63 Four Seasons Olympic Hotel
64 Pacific Plaza
68 Alexis Hotel
71 YMCA

PLACES TO EAT
1 Caffe Minnies
5 Restaurant Shilla
8 Marco's Supperclub
9 El Gaucho
11 Macrina
12 Lampreia
13 Shiro's Sushi Restaurant
15 Two Bells Tavern
21 Flying Fish
24 Mama's Mexican Kitchen
26 Noodle Ranch
28 Nikko
36 Queen City Grill
37 Betay Avone
38 Continental Cafe
45 ObaChine
46 Planet Hollywood
47 Fullers
49 Palomino Euro-Bistro
54 Wolfgang Puck Cafe
63 Georgian Room
69 Painted Table
74 McCormick's Fish House & Bar
75 House of Dumplings
78 Shanghai Garden
80 Hing Loon
81 See Garden
82 Sun-Ya Seafood

ENTERTAINMENT
2 Five Point Cafe
6 Timberline
10 Casbah
14 Speakeasy Café
17 Dimitriou's Jazz Alley
20 Belltown Pub
22 Lux Coffee House
25 Crocodile Cafe
27 Annex Theater
33 Cicud Rocm
35 Belltown Billiards
39 Vogue
83 Hart Brewery & Pub

OTHER
7 Victoria Clipper (Ferry to Victoria, EC and San Juan Islands)
16 Sit & Spin
19 Greyhound Bus Depot
29 American Express
31 Downtown Clinic
42 Bon Marché
43 Westlake Center
Thomas Cook Exchange, TicketMaster
44 Nordstrom
45 Visitor Information Center
48 City Centre Mall
5C Eddie Bauer
51 Virginia Mason Hospital
5E Hammering Mar
5E Benaroya Concert Hall
5i Cobb Building
5E Post Office
5S Rainier Square
60 Washington Mutual Building
6 Virginia Mason Fourth Ava Clinic
6S YWCA
6€ Frye Art Museum
6* The North Face
6S Legacy Ltd Gallery
70 Three Piece Sculpture: Vertebrae
72 Metro Transit Customer Service Office
73 Arctic Building
71 Columbia Seafirst Center
75 Wing Luke Asian Museum
77 Uwajimaya
79 Pacific Herb and Grocery

To Bainbridge Island
To Bremerton
To Vashon Island (foot-passengers only)
To Bremerton (foot-passengers only)
To Victoria, BC

Pier 52-53
Pier 51
Pier 50
Pier 48
Pier 46

Alaskan Fwy
Alaskan Way S

0   200   400 m
0   200   400 yards

The first area you will encounter is the classy shopping district that revolves around Nordstrom and the Westlake Center, both between 4th and 5th Aves. Here skateboarders and trench-coat-clad professionals tolerate each others' definition of fun. Right in the heart of the skateboard territory, there's a 'waterwall' that you can walk through without getting wet. If you're into the latest video games and virtual reality interactive systems, then make a detour into Gameworks, at 7th and Pike, a vast new future-is-now entertainment center.

The business district is to the south (just look for the looming buildings). There's not much to see there, except the buildings themselves and some sculpture. Most impressive is the **Columbia Seafirst Center** taking up the block between 4th and 5th Aves and Columbia and Cherry Sts. This Darth Vader of a building is the tallest on the West Coast. The observation deck on the 73rd floor is open weekdays 8:30 am to 4:30 pm and costs $5/4 adults/children. On the first level there's a food court with a plethora of fast food and frazzled bankers. Outside is the *Three Piece Sculpture: Vertebrae* by Henry Moore, a recipient of Seattle's '1% for art' clause. In the block around 5th Ave and Union St is the **Rainier Square Building**, a top-heavy structure that looks like a beaver started chipping away at its base. The beauty of the Seattle skyline is the blue-and-cream **Washington Mutual Building** at University St and 2nd Ave, which turns colors with the clouds and sunsets.

Check out the ornamental walruses on the **Arctic Building** at 3rd Ave and Cherry St, and the dour terra-cotta head of a Native American chief at the **Cobb Building** at University St and 4th Ave. Sixteen of these 800-lb heads once decorated the exterior of the White Henry-Stuart Building, one of the original structures near this site (it was torn down in 1976).

The distinctive, white 42-story **Smith Tower**, at the corner of 2nd Ave and Yesler Way near Pioneer Square, was built in 1914 by LC Smith, a man who made his fortune on typewriters. For many years, it was the tallest building in the world outside of New York City.

Heading down Pike or Union Sts, you'll notice the blocks between 3rd and 1st Aves are quite rundown – take extra precautions. Businesses move out frequently, panhandlers hover around bus stops and empty lots stand in contrast to the city's prosperity. Unfortunately, this is also where the main post office is and where buses en route to Capitol Hill and the University District stop (along Pike St). At the end of Pike St is Pike Place Market. From here, the Waterfront is directly below, Belltown and the Seattle Center are to the northwest and the Seattle Art Museum and Pioneer Square are to the southeast. (See below for these areas.)

Seattle Art Museum

Jonathan Borofsky's four-story action sculpture, *Hammering Man*, welcomes visitors to the Seattle Art Museum (☎ 206-654-3100), 100 University St, where the towering figure waves a mallet at the museum's front door.

The museum's collection, focusing on world art with an emphasis on Asian, African and Native American folk and tribal art, is greatly enhanced by the recent move to more spacious quarters. Especially good are the displays of masks, canoes and totem poles from Northwest Coastal tribes. Traveling shows are found in the Special Exhibits gallery; films and lectures take place in the 300-seat auditorium.

The museum is open 10 am to 5 pm Tuesday to Sunday, with hours extended to 9 pm on Thursday. Admission is $6/$4 adults/seniors and students. (Tickets are also good at the Seattle Asian Art Museum in Volunteer Park within one week of purchase.) On the first Thursday of the month, admission is free.

Pike Place Market

This expansive market began as a farmers' market in 1907. More than 90 years later, Pike Place is one of Seattle's most popular tourist attractions, and is noted as much for its exuberant theatricality and local crafts

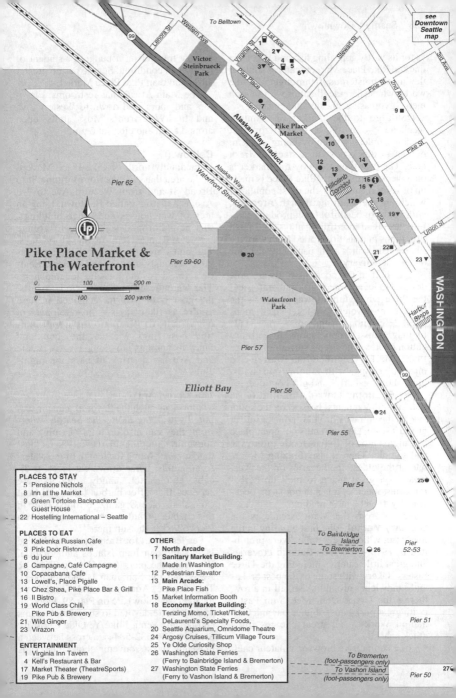

Pike Place Market & The Waterfront

To Belltown
To Bremerton
To Bainbridge Island
To Bremerton

99

1st Ave
Post Alley
2nd Ave
3rd Ave
Lenora St
Western Ave
Virginia St
Stewart St
Pike St
Post Alley
Union St

Victor Steinbrueck Park

Pike Place
Western Ave
Alaskan Way Viaduct
Alaskan Way
Waterfront Streetcar
Pike Place Market
Hillclimb Corridor

Pier 62
Pier 59-60
Waterfront Park
Pier 57
Pier 56
Pier 55
Pier 54
Pier 52-53
Pier 51
Pier 50

Elliott Bay

WASHINGTON
Harbor Steps

0   100   200 m
0   100   200 yards

To Bremerton
(foot-passengers only)
To Vashon Island
(foot-passengers only)

see
Downtown
Seattle
map

PLACES TO STAY
5 Pensione Nichols
8 Inn at the Market
9 Green Tortoise Backpackers'
   Guest House
22 Hostelling International – Seattle

PLACES TO EAT
2 Kaleenka Russian Cafe
3 Pink Door Ristorante
6 du jour
8 Campagne, Café Campagne
10 Copacabana Cafe
13 Lowell's, Place Pigalle
14 Chez Shea, Pike Place Bar & Grill
16 Il Bistro
19 World Class Chili,
   Pike Pub & Brewery
21 Wild Ginger
23 Virazon

ENTERTAINMENT
1 Virginia Inn Tavern
4 Kell's Restaurant & Bar
17 Market Theater (TheatreSports)
19 Pike Pub & Brewery

OTHER
7 North Arcade
11 Sanitary Market Building:
   Made In Washington
12 Pedestrian Elevator
13 Main Arcade:
   Pike Place Fish
15 Market Information Booth
18 Economy Market Building:
   Tenzing Momo, Ticket/Ticket,
   DeLaurenti's Specialty Foods,
20 Seattle Aquarium, Omnidome Theatre
24 Argosy Cruises, Tillicum Village Tours
25 Ye Olde Curiosity Shop
26 Washington State Ferries
   (Ferry to Bainbridge Island & Bremerton)
27 Washington State Ferries
   (Ferry to Vashon Island & Bremerton)

as for its vastly appealing fish and vegetable market. Pike Place Market features some of the most boisterous fishmongers in the world, whose dare-devil antics with salmon merge gymnastics, theater and cuisine.

Don't go to the market on summer weekends – or on a Friday for that matter – unless you enjoy being stuck in human gridlock next to a stack of fresh crab. The best time to enjoy the market is on a weekday morning. Pike Place is made up of several buildings, the most popular of which are the **Main** and **North Arcades**, with banks of beautiful fresh produce carefully arranged in artful displays, and fresh fish, crabs and shellfish piled high with ice (many fish stands will pack any fish for overnight delivery).

Over half of the open-air stalls are now devoted to locally made arts and crafts, and the three labyrinthine lower levels of the market are devoted to pocket-sized shops of all descriptions, from Indian spice stalls to magicians' supply shops to military button booths. The streets surrounding Pike Place Market continue the warren-like maze of shops, with ethnic food stalls, plant shops, galleries and gift boutiques.

The **Economy Market Building** (once a stable for merchants' horses) on the south side of the entrance has a wonderful Italian grocery store, De Laurenti's – a great place for aficionados of Italian foods to browse and sample. There's also Tenzing Momo, one of the oldest apothecaries on the West Coast – a great place to pick up herbal remedies, incense, oils and books or, occasionally, to get a tarot reading.

Across from the Main Arcade is the **Sanitary Market** – the first building in the market in which live animals were prohibited in 1910 – a maze of ethnic groceries and great little eateries including the Three Sisters Bakery with some of the best breads and sandwiches around. Also, all in a row, there's the Greek Deli, Mee Sum Pastry (with great pork buns), a juice bar and Cinnamon Works – all great choices for a quick snack.

For a compulsive browser, amateur chef, hungry traveler on a budget or student of the human condition, Seattle has no greater attraction than Pike Place Market.

The Main Arcade has restrooms. Elevators and stairs lead down to Western Ave and the Waterfront. Most stalls open around 8 am and close at 6 pm.

Belltown

Immediately north of Pike Place Market, in the area that reaches from Virginia St to Broad St and from Western Ave to 3rd Ave, is a district called Belltown. Long an area of warehouses and office buildings, this neighborhood was home to grunge music and musicians in the glory days. The clubs are still here, but the area has gone seriously upscale and some of Seattle's finest restaurants are located here. The warehouses are converting to lofts, designer boutiques have moved in, and you're as likely to see professionals in power suits as itinerant artists with multiple nose rings. Most of the shops and fancy restaurants are along 1st Ave, while 2nd Ave has a string of bars and nightclubs.

The Waterfront

Visitors can catch the flavor of a major seaport by walking along the Seattle waterfront; they can also do a lot of eating and souvenir shopping in the city's tackiest tourist zone. Along the length of the waterfront, amidst horse-drawn carriages, pedicabs and cotton candy vendors, are services that offer harbor tours and boat excursions (see Organized Tours, later in this chapter). Outdoor concerts are held on Piers 62/63 in the summer.

Ferries depart for Bremerton, Bainbridge Island, the San Juan Islands and Victoria, BC, from the piers (see Getting There & Away and the San Juan Islands chapter). The Seattle Aquarium and Omnidome theater (see below) are on Pier 59. Piers 54, 55 and 56 are devoted to shops, restaurants and novelty venues like Ye Olde Curiosity Shop (☎ 206-682-5844), a cross between a museum and a souvenir shop. Pier 57 is

WASHINGTON

now Waterfront Park, a small viewing area with benches.

The **Waterfront Streetcar** runs along Alaskan Way, the main thoroughfare along the waterfront. These little trolleys are especially handy for visitors, as they link the area near the Seattle Center (from the base of Broad St) to the Waterfront and Pike Place Market, going on to Pioneer Square and the International District. Tickets range between 85¢ and $1.10, and remain valid for an hour and a half.

While Hwy 99 in no way infringes upon getting from one place to the other, it is incredibly noisy and the parking areas under the freeway can be a bit scary at night. Luckily, savvy planners have created several walkways down to the water, the most recent of which are the Harbor Steps leading off from where University St ends at the Seattle Art Museum. In the middle of the steps is the rotating *Schubert's Sonata* sculpture by Mark di Suvero.

Seattle Aquarium This well-designed aquarium (☎ 206-386-4320, 206-386-4300), 1438 Alaskan Way, Pier 59, in Waterfront Park, offers a view into the underwater world of the Puget Sound and the northwestern Pacific Coast. Exhibits include re-creations of the many environments of bay and ocean, including tide pools, eelgrass beds, a coral reef and the sea floor. The centerpiece of the aquarium is a glass-domed room where – on the other side of the glass – sharks, octopi and other deep-water denizens lurk in the shadowy depths. Passages eventually lead outdoors to a salmon ladder, and to views over Elliott Bay and a pool where playful sea otters and seals await your attention.

The Seattle Aquarium is open 10 am to 7 pm daily from Memorial Day to Labor Day, and 10 am to 5 pm the rest of the year. Entrance is $7.50/6.75 for adults/seniors and disabled visitors, $5.00 for youths ages six to 18 and $1.90 for children ages three to five. Children under three are free. Combination tickets with the Omnidome theater are available; see below.

Omnidome Film Experience Adjacent to the aquarium is this 180° surround-screen movie theater (☎ 206-622-1868) on Pier 59. There are usually two shows available; the ongoing favorite is *The Eruption of Mt St Helens*, which features a helicopter ride over an exploding volcano (the film received an Academy Award nomination). Most features are 45 minutes long and begin showing at 10 am daily; call for show times. Tickets for one show are $6.95/5.95 adults/seniors and youths (six to 18), and $4.95 for children (ages three to 5). Children under three are free.

A combination ticket to the aquarium and to the Omnidome Film Experience is available at $13/11.25 adults/seniors; $9.50 for youths to 18, and $5.50 preschool to five.

Frye Art Museum
This small museum (☎ 206-622-9250), at 704 Terry Ave on First Hill, preserves the collection of Charles and Emma Frye. The Fryes collected over 1000 paintings, mostly 19th and early-20th-century European and American pieces, and a few Alaskan and Russian artworks. The museum is open 10 am to 5 pm Monday to Saturday, and noon to 5 pm Sunday. Admission is free.

Pioneer Square
The birthplace of Seattle, this red-brick district of historic buildings and totem pole-lined plazas is still a real crossroads of the modern city. For years this area was in decline until cheap rents and status on the National Register of Historic Places brought in what are now considered some of the city's best art galleries and antique shops. A number of restaurants also play up the frontier image while serving some of the city's best food.

Pioneer Square is most easily reached by foot or by bus (it's in the ride-free zone). For something more touristy-historic, take the Waterfront Streetcar which will put you smack dab in the heart of the square.

Walking from Pike Place Market, take either Alaskan Way along the Waterfront,

WASHINGTON

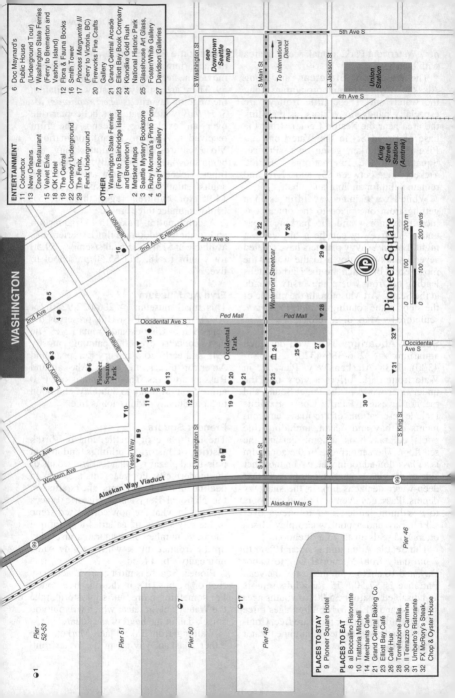

WASHINGTON

Pioneer Square

ENTERTAINMENT
11 Colourbox
13 New Orleans
    Creole Restaurant
15 Velvet Elvis
18 OK Hotel
19 The Central
22 Comedy Underground
29 The Fenix,
    Fenix Underground

OTHER
1 Washington State Ferries
  (Ferry to Bainbridge Island
  and Bremerton)
2 Metsker Maps
3 Seattle Mystery Bookstore
4 Ruby Montana's Pinto Pony
5 Greg Kucera Gallery

6 Doc Maynard's
  Public House
  (Underground Tour)
7 Washington State Ferries
  (Ferry to Bremerton and
  Vashon Island)
12 Flora & Fauna Books
16 Smith Tower
17 *Princess Marguerite III*
   (Ferry to Victoria, BC)
20 Fireworks Fine Crafts
   Gallery
21 Grand Central Arcade
23 Elliott Bay Book Company
24 Klondike Gold Rush
   National Historic Park
25 Glasshouse Art Glass,
   Foster/White Gallery
27 Davidson Galleries

PLACES TO STAY
9 Pioneer Square Hotel

PLACES TO EAT
8 al Boccalino Ristorante
10 Trattoria Mitchelli
14 Merchants Cafe
21 Grand Central Baking Co
23 Elliott Bay Café
26 Cafe Hue
28 Torrefazione Italia
30 Il Terrazzo Carmine
31 Umberto's Ristorante
32 FX McRory's Steak,
   Chop & Oyster House

or 1st Ave to pass by the art museum's *Hammering Man* and some unusual shops. The Pioneer Square area is bounded roughly by Cherry and S King Sts, 1st and 3rd Aves.

Right at the corner of Cherry St and 1st Ave you'll come to the original **Pioneer Square Park** – a cobblestoned triangular plaza with a totem pole and pergola. The original totem pole, so the story goes, was stolen from the Tlingit Indians in 1890 but subsequently burned down. When asked if they would carve another one, the Tlingit took the money offered, thanked the city for payment of the first totem pole, and waited for a better offer to carve the one now standing.

The pergola may look decorative, but its original purpose was to cover an underground lavatory and to protect people waiting for the cable car that went up and down Yesler Way. (Unfortunately, some homeless people and weekend partiers seem to be turning the area back into a lavatory.) Incidentally, Yesler Way was originally called Skid Road – logs would 'skid' down the road linking a logging area above town to Henry Yesler's mill on a pier. With the decline of the area, the street became a haven for homeless people. Soon the nickname 'Skid Row' was being used for equally destitute areas around the country.

Just south of Pioneer Square on Occidental Ave S, **Occidental Park** has a few more totem poles, all carved by Duane Pasco, a nationally respected Chinookan carver and artist from Poulsbo, on the Kitsap Peninsula. They depict the welcoming spirit of Kwakiutl, a totem bear, the tall Sun and Raven, and a man riding on the tail of a whale.

The **Grand Central Arcade**, with entrances from the park and 1st Ave S, has a good bakery cafe, plenty of tables, a cozy fire and an underground shopping arcade.

Between Main and Jackson Sts, the park turns into a tree-lined 'mall' full of galleries, some sculpture art and Torrefazione Italia, where you can drink one of Seattle's best lattes in a real ceramic Italian *tazza*.

The Great Fire

In Seattle's early days, the Pioneer Square area was a thrown-together village of wooden storefronts, log homes and lumber mills. Tide water lapped along 1st Ave, and many of the buildings and the boardwalks that led to them were raised up on stilts. No part of the original downtown was more than 4 feet above the bay at high tide, and the streets were frequently a quagmire.

When the Great Seattle Fire struck in 1889, the boardwalks throughout this district provided an unstoppable conduit for the flames, and most of the original town burned. What might have seemed a catastrophe was in fact a blessing, as the city rebuilt immediately with handsome structures of brick, steel and stone. This time, however, the streets were regraded, and ravines and inlets filled in. This raised the new city about a dozen feet above the old city; in some areas the regrading simply built over older ground-level buildings and streets. These are the catacombs explored in the famous Seattle Underground Tour (see Organized Tours, later in this chapter).

The rapid rebuilding of the Pioneer Square area also endowed the district with a rare architectural homogeneity. Most of the buildings around present-day Pioneer Square were built between 1890 and 1905. One architect, Elmer Fisher, was responsible for the plans of 50 buildings erected immediately after the fire. ■

Just south of Pioneer Square is the Kingdome, slated to be torn down to build two new, contentious sports stadiums for the city's football and baseball franchises.

Klondike Gold Rush Park Seattle's seminal position as the outfitting and transportation hub for the 1897 Alaskan and Yukon gold rush is recognized at this small national historical park/museum (☎ 206-553-7220), 117 S Main St. Exhibits document the abundance of gear and food necessary to stake a claim in the Klondike, which brought a boom to Seattle merchants. Park rangers demonstrate gold panning and there's a slide presentation about the gold rush. Admission is free and hours are 9 am to 5 pm daily.

INTERNATIONAL DISTRICT

Southeast of Pioneer Square is the International District, Seattle's Chinatown, where Asian groceries and restaurants line the streets. Chinese were among the first settlers in Seattle, and have been followed by Japanese, Filipinos, Vietnamese, Laotians and others.

The main center of the district is between 5th and 7th Aves and Weller and Jackson Sts. The best way to get there from Pioneer Square is to walk up Jackson St. You'll pass the outwardly handsome **King Street Station**, the old Italianate Great Northern Railroad depot, its stately brick tower long an integral (though now dwarfed) piece of the downtown skyline. It's presently in use as the Amtrak station. Go along Jackson St to 6th Ave and turn right to get to the heart of the small district.

Weller St is a good street to get a glimpse of it all. In addition to the many restaurants, there is Pacific Herb & Grocery (☎ 206-340-6411) at 610 S Weller St between 6th and Maynard Aves. The herbal medicine specialists there can tell you all about the uses of different roots, bones, flowers and teas. Right next door is a tofu shop where you can watch tofu being made and also buy some very cheaply. At about 7th Ave the district fizzles out for a few blocks then picks up at 10th Ave and continues uphill to 12th Ave with a hodgepodge of small malls and parking lots. This area has more Vietnamese influence than the area below it.

In case you've forgotten you're on the Pacific Rim, head to Uwajimaya (☎ 206-624-6248), 519 6th Ave S, the supermarket of the International District. At this large Asian department and grocery store – a cornerstone of Seattle's Asian community – you'll find exotic fruits and vegetables and cooking utensils, and come face to face with those dim sum ingredients you've always wondered about. It's a great place to browse.

Wing Luke Asian Museum

This pan-Asian museum (☎ 206-623-5124), 407 7th Ave S, is devoted solely to Asian and Pacific-American culture, history and art. Named after the first Asian elected official in Seattle, the museum examines the often difficult and violent meeting of Asian and Western cultures in Seattle. Particularly good are the photos and displays on the Chinese settlement in the 1880s and the retelling of Japanese internment during WWII. The museum is self-guided and open 11 am to 4:30 pm Tuesday to Friday, and noon to 4 pm weekends. Admission is $2.50/1.50 for adults/seniors and students, and 75¢ for children ages five to 12.

SEATTLE CENTER

In 1962, Seattle was confident and ready for company. The spirit of the city was perfectly captured in the 1962 World's Fair; Seattle, the home of high-tech jumbo jets, saw itself as the city of the future.

The World's Fair, also known as 'Century 21 Exposition,' was a summer-long exhibition that brought in nearly 10 million visitors from around the world to view the future, Seattle-style. A warehouse area north of downtown was leveled, and a futuristic international enclave of exhibition halls, arenas and public spaces sprang up. Never mind that today the Seattle Center, as we now term the World's Fair grounds, generates more nostalgia for the Jetsons than thoughts of the future.

Probably no other building in Seattle epitomizes the city as well as the Space Needle, the 605-foot-high futuristic observation station and restaurant. The Monorail, a 1½-mile experiment in mass transit, was another signature piece of the 1962 fair. The Flag Pavilion & Plaza and the International Fountain (with jets of water that pulse to the beat of music) point to the cosmopolitan sympathies of the fair. These landmarks have lived on: the Seattle Opera House

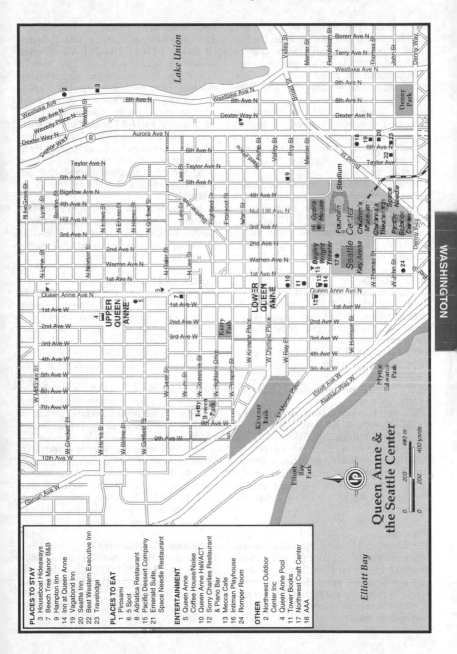

WASHINGTON

Queen Anne & the Seattle Center

PLACES TO STAY
3 Houseboat Hideaways
7 Beech Tree Manor B&B
9 Hampton Inn
14 Inn at Queen Anne
19 Vagabond Inn
20 Seattle Inn
22 Best Western Executive Inn
23 Travelodge

PLACES TO EAT
1 Pirosami
6 5 Spot
8 Adriatica Restaurant
15 Pacific Dessert Company
21 Emerald Suite,
    Space Needle Restaurant

ENTERTAINMENT
5 Queen Anne
   Coffee House/Noise
10 Queen Anne Hall/ACT
12 Sorry Charlies Restaurant
    & Piano Bar
13 Mecca Cafe
16 Intiman Playhouse
24 Romper Room

OTHER
2 Northwest Outdoor
   Center Inc
4 Queen Anne Pool
11 Tower Books
17 Northwest Craft Center
18 AAA

(home of the opera, symphony and ballet), two playhouses, two sports arenas, the Fun Forest Amusement Park (with carnival rides) and various museums and art spaces.

For information about the Seattle Center complex, call ☎ 206-684-8582, 206-684-7200; it's between Denny Way and Mercer St, and 1st and 5th Aves N. A number of fast-food venues, as well as bathrooms and other public facilities, are located in Center House near the Monorail terminal. No admission is charged to enter the complex.

Parking can be tight around the Seattle Center when more than one large event takes place. There are parking lots on Mercer St, between 3rd and 4th Aves N. There's easy access to the Waterfront Trolley at Broad St and Western Ave, if you want to continue the walking tour of downtown.

Space Needle

Seattle's signature monument, the Space Needle (☎ 206-443-2111), 219 4th Ave N, takes advantage of its 520-foot-high observation deck with 360° views of Seattle and surrounding areas to bombard visitors with historical information and interpretive displays. To zip to the top on the elevators (it takes 41 seconds) commands a charge of $8.50/7/5 adults/seniors/children ages five to 12.

Way back in 1962, the Space Needle surfed the wave of the future with its two revolving restaurants (☎ 206-443-2111); the Emerald Suite is much more expensive than the Space Needle Restaurant, though patrons at either one receive free passage on the elevators. There's also a lounge at the top, but there's no free passage for mere drinks.

Monorail

The futuristic Monorail provides fun and frequent transport between downtown's Westlake Center, at Pine St and 5th Ave, and the Seattle Center. Cars run about every 10 minutes, and tickets are $1/75¢/50¢ adults/children/seniors. The trip takes only two minutes.

Pacific Science Center

This museum of science and industry (☎ 206-443-2001), 200 2nd Ave N, once housed the science pavilion of the World's Fair. Today, the center offers virtual reality exhibits, laser shows, holograms, hands-on demonstrations and other wonders of science. Also on the premises is the vaulted-screen **IMAX Theater** and a planetarium. The Pacific Science Center is open 10 am to 5 pm weekdays, and 10 am to 6 pm weekends. Admission to the exhibit space is $7.50/5.50 adults/seniors and children ages six to 13, and $3.50 for children ages two to five.

Admission to the IMAX Theater and Laserium, a 'laser theater,' is $3 on top of the general admission price, or $3 per seat for the laser show only. An IMAX Theater-only ticket is $5.50 per person.

Children's Museum

This learning center (☎ 206-441-1768) in the basement of Center House offers a number of imaginative activities and displays, many focusing on cross-cultural awareness and hands-on art sessions. The play area includes a child-sized neighborhood, a play center and an area dedicated to blowing soap bubbles. The Children's Museum is open 10 am to 5 pm Tuesday to Sunday. During summer break, the museum is also open Monday. Admission is $5.50/4 adults/children; infants under one year are free.

Also for kids is the **Seattle Children's Theater** in the Charlotte Martin Theater. Call ☎ 206-443-0807 for performance information. The **Pacific Arts Center** (☎ 206-443-5437), in the same building, offers children's art classes and exhibits designed for young audiences.

Northwest Craft Center

Flanking the International Fountain, this gallery (☎ 206-728-1555) is mostly dedicated to ceramics by regional craftspeople. Exhibits change monthly; there's also a gift shop carrying other handmade crafts from the area.

QUEEN ANNE

Rising above the Seattle Center is Queen Anne Hill – a neighborhood of majestic red-brick houses and apartment buildings, sweeping lawns manicured to perfection and gorgeous views of the city and bay. There are two hubs along Queen Anne Ave – one at the base of the hill, the other at the top. Like all Seattle neighborhoods, there's a full array of cafes, trendy music clubs and shops.

The main reason to visit Queen Anne, however, is to check out the view. A **scenic overlook** in Kerry Park at 3rd Ave N and W Highland Drive is the best spot for it, especially at night or sunset.

From downtown take 1st Ave, which will turn into Queen Anne Ave N. Highland Drive can be accessed from here. Along W Olympic Place there's Kinnear Park, a nice expanse of grass and trees where people and dogs stroll along.

Bus Nos 2 and 13 go near the vista point; bus Nos 1, 3 and 4 also go up to Queen Anne. Bus No 1 travels on the west side of the hill, Nos 3 and 4 go up Taylor St on the east side.

CAPITOL HILL

Unlike other parts of the city, it's the throngs of people along the streets and not the buildings that really sets Capitol Hill apart from the other neighborhoods. Long a counterculture oasis, there are probably more nose rings and goatees on Capitol Hill than anywhere else in the Northwest. Also the principal gay and lesbian neighborhood in Seattle, the area has an unmatched vitality and creativity.

If you take bus Nos 7 or 10 from downtown, get off at **Broadway** – the main strip. Brass-inlaid dance steps along Broadway propel you into a rumba or a tango (actually, it's public art), but you'll never see a local learning the steps. And that's about as aesthetic as this street gets. East John St (the continuation of Olive Way) is the main corner of activity. Marked by a bubble machine outside, Twice Sold Tales (☎ 206-324-2421) at 905 E John St is

a rambling used-book store that stays open very late. Head north on Broadway to peruse the multitudes of shops.

Between E Harrison and E Republican Sts is the Broadway Market with two stories of shops, eateries and a cinema featuring some of the better Hollywood flicks. Across the street, Dilettante Chocolates (☎ 206-329-6463), 416 Broadway E, decked in pink and umbrellas, is well known for truffles and 'adult' milkshakes. A block past that, Pacific Dessert Co is another place for sugar and caffeine highs. The Broadway strip ends at E Roy St and the atmosphere turns to well-maintained houses with manicured lawns. Continue down Broadway until it turns into 10th Ave E and you'll be right by Volunteer Park (see below). Near the corner of 10th Ave E and Galer St is **St Marks Cathedral** (☎ 206-720-0217), where a chorus performs Gregorian chants (compline) on Sunday nights at 9:30 pm.

Seven blocks east of Broadway is **15th Ave E**, another strip, although much more tame than the former. The blocks between Thomas and Mercer hold the most interest, with bookstores, wine shops, bakeries and restaurants back to back.

At the south end of Broadway is the hip **Pike/Pine Corridor** which extends from 12th Ave to about 9th Ave (back near the convention center). Long considered the city's gay-bar district, the nightlife hot spot has diversified to include all-night coffeehouses, live-music clubs and rowdy, smoke-filled bars. If you're looking for late-night action, this is one of Seattle's most lively scenes.

If you're driving, your best bet is to park in the pay lot behind the Broadway Market west of Broadway on E Harrison St. Otherwise, you'll find the parking, crowds, and traffic on Capitol Hill very frustrating.

Volunteer Park

This stately 140-acre park above downtown Seattle on Capitol Hill began as pioneer Seattle's cemetery. However, as the city grew and the need for water became

WASHINGTON

WASHINGTON

to The
U District map

Interlaken
Park

Lakeview
Cemetery

Volunteer
Park

Reservoir

Lake
Union

see
Queen Anne &
the Seattle
Center map

PLACES TO STAY
3 B&B At Mildred's
6 Bacon Mansion B&B,
   Broadway Guesthouse
7 Salisbury House B&B
15 Vincent's Backpackers
   Guesthouse
31 American Backpackers
   Hostel
33 Hill House B&B
37 Gaslight Inn B&B

PLACES TO EAT
8 Surrogate Hostess
13 Siam on Broadway
14 Kitto Noodle House
16 Pacific Dessert Co

19th Ave E
18th Ave E
17th Ave E
16th Ave E
15th Ave E
14th Ave E
13th Ave E
12th Ave E
11th Ave E
10th Ave E

E Ward St
E Valley St
E Roy St
E Mercer St
E Republican St
E Aloha St
E Prospect St
E Highland Drive
E Galer St
Grandview Place E
Galer St

Malden Ave E
Federal Ave E
Broadway E
Harvard Ave E
Harvard Ave E
Boylston Ave E
Belmont Place E
Belmont Ave E
Summit Ave E
Bellevue Ct Place
Bellevue Pl E
Lakeview Blvd E
Eastlake Ave E
Fairview Ave E
Fairview Ave N
Franklin Ave E
E Garfield St

Aloha St
Valley St

Tashkent
Park

23	Broadway New
	American Grill
27	El Greco
29	Café Septieme

ENTERTAINMENT
5 Cucinal Cucinal
9 Cornish College
  of the Arts
11 The Harvard Exit
12 Deluxe Bar & Grill
17 Broadway Market
  Cinemas
24 Ileen's Sports Bar
  (formerly Ernie Steele's)
26 B&O Espresso
34 RKCNDY
38 Re-Bar
39 Puss-Puss Cafe
40 The Egyptian
41 Odd Fellows Hall
42 New City Theatre
43 Safari
44 Globe Cafe
45 Six Arms Pub
  & Brewery
47 Rosebud Espresso
48 Neighbours
49 The Easy
50 The Comet
51 Cafe Paradiso
52 Wildrose

OTHER
1 St Mark's Cathedral
2 Volunteer Park
  Conservatory
4 Seattle Asian
  Art Museum
10 Marco Polo
17 Broadway Market:
  Ticket/Ticket
18 Council Travel
19 Dilettante Chocolates
21 Red & Black Books
22 Bailey/Coy Books
25 REI
28 Pink Zone
30 Post Office
32 Twice Sold Tales
35 Central Co-op
36 12th Ave Laundry
46 Beyond the Closet
  Books
53 Donald Young Gallery

Capitol Hill

WASHINGTON

see
Downtown
Seattle map

more pressing (particularly after the Great Seattle Fire), Volunteer Park, with its water tower and reservoir, was created.

Roads and paths wind around the park, with manicured meadow-like lawns descending to the mansion-rich neighborhoods that flank the area. Because the park has existed in one form or another since 1876, the trees and landscaping here reflect a kind of maximum growth of the Seattle urban ecosystem. Keen seekers of views can climb the 75-foot 1907 watertower for wonderful vistas over the Space Needle and Elliott Bay. At night, the park is a popular gay pick-up spot.

The **Seattle Asian Art Museum** (☎ 206-654-3100) has re-opened in Volunteer Park and houses the extensive Asian art collection of Dr Richard Fuller, who donated this severe art moderne-style gallery to the city in 1932. The Asian Art Museum is administered by the Seattle Art Museum downtown, and tickets are good for both institutions if used within a week. Hours are 10 am to 5 pm Tuesday to Sunday, except on Thursday, when the museum stays open till 9 pm. Admission is $6/4 adults/seniors and students, and children under 12 are free.

The park is also home to the **Volunteer Park Conservatory**, a classic Victorian greenhouse built in 1910, that features five galleries filled with palms, cacti and tropical plants. The conservatory is free to the public.

To reach Volunteer Park, follow 15th Ave E to E Galer St, and turn west.

FREMONT

Unlike the flashy, urban disenfranchisement that gives Capitol Hill its spirit, life here is conducted with more humor and sense of community well-being. For the visitor, this neighborhood makes a nice change from the hectic pace of the city center. In the evenings, pubs, restaurants and coffeehouses fill with a lively mix of old hippies, young professionals and gregarious students from nearby University of Washington. If you're in a buying mood, shop the kitschy second-hand shops for that couch, mannequin or retro

sundress. A brewpub, several busy ethnic restaurants and a coffeehouse with a dramatic clientele keeps Fremont hopping until late in the evenings.

Fremont is located where Lake Union pours into the shipping canal. Probably the most fun-loving of the northern neighborhoods, Fremont is known for its unorthodox public sculpture, junk stores, summer outdoor film festivals and general high spirits.

Probably the most discussed piece of public art in the city, *Waiting for the Interurban* is a cast aluminum statue of ordinary people (whom locals like to dress up for seasonal events and occasions such as Christmas, a Huskies game, someone's birthday, etc) waiting for a commuter bus; the *Fremont Troll* (a mammoth cement figure consuming a whole VW bug carcass) lives under the Aurora Bridge; and a slightly zany-looking rocket that the community has adopted as its totem stands in the main business district. The latest addition to Fremont's public art is a statue of Lenin that made its way here from the former Soviet Union.

In summer, films are shown on the side of a Fremont-center building; filmgoers are encouraged to bring their own chairs and couches to set up in the parking lot. This **Fremont Almost-Free Outdoor Cinema** (☎ 206-632-0287) is held every Saturday night beginning in June and runs into September. A $5 donation is requested to help pay for the cinema and support charities. Films are shown in the U-Park parking lot behind the Red Door Ale House (35th St and Fremont Place).

In the same lot the **Fremont Sunday Market** runs from 10 am to 5 pm throughout summer and features an incredible variety of artists as well as people getting rid of junk. Call ☎ 206-282-5706 for information.

To get to Fremont from downtown, take Westlake Blvd north along Lake Union, and follow signs for the Fremont Bridge. The main strip, Fremont Ave N, is the focal point of the shops, pubs and restaurants. Bus Nos 6, 16, 26 and 28 go to Fremont.

WALLINGFORD

Wallingford has blossomed from an old working-class neighborhood into a pleasant district of interesting shops, bookstores and inexpensive eateries, all just across the freeway from the university. The main shopping area focuses on the old Wallingford school, at Wallingford and N 45 Sts, which has been remodeled into a boutique and restaurant mall. Just down the street are a couple of art and foreign-film cinemas, amid a clutch of ethnic restaurants.

The main hub is along N 45th St approximately between Stone Way and Corliss Ave. There's an incredible mix of stores – including the locally known Erotic Bakery (☎ 206-545-6969) 2323 N 45th St, where phallus-shaped desserts are made to order – and an amazing assortment of comic book stores (quite the rage in Seattle). Teahouse Kuan Yin is a great stop for a pot of exotic tea (see Coffeehouses and Teahouses under Entertainment), and Herbal Altar-Natives (☎ 206-545-2915) 1612 N 45th St, suite 1A, is an extremely weird head shop/gift boutique/coffeehouse/homeopathic center with free t'ai chi lessons, hemp products, 'psychic tea' and a 'vegan spiritual pasta line' (huh?).

To reach Wallingford from downtown, take I-5 north, exit at 45th St and turn west. Bus Nos 6, 16 and 26 go to Wallingford from downtown.

Gas Works Park

Urban reclamation has no greater monument in Seattle than Gas Works Park. On a grassy point on the north end of Lake Union, this factory produced heating and lighting gas from 1906 till 1956. The gas works was thereafter understandably considered an eyesore and environmental menace. Nonetheless, the beautiful location of the park – with its stellar views of downtown Seattle over Lake Union, and of sailboats and yachts to-ing and fro-ing from the shipping canal – induced the city government to convert the former industrial site into a public park in 1975.

Rather than tear down the factory, however, landscape architects preserved much of the old plant which is now painted black and highlighted with rather joyful graffiti. Gas Works Park is one of Seattle's best-loved parks; people come here to fly kites, picnic near the lake and simply take in the view. Be sure to climb the small hill to see the clever sundial.

Gas Works Park is at the southern end of Meridian Ave N at N Northlake Way. From downtown, take Bus No 26.

GREEN LAKE

Just north of Wallingford are a cluster of neighborhoods flanking the east shore of Green Lake. If you need to get away from the crowds along the lakefront, the requisite coffee shops and cheap restaurants in the old town (along Ravenna Blvd) make a good getaway. East a few blocks, near NE 65th St and Roosevelt Way NE, are a cluster of New Age bookstores and crystal shops.

Woodland & Green Lake Parks

This large park complex contains Seattle's highly acclaimed zoo, the civic rose gardens and Green Lake, a favorite with sunbathers, swimmers and windsurfers in summer. (Swimmers should note, however, that the lake's green color is due to algae blooms which can cause an unpleasant condition called 'swimmer's itch.') The paths that line the lake are very popular with joggers and bikers.

The **Woodland Park Zoo** (☎ 206-684-4800), 5500 Phinney Ave N, is rated one of the top zoos in the country. The Seattle zoo was one of the first in the country to free animals from their restrictive cages in favor of ecosystem enclosures, where animals from similar environments share large spaces that seek to replicate their natural surroundings. Feature exhibits include a tropical rain forest, two gorilla exhibits, an Asian elephant forest and an African savanna. It's open 9:30 am to dusk daily (roughly 6 pm from March 15 to October 14, or 4 pm at other times of the year). The cost is $8/7.25 adults/seniors, $5.50 for youth ages six to 17 and $3.25 for children ages three to five. Parking is an additional

WASHINGTON

WASHINGTON

see The
U District
map

Green Lake

Green Lake Park

GREEN LAKE

Woodland Park

PLACES TO EAT
8 Bizzarro
10 India Cuisine
11 Julia's
14 Jitterbug Cafe
15 My Brother's Pizza
16 Boulangerie
19 Taco del Mar
20 Triangle Lounge
21 El Camino
22 Longshoreman's Daughter
24 Still Life Cafe
25 Pontevecchio

ENTERTAINMENT
1 Bathhouse
   Theatre Company
4 The Latona
13 Teahouse Kuan Yin
18 Trolleyman Pub
20 Triangle Lounge

OTHER
2 Green Lake Boat Rental
3 Gregg's Greenlake Cycle
5 Green Lake
   Small Craft Center
6 Woodland Park Zoo
7 Seattle Rose Garden
9 Herbal Altar-Natives
12 Wallingford Center
13 Wide World Books
17 Erotic Bakery
23 Fremont Sunday Market,
   Outdoor Cinema
26 Waiting for the
   Interurban
27 Fremont Troll
28 Sailboat Rentals &
   Yacht Charters Inc

Fremont, Wallingford & Green Lake

WALLINGFORD

WASHINGTON

FREMONT

see Queen Anne & the Seattle Center map

8th Ave NE
7th Ave NE
5th Ave NE
4th Ave NE
Latona Ave NE
Thackery Place NE
2nd Ave NE
1st Ave NE

Eastern Ave N
Sunnyside Ave N
Corliss Ave N

Burke Ave N

Wallingford Ave N

Densmore Ave N

Woodlawn Ave N

Interlake Ave N

Midvale N
Woodland Park Ave N
Whitman Ave N
Winslow Place N
Aurora Ave N

Linden Ave N

Fremont Ave N
Evanston Ave N
Dayton Ave N
Francis Ave N
Phinney Ave N
Greenwood Ave N
Palatine Ave
1st Ave NW
2nd Ave NW
Baker Ave NW
3rd Ave NW

Bagley Ave N
Meridian Ave N

Densmore Ave N
Woodlawn Ave N

Greenlake Way
E Midvale Place

University Bridge
Furham Ave E
Franklin Ave E
E Allison St
E Gwinn Place
E Shelby St
E Hamlin St
E Edgar St   Roanoke
E Roanoke St   Park
E Miller St

Harvard Ave E
Boylston Ave E
Franklin Ave E

Yale Ter E   Yale
Ave E
E Edgar St

Minor Ave E

Fairview Ave E

Lake Washington Ship Canal Bridge

N Pacific St

Burke-Gilman Trail

Lake Union

Gas Works Park

N Northlake Way

Carr Place N
Ashworth Ave N
Interlake Ave N
Stone Way N

Woodland Park Ave N
Albion Place N

Aurora Bridge (George Washington Memorial Bridge)

Fremont Way N
N Northlake Way
Fremont Bridge

Wasatch Ave
Dexter Way N

4th Ave N
3rd Ave N
Mayfair Ave N
2nd Ave N
Warren Ave N
1st Ave N

Queen Anne Ave N

Fulton St
Aloha St

Newell St
Queen Anne Ave N

2nd Ave W

Rodgers Park
W Raye St

3rd Ave W
4th Ave W
5th Ave W

Seattle Pacific University

W Nickerson St

W Cremona St
W Dravus St
W Etruria St
W Florentia St

Queen Anne Ave N
3rd Ave W

Mt Pleasant Cemetery

W Dravus St

W Pleasant Place
W Smith St

W Barrett St
W Fulton St
W Armour St
W Newell St

Conkling Place

9th Ave W

Fremont Canal Park

N Canal St
W Ewing St

Lake Washington Ship Canal

NW Ewing St

Leary Way NW

NW Fern Pl

NW 41st St
9th Ave NW

NW 47th St
NW 46th St
NW 45th St
NW 44th St
NW Bright St

NW 41st St
NW 40th St
NW 39th St

NW Bowdoin Place

N 36th St
N 35th St
N 34th St

Fremont Place N

Phinney Ave N
Francis Ave N
Dayton Ave N
Evanston Ave N
Fremont Ave N
Fremont Ave N

N 43rd St
N 42nd St

N 47th St
N 45th St

N 44th St
N 43rd St
N 42nd St
N 41st St
N 40th St
N 39th St

N 46th St
N 45th St
N 43rd St
N 42nd St
N 41st St
N 40th St

N 38th St
N 35th St
N 34th St
N 37th St
N 36th St
N 35th St
N 34th St

Stone Way N
Bridge Way N

Aurora Ave N

400 m
400 yards
200
200

Body Art & Accessories

The practices of tattooing and body piercing exploded in popularity nationwide in the late 1980s, and Seattle is still one of the leaders in this trend. If you wish to join the trend or add to your collection of body embellishments, there are plenty of places throughout the city that would be happy to oblige you.

Before you go under the needles, however, you should check out the establishment carefully. Make sure it is licensed, that all equipment is autoclaved and that the general environment of the shop is clean. Don't make any hasty decisions, especially with tattoos. Think about the design you want and research the artists and their work. If after consulting with an artist you aren't satisfied, go somewhere else. Finally, if you're wondering about tattoo removal, you shouldn't get one in the first place; the technology of tattoo removal is expensive, painful and not very effective.

Most tattoo prices vary according to the color, location and difficulty of the design, though for most of the following businesses, rates range from $85 to $100 an hour, with a minimum cost of $35 to $50. Piercings generally run $30 per hole for things like eyebrows and cheeks, and you'll need to choose jewelry, which typically runs $15 and up. The more intimate the body part, the more dearly you're going to pay (possibly in more ways than one!).

Most shops are located in Capitol Hill, Pike Place Market and the U District. The following list includes those with the best reputation among young Seattle hipsters.

$3.50. Take bus No 5 from downtown to reach the zoo.

The 2½-acre **Seattle Rose Garden** (☎ 206-684-4040), near the entrance road to the zoo, contains 5000 plants. Varieties include heirloom roses, as well as new strains being tested for All-American Rose selections. Entrance is free.

Down the hill from the zoo is **Green Lake Park**, an incredibly popular park with recreationists and sunbathers. Two paths wind 2.8 miles around the artificial lake, but even these aren't enough to fill the needs of the hundreds of joggers, power walkers, bikers and in-line skaters who throng here daily. In fact, competition for space on the trails has led to altercations between speeding athletes; the city government has been called in to regulate traffic on the paths.

Tennis courts, a soccer field, bowling green and baseball diamond are some of the other recreational facilities at the park, and Green Lake Small Craft Center (☎ 206-684-4074), 5900 W Green Lake Way N, offers sailing, canoeing and kayaking instruction. In the summer, you can also rent boats (sailboats, canoes, kayaks, sailboards, paddleboats and rowboats) from Green Lake Boat Rental (☎ 206-527-0171), 7351 E Green Lake Drive N; they're open daily from about April to September. There are two swimming beaches along the north end of the lake, but on sunny days, the entire shoreline is massed with gleaming pale bodies. Bus Nos 6, 16 or 26 go to Green Lake from downtown.

U DISTRICT

The campus sits at the edge of a busy commercial area known as the U District. The

Fantasy Unlimited This notorious sex store (☎ 206-682-0167) at 102 Pike St across from the market, offers an immense variety of sex toys and lingerie, but is also well known and respected for its piercing and tattoo services. It's open 10 am to 7 pm Monday to Saturday, and 11 am to 6 pm Sunday.

Mind's Eye Tattoo & Body Piercing (☎ 206-522-7954), 5206 University Way NE. Co-owner Reverend Eric Eye performs a variety of services from weddings, baptisms and funerals to tattoos and body piercings. Although his shop has only been open since 1992, it was the first tattoo shop in the U District and remains the most reputable. Mind's Eye is open 1 to 10 pm weekdays and noon to 6 pm Sunday.

The Pink Zone This shop (☎ 206-325-0050) in the Broadway Market (in the heart of Capitol Hill) sells 'visible queer gear' in addition to performing tattoos and piercings. The friendly staff pride themselves on cleanliness and the shop attracts a diverse (but generally young) clientele. They are open for tattoos and piercings noon to 10 pm weekdays, noon to 9 pm Saturday and noon to 7 pm Sunday.

Rudy's Barbershop Wildly popular with gay men and other hipsters, Rudy's (☎ 206-329-3008), 614 E Pine St, is open 9 am to 9 pm Monday to Saturday and 11 am to 5 pm Sunday.

Skinprint Tattoo If you're looking for that special remembrance of Seattle, then consider a trip to Skinprint (☎ 206-547-0056), 403 NE 45th St, where in addition to a full range of tattoo and piercing options, you can elect to get branded or otherwise scarified.

Tattoo You This tattoo joint in the Corridor (☎ 206-324-6413), 1017 E Pike St, is open noon to 6 pm Wednesday to Saturday.

Vyvyn Lazonga Vyvyn Lazonga (☎ 206-622-1535), one of the first modern female tattoo artists, has nationwide name recognition. Her store at 1516 Western Ave, just below Pike Place Market, is open 11 am to 7 pm daily. ■

main streets here are University Way, also known as 'The Ave,' and NE 45 St. On these busy streets are innumerable cheap restaurants and cafes, student-oriented bars, cinemas and bookstores.

University of Washington
Established in 1861, the University of Washington was first built downtown, on the site of the present Four Seasons Olympic Hotel. There were originally 37 students, overseen by university president and carpenter Asa 'Here Come the Brides' Mercer (who in the 1860s masterminded the scheme to bring marriageable women to Seattle from the eastern USA).

The university moved to its present location above Lake Washington in 1895. Much of the 694-acre site was incorporated into the grounds of the Alaska-Yukon-Pacific Exposition, a world's fair-like gathering that built dozens of new buildings in the area and served to landscape the campus.

Today, the university is the largest in the Northwest, with around 35,000 students. Noted programs include law and medicine; it's also highly regarded for computer science and liberal arts. 'U Dub,' as most people refer to the university, is also notable for a state institution in that more than half of its students are in graduate programs.

The center of the campus is called **Central Plaza**, although everyone refers to it as Red Square due to its base of red brick. To the east is **Suzzalo Library**, a fanciful Gothic-revival cathedral of books. Beyond the library is the **Quad**, an area that contains many of the original buildings on campus. When the ivy turns red in the autumn, the effect is very New England-ish.

WASHINGTON

The
U District

49th Ave NE
48th Ave NE
47th Ave NE
47th Place NE
47th Ave NE
46th Ave NE
46th Ave N
46th Ave NE
45th Ave NE
44th Ave NE
44th Ave NE
43rd Ave NE
42nd Ave NE
41st Ave NE
41st Ave NE

Laurelhurst
Playfield

NE 45th St
NE 44th St
NE 43rd St
42nd St

Burke
Gilman
Park

NE 40th St
38th Ave NE
Surber Dr NE
NE Belvoir Pl
NE 38th St

44th St
43rd St
42nd St
41st St

40th Ave NE
39th Ave NE
38th Ave NE
37th Ave NE
36th Ave NE
35th Ave NE

NE 60th St
NE 57th St
NE 55th St
NE 52nd St
NE 50th St

39th Ave NE
36th Ave NE

14

34th Ave N

Mary Gates
Memorial Drive

34th Ave NE
33rd Ave NE
31st Ave NE
30th Ave NE
29th Ave NE

Calvary
Catholic
Cemetery

34th Ave NE
University View Place NE
Union Bay Place

NE 54th St
NE 53rd St

Clark Rd

27th Ave NE
26th Ave NE
25th Ave NE

NE Blakeley St
Burke Gilman Trail

NE 45th St

Walla Walla Rd

NE 62nd St

513

Montlake Blvd NE
Mason Rd

25th Ave NE
24th Ave NE

13

1

Ravenna Place
Ravenna Ave NE

22nd Ave NE

University
of
Washington

Ravenna
Park

NE 56th St
Park Rd

NE 55th St

21st Ave NE
20th Ave NE
19th Ave NE
18th Ave NE
17th Ave NE

Stevens Way

Husky
Union
Building

16th Ave NE
15th Ave NE

The Quad

Suzallo
Library
25

Cowen
Park

NE Ravenna Blvd

NE 58th St

NE 60th St

3

12

Meany
Hall

10
8   11
9   15   16
17
18
19

23

24

University Way NE
Brooklyn Ave NE
12th Ave NE
11th Ave NE

2
4

21
22

NE Campus Parkway
NE 40th St

NE 56th St
NE 55th St
NE 52nd St
NE 47th St
NE 45th St
NE 43rd St
NE 42nd St
NE 41st St

12th Ave NE

NE 61st St

Roosevelt Way NE

7

9th Ave NE
8th Ave NE
7th Ave NE

NE 56th St
NE 64th St
NE 63rd St
NE 62nd St
NE 58th St
NE 57th St
NE 56th St

see
Fremont, Wallingford
& Green Lake map

6

20

Roosevelt Way NE

11th Ave NE

NE 43rd St
NE 42nd St

6th Ave NE
Hillman Place NE
5th Ave NE

5

5th Ave NE
4th Ave NE

5

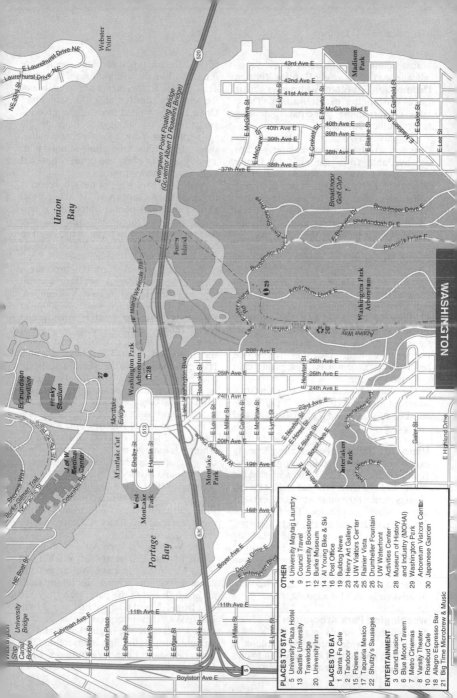

Union Bay

Webster Point

E Laurelhurst Drive NE

NE 45th St

Laurelhurst Drive NE

43rd Ave E
42nd Ave E
41st Ave E

Madison Park

McGilvra Blvd E

40th Ave E
39th Ave E
38th Ave E

37th Ave E

E McGilvra St
E Crockett St
E Newton St

E Garfield St
E Lee St
E Galer St
E Blaine St
E Lee St

E McGraw

Evergreen Point Floating Bridge
(Governor Albert D Rosellini Bridge)

Broadmoor Golf Club

Broadmoor Drive E

Shenandoah Dr E

E Shelby Drive
E Birchmont Dr E
Broadmoor Dr E

Parkside Drive E

Foster Island

29

Arboretum Drive E

Washington Park Arboretum

NE Island Wetlands Trail

Lake Washington Blvd E

Azalea Way

30

WASHINGTON

Washington Park Arboretum

28

26th Ave E

25th Ave E

24th Ave E

26th Ave E

26th Ave E

24th Ave E

E Newton St

23rd Ave E

Interlaken Blvd

Galer St

E Highland Drive

Edmundson Pavilion

27

Husky Stadium

Montlake Bridge

Montlake Cut

513

NE Pacific St

U of W Medical Center

Columbia Rd

E Shelby St

E Hamlin St

Lake Washington Blvd

Boyer Ave E

N Montlake

Boyhalt St
E Louisa St
E Miller St
E McGraw St
E Lynn St

24th Ave E
20th Ave E
19th Ave E

E Newton St
E Howe St
E Blaine St
Boyer Ave E

Interlaken Park

Interlaken Dr E

West MontLake Park

Montlake Park

16th Ave E

Stevens Way

Burke-Gilman Trail

NE Boat St

NE Pacific St

Portage Bay

Boyer Ave E

Delmar Drive E

E Interlaken Blvd

Washington Ship Canal Bridge

University Bridge

Fuhrman Ave E

11th Ave E

11th Ave E

E Allison St
E Gwinn Place
E Shelby St
E Hamlin St
E Edgar St
E Roanoke St

E Miller St

E Lynn St

Boylston Ave E

5

Just below Red Square is a wide promenade leading to lovely **Rainier Vista** at **Drumheller Fountain**, with views across Lake Washington to Mt Rainier. These sites comprise the principal remaining legacy of the 1909 Expo.

The university is a lively place and it's definitely worth touring the campus – maps are available from the visitors' center (☎ 206-543-9198) at 4014 University Way – especially in spring when flowering bulbs and azaleas paint the verdant campus with brilliant colors. Bus Nos 71, 72 and 73 offer the most direct routes from the downtown bus tunnel to the university.

Burke Museum This museum of natural history and anthropology (☎ 206-543-5590) is on the University of Washington campus near the junction of 16th Ave NE and NE 45th St. There's a good collection of dinosaur skeletons, but the real treasures here are the North Coast Indian artifacts, especially the collection of cedar canoes and totem poles. On the ground level of the museum is a pleasant patio cafe, the Boiserie.

The Burke Memorial Washington State Museum is open 10 am to 5 pm daily; admission is $2.50/1.50 adults/seniors and children over six.

Henry Art Gallery The university's newly expanded and renovated fine-art gallery, the Henry (☎ 206-543-2280), on campus at the corners of 15 Ave NE and NE 41st St, mounts some of the most intelligent exhibits and installations in Seattle. The focus is on 20th-century art and artists; there's a small permanent collection, but the changing shows – 35 a year – are usually noteworthy. There is also a cafe. The Henry is open 11 am to 5 pm Tuesday to Sunday, and 11 am to 8 pm Wednesday and Thursday. Admission is $5/3 for adults/seniors.

Washington Park Arboretum

This wild and lovely park (☎ 206-543-8800) has a wide variety of gardens, a waterfront nature trail and acres and acres of mature forest threaded by paths. Over 5500 different types of plant species are found within the arboretum's 200 acres. Trail guides to the plants are available at the **visitors' center** at 2300 Arboretum Drive E; free guided tours of the grounds are available on Sundays at 1 pm. In the spring, **Azalea Way**, a jogger-free trail that winds through the arboretum, is lined with a giddy array of pink- and orange-flowered azaleas and rhododendrons.

At the southern edge of the arboretum is the **Japanese Garden**, a 3½-acre formal garden with koi pools, waterfalls, a teahouse and manicured plantings. The garden is open 10 am to 6 pm daily, April to November. Entry is $2.50/1.50 adults/seniors and youths 19 and under.

The northern edge of the arboretum includes a wonderful **wetlands trail** around Foster Island in Lake Washington. The trail winds through wetlands and over floating bridges to smaller islands and reedy shoals. Bird watching is popular here, as is canoeing, fishing and swimming. It's just too bad that busy, elevated Hwy 520 roars above the island. The nature trail is best accessed from the parking lot near the visitors' center, or from the MOHAI parking lot, below.

At the northwest corner of the arboretum is the **Museum of History and Industry** (☎ 206-324-1125), 2700 24th Ave E, which, despite its name, is probably best thought of as a museum of Seattle and Puget Sound history. Usually called by its acronym, MOHAI is a likable collection of old planes, memorabilia from the Great Fire, and artifacts and lore from Seattle's great seafaring era. Entry is $5.50/3 adults/seniors and students.

The Washington Park Arboretum is just south of the University of Washington along Union Bay in Lake Washington. To reach the visitors' center and hiking trails at the north end of the park, take Hwy 520 east from I-5, and take the first exit (Montlake/UW). This intersection can be confusing: stay in the right lane, and go straight through the first intersection. This lane becomes Lake Washington Blvd. Follow this street for about a quarter of a mile, then turn east (left) onto E Foster Lake Rd (not 26th Ave). Follow signs for the visitors center. If you're trying to get to MOHAI, take the same exit and follow the signs toward Montlake and the university, but turn east (right) immediately on E Hamlin St or E Shelby St before crossing the Montlake Bridge.

Access from the south is somewhat less confusing. Follow Madison St from downtown for about 2½ miles until it intersects Lake Washington Blvd. Turn north (left) at the junction. Take Arboretum Drive E to the visitors' center. The No 11 Madison St bus delivers you to the base of the park at Lake Washington Blvd, but there's still quite a walk (albeit through the park) to the visitors' center.

BALLARD & THE CANAL

Northwest of Seattle, the waters of Lake Washington and Lake Union meet the Puget Sound in the 8-mile-long Lake Washington Ship Canal. The idea of linking the major lakes around Seattle to the salt water bay had been discussed since 1867, but it wasn't until 1911 that the Army Corps of Engineers, under the direction of Hiram Chittenden, began the unification of the waters. First, a channel was cut between Lake Washington and Lake Union, thereby lowering Lake Washington by nine feet. Then the canal was cut through from Salmon Harbor on Lake Union to the Puget Sound, where two locks were installed in 1917.

Now, 100,000 boats a year pass through the canal, and the locks, with their fish ladder and beautiful adjacent park, make a popular outing destination for families. This is also a restful spot for anyone needing some relief from the jangling of Seattle caffeine and traffic.

While Ballard has been the brunt of many a local's joke, it is fast becoming another hip neighborhood, centered mainly in its historic district along Ballard Ave NW between 20th and 22nd Aves. There are many good taverns and some fun budget gourmet restaurants. Market St is the main commercial drag. Bus No 17 from downtown goes to Ballard, and to the following sights along the ship canal.

Hiram M Chittenden Locks

Watching boats traverse the locks on the shipping canal offers a strange Zen-like attraction for locals and tourists alike. The process takes between 10 and 30 minutes, depending on whether the large or small lock is used. Walkways alongside the locks allow an intimate look at the workings of these water elevators and at the vessels passing through them.

On the southern side of the locks is a **fish ladder**, built in 1976 to assist salmon fighting their way to spawning grounds in the Cascade headwaters of the Sammamish River, which feeds Lake Washington. Visitors can watch the fish through underwater glass-sided tanks or from above (nets keep salmon from overleaping and stranding themselves on the pavement). You can also watch sea lions munch on the salmon while they thrash around trying to figure out how to negotiate the fish ladder (just what to do about the salmon-loving sea lions has stymied environmentalists, anglers and the local Fish & Wildlife Department). The best time to see the salmon is during spawning season, from mid-June to September.

On the northern entrance to the lock area is the **Carl English Jr Botanical Gardens**, a charming, small arboretum and specimen garden. Trails wind through gardens filled with mature trees (with identifying labels) and flower gardens; plan on communing with imploring squirrels and haughty Canadian geese.

Flanking the gardens is a small museum and visitors' center (☎ 206-783-7059) documenting the history of the locks. The visitors' center is open 10 am to 7 pm daily from July to September, and 11 am to 5 pm Thursday to Monday the rest of the year. Free tours of the locks are offered at 1 and 3:30 pm daily, June to September. From October to May, tours are offered at 2 pm weekends only. Access to all areas at the locks is free; the gardens are closed from 9 pm to 7 am, although the locks remain open 24 hours. The Chittenden Locks are northwest of downtown Seattle, at 3015 NW 54th St, about half a mile west of Ballard off Market St.

Fishermen's Terminal
Seattle's fishing fleet resides at Fishermen's Terminal, in a wide abayment in the shipping canal called Salmon Bay. About 700 fishing boats dock here, making this the largest halibut and salmon fleet in the world. One of the reasons for the popularity of Fisherman's Terminal with boat owners is that the facility lies in fresh water (above the Chittenden Locks), which is much less corrosive to boats than salt water.

It's great fun to wander the piers, watching crews unload their catch, clean boats and repair nets. Interpretive displays explain the history of Seattle's fishing fleet, and a statue of a fisherman at the base of the piers commemorates lost seamen.

In the two shed-like terminal buildings are a couple of good restaurants specializing in the freshest seafood in Seattle, a tobacconist, a ship's chandlers and a store devoted to navigational charts and nautical gifts. Stop at the **Wild Salmon Fish Market** (☎ 206-283-3366) to buy the pick of the day's catch.

The Fishermen's Terminal is on the south end of the Ballard Bridge, at 19th Ave and W Nickerson St.

Shilshole Bay & Golden Gardens
Continuing about 2 miles along Seaview Ave from the locks is Shilshole Bay Marina. There's not much here besides the touristy restaurants and shops that accompany harbors, but the boats are nice. Just a couple hundred yards more is Golden Gardens Park, a beach park with sandy beaches and pebbly shores. There are picnic facilities, bathrooms, basketball hoops, volleyball nets, gangs of Canadian geese and plenty of space to get away from all the activity.

DISCOVERY PARK
Discovery Park is 534 acres of urban wilderness. Locals love to come here to get away from the ever-present manicure of city gardens and get windswept along the many trails.

The park was originally Fort Lawton, an army base established in 1897 to protect Seattle from unnamed enemies. Fort Lawton didn't see much activity until WWII, when it was used as barracks for troops destined for the Pacific. When the fort was declared surplus property in the 1960s, the city of Seattle decided to turn the area into a park (although significant portions of the park are still used for military housing).

Discovery Park has over 7 miles of hiking trails, several of which lead to the **Daybreak Star Indian Cultural Center**, a community center for Seattle-area Native Americans. Except for a small art gallery, there are few facilities for outside visitors. The vista point here has beautiful views of the Sound, and several steep trails lead down through the forest to narrow, sandy beaches.

A paved road makes an almost 3-mile loop of the park, with trails sprawling out from it to other lookouts. About a mile out from the loop trail, a trail skirts the water edge of the park all the way to the **West Point Lighthouse**, a great scenic spot.

For a map of the trail and road system stop by the visitors' center (☎ 206-386-4236) near the Government Way entrance. The center is open 8:30 am to 5:30 pm daily. The park also runs educational programs ranging from nature walks on Saturdays to day camps for children to bird watching tours.

From downtown take Elliott Way north, which will turn into 15th Ave W. Take the Dravus St exit and turn left on Dravus St. Then go right on 20th Ave W and follow the road until it turns into Gilman Ave W and then W Government Way. Or simply take the bus; Nos 19 and 33 both leave from downtown and the Seattle Center for the park.

LAKE WASHINGTON
When it gets hot in the summer (yes, Seattle can get hot) people make the pilgrimage to this lake to sprawl out on the

small sandy/grassy beaches. Just driving cycling, or walking around the area is a good respite (see Hiking & Biking, below). The houses along Lake Washington Blvd boast of old money or new corporate wealth; this is the neighborhood of Microsoft's top dogs and was home to deceased singer Kurt Cobain.

Going north along Lake Washington Blvd, you'll find **Denny Blaine Park**, a predominantly lesbian beach, down a tree-lined lane. Continue along the boulevard and you'll end up at E Madison St right by the arboretum, and not far from *Cafe Flora* (☎ 206-325-9100), 2901 E Madison St, a favorite with vegetarians (closed on Monday). If you take E Madison St to the right, you'll get to **Madison Park**, another neighborhood with the usual hub of trendy restaurants and cafes. At the end of Howe St there's a public beach with picnic tables and a floating dock.

Madrona
Take Union or Cherry Sts from downtown to get to Madrona, once a never-heard-of neighborhood but now another destination for many, mainly to eat at one of the most popular brunch places in the city, the Hi Spot Cafe (☎ 206-325-7905), 1410 34th Ave.

The business district is on 34th Ave between Pike and Spring Sts. Madrona is one of Seattle's more ethnically diverse neighborhoods, blending elements of the largely African American Central District to the west with the predominantly white neighborhoods that ring Lake Washington proper. Madrona Beach, just down from the business district in Madrona Park, is one of the nicest along the lake. To reach Madrona via public transport, take outbound bus No 2 on Spring St from downtown.

Seward Park
For something wild – as in wilderness – go to Seward Park, a 277-acre promontory that juts into Lake Washington. The park preserves about the only old-growth forest anywhere in the vicinity of Seattle and is

home to wildlife, including a nesting pair of bald eagles. Hikers and bikers will be interested in the 2½-mile lakeside trail; other trails lead to a fish hatchery, beach access and several picnic areas. Seward Park can be dangerous after dark, so be attentive.

To reach the park, take I-5 south to I-90, exit 164. Once on I-90, take exit 1 to Rainier Ave S, or Hwy 900. Stay on Hwy 900 until the intersection with S Orcas St in about 2 miles. Turn east, and follow the signs to the park. From downtown, take bus No 39.

WEST SEATTLE & ALKI BEACH
For a more happening park, head out to Alki Beach in West Seattle. At the headland of Alki Point, Seattle's first settlers made their home; today, this 2-mile stretch of sandy beach is a madhouse in summer, when in emulation of southern California the volleyball nets go up, mass sunbathing occupies the strand and teens in souped-up cars prowl the streets. Still, it's Seattle's only real beach scene, and the views onto Seattle from Duwamish Head, at the northern end of the beach, are spectacular. You might want to avoid Alki on summer weekends, but the good beachside cafes, the quaint fish and chips joints, the miniature Statue of Liberty on the beach and the Alki Point Lighthouse make it a nice getaway most other times.

Take Hwy 99 or I-5 south of Seattle to the West Seattle Freeway; get off at Harbor Ave SW, the beach road that will take you all the way around the promontory. Bus Nos 37 and 56 go to Alki Beach.

ACTIVITIES
Hiking & Biking
In Seattle, it's possible to hike wilderness trails without ever leaving the city. There are several miles of trails in a remnant of the area's old-growth forest at **Seward Park**, and even longer trails are found in 534-acre **Discovery Park**, northwest of downtown (see Seward and Discovery Parks sections for more details).

For a long-distance path that's welcoming

to both hikers and bikers, try the **Burke-Gilman Trail**, a 12½-mile paved path that runs between Gas Works Park on Lake Union and Log Boom Park on the north end of Lake Washington in the suburb of Kenmore. The trail follows an old rail line along the shores of the lakes, all at an easy grade. The views are great, though on weekends the trail can be pretty busy. A convenient place to rent a bike is Al Young Bike and Ski (☎ 206-524-2642), 3615 NE 45th St, near both the university and the Burke-Gilman trail. Near Green Lake, you can rent bicycles, in-line skates and just about any other form of recreational conveyance at Gregg's Greenlake Cycle (☎ 206-523-1822), 7007 Woodlawn Ave NE.

Recreational Outings

The local branch of the Sierra Club (☎ 206-523-2019), 8511 15th St NE, is very busy, and with a little planning you can fit an outdoor adventure into your Seattle stay. Their extremely diverse offerings range from beachcombing and botany walks at Alki to enological bike tours of the Yakima Valley wine country, and from weekend canoe trips down the Olympic Peninsula's Bogachiel River to weekend day-hiking and car-camping trips along the Pacific Crest Trail. Call for a recording of future events. Most day trips are free; longer trips may have minimal fees.

The outdoor gear outfitter REI also organizes year-round training and recreational activities in the Seattle area. These include adventurous outings focused on climbing, hiking and rafting. For more information, call REI Adventure Travel at ☎ 800-622-2236 or 253-437-1100.

Boating & Kayaking

Northwest Outdoor Center Inc (☎ 206-281-9694), 2100 Westlake Ave N, on Lake Union (see Queen Anne map) offers instruction in sea and white-water kayaking, and rents kayaks there on the lake. Other services include houseboat and kayak tours, as well as sunset tours through the locks at Ballard.

The UW Waterfront Activities Center (☎ 206-543-9433) rents canoes and rowboats for $5 an hour. Bring along an ID – and a passport if you're from out of the country. You have to stay in the Lake Washington area; no cruising through the canal to the Puget Sound. The center is open 10 am to about 5:30 or 6:30 pm daily (about 7:30 pm in the summer), and is in the southeast corner of the Husky Stadium parking lot.

In good weather, the surface of Lake Union is covered with sailboats. Join the fun at Sailboat Rentals & Yacht Charters Inc (☎ 206-632-3302), 1301 N Northlake Way, Lake Union (see Wallingford map). Rentals include 14-foot to 32-foot models, available by the hour, day or week.

Swimming

The downtown YMCA (☎ 206-382-5010), 909 4th Ave, and the downtown YWCA (☎ 206-461-4868), 1118 5th Ave, have co-ed indoor pools. Also convenient to downtown is the Queen Anne Pool (☎ 206-386-4282), 1920 1st Ave W.

There are public beaches at Green Lake Park, Alki Beach and Lake Washington. For information about city pools throughout the Seattle, call the city park bureau at (☎ 206-684-4075).

Golf

Seattle's most popular course is Jackson Park (☎ 206-363-4747), 1000 NE 135th St, at the far northern edge of the city. This 18-hole course is best attempted on weekdays, when there are fewer lines at the first tee. Another convenient course is Jefferson Park (☎ 206-762-4513), 4101 Beacon Ave S (on Beacon Hill, south of I-90 and east of I-5), an 18-hole course with short fairways and lots of mature – but sometimes troublesome – trees and bushes.

Southwest of downtown is West Seattle Municipal Course (☎ 206-935-5187), 4470 35th Ave SW, with 18 holes, and superior views across Elliott Bay to Seattle.

Courses

Seattle's Experimental College (☎ 206-543-4375) is a funky alternative and continuing-

CAROLYN HUBBARD

KEVIN SCHAFER

TONY WHEELER

Top Left: Fremont mural by Patrick Gabriel, Seattle, WA   **Top Right:** Reflection of Space Needle, Seattle, WA
Bottom: Crabs at Pike Place Market, Seattle, WA

DAVE G HOUSER

NIK WHEELER

BILL MCRAE

Top Left: Sea kayaking, Rosario Harbor, Orcas
  Island, WA
Bottom: Washington State Ferry and Mt Baker, WA

Top Right: Roche Harbor, San Juan Island, WA

education institution with a variety of one-day and multi-day seminars. You can take a massage class or art workshop; or if you're heading off on a kayaking expedition in the Sound, call for their schedule of classes in advance of your trip. They're pretty cheap, lots of fun and a good way to meet locals who share your interests.

ORGANIZED TOURS
City Tours
Seattle suffers no shortage of tour organizers. Gray Line of Seattle (☎ 206-626-5208, 800-426-7532) has a whole catalog of Seattle-area bus and boat tours. The six-hour **Grand City Tour** operates from April to mid-October; tickets cost $33/16.50 adults/children. Their **Seattle City Tour** is an abbreviated version that runs year-round, lasts almost three hours and costs $24.

Seattle's **Underground Tour** starts from Doc Maynard's Public House (☎ 206-682-4646), 610 1st Ave, a restored 1890s saloon. The city's 'underground' was conveniently forgotten until the late 1960s, when businessman and raconteur Bill Speidel chanced onto the old subterranean storefronts near his office, and after a few years of courting headlines and permits, he was in business as a tour operator.

Most of these chambers date from the 1880s, before Seattle's fire and the rebuilding of the district elevated the city off the tide flats. Tour guides like to emphasize the underground nature of the tour with whimsical noting of historic bordellos and corrupt politicians, both of which flourished in early Seattle history. An hour long, three-block subterranean hike through a series of rather ordinary-looking basements follows the 20-minute introduction. Daily schedules vary seasonally, and reservations are recommended. Tickets are $6.50/5.50 adults/seniors, $5 for students ages 13 to 17, and $2.75 for children ages six to 12; cash only.

For personalized tours, contact Seattle & More Step-On Guides (☎ 206-244-7983), or Show Me Seattle (☎ 206-633-2489). For walking tours of Seattle, check with the visitors' center.

Boat Tours
There are a number of boat sightseeing trips offered along the Waterfront. One of the major operators is Argosy Cruises (☎ 206-623-4252), which offers a number of different tours daily from Pier 55. The Seattle Harbor Tour is a one-hour narrated tour of Elliott Bay, the Waterfront, and the Port of Seattle. Prices are $14.50/13 adults/seniors and students, and $7 for children ages five to 12 (kids under five are free). Their three-hour Lake Washington Cruise costs $18.50/17/9.50.

SPECIAL EVENTS
Chinese New Year
Seattle's first big ethnic festival of the year is Chinese New Year, held in the International District usually in January or late February; The first day is celebrated with parades, firecrackers, fireworks and lots of food. Call ☎ 206-623-8171 for more information.

Fat Tuesday
The Pioneer Square district embraces its somewhat rowdy reputation on Mardi Gras in February, when the area is convulsed with the Fat Tuesday celebration. Music and revelry in bars and restaurants obviously comprise the main events, although the special Seattle touch is lent by the annual, competitive **Spam-carving Contest**. Contact the visitors' center for more information.

Freedom Day Celebration
Seattle's lesbian and gay-pride event, the Freedom Day Celebration, is usually held the last Sunday in June on Capitol Hill. A parade begins along Broadway and continues to Volunteer Park, where there are speeches, music and a rally. For information, contact the Freedom Day Committee at ☎ 206-323-1229.

Northwest Folklife Festival
The Northwest Folklife Festival (☎ 206-684-7300), 305 Harrison St, takes over the Seattle Center during Memorial Day weekend. Over 5000 performers and artists

present music, dance, crafts, food and family activities representing over 100 countries. Admission is free.

The Bite

Seattle's restaurants and caterers cook up a culinary storm during the Bite of Seattle at the Seattle Center, usually held the second weekend in July. Visitors can sample foods from dozens of Seattle-area chefs, and taste local beers and wines. Entry to The Bite is free, but you will need to pay for servings of food from each vendor. The evening ends with live music. For more information, contact ☎ 206-232-2982.

Seafair

Seattle's biggest summer festival is Seafair, an extravagant civic celebration that began as a hydroplane race on Lake Washington. Old Seattle families jealously maintain their moorages on the lake in order to have the best possible views of these roaring jet boats. Today, however, all manner of festivities stretch the event to three weeks (from late July through early August) and extend all across the city; events include a torchlight parade, an airshow, lots of music, a carnival and even the arrival of the naval fleet and Blue Angels. Lodging is in short supply in Seattle on Seafair weekend, so plan accordingly. Unless you love unbridled revelry or really want to watch the hydroplane races, you might want to avoid Seattle on this weekend (usually the first in August), and don't plan to cross the I-90 or Hwy 520 bridges while the races are in progress. For more information, contact the festival office at ☎ 206-728-0123.

Bumbershoot

Seattle's biggest arts and music celebration is Bumbershoot, held at the Seattle Center over Labor Day weekend. In addition to an arts and crafts fair, there are special theatrical and musical events (past artists include Beck, Art Ensemble of Chicago and the Neville Brothers), a film festival and fine arts exhibitions. For more information, call ☎ 206-281-8111.

PLACES TO STAY

When Seattle is all booked up, you'll be glad to have the help of the Seattle Hotel Hotline (☎ 206-461-5882, 800-535-7071) which offers a free reservation service for area hotels.

The Seattle B&B Association (☎ 206-547-1020) has a brochure listing the association's member B&Bs; write to the SBBA at PO Box 31772, Seattle, WA 98103-1772.

Camping

Campers intending to visit downtown Seattle face lengthy commutes. Two suburban campgrounds offer the most convenient facilities. In Bellevue, *Trailers Inn* (☎ 206-747-9181, 800-659-4684), 15531 SE 37th St, has showers, an indoor pool, playground and laundry, but no tent facilities. To reach the campground, take I-90 exit 11, turn south to the frontage road and follow the signs for five blocks. In Kent, south of Seattle, is the *KOA Seattle-Tacoma* (☎ 206-872-8652, 800-659-4684), 5807 S 212th St. Facilities include a tent area, heated pool, car rentals, playground and laundry; sites are $21 to $27.

Tent campers are pretty much limited to *Saltwater State Park* (☎ 206-764-4128), a busy but pleasant beachfront park on the Puget Sound, about 20 miles south of Seattle. To reach the park, take I-5 exit 149 west toward Des Moines. At the junction of Hwy 99 (also called Pacific Hwy), turn south and drive to 240th St. Turn west and follow signs to the park.

Hostels

Hostelling International – Seattle (☎ 206-622-5443), 84 Union St, has 199 beds in dormitories, family rooms and double rooms. Kitchen and laundry facilities are provided, as well as a common area with a TV. Rates are $15/17 a night, members/non-members. The hostel is in a good location, central to the Waterfront and to Pike Place Market. Members only in summer.

Both men and women can stay at the *Central District YMCA* (☎ 206-382-5000), 909 4th Ave; rooms for singles/doubles start at $29/39. There are also beds in a dormitory reserved for card-carrying HI/ AYH members; the cost is $18.

The *Green Tortoise Backpackers Guesthouse* (☎ 206-322-1222, or 888-424-6783 from outside Seattle in the US or Canada), at 1525 2nd Ave near Pike Place Market, charges $15 a night for a dorm bed. They also have private rooms for $31/40 with a bathroom. Reservations are recommended as this place fills fast with travelers from the bus (see Getting There & Away). The *Commodore Motor Hotel* (☎ 206-448-8868, 800-714-8868), 2013 2nd Ave downtown, also has $14 hostel rooms.

Both of Capitol Hill's hostels cater to international student travelers, and offer cheap, decidedly unfussy accommodations These may not be for you if you value modesty or absolute cleanliness. *Vincent's Backpackers Guesthouse* (☎ 206-323-7849), 527 Malden Ave E, is more or less a dormitory, with beds going for $12 a night; private rooms (bath down the hall) are also available for $35 for up to three people. Free coffee and breakfast is provided; you share a kitchen, TV lounge, and laundry facilities.

In the thick of things on Broadway, the *American Backpackers Hostel* (☎ 206-720-2965), 126 Broadway E, has much the same amenities as Vincent's but focuses almost exclusively on non-US travelers. The hostel's 55 dorm-style beds go for $14. Enter via the alley beside the bubble machine at Twice Sold Tales bookstore.

B&Bs

The *Bacon Mansion B&B* (☎ 206-329-1864, 800-240-1864), 959 Broadway Ave E, on Capitol Hill has eight guest rooms, six with private bathrooms. Rates at this Tudor-style mansion range from $89 for a shared bathroom to $109 for a private room. *B&B at Mildred's* (☎ 206-325-6072), 1202 15th Ave E, is an old Victorian home across the street from Volunteer Park. The three guest rooms, each with private bath, are $75/95. *Salisbury House B&B* (☎ 206-328-8682), 750 16th Ave E, is also near the park. The four rooms at this 1904 home range from $65 to $119; all have private bathrooms. On a much larger scale is

Gaslight Inn B&B (☎ 206-325-3654), 1727 15th Ave E, with 15 rooms available in two neighboring homes; there's also a pool and hot tub. There is a mix of private and shared bathrooms; rooms range from $62 to $148. At the *Hill House B&B* (☎ 206-720-7161, 800-720-7161), 1113 E John St, there are five guest rooms in a restored 1903 home; three have private bathrooms. Rates range from $65 to $105.

There aren't many B&Bs right in downtown Seattle, which makes *Pensione Nichols* (☎ 206-441-7125), 1923 1st Ave, even more special. Right in the urban thick of things near Pike Place Market, this charmingly remodeled older hotel has rooms starting at $60/$85.

Just north of downtown on Queen Anne Hill is a cluster of nice older homes and some B&Bs; this area is convenient to events at the Seattle Center. The *Beech Tree Manor B&B* (☎ 206-281-7037), 1405 Queen Anne Ave N, is an early 20th-century mansion with six rooms ranging from $59 to $125; there's a mix of private and shared bathrooms.

Houseboats

For something uniquely Seattle, consider *Houseboat Hideaways* (☎ 206-323-5323), 2000 Westlake Ave N, at Lake Union's Westlake Marina (see Queen Anne and the Seattle Center map). Each of the two houseboats sleep one to six people; nightly rates begin at $125.

Hotels – downtown

Most of the following downtown motels offer some kind of parking program with in-and-out privileges, but you'll pay handsomely for it, usually between $12 and $20 a day. If you have a car, you'll need to factor the parking fees into the cost of staying downtown or else stay out near the Seattle Center where most lodgings offer free parking.

Budget Two large but modest older hotels offer inexpensive lodging right downtown; rooms here are best described as no-frills, but there's nothing scary about staying

WASHINGTON

here, and you can't argue with the rates. The *Commodore Motor Hotel* (☎ 206-448-8868, 800-714-8868), 2013 2nd Ave, has a mix of options, including $14 hostel rooms, private rooms with a shared bathroom down the hall ($49/59 for singles/doubles), and rooms with private bathrooms ($53/74). Near Pike Place Market and Belltown, the hotel also has its own free parking garage, always a plus in Seattle. The *Moore Hotel* (☎ 206-448-4851, 800-421-5508), 1926 2nd Ave, has rooms with private or shared bathrooms; this once-grand hotel has 135 rooms starting at $34/39. Consider that you can afford a suite here for the price of a closet at a remodeled hotel.

Middle There's no old-fashioned glamour at the *Sixth Avenue Inn* (☎ 206-441-8300, 800-648-6440), 2000 6th Ave, a motor inn centrally located downtown, but there is free parking, and it is a perfectly nice place to stay mid-way between downtown and the Seattle Center. Seasonal rates range between $96 and $120 for singles, $120 and $144 for doubles. *Days Inn Town Center* (☎ 206-448-3434, 800-225-7169), 2205 7th Ave, has rooms starting at $59/69, and *Loyal Inn Best Western* (☎ 206-682-0200), 2301 8th Ave, has some kitchenettes; rooms cost $72 to $110.

The *Pacific Plaza* (☎ 206-623-3900, 800-426-1165), 400 Spring St, is centrally located, just a block from the Four Seasons Olympic. Nicely remodeled rooms come with a big breakfast (in the breakfast lounge) and cost $80 to $110. There's no air conditioning, so it's not a good choice in summer. The *Inn at Virginia Mason* (☎ 206-583-6453, 800-283-6453), 1006 Spring St, is on First Hill, just above downtown near a complex of hospitals. This nicely maintained older hotel caters to families needing to stay near the medical facilities but also offers quiet rooms to other visitors. Rates begin at $95 for both singles and doubles; there are discounts if you are staying at the hotel for family medical reasons. At the *Hotel Seattle* (☎ 206-623-5110, 800-426-2439), 315

Seneca St, basic rooms run $80/110 for a single/double.

Long one of Seattle's landmarks, the *Camlin Hotel* (☎ 206-682-0100, 800-426-0670), 1619 9th Ave, has been remodeled and its beautiful lobby again sparkles (note that the Camlin plans to close temporarily for further renovations in the near future). The *WestCoast Vance Hotel* (☎ 206-441-4200), 620 Stewart St, is another nicely restored older hotel. Rooms at either of these hotels range from around $85 to $119. In winter, they both offer reduced rates and a free breakfast.

Top End Most large hotel chains have operations in Seattle, offering business travelers and conventioneers modern rooms with a wide range of facilities. The best of these is the *Seattle Sheraton Hotel & Towers* (☎ 206-621-9000, 800-325-3535), 1400 6th Ave; rooms range from $135 to $250. The *Westin Hotel Seattle* (☎ 206-728-1000, 800-228-3000), 1900 5th Ave, is another luxury business hotel with rooms starting at $220.

For a more unique Northwestern experience, stay at one of Seattle's local luxury hotels or one of the many historic grand hotels, many of which have been remodeled; both options offer gracious comforts of another era. The prices listed are standard midweek rates; at most hotels, weekend packages and off-season deals lower the prices considerably.

The *Alexis Hotel* (☎ 206-624-4844, 800-426-7033), 1007 1st Ave near Madison St, is a modern hotel tucked inside an old architectural exoskeleton. This is a hotel that emphasizes quiet rooms and high-quality service and amenities, so don't expect dramatic views or ostentatious glamour. Room prices range from $175 to $370. In addition to the main hotel building, there are more rooms and condo-style suites in the building next door. The suites start at $345, while hotel rooms start at $175/190. *The Paramount* (☎ 206-292-9500, 800-426-0670), 724 Pine St, is another gem of a hotel with rooms starting at $189/199.

The *Sorrento Hotel* (☎ 206-622-6400, 800-426-1265), 900 Madison St, was Seattle's finest hotel when it was built in 1909. After a substantial refurbishing, this beautiful hotel, lined with mahogany and hung with chandeliers, is again one of Seattle's best. Rooms start at $160/180. The other doyen of old money and elegance is the *Four Seasons Olympic Hotel* (☎ 206-621-1700, 800-821-8106 in Washington, 800-332-3442 elsewhere), 411 University St. Imposing and luxurious, the Olympic was built in 1924 and subsequent remodels have worked to maintain the period glamour of its architecture. This hotel could have been a set in an extra-suave Cary Grant movie. Rooms range from $190 to $245 for a single and $285 to $355 for a double.

Hotels – Pioneer Square
Stay in the historic heart of Seattle at *Pioneer Square Hotel* (☎ 206-340-1234), 77 Yesler Way, a recently refurbished older hotel with nicely appointed rooms at $119/129. Nightlife, restaurants, and shopping are just steps from the door.

Hotels – the Waterfront
Only one Seattle hotel actually faces onto Elliott Bay, and that's the *Edgewater* (☎ 206-728-7000, 800-624-0670), 2411 Alaskan Way, Pier 67 (see Downtown Seattle map). When this hotel was first built, people paid a premium to stay in the rooms that literally hang over the bay, in order to fish from the windows. Times have changed, and fishing is no longer allowed. If you came to Seattle to experience the tang of sea air, this might be the hotel for you. Prices begin at $99 but range quite a bit depending on whether you're right on the water.

Hotels – Pike Place Market
The *Inn at the Market* (☎ 206-443-3600, 800-446-4484), 86 Pine St, is in fact a modern and architecturally interesting hotel, and it's the only top-end lodging in the venerable Pike Place Market. Rooms are large, and most have grand views onto

market activity and the Puget Sound. Prices range from $130 to $325.

Hotels – Queen Anne
There are excellent reasons to stay near the Seattle Center. It's only five minutes from downtown on the Monorail or bus, and room prices are usually lower than those downtown. You can also park your vehicle for free at your hotel, no small matter in Seattle.

There's a cluster of mid-range motels near the Seattle Center. At the *Vagabond Inn* (near the Space Needle, ☎ 206-441-0400, 800-522-1555), 325 Aurora Ave N, children 18 and under can stay free when accompanied by their parents, which is especially great when you're trying to scrounge enough dough to send your herd up the Space Needle. Rooms start at $79/89. The *Seattle Inn* (☎ 206-728-7666, 800-255-7932), 225 Aurora Ave N, has rooms at $56/59. The *Travelodge* by the Space Needle (☎ 206-441-7878, 800-578-7878), 200 6th Ave N, has rooms that start at $99/109. The remodeled *Best Western Executive Inn* (☎ 206-448-9444, 800-351-9444), 200 Taylor Ave N, is in the shadow of the Space Needle, with rooms starting at $100/148.

On the lower Queen Anne side of the Seattle Center are a couple of good lodging choices. The *Inn at Queen Anne* (☎ 206-282-7357, 800-952-5043), 505 1st Ave N, is an old apartment building turned limited-service hotel. Rooms come with kitchenettes, continental breakfast, and voice mail. Studios start at $76/86. The *Hampton Inn* (☎ 206-282-7700), 700 5th Ave N, is a brand new lodging with nicely appointed rooms ($89/99).

Hotels – U District
Off I-5 exit 169 are a number of moderately priced motels near the University of Washington; only 3 miles from downtown, these accommodations are also close to eating and drinking in the Wallingford/Green Lake area. *University Plaza Hotel* (☎ 206-634-0100, 800-343-7040), 400 NE 45th St, is just across the freeway from

WASHINGTON

campus. Room rates vary seasonally and range from $70 to $95; there's a heated swimming pool, and pets are allowed. The *University Inn* (☎ 206-632-5055, 800-733-3855), 4140 Roosevelt Way NE, is adjacent to campus, offers a free continental breakfast and an outdoor pool, and children under 18 stay free with parents. Rooms start at $99/109. Just east of the university, *Seattle University Travelodge* (☎ 206-525-4612, 800-578-7878), 4725 25th Ave NE, is close to Children's Hospital and has an outdoor pool. Rooms start at $79/99.

Hotels – near the airport

If you're flying in or out of Sea-Tac, the following hotels all offer complimentary airport shuttles. *Airport Plaza Hotel* (☎ 206-433-0400), 18601 Pacific Hwy S, has basic rooms from $40/45. The new *Days Inn at Sea-Tac Airport,* (☎ 206-244-3600, 800-325-2525), 19015 International Blvd S, has more amenities and rooms at $64/74. If you're looking for something fancy, the *Radisson Hotel Seattle Airport* (☎ 206-244-6000, 800-333-3333), 17001 Pacific Hwy S, has rooms at $119/$129.

PLACES TO EAT

Seattle offers a bewildering array of inexpensive places to eat; it also boasts the most expensive restaurants in the Northwest. In the mean, prices are higher here than elsewhere in the Northwest; in the mid-range restaurants, a nice, medium-frills meal edges toward (and sometimes past) $25 a person. While entrées may not be expensive, you can often rack up quite a bill by the time you add an appetizer, salad, dessert or a few drinks.

Top-end restaurant have entrées or main dishes that usually top $20 per person. These restaurants often serve Northwest cuisine, or high-end French or Italian cooking. A leisurely meal with several courses and a bottle of wine can easily top $50 per person. (And don't forget the tip.) Some restaurants will offer prix-fixe menus that include a number of courses for a set price, usually from $40 to $60. If you need to justify such reckless expense, remember that

Seattle has one of the hottest restaurant scenes on the West Coast.

If you're looking for organic produce and healthy food, check out the listings for Puget Consumers Co-op in the phone book. There are seven locations in the Seattle area. Not far from downtown is the Central Co-op (☎ 206-329-1545), 1835 12th Ave E on Capitol Hill, with a good selection of organic groceries and macrobiotic products.

Downtown

There are a few noteworthy places to eat right in the central downtown area, but the majority of these restaurants are designed with business meetings and expense accounts in mind. In most cases, visitors or travelers on a budget will have more fun and selection in the Pike Place Market neighborhood, Belltown, or in and around Pioneer Square.

Budget *Restaurant Shilla* (☎ 206-623-9996), 2300 8th Ave, is probably the best Korean restaurant downtown, with brazier-grilled bulkogi (marinated thin-sliced beef) a specialty. If you're already downtown and just want something cheap and easy, go to the food court at Westlake Center at 5th Ave and Pine St where there are several dozen food vendors with pretty good take-out food (and a large seating area). Otherwise, head to Pike Place Market.

Middle When people think about Northwestern food, they often think of old-fashioned oyster bars and cavernous chop houses filled with rowdy yeomen. While the purveyors of Northwest cuisine have tried to expunge this food stereotype, and the frontier yeoman have been replaced with stockbrokers and professional athletes, the early 1900s steak and fish house still exists at a few entertaining Seattle restaurants. *McCormick's Fish House & Bar* (☎ 206-682-3900), 722 4th Ave, offers a full sheet of daily fresh fish specials, mostly grilled with zesty sauces, a fine selection of local oysters, chops and steak, all served in wood-lined, brass-outfitted chambers that give off the aura of a bustling Victorian men's club.

Or you could trade the Northwestern ambiance for slick California glamour. You may not want to admit that you hang around *Planet Hollywood* (☎ 206-287-0001), 1500 Sixth Ave, but actually the food – mostly upscale burgers and such – isn't too bad. Another recent Los Angeles import is *Oba-Chine* (☎ 206-749-9653), 1518 6th Ave, Wolfgang Puck's take on Oriental food. The decor – a wild Hong Kong art deco look – is at least as interesting as the food.

One of downtown's most stylish see-and-be-seen scenes is *Palomino Euro-Bistro* (☎ 206-623-1300), 1420 5th Ave, on the top floor of the City Centre Mall. The dining room is saturated with color and is always filled with gregarious, well-dressed diners, all of whom seem to know one another. Quite a feat in this mammoth restaurant. For entrées, stick to the upscale pasta and pizza selections.

Outside the confines of Pike Place Market, but still part of the scene is *Wolfgang Puck Café* (☎ 206-621-9653), 1225 1st Ave, the California food guru's casual, eye-poppingly decorated bistro. Pizza, salads, and pasta ($10 to $15) are the building blocks of the very international and well-priced menu.

Top End If Seattle is in fact home to a school of cuisine (as many here fervently presume), then the following restaurants are among the best practitioners. The *Dahlia Lounge* (☎ 206-682-4142), 1904 4th Ave, usually gets the credit for creating the reality and then the notion of Northwest cuisine. The *Painted Table* (☎ 206-624-3646), 92 Madison St, is an unpretentious, pretty restaurant in the Alexis Hotel, with Pacific Rim cuisine based on local ingredients. *Fullers* at the Seattle Sheraton Hotel (☎ 206-447-5544), 1400 6th Ave, is often considered the city's single best restaurant, with consistently inventive cuisine, unusual ingredients, and an extremely swank dining room.

The *Georgian Room* at the Four Seasons Olympic Hotel (☎ 206-621-7889), 411 University Ave, is one of the most imposing restaurants in the city, with equally stylish, regionally inspired food. *Nikko* (☎ 206-322-4641), 1900 5th Ave, in the Westin Hotel, is the city's best Japanese restaurant, with excellent sushi and inventive variations on Japanese standards.

Pioneer Square

Budget You can get inexpensive burgers and sandwiches at a number of Pioneer Square taverns, but for the same money you can eat good ethnic food. *Cafe Hue* (☎ 206-625-9833), 312 2nd Ave S, is a Vietnamese restaurant that preserves colonial French influences. Seattle's best bakery is also in Pioneer Square. In addition to peasant-style loaves and baguettes, *Grand Central Baking Co* (☎ 206-622-3644), 214 1st Ave S in the Grand Central Arcade, serves lunchtime salads and focaccia sandwiches cafeteria-style in its lobby-like dining area. The *Elliott Bay Café* (☎ 206-682-6664) 101 S Main St, in the bookstore of the same name, is a cozy place for soup, salad, and sandwiches.

Middle Purportedly the oldest restaurant still operating on the West Coast, *Merchants Cafe* (☎ 206-624-1515), 109 Yesler Way, serves a wide assortment of salads, hot sandwiches (about $5) and steak, seafood and chicken entrées between $9 and $12. The cafe is open for breakfast (omelets are the specialty), lunch and dinner and has a very reasonable beer and wine list. It's a good place to get a bite to eat or a drink, if only to check out the historic idiosyncrasies of the place, like the stand-up bar (all 30 feet of it) that came from the East Coast via the Horn.

For reasons not immediately apparent, Seattle has an inordinate number of Italian restaurants. Some of the best are in the Pioneer Square area. *Trattoria Mitchelli* (☎ 206-623-3883), 84 Yesler Way, serves good pasta, pizza and calzones, though its main attraction is that it stays open till 4 am Tuesday to Saturday nights to feed all those joint-cover revelers. Busy and engaging, *Umberto's Ristorante* (☎ 206-

621-0575), 100 S King St, is known for its outstanding pasta dishes (in the $13 range); however, the grilled meats are truly superior; pork tenderloin with Madeira and wild mushrooms is $17. A shade more expensive and dignified, *al Boccalino Ristorante* (☎ 206-622-7688), 1 Yesler Way, offers excellent pasta dishes but really delivers with innovative grilled fish and seafood dishes.

FX McRory's Steak, Chop & Oyster House (☎ 206-623-4800), 419 Occidental Ave S, is a vast Pioneer Square landmark across from the new sports stadiums. The bar, always full of jocks and sports fans, can get completely out of hand after home games. At other times, diners can admire the lovely architecture and enjoy well-prepared steak; the oysters are a must.

Top End Usually mentioned in discussions of Seattle's best restaurants, *Il Terrazzo Carmine* (☎ 206-467-7797), 411 1st Ave S, is a showcase of European luxury that serves excellent many-coursed Italian meals. Plan to spend a leisurely evening and quite a bit of money; entrées are usually over $25.

Pike Place Market
Budget For a wide selection of fresh produce, bakery products, deli items and take-out ethnic foods, head to Pike Place Market (see earlier section on Pike Place Market for more cheap eats). There's no reason to go away hungry from – or to spend much money at – this cacophonous market. If you want a sit-down meal, some of the market cafes are inexpensive.

Try *Lowell's* (☎ 206-622-2036) 1519 Pike Place, for eye-opening breakfasts and cheap-and-cheerful lunches. If for some reason you've been hankering for Bolivian cuisine, hanker no more. *Copacabana Cafe* (☎ 206-622-6359), 1502½ Pike Place, serves up inexpensive Andean dishes like pollo saltado (braised chicken with green peppers and tomatoes) for $9. However, perhaps the best reason to explore South American cuisine may be this convivial restaurant's great views over the Pike Place Market; at *du jour* (☎ 206-441-

DAVE PEEVERS

3354), 1919 1st Ave, the views from the back and the fancy salads make this a local hangout.

Just when you think that every restaurant niche has been explored, there's *World Class Chili* (☎ 206-623-3678), 93 Pike St, a restaurant devoted to the many faces and strengths of chili soup. Another option in the market is the *Pike Pub & Brewery* (☎ 206-622-6044), 1415 1st Ave, with burgers and better-than-average pub grub to accompany a pint of ale.

Middle *Place Pigalle* (☎ 206-624-1756), 81 Pike St, offers great views over the bay and inventive Latin- and Asian-influenced dishes. A Seattle institution, the *Pink Door Ristorante* (☎ 206-443-3241), 1919 Post Alley, titillates first-time visitors by posting no sign. Just head for the pink door (near the corner of Post Alley and Stewart St) with the amazing Italian smells wafting out, and *eccolo!* Lunch is mostly pasta dishes ($8), but there's also a soul-stirring cioppino ($9); dinner prices are slightly higher and reservations are recommended. *Café Campagne* (☎ 206-728-2233), 1600 Post Alley, is the casual younger sibling to upscale Campagne, and the quality of the French-style cooking is what you'd expect from this talented kitchen. However, the prices are manageable, and you don't have to dress up for dinner.

In the street below the market is *Wild Ginger* (☎ 206-623-4450), 1400 Western Ave, a wildly popular restaurant that features the fiery cuisines of Indochina, an attractive dining room and upscale clientele. If you shy away from spicy food, then the *Kaleenka Russian Cafe* (☎ 206-728-1278), 1933 1st Ave, might be a better bet. Good, solid dishes like Siberian beef dumplings are $9; Georgian pressed chicken is $13.

Top End At *Il Bistro* (☎ 206-682-3049), 93A Pike St, No 206, in Pike Place Market, the best and freshest of the market is incorporated into daily Italian-influenced specials, and served in an intimate, white-linen atmosphere. *Campagne* (☎ 206-728-2800), 86 Pine St, in the Inn at the Market, is Seattle's best traditional French restaurant, with an emphasis on the foods of Gascony (entrées top $25). *Chez Shea* (☎ 206-467-9990), 94 Pike St, is a treasure hidden away in Pike Place Market. Great views over the sound combine with Continental-style prix-fixe menus (four courses for $39) to make this one of the city's most romantic restaurants.

Just down the street from the market is *Virazon* (☎ 206-233-0123), 1329 1st Ave, a classy restaurant that introduces French techniques and sauces to the Northwest larder. Entrées are between $17 and $20, and there's a $49 five-course prix-fixe menu.

Belltown

Belltown isn't just for punk rockers and artists any more. In the past few years, this unprepossessing neighborhood flanking downtown has become the uncontested center of fine dining in Seattle. Luckily, to go with the new, upscale temples of haute cuisine, there's still an abundance of delis, inexpensive taverns with pub lunches and low-budget hangouts frequented by arty musicians and starving students. A lot of these venues are little cubby holes that serve soup, sandwiches and salads to eat in (there are always a few streetside tables) or take out.

Budget A favorite for soups is the *Continental Cafe* (☎ 206-728-8759), located at 2123 1st Ave.

Mama's Mexican Kitchen (☎ 206-728-6262), 2234 2nd Ave, is always packed. But that's no surprise for a place that serves $5 burritos, huge combination plates and – from 4 to 6 pm on weekdays – $2 margaritas, all surrounded in Mexican kitsch artifacts. The venerable *Two Bells Tavern* (☎ 206-441-3050), 2313 4th Ave, serves one of Seattle's best burgers – and a couple of dozen regional draft beers. *Noodle Ranch* (☎ 206-728-0463), 2228 2nd Ave, is a hip diner with Pan-Asian noodle dishes.

Macrina (☎ 206-448-4032), 2408 1st Ave at Battery St, is an artsy bakery that makes some of the best bread in town. Light lunches are also served.

Middle Belltown is a mini United Nations when it comes to moderately priced dining opportunities. One of the best places to go for excellent and well-priced sushi is *Shiro's Sushi Restaurant* (☎ 206-443-9844), 2401 2nd Ave. *Betay Avone* (☎ 206-448-5597), 113 Blanchard St, is one of Seattle's only kosher restaurants; comfortable and upscale, the focus is on Israeli-style Mediterranean cuisine.

Eating at *Marco's Supperclub* (☎ 206-441-7801), 2510 1st Ave, is a bit like traveling around the world. 'Multi-ethnic' only begins to describe the cooking at this very popular, boisterous restaurant; the deep-fried sage leaves are mandatory.

The handsomely austere *Queen City Grill* (☎ 206-443-0975), 2201 1st Ave, offers great seafood from its daily menu, and a solid and eclectic selection of meats and chicken from its seasonal menu. Try the crab cakes with bell pepper aioli for $15.

Keep going through Belltown and at the corner of 1st Ave and Denny Way there's *Caffè Minnies* (☎ 206-448-6263), a '50s-style diner open 24 hours – a blessing when you're still out on the town at 2 am.

Top End Easily one of the most exciting restaurants to open in Seattle recently, *Flying Fish* (☎ 206-728-8595), 2234 1st Ave, specializes in fish and seafood, as you'd expect. However, what you can't adequately anticipate is the expert transforming touch of spice and élan that turns just another piece of salmon or tuna into pure magic. The dining room is bustling and energetic, the service friendly and top-notch. *El Gaucho* (☎ 206-728-1337), 2505 1st Ave, is a modern, hip recreation of a '50s supper club, complete with massive steaks, a cigar room, dozens of single malt Scotches, and a very stylish clientele. Service is impeccable, and is an integral part of the show. A new contender for the title of Seattle's best Italian restaurant is *Lampreia* (☎ 206-443-3301), 2400 1st Ave, a high-toned and formal restaurant somewhat at odds with bohemian Belltown. Grilled fish and meats are the specialties and are complemented by a good wine list.

International District
Another neighborhood for cheap eats is the International District. The best deals are found in the many Vietnamese, Thai and Chinese restaurants that line Jackson St between 6th and 12th Aves. In many of these, you'll have trouble spending over $5 on lunch, and $7 can buy dinner if you're cautious. One thing you'll notice in this district is that there are places where the tourists go and places where everyone else goes. The following suggestions weed out the ones with lines (and consequently higher prices) in preference of local favorites.

Hing Loon (☎ 206-682-2828), 628 S Weller St, specializes in seafood dishes. The curry scallops cost $9 and are pleasantly spicy. Check out the selections on the walls as well. The place is clean and the service is fast. A bit pricier but higher quality is *Sea Garden* (☎ 206-623-2100) at 509 7th Ave S. Hot pots cost $8 to $9, huge bowls of noodle soup cost between $3 and $5. *Shanghai Garden* (☎ 206-625-1689), 524 6th Ave S, is one of the best Chinese restaurants in this neighborhood, with a selection of dishes that thankfully strays far from the usual sweet-and-sours and fu yungs. *Sun-Ya Seafood Restaurant* (☎ 206-623-1670), 605 7th Ave, is the best place to go for dim sum.

For a cheap snack or meal there's *House of Dumplings* (☎ 206-340-0774) across

from Uwajimaya on S King St. A serving of eight very good vegetable dumplings costs $5.

Up in the more Vietnamese sector, in Asian Plaza on the corner of S Jackson St and 12th Ave, there's *A Little Bit of Saigon* (☎ 206-325-3663), a huge restaurant serving some great food and imported beer. Spring rolls (not fried) served with peanut sauce cost $3. If you're really adventurous, try one of their desserts in a glass. *Saigon Bistro* (☎ 206-329-4939), 1032 S Jackson St, is a favorite for their filling soups and special 'dry' noodles.

Capitol Hill
Budget There's no end to good and inexpensive places to eat along Broadway, especially if you like ethnic food. Student favorites include the *Kitto Noodle House* (☎ 206-325-8486), 614 Broadway E for Asian noodles in the $8 range, and *El Greco* (☎ 206-328-4604), 219 Broadway E, for Mediterranean dishes. *Siam on Broadway* (☎ 206-324-0892) 616 Broadway E, is a favorite for Thai food. For vegetarian entrées and fresh fruit, wheatgrass and vegetable juices in a Jetson-like, futuristic interior, go to the *Gravity Bar* (☎ 206-325-7186), 415 Broadway E, in the Broadway Market. A popular place for coffee and dessert is the *Pacific Dessert Co* (☎ 206-328-1950), 516 Broadway E. On the east side of Capitol Hill, the *Surrogate Hostess* (☎ 206-324-1944), 746 19th Ave E, is a hip and health-conscious eatery where food is served cafeteria-style; most dishes are under $5.

Middle *Café Septieme* (☎ 206-860-8858), 214 Broadway E, is a very trendy, intensely spare and arty cafe with an attitude. The food – all homemade, sophisticated, but simple stuff – is very good. The *Broadway New American Grill* (☎ 206-328-7000), 314 Broadway E, mixes a rowdy bar scene with good burgers, ribs and other items from the grill.

Coastal Kitchen (☎ 206-322-1145), 429

15th Ave E serves up some of the best food in the neighborhood, with their eclectic mix of Cajun, Mayan and Mexican inspirations. They have a great 'blunch,' served between 8:30 am and 3 pm on weekends.

Queen Anne & the Seattle Center

Middle Everyone's favorite breakfast diner is the *5 Spot* (☎ 206-285-7768) at 1502 Queen Anne Ave N. Go early, and avoid the weekends when lines snake out the door.

Pacific Dessert Co (☎ 206-284-8100), 127 Mercer St, is famous in Seattle for its fabulous rich cakes and good coffee, and is a popular after opera spot for the well-dressed Seattle Center crowd.

Adriatica Restaurant (☎ 206-285-5000), 1107 Dexter Ave N at Ward St, always gets a mention when people talk about their favorite Italian restaurants. In an old home overlooking Lake Union at the top of a dizzying flight of stairs, Adriatica offers views to go with its excellent pasta, veal and fish dishes.

One of Seattle's most unusual ethnic restaurants is *Pirosami* (☎ 206-285-3360), 2220 Queen Anne Ave N. The specialty is food from Georgia and the Caucasus, which is similar to eastern Mediterranean cuisine but with more subtlety and earthiness. They also serve Northwest favorites cooked with Georgian overtones. Expect to pay $15 a person for dinner.

Top End No compilation of Seattle restaurants would be complete without a mention of the Space Needle (☎ 206-443-2111), 219 4th Ave N. There are two restaurants in the tower, the *Emerald Suite* (☎ 206-443-2150) and the *Space Needle Restaurant* (☎ 206-443-2100). Both serve their own versions of Northwest cuisine 500 feet in the air while providing a slowly rotating 360° view of the city. In fact, the restaurants are not as bad as their reputations, though The Emerald Suite is quite expensive, with entrées between $20 and $35; it also has a dress code. The ride up the elevator is free if you have meal reservations.

Fremont

An institution in Fremont, the *Still Life Cafe* (☎ 206-547-9850), 709 N 35th St, is a great spot to park at a table, drink coffee and nibble this and that. Most dishes are vegetarian; the soups are especially good. The place to be in Fremont is the *Triangle Lounge* (☎ 206-632-0880), 3507 Fremont Place N. Zippy American dishes make this arrowhead-shaped cafe a bustling crossroads. *El Camino* (☎ 206-632-7303), 607 N 35th St, has several things to recommend it: very good Mexican regional cooking, a stylish dining room, and a real bar (in strangely short supply in Fremont). *Pontevecchio* (☎ 206-633-3989), 710 N 34th St, is the local not-too-spendy Italian trattoria, with tasty food and a dose of that peculiar Fremont funkiness.

The *Longshoreman's Daughter* (☎ 206-633-5169), 3510 Fremont Place N, is the local breakfast spot of choice. At lunch try hearty plates of seasonal vegetables, seafood, meat and excellent garlic mashed potatoes at this urban-arty storefront. Down the street is a small walk-in burrito place, *Taco del Mar*, where an overflowing burrito will cost about $4.

Wallingford

In Wallingford, N 45th St stretches past a long strip of inexpensive, mostly ethnic restaurants.

Budget *Julia's* (☎ 206-633-1175), 4401 Wallingford Ave N, is the long-established place for breakfast in this part of Seattle, especially if your idea of an eye-opener is a stack of pancakes and gallons of coffee. If your idea of breakfast is a bloody mary and goat cheese and sun-dried tomato frittata, then you should try the zippy *Jitterbug Cafe* (☎ 206-547-6313), 2114 N 45th St. Don't pass up the *Boulangerie* (☎ 206-634-2211), 2200 N 45th St, as close as Seattle gets to a real French bakery.

My Brother's Pizza (☎ 206-547-3663), 2109 N 45th St, has some of the best pizza in the city and they have a unique way of serving it – upside down and in a bowl. It's

WASHINGTON

often packed, but there is a take-out window.

Middle *India Cuisine* (☎ 206-632-5307), 1718 N 45th St, is one of Seattle's best tandoor houses. Other good choices along the 45th St strip between I-5 and Stone Way N include a Thai cafe, a sushi bar, an Italian trattoria, as well as Mexican, Irish and even Afghani restaurants.

You'd never guess that with a name like *Bizzarro* (☎ 206-545-7327), 1307 N 46th St, this Wallingford hotbed is an excellent neighborhood Italian cafe. (Once you learn that it's housed in someone's garage, the name makes sense.)

U District

Budget Adjacent to the University of Washington is University Way, where you'd rightly expect to find a lot of inexpensive restaurants and cafes. During the day, it can be hard to park along 'The Ave,' as it's called, but at night the crowds are fewer and the food is still cheap.

Taquería Mexico (☎ 206-633-5256), 4226 University Way NE, can accommodate the smallest budget. *Flowers* (☎ 206-633-1903), 4247 University Way NE, offers vegetarian fare and a juice bar. *Schultzy's Sausages* (☎ 206-548-9461), 4142 University Way NE, is the place to go for all sorts of grilled sausage sandwiches: it's the 'best of the wurst.' *Tandoor* (☎ 206-523-7477), 5024 University Way NE, doesn't look like much, but the tandoor-roasted meats and other Indian dishes are a delight.

Middle North of the university is *Santa Fe Cafe* (☎ 206-524-7736), 2255 NE 65th, a converted storefront with New Mexican-style food.

Ballard

Ray's Boathouse (☎ 206-789-3770), 6049 Seaview Ave NW, has views over the Olympics, a nautical decor and an exhaustive fresh fish menu with reasonable prices: it's what tourists think of when they think of Seattle. But the food's great and the views are wondrous. If you can't

get reservations, at least come for a drink on the deck. Ray's is about a mile west of the Ballard locks.

Madrona

The *Hi Spot Cafe* (☎ 206-325-7905), 1410 34th Ave, has been known since it opened for incredible cinnamon rolls, Torrefazione coffee and filling breakfasts, including creative omelets served with potatoes. The sandwich and salad lunch ($3 to $6) is just as good, and at dinner most entrées stay under $10. On weekends, get there before 9 am for breakfast to avoid long waits.

Cafe Soleil (☎ 206-325-1126), down the street at 1400 34th Ave, is another good eatery with outdoor tables and friendly service. Egg frittatas with such tastes as sun-dried tomatoes, black olives and feta cheese cost $5.50.

ENTERTAINMENT

For a listing of Seattle's live entertainment, consult the *Seattle Weekly*, the *Stranger* or the arts sections of the daily papers. Tickets for most events are available at Ticket-Master (☎ 206-628-0888, 206-292-2787), which has ticket centers in several store chains, some independent stores, and one in Westlake Center. Chains include PayLess Drug Stores, Budget Tapes & Discs, Disc Jockey, Tower Records and The Wherehouse. Call to charge tickets by phone or to find the nearest location. TicketMaster is open 8 am to 9 pm Monday to Saturday, 10 am to 6 pm Sunday.

For rush seats, TicketMaster has its own Discount Ticket Booth (☎ 206-233-1111) at Westlake Center downtown. Day-of-performance tickets are extra cheap, but you have to pay cash. It opens at 10 am daily. Ticket/Ticket (☎ 206-324-2744) is another half-price, day-of-show ticket outlet; however, they won't give out ticket availability over the phone. There is a location at Pike Place Market and at the Broadway Market on Capitol Hill.

Coffeehouses & Teahouses

Seattle often gets credit for starting the US coffee craze. In the process, Seattle's coffee fanaticism has also served to revitalize the coffeehouse as a social meeting place that provides frequent poetry readings, theatrical entertainment and acoustic music, as well as a place to read, write letters and chat with friends. Coffeehouses also provide a largely alcohol-free place to hang out. There are coffeehouses all across Seattle; here are a few to get you started.

Belltown For a break from the Belltown 'scene,' head to *Lux Coffee House* (☎ 206-443-0962), 2226 1st Ave. The *Speakeasy Café* (☎ 206-728-9770), 2304 2nd Ave, is a full service Internet cafe with the other accouterments of modern life, like espresso, microbrews, and a cigar shop. If you tire of staring at the screen, then take in one of the performances or readings held here.

Queen Anne On Thursdays, *Noise* (☎ 206-938-5572) in the Queen Anne Coffeehouse at 1625 Queen Anne Ave N, is an open-mike venue devoted to the spoken word. You'll find slam poetry some nights, readings from novels and plays another.

Capitol Hill If you're near the dance clubs on Pine and Pike Sts, head to *Puss-Puss Cafe* (☎ 206-720-1883), 514 E Pine St, or *Cafe Paradiso* (☎ 206-322-6960), 1005 E Pike St; both are open very late on weekend nights. A couple of other favorites are *B&O Espresso* (☎ 206-322-5028) at 204 Belmont Ave E and *Rosebud Espresso* (☎ 206-323-6636), 719 E Pike St. The *Globe Cafe* (☎ 206-689-8661), 1531 14th Ave, has frequent literary events and musical performances.

U District Near the university, go to *Allegro Espresso Bar* (☎ 206-633-3030), 4214 University Way NE, or *Rosebud Cafe* (☎ 206-633-0801), 1411 NE 45th.

Wallingford For a caffeine switch, try the tea shop next to Wide World Books. *Teahouse Kuan Yin* (☎ 206-632-2055) at 1911 N 45th St, has an impressive selection of black, oolong, green and herbal teas and

paraphernalia to enjoy a pot. It's open 10 am to 11 pm every day but stays open until midnight on Fridays and Saturdays.

Cinemas

Although suburban multi-screen cinema complexes are common enough in Seattle, there are still quite a number of small independent theaters that go out of their way to find the unusual and obscure. At opposite ends of Capitol Hill are two of the best art cinemas, the *Egyptian* (☎ 206-323-4978), 801 E Pine St, and the *Harvard Exit* (☎ 206-323-8986), 807 E Roy St. Cineastes will like the off-beat fare at the *Grand Illusion* (☎ 206-523-3935), 1403 NE 50th St in the U District. The new *Casbah* (☎ 206-443-1533) at 70 Wall St in Belltown shows vintage films in a setting reminiscent of a '50s lounge.

Some first-run houses tend toward foreign and smaller independent films. *Broadway Market Cinemas* (☎ 206-323-0231), Broadway and E Harrison St on Capitol Hill, the *Varsity* (☎ 206-632-3131), 4329 University Way NE, and *Metro Cinemas* (☎ 206-633-0055), 4500 9th Ave NE at 45th St NE, near the university, offer first-run art and foreign films along with the regular mainstream smash hits.

The biggest event of the year for filmgoers is the Seattle International Film Festival (☎ 206-324-9996), a three-week-long extravaganza of films from around the world that usually includes many US debuts. The festival is usually held in late May and early June at the Harvard Exit and the Egyptian theaters.

Performing Arts

Theater Seattle has one of the most vibrant theater scenes on the West Coast. The following equity troupes present a range of classical and modern dramatic theater. Check the newspapers for openings (the *PI's* 'What's Happening' section, which comes out on Friday, has good theater listings).

A Contemporary Theater (ACT, ☎ 206-285-5110), 110 W Roy St, near the Seattle Center, is in historic Queen Anne Hall. The

WASHINGTON

season runs May to December. The box office is open noon to 6 pm Tuesday to Friday. The *Seattle Repertory Theatre* (☎ 206-443-2222), 155 Mercer St, performs in the Bagley Wright Theatre at the Seattle Center. Next door, the *Intiman Theatre Company*, Seattle's oldest and largest, performs at the Intiman Playhouse (☎ 206-626-0782), 2nd Ave N and Mercer St. The *Seattle Children's Theater* (☎ 206-441-3322) offers excellent productions for young theatergoers in the Charlotte Martin Theater at the Seattle Center.

The *Bathhouse Theatre Company* (☎ 206-524-9108), 7312 W Green Lake Drive N, takes risks with modern adaptations of classics and original contemporary drama. *Empty Space Theatre* (☎ 206-547-7500), 3509 Fremont Ave, presents offbeat shows and readings. Tickets for all the above venues are available through Ticket-Master. *The Annex Theatre* (☎ 206-728-0933) at 1916 4th Ave in Belltown and the *Velvet Elvis* (☎ 206-624-8477) at 107 Occidental Ave S in Pioneer Square are two alternative-theater venues.

On Pine St west of Broadway, there's the *Odd Fellows Hall* – a huge warehouse-turned-performance-space with numerous shows including the Allegro dance series. Check local newspapers for listings. *New City Theater* (☎ 206-323-6800), 1634 11th Ave, offers a wild mix of cabaret, regular plays, film and performance-art shenanigans. The Greek Active is a gay troupe that performs farces (this is the new drag art form) at *The Easy* (☎ 206-323-8343) on 916 E Pike St. Both the *Cornish College of the Arts* (☎ 206-323-1486) at 710 E Roy St, and the *UW School of Drama* (☎ 206-543-4880) churn out student productions; the UW has three different performance spaces, so call ahead to confirm locations.

Classical Music & Dance Under maestro Gerard Schwartz, the *Seattle Symphony* (☎ 206-443-4747) has risen to prominence as a major regional orchestra, and has released a series of critically acclaimed recordings. The symphony performs at the new Benaroya Concert Hall downtown at 2nd Ave and University St. The *Northwest Chamber Orchestra* (☎ 206-343-0045) is the Northwest's only orchestra that focuses on period chamber music; the group performs at various venues throughout the city.

The *Seattle Opera* (☎ 206-389-7676) has moved from strength to strength under the directorship of Speight Jenkins. For a regional company, the Seattle Opera isn't afraid to tackle weighty or non-traditional works; productions of Philip Glass and of Wagner's *Ring* cycle have given opera lovers a lot to mull over. However, the company is perhaps most noted for its unconventional stagings of the traditional repertoire. Performances are at the Opera House in the Seattle Center.

Also performing at the Opera House is the *Pacific Northwest Ballet* (☎ 206-441-9411), the foremost dance company in the Northwest. *Seattle Men's Chorus* (☎ 206-323-2992) is one of the nation's most active gay choral groups, with nearly three dozen engagements throughout the year. Their Christmas concert is a popular holiday sell-out.

Summer musical festivals include the Seattle International Music Festival (☎ 206-622-1392), the Seattle Chamber Music Festival (☎ 206-328-5606) and the International Chamber Music Series (☎ 206-543-4880).

Bars & Brewpubs
There's nothing sedate about nightlife in Seattle. While lots of attention is paid to live music clubs, the microbrew craze has served to establish neighborhood bars as lively and respectable places to while away the hours.

Downtown & Pioneer Square For a good overview of the 'scene' in Pioneer Square, get the joint cover ($8 on weekends, $5 on weeknights) that lets you into about 10 different clubs with live jazz and blues music. Most clubs are on 1st Ave S, but you'll be able to tell which places participate by the crowds, the signs and the coffee/pretzel carts outside.

The *Hart Brewery & Pub* (☎ 206-682-

3377), at 91 S Royal Brougham Way across from the site of the new sports stadiums, is where Hart Brewers make Thomas Kemper beers. Beer samplers are available as an introduction to the 20 different varieties on tap.

For an elegant cocktail with piano glissandos in the background, take the elevator to the *Cloud Room* (☎ 206-682-0100), 1619 9th Ave, atop the Camlin Hotel (note that the Camlin plans to close temporarily for further renovations in the near future).

Pike Place Market One of Seattle's most likable bars, the *Virginia Inn Tavern* (☎ 206-728-1937), 1937 1st Ave, manages to service many distinct groups of people at once (see Pike Place Market map). Lots of beers on tap, a nice interior and friendly help make this a good rendezvous spot and a great staging area for forays elsewhere. The *Pike Pub and Brewery* (☎ 206-622-6044), 1415 1st Ave, is in the South Arcade, and offers good pub grub in addition to hand-crafted ales.

Belltown Just down from the Virginia Inn is the *Belltown Pub* (☎ 206-728-4311), 2322 1st Ave, another friendly bar with tons of atmosphere.

Belltown Billiards (☎ 206-448-6779) is just down the street from the Queen City Grill at 90 Blanchard St. You can eat here if you want – they have a decent Italian menu – but the main draw is playing pool in a swanky location. This place draws all types, from club rats to corporate brats. There's live jazz on Sundays and Mondays and a Chardonnay happy hour from 4 to 7 pm weekdays with half-price pool.

The *Five Point Cafe* (☎ 206-448-9993) in Tillicum Square at 415 Cedar St, faces the statue of Chief Sealth. Around since 1929, this is a popular hangout for old-timers as well as bikers and young hipsters. (The urinal in the men's bathroom has a periscope-view of the Space Needle.) The Five Point is open 24 hours a day.

Capitol Hill The main gay-bar district is centered in 'the Corridor' around Pike and Pine Sts and Broadway, with a number of gay-oriented dance clubs as well as coffeehouses. This area is also home to arty live music clubs and taverns, so it's about as close to party central as it gets in Seattle.

Wild Rose (☎ 206-324-9210), 1201 E Pike St at 11th Ave, is one of the few bars for lesbians in the area. They serve sandwiches ($4 to $5) and have a wide selection of microbrews and pool tables.

The Comet (☎ 206-323-9853), 922 E Pike St, is an institution in the world of grunge music, where pool and surly attitudes still mandate. Next door *The Easy* (☎ 206-323-8343), 916 E Pike, is one of the other lesbian bars in the area.

On Broadway at the corner of Thomas St, *Ileen's Sports Bar* (☎ 206-324-0229) tries really hard to be sporty, but the locals, loyal to the former name of Ernie Steele's, maintain the mix of trendy clientele, alternative music and good, cheap drinks. The smoke, as well as mounted heads of moose and elk, reinforce the non-sportiness.

The *Deluxe Bar & Grill* (☎ 206-324-9697), 625 Broadway E, does, however, maintain a sports bar atmosphere with vinyl booths, tacky pop music, constant games on TV and a standard selection of beers and sophisticated diner food. There's a happy hour from 3 to 7 pm, and if you didn't get enough the first time, there's another from 11 pm to 1 am when the place closes.

Sure, you can get a meal at *Cucina! Cucina!* (☎ 206-447-2782), 901 Fairview Ave N, between Capitol Hill and the Seattle Center on Lake Union, but most people come here to drink. In summer there are outdoor tables overlooking the lake.

Six Arms Pub & Brewery (☎ 206-223-1698), 300 E Pike St, a branch of Portland's McMenimans brewpubs, is one of the most charming with a real neighborhood feel.

Queen Anne *Mecca Cafe* (☎ 206-285-9728), 526 Queen Anne Ave N, is one of

WASHINGTON

A History of Grunge

During the early 1990s, an unprecedented amount of media attention focused on Seattle's 'grunge rock' music scene. Practically every major newspaper and music publication in the world printed something about the new genre as it sprang to life. *Vogue* magazine (among others) ran photo spreads featuring super-models dressed in so-called grunge fashion, and the *New York Times* claimed the existence of a secret grunge patois and published a list of ridiculous insider slang terms under the heading, 'Lexicon of Grunge.'

Most Seattle musicians consider the term 'grunge' and all the media coverage of their once-obscure music scene laughable. After all, Seattle has always had a thriving local music scene. Pioneering Northwest rock bands like the Kingsmen and the Sonics – and of course, Seattle's own legendary Jimi Hendrix – helped define rock and roll in the '60s. Local groups Heart and The Steve Miller Band produced hits in the '70s, and blues man Robert Cray and saxophonist Kenny G gained notoriety in the '80s. But none of these artists were ever represented or known in the media as 'Seattle musicians' per se. It was not until the city spawned the decade of '90s grunge that the world turned to Seattle as the origin of a unique sound.

Bands like Nirvana, Pearl Jam, Soundgarden, Alice in Chains and Screaming Trees achieved tremendous commercial success and sold millions of records worldwide. Dozens of other bands were offered big-dollar recording contracts just because they were from Seattle or sounded similar to the handful of grunge bands that had the hits. Everyone wanted to sign a Seattle band and cash in on the grunge craze.

But the sound born of the Northwest punk underground was not so easily tamed by corporate America. Most bands that record companies were after had developed their music playing at rowdy house parties and tiny rock clubs, rehearsing in basements and garages in the low-rent districts where they lived. Of the bands that inked major label contracts, most were dropped within a year. Others broke up as a result of the rigors of touring, songwriting demands and constant partying.

Nirvana lived the quintessential rags-to-riches Seattle music story. Working-class kids from Aberdeen, WA, they started out playing at parties around Olympia and Seattle and saved up enough gig money to record a few songs for a cheap demo tape. The engineer at the studio liked their tape and passed it along to a friend who owned a then-small independent record label in Seattle called SubPop. For an estimated $600, Nirvana recorded and mixed the songs for what was to become their debut album, *Bleach*. Nirvana's second album, *Nevermind*, sold over 10 million copies.

The band's success brought unwelcome celebrity to Nirvana's lead singer Kurt Cobain, who – disillusioned with rock stardom and addicted to heroin – took his own life in April, 1994. The world press converged on Seattle in one final wave to cover the Cobain suicide and then they withdrew, apparently disinterested in what else Seattle musicians had to offer. ∎

– **Steve Moriarty** Seattle musician, formerly of the rock band 'The Gits'

Kurt Cobain

the latest trend-setting nightspots mixed with a diner atmosphere. At first, the Mecca appears to be an old-fashioned cafe for locals, but it gets more and more youthful and boisterous as the evening progresses and the drinks start flowing. *Sorry Charlies Restaurant & Piano Bar* (☎ 206-283-3245), 529 Queen Anne Ave N, has a great old-time Seattle 'tacky diner' atmosphere. The piano man comes in at 8 pm, Tuesday through Sunday, and everyone joins in singing.

Fremont & Green Lake The *Trolleyman Pub* (☎ 206-548-8000), 3400 Phinney Ave N, is at Redhook Brewery's first operation in Fremont. This old trolley barn makes for a very comfortable place for a pint or a light meal; the brewery also offers free tours of the operation between 2 and 6 pm weekdays, and on the hour from 10 am till 6 pm on weekends.

The *Triangle Lounge* (☎ 206-632-0880), 3507 Fremont Place N at 35th St, has eight beers on tap and a lively crowd.

If you're thirsty from too much sunbathing at Green Lake, head to *The Latona* (☎ 206-525-2238), 6423 Latona Ave NE at NE 65th St, to find one of the nicest pubs in the area. Thursday through Sunday nights there's live acoustic or light jazz music.

U District Near the university is rowdy *Big Time Microbrew & Music* (☎ 206-545-4509), 4133 University Way NE, with a good pub grub menu. The *Blue Moon Tavern* (no phone) at 712 NE 45th St, is a dive of an institution made famous by the people who drank here, like Kerouac and Ginsberg. This bar is especially popular on Sunday, as it's Grateful Dead night.

Live Music
The Northwest's gift to the music world – grunge rock – was a passing phase, albeit one of epic proportions. That doesn't mean that grunge bands like Pearl Jam and Mudhoney aren't still extraordinarily popular; they are. It's just that the grunge image lost much of its appeal for its progenitors when

impressionable suburban youth all over the country adopted its ratty, plaid-shirted style. You'll still find a cutting-edge music scene in Seattle, with new venues opening at an astonishing rate.

Don't miss *Crocodile Cafe* (☎ 206-441-5611), 2200 2nd Ave in Belltown, a springboard for local bands, and a real institution. There's multi-venue artistic anguish at the *OK Hotel* (☎ 206-621-7903), 212 Alaskan Way S, which is as likely to have slam poetry, bizarre films, or performance art as live bands. Other hot clubs are *RKCNDY* (☎ 206-667-0219), 1812 Yale St near the base of Capitol Hill, and *Colourbox* (☎ 206-340-4101), 113 1st Ave in Pioneer Square.

The center for clubbing in Pioneer Square is *The Fenix* and *Fenix Underground* (☎ 206-467-1111), 315 and 323 2nd Ave. The club owes its fame in part to owner John Corbett, who played Chris the DJ on TV's *Northern Exposure*. Ballard is another music hotbed; the center of things up here are *Tractor Tavern* (☎ 206-789-3599), 5213 Ballard Ave SW, and the *Ballard Firehouse* (☎ 206-784-3516), 5429 Russell Ave NW.

For jazz, head downtown to *Dimitriou's Jazz Alley* (☎ 206-441-9729), 2033 6th Ave at Lenora St, Seattle's most prestigious jazz club with many national acts passing through. The *New Orleans Creole Restaurant* (☎ 206-622-2563), 114 1st Ave S in Pioneer Square, also has good jazz. Just down the street is the city's best and oldest blues club, *The Central* (☎ 206-622-0209), 207 1st Ave S. *Kell's Restaurant & Bar* (☎ 206-728-1916), 1916 Post Alley in the Pike Place Market, has live Irish music Wednesday to Saturday evenings.

Summer Nights at the Pier (☎ 206-281-8111) hosts big national acts outdoors on Piers 62/63 during the summer.

Dance Clubs
There's a characteristic edge to the dance bar scene in Seattle, and many of the city's dance clubs double as live music venues.

Vogue (☎ 206-443-0673), 2018 1st Ave in Belltown, is one of the most enter-

WASHINGTON

The Seattle Music Scene Today

In the years of the grunge boom, hundreds of bands formed locally while others relocated to Seattle from different parts of the country. Small music venues sprang up all over town, creating the opportunity for all types of live music to develop an audience. Seattle's music fans are supportive of local talent, and nightclubbing has long been a favorite evening activity.

Jazz groups are exploring and reinventing old styles like swing and bebop, as well as combining their sounds with rock and funk. The bands Bebop and Destruction are a must-see for jazz lovers. Critters Buggin' play a danceable mix of funky jazz with African rhythms and The Black Cat Orchestra performs jazz with an Eastern European flavor. Young hipsters don vintage suits and dresses, sip martinis and dance to new swing bands like The Nightcaps, The Molestics, and Monty Banks and the High Rollers. Crash courses in swing dancing are sometimes offered prior to the appearance of a featured band.

Seattle's increasingly rich ethnic and cultural diversity is reflected in the wide variety of music heard in the city's clubs. Most dance clubs advertise different kinds of music on different nights. Musicians from the rapidly-growing East African population have brought their African music traditions to the area, combining them with pop and reggae to create an inspired world-beat sound. Check out the band Enzenze or the Jamaican rhythms of Clinton Fearon.

The growing Latino community has introduced salsa dancing to the city's nightlife. While people often dance to recorded music, it's not unusual to happen upon a live band, such as Latin Expressions.

Celtic music is also gaining a loyal legion of fans all around the US and Seattle is no exception. The Suffering Gales and The Stevedores play traditional Irish folk tunes while The Saint Bushmill's Choir is a rowdier Celtic rock band.

Inextricably woven into the fabric of Seattle culture, rock 'n' roll is also alive and well and the city's small clubs and bars are great places to hear it. Cover charges vary, but usually start around $5 – some places charge nothing at all, and one can choose from dozens of live performances on any given night of the week. Sycophant, Gerald Collier, Heroic Trio, Murder City Devils, The Fastbacks, The Posies, Mudhoney, Gas Huffer, Marc Olsen, and Supersuckers are just a few of the area's original rock bands.

While antiquated state liquor laws make it difficult for music venues to admit minors, there are a few places that cater to all ages. Such places don't serve alcohol and often have a hard time making enough revenue to keep their doors open. RKCNDY (pronounced 'rock candy') presents mainly quality national alternative rock acts and has a capacity of around 600. The Velvet Elvis is a little non-profit theater in Pioneer Square that sometimes allows kids to put on live music shows. All shows are listed and updated regularly in the local newspapers and weeklies.

Experience Music Project Rock 'n' roll has played a significant role in the development of Seattle's music culture. The EMP is a museum now under construction to document and celebrate the history of rock and other forms of popular American music in the Northwest. Founded by Microsoft co-founder Paul Allen and designed by architect Frank Geary, the non-profit museum is scheduled to open in early in the new century. EMP will combine the interpretive aspects of a traditional museum with educational programs and a specialized research center and library. The museum will also feature live performances and other special attractions. ■

– Steve Moriarty

taining dance halls around, not the least due to its theme nights (check out Fetish Night). The *Romper Room* (☎ 206-284-5003), 106 1st Ave N in lower Queen Anne, has live music alternating with DJ dance nights.

The hottest dance venues in Seattle are the gay clubs. For a mostly-gay disco scene, head to the Pike/Pine Corridor and go to *Neighbours* (☎ 206-324-5358), 1509 Broadway E (enter in the alley) or *The Easy* (☎ 206-323-8343), 916 E Pike St. *Safari* (☎ 206-328-4250), 1518 11th Ave, is the newest, most outrageous queer disco on Capitol Hill.

The always amusing *Re-Bar* (☎ 206-233-9873), 1114 Howell St at Boren Ave near the base of Capitol Hill, is a curious cross between a black hip-hop dance club and a lesbian/gay (in that order) disco. For something different, head to the nearby *Timberline* (☎ 206-622-6220), 2015 Boren Ave (see Downtown Seattle map), a gay country & western bar with line dancing.

Comedy Clubs
Seattle's main venue for stand-up comedy is the *Comedy Underground* (☎ 206-628-0303, 206 628 0888), located at 222 S Main St near Pioneer Square. If you've never seen *TheatreSports* (☎ 206-781-9213), then plan a wild evening of audience-inspired madness with these compulsive improvisational actors. The original Seattle troupe performs at the Market Theater in Pike Place Market at 1428 Post Alley.

Spectator Sports
Seattle has a full complement of professional sports teams. The Seattle Mariners (☎ 206-343-4600), the northwest's only major league baseball team, and the Seattle Seahawks (☎ 206-827-9777), the northwest's only NFL franchise, will play in the new sports stadiums just south of downtown.

Plenty of sports excitement is provided by the Seattle Supersonics (☎ 206-281-5850), Seattle's NBA franchise who play at the Key Arena. The Seattle Thunderbirds hockey club (☎ 206-448-7825) plays at the Seattle Center Arena from September to March.

Seattle Reign (☎ 206-285-5225) is the city's professional women's basketball club.

Tickets to games for all the above teams can be obtained through TicketMaster outlets (☎ 206-628-0888).

The University of Washington Huskies, who play football in Husky Stadium at the south end of campus, are wildly popular and their games can be great fun. Call ☎ 206-543-2200 for schedule and ticket information.

SHOPPING
The main shopping area in Seattle is downtown between 3rd and 6th Aves, between University and Stewart Sts. The Westlake Center at 4th Ave and Pine St, Rainier Square at 4th Ave and Union St, and City Centre Mall at 5th Ave between Pike and Union Sts, each host a plethora of small, interesting boutiques designed to get your wallet out of your pocket. The downtown Nordstrom (☎ 206 628-2111) at Pine St and 6th Ave, is the flagship store of the upscale clothing chain. The Bon Marché (☎ 206-344-2121) at 3rd Ave and Pine St, is Seattle's oldest and largest department store.

More downtown shopping is available in the streets surrounding Pike Place Market, a maze of food and craft stalls, galleries, and small, usually unique specialty shops. The Pioneer Square area and Capitol Hill are also good neighbourhoods for locally owned shops with a more individual selection of gifts and products.

Local Products & Fun Shops
Shopping for food is great fun in Pike Place Market; even if you don't have a kitchen handy, you can channel your shopping urges into buying local jams or syrups, into hunting for obscure spices and condiments, or picking out a bottle of local wine for drinking later.

Northwest food specialties make good gifts. Look for products made from local berries; cranberries especially are likely to turn up in unusual and delicious candies and snacks. Berry syrups and jams also make good gifts. Perhaps the gift that says

WASHINGTON

'I ♥ Seattle' the most is a whole salmon or other fish from the fish markets. All of the markets will prepare fish for transport on airplanes; or you can call and have them take care of overnight shipping. Jack's Fish Spot (☎ 206-467-0514) or Pike Place Fish (☎ 206-682-7181, 800-542-7732) are two of the best. If you're not up to buying a 15lb Chinook salmon, then perhaps a filet of smoked salmon would make a better remembrance of Seattle. Smoked salmon has a long – and delicious – history in the Pacific Northwest, as it was one of the primary foodstuffs of local Native Americans.

The North Arcade of Pike Place Market is given over to local artists and craftspeople, and you'll be able to find fun and inexpensive jewelry, clothing (watch for hand-knitted, Native Indian-designed Cowichan sweaters, made on Vancouver Island), wood and bone carvings, and a lot of other interesting (and not-so-interesting) things to buy. Most of the fun is in the browsing.

For other locally made souvenirs and gifts, head to the Made in Washington store (☎ 206-467-0788), in the Post Alley Building in Pike Place Market (there are also four other Seattle locations).

Ruby Montana's Pinto Pony (☎ 206-621-7669), 603 2nd Ave, is one of Seattle's most unique stores, a cross between a kitschy antique store and an outré gift shop. Ruby has one of the largest salt-and-pepper shaker collections in the known world; come here also for any Elvis paraphernalia you may be missing.

Art Galleries

Stop in at a few Seattle art galleries to get a better feel for Pacific Northwest art. On the first Thursday of every month, the galleries around Pioneer Square stay open late, enticing people with wine and snacks, and everyone goes to look at everyone else looking at the art. Known as **ArtWalk** or 'First Thursday,' this is the best time to be a part of the whole gallery scene.

The Seattle area is known for its Pilchuck Glass School, begun by Dale Chihuly. Both Glasshouse Art Glass (☎ 206-682-9939),

311 Occidental Ave S, and the Foster/White Gallery (☎ 206-622-2833) upstairs at 311½, feature glass works as well as paintings from mainstream Northwest artists.

Davidson Galleries (☎ 206-622-1554), 313 Occidental Ave S, is another Pioneer Square gallery with often eclectic groupings of old and new regional artists. Contemporary Northwest art is on display at Donald Young Gallery, (☎ 206-860-1651), 1103 E Pike, usually Seattle's most experimental gallery; and at Greg Kucera Gallery, (☎ 206-624-0770), 608 2nd Ave, where blue-chip contemporary artists hang with the best of the locals. Legacy Ltd (☎ 206-624-6350), 1003 1st Ave, is probably the city's best gallery for Northwest Indian and Inuit art and artifacts. Fireworks Fine Crafts Gallery (☎ 206-682-8707), 210 1st Ave S, is a great mixture of funky handmade jewelry, furniture, pottery, you name it. This is a good place to actually buy something artsy without spending your annual income.

Camping & Outdoor Gear

The new, state-of-the-art REI (Recreational Equipment Inc, ☎ 206-323-8333) is right by I-5 north of downtown at 222 Yale Ave N (see Capitol Hill map). This outdoor recreation megastore has actually become a tourist destination. It has its own climbing wall (more like a mountain), and you can check out the rainproofing of various brands of gear in a special rainstorm booth, or try out hiking boots on a simulated mountain trail. REI rents all forms of ski packages, climbing gear and camping equipment (call for daily/weekly rates), and also organizes adventure travel trips (see Activities section).

For hard-core climbing and hiking equipment, go to The North Face (☎ 206-622-4111), 1023 1st Ave, downtown. Another local outfitter-made-good is Eddie Bauer (☎ 206-622-2766), 1330 5th Ave. The flagship downtown store offers a large selection of rugged clothing (including things you don't find in the catalog) plus a decorator and home-wares department.

GETTING THERE & AWAY
Air
Seattle's airport, known as Sea-Tac, is the largest in the Northwest, with daily service to Europe, Asia and points throughout the USA and Canada on most national and regional airlines.

Sea-Tac is also a major hub for small commuter airlines with flights to the San Juan Islands, Bellingham, Wenatchee, Yakima and Spokane. Seattle is linked to Portland with flights almost every half-hour and there are hourly flights to and from Vancouver, BC. The airport is 13 miles south of the city on I-5.

The following airlines have offices downtown:

Alaska Airlines, 1301 4th Ave
  (☎ 206-433-3100, 800-426-0333)
American Airlines, 1400 6th Ave
  (☎ 800-433-7300); there's also a ticketing desk in the Sheraton Hotel
British Airways, 1304 4th Ave,
  (☎ 206-433-6714, 800-247-9297)
Continental Airlines, 400 University St
  (☎ 206-624-1740, 800-525-0280)
Delta Air Lines, 410 University St
  (☎ 206-625-0469, 800-221-1212)
Northwest Airlines, 402 University St
  (☎ 800-225-2525)
Scandinavian Airlines (SAS),1301 5th Ave,
  suite 2727 (☎ 800-221-2350)
TWA, 1001 4th Ave
  (☎ 800-221-2000)
United Airlines, 1225 4th Ave
  (☎ 206-441-3700, 800-241-6522)

Bus
Greyhound buses (☎ 206-628-5526, 800-231-2222), 811 Stewart St, link Seattle to Portland, Eugene and points in California along I-5 south, as well as to Bellingham and Vancouver, BC, on I-5 north. Buses also service the I-90 corridor from Seattle to Spokane and on through northern Idaho and Montana to Chicago, and the route from Seattle to Yakima, the Tri-Cities and points south along Hwy 97. One bus daily links Seattle to Port Angeles. The depot is at 8th Ave and Stewart St.

If you're heading to British Columbia, consider the Quick Shuttle (☎ 800-665-2122), which makes five daily express runs between Seattle and Vancouver, BC. Pick-up is either at Sea-Tac airport ($35 one way) or the downtown Travelodge, 200 6th Ave N ($29 one way).

Green Tortoise (☎ 800-867-8647 from the US or Canada, or 415-956-7500 from the San Francisco Bay Area) travels overnight to San Francisco for $59 (call to reserve a spot) and to Portland for $15. The schoolbus-turned-lounge leaves from the Greyhound depot at 8 am Sunday and Thursday.

Train
Amtrak offers train service to/from Seattle at King St Station (☎ 800-872-7245), 303 S Jackson St. Seattle is the terminus of three Amtrak train lines. With four departures weekly, the *Empire Builder* heads east through Spokane, eventually reaching Chicago; a roundtrip ticket from Chicago to Seattle ranges from $184 to $340, depending on availability.

The *Coast Starlight* runs daily between Seattle and Los Angeles, with stops in Tacoma, Olympia, Portland and points south; four trains daily run to Portland, and the roundtrip ticket can be as little as $30 with advance booking; to Los Angeles, fares range between $237 and $438. The *Mount Baker* travels between Seattle and Vancouver, BC. There's only one train a day, although Amtrak also operates three buses daily between the two cities; the fare is $19 one way.

Car
The AAA office (☎ 206-448-5353) is at 330 6th Ave N, near the Seattle Center.

Rental Most national car-rental firms have booths at the airport. The following also maintain offices in the downtown area.

Allstar Rent-a-Car, 2402 7th Ave
  (☎ 206-443-3368)
Avis, 1919 5th Ave
  (☎ 206-448-1700)
Budget,19030 28th Ave S
  (☎ 206-682-2277, 800-527-0700)

WASHINGTON

Dollar Rent A Car, 710 Stewart St
  (☎ 206-682-1316)
Hertz, 722 Pike St
  (☎ 206-682-5050, 800-654-3131)
National Car Rental, 1942 Westlake Ave
  (☎ 206-448-7368)
Xtra Car Discount Rentals, 1124 Denny Way
  (☎ 206-623-8646)

RV Rental   Adventure Werks (☎ 800-736-8897), 3713 Seeley St, Bellingham, specializes in VW camper rental. Camping packages and mountain bike rental are also available. There are also a handful of companies that rent motorhomes (RVs) in the Seattle area, but you'll have to go a bit out of town to find them.

Eastside Motorhome Rentals,
  3625 241st Ave SE, Issaquah
  (☎ 206-399-5878)
NW Van & Motor Home Rentals,
  14458 Ambaum Blvd SW, Burien
  (☎ 206-241-6111, 800-359-4306)
Western Motorhome Rentals,
  19303 Hwy 99, Lynnwood
  (☎ 206-775-1181, 800-800-1181)

Weather & Road Conditions   For a report of road conditions, call ☎ 425-455-7700. Call ☎ 206-368-4499 for a traffic report, and ☎ 206-442-2800 ext 2032 for a weather report.

Ferry
Ferries to most Washington destinations (Bremerton, and Vashon and Bainbridge Islands) are state-operated, and all ferry queries can be routed through a central information line (☎ 206-464-6400 or 800-843-3779 in Washington only). Reservations for the Washington State Ferry System are taken for vehicles only, and only for the Anacortes to Sidney, BC sailing.

To/From Victoria, BC, & the San Juan Islands   Clipper Navigation runs two ferry lines to Victoria, one of which stops in the San Juan Islands in the summer. The *Victoria Clipper* (☎ 206-448-5000) departs from Pier 69 in Seattle for Victoria at 8:30 am only in winter, with additional boats at 7:30 am, 8 am and 4 pm in high season (May 16 to September 13). This is a

high-speed, passenger-only ferry; adult fare for the two- to three-hour trip costs adults $58 to $66 one way, and $94 to $109 roundtrip in high season; children are half-price. The 7:30 am summer sailing also stops at Friday Harbor on San Juan Island ($39 one way, $59 roundtrip) and Rosario Resort on Orcas Island ($43 one way, $67 roundtrip).

One-way tickets on the slower 4½-hour car ferry, *Princess Marguerite III*, are $29 adults and $49 for a car and driver. This ferry departs from Pier 48 at 1 pm daily in summer only.

Reservations are recommended, and tickets for the *Victoria Clipper* or the *Princess Marguerite III* may be purchased at their respective terminals or by calling the above number; travelers should bring ID and be prepared to go through Canadian customs upon arrival.

GETTING AROUND
To/From the Airport
Gray Line runs an Airport Express (☎ 206-626-6088) every 15 minutes from 5 am to midnight between Sea-Tac and downtown Seattle's major hotels. The cost is $7.50 one way or $13 roundtrip. There's also the Shuttle Express (☎ 206-622-1424, 800-487-7433), which offers town car service to downtown hotels for $39.

Bus
Metro Transit (☎ 206-553-3000) serves the greater Seattle metropolitan area with 130 bus routes. Most of Seattle's buses run through downtown on 4th Ave, or in the Bus Tunnel, which has five entrances in the downtown area. In the immediate downtown area – between 6th Ave and the Waterfront, and between Jackson St in Pioneer Square and Battery St – all bus rides are free from 6 am to 7 pm. Note that the Seattle Center is outside of the ride-free zone.

Regular bus fare is $1.25 during peak hours (5 to 9 am and 3 to 6 pm) and $1 at other times. If you are catching a bus that's heading downtown, you purchase your ticket when you get on; however, if you board a bus downtown and head elsewhere, you pay when you get off. Bus drivers do not make change, so you need exact fare. Buy tickets in advance or get a weekend/holiday pass ($2) at the Metro Customer Service office at 821 2nd Ave, or at the Westlake Center bus tunnel station. Pick up a copy of various bus schedules at these offices, and also a Metro bus map for $2.

Frequently used buses include Nos 71, 72 and 73 between downtown and the university; bus No 7 climbs up to Capitol Hill and runs along Broadway before eventually ending up at the University of Washington; bus Nos 10 and 43 also go to Capitol Hill. To get to the Seattle Center, take bus Nos 1, 2, 3, 4, 6, 13, 15 or 18. Bus No 26 runs to Fremont, and then through Wallingford to Greenlake.

Trolley

Seattle Trolley Tours (☎ 206-626-5212) provide a great form of downtown transport, especially for sightseeing. Visitors are encouraged to get on and off at leisure, and tickets are good for the full day of operation. Stops, indicated by bright yellow sandwich boards, include Westlake Center, Space Needle, Pike Place, Waterfront, Pioneer Square, International District, Kingdome, Seattle Art Museum and Newmark Center (on 2nd Ave). The trolley runs every 30 minutes. Information centers are located across from the Westlake Center Nordstrom on Pine St and at Pier 57. One-day tickets cost $13/8 adults/seniors and students, and can be purchased either at the information center or upon boarding. The trolley operates 9:30 am to 6 pm daily from May 1 to October 15.

Monorail

The futuristic Monorail provides frequent transport between downtown's Westlake Center, at Pine St and 5th Ave, and Seattle Center. This 1½-mile experiment in mass transit was built in 1962 as a signature piece for the World's Fair. Cars run the two-minute trip about every 10 minutes, and tickets are $1/75¢ adults/children, and 50¢ for seniors. The Seattle Center depot is near the base of the Space Needle. The Monorail operates 7:30 am to 11 pm weekdays, and 9 am to 11 pm weekends.

Taxi

For a cab, call one of the following:

Farwest Taxi	☎ 206-622-1717
Graytop Cabs	☎ 206-282-8222
STITA Taxi	☎ 206-246-9980
Yellow Cabs	☎ 206-622-6500

Around Seattle

IN & ON THE SOUND
Blake Island
Blake Island is a state park whose only approach is by boat; this made it a safe place to host the 1993 APEC conference, where President Clinton met with 14 Asian leaders. The most popular facility on the Island is Tillicum Village with its Northwest Coast Indian Cultural Center & Restaurant. Tillicum Village and Tours (☎ 206-443-1244) charters boats which depart from Piers 55 and 56 in Seattle for a tour of the waterfront and an excursion to Blake Island. The package includes a traditional Indian salmon bake, traditional dancing and a film about Northwest Native Americans. After the meal, there's time for a short hike on the island or for gift shopping. Tours last four hours and depart daily from May to mid-October, and on weekends most of the rest of the year; $55/22 adults/children.

Bainbridge Island
The most popular ferry trip for tourists is between Seattle and Winslow, Bainbridge Island's primary town. Winslow has outfitted itself as a destination for day passengers by establishing an array of shops and restaurants within an easy walk of the dock. However, most tourists take the ferry simply for the ride and the great views of Seattle as the ferry negotiates Elliott Bay. The **Bainbridge Island Winery** (☎ 206-842-9463) in Winslow is a good destination for cyclists and wine-lovers.

Ferries to Bainbridge Island make trips around the clock, with at least one departure each hour during the day. Ferries board at Pier 52 for the 35-minute (one-way) trip; one-way fare (seasonal) costs $3.50 for passengers, $7.10 for autos (driver included). Passenger fares are collected on the westbound service only, which means that foot passengers and non-drivers travel free on eastbound ferries.

Vashon Island
More rural and countercultural than Bainbridge Island to the north, Vashon Island has resisted suburbanization – a rare accomplishment in the Puget Sound. Much of the island is covered with farms and gardens; the little community centers double as commercial hubs and artists' enclaves. Cascade views are great, with unencumbered vistas from Mt Rainier in the south to Mt Baker in the north.

Vashon is a good island to explore by bicycle, or to drive around, lazily stopping to pick berries or fruit at a 'u-pick' garden or orchard; or plan a hike in one of the county parks. Travelers from Seattle can make a visit to Vashon into a loop trip by taking the Tahlequah ferry from the southern end of the island to Fauntleroy in West Seattle, returning via the mainland's I-5.

From Pier 50 in Seattle, a passenger-only ferry leaves eight times daily for Vashon Island. However, the ferry will deposit you distant from the centers of Vashon commerce and culture, so you'll need to bring a bike or have a lift arranged. From Fauntleroy in West Seattle, a car ferry leaves almost 40 times daily for Vashon.

Bremerton
Seattle's other ferry destination is Bremerton, the largest town on the Kitsap Peninsula, and the Puget Sound's principal naval base. The main attraction here is the **Naval Museum** (☎ 206-479-7447), 130 Washington Ave, and *USS Turner Joy* (☎ 206-792-2457), 300 Washington Beach Ave. This historic US Naval destroyer is on the waterfront park, right next to the ferry

terminal. Tours are available 10 am to 6 pm daily May to October, and 11 am to 4 pm Thursday to Monday from November to April. Tickets cost $3 to $5.

The automobile ferry to Bremerton makes 13 trips daily from the terminal at Pier 52. There are also five weekday and four weekend passenger-only ferries. Boarding and ticket sales for this ferry are at Pier 50. The trip takes about an hour on either boat, and one-way tickets cost $3.50 for passengers and $7.10 for autos (driver included).

SOUTH OF SEATTLE
Rainier Brewing Company
It's a far cry from microbrew, but Rainier Beer is a northwest original. The brewery (☎ 206-622-2600), 3100 Airport Way S (off I-5), also makes a variety of other beers, from Henry Weinhard's and Heidelberg to Yakima Honey Wheat. Stop by for a free 30-minute factory tour between 1 and 6 pm Monday to Saturday. Bus No 30 goes here from downtown.

Museum of Flight
More interesting than it sounds, this vast museum of aviation (☎ 206-764-5720), 9494 E Marginal Way S, has over 50 historic aircraft on display. The museum is on Boeing Field, about 10 miles south of downtown, although it has no formal ties to Boeing. The museum presents the entire history of flight, from da Vinci to the Wright Brothers to the NASA space program. Twenty airplanes are suspended from the ceiling of the glass, six-story Great Gallery; vintage flyers reside on the grounds outside the buildings and the restored 1909 Red Barn – where Boeing had its beginnings – contains exhibits and displays. There's also a hands-on area where visitors get to sit in the pilot's seat and work the controls. Films about flight and aircraft history are shown in the small theater and there's also a gift shop and cafe.

The museum is open 10 am to 5 pm daily except Thursday, when it stays open until 9 pm. Admission is $8/7 adults/seniors, $4 for youths ages six to 15; kids under six are free. To find the museum, take I-5 exit 158 south of Seattle; turn west and follow East Marginal Way.

Puyallup
The Puget Sound remembers its agricultural underpinnings at the **Western Washington Fair** (☎ 206-845-1771), 110 9th Ave SW, south of Seattle in Puyallup. Held in mid-September, the fair offers a bewildering array of livestock and agricultural displays, a carnival, home and garden show and live entertainment. To reach Puyallup, take I-5 south toward Tacoma, leaving the freeway at exit No 135; Puyallup is 35 miles south of Seattle.

NORTH OF SEATTLE
Boeing Factory
Near the city of Everett is the facility where most of Boeing's wide bodied jets – the 747, 767, and 777s – are produced. Free 90-minute tours of the vast building (apparently the world's largest) and the production areas are offered on weekdays. No photography is allowed in the facility. Tour times change seasonally; call ahead to confirm, ☎ 206-544-1264, 800-464-1264. Tours are offered on a first-come, first-served basis and are quite popular, so plan to get to the plant with plenty of lead time; tickets are usually gone by noon.

To reach the Boeing factory, follow I-5 north to exit 189; turn west and drive 3 miles on Hwy 526.

Snohomish
The little community of Snohomish was once a mill town, but today its historic center has been totally given over to antique stores. If you like to shop for antiques you can easily spend a day here, as there are scores of malls, stalls and shops, all devoted to furniture and collectibles. To reach Snohomish, take I-5 north to Everett, take exit 194 and follow US 2.

EAST OF SEATTLE
'The Eastside'
Bellevue was long the suburb that Seattleites loved to disdain. However, mass immigration to the Seattle area has boosted the population of this city on the eastern shores of Lake Washington to the point where Bellevue is now the state's third-largest city, an upscale burg with high-cost housing and attractive parks. Civic and social life centers on **Bellevue Square**, the shopping mall that sets the tone for downtown and the surrounding communities. Even if you don't need to go shopping, the top floor's **Bellevue Art Museum** (☎ 206-454-6021) is worth a visit.

North of Bellevue on I-405 is Kirkland, a city known for its lakefront business district, marinas and antique shopping malls. Some of the best public access to Lake Washington is along Lake Ave; lots of waterfront restaurants are found here, some with docks for their boat-transported customers. **Hales Brewery** (☎ 206-827-4359), 109 Central Way, is one of the original Seattle area microbreweries.

East of Kirkland is Redmond, a sprawling suburb and the center of Seattle's high-tech industry. Computer giant Microsoft dominates life here.

To reach the Eastside, take I-90 east from downtown Seattle, or cross Lake Washington on the Evergreen Point Floating Bridge (Hwy 520) and turn north onto I-405 for Kirkland, south for Bellevue. Exit at NE 8th St for Bellevue Square.

Snoqualmie Falls
An hour's drive into the mountains east of Seattle is **The Salish Lodge at Snoqualmie Falls** (☎ 206-888-2556, 800-826-6124), PO Box 1109, Snoqualmie, WA 98065. This beautiful resort lodge sits atop 268-foot Snoqualmie Falls and was the locale for many of the scenes from the TV series *Twin Peaks*. The drive into the Cascades, views of the waterfall and short hikes in the area, followed by lunch at the lodge (jokes about cherry pie and a cup of joe are mandatory) make for a nice day away.

To reach Snoqualmie Falls, drive east on I-90 to North Bend, exit 31. The falls and resort are 4 miles northwest of town on Hwy 202.

WASHINGTON

Snoqualmie Pass
Seattle is fortunate to have several ski areas within an easy drive of the city. Closest are the ski slopes at Stevens Pass, 78 miles east of Seattle on US 2 (see the Central Washington chapter) and Snoqualmie Pass, 53 miles east on I-90.

The ski resort at Snoqualmie Pass is a popular excursion for Seattleites, and includes four different ski areas operated by the same company. The four ski areas, the **Summit at Snoqualmie** (☎ 206-232-8182; for a snow report, call ☎ 206-236-1600), **Alpental, Ski Acres** and **Hyak**, vary greatly in difficulty and somewhat in conditions. Alpental is generally considered the most difficult, with steep slopes and 2200 feet of vertical drop. Hyak is over the pass, and usually offers drier and faster snow. Ski Acres offers both downhill and groomed cross-country runs; snow tubing is available at the Snowflake Recreation Area. Snowboards are allowed on all slopes, and Hyak and Snoqualmie Pass have special snowboarding areas. Ski instruction and rental equpiment are available; night skiing is offered throughout the week. One lift ticket is good at all four areas and free buses link the runs. Tickets are $17 early-week; $31 on weekends and holidays.

In central Seattle, the most convenient place to rent skis is at REI (☎ 206-223-1944), 222 Yale Ave N (see Capitol Hill map). Convenient to neighborhoods near the university is Seattle Ski Rental Inc (206-548-1000) at 907 NE 45th St.

If you don't have a vehicle or don't want to face the drive, there are several options for getting to the ski areas. The Pass's ski buses (☎ 206-232-8182) leave from several locations in the Seattle area. While most seats are reserved by season-pass holders, single seats are often available, particularly during the week.

Woodinville
The suburban community of Woodinville, 14 miles north of Bellevue off I-405, is home to two popular wineries and a brewpub. **Chateau Ste Michelle** (☎ 206-488-3300), 14111 NE 145th St, was one of Washington's first wineries (though most of their wine production is in the Yakima area). This historic 87-acre estate lends itself easily to picnics and concerts in the summer. It's open for winetasting from 10 am to 4:30 pm daily. Next door is the **Columbia Winery** (☎ 206-488-2776), 14030 NE 145th St, which also has winetasting from 10 am to 5 pm daily, and tours 10:30 am to 4:30 pm on Saturday and Sunday.

Redhook was one of Washington's first microbreweries, and their Woodinville brewery and pub, called the *Forecasters Public House,* (☎ 206-482-3232), 14300 NE 145th St, offers tours at 2 and 4 pm weekdays, and on the hour from noon to 5 pm on weekends.

Tacoma & Olympia

Tacoma and Olympia are the two largest cities south of Seattle along the Puget Sound, and they can make nice alternatives as places to stay. Though it was once the principal city on the Sound, Tacoma has suffered a bad reputation for years – partly the result of too many pulp mills. But Tacoma has been cleaning up its act, and today it's much nicer than the many Northwest jokes about it would lead you to believe. It has the largest city park this side of New York City's Central Park, as well as some inexpensive accommodations.

Olympia, the state capital, is a smaller, cozier city that runs on politics but has a surprisingly hip, alternative side. In addition to being a pleasant place to visit in and of itself, Olympia makes a good base from which to explore the Olympic Peninsula, Pacific Coast beaches and Mt Rainier National Park.

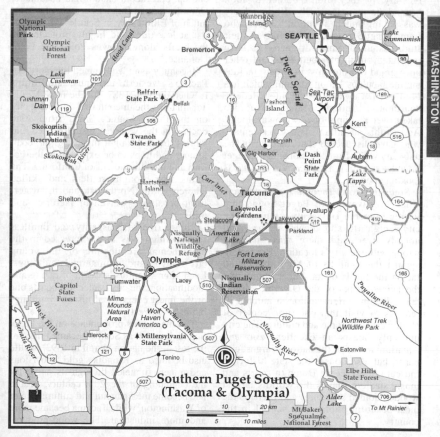

Southern Puget Sound
(Tacoma & Olympia)

WASHINGTON

TACOMA
Population 185,600

Long the object of every other northwest city's scorn, Tacoma has been known for years as a beleaguered mill town with a big domed stadium and a bombed-out (though architecturally notable) downtown. It didn't take a poet to coin the phrase 'the Tacoma aroma,' but the epitaph stuck: it's a coy euphemism for that certain unpleasant odor the area's pulp mills lend to the air.

However, Tacoma is turning itself around. People who speak ill of this Puget Sound city probably haven't been here recently, or they didn't bother to look beyond the shopping malls. While nobody was paying much attention, artists who found Seattle too expensive moved their studios south; community activists have renovated old theater buildings and other once-grand downtown structures – including the fabulous Union Station, which has been gussied up and turned into a federal courthouse. Antique dealers have also taken over a couple of downtown blocks. Add to this an influx of new residents – who have discovered that Tacoma is the only city with affordable housing on Puget Sound – and all of a sudden, Tacoma starts looking good.

Students from Tacoma's two universities – University of Puget Sound and Pacific Lutheran University – support the city's nightlife and theater scene. And nobody ever said there was anything wrong with the city's location. Backed up against the foothills of Mt Rainier, and facing the fjords of the Puget Sound and the jagged peaks of the Olympic Mountains, Tacoma offers visitors a number of reasons to visit this one-time center of Northwest commerce and culture. The city not only boasts an excellent zoo and aquarium in one of the nation's largest city parks, but also houses the state historical museum, the Tacoma Dome (a sports and music stadium that is the world's largest wooden domed structure) and perhaps the most beautiful public high school in the country.

History

Captain George Vancouver first came to Commencement Bay in 1792, and the site was thereafter visited by other early explorers. However, the usual settlement pattern of sawmills and farmlands was barely underway when local land speculators began to wager that Tacoma would end up as the Puget Sound rail terminus for the Northern Pacific Railroad, which by the late 1860s was looking for a northwest port city. Almost every settlement on the Puget Sound went through boom times as speculation rose about where the railroad would end up, but Tacoma had a real advantage: Commencement Bay was deep (at that time much of Elliott Bay in Seattle was a mud-flat at low tide) and highly protected by the bluffs along Browns Point and Point Defiance.

Tacoma was indeed named the Northern Pacific's western terminus, and trains reached there in 1887; for the next decade Tacoma was the uncontested dominant city on the Puget Sound. Ships from Asia docked at the wharves to unload tea and fabrics; trains brought metals, grain, coal, lumber and hops to be exported to the Far East and the boomtowns of California. The trains also brought settlers and skilled laborers to the Northwest, and the waterfront became a warren of factories and mills.

This period of prosperity and limitless self-confidence is best expressed in the monumental architecture of the young city's civic and commercial buildings. Even after a century's worth of razing and modification, the city center still boasts one of the finest enclaves of historic buildings in the Northwest.

Tacoma saw its prominence on the Puget Sound diminish as Seattle became linked to the rest of the nation by rail in 1893. Seattle also boomed as Klondike gold, provisions and miners funneled through its ports. By the beginning of the 20th century, Seattle had become the financial and cultural center of Washington, while Tacoma became more and more industrial. The wood-products giant Weyerhaeuser brought its mills – and eventually its corporate headquarters – to Tacoma in the early 1900s, and smelting, especially of aluminum, thrived on cheap hydropower. Tacoma also connected itself closely to the military by donating land in 1917 to build Fort Lewis and McChord Air Force Base just south of the city.

Beginning in the 1960s, Tacoma's industries slipped into Rust Belt-like decline, and the city began to merge into the suburban sprawl of the greater Puget Sound. Today, the city seems at the cusp of a second growth period as its architectural beauty and cheap rents lure small industries, artists, musicians and others looking for affordable housing into the boomland of western Washington.

Orientation

Tacoma is located on Commencement Bay, a deep harbor protected by Point Defiance, a thumb of land that sticks out into the Puget Sound. The busy Port of Tacoma is immediately north of downtown, on five artificial bays dredged out of the Puyallup River's estuary (there's a free Public Observation Tower off E 11th St, where you can view the Port of Tacoma at work). Directly northwest of downtown, along Tacoma Ave, is the Stadium Historic District, an enclave of Victorian homes and Stadium High School. Further northwest, centered on N 30th St, is the Old Town District. Along the Commencement Bay waterfront north of Old Town is Ruston, a tiny independent municipality totally engulfed by Tacoma and Point Defiance Park.

I-5 runs just to the east of city center. Tacoma is 32 miles south of Seattle, and 143 miles north of Portland. Highway 16 leaves I-5 at Tacoma and crosses the impressive Tacoma Narrows Bridge, leading to Gig Harbor and Bremerton on the Kitsap Peninsula.

A branch of the freeway, called I-705, departs I-5 at exit 133 and runs into the city center and the port area. Just to the east of the exit is the Tacoma Dome. Point Defiance Park is at the northern end of the city,

and is reached from downtown on Ruston Way, which is paralleled by a waterfront walking/biking path. From the end of Pearl St in Point Defiance Park, a ferry departs for Vashon Island.

Pacific Ave, Commerce St and Broadway are the main downtown arterials running north-south; the center of Tacoma is largely encompassed between east-west running 9th and 15th Sts. In general, east-west streets are numbered, north-south streets have names. Another main arterial is Division Ave, which divides north from south in street addresses, and turns into 6th Ave west of downtown.

Information

Look for tourist information at the visitors' center (☎ 253-627-2836, 800-272-7801) in Freighthouse Square at 430 E 25th St, just north of the Tacoma Dome, or downtown in the Convention and Visitors Bureau at 1001 Pacific Ave, suite 400. The main post office is at 4001 S Pine St; more convenient to downtown is the branch at 1102 A St. St Joseph's Medical Center (☎ 253-627-4101) is at 1717 South J St. To find out what's happening in Tacoma, check out the free *Tacoma City Paper*, or *Tacoma Voice*. The daily paper is the *Tacoma News Tribune*. Public radio is heard at 88.5, KPLU FM.

To clean your clothes, head to New Era Laundercenter (☎ 253-759-3501), 2621 N Proctor St. The best place for books on local history and travel is the Pacific Northwest Shop (☎ 253-798-5880) in the Washington State History Museum.

Union Station

Start a tour of downtown Tacoma at Union Station, on Pacific Ave at 19th St. This enormous, copper-domed neo-Baroque depot was designed by the same architects who built New York City's Grand Central Station, and it was completed in 1911. However, by the 1980s, Amtrak had pulled out, Union Station had been boarded up, and the surrounding red-brick warehouse neighborhood had become quite creepy, to say the least. The graceful train depot was

WASHINGTON

510   Tacoma

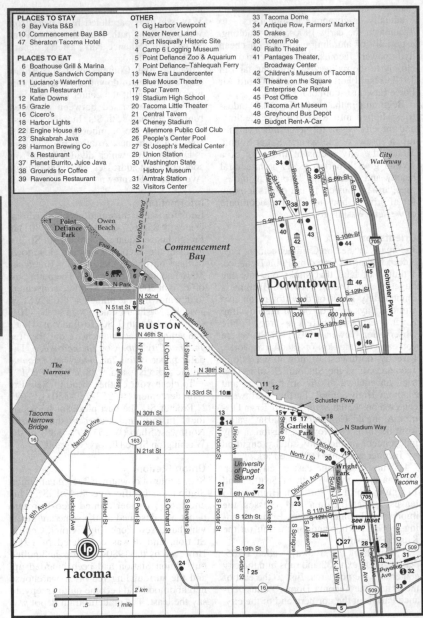

PLACES TO STAY
9 Bay Vista B&B
10 Commencement Bay B&B
47 Sheraton Tacoma Hotel

PLACES TO EAT
6 Boathouse Grill & Marina
8 Antique Sandwich Company
11 Luciano's Waterfront Italian Restaurant
12 Katie Downs
15 Grazie
16 Cicero's
18 Harbor Lights
22 Engine House #9
23 Shakabrah Java
28 Harmon Brewing Co & Restaurant
37 Planet Burrito, Juice Java
38 Grounds for Coffee
39 Ravenous Restaurant

OTHER
1 Gig Harbor Viewpoint
2 Never Never Land
3 Fort Nisqually Historic Site
4 Camp 6 Logging Museum
5 Point Defiance Zoo & Aquarium
7 Point Defiance–Tahlequah Ferry
13 New Era Laundercenter
14 Blue Mouse Theatre
17 Spar Tavern
19 Stadium High School
20 Tacoma Little Theater
21 Central Tavern
24 Cheney Stadium
25 Allenmore Public Golf Club
26 People's Center Pool
27 St Joseph's Medical Center
29 Union Station
30 Washington State History Museum
31 Amtrak Station
32 Visitors Center

33 Tacoma Dome
34 Antique Row, Farmers' Market
35 Drakes
36 Totem Pole
40 Rialto Theater
41 Pantages Theater, Broadway Center
42 Children's Museum of Tacoma
43 Theatre on the Square
44 Enterprise Car Rental
45 Post Office
46 Tacoma Art Museum
48 Greyhound Bus Depot
49 Budget Rent-A-Car

renovated in the early '90s and now houses the federal courts. Next door, an entirely new building constructed in the same domed style contains the Washington State History Museum.

Step inside the airy Union Station rotunda, which is dominated by several massive installations of glass art by Tacoma native Dale Chihuly. Hanging from the center of the rotunda is a translucent, three-story cluster of sensuous, deep-blue grapes; in the north-facing rosette is a collage of poppy-red glass.

To reach Union Station from downtown, take bus No 46 from Commercial St.

Washington State History Museum

Located next to Union Station, this is the state's leading museum of history (☎ 253-272-3500, 888-238-4373), 1911 Pacific Ave. The primary exhibit is the 'Hall of Washington History,' a chronological examination of the history of Washington, beginning with Native Americans and moving through the settlement era and up to the present. Particularly well done are the exhibits relating to the Northwest coastal tribes. Other galleries are devoted to changing exhibits, often the works of regional photographers. The lobby contains a good bookstore with an excellent selection of Northwest history and travel books, as well as a selection of quality crafts and gifts. It's open 9 am to 5 pm Tuesday to Saturday from Memorial Day weekend to Labor Day (10 am to 5 pm the rest of the year), and 11 am to 5 pm Sunday. Admission is $7/6 adults/seniors; students and youths are $5, children six to 12 are $4, aged five and under are free. The museum is open until 8 pm on Thursday, and there is free admission after 5 pm.

Tacoma Art Museum

After seeing the glass installation at Union Station, you'll probably want to see more of Chihuly's work. The Tacoma Art Museum (☎ 253-272-4258), 1123 Pacific Ave at 12th St, has a permanent display of some of Chihuly's more intimate (smaller) works, as well as a gallery devoted to traveling shows.

The museum is open 10 am to 5 pm Tuesday, Wednesday, Friday and Saturday, 10 am to 7 pm Thursday, and noon to 5 pm Sunday. Admission is $4/3 adults/students and seniors; children under 12 are free. Admission is free on the third Thursday of each month.

Broadway Theater District

Things began to look up for Tacoma's arts scene when the ornate **Pantages Theater**, 909 Broadway, was renovated in 1983. Now the blocks surrounding the Pantages are abuzz with a lively gentrification. The Pantages was once an elaborate vaudeville hall, famed for its acoustics; today it's Tacoma's primary performance stage. This theater, the refurbished **Rialto Theater** at the corner of Market and 9th Sts and the **Theatre on the Square**, 915 Broadway, are the primary components of the Broadway Center for the Performing Arts complex (see Entertainment, later in this section).

In the midst of the theater district is the **Children's Museum of Tacoma** (☎ 253-627-6031), 936 Broadway, a hands-on activity center specializing in science and technology exhibits for kids. It's open 10 am to 5 pm Tuesday to Friday, 10 am to 5 pm Saturday, and noon to 5 pm Sunday. Call for extended summer hours. Admission is $4.25 per person, children under two are free; the museum is also free on Friday evening from 5 to 9 pm.

Directly north of 9th St on Broadway is **Antique Row**, a two-block-long maze of antique and collectibles shops that antique lovers shouldn't miss. Along Broadway in the antique district, a **farmers' market** sets up every Thursday from June through September. Follow 9th St three blocks east toward the waterfront to reach Fireman's Park. The **totem pole** here is claimed to be, at 105 feet, the tallest in the world.

South on Broadway at 13th St is **Broadway Plaza**, a 1960s urban renewal project in the form of a pedestrian mall.

Stadium District

The Stadium neighborhood has always been Tacoma's nicest, and a walk down

N Tacoma Ave from Garfield Park passes by a number of nice **Victorian homes**. Turn down Division Ave and head to Wright Park at South G St, where the ornate, domed **Seymour Botanical Conservatory** (☎ 253-591-5330), 316 South G St, is filled with tropical plants in the middle of a park full of native Douglas firs. The conservatory is open 10 am to 4:30 pm daily.

The most amazing structure in this genteel old neighborhood is the turreted, ivy-covered **Stadium High School**, at the corner of N 1st St and Broadway (from downtown, follow Commercial St north until it becomes Stadium Way). Construction began in 1891, when the building was conceived as a monumental luxury hotel. However, a series of economic calamities waylaid the hotel's completion, and by 1902 the unfinished chateau-esque structure was slated to be dismantled. However, alert citizens petitioned to convert the building into a badly needed high school. The result is one of the most eye-catching and architecturally imposing public schools anywhere.

Point Defiance Park

One of Tacoma's preeminent attractions, this 700-acre park (☎ 253-305-1000), flanked by the waters of Puget Sound, contains a wealth of gardens, the city zoo and aquarium, and a number of recreational and historic sites.

The park contains 13.7 miles of hiking trails, which wind through groves of old-growth forests and lead to sheltered beaches. (It's unwise to hike the trails alone after dark.) The main paved road through the park is called Five Mile Drive; on Saturday this scenic road remains closed to motor vehicles until 1 pm, though it's open to bicycles, joggers and in-line skaters. Bicyclists are not allowed on any hiking trails, and must stay on the paved bike paths. Popular picnic areas include **Gig Harbor Viewpoint** and **Owen Beach**, which is a favorite of summer sunbathers.

Abundant **formal gardens** are maintained cooperatively by members of local garden clubs, with help from the Metropolitan Park District. Park gardens include the Japanese Garden, with a torii gate and Shinto shrine received as a gift from Kitakyushu, Tacoma's sister city in Japan, the Herb Garden and the Rhododendron Garden, which is a blaze of color in May. Just past the zoo entrance on Five Mile Drive is the civic Rose Garden, established in 1895, with more than an acre of bushes, many of heirloom varieties. A new addition is the Iris Garden, a small circular bed across from the Dahlia Trial Garden. The Northwest Native Garden, located near the park's main exit, presents a collection of indigenous plants ranging from trees to grasses.

The **Boathouse Marina** offers moorage and boat rentals, and sports a restaurant, *The Boathouse Grill* (☎ 253-756-7336), and a tackle shop. Find additional moorage and shower facilities at Breakwater Marina, east of the Vashon Island ferry dock.

To reach the park from downtown, take Schuster Parkway north and turn onto Ruston Way; it's about 5 miles to the park. From I-5, take exit 132 and follow Hwy 16 just past 6th Ave. Turn right on Pearl St, and follow Pearl St north 3 miles to the park entrance. If you're on public transport, take bus No 11 from Commerce St.

Point Defiance Zoo & Aquarium This award-winning zoo (☎ 253-591-5337) is often considered one of the best in the USA. It's unusual in that it focuses primarily on species from the Pacific Rim, including polar bears, musk ox and Arctic fox at the Arctic Tundra exhibit. Peer at coastline mammals through the underwater windows at Rocky Shores. No fewer than 30 huge sharks swim among tropical fish and eels in the lagoon at Discovery Reef Aquarium. Elephants and apes and other zoo favorites are housed in the Southeast Asia complex. The zoo and aquarium are open 10 am to 4 pm daily. Admission is $7/6.55 adults/seniors; children ages four to 13 are $5.30 and under four are free.

Fort Nisqually Historic Site In 1833, the Hudson's Bay Company trading post at

Napeequa River Valley, Glacier Peak Wilderness, WA

Top: Red heather and Mt Baker, WA

Bottom: Wildflower meadow and Fortress Mountain, Glacier Peak Wilderness, WA

Fort Nisqually was established 17 miles south of Tacoma near DuPont. This restoration of the HBC fort (☎ 253-591-5339) includes the factor's house, granary, trade store, blacksmith shop, laborers' quarters and corner bastions, all furnished to reflect life on the frontier in the 1850s at the height of the old fort's prominence. Nineteenth-century fur-trade artifacts are on exhibit in the small museum. Docents in period clothing demonstrate blacksmithing, spinning and beadwork.

Fort Nisqually is open 11 am to 6 pm daily, June 1st through Labor Day, with adult/child admissions at $1.50/75¢. The fort is open 11 am to 4 pm Wednesday through Sunday the rest of the year and admission is free.

Camp 6 Logging Museum
An open-air logging museum, Camp 6 (☎ 253-752-0047) is a reconstruction of a pioneer logging camp focusing on the steam powered equipment used from the 1880s to the 1940s. On spring and summer weekends only, ride on a logging train with a steam locomotive. The museum is open 10 am to 5 pm from mid-January through October 31 and is closed the rest of the year.

Never Never Land
If the kids didn't enjoy the steam donkey at Camp 6, then this 10-acre, storyland theme park (☎ 253-591-5845) in an outdoor forest setting might tickle their fancy. Wooded paths lead to oversized sculpted figures of nursery-rhyme characters; on summer weekends, kids can meet real costumed characters, such as Humpty Dumpty, Peter Rabbit, the Big Bad Wolf and Little Red Riding Hood. It's open 11 am to 6 pm daily May to Labor Day, and 11 am to 5 pm on weekends only in early spring and September. Admission is $2.75/1.25 adults/children.

Activities
Both convenient and challenging, Allenmore Public Golf Club (☎ 253-627-7211), 2125 S Cedar St, is a well-established 18-hole golf course just west of downtown. If you want to swim, go to People's Center

Pool (☎ 253-591-5323) at 1602 Martin Luther King, Jr Way, open year-round.

Places to Stay

Camping Five miles northeast of downtown Tacoma (off Hwy 509) is *Dash Point State Park* (☎ 253-593-2206), a beachfront state park with both tent sites ($11) and trailer hookups ($16). This is a popular place in summer, when the water warms up enough for swimming. Across the Hwy 16 Narrows Bridge is *Gig Harbor RV Resort* (☎ 253-858-8138), in Gig Harbor at 9515 Burnham Drive. Hookups ($25) and tent sites ($12.50) are available, as well as a pool, laundry and playground.

B&Bs *Bay Vista B&B* (☎ 253-759-8084), 4617 Darien Drive N (off 46th St), is near Point Defiance and the Vashon Island ferry; it has one suite ($85) and a bedroom for $75. *Commencement Bay B&B* (☎ 253-752-8175), 3312 N Union Ave, overlooks the bay and offers three guest rooms (two share a bathroom); there's even an office with a modem hook-up for business travelers. Room rates range from $85 to $105 in peak season.

For other B&Bs in Tacoma, contact Greater Tacoma B&B Reservations by phone at ☎ 253-759-4088, 800-406-4088. There's no added charge to make reservations using this service.

Hotels If you're on a budget and planning to visit Seattle, you can save a little money by staying in Tacoma and commuting the half-hour up I-5. However, almost all lodgings are now located along the freeway and don't offer much in the way of charm. Just east of Tacoma in Fife there are several, but the *Econo Lodge at the Port of Tacoma* (☎ 253-922-0550, 800-424-4777), off I-5 exit 136 at 3518 Pacific Hwy, has the best rates in the area. There's an outdoor pool and guest laundry, and pets are allowed; singles/doubles are $49/56.

South of Tacoma, between I-5 exit Nos 128 and 129, are a clutch of motels. The most attractive one is the *Best Western Tacoma Inn* (☎ 253-535-2880, 800-305-2880),

8726 S Hosmer St, with a courtyard pool, putting green and guest laundry. Rooms begin at $61/77. Next door, the *King Oscar Motel* (☎ 253-539-1153, 800-578-7878), 8820 S Hosmer St, has rooms at $60/65.

About the only place to stay downtown is the *Sheraton Tacoma Hotel* (☎ 253-572-3200, 800-845-9466) at 1320 Broadway Plaza. It's a convention-style hotel with rooms starting at $118/$133, and suites starting at $140.

Places to Eat

Grounds for Coffee (☎ 253-627-7742), 764 Broadway, is a friendly downtown cafe for morning coffee or sandwiches at lunch. There are lots of easy chairs and couches to kick back on. Another good, central place for lunch or an inexpensive dinner is *Ravenous Restaurant* (☎ 253-572-6374), 785 Broadway, with pizza, pasta, and urbane Italian entrées. Even if you're not on a budget, you'll enjoy *Planet Burrito* (☎ 253-272-4233), 754 St Helens St, with its zippy wraps; they've knocked out the wall between it and *Juice Java*, the coffee shop and juice bar next door.

In Ruston, on the way to Point Defiance Park, the *Antique Sandwich Company* (☎ 253-752-4069), 5102 N Pearl St, is a landmark luncheonette filled with students, young families and seniors who have been regulars for decades.

As in nearby Seattle, Italian food has become the dining standard in Tacoma. *Grazie* (☎ 253-627-0231), 2301 N 30th St, is an Italian hangout with great views of Commencement Bay; northern Italian specialties with veal, chicken and pasta are in the $12 to $16 range. Another Italian favorite with great views is *Luciano's Waterfront Italian Restaurant* (☎ 253-756-5611), 3327 Ruston Way, with a more traditional Italian menu in the same price range.

Amid the antique stores across from the new history museum, *Harmon Brewing Company & Restaurant* (☎ 253-383-2739), 1938 Pacific Ave S, offers up homemade ales and a full service menu; families are welcome.

A Tacoma original, *Harbor Lights* (☎ 253-752-8600), 2761 Ruston Way, is a former fishermen's eatery. The clientele has changed, but not the excellent quality, the old-fashioned seafood preparations nor the enormous workingman's portions. Call ahead for reservations.

Out in Point Defiance Park, *Anthony's at Point Defiance* (formerly the Boathouse Grill) (☎ 253-752-9700), 5910 N Waterfront Dr, near the park's Pearl St entrance, has great views over Commencement Bay, and features family-style seafood dining.

Entertainment

Coffeehouses *Shakabrah Java* (☎ 253-572-4369), 2618 6th Ave, offers a fine selection of loose-leaf teas as well as the standard coffee drinks; it has a living room with board games. *Cicero's* (☎ 253-272-2122), 2123 N 30th St, is the classy place in Old Town to swill lattes and hang out.

Cinemas For off-beat and foreign films, the restored *Blue Mouse Theatre* (☎ 253-752-9500), 2611 N Proctor St, is the place to go (the cool neon on the marquee was designed by omnipresent Dale Chihuly). Art films are shown at the *Rialto Theater* (☎ 253-591-0052), 310 9th St, as part of the Broadway Center series.

Performing Arts Tacoma has a long history of live theater. Tacoma Actors Guild (☎ 253-272-2145) makes its home at the *Theatre on the Square* (☎ 253-591-5890), 915 Broadway. The *Tacoma Little Theater* (☎ 253-272-2281), a community theater group established in 1909, stages productions for both children and adults at Beverly Center, 210 N I St. In the summer, outdoor drama and comedy productions are staged at Celebrations Meadow in Gig Harbor by the Performance Circle (☎ 253-851-7529).

The *Broadway Center for the Performing Arts* (☎ 253-591-5894), 901 Broadway, brings music, dance and theater to town. Shows are staged at the opulent 1100-seat Pantages Theater, 901 Broadway, and at the Rialto Theater, 310 9th St at Market St.

The *Tacoma Opera* (☎ 253-627-7789) is a community opera company whose works are all sung in English. The *Tacoma Philharmonic* (☎ 253-272-0809) is a presenting organization that brings outside symphony orchestras to the Pantages. *BalleTacoma* (☎ 253-272-9631) performs at Pantages, while the local *Tacoma Symphony* (☎ 253-272-7264) and the *Tacoma Youth Symphony* (☎ 253-627-2792) both perform at the Rialto.

Nightlife *Bob's Java Jive* (☎ 253-475-9843) at 2102 S Tacoma Way along an unattractive strip of car dealerships, is quite the institution in Tacoma. This pre-fab, larger-than-life coffeepot was built in 1927 by veterinarian Dr Button. Primarily a restaurant, the Jive served its days as a speakeasy – the entrance was through the ladies' room. Today the place is a scream of tacky furniture, pool tables, jukeboxes and a menu of cheap sandwiches, burgers and domestic beer.

Engine House No 9 (☎ 253-272-3435), 611 N Pine St by 6th St, has a great selection of beers and ciders on tap, and yes, it really was a fire engine house. They also have a full menu, including sandwiches, pizzas and salads – none of which are over $6.50. The Engine House is open 11 am to 2 am daily.

Katie Downs (☎ 253-756-0771) along the waterfront at 3211 Ruston Way, is a popular place to grab a beer (they have 22 kinds on tap) and a pizza or some steamer clams. There is seating on an outdoor deck with a great view of the Sound. Reservations are taken during the week, but not for weekend evenings, nor for deck seating. It's open 11 am to midnight daily.

If you're in Old Town, check out the *Spar Tavern* (☎ 253-627-8215), 2121 N 30th St, a classy early-20th-century bar that's now pouring local microbrews.

Tacoma's main dance club is *Drakes* (☎ 253-572-4144), 734 Pacific Ave. Check out the local music scene at the *Central Tavern* (☎ 253-756-0424), 3829 6th Ave.

Spectator Sports
Tacoma Rainiers (☎ 253-752-7707, 800-281-3834) is a Triple-A farm team of the Seattle Mariners; they play at Cheney Stadium, Hwy 16 at Stevens St.

Getting There & Away
Air Tacoma is served by Sea-Tac Airport, 15 miles north on I-5. For more information on air service to Sea-Tac, see the Seattle chapter.

Bus Greyhound (☎ 253-383-4621), 1319 Pacific Ave, links Tacoma to other cities along the I-5 corridor. Also, regional buses leave from the bus station for Port Angeles and Port Townsend; call the Greyhound number for information. One-way fare to Portland is $19; to Seattle it's $5.

Train Three Amtrak trains a day link Tacoma to Seattle and Portland from the depot (☎ 253-627-8141) at 1001 Puyallup Ave. One-way fare to Portland is $18; to Seattle it's $6.50.

Car For a rental vehicle, contact either Enterprise (☎ 253-566-6480), 455 St Helens, or Budget (☎ 253-383-4944), 1305 Pacific Ave, both in downtown Tacoma.

Ferry Sailings to Vashon Island via the Point Defiance-Tahlequah Ferry run from about 5 am to midnight daily. Vehicle-and-driver fares are $8 to $10 (low season or high season), and foot-passenger fares are $2.30. For information on Washington State Ferries, call ☎ 800-843-3779.

Getting Around
To/From the Airport Capital Aeroporter (☎ 253-927-6179) offers 15 buses daily between Tacoma-area stops and Sea-Tac. A one-way fare is $13; the downtown stop is at the Sheraton, 1320 Broadway.

Bus The local bus system is called Pierce Transit (☎ 253-581-8000, 800-562-8109), with service throughout the Tacoma area. Buses to note are the No 11, which runs from downtown to Point Defiance Park and

WASHINGTON

the Vashon Island ferry, and the No 100, which runs out to Gig Harbor. Local fare is 90¢. Pierce Transit also operates a number of express buses throughout the day to downtown Seattle.

Taxi For a taxi, call Yellow Cab (☎ 253-472-3303).

AROUND TACOMA
Lakewold Gardens
The Lakewold Gardens (☎ 253-584-3360), 12317 Gravelly Lake Drive, on a 10-acre estate from the early 1900s, is one of the Northwest's finest private gardens. Landscape architects from the Olmsted Bros firm, who also planned New York City's Central Park, were involved in the original planning of the garden, and in the successive 90 years it has evolved into a mature woodland estate. Especially notable are the rhododendrons, which number in the hundreds, exotic trees chosen for their multicolored and many-shaped foliage, and a formal garden with roses, statuary, fountains and parterres.

The garden is open 10 am to 4 pm from Saturday to Monday and on Thursday, and noon to 8 pm on Friday, from April to September; it's open 10 am to 3 pm on Friday, Saturday and Sunday in the off-season. Admission is $5/3 adults/seniors, and children under 12 are free. To get to the gardens, take I-5 south to exit 124, which leads onto Gravelly Lake Drive.

Northwest Trek Wildlife Park
This wildlife park (☎ 253-847-1901, 360-832-7152, 800-433-8735) allows Northwest native wildlife to roam freely on a 600-acre site. Species like grizzly bears, cougars and wolves live in large natural outdoor enclosures; bison, elk, deer and caribou range pretty much as they see fit in a 435-acre meadow and forest. Trams circle through much of the park, with naturalists leading an hour-long tour. Unlike mom-and-pop zoos with animals in stinky runs, Northwest Trek is a well-planned facility, and is administered by the Park Bureau of Tacoma. In addition to the wild-

life areas, there's a cafe and gift shop; picnic areas are also available.

At the **Cheney Discovery Center**, children learn about environmental issues and watch bees in a glass-sided hive; there's also a supervised touch tank with live reptiles and amphibians.

Northwest Trek is located 35 miles south of Tacoma, 6 miles north of Eatonville off Hwy 161 at 11610 Trek Drive E (take I-5 south to Hwy 512 east, which leads to Hwy 161 south). The park is open 9:30 am to dusk daily, March through October. The rest of the year the park is open Friday to Sunday only, the same hours. Admission is $8.25/7.75 adults/seniors; youth ages five to 17 are $5.75, and children (three and four) are $3.75.

Steilacoom
Founded in 1851 by a New England sea captain, Steilacoom is Washington's oldest incorporated town. After the establishment of a hotel, store and sawmill, the little town was up and running and for a couple of decades it was an important settlement for newly arriving settlers. It didn't take long for nearby Tacoma to overwhelm the little village, especially after the railroad brought a galloping pace of development to the area.

The old town center boasts 32 buildings on the National Register of Historic Places, most dating from the late 1800s; many buildings are open for viewing, including a museum of local history. **Town Hall Museum** (☎ 253-584-4133), is open 1 pm to 4 pm Tuesday through Sunday, March 1 to October 31.

The **Steilacoom Tribal Cultural Center** (☎ 253-584-6308), 1515 Lafayette St, commemorates the history of the local Salish tribe. The museum consists of three exhibition galleries, a gift shop and a snack bar serving Native American foods. The center is open 10 am to 4 pm Tuesday to Sunday. Admission is $2/1 adults/seniors and students; families are $6. Children six and under are free.

Steilacoom is 15 miles south of Tacoma on the Puget Sound. From I-5, take exit 128 and turn west, following Steilacoom Rd.

Fort Lewis Military Museum

Fort Lewis is a large army training camp that was established in 1917 as the USA entered WWI. Pacific Northwest military history from Lewis and Clark onward is retold at the Military Museum (☎ 253-967-7206) in Fort Lewis.

One of the most notable features of the museum – most of which consists of old uniforms and equipment – is the building itself. The chalet-like structure was built in 1919 by the Salvation Army as a 150-room inn to provide R&R for local military personnel and their guests, and it served as the social center of the fort for decades. The museum is open noon to 4 pm Wednesday to Sunday; admission is free. To get to Fort Lewis and the museum, take I-5 exit 120.

OLYMPIA
Population 38,650

Olympia is a city known to most for its beer and its politics, and as such, it may not initially seem like an obvious magnet for travelers. As Washington's oldest settlement and the state capital, Olympia could easily be just another one of those sleepy, 'insiders-only' towns whose most interesting moments occurred 100 years ago. In fact, Olympia is a vital city – together with sister cities Lacey and Tumwater, the urban area has a population of over 90,000 – with a strong alternative community.

Of course, part of the reason for the vitality of Olympia is the state capital, which keeps political issues in the forefront. But no small part of the equation is Evergreen State College, an innovative public university with 3100 students, which was founded in 1971 as a result of the student movements of the '60s. Classes, programs and degrees are usually inter-disciplinary, multi-ethnic and relatively unstructured, attracting students and faculty with progressive, out-of-the-mainstream ideas. When you find that Olympia offers better music, cinema, coffee and just-under-the-surface hipness than you might expect, thank Evergreen.

Olympia makes a good base for exploring western Washington. Both Mt Rainier and Olympic National Parks are within an hour's drive, and Pacific Coast beaches are just 60 miles away at Ocean Shores.

History

The lower reaches of the Puget Sound were home to the Nisqually, a Salish tribe. The Nisqually were unlike most coastal tribes in that they maintained large herds of horses, which they pastured in the lowlands of the Nisqually River valley.

The first US settlement in Washington was founded at Tumwater, along the falls of the Deschutes River, when a group of 32 Missourians arrived here in 1845. They chose to settle north of the Columbia in British-dominated territory because some members of the party were partly African American – including the group's leader, George Bush – and Oregon's territorial laws forbade settlement by blacks. Access to water power and to the harbor at Budd Inlet propelled the new settlement into industrialization. By 1850, the settlement (then called New Market) boasted a grist mill, sawmill, tannery and other small factories. Beer brewing was an early industry here as well. The original brewery in Tumwater was called Capital Brewing Company; in 1905, the company was bought out and renamed the Olympia Brewing Company.

Olympia was Washington's principal settlement when the village was named the territorial capital in 1853. The first meetings of the territory's legislature met above a bar, then were moved to a local Masonic lodge. The building of a permanent capitol building was not begun until 1893; however, due to economic vicissitudes, the capitol was not completed until 1928. During much of this time, the old Thurston County Courthouse served as Washington's state capitol building.

Orientation

Olympia is at the southern end of the Puget Sound. Immediately south of Olympia is Tumwater, and east on Hwy 510 is Lacey; these three separate towns make up an urban entity often referred to as the South Sound. Due to its location, Olympia is a

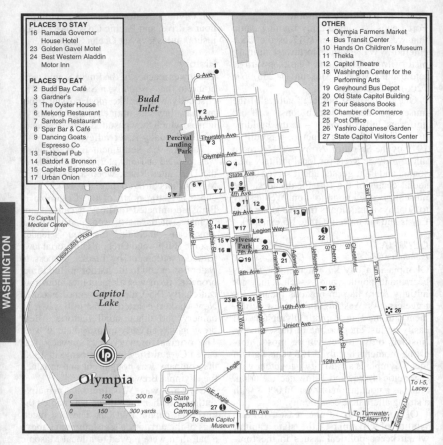

PLACES TO STAY
16 Ramada Governor
   House Hotel
23 Golden Gavel Motel
24 Best Western Aladdin
   Motor Inn

PLACES TO EAT
2 Budd Bay Café
3 Gardner's
5 The Oyster House
6 Mekong Restaurant
7 Santosh Restaurant
8 Spar Bar & Café
9 Dancing Goats
   Espresso Co
13 Fishbowl Pub
14 Batdorf & Bronson
15 Capitale Espresso & Grille
17 Urban Onion

OTHER
1 Olympia Farmers Market
4 Bus Transit Center
10 Hands On Children's Museum
11 Thekla
12 Capitol Theatre
18 Washington Center for the
   Performing Arts
19 Greyhound Bus Depot
20 Old State Capitol Building
21 Four Seasons Books
22 Chamber of Commerce
25 Post Office
26 Yashiro Japanese Garden
27 State Capitol Visitors Center

Olympia

division point for a number of road systems. I-5 passes through, running between Seattle (60 miles) and Portland (114 miles). Highway 101 runs north and west, leading to the Hood Canal and Olympic Peninsula; Port Angeles is 121 miles away. From Hwy 101, Hwy 8 to Aberdeen (50 miles) also leads out from Olympia.

Olympia is dominated by the Washington State Capitol campus which rises on a bluff above Capitol Lake (formed by damming the Deschutes River), Budd Inlet and downtown. I-5 exit 105 loops around and turns into 14th Ave and leads directly to the capitol and to Capitol Way, the main north-

south street through downtown. The main commercial area of Olympia is around 4th and 5th Aves along Capitol Way.

Local Olympians will often to refer to 'westside' and 'eastside' districts of the city. The finger-like intrusions of Budd Inlet and Capitol Lake serve to divide the city into eastern and western halves.

Information

Olympia/Thurston Chamber of Commerce (☎ 360-357-3362) is at 512 Legion Way. The State Capitol Visitors Center (☎ 360-586-3460) is right off the freeway at 14th Ave and Capitol Way. Information on the

Olympic National Forest, administered by the USFS, can be obtained from the USFS office (☎ 360-956-2300) at 1835 Black Lake Blvd NW, Olympia, WA 98512. You can also pick up free backcountry permits for wilderness camping in the Olympic National Park here.

Olympia's central post office is at 900 Jefferson St SE, 98507. For medical emergencies, go to Capital Medical Center (☎ 360-754-5858), 3900 Capital Mall Drive SW. Fireside Books (☎ 360-352-4006), 116 E Legion Way, is a good local independent bookstore. To do laundry, go to Eastside Laundry & Cleaners (☎ 360-352-2575), 122 Turner St NE, near the Thriftway store between 4th Ave and State St.

State Capitol Campus

The Washington State Capitol sits in a 30-acre, park-like setting above Capitol Lake, with beautiful views onto the Olympic Mountains across Budd Inlet. This campus holds the majority of the state's official buildings, including the vast domed **Legislative Building**, completed in 1927. At the time of its construction, the capitol's 287-foot dome was the fourth largest in the world (exceeded only by the US Capitol, St Paul's in London, and St Peter's in Rome); the chandelier hanging in the rotunda was made by Louis Tiffany. The Legislative Building is open 8 am to 4:30 pm daily; admission is free. Tours are usually offered on the hour from 9 am to 4 pm. To find out about tours and for general information, call the Capitol Visitors Center (☎ 360-586-3460) or stop by the office at 14th Ave and Capitol Way.

Across the plaza from the Legislative Building is the **Temple of Justice**, the supreme court building, flanked by sandstone colonnades and lined in the interior by an oppressive amount of marble. The **Capitol Conservatory** is just to the north. On display here is a large collection of tropical and subtropical plants; the flowers for official state occasions are also grown here. Both of these buildings are open to the public 8 am to 4:30 pm Monday to Friday throughout the year, and also on weekends (same hours) from Memorial Day to Labor Day.

The oldest building on the campus is the **Executive Mansion**, built in 1908. The home of the governor is open for tours only on Wednesdays; call to reserve a space. Outdoor attractions include the **Vietnam War Memorial**, a sunken rose garden and various fountains and monumental sculptures. A free guided tour covers all these sites; call ☎ 360-586-8687 for tour information and reservations.

State Capitol Museum

A few blocks south of the campus is the State Capitol Museum (☎ 360-753-2580), 211 W 21st Ave. Housed in the 1920s Lord Mansion, this museum commemorates the general history of Washington, focusing on the move toward statehood and the capital. Also included are displays re-creating aspects of the everyday life of the Nisqually Indians, including a longhouse. It's open 10 am to 4 pm Tuesday to Friday, and noon to 4 pm Saturday and Sunday. Admission is by donation.

Old State Capitol Building

In 1903, under the leadership of Populist governor John Rogers, the state government recycled the 1891 Thurston County Courthouse by turning it into the state capitol for nearly 25 years, while the current Legislative Building was very slowly being built. In its heyday, this Romanesque-revival structure was even more commanding: its nine-story central tower burned in 1928, and the building's 11 turrets fell off during a 1949 earthquake. The old capitol is now the office for the State Superintendent of Public Instruction; it's open for self-guided tours, or groups can call ahead for a guided tour (☎ 360-753-6725). The building, at 600 S Washington St across from Sylvester Park, is open to visitors 9 to 11:30 am and 1 to 4:30 pm Monday to Friday.

Percival Landing Park

When Olympia was established, its narrow harbor was a mudflat during low tides: after years of dredging, Olympia's harbor is still small potatoes compared to the busy ports of commerce at Tacoma and Seattle. This park, on Water St between Thurston St and 4th Ave, is essentially a boardwalk along the harbor, which is used mostly as a marina by pleasure boats. It's a pleasant half-mile walk, especially when the Olympic Mountains sparkle across the bay. At the north end of the boardwalk is an observation tower, from which one can see logs being loaded onto freighters at the Port of Olympia. At the 4th St end of the waterfront is a locally noted statue called *The Kiss*, which you don't need to see to imagine. Nearby is *Heritage Fountain*, popular in summer with over-heated kids.

Percival Park is the site of a number of festivities, including Harbor Days, when vessels as different as tug boats and Native American cedar canoes fill the harbor (see Special Events).

Olympia Farmers' Market

One of Olympia's pleasures is the Olympia Farmers' Market (☎ 360-352-9096), 700 Capitol Way N, at the north end of town. The market offers fresh local produce, crafts and food booths from the first weekend in April through December. The market is open 10 am to 3 pm, Thursday through Sunday, weekends only in April, November and December.

Yashiro Japanese Garden

This small, relatively new garden is a collaborative effort between Olympia and its Japanese sister city, Yashiro. Highlights include a bamboo grove, pagoda and a pond and waterfall; the grounds include stone lanterns and other gifts from Yashiro. The garden is near Plum St and Union Ave, across from Olympia City Hall and is open during daylight hours. Admission is free.

Hands On Children's Museum

Kids will be enthralled by this children's activity center (☎ 360-956-0818) at 108 Franklin St NE. Exhibits include a simulated tide pool, make-believe seafood diner and 'underseas' film theater – but what kids today really enjoy is playing on the

computers with multimedia CD-ROM programs. The museum is open 10 am to 5 pm Tuesday to Saturday. Admission is $3.50, infants under 12 months are free. During the academic year, the museum offers an after-school special with all admissions just $1 from 3 to 5 pm, Tuesday to Friday.

Golf

There are a number of good golf courses around Olympia. Two 18-hole courses to check out are Indian Summer Golf Course (☎ 360-438-6439), 5900 Troon Lane SE, and Capitol City Golf Club (☎ 360-491-5111), 5225 Yelm Hwy SE (take Capitol Way south of Olympia). It's one of the best winter courses in the Puget Sound area.

Canoeing and Sea Kayaking

Rent a canoe or sea kayak from Boston Harbor Marina (☎ 360-357-5670), 312 73rd Ave NE, and explore the bays of lower Puget Sound. To reach Boston Harbor, follow East Bay Rd from downtown; the marina is about 6 miles north.

Special Events

Throughout the summer, the **Music in the Park & Music in the Dark** series (☎ 360-943-2375) takes place in Sylvester Park in front of the Old State Capitol on Washington St and Legion Way. Concerts are held Friday at noon and Wednesday at 7 pm, mid-July to the end of August.

Olympia's big summer festival is **Harbor Days** (☎ 360-754-4557), held on Labor Day weekend, when Percival Landing Park becomes the site of various maritime events, like tub boat races and food and craft booths. The **Olympia Art Walk** (☎ 360-753-8380) is an arts and crafts fair held at several downtown locations in early October. Watch for special displays and exhibits, as well as discussions and events.

Places to Stay

Camping *Olympia Campground* (☎ 360-352-2551),1441 83rd Ave SW (off I-5 exit 101), promises shady sites and good TV reception. Among the full-service amenities are a heated pool (in summer), free showers, game room and movie rentals. Tent sites cost $17, hookups cost $23 and camper cabins are also available. It's open year-round. Only blocks away, and with similar facilities, is *American Heritage Campground* (☎ 360-943-8778), 9610 Kimmie St SW, with more wooded sites for tents ($18), RVs ($25) and cabins. Turn off I-5 at exit 99 and travel a quarter of a mile east to Kimmie St. It's open Memorial Day to Labor Day only.

Forego the RV-park scene for *Millersylvania State Park* (☎ 360-753-1519), 10 miles south of Olympia off I-5 exit 95. Activities at the park include hiking, lake fishing and swimming. Tent sites cost $11; RV hookups are $15.

B&Bs *Harbinger Inn B&B* (☎ 360-754-0389), 1136 E Bay Drive NE, is a circa 1910 home overlooking Budd Inlet. There are four guest rooms, three with private facilities. Children under 10 are not permitted. Rates are between $60 and $125.

Hotels Olympia is the state capital, and rooms tend to be expensive if you're not on a lobbyist's expense account. If you're just passing through, there's a cluster of motels out at I-5 exit 102, including most of the chains. Try the *Tyee Motel* (☎ 360-352-0511, 800-386-8933) 500 Tyee Drive, which has a pool and restaurant; single/double rooms are $73. The *Best Western Tumwater Inn Motel* (☎ 360-956-1235), 5188 Capital Blvd, has microwaves, guest laundry and free continental breakfast. Rooms are $66/77.

Stay right downtown at the *Golden Gavel Motel* (☎ 360-352-8533), 909 Capitol Way S, one of the less expensive places to stay at $39/46. Across the street, the *Best Western Aladdin Motor Inn* (☎ 360-352-7200), 900 Capitol Way S, is where many representatives have suites while the legislature is in session. There's a heated outdoor pool; rooms are $64/84. The *Ramada Governor House Hotel* (☎ 360-352-7700, 800-272-6232), 621 Capitol Way S, is Olympia's fanciest lodging, with a heated pool, guest laundry, fitness center,

restaurant and convention facilities. Room rates range from $70 to $105.

Places to Eat
If you're looking for a latte to start the day, head to *Batdorf & Bronson* (☎ 360-786-6717), 513 Capitol Way S, a comfortable espresso bar with breakfast pastries and a selection of regional papers. There's no better place for a traditional breakfast than the old fashioned, wood-paneled *Spar Bar & Cafe* (☎ 360-357-6444), 114 4th Ave E, a diner, cigar shop, newsstand and bar combo that hasn't changed since the 1930s.

If you're assembling organic food to cook yourself, head to *Olympia Food Co-op* at either of two locations: westside (☎ 360-754-7666), 921 Rogers St N, or eastside (☎ 360-956-3870), 3111 Pacific St SE. For picnic breads, go to *San Francisco Street Bakery* (☎ 360-753-8553), 1320 San Francisco St NE. Vegetarian and other healthy burritos are the draw at *Burrito Heaven* (☎ 360-956-3661), 2101 W Harrison Ave.

Olympia's long-standing vegetarian restaurant is the slightly dowdy *Urban Onion* (☎ 360-943-9242), 116 Legion Way E. Lunchtime salad and quiche go for $7. *Mekong Restaurant* (☎ 360-352-9620), 125 Columbia St NW, is the local favorite for Thai food, while *Capitale Espresso Grille* (☎ 360-352-8007), 609 Capitol Way S, offers a selection of spicy Italian pastas (penne alla puttanesca goes for $9). A new favorite is *Santosh* (☎ 360-943-3442), 116 4th Ave W, with an inexpensive Indian lunch buffet for under $5 at lunch.

Since it's the state capitol, there are a number of fine dining establishments – all the better to schmooze in. *Gardners* (☎ 360-786-8466), 111 Thurston Ave, serves the city's best seafood, pasta and steaks, with full dinners in the $12 to $17 range.

If you're looking for a table with a view, go to the *Budd Bay Cafe* (☎ 360-357-6963), 525 Columbia St NW, right above the marina on Percival Landing. Dinner entrées include steak, seafood, pasta and prime rib in the $13 range; on Sunday there's a popular champagne brunch. Harbor views are great at *The Oyster House* (☎ 360-753-7000), 320 West 4th Ave, though it's a better place for a drink than a full meal.

Entertainment

Coffeehouses In Olympia's coffeehouses you're more likely to spot local artists, students and stylishly disenfranchised youth than lobbyists; saunter down 4th Ave E to find handfuls of trendy coffee shops. For late-night espressos and post-concert discussions, the place to go is *Dancing Goats Espresso Co* (☎ 360-754-8187), 124 4th Ave E.

Brewpubs *Fishbowl Pub* (☎ 360-943-3650), 515 Jefferson St SE, serves their own Fish Tale ales, a tasty alternative to the ubiquitous Olympia brewery beers. In addition to the British-style ales, there's a snack menu.

Cinemas Olympia's art cinema par excellence is the *Capitol Theatre* (☎ 360-754-5378), 206 5th Ave E. This foreign and independent film cinema commands the kind of local devotion you'd expect in a small, intellectual community. For the latest major release films, go to the *Lacey Cinemas* (☎ 360-459-0960) at 4431 Martin Way E in Lacey.

Performing Arts Olympia's primary venue for national touring shows and other cultural activities is the *Washington Center for the Performing Arts* (☎ 360-753-8586), 512 Washington St SE.

Live Music On weekend evenings, the backstage of the *Capitol Theatre* (☎ 360-754-5378), 206 5th Ave E, is where to catch local bands delivered fresh from Evergreen College.

Dance Clubs For dancing, go to *Thekla* (☎ 360-352-1855), 116 5th Ave E; its entrance is in the alley (you can't miss the cartoon montage around the door). The music changes nightly, but the clientele remains a friendly, gay/straight hodge-podge.

Getting There & Away

Bus Six Greyhound buses a day link Olympia to other I-5-corridor cities from its station (☎ 360-357-5541) at 107 7th Ave E. One-way fare to Seattle is $9. Gray's Harbor Transportation Authority (☎ 360-532-2770, 800-562-9730) also offers bus service to Aberdeen on the Pacific coast.

Train Amtrak (☎ 360-923-4602) stops at its station in Lacey at 6600 Yelm Hwy SE; three trains a day link Olympia with Seattle and Portland. Bus No 94 stops at the station once an hour; however, the bus terminates at the Lacey Transit Center, not downtown Olympia. You'll need to catch another bus from Lacey to Olympia.

Getting Around

To/From the Airport The Capital Aeroporter (☎ 360-754-7113) operates 19 buses daily from the Ramada Governor House Hotel, 621 Capitol Way E, in Olympia to Sea-Tac airport. One-way fare is $20; reservations are suggested.

Bus Olympia's public transport system is called IT for Intercity Transit (☎ 360-786-1881, 800-287-6348); standard fare is 60¢. The downtown transit center is at State Ave and Capitol Way. Bus No 41 runs out to Evergreen College from downtown; Bus No 62 runs up to the Lacey Transit Center.

Taxi For a cab, call Capitol City Taxi at ☎ 360-357-3700.

AROUND OLYMPIA
Tumwater

At the lowest of the three falls on the Deschutes River, **Tumwater Historical Park** (☎ 360-754-4160) is situated at the site of Olympia's original pioneer settlement and has a playground, picnic area and nature trail along the river. Deschutes Falls is the site of a lot of anadromous activity in late August and September, when the Deschutes River Chinook salmon run begins. Stand on the viewing platform to watch the fish throw themselves up the falls and climb the fish ladders.

Although the passage of I-5 through this historic corridor has meant the destruction of many of the area's old homes and buildings, a few remain. The **Henderson House Museum** on Deschutes Way in the park, contains artifacts and displays of pioneer life and early industry in Tumwater.

Adjacent is **Crosby House**, a museum commemorating one of Olympia's first families. In 1847, 24 members of the Crosby family arrived from Maine, almost doubling the white population of the Tumwater/Olympia area. The Crosby House was built in 1858 and was the home of Nathaniel Crosby III, grandfather of Bing Crosby. Both museums are open noon to 4 pm Thursday to Sunday.

Forget regional microbrews for a moment and tour the **Olympia Brewing Co**, one of the largest breweries in the West. The brewery has been producing beer since 1896 (though in 1993 it was bought by Pabst), and the brewery ranks right up there with state government as the city's largest employer. The free, 40-minute tour through the fermentation tanks to the tasting room and gift shop is quite interesting. It's open 9 am to 4:30 pm daily April 1 to Labor Day Weekend, but call to confirm tours (☎ 360-754-5212), as the tour dates and times seem to change frequently. The brewery is located on Capitol Blvd, immediately east of I-5 exit 103 in Tumwater; you can't miss it. Take bus No 12 or 13.

Get an eyeful of Deschutes Falls (and the brewery) at *Falls Terrace* (☎ 360-943-7830), 106 S Deschutes Way, open for lunch and dinner and serving that Northwestern triumvirate of steak, pasta and seafood, all in the $15 range.

Nisqually National Wildlife Refuge
The estuary of the Nisqually River has been set aside as a preserve for wildlife, particularly for waterfowl and shore birds. The diverse habitat at the refuge, which includes saltwater and freshwater marshes, tide flats, grasslands and woodlands, is home to over 300 species of wildlife; about 20,000 migratory waterfowl winter here.

A number of hikes, ranging from half a mile to over 5 miles, lead out from the refuge parking area. For more information and a wildlife checklist, stop by the refuge headquarters (☎ 360-753-9467) at 100 Brown Farm Rd (take I-5 north to exit 114). The wildlife area is open during daylight hours; there is a $3 entry fee per family.

Wolf Haven America
Wolf Haven America is a 75-acre wolf rehabilitation center and permanent home for around 40 wolves no longer able to live in the wild. Associated with the center is the nonprofit Wolf Haven International (☎ 360-264-4695, 800-448-9653), which offers programs, tours and ecology classes at the interpretive center, all designed to provide a better understanding of the much-maligned wolf.

The center is open 10 am to 4 pm daily, May through September, and from 10 am

Gray wolves once inhabited much of North America, but are now found only in Canada and the northernmost areas of the USA.

to 3 pm Wednesday to Sunday, October through April. Tours of the grounds are available on the hour. Admission is $5/2.50 adults/children (ages five to 12). From May through September, there's the special Summer Howl, an evening campfire program from 6 to 9 pm on Friday and Saturday. Admission to Summer Howl costs $6/4 adults/children.

To reach Wolf Haven from Olympia, take I-5 south to exit 102 and follow signs to Tenino on Capitol Blvd. Continue south (the street becomes Old Hwy 99) about 6 miles and follow the signs; the center is located at 3111 Offut Lake Rd.

Mima Mounds Natural Area
These geological curiosities – acres and acres of dimpled prairies – once covered much of the lowlands around the southern Puget Sound. Early explorers assumed that these six- to eight-foot-high, 20- to 30-foot-wide earth mounds were burial chambers; however, modern researchers believe they are the result of ancient pocket gophers or Ice Age freeze-thaw patterns.

Whatever caused them, these formations are certainly very odd.

The Nature Conservancy bought one of the last remaining tracts of Mima Mounds (most have been leveled and plowed as farmland) and released the land to the state for preservation. The Mima Mounds Natural Area preserve encompasses a 500-acre clearing containing thousands of mounds and a number of trails – including a half-mile nature trail – wind through them. There's also an informational kiosk and picnic tables. The preserve is especially nice in spring, when the area is carpeted with wildflowers. It's open during daylight hours only; no overnight camping.

To reach the Mima Mounds, take I-5 exit 95 south of Olympia and turn west on Hwy 121 toward Littlerock. From Littlerock, follow 128th Ave SW 1 mile to the T-junction with Waddell Creek Rd. Turn north and drive for 1 mile to the preserve. For more information on the Mima Mounds Natural Area, contact the Washington Department of Natural Resources (☎ 360-748-2383).

Northwestern Washington & the San Juan Islands

In the northwestern corner of Washington, the Pacific Ocean washes into Georgia Strait, the Strait of Juan de Fuca and the Puget Sound, as well as into a thousand tiny inlets, fjords and channels. Rising above the mist and the blue-green waves is a mosaic of forested islands and peninsulas along the bay-dented mainland. The primary attraction here is the San Juan Islands, which, together with the Oregon coast, undoubtedly comprise the most beautiful and unique destination in the Pacific Northwest. These remote islands, accessible only by boat or air, range from tightly folded mountain peaks to rolling moors and farmland. Bicycles fill the roads, B&Bs nestle among the trees and sheep and cattle graze in grassy pastures. And everywhere, the Pacific encroaches.

Across from the islands and on the mainland, the largest city in this marine-oriented province is Bellingham, a delightful university town with lively street life and good restaurants. For the traveler, Bellingham is a welcome escape from the big-city stress of either Seattle or Vancouver, BC, and it is close to recreation on Mt Baker and in North Cascades National Park. Along the lower Skagit River, historic La Conner provides a relaxing respite from highway driving or for an overnight stay, and in the spring the fertile flood plains of this valley come alive with acres of tulips and other flowers in a not-to-be-missed display. Whidbey Island contains two of Washington's most popular (read: crowded) vacation spots, the beautiful Deception Pass State Park and the quaint, upscale town of Langley.

GETTING THERE & AWAY
Air Bellingham is served by United and Horizon Airlines with regularly scheduled flights. However, to get to the San Juans via air, you'll need to take commuter flights from Bellingham, Anacortes, or Sea-Tac to Friday Harbor. If you're more adventurous, catch a seaplane from Lake Union in Seattle to any of the three major islands; this is an especially popular way to get to the resorts at Rosario and Roche Harbor.

Bus Greyhound service sticks exclusively to I-5 stops such as Mount Vernon and Bellingham. The Airporter Shuttle (☎ 800-235-5247) is a small private carrier that links Sea-Tac to the San Juan ferry terminal, Whidbey Island and Anacortes ($30 one way, $54 roundtrip), to Mt Vernon/Burlington, Bellingham ($32 one way, $55 roundtrip) and to Blaine ($36 one way, $64 roundtrip). There are buses every two hours; reservations are requested. Although the fares aren't exactly cheap, this is the easiest way to get to slightly off-the-freeway locations in this part of the Northwest.

County bus services are good on the mainland; however, there is no public bus service on the islands. With advance notice, most resorts, B&Bs and hotels will pick up guests at ferry terminals.

Train Amtrak's *Mt Baker* line runs once daily (with two additional rail link buses) from Seattle to Vancouver, BC, with stops in Edmonds, Everett, Burlington/Mt Vernon, Bellingham, and the border crossing at Blaine.

Ferry Ferries are by far the most popular and simplest way to get to the San Juans. In addition to the Washington State car ferries, which run from Anacortes through the islands to Sidney, BC, a number of passenger ferries provide service to the islands from Bellingham and Seattle.

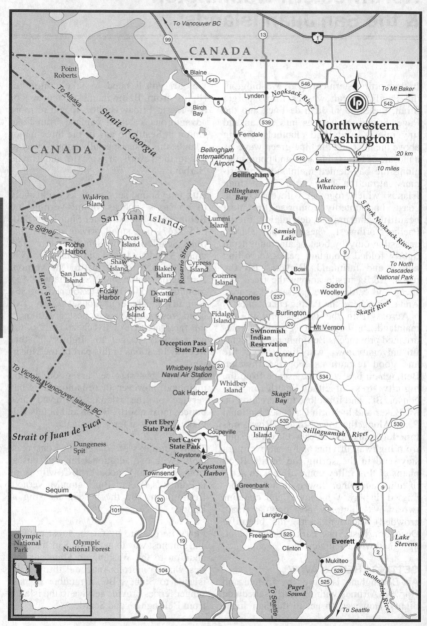

BELLINGHAM
Population 61,043

The handsome old port city of Bellingham is one of the Northwest's most appealing cultural centers. Perched on hills overlooking a busy harbor, Bellingham faces the southern end of Georgia Strait, which is here spangled with forested islands – Lummi, Samish, Orcas and Cypress. Rising immediately behind the city is Mt Baker, crowned with glaciers and horn-like peaks. Bellingham is home to Western Washington University, a busy nightlife scene that favors live bands and local brews, and a selection of restaurants that are all the more pleasing for their affordability. Bellingham is in many ways the Washington equivalent of Eugene, OR: a comfortable collegiate center of left-leaning politics and alternative lifestyles.

Bellingham derives a good deal of its charm from its mix of populations. Just 18 miles south of Canada, Bellingham's shopping malls and downtown streets are busy with Canadian shoppers and day-trippers. Toss in the mature hippie contingent that assembles in coffee shops, rowdy students massing in brewpubs, and patrician urban refugees seeking asylum from the pace of other Northwest cities, and you have a colorful, carefree citizenry.

Bellingham began as four separate communities – Fairhaven, Sehome, Whatcom and Bellingham – each of which developed along deep Bellingham Bay. Fairhaven grew up around speculation that it would be selected as the Great Northern Railroad's Pacific Coast port city, and a core of red brick storefronts and hotels sprang up in the 1880s. When the Great Northern chose Seattle instead, Fairhaven fell into a slumber. Recent renovation has turned the handsome old buildings into a shopping and dining precinct. Whatcom was the site of an early commune, Sehome was the site of a coal mine in the 1860s, and Bellingham was a busy port site. By 1903, the towns had consolidated into a single civic entity.

Orientation
Bellingham is 18 miles south of the international border crossing at Blaine and 54 miles from downtown Vancouver, BC. From Seattle, Bellingham is 89 miles north on I-5.

Because Bellingham is comprised of what were formerly several separate towns, the street systems are pretty confusing. The current city center is west of I-5; exit 253 leads to Holly St, a major downtown arterial and one of the few streets to cut through the area without getting caught up in conflicting street grids. Holly St intersects State St, another major arterial that runs south to the Fairhaven district and north to I-5 (exit 254). North of the intersection of State and Holly Sts is a quadrant of streets with a completely different grid; many city offices and businesses are located here.

Be sure to stop and get a map from the visitors' center. In many ways, it's probably easier just to park and explore Bellingham on foot. The grids are pretty hard to figure out from behind the wheel.

Information
Tourist Office For information about the area, contact the Bellingham/Whatcom County Convention & Visitors Bureau (☎ 360-671-3990, 800-487-2032), 904 Potter St, Bellingham, WA 98229. The visitors' center is off I-5 exit 253, but it's a little difficult to locate; it's open 9 am to 6 pm. To find it, turn north on King St from Lakeway Drive (following signs for I-5 north), and turn immediately right instead of entering the freeway.

For information about the Canadian/US border, contact the US Border Patrol at Blaine (☎ 360-332-8781) or the Canadian Immigration office (☎ 604-536-7671).

Post The post office is at 315 Prospect St.

Bookstores Bellingham's best bookstore is Village Books (☎ 360-671-2626, 800-392-2005), 1210 11th St at Harris Ave in Fairhaven, which sells new and used books. The store is a real community resource, with lots of author readings and literary activities, to say nothing of being home to the popular Colophon Cafe, a trendy coffee shop with service on both floors of the bookstore.

Media Bellingham offers a number of free publications that profile the local arts and entertainment scene. Pick up a handful in most bookstores or cafes. The best of these is called *Northwest Events* and is published monthly. The daily paper is the Bellingham *Herald*. For public radio, tune to KZAZ, 91.7 FM.

Laundry Convenient to Fairhaven and the university is Fairhaven Laundry & Cleaners (☎ 360-734-9647) at 1414 12th St. There's also Sunshine Cleaners (☎ 360-733-6610) in the impossible-to-miss Fred Meyer Shopping Center on Lakeway Drive immediately north of I-5 exit 253.

Medical Services For health emergencies, go to St Joseph Hospital (☎ 360-734-5400) at 2901 Squalicum Parkway, near I-5 exit 256. The hospital's South Campus (same phone number) is at 809 E Chestnut St and is more convenient to downtown.

Whatcom Museum of History & Art
The building itself is reason enough to visit this excellent regional museum (☎ 360-676-6981), 121 Prospect St. It's in the imposing and fanciful red-brick Whatcom City Hall, built in 1892. This large complex now boasts four separate units whose galleries contain a good collection of artifacts from local native tribes, a collection of vintage toys, a re-creation of a 19th-century Bellingham street scene and a large natural history section with hundreds of stuffed birds. Several galleries are devoted to traveling displays of fine art. The museum is open noon to 5 pm, Tuesday through Sunday; admission is by donation. Next door is the **Whatcom Children's Museum** (☎ 360-733-8769), 227 Prospect St, with interactive displays for the younger set. Hours for the Children's Museum are noon to 5 pm Sunday, Tuesday and Wednesday and 10 am to 5 pm Thursday to Saturday; admission is $2.

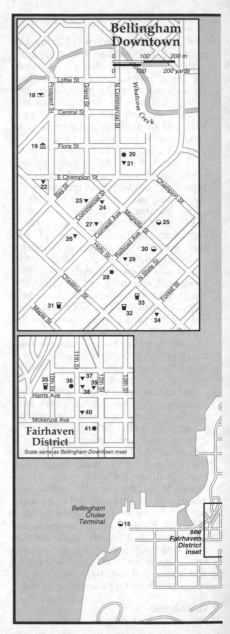

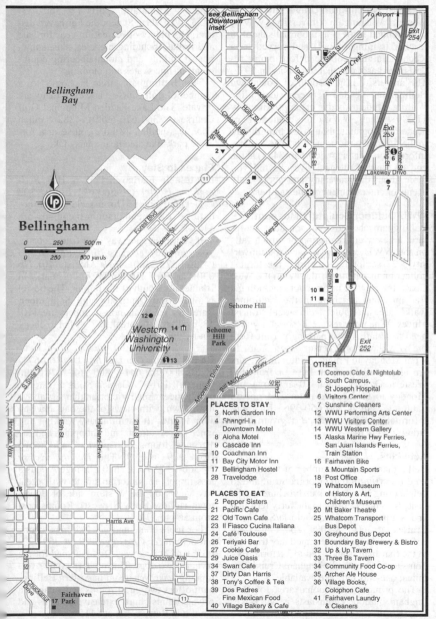

see Bellingham Downtown inset

To Airport

Exit 254

Bellingham Bay

Whatcom Creek

N State St

York St

Magnolia St

Holly St

Chestnut St

Maple St

Exit 253

Ellis St

King St

Potter St

Lakeway Drive

Bellingham

0   250   500 m
0   250   500 yards

High St

Indian St

Key St

Samish Way

Forest Blvd

Forest St

Garden St

Sehome Hill

Exit 252

Western Washington University

Sehome Hill Park

S State St

15th St

Highland Drive

21st St

24th St

Arboretum Drive

Bill McDonald Pkwy

32nd St

Finnegan Way

12th St

Chuckanut Drive

Harris Ave

Donovan Ave

Fairhaven Park

OTHER
1 Coomoo Cafe & Nightclub
5 South Campus,
   St Joseph Hospital
6 Visitors Center
7 Sunshine Cleaners
12 WWU Performing Arts Center
13 WWU Visitors Center
14 WWU Western Gallery
15 Alaska Marine Hwy Ferries,
   San Juan Islands Ferries,
   Train Station
16 Fairhaven Bike
   & Mountain Sports
18 Post Office
19 Whatcom Museum
   of History & Art,
   Children's Museum
20 Mt Baker Theatre
25 Whatcom Transport
   Bus Depot
30 Greyhound Bus Depot
31 Boundary Bay Brewery & Bistro
32 Up & Up Tavern
33 Three Bs Tavern
34 Community Food Co-op
35 Archer Ale House
36 Village Books,
   Colophon Cafe
41 Fairhaven Laundry
   & Cleaners

PLACES TO STAY
3 North Garden Inn
4 Shangri-La
   Downtown Motel
8 Aloha Motel
9 Cascade Inn
10 Coachman Inn
11 Bay City Motor Inn
17 Bellingham Hostel
28 Travelodge

PLACES TO EAT
2 Pepper Sisters
21 Pacific Cafe
22 Old Town Cafe
23 Il Fiasco Cucina Italiana
24 Café Toulouse
26 Teriyaki Bar
27 Cookie Cafe
29 Juice Oasis
34 Swan Cafe
37 Dirty Dan Harris
38 Tony's Coffee & Tea
39 Dos Padres
   Fine Mexican Food
40 Village Bakery & Cafe

WASHINGTON

Western Washington University

Western Washington University (WWU) was founded in 1893 as a normal school (a teacher training school) and served as a teacher training college before being redesignated as a regional university in 1977. The university is just south of downtown Bellingham, nestled between steep hills. With a student body of approximately 11,000 students, WWU offers a full range of academic programs, though its strengths are in the fine and performing arts. The Visitors Information Center (☎ 360-650-3424) at the end of South College Drive can tell you more about the university and about daily events or entertainment on the campus.

WWU Outdoor Sculpture Museum

Bellingham abounds with outdoor sculpture, a heavy concentration of which falls on the WWU campus. In fact, the university's 22 sculptures comprise the largest collection of outdoor sculpture on the West Coast. Interpretive information, including a free map and brochure of the 'sculpture walk' are available from local tourist offices. When classes are in session you'll need to obtain a free parking permit from the WWU visitors' center, open 7 am to 7 pm Monday to Friday. Audiophone tours are also available from here or from the Western Gallery, open 10 am to 4 pm Monday to Friday, and noon to 4 pm on Saturday. Call ☎ 360 650-3963 for more information or to arrange a group tour. Admission is free.

Activities

Bellingham offers a number of scenic and wildlife **cruises** into Georgia Strait and to neighboring islands; pick up brochures at the visitors' center or drive to the ferry terminal and shop the options. Victoria/San Juan Cruises (☎ 360-738-8099, 800-443-4552), 355 Harris Ave, offers narrated day trips out to the San Juan Islands and to Victoria, BC. Tours leave from the Bellingham Cruise Terminal; one-way fares are available.

The primary recreational area for Bellingham outdoor enthusiasts is Mt Baker (see North Cascades chapter). Fairhaven

Bike & Mountain Sports (☎ 360-733-4433), 1103 11th St near the Fairhaven district, has plenty of recreation gear for sale and rental, including bicycles, skis, snowboards, hiking and mountaineering equipment, in-line skates and clothing.

The Bellingham area is home to a number of **golf** courses; however, many are private. The Lake Padden Municipal Golf Course (☎ 360-676-6989), 4882 Samish Way, is a public, 18-hole course in a forested park-like area near a busy lake.

Places to Stay

Hostels In Fairhaven Park is HI's *Bellingham Hostel* (☎ 360-671-1750), 107 Chuckanut Drive. Dorm-style accommodations for members/non-members are $12/15.

If you're on your way to or from Canada, you can stay at HI's *Birch Bay Hostel* (☎ 360-371-2180), 4639 Alderson Rd, No 630, at Bay Horizon County Park in Blaine, just south of the border. The hostel is open from April through September. Rates for members/non-members are $10/13; cyclists get a break at $7. Plan to check out by 9:30 am.

B&Bs *North Garden Inn* (☎ 360-671-7828, 800-922-6414; 800-367-1676 from Canada), 1014 N Garden St, is a historic, 1897 Queen Anne Victorian that sits above downtown, with views of the bay and San Juan Islands. It's within easy walking distance of restaurants and shopping, and the 10 guest rooms with private baths range from $79 to $99. The *Decann House* (☎ 360-734-9172), 2610 Eldridge Ave, is a less-imposing Victorian home with great bay views on the western side of downtown (follow Holly St west). Rooms cost from $64 to $74.

For more contemporary lodgings, check out *Schnauzer Crossing B&B* (☎ 360-733-0055), 4421 Lakeway Drive, named for the owner's two dogs. This modern home overlooking Lake Whatcom in eastern Bellingham offers two guest rooms and a cabin, a private tennis court, extensive gardens and a hot tub. Rates begin at $115.

For a more extensive listing of area B&Bs, contact the Bed & Breakfast Guild of Whatcom County (☎ 360-676-4560), and ask for their brochure.

Hotels The majority of Bellingham's inexpensive motels are along Samish Way off exit 252, not far from WWU. If you're looking for something cheap, try the *Bell Motel* (☎ 360-733-2520), 208 N Samish Way, or the *Aloha Motel* (☎ 360-733-4900), 315 N Samish Way. Both have single/double rooms for $29/39, take pets and offer kitchen units. For a little more comfort, try the *Coachman Inn* (☎ 360-671-9000, 800-962-6641),120 Samish Way, with a pool and rooms at $45/65. The *Bay City Motor Inn* (☎ 360-676-0332, 800-538-8204), 116 N Samish Way, offers a workout room and a pool table; rooms are $40/45.

Out near the freeway exit 256, there's a *Quality Inn* (☎ 360-647-8000), 100 E Kellogg Rd, with a pool, laundry, hot tub and rooms for $65/75. The lodging of choice in these parts – if you judge by the number of Canadian license plates – is *Best Western Heritage Inn* (☎ 360-647-1912, 800-528-1234), 151 E McCloud Rd, off exit 256. Rooms (starting at $64/69) are large and nicely furnished, and there's a free continental breakfast.

If you want to enjoy downtown Bellingham, stay at one of the motels within walking distance of fine restaurants and entertainment. The *Shangri-La Downtown Motel* (☎ 360-733-7050), 611 E Holly St, is a trifle modest but a good deal at $32 a night. The *Travelodge* (☎ 360-734-1900, 800-578-7878), 202 E Holly St, is right downtown and a good value with rooms under $40 a night.

Places to Eat

For a town its size, Bellingham has a wide variety of very good restaurants, with most prices well below what you'll find in Seattle.

Downtown The *Old Town Cafe* (☎ 360-671-4431), 316 Holly St, has a happy-go-

lucky, hippie atmosphere, and vegetarian dishes are offered at breakfast and lunch, along with fresh pastries and espresso. *Café Toulouse* (☎ 360-733-8996), 114 W Magnolia St, No 102, is a nice street-side bistro with morning coffee and light lunch fare.

The place to go for organic produce and health foods is the *Community Food Co-op* (☎ 360-734-8158) at 1220 N Forest St. Inside, the *Swan Cafe* (☎ 360-734-0542), is open for breakfast, lunch and dinner. For a vegetarian snack, head to *The Juice Oasis* (☎ 360-647-4519), 207½ E Holly St. A popular student haunt is *The Teriyaki Bar* (☎ 360-733-0294) at 119 W Holly St, with table service, a drive-up window and delivery, and most dishes under $5.

For good Tex-Mex and Southwestern cooking, go to *Pepper Sisters* (☎ 360-671-3414), 1055 N State St, with dishes from $10 to $14. Although it's a brewpub, *Orchard Street Brewery* (☎ 360-647-1614), 709 W Orchard Dr, off I-5 exit 256, has high-quality Northwest cuisine to accompany its award-winning ales; the dining room is high design as well.

Bellingham's two best restaurants are downtown. The *Pacific Cafe* (☎ 360-647-0800), 100 N Commercial St, brings both Oriental and French influences to bear on local fish, seafood and meat. Plan on spending $15 to $20 for entrées. *Il Fiasco Cucina Italiana* (☎ 360-676-9136), 1309 Commercial St, is a superior Italian restaurant with excellent service and delicious food. Pasta dishes run from $12 to $14, while grilled dishes – like pork tenderloin with wild mushrooms – are in the $15 range. It's open for dinner daily and lunch weekdays only.

Fairhaven Housed inside Village Books in Fairhaven, the *Colophon Cafe* (☎ 360-647-0092), 1208 11th St, blends the features of a literary cafe with a multi-ethnic eatery. Espresso and pastries (especially the homemade pies) fuel book-shoppers, while the meals served at lunch and dinner – which include soups, entrées and salads – bring people in from the neighborhood for tasty

WASHINGTON

and inexpensive dining. Also in Fairhaven is *Dos Padres Fine Mexican Food* (☎ 360-733-9900), 1111 Harris Ave. Dishes reflect a mix of traditional and nuevo influences; a three-alarm, black-bean enchilada dinner is under $10. For something light, go to the *Village Bakery Cafe* (☎ 360-671-7258), 1307 11th St, with coffee and baked goods.

For steak, prime rib and seafood in a historic setting, go to *Dirty Dan Harris* (☎ 360-676-1011), 1211 11th St. Steaks range from $12 to $15.

Entertainment
Coffeehouses Relax in the locals' favorite coffee shop at *Tony's Coffee & Tea* (☎ 360-733-6319), 1101 Harris Ave, in Fairhaven. Students, unrepentant hippies and housewives come here to do some serious hanging out. In summer, there's a shady garden area to lounge in. The *Cookie Cafe* (☎ 360-671-8550), 1307 Cornwall Ave, has regularly scheduled poetry readings, music, and other performances.

Theater *Mt Baker Theatre*, at 106 N Commercial St, is a grand old historic theater built in 1925, which is both a cinema (☎ 360-734-4950) and live performance stage (☎ 360-734-6080) specializing in national touring acts. WWU's *Performing Arts Center* (☎ 360-650-3866), on campus, is another performance space featuring local and regional music and dance productions.

Cinemas You'll find Bellingham's movie theaters in outlying shopping malls. *Bellis Fair Cinemas* (☎ 360-676-9990), in the Bellis Fair shopping center north of town off I-5 exit 256, is the place for first-run films.

Bars & Brewpubs Bellingham's student population supports a number of friendly bars and taverns. Downtown, the *Three Bs Tavern* (☎ 360-734-1881) and the *Up & Up Tavern* (☎ 360-733-9739), next door to each other at 1226 and 1234 N State St, are both lively student hangouts with pool tables and draft beer; the Three Bs has live music on weekends. In Fairhaven, the

Archer Ale House (☎ 360-647-7002), 1212 10th St, has lots of regional microbrews on tap, features darts and is smoke-free.

The *Boundary Bay Brewery & Bistro* (☎ 360-647-5593), 1107 Railroad Ave, has live music on some nights; no minors. The *Cosmos Cafe & Nightclub* (☎ 360-734-1500), 1707 N State St, has a mix of DJ-driven and live music.

Getting There & Away
Air Bellingham International Airport (☎ 360-676-2500) is northwest of Bellingham off I-5 exit 258. The city is served by Horizon Air and United Express with service to Seattle and Vancouver, BC; a roundtrip from Seattle is around $100. Island Shuttle (☎ 800-475-3829) flies from Bellingham to Victoria, BC, and the San Juan Islands with both regularly scheduled flights and charters.

Bus Greyhound buses serve Bellingham on the Seattle-Vancouver run. Three buses pass through daily heading north to Vancouver, BC ($13), and four go south to Seattle ($13). There's a special Seattle-bound express on Fridays. The depot (☎ 360-733-5251) is at 1329 N State St.

Train Amtrak trains from Vancouver, BC, and Seattle stop at the train depot (☎ 360 734-8851), at the end of Harris Ave near the ferry terminal.

Ferry Bellingham is the terminal for the Alaska Marine Highway Ferries (☎ 360-676-8445, 800-642-0066), which travel once a week up the Inside Passage to Juneau, Skagway and other southeast Alaskan ports. Passenger fares to Skagway start at $240; add a small car (up to 15 feet) and the fare jumps to $586. Cabins for the three-day trip can be hard to come by, so reserve well in advance.

The San Juan Islands Shuttle Express (☎ 360-671-1137, 888-373-8522) travels daily in summer only from the Alaska ferry terminal in Fairhaven to San Juan and Orcas Islands. Bicycles are welcome on board with a $2 surcharge.

Getting Around

Bus service on Whatcom Transportation Authority (☎ 360-676-7433) is modest but functional. The fleet runs weekdays from around 6 am to 5 pm; service is reduced on Saturdays and nonexistent on Sundays. On weekday evenings the special 'Nightline' bus connects Fairhaven, WWU and Bellis Fair mall to downtown Bellingham. Bus No 1A goes south to the Bellingham Ferry Terminal every hour. Find the main bus terminal downtown on Railroad Ave, between E Champion and Magnolia Sts; the local fare is 35¢.

ANACORTES

Population 13,500

Noted principally as the departure point for the San Juan Islands ferries, Anacortes is actually quite a pleasant town, so all is not lost if you end up spending a night here. In fact, unintended layovers are not uncommon. Ferries can fill up on summer weekends and once they're full, they're full. Also, travelers who forget to check the ferry schedule or who suffer at the hands of the Seattle traffic gods sometimes show up too late and must wait until the following day to board.

The ferry terminal is 3 miles west of Anacortes, and lots of motels and fast food restaurants line Hwy 20 from the outskirts of town to the ferry dock. However, if you have time to kill or need to spend the night, head downtown, where there are good restaurants and inexpensive motels. The old downtown buildings are decorated with life-size cutouts of early Anacortes residents, inspired by historic photographs. While it sounds kind of cheesy, in fact the effect is pleasant and rather sweet.

Orientation & Information

Anacortes is itself on Fidalgo Island, separated from the mainland by a narrow channel, 17 miles west of I-5 on Hwy 20. The downtown harbor (as opposed to the Washington State Ferry Terminal) skirts the edge of the business district, giving the town a real maritime air. The chamber of commerce (☎ 360-293-3832) is at 819 Commercial Ave.

Places to Stay

B&Bs The *Nantucket Inn* (☎ 360-293-6007, 888-293-6007), 3402 Commercial Ave, is a grand old home with five guest rooms, most with private bath, ranging from $75 to $125. Past the ferry terminal, with views overlooking Rosario Strait, *Sunset Beach B&B* (☎ 360-293-5428), 100 Sunset Beach, has two guest rooms at $82 and $95.

Hotels There are a lot of motels along the Commercial Ave strip. The best deals are at *Gateway Motel* (☎ 360-293-2655), 2019 Commercial Ave, with single/double rooms at $35/50; and at *Paul's Motel* (☎ 360-293-3108), 3100 Commercial Ave, with rooms starting at $40. A couple of notches up in facilities, comfort and price (both start at around $65/75) are the *Anacortes Inn* (☎ 360-293-3153 or 800-327-7976), 3006 Commercial Ave, and the *Islands Inn* (☎ 360-293-4334), 3401 Commercial Ave, which has a good restaurant in the complex. Both have pools.

It's quieter to stay downtown, off the main strip, and it's an easy walk to good restaurants. The *Cap Sante Inn* (☎ 360-293-0602), 906 9th St, is a cozy motor inn with a guest laundry and rooms at $65/69. The *San Juan Motel* (☎ 360-293-5105), 1103 6th St, offers kitchenettes and rooms at $46/56.

Ship Harbor Inn (☎ 360-293-5177), 5316 Ferry Terminal Rd, offers the easiest access to the ferries, as it's just above the terminal; what's more, the rooms have fireplaces and are nicer than average. The motel also offers bike rentals for those heading to the San Juans. Double rooms start at $80.

By far the most stylish place to stay in the area is the *Majestic Hotel* (☎ 360-293-3355), 419 Commercial Ave, which has 23 antique-filled rooms in a beautifully restored 1889 hotel filled with wood paneling, marble and brass. The cozy downstairs bar is a great place for a drink, and the restaurant is excellent. Rates start at $98 and go to $225.

Places to Eat
Head to *Calico Cupboard Cafe & Bakery* (☎ 360-293-7315), 901 Commercial Ave, for old-fashioned breakfasts, or load up on French pastries at *La Vie en Rose* (☎ 360-299-9546), 416 Commercial Ave. There's a little of everything at friendly, boisterous *Gere-a-Deli* (☎ 360-293-7383), 502 Commercial Ave, from bowls of granola in the morning to all-you-can-eat pasta on Friday nights. Soups, salads and sandwiches are the staples at lunch. *El Jinete* (☎ 360-293-2631), 509½ Commercial Ave, is a cozy Mexican restaurant with traditional dishes under $7.

The *Anacortes Brewhouse* (☎ 360-293-2444), 320 Commercial Ave, is a delightful place to sample the local brews and to snack on wood-fired pizza. Located in a handsome old bar, the Brewhouse really packs 'em in at night, and with reason: the food is reasonably priced, and it's a friendly, youthful place to have a drink in a town where most bars are basically locals-only. *Bella Isola* (☎ 360-299-8398), 619 Commercial Ave, is a trattoria with traditional Italian fare and Northwest regional specials in the $10 to $12 price range.

The restaurant of note in Anacortes is the *Salmon Run* (☎ 360-299-2923) in the Majestic Hotel at 419 Commercial Ave. The dining room overlooks a lovely garden, and although it's updated with pastel colors and fish carvings, it retains the classy charm that was its birthright in 1889. Dinners are a melange of classic French and fresh Northwest flavors; local fish is featured. Expect to pay $15 to $20 for entrées.

Getting There & Away
The closest Greyhound bus service is to Burlington, 17 miles east of Anacortes at the junction of I-5 and Hwy 20. From here, Skagit County Transport buses (☎ 360-757-8801) continue to Anacortes and to the ferry terminal. The Airporter Shuttle (☎ 360-622-1424) offers frequent bus service between Sea-Tac airport, Anacortes and the San Juan ferries; one-way fare is $30, and reservations are appreciated.

Lower Skagit River Valley

The Skagit River originates far to the east in North Cascades National Park and flows west to meet the Pacific Ocean near the little port town of La Conner. For much of its journey between the national park and the town of Sedro Woolley, the road and river share a steep-sided glacial valley, a designated 'Wild & Scenic' route that nonetheless is joined by the undulating power lines of three upper Skagit hydroelectric dams.

Out of the canyon, the Skagit River leaves the mountains and flows through a low-lying flood plain. As in Holland, early settlers used dikes to channel the river, retrieving rich farmland from the Skagit's seasonal floods. Today, dairy farms and plant nurseries are the norm. In the early spring, lower Skagit Valley fields are a wild display of tulip blooms, as this area is one of the nation's primary sources of spring bulbs. In fact, more acreage is under tulip cultivation here than in Holland.

Most towns here – like Sedro Woolley and Mt Vernon – are small and serve local farmers; however, historic streets and boutique shopping make La Conner a major destination.

SEDRO WOOLLEY
Population 7506
An early settler wanted to name this forested town 'Bug,' but the local women lobbied hard for *'Sedro'* (Spanish for cedar) and won. 'Woolley' was tacked on when an entrepreneurial Mr Woolley started building a few miles away, where the railroad was planned to pass through. The towns and their names eventually merged, and Sedro Woolley developed into a thriving timber town. Though logging has

diminished in recent years, it's still a big part of the local economy.

For travelers, the town of Sedro Woolley isn't of consuming interest. It is, however, a good place to stop before heading into North Cascades National Park (see the North Cascades chapter), as it's the last town of consequence for a couple hundred miles on Hwy 20 as it winds east up the Skagit River canyon and into the wilds of the Cascade Range.

Information

The chamber of commerce (☎ 360-855-1841), 116 Woodworth St, is housed in a caboose at the west end of town. The Mt Baker-Snoqualmie National Forest Ranger Station (☎ 360-856-5700), 800 State St, is open 8 am to 4:30 pm Monday to Friday. This is a good place to get information about the North Cascades National Park if you're planning an excursion in that direction.

The post office in Sedro Woolley is at 111 Woodworth St. The laundromat, Crossroads Sparkle Shop (☎ 360-856-0700), is next to Thrifty Foods in Sedro Woolley's Crossroads Square. If you're headed east, this is the last laundromat you may see for a while.

Places to Stay & Eat

The *Three Rivers Inn & Restaurant* (☎ 360-855-2626, 800-221-5122), at 210 Ball St (on Hwy 20 near the Hwy 9 intersection), is not bad at all for a bed and a meal. Singles/doubles are $58/66 and up, and there's an outdoor pool. The other motel in town, the *Skagit Motel* (☎ 360-856-6001, 800-582-9121), is a few dollars less at $40/50; it's a mile west of town on Hwy 20.

MT VERNON
Population 22,059
The farming center of Mt Vernon sits along a wide curve in the Skagit River. When white settlers first arrived, they began to build dikes along the Skagit to channel the river out of its wide flood plain and sloughs. However, river travel and farming

above the Mt Vernon area was impeded by enormous natural log jams in the river. After the log jams were removed in the 1870s, the valley opened up for more farming.

The rich soil and abundant water in the Skagit River valley makes this one of the most productive agricultural areas in the Northwest. The valley is the nation's single largest source of peas and is noted also for its production of strawberries. The most famous crops of the valley, though, are tulips, daffodils and irises, which come into bloom in the spring and are the focus of April's annual Tulip Festival.

Information

The Mt Vernon Chamber of Commerce (☎ 360-855-0974) is at 200 E College Way, and the post office is at 1207 Cleveland St. For medical emergencies, go to Skagit Valley Hospital (☎ 360-424-4111), 1415 E Kincaid.

Skagit Valley Tulip Festival

Head to Mt Vernon around late March or early April for the Northwest's most colorful festival. While most people don't really think of this as a 'festival' per se – most simply drive the side roads between Mt Vernon and La Conner armed with a tulip field map – there is an ongoing roster of events: an arts and crafts fair, a salmon bake, parade, musical concerts and the like.

When the weather is clear, the roads through the tulip fields are jammed with cyclists. If possible, take in the festival backroads on a weekday, as weekend afternoons bring long lines of cars, bikes and pedestrians sure to spoil the pace of a leisurely drive. For more information about the festival, contact Mt Vernon's chamber of commerce.

Places to Stay & Eat

West Winds Motel (☎ 360-424-4224), 2020 Riverside Drive, is a modest, inexpensive lodging in a town with otherwise rather expensive motels. Pets are allowed, children under 10 stay for free, and singles/doubles are $40/48. The *Tulip Valley Inn*

(☎ 360-428-5969), 2200 Freeway Drive, is a new motel complex with rooms at $45/65. The *Motor Inn Best Western* (☎ 360-424-4287), 300 W College Way, with a pool, kitchen units and pets allowed, is a good deal at $60/70.

Although the intersection of Hwy 538 and I-5 at exit 227 sprouts forth a large variety of fast food restaurants, Mt Vernon has much better things to offer off the freeway. The *Longfellow Cafe Oldtown Bistro* (☎ 360-336-3684), 416 Maple St, is in a historic old granary, with lunchtime sandwiches, soups, light entrées and evening seafood specials. *Wildflowers* (☎ 360-424-9724), 2001 E College Way, is Mt Vernon's other restaurant of note. Located in a Victorian home, the restaurant's specialty is elaborate preparations of local seafood (from $14 to $22) as well as freshly made breads, salads and desserts.

LA CONNER
At first glance, La Conner is an unlikely little tourist mecca. However, situated just north of the mouth of the Skagit River, La Conner's well-maintained and stylish 1880s storefronts and pretty harbor became a magnet for artists and writers during the 1960s and '70s (the likes of Tom Robbins live here). The galleries and artistic coteries drew attention to the slumbering but handsome town, and soon boutiques, nice restaurants and antique shops took up residence. Not much later, the tour buses began rolling in.

La Conner is a charming and relaxing stop for anyone whose nerves are jangled by nearby I-5 traffic or for San Juan-bound travelers early for their ferry. Summer weekends bring hundreds of people to town, however, and the narrow streets become absolutely jammed. Time your visit carefully if you want to avoid the crowds.

Orientation & Information
La Conner is 11 miles west of I-5, and 9 miles from Anacortes. Directly across the Swinomish Channel from La Conner is a lobe of Fidalgo Island, home to the Swinomish Indian Reservation. For tourist information, contact the La Conner Chamber of Commerce (☎ 360-466-4778), PO Box 1610, La Conner, WA 98257.

Museum of Northwest Art
This new museum and gallery (☎ 360-466-4446), 121 S 1st St, has recently moved from its old location in the Gaches Mansion to this modern showcase. There are two floors of exhibition space: the ground floor is dedicated to changing shows featuring regional painters, glass artists and sculptors, while the second floor displays the museum's still small and unexceptional permanent collection. The museum is open Tuesday to Sunday, 10 am to 5 pm; admission is $3.

Skagit County Museum
In a modern building well away from the crush of tourists, this museum (☎ 360-466-3365), 501 4th St, offers well-presented displays of the usual dolls, vintage kitchen tools and medical equipment that you come to expect in regional museums. What makes this museum more interesting is the display of old photos, tools and mementos from the 1870s when dikes were built along the Skagit River to reclaim land. It is open 11 am to 5 pm Tuesday to Sunday. Admission is by donation.

Skagit Valley Nurseries
The reclaimed farmland along the Skagit River delta is home to a large number of plant nurseries, and if you're a gardener you'll enjoy stopping to browse through the wealth of plants on display and for sale. The oldest of the local nurseries is Tillinghurst Seed Co (☎ 360-466-3329) at 623 E Morris St, which is still doing business out of its 1885 storefront. Christianson's Nursery (☎ 360-466-3821), 1578 Best Rd, has a wide selection of nursery stock, including roses, rhododendrons, perennials and fruit and berry plants. RoozenGaarde Garden & Store (☎ 360-424-8531), 1587 Beaver Marsh Rd, near Mt Vernon, is one of the area's largest growers of tulips and daffodils, and it sells cut flowers in the spring and bulbs in the fall. Contact the

chamber of commerce for a complete list of regional nurseries.

Cruises

Mystic Sea Charters (☎ 360-466-3042, 800-308-9387) offers lunch, dinner, and sightseeing cruises from the docks at the end of Morris Street in downtown La Conner. Destinations include Deception Pass, the San Juan Islands and Fidalgo Island. Prices begin at $35 for a 2½ hour cruise. Cruises are in operation from late March through mid-October.

Places to Stay

Don't expect any lodging deals in La Conner: local inns and B&Bs take themselves seriously. A number of the B&Bs are old converted farmhouses in the area between La Conner and Mt Vernon. *Ridgeway B&B* (☎ 360 428 8068, 800 428-8068), 1292 McLean Rd, is situated in the midst of tulip fields and has five guest rooms, two with private facilities. Rooms range from $75 to $95; cottages are $250. The *White Swan Guest House* (☎ 360-445-6805), 1388 Moore Rd, has three rooms in a Victorian farmhouse and a two-story cottage with full kitchen. Rooms begin at $80.

Hotel Planter (☎ 360-466-4710, 800-488-5409), 715 1st St, is a refurbished hotel with renovated rooms and circa 1907 charm. Children are allowed on weekdays only; rooms start at $75 a night. *La Conner Channel Lodge* (☎ 360-466-1500), 205 N 1st St, is a newer lodging right on the channel, though this handsome luxury inn does its best to look in keeping with the rest of turn-of-the-century La Conner. The large and airy rooms have fireplaces and decks and cost in the neighborhood of $120 to $215. Run by the same owners, the *La Conner Country Inn* (☎ 360-466-3101), 107 S 2nd St, is a shingle-sided lodge-like inn just a few steps away from the busy waterfront, and it has comfortable rooms with fireplaces starting at $93 and going to $117.

Places to Eat

For breakfast, head to the *Calico Cupboard* (☎ 360-466-4451), 720 1st St, a bakery and cafe with fresh pastries, omelets and light lunches. Just down the street is *Legends* (☎ 360-466-5240), 708 1st St, an outdoor cafe which has Native American fast food – salmon tacos for less than $5.

Hungry Moon Delicatessen (☎ 360-466-1602), 110 N First St, has sandwiches, desserts and light meals to eat in or take out. *Lighthouse Inn* (☎ 360-446-3147), with outdoor seating overlooking the channel, serves grilled seafood, steak and other Northwest fare in the $10 to $12 range; there's also a streetside deli serving sandwiches.

La Conner Brewing Co (☎ 360-466-1415), 117 S 1st St, is the town's attractive brewpub, with wood-fired pizzas, snacks, and tasty ales. *Andiamo* (☎ 360-466-9111), 505 S First St, looks tiny, but there are three floors of seating. The cuisine is nouveau Italian, with prices in the $12 to $15 range. *Palmers Restaurant & Pub* (☎ 360-466 4261) is the local fine dining establishment, in the La Conner Country Inn, 205 E Washington. French-influenced entrées featuring veal, duck and seafood are in the $20 range.

San Juan Islands

The San Juan archipelago contains 457 islands sprawled across 750 sq miles of Pacific waters in the area where Puget Sound and the Straits of Juan de Fuca and Georgia meet between the US and Canada. Only about 200 of these islands are named, and of these, only a handful are inhabited. There are 172 islands in Washington, and Washington State Ferries provides service to the four largest – San Juan, Orcas, Shaw and Lopez Islands – while others are accessible only by private boat or plane.

In the 1860s, the islands were the subject of an odd and prolonged border dispute between the USA and Britain. Claimed by both nations, they were the site of the Pig War. Though both sides had very little at stake, they nearly came to blows over the shooting of a marauding pig. Eventually, the USA's claim of ownership prevailed without further bloodshed (see sidebar, The Pig War).

Only in the last twenty years have the San Juans been 'discovered,' as they were long considered an inaccessible backwater of farmers and fisherfolk. Nonetheless, in spite of the islands' pastoral setting – a patchwork of fields, forests, lakes and sheep pastures, and fishing boats setting sail from tiny rock-lined harbors – tourism is by far the mainstay of local economies.

The islands are now a major holiday destination without lodging enough to handle the crowds during the summer high season. And yet, despite the inevitable adulteration that commercialization brings, the islands retain their bucolic charm and make for a restful, almost unforgettable retreat.

In certain respects, the islands don't even feel like they belong to North America. The sense of remoteness from mainland life is palpable, the pace slower. A rocky field filled with sheep looks like it could be off the coast of Ireland; a steep, cliff-lined bay filled with old fishing boats could be in northern Scotland.

The islands are in a rain shadow created by Vancouver Island. They receive only 25 inches of rain and are sunny 250 days a year – substantially better weather than nearby Seattle. Summertime temperatures can reach 85°F; wintertime lows drop into the 30°s.

Subtle differences distinguish the four islands linked by the ferry system. Lopez is the most rural island, with fields and pastures stretching across the island's central plateau. Lopez also has the strongest sense of community; people seem to make their homes here, not just visit in the summer. Shaw is the smallest and most remote island, with almost no facilities for tourists. San Juan Island boasts the most history, the only incorporated town and a nice mixture of rural landscapes and resort facilities. Orcas Island is the rockiest and most mountainous island, and life is centered almost exclusively around the resorts.

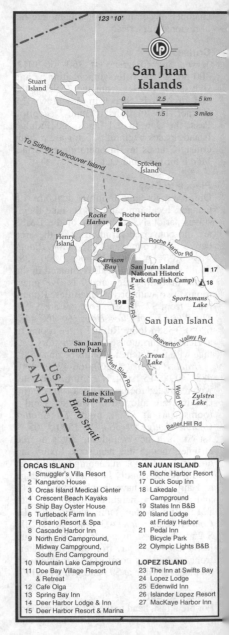

San Juan Islands

ORCAS ISLAND
1 Smuggler's Villa Resort
2 Kangaroo House
3 Orcas Island Medical Center
4 Crescent Beach Kayaks
5 Ship Bay Oyster House
6 Turtleback Farm Inn
7 Rosario Resort & Spa
8 Cascade Harbor Inn
9 North End Campground,
   Midway Campground,
   South End Campground
10 Mountain Lake Campground
11 Doe Bay Village Resort
   & Retreat
12 Cafe Olga
13 Spring Bay Inn
14 Deer Harbor Lodge & Inn
15 Deer Harbor Resort & Marina

SAN JUAN ISLAND
16 Roche Harbor Resort
17 Duck Soup Inn
18 Lakedale
   Campground
19 States Inn B&B
20 Island Lodge
   at Friday Harbor
21 Pedal Inn
   Bicycle Park
22 Olympic Lights B&B

LOPEZ ISLAND
23 The Inn at Swifts Bay
24 Lopez Lodge
25 Edenwild Inn
26 Islander Lopez Resort
27 MacKaye Harbor Inn

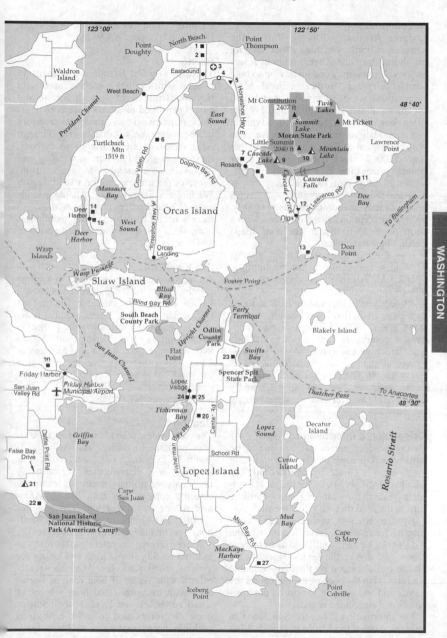

123°00'

122°50'

Waldron
Island

Point
Doughty

North Beach

Point
Thompson

Eastsound

West Beach

East
Sound

48°40'

Mt Constitution
2407 ft

Twin
Lakes

Turtleback
Mtn
1519 ft

Summit
Lake

Mt Pickett

Moran State Park

Little
Summit
2040 ft

Lawrence
Point

Massacre
Bay

Cascade
Lake

Mountain
Lake

Deer
Harbor

Orcas Island

Rosario

Cascade
Falls

West
Sound

Cascade Creek

Doe
Bay

Deer
Harbor

Olga

To Bellingham

Wasp
Islands

Orcas
Landing

Deer
Point

Wasp Passage

Shaw Island

Blind
Bay

Foster Point

Blind Bay Rd

South Beach
County Park

Blakely Island

Ferry
Terminal

Odlin
County
Park

Upright Channel

Flat
Point

Swifts
Bay

Friday Harbor

San Juan
Valley Rd

Friday Harbor
Municipal Airport

San Juan Channel

Spencer Spit
State Park

Lopez
Village

Thatcher Pass

To Anacortes
48°30'

Griffin
Bay

Fisherman
Bay

Lopez
Sound

Decatur
Island

False Bay
Drive

School Rd

Center
Island

Rosario Strait

Cape
San Juan

Lopez Island

San Juan Island
National Historic
Park (American Camp)

Mud Bay Rd

Mud
Bay

Cape
St Mary

MacKaye
Harbor

Iceberg
Point

Point
Colville

President Channel

Crow Valley Rd

Horseshoe Hwy W

Dolphin Bay Rd

Horseshoe Hwy E

Pt Lawrence Rd

Fisherman Bay Rd

Center Rd

Cattle Point Rd

Accommodations

Lodging frequently fills up during the summer, so don't even think about heading out during July and August without reservations – or you may end up having to take the last ferry back to the mainland. Most reservations are filled months ahead, and the most attractive lodging options are often booked even further in advance. Accommodations are also expensive: you will be pressed to find something for less than $100 a night during the summer (though prices often drop by half in the off-season). During high season, many resorts also demand multiple-day stays. Campsites aren't exactly numerous, either. Happily, there are exceptions to the rule, and with a little planning a trip to the San Juans needn't bust the budget.

If you're having trouble finding rooms, or want someone else to do the hunting, contact All Island Reservations (☎ 360-378-6977).

Also, if you're heading to the San Juans expecting to find miles of public beach, think again. In Washington, private land-owners control the land down to the tide line, which means that access to beaches, except at state or county parks, is effectively barred. The beach from the tide line to the water *is* public, but you will usually find several 'No Trespassing' signs barring your way.

Orientation & Information

Before heading out to the San Juans, be sure to pick a copy of *The Essential San Juan Islands Guide* by Marge and Ted Mueller (JASI, 1994), by far the most complete guide to the islands. There's hardly a turn in the road that isn't documented.

By all means, pick up the San Juan Islands map by International Travel Maps, with the red and black cover; you'll find them in most stores, and also on the ferries. Not only are all the roads covered on the map (valuable for bikers) but the back of the map gives the names and addresses of almost all the businesses and sites in the islands.

For information about the San Juans in general, contact the San Juan Islands Visitor Information Center (☎ 360-468-3663), PO Box 65, Lopez, WA 98261.

Biking

These mostly-flat islands are immensely popular with cyclists – each is laced with tiny roads that wind through forests and past sheep-filled meadows to remote bays. On summer weekends, there are probably more people on bikes than in cars. Though most motorists are courteous to cyclists, these roads are often narrow, winding and overused, so remember to use caution. Bicycles are transported for a small fee on Washington State Ferries. All the islands except Shaw offer bicycle rentals, so there's no need to bring your own; most companies will meet your ferry if you have a bike reserved.

Sea Kayaking

An increasingly popular means of exploring the shores of the San Juans is by sea kayak. Kayaks are available for rent on Orcas, San Juan and Lopez islands; tours and lessons are available also. Expect a guided half-day trip to cost around $30 to $40. An overnighter might cost as much as $200, and a three- to five-day excursion can run $220 to $450. Kayaks can be transported on ferries, both by vehicles and accompanying pedestrians.

Boating

The calm waters around the San Juans are a popular place for sailing and yachting. If you're lucky enough to have a boat at your disposal, or if you are planning on using boats as your primary means of transport, obtain a copy of *San Juan Islands, Afoot and Afloat* by Marge and Ted Mueller (Seattle, The Mountaineers, 1988), a handbook for the independent boat traveler.

More likely, travelers will turn to marinas on San Juan, Orcas and Lopez for various rental packages. Marinas usually offer a wide range of boat rentals, beginning with uncomplicated hourly hires of small rowboats and kayaks, to lunch or cocktail cruises and to more ambitious multiple-day excursions on yachts and sailboats. For the latter, you'll generally choose between a skippered charter (hiring a boat with crew by the day or week) or a self-navigated 'bare-boat' charter. Depending on your needs, tastes and size of party, a skippered charter can cost between $100 a day per person to several thousand dollars a week; meals, bedding and other niceties are usually included. See the individual island listings below for whom to contact about packages.

Prices for bare-boat rentals are equally broad and depend largely on the size and type of boat hired. Bare-boat charters provide all the on-board equipment and gear required or necessary for a safe trip. Food,

itinerary, bedding and other personal items are left to you. Before you are allowed to rent a bare-boat charter, companies will probably ask you to participate in a short checkout cruise to familiarize you with the vessel and to ascertain that you're competent to handle the boat. Prices for rentals begin at around $100 a day for a basic, comfortable sailboat.

Getting There & Away

Air Three airlines fly from the mainland to the San Juans. Harbor Air Lines (☎ 253-851-2381, 800-359-3220) offers flights from Sea-Tac Airport to Friday Harbor Municipal Airport, 1 mile west of Friday

---

The 'Pig War'

San Juan Island was the scene of an odd battle that occurred during the San Juan Border Dispute between the US and Britain from 1855 to 1872.

In 1846, both nations had agreed to split North America along the 49th parallel, with Britain retaining Vancouver Island. However, ownership of the San Juan Islands was left unresolved, as the treaty had divided the islands through 'the middle of the channel.' The British thought the channel in question was Rosario Strait to the east, while the US believed it was Haro Strait, to the west. The San Juan Islands lay in between.

The misunderstanding wasn't terribly important until American settlement began to take hold in the islands. The British Hudson's Bay Company (HBC) had maintained a fishery and various farms on San Juan Island for many years, then in 1855, a US magistrate attempted to levy import duties on goods from the HBC farms.

Official indignation was expressed by both sides, while US settlers continued to stream onto the islands. Finally, in 1859, shots were fired. A pig from the HBC farms had taken to wandering from its pens and rooting in the potato patch of a nearby US settler. The American shot the pig, the British demanded compensation, and after more mutual indignation the US sent troops to occupy the island and found Fort Pickett (now known as the American Camp). In retaliation, the British sent war ships from Victoria, BC to the island to protect HBC interests.

Cooler heads prevailed in London and Washington, DC, and a treaty declaring joint military occupation was eventually agreed upon. Meanwhile, attempts to procure a neutral arbitrator for the border dispute were continually thwarted by the US Senate until the Washington Treaty of 1871. In 1872, 13 years after the 'Pig War,' Kaiser Wilhelm I of Germany judged in favor of the US and the international boundary was established through Haro Strait. ■

Harbor off Spring St. Kenmore Air (☎ 360-486-1257, 800-543-9595) flies to Lopez, Orcas and San Juan islands on seaplanes from Lake Union and Lake Washington in Seattle; charter flights are available. If the ferry seems too slow, West Isle Air (☎ 800-874-4434) flies between Anacortes and the San Juans, with stops on Lopez, Orcas and San Juan islands; there are also links between Orcas and Friday Harbor. West Isle Air also has flights from Bellingham and Boeing Field in Seattle to the San Juans.

Flights from Seattle to the San Juans usually range from $80 to $100 one way.

Ferry By far the majority of people who visit the San Juans arrive on Washington State Ferries (☎ 800-843-3779), the state-owned ferry system that serves the islands of the Puget Sound and western Washington. From the mainland, car ferries

---

Riding the Ferries

Washington State Ferries is the largest publicly owned ferry system in the US, with 25 ships serving 20 different ports of call in the islands and coastal cities of the Puget Sound. Exploring northwestern Washington is nearly impossible without at some point boarding a ferry, but chances are that most travelers aren't used to the notion of boats as public transportation. Here are a few things to consider before your first ferry ride:

Reservations Except for the international sailings between Victoria and Seattle and Sidney and Anacortes (which recommend reservations), all other ferry service in the Puget Sound is offered on a first-come, first-served basis. Drivers should plan to be at the ferry docks an hour before sailing, and foot passengers at least a half-hour in advance, especially on weekends and in high season. If you don't get on the ferry you had planned for, you just have to wait for the next. It's not unusual to wait for more than one ferry in high season.

Boarding After buying your ticket (for all in-state ferries, fares are only charged going in one direction), you will be told to park in a specific lane. The lanes represent various destinations (especially in the San Juans, where ferries stop at several islands) or size and weight restrictions for vehicles. After you park, you are free to wander as long as you heed the call to return to your vehicle for boarding. You may be asked to back your vehicle onto the boat in some instances.

Note that ferries may leave a port of call without being completely full, as they often have to pick up vehicles at other destinations along the way.

Foot and bicycle passengers usually board first, and the crew will indicate when each lane should drive down the dock and load. After loading, car passengers can leave their vehicles and walk around on deck (on small ferries), or go upstairs to sitting and eating areas (on larger boats). On some ferries there's not much other than coffee to drink, while on larger vessels full food service is available. Smoking is prohibited on the vehicle decks and inside the cabins.

Pets (except seeing-eye dogs) must stay in vehicles on the lower decks.

Before boarding, disabled passengers should notify the terminal for instructions and assistance.

Disembarking When disembarking from ferries at night, don't turn on your headlights until signs say it's OK. A succession of headlights can blind the crew whose job is to guide you off the vessel. Drivers should be courteous to pedestrian and local traffic after disembarking by slowing down and letting people cross the street and allowing cars to make turns. Remember that you are part of a caravan of many – often as many as 50 – vehicles that can really clog up local intersections. ■

leave from Anacortes and depart for the four principal islands. At least one Washington State Ferry a day continues on to Sidney, near Victoria, BC, on Vancouver Island. Additionally, in the summer privately owned passenger-only ferries depart from Bellingham, Seattle, Port Townsend, and Victoria, bound for the San Juans.

If this is your first time on the Washington State Ferries, pick up the small, widely available timetable in advance and take a few minutes to get used to reading the schedules and fares. The system is a little complicated and can be hard to figure out at first.

Generally speaking, there are three different kinds of state ferry runs. The international ferry run travels between Anacortes and Sidney, with stops at Orcas and/or Friday Harbor, depending on the season and the ferry. Since this is an international run, note that if you board this ferry in the San Juans to return to Anacortes, you will be subject to a customs and immigrations inspection in Anacortes. The Anacortes/ Sidney crossing takes three hours. The regular domestic ferry run originates in Anacortes and travels to some if not all of the islands. *Not all ferries stop at all four islands.* Make certain that the ferry you take is scheduled to stop at the island you want. Travel time to the closest island, Lopez, takes 45 minutes; the most distant port, Friday Harbor on San Juan, takes 1¼ hours. Inter-island ferries travel a circular route exclusively between the four islands.

Passenger-only privately owned ferries are available from other points of departure. San Juan Shuttle Express (☎ 888-373-8522) travels from Bellingham to Orcas and Friday Harbor. In summer, the *Victoria Clipper* (☎ 360-448-5000) links Seattle with Friday Harbor on San Juan Island and Rosario Resort on Orcas Island, with service on to Victoria, BC. In the winter, a weekend-only service goes from Seattle to the San Juans, but with no continuation on to Victoria. Puget Sound Express (☎ 360-385-5288) offers service from Port Townsend to the San Juans.

On Washington State Ferries, fares are collected on westbound journeys only; that is, all westbound tickets are considered roundtrip. Hence, if you plan to visit all the islands, it's cheapest to go all the way to westernmost Friday Harbor initially and then work your way back through the other islands, since you won't have to buy another ticket. The exception is the international crossing from Sidney to Anacortes: if you board this ferry, you'll need to pay for the eastbound journey.

Fares between Anacortes and all San Juan Island destinations are $5.10 for a foot passenger, $21.75 high season for a car and driver, and $5.10 for each additional car passenger. Bicycles that are wheeled on in Anacortes incur a $2.90 surcharge, unless they are attached to a vehicle; in this case they ride free. The same rules apply to kayaks. However, foot passengers, bicycles and kayaks ride the inter-island ferries for free.

The international ferry between Anacortes and Sidney is $8.90 for foot passengers, $39.75 for car and driver, both high season, one way.

Getting Around

There is no public transport on the San Juans Islands. However, most motels and inns will pick up registered guests at the ferry, if they are notified in advance.

Lopez, Orcas and San Juan islands each have a taxi service (call to reserve it if you know what ferry you're coming in on). Rental cars are available in Friday Harbor, and of course, bike rentals shops are almost more common than cafes on the islands.

SAN JUAN ISLAND

Most visitors will find that San Juan Island, of all the islands, offers the most hospitable blend of sophisticated amenities, rural landscapes, bustling harbors and cultural facilities. A large part of the island's draw is Friday Harbor: with a population of about 1730, it's the only sizable town in all the San Juan Islands. But follow any of the streets out of Friday Harbor and you're soon on a central plateau, where small farms, dairies and lakes fill the verdant landscape.

The only other community of any size is Roche Harbor, on a beautiful bay to the northwest. This used to be the center of a lime-processing operation, an early San Juan Island industry. John McMillin, a onetime attorney from Tacoma, built an imposing complex that included lime kilns, a grand hotel, a private estate, workers' cottages, a small railway, a company store, a chapel and a shipping wharf. The lime factory closed in the 1950s, and the extensive buildings are now part of Roche Harbor Resort.

Orientation & Information

San Juan is the most westerly of the ferry-accessible San Juan Islands. The ferry terminal is at Friday Harbor on the eastern side of the island. From Friday Harbor, take 2nd St to Guard St, then turn right on Tucker Ave which will turn into Roche Harbor Rd and lead to the resort there in 10 miles. The main road from Friday Harbor south is Cattle Point Rd.

For more information, contact the San Juan Island Chamber of Commerce (☎ 360-378-5240), PO Box 98, San Juan Island, WA 98250. In summer, there's a visitors' information booth just across from the ferry landing. The visitors' center at 1st and Spring Sts can fill you in on the San Juan Island National Historic Park.

The post office (☎ 360-378-4511) is at 220 Blair Ave. For medical emergencies, go to the Inter-Island Medical Center (☎ 360-378-2141), 550 Spring St. Clean up those dirty clothes at the Wash Tub Laundromat (☎ 360-378-2070), just off Spring St at Front St, behind the San Juan Inn.

San Juan Island National Historic Park

The so-called 'Pig War' between the USA and Britain is the focus of this slightly gratuitous NPS-administered facility. There are three components to the park.

In Friday Harbor, at 125 Spring St, there's a visitors' center (☎ 360-378-2240) with information about the dispute and the historic sites. At the **English Camp**, 10 miles northwest of Friday Harbor off Beaverton Valley Rd, are the remains of the British military facilities dating from the 1860s. A path from the parking area leads down to the small site, which includes a blockhouse and a small museum containing artifacts of the island's native Indian culture. On a nice day, it's worth the detour just for the views over Garrison Bay.

On the southern flank of the island is the **American Camp**, 5 miles south of Friday Harbor off Cattle Point Rd, which has slightly more developed facilities. The sole remains of the 1859 fort are the officers' barracks and a laundress's house, though a series of interpretive trails lead to earthwork fortifications, a British farm from the dispute era and the beach. Near the trailhead is a small visitors' center.

Lime Kiln State Park

Set on the western shore of San Juan Island, off scenic West Side Rd, this is apparently the only park in the world devoted to whale watching. Most sightings are of killer or minke whales who gather to dine on the June salmon runs through Haro Strait. A trail leads from the parking lot to the main viewing area, which is equipped with picnic tables and interpretive panels explaining the whales' movements and natural history. Be sure to bring binoculars (even though whales are frequently spotted quite close to shore) and a little patience.

Friday Harbor

Friday Harbor offers a lively restaurant scene and more culture than you'd expect in this distant outpost of the USA. There are several unusual museums and plenty of lodging options and outdoor outfitters to round out your stay.

Friday Harbor is a popular stop for Canadians coming over from Victoria to shop and relax. During summer, there are a number of festivals and events – particularly the Dixieland Jazz Festival – that fill the streets (and most available lodging).

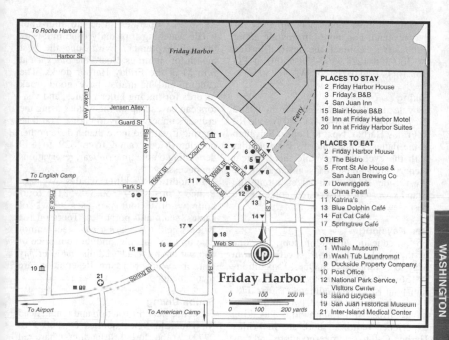

PLACES TO STAY
2 Friday Harbor House
3 Friday's B&B
4 San Juan Inn
15 Blair House B&B
16 Inn at Friday Harbor Motel
20 Inn at Friday Harbor Suites

PLACES TO EAT
2 Friday Harbor House
3 The Bistro
5 Front St Ale House &
   San Juan Brewing Co
6 Downriggers
8 China Pearl
11 Katrina's
13 Blue Dolphin Café
14 Fat Cat Café
17 Springtree Café

OTHER
1 Whale Museum
8 Wash Tub Laundromat
9 Duckside Property Company
10 Post Office
12 National Park Service,
   Visitors Center
18 Island Bicycles
19 San Juan Historical Museum
21 Inter-Island Medical Center

Friday Harbor

WASHINGTON

San Juan Historical Museum In an 1890s farmhouse now on the outskirts of Friday Harbor, this museum (☎ 360-378-3949), 405 Price St, commemorates early pioneer life on San Juan Island. While the building itself is interesting for its vernacular farmhouse architecture, the displays featuring kitchen and parlor furnishings – like the pump organ and massive wood range – are also worth checking out. The museum is open 1 to 4:30 pm Wednesday to Saturday from May through September. The rest of the year the museum is open the same hours Thursday and Friday only. Admission is by donation.

Whale Museum If the San Juan Islands had a mascot, it would surely be the killer whale. Indeed, these 25-foot-long whales are sometimes seen by lucky ferry passengers traveling through the islands. These and other sea mammals have been given their own natural history museum (☎ 360-378-4710) at 62 1st St. There are a number

of whale skeletons and life-size models as well as displays about marine life in general, Native American legends and recordings of ocean mammal songs. Children are welcome; there's even a hands-on children's room with puzzles and the like. For the truly serious whale lover, the museum offers courses concerning marine ecology and natural history.

The Whale Museum is open 10 am to 5 pm daily from Memorial Day to September 30, and 11 am to 4 pm daily the rest of the year. Admission is $4/$3.50 adults/seniors, and children are $1.

Dixieland Jazz Festival Friday Harbor's biggest party of the year is the annual jazz festival, held on the last weekend of July. More than a dozen jazz bands play the weekend long on a number of indoor and outdoor stages, with a special kids' concert on Saturday and a jazz church service on Sunday. Food and crafts booths line most downtown streets. Plan well in advance for lodging, as most rooms book up early for the weekend. For more information about the festival, contact the festival office (☎ 360-378-4224, 360-378-5509) at PO Box 1666, Friday Harbor, WA 98250.

Biking

Bicycle rentals are available from Island Bicycles (☎ 360-378-4941), 380 Argyle Rd in Friday Harbor. Next to Lopez, San Juan is the flattest island, and it's very popular with the cycling set. While there's great scenery along all the roads on San Juan, the West Side Rd, which edges along the island's western coast, offers some of the best views.

Sea Kayaking

For an educational wildlife tour, take one of the day-long kayak trips offered from May to October by Sea Quest Expeditions (☎ 360-378-5767). Both Sea Quest and San Juan Kayak Expeditions (☎ 360-378-4436) offer fully outfitted, two- to five-day kayak trips with no previous kayaking experience required; both are in Friday Harbor. Call to set up reservations and they will meet you at the ferry landing. For kayak rentals, contact Emerald Sea Aquatics (☎ 360-378-2772).

Boat Charters

Most charter companies offer 30- to 55-foot sailboats for scenic day trips, instruction and weeklong cruises, either skippered or bare-boat. Most rent year-round, but keep in mind that you'll save heaps if you sail in the off-season. For sailboats, contact Trophy Charters (☎ 360-378-2110) or Captain Howard's Charters (☎ 360-378-3958). Sailboats and powered yachts are both available from Charters Northwest (☎ 360-378-7196), 189 1st St S.

For more charters contact Dolphin Yacht Charters (☎ 360-378-4829), a chartering agency brokering skippered and bare-boat yachts between Seattle and Alaska.

Whale Watching

In the summer season, San Juan Boat Rentals & Tours (☎ 360-378-3499, 800-232-6722) operates three- to four-hour whale-watching trips daily from mid-May through September, with June the best month for sightings. Board the *Blackfish* at Slip M at the Friday Harbor docks. The captain and naturalist have good track records for finding killer whales, and visitors can eavesdrop on the whales using the cruiser's underwater hydrophone. You'll be sharing it with no more than a dozen other people. Prices range from $29 to $49 depending on the time of year; reservations are necessary.

In addition to killer whales, Western Prince Cruises' (☎ 360-378-5315) four-hour wildlife tour promises views of eagles, seals and porpoises. Tours on the twice-weekly *Western Prince* accommodate up to 33 people, and the tour price of $45 per adult includes admission to Friday Harbor's Whale Museum. Reservations are recommended.

Scuba Diving

For scuba gear, instruction and rental, head for Emerald Sea Aquatics (☎ 360-378-2772), at the Spring St landing. Chartered half-day dives cost $55. Full-day dives for four to six passengers cost $500 to $600.

Places to Stay

Camping Five miles from Friday Harbor, the versatile *Lakedale Campground* (☎ 360-378-2350), 2627 Roche Harbor Rd, has 115 tent sites, 15 bicycle sites and 19 RV sites (no hookups), plus three tent cabins. Sites ($16 to $22) nestled among woods and grassy fields between the campground's three trout and bass-stocked lakes are available from April 1 to October 15. There are also showers, boat rentals and a grocery store that has camping equipment and fishing tackle for sale or rental.

Cyclists will love *Pedal Inn Bicycle Park* (☎ 360-378-3049), 1300 False Bay Drive, a campground exclusively for cyclists. The campground lies south of Friday Harbor. Reach False Bay Drive from Cattle Point Rd, or from False Bay Rd off Bailer Hill Rd. Purchase staple food items from the small grocery store.

Killer whales, also called orcas, are often spotted around the islands in the summer.

The small campground at *San Juan County Park* (☎ 360-378-2992), 380 Westside Rd N, on San Juan's west shore, offers access to excellent scuba diving and views of Victoria, BC. It gets crowded during the summer, so plan accordingly. Groceries and tackle are available near the boat launch.

B&Bs There's a proliferation of B&Bs on San Juan Island. For a more complete listing, contact the B&B Association of San Juan Island, PO Box 3016, Friday Harbor, WA, 98250. The association also operates a room availability hotline at ☎ 360-378-3030.

On the hill above the harbor, *Blair House B&B* (☎ 360-378-5907), 345 Blair Ave, is a woodsy, 1909 home offering five rooms with shared baths and a cottage with private facilities. All rooms share access to a swimming pool and hot tub. Room rates are $75 to $110, while the cottage goes for $155 for two people.

In Friday Harbor, two old downtown hotels have been turned into B&Bs. *Friday's B&B* (☎ 360-378-5848, 800-352-2632), 35 1st St, first opened its doors in 1891. Renovated in 1992, Friday's now has seven double rooms with shared bathroom, three suites with private baths and one kitchenette. Rooms cost $90 to $160; a continental breakfast is included. The Bistro Restaurant is on the main floor.

The *San Juan Inn* (☎ 360-378-2070), 50 Spring St, is another historic hotel that's been updated with modern conveniences without losing its 1879 Victorian charm. There are four double rooms with private baths and six rooms that share three baths. All rooms share a 2nd-floor sitting room and dining room. High-season rates are $78 to $102.

On the far western side of the island is the *States Inn B&B* (☎ 360-378-6240, 360-378-4243), 2039 W Valley Rd, which was once a country schoolhouse. It is now on a working horse ranch and the old school has been remodeled into nine guest rooms, all with private facilities; guided horseback rides are available to guests. Rooms cost $85 to $125. On the southern edge of the island is *Olympic Lights B&B* (☎ 360-378-3186), 4531-A Cattle Point Rd, a restored 1895 farmhouse standing on an open bluff with views south onto the Strait of Juan de Fuca and the Olympic Mountains. There are five guest rooms ($70 to $105) in the sparely elegant inn, with a mix of private and shared baths.

Hotels As the plural name intimates, *The Inns at Friday Harbor* (☎ 360-378-4000, 800-752-5752) are in fact two different lodgings two blocks away from each other. The first, at 410 Spring St, is an older but well-maintained motel with a pool, while the second, at 680 Spring St, is a more modern complex with suite-style rooms and a restaurant. If roomy and modern facilities are important to you, this is probably the best bet in Friday Harbor. Motel rooms start at $99 and the suites start at $135. The hotel also runs a double-decker bus tour.

On a quiet side street half a mile from the town center, *Island Lodge at Friday Harbor* (☎ 360-378-2000, 800-822-4753), 1016 Guard St, is another modern, comfortable motel facility with a hot tub and sauna; it's also a rare good deal for the San Juans. The spacious motel rooms go for $99/110. As if that weren't enough, the motel also overlooks a llama pasture.

The newest and most exclusive lodging in Friday Harbor is *Friday Harbor House* (☎ 360-378-8455), 130 West St, a modern boutique hotel with great views over the harbor. All rooms have a fireplace, Jacuzzi and other upscale niceties. The rates, from $195 upwards, include a full breakfast.

Resorts Located on the site of a former lime kiln and country estate, *Roche Harbor Resort* (☎ 360-378-2155, 800-451-8910), in Roche Harbor, is just about the nicest place to stay in all the San Juans. Certainly there's no more beautiful harbor, and the slightly weird accouterments left over from the limestone mining days (check out the family mausoleum festooned with arcane Masonic symbolism) only add to the charm. In 1886, limestone king John McMillin built the imposing Hotel de Haro – with wide, ivy-covered verandahs and formal gardens – as the company hotel. Over 100 years later, it's still taking guests, who enjoy its slightly faded gentility; rooms at this landmark inn begin at $84.

A number of refurbished workers' cottages fill a grassy meadow above the harbor, just a few yards from the swimming pool and playground, and rent for $130 to $195. Fully modern condominiums are discreetly tucked behind a stand of trees; rates begin at $155 for a one-bedroom condo, $195 for two bedrooms. In addition to the lodgings, there's a marina with boat rentals, restaurant, lounge and old general store on the dock. You can even land your private jet on the air strip.

Vacation Home Rentals *Dockside Property Company* (☎ 360-378-5060, 800-992-1904), 285 Blair Ave, manages around 60 year-round vacation homes in the islands, most of which are on San Juan. Call to request a brochure with pictures of all the homes and their rates, which start at $700 weekly.

Places to Eat
Friday Harbor is filled with good places to eat and most are pretty easy on the wallet. In addition, you can walk the downtown area in less than 10 minutes and survey all your choices. If you can't make up your mind, here are a few sure bets.

Breakfast is a big deal in a holiday destination like Friday Harbor, and there are good choices for a leisurely brunch. *Blue Dolphin Cafe* (☎ 360-378-6116), 185 1st St, is right by the ferry, and has good traditional, egg-rich breakfasts. The *Fat Cat Cafe* (☎ 360-378-8646), 275 A St S, has traditional breakfasts plus a bakery, and patio seating in decent weather. *Katrina's* (☎ 360-378-7290), 135 2nd St, is an informal little cafe with vegetarian dishes, bakery items and a strong alternative feel.

For deep-dish pizza, head to *The Bistro* (☎ 360-378-3076), 35 1st St, open for lunch and dinner on the main floor at Friday's B&B. They also have a good selection of sandwiches, salads and pasta. *China Pearl* (☎ 360-378-5254), 51 Spring St, is a good place to go for inexpensive traditional and Sichuan food. You'll spend less than $10 a head for dinner at either of these restaurants. There's live jazz on the weekends and karaoke whenever anyone has the nerve.

Down along the waterfront are several supper clubs, such as *Downriggers* (☎ 360-378-2700) at the base of Spring St, that offer Northwest cuisine – good steak and grilled seafood ($10 to $22) – along with views over the harbor.

Front St Ale House & San Juan Brewing Company (☎ 360-378-2337), 1 Front St, is the island's only brewery serving up British-style beers in a real pub atmosphere – a table full of real fishermen does wonders for the ambiance. The food's good, too: traditional British favorites like steak-and-kidney pie and bangers and mash keep company with such standbys as chili, chowder and hamburgers.

Springtree Cafe (☎ 360-378-4848), 310 Spring St, offers casual bistro-style dining in a spare but comfortable cafe. The menu tends toward seafood and vegetarian dishes ($10 to $12), cooked with Northwest élan but with an eye for health. In summer, there's dining in the courtyard. The dining room at the *Friday Harbor House* (☎ 360-378-8455), 130 West St, is an intimate room with a fireplace and great views. The menu is small but tempting, with seasonal Northwest cuisine in the $15 to $20 range.

While there's both a fine dining room and a family cafe at Roche Harbor Resort, the only good reason to leave Friday Harbor looking for food is to go to the *Duck Soup Inn* (☎ 360-378-4878), 3090 Roche Harbor Rd. About 4½ miles northeast of Friday Harbor, this friendly establishment serves local seafood and meats with Continental aplomb in a handsome, fireplace-dominated dining room. Open for dinner only; prices range from $15 to $18.

Getting Around

Friday Harbor Car Rentals (☎ 360-378-4351) operates out of the Inns of Friday Harbor, 410 Spring St. There are also car rentals at the Friday Harbor airport from Practical Rent-A-Car (☎ 360-293-6750).

You can rent mopeds from Susie's Mopeds (☎ 360-378-5244), at Nichols and A St, and call Primo Taxi (☎ 360-378-3550) for a cab.

ORCAS ISLAND

Orcas is the largest of the San Juan Islands, and in some ways it is the most exclusive. The mountainous landscape isn't particularly friendly to agriculture, the backbone of local economies on the other islands. However, the rocky promontories and isolated harbors look good in real estate brochures, so retirement homes, resort communities and weekend manses generally take up the void.

In terms of rugged physical beauty, Orcas is probably the most fetching of the islands. Mt Constitution is the highest point in the San Juans, and from its peak views stretch from Mt Baker to the Olympic Mountains and Vancouver Island. Mt Constitution is only one of several forested peaks on Orcas, around which the rest of the island folds in steep valleys. Along the rocky coast, narrow cliff-lined inlets do service as harbors for small pleasure boats.

Orcas Island offers a wide array of tourist facilities, including the San Juans' largest state park and campground. However, it still retains a palpable sense of being an insider's destination, perhaps because there isn't much of a town on the island. You need to know where you're going before you get there because lodgings, restaurants and recreation are scattered all over. Orcas is the kind of place where families return to pass the summer generation after generation (some lodgings have a week-long minimum stay in high season), which only adds to the purposeful insularity of the island.

Orientation & Information

Orcas Island is shaped like a saddlebag, with two distinct lobes very nearly cleaved by East Sound. The ferry terminal is at the tiny community of Orcas Landing, on the western half of the island. Roads lead north and then west to the village of Deer Harbor and, on the other side of Turtleback Mountain, to West Beach. The island's main

WASHINGTON

population center is Eastsound, at the northern extreme of East Sound, where the two halves of the island meet. Most tourist and commercial facilities are available here, including a post office, laundry, bank, grocery store and gas station. The eastern half of the island is essentially comprised of Moran State Park and of resorts scattered along the coastline. The most noted of these is Rosario Resort, whose centerpiece is a mansion and spa built in 1910 by a former mayor of Seattle.

For more information, contact the Orcas Island Chamber of Commerce (☎ 360-376-2273), PO Box 252, Eastsound, WA 98245. Orcas Island Medical Center (☎ 360-376-2561) is in Eastsound off Mt Baker Rd.

Orcas Island Historical Museum
This interesting series of six log cabins-cum-museums (☎ 360-376-4849) relates the pioneer and local history of Orcas and the San Juan Islands. Besides the usual collection of household goods, tools, weapons and photographs, there's a good display of native Indian artifacts. A curious collection of Chinese 'coolie' hats commemorates the San Juan Islands' role as a passageway for illegal Asian immigrants in the 1880s.

The museum is on N Beach Rd in Eastsound. It's open 1 to 4 pm Monday to Saturday, from Memorial Day to Labor Day, and on Friday and Saturday only from Labor Day to October 15. At other times you can see it by appointment. Admission is by donation.

Moran State Park
The fourth-largest state park in Washington, 7-sq-mile Moran State Park (☎ 360-376-2326) is southeast of Eastsound on Horseshoe Hwy. The park is dominated by **Mt Constitution**, the highest peak in the San Juans at 2407 feet, which is graced with lakes and waterfalls, hiking and mountain biking trails, and interpretive displays.

Nearly everyone who visits Orcas Island makes their way up the steep and winding paved road to the summit of Mt Constitution; in summer, this can be a busy place. The road up the mountain turns off Horseshoe Hwy just past Cascade Lake. This 5-mile ascent is not a road for trailers or large mobile homes, or for the vast majority of cyclists, as the grade is a persistent 7% with frequent hairpin turns. At the top, beside an unfortunately situated microwave receiver, is a three-story stone tower whose summit affords great views over all of northwestern Washington.

There are two major bodies of water in the park, **Cascade Lake** and **Mountain Lake**, which offer campgrounds, good trout fishing, non-motorized boating (both lakes offer boat rentals), picnic areas and swimming beaches.

There are nearly 40 miles of trails in Moran State Park, and about half of them are open seasonally for mountain biking. Get a trail map from the park headquarters to find out current trails open to bikers.

Both Cascade and Mountain Lakes are ringed by hiking trails, and a 3-mile trail links the two. This trail passes by the 100-foot **Cascade Falls** and two smaller falls.

Smuggling in the San Juans
Because the San Juan Islands and northwestern Washington were remote, unpatrolled regions between two nations for many years, there was a long history of smuggling in the area. In the 1880s, the smuggling of wool bundles and Chinese laborers from Canada into the US was commonplace. (Under the Chinese Exclusion Act of 1882, Chinese immigrants were forbidden to enter the US because of anti-Chinese prejudice stemming from job competition.)

During Prohibition in the 1920s, a flood of alcohol flowed from Canada through these US waters. Ironically, the most famous hooch smuggler of all was Seattle police captain Ray Olmstead, who brought in some 200 cases of booze a day and evaded capture by using a network of shrewd locals to move his goods for him. ∎

Cascade Falls is more easily reached from a trailhead off the Mt Constitution road, about half a mile uphill from the junction with Horseshoe Hwy. From here, it's only a quarter of a mile to the falls.

Trails lead from Cascade Lake's North End Campground and climb 4.3 miles up to Mt Constitution; however, it's a lot easier to catch a ride to the summit and take in the views on the way downhill. A portion of this trail is fairly flat: from the viewing tower, past marshy Summit Lake, to Little Summit, where the trail crosses the road before making the descent to Cascade Lake.

Biking

For foot passengers getting off at Orcas landing, nothing could be more convenient than Dolphin Bay Bicycles (☎ 360-376-4157, 360-376-3093), two blocks from the ferry landing. Rates vary depending on the duration of the rental, and there is no charge for helmets. Racks and touring packs are also available. In Eastsound, head to Wildlife Cycles (☎ 360-376-4708), just off North Beach Rd, for bike rentals.

Sea Kayaking

The protected shoreline of East Sound is a good place for beginners to learn the craft of sea kayaking, or for veterans to view wildlife along the rocky coastline. Crescent Beach Kayaks (☎ 360-376-2464), directly across the road from Crescent Beach near Eastsound, has a limited number of double and single kayaks for rent.

Both of the following kayak outfitters also offer a variety of guided trips in two-person kayaks, from a half day to several days, as well as beginner classes. Contact Shearwater Adventures (☎ 360-376-4699) in Eastsound for guided half-day trips of Eastsound, the Wasp Islands or the north shore. Island Kayak Guides (☎ 360-376-4755, 360-376-2291), at Doe Bay Village Resort & Retreat, offers guided tours of Peapod Island Wildlife Refuge and Gorilla Rock. Beginners will like the introductory trip around Doe Bay and Doe Island. There's also a full-moon evening trip.

In addition to these outfitters, a good number of places with overnight lodgings also facilitate kayaking and offer rental, instruction and excursions.

Boating & Whale Watching

Deer Harbor Charters (☎ 360-376-5989, 800-544-5758), at Deer Harbor Resort, has loads of nautical offerings. Rent a small rowboat with an outboard motor for fishing or exploring, or get outfitted with fishing gear and a guide. Take a sailing excursion, or lounge around East Sound on a luxury yacht. Whale-watching excursions may include sightings of eagles, seals and sea lions, as well as killer whales (or 'orcas'), minke whales and porpoises. Bare-boat charters are also available.

Places to Stay

If you're having trouble locating a room, the chamber of commerce offers an accommodations availability hotline at ☎ 360-376-8888.

Camping *Moran State Park* (☎ 360-376-2326), southeast of Eastsound on Horseshoe Hwy, is the largest camping area in the San Juans. There are more than 150 campsites (no hookups) in four different lakeside locations: Mountain Lake Campground at Mountain Lake, and North End, Midway and South End Campgrounds at Cascade Lake. Sites are $10 and reservations are strongly recommended during the summer.

Tent and RV campers can also stay at *Doe Bay Village Resort & Retreat* on the Horseshoe Hwy at Doe Bay (see Resorts, below).

B&Bs *Kangaroo House* (☎ 360-376-2175), on N Beach Rd in Eastsound, is a 1907 Craftsman-style B&B set on 3 acres. There are five guest rooms ($75 to $125), two with private baths. On Crow Valley Rd, off Deer Harbor Rd, is *Turtleback Farm Inn* (☎ 360-376-4914). This lovely old farmhouse overlooks a wide meadow and lake and offers seven guest rooms ($80 to $160). All have private baths and share a sitting room and dining room.

South of Olga on Obstruction Pass Rd is a unique B&B, the *Spring Bay Inn* (☎ 360-376-5531). This B&B is run by two former park rangers, who include a program of basic kayak instruction in the price of the stay ($175 to $225). Hungry kayakers returning from a morning tour are greeted with a full breakfast. All equipment is provided. A two-night minimum stay applies during the summer season; the inn is set just back from the water, with a beach-side hot tub. The Spring Bay Inn is quite isolated – not only is it in the forest, it is also quite a ways from the ferry and Eastsound.

Hotels At Orcas Landing, the historic *Orcas Hotel* (☎ 360-376-4300) was built in 1904 and is listed on the National Register of Historic Places. The old hotel was completely refurbished in 1985, and it now offers a dozen rooms, some with private facilities; rates range between $69 and $170. This handsome inn, with wraparound porches and great views, also has an espresso bar, restaurant and lounge.

Deer Harbor, west of Orcas Landing, is one of the most beautiful harbors on the island. *Deer Harbor Resort & Marina* (☎ 360-376-4420) seems to own – and rent – pretty much every building in this little hamlet. There's a wide array of accommodations, ranging from cottages to motel-style bungalows ($189 to $229) and small houses right on the water ($239 to $299). The resort also offers full boat rental facilities, tennis courts, bike rentals and a small restaurant and market.

Just half a mile from Deer Harbor is the *Deer Harbor Lodge & Inn* (☎ 360-376-4110), on Deer Harbor Rd. Rooms aren't offered in the old lodge any longer (though the restaurant is open during high season); instead, there are eight rooms in a newer, adjacent log-cabin-like building ($99 to $169 for double occupancy).

In Eastsound, the *Outlook Inn* (☎ 360-376-2200), on Horseshoe Hwy, is now a lodging complex that has at its heart a venerable old hotel from the 1890s. While most rooms in the original hotel share bathrooms (starting at $79), there's a motel-like

wing attached to the old hotel with modern rooms (starting at $120). Brand new is a suites-only addition on the bluff just above the old hotel ($220 and up). The restaurant at the Outlook is notable because it offers Thai food (including vegetarian dishes) alongside more stalwart Northwest fare. Just next door is the *Landmark Inn* (☎ 360-376-2423), on Horseshoe Hwy, a modern lodging with spacious suites, all with full kitchens, fireplaces, and balconies. Views from the front are wonderful and prices aren't bad at $130 to $150, depending on the view.

Sharing the view with Rosario Resort, *Cascade Harbor Inn* (☎ 360-376-6350), 4 miles south of East Sound, offers standard motel rooms ($90) and upscale condo-like suites with balconies, fireplaces, kitchens, and 'location location location.' One-bedroom suites are $190.

Resorts If you're taking a family or group of friends to Orcas, consider the *Smuggler's Villa Resort* (☎ 360-376-2297, 800-488-2097) on the northern coast just north of Eastsound on N Beach Rd. The resort is a complex of 20 small and medium-sized, architecturally innovative, two-bedroom homes with fireplaces, right on the beach. Facilities include a marina, an outdoor pool, a tennis court and other recreation facilities. Rates range from $180 to $250.

For years, the place for upscale Orcas visitors was *Rosario Resort & Spa* (☎ 360-376-2222, 800-562-8820) on Rosario Way, 4 miles south of Eastsound off Horseshoe Hwy. Built in the 1910s as the middle-age folly of one-time Seattle mayor Robert Moran, the old mansion is the centerpiece of a resort complex that includes almost 180 modern rooms, tennis courts, swimming pools, a marina and elaborate tiled spa facilities in the basement. The old mansion houses a fine dining restaurant, family dining room, and lounge, all with exquisite views over East Sound. Accommodations aren't cheap ($219 to $294), and the nouveau riche crowd can be quite snooty.

There are resorts, and then there's *Doe Bay Village Resort & Retreat* (☎ 360-376-

2291, 360-376-4755), on Doe Bay on the island's easternmost shore, 18 miles east of Eastsound on the Horseshoe Hwy. This slightly shabby, comfortable and welcoming vacation spot is by far the least expensive and most 'alternative' lodging in the San Juans. The resort overlooks Doe Bay, as lovely a spot as any on Orcas, and has at once the atmosphere of an artists' commune, hippie retreat and New Age center. Doe Bay also has hot and cold tubs and a beachfront sauna.

The lodgings here include campsites ($18), dorm and hostel rooms ($15.50), a tree house and various levels of cabins and yurts. Cabins without a bathroom or a kitchen start at $44.50, moving up to $100 as bathrooms, kitchens, wood stoves, beds and extra rooms are added. Rates are for double occupancy; each additional person adds $11. Most lodging facilities are in a grassy swale with views of the water, while others are tucked into the surrounding woods. The clothing-optional hot tub is set apart on one side of a creek, and there is also a restaurant where healthy meals are served up family-style, according to the whim of the cook.

Vacation Home Rentals *Dockside Properties* (☎ 360-378-5060, 800-992-1904), PO Box 1459, Friday Harbor, WA 98250, on San Juan Island, has a handful of vacation homes available for rent. Call the 800 number for an illustrated brochure with detailed rates.

Places to Eat
There are dining rooms at most resorts and marinas, and some are noted above. The following restaurants deserve special notice. At Orcas landing, *The Boardwalk* (☎ 360-376-2971) is a string of cottages-cum-boutiques with several eating options, including burgers and fish and chips. The *Orcas Hotel* (☎ 360-376-4300) is open for breakfast, lunch and dinner. The old hotel's dining room combines a pub ambiance with Northwest cuisine. There's also a small coffee shop tucked into the westside corner of the building for espresso and pastries.

There are more good places to eat in Eastsound than the size of the place could possibly justify. *Doty's A-1 Cafe & Bakery* (☎ 360-376-2593), off North Beach Rd, is the place to go for that all-important jelly doughnut or deli sandwich; there's also indoor seating for an inexpensive breakfast or lunch. *Comet Cafe* (no phone), in East Sound Square, combines the qualities of a healthy bakery and coffee shop.

La Famiglia Ristorante (☎ 360-376-2335), on Prune Alley, features good, nicely-priced Italian favorites, while *Bilbo's Festivo* (☎ 360-376-4728), off North Beach Rd, has Mexican and Southwest cuisine. Dinner at either of these restaurants will run about $10. For highbrow cuisine, go to *Christina's* (☎ 360-376-4904), along Horseshoe Hwy in Eastsound. Fresh seafood is the major item on the highly eclectic, rather French-by-Northwest menu (grilled sturgeon with beurre blanc is $19).

Following Horseshoe Hwy 2 miles south from Eastsound, the *Ship Bay Oyster House* (☎ 360-376-5886) is in an attractive, early 1900s sea captain's home. Offerings include oysters, scallops, mussels, shrimp, and catch-of-the-day specials from $12 to $17. Steak, chicken and ribs are also available.

At the *Orcas Room* at Rosario Resort (☎ 360-376-2222), 1 Rosario Way, there's a lot to like, including the views, the food (French-influenced Northwest cuisine like leg of lamb and veal scallops in the $20 range), and the handsome old mansion.

In the tiny community of Olga, find *Cafe Olga* (☎ 360-376-5098) in the Orcas Island Artworks building. At this homey restaurant and gallery, light meals and bakery goods are served at breakfast, lunch and for early dinner.

Getting Around
Orcas Island Taxi (☎ 360-376-8294), has regular taxi service as well as rental cars. The Orcas Shuttle (☎ 360-376-8887) provides tours and transit service to Moran State Park and other destinations; the fare is based on your destination.

WASHINGTON

LOPEZ ISLAND

Lopez is the most agricultural of the San Juan Islands and the closest to the mainland. For both of these reasons, it is somewhat overlooked in the free-for-all that is tourism in the San Juans. However, if you want quiet, pastoral charm and don't need organized fun, it's hard to beat Lopez Island.

One of the first things you'll note as you drive around the island is that all the locals wave as they pass – they don't automatically assume you're a stranger. This friendly, rather agrarian bonhomie makes Lopez seem more like a green corner of Iowa than a Pacific Northwest tourist destination. Lopez has also resisted the commercialization of its farmland somewhat better than the other islands. Here, pastures are for grazing sheep or hay-making – they aren't merely the aesthetic property of quaint country inns and B&Bs.

The island gets rockier and more rural toward the south; near MacKaye Harbor, the stony fields and cliff-lined bay look for all the world like the Hebrides.

Orientation & Information

The ferry terminal is in a purely functional harbor on the extreme north end of the island. The closest Lopez comes to having a town is Lopez Village, no more than a collection of houses and a tiny business district overlooking a shallow bay. Most businesses, including one gas station and a grocery store, are here. In summer, a farmers' market takes over the village. Just to the south of Lopez Village is Fisherman Bay, a hotel and marina complex.

For information about businesses and recreation on Lopez Island, contact Lopez Island Chamber of Commerce (☎ 360-468-3663), PO Box 121, Lopez Island, WA 98261. If you want a taxi, call Angie's Cab (☎ 360-468-2227).

Biking

Except for the long uphill slope leading from the ferry, Lopez is exceptionally flat, making this a good choice for island cyclists. The few roads that wind around the island also have very little car traffic. Rent a bike at Lopez Bicycle Works (☎ 360-468-2847) at the marina; you can also rent a sea kayak here. Good cycling destinations are Agate Beach or Shark Reef Park, a good spot for picnicking, whale watching and sea-lion viewing.

Charter Fishing

Skippered day and overnight fishing trips are available from Harmony Charters (☎ 360-468-3310), Mystic Sea Charters (☎ 360-468-2032) and Kismet Sailing Charters (☎ 360-468-2435), all of which operate out of Fisherman Bay. Visitors select from a number of organized packages, or they can schedule individualized tours or cruises.

Places to Stay

Camping Just 1.3 miles south of the ferry landing, *Odlin County Park* (☎ 360-468-2496) is a pleasant waterfront campground, picnic area and public dock. Facilities are minimal – running water, pit toilets – but you can't beat the location. Sites are $12. *Spencer Spit State Park* (☎ 360-468-2251), 5 miles southeast of the ferry landing on Baker View Rd, can be reached by both boat and car. This can be a pretty busy place during midsummer, as it is one of the few state parks in the islands. There are nearly 50 sites (no hookups), with flush toilets, running water, picnic area and beach access. Sites are $16.

B&Bs Built to resemble a Victorian mansion, the *Edenwild Inn* (☎ 360-468-3238) in Lopez Village is the most eye-catching building on Lopez Island, with its lovely formal gardens, wide porch and gables. Popular with honeymooners, the mansion has eight guest rooms for $100 and up, some with fireplaces, all with private baths.

On the other side of the island is the *Inn at Swifts Bay* (☎ 360-468-3636), east on Port Stanley Rd (look for mailbox No 3402 and the banners hanging from the decks). In a quiet corner on a quiet island, this graceful inn offers a hot tub, easy beach access and three acres of surrounding woods for solitude. There are five guest rooms, three with private baths, costing $95 to $175.

Standing stalwart and white at the edge of a shallow bay, the *MacKaye Harbor Inn* (☎ 360-468-2253), on MacKaye Harbor Rd, is near the south end of the island. This 1920s sea captain's home has four bedrooms and one suite ($99 to $175), and provides bicycles, rowboats and kayaks for guests. It's very popular and usually heavily booked.

Hotels Easily the cheapest place to stay on Lopez (and just about anywhere in the islands) is the *Lopez Lodge* (☎ 360-468-2500), above the video store in Lopez Village. Don't go looking for quaint charm: these three rooms are spacious and clean and offer views of the bay for $59 to $99. If you plan to spend most of your time outdoors, then these utilitarian digs might be just the ticket.

The Islander Lopez Resort (☎ 360-468-2233, 800-736-3434), on Fisherman Bay Rd, south of Lopez Village, is as close to a bona fide motel as one will find in the San Juans. The rooms are attractive; most have great views over Fisherman Bay, some have kitchenettes and there's also a hot tub. A night here should set you back $75 to $155. Across from the units is a bar and restaurant, which open onto a marina.

Places to Eat
All of the following are less than a block from each other in Lopez Village (in fact, they practically constitute Lopez Village).

Holly B's Bakery (☎ 360-468-2133) is the early morning latte and pastry stop; it's open only in summer. Right across the street is *Gail's* (☎ 360-468-2150), which serves breakfast and lunch daily and dinners from Thursday to Sunday. Summer vegetables are grown in the adjacent garden. Pasta dishes, salads and sandwiches are served at lunch, while at night steak, seafood and chicken round out the menu; meals begin at $12. In good weather, sit on the verandah below the grape arbor and watch the boats in the harbor. The most noted restaurant on

The brown pelican, common in the San Juan Islands, scoops fish out of the water with an expansible pouch attached to its beak.

Lopez is *The Bay Cafe* (☎ 360-468-3700), in an old storefront, with inventive, ethnic seafood dishes headlining the menu. Prices are in the $12 to $15 range. For a microbrew and burger, there's *Bucky's Lopez Island Grill* (☎ 360-468-2595).

Shopping
Chimera Gallery (☎ 360-468-3265) in Lopez Village is also known as the Lopez Artist Cooperative. This small and amusing gallery features works from local artists and craftspeople, including pottery, handblown glass, Northwest Indian carvings, paintings, jewelry, woodblock prints, photography and weaving.

SHAW ISLAND
Shaw Island is the smallest of the San Juan Islands with ferry service, and it has the fewest facilities for travelers. South Beach County Park is really the only place to stay, and the only business on the island is a tiny store near the ferry landing. But don't get the idea that Shaw is uninhabited: in fact, it's as full of weekend and resort homes as the other islands, and in some ways an address on Shaw is enviable simply because there aren't many tourists clotting up the roads and beaches.

WASHINGTON

There are good reasons to disembark at Shaw, especially if you're on two wheels. The lack of an organized tourist industry means that the island's roads are mostly free of traffic. The rolling hills are covered with sheep, whose wool plays a large part in one of Shaw's major cottage industries, spinning and knitting.

The one thing that nearly everyone notes about the ferry landing at Shaw is the fact that it is operated by Franciscan nuns. The nuns also operate the small general store and sell gas at the tiny marina near the ferry landing.

Places to Stay

To reach *South Beach County Park* (☎ 360-378-4953), head south of the ferry landing on Blind Bay Rd and turn left on Squaw Bay Rd. There are a dozen campsites, with pit toilets only, costing $12 a night. The beach is popular with picnickers in summer and the water is often warm enough for swimming. The only other lodging option is one vacation home rental maintained by *Dockside Properties* (☎ 360-378-5060, 800-992-1904), PO Box 1459, Friday Harbor, WA 98250, a San Juan Island-based company.

Whidbey Island

Green, low-lying Whidbey Island snakes along the northern Washington mainland from the northern suburbs of Seattle to Deception Pass at Fidalgo Island. The sea is never far away on this long, narrow island, but unlike the San Juan Islands, there is no impression of remoteness here. Weekend visitors from Seattle can make the attractive harbor towns on Whidbey as congested as the mainland suburbs. Langley and Deception Pass State Park are immensely popular vacation spots; the metropolitan sprawl of Puget Sound cities is quite close and Oak Harbor contains an active naval air base. However, if you don't have time for a trip to the San Juans and hanker for a ferry ride and an island seascape, then a detour across

Whidbey is a fine introduction to historic maritime Washington – and don't forget to pick up a bottle of loganberry liqueur near Greenbank and a plate of fresh oysters in Coupeville.

Orientation & Information

Whidbey Island, at 45 miles in length, is the longest island in the USA. It's threaded by Hwy 525, which links ferries at Clinton to the mainland suburb of Mukilteo, and Hwy 20, which links Keystone by ferry to Port Townsend and Hwy 20 on the Olympic Peninsula. On the island, Hwy 20 continues north to Oak Harbor and crosses dramatic Deception Pass on two narrow bridges. Anacortes and the San Juan Island ferries are immediately north, and I-5 and the North Cascades National Park are to the west.

Getting There & Away

Commuter flights on Harbor Airlines (☎ 360-675-6666, 800-359-3220), Monroe Landing Rd, Oak Harbor, depart daily from Oak Harbor Airport for Sea-Tac Airport and the San Juan Islands. Alternatively, the Airporter Shuttle (☎ 800-235-5247) offers frequent bus service from Sea-Tac to Oak Harbor. Tickets are $33 one way, $59 roundtrip.

Washington State Ferries operates ferries between Clinton and Mukilteo (on the mainland) and between Keystone and Port Townsend (on the Olympic Peninsula). The automobile/driver fare for the 20-minute Mukilteo-Clinton ferry is $4.80, passengers cost $2.30; the ferry runs every half hour. Respective fares for the 30-minute Keystone-Port Townsend ferry are $7.10/ 1.75; the ferry runs about every 45 minutes.

Getting Around

Island Transit buses run the length of the island every hour for free, daily except Sunday, from the Clinton ferry dock to Langley, Freeland, Greenbank, the Keystone ferry dock, Coupeville, Oak Harbor and Deception Pass. For more information call ☎ 360-321-6688.

There are two Budget car-rental agencies in Oak Harbor, downtown (☎ 360-675-

2000), 133 W Pioneer Way, and at the airport (☎ 360-675-6666).

DECEPTION PASS STATE PARK

Early explorers of the Puget Sound believed that Whidbey Island was a peninsula, and it wasn't until 1792 that Captain George Vancouver found the narrow cliff-lined crevasse, churned by rushing water, between Fidalgo and Whidbey Islands. Passage through the channel was nearly impossible in the days of sailing ships, and it remains a challenge today even to motorized boats: high tides charge through the pass at better than nine knots.

Visitors to the 5.6 sq-mile park (☎ 360-675-2417) usually begin their acquaintance with this dramatic land and seascape by parking at the shoulders on either side of the bridge and walking across the spans that arch the chasm. The bridge was built during the 1930s by the Civilian Conservation Corps (CCC) and was considered an engineering feat in its day. The park itself also spans the channel, with facilities – including campgrounds – on both the north and south flanks of the passage.

More than 3.5 million visitors per year visit Deception Pass, which makes it Washington's most popular state park. Besides the dramatic bridge overviews, there are over 17 miles of saltwater shoreline and seven nearby islands, three freshwater lakes, boat docks, hundreds of picnic sites and 27 miles of forest trails available to both hikers and bikers. The park is especially popular with scuba divers and sea kayakers, who explore the park's reefs and cliff-edge shores.

Especially popular here are the campgrounds. Well over 250 campsites are nestled in the forests beside a lake and a saltwater bay. However, all sites are allocated on a first-come, first-served basis, which means that competition for the sites on summer weekends can be fierce. Late-arriving cyclists should ride past the disheartening rows of cars and ask about walk-in sites. Rates for standard sites during the summer are $11 to $16; facilities include running water, flush toilets and snack concessions.

OAK HARBOR
Population 19,356
Boosters of Oak Harbor have recently gone to a lot of trouble to promote the virtues of this, the largest town on Whidbey Island. However, Oak Harbor remains mostly charmless, dominated as it is by the Naval Air Station Whidbey Island. Built during WWII to re-arm planes defending the West Coast from attack, the post currently maintains a staff of 9000 personnel and is largely a flight-training facility for reservists and home to a number of defensive air squadrons. For tours of the base, call ☎ 360 257-2286.

Orientation & Information
Oak Harbor is 38 miles from the ferry at Clinton, 9 miles from Deception Pass and 21 miles from Anacortes. Hwy 20 is the main drag through the town, although an old downtown area along the harbor, bypassed by the highway, is just east of the Pioneer Way junction. The Greater Oak Harbor Chamber of Commerce (☎ 360-675-3535), 5506 Hwy 20, can provide tourist information.

Places to Stay & Eat
Several modern motels are scattered along the strip north of town. However, the most noteworthy is the *Auld Holland Inn* (☎ 360-675-0724, 800-228-0148), 5861 Hwy 20, with its operating windmill and old-world Dutch motif. Lodgings are offered complete with kitchenettes, outdoor pool, sauna, spa and tennis and basketball courts; rooms begin at $55, and children and pets are welcome. Some of the best food in Oak Harbor is served at the inn's *Kasteel Franssen Restaurant & Lounge,* which serves Dutch, French and some Northwest cuisine (from $13 to $19) in a pleasantly ersatz Euro-kitsch dining room.

COUPEVILLE
Population 1632
One of the oldest towns in Washington, Coupeville has an attractive old seafront filled with shops, antique stores and old

inns facing onto Penn Cove, noted for its oyster and mussel production. The town's founder, Captain Thomas Coupe, is noted as the only captain to have sailed a four-rigger through Deception Pass; he settled here along the shallow bay and claimed land for a farm. Other seafarers followed suit, and Coupeville, then a farming community, began to thrive. Although the old town, especially along Front St, remains attractive and is great for a stroll or a weekend getaway, the urban sprawl from Oak Harbor and the influx of refugee Seattleites have begun to take a toll.

Stop by the visitors' center for a walking-tour map of the town's old homes and business district; Coupe's original home is still standing at Grange St and the waterfront. The **Island County Historical Society Museum** (☎ 360-678-3310), on the waterfront at Front and Alexander Sts, tells the story of the community's shipping and farming history and is open 11 am to 5 pm weekdays, and 10 am to 5 pm weekends. Admission is $2/1.50 adults/seniors and students.

Orientation & Information
Coupeville is 10 miles south of Oak Harbor. For more information about the area, contact the Central Whidbey Chamber of Commerce (☎ 360-678-5434) at 5 S Main St, Coupeville, WA 98239.

Places to Stay
A number of old Coupeville homes and inns remain in service as B&Bs. The *Inn at Penn Cove* (☎ 360-678-8000, 800-688-2683), 702 N Main St, is made up of two side-by-side Victorian farmhouses that offer B&B lodgings just three blocks from the harbor. Rates for the six rooms range from $60 to $125. The *Anchorage Inn* (☎ 360-678-5581), 807 N Main St, isn't as old as it looks: it is in fact a painstaking reproduction of a Victorian mansion. While history buffs may object, at least all five rooms have private baths and the floors don't squeak. Rooms range from $75 to $95.

The Coupeville Inn (☎ 360-678-6668, 800-247-6162), 200 Coveland St, is conve-

nient to harborfront shopping and strolling, and some of the inn's rooms offer balconies overlooking Penn Cove. Double rooms cost $64 to $95, which includes a continental breakfast.

For history, you can't beat the *Captain Whidbey Inn* (☎ 360-678-4097, 800-366-4097), 2072 W Captain Whidbey Inn Rd, 3 miles west of Coupeville on Madrona Way. This madrona-log inn overlooking Penn Cove was built in 1907 and is a showcase of old-fashioned – almost medieval – charms. Lodging is in 12 low-slung guest rooms in the main lodge (some with bathroom down the hall), as well as cottages (some with kitchens), and a more modern building with verandahs facing onto a pond. Rates range between $85 and $160, with a two- to three-night minimum stay on weekends; prices include continental breakfast.

On a more functional level, the *Tyee Motel* (☎ 360-678-6616), 405 S Main St, is a modest, standard motel with rates starting at $43.

Places to Eat
A good place to go for fresh bread and pastries, as well as deli-style salads and soups, is *Knead & Feed* (☎ 360-678-5431), below 4 Front St. The *Captain's Galley* (☎ 360-678-0241), 10 Front St, is the place to head for sampling local oysters and mussels; they also have steak and pasta. There are great views over the harbor and an outdoor deck. The trendy spot for Northwest cuisine is *Christopher's* (☎ 360-678-5480), 23 Front St, open Wednesday to Sunday only for lunch and dinner.

For a romantic dinner, there's no cozier place than the wood-lined dining room at *Captain Whidbey Inn* (☎ 360-678-4097, 800-366-4097), 2072 W Captain Whidbey Inn Rd. Fresh seafood – especially mussels – is featured in the inn's noted Northwest-style dining room; meals run between $15 and $20.

Shopping
Ten miles south of Coupeville on Hwy 525, off Wonn Rd, is Whidbey's Greenbank

Berry Farm (☎ 360-678-7700). This farm is the world's largest producer of loganberries, a sweet, blackish berry rather like a boysenberry or black raspberry. The farm offers tours through the old farm buildings, and it sells fruit and fixings for picnics on the grounds. The farm is most noted for its loganberry liqueur, called Whidbeys, which is distilled from local berries and is used as an aperitif and to make kirs a la Northwest. As Whidbeys is Washington's only home-grown liqueur, it makes a good gift or souvenir. The winery-style farm is open 10 am to 5 pm daily for touring, tasting and picnicking.

FORT CASEY &
FORT EBEY STATE PARKS
Along with Fort Flagler and Fort Worden across Admiralty Inlet and Fort Ebey to the north, Fort Casey was part of the early 1900s military defense system that once guarded the entrance to Puget Sound. These fixed-gun fortresses became obsolete after WWI, and the fort is now a historic state park (☎ 360-678-4519), with facilities for camping and picnicking. Investigating the old cement batteries and underground tunnels that line the coast brings out the explorer in everyone, even those who excuse their delving in the name of gorgeous scenic views. **Admiralty Head Lighthouse** was built in 1861 and now houses the park's interpretive center.

Recreation at the park includes hiking, scuba diving, boat launching and beachcombing. It's a 4-mile walk north along the beach to Fort Ebey State Park, a WWII-era defensive fort, which has much the same facilities as Fort Casey. For more information, call the ranger station (☎ 360-678-4636) in Coupeville.

Places to Stay
Fort Casey State Park offers 35 campsites overlooking Keystone Harbor, busy with ferries to Port Townsend, and *Fort Ebey* has 50 campsites. Sites are $11, and facilities include flush toilets and running water. There are some beachside sites but no RV hookups.

One of the more unique and affordable places to stay in this part of the state is the *Fort Casey Inn* (☎ 360-678-8792), 1124 S Engle Rd, a series of four officers' duplexes from 1909 that are now rented as overnight accommodations. Each unit has two bedrooms, a kitchen, bathroom and fireplace in the sitting room. Although the rooms are rather plain, they are perfectly comfortable, and the makings for breakfast are provided in each room. Rates begin at $120 for two people and $150 for four.

LANGLEY
Population 1033
The most popular getaway on Whidbey Island is Langley, a seaside town that epitomizes the adjectives 'quaint' and 'cute.' However, the feeling is a bit manufactured. Langley *is* an attractive town – its harbor overlooks Saratoga Sound and the distant peaks of the Cascades – and it has a reputation as an artists' colony. But these things merely serve as the bow that wraps Langley's twee commercialism – the upscale boutiques, gift shops and cafes are designed to enchant those whose idea of a rapturous weekend away is not complete without shopping. If you're unencumbered by kids, all the better – very few of the expensive B&Bs and inns that have sprung up here allow children.

Orientation & Information
Langley is 8 miles north of Clinton and the ferry service from Mukilteo, making this the closest of the Whidbey Island communities to the urban areas of northern Seattle. For more information about the Langley area, contact the Langley Chamber of Commerce (☎ 360-221-6765) at 124½ 2nd St, Langley, WA 98260.

Places to Stay & Eat
Just about the only reasonably-priced place to stay in Langley is *Drake's Landing* (☎ 360-221-3999), 203 Wharf St, across from the boat harbor. Rooms begin at $65. Children and pets are allowed by prior arrangement.

Otherwise, expect to spend in the neighborhood of $100 a night. Probably the most noted of the many B&Bs in Langley is the *Eagles Nest* (☎ 360-221-5331), 3236 E Saratoga Rd, a contemporary B&B perched on a hill, with views of Saratoga Passage and Mt Baker. The four guest rooms range from $95 to $125; children over 12 are allowed.

The trendsetter in style and expense is the contemporary, condo-esque *Inn at Langley* (☎ 360-221-3033), 400 1st St. The beautifully furnished, waterfront rooms have large windows, whirlpool tubs and fireplaces. Rooms range from $189 to $279. Five-course dinners are served in the gallery-like *Country Kitchen*. Expect entrées to cost upwards of $20.

The most popular place to eat in these parts is *Cafe Langley* (☎ 360-221-3090), 113 1st St, which offers eastern Mediterranean cuisine, often zipped up with fresh Northwest seafood. Lunch can be had for less than $7, dinner for $13 to $16. For a beer and a burger, head up the stairs to the *Star Bistro* (☎ 360-221-2627), 201½ 1st St, which serves lunch and dinner. It's a relaxed place to have a drink and recover from a shopping spree.

Even more fundamental is the *Whidbey Island Brewery*, (☎ 360-221-8373), 620 2nd St, whose tasting room is open noon to 6 pm daily during summer, and Thursday to Monday only in the off-season. Beer's the thing here: the modest lunch menu is mostly hot dogs and locally baked focaccia.

Olympic Peninsula

A remote and rugged area of wild coast-lines, deep old-growth forests and craggy mountains, the Olympic Peninsula sticks out like a massive thumb from the mainland into the Pacific. It's also surrounded on the north and east by the Strait of Juan de Fuca and Hood Canal, respectively, and bordered by the Chehalis River to the south. This moat-like isolation has allowed the Olympic Peninsula to develop its own ecological and human history.

The peninsula contains the Olympic National Park, one of the nation's showcase parks, which harbors the continent's only temperate rain forests, but you will also find mile after mile of clear-cut forests. One of the least populated parts of Washington, the peninsula is home to genteel Victorian seaports and a number of Native American tribes.

The Olympic Peninsula also has some of the most extreme weather in the USA. Because the towering peaks of the Olympic Mountains trap moist Pacific air, rainfall on the western slopes is massive. At any time of year, visitors should anticipate rain or at least clouds while visiting the Olympic National Park. However, because the Olympics do such a thorough job of wringing out moisture, the land to the east is remarkably dry and sunny. Sequim, only a few dozen miles from the rain forests, receives only 16 inches of rain a year, with 300 days of sunshine.

History

Seafaring Native Americans have lived along the Olympic Peninsula for thousands of years, and the rich bounty from the ocean, forest and rivers made native life here relatively comfortable. Tribes like the Makah, Quileute and Quinault became expert seafarers in their cedar canoes, hunting whales and seals, and attained one of the highest levels of cultural sophistication of any Native American tribe.

European sailors had been exploring the Northwest coast since 1592, when Juan de Fuca, a Greek sailing under the Spanish flag, discovered the strait that now bears his name. But the first documented contact between the natives on the Olympic Peninsula and European explorers wasn't until 1790, when the Spaniard Manuel Quimper sailed into Neah Bay, traded with the Makahs and claimed the surrounding land for Spain. Two years later, a colonizing force arrived from Mexico and established a garrison at Neah Bay, where the Spanish planted gardens and built barns for their goats, cows, sheep and pigs. Soon after, the Spaniards moved the colony to Nootka Bay on Vancouver Island.

The wild mountains and inhospitable coast of the Olympic Peninsula didn't immediately attract settlers, even after nearby Puget Sound began to fill with people. By 1851, Port Townsend was established, and farmers and fisherfolk began to eke livings from the coastal verge. The expanse of virgin forests on the peninsula began to fall to the saw in the 1880s, as mill towns like Aberdeen and Hoquiam sprang up to the south. By the turn of the century, determined pioneers were penetrating the forests of the western peninsula, seeking to clear timber from homesteads in order to till the soil.

The interior of the peninsula remained uncharted until 1885, when an army expedition under the command of Lieutenant Joseph O'Neil explored the northern ranges. The most famous exploration of the Olympics was the so-called Press Expedition, sponsored by the *Seattle Press* newspaper. In mid-winter the Scottish explorer James Christie led five men into the Elwha Valley, where they spent over five months trying to cross the heart of the peninsula in boats and sleds that they fashioned as they went – though their spirit was unfortunately

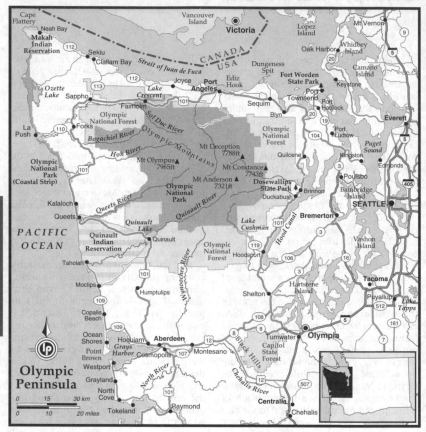

WASHINGTON

Olympic
Peninsula

0   15   30 km
0   10   20 miles

not equaled by their carpentry skills. Following a long tradition, these explorers named new peaks for their patrons – in this case, newspaper editors.

In general, the inclement weather eventually doomed the efforts of all but the most single-minded of these homesteaders. The peninsula remained wild and isolated until the 1930s, when US 101 pushed through the deep forests, linking longtime coastal communities by road for the first time. Then, in 1938, after a 40-year struggle between conservationists, industrialists and logging companies, the Olympic National Park was established in the heart of the peninsula.

Orientation

Only one road, US 101, rings the Olympic Peninsula. Even though the road is in excellent condition, it bears repeating that distances are great, and first-time visitors to the peninsula almost always find that it takes a lot longer to get where they're going than expected – you should always allow extra time.

The most northwesterly point in the continental USA is Cape Flattery near Neah Bay, at the tip of the Olympic Peninsula.

Information

There are a number of excellent local publications available that discuss tourist sites, lodging and restaurants on the peninsula. The Port Angeles *Peninsula Daily News* publishes the free *Olympic Peninsula Visitor Guide* twice a year. Also worth picking up is *Dan Youra's Olympic Peninsula Guide*, which is jammed full of all sorts of information about the peninsula and includes a good map. Priced at $1, the publication is usually available free from visitors' centers. To obtain a copy by mail, contact Olympic Publishing (☎ 360-437-2277), 7450 Oak Bay Rd, Port Ludlow, WA 98365.

Getting There & Away

Severe weather can sometimes close down the Hood Canal Bridge. Call ☎ 360-437-2288 for bridge information.

Air Horizon Air (☎ 360-547-9308) has service to Fairchild International Airport, on the outskirts of Port Angeles, from Portland, Seattle and Victoria, BC.

Bus Buses are the best means of public transportation along the northern Olympic Peninsula, but the service is a bit complicated. Port Angeles is the main hub of transportation and the visitors' center there (☎ 360-452-2363) can help if you get confused.

Olympic Bus Lines (☎ 360-452-3858) provides service between Sea-Tac Airport, Seattle and Port Angeles. From Port Angeles, Clallam Transit buses (☎ 360-452-4511, 800-858-3747) depart to Forks and destinations on the western half of the peninsula (including Neah Bay), and east to Sequim.

To reach Port Townsend, take the ferry from downtown Seattle to Bainbridge Island, and at the ferry dock catch the No 90 Kitsap Transit bus (☎ 360-479-6962) to Poulsbo (a bus meets every sailing). From

Poulsbo, pick up a Jefferson Transit bus (☎ 360-385-4777) to Port Townsend. Jefferson Transit also runs to Sequim, where you can pick up Clallam Transit buses for points west.

Grayline Buses (☎ 360-452-5112) offers sightseeing tours and overnight packages from Port Angeles to Victoria.

Ferry To/from Seattle, the fastest access to the Olympic Peninsula involves taking either the Seattle-Bainbridge Island ferry or the Edmonds-Kingston ferry and driving from there. You can also take the Whidbey Island ferry from Keystone to Port Townsend, and continue on from there. From Seattle to Port Angeles is only 77 miles, but because of ferry schedules and traffic, the journey can easily take half a day.

To/from Victoria, Black Ball Transport (☎ 360-457-4491), provides passenger and automobile service from Port Angeles. Also from Port Angeles to Victoria, the Victoria Express (☎ 360-452-8088, 800-633-1589) offers one-hour service for passengers and cyclists only; it runs from late May to mid-October. Frequency and schedules vary seasonally for both ferries.

Olympic National Park

One of the most popular national parks in the US, Olympic National Park is noted for its wilderness hiking, dramatic scenery and widely varying ecosystems. The heavily-glaciered Olympic Mountains rise to nearly 8000 feet in only 25 miles from sea level, and were one of the last explored areas of Washington, despite their proximity to major population centers. Calls for the Olympics to be preserved as a national park were made as early as 1897; however, the area was initially declared a forest reserve, and then, in 1909, a national monument by President Theodore Roosevelt.

WASHINGTON

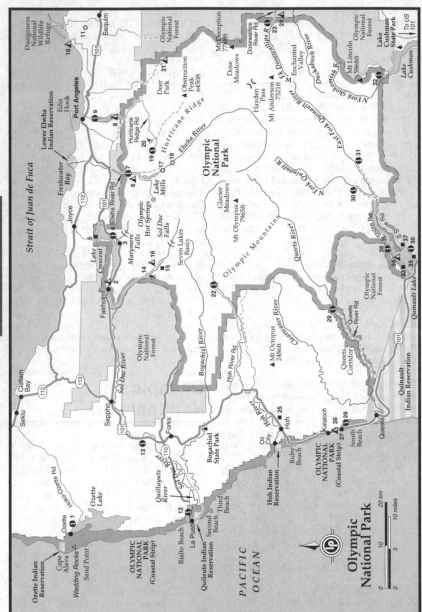

PLACES TO STAY	27	Kalaloch Lodge	13	USFS/NPS Information Station
1 Lake Ozette Campground	29	Queets Campground	14	Ancient Groves Nature Trail
2 Fairholm Campground	30	North Fork Campground		
3 Lake Crescent Lodge	31	Graves Creek Campground	17	Whiskey Bend
5 Log Cabin Resort	32	Staircase Campground	18	Humes Ranch
6 Altaire Campground	33	Lochaerie Resort	19	Hurricane Ridge Visitors' Center
7 Elwha Campground	34	July Creek Campground		
8 Heart O' the Hills Campground	35	Lake Quinault Lodge	20	Hurricane Ridge Ski Area
	37	Rain Forest Resort Village	22	Hoh Rain Forest Visitors' Center
10 Dungeness Recreation Area				
	OTHER		23	Dosewallips Ranger Station
12 Mora Campground				
15 Sol Duc Hot Springs Resort	1	Lake Ozette Ranger Station	28	Kalaloch Information Station
16 Sol Duc Campground				
21 Deer Park Campground	4	Storm King Information Station	29	Queets Ranger Station
22 Hoh Campground			30	North Fork Hanger Station
24 Elkhorn Campground, Boulder Creek Campground	7	Elwha Ranger Station	31	Graves Creek Ranger Station
	9	Pioneer Memorial Museum & Visitor Center	32	Staircase Ranger Station
25 Rain Forest Hostel	11	Olympic Game Farm	36	Quinault USFS Office
26 Kalaloch Campground	12	Mora Ranger Station	38	Quinalt Ranger Station

Such designations didn't save large portions of these federal lands from falling into private and state hands. During WWI, almost half of the original national monument was opened up for mining and logging. Earlier attempts to create the Elk National Park to preserve the indigenous Roosevelt elk had failed. President Franklin Roosevelt succeeded in pushing a bill through Congress in 1938 authorizing the Olympic National Forest. The original 1012-sq-mile park consisted only of the highest and most rugged peaks in the range; in later years the lowland rain forests and coastal strip were added, bringing the total area to nearly 1406 sq miles.

Olympic National Park is best thought of as a wilderness preserve. Many of the best and most spectacular sights are reserved for long-distance walkers who trek across the park's interior. Camping in the park is easy, with 17 large campgrounds accessible by car as well as 95 backcountry campgrounds. Magnificent waterfalls, wide alpine meadows sparkling with summer wildflowers, eerie moss-bearded forests dripping with fog, and remote lakes shimmering beneath glaciers are among the destinations available to those willing to get out of their cars and hike a few miles.

Orientation

Access to Olympic National Park is mostly by foot, as most roads open to vehicles terminate shortly after entering park lands. In the following descriptions, information is laid out by entrance road. Be sure to pick up a current map of the park before heading into the wilderness.

Entrance fees to the park are $10 per vehicle and $5 per person for pedestrians, cyclists and bus passengers. Fees are collected at Hurricane Ridge, Elwha, Hoh, Sol Duc and Staircase entrance points, May to September only, with entrance fees charged for access to Hurricane Ridge on winter weekends and during the Christmas and New Year holidays. Entrance passes are good for one week.

Information

For information about the park, contact the Olympic National Park Headquarters (☎ 360-452-0330, 360-452-4501), at 600 E Park Ave, Port Angeles, WA 98362. If you know what forms of recreation you're interested in, or even what valleys you plan to visit, then let the rangers know: a

WASHINGTON

lot of the free information available is specific to certain valleys and activities. Backcountry permits and information on the Olympic National Forest, administered by the USFS, can be obtained from the USFS office (☎ 360-956-2300), 1835 Black Lake Blvd NW, Olympia, WA 98512. Many national park visitors' centers double as USFS ranger stations, where you can pick up free backcountry permits for wilderness camping in the park.

The park headquarters (☎ 360-452-0330) can provide some road and weather information. Call ☎ 360-452-0329 for weather information on Hurricane Ridge.

Activities

Olympic National Park is roughly 40 miles in diameter, and few roads penetrate more than a few miles into the park proper. The rest of the park is the province of hikers, especially those willing to traverse the wilderness on one of the many long-distance trails. Pack horses are allowed on nearly all trails and are often used for carrying gear on cross-park expeditions. The 57-mile Olympic Coastal Strip, a parcel of the national park unconnected to the park's main body, is accessible only to hikers, who can marvel at the wildlife, ancient petroglyphs and remarkable scenery of this rugged coastline.

Mt Olympus and Mt Deception are the highest mountains in the park and are popular for **climbing**; both involve considerable cross-glacier traverses and should only be attempted after consultation with authorities and with the appropriate equipment. Though many of the craggy peaks elsewhere require technical climbing skills, it's weather, and not difficulty per se, that often enforces limits on climbers, as conditions can change dramatically in no time at all.

A number of outfitters run **white-water rafting** trips on the park's rivers, including the Hoh, Elwha and Queets. The Olympic Outdoor Center (☎ 360-697-6095, 800-659-6095), 26469 Circle Place NW, in Poulsbo (just north of Bremerton), operates several white-water rafting and **sea-kayaking** trips at different times of year, on bays and rivers throughout the peninsula. They also offer equipment sales and rentals and teach classes.

Rivers and lakes in the park are noted for their trout and salmon **fishing**. No license is needed to fish in the park, although other regulations may be in place – check with a park ranger. Canoe and kayak rentals are available at many of the larger lakes.

The Formation of the Olympic Mountains

The mountains of the Olympic Peninsula began as sea-floor sediments deep in the Pacific Ocean about 70 million years ago. Undersea volcanoes eventually pushed up through these formations to form seamounts, or underwater mountains. As the North American continent drifted across the Pacific Ocean, the heavier ocean floor slid under the leading edge of the continent and this marine mountain chain was partially scraped off the ocean floor.

About 30 million years ago, the ocean-floor plate bearing the old seamount range completely disappeared beneath the continent and with nothing to anchor the jumbled mass of rock, it began to rise up along the continent's edge. Over the course of millions of years, the old mountains formed at sea punched up through the level landmass of the Olympic Peninsula to tower almost 8000 feet above the Pacific.

During the most recent ice age, glaciers flowing down from the Arctic filled the Puget Sound and the valleys of the rising Olympic Mountains; some glaciers stretched from the peaks all the way to the Pacific Coast. ■

The park remains open in winter, and the area around Hurricane Ridge is popular for **cross-country skiing** and **sledding**. Free **snowshoe tours** are led by rangers on the weekends. Most lower valley trails are passable year-round.

Olympic Park Institute This environmentally oriented foundation offers seminars in a wide variety of fields, including geology, wildflowers, marine mammals, Northwest Native American art and forest ecology. Most courses involve outdoor field trips and excursions, but are headquartered out of the institute's facility on Lake Crescent. Courses are held in spring, summer and winter, and most take place over a weekend. Fees vary from course to course (anticipate fees from $180 to $250) and include food and lodging (the institute owns a lodge and cabins along the lake). For more information, contact Olympic Park Institute (☎ 360-928-3720), HC 62 Box 9T, Port Angeles, WA 98362.

NORTHERN ENTRANCES
The most popular access to Olympic National Park is from the north. Port Angeles and Sequim are good jumping off points for valley hikes and for visiting Hurricane Ridge and Deer Park. The park's largest lake, Lake Crescent, is popular with anglers and boaters and sports two of the park's five lodges.

Pioneer Memorial Museum & Visitor Center
The park's main information and visitors' center (☎ 360-452-0330) is located at 3002 Mt Angeles Rd in Port Angeles, about 1 mile south of US 101 off Race St; this same road leads up to Hurricane Ridge (watch for signs). The center offers a children's discovery center, a slide presentation, a bookstore and several interactive displays regarding plant and animal life. A replica of a prehistoric Makah seal-hunting canoe is worth the stop, especially if you won't make it out to Neah Bay to see the originals at the Makah Museum. Park rangers are on hand to answer any ques-

tions. The center is open 9 am to 4 pm daily, year-round.

Hurricane Ridge
Beginning at sea level in Port Angeles, the 18-mile Hurricane Ridge Rd climbs up 5300 feet into the Olympic peaks to extensive wildflower meadows and expansive vistas. On a clear day, the rugged peaks and glaciers of Mt Olympus loom spectacularly across the deep, and frequently cloud-filled, Elwha River valley.

The Hurricane Ridge visitors' center (☎ 360-452-0329, for a recorded message about activities and access) is usually open 9 am to 4 pm daily, except in midwinter when it's open only on weekends. The center has a snack bar, gift shop, toilets and ski (both downhill and cross-country) and snowshoe rentals.

Hurricane Ridge is a good base for many activities, though there is no camping. In summer, rangers conduct a number of open-air informational discussions and hikes. During the winter, cross-country and downhill skiing and sledding take over; on weekends, rangers lead free guided snowshoe tours.

Hiking Hurricane Ridge is one of the highest points accessible to vehicles in the park, so it is understandably a popular trailhead for hikers wanting to explore the park's high country. A number of short hikes lead through meadows to spectacular vista points. **Hurricane Hill Trail**, which begins in the parking area, and the network of trails known as the **Meadow Loops**, beginning at the visitors' center, are popular, moderately easy hikes through gorgeous scenery. The first half-mile of both of these trails is wheelchair accessible.

From Hurricane Ridge, you can drive a rough and frequently steep 8.4-mile road to **Obstruction Peak**, another vista point with even better views of the Olympic peaks. Here, hikers looking for long-distance treks can pick up the **Grand Ridge Trail**, which leads to Deer Park (see below), and the **Wolf Creek Trail**, an

8½-mile downhill jaunt to Whiskey Bend, where it picks up the Elwha Trail.

Skiing Hurricane Ridge is a great departure point for cross-country skiers, who can explore pristine high meadows and mountain ridges without a dreary uphill slog. The road to the ridge is plowed every weekend, and it stays open during the week, weather permitting. A number of ski trails are indicated in a brochure available from park rangers, or you can follow trail signs (most of the trails follow the hiking trails). However, avalanche conditions can make some of these trails dangerous. Check with park rangers before departing on long trails.

The downhill ski area is open during the Christmas holidays and on weekends only from January through March. Although the ski area doesn't offer many challenges for advanced skiers, the gentle 1600-foot slope is a good place for families and beginners. All-day lift tickets are $15. Folks on inner tubes and sleds have a separate area behind the ski hill.

Deer Park

The park's highest access road departs from US 101, 5 miles east of Port Angeles and climbs up a steep, graveled road to alpine meadows, a campground and a 5850-foot trailhead. There are a couple of good reasons to lurch your way up this 17-mile grade, which closes during snowy weather and is not advised for trailer or RV traffic. From the Deer Park trailhead, the 7½-mile **Grand Ridge Trail** sets off toward Obstruction Peak, east of Hurricane Ridge. With much of the trail above timberline, it has some of the best views in the park. Deer Park also tends to get far less traffic than Hurricane Ridge, which in summer is almost a carnival of activity. Comparably, visitors and campers here have the wildflowers and vistas to themselves – and frequently have better weather.

Elwha River Valley

The Elwha, the largest river on the Olympic Peninsula, and Lake Mills (actu-

ally a reservoir) are popular for **trout fishing**. The Elwha River Rd turns south from US 101 about 8 miles west of Port Angeles. Follow it for 10 miles to the Elwha Ranger Station (☎ 360-452-9191). The road immediately forks. Turn west to reach the Olympic Hot Springs trailhead, or turn east and continue toward Whiskey Bend to reach the Elwha River and other long-distance trailheads.

Hiking Commercially developed as a resort in the 1930s, the **Olympic Hot Springs** once featured pools and cabins that have long since disappeared. Park supervisors closed the road to the hot springs in order to limit access somewhat and to preserve the area; the area's springs have now returned to nature. Note that official maps don't even show the hot springs (though it's adjacent to Boulder Creek Campground). The 2.2-mile hike, which follows the old road bed, is well worth it – a series of hot pools steam alongside the rushing Boulder Creek, all in a verdant deep-forest grove. (You'll need a backcountry permit to camp overnight at Boulder.)

From Whisky Bend, the **Elwha Trail** leads up the main branch of the Elwha River and is one of the primary cross-park trails, leading to Dosewallips and, over Low Divide, to the North Fork Quinault River entrance. Day-hikers may elect to follow the trail for 2 miles to Humes Ranch, the remains of a homestead-era ranch.

Lake Crescent

Eight-and-a-half miles long and 624 feet deep, Lake Crescent is one of the most popular stops in the park due to its beautiful vistas, its boating and fishing, and Lake Crescent Lodge, one of the park's venerable lakeside resorts. For information about the Lake Crescent area, contact the Storm King Information Station (☎ 360-928-3380), just east of Lake Crescent Lodge off US 101. It's open in summer only.

Hiking One of the most popular short hikes in the park goes to **Marymere Falls**, a

90-foot cascade that drapes down a basalt cliff. This 1¹/₂-mile roundtrip leads out from the Storm King Information Station along the Barnes Creek Trail. The trail is wheelchair accessible.

For a more energetic hike, climb up the side of **Mt Storm King**, the peak that rises to the east of Lake Crescent. The steep, 3¹/₂-mile trail splits off the Barnes Creek Trail.

Fishing & Boating Lake Crescent was once home to two indigenous trout subspecies, the Beardslee (a cousin of the rainbow) and the *crescentii*, a variation on the cutthroat. Both have become hybridized with the introduction of hatchery-bred fish. The fishing is good, however, as the lake is very deep with steep shorelines; no bait-fishing is allowed. Boat rentals are available at Lake Crescent Lodge, the Log Cabin Resort (see Places to Stay below), and the Fairholm General Store (☎ 360-928-3020).

Paddleboat Tours Paddleboats once plied Lake Crescent in the early 1900s, serving the many resorts and lodges that lined its shores. Paddleboats again cruise the lake, now offering interpretive tours. Cruises depart from near Crescent Lake Lodge at 10 am, noon, 2 and 4 pm, but ticketing, free parking, and a shuttle are available at the Storm King Ranger Station. Arrive at the shuttle a half-hour before your desired departure time. Tickets are $15/14 adults/ seniors and $10 for youths age 17 and

younger. Reservations are recommended (☎ 360-452-4520).

Sol Duc River Valley
Just west of Lake Crescent, the Sol Duc River flows toward the Pacific Coast. The headwaters of the river fall within the national park boundaries and offer a developed hot springs resort and some of the best day hiking in the Olympics. A paved road follows the Sol Duc River from US 101 for nearly 14 miles, passing the hot springs and ending at a trailhead. The summer-only Sol Duc Ranger Station (☎ 360-327-3534) is located at the hot springs.

Sol Duc Hot Springs Indian legend recounts the battle of two lightning fish who engaged in bitter combat; however, neither won the contest. Each crawled into the earth and shed hot tears, thereby creating Sol Duc and Olympic Hot Springs. The mineral springs at Sol Duc are much more developed than the natural pools at Olympic. The hot water has been diverted into three large tiled pools and there's also a regular swimming pool to cool off in. Access to the hot springs at Sol Duc Hot Springs Resort is $5. In addition to cabins, the resort contains a restaurant and snack bar, a gift shop and a grocery store. In summer there are ranger-led programs and activities.

Hiking Two miles past the resort, the Sol Duc road terminates, and trails lead into the forest. The most popular hike here is to **Sol Duc Falls**, where the Sol Duc River drops 40 feet into a narrow gorge. The three-quarter-mile, one-way hike follows a gentle grade through a mossy old-growth cedar forest before crossing a bridge above the falls.

For a more strenuous hike, cross the bridge at the falls and climb the **Canyon Creek Trail** up to Deer Lake. This sometimes steep, 3-mile (one-way) trail reaches the tree-rimmed lake (where you will indeed often see deer). It then joins **High Divide Trail**, which leads to the Seven Lakes Basin, a popular overnight destination.

Another good leg-stretcher is the **Mink Lake Trail**, departing from the resort. This 2¹/₂-mile (one way) trail leads up to marshy Mink Lake, noted for its bird and wildlife viewing.

For a short, interpretive hike through old-growth forest, take the **Ancient Groves Nature Trail**, located 8 miles from US 101 along the Sol Duc Rd. Along this 1-mile loop trail there are signs labeling tree and plant species and explaining rain forest ecology.

Places to Stay & Eat

Camping Nearly all of the national park campgrounds have running water and toilets and allow pets, but there are no hookups for RVs and no showers. Unless otherwise noted, fees are $10 a night. There is no camping allowed at Hurricane Ridge; the closest national park campground is *Heart O' the Hills*, 5 miles south of Port Angeles on Hurricane Ridge Rd, with 105 sites. The *Deer Park Campground* offers 18 campsites and has no fee. There are two campgrounds just inside the park along the Elwha River: the *Elwha Campground* with 41 campsites and the *Altaire Campground* with 30. The only national park campground on Lake Crescent is *Fairholm Campground*, 28 miles west of Port Angeles on US 101, with 87 campsites. Along the Sol Duc River, immediately upstream from the Sol Duc Hot Springs Resort, is *Sol Duc Campground* with 80 sites.

Lodges & Cabins There are two lodges at Lake Crescent. The preeminent one is *Lake Crescent Lodge* (☎ 360-928-3211), 416 Lake Crescent Rd, which is 20 miles west of Port Angeles off US 101 (look for signs to the lodge). This old-fashioned inn was built in 1915 as a fishing resort. The original shake-sided lodge still stands and operates as the main lodging, restaurant and bar, though a number of lakeside cabins have been added to accommodate more guests. Most room rates range between $120 and $160 a night. Call well in advance for accommodations; the lodge

is open from the last weekend in April to the end of October.

The *Log Cabin Resort* (☎ 360-928-3325), 3183 E Beach Rd, on the north bank of Lake Crescent, has cabins, chalets (which sleep six), lodge rooms and RV hookups; accommodations range from $61 to $101 a night. The restaurant is favored by anglers and other hungry outdoor types. It's open from May 15 to October 1.

Along the Sol Duc River is the *Sol Duc Hot Springs Resort* (☎ 360-327-3583). Thirty-two modern and rather unromantic cabins, six with kitchens and all with private baths, are scattered around a meadow. There is also a restaurant, snack bar and grocery store. Room rates range between $85 and $100; the resort is open from May 15 to October 1.

EASTERN ENTRANCES

The eastern entrances to Olympic National Park aren't as developed with lodges and interpretive sites as other access points, but they are the closest to major population centers and serve as access points for long-distance hikers from the Puget Sound area.

Dosewallips River Valley

This narrow valley (pronounced *DOE-sey-WAL-ups*) is surrounded by some of the highest mountains in the Olympics, including Mt Anderson and Mt Deception. The graveled Dosewallips River Rd follows the Dosewallips River from US 101 for 15 miles to the Dosewallips Ranger Station, where the road terminates and trails begin.

Hiking Day-hikers won't find many satisfying short loop trails here, but hiking portions of the two long-distance paths – with increasingly impressive views of heavily-glaciered Mt Anderson – is reason enough to visit the valley. From the Dosewallips Ranger Station, a wide trail leads upriver for 1.4 miles to Dose Forks, where the path divides into two major trans-park trails.

The northbound trail is called the **Dosewallips Trail**, and it climbs up to beautiful Dose Meadows (10 miles from

Dose Forks) before crossing Hayden Pass and dropping into the Elwha Valley and the Elwha Trail. The southerly trail is called **West Fork Dosewallips Trail** and it leads to Honeymoon Meadows (9 miles from Dose Forks), a spring-filled basin immediately beneath the glaciers of precipitous 7321-foot Mt Anderson. The trail continues up to Anderson Pass and into the East Fork Quinault River trail system.

Staircase

This is another favorite entrance for hikers, in part because the national park trail system nearly abuts Lake Cushman State Park, immensely popular with families, anglers and boaters from the Tacoma area. The Staircase Ranger Station (☎ 360-877-5569) is just inside the national park boundary, 15 miles from US 101 at the small town of Hoodsport.

Hiking The trail system here follows the drainage of the North Fork Skokomish River, which is flanked by some of the most rugged peaks in the Olympics, including those in the aptly named Sawtooth Range. The principal long-distance trail is the **North Fork Skokomish Trail**, which leads up this beautiful, heavily-forested valley, eventually crossing into the Duckabush River valley to intercept other trans-park trail systems. Ambitious day-hikers might consider following this trail 3.7 miles to find the **Flapjack Lakes Trail**, an easy 4-mile climb up to several small lakes that shimmer beneath the awesome crags of the Sawtooth peaks.

A popular short hike follows the south bank of the North Fork Skokomish River along the **Staircase Rapids Trail**, which leads through lush old-growth forest to the rapids. Continue up the trail a short distance to the Rapids Bridge, which crosses over to the North Fork Skokomish Trail and makes for a nice 2-mile loop trip.

Places to Stay

There are two popular state parks along the east edge of the national park; both have running water, flush toilets and some RV hookups. Near the mouth of Dosewallips River, near Brinnon along US 101, is *Dosewallips State Park* (☎ 360-796-4415), a large and attractive park with 130 campsites. At both, tent sites cost $10, hookups are $15. Eleven miles up the Dosewallips River in the national forest is *Elkhorn Campground*, a USFS site with running water. At the end of the road, at *Dosewallips Campground*, there are 32 primitive sites, no fees.

Lake Cushman State Park (☎ 360-877-5491), 8 miles west of Hoodsport, is centered on a large reservoir on the Skokomish River, in the scenic southern Olympic Mountains. It's popular with anglers, water-skiers and campers. There are 80 campsites, some with hookups; running water and flush toilets are provided. Past Lake Cushman along the North Fork Skokomish River, inside the national park, *Staircase Campground* has 59 sites. Tent sites are $10 at both places.

WESTERN ENTRANCES

The Pacific side of the Olympics is the most remote part of the park and home to the noted temperate rain forests. Three mighty rivers drain this face of the Olympics; their valleys fill with the full force of the Pacific's clouds and moisture, guaranteeing the annual 12 feet of rain necessary for the region's fabulously luxuriant plant growth.

US 101 is the only road that accesses this vast, heavily-wooded area, which in part accounts for its isolation (foul weather is another reason). By car, it's a long drive to Queets or Hoh from the Puget Sound area.

Hoh Rain Forest

The most famous of the Olympic rain forests, the Hoh River area offers a variety of hikes and an interpretive center. If you have room for only one stop on the western side, this should be it. The following sites are off Hoh River Rd, a paved all-weather road that winds through clear-cuts before reaching the national park boundary, 12 miles from US 101. While driving toward the visitors'

WASHINGTON

Washington's Own 'Jurassic Park'

Because of the Olympic Peninsula's geologic isolation – it was cut off from the mainland by ice-age glaciers – and its current separation from the mainland by the Puget Sound and Strait of Juan de Fuca, a number of plants and animals are unique to the area. In addition to the peninsula's noted rain forests, which include some of the largest, oldest and densest virgin forests remaining in North America, there are over 40 sizable river valleys and some 60 glaciers in its rugged mountain range.

Temperate Rain Forests The main thing that produces the rain forests of the Olympic Peninsula is moisture, and lots of it. Rainfall in this area ranges from 140 to nearly 200 inches a year. Coupled with mild temperatures, these conditions allow the trees and plants to grow to massive size. Additionally, the heavily contorted valleys of the west-facing Olympic Mountains trap moist air, producing heavy fogs during summer. This feeds a group of plants called epiphytes, vegetation that hangs from trees and gleans moisture and sustenance from the humid air. The most noticeable of these plants is the club moss, a long, green whiskery growth that attaches itself to branches in the forest. Sword and licorice ferns also sprout along the length of tree trunks, adding to their shaggy appearances.

The most common trees in the rain forests are the Sitka spruce, hemlock, red cedar, maple and red alder. Trees up to 300 feet tall, with girths of up to 20 feet, are not uncommon. In fact, the Olympic Peninsula boasts record-sized trees in eight different species.

Mountain Lions The survival of the mountain lion is a conservation success story. Once considered threatened in much of its natural territory, mountain lions are today becoming more and more common in the Olympics. Although there have been a few cases of mountain lions mauling or killing humans in other areas of the American West, no serious incidents have occurred yet in the park. Nonetheless, you should be especially careful not to

center, stop at the **giant spruce tree** just beside the road. This lord of the forest is 270 feet high and over 700 years old. There's a ranger station near the visitors' center.

Information At the end of Hoh River Rd, the visitors' center (☎ 360-374-6925) offers a series of displays that explain the ecology of the rain forest and describe the plants and animals that comprise it. There's also a bookstore. Rangers lead guided walks twice a day during summer; call ahead for times. Just outside of the center is a very short, wheelchair-accessible nature trail through a rain forest marsh. The visitors' center is open 9 am to 4 pm daily; in July and August it closes at 6:30 pm.

Hiking Leading out from the visitors' center are several excellent day hikes into

virgin rain forest. The most popular of these is the justly famous **Hall of Moss Trail**, an easy three-quarter-mile loop through some of the shaggiest trees you'll ever see. Epiphytic club moss, ferns and lichens completely overwhelm the massive trunks of maples and Sitka spruce in this misty forest. The 1¼-mile **Spruce Nature Trail** is another short interpreted loop trail leading out from the visitors' center.

The **Hoh Trail** is the major entry trail into the wide, glacier-channeled Hoh River valley, and it is the principal access to the park's highest peak, Mt Olympus. The trail follows an easy grade for 12 miles, and day-hikers will find this a very pleasant if undramatic hike: just keep going until you need to turn back. If you are tempted to make this an overnight trip (there are numerous formal and informal

make sudden movements when hiking alone, and you should never leave children unsupervised.

Mountain Goats In the 1920s these large, white-haired goats were introduced from the Rockies to the Olympic Mountains, where they have thrived. However, mountain goats now exist in such numbers in the Olympic high country that they present a threat to delicate plants of alpine meadows. In recent years, park rangers have been euphemistically 'removing' goats from areas adversely affected by goat overpopulation, which has become an issue of some controversy.

Roosevelt Elk This species of elk is found only in the coastal mountains of the Pacific Northwest, and protection of the herds in the Olympic Mountains was one of the initial reasons for establishing the national park. Roosevelt elk – named after Teddy, who assisted in their preservation – are light brown in color, with dark brown underparts. They are larger than the Rocky Mountain wapiti (American elk); bull elks can weigh upwards of 1000lb, and have dark brown manes and antlers up to 5 feet across. They are also more social animals, often running in herds of up to 50. However, Roosevelt elk are notoriously shy animals, and even though an estimated 7000 live on the peninsula, it is unlikely that hikers will sight one. ■

campsites along the way), be sure to pick up a backcountry permit from the ranger station.

Climbing The highest peak in the Olympics, rugged **Mt Olympus**, at 7965 feet, is the most commonly climbed peak in the range. However, don't let its relative lack of stature fool you. Mt Olympus is the first major peak that Pacific storms encounter. A lot of snow – and harsh weather in general – falls here. In the continental USA, only Mt Rainier and Mt Baker have more extensive glacial formations.

The Hoh Trail basically ends at Glacier Meadows, 17 miles from the Hoh visitors' center. The campground here is frequently used as a base camp for ascents of the mountain. From here on, much of the remaining climb is on glaciers and along craggy escarpments. Most people make the ascent between June and early September, although adventurous souls begin to climb as early as April.

Guided climbs and mountaineering schools for would-be climbers are available and are suggested for novices. Each year Mt Olympus claims several lives and causes injuries, usually from falls into glacial crevasses or exposure during storms. For information on guided climbs, contact Olympic Mountaineering (☎ 360-452-0240), 221 S Peabody St in Port Angeles. They also rent out climbing equipment as do REI outlets in the Seattle area. For further reference, get hold of Custom Correct maps for the peak as well as the book, *Climber's Guide to the Olympic Mountains*, published by The Mountaineers.

WASHINGTON

Queets River Valley

The Queets River valley is the most remote part of the Olympic National Park. Part of this isolation is intentional; the park service has made access to the valley rather challenging and trails in the Queets don't link up with any other trans-park trails. This means, however, that the Queets valley is the most pristine area in the park.

The so-called Queets Corridor – the thin finger of land that juts out of the southern end of the park along the river – was added to the park in 1953. This narrow corridor, which nearly reaches the Pacific, is meant to preserve one of the peninsula's river valleys all the way from its glacial beginnings to the coast.

Hiking Queets River Rd leaves US 101 and almost immediately drops into the national park. The road follows the Queets River for 13 miles before ending at Queets Campground & Ranger Station. From here, there is one popular day hike, the gentle, 3-mile **Queets Campground Loop Trail**.

Experienced or adventurous hikers can elect to ford the Queets River and explore the **Queets Trail**, which leads up the river for 15 miles before petering out in heavy forest. The trail passes through some of the most spectacular old-growth rain forest in the park – the trees are sometimes so large as to be disquieting – and past great fishing holes (the Queets is noted for both salmon and steelhead). However, the fording of the Queets remains an obstacle to many and is safely contemplated by the wary only in late summer or fall.

Quinault River Valley

The focus of the Quinault Valley is Lake Quinault, a beautiful glacial lake surrounded by forested peaks. The resorts and homes along the lakeshore make this a very popular retreat; the charming Lake Quinault Lodge is one of the few original Olympic lodges still in business. Upstream from Lake Quinault, the river divides into the North Fork and East Fork Quinault Rivers. Both valleys harbor important trans-park trails.

Lake Quinault The second-largest lake in Olympic National Park, this deep-blue gem offers fishing, boating and swimming. Two lodges face onto the lake, and there are three public campgrounds. The lake is accessed by two different roads. The South Shore Rd leads to the tiny village of Quinault with lodges and a USFS ranger station (☎ 360-288-2525) before climbing up into the park proper to the trailhead of the famed Enchanted Valley in the East Fork Quinault valley. The North Shore Rd enters the national park and winds along the lake's north shore, accessing the Quinault Ranger Station before climbing up to the North Fork Quinault trailhead. (A bridge links the two roads about 13 miles up the valley.)

Lake Quinault is part of the Quinault Indian Reservation, and fishing is regulated by the tribe; check locally for tribal licenses and regulations. Boat rentals are available from Lake Quinault Lodge and boat slips are offered at both south shore public campgrounds and at Rain Forest Resort.

There is plenty of hiking – a number of short trails begin just below the Lake Quinault Lodge on South Shore Rd. This trail system is accessed by any number of points in the Quinault village area; pick up a free map of the trails from the USFS office. The shortest trail is the **Quinault Rain Forest Nature Trail**, a half-mile trail through 500-year-old Douglas firs. This short trail adjoins the 3-mile **Quinault Loop Trail**, which meanders through the rain forests before looping back to the lake.

East Fork Quinault River Leading to arguably the most famous – and certainly one of the most photographed – parts of the park, the **Enchanted Valley Trail** climbs up to a large meadow (a former glacial lakebed) percolated by streams and springs and resplendent with wildflowers and copses of alder trees. To the north there are sheer cliff faces and peaks rising 2000 feet from the valley floor; during spring snowmelt, the 3-mile-long precipice is drizzled by thousands of small waterfalls.

The aptly named Enchanted Valley is reached after a long hike from the Graves Creek Ranger Station and trailhead at the end of the South Shore Rd, 19 miles from US 101. The first 12 miles of the trail pass through old-growth forests and are narrowly walled in by forested ridges. After attaining the Enchanted Valley, the trail is mostly level for 2¹/₂ miles, before it arches up to Anderson Pass (19 miles from Graves Creek). Here, long-distance hikers can continue down the **West Fork Dosewallips Trail** to complete a popular trans-park trek.

North Fork Quinault River Another popular cross-park path passes through this valley to join the lengthy Elwha River valley and its trail system; the **North Fork Quinault Trail** begins at the end of the North Shore Rd, at the North Fork Campground & Ranger Station, 17 miles from US 101. This major trail is not as picturesque as the East Fork, as much of the lower terrain is heavily forested.

Places to Stay & Eat
Camping Unless otherwise noted, the USFS campgrounds have running water and toilets but no RV hookups, and are $10 to $12 a night. The *Hoh Campground*, adjacent to the Hoh Rain Forest Visitors Center, offers 89 sites. The *Queets Campground*, at the end of Queets River Rd, offers 20 primitive sites with no fee. The *North Fork Campground*, on the North Fork Quinault River, has seven sites, and *Graves Creek Campground*, at the trailhead for the East Fork Quinault River trail, has 30 sites. There is a nice tents-only campground called *July Creek*, with 29 sites, on the north shore of Lake Quinault.

There's a hostel on the Hoh River; see Forks, later in this chapter, for details.

Lodges & Cabins The justly famous and entirely charming *Lake Quinault Lodge* (☎ 360-288-2571, 800-562-6672), 345 S Shore Rd, was built in 1926, and its classic fireplace lobby has greeted visitors ever since. There are a variety of lodging options. Rooms are available in the old,

shake-sided log lodge (starting at $100) and in a number of detached cabins and annexes (beginning at $150). Prices drop by half in the off-season or with promotional specials. Call well in advance for rooms. Facilities include a heated pool, a gift shop and boat rentals. The lodge's lake-view dining room offers lunches from $6 and dinners, which feature local fish, seafood and steak, from $12 to $16.

Rain Forest Resort Village (☎ 360-288-2535, 800-255-6936), 516 S Shore Rd, about 3¹/₂ miles east of US 101, is a more modern, less charming lodging option with rooms in cabins with fireplaces ($115 to $185) or in a motel wing (starting at $82). The *Salmon House* is the resort's restaurant, with family dining, steak and seafood. Other facilities include a general store, laundry and boat rentals. RV hookups are also available.

On the north shore of Lake Quinault is *Lochaerie Resort* (☎ 360-288-2215), 638 N Shore Rd, 4 miles north of US 101. This venerable resort offers lodging in six comfortable cabins ($60 to $70), each named after different Olympic peaks and each with its own character.

OLYMPIC COASTAL STRIP
Fifty-seven miles of the Olympic Peninsula coast were added to the national park in 1953, making this the longest wilderness coastline in the continental USA. Known officially as the Olympic Coastal Strip, this is some of the most rugged and picturesque coastline anywhere: sea stacks and islands parade out into the pounding surf, often capped by miniature forests (remnants of when these rocks were still part of the headland). Wildlife, including many marine mammals such as sea otters found almost nowhere else in the USA, is frequently seen. There's a wealth of life in tide pools and on rocky aviaries, and gray whales spout offshore.

The coastline is accessed by roads at only a few places; otherwise this expanse of rock, sea water and sand belongs to hardy trekkers who negotiate the tides, waves and treacherous headlands on foot.

WASHINGTON

Long-distance hiking along the Pacific Ocean should not be entered into lightly: it's more than just a saunter down a sandy strand.

If you are contemplating a long trek along the coast, request information from the NPS (see Information in Port Angeles and Forks), buy good maps and learn to read tide tables. Many portions of the coastline can only be negotiated at low tide, while other areas can't be rounded on foot at any time. These promontories require strenuous climbs up and down (often on rope ladders, or sometimes just on ropes) and cross-country excursions to the next safe beach-walking area. Fast-moving waves can easily isolate hikers on rocky points or headlands, and the weather can change quickly. In all but the height of summer, hikers need to be prepared for all kinds of weather.

The most popular long-distance beach hike is the section between Ozette and Rialto Beach, a 20-mile trek that usually requires three or four days. Another favorite three-nighter is the beach hike between Third Beach (near La Push) and Oil City, a 17-mile hike along one of the most rugged stretches of the Olympic Peninsula's coast. Remember that you'll need a backcountry permit to camp overnight along the coast (except at official campgrounds). Also pick up a copy of The Mountaineers' *Exploring Washington's Wild Olympic Coast* by David Hooper, which admirably describes the challenges and pleasures of these coastal hikes.

Although the Olympic Coastal Strip is, in terms of recreation, set up for long-distance hikers, there are a number of areas where less ardent explorers and beach-combers can sample this wonderful wilderness coastline.

Ozette

Most noted as the site of an ancient Makah village (see Neah Bay, later in this chapter), the Ozette area is one of the most accessible parts of the Olympic coast. Except on the busiest summer weekends, it's easy to get away from the crowds and experience these beaches as wilderness.

The Hoko-Ozette Rd leaves Hwy 112 about 2 miles west of Sekiu and proceeds 20 miles down a paved and graveled road to Lake Ozette Ranger Station & Campground (☎ 360-963-2725) on Ozette Lake. Ozette Lake is the third-largest lake in Washington and is a popular spot for water-skiers and anglers.

Hiking From the ranger station, two board-walk trails lead out to the beach. To the north, the 3-mile **Cape Alava Trail** leads to a section of sandy beach that has a jumble of offshore rocks and islands, making this a lovely place for a picnic or beachcombing.

It was along this coast that the 15th-century village known as Ozette was unearthed. Nothing remains of the excavation today except a commemorative plaque, though many of the artifacts are on display at the Makah Museum at Neah Bay. The southern **Sand Point Trail** from Ozette Ranger Station leads 2.8 miles to beaches below a low bluff; whale watchers often come here in the migration season.

The two Ozette trails can easily be linked as a long day hike. It's a little over 3 miles between Cape Alava and Sand Point along the beach, and no dangerous head-lands impede hikers, even at high tide, though the rather coarse, rocky beach can make this hike strenuous.

The high point of this hike is the **Wedding Rocks**, the most significant group of petroglyphs on the Olympic Peninsula. About a mile south of Cape Alava, the small outcropping contains over 100 superb rock carvings, including noted carvings of whales, a European square-rigger and fertility figures. The site was traditionally used for Makah weddings and is still considered sacred, and not just by Native Americans – a lot of New Age worship goes on here as well.

Rialto Beach

One of the few Olympic beaches easily accessed by vehicle, Rialto is a popular place for day excursions. Located at the mouth of the Quillayute River across from La Push, the log-littered, stony beach faces a profusion of flat-topped offshore islands. Hikers with an eye on the tide table can trek up to **Hole-in-the-Wall**, a bluff with a wave-weathered hole in it, about 2 miles north of the parking area. This is a wild place to visit after a storm, when waves barrel up to the edge of the forest, dragging logs out to sea.

Facilities at Rialto Beach include flush toilets and picnic tables. Mora Ranger Station (☎ 360-374-5460) can issue backcountry permits and information; in summer there are also naturalist-led walks along the beach.

To reach Rialto Beach, turn west 1 mile north of Forks off US 101 and follow the La Push road (Hwy 110). In 13 miles the road divides, with Mora and Rialto Beach on the northern fork. It's 4 miles from there to the beach.

Ruby Beach to South Beach

This most southerly area of the Olympic Coastal Strip is located between the Hoh and Quinault Indian Reservations. The beach along this stretch is generally much less dramatic than that farther north, and there is regular beach access from US 101. Probably the most attractive coastal areas are found at Ruby Beach, where the beach is made up of polished black stones the size of silver dollars, and at Kalaloch (pronounced *Klay-lock*). Other beachfronts (unimaginatively named Beaches One through Six) are sandy strands popular with beachcombers. For information about this area, contact the Kalaloch Information Station (☎ 360-962-2283).

Places to Stay & Eat

Camping With a wilderness permit, there are plenty of informal campsites along the beach at both Cape Alava and Sand Point. At *Lake Ozette Campground*, there are 14 free sites, but no hookups. Along the Quillayute River, 3 miles east of La Push and Rialto Beach, *Mora Campground* offers 94 regular sites with a $11 fee. No beach camping is allowed along Rialto Beach between the Quillayute River and Ellen

Creek, about a mile above the beach parking area. The *Kalaloch Campground* has 177 regular sites.

There's a hostel on the Hoh River; see Places to Stay under Forks for more information.

Lodges & Cabins The *Kalaloch Lodge* (☎ 360-962-2271), 157151 US 101 in Kalaloch, is the only lodging and restaurant between Ruby Beach and Queets. Built in 1953 as an anglers' retreat, the lodge was included in the park's coastal strip and is now operated by park concessionaires. In addition to rooms in the old lodge, there are over 40 log cabins scattered along the headlands above the beach. Some cabins and rooms sleep up to six people. In peak season, cabins run between $122 and $187. There's also an RV park and tent sites in an adjacent campground. The lodge restaurant has family-style meals in beach-view dining rooms (the best views are from the upstairs lounge).

Northeastern Olympic Peninsula

The northeast corner of the Olympic Peninsula is where most of the region's population lives, along a stretch of the Strait of Juan de Fuca from Port Townsend to Port Angeles. Outdoor recreationists love this part of the peninsula because of the much-discussed rain shadow: here you get the beauty of the Olympics without all of the rain. Sea kayaking, sailing, fishing and golf are all popular pastimes here.

Port Townsend is one of the oldest towns in Washington. It went through a notable building boom in 1890, followed by an immediate bust, which preserved the town as an architectural showpiece. Most of the town is on the National Register of Historic Places. Port Angeles is just a ferry ride from Canada and is on the doorstep to Olympic Mountain high country. This comfortable port town is a convenient center for Olympic Peninsula exploration.

Getting Around

Public transportation between the communities in the northeast peninsula is limited to buses. Since each of the two northern counties (Clallam and Jefferson) has its own system, you have to change lines in order to get from Port Townsend to Port Angeles by bus. If the following service seems confusing, check a map for the county boundaries, and it all becomes a bit clearer.

Jefferson Transit (☎ 360-385-4777) serves Port Townsend and outlying areas in Jefferson County, the easternmost corner of the peninsula. Buses travel as far west as Sequim. Connections can be made from there to Port Angeles and points west on The Bus, Clallam County's intercity transit system. The fare is 50¢. (Another branch of Jefferson Transit's service runs between Lake Quinault and Grays Harbor on the west side of the peninsula).

Clallam County's The Bus (☎ 360-452-4511, 800-858-3747) travels as far west as Neah Bay and La Push and as far east as Diamond Point. Eastbound, the No 30 bus travels between Port Angeles and Sequim, where you can connect with Jefferson Transit buses to Port Townsend and points east. To head west, take the No 14 bus to Sappho, and from there pick up connections to either La Push or Neah Bay. In Port Angeles, the main transfer center is at Oak and Front Sts, conveniently located near the ferry dock and visitors' center. Fares start at 75¢ for adults. Call for detailed route and schedule information.

PORT TOWNSEND

Population 8727

One of the best preserved Victorian-era seaports in the USA, Port Townsend is one of the few urban must-sees in a region otherwise dedicated to the marvels of nature. Block after block of elaborate storefronts line the harbor, and on the hill above the port are ornate mansions (many of which are now B&Bs) built for the merchant

kings of the early Washington Territory. On a clear day, views from Port Townsend are stunning, as the town looks across deep-blue Admiralty Inlet, filled with sailboats and ferries, to Whidbey Island and on to the white-glaciered mass of Mt Baker.

Port Townsend was first settled in 1851, the same year that Seattle was established, and for years the two struggling port cities maintained a strident competition for supremacy in Puget Sound trade. Then, in 1888, a subsidiary of Union Pacific announced plans to build rails from Portland to Port Townsend. With its dominance in the Puget Sound now seemingly assured, the citizens of Port Townsend went into a frenzy of commercial development, building a handsome retail core along the harbor and establishing opulent uptown mansions for the elite of trade and industry. However, in 1890, the rail link with Portland evaporated, and within three years the city was all but deserted. At the time, a local wag maintained that the town was still standing only because no one had the money to tear the buildings down.

Today, a new generation of merchant kings has restored historic Port Townsend, turning the downtown district into a shopper's destination for antiques, rare books, upscale clothing and regional art. While Port Townsend hovers at the brink of over-commercialization, it remains a great place to spend an afternoon browsing and an unparalleled place to spend a night or two in a B&B or vintage hotel.

Information & Orientation

The Port Townsend Chamber of Commerce visitors' center (☎ 360-385-2722), 2437 E Sims Way, Port Townsend, WA 98368, is open 9 am to 5 pm weekdays, 10 am to 4 pm Saturday, and 11 am to 4 pm Sunday.

The chamber of commerce puts out a useful map and guide to the downtown historic district, which abounds with Victorian-era architecture. The white birds found painted on the pavement all over town mark the Port Townsend Seagull Tour

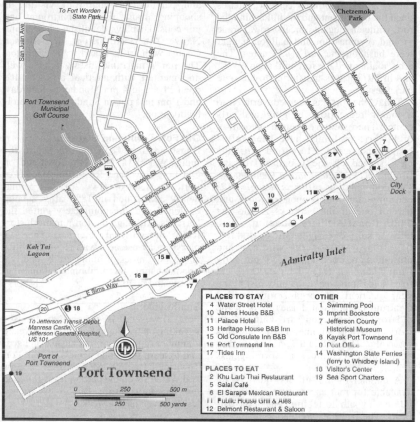

PLACES TO STAY
4   Water Street Hotel
10 James House B&B
11 Palace Hotel
13 Heritage House B&B Inn
15 Old Consulate Inn B&B
16 Port Townsend Inn
17 Tides Inn

PLACES TO EAT
2   Khu Larb Thai Restaurant
5   Salal Café
6   El Sarape Mexican Restaurant
11 Public House Grill & Ales
12 Belmont Restaurant & Saloon

OTHER
1   Swimming Pool
3   Imprint Bookstore
7   Jefferson County
    Historical Museum
8   Kayak Port Townsend
9   Post Office
14 Washington State Ferries
    (ferry to Whidbey Island)
18 Visitor's Center
19 Sea Sport Charters

route, an auto tour of sites and historic structures (see also Special Events, below).

Generally speaking, there are two vintage commercial districts in Port Townsend, both filled with Victorian-era structures. Downtown is the main commercial area; it stretches down Water Street along the waterfront. Uptown is atop the bluff and there's another commercial center on Lawrence St at Polk and Tyler Sts.

The post office, at Washington and Van Buren Sts uptown, is in an amazing stone edifice which was formerly the Customs House. Port Townsend offers a number of used- and rare-book stores. For travel information, go to Imprint Bookstore (☎ 360-385-3643) at 820 Water St.

Do your laundry at the Port Townsend Laundromat/Car Wash (☎ 360-385-5755), 2115 W Sims Way, and wash your car while you wait. Jefferson General Hospital (☎ 360-385-2200, 800-244-8917) is at 834 Sheridan St.

Fort Worden State Park
Fort Worden (☎ 360-385-4730), 200 Battery Way (off Cherry St), was built in 1900 as one of three major fortifications on Puget Sound to defend the area from

enemy attack. Enormous cement batteries lined the beachfront and the hill behind the fort, while an elegant officers' row, parade ground, gymnasium and balloon hangar were built on the fort's 433 acres. The army maintained the fort until after WWII, and in 1972 it was transferred to the state parks service.

Today, the fort has been converted into a major recreation, lodging and arts center. The extensive grounds and array of historic buildings have been refurbished and returned to period spiff (the park served as the backdrop for the filming of *An Officer and a Gentleman*). The commanding officer's home, a 12-bedroom mansion, is open for tours, and part of one of the barracks is now the **248th Coast Artillery Museum**, which tells the story of early Pacific coastal fortifications. Most park buildings and museums are open 11 am to 4 pm daily from Memorial Day to Labor Day, and from 1 to 4 pm weekends only rest of the year. A local arts organization, called Centrum Foundation, leases parts of the old fort for numerous art conferences, workshops and summer music and arts festivals. The old balloon hangar has been converted into a performing arts center.

A number of the officers' quarters are available for rent as vacation homes, and HI runs a youth hostel from one of the barracks. The facilities are also available for conferences and meetings. In addition, there are 80 campsites, boat launches, picnic sites and a beach access. Hikes lead along the headland to Point Wilson Light Station.

The **Port Townsend Marine Science Center** (☎ 360-385-5582) is on the park's fishing pier and features a touch tank. This aquarium is open noon to 6 pm Tuesday to Sunday, June 15 through Labor Day, weekends only from March 1 through June 14 and from Labor Day through October 31.

Jefferson County Historical Museum

The local museum (☎ 360-385-1003), 210 Madison St, is in the old city hall building, and part of the charm of visiting is snooping around the old courtrooms and jail cells. Displays detail the pioneer and Native American history of Jefferson County with artifacts and scads of photos. The port's maritime history is also well documented with nautical artifacts. It's open 11 am to 4 pm Monday to Saturday, and 1 pm to 4 pm on Sunday; admission is by donation.

Old Fort Townsend State Park

Constructed in 1856 in response to the Indian War of 1855-56, Fort Townsend, on Old Fort Townsend Rd (4 miles south of Port Townsend on Hwy 20), was permanently abandoned in 1895 after a lamp exploded and fire completely gutted the barracks. Although the fort remains historically insignificant, the park sports a pleasant day-use area with picnic facilities and over 6 miles of hiking trails, and is a popular spot for crabbing, clamming, fishing and boating.

Sea Kayaking

Port Townsend is the center for sea kayaking on the Puget Sound, and there are a number of places to rent kayaks and gear and to learn the fundamentals. Kayak Port Townsend (☎ 360-385-6240), at Monroe and Water Sts on the harbor, leads full- and half-day kayak trips for all experience levels, seven days a week.

Other Activities

Sea Sport Charters (☎ 360-385-7031) offers salmon **fishing** and bottom-fishing excursions as well as wildlife tours along the Strait of Juan de Fuca. They operate out of Port Townsend Boat Haven (☎ 360-385-2355), the local marina. Play nine holes of golf at Chevy Chase Golf Club (☎ 360-385-0704), 7401 Cape George Rd, the state's oldest public golf course, or at Port Townsend Golf Course (☎ 360-385-0752), 1948 Blaine St. The swimming pool at Mountain View Elementary School (☎ 360-385-7665) on Walker St at Blaine St, is open to the public; call for the schedule.

Special Events

Those enticed by Port Townsend's Victorian charm will want to be in town for the semi-annual Historic Homes Tours, held once in the spring, the first week of May, and again in the third week of September. Most of these homes are private residences and are not available for public viewing at any other time. Call the chamber of commerce for more information.

Centrum, a nonprofit arts foundation based at Fort Worden State Park, sponsors an endless stream of arts and music festivals and seminars year round. One of the most popular festivals at Fort Worden is Jazz Port Townsend, a late-July event with national acts. Call Centrum (☎ 360-385-3102, 800-733-3608) for a schedule or write PO Box 1158, Port Townsend, WA 98368.

Places to Stay

Camping RV campers can hook up at *Sea Breeze Center* (☎ 360-385-7753), 1408 Sims Way, a full-service RV village with hookup sites at $19, or at the *Jefferson County Fairgrounds* (☎ 360-385-1013), north of Port Townsend near Fort Worden, where sites are $6 to $8.

Campsites are only one of several accommodation options at *Fort Worden State Park* (☎ 360-385-4730), 200 Battery Way in Port Townsend. Regular sites are $11 and hookups cost $15. Campers can make reservations by contacting the park directly. Visitors can also pass up the campsites for a stay in one of the park's vacation homes or in the youth hostel (see below). There's more camping at *Old Fort Townsend State Park* (☎ 360-385-3595) on Old Fort Townsend Rd, 4 miles south of Port Townsend on Hwy 20, where sites ($10) are lined up on the old parade field (no hookups though). It's open from May to mid-September.

Hostels The *AYH/HI Olympic Hostel* in the historic barracks at Fort Worden State Park (☎ 360-385-0655), 272 Battery Way. The hostel is normally open year-round, even though it has been closed during January

and February for maintenance in the past. Rates are $12 to $15.

B&Bs There are dozens of B&Bs in Port Townsend; if you're really into it, contact the chamber of commerce for a full listing. The following are especially nice: The *James House B&B* (☎ 360-385-1238), 1238 Washington St, offers 12 rooms, some with private baths and many with great views over the harbor. Rooms range from $75 to 125. The *Heritage House B&B Inn* (☎ 360-385-6800), 305 Pierce St, is an Italianate mansion with six guest rooms (four with private bathroom) ranging from $70 to $142.

The former German ambassador lived at the *Old Consulate Inn B&B* (☎ 360-385-6753), 313 Walker St at Washington St, a lovely Victorian with a wraparound porch and six rooms (all with private baths) from $96 to $195. Of all the astonishing homes built in Port Townsend, none can top the *Manresa Castle* (☎ 360-385-5750, 800-732-1281), 7th and Sheridan Sts (off E Sims Way), built by the first mayor of Port Townsend as a home for his new bride. The 40-room mansion looks like a castle out of a fairy tale, sitting high above the town, with views on all sides. Rooms range from $68 to $180 (for a turret!) in the high season.

Hotels Some of the Victorian-era hotels have also been restored. The *Palace Hotel* (☎ 360-385-0773, 800-962-0741), 1004 Water St, built in 1890, has been brought back to its original spit and polish. Some rooms have been remodeled into suites with private baths while others are still authentic (bathroom down the hall). Rates range from $54 to $175. Another refurbished inn is the *Water Street Hotel* (☎ 360-385-5467, 800-735-9810), 635 Water St, with rooms starting at $50.

Not all lodging in Port Townsend is antique. The *Port Townsend Inn* (☎ 360-385-2211, 800-822-8696), 2020 Washington St, is an attractive motel on the edge of the historic district with single/double rooms starting at $68/78. At the

Tides Inn (☎ 360-385-0595, 800-822-8696), 1807 Water St, the view rooms overlook Admiralty Inlet and Whidbey Island; singles/doubles are $58/78.

Vacation Home Rentals *Officers' Row Vacation Homes* at Fort Worden State Park (☎ 360-385-4730), 200 Battery Way, date from 1904 and were formerly the officers' quarters at Fort Worden. Most of the kitchens are modern, though the houses retain period charm; some have up to six bedrooms. These houses are very popular, and with prices starting at $85, they're a great bargain. Plan to make reservations up to a year in advance if you want a chance at the prime houses.

Places to Eat
The center of Port Townsend is packed with trendy cafes and restaurants. You'll have no problem finding some place to eat, but here are some favorites. For big breakfast omelets or a zippy lunch, head to *Salal Café* (☎ 360-385-6532), 634 Water St. The seafood tacos are notable at *El Serape Mexican Restaurant* (☎ 360-379-9343), 628 Water St. *Public House Grill & Ales* (☎ 360-385-9708), 1038 Water St in the Palace Hotel, offers an informal, pub-like atmosphere, with a menu of grilled items ranging from burgers to steak.

Belmont Restaurant & Saloon (☎ 360-385-3007), 925 Water St, has a lovely dining room (the Belmont Hotel was established in 1889), with a wide international menu featuring local seafood and produce. *Khu Larb Thai Restaurant* (☎ 360-385-5023), 225 Adams St, has excellent Thai food and an extensive menu of specialties.

For Port Townsend's most romantic meal, go to *Manresa Castle Victorian Restaurant* (☎ 360-385-5750), at 7th and Sheridan Sts. There's nothing ordinary about the setting – a Bavarian castle on a bluff above the town – and the food is also exceptional, with an emphasis on up-to-date international preparations of local seafood, meats, and produce.

Getting There & Away
Bus Jefferson Transit (☎ 360-385-4777) at 1615 W Sims Way, runs buses to Sequim, where you can pick up Clallam Transit buses for points west, and to Poulsbo, a connection point for Seattle (see Getting There & Away at the beginning of this chapter).

Ferry Washington State Ferries (☎ 800-344-4352) operates about 10 half-hour trips a day to Keystone on Whidbey Island from the downtown terminal, on the east end of Harrison St. Rates and schedules vary seasonally, with high-season fares starting at $7.10 for a car and driver and $1.75 for passengers. Service is occasionally disrupted by severe low tides or stormy seas.

Getting Around
Jefferson Transit (☎ 360-385-4777) has local bus service along Water St downtown and Lawrence St uptown. Buses to Fort Worden travel along Cherry St. To rent a car, contact Budget Rent-a-Car (☎ 360-385-7766), 3049 E Sims Way. For a taxi, call Key City Transport (☎ 360-385-5972).

SEQUIM
Pop 4138
When people say, 'It's the climate,' it's partly because there's not much else to recommend this anomalous little boomtown. Directly in the path of the Olympics rain shadow, Sequim gets less than 20 inches of rain a year, quite a feat on this otherwise sodden peninsula. Initially, irrigation projects brought settlement to this area, then retirees and others looking for sunshine and Shangri-La on the Puget Sound planted themselves here as well. Predictably, the next step was golf courses, which currently ring the town.

The downtown area is a long, inelegant stretch of old strip malls; nonetheless, boutiques are rapidly squeezing in. Traffic really jams up on US 101 behind Sequim's traffic light, so you may get a chance to window shop from your car.

Information

The visitors' center (☎ 360-683-6197, 800-737-8462) is on the east end of town on US 101 at 1192 E Washington St. Direct correspondence to the Sequim-Dungeness Valley Chamber of Commerce, PO Box 907, Sequim, WA 98382.

Dungeness Spit

Immediately north of town is the Dungeness Spit, a sandy arm that extends 5½ miles into the Strait of Juan de Fuca; it's the longest natural sand hook in the nation. Now part of Dungeness National Wildlife Refuge, it's a great place to hike and get a closer look at the marine environment of the northern Pacific Coast.

The primary wildlife you'll see here are shorebirds, especially herons, various kinds of ducks and loons, and raptors like bald eagles. Seals also crawl up on the sandy beach to sun; look for them bobbing offshore, watching you.

To reach the refuge from Sequim, head north up Sequim Ave (which turns into Sequim Dungeness Way) to Dungeness Bay, or take bus No 44 from downtown. The Dungeness School House, built in 1892, is on the left side of the road right before the road crosses the Dungeness River. Access to the Dungeness Spit is at the Dungeness Recreation Area, a county park. You'll have to park here, as access to the spit is by foot or horseback only. There's a $3 per person fee to enter the refuge and hike the spit. From the park, it's a 12-mile roundtrip walk to **Dungeness Lighthouse**, which was built in 1857 at the end of the spit.

Olympic Game Farm

If you feel like going on a safari, head to the Olympic Game Farm (☎ 360-683-4295, 800-778-4295), 1423 Ward Rd, which offers driving and walking tours through a 90-acre open-air zoo. Most of the 'wildlife' here is semi-domesticated, as many of the animals were trained as 'actors' for wildlife films for Disney Studios. The farm also breeds endangered species (like timber wolves and jaguars) for other zoos. It's open 9 am to 4 pm daily,

year-round; admission is $7/6 adults/children. From Sequim, take Sequim-Dungeness Way northward about a mile, then turn left (west) on Woodcock Lane. In about a mile, turn north again on Ward Way and follow it half a mile to the game farm.

Sequim Bay State Park

This pleasant state park (☎ 360-683-4235) is on Sequim Bay, a shallow bay protected by sand spits from the turbulence of the strait, making it a favorite for kayakers and canoers. On the other hand, at low tide, captains of motorized craft are in for a navigational nightmare. There's also camping and picnicking. The park is located 4 miles southwest of Sequim on US 101.

Wineries

The near Mediterranean climate of Sequim has prompted a couple of wineries to spring up. **Neuharth Winery** (☎ 360-683-9652), 885 Still Rd, Sequim, WA 98382, is open 9:30 am to 5:30 pm daily from May 15 to October 1; noon to 5 pm Wednesday to Sunday the rest of the year. It has an attractive tasting room and high-quality wines. **Lost Mountain Winery** (☎ 360-683-5229), at 3174 Lost Mountain Rd, Sequim, WA 98382, makes hearty red wines their specialty; call ahead for hours.

Golf

The sun shines bright in Sequim, and a number of golf courses have sprung up with the retirement community mostly in mind. The only fully public course here is Dungeness Golf and Country Club (☎ 360-683-6344), 491 Woodcock Rd, an 18-hole course on the road to Dungeness Spit.

Places to Stay

Camping There are both tent and RV sites ($11/16) at *Sequim Bay State Park* (☎ 360-683-4235), 4 miles south of Sequim on US 101. *Dungeness Recreation Area* is adjacent to the Dungeness National Wildlife Refuge, and is operated by Clallam County Parks (☎ 360-417-2291), with 65 campsites ($12), showers and flush toilets, but no hookups.

WASHINGTON

Hotels All of the following hotels are in the $60 to $80 range, and are along busy US 101, which is essentially all there is to Sequim. The very red *Red Ranch Inn* (☎ 360-683-4195), 830 W Washington St, can't be missed on the western edge of Sequim; kids under 12 are free. There's an equally red restaurant on the premises. The *Sundowner Motel* (☎ 360-683-5532, 800-325-6966), 364 W Washington St, has some rooms with kitchens. *Sequim Econo Lodge* (☎ 360-683-7113, 800-488-7113), 801 E Washington St, has free continental breakfast and in-room microwaves and fridges.

Stay outside of town at the *Sequim Bay Lodge Best Western* (☎ 360-683-0691, 800-622-0691), 268522 US 101, near John Wayne Marina. Rooms begin at $70/80; there's a restaurant and a nine-hole golf course.

Places to Eat
For breakfast, the place to go is the *Oak Table Cafe* (☎ 360-683-2179), 292 W Bell St, for apple pancakes, great omelets and espresso drinks. *The Three Crabs* (☎ 360-683-4264), 101 Three Crabs Rd, at the harbor at Dungeness, is an institution. This is the place to fill up on namesake Dungeness crab. It's worth visiting *El Cazador* (360-683-4788), 535 W Washington St, a local Mexican chain, if for no other reason than that the Sequim branch is in a renovated grain elevator. For more traditional Northwest-style cuisine, go to *Buckhorn Grill* (☎ 360-683-9010), 268522 US 101, at the Sequim Bay Lodge east of town.

Shopping
Northwest Native Expressions (☎ 360-681-4640), 1033 Old Blyn Hwy, is a gallery of Native American art located in the tiny S'Klallam Indian community on Sequim Bay. Masks, bentwood boxes and bowls, basketry, blankets and jewelry by artists from many Northwest tribes are on display. There's also a good selection of books and small gifts. Proceeds from sales go to support native tribal cultural programs. The gallery is 6 miles east of Sequim near Blyn.

PORT ANGELES
Population 18,674

Although Port Angeles is mostly known as a place you pass through to get elsewhere – in this case to Canada or to Olympic National Park – it's a pleasant enough town with inexpensive motels and good restaurants and a real nautical air. All in all, it's a good base for exploring the peninsula.

The natural harbor at Port Angeles attracted the attention of land speculators in the 1860s, but President Abraham Lincoln placed the land around the bay under federal ownership as a 'Navy and Military Reserve,' in case the USA needed to build defenses against the pesky British installations directly across the strait in Victoria. However, by the 1890s, fear of the British had been largely replaced by the desire to homestead the land, and a flood of squatters moved onto the military reservation and settled. Eventually the US government recognized the squatters' land claims and opened the remainder of the reservation to settlement.

In the 1910s and 1920s, dams were built on the Elwha River, at the base of the Olympic Mountains. The power they generated was designed to run Port Angeles' saw and pulp mills, which still line the waterfront. However, the dams stopped migration of native salmon and steelhead trout to the upper Elwha, formerly the peninsula's greatest spawning grounds. In recent years, environmentalists have attempted to use the Endangered Species Act to force the state to remove the dams and restore the fish to their native habitat.

Information
The Port Angeles Visitor Center (☎ 360-452-2363), 121 E Railroad Ave, Port Angeles, WA 98362, is adjacent to the ferry terminal on the waterfront. Sharing the same office is a visitors' center for Victoria, BC (☎ 360-998-1224). The visitors' center for Olympic National Park (☎ 360-452-0330) is 1 mile south of town, off Race St at 3002 Mt Angeles Rd.

The post office is at 424 E 1st St, Port Angeles, WA 97362. Port Book & News

PLACES TO STAY
7   DoubleTree Hotel
    Port Angeles
12 Uptown Motel
13 Hill Haus Motel
19 Flagstone Motel
21 Royal Victorian Motel
23 Tudor Inn

PLACES TO EAT
4   The Downrigger
9   First St Haven
10 The Coffee House
11 Bella Italia
14 Bonny's Bakery

OTHER
1   Bus Depot
2   Victoria Express,
    Black Ball Transport
3   Visitors' Center
5   Feiro Marine Laboratory
6   Budget Rent-a-Car
8   Port Book & News
15 Clallam County Museum
16 Peabody St Coin Laundry
17 Olympic Mountaineering
18 Post Office
20 Landmark Property
    Management
22 Star Rent-a-Car

Port Angeles

Port Angeles Harbor

0   250   500 m
0   250   500 yards

WASHINGTON

(☎ 360-452-6367), 104 E 1st St, offers a vast selection of magazines and both new and used books. The local travel section is also good. It's open until 9 pm. Peabody Street Coin Laundry, 212 S Peabody St, is open 24 hours a day.

City Pier
This pier, off the end of Lincoln St, allows pedestrians a chance to venture out into the harbor, where there's an observation tower and picnic area. Also on the pier is the **Feiro Marine Laboratory** (☎ 360-452-3940), operated by the marine studies facility of local Peninsula College. Kids will love the hands-on touch tank filled with the aquatic denizens of the strait. There's a staff person on hand to answer questions and to protect the octopus. The lab is open 10 am to 8 pm daily from Memorial Day to Labor Day, and noon to 4 pm weekends only the rest of the year; admission is $1/50¢ adults/children.

Clallam County Museum
This local museum (☎ 360-417-2364), 319 Lincoln St, is housed in the handsome old

Early Utopia

The land just east of Port Angeles was formerly a utopian colony, established in 1887 by a Seattle attorney named George Smith. The Puget Sound Cooperative Colony was founded on the principle that 'everyone shall act as a civilized being, shall avoid all excesses, be just and undeceiving to all.'

With these good intentions, the colony established a school, sawmill and shipyard, and cleared land. However, as the town of Port Angeles became more and more of an economic and cultural entity in the late 1890s, the distinction between the citizens of town and colony increasingly blurred and eventually disappeared. ■

county courthouse and retells the story of the community's growth. It's largely a tale of logging, milling and shipping, but the building is lovely. The museum is open 10 am to 4 pm Monday to Saturday in summer; it's open weekdays only in winter. Admission is free.

Port Angeles Fine Arts Center

The Olympic Peninsula has a long history as an art-producing area, dating back as far as the Makahs and other artistically inclined native peoples. Today, dozens of professional artists live on the peninsula, and this small regional gallery (☎ 360-457-3532), 1203 E Lauridsen St, usually has exhibits of local work. The gallery is high above the city in a 5-acre garden with beautiful views over the strait. The center is open from 11 am to 5 pm Thursday to Sunday.

Waterfront Trail

If you want to limber up before taking on a mountain trail in the Olympics, try the trail that stretches 6 miles along the Port Angeles waterfront out to the end of **Ediz Hook**, the sand spit that loops around the bay. This is a popular picnic spot. A good place to pick up the trail is at the base of City Pier.

Activities

Look into guided climbs or get outdoor gear and supplies at Olympic Mountaineering (☎ 360-452-0240), 221 S Peabody St. It's a great clearing-house for classes and lessons in many sports, with a very friendly and enthusiastic staff. The store also rents gear such as stoves, packs, tents, skis and so on.

For guided **ecotours** of Olympic National Park, contact Olympic Van Tours & Shuttles (☎ 360-452-3858), PO Box 2201, Port Angeles, WA 98362. You can also arrange to be picked up after transpark hikes or from Sea-Tac Airport. Contact Rite Bros Aviation (☎ 360-452-6226, 360-452-7227), at the west end of Fairchild Airport, for information about **scenic flights** over Olympic National Park and other parts of the peninsula.

Places to Stay

Camping The *Port Angeles/Sequim KOA* (☎ 360-457-5916), 80 O'Brien Rd, 7 miles east of Port Angeles on US 101, has both RV and tent sites, with a laundry, showers and a heated pool. Open from April through October; sites begin at $19.

B&Bs *Domaine Madeleine* (☎ 360-457-4174), 146 Wildflower Lane, east of Port Angeles, is a perennial favorite with couples who come here for the wonderful views of the strait and Vancouver Island, the French-inspired 5-acre garden and the comforts of a well-run B&B. There are three guest rooms and one suite, all with views; rooms range from $125 to $165. *Tudor Inn* (☎ 360-452-3138), 1108 S Oak St, is a 1910 home with five bedrooms (two with private baths) and a library and sitting room for guests. Room rates range from $85 to $110.

Hotels Port Angeles sees a lot of travelers due to the ferries, and there are a number of good, reasonably priced motels with rooms starting under $40. Three of the best deals here are the *Traveler's Motel* (☎ 360-452-2303), 1133 E 1st St, the *All View Motel* (☎ 360-457-7779), 214 E Lauridsen Blvd (off Lincoln St), and the *Royal Victorian Motel* (☎ 360-452-2316), 521 E 1st St. Only slightly more expensive is the *Flagstone Motel* (☎ 360-457-9494), at 415 E 1st St.

For a quieter location, head to the *Hill Haus Motel* (☎ 360-452-9285), 111 W 2nd St, $55/59 single/double, or the *Uptown Motel* (☎ 360-457-9434), 2nd and Laurel Sts, $65 per room, which sit beside each other on the bluff above downtown. Both have views over the harbor and of the Olympics, and both are clean and friendly.

For something a bit more upscale, go to the *DoubleTree Hotel Port Angeles* (☎ 360-452-9215, 800-547-8010), 221 N Lincoln St, right on the waterfront. This is a large development with 187 rooms and the kinds of comforts – like a heated pool, spa and balconies over the harbor – that you'd expect for upward of $119 a night. You'll also find comfort at the *Best Western Olympic Lodge* (☎ 360-452-2993, 800-600-2993), 140 Del Guzzi Drive, in a country setting 1 mile east of Port Angeles on US 101. They have a heated pool, Jacuzzi and small conference facilities; rooms begin at $79.

Vacation Home Rentals If you're looking for private homes available for short-term vacation rentals in the Port Angeles area, try Landmark Property Management (☎ 360-452-1326), 501 E 1st St.

Places to Eat

There's a sly kind of countercultural bent to Port Angeles, but it's hard to put your finger on it. Hang out at some of the local cafes and you begin to get a sense of it. The extra-narrow *First St Haven* (☎ 360-457-0352), 107 E 1st St, is the place to go for traditional diner-style breakfasts. Stop at *Bonny's Bakery* (☎ 360-457-3585), 215 S Lincoln St, in an old firehall. Bonny's specializes in French pastries, fresh Danishes and cinnamon rolls; there's espresso, too.

The Coffee House (☎ 360-452-1459), 118 E 1st St, is an art gallery-cum-coffeehouse and restaurant that offers a large and eclectic, world-cuisine menu.

There are plenty of vegetarian dishes, most less than $10. On weekends, there's local acoustic entertainment. For Italian food, go to *Bella Italia* (☎ 360-457-5442), 117-B 1st St, which specializes in local seafood. You need to enter the restaurant from the alley behind and below the store.

If you're looking for a traditional steakhouse and nightclub, head to *Bushwhacker Restaurant* (☎ 360-457-4113), 1527 E 1st St. This is also a good place to find fresh local seafood. Locals are fond of recommending *The Downrigger* (☎ 360-452-2700), 115 Railroad Ave (on the wharf next to the ferry terminal), which has great views over the harbor and out to Victoria, BC. Go for the views – or a drink – but steer clear of what purports to be cuisine.

Getting There & Around

Air Horizon Air (☎ 360-547-9308) has service to Portland, Seattle and Victoria, BC, from Fairchild International Airport.

Bus Olympic Bus Lines (☎ 360-452-3858) has two buses a day between Sea-Tac Airport, Seattle and Port Angeles. Buses arrive/depart from Crazy Mike's at 6th and Lincoln Sts. One-way fare to Seattle is $20. Clallam Transit buses (☎ 360-452-4511, 800-858-3747) depart to Forks and destinations on the western half of the peninsula (including Neah Bay), and east to Sequim. The bus depot is at the corner of Oak and Front Sts.

Grayline Buses (☎ 360-452-5112) offers sightseeing tours to/from Victoria and overnight packages from Port Angeles. They'll even pick you up at your RV park.

Ferry Black Ball Transport (☎ 360-457-4491), also known as the Coho Ferry, provides passenger and automobile service to Victoria. The 1½-hour trip costs $27.25 one way for a car and driver; adult/child passengers cost $6.75/3.25. This ferry makes a brief closure in January for maintenance. The Victoria Express (☎ 360-452-8088, 800-633-1589) also offers one-hour service for passengers and cyclists only; it runs from late May to mid-October.

Reservations are recommended. Roundtrip fare is $25/12 adults/children; seniors receive a 10% discount. Bicycles cost an extra $2. Frequency and schedules vary seasonally for both ferries.

Car Budget Rent-a-Car (☎ 360-452-4774) has two locations, one directly across from the ferry terminal at 111 W Front St, and one at Fairchild International Airport (☎ 360-457-4246). Rentals are also available from Star Rent-a-Car (☎ 360-452-8001), 602 E Front St.

If you need a taxi, call Blue Top Cab Co (☎ 360-452-2223).

Northwestern Olympic Peninsula

In the northwest section of the Olympic Peninsula, US 101 winds through some of the most remote land this side of the Puget Sound. The land that's not part of Olympic National Park is heavily logged and mostly unpopulated, due to extremes in weather and isolation. Four Indian reservations cling to the edge of the continent at the western brink of the peninsula, and each welcomes respectful visitors.

The major town out here is Forks, which has ample numbers of motel rooms and restaurants. If you're traveling in the northwestern peninsula, reservations are a good idea – even in Forks – because it's a long way to the next town. Don't let these considerations inhibit you from visiting other areas: the museum in Neah Bay is world-class, and the bay at La Push is beautiful and primordial. Just plan ahead. Other towns – Clallam Bay and Sekiu – have little to offer visitors who aren't charter fishers.

It's worth noting that the restaurants and lodgings in Forks are open year-round, while many of the other smaller towns on the northwest corner essentially shut down outside of tourist season.

NEAH BAY
Population 1214
The center of the Makah Indian Reservation, this old fishing town features one of the best Native American museums in the USA, but otherwise it has pretty basic amenities for the traveler. It's a long and increasingly winding cliff-side road that links Neah Bay to the rest of the peninsula, and from here roads press even farther west through forests to Cape Flattery, the most northwesterly point in the continental USA. Neah Bay sits alongside a wide, wind-frothed harbor overlooked by totem poles. There's more than just a sense of history here; in Neah Bay, at the perimeter of the continent, there's also a sense of timelessness.

Orientation & Information
On Hwy 112, Neah Bay is 18 miles west of Sekiu and 75 miles west of Port Angeles. For more information about the Makah Reservation, contact the Makah Tribal Council (☎ 360-645-2201), PO Box 115, Neah Bay, WA 98357.

Makah Cultural & Research Center
This transfixing museum and cultural center (☎ 360-645-2711), on the east end of Neah Bay off Hwy 112, is one of the USA's greatest collections of Native American archaeology and the sole repository of the Ozette artifacts. Excellent displays interpret the many objects found at the Ozette site and fit them together into a whole that illustrates the day-to-day life of the ancient Makah.

Especially impressive is the ingenious use that the Ozettes made of their environment; everything they needed was fashioned from bone, stone, wood or grasses. Also notable is their intricate use of design. Not only would they carve a comb from a piece of bone, but its handle would be fashioned to represent a grimacing human face. They felled cedar trees and cut boards (all without the use of any metal tools), and etched house planks with ceremonial shapes like whales and owls.

Ozette: The American Pompeii

The Makah tribe has dwelt at the mouth of the Strait of Juan de Fuca for centuries, and its members were among the greatest of the seafaring Northwest Indians. Hunters would put to sea on large dugout cedar canoes to hunt gray whales, which annually migrate past these shores. Sometimes the whalers would paddle out 40 miles into the Pacific in search of their quarry. After harpooning the animal, the Makah hunters would lance the whale with floats made of inflated seal skins to keep it from diving. After the whale was killed, it was towed back to the village, where it was processed into food and its bones were made into tools.

The Makah also hunted seals, halibut and other marine fish. From the forests and meadows, they made canoes, baskets, bentwood boxes and other everyday items, all artistically designed and most carved with ceremonial or amusing details.

The reason we know so much about Makah prehistory is due to one of the great accidents of archaeology. Situated on the western side of the Olympic Peninsula, Ozette was one of five original ancient Makah villages. It was built on a grassy ledge above the beach and below a steep dirt slope. Apparently, about 500 years ago, after a powerful rainstorm, the slope above the village gave way and a massive mud slide buried the village.

The Ozette villagers apparently never attempted to retrieve the objects from the settlement, and the site remained undisturbed for centuries. After another lashing storm in the early 1970s, a hiker along the beach noticed timbers and boards sticking out of a recently exposed hillside. The tribe and archaeologists were contacted, and a decade-long excavation of the site ensued.

Ozette is often referred to as the American Pompeii, for the wealth of items recovered and the view it gives into the everyday life of the ancient Makah. Entire longhouses, with all the tools, toys, weapons, baskets and implements intact, were uncovered. After the artifacts were cataloged and interpreted (often with the help of Makah elders, who were sometimes the only source of information on the use of certain tools or objects), the Makah erected a huge new museum at Neah Bay to exhibit the artifacts and tell the story of their ancestors. ■

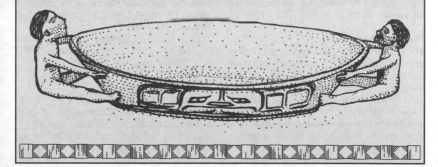

Among the displays are a number of Makah canoes, complete with whaling weapons, and a replica of an Ozette longhouse, which is filled with the tools, baskets, and goods of everyday life. In the museum theater, the film *A Gift from the Past* is shown twice daily at 10 am and 2 pm, and recounts the discovery, excavation and importance of the Ozette site. The sophistication of ancient Makah life is quite remarkable, and to walk out of the museum and find yourself in the same environment where the ancient Makah lived produces a profound and thoughtful respect.

The museum is open 10 am to 5 pm daily, June 1 through September 15, and 10 am to 5 pm Wednesday to Sunday the rest of the year. Admission is $4/$3 adults/seniors and children.

Cape Flattery

Although no roads lead directly to Cape Flattery, the most northwesterly point in the lower 48 states, a mile-long hiking path leads to this dramatic 300-foot promontory. From Neah Bay, take the main street through town and follow a sign stating 'Cove Trails' that points up a hill (at this point stop following the roads that say Cape Flattery Resort). The 8-mile road to the Cape Flattery trailhead is pretty rough but it can be negotiated by most vehicles.

From the top of this wild, wind-buffeted point, cliffs fall away to the raging Pacific. Just offshore is Tatoosh Island, with a lighthouse and Coast Guard station. This is a good place to watch for whales during migration season.

Places to Stay & Eat

Most facilities were designed with anglers in mind, who used to come here in droves for the salmon fishing. Of the bayside lodgings, probably the best is *Silver Salmon Resort* (☎ 360-645-2388), on Bay View Ave (Hwy 112), with rooms starting at $39. On the waterfront is the *Bay View Restaurant* (☎ 360-645-2872), which is open year-round.

The best lodging and dining option for most people is also the most unique: the Air Force built a small air base near Neah Bay during WWII to defend the mouth of the Strait of Juan de Fuca. Years later, the base was closed, and the land – including five barracks and various recreational facilities – reverted to the tribe. The Makah have converted the style-less base facilities into the year-round *Cape Flattery Resort* (☎ 360-645-2201), about 2 miles west of Neah Bay on Hwy 112. In addition to lodging units and dormitory-type accommodations, there's a conference center, bowling alley, gymnasium and restaurant, the *Makah Bay Cafe*. Room rates range between $40 to $60.

FORKS

Forks is unabashedly a lumber town, but it doesn't seem as down on its luck as many other logging communities in the Northwest. This is by far the largest and friendliest place to stay on the western half of the Olympic Peninsula, as there are lots of hotels and several good places to eat. Forks is convenient to the Hoh Rain Forest, Neah Bay and the Olympic coastline.

Orientation & Information

Many roads lead off Forks to interesting places. From Forks, it's 17 miles west to La Push and Rialto Beach, and 57 miles north to Neah Bay. The Hoh Rain Forest Visitors Center is 24 miles south on US 101, and Kalaloch is 35 miles south. The Olympic National Park maintains an information station (☎ 360-452-0330) 7 miles north of Forks on Hwy 101.

The Forks Chamber of Commerce (☎ 360-374-2531) can be contacted at PO Box 1249, Forks, WA 98331.

Forks Timber Museum

One mile south of Forks on US 101 next to the visitors' center, this museum (☎ 360-374-9663) remembers the early settlers and loggers of the west end. Included in the collection is a steam donkey – used to transport logs – and pioneer farming imple-

WASHINGTON

ments. The local Native Americans are represented with a dugout canoe. Open daily 10 am to 4 pm, May through October; admission is by donation.

Places to Stay

Camping There's easy access to a number of public campgrounds; check the map from the national park. Most convenient is *Bogachiel State Park* (☎ 360-374-6356), 6 miles south of Forks on US 101, with 41 sites, piped water and flush toilets, right on the Bogachiel River. Otherwise, there's *Forks 101 RV Park* (☎ 360-374-507, 800-962-9964), a half-mile south of town on US 101.

Hostels The *Rain Forest Hostel* (☎ 360-374-2270), HC 80, Box 870, Forks, WA 98331, 23 miles south of Forks on US 101, is a private home with four dorm rooms. Facilities include a full kitchen, common room and fireplace. Lodging is $10 per night.

B&Bs *Miller Tree Inn B&B* (☎ 360-374-6806), 654 E Division St (next to city hall), offers six guest rooms, two with private baths. This old farmhouse sits on three acres, and rooms begin at $55.

Hotels *Forks Motel* (☎ 360-374-6243, 800-544-3416), 432 Forks Ave S, is a pleasant place with many rooms, a laundry, some kitchenettes and a pool; singles/doubles are $47/50. Across the street is *Pacific Inn Motel* (☎ 360-374-9400, 800-235-7344), 352 US 101 S, where kids under 12 are free and there's a guest laundry. Rooms cost $48/57. *Town Motel* (☎ 360-374-6231), 1080 S Forks Ave, has large family units, some kitchen units, and pets are OK; rates begin at $35/39.

Places to Eat

For breakfast, follow the locals to *The Coffee Shop* (☎ 360-374-6321), 241 Forks Ave, just next to the Pay & Save supermarket. Mountains of eggs, hash browns and pancakes sustain logger and tourist alike.

At *South North Garden* (☎ 360-374-9779), 219 Sol Duc Way, expert cooks serve up Asian food, the quality of which rivals that found in Seattle or Portland. An extensive selection of both Mandarin and Sichuan food is available, with most dinner entrées ranging from $6 to $9. The *Smokehouse Restaurant* (☎ 360-372-6258), a mile north of Forks at the La Push junction, is the local steak and seafood house.

LA PUSH

La Push is a tiny fishing village at the mouth of the Quillayute River and the principal settlement in the Quileute Indian Reservation. La Push looks out onto a jumble of towering, tree-topped islands, which serve to protect its small, busy harbor. It's worth the 17-mile drive down from US 101 just to watch the fishing boats setting out to sea from this beautiful and rugged bay. The Quileute have done more to attract tourism than many of the tribes on the peninsula by building a somewhat funky resort in La Push, above a magnificent stretch of beach.

Orientation & Information

Hwy 110, the road down from US 101, divides at the point where the Bogachiel and Sol Duc Rivers join. The northerly road continues to Mora and Rialto Beach on the Olympic Coastal Strip, while the road to the south continues to La Push. Just outside of town are the trailheads to Third and Second Beaches, also part of the park. Both offer a scenic beachfront; however, the coast is so rugged here that it's not possible to walk from one to the other along the Pacific. Third Beach is the starting point for a popular three-day beach hike to Oil City, 17 miles south near Hoh.

For more information, contact the Quileute Tribal Council (☎ 360-374-6163), PO Box 279, La Push, WA 98350.

Places to Stay & Eat

At the tribally owned and operated *La Push Ocean Park Resort* (☎ 360-374-5267, 800-487-1267), lodgings range from comfortable to pretty rustic and include a motel unit, a lodge and a variety of cabins. The lodge sits above one of the most beautiful beaches in Washington, but before setting out be sure you know what class of lodging you're getting. Ask specific questions – not all cabins have private bathrooms. Rooms range from $40 Camper's Cabins (no toilet) to $125 deluxe cabins with stone fireplaces. The resort also offers tent and RV camping for $10 to $12.

There's no restaurant in La Push, though there is a small market, and fresh seafood is available from fishing terminals near the harbor. You may want to request a kitchenette at the resort if you're going to spend any amount of time at La Push.

North Beach Area

These extensive sandy beaches – there's almost 30 miles of public access shoreline between Moclips and Point Brown – certainly offer beachcombers plenty of opportunity to explore, and in midsummer, temperatures invite sunbathing and dips into the chilly Pacific. These are the closest coastal beaches to Puget Sound population centers, and they can be very busy with family vacationers. In the fall, the beaches come alive with razor-clam diggers, who at low tide hunt the wily and succulent bivalves.

However, there's little else to recommend this area. If you're looking for wild and isolated coastline, or a mystic oneness with the sea, this probably isn't your stretch of beach. Washington State beaches are administered by the state highway department and are maintained as public roadways. Here, vehicles are allowed on the beaches, and you'll have to watch your children and dogs lest they be struck by speeding motorists; hardly anyone obeys the 25-mph speed limit. By late afternoon, after the hot-rod beach bums have had a few beers, lolling on the beach is – at the very least – unpleasant, if not unsafe. If you're heading to the Northwest for a

beach holiday, you'll generally be much happier in Oregon, where vehicles are kept off the beaches.

Orientation
South of Queets, at the southern end of the Olympic National Park Coastal Strip, US 101 heads inland to circumvent the Quinault Indian Reservation. The road passes by Lake Quinault, and then heads south to Hoquiam. An alternative route is to take a good, 17-mile-long, paved and gravel road 7 miles south of Lake Quinault, which joins Hwy 109 at Moclips. From here, travelers can continue south past modest beachside towns to Ocean Shores, or drive north into Taholah, a fishing village on the Quinault Reservation. It's 24 miles between Lake Quinault and Moclips, and 23 miles between Moclips and Ocean Shores.

Information
For information about this stretch of beach, contact the Washington Coast Chamber of Commerce (☎ 360-289-4552, 800-286-4552), on Hwy 109 in Ocean City. For information about the Quinault Reservation, contact the Quinault Indian Nation (☎ 360-276-8211), PO Box 189, Taholah, WA 98587.

MOCLIPS
Moclips, just south of the Quinault Indian Reservation, is kind of a dead end for northbound beach holiday makers – from here the road turns inland to Lake Quinault. The isolation suits most visitors. The beach here is more rugged and picturesque than farther south: cliffs line the beach, and a few rocky tide pools sit at tide line. Along Hwy 109, between Moclips and the development at Ocean Shores, are a number of desultory beach towns and beach access points. The farther south you go, the busier and more developed it gets.

Places to Stay & Eat
Pacific Beach State Park (☎ 360-289-3553) on Hwy 109, 2 miles south of Moclips at Pacific Beach, offers 118 tent sites ($10) and 20 RV sites with hookups ($15). There's no

vehicle access to the beach at this park, which means that you'll usually find more people than pickups crossing the sand.

Moclips has a couple of fairly basic oceanfront motels and one charming resort. The best of the motels is the *Hi-Tide Ocean Beach Resort* (☎ 360-276-4142), 4890 Railroad Ave, which offers new condo-type units above the mouth of the Moclips River. Rates are $84/94 single/double.

For something special, go to the *Ocean Crest Resort* (☎ 360-276-4465), at Sunset Beach, 1 mile south of Moclips off Hwy 109; this is the nicest place to stay along this stretch of coast. There are a number of lodging options, ranging from studio apartments to two-bedroom suites. All rooms in this rambling complex have cable TV and maid service; kitchenettes and fireplaces are also available. There is a two-night minimum stay on weekends. In addition to the handsome rooms, there's a heated indoor pool, a sauna and an exercise room. The restaurant is noted for its outstanding food – steak and seafood – and for its long views of the Pacific shore. The upstairs lounge is a great place for a snug drink while watching for whales. The resort has private beach access down a winding, wooded path. Rooms range from $56 to $123; in the off season, the resort offers three nights for the price of two. Call for other specials.

There are no other restaurants in the area, but there's a small market in town.

OCEAN SHORES
Population 3019

Ocean Shores is what's left of a huge development gone bust. In the 1960s, developers divided 9 sq miles of this land into lots in anticipation of a land rush. Four-lane roads and an airport went in, but the boom never happened and after a decade the company went bankrupt.

The moral of the story is that it's hard to make a real estate boom out of the most characterless beach in the entire Northwest. The views from this finger of land north of the mouth of Grays Harbor are limited to mile after mile of marshy coastal plains covered with scrubby pines and beach grass, with houses stuck here and there.

However, these aesthetic considerations don't stop Ocean Shores from being a major beach resort. People come for the sandy beaches, and there are certainly a lot of them. They double as sand-lot speedways, so watch out for revved-up pickups careening along the shoreline. There are also many motels and beach-type concessions near the 'gates' to Ocean Shores. A bit farther south some quite upscale resorts face onto the Pacific. From the marina, a summer-only car ferry crosses over to Westport, across Grays Harbor.

Orientation & Information
Ocean Shores is on Hwy 115, 18 miles west of Hoquiam on Hwy 109. For more information, contact the Ocean Shores Chamber of Commerce (☎ 360-289-2451, 800-762-3224), in the Catala Mall, 899 Point Brown Ave, which is the main street in Ocean Shores.

Places to Stay & Eat
Ocean Shores Visitors Center offers a reservation service (☎ 800-562-8612) to the many motels and campgrounds lining the beach.

For camping, go to *Ocean City State Park* (☎ 360-289-3553), 148 Hwy 115, which offers almost 200 campsites (from $10 to $15) right on the beach.

Following are a couple of dandy motels in Ocean Shores, but there are dozens of others. *Gitchee Gumee Motel* (☎ 360-289-3323, 800-448-2433) has kitchens in non-smoking and pet-friendly units, and indoor and outdoor swimming pools. Rooms in the high season begin at $55. The *Polynesian Condominium Resort* (☎ 360-289-3361, 800-562-4836) has a variety of room types, from motel rooms ($69 and up) to a three-bedroom penthouse ($104). Most rooms have balconies and kitchen facilities. There's also an indoor pool and exercise room. Children under 12 are free. *Mariah's Restaurant*, in the complex, is one of the better places to eat in Ocean Shores.

However, you'll be disappointed if you expect to find fine cuisine at Ocean Shores. Be happy that the *Home Port Restaurant* (☎ 360-289-2600), 857 Point Brown Ave, offers chowders, steak, seafood and a salad bar. If you were far-sighted enough to get a kitchen motel unit, then head to *Mike's Seafood* (☎ 360-289-0532), 830 Point Brown Ave, to buy a crab or some razor clams.

Southwestern Washington

Separated from the rest of the Pacific Northwest by deep forests, I-5 and the Columbia River, southwestern Washington is an isolated network of mountains, bays and sandy peninsulas that contains some of the state's most popular beaches and farm country.

The mouth of the Columbia River is the region's prominent geographical feature, and it is responsible for the local climate as well as for most of the area's history. The great river is over 7 miles wide when it reaches the Pacific Ocean at Cape Disappointment, its valley forming a trough between Oregon's Coast Range and the Olympic Mountains farther north. Through this gap in the coastal mountains, the clouds, rain and winds of the Pacific flow unhindered, spreading far inland, creating one of the mildest climates in the continental USA. Summers are cool, and winters are wet but not cold. The frequent fog and rain (up to 100 inches yearly) favor dense forests and dairy farms.

The Columbia River, a great navigational thoroughfare, attracted the first white settlers to this region and is home to Longview, one of the largest timber ports in the world. The old-growth forests of southwestern Washington once rivaled those of the Olympic Peninsula, but they fell to the logger early because of easy access to the river. Once prominent salmon-fishing ports at the mouth of the Columbia River and at Grays Harbor have declined along with the salmon, though Westport is still a center for Northwest charter fishing.

In the late 18th century, American and European traders arrived and established long-standing trade relationships with the native Chinook tribes along the river and at Grays Harbor. Lewis and Clark tarried here as well, partaking of Chinook hospitality during the hard winter of 1805. Access to the Columbia River's trade routes was important to the Hudson's Bay Company, which established Fort Vancouver across from the confluence of the Willamette River in 1824. This fur-trading outpost was the first real settlement in the Pacific Northwest, and it became the unwitting nucleus of pioneer migration.

The Columbia River is also responsible for the 28 miles of beaches along the Long Beach Peninsula and for those at Grayland, as its mighty burden of sediment flows out into the Pacific and is swept northward by currents, dumping its sand. Protected by this spit of land, the shoals and backwaters of Willapa Bay are perfect for raising oysters, and this remote corner of Washington is one of the most famed oyster-raising areas in the USA.

Orientation

I-5 runs along the Columbia and Cowlitz Rivers as it threads its way between Portland and Seattle. Between this transportation corridor and the Pacific Ocean runs Hwy 4, which continues to parallel the Columbia from Longview, and Hwy 6, which links Chehalis and Raymond. Both are slow roads that pass lots of clear-cuts and low mountains. This remoteness means that the western parts of this region, in particular the Long Beach Peninsula, are more accessible from Oregon than from the rest of Washington, and historically, Oregonians have played a large role in developing the area as a beach resort. From the south, the quickest access to Long Beach is on Oregon's US 30, crossing the Columbia at Astoria.

CENTRALIA & CHEHALIS

These two old farm and mill communities lodged between logged-off hills on the upper Chehalis River were once separated by 5 miles of fields, but they have practically grown together to form a single elongated town. While Centralia (population 13,480)

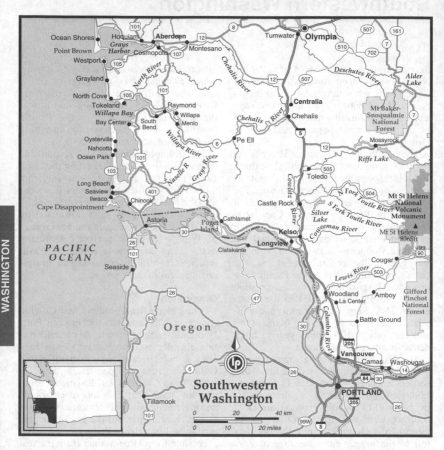

and Chehalis (population 7035) each boasts a historic red-brick center oriented to the railroad tracks, they both also have new business districts strung alongside I-5.

There's more here than meets the eye: Centralia has established a new-found reputation as a shopping destination. There are dozens of factory outlets, shops and discount malls just west of exit 82, and the old downtown is packed with excellent antique malls. It that isn't enough to lure you off the freeway for a break (these towns are exactly half-way between Seattle and Portland, 84 miles either direction), then consider stopping at one of the

region's most historic and charming brewpubs, the Olympic Club. Chehalis is more down on its luck; besides the county museum, there's little here that will beguile the traveler.

Centralia has the honor of being the only community in the Northwest founded by an African American. A former slave, George Washington was born in Virginia, but moved out West from Missouri with the family who first owned him and then freed and adopted him. Washington was able to establish a land claim in 1852 near the Chehalis River, which now includes most of downtown Centralia.

Orientation & Information

Both Centralia and Chehalis are a little odd to navigate for first-time visitors. In Chehalis, be prepared for a seemingly gratuitous one-way system and oddly angled streets; the principal street is called Market St. In Centralia, be prepared for an address numbering system that doesn't follow the numbered streets. Addresses are numbered from Main St; 1st St is actually the 700 block, as far as addresses go.

For more information about the area, contact Tourism Lewis County (☎ 360-525-3323, 800-525-3323), at 500 NW Chamber of Commerce Way, Chehalis, WA 98532.

Lewis County Historical Museum

The Lewis County Historical Museum (☎ 360-748-0831), 599 NW Front St, in the old railway depot in Chehalis, offers a wide perspective on the sometimes violent his-

WASHINGTON

The Centralia Massacre

By the 1900s, Centralia and Chehalis were both boomtowns, with logging, mining and farming in the ascendancy. Since both pay and working conditions in the logging and mining camps were poor, several unions quickly took root, the dominant one being the Chicago-based International Workers of the World, known as the IWW or the 'Wobblies.' The IWW subscribed to revolutionary goals like a single worldwide union and a worker takeover of production, which was to be achieved by class

From the IWW paper, *Industrial Worker*, Dec 26, 1912

warfare and armed resistance to the forces of capitalist oppression. However, the IWW also spoke out against US involvement in World War I, favoring pacifism.

In Centralia, the IWW enjoyed support from the working classes; but during WWI, the union's practice of labor slowdowns and strikes angered many who felt that such labor agitations were unpatriotic during wartime.

In 1919, after the return of local soldiers from Europe, the American Legion held an Armistice Day parade to honor the returned veterans. As they had in the past, the Legionnaires boasted of their intent to raid the IWW union hall, but this time the IWW intended to meet fire with fire.

A group of armed veterans assembled in front of the IWW union hall and rushed the building in a raid. Armed IWW supporters then fired into the crowd, killing three Legionnaires; a fourth was killed in a later skirmish. In the melée, most of the IWW assailants escaped, though one, Wesley Everest, was apprehended after a long chase.

Not knowing who had fired the fatal shots, law enforcement rounded up the local leaders of the IWW and jailed them. That night, vigilante Legionnaires broke into the jail and abducted Everest. The next day, he was found beaten, castrated and shot, hanging from a railway bridge. His body was brought back to the jail and put on display in front of the remaining IWW members.

Nine IWW members were tried, found guilty of first-degree murder and sentenced to lengthy jail terms. No investigation or charges ever followed the death of Everest.

The IWW union hall still stands at 807 N Tower St, and the Lewis County Museum has a good exhibit of the documents and history of this traumatic incident, a seminal chapter in the history of the US labor movement. ■

tory of the area. In addition to the usual re-creation of a frontier school room, kitchen and doctor's office, there are baskets and artifacts from the local Chehalis tribe, vintage logging equipment and displays relating to George Washington's founding of Centralia. The central exhibit deals with the so-called Centralia Massacre. The museum does a good job of presenting the case from all points of view. However, most of the exhibits are lengthy documents and texts that have to be read, so plan to spend some time if you want to take in this exhibit.

The museum is open 9 am to 5 pm Tuesday to Saturday and 1 to 5 pm on Sunday. Admission is $2/1.50 adults/seniors and $1 for children; families $5.

Places to Stay

Camping Two nice state parks are within an easy drive of Centralia and Chehalis. *Lewis & Clark State Park* (☎ 360-864-2643) contains a magnificent stand of old-growth forest. To reach the park, drive 10 miles south of Chehalis on I-5 and take US 12 east for 2¹/₂ miles. Turn south onto Jackson Hwy, which leads immediately to the park. *Rainbow Falls State Park* (☎ 360-291-3767) is on the Chehalis River, 17 miles west of Chehalis on Hwy 6. Facilities at both parks include running water, flush toilets, picnic areas and hiking trails; campsites are $15 RV, $10 tent.

B&Bs Like many Northwest towns, Centralia and Chehalis have their share of grand old homes built by early logging barons and industrialists. The *Candalite Mansion B&B* (☎ 360-736-4749, 800-489-4749), 402 N Rock St in Centralia, is a 1903 mansion with six guest rooms, some of which have private bathrooms. Rooms are $50 to $65.

Hotels There are a number of inexpensive motels off I-5 exit 82 in Centralia, convenient to the factory outlet stores. The *Park Motel* (☎ 360-736-9333), 1011 Belmont, has single/double rooms for $32/42. At the *Centralia Days Inn* (☎ 360-736-2875), 702

W Harrison Ave, there's an outdoor pool and free continental breakfast. Rooms are $54/64. The *Ferryman's Inn* (☎ 360-330-2094), 1003 Eckerson Rd, offers a pool, hot tub, guest laundry and continental breakfast. Rates are $45/51.

If you want to stay in Chehalis, head to the *Relax Inn* (☎ 360-748-8608), 550 SW Parkland Drive, off I-5 exit 76, where rooms are $39/50.

Places to Eat

There's a concentration of fast-food and chain restaurants near the outlet stores at I-5 exit 82. If you head into town to go antique shopping, stop off at the *Berry Fields Cafe* (☎ 360-736-1183), in the Centralia Square Antique Mall at 201 S Pearl St, for soup, sandwiches and light entrées. In Chehalis, go to *Sweet Inspirations* (☎ 360-748-7102), 514 N Market Blvd, which serves lunchtime sandwiches and light meals at a refurbished soda fountain.

Only slightly more expensive is much-beloved *Mary McCranks* (☎ 360-748-3662), 4 miles south of Chehalis on Jackson Hwy. This old-fashioned dinner house has been serving up tasty, home-style cooking since the 1930s – so long, in fact, that its traditional menu of chicken and dumplings, steak and gravy, and the like, has come back into style as regional cooking.

For a piece of history and a pint of ale, be sure to stop at the *Olympic Club* (☎ 360-736-5164), 112 N Tower Ave. This fantastic old bar and cafe dates from the 1910s; when Portland brewers, the McMenamins, took over the club in 1996, they retained the leaded-glass windows, mahogany backbar, handmade Tiffany lampshades and sky-lights, and the art deco murals. It's a fantastic place for lunch or dinner; the Olympic alone justifies a stop in Centralia.

Getting There & Away

Greyhound buses stop five times daily both north- and southbound between Portland and Seattle at the depot (☎ 360-736-9810), 1232 Mellen St in Centralia; the one-way fare from either city is $18. Amtrak stops at the station on Railway Ave at W Maple St, in downtown Centralia.

Lower Columbia River

Near Portland, the Columbia River picks up the waters of the Willamette River and turns north to catch the waters of the Lewis and Cowlitz Rivers. Downstream from Longview, the river cuts west again, becoming truly enormous. Steep hills and cliffs line the Columbia River, islands and shoals slow the current, and the river continually widens until, near Grays Bay, it occupies a channel over 7 miles across.

Throughout most of the history of the Northwest, the Columbia River has been one of the region's principal avenues of entrance and exploration. Historic villages and military forts line its shores, and enormous ships still ply the river, headed from Portland or Longview to ports around the world. While many of the Washington towns along the Columbia River are industrial and don't offer much for the traveler, others retain the charm of small fishing ports. Hwy 4 from Longview to the Long Beach Peninsula clings to the cliffs along the river and offers dramatic views of wooded islands and the green, deforested hills of Oregon.

History

Chinook villages once stretched along the northern bank of the Columbia River. Because the lower Columbia was the crossroads for the transportation of goods north and south, as well as east to the Native American trade center at Celilo Falls, the Chinook became one of the most prominent mercantile tribes in the Northwest.

The area where the fast-moving waters of the Columbia meets the roiling surf of the Pacific is called the Columbia Bar, and it is a notoriously treacherous crossing for ships. The first of the white explorers to penetrate from the Pacific Ocean across the

bar and up the Columbia River was the American Robert Gray in 1792, closely followed by various British explorers. For the next decade, trade flourished between the Chinook and other tribes along the northern Pacific Coast and the British and US traders. Chinook women took the lead in these trading ventures, which elevated them to dominant positions within the tribe.

When Lewis and Clark arrived at the mouth of the Columbia in 1805, they initially worked their way up the Washington side of the river in a dismal winter storm so unsparing that the captains recorded heavy rainfall and gales for 31 days in a row. The US party traded with the Chinooks before crossing over to Oregon.

Disease decimated the Chinook population as contact with whites increased, leaving the mouth of the Columbia River open to settlement. Ilwaco was the first encampment along the river. Founded in the 1840s, it became the transportation link between the river steamers, ocean-going riggers and the new-born communities of Willapa Bay. Soon the Civil War brought fortifications to the mouth of the river. Fort Canby was established in 1852 and quickly upgraded to prevent Confederate gunboats from entering the river. Later in the century, Fort Columbia was established nearby to provide further protection to Columbia River ports.

As better shipping and rail links provided a market for Northwest products in the 1880s, industrial fishing and canning of salmon became the dominant trade of Ilwaco and the town of Chinook. At its peak, 34 fish-canning operations lined the waterfront of the lower Columbia towns.

VANCOUVER
Population 59,982

Vancouver (and much of quickly-urbanizing Clark County) is immediately across the Columbia River from Portland and it is best thought of as a suburb of Oregon's largest city. As anyone who has tried to get across the bridges during rush hour can testify, a *lot* of people commute

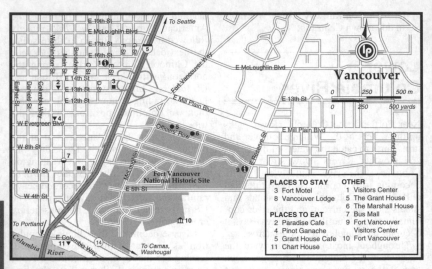

E 19th St
E McLoughlin Blvd
E 17th St
E 16th St
To Seattle
Washington
Broadway
Main St
Esther St
Daniels St
Columbia Way
E 14th St
E 13th St
E 12th St
W Evergreen Blvd
W 8th St
W 6th St
W 4th St
To Portland
Columbia River
E Columbia Way
E McLoughlin Blvd
Fort Vancouver Way
E Mill Plain Blvd
Officers' Row
Fort Vancouver
National Historic Site
E 5th St
Vancouver
E 13th St
E Mill Plain Blvd
Reserve St
Grand Blvd
To Camas,
Washougal

0   250   500 m
0   250   500 yards

PLACES TO STAY
3 Fort Motel
8 Vancouver Lodge

PLACES TO EAT
2 Paradise Cafe
4 Pinot Ganache
5 Grant House Cafe
11 Chart House

OTHER
1 Visitors Center
5 The Grant House
6 The Marshall House
7 Bus Mall
9 Fort Vancouver
   Visitors Center
10 Fort Vancouver

between homes in southwest Washington and jobs or shopping in Portland. The reason for this border jumping is partly due to the two states' tax codes: Oregon doesn't have a sales tax and Washington has a marginal property tax. With a little ambition, the savvy local can do a little more driving and pay a little (or a lot) less tax.

Present-day Vancouver is a fairly drab place, despite the fact that it is the oldest settlement in the Pacific Northwest and is currently one of the fastest-growing areas of Washington State. Vancouver's major appeal to travelers is reconstructed Fort Vancouver, the old Hudson's Bay Company trading post. The adjoining US Army's Officers' Row is also a lovely place for a stroll. However, most travelers will find dining, lodging and nightlife options more appealing in nearby Portland.

Orientation

Vancouver is on the northern bank of the Columbia River, not far from the confluence of the Willamette River. Vancouver is 164 miles from Seattle on I-5, but only 8 from downtown Portland across the I-5 Bridge. A second freeway, I-205, leaves

I-5 just northeast of Vancouver and links eastern Vancouver communities with east Portland, Portland International Airport (PDX), and I-84 eastbound (which runs along the north side of the river) before it rejoins I-5 south of Portland. Hwy 14 follows the north bank of the river, joining the two freeways and continuing east to Camas, Washougal and the Columbia River Gorge.

Downtown Vancouver is directly west of I-5. The principal streets through downtown are Main St and Broadway, which parallel I-5.

Information

For information about the Vancouver area, contact the Vancouver/Clark County Visitors & Convention Services (☎ 360-693-1313, 800-377-7084), 404 E 15th St, suite 11, Vancouver, WA 98663.

The headquarters for the Gifford-Pinchot National Forest (☎ 360-750-5000), which administers most of the forests in southwestern Washington, is at 6926 E Fourth Plain Blvd. This is a good place to pick up maps and get information on hiking and camping in the public lands of the Gifford Pinchot.

WASHINGTON

The post office is at 2700 Caples Ave. For clean clothes and that just-tanned look, go to Wash 'n Tan (☎ 360-693-2954) at the corner of Fourth Plain Blvd and Kauffman St. It has drop-off service, dry cleaning and tanning booths. The Southwest Washington Medical Center (☎ 360-256-2000) is at 3400 Main St.

Fort Vancouver

Administered by the NPS, the reconstruction of Fort Vancouver (☎ 360-696-7655), the Hudson's Bay Company trading post, is an engaging stop for families or anyone curious about Northwest history. A living history program with instructive docents in period costume, an interpretive center and museum, and the buildings and stockaded grounds provide a vital insight into life on the Pacific frontier. Even if you're just looking for a place to park the car and stretch your legs or have a picnic, this is a good stop: between the old parade grounds, Officers' Row and the fort area is a major green space with lovely trees and manicured lawns.

Fort Vancouver National Historic Site

In 1948, archaeologists began to excavate the site of old Fort Vancouver. With contemporary drawings and material gleaned from the site, they reconstructed several portions, with other buildings slated for reconstruction. A 15-foot-high stockade with a three-story corner turret encloses an area of roughly 700 by 300 feet. Inside the stockade are reconstructions of the Chief Factor's residence, bakery, foundry, trade shop, kitchen and other buildings. Children will enjoy climbing up into the bastion for views of the fort, the Columbia River and Mt Hood.

The reconstructed fort is open 9 am to 5 pm daily from Memorial Day to Labor Day, and 9 am to 4 pm the rest of the year. Tours leave on the hour and group tours can be booked on the half-hour. Call ☎ 360-696-7655 to schedule. Interpreters in period dress present daily cultural demonstrations in the fort's kitchen, and also in the forge from Thursday to Monday.

Other demonstrations are available on summer weekends. Entrance fees for adults/families are $2/4; children under 16 are free. The visitors' center, on E Reserve St, is free and features a small museum, gift shop and interpretive information, including a 15-minute film.

Officers' Row On the north side of E Evergreen Blvd and the old parade grounds is Officers' Row, a park-like boulevard of historic and glamorous officers' homes built between 1850 and 1906 by the US Army. These handsome buildings are owned by the city of Vancouver and are rented out as offices and apartments. Two of the buildings are open to the public. The **Grant House** (☎ 360-694-5252), 1101 Officers' Row, is the oldest – built in 1850 from logs and later covered with clapboard – and it now houses a cafe and the Grant House Folk Art Center, a small exhibition space and gallery. The **Marshall House**, built in 1886 and home to General George Marshall in the 1930s, is a grand, Queen Anne-style mansion. Tours are available; call ☎ 360-693-3103 for schedules.

Places to Stay

Although Vancouver is a fairly large city – it's Washington's fourth-largest metropolitan area – most people visit it as a side trip from Portland. If you want to stay north of the Columbia River, Vancouver offers a couple of inexpensive lodging options, though both back up to the freeway. The *Fort Motel* (☎ 360-694-3327), 500 E 13th St, is in downtown Vancouver and is convenient to tours at its namesake Fort Vancouver. The *Vancouver Lodge* (☎ 360-693-3668), 601 Broadway, is also downtown. Both offer kitchenettes and non smoking rooms and take pets; singles/doubles at each place start at $40/48.

Places to Eat

Restaurants in Vancouver offer a bit more of a selection. *Paradise Cafe* (☎ 360-696-1612), 1304 Main St, is an espresso bar with a good selection of pastries, salads and light entrées for lunch. You can experience

Fort Vancouver: On the Edge of the Frontier

Fort Vancouver was founded in 1824 as the British administrative headquarters and principal trading post in the Oregon Country, which then included all of present-day Oregon, Washington, Idaho and parts of Montana and British Columbia. The stockaded fort – which did not serve a military function – was also the center of civilized life in the region, and saw the Northwest's first farms, dairy operations, orchards, saw mills, foundries, hospital and commercial bakery.

The Hudson's Bay Company (HBC) employed its own trappers to trap beaver, mink, otter and wolf, among other animals, and traded with Native American hunters for furs. The principal items of trade included blankets, glass beads and fabric, all produced in Europe. The local smithy, bakery, farms and gardens soon created other items for trade and sale, mainly to other HBC forts and to the increasing number of Americans settling in Oregon.

Life at Fort Vancouver was conducted with a great deal of civility. Dr John McLoughlin, a Scots-Canadian physician, was the chief factor (or presiding officer), and he and his Iroquois wife lived in a large, white clapboard home with all the niceties and elegance of a contemporary home in Boston or Britain. There were separate dining rooms for male guests and for their wives. Employees lived in barracks within the stockade, while the substantial numbers of hangers-on – farmers, day laborers and Indian traders – lived outside the barricade.

Farms spread out for 20 miles along the flat Columbia flood plane, extending 10 miles inland from the river. At its height, the population of the fort and environs reached about 1000 inhabitants.

When pioneers arrived at the end of the Oregon Trail in the early 1840s, most were penniless, hungry and facing a long dreary winter. For reasons that are at best conjectural, McLoughlin seemed attracted to the American pioneers, and he welcomed them to Fort Vancouver where – despite strict HBC regulations to the contrary – he extended them credit, sold them seed grain and livestock, and helped them settle along the Willamette River.

McLoughlin's generosity eventually landed him in trouble with his superiors. When Britain ceded the Oregon Country to the USA in 1846, eventually moving the HBC headquarters to Fort Victoria in British Columbia, McLoughlin was relieved of his duties. He chose to stay in US territory and moved to Oregon City.

Fort Vancouver remained an HBC property until 1860, although the heyday of the fur trade was long over. Much of the fort burned down in 1863. Meanwhile, the US Army established an adjacent garrison called Vancouver Barracks, and in time this served as the military headquarters for the army's Department of the Columbia. The clapboard barracks along the current parade grounds and the beautiful homes along Officers' Row date largely from the 1870s and '80s, though the Vancouver Barracks remained in military operation through both world wars. The Vancouver Barracks were decommissioned in 1947. ■

the splendor of old Officers' Row if you eat at the *Grant House Cafe* (☎ 360-699-1213), 1101 Officers' Row. For weekday lunches, salads and sandwiches are offered, while on Thursday to Sunday night the restaurant is open for dinner with a menu offering steak, lamb and seafood à la Northwest ($12 to $15). Trendy *Pinot Ganache* (☎ 360-695-7786), 1004 Washington St, offers a wide

variety of dishes in a busy bistro atmosphere. One of Vancouver's most popular places to eat is right on the banks of the Columbia River.

Although the food at the *Chart House* (☎ 360-693-9211), 101 E Columbia Way, doesn't involve any surprises – they offer the basic chicken, pasta and steak – on a warm evening this is a great place to enjoy a drink or dinner on the waterside deck and watch the sunset.

Shopping

Most of the woolen products from the renowned Pendleton Woolen Mill are made not in Pendleton but in Washougal, 16 miles east of Vancouver on Hwy 14. Free tours of the mill (☎ 360-835-2131), at 2 17th St in Washougal, are offered at 9, 10 and 11 am, and 1:30 pm weekdays. The outlet store here sells fabric, clothing and blankets at substantial discounts.

Getting There & Around

Vancouver's public transport system is called C-Tran (☎ 360-695-0123), and it offers service throughout Clark County. Bus Nos 5, 14 and 134 travel along I-5 to Portland. The downtown bus mall is along 7th St between Broadway and Washington St.

LONGVIEW & KELSO

After driving through the mossy woods along the Cowlitz or Lewis Rivers, or coming in from the west along the Columbia River, it's a little surprising to come upon Longview (population 33,767) and its twin, Kelso (population 12,226). These thoroughly industrial small towns are at the westward turn of the Columbia, where it meets the Cowlitz River.

Longview was founded as a planned community – one of the first in the American West – for employees of the Long-Bell Lumber Company, which built a huge mill here in 1924. The town was laid out in a series of concentric rings, through which meanders an artificial lake and a park. Take a walk along Broadway St or through Sacajawea Park to get a sense of the grand aspirations of Longview's civic planners.

Longview is where the majority of the logs cut from the southwest Washington forests go to be milled and shipped overseas. Despite attempts to ban the shipping of raw logs from Northwest forests (in order to keep mill jobs stateside), nearly two million tons of logs leave the port of Longview each year, bound mostly for Japan. Cross Longview's high-arching bridge over the Columbia River and look down to see acres and acres of unmilled logs awaiting export.

There's little here to divert the modern traveler, save convenient hotels and refueling needs.

If you're driving I-5, you'll note huge piles of white soil overgrown with gorse along the Cowlitz River near Castle Rock. These immense dikes are composed of volcanic dust from Mt St Helens which was dredged from the Toutle and Cowlitz Rivers shortly after the volcano erupted in 1980.

Places to Stay & Eat

There are a number of motels in Kelso, just off I-5 exit 39. Convenient to the freeway is the new *Comfort Inn* (☎ 360-425-4600), 440 Three Rivers Drive, with indoor pool, spa and free continental breakfast. Rooms are $65/70 for a single/double. The *Best Western Aladdin Motor Inn* (☎ 360-425-9660, 800-764-7378), 310 Long Ave, has kitchen units, a pool, restaurant and lounge; rates are $58/68.

The inevitable and easily-spotted fast-food emporiums are also near the freeway. For something more interesting, head into Longview proper. For coffee, soup and sandwiches, stop by the *Bookshop Cafe* (☎ 360-425-8707), 1203 14th Ave. For the area's best meal, head to *Henri's* (☎ 360-425-7970), 4545 Ocean Beach Hwy, on Hwy 4 toward Cathlamet. The steak, seafood and lamb dishes ($12 to $16) are meant to be continental, but in this blue collar town, portion size matters more than refinement.

CATHLAMET

Population 536

The old logging and fishing town of Cathlamet occupies a position above the Columbia River and Puget Island, a low-lying agricultural island dedicated to dairy farms. The little-changed downtown area is a pleasant stop for travelers looking for a break from the persistent curves of Hwy 4. The harbor is usually filled with pleasure boats, whose crews tie up here to enjoy the tranquillity and historic atmosphere.

Cathlamet was originally the site of a Chinook village. The first white settler arrived in 1846 and the town prospered early as a salmon-packing center, then boomed in the 1910s as a logging and mill town. Not much has changed the handsome, red-brick center of town since these heydays.

A bridge leads from Cathlamet to Puget Island, the largest island in the Columbia River. This flat, rural island is popular with cyclists. Follow Hwy 409 across the island and take a car ferry – the last on the lower Columbia – to Oregon (see Getting There & Away).

Cathlamet is 26 miles west of Longview and Kelso on Hwy 4; from Cathlamet, it's 40 miles to Long Beach.

Places to Stay & Eat
If you're looking for a quiet retreat, consider the *Bradley House Country Keeper B&B* (☎ 360-795-3030), 61 Main St, a 1907 mansion that once served as the county library. The four guest rooms (two with private bathrooms) are filled with antiques; rooms range from $65 to $95. Some of the cheapest rooms hereabout are at *Nassa Point Motel* (☎ 360-795-3941), 3 miles east of Cathlamet on Hwy 4. With the Columbia River practically in the front yard, this is a popular stop for anglers, windsurfers and boaters. Rooms start at $35 a night.

There are several homey cafes in Cathlamet, and the best of the lot is *Birnie's Retreat* (☎ 360-795-3432), 88 Main St. It's open for three meals a day, and it offers a selection of seafood and Cajun dishes at dinner.

Getting There & Away
Car Ferries (☎ 360-849-4277) cross the Columbia River between Westport, OR, and Puget Island, along the Columbia's north bank. The ferry leaves from Puget Island on the hour, and from Westport at 15 minutes after the hour. The fare is $2 for a car and driver, 50¢ per additional passenger,

and $1 per cyclist or foot passenger. The passage takes 15 minutes.

CHINOOK
The small town of Chinook is named for the Native American tribe whose villages once lined these shores, but the community might well have been named for the Chinook salmon. By the 1880s, Chinook was one of the region's major fish-canning centers, and this affluence is easily seen in the handsome turn-of-the-century fishermen's homes and the false-fronted downtown.

Chinook is still an active fishing port, but most travelers will remember Chinook for its HI/AYH hostel, one of the few along the northwest Pacific Coast. Chinook is 5 miles west of the base of the Astoria Bridge on US 101 and 9 miles southeast of Long Beach.

Fort Columbia State Park
Fort Columbia State Park (☎ 360-642-3078), on a rocky bluff above the Columbia River 1 mile south of Chinook, is a well-preserved military fort built between 1898 and 1905 during the Spanish-American War. Although the fort maintained its defensive purpose through WWII, it was demilitarized shortly thereafter.

The fort is largely unchanged from the glory days of 1900, with the barracks now serving as an **interpretive center** and **museum**. Other buildings open to the public include **Columbia House,** the commanding officer's residence. The old hospital is now operated as a hostel. Trails lead to cement artillery fortifications and batteries, which once housed guns that protected shipping channels on the Columbia River.

Park hours are 8 am to dusk daily, from May 15 to October 1; it's closed Monday and Tuesday the rest of the year. The interpretive center is open from 10 am to 5 pm Wednesday to Sunday, May through October, and 10 am to 4 pm the rest of the year; admission is free.

Places to Stay & Eat
Fort Columbia Hostel (☎ 360-777-8755) in Fort Columbia State Park is 1 mile south of

Chinook on US 101. The hostel offers a fully-equipped kitchen, an all-you-can-eat pancake breakfast for 50¢, and a combination of family and dorm-style rooms in the fort's old hospital. Facilities include a game room, lounge area and fireplace, and there are hiking trails nearby. Rates are $8 for HI/AYH members, $13 for non-members.

Chinook's most noted restaurant, and in fact a favorite throughout the Northwest, is *The Sanctuary* (☎ 360-777-8380), US 101 at Hazel St. In an old Methodist church built in 1906, the Sanctuary prepares local seafood, steak and pasta ($10 to $17) in an eclectic multi-ethnic manner that's always interesting and often excellent. Pizza is available in the Sanctuary's Garden Annex.

ILWACO
Population 848

The major fishing port on Washington's southern coast, Ilwaco still bustles with charter and commercial fishing. The early growth of the salmon-canning industry here was aided by the development of salmon traps, a method of catching the fish that was made illegal in the 1930s.

Unlike the flat Long Beach Peninsula that stretches to the north from here, Ilwaco is hemmed in by rocky hills. West of town, on a rugged promontory above the mouth of the Columbia River, are the remains of Fort Canby, a Civil War-era military fort that was designed to protect Columbia River shipping from Confederate interference. After WWII, part of the fort's land passed into the hands of the state, which dedicated it to the city as a park.

Fort Canby State Park

Although little remains of the original fort, this state park (☎ 360-642-3078) is of considerable interest because of its interpretive center, nice beach area and hiking trails to dramatic lighthouses.

Established in 1852, Fort Canby wasn't heavily fortified until the 1860s, during the Civil War. The fort was upgraded dramatically during WWII, when it and Fort Stephens on the Oregon side of the Columbia River stood as the principal

defenders of the river from enemy infiltration. The mouth of the Columbia River was webbed with mines during the war. Although no shots were fired from Fort Canby, a Japanese submarine did manage to penetrate close enough to the Oregon side to fire on Fort Stephens in 1942.

Lewis and Clark camped near here in 1805 and climbed up onto the bluff for their first real glimpse of the Pacific Ocean. The **Lewis & Clark Interpretive Center** offers a timeline of their entire journey that discusses the reasons for the expedition, followed by a retelling of their adventure with diary entries, mementos and illustrations. A multimedia theater shows short films about the journey. The center also documents the history of navigation on the Columbia, focusing on the dangerous Columbia bar, seen from the building's expanse of windows. It's open 10 am to 5 pm daily, and donations are appreciated.

From the interpretive center, a hiking trail leads 1.8 miles to **Cape Disappointment Lighthouse**. On a steep bluff above the Columbia, the lighthouse was built in 1856, the first lighthouse in the Northwest. A second lighthouse, **North Head Lighthouse**, is off the park's main access road and is accessed by a short hiking trail from the parking area. Neither lighthouse is open for tours.

Waikiki Beach is immediately south of the camping area, or it can be reached by turning west on Jetty Rd. Continue on this road until you reach the end of the riprap jetty, a half-mile-long rock spit that extends out into the Pacific.

Fort Canby State Park is open daily, with no admission charged for day-use areas. See Places to Stay & Eat for camping information. To reach Fort Canby, follow US 101 through Ilwaco and turn onto Robert Gray Drive at the flashing light. The interpretive center is 3^1/$_2$ miles south of the intersection.

Ilwaco Heritage Museum

Ilwaco's maritime past is on display in this good regional museum (☎ 360-642-3446), 115 SE Lake St. There are displays on the

WASHINGTON

local Chinook, and other exhibits explain the history of the local cranberry and logging industries. A toy-sized version of the old Clamshell Railway that ran from Ilwaco to Nahcotta in the late 1880s still runs on a 50-foot scale model of the Long Beach Peninsula in the line's old former depot, also a part of the museum. The museum is open 9 am to 5 pm Monday through Saturday, and 10 am to 4 pm on Sunday, Memorial Day through Labor Day. The rest of the year it's open 10 am to 4 pm Monday to Saturday, and 10 am to 2 pm on Sunday. Admission is $2/1.75 for adults/seniors and 75¢ for children.

Charter Fishing

Ilwaco has plenty of charter-fishing options, including salmon (during season), sturgeon, tuna and bottom fish. Contact one of the following for prices and packages, or contact the Long Beach Peninsula Chamber of Commerce (☎ 360-642-3145, 800-642-2400) for a full listing of outfitters. Sea Breeze Charters (☎ 360-642-2300), Beacon Charters (☎ 360-642-2138) and Ilwaco Charter Service (☎ 360-642-3232) are all along the harbor, off Howerton Ave.

Places to Stay & Eat

Fort Canby State Park (☎ 360-642-3078) has more than 250 campsites with piped water, flush toilets and access to beach recreation. Sites are $10 and $15. *Beacon Charters & RV Park* (☎ 360-642-2138), along the waterfront, has RV sites with showers and some full hookups for $13 to $17.

The *Chick-A-Dee Inn* (☎ 360-642-8686), 122 Williams St NE, on a wooded rise above town, was once the Ilwaco Presbyterian Church but is now a handsome inn with nine guest rooms in the old parsonage and vestry. The church proper is a community arts center. The rooms range from $86 to $116.

Kola House B&B (☎ 360-642-2819), 211 Pearl Ave, has five rooms, one with a fireplace and sauna, and a cabin. There's also a hot tub in the basement. Be sure to book early for the small cabin. Rooms cost $65 to $75.

Heidi's Inn (☎ 360-642-2387), at 126 Spruce St, is a modest but comfortable motel with kitchen units and guest laundry; pets are OK. Single rooms start at $39 and apartment-like kitchenettes at $65, and discounts are offered for midweek or week-long stays. The *Tidewind Cafe* (☎ 360-642-2111) overlooks the harbor off Howerton St, and offers home cooking and breakfast anytime.

Long Beach Peninsula & Willapa Bay

Long Beach Peninsula, the thin sand spit just north of the mouth of the Columbia River, claims to have the world's longest beach. And with 28 unbroken miles of it, the boast has to be taken seriously. However, the beautiful beach is disappointingly adjoined with 28 miles of rather lackluster development, and the beach itself is overrun with pickup trucks (as Washington State beaches are considered highways). Purists might prefer the Willapa Bay side of the peninsula, with its old towns, oyster beds and wildlife viewing.

The beach resorts here have a long pedigree, dating from the 1880s, when Portland families journeyed down the Columbia River by steamboat to summer at the coast. A rail line, referred to as the Clamshell Railway, linked the oyster beds at Nahcotta to boats at Ilwaco in 1888. While the oyster beds on the bay side of the Long Beach Peninsula were the main economic force, the railroad also carried summer holiday-makers to the sandy beaches on the Pacific side of the spit. Soon the beach towns of Seaview and Long Beach sprang up, and across the bay beach resorts at Tokeland and North Cove were established.

Willapa Bay is known to oyster-lovers around the country for the excellent bivalves that grow in this shallow inlet, which is fed by six rivers. The first industry founded here was oyster production, and while logging and dairy farms have each had their day, oyster farming remains the area's major industry.

Getting Around
Pacific Transit System (☎ 360-642-9418) is the local bus company, and it runs buses throughout Pacific County, from Aberdeen and Westport to towns along the Long Beach Peninsula. Pacific buses also run as far south as Astoria, OR.

For a cab on the Long Beach Peninsula, call Beach Cab (☎ 360-642-3905).

LONG BEACH & SEAVIEW
Population 1345
Long Beach and Seaview comprise the major population center on the peninsula. Both began as beach resorts in the late 1880s. A few old inns from this era have been beautifully restored, but most visitors will probably find that much of the area's local charm has been overrun by aggressive commercialization. Hwy 103 stretches out to form the main – and nearly the only – street for both Long Beach and Seaview, and it's lined with the sorts of T-shirt shops, middle-brow boutiques, fast-food mills and bumper-car arenas that somehow always find their way to beach towns. However, the endless beach that brings in multitudes of sunbathers and vacationers during the summer is appealing, if characterless.

Orientation
The Long Beach Peninsula has two main arteries. On the west side of the peninsula is Hwy 103 (also known as Pacific Hwy), which runs from Seaview to Leadbetter Point State Park. On the east, or bay side, an alternative route called Sandridge Rd runs from just east of Seaview to Oysterville. Both of these roads are heavily used and slow going, especially during the high season. Many local access roads cross the peninsula, linking these arterials. Numbered streets north of Bolstad Ave in Long Beach are labeled 'north,' and those south are labeled 'south;' because the communities are so small, few people pay attention to addresses.

From Portland to Long Beach is 126 miles; from Seattle, it's 146 miles.

Information
The Long Beach Peninsula Visitors Bureau (☎ 360-642-2400, 800-451-2542) can be reached at PO Box 562, Long Beach, WA 98631. This office can also help you get reservations for area motels and lodgings. There's a visitors' center at the corner of US 101 and Pacific Hwy (Hwy 103) in Seaview.

The local *Chinook Observer* (☎ 360-642-8181) puts out an excellent annual guide to services, activities and business on the peninsula. Their *Visitor's Guide* is available free at visitors' centers, or get one by mail by sending $2 to the *Chinook Observer*, PO Box 427, Long Beach, WA 98631.

The peninsula's only hospital is Ocean Beach Hospital (☎ 360-642-3181) at 1st and Fir Sts in Ilwaco.

Beaches
Primary beach-access sites in Long Beach are west off 10th St SW and Bolstad Ave. An all-abilities, quarter-mile-long boardwalk links the two access points. In Seaview, the primary public access point is off 38th St. The beach in this area is now closed to vehicles from April 15 to Labor Day weekend. The beach north of Bolstad Ave to Ocean Park is open to vehicles year-round; during razor clam seasons, vehicles are permitted on all beaches.

Remember that surf-swimming here is dangerous and is prohibited along the beach due to strong waves and quickly changing tides.

World Kite Museum & Hall of Fame
Long Beach is noted worldwide for its kite festival, so it was just a matter of time before someone opened a kite museum here (☎ 360-642-4020), at 3rd St and Pacific Hwy. If you think that a museum devoted to the history and artistry of kites might be a bore, think again. Kites have been used for scientific research, aerial photography, mail

WASHINGTON

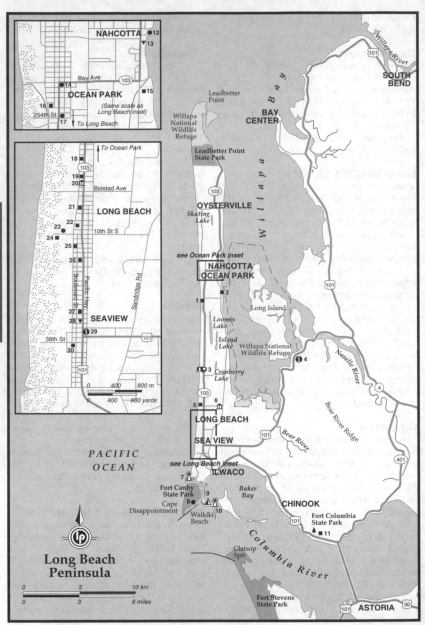

NAHCOTTA

12
13

Bay Ave
103

14

OCEAN PARK
(Same scale as
Long Beach inset)

16
254th St
17
To Long Beach

15

To Ocean Park

18
103
19
20
Bolstad Ave

21
22
LONG BEACH
23
10th St S
24
25
26

Pacific Hwy
Boulevard St

27
28
SEAVIEW
29
38th St
30
101

Sandridge Rd

0   400   800 m
0   400   600 yards

Willapa
River

101

SOUTH
BEND

W i l l a p a   B a y

Leadbetter
Point

Willapa
National
Wildlife
Refuge

Leadbetter Point
State Park

103

OYSTERVILLE

Skating
Lake

see Ocean Park inset

NAHCOTTA
OCEAN PARK

1   2

Loomis
Lake

Island
Lake

3
Cranberry
Lake

103

5   6

LONG BEACH

SEA VIEW

see Long Beach inset

PACIFIC
OCEAN

7
Fort Canby
State Park
8
Cape
Disappointment

9

10
Waikiki
Beach

ILWACO

101

Bear River

BAY
CENTER

W i l l a p a   R i v e r

Long Island

Willapa National
Wildlife Refuge

4

Naselle River

Bear River Ridge

101

4

401

Baker
Bay

CHINOOK

101
Fort Columbia
State Park

11

C o l u m b i a   R i v e r

Clatsop
Spit

Fort Stevens
State Park

101   30

ASTORIA

LP

Long Beach
Peninsula

0   5   10 km
0   3   6 miles

PLACES TO STAY	26 Scandinavian Gardens Inn B&B	7 North Head Lighthouse
1 Klipson Beach Cottages	27 Shelburne Inn	8 Lewis & Clark Interpretive Center
2 Caswell's on the Bay B&B	30 Sou'Wester Lodge	10 Cape Disappointment Lighthouse
3 Anderson's on the Ocean RV Park		12 Willapa Bay Excursions, Willapa Bay Kayak Rental
5 The Breakers	PLACES TO EAT	
9 Fort Canby Campground	13 The Ark	14 Jack's Country Market
11 Fort Columbia Hostel	24 Lightship Restaurant	17 P&K Crab & Seafood Market
15 Moby Dick Hotel	27 Shoalwater Restaurant	
16 Sunset View Resort	28 42nd Street Cafe	20 World Kite Museum & Hall of Fame
18 Boreas B&B		
19 Arcadia Court	OTHER	23 Skippers Horse Rental
21 Shaman Motel	4 Willapa National Wildlife Refuge Headquarters	29 Visitors' Center
22 Boardwalk Cottages		
24 Nendel's Edgewater Inn	6 Cranberry Museum & Gift Shop	
25 Our Place at the Beach		

delivery and reconnaissance – as well as for amusement – for centuries. The whole story's here, along with the largest, smallest and wackiest kites.

The museum is open 11 am to 5 pm daily, from June to August; September and October it's closed Tuesday to Thursday. The rest of the year, it's open 11 am to 4 pm, weekends only. Admission is $1/50¢ adults/children and $3 for families.

Activities
Sports rental outlets are scattered around the various communities on the peninsula. Willapa Bay Excursions (☎ 360-665-4449), 270th St and Sandridge Rd in Nahcotta, rents kayaks and bikes and gives boat tours of the peninsula; they also offer trips around Long Island. A number of outfitters offer **horseback riding** along the beach. Skippers Horse Rental (☎ 360-642-3676) along 10th St S in Long Beach is open year-round.

International Kite Festival
Thousands of people descend on Long Beach each year for the Washington State International Kite Festival, which is billed as the largest kite festival in the western hemisphere. The festival is held during the third week of August and includes participants from all over the world. Events include stunt-kite flying and competitions between individuals and teams.

Each year, festival-goers seek to gain new world records: the greatest number of kites in flight at one time, the largest kite flown, the longest flight time for a kite and so on.

Long Beach is busy during the festival – approximately 150,000 people visit during the week-long event – so make plans early to attend.

Places to Stay
Long Beach and Seaview offer quite a mix of old-fashioned inns, resort condos and cheesy motels. The places listed below are all good choices; for more options, contact the chamber of commerce (☎ 360-642-2400, 800-451-2542), which offers a room-reservation service.

Camping Sites at the following range from $14 to $20. *Anderson's On The Ocean RV Park* (☎ 360-642-2231, 800-645-6795), 3½ miles north of Long Beach on Hwy 103, has 60 hookups with hot showers. The *Sou'Wester* (☎ 360-642-2542), also has sites for both tents and RVs, with hot showers and laundry. For more information, see Sou'Wester Lodge below.

B&Bs The *Boreas Bed & Breakfast* (☎ 360-642-8069, 888-642-8069), 607 N Boulevard in Long Beach, is a historic beach-view home with five guest rooms (three with private bathroom) and a spa.

WASHINGTON

The *Scandinavian Gardens Inn B&B* (☎ 360-642-8763), 1610 California St S, offers four guest rooms and one suite, each with private bathroom. Facilities include a sauna and spa. Rooms range from $65 to $110 and include a Scandinavian-style breakfast.

Hotels Just a quick walk from the beach, *Arcadia Court* (☎ 360-642-2613), N 4th at Boulevard St, has eight well-kept cabins, most with kitchen facilities; pets are OK. Prices range from $35 to $83 a night. At *Boardwalk Cottages* (☎ 360-642-2305), 800 S Boulevard St, all units have kitchens; one- and two-bedroom cottages cost from $49 to $76.

One of the better deals for motels in Long Beach is *Our Place at the Beach* (☎ 360-642-3793, 800-538-5107), 1309 S Boulevard St, a small older motel with some kitchen units, a fitness center, hot tubs and a sauna. Single/double rooms are $45/59. Slightly newer and spiffier is the *Shaman Motel* (☎ 360-642-3714, 800-753-3750), 115 3rd St SW, which offers large rooms in a motel complex. Some units offer ocean views and fireplaces; there's also a swimming pool and pets are OK. Rates are $74/84.

Long Beach's only real beachfront lodging is *Nendel's Edgewater Inn* (☎ 360-642-2311, 800-547-0106), 409 10th St SW, which abuts the boardwalk and the beach. Facilities include a good restaurant, lounge and hot tub. During the high season, rooms begin at $65 to $98. *The Breakers* (☎ 360-642-4414, 800-288-8890) is a condominium resort 1 mile north of Long Beach on Hwy 103. The Breakers offers suite-style rooms with fireplaces, kitchens and balconies, with an indoor pool and spa on the premises. Basic one-bedroom units start at $57, more deluxe units with views top out at $183.

Sou'Wester Lodge (☎ 360-642-2542) on 38th St (or Beach Access Rd) in Seaview is a historic three-story lodge built in 1892 by an Oregon senator. The Sou'Wester is heavy on irreverence: the owners insist that the establishment is a B&(MYOD)B, or 'bed and make your own damn breakfast.' Unlike the upscale Shelburne Inn, which it otherwise resembles, the Sou'Wester has a self-amused air of funkiness, eclecticism and nonchalance. In the original lodge, there are both simple bedroom units that share kitchen, bathroom and living area ($51 to $54) and apartment-style units ($61 to $99). There are also a number of cabins

Northwest Cranberries

The Long Beach Peninsula is a major producer of cranberries; many of the roads that crisscross the peninsula pass by fields filled with these low-growing bushes covered with brilliant red, tart berries.

Cranberry production began on the Long Beach Peninsula in the 1890s, when plants were shipped from Massachusetts and planted in low-lying bogs. Cranberry bushes are very long-lived; some plants in today's farms are originals – over 100 years old. Today there are about 130 cranberry growers in southwestern Washington, which produce 15 million pounds of berries yearly. Bandon, in southern Oregon, is another major cranberry growing area in the Northwest.

Cranberry harvest is a colorful time. In October, the fields are flooded and the bright red berries float to the surface. Workers drag floating booms across the water surface to corral the berries, which are then processed.

Tour cranberry bogs and a historic cranberry research center at the Cranberry Museum and Gift Shop, along Pioneer Rd north of Long Beach. The museum is open from 10 am to 3 pm Friday, Saturday and Sunday. Admission is free. ■

($46 to $86) and TCH units, or Trailer Classics Hodgepodge – a collection of 1950s Spartan house trailers, each one renovated and individually decorated à la Sou'Wester ($65).

If the Sou'Wester isn't quite your style, then head to the *Shelburne Inn* (☎ 360-642-2442), 4415 Pacific Hwy in Seaview, a historic building on the National Register and one of the original lodgings on the Long Beach Peninsula. Built in 1896 as a stage-coach inn, this hotel is also home to one of the top restaurants in the Northwest. The entire building is a jewel of late-19th-century artisanship that has been carefully preserved and refurbished with period fixtures. Each of the 15 guest rooms has a private bathroom and is decorated with antiques. Rooms vary greatly in size, and range from $99 to $169 a night, including breakfast.

Places to Eat

There are any number of fast-food restaurants, chowder houses and assorted eateries along the Hwy 103 stretch. The area has several restaurants of note, however. The *42nd Street Cafe* (☎ 360-642-2323), 42nd St and Pacific Hwy in Seaview, serves old-fashioned home-style food, like pot roast and pan fried chicken, as well as hearty preparations of local seafood and oysters. Most dishes range from $10 to $12.

The *Lightship Restaurant* (☎ 360-642-3252) offers great views of the beach (from the top floor of Nendel's Inn), with fresh local seafood, steak, prime rib and home-made desserts.

Most people consider the *Shoalwater Restaurant* (☎ 360-642-4142), 4415 Pacific Hwy at the Shelburne Inn, one of the show-places of Northwest cuisine. The dining room, dominated by arched stained-glass windows and old wainscot panels, is certainly one of the most charming you'll find. Local seafood, fish, poultry and lamb are served with a consistently inventive flair; dishes are in the $20 range. At lunch, pub meals only are served in the bar, and breakfasts are for guests only.

OCEAN PARK

Ocean Park began its existence as a Methodist church camp in the 1880s. Camp meetings gave way to a Christian resort community in the 1890s (when permanent homes were first built here), and restrictive covenants limited sales of alcohol and gambling. Even though times have changed and Ocean Park seeks to attract as many weekenders as possible, the sale of alcohol is still limited to the parts of town south of Bay Avenue.

Today, Ocean Park is a quieter, less-developed version of the resort towns to the south. It feels much more like a town where people actually live rather than just visit. However, in terms of lodging, restaurants and activities, there are decidedly fewer choices – a trade-off that may be attractive if you want to avoid the manic congestion of Long Beach.

Ocean Park is 10 miles north of Long Beach along Hwy 103.

Places to Stay & Eat

Klipson Beach Cottages (☎ 360-665-4888), 22617 Pacific Hwy, south of Ocean Park, are attractive cabins with decks, kitchens, barbecues and fireplaces or wood stoves. Weekday/weekend rates for single rooms start at $80/90. *Sunset View Resort* (☎ 360-665-4494, 800-272-9199), 256th St and Park Ave, is a handsome motel resort with ocean views, hot tubs and easy beach access, tucked in the dunes just south of Ocean Park. Rooms start at $64.

Most of the food in Ocean Park is perfunctory. You'll find a good deli and just about everything else – at *Jack's Country Market*, at Hwy 103 and Bay Ave. Stop by *P&K Crab & Seafood Market* (☎ 360-665-6800), Hwy 103 and 254th St, for fresh crab, clams and other seasonal seafood.

OYSTERVILLE & NAHCOTTA

The charm of these old settlements – the only settlements on the bay side of the Long Beach Peninsula – derives not just from their history but also from the absence of the carnival atmosphere of the

WASHINGTON

The Oysters of Willapa Bay

In 1854, entrepreneurs RH Espy and IA Clark journeyed to the mouth of the Columbia River, looking for a place to begin an oyster business. They asked Chinook Chief Nahcati for advice, and he directed them north to what was then called Shoalwater Bay, where for centuries the Chinook had harvested wild oysters. At that time, native oysters filled the bay. The Chinook harvested oysters seasonally and dried the flesh of the bivalves for use throughout the year. Dried oysters were so prevalent and popular with coastal tribes that they functioned in trade as a form of currency.

Finding that the oysters were indeed abundant, Espy and Clark began a settlement near the Chinook camp. The oyster business they started experienced immediate success: wealthy prospectors in San Francisco would pay over $40 a plate for fresh oysters. Ice-filled freighters began calling at Oysterville and later Nahcotta (which had a deeper port) to transport the oysters to the booming gold rush center. Within two years, Oysterville grew to 500 inhabitants and became the seat of Pacific County.

By 1888 the 'Clamshell Line,' a branch of the Ilwaco Railway & Navigation Company, reached Nahcotta and linked the two oyster-producing towns to the Columbia River navigation system.

However, the native oysters weren't able to sustain such over-harvesting, and the oyster boom went bust. By 1893, Oysterville's future was so blighted that partisans of South Bend, across Willapa Bay, rowed over and stole the county documents, thereby establishing South Bend as the new county seat.

The oyster industry remained in major decline until the 1940s, when Japanese oysters were imported and intensive oyster farming techniques were introduced. Oysterville and Nahcotta were revived and are once again major producers of oysters; watch for shallow-bottomed oyster boats harvesting shellfish at high tides and note the gleaming pile of white shells beside the wharfs. ■

beachfront towns. Here, wildlife viewing, oyster harvesting and gracious dining occupies the time of residents and visitors alike. Oysterville stands largely unchanged since its heyday in the 1880s, when the oyster boom was at its peak. The entire town was placed on the National Register of Historic Places in 1976.

Just off Hwy 103, Oysterville is filled with well-preserved Victorian homes. The oldest, built in 1863, is the **Red Cottage**, near Clay St and Territory Rd. The **Big Red House**, the original home of Oysterville co-founder RH Espy, was built in 1871, and it stands at Division St and Territory Rd. If you walk down Clay St toward the bay and look back, you can see the house facades that were once the town-front: since initially there was no overland transport, the town was originally oriented toward the bay. Other historic buildings include a one-room schoolhouse and the

1892 **Oysterville Church**, which is open daily during the summer and on weekends the rest of the year; pick up a copy of the historic-walking-tour brochure here. A family-owned oyster plant still operates at the docks on Pacific St; if you have access to a kitchen, a campfire, or even just an oyster knife, pick up some oysters for later.

Leadbetter Point State Park

This 807-acre park is a kind of buffer between the straggling developments of Long Beach Peninsula and a section of the Willapa National Wildlife Refuge, which is here a narrowing band of dunes increasingly breached by Pacific waves. The park has a couple of informal hiking trails through forest and marshes, with good bird-watching. However, most people meander down to the shores of Willapa Bay. At low tide, mile after mile of reed-covered shoals are exposed, riven with narrow channels.

Stroll north along the lowering dunes and keep an eye open for unusual birds. This is one of the best places to watch for shorebirds in the Northwest. Snowy plovers, Lapland longspurs, sooty shearwaters and brown pelicans are just some of the many varieties an alert bird-watcher can spot here.

Jazz & Oysters

Jazz & Oysters, one of Oysterville's big summer events, is held in mid-August. In addition to live jazz on the grounds of the historic Oysterville Schoolhouse, there's lots of grilled oysters and other seafood to sample. For information, call ☎ 360-642-2400.

Places to Stay & Eat

Moby Dick Hotel (☎ 360-665-4543), in Nahcotta, is an old Coast Guard barracks turned B&B. The Moby Dick doesn't look like much from the outside, but it's actually a nice place to spend the night. There are 10 rooms in all, with rates ranging from $65 to $95. Also notable is *Caswell's on the Bay Bed & Breakfast Inn* (☎ 360-665-6535, 888-553-2319), 25204 Sandridge Road, just south of Nahcotta. This lovely new period-designed home offers wonderful views onto Willapa Bay from its wrap around porches. There are five guest rooms, with private baths, starting at $85.

The Ark (☎ 360-665-4133), on the oyster wharf in Nahcotta, is considered one of the best restaurants in the Pacific Northwest. The dining room is unostentatious but comfortable – however, what's been bringing diners here for the last two decades is the Ark's sophisticated yet adventurous way with fish. The restaurant was begun with help from local-boy-made-good James Beard, whose culinary convictions wed classical French techniques to fresh and sometimes unusual local products. The result is grilled fish, like salmon, sturgeon, swordfish – or whatever comes off the fishing boats – with rarefied sauces, fresh wild mushrooms, local vegetables, and nuts. And of course, oysters: raised within yards of the restaurant, and pan-fried for an all-you-can-eat feast, this simple delicacy alone ensures the Ark's reputation. The pastries are usually rich with local fruit and heavy with cream. It's worth keeping in mind that the Ark's bakery is open daily for goodies like cookies, cinnamon rolls and whole-wheat breads. Entrée prices range from $15 to $20, but for a full dinner plan on $25 to $30. Closed Monday evenings in summer; open weekends only in winter.

WILLAPA NATIONAL WILDLIFE REFUGE

Willapa Bay is an extremely shallow body of water and during low tides the salt water retreats, leaving only a few channels filled with water, surrounded by miles of mud flats, salt marshes and reedy estuaries. The bay provides a habitat for a great diversity of wildlife, notably shorebirds in migration (256 varieties have been sighted in Willapa Bay and 86 species are known to nest here), as well as birds of prey and songbirds. **Long Island**, an 8-mile-long rocky island in the bay, is home to many large mammals, like Roosevelt elk, black bear, otter and coyote, all of which are now rare on the mainland near the bay.

The refuge is made up of five parts including Long Island, an area at the mouth of the Bear River and the extreme tip of the Long Beach Peninsula beyond Leadbetter Point State Park. To reach Long Island you'll need a canoe or kayak; there's a boat dock on the island across from the refuge headquarters. Be sure to inquire about tides before embarking; it's easy to get stranded during low tide. Long Island offers seven primitive campgrounds as well as a network of hiking trails. Contact the refuge for a map.

The refuge headquarters are across from Long Island off US 101, 8 miles northeast of Seaview, and can be contacted by writing to Willapa National Wildlife Refuge (☎ 360-484-3482), Ilwaco, WA 98624. For kayaks and canoes, contact Willapa Bay Kayak Rentals (☎ 360-642-4892) at the marina in Nahcotta near Ocean Park.

SOUTH BEND & RAYMOND

The little towns on the east side of Willapa Bay are some of Washington's earliest, and they have changed little over the last 50 years. South Bend (population 1719) is fond of calling itself the Oyster Capital of the World; with the world's largest oyster plant and six major oyster companies here, it's hard to dispute the title.

The first things you'll notice as you enter South Bend are the mountains of oyster shells piled by the aging harbor and the briny scent of the sea. The next thing you'll notice is the opulent Pacific County Courthouse, a Jeffersonian monument exemplifying the region's turn-of-the-century pride. Raymond (population 3019), 4 miles up the bay from South Bend, is another historic waterfront at the mouth of the sluggish Willapa River.

Orientation

South Bend and Raymond are near the confluence of the Willapa River and Willapa Bay. US 101 is the main street of South Bend, though it's referred to as Robert Bush Drive. Most of Raymond's historic town center is a few blocks west of US 101, near the harbor.

Information

For information on the Willapa Bay area, contact the South Bend Chamber of Commerce (☎ 360-875-5231), PO Box 335, South Bend, WA 98586, or visit the information booth at the corner of US 101 and A St. You can contact the Raymond Chamber of Commerce (☎ 360-942-5419) at PO Box 86, Raymond, WA 98577, or stop at the visitors' center at Commercial and 5th Sts.

The Grave of Willie Keil

One of the more macabre tales of the Oregon Trail is the story of Dr William Keil, the charismatic leader of the utopian Aurora Colony in Oregon's Willamette Valley. Keil and his followers had moved from New England to Missouri in the 1850s, where they established a commune called Bethal Colony. However, the climate and their reception by the local people filled Keil with foreboding and the group decided to emigrate in 1855 to the Oregon Country, where they planned to re-establish their colony on Willapa Bay.

As plans to begin the 2000-mile journey started to take shape, Keil promised his 19-year-old son Willie that he could lead the wagon train on the trip west from Missouri. Sadly, Willie died of malaria four days before their departure. Dr Keil was determined to fulfill his promise nonetheless, and had his son's body sealed in a zinc-lined coffin filled with whiskey, which he then placed in a hearsified wagon at the head of the 250-person train.

Willie's brandied body was finally buried along what is now Hwy 6, one mile west of Menlo, on the night of the party's arrival, November 26, 1855. You can visit the grave site, now a state monument, and reflect on the determination of the Oregon Trail pioneers.

Although a handful of the colonists chose to remain on Willapa Bay, most, including Dr Keil himself, found the climate here too damp and instead moved south of Portland to establish the Aurora Colony. (See also The Aurora Colony sidebar in the Willamette Valley, OR, chapter.) ■

In a medical emergency, head to Willapa Harbor Hospital (☎ 360-875-5526) at Alder and Cedar Sts in South Bend.

Pacific County Museum
This community museum (☎ 360-875-5224), 1008 W Robert Bush Drive in South Bend, is a repository of local history spanning the periods of Native American prehistory through the pioneer fish and oyster industry of the mid-1800s. The museum has an especially good selection of historic fishing and logging equipment, as well as a bookstore. The museum is open from 11 am to 4 pm daily; admission is free.

Special Events
South Bend's big event is the Oyster Stampede, held on Memorial Day weekend. There are tons of oysters to sample in the large tent along the harbor. If you're handy with an oyster knife, consider competing in the oyster shucking contest. For more information call the chamber of commerce (☎ 360-875-5231).

Raymond pulls out the stops for the Willapa Harbor Festival (formerly known as the Loggers' Festival), held the first weekend of August. Event sponsors have toned down the logging theme and the festival instead focuses on parades, a salmon barbecue, a quilt and flower show and musical events. For more information contact the Raymond Chamber of Commerce (☎ 360-942-5419).

Places to Stay
Maring's Courthouse Hill B&B (☎ 360-875-6519, 800-875-6519), 600 W 2nd St, South Bend, is an 1892 vintage home just a block from the Pacific County Courthouse, with river-view rooms. The three guest rooms, two with private bathroom, range from $55 to $65.

It's nothing fancy, but the *H & H Motel* (☎ 360-875-5523), E Water and Pennsylvania Sts, north of South Bend on US 101, is a perfectly adequate motor inn, with a good bar and diner next door. Single/double rooms are $37/47.

Places to Eat
In South Bend, expect to find oysters on every menu. For a quick beer and an oyster shooter, go to *O'Sheridan's Tavern* (☎ 360-875-5791), 1011 W Robert Bush Drive, an old saloon turned oyster bar. *Gardners'* (☎ 360-875-5154), 702 W Robert Bush Drive, is a bit more homey, with seafood and pasta dishes mostly under $10. It's open for dinner Thursday to Sunday and for lunch on Thursday and Friday. Fine dining in South Bend means *Boondocks Restaurant* (☎ 360-875-5155), at the corner of Willapa St and Robert Bush Drive. Oysters join steak, prime rib and other grilled items; prices range from $10 to $15.

TOKELAND
The tiny community of Tokeland is on a spit of sand that reaches out into the north end of Willapa Bay. Although the resort community here reached its peak almost a century ago, and has been in gentle decline pretty much ever since, there's a good reason to turn off Hwy 105 and make your way to the old village. The *Tokeland Hotel* (☎ 360-267-7006), 100 Hotel Rd, is a handsome old resort hotel established in 1885, and notwithstanding a few updates in plumbing, it's still offering the same rooms and hospitality as the day it opened. The rooms are small and bathrooms are down the hall, but the charm and authenticity of this well-kept old inn will delight most visitors. Well-behaved pets also get an invite. Single/double rooms are $55/65. Three meals a day are served in the dining room.

Grays Harbor Area

The large, highly protected bay known as Grays Harbor was a natural for both native and early European settlement. The bay, which receives the waters of six major rivers, saw the development of Aberdeen and Hoquiam in the late 19th century. During these early years of Washington, when most commerce was maritime, the mills, factories and shipping lines of Grays Harbor were among the most important in the Northwest. Now a sleepy backwater, the Grays Harbor area is doing its best to lure in tourism by stressing charter fishing and access to the beaches along the Pacific Coast.

ABERDEEN & HOQUIAM

In some cities, history looks distinguished, in others, is just looks old. There's as much history here as anywhere in Washington, but unfortunately the faded old mill towns of Aberdeen (population 16,598) and Hoquiam (population 9178) have seen better days. The good news is that beneath the shabby exterior are some inexpensive rooms, a few good restaurants and pleasant, hard-working people.

Originally, Grays Harbor was home to the Chehalis tribe, who maintained villages along the bay and the riverbanks. The first white explorer to discover this large harbor was the American Robert Gray, in 1792, but white settlement didn't get under way until 1848.

The industrial engines of Aberdeen were fired in 1877 when a salmon packing plant opened, and Hoquiam's first lumber mill opened in 1882. By 1910, 34 lumber mills ringed Grays Harbor, with dozens of

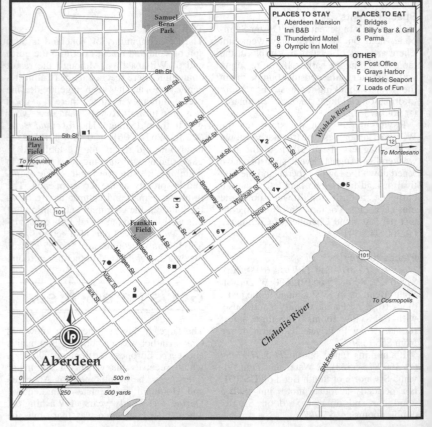

PLACES TO STAY
1 Aberdeen Mansion Inn B&B
8 Thunderbird Motel
9 Olympic Inn Motel

PLACES TO EAT
2 Bridges
4 Billy's Bar & Grill
6 Parma

OTHER
3 Post Office
5 Grays Harbor Historic Seaport
7 Loads of Fun

Aberdeen

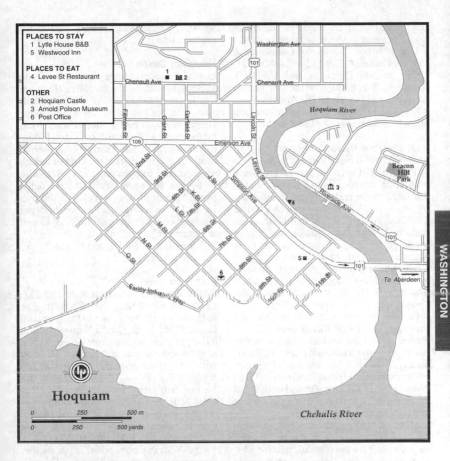

PLACES TO STAY
1 Lytle House B&B
5 Westwood Inn

PLACES TO EAT
4 Levee St Restaurant

OTHER
2 Hoquiam Castle
3 Arnold Polson Museum
6 Post Office

Washington Ave

Chenault Ave

Chenault Ave

Hoquiam River

Beacon Hill Park

Emerson Ave

Fillmore St

Grant St

Garfield St

Lincoln St

Levee St

Simpson Ave

Riverside Ave

2nd St

3rd St

4th St

L St

K St

Fifth St

M St

6th St

N St

7th St

Q St

8th St

9th St

10th St

11th St

Earley Industrial Way

To Aberdeen

Hoquiam

0   250   500 m
0   250   500 yards

Chehalis River

WASHINGTON

ships docked and waiting to freight the lumber to other parts of the nation. Aberdeen and Hoquiam were especially known for their large immigrant populations, who worked the shipyards, fishing boats, forests and mills, as well as for their wealthy captains of industry, whose elaborate homes still watch over Grays Harbor. The boom went bust during the 1930s, and these once-thriving port cities have been in gentle decline ever since. Efforts to lure retirees and new small business ventures to the area have partially succeeded; several years ago Hoquiam/Aberdeen was selected as one of the top 10 'micropolitan areas' in the USA.

Orientation & Information
Aberdeen is at the extreme eastern end of Grays Harbor, on the banks of the Chehalis and Wishkah Rivers. Hoquiam is just to the west, on the banks of the Hoquiam River. A third population center, Cosmopolis (population 1416), sits across the Chehalis River from Aberdeen.

Getting around in this thrown-together urban area can be pretty confusing, as each community has a different street grid. Stop and get a free map from the visitors' center if you're going to spend any time here.

Grays Harbor Chamber of Commerce & Visitors Center (☎ 360-532-1924, 800-321-1924), at 506 Duffy St (off US 101), Aberdeen, WA 98520, is on the strip linking Aberdeen and Hoquiam. The Aberdeen post office is at 115 K St. In Hoquiam, the post office is at the corner of M and 8th Sts.

Grays Harbor Historic Seaport

This nonprofit association (☎ 360-532-8611), 813 E Heron St, has taken over a portion of Aberdeen's old harbor, and is dedicated to the region's maritime history. In honor of Washington's centennial in 1989, the group designed and built a full-scale replica of *Lady Washington*, one of the ships piloted by Captain Robert Gray when he first sailed into Grays Harbor in 1792. Other Historic Seaport projects include building a replica of Gray's other ship, the *Columbia Rediviva* and developing a wetlands interpretive center.

For the traveler with a little time and curiosity, the *Lady Washington* offers a chance to sail on an 18th-century sailing vessel. This isn't a museum piece: the ship is usually on the go and is used for sail training, day excursions and other hands-on sail programs – it has sailed as far as Hawaii, and interested individuals can sign on as crew or as passengers on extended trips.

Much of the year, the *Lady Washington* sits at harbor in Aberdeen, where it is open for tours; call for the schedule and for a list of programs. The ship also sails up to Seattle during the summer, so be sure to call before heading out to see it.

Arnold Polson Museum

Built in 1923 by one of the timber barons of Hoquiam, this 26-room mansion-cum-museum (☎ 360-533-5862), 1611 Riverside Ave in Hoquiam, is filled with period furniture, clothing, a doll collection and logging implements. Next door is the civic rose garden. The museum is open 11 am to 4 pm, Wednesday through Sunday from June 1 through Labor Day weekend; the rest of the year it's open noon to 4 pm weekends only. Admission is $2/50¢ for adults/children.

Hoquiam Castle

Less a museum than a showcase of late Victorian-era taste, the so-called Hoquiam Castle (☎ 360-533-2005), 515 Chenault Ave, was built in 1897 on a hill above Hoquiam by Robert Lytle, another local lumber tycoon. The lavish cut glass, formal rooms paneled with oak and ornate period furnishings demonstrate the kind of wealth and opulence found along Grays Harbor in its heyday. It's open 10 am to 5 pm daily, from Memorial Day weekend through Labor Day weekend, and 11 am to 5 pm weekends only the rest of the year; closed in December.

Admission is $4 for adults and $1 for children under 11.

Places to Stay

B&Bs The *Lytle House B&B* (☎ 360-533-2320, 800-677-2320), 509 Chenault Ave in Hoquiam, sits next door to the Hoquiam Castle. This large Queen Anne mansion has eight guest rooms (from $65 to $150), public sitting rooms and parlors, all filled with antiques. *Aberdeen Mansion Inn B&B* (☎ 360-533-7079), 807 M St at 5th St, has five guest rooms, all with king-sized beds, in a 1905 mansion with wrap-around porches and a large formal garden. Rooms range from $95 to $125. The *Cooney Mansion B&B* (☎ 360-533-0602), 1705 5th St, in Cosmopolis, is yet another lumber baron's private Xanadu. This 37-room Craftsman-style mansion has nine guest rooms, five with private baths (doubles cost from $55 to $85), and the modern luxury of a hot tub, sauna and exercise room.

Hotels The place to stay in Aberdeen is *Olympic Inn Motel* (☎ 360-533-4200, 800-562-8618), at 616 W Heron St. The Olympic offers senior and commercial rates, kitchen units and laundry, and most units are non-smoking; singles range from $44 to $68; doubles from $58 to $78. The *Thunderbird Motel* (☎ 360-532-3153), 410

Heron St, is right in the center of town, with singles/doubles for $38/48. Over in Hoquiam, the best bet is the *Westwood Inn* (☎ 360-532-8161, 800-562 0994), 910 Simpson Ave, a sprawling complex near the center of town with large rooms starting at $65.

Places to Eat
Don't let the run-down looks of Aberdeen and Hoquiam fool you, as they have some surprisingly good restaurants.

Duffy's is a locally owned family dining chain, with three locations in Aberdeen and Hoquiam. They're a good place to go for breakfast or light meals.

In the rootin' tootin' days of yore, the bars in Aberdeen were haunted by Billy Gohl, a murderous fellow who robbed and killed drunken sailors and loggers. Billy and the era are both commemorated at *Billy's Bar & Grill* (☎ 360-533-7144), 322 E Heron St in Aberdeen, a handsome old bar and restaurant with good sandwiches, full dinners, and regional microbrews.

Aberdeen's best restaurant is Italian. *Parma* (☎ 360-532-3166), at 116 W Heron St, may be informal in decor but the food is top notch. Homemade bread, pasta and gnocchi are among the specialties. For much more traditional Northwest cuisine, including local seafood, go to the *Levee St Restaurant* (☎ 360-532-1959), 709 Levee St in Hoquiam, right on the waterfront, or *Bridges* (☎ 360-532-6563) 112 North G St in Aberdeen, for the area's best steak and prime rib.

Getting There & Away
Gray's Harbor Transportation Authority (☎ 360-532-2770, 800-562-9730), 3000 Bay Ave in Aberdeen, operates the local bus system and provides the public link to Puget Sound cities. There are six buses a day between Aberdeen and Olympia, and the fare is only $1.

WESTPORT
Population 2124
Westport was for years the largest whaling port on the West Coast and the largest

charter-fishing center in the Northwest. However, whaling ended long ago and current restrictions on salmon fishing have crippled the economy of this community. A lot of charter fishing still goes on – as there are plenty of other fish in the sea – and boats run whale-watching expeditions during migration. However, without the huge runs of salmon in Grays Harbor, the backbone of the fishing industry seems to have disappeared.

The stretch of beach between Westport on Grays Harbor and North Cove at the mouth of Willapa Bay is a study in drabness. There are miles of beach here, certainly, and the pace is slower and the atmosphere more tranquil than at Ocean Shores to the north or on the Long Beach Peninsula. However, it seems like beach resorts ought to be more fun than this. Mile after mile of flat beach is flanked by scrubby pines and beach grass, with near-derelict cottages and RV parks inserted here and there. This is a forlorn kind of place, in keeping with the Pacific pall that's common here much of the year. If you're fond of ennui, this might be your beach.

Orientation & Information
The area known as South Beach is the sandy headland from Westport to North Cove – in other words, the thrust of land between Grays Harbor and Willapa Bay. Westport is at the northern tip of a sandy peninsula and is really the only town in this area, although civilization clings desultorily to Hwy 105 as it rounds the cape toward the south. Westport is 22 miles southwest of Aberdeen.

For more information, contact the Westport-Grayland Chamber of Commerce (☎ 360-268-9422) at PO Box 306, Westport, WA 98595.

Westport Light State Park
Head out West Ocean Ave to Westport Light, the tallest lighthouse on the West Coast at 107 feet, and one of the few lighthouses in the nation that retains most of its original lighting system. Today, a 1000-watt electric lamp burns through an 1895

French-built Fresnel lens. Note that West-port Light isn't in the day-use park itself but on the Coast Guard property that's immediately adjacent; there are no tours. The year-round park has wind-screened picnic sites and access to a stretch of beach that's closed to motor vehicles from April 15 to Labor Day.

Westport Maritime Museum
This Coast-Guard-station-turned-museum (☎ 360-268-0078), 2201 Westhaven Drive, boasts some great period photos and arti-facts of seafaring days gone by. A complete skeleton of a gray whale is outside and can be viewed anytime. The museum is open 10 am to 4 pm daily from June to Sep-tember; the rest of the year it's open noon to 4 pm, Wednesday to Sunday. Admission is $2/1 adults/children, or $5 for a family.

Charter Fishing
Charter fishing is not what it once was in Westport, but it is still going strong. Though Northwest salmon populations have declined rapidly, not all runs of salmon are equally threatened, so salmon fishing is regulated and restricted on a sea-sonal basis. If you want to fish for salmon, call one of the following charter-fishing operations to find out when a season is going to open.

Nonetheless, charter boats head out reg-ularly in search of bottom fish, tuna, shark, halibut and rockfish – all worthy quarry for the angler, offering much the same thrill and adventure as salmon fishing. Some sort of discount is usually available in the form of package deals with lodging, or group and weekday discounts, so don't be shy about asking. Keep your eyes peeled for discount coupons in local papers and tourist brochures.

For information about charter fishing from Westport, contact one of the fol-lowing outfitters, or request a full listing of outfitters from the chamber of commerce. Westport Charters (☎ 360-268-9120, 800-562-0157) at the marina is a well-established outfit with a fleet of nine vessels. Deep Sea Charters (☎ 360-268-9300, 800-562-0151) is right across from Float 6. Coho Charters (☎ 360-268-0111, 800-572-0177), 2501 N Nyhus, is part of a large year-round motel and RV park com-plex (see below).

Whale Watching
Most charter companies listed above also run whale-watching excursions in the spring. Stroll along the marina and check the offerings usually posted on chalk board signs near the boats. An hour-long excur-sion will cost around $12.

Places to Stay
Camping RV campers are welcome at the *Coho Charters Motel & RV Park* (see below), where full hook-up sites are $18; no tents. Tent campers will want to go to *Twin Harbors State Park* (☎ 360-268-9717), 3 miles south of Westport on Hwy 105, a vast campground with 321 sites. Facilities include piped water and flush toi-lets; $10 tents, $15 RVs.

B&Bs *Glenacres Inn B&B* (☎ 360-268-9391), 222 N Montesano St, is a historic inn built in 1898 on a wooded estate. Facil-ities include an outdoor hot tub and gazebo. There are five B&B rooms in the main lodge, as well as motel-like rooms in a separate building. Rooms are $75.

Hotels The most inexpensive places to stay in Westport are back away from the harbor along Hwy 105, known here as Montesano St. *McBee's Silver Sands Motel* (☎ 360-268-9029), 1001 S Montesano St, has 19 small units that don't offer much above the basics, but it's cheap, with rooms starting at $49. The *Frank L Motel* (☎ 360-268-9200), 725 S Montesano St, is com-fortable and clean and offers kitchenettes; you can cook clams, crabs and oysters on the patio barbecue. Room rates are $48/52 for singles/doubles.

Coho Charters Motel & RV Park (☎ 360-268-0111, 800-572-0177), 2501 N Nyhus St, is only one block away from the beach and harbor. The motel rents crab pots, sells bait and offers charter packages. Rooms are

$56/63. *Islander Charters & Motel* (☎ 360-268-9166, 800-322-1740), 421 E Neddie Rose Drive, is right on the harbor with ocean-view and kitchen-equipped rooms; there's also an outdoor pool, restaurant and charter office. Rooms start at $65/70.

Chateau Westport (☎ 360-268-9101, 800-255-9101), 710 W Hancock St at Forrest St, a resort motel on the beach, is the fanciest lodging in the area. There's an indoor pool, most rooms come with balconies and kitchens are available. Ocean-view rooms start at $67/72.

Places to Eat

Along the harbor are a lot of fish-and-chips restaurants and other takeout food establishments. For the best views and food, try the following places. The *Islander Restaurant* (☎ 360-268-9166), 421-E Neddie Rose Drive, is the harbor-view dining room of a motel complex. That being said, the food – mostly burgers, steak and local seafood costing between $10 and $15 – isn't bad. Only a few yards away is *Pelican*

Point (☎ 360-268-1333), 2681 Westhaven Drive, which is Westport's fine-dining establishment, or as close as it gets around here. Expect seafood, steak and ribs from $12 to $17. It's open for lunch and dinner.

Getting There & Away

Bus Grays Harbor Transit (☎ 360-532-2770, 800-562-9730) is the county-operated bus system. Southbound buses from Aberdeen connect at Westport with Pacific Transit System buses serving South Bend, Raymond and the Long Beach Peninsula. Grays Harbor Transit also offers the only bus service to Aberdeen and Olympia.

Ferry In the summer only, a passenger ferry crosses from Westport to Ocean Shores six times daily. The fare is $10 roundtrip, $5.50 one way, with children under six free. Call Westport/Ocean Shores Ferry (☎ 360-268-0047 in Westport, ☎ 360-289-3391 in Ocean Shores) for information.

WASHINGTON

South Cascades

The mightiest and most explosive of the Pacific Northwest peaks are found in southern Washington. Mt Rainier, one of the highest peaks in the USA, towers above Tacoma and the Puget Sound. One of the first national parks, this massive peak is extremely popular with hikers, climbers, skiers and onlookers, who wind along the area's roads in summer and fall, exultant with the majestic surroundings.

A mountain experience of a completely different sort comes at Mt St Helens, the sawed-off peak whose 1980 eruption showed the world what tremendous forces lay hidden in Northwest landscapes. Two viewpoints and an interpretive center provide a look at the devastation wrought by the explosion of this volcanic peak.

Tucked into a little-visited corner of southern Washington is Mt Adams, in many ways the neglected sibling in this family of peaks. Fans of this mountain's many marvels hope it stays that way. An easy summit climb, wildflower meadows, berry fields and – most uniquely – relative solitude recommend Mt Adams to the explorer who likes a little wilderness in their outdoor experience.

Geologically speaking, the Cascade peaks are all very young. Mt Rainier began erupting about a million years ago, although it and Mt Adams have been very active in the last 20,000 years. Youthful Mt St Helens is still in the process of expressing itself.

Mt Rainier is big enough, it is often said, to create its own weather, which basically means *bad* weather. At times it seems to snare any passing cloud and make a storm out of it. In fact, weather is very changeable on and near all the Cascade peaks. Lovely summer days can turn blustery in an instant, so pack a warm sweater and rain gear. Summer temperatures average in the mid-70s; in the winter, temperatures run toward the mid-20s, and snowstorms are common.

Summer comes late to the South Cascades, but it comes with a bang, as high-elevation meadows explode with wildflowers. By mid-August, the huckleberries are ready for picking, and it's almost worth a special trip – the Mt Adams area has huckleberry fields designated especially for harvesters. And while most visitors never see the black bears and cougars that live in the backcountry, day hikers have a good chance of spotting hoary marmots, pine martens and mountain goats.

Mt Rainier National Park Area

Mt Rainier, at 14,411 feet, is the Cascades' highest peak, and it is imbued with more myth than any other mountain in the Northwest. Seattleites simply call it 'the Mountain' and judge the weather by its visibility. If you can see the peak for a few days running, the weather is good. But the flat, flying-saucer shaped, lenticular clouds that hover around the summit often herald fierce mountain storms – even on days when hikers at the lower elevations of Paradise or Sunrise are enjoying good weather. With its 26 glaciers, Mt Rainier is the most heavily glaciated peak in the USA outside of Alaska.

The Nisquallies, Yakamas, Puyallups and other local native people knew this volcanic peak as Tahoma. They made regular trips to its foothills to hunt, fish and pick huckleberries, but they were generally uneasy about climbing the mountain.

When British captain George Vancouver spotted the peak from the Puget Sound in 1792, he named it for his friend Rear Admiral Peter Rainier. This name was not easily accepted by all Euro-Americans who moved to the northwest; even in the late

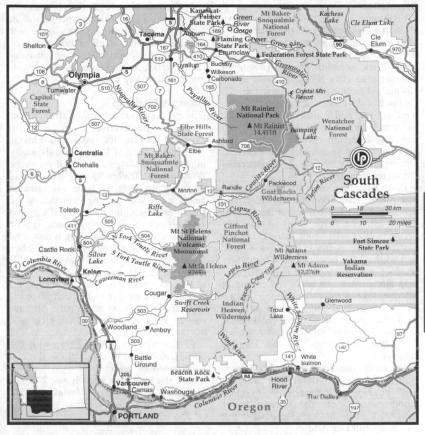

1800s, many felt Tahoma was a far more appropriate name.

When Mt Rainier was declared a national park in 1899, some of the land was obtained through a swap with the Northern Pacific Railroad. Railroad lands were originally granted by the federal government as incentive for railroad companies to build a transcontinental line. Northern Pacific swapped some of its grant lands within the new park for timber-rich land elsewhere, which they subsequently sold to timber companies. During the 1930s, Depression-era CCC workers built many of the still-existing park structures and trails.

Still a fairly potent volcano, Mt Rainier was created by repeated episodes of lava and mudflow and many eruptions of ash and rock. Before blasting its top some 5800 years ago, Mt Rainier reached as high as 16,000 feet. The 2-mile crater from that eruption was joined by another large crater after a blast 2500 years ago; these two craters mark Mt Rainier's summit now, where gas from mountaintop steam vents creates toasty-warm fern caves.

Orientation

Mt Rainier – so visible from the windows of Seattle – is actually 95 miles southeast of that city. There is no ring road encircling the park, and the four entrances by and large mark separate roads. The main entrance road, Hwy 706 (also known as the Nisqually-Longmire Rd), comes in through the town of Ashford, near the park's southwest ·corner, and follows the Nisqually River into the park. Past the Nisqually entrance is Longmire, which contains the only hotel open year-round, and Paradise, where the park's other hotel operates during the summer.

East of Paradise, near the park's southeast corner, Hwy 706 runs into Hwy 123; drive south and you'll arrive at the Ohanapecosh entrance. Drive north and Hwy 123 becomes Hwy 410 about halfway up the eastern park boundary at the Cayuse Pass. Just north of that junction, the White River entrance road cuts west off Hwy 410, running along the White River and ending at Sunrise, known for its great views. Hwy 410 bends around and becomes an east-west road across the northern outskirts of the park, passing through the town of Enumclaw before reaching the Tacoma suburbs.

The most remote entrance to Mt Rainier National Park is the Carbon River entrance, south of Hwy 410 in the northwest corner. Another road near the Carbon River entrance leads to Mowich Lake but is not an official entrance road.

Information

For information on the park, call or write the superintendent's office (☎ 360-569-2211) at Mt Rainier National Park, Ashford, WA 98304.

Park entrance fees are $10 per car and $5 for pedestrians and cyclists (those under 17 are free). Backcountry permits – once free – now cost $5 per day.

All roads but the Hwy 706 Nisqually entrance road to Paradise close down in the winter. Pay phones are available at all the park's fee campgrounds as well as at ranger stations and visitors' centers.

Mt Rainier National Park publishes two newspapers a year, *Tahoma* and *Snowdrift*, which are dispensed upon entry to the park and are available at all visitors' centers. These have current information on naturalist walks, evening campground programs and park news.

Hiking & Climbing

Hiking opportunities range from short walks on interpretive nature trails to extended backcountry jaunts. Once hikers have had a taste of Rainier's trails, many pine to circumnavigate the mountain on the **Wonderland Trail**, a 93-mile loop around the mountain. The trail changes elevation at nearly every turn, passing through lowland forests and subalpine meadows. It's a good 10-day trek, with campgrounds spaced about every 10 miles. Camping is restricted to the designated campgrounds. Remember, before any overnight backpacking trip, it's necessary to stop by an NPS ranger station or visitors' center to obtain a backcountry permit. There are five regular campgrounds (a total of 577 sites) in the park; all have running water and either flush or pit toilets, but no RV hookups.

Climbers must also register with the NPS. Guided climbs are available through Rainier Mountaineering, based in the summer at the Paradise Guide House (☎ 360-569-2227) and during the winter at 535 Dock St, suite 209, Tacoma, WA 98402 (☎ 253-627-6242).

Organized Tours

Gray Line (☎ 206-626-7532, 800-426-7532) runs bus tours of the park from the Seattle Sheraton Hotel. The 10-hour tour leaves the hotel at 8:15 am daily during the summer and costs $45.

Camping

Mt Rainier National Park has a new reservations system for its campgrounds. From July 1 through Labor Day, sites at Ohanapecosh and Cougar Rock Campgrounds can be reserved by calling ☎ 800-365-2267. During this time, sites at these campgrounds cost $14, which includes the

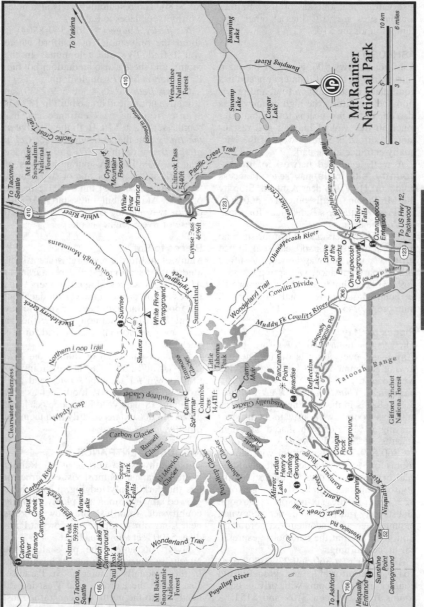

reservation fee; outside of the summer season, sites are $12. Sites at other park campgrounds are $10.

ASHFORD

Ashford, on Hwy 706, is one of the main entry points to the Mt Rainier area and is a good place to stock up on food and provisions before hitting the high country. It is also one of the few nearby towns that offer much in the way of lodging and restaurants. Ashford is 5 miles west of the Nisqually entrance to the park.

A well-developed network of **cross-country ski trails** has several access points off Hwy 706 near Ashford. Stop by the Mt Tacoma Trails office (☎ 360-569-2451) at Whittaker's Bunkhouse for a trail map of the area.

Climbers, hikers and auto tourists who may be a little stiff or sore can soak in **hot tubs** at a spot halfway between Ashford and the park entrance. Wellspring (☎ 360-569-2514) has hot tubs and a sauna for $10 an hour. Massages for a half-hour or full hour are $25/45.

Places to Stay

There is one main road in Ashford – Hwy 706 – and everything is on it. The following accommodations are found driving west to east.

Jasmer's Guesthouse & B&B (☎ 360-569-2682) is in the quiet heart of Ashford, and has rooms with private bathrooms starting at $115, or with shared bathroom starting at $76. *Whittaker's Bunkhouse* (☎ 360-569-2439) is a motel with simple rooms for $65 a single/double; the building was originally used as a logger's bunkhouse. Mountain climbers often go for a $25 bunk in the six-person bunkroom. Guests may run into the owner, renowned mountaineer and raconteur-extraordinaire Lou Whittaker, at the bunkhouse espresso bar in the morning.

Alexander's (☎ 360-569-2300, 800-654-7615), a comfortable and graceful old country inn, has rooms with private bathrooms from between $109 and $151. A separate guesthouse sleeps eight and rents

for $180. The restaurant here is also noteworthy (see Places to Eat).

Nisqually Lodge (☎ 360-569-8804) is about the only motel in Ashford where you'll find TVs and telephones in the rooms, and there's also an outdoor hot tub. Rates start at $69/79 single/double.

Growly Bear B&B (☎ 360-569-2339), an attractive homestead house built in 1890, is a mile from the park entrance and has rooms starting at $76. Both the *Cottage at the Berry* and the somewhat larger *Cabin at the Berry* (both ☎ 360-569-2628) are near the Wild Berry restaurant just west of the park entrance. For one or two people, the cottage costs $65; three to five people pay $80. At the cabin, rates start at $65 for one or two and top out at $125 for a full house of five to eight people.

Places to Eat

Many of Ashford's restaurants are associated with its lodgings; the restaurant at *Alexander's* serves elegant dinners – its prices are on par with the park lodges' but the food is a far sight better. Expect to pay about $18 for a salmon dinner, though early evening specials can be had for less than $10.

For a casual lunch or dinner, the *Wild Berry* (☎ 360-569-2628) is a local institution known for friendly service and generous portions of hearty food, such as stew for about $8. The Wild Berry cooks a lot of pizza, but doesn't necessarily turn them out quickly.

NISQUALLY ENTRANCE

This southwestern corner of Mt Rainier National Park is its most visited corner: it has the park's only lodging, a road that's plowed all winter long and plenty of lovely countryside, from lush old-growth forests near Longmire to alpine meadows at Paradise, 5400 feet above sea level.

Hwy 706 enters the park along the Nisqually River, which has its headwaters in the Nisqually Glacier above Paradise. Just inside the entrance, the Westside Rd heads off to the north, and car traffic must stop after 3 miles but cyclists and hikers can keep on going. Cyclists must stick to the old roadbed, but hikers can strike out on trails, most of which lead up drainages toward the mountain. If you plan to camp anywhere along the Westside Rd, be sure to pick up a backcountry permit at Longmire. It's also a good idea to inquire about road and trail conditions, as they are often damaged by floods.

Continuing east on Hwy 706, the first good views of the mountain come at Kautz Creek, one of several glacier-fed streams that contribute to the Nisqually River. After passing Longmire, the road begins to climb steadily, passing several good viewpoints and some sharp hairpin turns on the way to Paradise. Allow *at least* 45 minutes to drive from the park entrance to Paradise – and that's without making any stops.

From Paradise, the road heads east through waterfall-bedecked Stevens Canyon on the way to the Ohanapecosh entrance.

Information
Backpackers and hikers should stop by the Longmire Hiker Information Center (☎ 360-569-2211, ext 3317) for trail information and backcountry permits. Park rangers at the Jackson Visitor Center (☎ 360-569-2211, ext 2328) at Paradise dispense trail maps and can recommend good hikes and campsites. This is another place to get backcountry permits and to register if you're climbing the mountain.

Longmire
During an 1883 climbing trip, James Longmire noticed a mineral hot springs and a lovely meadow near the base of Mt Rainier. He and his family returned the following year and established Longmire's Medical Springs, and in 1890, he built the Longmire Springs Hotel. (See Climbing Mt Rainier sidebar.) When Mt Rainier became a national park in 1899, the Longmire area was the hub of activity and the original park headquarters.

The **Longmire Museum** (☎ 360-569-2211, ext 3314), open 9 am to 5:30 pm daily, has exhibits on natural history, Native

Climbing Mt Rainier: Because it's There
The first documented climb to the summit of Mt Rainier was accomplished in 1870. A Yakama guide named Sluiskin led a group of four men as far as present-day Paradise, but there refused to go any farther as Native American legend told of a fiery spirit who lived in the mountain. Two of the men, Hazard Stevens and Philemon Van Trump, continued without their guide up past Camp Muir and along the Gibraltar Ledge to the summit, where they spent the night in a sulpherous hot-springs cave. When they returned to base camp, Sluiskin initially took them for ghosts.

James Longmire, one of the members who had turned back, later settled near a mineral spring at the base of the mountain in the 1880s. Once Longmire had established a trail up the mountain, Mt Rainier started to be visited regularly by aspiring mountain climbers. In 1884, Longmire opened a mineral spring resort and began building access roads for visitors to his establishment and up the mountain to Paradise.

In 1890, Fay Fuller, a Puget Sound schoolteacher, became the first woman to climb Mt Rainier. Fuller climbed in bloomers, a straw hat and leather oxfords, which she customized by driving 'long caulks and brads' into the soles. She spent a night in an ice cave in the summit crater with her five male climbing partners, and later wrote that she expected many women to follow in her footsteps, which indeed they did. By the early 20th century, husband-and-wife climbing teams were fairly common, and subsequent mountaineers' expeditions to the Cascades summits were close to 50% women. ■

American culture and early white exploration of the area. Admission is free. To stretch your legs from the long drive in, wander the **Trail of the Shadows**, a 1.8-mile trail across the road from the Longmire Lodge. As steeped in history as it is in nature, the trail passes the mineral springs that spurred the hot springs resort in 1884 (when the water ran considerably warmer than it does now) and a cabin built in 1888 by Longmire's son.

Paradise

Late-summer visitors to Paradise can expect dazzling wildflowers. The first to bloom, even before the snow has completely melted, are avalanche lilies, glacier lilies and western anemones. They're followed by lupine, mountain bog gentian and paintbrush, creating broad washes of blue and red across the slopes. The Nisqually Glacier dips down toward Paradise; follow the **Skyline Trail** to the Glacier Overlook for a good look at the glacier and Nisqually Icefall, huge chunks of ice moving slowly down the glacier.

Even if you're not staying at the **Paradise Inn** (see Places to Stay below), the lobby of this classic national park lodge is worth a visit. Huge fireplaces anchor each end of the lobby, massive timbers hold up the ceiling, and comfortable leather sofas and chairs make relaxing with a good mystery novel as alluring as hiking Paradise's trails.

A shop in the Jackson Visitor Center sells books on Rainier and the Cascades, and there's a post office in the lobby of the Paradise Inn.

Hiking

A couple of trails lead to **Indian Henry's Hunting Grounds**, a magnificent flower-lit meadow with (on the right days) perfect views of Mt Rainier reflected in Mirror Lake. It's a 5½-mile hike in through meadow after meadow from the Kautz Creek Trailhead, which is 3½ miles from the park entrance, about halfway between the entrance and Longmire. Another route to Indian Henry's Hunting Grounds starts near Longmire and follows the **Wonderland Trail** (see Hiking and Climbing, above) over **Rampart Ridge**; this 6½-mile hike to the meadows is not easy, as the 2400-foot elevation gain is accomplished with lots of ups and downs.

Paradise is laced with trails, many of them paved for the first mile or so, and it's easy enough to wander out from the parking lot and make up an impromptu loop just by following the trail markers. But for a decent leg-stretch and a close-up look at wildflowers, marmots and the Nisqually Glacier, hike the 6-mile **Skyline Trail**, starting at the Paradise Inn and climbing about 1600 feet to **Panorama Point**, with good views of Rainier and the neighboring Tatoosh Range. The trails are usually crowded near the lodge, but traffic drops off after the first hill leaves unconditioned hikers sucking thin air. For a steep shortcut on the return part of the loop, hike down **Golden Gate Trail**.

Ambitious day hikers can continue up the mountain from Panorama Point and follow the **Pebble Creek Trail** to the snow-field track leading to **Camp Muir**. Camp Muir is the main overnight bivouac spot for climbing parties, and it has stupendous views south to Mt Adams, Mt St Helens and Mt Hood. Camp Muir is at 10,000 feet, so it's not a hike to be taken lightly, and it requires sufficient clothing for all sorts of weather and a good supply of food and water.

A lower elevation trail, the **Lakes Trail**, starts at Paradise and heads a little way down the mountain, making a 5-mile loop through subalpine meadows and passing Reflection Lakes, with views of the Tatoosh Range. In the fall, trailside huckleberry bushes redden, making this a lovely, not overly-strenuous hike.

Cross-Country Skiing

During the winter, the road is plowed as far as Paradise, and people take to the trails on cross-country skis and snowshoes. There is also a designated 'snow play' area, which is groomed for inner-tube riders.

It can be a hairy drive up the mountain in bad weather, though. If it seems safer to stay at lower elevations, ski the Westside Road, just inside the Nisqually entrance (though you may encounter snowmobilers).

The Longmire Ski Touring Center (☎ 360-569-2411), with trail information and cross-country ski and snowshoe rentals, is open at Longmire from mid-December to April.

Climbing

The most popular route to the summit of Mt Rainier starts at Paradise. It involves a brief night's rest at Camp Muir before rising between midnight and 2 am to don crampons, rope up, climb over Disappointment Cleaver and ascend the Ingraham Glacier to the summit. All climbers going higher than Camp Muir must register at the Paradise Ranger Station. Inexperienced climbers should not attempt this rigorous ascent independently: climb instead with the guide service.

Rainier Mountaineering (☎ 360-569-2227, 253-627-6242 in the winter) offers climbing classes and guided climbs to Mt Rainier's summit in late summer and fall, as well as a variety of specialized seminars. Unless you are an expert mountain climber, it is prudent to spend $465 for a day of climbing school and a two-day summit climb. Rainier Mountaineering's base is the Guide House across from the Paradise Inn. Rent ice axes, crampons and plastic mountaineering boots from the Guide House, open 9 am to 5 pm daily.

Other Activities

Park naturalists present slide shows at the Paradise Inn and the Cougar Rock Campground amphitheater every summer evening at 8:30 or 9 pm. Check the bulletin boards at the inn and campground for a schedule of topics.

Children ages six to 11 can join a park ranger for 'Junior Ranger' hikes and nature activities at the Cougar Rock Campground. The 1½-hour program is repeated several times a week; check the campground bulletin board for the schedule.

Movies and slide shows about the mountain and the preservation of Paradise's meadows are shown throughout the day at the Jackson Visitor Center.

Places to Stay

Camping *Sunshine Point Campground*, just inside the park near the Nisqually entrance, is one of the park's smaller campgrounds. Its 18 riverside sites go for $10 a night, and it's the only campground open year-round. *Cougar Rock Campground*, 2½ miles uphill from Longmire on the way to Paradise, has 200 sites costing $12 to $14, and is open until mid-October. See Camping, above, for reservation information.

Lodges Of the park's two lodges, *Paradise Inn* (☎ 360-569-2413) and the *Longmire National Park Inn* (☎ 360-569-2411), Paradise is grander and has the more spectacular setting, with prices at $80 for one-bed rooms, or $109 for two-bed rooms. But Longmire – which stands on the site of the old Longmire Springs Hotel – is cozier and, conveniently for cross-country skiers, is open year-round; prices here start at $66 for a room with one bed and a shared bath, or $91 for a private bath. The season at Paradise runs from late May to early October. Call for reservations at either place (☎ 360-569-2275), as rooms fill up fast. It's best to book far in advance, but cancellations occur frequently, so it pays to keep calling even if initially there are no openings. It's also a good idea to ask for a confirmation, as booking foul-ups happen easily. If the park lodges are full, the closest accommodations outside the park are in Ashford.

Climbers often begin mountain ascents long before sunrise.

DAVE SKIBINSKI

Mt Rainier

Places to Eat

A snack bar at the Paradise Inn and a cafeteria in the Jackson Visitor Center at Paradise offer the most basic sustenance. But even cafeteria chili is welcome after a winter snowshoe expedition. The visitors' center cafeteria is open daily from May to September and on weekends and holidays the rest of the year.

The dining room at *Paradise Inn* (☎ 360-569-2413) is pretty good if you're just there for one or two meals. After that, even the salmon seems a little institutional and requires some vigorous hiking to make it worth the $15 or so it'll set you back. The Paradise Inn is open from late May to early October. Down the hill at Longmire, Glacier Park Services (the park concessionaire) serves essentially the same meals at the *Longmire National Park Inn* (☎ 360-569-2411); they serve three meals a day and are open year-round.

PACKWOOD

Packwood, with its abundance of motels and restaurants, is a convenient base for exploring the east side of Mt Rainier and for launching a trip into the Goat Rocks Wilderness Area to the south.

Twelve miles southwest of Ohanapecosh on US 12, Packwood is the closest real town to the Ohanapecosh and White River entrances to Mt Rainier National Park. It's also on the well-traveled route between Mt Rainier and Mt St Helens, with the less-visited Mt Adams also in the neighborhood. To reach Mt St Helens, head west on

US 12 to Randle, then south on Hwy 131 to the turnoff for the Windy Ridge viewpoint. You can get to trailheads on the north side of Mt Adams by heading south on USFS Rd 21, a few miles south of Packwood.

The Packwood Ranger Station (☎ 360-494-5515), on US 12 near the north end of town, is a good source of information on the Goat Rocks Wilderness Area.

Places to Stay

The *Packwood RV Park & Campground* (☎ 360-494-5145) has a few tent sites and full amenities, including a laundromat, a store and a cafe. It's right in the heart of Packwood, set back just a bit from US 12. Rates run from $12 to $17. *La Wis Wis Campground* (☎ 360-494-5515), a USFS campground on US 12 halfway between Packwood and Ohanapecosh, is a good place to look for a campsite in the summer when the national park fills up. It has about 100 sites with running water and flush toilets for $12.

Old Hotel Packwood (☎ 360-494-5431) is a renovated log hotel with a big porch and shared baths for most of the rooms; singles/doubles are $21/40. Unfortunately, the place hasn't changed much since it was built in 1912. The *Tatoosh Motel* (☎ 360-494-6710), on the west side of town, has homey duplex cabin-type units; several have kitchenettes and there is an outdoor hot tub. Single/double rooms are $45/48.

Another good choice in Packwood is the *Mountain View Lodge Motel* (☎ 360-494-5555), with rooms at $34/45. It's on the east side of town. The *Inn of Packwood* (☎ 360-494-5500) has an indoor pool and an outdoor spa, and singles/doubles for $60/80. The *Cowlitz Lodge* (☎ 360-494-4444), also right on US 12, has rooms from $57/67, a free continental breakfast and a hot tub.

Places to Eat

Packwood is home to a number of drive-ins and unprepossessing diners. Probably the best of the lot is *The Club Cafe* (☎ 360-494-5977), a chicken-fried-steak kind of place. A bit more upscale is *Peter's Inn*

(☎ 360-494-4000), a steak house with a good salad bar.

OHANAPECOSH ENTRANCE

Ohanapecosh means 'clear waters' to the local Native Americans, and this southeastern entry road certainly provides beautiful views of the rushing Ohanapecosh River. There are also a couple of popular trails into the dense forests here.

From Ohanapecosh, there's good access (via US 12) to the Goat Rocks Wilderness Area and Mt St Helens. To reach Mt St Helens, take US 12 west to Randle, then head south on Hwy 131, which shortly becomes USFS Rd 25. This will put you on the east side of Mt St Helens.

Information

The Ohanapecosh Visitor Center (☎ 360 569-2211, ext 2352), on Hwy 123 at the park's southeastern corner, is open 9 am to 6 pm daily during the summer. The displays here focus on tree identification and the local old-growth forest. Rangers also offer information on hiking trails.

Hiking

The 1½-mile trail into the **Grove of the Patriarchs** is one of Mt Rainier's most popular hikes, and it's worth the walk for a look at some truly large trees. The mostly level trail crosses the Ohanapecosh River to a small island where thousand-year-old Douglas firs and cedars grow. Find the trailhead just north of the Ohanapecosh Visitor Center.

Just outside the Ohanapecosh Visitor Center, the half-mile **Ohanapecosh Nature Trail** winds through the forest and visits a small natural hot spring. The hot spring along the trail is more of a seep than a wallow, but there is a tiny trailside bench that allows weary hikers to soak their sore feet in a six-inch-deep pool. Below the springs, bright green grass grows lushly in a meadow that was once the site of a hot-springs spa.

If the Ohanapecosh Nature Trail seems like just a starting point for a hike, follow the signpost just past the hot springs for the

Silver Falls Loop. The easy 3-mile loop visits noisy Silver Falls and, at its north end, can hook up with the trail to the Grove of the Patriarchs.

The **Pacific Crest Trail** runs along the eastern edge of Mt Rainier National Park, and trailheads at Ohanapecosh and Chinook Pass, on Hwy 123 a few miles south of the park's White River entrance, provide local access to the high mountain trail. It's best to make this fine 19-mile stretch into a two-day, north-to-south hike, starting at Chinook Pass. Plan for cool weather; the trail runs at 5000 feet and above, with peeks at Mt Rainier and plenty of wildlife and late-season huckleberries.

Places to Stay & Eat

The 208-site *Ohanapecosh Campground* charges $12 to $14 a night and is open from June to late October (see Camping, above, for information on reservations). If it's full, head out of the park and go south a few miles to *La Wis Wis Campground*, a Gifford Pinchot National Forest campground (see Places to Stay under Packwood, above).

There are no food services at Ohanapecosh. The closest place for groceries or a meal is in the town of Packwood, about 12 miles to the southwest on US 12.

WHITE RIVER ENTRANCE

Some of the best views of Mt Rainier – with Emmons Glacier sliding down its face, Little Tahoma Peak in the foreground, and the craggy Goat Rocks Wilderness Area off to the southeast – are from Sunrise. Sunrise's 6400-foot high open meadows are scattered with trees and laced with hiking trails. Since it's on the mountain's east side, the whole White River-Sunrise area benefits from Mt Rainier's 'rain shadow' and receives less precipitation than the damp west side.

Basic visitor facilities, including meals and restrooms, are available at the Sunrise Lodge. There's also a visitors' information desk to answer questions and issue backcountry permits.

WASHINGTON

Orientation & Information

The White River entrance road, off Hwy 410, follows the river valley to the White River Campground on a spur off the main road about 7 miles from the park entrance. The main road leaves the river and begins climbing after the turnoff for the campground, ascending another 2400 feet in the 10-mile stretch to Sunrise.

The ranger station (☎ 360-569-2211, ext 2356) at the White River entrance dispenses backcountry permits and hiking information. It's open 8 am to 4:30 pm Sunday to Thursday, 8 am to 9 pm Friday, and 7 am to 7 pm Saturday. Sunrise Visitor Center (☎ 360-569-2211, ext 2357) is open 9 am to 6 pm Sunday to Friday, and 9 am to 7 pm on Saturday.

Mountain Goat Walk

Park naturalists lead a 1½-mile hike each Sunday afternoon from the Sourdough Ridge Trailhead at Sunrise to explore the mountain goat habitat. If this doesn't fit your schedule, make it a self-guided walk. Pick up the trail at the picnic area behind the visitors' center and either hike the nature trail loop (there is some uphill walking) or blast off onto a longer trail along Sourdough Ridge.

Hiking

It doesn't take long for hikers to become enraptured with the White River-Sunrise area. The only glitch may be the crowds. Try to hike on a weekday, and hit the trail early in the morning.

A trailhead directly across the parking lot from the Sunrise Lodge provides access to several short walks and a plethora of longer hikes. It's an easy stroll to the **Emmons Vista**, with good views of Mt Rainier, Little Tahoma and the Emmons Glacier. For a longer – but level – walk, turn right just before the Emmons Vista onto the **Sunrise Rim Trail**, which takes about 1½ miles to reach **Shadow Lake** and Sunrise Camp, a walk-in backcountry campground. From here, an old service road provides a short route back to the lodge parking lot.

Three miles from the White River entrance, the trail to **Summerland** takes off along Fryingpan Creek. The 4.3-mile hike climbs gradually through forest, then through brush, before reaching Summerland's open subalpine meadows with views of Mt Rainier and pointy, glacier-chiseled Little Tahoma peak. Mountain goats and elk are often visible from this extremely popular trail.

To get to **Emmons Glacier**, a less-spectacular, but perfectly pleasant trail starts from the far end of the White River Campground and follows a fork of the White River for 3½ miles to Glacier Basin, a meadow surrounded by slopes that are home to mountain goats and form a corridor for mountain climbers. For a view of Emmons Glacier, the largest glacier in the lower 48 states, turn off the **Glacier Basin Trail** after 1 mile and hike another half-mile along the glacier's lateral moraine to the overlook. (Actually, the official viewpoint doesn't have much over the many informal tracks up to the moraine's crest that precede it.)

Though most people drive from White River to Sunrise, sturdy hikers can leave their cars at the White River Campground and take the 3-mile trek from the campground's 'C' loop up the **Wonderland Trail** (see Hiking and Climbing, above) to the **Sunrise Rim Trail**. The steep trail is forested for the first couple of miles, then it breaks into steep-walled subalpine meadows and good mountain views. At Sunrise, the trail hooks up with a bevy of nature trails.

Climbing

From the White River Campground, climbers hike the Glacier Basin Trail to the Inter Glacier, then rope up into teams and continue to the 9500-foot bivouac at Camp Schurman, where rocky Steamboat Prow juts up and separates the Emmons and Winthrop Glaciers. Most climbers follow Emmons' crevasse-free 'corridor' as far as possible, then skirt crevasses, including the gaping bergschrund where the top of the glacier pulls away from the mountain's ice cap, to reach the summit.

Places to Stay & Eat
The 117-site *White River Campground* is 10 road miles or 3½ steep trail miles downhill from Sunrise. Campground fees are $10, which buys flush toilets, running water and crowded, though not unpleasant, camping spaces. It's open only in summer.

For campers who are willing to dispense with such amenities as running water and pack in their gear 1½ miles, *Sunrise Camp* is just down the Sunrise Rim Trail from the lodge parking lot. This is backcountry camping, so a permit is required.

There is no indoor lodging at Sunrise. The closest motel rooms are at *Crystal Mountain Resort* (see Crystal Mountain Resort later in this section) or in Enumclaw or Packwood.

The *Sunrise Lodge* restaurant is open for meals 10 am to 7 pm daily from late June through early September. Don't expect anything fancy – it's a hamburger and hot dog sort of place.

CARBON RIVER ENTRANCE
This remote northwest corner of Mt Rainier National Park is a dense green pocket, made all the more striking by the intensive clear-cutting that has gone on in the Carbon River valley outside the park boundaries. There's lots of water, mushrooms, moss and several hikes to waterfalls. There's also the park's lowest reaching glacier, a river cloudy with glacial till, and a remarkable inland rain forest. The Carbon River area has very few glimpses of Mt Rainier; for big mountain views, head to Mowich Lake.

Orientation
To get to Carbon River and Mowich Lake from the I-5 corridor, it's easiest to take Hwy 167 south to Puyallup and from there pick up Hwy 410 east to Buckley. From there take Hwy 165 south past the small towns of Wilkeson and Carbonado; the road forks a few miles past Carbonado. The left fork follows the Carbon River and is paved to just inside the park entrance. The right fork is paved for a couple of miles, and then becomes a well-graded gravel road, which climbs above the Carbon River valley and terminates about 18 miles from the fork at Mowich Lake. Neither road is plowed in the winter.

Information
The Carbon River Ranger Station (☎ 360-569-2211, ext 2358) is open 9 am to 5 pm daily during the summer; it's just inside the park entrance. This is the only reliable place in the park's northwest corner to get a backcountry permit. During the summer, a park service volunteer patrols the Mowich Lake Campground and can answer questions about the local trails.

Carbon River Rain Forest
Though there are plenty of times when all of Mt Rainier seems like a rain forest, the short **Carbon River Trail** just inside the park entrance loops through the only true inland rain forest in the park – indeed, in all of North America. Huge-leafed plants grow alongside the boardwalk that elevates the trail from the frequently steaming ground below, and the moist air condenses into droplets hanging from big Douglas firs and cedars.

Hiking
At 3820 feet, the **Carbon Glacier** reaches a lower elevation than any other glacier on Mt Rainier. A trail starts at the Ipsut Creek Campground, and 3½ miles away it passes the glacier's leading edge. Hikers are warned not to approach the glacier too closely, as rockfall from the glacier's surface is unpredictable and dangerous. The same trailhead also provides access to the **Wonderland Trail** (see Hiking and Climbing, above), which crosses Ipsut Pass on the way to Mowich Lake (a 5.3-mile hike from the Ipsut Creek Trailhead).

A 35-mile, three- or four-day trip, the **Northern Loop Trail** passes through some of the park's least-traveled areas. The loop starts at Ipsut Creek and follows the Carbon River Glacier Trail for a couple of miles before taking off to the east and passing through Windy Gap on its steep, up-and-down path toward Sunrise. Just

WASHINGTON

west of Sunrise, the Northern Loop Trail joins up with the Wonderland Trail, which returns hikers to Ipsut Creek or continues around the mountain.

To reach **Summit Lake**, just outside the park's Carbon River entrance, turn north on USFS Rd 7810 and follow it to the end. The 2½-mile trail to Summit Lake is in the Clearwater Wilderness Area. Like the national park, this wilderness area has areas of old-growth forest. Mt Rainier's north face – including the nearly unclimbable Willis Wall, a sheer wall of loose rock and ice – comes into good view at Summit Lake.

From trailheads at Mowich Lake, one extremely popular trail heads south and passes **Spray Falls** on its way to **Spray Park**, flush with wildflowers late in the summer. It's just under 3 miles to Spray Park. As popular as this trail is, it's not all that easy. A dizzying run of switchbacks just past the falls pulls the trail out of the forest to the Spray Park meadows.

For views of Mt Rainier, try going to **Tolmie Peak lookout**. Head north on the Wonderland Trail from Mowich Lake, then turn off at Ipsut Pass and climb to the lookout at 5939-foot Tolmie Peak. If the final chug up Tolmie Peak seems too daunting, Eunice Lake at its base is a perfectly good place to relax.

The **Paul Peak Trail** hooks up with the Wonderland Trail 3 miles from its trailhead on the Mowich Lake Rd. It joins the Mowich River Trail in 5.8 miles. Try this trail on summer weekends when hikers choke Spray Park.

Places to Stay & Eat
Ipsut Creek Campground, at the end of the Carbon River Rd, has 29 sites for $10 a night, and is open only in summer. There's also the small, free walk-in *Mowich Lake Campground* just past the Mowich Lake parking lot, but the campground itself is far less inviting than its surroundings, and there's no water. The *Mountain View Inn* (☎ 360-829-1100), at the junction of Hwys 165 and 410 in Buckley, is the closest motel, with rooms at $63/69 single/double.

Clark's nutcracker, with its distinctive black and white wings, can be found in the high Cascades.

The closest place to the Carbon River area to buy food is the small town of Wilkeson, about 18 miles from the park entrance. There are a couple of small stores and a restaurant, the *Pick & Shovel*.

ENUMCLAW
Seattleites almost always pass through Enumclaw on their way to Mt Rainier; this is where the mountain really starts to tower and the towns quit seeming like passably attractive suburbs of Seattle. Even though there are places to drink espresso and get a decent lunch in Enumclaw, it's a pretty rural place and is justifiably called a gateway to Mt Rainier National Park. It's a good place to stock up on food before getting to remote northern areas of the park.

Hwy 410 from Enumclaw leads to the park's White River entrance; Hwy 165, accessible to the southwest of town, is the route to the Carbon River entrance. White River Ranger Station (☎ 360-825-6585), on Hwy 410 just east of downtown, has information on trails in Mt Rainier National Park and the surrounding national and state forest lands.

Places to Stay & Eat
The *Kanaskat-Palmer State Park* (☎ 360-886-0148), 11 miles northeast of Enumclaw via Farman Rd, has 50 campsites (and

WASHINGTON

showers!) for $11 to $16. It's a popular put-in spot for floating the Green River Gorge (see below).

The White Rose Inn (☎ 360-825-7194, 800-404-7194), 1610 Griffin Ave, is a B&B with rooms from $85 to $95, all with private baths. *Best Western Park Center Hotel* (☎ 360-825-4490), 1000 Griffin Ave, has singles/doubles for $64/68. It's downtown on Enumclaw's main street (paralleling Hwy 410, one block to the north).

Baumgartner's Deli (☎ 360-825-1067), 1008 E Roosevelt (also known as Hwy 410), is known to locals and park-goers as a place for delicious sandwiches and cheesecake. Have them make a couple of extra sandwiches to eat on the trail – and save those energy bars and dehydrated dinners for another trip.

GREEN RIVER GORGE

This river preserve, 12 miles north of Enumclaw on Hwy 169, has hiking trails, caves and fossils, not to mention great canoeing (there are several put-in spots). At Flaming Geyser State Park (☎ 360-931-3930), a subset of the recreation area, methane fuels two geysers, which were originally test holes for gas and coal exploration. There is a six-inch flame on one geyser; the other one bubbles away in a spring, where its methane has dyed the creekbed gray. There are more opportunities for floating or fishing the Green River at the park.

FEDERATION FOREST STATE PARK

Federation Forest State Park's 612 acres of virgin forest provide a respite from the heavily logged Weyerhaeuser land nearby. The park, 17 miles east of Enumclaw on Hwy 410, is a pleasant spot for a low-key picnic or nature walk; it has an interpretive center and a couple of miles of trails, partly incorporating the historic Naches Trail. The Naches Trail, between Fort Walla Walla and Fort Steilacoom, was used by pioneers from 1853 – when the Longmire party crossed the mountains – until about 1884, when easier routes across the Cascades gained favor.

CRYSTAL MOUNTAIN RESORT

One of the largest and most popular ski areas in Washington, Crystal Mountain Resort (☎ 360-663-2265, 800-852-1444) offers year-round recreational activities. This downhill ski resort is just outside the boundaries of Mt Rainier National Park on the northeast corner. It's 6 miles north on Hwy 410 and about 36 miles east of the town of Enumclaw.

Downhill skiers give Crystal Mountain high marks for its variety of terrain, which includes some very steep chutes and remote, unpatrolled backcountry trails. The vertical drop is 3120 feet and is served by 10 lifts. There are also 34 backcountry trails for advanced skiers. Lift tickets are $35 adult, $30 for youths 11 to 17. There's night skiing Friday through Sunday till 10 pm. The resort has a full range of rentals (including cross-country skis) and ski instruction classes. Snowboarding is also very popular.

During the summer, a $10 chairlift ride leads to several fairly easy hiking and mountain biking trails. Resort staff can provide complete trail information. The popular lift-top restaurant has a good view of Mt Rainier.

You can rent a mountain bike at the resort's sport shop (☎ 800-766-9297) for $6 an hour, or for $15/20 for a half/full day. Just downhill from the base of the lifts, a swimming pool and hot tub ($2 admission) may be enticing to park-goers who have been camping a little too long and hiking a little too vigorously.

Places to Stay & Eat

As you might expect, accommodations are all managed by the resort and there are a bewildering array of package deals, with cut-rate prices during the off-season. Since there are so many price variations, it's best just to call either the *Alpine Inn* (☎ 360-663-2262) or the telephone operator who services all the other lodgings (☎ 360-663-2558) and ask their advice. In a nutshell, the *Alpine Inn* is the budget place, with no-frills rooms from $40 (shared bathroom) or $85 (private shower). The *Village Inn*, from

WASHINGTON

$70 to $77, and the *Quicksilver Lodge*, a touch fancier at $80 to $95, have rooms with TV, VCR and refrigerator. Groups of four or more should look into renting a condominium; one-bedroom apartments at *Silver Skis Chalet* or *Crystal Chalets* range from $110 to $160.

A full range of cafes, restaurants and bars cater to skiers. During the winter, the restaurant in the *Alpine Inn* (☎ 360-663-2262) has the best food, but it closes down in the summer. If you're here then, go to the *Summit House* (☎ 360-663-2300) at the top of the lift, which replaces its winter-time cafeteria food with sit-down 'sunset dinners' in the summer.

GOAT ROCKS WILDERNESS AREA

The Goat Rocks Wilderness Area is wonderful high country, with great craggy rocks, mountain goats and views of the surrounding Cascade peaks. Goat Rocks was originally a 12,000-foot-high volcano; long extinct, it has eroded into several peaks averaging 8000 feet. Since it's largely above the timberline, hiking season starts late (July) and ends early (late September). The **Pacific Crest Trail** (PCT) passes through the most spectacular section of the wilderness area. It's a huge hike from one side to the other, 25 to 30 miles total, with the best parts coming about halfway in, making for no easy in-and-out trip.

However, for experienced hikers, there is a shorter way to get to the heart of the Goat Rocks. From Packwood, drive a few miles west on US 12, then turn south on USFS Rd 21, take a left just past Hugo Lake onto USFS Rd 2150, which goes to the trailhead at Chambers Lake, some 21 miles from Packwood. Begin hiking at Chambers Lake to Snowgrass Flat (trail No 96), then cut over on a side trail to the PCT. It's about 5 miles from the trailhead to the PCT, and at that point you're within a mile of good camping spots near some glaciers. The Goat Rocks themselves are stunning, and another 3 miles up to **Elks Pass** on the PCT leads to magnificent mountain vistas.

To make a loop back to Chambers Lake, cut cross-country from the glacier-side camp over to Goat Lake. Pick up trail No 86 at Goat Lake; it turns into trail No 95 and returns via a very nice but rugged trail back to the Chambers Lake Trailhead. Water is limited along this route; take a good filter and get streamflow or snow off the glaciers.

For more hikes in Goat Rocks, see *100 Hikes in the South Cascades and Olympics* by Ira Spring and Harvey Manning (The Mountaineers, Seattle, 1992).

RANDLE

Randle, a crossroads town between Mt Rainier and Mt St Helens, doesn't pretend to be anything fancy or upscale. Stay here if 'convenient' and 'cheap' are important words in your vocabulary.

Maple Grove Campground & RV Park (☎ 360-497-2741) is on US 12 in Randle and has sites for $12 (tents) to $20 (full hookups).

Tall Timber Motel (☎ 360-497-2991), on US 12 in Randle, has an attached coffee-shop and single/double rooms for $30/40. *Medici Motel* (☎ 360-497-7700), 3 miles south of US 12 on Hwy 131, is a modest place with kitchenette rooms for $45. Two of the four rooms share a bathroom.

Randle's *Big Bottom Cafe* (☎ 360-497-9982) may seem a little intimidating – the parking lot is full of huge American pick-ups and the bar is full of giant men – but it is *the* place to get a decent steak in town, and they are used to serving people who are just passing through.

Mt St Helens

Where were you when Mt St Helens blew? For most people in the Pacific Northwest, the events of May 18, 1980, are as welded into memory as the dates of the bombing of Pearl Harbor and the assassination of John F Kennedy. Mt St Helens erupted with the force of 21,000 atomic bombs, leveling hundreds of square miles of forest and

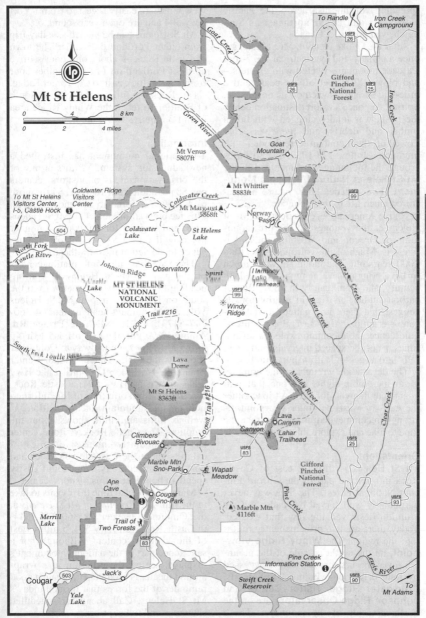

Mt St Helens

0   4   8 km
0   2   4 miles

To Randle
Iron Creek
Campground
USFS 26

Goat Creek

Gifford
Pinchot
National
Forest

USFS 26

USFS 25

Iron Creek

Green River

Mt Venus
5807ft

Goat
Mountain

USFS 99

Mt Whittier
5883ft

To Mt St Helens
Visitors Center,
I-5, Castle Hock

Coldwater Ridge
Visitors
Center

Coldwater Creek

Mt Margaret
5868ft

Norway
Pass

504

Coldwater
Lake

St Helens
Lake

Chakwin Creek

North Fork
Toutle River

Johnson Ridge

Observatory

Independence Pass

Spirit
Lake

Harmony
Lake
Trailhead

Bean Creek

Castle
Lake

MT ST HELENS
NATIONAL
VOLCANIC
MONUMENT

USFS 99

Windy
Ridge

Loowit Trail #216

South Fork Toutle River

Lava
Dome

Muddy River

Mt St Helens
8363ft

Loowit Trail #216

Climbers'
Bivouac

Ape
Canyon

Lava
Canyon

Lahar
Trailhead

USFS 25

Marble Mtn
Sno-Park

USFS 83

Wapati
Meadow

Gifford
Pinchot
National
Forest

Pine Creek

Clear Creek

USFS 93

Ape
Cave

Cougar
Sno-Park

Merrill
Lake

Marble Mtn
4116ft

Trail of Two Forests

USFS 83

Pine Creek
Information Station

USFS 90

Lewis River

Cougar

503

Jack's

Swift Creek
Reservoir

To
Mt Adams

Yale
Lake

WASHINGTON

spreading volcanic ash across the Pacific Northwest and as far northeast as Saskatchewan province, Canada.

After the smoke cleared, Mt St Helens – once a comely and symmetrical 9677-foot Cascade mountain covered with glaciers – had blown 1300 feet off its peak, and a mile-wide crater yawned on its north side. Spirit Lake, once a resort destination below the peak, was totally clogged with fallen timber and debris, and the rivers that flowed off the mountain were flooded with mud and ash flows. In 1982, 172 sq miles around the mountain were included in the **Mt St Helens National Volcanic Monument**. Two decades later, nature has restored much life to the mountain.

Native American legends depicted Mt St Helens as the youngest of the fire mountains of Oregon and Washington, and it likely is. Much of the volcano is less than 2000 years old. The mountain was known to have erupted several times in the 19th century, and significantly in 1857. Radiocarbon studies of trees in nearby forests suggest that there is a pattern to the volcano's eruption. After several centuries of quiescence, the mountain explodes several times in decade-spaced intervals, and again falls into a (geologically) short slumber.

The devastation wrought by the eruption is an incredible sight, and one that will haunt your thoughts for days. A trip to either the east- or westside crater viewpoints is strongly recommended; if you can, take the time to hike and explore this unique area.

Orientation

Mt St Helens is directly east of Castle Rock in a remote part of the Gifford Pinchot National Forest. The area was never particularly well served by roads, and the eruption destroyed the few that existed. Today, there are two principal entry routes into the region. The **Windy Ridge viewpoint**, on the northeast side of the mountain, was the first opened and is accessed by long drives on winding USFS roads. **Coldwater Ridge Visitor Center** and **Johnson Ridge Observatory** are on the northwest side of the mountain. These

viewpoints are easily accessed from I-5 off Hwy 504 and are open year-round.

Mt St Helens can be visited as a day-trip from either Portland or Seattle. The town of Castle Rock is about one hour's drive north of Portland on I-5; it's another hour from Castle Rock east to Coldwater Ridge. Castle Rock is a little over two hours south of Seattle. To reach the Windy Ridge area from I-5 requires two more hours.

Information

The national monument has instituted a new admission system. Visitors at any of the observation areas or visitors' centers pay $8 per adult from 16 to 61, $4 for those 62 and over, children 15 and under are free. This fee buys admission at all Mt St Helens sites, and is good for one week. Summer hikers will find a $3 per vehicle maintenance fee levied at most trailheads.

There are two major information centers on the way to Mt St Helens. If you are heading to the Windy Ridge area from the south on Hwy 503, stop at Mt St Helens Volcanic Monument headquarters (☎ 360-247-5473), 42218 NE Yale Bridge Rd, Amboy, WA 98601. Just off I-5 exit 49 near Castle Rock, on the way to Coldwater Ridge, is the Mt St Helens Visitor Center (☎ 360-274-2103), 3029 Spirit Lake Hwy (also known as Hwy 504), Castle Rock, WA 98611. Both offer lots of free information on the mountain and recreation, as well as films and slide shows about the eruption. The Castle Rock visitors' center has a particularly impressive series of exhibits about the Cascade volcanoes and post-eruption ecology. You could easily spend an hour just at this visitors' center.

Many people also time their visits to take in the film *The Eruption of Mt St Helens* at the Omnimax Theater (☎ 360-274-9844) in Castle Rock (on Hwy 504, 5 miles west of the visitors' center). Although not a sanctioned part of the national monument's displays, seeing the eruption in a wraparound theater is pretty exciting and a good reminder of the forces that formed today's Mt St Helens. Call ahead for scheduled showings and ticket prices.

When Mt St Helens Blew Her Stack

The most recent Mt St Helens eruption was first anticipated in March 1980, when small steam clouds began to build above the mountain and earthquakes rocked the area. Initially, geologists thought that the pyrotechnics were simply the result of ground water reaching the molten core of the mountain and not of rising lava. In fact, it wasn't until late in the game that scientists realized a major eruption was imminent.

Even though the state police worked to evacuate the Mt St Helens area prior to the eruption, some people who had always lived near the mountain simply chose to stay and take their chances, while others ignored the warnings and sneaked in to watch the volcano. The most well-known of those who stayed behind was Harry Truman, the proprietor of a resort on Spirit Lake. He was among the people killed on the mountain when the blast took place.

The 1980 eruption was one of steam, not lava. The molten rock that rose to the surface of the volcano was heavily infused with water, which at temperatures of 750°F is capable of enormous explosive power. As this piston of lava pushed closer and closer to the surface, it created a bulge on the north side of the peak that grew larger and more unstable with each passing day.

On May 18, the rock finally gave way; the entire north face of Mt St Helens slid down the mountain in what geologist believe was the largest landslide in recorded history. The landslide carried mud, snow, ice and rock at speeds of 200 mph, dumping them into Spirit Lake and 17 miles down the North Fork Toutle River valley. At over 800°F, the mudflows turned Spirit Lake into a boiling cauldron that instantly killed all fish and animal life.

Without the rock cover to hold them back, super-heated steam and gases finally broke through to the surface of the volcano, blasting a 15 mile high cloud of ash and rock into the air at speeds of 500 mph. The blast, carrying scorching temperatures and poisonous gases, hurtled through the forests north of the crater at speeds of 200 mph, leveling 150 sq miles of forest in an instant.

The amount of mud and ash that was eventually carried downriver was enormous; look for 100-foot-high banks of dredged white ash (now covered with gorse) along the Toutle River near I-5 exit 52. Even navigation on the Columbia River was affected, as huge deposits of mud and ash closed the shipping channels between Portland and the Pacific for many weeks.

In the end, 59 people were killed in the blast while another 190 who were within the affected zone lived through the eruption, but almost 1000 people who lived mainly along the Toutle River were left homeless. Downwind from the eruption, several inches of ash settled between Yakima and Spokane, disrupting businesses, schools and life in general for months. Many years later, drifts of ash left by the region's snowplows were still visible along the roadsides. While Mt St Helens has remained calm since 1980, geologists concur that another explosion is only a matter of time. ■

Coldwater Ridge Visitors Center & Johnson Ridge Observatory

Coldwater Ridge Visitors Center (☎ 360-274-2131), 45 miles east of Castle Rock and I-5 on Hwy 504, was completed in 1993. After leaving Castle Rock, Hwy 504 climbs steadily to Coldwater Ridge, a 5000-foot-high spur with views directly into the mouth of Mt St Helens' north-facing crater.

The interpretive center is a modern lodge overlooking Coldwater Lake, a long and narrow body of water created by a massive landslide during the 1980 eruption. The facility provides a wonderful glassed-in viewing area, a theater where a dozen video screens re-create the explosion of Mt St Helens and the rebirth of nature on the mountain, and rooms with interactive displays focusing on the cycles of nature. A rather creepy android gives final benediction to hikers before they set out. There's also a bookstore and a cafeteria. A short nature trail called the **Winds of Change** leads from the visitors' center and demonstrates the re-growth of vegetation in the area. Interpretive talks and hikes are offered year-round; call ahead for the schedule.

Roads lead from Coldwater Ridge Visitors Center down to the lake, and then climb up nearly 3000 feet to Johnson Ridge Observatory, another visitors' center and viewing area that looks directly into the mouth of the crater.

The visitors' center and the observatory are both open year-round; 9 am to 6 pm from April 1 to September 30, and 9 am to 5 pm the rest of the year.

Windy Ridge Viewpoint

A somewhat more remote vista point is on the northeastern side of the mountain, along Windy Ridge. Partisans often hold that this viewpoint is more impressive than that at Coldwater Ridge; while this is probably true, you will also spend more time on winding roads to get there.

Windy Ridge is at the terminus of USFS Rd 99, at a parking lot overlooking log-jammed Spirit Lake and looking directly at the lava dome in the mouth of the crater. The reality of the volcano's power and destruction is everywhere apparent. The road passes by entire forests that were blown down by the tremendous blast of the eruption, and boulders and ash are strewn about the mountainside. Trails lead to other viewpoints and down to Spirit Lake. There are toilets and a snack bar at the viewpoint, but no phone or visitors' center. Rangers offer interpretive talks and hikes on summer weekends.

To reach Windy Ridge from the north, turn onto USFS Rd 25 at Randle, on US 12 (48 miles east of I-5 exit 68). Travel 20 miles to the junction of USFS Rd 99. Follow this frequently winding, and – in summer – heavily traveled, gravel road for another 17 miles to the viewpoint. From the southwest, turn east off I-5 at Woodland (exit 21) onto Hwy 503, which leads to USFS Rd 90 and the Pine Creek Information Station at the intersection with USFS Rd 25 (in total about 45 miles). Follow USFS Rd 25 for 25 miles, and turn west on USFS Rd 99; the viewpoint is 17 miles distant. Allow at least 1¼ hours for the drive from either Randle or Pine Creek.

Ape Cave

The longest lava tube in the continental USA, the Ape Cave is also, at 12,810 feet in length, one of the longest underground hiking trails in the USFS trail system. Lava tubes are formed when the exterior of a deep lava flow hardens while the interior continues to flow. Eventually the liquid lava empties out of the crust, leaving a hollow tube with lava walls. In the case of the Ape Cave, the lava flowed down a deep watercourse; the top of the ravine sealed, but the lava continued to flow underground.

Hikers can walk and scramble the length of the Ape Cave on two trails, both beginning at an informational kiosk just off USFS Rd 8303. The three-quarter-mile **Lower Ape Cave Trail** follows the cave downstream from the main entrance. This part of the cave has a dry sandy bottom and nearly 20-foot-high ceilings, and it is by far the easier walk. There is no exit at this end of the cave, so you need to retrace your steps to get out. The 1½-mile **Upper Ape Cave Trail** requires a lot of scrambling over rock piles and narrower passages. The trail eventually exits at the upper entrance. Hikers can rent lanterns at the Ape Cave headquarters for $3.

Free half-hour, ranger-led explorations of the Ape Cave are offered daily from June 15 through September 5. These Ape Cave lantern walks are offered at 12:30, 1.30 and 2:30 pm weekdays, and on the half-hour from 11:30 am to 4:30 pm on weekends.

Also in the Ape Cave area is the wheel-chair-accessible **Trail of Two Forests**, a quarter-mile boardwalk along a stream and a lava cast forest. Interpretive displays explain the process of reforestation at this ancient lava flow.

By the way, the reference to 'ape' in the name of this cave and a nearby canyon has little to do with primates. A group of boy-scout adventurers took to calling themselves the Mt St Helens Apes after a purported sighting of Big Foot in Ape Canyon in 1924. Members of this group discovered this cave in 1946, hence the name.

Hiking

A number of short interpretive hikes leave from Coldwater Ridge and the lake, though to reach the principal Mt St Helens trail network from here requires a long slog across desolate pumice fields and mudflows, which can be oppressively hot on a sunny day. Hikers are better advised to begin hikes from Windy Ridge or the south side of the mountain. In either case, take along plenty of water, as there is very little natural water along these barren, dry trails.

Named after the female spirit that inhabits Mt St Helens in Native American myth, the **Loowit Trail No 216** is a 27-mile trail system that circles the mountain. Because of the extremely rugged terrain, be sure to check with rangers before setting out for an extended hike, as washouts and landslides are common. The most popular portion of the trail crosses the face of the

crater on the mountain's north side. The easiest access to the Loowit Trail is from Windy Ridge viewpoint.

The **Lahar Trailhead** in Ape Canyon, at the end of USFS Rd 83, provides access to a number of different hikes into wild volcanic landscapes, including a barrier-free path along a recent mudflow to a waterfall vista. The all-abilities trail is the beginning portion of the 2.4-mile **Lava Canyon Trail**; however, after the first half-mile the trail drops down into a steep canyon scoured out by the Mt St Helens eruption. The trail is for the intrepid, but it's great fun. A second trail ascends along a wooded ridge top beside a barren mudflow. The **Ape Canyon Trail** passes through patches of old-growth forest before reaching a deep and narrow chasm cut in the flanks of the mountain. At 5½ miles, the trail ties into the Loowit Trail No 216.

The long access roads leading into Spirit Lake and Windy Ridge have several trail heads, some of which access the following day hikes. The most popular hike in the area is called the **Harmony Lake Trail**, which leads down past scorched tree stumps to the shores of Spirit Lake. Although the hike is just over a mile in length, it is fairly steep going. The trail head is about 2 miles north of Windy Ridge viewpoint on USFS Rd 99.

The views from **Norway Pass** are among the best in the monument, with Mt St Helens and its open-jawed crater rising directly above the timber-cluttered Spirit Lake. To reach this overview, take the 2½-mile **Norway Pass Trail** from the trailhead on USFS Rd 26, 1 mile north of the junction with USFS Rds 99. Hikers with a shuttle can make a loop by returning along the **Independence Pass Trail** from Norway Ridge. This 3½-mile trail begins on USFS Rd 99 at the Independence Pass Trailhead, 2½ miles south of the junction of USFS Rd 99 and 26.

From Windy Ridge viewpoint itself, the **Truman Trail** leads directly toward the mountain, offering the quickest approach to the crater itself and to the around-mountain Loowit Trail. Even so, it's a hot and desolate 4-mile trudge before you reach the crater.

Cross-Country Skiing

The southern part of the monument has a number of Sno-Parks off USFS Rd 83. In winter, Cougar Sno-Park accesses a number of snowed-in USFS roads near the Ape Cave; Marble Mountain Sno-Park offers access to more snowbound roads and to Wapiti Meadows, with many miles of groomed trails. (The NPS does not rent cross-country skis in this area, but Jack's Restaurant does; see Climbing, below.)

Climbing

Because Mt St Helens is a very delicate and sometimes dangerous mountain, climbers must obtain a permit to ascend the peak between May 15 and October 31. The permit itself is free, but each hiker pays $15; one permit can cover up to 12 people and is good for 24 hours. Because the number of climbers with advance permits is limited to 100 people per day, competition is fierce for summer weekends. Permits are available by contacting the monument headquarters in Amboy (see the preceding Information section. For up-to-the-minute information on climbing Mt St Helens, call the Climbers Hotline at ☎ 360-247-3961.

Permits for an additional 50 climbers are available on a first-come, first-served basis from Jack's Restaurant & Store (☎ 360-231-4276), 5 miles west of Cougar on USFS Rd 90, which serves as a de facto headquarters for Mt St Helens climbs. The day before you want to climb, you need to sign up at Jack's; they start taking names at 11 am and issue the permits at 6 pm, and you must be present to receive them. All climbers are required to sign in at the climber's register at Jack's both before and after the climb.

Most climbers leave from trailhead No 216B at the end of USFS Rd 830, off USFS Rd 83, a total of 14 miles northeast of Cougar. No technical climbing abilities are needed, particularly in late summer after all the snow has melted. However, the climb isn't fun and games, as most of the quite steep ascent involves struggling up loose pumice fields. The 5-mile trail ends at the summit cliffs, with astonishing views down onto the smoking lava dome and the incinerated viscera of the mountain. Be very careful of the lip of the crater, as the rock here is unstable. Allow at least eight hours to make the roundtrip. Early in the season, bring along a sheet of plastic and slide down the snow fields for a fast descent.

Places to Stay & Eat

Mt St Helens is a pretty remote area and facilities are quite limited. There are a couple of diners and motels in Castle Rock, and a rustic lodge at Cougar, but most people will choose to camp or to make this a day-trip from a larger center.

Campgrounds aren't all that easy to find in this burned-up landscape, either. Campsites are most abundant on the south side of the monument, away from the main force of the explosion. *Yale Lake* and *Swift Creek Reservoir*, on the Lewis River, are both just south of the mountain and offer five lakeside campgrounds popular with motor boaters. Since the slopes along the Lewis River have recently been clear-cut, this is a fairly unenthralling place to get away from it all. To the north of Mt St Helens (on USFS Rd 25 near the junction with USFS Rd 26) is *Iron Creek Campground*, the only campground in the monument itself. Facilities include running water and pit toilets. The $12 sites, of which there are nearly 100, go quickly in summer, and can be reserved by calling US Forest Service reservations at ☎ 800-280-2267.

To the east at Castle Rock is *Seaquest State Park*, open year-round with nearly 100 campsites, running water and flush toilets ($11-$16). Seaquest is directly across from the entrance to the Mt St Helens Visitor Center, 5 miles west of I-5 exit 49 on Hwy 504.

The nicest place to stay in Castle Rock is the *Mt St Helens Motel* (☎ 360-274-7721), 1340 Mt St Helens Way NE, where single/double rooms are $48/58. There are a number of family restaurants adjacent.

Mt Adams

Mt Adams, at 12,276 feet, is the second-highest peak in Washington, and it towers over the beautiful and mostly undeveloped meadows and valleys of south-central Washington. It is one of the most beautiful of the Cascade peaks, with some enchanting hikes and an easy ascent to the mountain's summit. However, Mt Adams also has the distinction of being one of the least-visited and under-utilized mountain areas in the Northwest. Oregonians, who have the easiest access to Mt Adams from Portland and I-84, prefer to visit their own peaks, particularly Mt Hood, and getting to Mt Adams from most parts of Washington requires a lot of driving, much of it right past other alluring mountains. Also, the entire eastern slope of Mt Adams is enclosed in the Yakama Indian Reservation, and with a few specific exceptions, the land is not open to non-tribal members.

What this means is that hikers and campers will find Mt Adams relatively secluded, certainly compared with the throngs visiting its more popular and famous siblings. During the winter, snowed-in logging roads yield miles of cross-country ski trails near Trout Lake. Routes are well-signed and trail maps are available at the ranger station.

The **Mt Adams Wilderness Area**, a 66-sq-mile preserve, includes the mountain's summit and the western half of the mountain. While hiking, climbing and cross-country skiing are popular pastimes here, a more unique activity in the Mt Adams area is huckleberry picking. The high meadows around the mountain are famed for their late summer crop of this wild blueberry.

Mt Adams was known to early native tribes as Klickitat or Pah-to. Many myths and legends pit the spirit of Mt Adams against that of Mt Hood, directly south in Oregon. Inevitably, their conflicts ended with each shooting fire and smoke at the other. Mt Adams is considered a sacred site to the Yakama tribe.

Mt Adams is also geologically unique among Cascade peaks; it's composed of a number of separate volcanic cones, each of which erupted at different times, whereas most volcanoes erupt from a single cone. These multiple cones lend Mt Adams its distinctive broadly domed appearance. Mt Adams first began erupting about 450,000 years ago, though the peak we see today was largely formed about 15,000 years ago, toward the end of the most recent ice age. Ten major glaciers still cling to the mountain.

Orientation

The easiest access to Mt Adams is from the Columbia River Gorge, from either I-84 or Hwy 14. From Hood River or White Salmon to the south, take Hwy 141 north (about 25 miles) to Trout Lake, a tiny community that's nonetheless the head of recreation in the area. In summer, USFS Rd 23, a fair graveled road, is open between Randle, south of Mt Rainier on US 12, and Trout Lake (a three-hour drive).

Information

For information on hiking or climbing, consult the Gifford Pinchot National Forest ranger stations, at 2455 Hwy 141 in Trout Lake (☎ 509-395-2501) and in Randle (☎ 509-497-1100). If you plan to pick huckleberries or mushrooms in the national forest, stop here to get permits. Maps of the Mt Adams Wilderness Area and the Indian Heaven Wilderness Area can be picked up for $1 each. They can also be mail-ordered through the Forest Supervisor, Gifford Pinchot National Forest, 500 West 12th St, Vancouver, WA 98660.

Hiking

Two famous trails capture the beauty and vastness of Mt Adams. The slightly mis-named **Around the Mountain Trail**, also known as Trail 9, skirts the southern base of the peak for 8.3 miles between the Bird Creek area, at the trailhead off USFS Rd 8290, and the **Pacific Crest Trail** (PCT), which enters the wilderness from the southwest. The PCT continues around to

Stalking the Wild Huckleberry

The blue huckleberry is a wild blueberry, admired for its tangy flavor. It can be eaten fresh, made up into pies, jams and any number of ice-cream and chocolate confections. The huckleberry was an integral part of the Native American diet. Tribes made summer excursions to the high mountain meadows where these low, bushy huckleberry plants flourish; the berries were often dried for winter use.

Southwest of Mt Adams are some of the largest and most productive wild huckleberry meadows in the Northwest. The elevation is high – usually above 4000 feet – but quite flat due to the underlying lava flows. This land of marsh and lake is perfect for huckleberries – as it is for mosquitoes, so be warned.

Huckleberry season is usually August through September, and a number of USFS-administered areas are open for berry picking. Free USFS permits are necessary, and rangers will also offer advice and maps indicating where the harvest is most productive. Traditionally, the best berry picking is in the Sawtooth Berryfields, an area immediately north of the Indian Heaven Wilderness Area. Follow signs for the Surprise Lakes or Cold Springs campgrounds, off USFS Rd 24, about 21 miles west of Trout Lake. ■

the north side of Mt Adams and branches north before entering the Yakama Indian Reservation. These two trails manage to traverse about half of the mountain's girth, mostly at timberline and mostly at a gentle grade. The views of surrounding Cascade peaks are incredible. It's about 25 miles from the Bird Creek Trailhead to the northern border of the wilderness area (via the PCT). There are no base trails on the mountain's east side, which belongs to the tribe.

To those who know it, the **Bird Creek Meadow Trail** is one of the best-loved hikes in the Northwest. The 3-mile loop trail leads from the Bird Creek Trailhead

and gently climbs to an alpine meadow showered by waterfalls and ablaze with wildflowers. Looming above are the cliffs and glaciers of Mt Adams' summit. After ascending to a ridge-top viewpoint, the trail loops back beside tiny lakes and yet more wildflowers. The best time to hike the trail is in July, when blooms are at their peak and most of the trails will be free of ice.

Both of the above trails begin in a small, western portion of the Yakama Indian Reservation that is open to non-Yakamas. However, to hike or camp in this area requires paying a $10-per-vehicle fee to the tribe. The Around the Mountain Trail can also be accessed from the Morrison Creek or Cold Creek Campground trailheads, outside the reservation, but Bird Creek Meadows is entirely within the reservation and subject to the fee.

Climbing

Mt Adams is known as one of the easiest Cascade peaks to climb, and it's often used as a trial peak for beginners. While most climbs on Mt Adams are non-technical slogs up a glacier, even these require basic climbing gear. Altitude sickness and severe weather changes are the biggest threats to novice climbers.

The easiest approaches (Grade II) are from the south, via Cold Creek Campground, and up the South Spur to the summit. These approaches are good between May and August. There's a more difficult route (Grade III) from the north over Adams Glacier via Takhlakh Lake Campground. Climbers should sign in and out at the USFS ranger station at either Trout Lake or Randle.

Places to Stay & Eat

Though there are some lovely campgrounds on Mt Adams, be prepared for insect pests during the summer. Near Bird Creek Meadows are three lakeside campgrounds in the Yakama Indian Reservation (☎ 509-865-5121, ext 657). Sites are $15 a night in addition to the $10 entrance fee and all have running water and pit toilets. The campgrounds at *Bird Lake*, 20 sites, and *Mirror Lake*, 12 sites, are about 16 miles east of Trout Lake on USFS Rds 82 and 8290. Two miles farther down this rough road is *Bench Lake Campground*, with 44 sites and great views of Mt Adams.

There's another cluster of lakeside USFS campgrounds about 25 miles north along USFS Rd 23. The nicest of these is *Takhlakh Lake Campground*, which has 54 sites with running water and pit toilets. It costs $5 a night. From here, you can hike into the *Chain of Lakes Campground*, less than a mile away, for more seclusion; this free primitive campground has three sites.

The *Trout Lake Country Inn* (☎ 509-395-2894), 15 Guler Rd has rooms in the inn for $65, and a cabin for $85. *Serenity* (☎ 509-395-2500), 1 mile south of Trout

Lake on Hwy 141, has four luxury cabins in the woods ($75 to $125), each with kitchen and bathrooms, and great views of Mt Adams.

Flying L Ranch (☎ 509-364-3488), 25 Flying L Lane in Glenwood, is about 18 miles from Trout Lake off Glenwood Rd. Rooms in the lodge and guesthouse cost $80 to $110; cabins are $110 to $140. Prices include breakfast and use of a common kitchen. Recreation packages are available in the summer.

The other option for food in Trout Lake is *Bonnie's Place Cafe* (☎ 509-395-2747), 2376 Hwy 141, a traditional diner. *Tsugali's Deli* (☎ 509-395-2269), 2385 Hwy 141, has picnic supplies and heaping scoops of huckleberry ice cream.

North Cascades

The Cascade Range starts in Canada and runs all the way south to northern California, but the North Cascades refer specifically to the rugged, chiseled alpine peaks in northern Washington. Indeed, with their hanging glaciers and valleys, their icefalls and cirque-cradled lakes, these particular mountains are so thoroughly alpine in character that it's tempting to call them (as John Muir did) the 'American Alps.'

Rocky, glaciated and wild, the North Cascades are well known to Northwest climbers, hikers, bicyclists, anglers and auto tourists, all of whom tend to give a little sigh of awe before they launch into descriptions of this majestic land. However, don't expect to happen across a motel or lodge, or even much of a cabin resort, between Marblemount and Mazama. Due to the lack of facilities, most people merely drive through, but as with the Olympic Mountains, the most beautiful and dramatic sights of this rocky terrain are found off-road – by hiking one of the numerous trails or climbing to the crests of the mountains' ridges. Campgrounds, both formal and de facto, abound in the North Cascades. And it's best to come prepared with enough food to see you through your stay, be that a bag of chips to nibble as you drive or a week's worth of camp chow.

Mt Baker, just west of the national park, is extremely popular, not only because it offers some of the best hiking, climbing and skiing in the state, but also because there's a little more in the way of accommodations and there are even a few good restaurants nearby. Farther south, the area around Darrington is another major access to the North Cascades; it has plenty of hiking, and climbers head for Glacier Peak.

The Cascades are the spine of the Northwest, wringing out Pacific storm fronts like a wet sponge. They divide the land and the state, creating wet, forested slopes and valleys to the west, and leaving the eastern plains bone dry. Go prepared for snow, expect rain, and with some luck, the sun will shine long enough to see the peaks. If anything, the weather is changeable. Hikers should take this seriously, and pack for rain and cold weather even in summer.

On the east side of the mountains, the Stehekin River flows down out of the mountains and feeds into Lake Chelan, the third-deepest lake in the USA and another beautiful center for recreation or relaxation in this gorgeous corner of the state. Cross-country skiers flock to the Methow Valley in the winter from miles around – the trails here are excellent and the weather is generally much better than at Mt Baker.

History

Native peoples, like most modern folks, didn't make year-round homes in the North Cascades. Though Native Americans traveled to the North Cascades in the summer for roots, berries, hunting and fishing, they didn't really stick around once the snow began to pile up. Trails first traveled by Native Americans between the Puget Sound and the Columbia Basin are still hiked today; the popular Cascade Pass Trail was one link in this traders' route.

When whites arrived, it took them about 70 years to find a way into and through the mountains. The first to make it through was a cartographer employed by the army. Miners kept hoping to strike it rich in the mountains, but few managed to eke out any type of living from the rocky, remote streams.

It took power-thirsty Seattle to put any kind of reins on this rugged country. The abundant water cascading down steep drops caught the eyes of engineers, and in the 1920s and '30s a series of dams were built along the Upper Skagit River, turning this section of the river into reservoirs and stringing the valleys with power lines. The

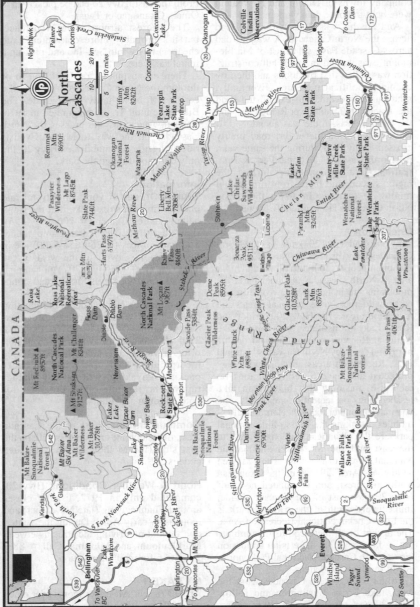

company towns of Diablo and Newhalem were built to house dam workers.

And all this was done without a road across the North Cascades. A wagon road across Cascade Pass, southeast of Marblemount, was started in 1896, but construction was halted first by floods and then by changing political pressures. Eventually, road builders decided to extend the road that reached to Diablo over Rainy Pass, and the Cascade Pass route was abandoned. It wasn't until 1968 that a dirt road finally crossed Rainy Pass; during the same year, the North Cascades National Park & Recreation Area was created, shifting the region's economic focus from timber and mining to tourism. In 1972, the paved North Cascades Hwy officially opened.

Orientation

Only one road, Hwy 20 (known as the North Cascades Hwy) crosses the North Cascades. Although people refer casually to the entire area as North Cascades National Park, the mountains are in fact a jigsaw of different parks, wilderness areas, national forests and recreation areas. The Hwy 20 corridor and Ross Lake constitute the Ross Lake National Recreation Area, flanked on the north and south by North Cascades National Park. Recreation areas are somewhat less protected and have fewer restrictions on their use, meaning that hikers can take leashed dogs on recreation-area trails, and you may encounter four-wheelers and snowmobiles. Flanking the 781-sq-mile national park are the Okanogan National Forest to the east and the Mt Baker-Snoqualmie National Forest to the west. The Pasayten Wilderness Area falls within the Okanogan National Forest, and is situated north of Hwy 20, just east of the Cascade divide. Immediately south of the national park is the Lake Chelan National Recreation Area. The upshot of all these confusing administrative factors is that there is no admission fee to North Cascades National Park, nor to any of the associated areas.

To get to the North Cascades from the west, take I-5 to Burlington and follow Hwy 20 east up the Skagit River valley.

From the east, Hwy 20 can be picked up at Omak, Okanogan or Twisp.

The nearest airport is in Wenatchee, but it's probably more convenient (and cheaper) to fly into Sea-Tac and pick up a rental car there.

There is no public transportation to or through the North Cascades. You'll need a car or – for the hardy – a bicycle. The Bikecentennial Trail, inaugurated in 1976, starts in Anacortes and crosses the North Cascades on the way to Maine. Cyclists ride alongside automobiles on Hwy 20, the only corridor through the park.

Information

Tourist Offices If you can only tolerate one information stop, make it at the Newhalem Visitor Center (☎ 206-386-4495), right next to the Newhalem Campground. The park offices (☎ 360-856-5700) are in Sedro Woolley, well to the west of the mountains, at 2105 Hwy 20. You can pick up backcountry permits for off-road camping at either place.

If you want a more in-depth introduction to the area's wilderness, the North Cascades Institute (☎ 360-856-5700, ext 209), 2105 Hwy 20, Sedro Woolley, WA 98284, offers a variety of natural history classes incorporating activities such as backpacking, kayaking, writing and photography. The institute offers programs for both children and adults.

Communications West of the Cascade crest, the telephone area code is 360; on the east side (the Methow Valley), the area code is 509.

Road & Weather Conditions Hwy 20, completed only in 1972, usually closes around Thanksgiving (late November) and reopens in early April. During the winter, don't count on driving the stretch between Marblemount and Mazama. Call ☎ 888-766-4636 for road information.

MT BAKER

At 10,778 feet, Mt Baker looms over much of northern Washington and provides a

The North Cascades Volcanoes

Washington's North Cascades started off as the southern tip of a volcanic micro-continent that included part of present-day British Columbia. Tropical fossils in the North Cascades hint that the erstwhile island had its start in the South Pacific, then drifted north and ran into the Okanogan, which then formed the western edge of North America. As the two bodies of land joined, rocks crumpled to form long north-south ridges, stretching and faulting along the same axis.

The volcanoes, present before the micro-continent ever drifted into North America, continued to erupt, but not all of the intensely hot rocks spewed outward; many were subjected to great pressures and crystalized beneath the earth's surface to form granite. Much of this granite was ultimately pushed upward into new mountains, the metamorphic forces of pressure and heat creating 'gneisses' (banded or foliated rocks), which form the North Cascades' characteristic spires and horns. These were carved during several waves of ice ages, beginning about 500,000 years ago. Glaciers carved out long, straight, U-shaped river valleys with exceptionally steep walls, giving the Cascades their distinctive chiseled look. Even today, 318 glaciers continue to work on the rocks. For a good look at rocks and informative park displays, pull off at the Diablo Lake Overlook, milepost 132.

The highest of the North Cascade peaks, Mt Baker is on the edge of the Northern Cascade province. As the Cascade Range began to rise, volcanoes shot up through this older formation. Mount Baker began to erupt about one million years ago, although its present cone was probably built in the last 20,000 years.

Mt Baker is still an active volcano. A summit cinder cone and a 12 mile long lava flow down Sulfur Creek are probably only 1000 years old, and eruptions of ash were reported in 1843 and 1859. More recently, Mt Baker produced significant steam and ash eruptions in 1975, leading to speculation that the volcano was building up to a major eruption. ■

craggy, glacier-hung backdrop to Bellingham. The peak was heavily glaciated during the last ice age; after these large glaciers retreated, the mountain was incised with cirques and deep notch-like valleys. Glaciers are still gnawing away at Mt Baker and 10,000 acres of permanent snowfields still cling to the mountain's flanks.

This rugged birthright makes Mt Baker and nearby 9127-foot Mt Shuksan popular destinations for hikers, skiers and climbers. It also means that many of the trails up and around Mt Baker and the surrounding peaks require pretty steep ascents and descents. Also, Mt Baker's far northwest location (only 15 miles south of the Canadian border) means that precipitation – mostly snow – positively dumps here. Hiking trails may not be free of snowpack until August. But all that snow is good news to skiers – the Mt

Baker Ski Area has the deepest base in the state, and informal cross-country trails open up the wilderness to adventurous Nordic skiers.

The rugged and snow-bound territory around Mt Baker wasn't of much interest to either Native Americans or white settlers until rumors of gold brought prospectors swarming into the North Fork Nooksack River in the 1890s and 1900s. Although hard rock mining did briefly flourish in the area, the difficult climate made transportation and exploration difficult. Logging soon replaced mining as the primary economic force in the area.

Mt Baker was first climbed in 1868, and by 1911 ascents of the mountain were common enough for the Bellingham Chamber of Commerce to sponsor a marathon race that included a climb up and down the peak. The annual race was canceled two years later, when one contestant fell into a glacial crevasse and had to be rescued.

There were frequent calls throughout the 1900s for the Mt Baker area to be declared a national park, but it wasn't until 1984 that the region was made a wilderness area.

The peak itself, and 184 sq miles of surrounding public land, are enclosed in the Mt Baker Wilderness Area; adjacent to this is the 8600-acre Mt Baker National Recreation Area. Paved Hwy 542, which climbs up to 5200 feet to a breathtaking vista called Artist Point, has been designated a National Forest Scenic Byway. However, the final 10 miles are very steep and narrow – you may find that some of the switchbacks are themselves breathtaking. If you're pulling a trailer, it's a good idea to leave it at the base of the mountain.

The little community of Glacier (population 200) on Hwy 542 is basically a smattering of motels and restaurants designed to service skiers. No gasoline is available, so tank up at either Kendall or Maple Falls.

Orientation

Generally speaking, there are two ways to get to Mt Baker. The most popular is on Hwy 542, which travels east from Bellingham via Kendall; it's 62 miles to the Mt Baker Ski Area. This road is open year-round and offers the highest-altitude access point. A second access road, Baker Lake Rd off Hwy 20 at Concrete, dead-ends at the northern end of Baker Lake.

Information

The Forest Service's Glacier Public Service Center (☎ 360-599-2714), just east of Glacier, is open 8:30 am to 4:30 pm daily. At this handsome CCC-built stone lodge is a small bookshop, interpretive displays on the park, and a ranger to answer questions; you can also call here to find out about road closures. In the summer you can also ask questions at the Heather Meadows Visitors Center.

The wilderness area is administered by the Mt Baker-Snoqualmie National Forest (☎ 360-856-5700), 2105 Hwy 20, Sedro

Woolley, WA 98284; contact this office for more information about the wilderness, and hiking and skiing trails.

Mt Baker Hwy Scenic Byway

Even if you're a travel purist and spurn popular vista points, you'll probably want to join the parade of RVs on Hwy 542 and drive up to Artist Point, with its incredible views onto Mt Baker and Mt Shuksan. It's a great introduction to this magnificent area, and hiking trails split off from the highway and lead to less thronged viewpoints and hidden lakes. This route is open all winter as far as Mt Baker Ski Area; the remaining 2.6 miles to Artist Point are open from mid-July to late October, or until snowfall. Also bear in mind that the final 10 miles of the highway climb 3200 feet. This is a steep and very winding road.

From Glacier, the first 14 miles climb through old-growth fir forests along the North Fork Nooksack River. One stop along this stretch of road ought to be **Nooksack Falls**, which drop 175 feet into a deep gorge. After Silver Fir Campground, the road begins to climb in earnest. Mt Shuksan looms to the east, its glaciers seemingly held back by horn-like peaks. At **Heather Meadows**, the upward climb slows for a moment. The Mt Baker Ski Area is here, and just up the road is **Austin Pass**, a picnic area and the beginning point of several hiking trails.

The road ends 34 miles east of Glacier at **Artist Point**, at 5200 feet, with views onto the face of both Mt Baker and Mt Shuksan across a tiny reflecting pond. To the north rear the rugged Canadian peaks. This is a magical spot; it's like being at the top of the world.

Hiking

Many hiking trails around Mt Baker require fairly strenuous climbs up glacier-carved valleys to viewpoints and wildflower meadows; however, several hikes leave from trailheads at the end of lengthy backroad drives and reach the high country in relatively short order.

Heliotrope Ridge Most climbers ascend to the top of Mt Baker from Heliotrope Ridge and onto Coleman Glacier. The 3-mile, one-way trail to the edge of the glacier is also popular with day-hikers in August when the meadows, at 6200 feet, are ablaze with wildflowers.

To reach this trail, designated as No 677, turn south onto USFS Rd 39, 1 mile east of Glacier. This unpaved road climbs up the side of Mt Baker for 8 miles to the trailhead. After a 2-mile hike through forest, the trail reaches timberline and then crosses several glacial streams and wildflower meadows. The trail then climbs up onto a moraine and suddenly overlooks Coleman Glacier. The views onto the face of Mt Baker and onto the massive, deeply rivened glacier are incredible. Unless you have climbing gear, don't attempt to make your way onto the glacier or to climb any higher along the frequently snow-packed morainal ridge.

Excelsior Mountain From this 5700-foot peak, hikers and Mt Baker view each other eye-to-eye across the narrow North Fork Nooksack valley. Several steep trails lead to this vantage point from Hwy 542. The following route lets your vehicle do most of the climbing. Drive 2 miles east of Glacier, and turn at the Douglas Fir Campground onto USFS Rd 31, also called Canyon Creek Rd. Follow this road for almost 15 miles around to the back of Excelsior Mountain. Park at the head of trail No 625, and hike 2½ miles past Damfino Lakes and meadows to Excelsior Pass. A quarter-mile to the east, at the end of an easy path, is Excelsior Peak.

Lake Ann One of the most popular hikes in the area is the 8-mile, roundtrip hike up to Lake Ann, shimmering beneath the massive hanging glaciers of Mt Shuksan. The trail to Lake Ann leaves from Austin Pass Picnic Area.

Chain Lakes Loop Beginning at the Artist Point parking lot and circling a high plateau, this beautiful 6-mile loop trail passes a half-dozen icy lakes surrounded by huckleberry meadows. The trail begins at the west end of the parking lot, and the tree-shaded trailhead is sometimes covered by snow; take the trail that drops into the forest, not the one that climbs the plateau.

The trail passes Mazama, Iceberg and Hayes Lakes, then climbs a ridge to drop onto the first of the two Bagley Lakes. Between the two lakes, a trail cuts south and climbs up to Hwy 542, and a short climb up the road returns hikers to their vehicles at Artist Point. Hikers can also continue on the loop trail past the second Bagley Lake, shortly arriving at Mt Baker Ski Area.

Skiing

Downhill Mt Baker Ski Area (☎ 360-734-6771) has alpine ski runs with a vertical rise of 1500 feet on the dry, eastern side of the mountain. An exciting variety of chutes, half-pipes, cliffs and excellent powder has gained Mt Baker national distinction among snowboarders, though it's still more or less undiscovered by the masses. The lodge offers complete rental and instruction facilities. Snowboard rentals from the Mt Baker Snowboard Shop (☎ 360-599-2008), 9996 Forest St, behind Milano's Restaurant in Glacier are less expensive. Lift tickets are $29 weekends and holidays and $17 to $20 midweek. Better hit the slopes early, as the ski area shuts down at 3:30 pm. Call ☎ 360-671-0211 for a snow report.

Cross-Country The heavy falls of fine, dry snow also make Mt Baker the most popular cross-country ski destination in Washington. In addition to downhill runs, Mt Baker Ski Area also offers groomed cross-country trails. From the ski area, snowed-in Hwy 542 up to Artist Point and the trail around the Chain Lakes open up great vistas of the snowy peaks. Other popular cross-country ski trails start at Silver Fir Campground, and run through meadows along Anderson Creek.

Cross-country ski rentals are available from the ski shop at the Mt Baker Ski Area, or from the Base Camp (☎ 360-733-5461), 901 W Holly St in Bellingham. State Sno-Park permits are mandatory at plowed trailheads and are available at local businesses.

Climbing

The two principal routes up Mt Baker ascend Coleman Glacier, on the northwest side of the mountain, and Easton Glacier, on the south side. Both require two days, with a night spent camping at the base of the glaciered peak.

The easiest route is from the south, up Easton Glacier from the Shreiber Meadow trailhead. Although technical equipment is highly recommended, snowmobiles have been known to ascend Mt Baker along this route. The northern ascent begins at the Heliotrope Ridge trailhead (see Hiking, above) and continues across Coleman and Roosevelt Glaciers for a final steep and icy climb up the North Ridge to the summit.

In addition to the usual dangers from altitude sickness and glacial crevasses, Mt Baker carries the threat of extremely changeable weather. As the peak is only 35 miles from sea level in Puget Sound, moist air can belt across the hills and shroud the peak in clouds and storms in minutes. Take navigational tools along on any high elevation hike, and know how to use them.

Novice climbers should consider classes and guided climbs with the American Alpine Institute (☎ 360-671-1505), 1515 12th St, Bellingham, WA 98225. AAI is one of the nation's best climbing schools, and offers a variety of weekend classes as well as longer programs focusing on rock, ice and snow climbing. A three-day ascent of Mt Baker, including instruction in glacier travel, costs around $230, depending on the number of students per guide. They lead two to three climbs weekly during the climbing season (mid-May to September).

White-Water Rafting

White-water rafters put in just above the Douglas Fir Campground and raft the North Fork Nooksack, a Class III river, to Maple Falls, a total of 10 miles. For a guided raft trip, contact either River Riders at ☎ 800-448-7238, or Blue Sky Outfitters (☎ 206-931-0637), PO Box 124, Pacific, WA 98047.

Places to Stay & Eat

Several attractive USFS campgrounds are positioned along Hwy 542 and the North Fork Nooksack River. *Douglas Fir Campground* is 2 miles east of Glacier and *Silver Fir Campground* is 12 miles east of Glacier. Sites cost $10 and have drinking water and pit toilets.

The new *Mt Baker RV Park & Campground* (☎ 360-599-1908, 888-250-7077), 10443 Mt Baker Hwy, near the Snowline Inn, is the only campground on Mt Baker with RV hookups. It also stays open during the winter for the ski season.

Glacier Creek Motel & Cabins (☎ 360-599-2991), 10036 Mt Baker Hwy in Glacier, offers lodging in motel rooms ($42 to $50) or in creekside cabins starting at $60.

The *Snowline Inn* (☎ 800-228-0119), 10433 Mt Baker Hwy in Glacier, has condominiums with full kitchen facilities. One-bedroom units start at $65; larger loft units start at $85.

Food is surprisingly good in Glacier. *Milano's Restaurant & Deli* (☎ 360-599-2863), 9990 Mt Baker Hwy, offers fresh pasta – no surprise – in an attractive bistro atmosphere; dinner entrées run $9 to $11. The portions are huge and there's usually a line out the door, but hang in there – it's well worth the wait. It's also open for breakfast on weekends. *Mountain Laurel*

Cafe (☎ 360-599-1002), 9393 Mt Baker Hwy, another 1½ miles west of Glacier, specializes in organically grown vegetarian and seafood preparations for lunch and dinner. The *Chandelier* (☎ 360-599-2233), east of Glacier, has family-style cooking and late-night dancing.

MOUNTAIN LOOP HWY
The Mountain Loop Hwy (USFS Rd 20) is a woodsy corridor linking Hwys 92 and 530 that's strewn with trailheads and peppered with the dregs of old mines. Miners went after galena ore, a conglomeration of silver and lead, but the plethora of faulted rock in the nearby hills made it difficult to follow veins very far. If you're traveling from the Seattle area, this is a good alternative approach to North Cascades National Park. From here, most people head to the **Glacier Peak Wilderness Area** and to 10,541-foot Glacier Peak itself.

To reach the loop highway, get off I 5 at Arlington (Hwy 530), then head south on Jordan Rd to Granite Falls and Hwy 92. Turn east onto USFS Rd 92, and turn north at the Sauk River for the Mountain Loop Hwy, a gravel road for the first 12 miles (to the White Chuck River); this road rejoins Hwy 530 at Darrington, the northern terminus of the Mountain Loop Hwy. From Darrington it's 19 miles north to the North Cascade Hwy at Rockport on Hwy 530, and 28 miles west back to Arlington.

Stop by the Darrington Ranger Station (☎ 360-436-1155), 1405 Emmons St, for hiking information. If you're driving the Mountain Loop Hwy en route to Darrington you can stop by the Ranger Station in Verlot (☎ 360-691-7791).

Hiking & Climbing
One deservedly popular local hike is to **Kennedy Hot Springs** in the Glacier Peak Wilderness Area. Eight miles south of Darrington, at the White Chuck Campground, turn onto USFS Rd 23 and continue to the road's end. Park and start hiking along the White Chuck River Trail (No 643). The 96°F hot springs are 5 miles in from the trailhead.

To climb **Glacier Peak**, follow the White Chuck Trail another 1½ miles past the hot springs to the Pacific Crest Trail. Turn north and hike about a half-mile to the Glacier Trail and Sitkum Ridge and the timberline base camp. It's a long approach – about 10 miles all told – before you get onto the Sitkum Glacier, a relatively untechnical but steep route to the 10,541-foot summit.

Places to Stay & Eat
There are about a dozen USFS campgrounds along the Mountain Loop Hwy. *Turlo Campground, Verlot Campground* and *Gold Basin Campground* (the area's largest), are all clustered around Verlot on the south fork of the Stillaguamish. Eight miles south of Darrington on the Sauk River is *White Chuck Campground*, which is convenient to the White Chuck Trail. Further south is *Bedal Campground* at the confluence of the Sauk River's north and south forks. Expect pit toilets, running water and an $8 camping fee.

The *Stagecoach Inn* (☎ 360-436-1776, 800-428-1776), 1100 Seaman, is Darrington's only real motel, with rooms for $65. There's a paucity of restaurants in Darrington, so it helps that the Stagecoach serves a continental breakfast. Your best bet for a meal is to cook it yourself.

UPPER SKAGIT RIVER VALLEY
From Sedro Woolley, Hwy 20 makes its subtle ascent along this pretty Cascade river valley en route to the North Cascades National Park. It's Bible camps, logging outfits, and counter-culturalist homesteads for most of the way, much like any other forest corridor in this part of the state. Concrete (population 847), 23 miles east of Sedro Woolley, is the Upper Skagit Valley's largest town, and serves as a base for people headed up to Baker Lake or to climbs around Mt Baker. Rockport (population 300), at the junction of Hwys 20 and 530, sits where the Sauk River joins the Skagit River, and has become known as one of the Northwest's best bald eagle viewing sites. It's

also popular with river rafters and anglers.

Stop and fill the car with gas and snack food at Marblemount, the region's oldest town – it's the last real town on Hwy 20 for 69 miles (and it has the last tavern for 89 miles). In the winter, Hwy 20 is plowed as far east as Marblemount, 40 miles east of Sedro Woolley; the stretch between Marblemount and Mazama is usually closed between mid-November and early April. The highway turns north just past Marblemount, and Cascade River Rd heads east across the Skagit River, past a fish hatchery and some campgrounds, to the Cascade Pass Trailhead, some 25 miles from Marblemount.

Information
Marblemount Wilderness Center (☎ 360-873-4500, ext 37 or 39) issues backcountry permits and answers questions about trails. It's open daily during the summer and has extended hours. Call ☎ 888-766-4636 for road information if you want to travel past Marblemount near the beginning or end of winter.

There's a post office in Concrete (☎ 360-853-8201) at 5085 Railroad Ave, and in Marblemount (☎ 360-873-2125) at 5868 Hwy 20.

You may also want to take advantage of the Wilderness Village Laundromat (☎ 360-873-2571) east of Rockport on Hwy 20, next to the Wilderness Village RV Park.

Baker Lake & Lake Shannon
Just north of Concrete is Baker Lake, a natural lake that was enlarged by the backwaters from Upper Baker Lake Dam in the early 1960s. Below it is Lake Shannon, held back by Lower Baker Lake Dam. Washington's largest colony of nesting osprey is found at Lake Shannon.

Baker Lake is a popular place to launch a boat and fish for Kokanee salmon or lake and rainbow trout, and there's a small vacation resort at the north end of the lake. There are also several hiking trails. Baker Lake Rd runs along the west side of the lake, passing several campgrounds and the

Shadow of the Sentinels, a nature trail through old-growth Douglas firs, before ending at USFS Rd 1168, which leads to the **Baker River Trail**. This relatively flat trail runs 3 miles up the jade green river past huge old cedars and beaver ponds; it makes a good family hike.

The trail to **Baker Hot Springs** is about 3 miles west of the Park Creek Campground on Baker Lake's north end. Take USFS Rd 1144 (just past the campground) for 3.2 miles to a large parking area. A short trail from the north end of the parking lot leads to the 109°F natural pool. Don't expect bathing suits.

To reach the lakes, turn north off Hwy 20 onto Baker Lake Rd, 6 miles west of Concrete.

Upper Skagit Bald Eagle Area
The bald eagle area is essentially the 10-mile stretch of the Skagit River between Rockport and Marblemount. After salmon spawn, their spent carcasses become meals for the more than 600 eagles who winter here. January is the best time to view the eagles, which are present from November through early March.

In Rockport, the **Howard Miller Steelhead Park** makes a good base for a morning of eagle-watching. The riverside setting, near the confluence of the Sauk and Skagit Rivers, and the name of this park will lure anglers, but even passersby should stop and take a look at the 30-foot-long cedar dugout canoe. Native Americans traveled the local rivers in such canoes, which they poled from a standing position, rather than kneeling to paddle.

Climbing
North Cascades climbers get to choose from glaciers, rock and ice; many climbs, including **Mt Shuksan**, a 9127-foot peak north of Baker Lake in the Mt Baker Wilderness Area, contain a mix of all three. Shuksan is an exception among the local peaks in that its approach is easy; most North Cascades climbs require several

days, largely because the approach hikes are quite long. Reach the Sulfide Glacier route by driving almost all the way up Baker Lake Rd, turning onto Shannon Creek Rd (USFS Rd 1152) at the campground and, after 3 miles, taking the high road until it ends (4½ miles). Hike the **Shannon Ridge Trail** to the timberline. This route is best climbed during the summer, and it's a favorite with ski mountaineers. For complete route information, see Fred Beckey's *Cascade Alpine Guide*, volume 3.

Hiking

The **Sauk Mountain Trail** leads to an old fire lookout with great views of Mt Baker and the North Cascades. This 2.1-mile hike from USFS Rd 1030 (which is well marked by signs near Rockport State Park) climbs 1200 feet, is not too steep for average hikers and passes wildflowers galore in the spring and a side trail to Sauk Lake.

Rafting

The upper part of the Skagit River is an easy float. Reach the standard put-in spot by taking Cascade River Rd out of Marblemount and turning left just after the bridge over the Skagit River. Take out at Howard Miller Steelhead Park in Rockport. Several outfitters run **eagle-watching** float trips. Call Chinook Expeditions (☎ 206-793-3451, 800-241-3451), Orion Expeditions (☎ 206-547-6715, 800-553-7466), or Wildwater River Tours (☎ 206-939-2151, 800-522-9453). Eagle-watching trips usually run from mid-November to January and cost about $60 per person.

Special Events

The Upper Skagit Bald Eagle Festival (☎ 360-853-7009) is held the first weekend in February in Concrete, Rockport and Marblemount.

Places to Stay

Camping Baker Lake has seven campgrounds, mostly on the lake's west bank. If it's hot out, bear in mind that *Horseshoe*

Cove Campground, 13 miles north of Concrete, has a swimming beach, and that glacier-fed Baker Lake warms up enough for swimming in the summer; there is running water, mostly pit toilets and sites cost $10. The spacious wooded sites here are quickly packed with large, extended family groups; call ☎ 800-280-2267 for reservations. Campgrounds are smaller and quieter further up the Baker Lake Rd. On the east side of Baker Lake is *Maple Grove Campground*, a free boat-in, hike-in campground with no running water. It's at the end of the East Bank Trail, an easy 4-mile hike past burn scars from Mt Baker's 1843 eruption.

The riverside *Howard Miller Steelhead Park* (☎ 360-853-8808) has an expanse of grassy sites for tents ($12) and RVs ($16); this county-owned campground, where Hwy 530 joins Hwy 20, is open year-round (handy for winter steelhead anglers) and it has showers. *Rockport State Park* (☎ 360-853-8461) is about a mile west of Howard Miller, set in a lush old-growth forest with several hiking trails. Fees range from $10 to $15; showers and RV hookups are among the amenities. There are also CCC-built A-frame shelters for groups. Camping season runs from April to October.

East of Rockport on Hwy 20, the *Wilderness Village RV Park* (☎ 360-873-2571), at 5550 Hwy 20, has sites with full hookups for $16.

Hotels The closest motel lodgings are at Concrete. The *North Cascade Inn* (☎ 360-853-8870, 800-251-3054), 4284 Hwy 20, is a motel and restaurant just west of Concrete; rooms start at $45.

Lodges A bright yellow taxi flags travelers to stop for the night at *A Cab-in the Woods* (☎ 360-873-4106) on Hwy 20, about 3 miles west of Marblemount. Cedar log cabins with kitchens cost $65, and there's a trail from the cabins to the river. Also west of Marblemount, the area's nicest cabins are at *Clark's Skagit River*

Cabins (☎ 360-873-2250, 800-273-2606), 5675 Hwy 20, between mileposts 103 and 104, by the funky Eatery Drive-In Restaurant & Museum. Cabins go for $49 to $109 a night.

Resorts The *Baker Lake Resort* (☎ 360-757-2262) is open year-round at milepost 20 on Baker Lake Rd; it has cabins, campsites, boat rentals and a small store. Cabins are $40 to $85, with the less expensive ones sharing bathroom facilities. All the cabins include kitchenettes, but guests are expected to bring their own linens and towels.

Places to Eat
Aside from the small store at Baker Lake Resort, there is no place to buy food at Baker Lake. Stock up or chow down in Concrete, where the *Baker St Bar & Grill* (☎ 360-853-7002) brings microbrew beers and tasty, trendy food to Concrete's main drag. Every year, on the 4th Saturday of July, the restaurant sponsors a Skagit River raft race from Rockport to Concrete, where style is as important as speed. *Annie's Pizza Station* (☎ 360-853-7227), 4280 Hwy 20, in uptown Concrete, serves pizza and sandwiches from a renovated gas station. Next door, the *Java House & Creamery* (☎ 360-853-8295), 4280 Hwy 20 serves homemade soup and ice cream. The *North Cascade Inn* (☎ 360-853-8771), 4284 Hwy 20, has an antique-bedecked restaurant with especially good pie.

Head 3 miles east of Rockport for a berry shake at *Cascadian Farms* (☎ 360-853-8173). It's a tiny roadside stand with coffee, homemade ice cream and local organic berries, juice and pickles.

In Marblemount, the pine lodge-styled *Buffalo Run Restaurant* (☎ 360-873-2461), 5860 Hwy 20, features gamey burgers made with venison, buffalo and ostrich ($7), as well as the usual sandwiches. The dinners here are the closest thing you'll find to fine dining in these parts, with New Zealand wild hare going for $12.95. During the winter, grab a meal at the *Log House Inn* (☎ 360-873-4311), Marblemount's less hip restaurant.

North Cascades National Park

For the backcountry hiker and adventurer, North Cascades National Park is paradise. The North Cascades Hwy is really the only road, and there are precious few facilities. Though there are plenty of scenic pull-offs along the highway and easily accessible, short interpretive hikes, a whole new world of craggy, rugged mountains awaits those who venture a few miles off the road to the first pass. Come with a backpack, pick up a map and backcountry permit at one of the visitors' centers or ranger stations, and strike out into some of the most dramatic scenery Washington has to offer.

The Hwy 20 corridor and Diablo and Ross Lakes are actually in the Ross Lake National Recreation Area, while North Cascades National Park straddles this strip to the north and south. Newhalem, a utilitarian dam-workers' town, is the jumping-off point for recreation in the area, and the visitors' center here is definitely worth a stop. Many people also come for tours of the Diablo and Ross dams, for rafting the Skagit River and for fishing in the river and lakes.

On the east side of the park, the North Cascades Hwy crests two passes, the 4860-foot Rainy Pass and, 5 miles to the east, the slightly higher 5477-foot Washington Pass. A big hairpin loop in the highway at Washington Pass marks the striking climatic between west and east. Two geological landmarks of the North Cascades – Early Winters Spires and Liberty Bell Mountain (a favorite of rock climbers) – are visible from the Washington Pass overlook, just west of the hairpin.

The relatively large expanse of wilderness and the alpine character of the North Cascades make this home to a variety of wildlife. Small populations of gray wolves and grizzly bears keep a foothold in the remote backcountry of the North Cascades. Black bears are more common, as are

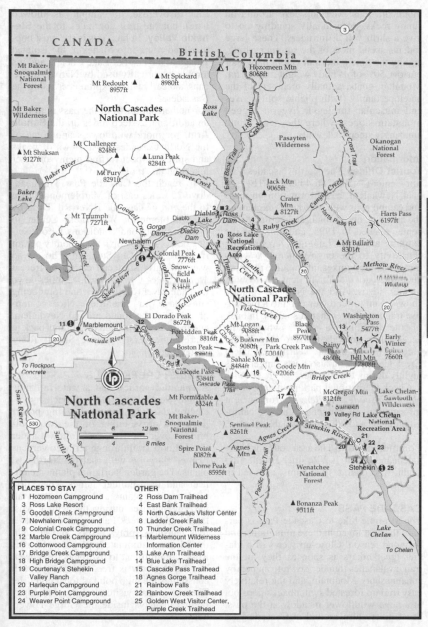

WASHINGTON

PLACES TO STAY
1 Hozomeen Campground
3 Ross Lake Resort
5 Goodell Creek Campground
8 Newhalem Campground
9 Colonial Creek Campground
12 Marble Creek Campground
16 Cottonwood Campground
17 Bridge Creek Campground
18 High Bridge Campground
19 Courtenay's Stehekin
    Valley Ranch
20 Harlequin Campground
23 Purple Point Campground
24 Weaver Point Campground

OTHER
2 Ross Dam Trailhead
4 East Bank Trailhead
6 North Cascades Visitor Center
7 Ladder Creek Falls
10 Thunder Creek Trailhead
11 Marblemount Wilderness
    Information Center
13 Lake Ann Trailhead
14 Blue Lake Trailhead
15 Cascade Pass Trailhead
18 Agnes Gorge Trailhead
21 Rainbow Falls
22 Rainbow Creek Trailhead
25 Golden West Visitor Center,
    Purple Creek Trailhead

mountain lions. Marmots laze around on sunny rocks, occasionally standing up to give a shrill yell at intruders. These large rodents spend most of the summer eating, and by the time a marmot enters its winter burrow, 50% of its body weight may be fat. Mountain goats, actually members of the antelope family (with pliable split hooves and muscular forelegs), live on rugged mountain slopes, where they can climb amazingly steep rock walls.

Information

Tourist Offices The North Cascades Visitor Center (☎ 206-386-4495), on Hwy 20 near Newhalem, has information on trails and camping, as well as exhibits explaining the area's plants, animals and geology. The center opened in 1993, and some of the exhibits are quite imaginative, stressing sensitivity to the environment. A walk-through exhibit mixes informative placards about the park's different ecosystems with nature videos. And the New Agey slide show, meant to send viewers into a meditative trance, is better than it sounds. In back of the building, a short, wheelchair-accessible boardwalk leads to magnificent views of the mountains. Nearby Newhalem Creek Campground also hosts ranger talks nightly during the summer.

Check the national park publication, the *North Cascade Challenger*, for current information on ranger-led hikes, campground fees and other park-related news.

Communications The area code for Newhalem and Diablo is 206, since Seattle City Light, who operates the dams, is based in Seattle.

CASCADE PASS

The 3½-mile hike to Cascade Pass is perhaps the best loved in these mountains, and for good reason. Close-up views of a glacier greet hikers as soon as they hit the trail, avalanches thunder down from nearby Johannesburg Mountain, and the relatively easy trail up forested switchbacks pops out at a huge wildflower meadow at the pass. Most hikers turn around at Cascade Pass

(due to overuse, no camping is allowed here), but the trail continues to the **Stehekin Valley**. In fact, this is the most popular land route into Stehekin, the isolated village at the head of Lake Chelan, and it's a route historically used by Native Americans and early white explorers crossing the Cascades.

Another option from the pass is to hike an additional 2 steep miles up the **Sahale Arm**, for more wildflowers and some of the North Cascades' best views of peaks and spires. Expect to find plenty of other hikers on this trail.

To reach the Cascade Pass Trailhead, drive 25 miles east of Marblemount down to the end of Cascade River Rd. Drop by the Marblemount Wilderness Center to inquire about road conditions before setting out, or to pick up a backcountry permit if you're headed to Stehekin. Those who want an early start can camp for free at *Marble Creek Campground*, 12 miles down Cascade River Rd; the dark and foreboding sites have no amenities. Nicer campgrounds can be found around Newhalem, and there are cabins and restaurants back in Marblemount (see Upper Skagit River Valley, above).

LADDER CREEK FALLS

A splendid garden and a waterfall hide behind Newhalem's old-fashioned hydroelectric dam. Ignore the buzzing power lines and cross either of the two footbridges over the river and follow Ladder Creek Loop Trail through terraced gardens planted largely with native Northwest plants. The garden's original planner, engineer and dam-builder James Ross, first used tropical plants and moved them all into greenhouses during the winter. Mist from Ladder Creek Falls – cut deep into a rock chasm – sprays hikers, and at night the falls are illuminated, a legacy of James Ross' commitment to hydroelectric power. The **light show** is free, and pretty much constitutes the high point of local nightlife. There is a small visitors' center with interpretive displays inside the Gorge Powerhouse.

Bigfoot Territory

Bigfoot (or Sasquatch) is a legendary resident of the Pacific Northwest. While sightings have been reported all over North America, this area seems to be the creature's favorite stomping ground. Tales of Bigfoot abound, especially among loggers and hunters, but several Native American legends also contain a *Sasquatch* or *Omah* – a similar 'wild man of the woods.' The creature is actually sought after by some scientists and wildlife biologists who take Bigfoot research seriously.

Could the animal be a link in the evolutionary process?

Commonly described as looking like a large ape, Bigfoot stands about 7½ feet tall and walks upright while swinging its arms; it weighs 400 to 500lb, is covered in hair (from gray to reddish-brown or black), has dark brown or yellow eyes and possesses a foul, overpowering odor. Photos and plaster casts of its tracks show human-like, five-toed footprints averaging 16 inches in length (approximately a shoe-size 21; think Shaquille O'Neal).

According to most reports, Bigfoot is non-aggressive and usually flees from people when sighted, but he's also been said to occasionally throw rocks, shake cars or chase people. In general, Bigfoot seems to stick to the woods, but he has been spotted crossing highways and wandering through campgrounds, backyards and other unlikely places.

Despite a variety of 'evidence' – blurred photos and video footage, hair samples, plaster casts of footprints and audio recordings of Bigfoot's call (a loud roaring or growling sound) – the creature's existence has never been confirmed. To catch a virtual glimpse of the big guy (and hear an audio file), check out the Washington State Sasquatch Homepage: www.angelfire.com/wa/sasquatchsearch. ■

WASHINGTON

ROSS & DIABLO LAKES

Ross Lake stretches out for 24 miles, all the way across the Canadian border, but there are no roads along it from the south. To get to any of the lakeside trailheads, or to the Ross Lake Resort, you must take the resort-run water taxi (see Places to Stay below). Trout live in Ross Lake, and boat rentals for fishing can be had at the resort.

Just below Ross Lake, blue-green Diablo Lake is held back by the 389-foot-high Diablo Dam, which was the world's highest arch-type dam when it was completed in 1930. Perhaps more interesting than its size is the amount of trouble James Ross and the city of Seattle went to for its construction. Since there was still no road here in the '20s, a narrow-gauge railroad ferried workers and their supplies from Rockport through the rocky Skagit River Canyon to Diablo, where, one by one, the railroad cars were hoisted 560 feet up the steep hillside to the dam by an incline lift, which consisted of two parallel sets of tracks and a counterweight. At the top of the hill, a locomotive carried the railroad cars a few hundred yards to Diablo Lake, which they crossed on a barge to the Ross Dam construction site.

In another bit of area history, Jack Kerouac spent the summer of 1956 as a fire lookout on Desolation Peak north of here – he hated it.

Organized Tours

Skagit Tours (☎ 206-684-3030) operates several tours of Diablo and the vicinity. On the popular, four-hour deluxe tour, visitors are hauled up the hillside on the Incline Railroad, shown around the hilltop hydro-electric project, ferried across Diablo Lake for a walk through the turbines of Ross Dam, and returned to Diablo for a big fried-chicken dinner (there's spaghetti for vegetarians). The deluxe tour costs $25/22 adults/seniors; children are $12.50 and reservations are required. The tour provides a good insight into local history and geography.

Less ambitious is the 90-minute, $5 tour, which eliminates the boat ride to Ross Dam and the chicken dinner and substitutes a walk across the top of Diablo Dam. Reservations are not required for this tour, which leaves at 11 am and 1:15 pm daily from mid-June to Labor Day.

Even the thriftiest travelers can stop for a ride up the **Incline Railway**. This brief trip costs a mere 25¢, and it's an easy way to get some views.

Hiking

The North Cascades are a wonder of riches, and the essential reference guide for hikers is *100 Hikes in the North Cascades* by Ira Spring and Harvey Manning (The Mountaineers, Seattle, 1994). The hikes listed below are only a smattering of what's available; stop by the visitors' center for a full listing and for advice on an appropriate trek.

From the Newhalem Creek Campground, 40 yards past the Newhalem Creek bridge, the less-trafficked **Lower Newhalem Creek Trail** passes hemlocks, cedars and firs on its nearly half-mile path to a creek-side glade.

From the south end of the Colonial Creek Campground (4 miles east of Diablo Dam), the long **Thunder Creek Trail** leads to a number of interesting sights. Park Creek Pass, 19½ miles from the trailhead, offers views and a passageway to the Stehekin River. It's only a 1.3-mile jaunt from the campground to Thunder Creek, where a surprising number of wildflowers flourish in the dank creek-bottom forest.

Wheelchair-Accessible Trails

While ardent hikers may not feel a trek has even begun until they've walked a few miles, the North Cascades offer plenty of short, beautiful trails that are accessible to hikers of all abilities. At the back of the North Cascades National Park Visitor Center in Newhalem, a short boardwalk leads to views of the Picket Range, some of the most spectacular peaks in the North Cascades.

To get a feel for the frequently drippy west-side forests, try the half-mile **Riverside Nature Trail**, which skirts Newhalem Campground. This 'To Know a Tree' trail is graded and graveled for wheelchair use.

At the end of Main St in Newhalem, the **Trail of the Cedars** is a half-mile loop across a suspension bridge to the Skagit River's forested south shore. A boardwalk trail, the **Happy Creek Forest Walk** makes a three-mile loop through old-growth forests off Hwy 20, milepost 134, right between Diablo and Ross Lakes (about eight miles east of Diablo). Even to seasoned nature-trail walkers, the interpretive signs are quite good.

At Rainy Pass on Hwy 20, milepost 161, there is the **Rainy Lake Trail**, a mile-long paved trail through the woods to Rainy Lake. ■

To reach the **Thunder Woods Nature Trail**, head 300 yards down the Thunder Creek Trail, then turn off for the partly steep 1.8-mile loop. A little over a mile down the Thunder Creek Trail, there's a junction for Fourth of July Pass and **Panther Creek Trail**. A moderately steep trail reaches Fourth of July Pass in 3.2 miles. Panther Creek Trail continues 5 miles back to Hwy 20, east of Ross Lake.

From its Hwy 20 trailhead (milepost 134), the **Ross Dam Trail** descends 1 mile, crosses over the top of Ross Dam and follows the west bank of Ross Lake to Ross Lake Resort (1½ miles), Big Beaver Creek and backcountry.

After a quick descent from the highway (milepost 138) to Ruby Creek, the **East Bank Trail** cruises along the creek and Ross Lake north to the Pasayten Wilderness. There are no big expansive views, but if you're in the mood for a dark forest hike, this is the ticket. It's also one way to get to Hozomeen, a remote lakeside campground 28 miles to the north, near the Canadian border.

At Rainy Pass, the **Pacific Crest Trail** crosses Hwy 20. To sample the trail, strike out north from here for 6820-foot Cutthroat Pass (4 miles). Several more leisurely hikes also start from Rainy Pass. Try the easy 2-mile trail to green, cirque-cradled **Lake Ann**, from which it's another mile to **Heather Pass**, and yet an additional mile to 6600-foot **Maple Pass**.

Just to the west of Washington Pass, between mileposts 161 and 162, **Blue Lake Trail** is an ambling 2-mile climb through subalpine meadows to Blue Lake, at 6250 feet. Snow blocks the trail's upper reaches until at least July, and once it melts, there can be lots of bugs and almost as many hikers. Nevertheless, the views onto Whistler Mountain, Cutthroat Peak and Liberty Bell Mountain make a hiker willing to put up with a few minor inconveniences.

Rafting

You can book rafting trips on the Skagit River with Alpine Adventures (☎ 800-926-7238), Osprey River Adventures (☎ 509-997-4116, 800-997-4116), Northwest Wilderness River Riders (☎ 800-448-7238), or Wildwater River Tours (☎ 206-939-2151, 800-522-9453). Expect to pay around $75 for a day on the river. Though the dam-controlled water levels make the Skagit runnable year-round, outfitters tend to concentrate on summer white-water trips.

Floaters usually put in at Goodell Creek Campground and float to Bacon Creek or Copper Creek, about 10 miles downriver. Conditions depend on what's going on at the dams upriver, but it's usually a Class II or III trip. The waters are a little quieter downriver from Marblemount.

Places to Stay & Eat

Camping *Newhalem Creek Campground*, a big USFS campground near the North Cascades visitors' center, is open mid-June to Labor Day. There are 127 sites (no hookups) and the fee is $10; amenities include flush toilets, running water and regularly scheduled talks and hikes with park naturalists.

Sites are also nice at the smaller, less-developed *Goodell Creek Campground*, on the Skagit River west of Newhalem, near milepost 119. Expect to find pit toilets, drinking water and a $7 fee; it's open year-round. The informal *Gorge Creek Campground* has no amenities and only a few spaces, but it's a reasonable alternative to the big, crowded park campgrounds. It's right off the highway on the road to Diablo.

The *Colonial Creek Campground* near Diablo has 167 sites – flush toilets, running water, no hookups – on the Thunder Arm of Diablo Lake on either side of the highway. On the south side, several walk-in sites set on a bluff among big trees offer a chance to get away from the cars; the lakeside spots are the most coveted, and the most crowded.

Lodges The floating cabins at secluded *Ross Lake Resort* (☎ 206-386-4437), on the west side of the lake just north of Ross Dam, were built in the 1930s for loggers working in the valley soon to be flooded by Ross Dam. There's no road to the resort – guests can either hike the 2-mile trail from Hwy 20 or take the resort's tugboat taxi and truck shuttle from the parking area near Diablo Dam. The houseboat cabins are rustic, but they do have plumbing, electricity and kitchenettes. The smallest, least expensive cabins share a bathroom with one other cabin. Since there's no restaurant, guests should remember to bring food for all their meals. Cabins range from $58 to $111 a night (the most expensive are bunkhouse cabins with room for six). The resort rents canoes, kayaks and motorboats ($20 to $50 a day), and operates a water taxi service for hikers destined for trailheads around the lake ($5 roundtrip).

If you need to pick up some food, stop by the store in Newhalem.

Methow Valley

East of Washington Pass, the land dries up a bit and the sky is typically less choked with clouds. The Methow (pronounced *MET-how*) River valley is the land of cross-country skiing, where the snow is more powdery than the 'cement' that falls west of the Cascades. Recreationally, the Methow comes into its own in the winter, but summer's no let-down. When the snow melts, the valley becomes spectacularly green, and there's plenty of hiking, mountain biking, rafting and fishing.

The Upper Methow River flows through a straight, steep-walled valley cut by a glacier during the most recent ice age. The valley begins to widen around Mazama and becomes fairly open by the time it hits Winthrop and Twisp. Off to the southwest is the Sawtooth Ridge and the Lake Chelan-Sawtooth Wilderness Area. To the north and east, the Okanogan hills reach into Canada. At Pateros, the Methow River flows into the Columbia River.

Native Americans have lived along the Methow, Twisp and Chewuch Rivers some

9000 years. In 1811, David Thompson, the North West Company trader and geographer (see the David Thompson sidebar in the Northeastern Washington chapter), visited the Salish-speaking Methows along the river named for them and observed tribal members fishing for salmon at the river's mouth. A small tribe, the Methow were more or less swallowed up when they were sent to the Colville Reservation in 1883.

For whites, 1883 marked the beginning of Methow Valley settlements. Gold was the original lure, commerce proved more permanent, but nothing really boomed until Hwy 20 opened in 1972, bringing a steady stream of visitors. Winthrop especially has tried to capitalize on tourism, turning itself into a living version of the 'Old West' – you will also find most of the area's accommodations here.

Orientation & Information
Winter snows block the highest stretch of Hwy 20 between Marblemount and Mazama from late November to early April. To check on the status of the road, call ☎ 888-766-4636. Methow-bound skiers make their approach from western Washington by taking US 2 to Wenatchee, then heading north on US 97 past Lake Chelan to Pateros, where Hwy 153 traces the Methow River northwest to Twisp and Hwy 20.

MAZAMA
Population 60
There's not much to the town of Mazama – just a couple of gas pumps and a general store with one of the state's busiest pay phones in front – but there are several small resorts in the area. The village of Early Winters, a stone's throw up the highway from Mazama, is home to an upscale vacation resort at Wilson Ranch meadow, though for the most part it's small and exceedingly quiet.

The USFS runs a visitors' center (☎ 509-996-2534) near milepost 178 on Hwy 20 in Early Winters. Though 911 will summon police or an ambulance, call ☎ 509-997-2106 to report a fire.

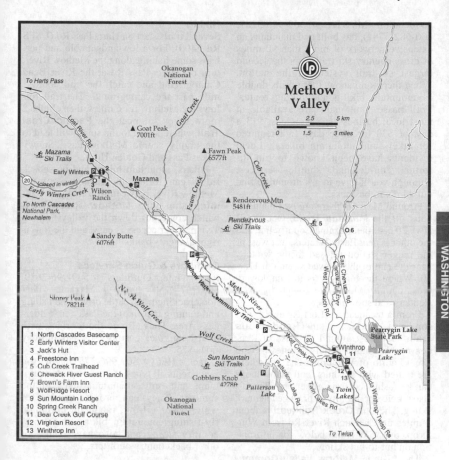

To Harts Pass

Okanogan
National
Forest

**Methow
Valley**

Lost River Rd

Goat Creek

▲ Goat Peak
7001ft

▲ Fawn Peak
6577ft

Cub Creek

0   2.5   5 km
0   1.5   3 miles

⛷ Mazama
Ski Trails

Early Winters
(closed in winter)

20

Early Winters Creek

Mazama

Wilson
Ranch

Fawn Creek

▲ Rendezvous Mtn
5481ft

To North Cascades
National Park,
Newhalem

Rendezvous
Ski Trails

⛷ 5

6

▲ Sandy Butte
6076ft

WASHINGTON

Methow Valley Community Trail

Methow River

East Chewuch Rd

West Chewuch Rd

Storey Peak ▲
7821ft

Nk Yk Wolf Creek

Wolf Creek

8

Pearrygin Lake
State Park

9

Wolf Creek Rd

20

Winthrop

11

Pearrygin
Lake

Sun Mountain
Ski Trails

Sun Mountain
Ski Trails

Gobblers Knob
4278ft

Patterson Lake Rd

10

12

13

Eastside Winthrop-Twisp Rd

Twin
Lakes

Patterson Lake

Okanogan
National
Forest

Twin Lakes Rd

To Twisp

1 North Cascades Basecamp
2 Early Winters Visitor Center
3 Jack's Hut
4 Freestone Inn
5 Cub Creek Trailhead
6 Chewack River Guest Ranch
7 Brown's Farm Inn
8 WolfRidge Resort
9 Sun Mountain Lodge
10 Spring Creek Ranch
11 Bear Creek Golf Course
12 Virginian Resort
13 Winthrop Inn

Harts Pass

Near the end of what may be the state's most terrifying road – a steep one-laner with long, deadly drop-offs and no guard rails – is Harts Pass (6197 feet). Suck in your breath and drive, for the views from the top are outstanding. Catch the road to Harts Pass by heading northwest on Lost River Rd (also known as Mazama Rd) past the Mazama Country Inn to USFS Rd 5400. The road is paved for the first 12 miles, and the last dozen miles are gravel. At Harts Pass, there's still more of a climb for the intrepid driver; head another 2½

miles up to **Slate Peak**, where, a short hike from the road's end, the view from an abandoned fire lookout is a true panorama. At its 7800-foot terminus, this is the state's highest roadside spot. Slate Peak is also the site of the northernmost road access to the Pacific Crest Trail in the USA; north of the road's end, the Pasayten Wilderness reaches to Canada.

Cross-Country Skiing

This is what the Methow Valley is famous for – good, dry snow and plenty of places to ski. The Methow Valley Sports Trails

Association (MVSTA; ☎ 509-996-3287, 800-682-5787), has built and maintains an extensive network of more than 90 miles of cross-country ski trails; it's the second largest ski-trail system in the nation. When there's no snow, these trails double as mountain biking and hiking routes. Trail passes and maps are available at most local businesses; passes cost $13 a day, or $30 for three days (not required for hikers and mountain bikers). Local residents have been known to run informal, on-demand shuttle services, although you'll have to ask around to find out who's in business.

Around Mazama there are two main ski hubs for the **Mazama Trails**. One is off Hwy 20 near the Mazama Country Inn, and the other is near Early Winters, just west of the ranger station (closed in the winter), near the end of the plowed stretch of Hwy 20. Where the highway is left unplowed, cross-country skiers are joined by dog-sledders and snowmobilers.

From a trailhead on Lost River Rd, just southeast of Mazama, the **Rendezvous Trails** skirt east around the base of Rendezvous Mountain about 21 miles to Cub Creek, north of Winthrop. The trails here are dotted with ski huts, and many loops can be fashioned from either end. There's also ample opportunity to practice telemark skiing. The **Cub Creek Trailhead** is about 5 miles up Chewuch River Rd from Winthrop. See 'Ski Huts' below for information on hut-to-hut skiing.

The 17-mile **Methow Valley Community Trail** runs along the Methow River between Mazama and Winthrop. You can also pick it up 6 miles south of Mazama, from a trailhead near Brown's Farm Inn.

Passes, maps, and ski rentals are available from The Mazama Country Inn (☎ 509-996-2681), or from Jack's Hut (☎ 509-996-2752), near the Freestone Inn at Wilson Ranch. Jack's Hut also offers instruction and private guides for all kinds of skiing and does bookings for North Cascade Heli-Skiing; one day of helicopter skiing costs around $525.

For a snow report call ☎ 800-682-5787.

Hiking

Several trails start on Harts Pass Rd (USFS Rd 5400). For a lowlands amble and perhaps some fishing along the Methow River, turn off Harts Pass Rd at the River Bend Campground and catch the trail about 1 mile past the campground. The trail follows the Methow for 6 miles, then climbs 2 more miles to meet the **Pacific Crest Trail**, where a turn to the south will lead to the highly scenic Methow Pass, Snowy Lakes Pass and Golden Horn.

Hikers, mountain bikers and horseback riders can follow the meanders of the Methow River between Mazama and Winthrop along the **Methow River Trail**, which continues down the valley floor to Twisp. River access is easy, and the trail is right along its banks.

Outfitters & Guide Services

Early Winters Outfitters (☎ 509-996-2659, 800-737-8750), based in Mazama, offers horsepacking trips, cattle drives and fishing and hunting trips into the Pasayten Wilderness Area. They also do shorter rides, with hour-long rides costing $15 and full-day rides $75.

Jack's Hut (☎ 509-996-2752) at Wilson ranch rents all types of winter sports equipment and rents mountain bikes in the summer. They can provide guides for white-water rafting, mountain climbing, fly-fishing, mountain biking and cross-country skiing and also have names of other backcountry outfitters.

Places to Stay

Methow Valley Central Reservations (☎ 509-996-2148, 800-422-3048) runs an especially helpful reservation service that books accommodations in the region's inns, lodges, B&Bs and cabins, as well as in vacation home rentals.

Camping Three USFS campgrounds are just off Hwy 20 on Early Winters Creek. *Lone Fir Campground* (milepost 168) has pit toilets, running water and an $8 fee. *Klipchuck Campground* (milepost 175, then about a mile up the side road) and

Early Winters Campground (milepost 177) have similar amenities.

Ski Huts A series of four ski huts, accessible only from trails, dot the Rendezvous area outside Winthrop. Call the Methow Valley Central Reservations (☎ 509-996-2148, 800-422-3048) to book a bunk ($25) or an entire eight-person hut ($140). If you're not up to skiing with a pack, freight haul is available through Rendezvous Outfitters for $70 a leg.

B&Bs *Chokecherry Inn B&B* (☎ 509-996-2049) is on the Methow River about three-quarters of a mile east of the Early Winters ranger station. The two rooms each have private bathrooms, and there's a hot tub on the deck. Rooms cost $75.

Lodges The *Mazama Country Inn* (☎ 509-996-2681, 800-843-7951), off Hwy 20 in Mazama, is a favorite place for skiers in the Upper Methow Valley. Rooms in the lodge start at $75; cabins with kitchens run up to $170. Ski trails radiate out from the lodge, and the restaurant serves the best food for miles around. In the winter, all meals are included in room rates.

The newest addition to the Methow Valley is the *Freestone Inn* (☎ 800-639-3809), 17798 Hwy 20, a beautifully designed lodge-style luxury hotel at Wilson Ranch in Early Winters. Hotel rooms all feature stone fireplaces (with easy push-button ignition) and have private, wood-slated balconies fronting onto a quiet lake; peak-season rates run $130 to $170. They also have lakefront cabins. A trail from the cross-country ski area at Early Winters leads right up to the doorstep, and non-guests are welcome to warm up in the hotel lobby or dine at the gourmet restaurant (reservations required).

The inn also runs the *Early Winters Cabins* (☎ 509-996-2355, 509-996-2843), which pretend to be rustic, but are a far cry from the old horsepacker cabins they used to be. Rates run $95 to $165 for these woodsy, creekfront cabins.

North Cascades Basecamp (☎ 509-996-2334), 255 Lost River Rd, is a small inn with six lodge rooms (all with shared bathrooms) and a housekeeping cabin (which sleeps up to six), a hot tub, trails and a pond. This is a good place to bring kids, as several of the rooms have bunk beds or twin beds in addition to a double or queen, and there's a playroom in the lodge. Lodge rooms start at $130 for doubles, which include all meals. During the summer, the rooms are rented out at a less expensive B&B rate of $75.

At *Brown's Farm Inn* (☎ 509-996-2571), about 6 miles south on Hwy 20 on Wolf Creek Rd, fresh eggs come with a cabin rental. Cabins with complete kitchens start at $65.

Places to Eat

There are only two restaurants in Mazama, and if you're staying at one of the lodges here chances are that your meals will be included. If they're not, be sure to make reservations. The *Mazama Country Inn* (☎ 509-996-2681, 800-843-7951) features hearty home-style fare that skiers love. For fine dining head to the *Freestone Inn* (☎ 800-639-3809) for entrées like pan-seared duck breast ($17). They also sell packed lunches.

WINTHROP
Population 365

Winthrop has been done over as an upscale Western town, where espresso is sold from false-fronted shops and flower baskets line the streets. As with its sister theme town, Leavenworth, it's easy to curl a lip or roll the eyes when describing Winthrop, but the fact is, it works. What was once a struggling east-slope town is now a thriving part of the new Old West.

The town was first settled in 1891 by Harvard-educated Guy Waring, who built a trading post at the confluence of the Chewuch and Methow Rivers. After a couple of visits to Winthrop, Waring's Harvard classmate Owen Wister settled down and wrote the best-selling book *The Virginian*, whose characters are supposedly based on Winthropians.

When the North Cascades Hwy opened in 1972, Winthrop was ready and waiting, with many of its frontier-era buildings spiffed up for the tourist trade. You know the routine: stroll the wood-plank sidewalk downtown and browse the gift shops. Be sure to stop and watch the blacksmith if he's at work forging wrought-iron hooks and trivets. Early in the century, Guy Waring owned every building on the main street except the log town hall; several of these buildings are still standing, though many have changed function. One, the Duck Brand Saloon, was built by Waring and bears the name of his cattle brand. It now serves as the community center. (The Duck Brand Saloon that serves up beer and nachos today is not the original.) What is now the Winthrop Palace Restaurant, at 149 Riverside Ave, was built in 1909 as the Winthrop Hotel.

Orientation

About 13 miles south of Mazama at Winthrop, the Chewuch River flows in from the north to join the Methow River, which runs down the sparsely-treed eastern flanks of the Cascades toward the Columbia River. The highway makes a 90° turn as it enters Winthrop from the west, and in the town center is sometimes referred to as Riverside Ave.

From Winthrop it's 40 miles to Okanogan on Hwy 20, and 61 miles south to Chelan.

Information

The Winthrop Chamber of Commerce (☎ 509-996-2125), PO Box 39, Winthrop, WA 98862, is on Hwy 20 right where it turns the corner in downtown. The Winthrop Ranger Station (☎ 509-996-2266) is on the west side of town, up the hill from the baseball diamond on West Chewuch Rd.

The post office (☎ 509-996-2282) is at 1110 Hwy 20. For ambulance services, call ☎ 509-996-2888. You can reach the police at ☎ 911 or ☎ 509-996-2160, and report fires by calling ☎ 509-997-2106.

Shafer Museum

Guy Waring built the log house that is now the centerpiece of the local historical museum (☎ 509-996-2712), 285 Castle Ave at Bridge St, one block up the hill from Riverside Ave. The well-built log home, known to Winthropians since its construction in 1897 as 'The Castle,' was Waring's payback to his wife for moving west. It's open daily 10 am to 5 pm, Memorial Day to Labor Day, and donations are appreciated.

Cascades Smoke Jumpers Base

Before a local cobbler teamed up with the USFS to make padded, multi-pocketed jumpsuits, nobody had ever jumped from a plane to extinguish a forest fire. Now that smoke jumpers have become elevated to heroes of modern western mythology, the Cascades Smoke Jumpers Base is open for tours. It's on Eastside Winthrop-Twisp Rd, halfway between the two towns. Call ahead to the Twisp Ranger Station (☎ 509-997-2131) to check on the schedule; visitors are usually welcome 9 am to 7 pm daily, June to October. Admission is free.

Pearrygin Lake State Park

If downtown Winthrop's crowds start to close in on you, skip out of town to Pearrygin Lake. The state park has a swimming beach and boat launch on the pretty aqua-colored lake, which is actually warm enough to swim in during the summer. During the winter, snowmobilers come here to get away from the cross-country skiers. The park also has facilities for tent camping and RVs, and the lake is stocked with trout. It's just under 5 miles northeast of town on Pearrygin Lake Rd (follow the signs from Hwy 20).

Cross-Country Skiing

West of Winthrop there's a network of cross-country ski trails just below the Sun Mountain Lodge (☎ 509-996-2211, 800-572-0493). If you aren't a lodge guest, park at the day-ski lot, just above Patterson Lake. The elevation here is 2600 feet, nearly 1000 feet higher than Winthrop, and the trails climb to 3600 feet on the **Thompson Ridge Rd Trail**. As with other trails maintained by the Methow Valley Sport Trail Association (MVSTA; ☎ 509-996-

3287, 800-682-5787) you'll need to purchase a trail pass.

Skiers can pick up the **Rendezvous Trails** (see Mazama above) from Winthrop by heading 5 miles north up the Chewuch River Rd to the Cub Creek Trailhead.

Winthrop is also the southeast terminus of the 17-mile **Methow Valley Community Trail**, which follows the river up to Mazama and Early Winters. There are trailheads near Winthrop at the Spring Creek Ranch, or at the WolfRidge Resort, about 5½ miles north of town off of Twin Lakes Rd.

In Winthrop, rent skis and purchase trail passes from Winthrop Mountain Sports (☎ 509-996-2886), 257 Riverside Ave.

Mountain Biking

Mountain bikers hit the ski trails once the snow clears in the summer. Sun Mountain offers 30 some miles of trail riding. One popular ride from Winthrop is an easy 12-mile loop to Pearrygin Lake. Start by following the well-marked road to Pearrygin Lake State Park. After 4 miles of paved-road cycling, continue straight up the dirt Pearrygin Lake Rd rather than turning right onto the paved entrance to the state park. The road climbs gently for 2 miles, affording good views of the valley and surrounding mountains. At the T-intersection, turn right and coast, hitting pavement again at the Bear Creek Golf Course. At the valley floor, turn right and pedal 3 miles back to town.

Both Winthrop Mountain Sports (☎ 509-996-2886) and the Sun Mountain Lodge (☎ 509-996-2211) rent mountain bikes. You can pick up a booklet describing local mountain bike routes at Winthrop Mountain Sports and at the ranger station.

Other Activities

While cross-country skiing is the area's main draw, summer still finds plenty to do around here. **Fishing** for trout and steelhead is popular in the Methow River, and Moccasin Lake – a mile-long hike from Patterson Lake Rd (the trailhead is about halfway up the road to Sun Mountain Lodge) – has very good fly-fishing. Aspiring climbers can find **rock-climbing**

instruction from the folks at Winthrop Mountain Sports (☎ 509-996-2886).

Horseback riding is also popular in the Methow Valley – the Chewack River Guest Ranch (☎ 509-996-2497) on East Chewuch River Rd has hour-long rides for $18, half-day lunch rides for $55, and overnight trips. They also offer horse boarding. If **golf** is more your speed, Bear Creek Golf Course (☎ 509-996-2284) on East County Rd has nine holes on a course noted for its lovely surroundings and for the wild animals that may stroll across the fairway.

Special Events

Winthrop's Memorial Day weekend rodeo makes you remember that Winthrop really is a western town, and not just a made-up one. The summer season is highlighted by the Winthrop Rhythm & Blues Festival (☎ 509-996-2541) – national acts come to town for three days in late July, and the concerts, held a mile north of town at The Blues Ranch, can get pretty wild. Tickets cost $35 to $45.

Call the MVSTA (☎ 800-682-5787) for details on their early-October Methow Valley Mountain Bike Festival.

And, if you're in town over President's Day weekend, be prepared for the big snowshoe softball tournament.

Places to Stay

Camping *Pearrygin Lake State Park* (☎ 509-996-2370) is 5 miles northeast of town on Pearrygin Lake Rd. Showers, boat launch, swimming and fishing make this a popular and usually crowded spot; campsites are $10. *Derry's Resort* (☎ 509-996-2322), 985 Bear Creek Rd, is also on Pearrygin Lake, and has campsites, cabins, boat rentals and laundry facilities. Campsites with RV hookups are $17.

There's also a large *KOA* (☎ 509-996-2258), 1114 Hwy 20, just east of town with fees ranging between $15 and $20. It's on the Methow River, which means it's more pleasant than the average KOA.

Ski Huts Rendezvous Outfitters maintains a series of cabins and runs freight haul for hut-to-hut skiing on the Rendezvous Trails; see Ski Huts under Mazama for details.

Hotels The cheapest place to stay in Winthrop is the *Farmhouse Inn* (☎ 509-996-2191, 888-996-2525), off Hwy 20 just south of town, operated by the owners of the Duck Brand Hotel and Cantina (see below). Three rooms at the six-room guesthouse have private bathrooms, the other three rooms share two bathrooms. Rooms run $39 to $64 and include a continental breakfast.

The *Trail's End Motel* (☎ 509-996-2303), 130 Riverside Ave, a small, false-fronted downtown motel, has double rooms starting at $58. At the *Duck Brand Hotel* (☎ 509-996-2192), 248 Riverside Ave, several rooms are above the very popular restaurant, which can make for noisy evenings (till the restaurant closes at 9:30 pm); rates are $65/75. The *Hotel Rio Vista* (☎ 509-996-3535), 285 Riverside Ave, has a typical Winthropian false-front and each room has a deck with a view of the Methow and Chewuch Rivers; double rooms run $85.

At the south end of town, the *Virginian Resort* (☎ 509-996-2535, 800-854-2834), 808 Hwy 20, has comfortable riverside motel rooms ($55 to $75), kitchenette cabins ($75) and a heated outdoor pool. The adjoining restaurant serves reasonably good Northwest cuisine. The *Best Western Cascade Inn Motel* (☎ 509-996-3100, 800-468-6754), 960 Hwy 20, has a hot tub and washers and dryers; double rooms start at $65 and go to $75 on weekends. The *Winthrop Inn* (☎ 509-996-2217, 800-444-1972), further south on Hwy 20, has a heated pool and hot tub, with single/double rooms starting at $60/65. It's right on the Methow River and has good access to cross-country ski trails. *Winthrop Mountain View Chalets* (☎ 509-996-3113, 800-527-3113), on Hwy 20 at the KOA, has cute two-person cabins with microwave ovens and nice decks (but no phones in the rooms) for $65 a night.

Resorts *Sun Mountain Lodge* (☎ 509-996-2211, 800-572-0493), 9 miles southwest of

town via Twin Lakes and Patterson Lake Rds, is the region's premier resort. Its rather grand mountaintop setting offers expansive views of the Methow Valley. The high-gloss rustic lodge has very comfortable rooms and a great restaurant. Cabins, a little ways down the hill at Patterson Lake, are somewhat removed from the hub of activity. Hiking, mountain bike and cross-country ski trails lead out from the lodge, and the resort also has horseback riding, canoeing, sailing, tennis courts and a pool.

In short, it's kind of a recreational fantasyland – very comfortable, with lots of good food waiting at the end of the day. During the winter, lodge rooms start at around $125; during the summer, expect to pay $160. Midweek stays always bring a price break of $15 to $20. The Patterson Lake cabins sleep four starting at $130 in winter, $165 in summer.

WolfRidge Resort (☎ 509-996-2828, 800-237-2388) is on Wolf Creek Rd, 5½ miles northwest of town; reach it via Twin Lakes Rd, which is just south of downtown and doubles back north. The resort has a wide variety of accommodations, ranging from hotel rooms to log townhouse suites; there's a heated outdoor pool and hot tub and cross-country ski trails. Rates start at $59 for a hotel room and run to $144 for a two-bedroom townhouse.

Chewack River Guest Ranch (☎ 509-996-2497), 6 miles north of Winthrop on East Chewuch River Rd, specializes in horseback riding, both for ranch guests and day-riders. Several guest rooms are available for $65, and a two-bedroom house rents for around $80.

Spring Creek Ranch (☎ 509-996-2495, 509-996-2510), across the Methow River from downtown at 491 Twin Lakes Rd, is a nicely-renovated 1929 farmhouse with kitchen facilities and a washer and dryer. Skiers will appreciate the Methow Valley Community Trail running right past the front door. Double rooms start at $180.

Vacation Home Rentals *Westar Lodge & Retreat* (☎ 509-996-2697) is 4 miles north of town on West Chewuch River Rd. The

Westar is geared toward housing groups, and it's a good place to come with a handful of friends for a cross-country ski vacation. Call Methow Valley Central Reservations (☎ 509-996-2148, 800-422-3048) for other cabins or vacation homes.

Places to Eat
If you just want a drink, the *Winthrop Brewing Company* (☎ 509-996-3183), 155 Riverside Ave, has a riverfront deck and microbrews on tap in the little red schoolhouse on Winthrop's main street. The lively, faux-Western *Cantina* (☎ 509-996-2192), in the Duck Brand Hotel, 248 Riverside Ave, serves up everything from Mexican food to apple pie.

At the *Winthrop Palace* (☎ 509-996-2245), 149 Riverside Ave, you're dining in the erstwhile Winthrop Hotel, which, from the looks of it, wasn't a bad place to spend a night in 1909. Both the setting and the food here are a little bit fancier than the other downtown Winthrop restaurants (which isn't really saying much).

If fancy is what you want, the restaurant at *Sun Mountain Lodge* (☎ 509-996-2211) is as close as you're going to get in this town. The food, which focuses on Northwest cuisine, really is worth the drive, and the Sunday brunch draws hungry hikers and cross-country skiers from all over the Methow Valley – the dress code is casual.

Shopping
DJ's Forge & Iron (☎ 509-996-2703), on Riverside Ave, showcases hand-forged ornamental iron made by Northwest blacksmiths. Hand-forged hooks, handles and letter openers make affordable souvenirs, and the selection of unique decorative home and kitchen hardware is sure to entice anyone with an interest in western craft or design.

TWISP
Population 990
In the past, Native Americans set up fish-drying camps at the junction of the Methow and Twisp Rivers, and the women who prepared the salmon were often plagued by yellow jackets, or *twips*, setting the stage for one of Washington's most charming town names. Twisp isn't loaded with prepackaged entertainment, but if small and unpretentious strikes your fancy, spend a night here, a more genuine version of the West than its false-fronted neighbor.

Orientation & Information
Twisp is 11 miles south of Winthrop on Hwy 20. Past Twisp, Hwy 20 turns east through the Okanogan National Forest for 29 miles to the towns of Omak and Okanogan in the Okanogan Valley. Hwy 153 splits off and follows the Methow River south, joining US 97 and the Columbia River at Pateros.

The Twisp Chamber of Commerce (☎ 509-997-2926), 201 S Methow Valley Hwy, operates out of the Methow Valley Community Center at the south edge of town, next to the tennis courts. Twisp Ranger Station (☎ 509-997-2131), 502 Glover St (Twisp's main street), has information on trails and campgrounds in the Okanogan National Forest. You'll find the post office (☎ 509-997-3777) at 205 Glover St. For medical emergencies (or fire), call ☎ 509-997-2106 for an ambulance.

Things to See
For a small town, Twisp has a pretty lively cultural scene, anchored in large part by the **Confluence Gallery & Art Center** (☎ 509-997-2787), 104 Glover St. The gallery mounts a new exhibit every six weeks or so, with a focus on work by regional artists.

Every Saturday morning from April to October, a Twispian mix of ranchers and hippies gather at the Methow Valley Community Center, next to the tennis courts on Hwy 20, for a **farmer's market**. Stop by for baked goods, produce or a handcrafted knife.

Hiking
Trails abound along the Twisp River. Follow Twisp River Rd west of town for about 11 miles, and veer left onto USFS Rd 4420 (West Buttermilk Creek Rd) to reach

a trail up Eagle Creek, which sprouts a trail along Oval Creek 2 miles from the trailhead. The 7-mile **Eagle Creek Trail** is fairly level; there's more uphill on the Oval Creek route, but it does have the reward of three high mountain lakes starting about 6½ miles in. Both of these trails can be the first leg of a backpacking trip into the **Lake Chelan-Sawtooth Wilderness Area**. There are many trails in the area, with many opportunities to hike over to Lake Chelan. If, at the end of the Twisp River Rd, you follow USFS Rd 44, you'll pass several campgrounds, each with hiking trails nearby (see Camping below).

There is a wheelchair-accessible paved walkway surrounding **Black Pine Lake**, a remote lake southwest of Twisp. From Hwy 20, follow the Twisp River Rd west 11 miles to USFS Rd 300, which heads south and reaches Black Pine Lake after 6½ miles.

Rafting

Rafters divide the Methow River into two floatable stretches. The upper stretch, from the town of Carlton to McFarland Creek (3 miles north of Methow) provides an easy-going float; the lower Methow, from McFarland Creek to Pateros, runs through the Black Canyon with more challenging white-water. Osprey River Adventures (☎ 509-997-4116, 800-997-4116) runs white-water trips on the Methow River from $50.

Other Activities

If you don't mind a few snowmobiles, **cross-country skiing** is easy along the flat Twisp River Rd, just out of Twisp. Just drive to the end of the plowed road, and ski as far as you like. Nearer to downtown, trails start at the Idle-A-While Motel and tool around Twisp and along the Methow River.

North Cascade Outfitters (☎ 509-997-1015) offers **horseback riding**. A 1½-hour ride costs $15 and a 2½-hour rides costs $25. Customized pack trips are also available. Or for something a little different, the Malamute Express (☎ 509-997-6402) runs **dog-sledding** trips; a half-day costs $112, while a full day with lunch costs $224.

Places to Stay

As with most of the recreation around Twisp, the Twisp River is the place to look for campsites. There are four campgrounds up Twisp River Rd (USFS Rd 44 and 4400) in the Okanogan National Forest, all at trailheads for the Lake Chelan-Sawtooth Wilderness Area. *War Creek Campground*, 14½ miles up the road, is right on the river, and has running water and a $7 fee. *Black Pine Lake Campground*, is 17½ miles southwest of Twisp at the end of the Poorman Creek Rd (USFS Rd 300) at Black Pine Lake.

You won't find any place particularly fancy or upscale to stay in Twisp, but there are several reasonably priced, basic motels. The *Sportsman Motel* (☎ 509-997-2911), 11010 E Hwy 20, has perfectly good knotty-pine rooms; singles/doubles are $39/41. At the *Idle-A-While Motel* (☎ 509-997-3222), 505 N Hwy 20, kitchenette cottages and regular motel rooms start at $45/51. It's not a bad place to while away a quiet Twisp evening – the motel has a hot tub and sauna, and rents VCRs and movies. There's easy access to cross-country ski trails in the wintertime.

A few miles southeast in Carlton, on Hwy 20, the *Country Town Motel* (☎ 509-997-3432) is one of the nicer motels between Winthrop and Chelan. There's an outdoor pool, a hot tub and a tiny golf course. Rooms are $50, and the motel is right across the road from the Methow River and the town's only other attraction: a guy who does chainsaw sculptures, seemingly 24 hours a day.

Up the Twisp River, the *Log House Inn B&B* (☎ 509-997-5001), 894 Twisp River Rd (9 miles west of Twisp), is convenient to recreation on the Twisp River Trail or the Lake Clean-Sawtooth Wilderness; they also offer boarding for horses. Rooms start at $55.

Places to Eat

The *Cinnamon Twisp Bakery* (☎ 509-997-5030), 102 Glover St, has excellent cinnamon twists and bagels. Your best bet for a meal is the *Glover St Cafe* (☎ 509-997-

1323), 104 Glover St, next door to the Confluence Gallery, though it's open limited hours. Unless you can warm up to deep-fried chicken and potatoes at the *Roadhouse Diner* (☎ 509-997-4015), downtown on Hwy 20, or whatever's cooking in a local bar, keep driving; Winthrop is only 11 miles north.

Lake Chelan

The glaciers that carved Lake Chelan were powerful excavators, leaving the third-deepest lake in the USA, after Oregon's Crater Lake and Lake Tahoe on the California/Nevada border. Both glaciers and mountain streams feed water into Lake Chelan, which is 55 miles long and 1500 feet deep.

Chelan, at the southeastern tip of the lake, is the primary base for transportation, accommodations, restaurants, recreational services and entertainment. Farther up the lake, mountains rise and trees fill in the lakeshore; by the time you reach Stehekin, a remote village near the lake's head, mountains jut up beyond the dense forest.

Lake Chelan is central Washington's playground. Anything you can do in or on water – swim, fish, sail, canoe, kayak, water-ski and jet-ski – is permitted. Windsurfers will have the most luck up near Stehekin or Lucerne, where the wind is stronger.

Orientation

The town of Chelan serves as the gateway to Lake Chelan. Stehekin, 55 miles northwest of Chelan at the north end of the lake, is on the southern edge of the North Cascades, and is connected to Chelan by *The Lady of the Lake II*, a passenger boat that runs regularly up and down the lake. Other than a boat, only a float plane or hiking trail will get you to Stehekin.

South Shore Rd follows Lake Chelan's western shore up as far as Twenty-five Mile Creek State Park; on the opposite side of the lake, the road stops at Greens Landing, a few miles past the town of Manson.

Getting There & Around

Air Pangborn Memorial Airport, 38 miles south at Wenatchee, is the nearest airport and is serviced by Horizon Air and United Express. Chelan Airways (☎ 509-682-5555) operates a daily seaplane service from Chelan to Stehekin and all points in between. A roundtrip flight to Stehekin costs $120.

Bus The free Link buses (☎ 509-662-1155) connect Chelan with Wenatchee and Leavenworth.

Ferry The Lake Chelan Boat Company (☎ 509-682-2224), PO Box 457, Chelan, WA 98816, operates boat service up and down Lake Chelan. A ride on the *Lady of the Lake II* is the most common way to reach Stehekin and Lucerne, and is popular with tourists who simply want to cruise the lake with a 90-minute stop in Stehekin. Another option is the *Lady Express*, which cuts the four-hour (one-way) boat trip down to just over two hours. During the summer, boats leave Chelan every morning at 8:30 am, and the last boat leaves Stehekin at 2 pm, returning to Chelan by 6 pm. If your destination is Holden Village (Lucerne) or one of the lakeside campgrounds, check with the tour company as to which boat best suits your needs.

Fares vary seasonally and in the high season can cost up to $22 or $41 for a roundtrip ticket; children under age 11 pay half price. Bring a bicycle along for $13 roundtrip (or rent one in Stehekin). Complete timetable and fare information is also available from the Lake Chelan visitors' center. The boats do not transport cars.

Dogs aren't permitted on the tour boat from March 15 to October 31, but there is a kennel in Manson; the Animal Inn Boarding Kennel (☎ 509-687-9497) is at 712 Wapato Way. During the off-season, a caged pet can ride for $24 roundtrip.

CHELAN
Population 3097

This town at the southeastern tip of Lake Chelan is flush with lakeside condos and

WASHINGTON

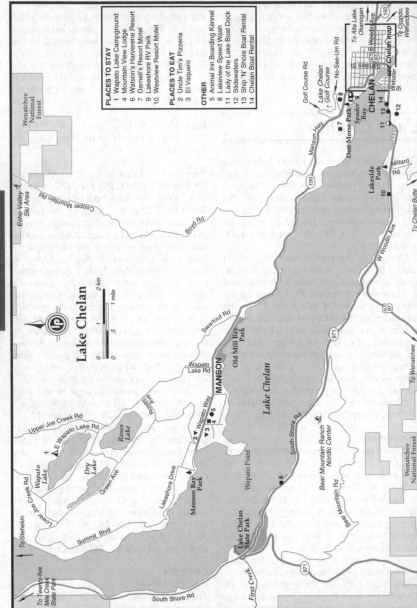

PLACES TO STAY
1 Wapato Lake Campground
4 Mountain View Lodge
6 Watson's Harverene Resort
7 Darnell's Resort Motel
9 Lakeshore RV Park
10 Westview Resort Motel

PLACES TO EAT
2 Uncle Tim's Pizzeria
3 El Vaquero

OTHER
5 Animal Inn Boarding Kennel
8 Lakeview Speed Wash
11 Lady of the Lake Boat Dock
12 Slidewaters
13 Ship 'N' Shore Boat Rental
14 Chelan Boat Rental

Lake Chelan

views of the North Cascades. Chelan is the hub of commercial and resort traffic on the lake, and is only appealing in a strictly functional way. The town is flanked by dry hills with scattered pines, lots of scrabble and scree, yellow balsamroot in spring and apple trees galore. The apples grown here are supposedly the state's finest, and no one who stops by a roadside fruit stand in late October is apt to argue the point.

The rural community of Manson (population 1800), 8 miles west of Chelan, makes a scenic drive or bike ride past apple orchards and views of the lake. Manson Bay Park is a popular swimming and picnic area on the north shore of Lake Chelan. There's also a boat ramp and picnic area at Old Mill Park, 2 miles east of town on Hwy 150, and a small gambling casino.

Orientation

Chelan is 37 miles northeast of Wenatchee via US 97 and 54 miles southwest of Omak on the same road. From Seattle, it's 166 miles via Stevens Pass and 173 miles via Snoqualmie Pass.

On either end, Woodin Ave (US 97) is the main drag into town. From Wenatchee, Alt US 97 intercepts US 971 on the west side of town and travels east along the lake's south shore to the city center. South Shore Rd (US 971) continues west, past the Alt US 97 cutoff to Wenatchee, to Lake Chelan State Park and Twenty five Mile Creek.

US 97 north from Okanogan (or south from Orondo) enters town from the east. As it reaches downtown, Hwy 150 (the Manson Hwy) splits off US 97 at Columbia St and continues for another 8 miles along the north shore to Manson, past a seemingly endless strip of time-share condominiums and private RV parks. From Manson, there's more scenery out Wapato Lake Rd (turn at the golf course) past Roses Lake, Wapato Lake, and Dry Lake.

Information

If it's tourist information you seek, don't miss the Lake Chelan Chamber of Commerce visitors' bureau (☎ 509-682-3503,

800-424-3526), 102 E Johnson Ave, or write them at PO Box 216, Chelan, WA 98816. The Chelan Ranger Station (☎ 509-682-2576), 428 W Woodin Ave, provides copious amounts of information on the Wenatchee National Forest, Lake Chelan State Park, the Lake Chelan National Recreation Area, and North Cascades National Park. Call ☎ 509-682-2549 to reach the NPS desk direct.

The post office (☎ 509-682-2625) is at 144 E Johnson Ave. Riverwalk Books (☎ 509-682-8901), downtown at 113 S Emerson St, is a nice place to browse for beach reading. For laundry, head to Lakeview Speed Wash (☎ 509-682-5023), near the Chelan Plaza at 504 Manson Rd.

The Lake Chelan Community Hospital (☎ 509-682-2531) is at 503 E Highland Ave.

Downtown

The **Campbell House Hotel**, at Columbia St and Woodin Ave, first did business in 1900, and some of the Campbell family furniture, which journeyed with its owners from Iowa to Chelan, is still in the hotel. The hotel now serves as the restaurant at Campbell's Resort & Conference Center (see Places to Stay). Another historic structure is **St Andrews Church**, a log building with stained glass windows at 120 E Woodin Ave.

Catch the mile-long paved path in **Riverwalk Park** at Emerson and Wapato Sts, and stroll along the short Chelan River.

Swimming & Boating

Water recreation is what Lake Chelan is all about. The lake is open to all manner of watercraft, though speedboats and jet-skis are the predominant choices at this end of the lake. Afternoon winds also make the lake suitable for sailing or windsurfing. Ship n' Shore Boat Rental (☎ 509-682-5125), 1230 W Woodin Ave, rents ski boats and jet-skis, as does neighboring Chelan Boat Rentals (☎ 509-682-4444), 1210 W Woodin Ave. Most places include delivery in the rental price.

A guarded swimming area, picnic areas and a boat launch, in addition to nearly 150

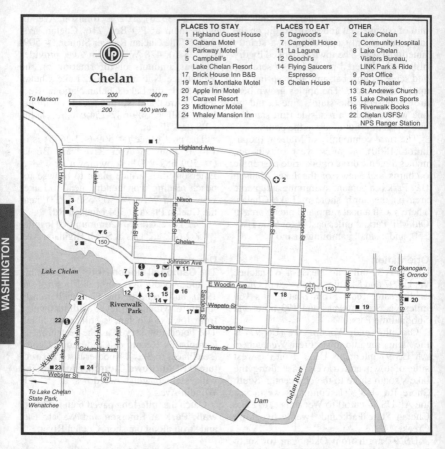

Chelan

To Manson

0   200   400 m
0   200   400 yards

PLACES TO STAY
1 Highland Guest House
3 Cabana Motel
4 Parkway Motel
5 Campbell's
  Lake Chelan Resort
17 Brick House Inn B&B
19 Mom's Montlake Motel
20 Apple Inn Motel
21 Caravel Resort
23 Midtowner Motel
24 Whaley Mansion Inn

PLACES TO EAT
6 Dagwood's
7 Campbell House
11 La Laguna
12 Goochi's
14 Flying Saucers
   Espresso
18 Chelan House

OTHER
2 Lake Chelan
  Community Hospital
8 Lake Chelan
  Visitors Bureau,
  LINK Park & Ride
9 Post Office
10 Ruby Theater
13 St Andrews Church
15 Lake Chelan Sports
16 Riverwalk Books
22 Chelan USFS/
   NPS Ranger Station

Highland Ave

Gibson

Nixon

Allen

Chelan

Johnson Ave

Lake Chelan

Manson Hwy

Lake

Columbia St

Emerson St

To Okanogan, Orondo

Navarre St

Robinson St

Wilson St

Washington St

E Woodin Ave

Wapato St

Okanogan St

Trow St

Sanders St

ALT 97   150

Riverwalk Park

W Woodin Ave

Lake Ave

3rd Ave

2nd Ave

1st Ave

Columbia Ave

Webster St

ALT 97

To Lake Chelan State Park, Wenatchee

Chelan River

Dam

WASHINGTON

campsites, make **Lake Chelan State Park** a busy lakeside spot. To get there, head west of Chelan on South Shore Rd for 9 miles, or cut north on the Navarre Coulee Rd (US 971) from US 97 between Entiat and Chelan.

Closer to town, there are more public beaches off US 97 at **Lakeside Park**, near the west side of Chelan. On the north shore, **Don Morse Memorial Park** on the Manson Hwy also has a boat launch and is adjacent to Lakeshore RV Park. In downtown Manson, the swimming area at **Manson Bay Park** features several floating docks, and there's a four-lane boat

launch at **Old Mill Bay Park** just south of town near Wapato Point.

There are other boat launches at **Twenty-five Mile Creek State Park**, another 11 miles west of Lake Chelan State Park at the end of South Shore Rd. Up the lake, beyond the reach of roads, are another 11 boat docks, most of which are associated with campgrounds.

If you have kids, don't even think they'll let you sneak past **Slidewaters Water Park** (☎ 509-682-5751), 102 Waterslide Drive off W Woodin Ave, on a hill above the Lady of the Lake boat dock. A day-long pass costs $10.95, or $7.95 for children ages four to seven. After 5 pm, the rates drop to $7.95/4.95.

Fishing

In Lake Chelan, fish for lake, rainbow and cutthroat trout, Kokanee and Chinook salmon, ling cod and smallmouth bass. Just north of Manson, Wapato Lake has good early summer fly-fishing for rainbow trout, and a fair number of bluegill and large-mouth bass. Nearby Roses Lake is open from December 1 to March 31 for rainbow trout, brown trout and catfish. Antillon Lake, another 3 miles north from Wapato Lake, is popular with families, as the resident bluegills, pumpkinseed and crappies are fairly easy to hook. Contact Rush's Fishing Guide Service (☎ 509-682-2802, 800-626-7874), PO Box 1481, Chelan 98816, for guided fishing excursions. Graybill's Guide Service (☎ 509-682-4294) specializes in salmon, steelhead and lake trout fishing.

Hang-Gliding & Paragliding

The warm thermals rising from the Columbia Basin provide good conditions for hang gliders and paragliders, and it's not unusual to see gliders launching off 3800-foot Chelan Butte, just southwest of town. Take Chelan Butte Rd at the west end of town, near Lakeside Park. For rentals and instruction contact Chelan Paragliding (☎ 509-682-7777).

Golf

Lake Chelan Golf Course (☎ 509-682-8026, 800-246-5361), 1501 Golf Course Drive, is a public 18-hole course, on a bluff overlooking the lake, surrounded by lovely scenery. About 17 miles south of Chelan on US 97 in Orondo is Desert Canyon Golf Course (☎ 509-784-1111, 800-852-5238), Central Washington's most deluxe course.

Other Activities

Mountain bikers should stop by the ranger station and pick up a map of USFS roads open to **cycling**. One popular mountain biking trail starts at Twenty-five Mile

Creek State Park and follows the north fork of Twenty-five Mile Creek. There are also trails on Echo Ridge Ski Area near Manson (see below). Road cyclists can ride a loop up to Manson along Wapato Lake Rd, past Roses, Wapato, and Dry Lakes.

There are plenty of good places to go **cross-country skiing** around Chelan, though most are run as off-season business ventures. (Chelan's ski season typically runs only from Christmas to mid-February or early-March.) Bear Mountain Ranch Nordic Center (☎ 509-682-5444), on Bear Mountain Rd, 5 miles west of Chelan off Alt US 97, maintains 34 miles of cross-country trails with telemark areas and good views of the lake. The trails are open daylight hours Friday to Monday and holidays; a slight trail fee is charged.

When snow makes it impossible to tee off, meet your golf partner for cross-country skiing or sledding at the Lake Chelan Golf Course, 1501 Golf Course Drive, which has 3 miles of groomed Nordic trails. For **downhill skiing** and **snowmobiling** check out the Echo Valley Ski Area (☎ 509-682-4002), off Hwy 150 between Chelan and Manson, on Cooper Mountain Rd, which features three tow-ropes and one pommel lift, in operation on Wednesday, Saturday and Sunday. There are more cross-country skiing and snowmobile trails next door at Echo Ridge.

For rentals, head to Lake Chelan Sports (☎ 509-682-2629), downtown at 132 E

Flies are used to catch trout in Wapato Lake.

Woodin Ave, or Lakeland Ski (☎ 509-687-3204) at the Echo Valley Ski Area.

Special Events
Manson's mid-May Apple Blossom Festival is highlighted by a parade and a chicken noodle dinner. Various hang-gliding events are held in Chelan throughout the spring and summer. Chelan's best festival is the mid-July Bach Feste, a 10-day series of concerts. Call the visitors' center (☎ 509-682-3503, 800-424-3526) for exact schedules.

Places to Stay
If Chelan is fully booked or seems too expensive, look in Wenatchee, where there are plenty of motel rooms for around $50. Free public transportation links Wenatchee with Chelan.

The tourist season peaks in the summer and in most places off-season rates drop at least a little bit. Prices in the listings below reflect the high-season summer months, and winter visitors to Chelan can count on room rates being considerably cheaper – up to 40% or even 50% lower at motels.

Camping If you're looking for a spot on Lake Chelan, then aim for *Lake Chelan State Park* (☎ 509-687-3710), on South Shore Rd, a large campground with nice lakeside spots (no hookups) 9 miles west of town. Reservations are a necessity during the summer. If you don't have reservations, try *Twenty-five Mile Creek State Park* (☎ 509-687-3610), 20 miles west of Chelan on South Shore Rd, just about at road's end. Even though it's fairly remote, the campground here can also fill up early on summer weekends. Make reservations for either by calling ☎ 800-452-5687; there's an extra reservation fee in addition to the $12 camping fee.

Lakeshore RV Park (☎ 509-682-8023), 619 W Manson Hwy next to Don Morse City Park in downtown Chelan has sites with full hookups for $26, and a few tent sites for $22. Inland around Manson there's less of a scene at *Wapato Lake Campground* (☎ 509-687-6037), on E Wapato Lake Rd, which has showers, flush toilets, and sites for either RVs or tents at $15.

A number of campgrounds accessible only by boat line the shores of Lake Chelan. Boaters should check at the ranger station for details.

B&Bs *Brick House Inn B&B* (☎ 509-682-4791, 800-799-2332), 302 Wapato St, is a downtown-Chelan Victorian home with rooms for $68. *Highland Guest House* (☎ 509-682-2892, 800-681-2892), 121 E Highland Ave, is a 1902 Victorian with good views. Rooms start at $90 but drop to $75 in the winter. *Mary Kay's Romantic Whaley Mansion Inn* (☎ 509-682-5735, 800-729-2408), 415 S 3rd Ave, is elegantly decorated, and rooms easily clear the $100 hurdle.

Up the lake, *Holden Village B&B* (☎ 509-687-9695), on Twenty-five Mile Creek at the end of South Shore Rd, offers inexpensive no-frills rooms from $35/45 during the summer, with lower winter rates and a three-bed dorm with bunks for $19 each. Many of the guests here are headed to Holden Village, a church-based retreat up the lake, but the B&B is open to anyone who's willing to change their own bed linens in the morning.

Hotels *Parkway Motel* (☎ 509-682-2822), 402 N Manson Rd, across from Lake Shore Park, charges only $40 for a basic room or $65 for a kitchenette. *Mom's Montlake Motel* (☎ 509-682-5715), 823 Wapato St, one block off the main drag at the east end of town, is a quiet, inexpensive place; single/double rooms start at $45/48.

The box-like *Apple Inn Motel* (☎ 509-682-4044), 1002 E Woodin Ave, has a heated outdoor pool and indoor hot tub. In the summer, rooms start at $49, or $55 with kitchenette. The *Midtowner Motel* (☎ 509-682-4051), 721 W Woodin Ave, isn't quite on the lake, but it's a well-rounded place, with indoor and outdoor pools, a hot tub, laundry facilities and kitchenette rooms for a mere $50/65.

The Cabana Motel (☎ 509-682-2233, 800-799-2332), 420 Manson Rd, is across from the city park and marina. Doubles start at $68, and poolside kitchenettes start at $83.

Up the road in Manson, the *Mountain View Lodge* (☎ 509-687-9505, 800-967-8105), 25 Wapato Point Parkway, has a heated pool, hot tub and picnic area, and houses more than the occasional tour group. Rooms start at $79 weekdays, or $91 on weekends.

Resorts Though they're not quite full-fledged destination resorts, all of these 'resort motels' offer more than the average motel. They're all on the lake, have private beaches with boat moorage, and are equipped to deal with small conventions or large families.

The sprawling *Campbell's Lake Chelan Resort & Conference Center* (☎ 509-682-2561, 800-553-8225), 104 W Woodin Ave, has swallowed up the historic Campbell Hotel, established in 1901. This is Chelan's premier resort. During peak season rooms start at $98/112. Rooms or cottages with kitchens cost anywhere from $120 to $180. Across the bay, the lakeside *Caravel Resort* (☎ 509-682-2582, 800-962-8723), 332 W Woodin Ave, is right downtown; rooms start at $92. *Westview Resort Motel* (☎ 509-682-4396), 2312 W Woodin Ave, on the outskirts of town by Lakeside Park, has an outdoor pool and spa, private beach and dock. Summer rates start at $89 for doubles.

Darnell's Resort Motel (☎ 509-682-2015, 800-967-8149), 901 Spader Bay Rd, off the road to Manson on the north side of Chelan, is another upscale lakeside motel, with an emphasis on family vacationers. Besides the beach, there are paddleboat rentals, tennis courts, an exercise room, a nine-hole putting golf course and bicycles. Rates start at $82 for a double. There are also two-bedroom units which sleep six, starting at $105.

Near Lake Chelan State Park, *Watson's Harverene Resort* (☎ 509-687-3720, 800-697-3720), 7750 South Shore Rd, has lakefront cottages for four people from $95. Boat storage and moorage are also available. *Kelly's Resort* (☎ 509-687-3220, 800-

567-8978), 12801 South Shore Rd, is about 5 miles past Lake Chelan State Park on Hwy 971. Woodsy cottages across the road from the lake cost $100 to $170.

Vacation Home Rentals Chelan Vacation Rentals (☎ 509-682-4011, 800-560-7829) has condos in a development with pool, hot tub and racquetball courts. Golf packages at Desert Canyon are also available.

Places to Eat
Early in the morning, *Flying Saucers Espresso* (☎ 509-682-5129), 116 S Emerson St, is the place to engage in local gossip and swill espresso. If it's 'hip' you're craving, there's a touch of it here, and a good dose of local color, but never so much of either as to make an outsider feel unwelcome. There's an astounding variety of homemade muffins, as well as cookies and pastries for later in the day.

Make a quick stop at *Dagwood's* (☎ 509-682-8630), 246 W Manson Hwy in Chelan Plaza, for inexpensive Thai food and stir-fry. There's good Mexican for lunch or dinner downtown at *La Laguna* (☎ 509-682-5553), 114 N Emerson St.

Goochi's (☎ 682-2436), 104 E Woodin Ave, tries for a brewpub atmosphere (though big-screen TV is not a typical brewpub installation) and does have many Northwest microbrews on tap. Burgers ($5 to $7.50) highlight the lunch menu, and for dinner, it's the sort of place where you follow your oyster shooters with a steak (about $15). Even if you're not up for a drink, stop in for a look at the cherrywood bar, brought around Cape Horn from Europe in the late 1800s, and previously installed in a Montana bar.

Campbell House Restaurant (☎ 509-682-4250), 104 W Woodin Ave, is the fanciest dining spot in town, and though the meals aren't generally what you'd call innovative, vegetarians will have to give the place credit for serving a stuffed squash entrée. Dinner at the *Chelan House* (☎ 509-682-2013), 502 E Woodin Ave, is the standard American meat with salad bar, but it opens early for breakfast.

There are a couple of decent places to eat in Manson. *Uncle Tim's Pizzeria* (☎ 509-687-3035), 76 Wapato Way, has huge, meaty pizzas and several pasta dishes (with prices topping out at $12.95 for shrimp tortellini). For Mexican food, *El Vaquero* (☎ 509-687-3179), 75 Wapato Way, is more authentic and tastier than the other nacho joints in the area, and it's easy to eat your fill for less than $10.

Entertainment
Catch a movie at the *Ruby Theater* (☎ 509-682-5016), 135 E Woodin Ave. The theater dates from 1913, and is named for the original owner's daughter.

Goochi's (☎ 509-682-2436), at 104 E Woodin Ave, brings in blues bands from around the Northwest on most Friday nights.

Getting There & Away
Chelan Airways (☎ 509-682-5555) operates a daily seaplane service between Chelan and Stehekin for $120 roundtrip. The airfield is northeast of town on Alt US 97. Ticket information is also available from the Lady of the Lake boat dock.

The *Lady of the Lake II* and *Lady Express* board once daily for trips across Lake Chelan to Lucerne and Stehekin. The Lady of the Lake boat dock (☎ 509-682-4584) is located on the south shore of the lake, a mile west of downtown on Alt US 97. See Getting There & Around at the beginning of this chapter for more details.

Getting Around
During the summer, a shuttle runs up to Lake Chelan State Park (though this service may be suspended). Wenatchee-based Link (☎ 509-662-1155, 800-851-5465) provides free bus service between Manson, Chelan, and Wenatchee on bus No 21. Buses stop throughout downtown Chelan and along Hwy 150; the park-and-ride at Columbia St and Johnson Ave, next to the chamber of commerce, is a convenient place to catch one.

AROUND CHELAN
Holden Village
Holden Village (☎ 509-687-3644), a retreat center operated by the Lutheran church, offers programs on theology, literature, the environment, Bible study, race and culture, as well as arts and crafts, for people of all religious backgrounds. Holden Village is open year-round, and during the winter, the schedule is less structured. Several trails lead into the adjacent Glacier Peak Wilderness Area. Holden Village is connected by a road to the Lucerne boat landing, and most visitors arrive on the *Lady of the Lake II* tour boat. (You can't drive there.) Rates start at $48 per person for one night with a discount given for subsequent nights stayed, or $226 a week. Prices include all meals and seminars. For information, write to the Registrar, Holden Village, Chelan, WA 98816.

Alta Lake
Alta Lake, 17 miles north of Chelan near Pateros (population 585), is home to Alta Lake State Park and a couple of small resorts, one with an attractive 18-hole golf course. Boaters and anglers like the lake, which is stocked with rainbow trout, and there is a swimming beach.

There are plenty of $11 campsites at *Alta Lake State Park* (☎ 509-923-2473). The *Alta Lake Golf Resort* (☎ 509-923-2359, 923-2033 for the motel) is connected with the golf course just north of Alta Lake and is, not surprisingly, particularly geared to golfers. Single/double rooms start at $48/52, and kitchenettes run $78. *Whistlin' Pine Resort* (☎ 509-923-2548), also on Alta Lake, has rustic two- or four-person cabins for $30/40; tent and RV sites start at $13. Whistlin' Pine is as close as you'll get to a dude ranch around here, as they offer horseback riding and fishing.

To reach Alta Lake from Chelan, head 17 miles north on US 97 to Pateros, and then turn west onto Hwy 153 for 2 miles to Alta Lake Rd.

STEHEKIN
Population 100

Of all the wonderful spots in the North Cascades, Stehekin is especially charmed. Part of the charm comes from its remoteness, as the tiny community is only accessible by boat, plane, or a long hike, most often across Cascade Pass. An equal amount of charm accrues from the beauty of its location at the head of Lake Chelan, on the southern edge of the North Cascades National Park. Plenty of hiking trails lead

A Tale of Two Forests
The North Cascades contain a rich variety of flora that varies dramatically between the wet west slopes and drier east slopes, as well as with elevation. The lower elevation, west-side slopes are forested with Western hemlocks and Western red cedar, like those on the short Happy Creek Forest boardwalk near Ross Lake and the Thunder River Trail at Colonial Creek Campground. Higher up, Douglas firs and Pacific silver firs join these trees. Such a forest can be seen on Hwy 20 at Rainy Pass. As the elevation increases, mountain hemlock and Pacific silver fir predominate until, at subalpine levels (such as at Washington Pass or along the Cascade Pass Trail), subalpine fir replaces silver fir. The wildflower meadows at Cascade Pass and Sahale Arm are examples of the highest, west-side subalpine zones. Above them, many rocky Cascade peaks are cloaked only with snow and ice.

On the east side of the Cascades, in places such as Blue Lake and Cutthroat Pass, subalpine larch and whitebark pine grow in the high, relatively dry subalpine forest. The Douglas fir and lodgepole pine forest along the Stehekin River is characteristic of east-side, mid-elevation growth, while lower on the Stehekin and at Bridge Creek, the lowlands forest is comprised of ponderosa pine and Douglas fir, which is particularly abundant due to years of fire suppression. ∎

into the mountains. If possible, stay here for a day or two rather than making a quick up-and-back tour-boat excursion.

Virtually all the tours, activities, places to eat and accommodations are limited to the summer season, which runs from mid-June to mid-September. In the winter, the North Cascades Stehekin Lodge has a few kitchenette units available, but visitors should bring their own food from Chelan.

'Stehekin' is roughly translated as 'the way through,' and though Native Americans didn't have villages at the north end of Lake Chelan, they did use nearby Cascade Pass as a route across the Cascades.

Miners after North Cascades gold figured a boat ride up Lake Chelan was easier than foot travel across the mountains, and prospectors began tramping through the area in the 1850s. Even Clara Barton, founder of the American Red Cross, visited Stehekin on a wood-fired steamboat in 1891 and filed a mining claim. However, Barton's visit was far upstaged when, in 1944, young Elizabeth Taylor filmed *The Courage of Lassie* in Stehekin. Subsistence farmers began putting down roots in the 1880s, and in 1905 a six-story, Swiss-style hotel opened, catering to hunters and anglers. In 1927, a dam at the lake's foot raised the water level by 21 feet, flooding many buildings, including Stehekin's original 1892 hotel.

Orientation
Stehekin is 55 miles north of Chelan, at the north end of Lake Chelan. See the North Cascades National Park map, earlier in this chapter, for sites in and around Stehekin.

Stehekin Valley Rd (the town's only road) is referred to most often as just 'the road.' From the boat landing, the road continues to the northwest for 23 miles, only five of which are paved. The road is clear of snow from High Bridge Campground (11 miles up) to the end from around late June, though severe flooding in past years has been known to close the road for an entire season. Be sure to check the road status with the NPS before making plans.

East of Stehekin the road dead-ends after 4 miles. Destinations at the landing are all within walking distance, and it's easy to rent a bike or catch a bus to travel up the road.

Information

Tourist Offices The Courtney Log Office, 150 yards past the post office, has information about the valley and serves as a sort of activities center and booking office. Write to Stehekin Heritage, PO Box 1, Stehekin, WA 98852, to obtain a copy of *The Stehekin Guidebook*, a useful tourist publication.

The Golden West Visitor Center houses the NPS Information Center, which is also an interpretive museum and art gallery. It's open 12:30 to 2 pm (the hours of the tour boat's layover in Stehekin) daily, March 15 to May 14; 8 am to 4:30 pm May 15 to September 15; and 10:30 am to 2 pm September 16 to mid-October. Backpackers and campers will need an overnight camping permit, which can be obtained here or from the Chelan Ranger Station. A limited number of permits are issued free, on a first-come, first-served basis, no more than 24 hours before departure. The NPS ranger station behind the North Cascades Stehekin Lodge serves as the off-season information center.

Post & Communications The post office is in the lower level of the ranger station.

Telephone service in Stehekin is via expensive radio-telephone, so most business listings are for answering services or voice mailboxes in Chelan. There's a regular credit card phone for outgoing calls in front of the public laundromat and shower house. Other telephone arrangements can be made at the Courtney Log Office, or the North Cascades Stehekin Lodge.

Media The *Stehekin Choice*, put out every two months, is a great way to gain insight into the life and culture of the 100 or so people who live here year-round.

Laundry There's a public laundry and shower house building on the main road, about 50 yards beyond the post office.

Medical Services The nearest hospital is in Chelan. The valley has its own network of individuals and NPS personnel certified in first-aid, so ask locals for a reference. Contact the ranger station in an emergency; most businesses and NPS employees carry radios for this purpose.

Hiking

If you're not staying overnight, it's hard to get very far on a hike with a layover of only a few hours. The way to **Buckner Orchard**, one of the Stehekin area's oldest settlements, makes for a nice walk. Once there you'll find a homestead cabin built in 1889, plenty of old farm equipment and trees that keep on bearing apples. Head 3.4 miles up the northwest branch of Stehekin Valley Rd, turn left at the far end of the Rainbow Creek bridge and look for a sign about 20 yards off the road, marking the Buckner Orchard Walk, an easy 1-mile roundtrip to the apple orchards. From just past the bridge, there's also a short path leading to the 312-foot **Rainbow Falls**.

The easy **Lakeshore Trail** starts at the Golden West Visitor Center and heads south near Lake Chelan's shore. There's a campground just a short way down the forested trail. It's 6 miles to views of the lake and valley at Hunts Bluff. It's also possible to make this into a backpacking trip; Moore Point is 7 miles from the trailhead while Prince Creek is 17 miles.

The relatively flat **Stehekin River Trail** starts at Harlequin Campground (4½ miles upvalley from the landing) and heads upriver through the forest, past many fishing holes. It's a cool, shady walk – perfect for a hot day.

A steady uphill hike from the **Rainbow Creek Trailhead**, 2½ miles from the landing, leads to great lake and valley views. There's a campground 2 miles from the trailhead at Rainbow Bridge. Take the left fork past the campground to complete the 5-mile **Rainbow Loop Trail**, which includes the initial climb to great views, with a fairly quick return to the valley. Take the right fork 1 mile to reach an incredible viewpoint of the lake and the Cascades;

this trail continues for another 10 miles to McAlester Pass.

Head east from the Golden West Visitor Center and immediately begin climbing the **Purple Creek Trail** toward 6884-foot Purple Pass, 7.4 miles away. Since it starts at the landing, hikers who are looking for a short, vigorous hike with good views of the lake and mountains can grunt uphill for a hour or so, and then return for the afternoon boat to Chelan. The forest yields to views after about 3 miles.

Just past the turnoff for High Bridge Campground (11 miles from the landing) pick up the **Agnes Gorge Trail** for an easy 2½-mile hike to a 210-foot gorge, past views of 8115-foot Agnes Mountain.

Biking
You can rent bikes from the store at the North Cascades Stehekin Lodge or from Discovery Bikes (☎ 509-884-4844) at the Courtney Log Office. Mountain bikes (for road riding only) rent for $3.50 an hour or $20 a day. They can also shuttle cyclists and their bikes up the road to the Stehekin Valley Ranch, which is just far enough to bike back down the valley in time to catch the 2 pm boat back to Chelan.

Fishing
The lower Stehekin River is open for catch-and-release fishing from March 1 to June 30, with the regular fishing season running from July 1 to October 31. Both cutthroat and rainbow trout live in the upper river and the creeks feeding into it. Kokanee (landlocked sockeye) salmon begin the run from Lake Chelan up the Stehekin in late August, and continue through September. Stop by McGregor Mountain Outdoor Company at the landing for fishing advice, supplies and regulation updates.

Other Activities
The Stehekin Adventure Company (one of the Courtney family's many ventures) offers **raft trips** on the Stehekin River in the spring and summer; day trips cost adults/children $40/30. Stehekin Valley Ranch's Cascade Corrals leads three-hour

horseback rides to Coon Lake; cost is $30 per person. Contact the Courtney Log Office (☎ 509-682-4677) to make reservations for both activities.

Be sure to check at the Golden West Visitor Center for the current listing of interpretive **nature walks** and hikes led by the NPS.

Organized Tours
Stehekin Valley Wagon Tours offers narrated tours to the Buckner Orchard, one-room Stehekin School, and Rainbow Falls in horse-drawn wagons. Tours depart from the Stehekin Pastry Company at 9:45 am; $10/5 for adults/children. Sign up at the Courtney Log Office.

The North Cascades Stehekin Lodge leads a daily bus trip to Rainbow Falls. Buses leave upon arrival of the *Lady Express* (around 10:45 am) and the *Lady of the Lake II* (around 12:30 pm). The 45-minute tour costs $5. They also offer a lunch tour to High Bridge ($20).

Places to Stay
Camping The NPS maintains 11 primitive campsites along the road up the valley, as well as a good number of hike-in campgrounds. First, you'll need to obtain a free camping permit from the NPS Information Center. *Purple Point Campground* is right at the landing, 200 yards upvalley from the dock. *Weaver Point Campground* is a boaters' campground, 1 mile from the landing by boat.

Four miles up the road at Harlequin Bridge is *Harlequin Campground*, which has great views of the river. You'll have direct access to trailheads for Agnes Gorge and the Pacific Crest Trail at *High Bridge Campground*, 11 miles from the landing. At the end of the line is *Cottonwood Campground*, 23 miles from the landing, the last campground accessible from the road. Don't forget this stretch stays snowed-in until late June.

B&Bs *Silver Bay Lodging & Cabins* (☎ 509-682-2212), Box 43, Stehekin, WA 98852, has one large, solar-heated B&B

room and several housekeeping cabins 2 miles up the road near the Stehekin Pastry Company. They may require a minimum stay, depending on where you'll be sleeping; rates run around $80 to $135, with seasonal variations.

Lodges *North Cascades Stehekin Lodge* (☎ 509-682-4494), PO Box 457, Chelan, WA 98816, is in town on the lakefront. Rooms start at $75, kitchenettes at $90. This is the 'modern' (ie, non-rustic) place to stay in Stehekin. They also offer boat moorage in Stehekin's new 30-slip marina.

Courtney's Stehekin Valley Ranch (☎ 509-682-4677), PO Box 36, Stehekin, WA 98852, provides lodging in rustic cabins. The cost is $60 per person, and includes all meals (plus lunch the day you leave), and transportation around the lower valley.

Cabins & Vacation Homes Home rentals around Stehekin typically require a minimum stay of at least two nights and rent for around $80 to $90 per night for two people, or about $475 to $550 per week.

The rustic *Stehekin Mountain Cabin* rents for $80 per night, or $360 per week. Write to Don and Roberta Pitts, PO Box 272, Stehekin, WA 98852.

Contact Mike and Nancy Barnhart (☎ 509-884-1730), PO Box 25, Stehekin, WA 98852, for information on how to rent the *Flick Creek House* or *Stehekin House*. *Rainbow's End Cabin* (☎ 509-682-3014), Box 8, Stehekin, WA 98852, near the Rainbow Creek Trailhead and Buckner Orchard sleeps three to four.

Cragg and Roberta Courtney (☎ 509-682-4677), PO Box 67, Stehekin, WA 98852, rent out the *Stehekin Log Cabin*, a comfortable log housekeeping cabin that sleeps up to 10 people. The *Stehekin Lindal Cedar Home* accommodates six people, and is available for monthly lease at around $1000 a month. Write to Walter Winkel, PO Box 14, Stehekin, WA 98852.

Places to Eat
The *North Cascades Stehekin Lodge Restaurant*, opposite the public docks, serves breakfast, lunch, and dinner – grilled halibut and blackened chicken are around $12. At the *Stehekin Valley Ranch* reservations are required, and there's a set dinner menu each day ($12 to $15). If you're cooking your own meals, there's a very limited stock of groceries at the landing, so you'd be wise to stock up in Chelan. The *Silver Bay Inn* serves breakfast, and the *Stehekin Pastry Company*, 2 miles upvalley from the landing, serves good pastries, espresso and ice cream.

Entertainment
The NPS has evening presentations on topics of natural and human history on weekends in July and August at the Golden West Visitor Center. Local residents sometimes supplement the programs with presentations on local cultural history. Ask at the visitors' center for a schedule.

Getting There & Away
Air Chelan Airways (☎ 509-682-5555) provides service to Stehekin from Chelan by seaplane. A roundtrip flight costs $120.

Ferry The most common way of getting to Stehekin is on either the *Lady of the Lake II* or *Lady Express* from Chelan. At least one boat makes the 55-mile trip daily, year-round. Fares and timetables vary seasonally, and a roundtrip ticket can cost as much as $41 in the high season. See Getting There & Around at the beginning of this chapter for specifics.

On Foot The Pacific Crest Trail passes by Stehekin, making it possible to hike 12 miles from Rainy Pass on Hwy 20 to the Bridge Creek Campground on the Stehekin Valley Rd, where you could then (depending upon the time of the year) be picked up by the NPS shuttle van (see below). Or you could just hike the 15 miles down the road into town (there are other campgrounds along the way). Alternatively, you could hike the 6½-mile Cascade Pass Trail from the northwest to the Cottonwood Campground at the end of the road, which is the most popular overland route to Stehekin (see Cascade Pass Trail under North Cascades National Park, above).

Getting Around

Although there are roads and cars in Stehekin, there are no roads *to* Stehekin. Courtesy transportation to and from the boat landing is included in most lodging prices.

Shuttle Bus The NPS operates a shuttle van up and down Stehekin Valley Rd twice daily, from the boat landing to Cottonwood Campground (weather permitting). It costs $5 each way, and passengers get a narrated tour. Day-trippers can make a reservation in person at the Golden West Visitor Center (☎ 360-856-5703, ext 14). Backpackers and campers should make their reservations at the same time they pick up their backcountry permits from the ranger stations in

Stehekin, Chelan, Marblemount, the North Cascades visitors' center (in Newhalem) or the Sedro Woolley Information Station.

During the summer the Stehekin Adventure Company takes over the service and runs four buses daily from the landing as far as High Bridge for $4 each way. The bus accommodates both bikes and backpacks. The bus also runs a 'bakery special,' charging $1 each way for those going only as far as the Stehekin Pastry Company.

Bicycle Bicycles are the easiest way to get around. Some lodges rent bicycles, while others simply let their guests borrow them. Rentals are available from Discovery Bikes (☎ 509-884-4844), at the Courtney Log Office. The Lake Chelan Boat Company charges $13 roundtrip for bike transport, if you'd prefer to bring your own.

WASHINGTON

Central Washington

If there are any defining images of central Washington, they may well be an apple tree and an irrigation ditch. There wouldn't be much out here it if weren't for the dams on the Columbia and Yakima Rivers. The resulting irrigation projects have turned this once-barren desert into one of the nation's greatest agricultural areas. There is still plenty of outback country here too, where farmers get by with dry-land wheat farms and a next-year mentality.

Central Washington's geography is dominated by the Columbia River and its dams. During the Ice Age, glaciers crept down from the north and overtook the Columbia River's channel, forcing the river water to cut a new southerly path. When the glaciers receded, the river went back to its original streambed, leaving a large area of central Washington with a big, dry river channel, known today as the Grand Coulee. This chapter covers the region east of the Cascade Mountains that stretches from the Grand Coulee in the northeast to the Yakama Indian Reservation in the southwest.

The long rain shadow cast by the Cascades over the entire area makes for a dry climate and warm summer temperatures. This lack of Pacific-slope gloom has changed a number of communities from agricultural trading centers or mining ghost towns into retirement and recreational communities. The city of Yakima has grown in stature and sophistication as retirees have settled here, and the local wine-making industry now attracts national attention. The Yakima Valley is home to the Yakama Indian Reservation and more apple orchards than you ever imagined possible.

Despite – or perhaps because of – the general aridity of the region, lakes are some of the prime destinations for travelers. The Bavarian village of Leavenworth (the concept may be a little hokey, but the setting is lovely) makes its mark as a faux-Alpine burg; it's a hub for lots of cross-country skiing, summer hiking and rock climbing, and water sports on nearby Lake Wenatchee. The Potholes is a curious area south of Moses Lake created when irrigation dams flooded desert sand dunes, which remain as islands above the water. Birds flock here, as do canoeists and anglers.

Two highways cross the Cascades from the west side into central Washington. US 2 heads east from Everett and crosses Stevens Pass to Leavenworth, then heads on to Spokane. From Seattle, I-90 cuts across Snoqualmie Pass and leads to Ellensburg, where I-82 splits off and heads south to Yakima.

From Ellensburg, I-90 continues west to Moses Lake and Spokane.

Wenatchee River Valley

As the Wenatchee River makes its way east from Lake Wenatchee to the Columbia River, there are remarkable changes in the valley's geography and culture. The area around Lake Wenatchee and Leavenworth is absolutely alpine, craggy and wild. The odd, faux-Bavarian town of Leavenworth itself was remodeled to fit into its landscape and lure visitors who wouldn't come for the great mountain and river recreation alone.

Halfway between Leavenworth and Wenatchee is Cashmere, a quiet riverside town, known mostly for its candy factory – Aplets & Cotlets – which produces sugary confections with some fame in the Northwest (every office must get a box of them at Christmas); they're sort of like ultra-sticky gum drops (but more expensive) made from boiled-down fruit, with walnuts

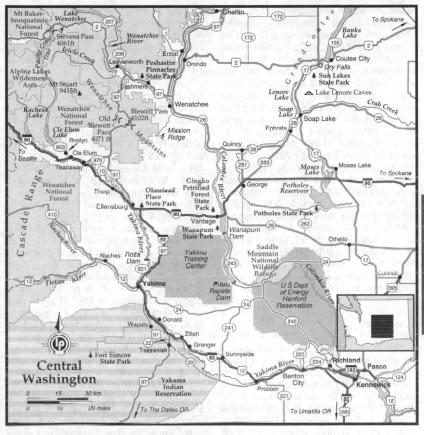

mixed in. The factory tour is the town's biggest attraction.

By the time the Wenatchee River pours into the Columbia River at Wenatchee, the scenery is dominated by apple trees. Wenatchee is the area's urban hub, with an easygoing sort of bustle and lodging that's slightly less expensive than up the road in touristy Leavenworth.

Getting There & Away

The Wenatchee Pangborn Memorial Airport is in East Wenatchee, 21 miles east of Leavenworth. Horizon Air and United Express have flights to Seattle and other northwestern cities. Local Link buses generously serve Wenatchee Valley's transit needs with free bus service between Wenatchee, Leavenworth, Chelan and local ski areas.

To check road conditions during the winter call ☎ 888-766-4636.

LEAVENWORTH
Population 1801

There are two ways of thinking about Leavenworth. Some people see it as the town that went Bavarian back in the '60s – the place where downtown shopkeepers pull on lederhosen and dirndl skirts every morning. Others visualize white-water rafting, rock climbing, and hiking trails. No matter what your point of view, there's so much going on here that just about everybody will find *something* of interest. Leavenworth's spectacular mountain setting – perched 1164 feet above sea level on the east slope of the Cascades, with the Wenatchee River rushing through town – is bound to appeal.

In the fall, salmon travel to their spawning grounds up the Wenatchee River. The Wenatchee is the only river in the state with three fairly strong wild salmon stocks: approximately 5000 spring Chinook, 9000 summer Chinook, and 40,000 sockeye salmon spawn up the Wenatchee every year.

Wildfires that ripped through several nearby canyons came close to Leavenworth's downtown during the summer of 1994. Trails in both Icicle and Tumwater Canyons have since reopened, but the barren stands of charred forest still remain.

Orientation

Icicle Rd, on the west side of town, traces Icicle Creek south to lots of recreational possibilities bordering the Alpine Lakes Wilderness Area. Another good road to cruise in search of random trailheads, de facto cross-country ski areas or a pretty drive, is the Chumstick Hwy (also called Chumstick Rd, or sometimes Hwy 209, as it used to be known), which heads north along Chumstick Creek (eventually it reaches Lake Wenatchee) at the east end of town. Blewett Pass is yet another recreation gateway, with plenty of trails and campgrounds to discover off of US 97, south of the junction with US 2.

Information

Drop by the Leavenworth Chamber of Commerce (☎ 509-548-5807), 894 US 2, in the Clocktower Building, or write them at PO Box 327, Leavenworth, WA 98826. The Leavenworth Ranger Station (☎ 509-782-1413), 600 Sherbourne, off US 2 at the east end of town, has a wealth of information on recreational opportunities in the Wenatchee National Forest, and has all types of use permits. There is another ranger station located at Lake Wenatchee (☎ 509-763-3103).

The post office (☎ 509-548-7212), 960 US 2, is next door to the Safeway. Two bookstores operate in Leavenworth's Bavarian downtown: A Book for All Seasons (☎ 509-548-1451), 639 Front St, and A Village Books & Music (☎ 509-548-5911), at 215 9th St.

Cascade Medical Center (☎ 509-548-5815), 817 Commercial St, is downtown near Waterfront Park.

Bavarian Village

Discover the heart of Leavenworth by cutting south from US 2 onto Front St, which leads into the Bavarian Village. A wander through this ersatz Bavarian village, with its steeply pitched roofs, painted flower boxes and endless gift shops can be either enjoyable, amusing or both. (Cynics may say otherwise, but we'll let a generous spirit prevail.) The **Gingerbread Factory** (see Places to Eat) is worth a stop for a snack and an earful of local gossip.

If you'd rather stroll than shop, pocket an extra gingerbread muffin and cut down 9th St to **Waterfront Park**. Paths trace the riverfront and a footbridge crosses over to Blackbird Island at the park's west end, where Icicle Creek meets the Wenatchee River. On a clear day, there are great views of Sleeping Lady Mountain, up Icicle Canyon southwest of town. To finish off a walking tour, return to town via 8th St for more food and gifts.

Leavenworth National Fish Hatchery

When the Grand Coulee and Chief Joseph Dams blocked salmon from migrating to their upstream spawning grounds, the government tried to ameliorate the loss of these populations by building hatcheries downstream from the dams. At the Leavenworth Hatchery (☎ 509-548-7641), off Icicle Rd at 12790 Fish Hatchery Rd,

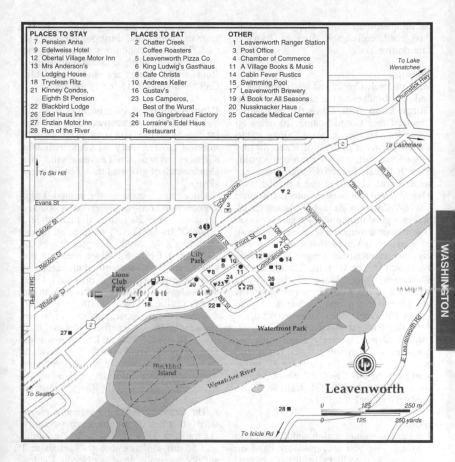

PLACES TO STAY
7   Pension Anna
9   Edelweiss Hotel
12 Obertal Village Motor Inn
13 Mrs Anderson's
    Lodging House
18 Tryolean Ritz
21 Kinney Condos,
    Eighth St Pension
22 Blackbird Lodge
26 Edel Haus Inn
27 Enzian Motor Inn
28 Run of the River

PLACES TO EAT
2   Chatter Creek
    Coffee Roasters
5   Leavenworth Pizza Co
6   King Ludwig's Gasthaus
8   Cafe Christa
10 Andreas Keller
16 Gustav's
23 Los Camperos,
    Best of the Wurst
24 The Gingerbread Factory
26 Lorraine's Edel Haus
    Restaurant

OTHER
1   Leavenworth Ranger Station
3   Post Office
4   Chamber of Commerce
11 A Village Books & Music
14 Cabin Fever Rustics
15 Swimming Pool
17 Leavenworth Brewery
19 A Book for All Seasons
20 Nussknacker Haus
25 Cascade Medical Center

about 2.5 million spring Chinook salmon are reared each year. The hatchery also raises some steelhead trout, a related anadromous fish. Both species of fish are released to migrate to the ocean in mid-April, when the rivers are running full force. The Chinook begin returning to spawn at the hatchery around August 10, and continue into the first week of September. (See Special Events below for information on the salmon festival.) The hatchery is open for a self-guided tour 7:30 am to 4 pm daily.

From the hatchery, hike the mile-long **Icicle Creek Interpretive Trail** and learn about the local ecology and history.

Tumwater Dam

Railroad buffs should stop about 4 miles northwest of town, on US 2, and examine the Tumwater Dam, built in 1907 to provide electricity to train engines passing through the long tunnels at Stevens Pass. The dam's power plant is in a separate location 2 miles downstream. Ask at the Leavenworth Ranger Station for a brochure detailing railroad history along the Stevens Pass road, called the 'Bygone Byways Interpretive Trail.'

Hiking

Walk up Icicle Creek, past waterfalls, pools and little beaches on the easy 3-mile **Icicle Gorge Loop Trail**. Catch the trail at the Chatter Creek Guard Station, 16 miles up Icicle Rd. Another easy trail along **Icicle Creek** begins at the end of Icicle Rd and follows the valley bottom through an old-growth forest. French Creek flows into Icicle Creek about 1½ miles up the trail. The trail continues deep into the Alpine Lakes Wilderness Area, but French Creek makes a good turnaround for an easy hike. If you want a longer hike, there are plenty of trails in the area that can be strung together to construct longer, more satisfying day hikes into the Alpine Lakes Wilderness Area. Many of these trails require a permit from the ranger station if you plan to stay overnight. See the Alpine Lakes Wilderness Area below for details.

In the Blewett Pass area off US 97, **Ingalls Creek**, a pretty creek with big boulders and swimming holes, has a trail running along it for miles and miles starting at Ingalls Creek Rd, about 7 miles south of US 2. Several side trails feed into the Ingalls Creek Trail.

Skiing

Rent cross-country and downhill skis, and anything else you may possibly need on your way to the slopes from the Leavenworth Outfitters Outdoor Center (☎ 509-763-3733, 800-347-7934), 21312 Hwy 207; or from Leavenworth Ski & Sports Center (☎ 509-548-7864), at the Icicle Junction Theme Park near Icicle Rd on US 2, which also offers instruction and guided tours.

Downhill The biggest ski area close to Leavenworth is **Stevens Pass** (☎ 360-973-2441), 37 miles west of town on US 2. With 36 runs, 11 lifts and a vertical drop of 1774 feet, this is the state's second-largest downhill venue. Lift tickets run $34 per weekend day for adults, with lower prices later in the day and during midweek ($18 to $23). When conditions permit, several lifts are open for night skiing until 10 pm. Rentals and classes are readily available. Call ☎ 360-663-7711 for a snow report.

Cross-Country A mile north of town up Ski Hill Drive, **Leavenworth's Ski Hill** (☎ 509-548-5115) is a small place with 25 miles of cross-country ski trails, including a link to downtown Leavenworth. One short stretch of groomed trail is lit for night skiing.

Once there's snow on the ground, **Lake Wenatchee** becomes a great cross-country ski area, with 20 miles of marked and groomed trails. There's another 36 miles, including a See & Ski interpretive area, in the Lower Chiwawa River area off the Chumstick Hwy, just north of the hamlet of Plain (between Leavenworth and Lake Wenatchee). Get maps and details from the ranger station in Leavenworth.

Cross-country skiers can expect to see snowmobilers at another popular trail area – **Blewett Pass**, on US 97. Roadside signs indicate Sno-Parks (buy a Sno-Park pass at any local grocery or sporting goods store) and trails; information is available from the Leavenworth Ranger District office.

The **Stevens Pass** ski area also maintains 16 miles of groomed cross-country ski trails. A daily pass costs $6 for adults and $5 for children/seniors. Rentals and snacks are available at the Nordic Center, which is 5 miles east of the downhill ski area and open 9 am to 4 pm, Friday to Sunday and holidays.

Rafting

Leavenworth's close proximity to the Wenatchee River makes it a popular destination for adventure-deprived urbanites. The uppermost stretch of the river, from Lake Wenatchee to Tumwater Campground, is an easy 19-mile, day-long float in a kayak or raft. The water is highest in May and June, when snowmelt contributes generously, but there is more wildlife (including salmon) in and around the river in September and October. All but expert kayakers should be sure to pull out at Tumwater Campground, as the next stretch of the Wenatchee to Leavenworth roils with rapids, big drops and sucking holes.

The following outfitters offer day trips on the river's third and most popular stretch – the 18½ miles from Leavenworth to Monitor. This section of the Wenatchee is typically run April to July, and its waves and holes earn it a Class III rating. Prices range from $45 to $75.

Leavenworth Outfitters – has floating, rafting, fishing and canoe trips and rentals (including inner tubes); 21312 Hwy 207, Leavenworth, WA 98826 (☎ 509-763-3733, 800-347-7934)

Alpine Adventures – has guided rafting trips; PO Box 253, Leavenworth, WA 98826 (☎ 509-548-4159, 800-926-7238)

Osprey Rafting Co – has guided rafting trips; PO Box 668, Leavenworth, WA 98826 (☎ 509-548-6400, 800-743-6269)

All Rivers Adventures – has white-water trips in rafts or inflatable kayaks; PO Box 12, Cashmere, WA 98815 (☎ 509-548-6400, 800-743-6269)

Climbing

In Tumwater Canyon **Castle Rock** is a popular rock-climbing area, partly because of its easy access – it's only about 3 miles northwest of town off US 2.

East of town at the **Peshastin Pinnacles State Park** (☎ 509-664-6373), a nice day will find rock climbers creeping up a cluster of 200-foot sandstone spires. Hikers can get to the top via steep, but quite manageable trails. Either way, you will be rewarded with great views of the Wenatchee River valley. The pinnacles are north of US 2 at the end of North Dryden Rd, just 2 miles west of Cashmere.

Serious climbers will no doubt focus on the Alpine Lakes Wilderness Area (see Alpine Lakes Wilderness Area later in this section), where challenging rock climbing in the Enchantment Lakes area requires a USFS permit. You can obtain a permit at the Leavenworth Ranger Station. To reach climbs on the **Snow Creek Wall**, including

Orbit (rated 5.8) and Outer Space (rated 5.9), follow the Snow Creek Trail a little more than a mile through a dismal burn into the Enchantment Lakes area. Rather than climbing all the way to the lakes, you should turn off onto the climbers' path where the trail and Snow Creek approach the steep wall.

Biking

Road bikers can decide if they're up to the 50-mile Leavenworth-Lake Wenatchee Loop. The hilly ride goes up Chumstick Hwy to the lake, then returns to town via Hwy 207 and US 2. It's not for the easily fatigued. When there's no snow on Ski Hill, this area just northwest of town becomes 'mountain bike hill.' Two loop trails, used for cross-country skiing in the winter, are open to bikers and hikers in the summer.

Several roads in the Icicle Creek area, off Icicle Rd, have become popular mountain-biking destinations. The USFS ranger station has information on suggested loops and routes in this area, as well as trips through the Chumstick, Blewett Pass and Mission Creek/Devil's Gulch areas. Leavenworth Outfitters Outdoor Center (☎ 509-763-3733, 800-347-7934), 21312 Hwy 207 near Lake Wenatchee, rents mountain bicycles and has a shuttle service.

Fishing

Rainbow and cutthroat trout are found in many lakes and streams (try some of the streams that feed the Chiwawa River), and the Wenatchee River is a good place to fish for winter steelhead. North of Leavenworth, both Lake Wenatchee and Fish Lake, a smaller lake just northeast of Lake Wenatchee, are popular lake fishing spots. Contact Leavenworth Outfitters for a guide (see Rafting, above).

Sleigh & Hay Rides

Capitalizing on the Bavarian theme, Red-Tail Canyon Farm (☎ 509-548-4512, 800-678-4512), 11780 Freund Canyon Rd, about 2½ miles up the Chumstick Hwy, gives rides in old-fashioned sleighs drawn by Belgian draft horses during the winter months, and hay rides at all other times of the year; adults/children $12/6.

Other Activities

The Eagle Creek Ranch (☎ 509-548-7798), PO Box 719, Leavenworth, WA 98826, has **horseback riding** with a variety of pack, hike/pack or drop-camp combination trips. Trail rides range from 1½ hours to six hours and cost $20 to $75. Icicle Outfitters & Guides Inc (☎ 800-497-3912), PO Box 322, Leavenworth, WA 98826, offers more extensive four- to seven-day pack trips.

For **dog-sledding** tours, contact Enchanted Mountain Tours (☎ 360-856-9168, 800-521-1694), 18555 Hazel Lane. Count on spending $135 for a half-day trip.

Good views of the mountains and the Wenatchee River are reason enough to **golf** at the 18-hole Leavenworth Golf Course (☎ 509-548-7267), 9101 Icicle Rd. The public pool (☎ 509-548-4142), 500 US 2, by the Lions Club Park, is open for **swimming** during the summer.

Special Events

Festivals are a part of life in any theme town, and Leavenworth doesn't skimp on them. Whenever there's a festival, lodgings fill up, so don't count on rolling into town without a reservation during the Mai Fest or Christmas tree-lighting weekends.

Spring comes late to Leavenworth, but by mid-May it's time to dance around a May pole, listen to 'oompah' music and flirt with strolling accordion players. During the Mai Fest there's a parade and a Saturday night street dance, both of which jam the streets of the Bavarian Village. Though some locals call the Mai Fest 'snooty,' plenty of people make annual oompah pilgrimages.

The International Folk Dance Festival is just a one-day festival in mid-June, but the costumes are great and the dances exciting. Summer at Leavenworth climaxes in mid-August with the Leavenworth International Accordion Celebration. Look for accordion competitions, workshops and dances. Applications are available through the chamber of commerce, and if you start practicing now, who knows what fame awaits.

The Leavenworth Fish Hatchery is the site of the Wenatchee River Salmon Festival in mid-September, which celebrates the return of thousands of salmon to the Wenatchee River. Field trips, including wetlands ecology tours and fishing clinics are part of the festival, and there's a crafts fair scheduled to coincide with the salmon events.

Leavenworth looks great at Christmas time, and makes the most of the season by holding Christmas tree-lighting festivals during the first two weekends of December. There's usually a good bit of snow on the ground, and plenty of opportunity for organized snowman-building contests, sledding in the park and hay rides.

Places to Stay

If Leavenworth is all booked up or seems too expensive, try Wenatchee, where there are plenty of motel rooms for around $50. There's free public transportation linking Wenatchee with Leavenworth (see Getting There & Away, below).

The tourist season peaks in the summer and picks up again around Christmas. At most places, off-season rates drop at least a little bit.

Camping There are scads of campgrounds around Leavenworth, making it easy to avoid expensive in-town accommodations. Of course, winter is hard and long hereabouts, so don't plan on too much early or late-season camping; campgrounds are generally open from May to late October. Icicle Rd and Blewett Pass (on US 97 south of US 2) are the main camping corridors. There's more camping north at Lake Wenatchee.

Tumwater Campground, 10 miles west of Leavenworth on US 2, is a convenient spot between Leavenworth and Lake Wenatchee. It's about what you'd expect from a busy roadside spot: flush toilets, running water, a $10 fee and crowds. Call ☎ 800-280-2267 to make a reservation.

Up Icicle Road there are seven USFS campgrounds, all with hand-pumped well water, pit toilets and fees of $7 to $8. *Eightmile Campground* is the closest to Leavenworth with 45 sites, and a few wheelchair-accessible ones. *Johnny Creek Campground*, further up, is in a beautiful forested spot with sites right on Icicle Creek. *Black Pine Creek Campground*, 15 miles from US 2 at the end of Icicle Rd, has facilities for horsepackers and sites for only $6.

A number of RV campgrounds have full hookups from $22 to $25. *Pine Village KOA Kampground* (☎ 509-548-7709), is a mile east of Leavenworth, just north of US 2 at 11401 River Bend Drive. Up Icicle Rd, the first campground you come to is a private one, *Icicle River RV Park* (☎ 509-548-5420), 7305 Icicle Rd. Near Blewett Pass, *Blu Shastin RV Park* (☎ 509-548-4184), 3300 US 97, is a tranquil creekside spot 7 miles south of US 2. It's open year-round and has a swimming pool.

B&Bs *Mrs Anderson's Lodging House* (☎ 509-548-6173, 800-253-8990), at 917 Commercial St, is right downtown. At $47 for a room with a shared bathroom, and $58 for a private bathroom, these are some of the least expensive rooms you'll find. Fortunately, the place has some charm and has been providing room and board for many years.

Another downtown inn, the *Edel Haus Inn* (☎ 509-548-4412, 800-487-3335), 320 9th St, is an attractive Bavarian-style place just across from Waterfront Park. Breakfast is not included in the $60 to $105 rate, but you do get a 50% discount on lunch or dinner at the inn's restaurant (which is, incidentally, one of the best in town).

Run of the River (☎ 509-548-7171, 800-288-6491), 9308 E Leavenworth Rd, has good views of Icicle Canyon. This log B&B inn forgoes Bavarian style in favor of traditional Northwest hewn-log decor. Rooms run $95 to $150; all have private bathrooms and are equipped with binoculars for bird and wildlife viewing. The inn also has a fleet of mountain bikes for

guests' use. *All Seasons River Inn* (☎ 509-548-1425, 800-254-0555), 8751 Icicle Rd, has rooms with private bathrooms and riverfront decks from $95 to $135. You can go hiking and cycling close by, and the inn can provide bikes.

Hotels Budget lodgings are hard to come by in Leavenworth. Perhaps the best bet is the *Edelweiss Hotel* (☎ 509-548-7015), 843 Front St, which has modest rooms with shared bathroom for as little as $18. If a private bathroom is important to you, cough up $43.

Three miles east of Leavenworth on the way to Wenatchee, the *River's Edge Motel* (☎ 509-548-7612, 800-451-5285), 8401 US 2, has a nice setting on the Wenatchee River. Rooms all have balconies overlooking the river, and several are equipped with kitchens. There's also a pool and hot tub. Standard rooms start at $57.

If you want to get into the thick of things, the *Tyrolean Ritz* (☎ 509-548-5455, 800-854-6365), 633 Front St, is a small hotel right in the heart of downtown Leavenworth with rooms starting at $65. The *Obertal Village Motor Inn* (☎ 509-548-5204, 800-537-9382), 922 Commercial St, is a European-style motel with slightly frou-frou decor. Rates for single/double rooms start at $63/67.

A particularly charming small inn, the *Pension Anna* (☎ 509-548-6273, 800-509-2662), 926 Commercial St, is next door to the Obertal, with rooms starting at $80. The Austrian decor is well-executed, and the proprietors recently bought and renovated an old chapel, which is now a suite ($150 to $170). Another non-kitschy European-style inn is the *Blackbird Lodge* (☎ 509-548-5800, 800-446-0240), 309 8th St, overlooking Blackbird Island. Rooms start at $79, and suites are $98.

A couple of modern, conference-style motels along US 2 have rooms for $78/88. The *Enzian Motor Inn* (☎ 509-548-5269, 800-223-8511), 590 US 2, a large, meticulously detailed motel has an exercise room, indoor/outdoor pools and hot tubs and cross-country skis to lend to guests. Give

WASHINGTON

692 Central Washington – Wenatchee River Valley

this place a second look – it's much nicer than the standard chain motel. The *Best Western Icicle Inn* (☎ 509-548-7000, 800-528-1234), 505 US 2 (at Icicle Rd), may not be as charming as the Enzian, but it's a comfortable motel with a pool, hot tub and exercise facilities.

Lodges On the road to Blewett Pass the *Ingalls Creek Trading Post* (☎ 509-548-5142), 3057 US 97, has more basic rooms with shared bathroom for $40. It's right near the Ingalls Creek Trail.

Resorts Three miles east of Leavenworth the *Mountain Home Lodge* (☎ 509-548-7077, 800-414-2378) at 8201 Mountain Home Rd, in a meadow surrounded by high trees, is a small and very attractive country inn that's especially popular with cross-country skiers. During the winter, all meals are included in the $195 to $305 fee (two nights minimum) for suites, or up to eight guests can be taken by Sno-Cat to a secluded cabin and cook their own meals in a fully equipped chef's kitchen ($350 to $800). In the summer, rates are about $90 less but meals are extra. Trails are close at hand, and the lodge has an outdoor pool, hot tub and tennis courts.

Vacation-Home Rentals Three booking services offer a bevy of vacation-home and condominium referrals, among them Bed-finders (☎ 509-548-4410, 800-323-2920), Destination Leavenworth (☎ 509-548-5802, 800-962-7359) and Leavenworth Vacation Getaways (☎ 509-548-4171, 800-548-4808).

Several condos and apartments are available around Leavenworth, and they're particularly suited to larger groups. The *Eighth St Pension* (☎ 548-4662) at 219 8th St is a two-bedroom apartment that sleeps six. Next door, the *Kinney Condos* (☎ 509-548-5585, 800-621-9676), at 217 8th St, can also house groups.

Places to Eat
Leavenworth has plenty of places to eat, especially if you like sausage and Wiener schnitzel. Drive towards Wenatchee to find roadside stands brimming with fresh fruit, especially locally grown apples and pears.

Budget East of Leavenworth, where US 97 meets US 2, stop and eat at the *Big Y Cafe* (☎ 509-548-5012) – everybody else does. It's open 24 hours and is best for a basic breakfast. If you need a jolt to even make it to the Big Y, pull off at *Chatter*

Going Bavarian
Leavenworth grew up as a railroad town, and when the Great Northern re-routed its tracks in the 1920s, bypassing the town, Leavenworth foundered. It wasn't long before the other substantial local business, the sawmill, closed, leaving the town badly equipped to handle the Great Depression. Downtown was pretty much boarded up for a few decades.

A local tourism committee, seeking to rejuvenate their town, noted that the California town of Solvang had done well by emphasizing its Danish heritage. A fair number of Russian Germans had pioneered much of eastern Washington, and the mountain setting seemed alpine enough to support a little Bavaria.

Though it took considerable boosterism to get the community to go along with the scheme, economics won out, and in the 1960s Leavenworth's downtown began to lay on the frills. Today's Leavenworth is Washington's favorite place to go for a family outing – there's something here for everyone, and it's a reasonable day trip from Seattle. Who would've guessed that busloads of tourists would one day jam the streets of this unlikely milltown, just for a day of eating sausages and snapping photos of accordion players? ■

WASHINGTON

Creek Coffee Roasters (☎ 509-782-4969), 894 US 2 at the east end of the town, which also has a drive-up joint. They really do have the best java in little Bavaria.

The *Gingerbread Factory* (☎ 509-548-6592), on Commercial St, known to locals as the GBF, is a funny combination of a tourist spot and locals' hangout. Gingerbread and other sweet baked goods are about all the food that's offered, but evening poetry readings add extra flavor. For more nutritious baked goods, head to *Homefires Bakery* (☎ 509-548-7362), at 13013 Bayne Rd, right off Icicle Rd near the fish hatchery. Stop by 9 am to 5 pm, Thursday to Monday, for homemade bread, cinnamon rolls and cookies.

Leavenworth Pizza Company (☎ 509-548-7766) is housed in the Clocktower Building at 894 US 2. It's a reasonably good and inexpensive place for a post-hike pizza and beer. *Best of the Wurst* (☎ 509-548-7580), 220 8th St, serves grilled sausages and burgers out of a sidewalk food stall for under $5, and is one of the only snack shops with iced tea.

If even the smell of sauerkraut wafting down Front St is making your stomach churn, head for *Los Camparos* (☎ 509-548-3314), 200 8th St, Leavenworth's only Mexican restaurant. There's a pleasant rooftop garden at this upstairs alleyway restaurant, which serves a tasty cabbage salsa as its own little hint of Bavaria.

Middle to Top End *Lorraine's Edel Haus Restaurant* (☎ 509-548-4412), 320 9th St, has some of Leavenworth's best food, including good salmon dinners ($16), in a quietly elegant dining room on the downstairs floor of a B&B. Entrées run $9 to $19, lunches run about $8.

Up by Lake Wenatchee, the *Cougar Inn* (☎ 509-763-3354), 23379 Hwy 207, is known for its Friday-night seafood buffet and its Sunday brunch buffet.

Bavarian-Theme Restaurants There are plenty, but *Gustav's* (☎ 509-548-4509), 617 US 2 (right where Front St splits off) has a rooftop beer garden, with lots of northwest beers on tap to complement the sausages and burgers. *Andreas Keller* (☎ 509-548-6000), 829 Front St, has the full array of sausages, sauerkraut and German potato salad. It might only be outdone by its neighbor, *King Ludwig's Gasthaus* (☎ 509-548-6625), 921 Front St, where there's dancing to go along with the Bavarian menu. *Cafe Christa* (☎ 509-548-5074) is upstairs at 801 Front St.

Entertainment
The *Leavenworth Brewery* (☎ 509-548-4545) at 636 Front St, brews its own, including root beer. Beer names are half the fun here – order up a Dirty Face Stout, Whistling Pig Wheat, Barking Dog Bitter or a Blind Pig Dunkelweizen. Pub food and full dinners are served (dinners cost around $10, beer-braised German sausage is $9), and people do come here to eat as well as to drink. Live music is performed on the weekends and free brewery tours start at 2 pm daily.

No trip to Washington's little Bavaria is quite complete without attending Leavenworth Summer Theater's full-length production of *The Sound of Music*. Shows are held Thursdays and Saturdays in August at Hatchery Park, on East Leavenworth Rd; the box office (☎ 509-548-2000), 565 US 2, is at the Icicle Junction Family Fun Center.

Shopping
If a stroll around Leavenworth inspires you to buy a dirndl skirt, stop by the Nussknacker Haus (☎ 509-548-4708), 735 Front St. Though they sell clothing, their specialty is actually nutcracker dolls.

Less Bavarian, but still a good place to shop for household gifts, is Cabin Fever Rustics (☎ 509-548-4238) at 923 Commercial St.

Getting There & Away
Northwestern Trailways buses stop in Leavenworth on their way between Seattle and Wenatchee. Call ☎ 800-366-3830 (in Washington only) for schedule and fare information.

The Link (☎ 509-662-1155, 800-851 5465) bus No 22 passes up US 2 between Leavenworth and Wenatchee several times daily, except on Sunday. The No 27 bus travels between Leavenworth and Lake Wenatchee. Buses are free (yes, free) and some buses have bike racks in the summer and ski racks in the winter. Pick up a schedule from the visitors' center.

Getting Around
Leavenworth Outfitters (☎ 509-763-3733, 800-347-7934) offers livery service with any mountain bike, raft or canoe rental. Skiers should contact Vertical Adventures (☎ 509-548-9104) for shuttle service to Stevens Pass and cross-country ski areas.

ALPINE LAKES WILDERNESS AREA
The Alpine Lakes, 614 sq miles of pieced-together alpine wilderness, got its patchwork shape from a history of mining and railroad land grants. It is best known for its Enchantment Lakes area, an especially compelling region with glacier-carved cirques and reflective alpine pools accessible from Icicle Canyon. Though more than 100,000 people visit the Alpine Lakes Wilderness each year, its most magical destinations are much further than a casual day-hike. Steep climbs and scrabbly trails demand intermediate-level backpacking skills and top physical condition.

Hiking
You can reach one of the **Enchantment Lakes Trailheads** by heading out of Leavenworth on Icicle Rd (USFS Rd 7600) to Snow Creek, just a couple of miles past the fish hatchery. Hike in (it's uphill) past Nada and Snow Lakes (5½ and 6¾ miles, respectively), and continue to climb to the basins dotted with the high Enchantment Lakes (10 miles).

Another entrance to the Alpine Lakes Wilderness Area begins on a dirt road just north of Tumwater Campground on US 2. Turn west from the highway to the **Chiwaukum Creek Trailhead** and hike the road for 1½ miles until you hit the wilderness boundary. Once you're on the trail, a

pine and Douglas-fir forest shades the creek as far as a trail junction, 5½ miles in. The right-hand fork (trail No 1591) continues up Chiwaukum Creek through increasingly patchy forest, giving way to meadows and, ultimately, to Chiwaukum and other alpine lakes. The hike to the trail's fork is a reasonable day hike; allow at least two days for a roundtrip hike to the lakes.

Due to heavy use of this fragile area, the USFS requires $5 permits for overnight trips to the Enchantment Lakes between June 15 and October 15. You'll want to plan well in advance if you want one, as there's lots of competition. Advance reservations for permits can be obtained over the phone by calling ☎ 888-953-7677, though the first year telephone reservations became available the entire season sold out within two hours – in February! An extra reservation charge applies. Not all is lost if you're beaten out of the reservation pool, since 25% of the permits are reserved for same-day use, and many reserved permits are canceled. Get yours at the Leavenworth Ranger Station (☎ 509-782-1413), 600 Sherbourne at US 2 in Leavenworth, open 7:45 am to 4:30 pm, Monday to Saturday. Special-use permits are also required for the Snoqualmie Pass and West Foss areas of the wilderness.

LAKE WENATCHEE
Lake Wenatchee, 23 miles north of the city of Wenatchee, is actually much closer to Leavenworth. There are two good routes to the lake: either head north on Chumstick Hwy or take US 2 west of town, then turn north onto Hwy 207. Once you get there, be prepared for a full array of activities. During the summer, there's swimming, boating and fishing; you can also hike the 4½-mile trail up Dirtyface Peak, cycle around the lake, or sign on with one of the rafting companies on Hwy 207 for a float trip.

In the winter, the lakeside becomes the domain of cross-country skiers. The best part here is that you don't have to drive up in the snow – just catch a free Link bus

(☎ 509-662-1155, 800-851-5565) from Leavenworth and throw your skis on the rack.

The Lake Wenatchee Ranger Station (☎ 509-763-3103) is at 22976 Hwy 207 in Lake Wenatchee.

Places to Stay & Eat

The woodsy *Lake Wenatchee State Park* (☎ 509-763-3101) is a large campground right on the lake with showers, a restaurant, a swimming beach, horseback rides and it has some wheelchair-accessible sites. Campsites cost $11 (no hookups) and hardy campers can pitch a tent (or pull up an RV) year-round. It's convenient, convivial and a good place for families. If you want more serenity, head around to the lake's south shore to *Glacier View Campground*, a smaller, lakeside USFS campground with pit toilets, running water and $7 sites.

While it's not on the lakeshore, the *Nason Creek Campground* is less than a mile away on Hwy 207, between Lake Wenatchee and US 2. For the $10 fee, you get flush toilets, running water and easy access to the Nason Ridge Trail. There are a few other hiking trails nearby, including one up Chiwaukum Creek (see Alpine Lakes Wilderness Area above).

A handful of secluded resorts along Hwy 207 make great hideaways for ski vacations. *Pine River Ranch* (☎ 509-763-3959, 800-669-3877), at 19668 Hwy 207, is a lovely old farmhouse with four B&B rooms (private bathrooms) and a cottage outfitted with two suites, from $85 to $130. The *Cougar Inn Resort* (☎ 509-763-3354), 23379 Hwy 207, has cabins for $75 and lodge rooms with shared bathrooms starting at $45, and is locally known for its restaurant. Show up Friday night for the seafood buffet, or Sunday morning for a huge brunch.

The *Mountain Springs Lodge* (☎ 509-763-2713, 800-858-2276), 19115 Chiwawa Loop Rd, is not far from Lake Wenatchee. Its rooms and lodges (they don't call them cabins here) are more upscale than the Cougar Inn and cost $80. There's also a hot tub. All of these places have good access to hiking and cross-country ski trails.

HENRY M JACKSON WILDERNESS AREA

Up near the Cascades crest, the Henry M Jackson Wilderness Area lies north of US 2 and south of the Glacier Peak Wilderness Area. Here, up the headwaters of Little Wenatchee River, are lots of great hikes. From Leavenworth, trailheads are best reached via Lake Wenatchee; continue on Hwy 207 past the head of the lake to USFS Rd 6500. Follow this road up the Little Wenatchee, take the right fork at Riverside Campground and continue to Little Wenatchee Ford Campground at road's end, where there are four trails to choose from.

Three of the four trails here – **Cady Pass, Cady Ridge** and **Little Wenatchee River Trails** – eventually hook up with the **Pacific Crest Trail**, making good loops for a two- or three-day backpacking trip. Day-hikers should choose the **Little Wenatchee Trail**, which follows the river for about 5 miles before climbing to a wildflower meadow. After about a quarter of a mile down this trail, a fourth trail branches off and heads up to great views at the top of **Poe Mountain**. Keep an eye peeled along the roadside for soapstone deposits; if you want to pocket more than a rock or two, get a mineral permit from the Lake Wenatchee Ranger Station.

WENATCHEE
Population 23,310

All over the Northwest, folks who hear 'Wenatchee' will predictably free-associate the name with 'apples.' That's the way it's been since central Washington's semi-arid lands were 'reclaimed' for apple orchards between 1890 and 1900, and that's the way it's likely to stay. As if to prove it, the Washington Apple Commission Visitor Center is right there as you roll into town, ready to toast you with swigs of cider.

Although the Wenatchee River valley has a history of Native American settlement stretching back at least 11,000 years, the area's development as an agricultural

WASHINGTON

center began quite recently. A Father DeGrassi, who taught farming to the Wenatchee tribe, is credited as being the first person to irrigate the valley. More small-scale irrigation projects started before the beginning of the 20th century, when farmers began to divert river water through ditches to their fields. In 1903 the Highline Canal carried water from west of Cashmere all the way to East Wenatchee. Within a few years, young fruit trees were growing everywhere that ditch water could reach. Once the trees matured, Wenatchee became the certified center of the apple world.

Orientation

Wenatchee is in almost the exact center of Washington. The Wenatchee River comes in from the northwest, the Columbia River from the north, and the confluence of the two rivers is at the north end of town. To the east and west are hills topped with the remains of ancient volcanoes (Saddle Rock, Black Rock and Castle Rock). Hwy 97 and US 2 (called Wenatchee Ave in town) go up the east side of the Columbia, while Alt US 97 goes up the west side. Two bridges and a pedestrian bridge over the Columbia connect Wenatchee with East Wenatchee. The big river valleys lend an openness to the landscape in striking contrast to the tight Cascade Canyons of Leavenworth, 22 miles to the west.

Information

Stop by the Wenatchee Area Visitor & Convention Bureau (☎ 509-622-2116, 800-572-7753), 2 S Chelan Ave, or write to PO Box 850, Wenatchee, WA 98801. The Wenatchee National Forest supervisor's office (☎ 509-622-4335), is at 215 Melody Lane. The downtown post office is at 301 Yakima St.

The *Wenatchee World* is published daily except Sunday in (as it says on the masthead) 'the Apple Capital of the World and the Buckle of the Power Belt of the Great Northwest.' Several translators broadcast Northwest Public Radio at FM 90.1, 90.3,

90.7 and 91.3. Laundry gets done at Wash Works Laundromat (☎ 509-662-3582), 907 S Wenatchee Ave. For medical emergencies go to Central Washington Hospital (☎ 509-662-1511), 1300 Fuller St.

North Central Washington Museum

The North Central Washington Museum (☎ 509-664-3340), downtown at 127 S Mission St, distinguishes itself from other historical museums by its apple exhibits, model trains and good visiting exhibits (past summers have brought a wonderful show of Dale Chihuly's glass). It's open daily except major holidays, Monday to Friday from 10 am to 4 pm, and weekends from 1 to 4 pm. It's closed on weekends in January. Admission is $3/1 adults/children.

Washington Apple Commission Visitor Center

Go for a taste of apple culture and maybe a nibble of the valley's latest crop at the Washington Apple Commission Visitor Center (☎ 509-663-9600), 2900 Euclid Ave, near the Wenatchee Confluence State Park at the northern edge of town. It's obviously an industry effort, but if you're into technical tourism, this is the place to learn how apples are grown, picked and processed. Hours are 8 am to 5 pm weekdays, 9 am to 5 pm on Saturday, and 11 am to 5 pm on Sunday and holidays. It's open Monday through Friday only from January to April.

Ohme Gardens

These acres of terraced woodland gardens (☎ 509-662-5785) at 3327 Ohme Rd, are carved into a bluff about 3 miles north of town, high above the confluence of the Wenatchee and Columbia Rivers. You can get to the Ohme Gardens via Alt US 97.

This carpet of green amid all the brown landscape is, as clearly as the valley's apple trees are, a testament to irrigation. The gardens are open 9 am to 6 pm daily from April 15 to October 15, and 9 am to 7 pm in the summer. Admission costs adults/children $5/3, which seems a little steep, but is well worth it. It's easy to spend a couple of peaceful hours in this cool oasis, wandering through the gardens and peering down at the Columbia River.

Rocky Reach Dam
Six miles north of town on US 97, Rocky Reach Dam has fish-viewing windows, a playground and large picnic area and two museums – one historical, the other paying homage to electricity. The historical museum, which is under water in the belly of the dam, is a little creepy, though moderately interesting. Behind the dam, the Columbia widens into flat and glassy Lake Entiat. The thing the kids will remember most is chasing the resident rabbits across the lawn. Opening hours are 8 am to dusk daily from mid-February to December.

Skiing
Mission Ridge (☎ 509-663-7631), 13 miles southwest of Wenatchee on Squilchuck Rd, has a vertical drop of 2200 feet, and 33 runs with four lifts and two rope-tows. It's open from late November to late April; full-day adult lift tickets are $20 to $30. There are also some cross-country and telemark trails at Mission Ridge, including some that are lit for night skiing. A free SkiLINK bus (☎ 509-662-1155, 800-851-5465) runs between Wenatchee and the ski area. Call ☎ 800-374-1693 for the latest snow conditions.

Golf
Golfers should have no problem keeping busy in the Wenatchee area. Desert Canyon (☎ 509-784-1111) is a particularly challenging championship 18-hole course, 12 miles north of East Wenatchee in Orondo. For a more casual game of golf, head to the 18-hole Three Lakes Golf Course (☎ 509-663-5448), 2695 Golf Dr, south of Wenatchee near Malaga.

Other Activities
Riverfront Park stretches along the Columbia River on the edge of downtown Wenatchee. Seven miles of trails on the Wenatchee side of the river, between Riverfront Park and the Columbia and Wenatchee

River confluence, link with a 4-mile trail along the Columbia's east bank. It's rather industrial down by the park, so don't be surprised to hear machinery clanking as you **stroll, cycle** or **rollerblade** along the river. Any number of downtown streets lead to the park: head down 5th St to come out by the skating rink, or go down Orondo Ave to reach the boat launch. Once on the trail, head north to Wenatchee Confluence State Park, or south to reach a footbridge across to East Wenatchee.

For **river swimming**, follow the signs at the north end of town through a few tricky intersections to the Wenatchee Confluence State Park. Besides the swimming beach, there are athletic fields, tennis and basketball courts, a campground and a boat launch.

If you feel like **ice skating**, the Riverfront Park Ice Arena (☎ 509-664-3396), 2 5th St, is open for public skating October to May. Rent city or mountain bikes at Second Wind (☎ 509-884-0821), 85 NE 9th Ave in East Wenatchee. Arlberg Sports (☎ 509-663-7401), 25 N Wenatchee Ave, also rents bikes and in-line skates.

Special Events
Wenatchee's big hoopla is the Washington State Apple Blossom Festival (☎ 509-662-3616), which takes place in late April to early May. Parades, a crafts show, a carnival, concerts, dances, a swim meet, a 10 K run and the crowning of the Apple Queen make the first week of May a busy time in Wenatchee. The other big event is the Ridge to River Relay (☎ 509-662-8799), a 35-mile foot, ski, bike, canoe and kayak race from Mission Ridge to Wenatchee. It is held just before the Apple Blossom Festival, around the third weekend in April.

Places to Stay
Camping A number of campgrounds on the Columbia River are well-developed to meet the needs (and lifestyles) of boaters, and feature flush toilets, showers, RV hookups and a boat launch. There's not much in the way of cover, and sites can be

windy. *Wenatchee Confluence State Park* (☎ 509-664-6373), on Olds Station Rd, marks the junction of the Wenatchee and Columbia Rivers. Follow signs from US 2 or US 97 at the north end of town to reach the park in a well-marked but roundabout way. On the east bank, 7 miles north of Wenatchee on US 2 is *Lincoln Rock State Park* (☎ 509-884-8702), on Lake Entiat, part of the Columbia River. Supposedly, a rock across the river from the park looks like Abraham Lincoln. Sites cost $11 to $16 and can be reserved by calling ☎ 800-452-5687. Some sites are wheelchair-accessible.

In Entiat, 16 miles north of Wenatchee on US 97 Alt, there's camping at *Entiat City Park* (☎ 509-784-1500), which has a popular swimming beach and a laundromat. Sites cost $10 to $12.

Towards Cashmere, *Wenatchee River County Park* (☎ 509-662-2525) is about 5 miles northwest of town on US 2 by the Wenatchee River. Manicured grassy lawns surround the campsites, which go for $12 to $16.

B&Bs *Rose Manor B&B* (☎ 509-662-1093), 156 S Emerson, is a huge old home close to downtown. Three of the five rooms have private bathrooms. A basic room with a shared bathroom is $50; the fourth-floor suite with all the extras is $95.

Children are welcome at the antique-filled *Cherub Inn B&B* (☎ 509-662-6011), 410 N Miller, and they'll be glad to hear that there's a pool. The proprietors offer airport pick-up. Rooms start at $65.

Hotels If ever there was a motel strip, N Wenatchee Ave is it. Some of the city's best motels are here, cheek-by-jowl with no-frills budget motels, which – incidentally – are only inexpensive in the off-season. During the summer and winter seasons don't be surprised to pay $50 for basic digs. Wenatchee does bake in the summer, so even the cheapest places have swimming pools.

Wenatchee's cheapest place to stay is the *Welcome Inn* (☎ 509-663-7121), 232 N Wenatchee Ave, a fairly basic, though well-situated motel with rates starting at $40. Single/double rooms are $47/53 at the well-established *Chieftain Motel & Restaurant* (☎ 509-663-8141, 800-572-4466), 1005 N Wenatchee Ave, a faded 70s luxury hotel. It's still the first place locals come when they need to house visitors, but it's not the shag carpeting that draws them in – it's the friendly staff, who just might cut you a cheaper rate.

You'll find rooms for $45 to $55 at the *Travelodge* (☎ 509-662-8165, 800-235-8165), 1004 N Wenatchee Ave, which has a hot tub, sauna, and ski-wax room; the *Avenue Motel* (☎ 509-663-7161, 800-733-8981), 720 N Wenatchee Ave, which has a hot tub and kitchenettes; and the *Vagabond Inn* (☎ 509-663-8133, 800-424-4777), 700 N Wenatchee Ave.

In the $60 range there's the *Holiday Lodge* (☎ 509-663-8167, 800-722-0852), 610 N Wenatchee Ave, with a hot tub, sauna, exercise room and laundry facilities. One block off busy Wenatchee Ave is the *Orchard Inn* (☎ 509-662-3443, 800-368-4571), 1401 N Miller, a large motel with an indoor pool and hot tub.

At the top end, the *WestCoast Wenatchee Center Hotel* (☎ 509-662-1234, 800-426-0670), 201 N Wenatchee Ave, has a fitness center and indoor/outdoor pool. It seems like an expense-account place, and indeed is the home of the Wenatchee Convention Center. There's more of the same at the *DoubleTree Hotel* (☎ 509-663-0711, 800-547-8010), 1225 N Wenatchee Ave. Rooms start at $80 at both hotels.

The *Rivers Inn* (☎ 509-884-1474, 800-922-3199), 580 Valley Mall Parkway in East Wenatchee, across from the region's largest mall, is an indication that for many people who live in rural central Washington, Wenatchee is a place to come shopping. The continental breakfast is free, and rooms start at $47/52.

Places to Eat
Budget-conscious street-food connoisseurs will look for Mexican food trucks to appear along Wenatchee Ave at lunchtime. Count

on being able to get a couple of beef tacos with fresh toppings for $2. *Dusty's In-N-Out* (☎ 509-662-7805), 1427 N Wenatchee Ave, is a classic drive-through or sit-down joint with Dusty burgers and Dusty dogs. Few things cost more than $3.

If you're in the mood for a decent milk-shake, stop by *Bellmore's Owl Drug Co* (☎ 509-662-7133), 39 S Wenatchee Ave, right downtown. *Bob's Classic Brass & Brew* (☎ 509-663-3954), 110 2nd St, has the best burgers in town and huge helpings of fries. Burgers start around $5. For a more nutritious lunch there's *Lemolo's Cafe & Deli* (☎ 509-664-6576), 114 N Wenatchee Ave, which serves salads and sandwiches.

The Vietnamese *Cuc Tran Cafe* (☎ 509-663-6281), 7 N Wenatchee Ave, is convenient, offers tasty food and is easy on the pocketbook. For more Southeast Asian cuisine head up to Mission St, where the *Thai Restaurant* (☎ 509-662-8077), 1211 N Mission St, is very popular with the locals.

The Windmill (☎ 509-663-3478), at 1501 N Wenatchee Ave, is an excellent, well-established steak house, while *Visconti's* (☎ 509-662-5013), 1737 N Wenatchee Ave, serves spaghetti dinners for $10, and is the best traditional Italian restaurant in town.

Wenatchee Roaster & Ale House (☎ 509-662-1234), 201 N Wenatchee Ave, one of Wenatchee's fancier restaurants, peers down condescendingly at the competition from the top of the convention center. However, Wenatchee's true top-end restaurant is *Steven's at Mission Square* (☎ 509-663-6573), 218 N Mission St. It is a good idea to book a couple of days in advance here. Expect good, fresh pasta and seafood dinners. Wenatchee's other really nice spot, the *Horan House* (☎ 509-663-0018), is tucked down by the river at 2 Horan Rd.

In East Wenatchee, look for *Garlini's Italian Restaurant* (☎ 509-884-1707), 810 Valley Mall Parkway.

Entertainment
During summer, look for lunchtime entertainment on Wednesdays at noon at the downtown convention center fountain (☎ 509-662-0059), 121 N Wenatchee Ave. *McGlinn's Public House* (☎ 509-663-9073), 111 Orondo Ave, serves microbrews and espresso – the two staples of a Northwest diet – and is a big after-work place.

Getting There & Away
Air Horizon Air and United Express serve the Pangborn Memorial Airport (☎ 509-884-2494) in East Wenatchee, with flights operating to and from Seattle. The cheapest one-way fare is $52.

Bus Northwestern Trailways (☎ 800-366-3830 in Washington) runs two daily buses west to Leavenworth and Seattle, and east to Moses Lake and Spokane. One-way fare to Seattle is $9. The bus station (☎ 509-662-2183), 300 S Columbia Ave, is at a new combined train-and-bus station off Wenatchee Ave at Kittitas St. You can also get to the nearby towns of Leavenworth and Chelan on free Link buses (see Getting Around, below).

Train Amtrak's *Empire Builder* stops daily in Wenatchee on its way between Seattle and Chicago, westbound at 4:25 am, and eastbound at 8:51 pm. The train station is at the foot of Kittitas St.

Car At the airport, rentals are available from Budget (☎ 509-663-2626) and Hertz (☎ 509-884-6900). U Save Auto Rental (☎ 509-663-0587) is in town at John Clark Motors, 908 S Wenatchee Ave.

Getting Around
Undoubtedly the best public transport deal in the Northwest, Link (☎ 509-662-1155, 800-851-5465) operates 20 lines around town and to adjoining communities such as Lake Wenatchee, Lake Chelan, Cashmere and Leavenworth. There's no fare, and buses run until 8 pm daily except on Sunday. Buses headed to the above destinations are equipped with bike racks. Skiers should inquire about the SkiLINK service to Mission Ridge on buses with specially mounted ski racks. The main

transit station is downtown on Wenatchee Ave and Kittitas St.

Taxi If you need a taxi, call Courtesy Cab (☎ 509-662-2126) or Woody's Cab (☎ 509-884-0358).

GLACIER PEAK WILDERNESS AREA
The small town of Entiat, 15 miles north of Wenatchee, is the eastern access point to the Glacier Peak Wilderness Area (Darrington is the western entrance). It's 38 miles from US 97 at Entiat to the road's end, with many campgrounds along the way. Over 211 sq miles burned in the Entiat drainage during 1994; this Tyee Creek fire was the largest single fire ever in the Wenatchee National Forest. Trails and roads have since reopened, though the dense and shrubby forests that once flanked the lower elevations are still in recovery.

Follow the Entiat River Rd (which becomes USFS Rd 51) to reach trails from Cottonwood Campground. Glacier views await at the end of a 10.5-mile hike up the **Entiat River Trail**, which passes through dense forest and alpine meadows before terminating on a cliff before Mount Maude and Seven Fingered Jack. Day-hikers should explore **Cow Creek Meadows**, on a wildflower-laden loop hike past Fifth of July Mt and Larch Lakes.

If you want hiking and camping advice, stop by the Entiat Ranger Station (☎ 509-784-1511), 2108 Entiat Way. Four USFS campgrounds up the Entiat River appear after the first 25 miles of USFS Rd 51, the *Fox Creek*, *Silver Falls*, *North Fork* and *Cottonwood* campgrounds.

Grand Coulee & Moses Lake

One of northeastern Washington's most spectacular geological events occurred about 10,000 years ago when glaciers filled the Pend Oreille River valley and much of northern Idaho, creating a huge ice dam that held back a glacial lake so large it covered most of western Montana. It also blocked the Columbia River, forcing it into a new channel. When the dam finally gave way (bobbing up like an ice cube in a glass of water), torrents of water rushed over eastern Washington, scouring topsoil and enlarging river channels. When the glaciers receded, the Columbia returned to its original channel, leaving a network of dry riverbeds called 'coulees.' Grand Coulee is the largest of these. Moses Coulee, which crosses US 2 about 12 miles west of Coulee City, is another. The Grand Coulee starts near the dam and extends south past Dry Falls, through Sun Lakes State Park, till it peters out somewhere north of Soap Lake.

Moses Lake is another ancient product of the flooded Columbia Basin. As for a vacation destination, Moses Lake appeals mostly to local motorboaters, but it can be a convenient place to spend the night along I-90 (it's about halfway between Seattle and Spokane) or to take an afternoon dip in the big community swimming pool. South of Moses Lake, the Potholes, an even more obscure destination to the average traveler, attract avid bird watchers from all over the Northwest.

GRAND COULEE
For 53 miles between the Grand Coulee Dam and Soap Lake, Hwys 155 and 17 pass through the Grand Coulee, a vast basalt canyon carved into rocky islands and spires reflecting onto small, shallow lakes. US 2 intercepts the Grand Coulee at the small town of Coulee City, separating the Grand Coulee's reservoir-dominated upper half from its more scenic lower portion. Coulee City is 26 miles south of Coulee Dam on Hwy 155.

Banks Lake
The 31-mile-long Banks Lake is a reservoir filled with water shuttled over from the Columbia River via Grand Coulee Dam. At the southern end of Banks Lake, near Coulee City, Dry Falls Dam controls the flow of water out of Banks Lake into the

Main Canal, which sends irrigation water out to Columbia Basin farms and orchards.

Steamboat Rock, a 700-foot-high basalt butte rises out of Banks Lake and dominates **Steamboat Rock State Park**. The park (☎ 509-633-1304) contains a swimming beach, campground and nine-hole golf course.

A sometimes steep **hiking** trail, which bursts with wildflowers in the spring, leads from the campground to the top of the butte, providing a wonderful view down the Grand Coulee (watch out for rattlesnakes here). The Northrup Canyon Trail begins in a sheltered canyon across the road from the state park and passes through Grand County's only forest. Northrup Lake, at the top of the canyon, is stocked with trout. Some homestead cabins remain near the trail. Check in at the Steamboat Rock Ranger Station before hiking this trail.

Dry Falls

Dry Falls, which cuts across the Grand Coulee, is 3½ miles wide and over 400 feet high. These scalloped cliffs are the remnants of what was once the world's largest waterfall. An interpretive center (☎ 509-632-5214) about 2 miles south of US 2 on Hwy 17 has exhibits depicting the region's geological history. It's open 10 am to 5 pm weekdays.

The coulee at the bottom of the falls is dotted with lakes which are stocked with trout and popular with flycasters. Reach these lakes via **Sun Lakes State Park** (☎ 509-632-5583), 4 miles south of US 2 on Hwy 17, a large park with camping, cabins, a golf course, horseback riding and boat and bicycle rentals.

Lake Lenore Caves

Ten miles south of Dry Falls, the Lake Lenore Caves were formed as the force of water from melting glaciers plucked out chunks of basalt from the coulee walls. Prehistoric hunters used these caves as shelters, and Native Americans left pictographs, many of which are still visible near the caves' entrances. A marked trail from the north end of Lenore Lake leads to the caves.

Places to Stay

Steamboat Rock State Park on Banks Lake has camping. Just south of Dry Falls the *Sun Lakes Park Resort* (☎ 509-632-5291) at Sun Lakes State Park has rustic cabins and a handful of mobile homes. Lodgers enjoy a heated pool, nine-hole and miniature golf courses and activities in a striking setting on Sun Lake. Cabins have kitchenettes, but you'll need to supply your own cookware and dishes. Towels and bedding are supplied. Rates for cabins start at $59, mobile homes at $91. There are also plenty of campsites here for tents ($11) and sites for RVs ($16).

There's little reason anyone would ever need (or want) to stay in Coulee City. But if you happen to find yourself stranded here the *Blue Top Motel* (☎ 509-632-5596), 109 N 6th, is basic and cheap, with rooms starting at $29/35. *Ala Cozy Motel* (☎ 509-632-5703, 800-321-7649), 9988 US 2 E, has an outdoor pool and spa, miniature golf and views of Banks Lake; rooms here are $38/43.

Places to Eat

Restaurants in Coulee City aren't much to look forward to. *The Crossing Dinner House* (☎ 509-632-5667), at 5th and Main Sts, serves Korean and American food, while right next door, *Steamboat Rock Restaurant* (☎ 509-632-5452) at 420 W Main St serves steak and seafood. If you're staying at nearby Sun Lakes State Park and get tired of camp cooking, try the *Dry Falls Cafe* (☎ 509-632-5634) at the intersection of Hwys 2 and 155. They have a breakfast special on weekdays.

SOAP LAKE
Population 1666

The Grand Coulee peters out at Soap Lake, ending the dramatic river-cut geology and entering a vast flat region. Soap Lake contains 17 minerals and – according to the lakeside sign – an 'ichthyological (fish)-like' oil, making it similar in content to

WASHINGTON

that of Germany's Baden-Baden. The water in the lake itself is funny-smelling and mildly slippery, and white foam gathers at the shoreline.

The lakeside town of Soap Lake is an odd assortment of dilapidation, antiques and upscale lodgings. It lies north of Moses Lake, south of US 2 and north of I-90 near the crossroads of Hwys 17 and 28. The Soap Lake Visitor Information Center (☎ 509-246-1821) is near the foot of the lake at 300 Beach St E. Other than taking a dip in the pungent lake, there's not much to do in these parts.

Native Americans camped on the banks of Soap Lake each summer to gamble, race horses and soak in the lake water. Early in the 1900s, pioneers began frequenting the lake, and it became something of a medical resort. The chamber of commerce keeps a file of letters attesting to the ameliorative effect of the water on psoriasis, arthritis and various circulatory disorders.

Drink your fill of the mineral water at the fountain next to the Inn at Soap Lake or take a swim at the public beach adjacent to the visitors' center at the south end of the lake.

Soap Lake's big summer event is the Great Canoe Race, which is held the second Saturday in July.

Places to Stay

RV Campers should head a couple of miles north to *American Adventures Soap Lake Resort* (☎ 509-246-1103), 22818 Hwy 17, for nice tree-shaded hookups on the lake.

Notaras Lodge (☎ 509-246-0462), 236 Main Ave E, is a rustic log lodge, and aside from the lake, is the only thing most Northwesterners have ever heard of in Soap Lake. Norma Zimmer, the Lawrence Welk Show's Champagne Lady, used to stay here a lot. Decorated theme rooms maintain a fine line between eccentricity and dopiness. Soap Lake water is piped into the tubs. Rooms run from $58/65, whirlpool suites from $91/98.

Inn at Soap Lake (☎ 509-246-1132), 226 Main Ave E, is a big stone building next to Notaras Lodge. Rooms at this surprisingly elegant, Euro-style hotel start at $50/55 for singles/doubles. Soap Lake water fills the bathtubs.

Besides these two showpieces, there's a handful of other motels in town. The nicest among them, *Tolo Vista Motel* (☎ 509-246-1512), 22 Daisy St N, has comfortable log cabins with mineral baths at $44 and up. The no-frills *Lake Motel* (☎ 509-246-1903), 322 Daisy St S, has doubles for $30 and a swimming pool.

Places to Eat

After a hot drive down the Grand Coulee, ice cream may be all that you care to eat; you'll find that and more in Soap Lake. *Nan's Ice Cream Parlor & Pizza* (☎ 509-246-0470) is at 27 Daisy St S. *Don's Restaurant* (☎ 509-246-1217), across from the Notaras at 14 Canna St N, is the best bet for dinner. They put a Greek twist on American food.

EPHRATA

Population 6323

Ephrata is not a particularly exciting place, but it can be a practical place to spend a night or grab a bite if you're passing through on your way to Grand Coulee Dam or Spokane.

Ephrata is 6 miles southwest of Soap Lake on US 28. The Ephrata Chamber of Commerce (☎ 509-754-4656) is next to the City of Ephrata Transportation Center at 90 NW Basin St. There are **hot springs** in Ephrata as well as the **Grant County Museum**, but that's about it.

Places to Stay & Eat

You can camp at *Oasis RV Park* (☎ 509-754-5102), just west of town at 2541 Basin St SW, an RV park with some tent sites, a swimming pool and a kids' fishing pond. It costs about $10 a night.

All of Ephrata's indoor lodgings are within a few blocks of each other on Basin St, the main drag. *Lariat Motel* (☎ 509-754-2437), 1639 Basin St SW, has a swimming pool – an important consideration in Ephrata in the summertime – and singles/doubles for $35/40. The *Columbia Motel* (☎ 509-754-

5226), near the turnoff to Moses Lake at 1257 Basin St SW, has kitchenette rooms for $36/40. *Sharlyn Motel* (☎ 509-754-3575), 848 Basin St SW, is small but decent, with rooms from $35/50. The *Travelodge* (☎ 509-754-4651), 31 Basin St SW, also has a pool; rooms run $55/65.

As for food, there's nothing fancy here, but at the *Reel Pizza Place* (☎ 509-754-0103), 347 Basin St NW you can take in a movie while you eat. *Lee's Landmark II Cafe* (☎ 509-754-2808), 130 NW 1st St, serves home-style meals for breakfast and lunch in a river-rock building downtown. Informal *Kafe Athens* (☎ 509-754-2839), 459 Basin St NW, is the best place in town for lunch or dinner, with excellent Greek food served cantina-style for under $5.

Getting There & Away
Amtrak's *Empire Builder* stops daily in Ephrata at the new City of Ephrata Transportation Center at 90 Alder St NW. The eastbound train stops at 9:48 pm, and the westbound one comes through at 3:20 am. This is also the place to catch the Northwestern Trailways (☎ 800-366-3830 in Washington) bus west to Wenatchee, Leavenworth and Seattle, or east to Moses Lake and Spokane. Local Grant Transit (☎ 509-765-0898) buses go to Soap Lake and Moses Lake.

MOSES LAKE
Population 13,503
The town of Moses Lake sprawls and is not burdened with an excess of charm. Most travelers know it as a stop on I-90 between Seattle and Spokane. There are few reasons besides hunger, fatigue and need of gas or a bathroom to stop in Moses Lake. The sinuous 17-mile-long Moses Lake draws lots of boaters and jet-skiers. The natural lake was augmented by water from the Columbia Basin Irrigation Project, which also feeds the Potholes Reservoir to the south.

Orientation & Information
Moses Lake is 178 miles east of Seattle, and 105 miles west of Spokane on I-90.

Hwy 17 heads south from Soap Lake and cuts northwest-southeast through Moses Lake on its way south to Eltopia, where it joins US 395 to the Tri-Cities. The main part of downtown Moses Lake is squeezed between the lake's Parker and Pelican Horns, which extend east from the main body of water. Broadway backs up onto the Parker Horn of Moses Lake. The town's awkward layout around these lakes can be disorienting. Broadway and Pioneer Way are both names for the I-90 business loop. From downtown, Stratford Road cuts across the lake to Hwy 17.

The Moses Lake Visitor & Information Center (☎ 509-765-7888, 800-992-6234) is at 324 S Pioneer Way. The main post office is on 3rd Ave between Ash and Beech Sts. Bob's Laundry (☎ 509-766-0464) is next to the Excell Shopping Center at 415 E 5th Ave. The Samaritan Hospital (☎ 509-765-5606) is at 801 E Wheeler Rd, just east of downtown.

Things to See & Do
Moses Lake itself is appealing mostly to motorboaters, but there are also a number of swimming beaches. Most of the activity is centered on **Moses Lake State Park**, a pleasant, tree-shaded day-use park west of town off I 90 exit 174.

More subtly interesting are the Pothole Lakes southwest of town (see below), and more blatantly fun for hot, car-weary kids is the giant **aquatics center** in downtown Moses Lake at McCosh Park (Dogwood and 4th Sts). Free summertime concerts and other events are held in the park at Centennial Theater (☎ 509-766-9240, 800-992-6234), the city's outdoor amphitheater.

Even if you've stopped just to get gas, don't miss the whimsical **Adam East Museum & Art Center** (☎ 509-766-9395), 122 W 3rd Ave, which exhibits the work of prominent Northwest folk artists (scrap metal sculpture was featured in a past exhibit). In the museum's history section, migration patterns of different Native American tribes are traced out in an interesting collection of ceremonial pipes. It's open 11 am to 5 pm, Tuesday to Saturday.

WASHINGTON

Places to Stay
Camping *Big Sun Resort* (☎ 509-765-8294), 2300 W Marina Dr, just off I-90 near Moses Lake State Park (a day-use park), is an RV park with a few tent sites ($12), lake access and boat docks; full hookups cost $17.50. Campers can access the state park via a footbridge across the freeway.

A prime RV spot near the Potholes Reservoir is *Mar Don Resort* (☎ 509-765-5061, 800-416-2736), 8198 HWY 262 E, near the O'Sullivan Dam on the south side of the reservoir, where tent and RV sites run $15 to $18. There are also motel rooms and a restaurant. Also on Hwy 262, there's *Potholes State Park* (☎ 509-346-2759), 25 miles southwest of Moses Lake at 670 O'Sullivan Dam Rd, a marina-type campground that's open year-round with sites from $7 to $16. This is a good base for bird watchers or canoeists bent on exploring the Potholes. It's 25 miles southwest of Moses Lake.

Hotels Most of Moses Lake's motels are clustered around the freeway exits, though there are also a few places to stay downtown. Virtually all of these motels have pools.

The *Maples Motel* (☎ 509-765-5665), 1006 W 3rd St, is near downtown parks, and has rooms for $24/30. Nearby is the *Sage 'n Sand Motel* (☎ 509-765-1755, 800-336-0454), 1011 S Pioneer Way, with rooms starting at $36. The *Travelodge* (☎ 509-765-8631), 316 S Pioneer Way at 3rd St, is also downtown and has rooms for $42.

Several chain motels are just off I-90 exit 176. The *Motel 6* (☎ 509-766-0250), 2822 Wapato Drive, has singles/doubles starting at $29/35. *Lakeshore Resort* (☎ 509-765-9201), 3206 W Lakeshore Drive, has a marina with rowboat rentals and a pool; singles/doubles start at $28/33. *Best Western Hallmark Inn on the Lake* (☎ 509-765-9211, 800-235-4255), 3000 Marina Drive, is one of Moses Lake's better motels, with boat docks, a pool and tennis courts; rooms cost $65 to $125.

At the freeway junction of I-90 and Hwy 17 (I-90 exit 179), the *Shilo Inn Motel* (☎ 509-765-9317, 800-222-2244), 1819 E Kittleson St, charges $75/79, and is pretty fancy by local standards.

Places to Eat
Moses Lake is mostly an American-food sort of place, with no particularly outstanding restaurants. Look for fast-food and family-style restaurants at the freeway exits. For something different there's *Thai Cuisine* (☎ 509-766-1489) in the shopping center at 627 Pioneer Way. For Mexican try *El Abuelo*, 1075 W Broadway.

Trying its darnedest to be Moses Lake's fancy steak-and-seafood place, *Michael's on the Lake* (☎ 509-765-1611), 910 W Broadway, features dining on a deck overlooking the lake. It's not incredibly expensive, and a salmon dinner runs $13.

Getting There & Around
Greyhound (☎ 509-766-1351) stops near I 90 exit 179 at the Shilo Inn, 1819 E Kittleson. Get around town in a taxi from Moses Lake Cab (☎ 509-766-7803).

POTHOLES WILDLIFE & RECREATION AREA
If you like odd geography, or yearn to see ruddy ducks swimming past sand-dune islands, spend a morning knocking around the Potholes or the Wildlife Area south and west of Potholes Reservoir. The reservoir, held back by O'Sullivan Dam, is just south of Moses Lake on Hwy 262. (Those seeking knowledge of irrigation systems will find a prime example of an irrigation canal flowing from the foot of the Potholes Reservoir.)

The land is surprisingly lush and green, with lots of water and wetlands surrounded by sand dunes, which sometimes pop up through the streams as islands. The Columbia Basin Irrigation Project is responsible for this weird ecology – O'Sullivan Dam and various irrigation schemes have filled any shallow spot with irrigation water, which courses through the native desert and turns some of the high sand

NIK WHEELER

KEVIN SCHAFER

JENNIFER SNARSKI

Top Left: Poppies and fence, Whatcom County, WA
Bottom: *The Joy of Running Together,* Riverfront Park,
Spokane, WA

Top Right: View from Mariella Inn, Friday Harbor, San
Juan Island, WA

Top: Wheat fields near Colfax, WA
Bottom Left: Ancient cedars in Kaniksu National
Forest, WA

Bottom Right: Monkey flowers, Edith Creek and Mt
Rainier, WA

dunes into islands. Canoeists can put in at **Potholes State Park**, 25 miles southwest of Moses Lake, and paddle the waterways. Bird watchers figure this to be a real oasis; come prepared to spot waterfowl, geese, avocets, herons, egrets, burrowing owls and songbirds. The Potholes aren't particularly well known, but most serious Northwest bird watchers have made springtime pilgrimages here.

Lots of the **hiking** here is on causeways running alongside water ditches. Hike beside the Frenchman Hills Wasteway, which leads water away from the Potholes Reservoir. There's a path to it leading out from the end of a gravel road, west from the Potholes State Park camping area. Remember this is a desert; hiking can be unpleasant in hot weather.

The best access to Potholes Reservoir is from the south. From Moses Lake take Hwy 17 southeast 10 miles to Hwy 262. Turn west on Hwy 262, which runs along the foot of the reservoir past O'Sullivan Dam, Potholes State Park and other informal access points. An 80-mile scenic drive past potholes, coulees and sand dunes traces a rectangular route around lake, bordered on the north by I-90's Frontage Road, on the west by Dodson Rd, on the south by Frenchman Hills Rd and Hwy 262, and on the east by Rd M (which runs into Hwy 17 just south of Moses Lake).

Yakima Valley

The Yakima River arises from the slopes of Snoqualmie Pass, far to the west. By the time the river gets to Yakima, most of its mountain freshness is gone and dams have slowed it down, diverting its waters into immense irrigation projects. When viewed on a sweltering hot day (of which there are many), the Yakima seems as life-giving as the Nile. The river flows through scorched ochre-colored hills, but where its water touches the soil, a bounty of life springs forth.

The Yakima Valley is the single largest producer of apples in the world, though hops, cherries, peaches and other tree fruits – as well as vegetables – are also found in abundance. In the last 20 years, wine grapes have taken their place on the hillsides, making this one of the Northwest's major wine areas. The lower Yakima Valley in particular is filled with irrigated fields and little towns dedicated to serving the needs of farmers.

There's no getting around the fact that it's hot and dry here – only eight inches of rain fall a year, summer highs hover around 100°F and there are over 300 days of sunshine annually. These climatic extremes make this area a mecca for sunlovers. Yakima is noted as a retirement center, especially for the career military, while the sunny weather and access to skiing and fishing serve to attract young recreation enthusiasts.

The preponderance of orchard work has also brought in a large Hispanic population from Mexico and Latin America; people of Hispanic origin compose 30% of the valley's population. The vast Yakama Indian Reservation to the southwest adds a strong Native American presence to the population mix.

At Yakima, the Yakima River suddenly passes out of the Yakima Canyon into a wide basin surrounded by brown hills. South of the city is the Yakama Indian Reservation and mile after mile of orchards and farms, which flank the Yakima River to its confluence with the Columbia at Richland. I-82 runs the length of the valley. Paralleling the freeway for much of the way is US 12, also known somewhat fancifully as the Wine Country Road. At Toppenish, US 97 splits off, heading south to Oregon and I-84. Seattle is 142 miles west of Yakima; Richland is 76 miles east.

ELLENSBURG
Population 13,498
Even if you're not going to stop in Ellensburg, at least slow down for it – it's the site of the state police training academy. Students

like to practice catching speeding motorists and writing up tickets.

The other college in town, Central Washington University (CWU), is large enough to give a relaxed collegiate feel to this agricultural hub town. Ellensburg's well-preserved downtown has lots of brick buildings, which were built after a fire burned nine downtown blocks and more than 200 homes in 1889. Ellensburg then thought itself on the way to becoming both the 'Pittsburgh of the West' (because of nearby iron ore and coal deposits) and the capital city of Washington. For better or worse, the iron and coal proved to be very low grade, and Olympia got the state capitol building, leaving Ellensburg the state normal school as a consolation prize.

Today, Ellensburg is a pleasant enough place to while away an afternoon or spend a night, with the old brick downtown and a couple of good restaurants, not to mention the signing chimps at the university's primate center. There is an easygoing, cowboy-poetry brand of sophistication here, which lapses just long enough each year for Ellensburg to become a rowdy cowtown during the Ellensburg Rodeo, one of the nation's largest.

Orientation
The Yakima River runs down the west side of Ellensburg; the Yakima Canyon is bordered by scenic Hwy 821.

I-90 sticks close to the Yakima River and runs more or less west of town. Hop off the freeway either northwest (at the West Ellensburg interchange) or southeast (at the South Ellensburg interchange) of town, and let the flow of traffic take you to Main St. Main St forms a T-junction with 8th St, which runs east to the university.

Information
For visitor and Forest Service information drop by the Ellensburg Chamber of Commerce (☎ 509-925-3137), 436 N Sprague, Ellensburg, WA 98926. You'll find the main post office at Pearl St and 3rd Ave. Old Fools Bookstore (☎ 509-925-4480),

112 E 3rd Ave, is a good new and used bookstore, while Four Winds Bookstore & Cafe (☎ 509-962-2375), 200 E 4th Ave, is kind of a student hangout with new and used books and a heavy New-Age emphasis. Catch the *Daily Record* for local news.

One laundromat, Model-Ke Cleaners (☎ 509-925-5389), is downtown at 207 N Pine St, and another, College Coin Laundry (☎ 509-962-6000), is close to the university at 8th and Walnut Sts. Kittitas Valley Community Hospital (☎ 509-962-9841) is at 603 S Chestnut St.

Historic District
The chamber of commerce has maps of the downtown historic district, which is roughly contained between 5th and 3rd Aves on one side, Main and Pine Sts on the other. The historic district is peppered with antique shops and galleries, making it a tempting place to spend an afternoon. Then there's the **cowboy sculpture** at 5th Ave and Pearl St and the oversize, cartoony **Ellensburg bull** lounging on a bench in the historic district. Don't miss **Dick & Jane's Spot**, out front at 101 N Pearl St, a funkified folk garden, crammed with bizarre lawn ornaments made from bicycle reflectors and other found objects.

Museums
The **Kittitas County Museum** (☎ 509-925-3778), 114 E 3rd Ave, in the 1889 Cadwell Building, is known mostly for its gemstone and petrified wood collections, as well as its horseshoe-arched windows. The museum is open 10 am to 4 pm, Monday to Saturday, May through September; the rest of the year it's open 11 am to 3 pm, Tuesday to Saturday. See the **Clymer Museum** (☎ 509-962-6416), 416 N Pearl St, for a collection of native-son John Clymer and other Northwest artists' works. It's open 10 am to 5 pm weekdays, and noon to 5 pm weekends.

The very engaging **Children's Activity Museum** (☎ 509-925-6789), 400 N Main St, has a miniature city to play in, a puppet theater and other incredibly popular hands-on activities. Visit the museum from 10 am to 4 pm, Wednesday to Saturday, and 1 pm to 5 pm on Sunday; weekday hours during the winter are 10 am to 3 pm.

Olmstead Place State Park
A family farm is preserved at this heritage park, 4½ miles southeast of Ellensburg off I-90, where you'll find a log cabin, pioneer barns and other farm buildings dating from 1875 to 1890. The buildings are open to the public on summer weekends. Contact the park ranger (☎ 509-925-1943) for more information.

Central Washington University
As with most small-town college campuses, this one is a good place for a student-watching stroll, but there are a couple of other attractions here as well.

Chimposiums CWU has gained some renown for its studies of chimpanzee-human communication. Yes, this is the home of the chimps who communicate using American Sign Language. On weekends the Chimpanzee and Human Communication Institute, at 13th Ave and D St, presents an informative, hour-long 'Chimposium' workshop that includes an audience with the chimps. The discussions on linguistics and primate behavior are interesting, but don't expect to have any elaborate conversations with the chimps – chimpanzee-human communication typically takes a lot of time and patience. Call ☎ 509-963-2244 for workshop times and to reserve tickets, which cost adult/students $10/7.50.

Japanese Garden Formal Japanese dry-landscape gardens offer a restful place for a stroll on the CWU campus. Find the garden's entry gate on the Walnut St Pedestrian Mall. It's open year-round, from daybreak to dusk. There's no admission other than your contribution to a donation box.

Thorp Grist Mill
This historic grist mill was once a de facto meeting place for local farmers and is now a rural museum with a multimedia presentation shown in a grain storage bin. The mill is open for viewing during the summer, and at other times by appointment. Thorp Mill Town Preservation Society (☎ 509-964-9640) has more information. West of Ellensburg, take I-90 exit 101 and travel through Thorp to reach the mill and stream park.

Yakima Canyon
South of Ellensburg, Hwy 821 follows the Yakima River through Yakima Canyon. The 25-mile backroad is a winding scenic route to Yakima and, unless you hit it on a busy weekend, is quiet enough for a bike ride. Watch out for drunk drivers.

Rafting Some people put their inflatable rafts in around Ellensburg and float down the Yakima River. Supreme Court Justice William O Douglas did. In the '60s he joined a concerned citizens group called the Yakima River Conservancy on a float down the river to rally support for their scenic-preservation plan.

It's possible to access the river on its designated scenic stretch along Hwy 821, south of Ellensburg, and spend three to four hours on a float to the Roza Dam. There's also a public put-in north on Hwy 10, below Cle Elum, for a lazy 15-mile, five- to six-hour float to the diversion

dam near Thorp. If you want to rent a raft, head to River Raft Rentals (☎ 509-964-2145), 7 miles west of Ellensburg at 9801 Hwy 10.

Hiking Though floating may be the ideal way to see the Yakima Canyon, there are hiking trails around and above the river. At the Umtanum Creek Recreation Area, about 12 miles south of Ellensburg on Hwy 821, a suspension footbridge crosses the river to trails leading up to a ridge-top viewpoint and along Umtanum Creek. (Remember: this is rattlesnake country.)

Fishing The Yakima River is also a big deal for fly-fishing. Contact the Evening Hatch (☎ 509-962-5959), for fly-fishing guide service. Cooper's Fly Shop (☎ 509-962-5259), 413 N Main St, has tackle and gear.

Paragliding The hot afternoon sun creates strong thermal updrafts, which keep paragliders well aloft above the Yakima River canyon. North American Paragliding (☎ 509-925-5565) has sales, service and tours.

Elk Feeding

Once the snow covers the natural forage, the Department of Wildlife (☎ 509-575-2740) takes it upon itself to feed approximately 750 elk each day at Watt Canyon, 15 miles north of Ellensburg. To watch this spectacle, put on some warm clothes and show up promptly at 8 am at the feeding station. Take I-90 exit 102, west of Ellensburg, cross left over the freeway and at the top of the hill turn right onto Old Thorp Cemetery Rd. Continue to Watt Canyon Rd and turn left. The feeding station is at the end of the road, about 1 mile away.

Special Events

The annual National Western Art Show & Auction (☎ 509-962-2934), held each May, brings some of the best Western artists to the local Best Western motel to sell their paintings, prints, sculpture and jewelry.

Ask for details at the Clymer Museum (see Museums, above).

The Whisky Dick Triathlon in late July starts off with a mile-long swim in the Columbia River, followed by a 26-mile bike ride up steep Whisky Dick Ridge and an 8.9-mile run back to Ellensburg.

Ellensburg's ultimate festival, the Ellensburg Rodeo (☎ 509-962-7830, 800-637-2444), starts on the Thursday of Labor Day weekend and runs for four days at the Kittitas County Fairgrounds. It's ranked among the top 10 rodeos in the nation and is one of central Washington's biggest events. Come prepared to see some hard riding and roping – participants take this rodeo very seriously, as there is big money at stake.

The Kittitas County Fair takes place at the same time as the rodeo and is also held at the same location.

Places to Stay

Camping *KOA Campground* (☎ 509-925-9319), off I-90 exit 106, has the only camping around Ellensburg. Fortunately, it's on the Yakima River. Sites start at $21, and it's a typically spiffy KOA, with a laundromat, pool, playground and showers.

B&Bs *Murphy's Country B&B* (☎ 509-925-7986), 2830 Thorp Hwy S, is a restored farmhouse just southwest of town across from the golf course. The two guest rooms go for $65/60.

Hotels The *Rainbow Motel* (☎ 509-925-3544), 1025 Cascade Way, is a pretty basic place, but it does have some of the cheapest rooms in town ($38). The *I-90 Inn Motel* (☎ 509-925-9844), 1390 Dollarway Rd, near I-90 exit 106 is convenient, inexpensive, and a good value with rooms starting at $42/46.

In town, the *Thunderbird Motel* (☎ 509-962-9856, 800-843-3492), 403 W 8th St, is a big motel with an outdoor pool and rooms from $41/45.

Near the freeway's South Ellensburg exchange (I-90 exit 109) there's a *Super 8 Motel* (☎ 509-962-6888, 800-800-8000) at

1500 Canyon Rd, with rooms and a pool for $50/54. The *Best Western Ellensburg Inn* (☎ 509-925-9801, 800-321-8791) is nearby at 1700 Canyon Rd. With room at $62/67, and an indoor pool, fitness center and hot tub, this is Ellensburg's most deluxe motel.

Places to Eat
In addition to all the usual fast-food restaurants, any college town in Washington is bound to have a few hip coffee joints. In Ellensburg, *D&M Coffee Station* (☎ 509-962-6333), 408 S Main St, is one of the best. It's an old gas station turned drive-through espresso shop, with brightly-painted gas pumps and a deck out back. It's near the turnoff for the hospital. If you want to sit down with your coffee, head to *The Coffee House* (☎ 509-925-5282), 211 E 8th Ave, which features a light breakfast and lunch menu, patio seating, and music on occasional evenings.

Out near I-90 exit 106, the space-themed *Roswell Cafe* (☎ 509-962-5436), 1600 N Currier St, has the eerie desertedness of a UFO crash, but the burgers and burritos are good and there's a number of microbrewed beers on tap.

Valley Cafe (☎ 509-925-3050), 105 W 3rd Ave, is a striking art-deco cafe that turns out remarkably good food. At lunch, a bowl of cioppino goes for $7.95 and a spinach salad for $4.95. Order a huge boxed lunch from their take-out menu for $7.25, or stop by the take-out shop next door to the restaurant for a muffin or cinnamon roll.

Bar 14 Ranch House Restaurant (☎ 509-962-6222), 1800 Canyon Rd, is a steak place convenient to I-90 exit 109.

If you're heading north of town on US 97, the *Mineral Springs Resort Restaurant* (☎ 509-857-2361), between Ellensburg and Blewett Pass, has huge portions and great pie (skip the ice cream). The local mineral water used here is strong enough to overpower the flavor of your iced tea.

Shopping
Jewelry made from Ellensburg blue agate makes an appropriate souvenir. This stone is unique to the Ellensburg area, but most of the prime agate territory is on private land. Fortunately, Ellensburg is studded with gem shops, all peddling blue agates. They're the focus at the Ellensburg Agate Shop (☎ 509-925-4998), 201 S Main St.

Gallery-hoppers should start at Gallery One (☎ 509-925-2670), 408½ N Pearl St, featuring contemporary arts and crafts.

Getting There & Away
The Greyhound station (☎ 509-925-1177), at 8th Ave and Okanogan St is a busy place, and has two buses a day to Seattle ($17.50 one way). There are also buses north to Wenatchee via both Cashmere and Quincy, and south to Yakima, Pasco, and Walla Walla. The one-way fare to Yakima costs $8.

AROUND ELLENSBURG
Roslyn
Population 1037
Roslyn, a tiny town on Hwy 903, is a couple of miles off I-90, about 25 miles northwest of Ellensburg. This is (and they won't let you forget it) where the TV show *Northern Exposure* was filmed; on TV, it's supposed to be a small town in the Alaskan bush.

Roslyn is yet another gateway to the popular **Alpine Lakes Wilderness Area**. Hwy 903 leads northwest of Roslyn and becomes Salmon la Sac Rd, passing by resort-rimmed Cle Elum Lake and ending some 25 miles later in the heart of the wilderness, just south of Deception Pass. This area gets less use than Snoqualmie Pass or Leavenworth, but don't expect solitude – over 100,000 people visit the Alpine Lakes every year. From the end of USFS Rd 4330 it's a hearty 4½-mile hike to the **Pacific Crest Trail** and 6724-foot **Cathedral Rock**. Contact the Cle Elum Ranger Station, (☎ 509-674-4411), 803 W 2nd St, on Hwy 903 in Cle Elum for more information.

Places to Stay & Eat The *Roslyn Cafe* (☎ 509-649-2763), at 2nd St and Pennsylvania Ave, is the place to eat, and the *Brick*

Tavern (☎ 509-649-2643), a block down at 1 Pennsylvania Ave, is the place to drink. (It's one of the several places that claim to be Washington's oldest saloon, but gains more cachet for its 'dogs welcome' policy.) Ask for a glass of Roslyn Beer, brewed ultra-locally at the Roslyn Brewing Company (☎ 509-649-2232), 33 Pennsylvania Ave. The brewery is open to visitors noon to 5 pm on weekends.

On your way to Roslyn from Ellensburg, you'll pass Cle Elum, home of the *Cle Elum Bakery* (☎ 509-674-2233), E 1st St. This bakery is a ritual stop for many I-90 travelers, but other than that, Cle Elum is a pretty quiet logging town with lots of empty storefronts. Of Cle Elum's several motels *The Cedar's Motel* (☎ 509-674-5535), 1001 E 1st St, isn't a bad choice; rooms cost $34/36. *MaMa Vallone's* (☎ 509-674-5174), 302 E 1st St, is the town's somewhat-renowned steak house and B&B inn with rooms for $57. Popular *Salmon La Sac Campground*, 12 miles north of Ronald on Salmon La Sac Rd, is a pleasant place to pitch a tent.

Vantage

I-90 crosses the Columbia River (which is called Wanapum Lake here, thanks to the

Wanapum Dam) at the town of Vantage. If you're even reading this, chances are that you've got tickets to a big-name concert at the spectacular Gorge Amphitheater in nearby George. Vantage is 42 miles southwest of Moses Lake and about 30 miles east of Ellensburg.

Fossilized trees and leaves dot the trails at the **Gingko Petrified Forest State Park & Interpretive Center**, and there are many species besides gingkos. A three-quarter-mile interpretive trail and a 3-mile hiking trail pass Douglas fir, spruce, maple, elm, gingko and gum trees, which are safely preserved behind steel grates. The trailheads are a couple of miles north of the freeway, but there's a small visitors' center on the west side of the freeway bridge. Take a moment to walk around here – several pictographs have been salvaged from the Wanapum Dam's backwaters, and are displayed on the river side of the visitors' center. The park is about 1 mile north of I-90 at Vantage, on the west bank of the Columbia River.

The **Wild Horse Monument** is across the Columbia from Vantage, and has good views of the river. This is a good place to stop the car and wander if the freeway is

---

Grandfather Cuts Loose the Ponies

Stop by the Wild Horse Monument, off I-90 near the Vantage Bridge, to see a sculpture of wild horses careening recklessly toward the edge of a cliff. The work of Northwest sculptor David Govedare (creator of the *Bloomsday Run* sculpture in Spokane), this sculpture, entitled *Grandfather Cuts Loose the Ponies*, represents a Native American creation story. Inspiring views overlooking the Columbia River make the monument a good place to pause from driving, and the story that accompanies Govedare's powerful image makes it hard not to reflect.

The monument's legend reads:

'Creatures of the planet, behold a Great Basket! I send this basket, bearing the gift of life, to all corners of the universe. Now take these ponies, I am cutting them loose. They will inspire a spirit of free will. They will be a companion for work and play on this planet... From the center of my Basket burns the fire of our collective souls. Humans you are responsible. You have the power of reasoning and the gift of free will. Use them wisely. Always be aware of the limitless nature of this ever-expanding universe. Let us live to inspire each other.' ■

getting to you. Don't expect to see wild horses here, it's just a statue.

To reach the **Wanapum Dam** (☎ 509-754-3541), with its fish-viewing windows and exhibits of Native American history, head south along the east bank of the Columbia River on Hwy 26 (which becomes Hwy 243). The dam is 5 miles south of I-90.

Places to Stay & Eat There's camping at *Wanapum State Park* (☎ 509-856-2700), 3 miles south of the freeway on the west side of the Columbia with tent/RV sites for $11/16. The other option is the *Vantage KOA & Motel* (☎ 509 856 2230), on the west side of the I-90 bridge, just north of the freeway. This is the closest lodging for people attending concerts at the Gorge Amphitheater in nearby George, so concert-goers should reserve early. During the peak summer season, motel rooms start at $54 and houses at $84 – except on concert nights when rooms are $84 and houses $110. Campsites start at $17 for two people, concert or not. Believe it or not, the KOA is better for tent campers than the RV-oriented state park campground.

If you're really concerned about dining, hop on over to Ellensburg, but if you just need sustenance, there are a couple of restaurants in Vantage, including the riverside *Wanapum Inn* (☎ 509-856-2244). Concert-goers will find plenty of food vendors at the show.

YAKIMA
Population 61,976
Yakima is the preeminent city of central Washington, and the trading center of an immense agricultural area. The city reflects this prosperity with a converted downtown-cum-mall development, massive commercial strips and some very conspicuous golf courses. Yakima likes to boast that it is the 'Palm Springs of the North.'

Yakima is the seat of local government, and many of the prominent older buildings in the downtown core are courthouses and such. Two particularly attractive buildings are the **Larson Building**, at Yakima Ave

and 2nd St, an art-deco marvel with 13 different shades of brick in its facade; check out the building's lobby. The grand, Italianate **Capitol Theatre**, at 19 S 3rd St, is another landmark of Yakima's boom years. Built in 1920 as a movie theater, the building is now a performing arts center.

A single block makes up Yakima's much-touted historic district. North Front St contains several good restaurants, a wine-tasting room, and boutiques. Most of the old Northern Pacific Depot across the street has been converted into the brewpub of the Northwest's oldest microbrewery.

Yakima does offer a few noteworthy restaurants, and an abundance of cheap motel rooms. The riverside Greenway, arboretum and adjacent parks make a good place to unload hot passengers and stretch weary muscles.

Orientation
I-82 runs along the Yakima River, east of Yakima's main downtown area; I-82 exit 33 leads to Yakima Ave which runs east-west and is the quickest route to downtown. The main north-south strip running through town is 1st St, which can be accessed from the N 1st St exit off I-82. Yakima Ave and Front St (essentially the train tracks) divide the city into directional quadrants.

There are both numbered streets and avenues in Yakima, so pay attention when people give addresses (numbered streets are east of the tracks and numbered avenues are west).

Information
The Yakima Valley Visitors & Convention Bureau (☎ 509-575-1300) is at 10 N 8th St, Yakima, WA 98901. The main post office is at 205 W Washington Ave, though the station at 112 S 3rd St is more convenient to downtown. The Booknook (☎ 509-453-3762), 722 Summitview Ave, is Yakima's best bookstore, with a good general selection tied to New-Age and self-help titles. The daily paper is the *Yakima Herald Republic*.

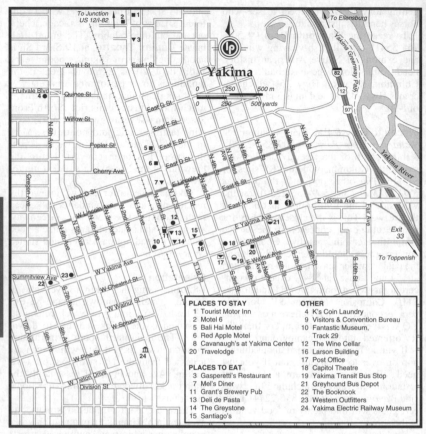

Yakima

0   250   500 m
0   250   500 yards

PLACES TO STAY
1   Tourist Motor Inn
2   Motel 6
5   Bali Hai Motel
6   Red Apple Motel
8   Cavanaugh's at Yakima Center
20 Travelodge

PLACES TO EAT
3   Gasperetti's Restaurant
7   Mel's Diner
11 Grant's Brewery Pub
13 Deli de Pasta
14 The Greystone
15 Santiago's

OTHER
4   K's Coin Laundry
9   Visitors & Convention Bureau
10 Fantastic Museum,
    Track 29
12 The Wine Cellar
16 Larson Building
17 Post Office
18 Capitol Theatre
19 Yakima Transit Bus Stop
21 Greyhound Bus Depot
22 The Booknook
23 Western Outfitters
24 Yakima Electric Railway Museum

K's Coin Laundry (☎ 509-452-5335) is at the corner of N 6th Ave and Fruitvale Blvd. Yakima Valley Memorial Hospital (☎ 509-575-8000) is at 2811 Tieton Drive. To check road conditions during the winter, call ☎ 888-766-4636.

Yakima Greenway & Parks
The Yakima Greenway is a scraggly string of parks and recreation areas that stretches the length of the Yakima River throughout the city, passing through natural wetlands and native vegetation. **Sarg Hubbard Park**, next to Washington's Fruit Place Visitor Center at I-82 exit 33, is a popular place to pick up the walking, hiking and biking path that follows the river for 7 miles. At the southern end of the Greenway is the **Yakima Arboretum**, a landscaped garden containing over 400 species of trees and shrubs. Stop at the Jewett Interpretive Center (☎ 509-248-7337) for a walking-tour brochure. The arboretum is just east of I-82 exit 34.

Yakima Valley Museum
This excellent regional museum (☎ 509-248-0747), 2105 Tieton Drive, together with adjacent Franklin Park, makes a great stop for visitors. The centerpiece of the

museum is its collection of horse-drawn conveyances, the largest such on the US West Coast. Other features of note include artifacts and exhibits about native Yakama culture and a replica of the office of late US Supreme Court Justice William O Douglas. Douglas, Yakima's most-noted native son, was the eminent jurist and US Supreme Court justice appointed to the court by Franklin D Roosevelt in 1939. He served until 1975, making him the longest-serving justice in the court's history. Although he's honored here and elsewhere around town with plaques and commemoratives, during his tenure on the court, his progressive politics usually rankled his home-town neighbors.

Not surprisingly, another section of the museum tells the story of apple production in the Yakima Valley. In yet another section, the **Children's Underground** does a good job of incorporating Yakima's human and natural history into a number of hands-on exhibits for kids. The museum is open from 10 am to 5 pm weekdays, and noon to 5 pm weekends. The Children's Underground is open 1 to 5 pm, Wednesday to Sunday, and admission is $3/1.50 adults/seniors and students, or $7 for a whole family.

Indian Painted Rocks

The Yakima River cuts narrow passages through the hills that flank the city. For the Native Americans who lived in the valley in prehistoric times, these cliff-lined ravines were natural avenues of transportation, as they are today. At the northern edge of Yakima, along an old foot trail, a large number of pictographs can still be seen. Many are of stylized humans with fantastic headdresses. It's easy to imagine that these images conveyed either a warning or a mark of territory to the natives who passed through this narrow gap.

To visit the Indian Painted Rocks, northwest of town, take the 40th Ave/Fruitvale exit off of US 12 and turn left onto old US 12, now called Powerhouse Rd. In about a mile, watch for a small plaque near a road-side parking area. Concrete steps lead up to the edge of the cliffs; watch for snakes.

Other Attractions

Adjacent to the museum is **Franklin Park**, with a playground, picnic tables, and – an important feature in sun-baked Yakima – a swimming pool .

Railroad buffs can hitch a ride to Selah on Yakima's **historic trolley.** Trips depart from the Yakima Electric Railway Museum (☎ 509-575-1700), 309 W Pine St at 3rd Ave, on weekends from May to early October. If you still have time to kill, then drop by the **World Famous Fantastic Museum** (☎ 509-575-0100), 15 W Yakima Ave, at the Track 29 antique mall, which has a goofy collection of celebrity exotica, like a pink Cadillac that once belonged to Elvis.

Skiing

White Pass Ski Area is 50 miles west of Yakima on US 12, on the southeast side of Mt Rainier. This popular ski resort offers 14 runs with a total vertical drop of 1505 feet. Lift tickets range from $18 to $20 on weekdays and $31 on weekends. There are also 9 miles of groomed cross-country trails. Call ☎ 509-453-8731 for general information, or ☎ 509 672 3100 for the Snowline.

Fishing

The Yakima River above Roza Dam (15 miles north) in the rugged Yakima Canyon is a spectacular place to fly-fish for trout. A good spot to start out is at Umtanum Creek, where a footbridge gives access to both sides of the river. Chinook Sporting Goods (☎ 509-452-8205), 901 S 1st St, has tackle and advice.

Rafting

Between the town of Ellensburg and the Roza Dam the Yakima River is gentle enough for novice floaters, but the scenery is impressive enough to make this an enjoyable trip. Contact Richie's River Rentals (☎ 509-453-2112) for rafts, guided trips and shuttles.

Golf

The Apple Tree Golf Course (☎ 509-966-5877), at 8804 Occidental Ave, offers 18 holes nestled in an apple orchard (what else?). The signature 17th hole is an island shaped like an apple. Suntides Golf Course (☎ 509-966-9065), 231 Pence Rd, 4 miles west on US 12, is the other 18-hole public standby.

Special Events

The Central Washington State Fair (☎ 509-452-0889) runs from the end of September to the first week in October and is known as one of the Northwest's best agricultural exhibitions. If you've passed them up everywhere else, this would be the place to give in and try one out. The fairgrounds are at Nob Hill Blvd and S 10th St.

There's a large Mexican population in the valley, and the Cinco de Mayo Fiesta is understandably a big celebration hereabouts. Usually held on the first weekend of May, the largest Cinco de Mayo celebrations are in nearby Sunnyside and Wapato.

For something completely different, try the Country Christmas Lighted Farm Implement Parade in neighboring Sunnyside, held the first Friday in December. Farmers dress their combines and threshers with festive lights and drive through town; watch for Rudolph and his nose so bright as he mingles with the mower blades, a favorite holiday jest. For more information contact the Sunnyside Chamber of Commerce at ☎ 509-837-5939.

Places to Stay

Camping There are campsites at *Yakima Sportsman State Park* (☎ 509-575-2774), 904 Keyes Rd, just across the Yakima River off Hwy 24. About half the sites have RV hookups ($16), and there are hot showers and flush toilets; tent sites cost $11. To reach it take I-82 exit 32 and follow Hwy 24 east, turning left onto Keyes Rd. As you make this turn you'll pass the *Yakima KOA* (☎ 509-248-5882), 1500 Keyes Rd, which has 140 full hookup sites for $22, a laundry, play area, showers and game room.

B&Bs Yakima's early and continued prosperity is reflected in the stately homes throughout the city. One of these has been turned into an attractive B&B and restaurant. The *Birchfield Manor* (☎ 509-452-1960, 800-375-3420), 2018 Birchfield Rd, east of Yakima off Hwy 24, also one of the best places to eat in the area, has five guest rooms, all with private bathrooms, starting from $80; suites top out at $175.

Hotels If you're looking for the motel strip, head to N 1st St, where there's a major concentration of inexpensive motels and fast-food outlets. All of the following have pools and kitchenettes, and rooms from $30 to $45. Check out the *Bali Hai Motel* (☎ 509-452-7178), 710 N 1st St (if for no other reason than its cool neon); the *Tourist Motor Inn* (☎ 509-452-6551), 1223 N 1st St, or the *Motel 6* (☎ 509-454-0080), 1104 N 1st St. You'll pay slightly more to stay at the *Red Apple Motel* (☎ 509-248-7150), 416 N 1st St, which features an apple-shaped pool and rooms for $43/48. A bit more upscale is the *DoubleTree Hotel* (☎ 509-248-7850, 800-547-8010) at 1507 N 1st St, which caters to business travelers. It has meeting rooms, two pools and airport pickup. Rooms begin at $81.

Stay closer to downtown at the *Yakima Travelodge* (☎ 509-453-7151, 800-578-7878), 110 S Naches Ave, on a quiet side street with rooms for $45/51. Yakima's downtown Convention Center is right next to *Cavanaugh's at Yakima Center* (☎ 509-248-5900, 800-843-4667), 697 E Yakima Ave, which offers rooms for $75/85. Just off I-82 exit 33 is the *Best Western Oxford Inn* (☎ 509-457-4444, 800-521-3050), 1603 Terrace Heights Drive. All rooms have views of the Yakima River and easy access to the Greenway; there are also exercise facilities. Rates are $61/67.

Places to Eat

For a traditional breakfast go to *Mel's Diner* (☎ 509-248-5382), 314 N 1st St. If you just need coffee, go to the *Lincoln Ave Espresso Bar* (☎ 509-576-6086), 1801 W

Lincoln Ave, which offers drive-through service.

Everyone's favorite Mexican restaurant is *Santiago's* (☎ 509-453-1644), 111 E Yakima Ave, where both traditional and specialty dishes are served in a stylish, somewhat boisterous, atmosphere. The *Deli de Pasta* (☎ 509-453-0571), 7 N Front St, is a casual Italian bistro, which lets diners match a variety of fresh pasta with the sauce of their choice – try the creamy lemon linguini. Lunch prices are in the $7 range and full dinners with salad and breadsticks run $15.

Yakima also boasts several restaurants that offer quality local wines and the kind of cuisine and high prices that you might not expect to find east of the Cascades. There's *Gasperetti's Restaurant* (☎ 509-248-0628), 1013 N 1st St, an outstanding northern Italian restaurant with an excellent wine list. Pasta dishes like penne with shrimp and tomato pepper salsa are $12.50; meat dishes like scaloppini alla romana (veal with prosciutto and wine sauce) go for $22. *The Greystone* (☎ 509-248-9801), 5 N Front St, in the historic district, is one of Yakima's original bars converted into a fine restaurant. Three-course dinners start at around $18; the excellent rack of lamb goes for $28.50.

Drive out into the country to find *Birchfield Manor* (☎ 509-452-1960), 2018 Birchfield Rd, east of Yakima off US 24. French-influenced cuisine and an extensive local wine list make this country inn a favorite with serious eaters. Dinner is served Thursday, Friday and Saturday only; reservations are required.

Entertainment

The Northwest boom in microbreweries began in Yakima in 1982, when *Grant's Brewery Pub* (☎ 509-575-2922), 32 N Front St, first released its British-style ales. Since that day, Grant's has remained in the forefront of regional brewing, and has expanded from the former brewery into the old train station across the street. Grant's ales are among the very best of Northwest beers: try the Scottish Ale and the IPA

(India Pale Ale). There's also a light menu with sandwiches and homemade soups.

First-run films are shown at the *Yakima Cinema* (☎ 509-248-0234), 1305 N 16th Ave, and the *Mercy 6-Plex* (☎ 509-248-0242), Valley Mall Blvd in Union Gap.

The Yakima Bears (☎ 509-457-5151) are a class-A baseball team. Games are played at the Central Washington Fairgrounds. The Yakima Sun Kings basketball club (☎ 509-248-1222) is a CBA team and plays in the SunDome, 1301 S Fair Ave, at the fairgrounds.

Shopping

Washington's Fruit Place Visitors Center (☎ 509-576-3090), 105 S 18th St, on the river at I-82 exit 33 has one-stop shopping for apple-shaped gifts and souvenirs.

If you're beginning to like the looks of those pearl-snap shirts and Wranglers jeans, head to Western Outfitters (☎ 509-248-5400), 601 W Yakima Ave, a large western clothing store. You'll find everything from cowboy hats to cattle prods.

Ouch Cactus Greenhouse (☎ 509-877-4740), 375 Parker Bridge Rd, just south of Yakima in Wapato, is a collector's outlet for cactus, succulents, bonsai trees and carnivorous plants. The cactus selection is enormous, as are some of the individual plants. The owners' personal display of live scorpions, poisonous snakes and alligators sets the ambiance.

If you don't have time to make the rounds of Yakima Valley wineries, head to The Wine Cellar (☎ 509-248-3590), 25 N Front St in the old opera house. A number of local wines are usually available for sampling and can be packed for shipping.

Getting There & Away

Commercial flights operate out of Yakima Air Terminal (☎ 509-575-6149), 2300 W Washington Ave. Horizon Air and United Express both fly between Seattle and Yakima for about $65 one way.

The Greyhound bus station (☎ 509-457-5131) is at 602 E Yakima Ave at the corner of 6th St. A trip to Seattle costs $21 one-way. Other buses continue on to Portland,

Bend, The Tri-Cities, Walla Walla and Spokane.

Rentals are available from Enterprise (☎ 509-248-2170), 312 W Nob Hill Blvd, or U-Save Auto Rental (☎ 509-452-5555) at 1117 W Lincoln Ave.

Getting Around

Yakima Transit (☎ 509-575-6175) runs Monday to Saturday, until around 6:30 pm. The transit center is on the corner of S 4th St and E Chestnut Ave. Adult fare is 50¢; exact change required. Bus No 9 runs hourly and half-hourly down S 1st St on its way to the airport.

If you're after a taxi, call Diamond Cab at ☎ 509-453-3113.

YAKIMA VALLEY WINE COUNTRY

Directly south of Yakima, the Yakima River passes through a narrow gap in the hills before coursing out into the wide, amazingly fertile lower Yakima Valley. Apples, hops, vegetables and grapes are everywhere. Stop by roadside stands or wineries to sample the local bounty.

There are nearly 25 long-established wineries between Yakima and Benton City. Most have tasting rooms with a full array of local wines and gift packages. I-82 stretches southeast from Yakima to the Tri-Cities to connect a number of small wine-making communities; Zillah is 24 miles east of Yakima, and Sunnyside is 36. Prosser is 49 miles east of Yakima, or 25 miles west of Richland. The Yakima Valley Hwy (old US 12), also called Wine Country Rd, parallels the freeway for most of the way, providing a pastoral alternative to I-82. For a free map and guide to all the wineries in the valley, send a stamped, self-addressed envelope to the Yakima Valley Wine Growers Association, PO Box 39, Grandview, WA 98930.

Wineries

There are a couple of wineries in Zillah worth visiting. **Bonair Winery** (☎ 509-829-6027), 500 S Bonair Rd, is open for tasting 10 am to 5 pm daily, and 10 am to 4:30 pm weekends only during the winter.

The cabernet is notable. You can picnic in the gazebo.

The second, **Covey Run** (☎ 509-829-6235), 1500 Vintage Rd, opens from 10 am to 5 pm Monday to Saturday, and noon to 5 pm Sunday from April 1 to November 30; it's open from 11 am to 4:30 pm Monday to Saturday, and from noon to 4:30 pm Sunday the rest of the year. Covey Run has a lovely tasting room and is a popular wedding location. As far as the wine goes, stick with the Semillon.

Stewart Vineyards (☎ 509-854-1882) at 1711 Cherry Hill Rd in the town of Granger, is one of the best in the Yakima Valley; just about everything is good here, even the Riesling. Tasting room hours are 10 am to 5 pm Monday to Saturday, and noon to 5 pm on Sunday.

One of the most noted Washington wineries, especially for its cabernet, is **The Hogue Cellars** (☎ 509-786-4557), Wine Country Rd in Prosser, which also makes one of the best chardonnays east of the Cascades. Their tasting room hours are 10 am to 5 pm daily. **Chinook Wines** (☎ 509-786-2725), also in Prosser on Wine Country Rd, is a small-scale winery known for producing the state's finest sauvignon blanc. Drop by their tasting room noon to 5 pm, Friday to Sunday.

The **Yakima River Winery** (☎ 509-786-2805), 143302 N River Rd, is 1½ miles west on N River Rd, right off Wine Country Rd in Prosser. The tasting room is open 10 am to 5 pm daily during the summer. Ask to try John's Port and the Lemberger, an otherwise obscure red varietal that likes the heat of central Washington. A final choice for the Prosser area is **Hinzerling Winery** (☎ 509-786-2163) at 1520 Sheridan Rd. It has picnic facilities and is open for tasting 11 am to 5 pm Monday to Saturday, and 11 am to 4 pm Sunday, from March to Christmas Eve. The cabernet from Hinzerling is about as good as Washington red wine gets.

Shopping

It goes without saying that you'll probably want to pick up a few bottles of wine. But for the unlikely, go to the Hangups Gallery (☎ 509-786-1149), 719 6th St, in Prosser. It features contemporary art, watercolor, mixed media, basket weaving and Japanese washi designs, though the work of a WSU Emeritus Professor of Entomology, who incorporates dead bugs into his glass-on-metal enamel jewelry, belt buckles and sculptures might be just the souvenir you have been looking for.

YAKAMA INDIAN RESERVATION

The Yakima Valley is also home to the Yakama Indian Reservation, Washington state's largest. Sixteen miles south of Yakima at Toppenish (population 8748), the primary town on the reservation, the Yakamas have built a pleasant interpretive center that seeks to explain and demonstrate the tribes' ancient cultural traditions. At Fort Simcoe there are the remains of an army outpost constructed in 1856 to quash Yakama Indian resistance to life on the reservation.

Toppenish is also doing its best to make itself a tourist destination on the basis of its historic murals. The Toppenish Chamber of Commerce (☎ 509-865-3262) can be contacted at PO Box 28, Toppenish, WA 98948.

Downtown Murals

Most buildings in downtown Toppenish are now covered with a variety of large murals, depicting some event or episode from Yakama or Northwest history. Several contain clever visual tricks. On the first weekend of June is the Mural-in-a-Day Festival, during which a group of painters work together to complete a mural in an eight-hour period.

However, given that the city appears dedicated to covering every available surface with a mural, visitors on *any* day

Yakama Indians

The Yakama Indians were one of the most populous and powerful of the inland plateau tribes. Their subsistence depended on the Yakima River, a major salmon fishery. Although the Yakamas were among the first Native Americans in the Northwest to have horses, they didn't use them extensively for hunting, and preferred fishing to hunting big game.

The Yakamas were among the natives that met Lewis and Clark at Celilo Falls in 1805, and were also among the 14 tribes that signed an 1855 treaty creating the Yakama Reservations. These tribes, which also included Klickatats and Wenatchees, went on to form the Yakama Nation.

However, the treaty was not ratified by the US Congress, and white settlers and miners continued to stream across the Yakama homelands. Conflicts between the Yakamas and the army escalated. In late 1855, the so-called Yakima War began, which involved Yakama attacks on settlements in the Columbia River Gorge and reprisals by Federal troops and Willamette Valley volunteers. The Yakamas were consigned to US Federal control after the army defeated a war party in a key battle at Union Gap in 1856. Fort Simcoe was established to maintain control over the reservation.

The Indian Agent responsible for the Yakamas throughout much of the later 1800s was a Methodist preacher who was a strong advocate of turning the Yakamas from fishers into farmers. Thus, a major fishing area on the Yakima River was sold out from the reservation and the money was used to establish the reservation's first irrigation canal. After the reservation was allotted to individual Yakamas in homestead-sized units, according to the Dawes Act, much of the most fertile and easily irrigated land passed into the hands of white farmers. ■

during the summer months can usually find a painter in action. Get information on murals in progress from the Toppenish Mural Society's visitors' center (☎ 509-865-6515) at 11A S Toppenish Ave.

Yakama Indian Nation Cultural Center

At this 12,000-sq-foot interpretive center and museum (☎ 509-865-2800), displays, dioramas and audio-visual exhibits explain the traditions and culture of the Yakama people. The museum focuses on the challenge of Spilyay, the trickster coyote whose legends taught the Yakama how to understand and interact harmoniously with nature. Most of the displays detail the seasonal and daily life of the tribe, from fishing at Celilo Falls to a re-creation of a tule mat longhouse. The usual collections of arrowheads and tools aren't much in evidence here. Instead, the dioramas and exhibits, with their accompanying music and sound effects, are meant to evoke a mood or impression of traditional life and spirituality.

The center also houses collections of traditional basketry, as well as a theater, gift shop, ceremonial longhouse, library and restaurant. The cultural center is at 280 Buster Rd, immediately north of Toppenish on US 97; it is designed to look like a traditional teepee, so you can't miss it. The center is open 9 am to 5 pm daily; adults/seniors $4/2, children $1.

Toppenish Museum

If you want to see the kinds of Native American artifacts that are largely absent from the tribe's cultural center, go to the Toppenish Museum (☎ 509-865-4510) on the 2nd floor of the public library at S Elm and Washington Ave. The high point of this community museum is the Estell Reel Meyer Indian Artifact Collection. Ms Meyer was one of the first women ever to be employed by the Federal government, and as Federal Superintendent of Indian Affairs from 1898 to 1910 she collected native crafts and artifacts in her travels. The museum is open 1 to 4:30 pm,

Monday to Thursday, and 2 to 4:30 pm Friday; admission is $1.50/50¢ adults/children.

American Hop Museum

This museum (☎ 509-865-4677) pays tribute to the fact that 75% of the US hops crop is grown in the Yakima Valley. The museum's focus is on hop-growing, from the 1600's to the present. It's in the restored Hop Growers Supply building at 22 S B St in Toppenish, and is open 10 am to 3 pm, Wednesday to Sunday.

Fort Simcoe State Park

The site of Fort Simcoe long served as a camp for the Yakamas, who stopped at the natural springs here on their way to their fishing camps at Celilo Falls. After the Yakama War, the army built this fort at the springs in order to keep the peace and to settle ongoing treaty violations. At its peak, Fort Simcoe consisted of officers' quarters, a blockhouse, an enclosing stockade and an enlisted mens' barracks. After the treaty creating the Yakama Reservation was ratified in 1859, Fort Simcoe was decommissioned and used as a boarding school for Native American children until 1923.

Today, Fort Simcoe State Park (☎ 509-874-2372) takes in 200 acres of the old fort grounds. The blockhouse and barracks have been rebuilt, and the original white clapboard officers' quarters have been restored and opened for tours. The old Indian Agency building is now an interpretive center that retells the story of the fort and the wars.

Almost as striking as the old fort buildings is the surprising midsummer green of the grounds and the ample shade from old oak trees. It's no wonder that both the Yakamas and the army coveted this oasis in the midst of scorched desert hills. The state park is understandably a popular place for summer picnics, with the grounds open from April through September. Fort Simcoe is 27 miles west of Toppenish, at the end of Hwy 220.

Special Events

The first weekend in June is the big Mural-in-a-Day Festival, when you can watch western artists paint like mad to complete a same-day work of art.

The Yakama Nation Cultural Powwow & Rodeo is held in Toppenish around the Fourth of July, and is the Yakama tribe's largest celebration. The four-day festival includes dancing, a parade and an 'Indian Village' with teepees, Indian food booths and stick games. For rodeo tickets contact ☎ 509-865-5315.

Places to Stay & Eat

The Yakama Tribes operate the *Yakama Nation RV Resort* (☎ 509-865-2000, 800-874-3087) adjacent to the Cultural Center at 280 Buster Rd, north of Toppenish. In addition to RV hookups ($18), there is a separate tent area and teepees for rent ($30). Facilities include a swimming pool, laundry, showers and playground.

Toppenish offers the usual kind of roadside motels. Try the *Oxbow Motor Inn* (☎ 509-865-5800, 888-865-5855), 511 S Elm St, with its own mural! Singles/doubles are $37/39. At the junction of US 97 and US 22, the *Toppenish Inn* (☎ 509-865-7444, 800-222-3161), 515 S Elm St, offers free continental breakfast, a pool and newer rooms for $53/61.

If you find yourself hungry in this part of the valley, do as the locals do and eat Mexican. There are good, inexpensive places to eat at just about every junction. In Toppenish, there's *Los Murales Restaurant* (☎ 509-865-7555), 202 W 1st Ave. For muffins and espresso drop by *La Hacienda Gardens* (☎ 509-865-1992), 207 S Toppenish Ave. Another good Mexican place is *El Ranchito* (☎ 509-829-5880), 1319 1st Ave, a tortilla factory and restaurant off I-82 exit 54 in Zillah.

Getting There & Away

Greyhound buses connect all the stops along the Yakima Valley between Yakima and The Tri-Cities. In Toppenish the bus stops at Branding Iron Restaurant at 61311 US 97.

Northeastern Washington

Northeastern Washington's mountains – the Kettle River and Selkirk Ranges – are the far western foothills of the Rockies. Ground down by several successive waves of glaciers, these forested slopes are now more rolling hills than jagged peaks. The Columbia River winds south through these mountains, widening into Lake Roosevelt as it turns west and backs up behind the Grand Coulee Dam. The Columbia then turns south again before its final journey to the sea, and the river here marks the northern boundary of the central Washington steppe. South of the Columbia, the land is flat and dry – the immense, lonesome geography of the mythic West.

Northeastern Washington lacks the developed recreation that's abundant in the western part of the state, but there are many good places to hike, fish and cross-country ski, especially in the Okanogan and Colville National Forests. The rugged, dramatic landscape of the Columbia Basin, scoured by ice-age floods, provides a suitably dramatic setting for the Grand Coulee Dam, one of the world's largest producers of hydroelectric power and a towering structure. Lake Roosevelt is a popular vacation spot for boating and fishing. Spokane is the best place to begin exploring these regions – it's the largest city for many a dry mile and a shopping mecca for the smaller communities of the Inland Northwest. It is also the only place where you have a chance of seeing the opera or eating a good Thai meal.

In terms of weather, the Cascades take the brunt of Pacific storms, which is why the land to the east receives so little rainfall. But at the state's northeastern edge, the Selkirks catch storms anew, receiving up to 80 inches of precipitation a year and creating an undeniable winter. Spokane misses the heavy rain and snow that falls in the nearby mountains, but it still gets its fair share.

History

Originally, Native Americans lived mainly around the Columbia River and its tributaries. Places like Kettle Falls and Spokane Falls were especially good spots for salmon fishing, and communities grew up around them. David Thompson, a Canadian explorer and fur trader, was the first white person to navigate the entire length of the Columbia River, and his reports and his excellent maps of the Inland Northwest laid the way for more fur traders.

Eventually, the Native American tribes were confined to the Colville and Spokane reservations. These reservations were large at first, but disease decimated the native populations and European settlers took back more of the land as mineral resources – especially gold – were found in the remote hills to the north. Life was pretty rugged, even after the Northern Pacific Railroad came through in 1881, spurring Spokane's growth. It wasn't until the Columbia Basin Irrigation Project in the 1930s, whose centerpiece was the building of the Grand Coulee Dam, that life began to change significantly. The irrigation project turned the nearby desert into wheat fields, and the electricity these dams produced helped support Washington's post-WWII industrial boom.

Orientation

US 2 runs across the southern edge of northeastern Washington, and it's roughly paralleled by Hwy 20 to the north. Bicycle tourists use Hwy 20 pretty heavily in the summer; it's part of a coast-to-coast route across the northern tier of the USA.

US 97 courses down the Okanogan Valley and joins up with the Columbia River near Brewster and the Chief Joseph Dam. Even more remote, Hwy 21 cuts north-south through the Colville Indian Reservation between US 2 at Wilbur and the Canadian border.

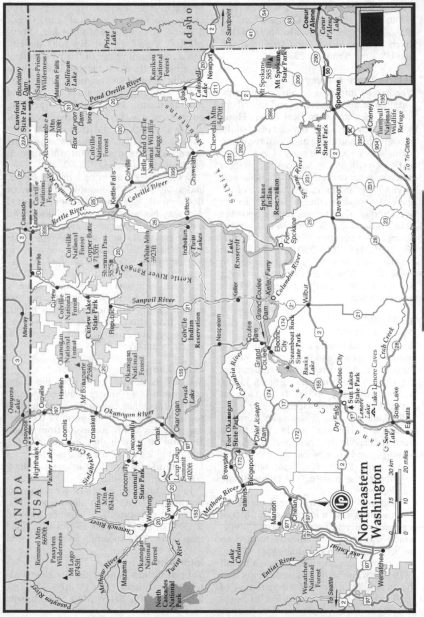

Northeastern Washington

From Spokane, take US 2 west to Hwy 174 to get to the Grand Coulee Dam. US 395 north traces the Kettle and Colville Rivers. To get to the Pend Oreille River, take US 2 north to Hwy 20. ·

Getting There & Away
Whether by air, train or bus, most transportation heads to Spokane, and from there you can pick up other local buses. However, Amtrak's *Empire Builder* only slinks through Spokane in the middle of the night.

Bus service to these parts is essentially tied to Greyhound, who contracts with a bunch of local carriers to supplement their service. The result is a confusing mishmash of companies that all sell tickets for one another. Greyhound serves Spokane from Portland and Seattle and a few other places. Northwestern Trailways (☎ 509-838-5626, 800-366-3830 in Washington) has the same service, plus service east to Boise. Borderline Stage (☎ 509-624-7192) has service to Colville and Kettle Falls from Spokane.

SPOKANE
Population 375,000
Spokane is the largest city between Seattle and Minneapolis, and it is the trade center for the Inland Northwest, an area comprising eastern Washington, northern Idaho, western Montana and parts of Oregon, British Columbia and Alberta.

Spokan Indians, whose name means 'children of the sun,' settled and fished from Spokane Falls. They spoke a Salishan language, and after procuring horses, they crossed the Rockies to hunt with their neighbors, the Kalispels, Flatheads and Nez Perce.

Though Spokane was the location of Washington's first trading post in 1810, it was eventually replaced by Fort Colvile, which was more conveniently located on the Columbia River. Indian wars slowed the region's development; it wasn't until 1879 that white settlers staked claims near the falls. The town had a population of 1000 in 1881, when Northern Pacific began building a transcontinental rail line through Spokane. After the discovery of gold and other precious metals around Coeur d'Alene, ID, in the 1880s, Spokane flourished as a gold capital. By 1883 the city was a major rail center of the West, served by several transcontinental lines which brought thousands of new immigrants eager for fresh opportunities in trade and manufacturing. In 1889, the burgeoning business area was destroyed by fire. A tent city was quickly constructed, and merchants continued operations while the downtown area was rebuilt, this time in brick rather than wood.

Spokane grew up to be a market center, and today the city is inordinately proud of its skywalk, an above-ground, covered walkway between a number of downtown buildings and department stores. Gigantic shopping malls and strip developments govern activities on the north side of town. But despite this kind of commercial success, Spokane fails to exude any of the prosperity that was so abundant in its early history. The downtown area in particular appears sadly afflicted by urban blight. Aside from shopping, Spokane also offers a few popular golf courses and several large city parks.

Orientation
Spokane is just 18 miles from the Idaho border and is 110 miles south of Canada. I-90 is the main east-west route through town; Sprague Ave, just north of the freeway, divides north addresses from south. Division St is the main north-south street, and it divides east from west and becomes US 2 north of town. It's a long, nasty drag, but often unavoidable.

In general, avenues run east-west, streets north-south. The main downtown area, including the skywalk, is between I-90 and Riverfront Park. Be sure to pick up a good map if you'll be spending some time here.

Information
Tourist Office Stop by the Spokane Visitors Information Center (☎ 509-747-3230, 800-248-3230), 201 W Main St at Browne St, for a raft of information.

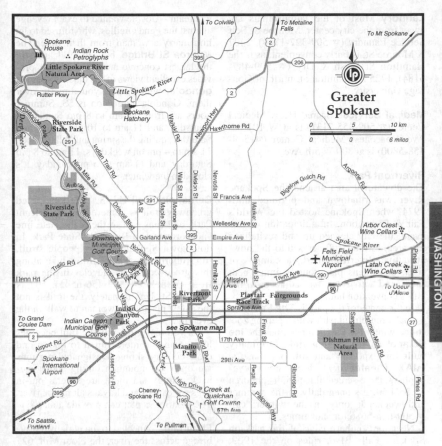

Money The American Express outlet at House of Travel, (☎ 509-467-5535), 1322 N Monroe St, can exchange foreign currency.

Post The main post office (☎ 509-459-0274) is at 703 E Trent Ave, although the location at 904 W Riverside Ave is more convenient to downtown.

Bookstores Auntie's Bookstore (☎ 509-838-0206), 402 W Main Ave, is northeastern Washington's best bookstore. It's large, with a good mix of regional titles and a nice cafe. Readings and other events are scheduled several times a week (Spo-

kane native Sherman Alexie, who reads here from time to time, is a don't-miss).

For a great selection of national park maps and travel books, Northwest Map & Travel Books (☎ 509-455-6981), 525 W Sprague Ave, is the place to go. The American Institute of Architects runs the AIA Bookstore (☎ 509-747-5498) at 335 W Sprague Ave. It's only open 10 am to 2 pm on weekdays.

Media The *Spokesman-Review* is the local daily newspaper, and the *Inlander*, a free weekly, covers the arts. The public radio station is at 91.1 FM.

Laundry Most of the laundromats are away from the city center. Monroe St Self Service Laundry (☎ 509-327-1769), 2407 N Monroe St, is fairly convenient, as is the Hamilton St Wash & Dry (☎ 509-487-6184), 1725 N Hamilton St, north of Gonzaga University.

Medical Services Sacred Heart Medical Center (☎ 509-455-3131) is at W 101 8th Ave. Deaconess Medical Center (☎ 509-458-5800) is at 800 W 5th Ave.

Riverfront Park

The downtown area around the Spokane River was rundown and polluted until 1974, when Spokane hosted the World's Fair & Exposition. In anticipation of that event, the city cleaned up and revitalized the area, turning 100 acres into the now-attractive Riverfront Park, a campus of riverside gardens, playgrounds, amusement rides, and activity centers adjacent to the city's convention hall.

In the center of the park is **The Pavilion**, a small amusement park with a petting zoo. In the winter the Pavilion becomes the **Ice Palace**, an ice skating rink. Originally built for Expo '74 and still popular, the **IMAX Theater** next door shows eye-popping, large-screen films; adults/children $5.25/4.50. It's open daily in the summer and weekends only in the winter; call ☎ 509-625-6686 for showtimes.

Near the southern edge of the park on Spokane Falls Blvd, rides on the 1909, hand-carved **carousel**, built with painstaking care by Charles Looff, are less of a thrill but still fun at any age. West of here at Post St, statues of runners pay playful tribute to the Bloomsday race runners. Pavilion rides and other activities are all charged separately, or you can get a comprehensive day pass for around $10; call the park (☎ 509-456-4386 or 800-336-7275) for all information on park activities.

Spokane Falls This is a good place to relax or to start exploring. Indian legend says that the multi-tiered falls were created by Coyote in order to keep salmon from swimming

upstream – Coyote wanted to exact revenge against the Pend Oreilles, who refused to let him marry a woman from their tribe. The **Monroe St Bridge**, built in 1911 and still the largest concrete arch in the USA, provides excellent views of the falls, as does the **gondola**, which takes you directly over them. Gondola admission is $3. Summer hours are from 11 am to 8 pm Sunday to Thursday, and 11 am to 10 pm Friday and Saturday; during the spring and fall it's open 11 am to 4 pm on weekdays, 11 am to 8 pm Saturday, and 11 am to 5 pm Sunday. It's closed in the winter.

Centennial Trail This 39-mile-long paved greenway trail is centered on Riverfront Park, and runs east to the Idaho state line and northwest to Riverside State Park. In downtown Spokane, many people stroll, run, rollerblade, skateboard or bike along this greenway. Rent bicycles in the park from Quinn's (☎ 509-456-6545), 507 N Howard St. Unfortunately, the trail is not the safest place for a woman to walk in the evening.

As you leave the city, the trail becomes less urban and more suited to hiking and cross-country skiing. Designated portions are open for mountain biking and horseback riding, and there are several put-in sites for canoes and kayaks along the river. The visitors' center can provide a map.

Flour Mill Connected to the park by a footbridge across the river, the Flour Mill, 621 W Mallon Ave, was built in 1890 as the region's most modern mill. Remodeled in 1973, the mill now houses shops and restaurants.

Gonzaga University

Founded in 1887 by the Jesuit Order, Gonzaga University has a reputation as one of the West Coast's top liberal arts institutions. Over 5000 students attend this privately-run Catholic university, which has a law and graduate school in addition to a full plate of undergraduate programs. Gonzaga's most famous alumni, Bing Crosby, donated a comprehensive collection of his recordings and a good deal of memorabilia to his alma mater. You'll find much of it on display in the **Bing Crosby Memorabilia Room** (☎ 509-328-4220 ext 4297), 502 E Boone Ave, in the university's Crosby Student Center, where a bronze statue of the famous crooner stands out front. It's open 8:30 am to 4:30 pm daily during the school year, and on weekdays during the summer.

The **Jundt Art Center & Museum** (☎ 509-328-4220 ext 3211), at the end of Pearl St, includes a surprisingly good collection of classical sculpture and painting. There are also substantial works of art glass by Dale Chihuly, who produced a startling installation for the center – an 18-foot chandelier comprised of 800 snakey, red glass shapes.

Gonzaga sits on the north bank of the Spokane River across from downtown, and is easily reached by turning east onto Boone Ave, from either Division or Ruby Sts.

Cheney Cowles Museum

The Eastern Washington State Historical Society runs the well-curated Cheney Cowles Museum (☎ 509-456-3931), 2316 W 1st Ave, which features regional history and rotating art exhibits. Hours are 10 am to 5 pm Tuesday to Saturday, and 1 to 5 pm on Sunday. On Wednesday the museum stays open until 10 pm with free admission during the evening and half price admission during the afternoon. Admission at all other times is adults/seniors $4/3, children $2.50. The price includes admission to the 1898 **Campbell House** next door – the Tudor-style estate of mining tycoon Amasa Campbell, which was built during Spokane's 'Age of Elegance.'

Manito Park

Located in the South Hill neighborhood, half a dozen different flower gardens, a small wading pool and a conservatory make Manito Park (☎ 509-625-6622) a good place to relax for a couple of hours. There are a number of formal gardens, a lilac garden, rose garden, perennial garden

and a peaceful Japanese garden with a pond. To reach the park from downtown, take Stevens St south (which turns into Bernard St) to 21st Ave, then take a left to reach the park entrance. Bus Nos 34 or 33 will also get you there.

Riverside State Park

Six miles northwest of town on the Spokane River is Riverside State Park (☎ 509-456-3964). The highlight of the nearly 12-sq-mile park is the **Centennial Trail**, which stretches 39 miles from Spokane House at the northern edge of Riverside Park, through downtown Spokane and on to the Idaho state line. Many people hike and bike this trail, and it has numerous put-in spots for canoes or kayaks. There are also other hiking and equestrian trails here; contact Trailtown Riding Stables (☎ 509-456-8249), for **horseback riding**. Highlights in the southern end of the park near the campground include the **Bowl & Pitcher**, a deep gorge with huge boulders, and **fossil beds** on the west side of the river near Deep Creek.

At the northern edge of the park, find **petroglyphs** on Indian Rock close to where the Little Spokane River flows into the Spokane. Nearby, there's the **Spokane House Interpretive Center**, at the site where fur trader David Thompson of the North West Company built a trading post in 1810. Today there are few traces of the trading post, and even the interpretive center has trouble staying open due to lack of funds. It's open summer weekends most years.

Little Spokane River Natural Area At the north end of Riverside State Park, a 6-mile trail for hikers or cross-country skiers runs along the exceptionally peaceful Little Spokane River, between the Spokane Hatchery (on Waikiki Rd) and the mouth of the river. This is also a good place to canoe (put in by the hatchery). Great blue herons nest here, and bald eagles commonly winter at the river's mouth.

To reach the park, head west and then north on Hwy 291 (called Francis Ave in

WASHINGTON

WASHINGTON

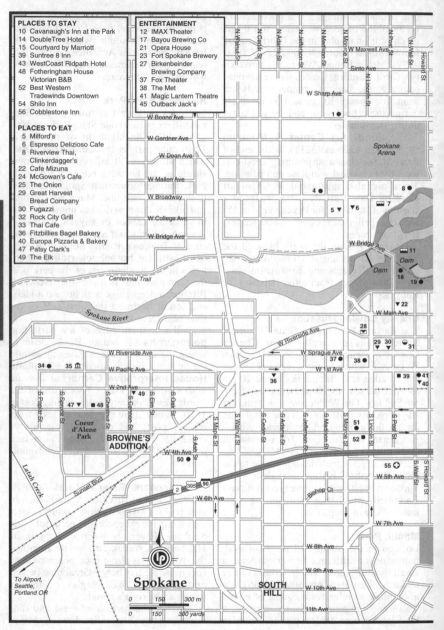

PLACES TO STAY
10 Cavanaugh's Inn at the Park
14 DoubleTree Hotel
15 Courtyard by Marriott
39 Suntree 8 Inn
43 WestCoast Ridpath Hotel
48 Fotheringham House
   Victorian B&B
52 Best Western
   Tradewinds Downtown
54 Shilo Inn
56 Cobblestone Inn

PLACES TO EAT
5 Milford's
6 Espresso Delizioso Cafe
8 Riverview Thai,
   Clinkerdagger's
22 Cafe Mizuna
24 McGowan's Cafe
25 The Onion
29 Great Harvest
   Bread Company
30 Fugazzi
32 Rock City Grill
33 Thai Cafe
36 Fitzbillies Bagel Bakery
47 Europa Pizzaria & Bakery
49 Patsy Clark's
49 The Elk

ENTERTAINMENT
12 IMAX Theater
17 Bayou Brewing Co
21 Opera House
23 Fort Spokane Brewery
27 Birkenbeinder
   Brewing Company
37 Fox Theater
38 The Met
41 Magic Lantern Theatre
45 Outback Jack's

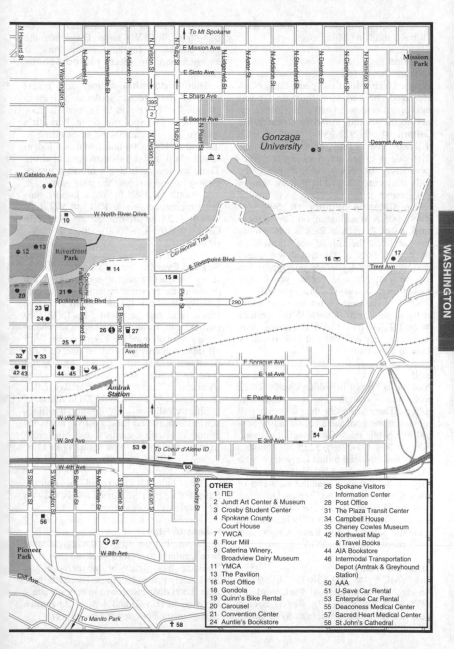

OTHER
1 REI
2 Jundt Art Center & Museum
3 Crosby Student Center
4 Spokane County
   Court House
7 YWCA
8 Flour Mill
9 Caterina Winery,
   Broadview Dairy Museum
11 YMCA
13 The Pavilion
16 Post Office
18 Gondola
19 Quinn's Bike Rental
20 Carousel
21 Convention Center
24 Auntie's Bookstore

26 Spokane Visitors
   Information Center
28 Post Office
31 The Plaza Transit Center
34 Campbell House
35 Cheney Cowles Museum
42 Northwest Map
   & Travel Books
44 AIA Bookstore
46 Intermodal Transportation
   Depot (Amtrak & Greyhound
   Station)
50 AAA
51 U-Save Car Rental
53 Enterprise Car Rental
55 Deaconess Medical Center
57 Sacred Heart Medical Center
58 St John's Cathedral

town) which passes park entrances at Rifle Club Rd and Nine Mile Falls.

Wineries

Spokane has a few wineries, which are mostly notable for their good merlots. A life-sized checkerboard, fountains, pools and formal gardens impart a sense of fairyland to the grounds at **Arbor Crest Wine Cellars** (☎ 509-927-9894), 4705 N Fruit Hill Rd. The tasting room, housed in a cliff-side mansion overlooking the Spokane River, is open noon to 5 pm daily. Only adults are allowed to visit the winery and grounds.

The **Caterina Winery** (☎ 509-328-5069), 905 N Washington, on the northern outskirts of Riverfront Park is one winery you *can* bring the kids to – it's housed on the bottom floor of the Broadview Dairy Museum. Their Cabernet sauvignon has received attention in recent years. The tasting room is open noon to 5 pm daily.

Riesling and chardonnay are good wines to try at the **Latah Creek Wine Cellars** (☎ 509-926-0164), 13030 E Indiana Ave, east of the city off I-90 exit 289. It's open 9 am to 5 pm daily.

Golf

Spokane is known in golfing circles for its profusion of courses and its enthusiastic golfers. There are more than a dozen golf courses in the Spokane area, including several fine public ones. Gently rolling Downriver (☎ 509-327-5269), 3225 N Columbia Circle, and top-rated Indian Canyon (☎ 509-747-5353), 4304 W West Drive, are both hilly, 18-hole courses near the west end of town. South of town, The Creek at Qualchan (☎ 448-9317), 301 E Meadow Lane Rd (I-90 exit 279), is a challenging 18-hole course in a natural setting along Latah Creek, and was a recent stop on the PGA golf tour.

Other Activities

The YMCA (☎ 509-838-3577), 507 N Howard St, in Riverfront Park, and the YWCA (☎ 509-326-1190), 829 W Broadway, just across the river, both have indoor **swimming** pools.

Indian Canyon Riding Stables (☎ 509-624-4646), 4812 W Canyon Drive, near the golf course at Indian Canyon Park, is another popular place for **horseback riding**.

There's **downhill skiing** sans resort hype at the Mount Spokane Ski Area (☎ 509-238-6281), on 5878-foot Mt Spokane near Mt Spokane State Park. It's located 31 miles northeast of Spokane at the end of Hwy 206 and features a lodge, rental shop and 2100-foot vertical drop. There are several trails for **cross-country skiing** in, and just past the state park.

To outfit yourself for more intense outdoor recreation, go to REI (☎ 509-328-9900), 1125 N Monroe St, or Mountain Gear (☎ 509-325-9000), 2002 N Division St.

Special Events

If Spokane is famous for any one thing, it's probably the Bloomsday Run (held the first Sunday in May). It's the world's biggest timed road race, attracting up to 60,000 participants. Runners, walkers and wheelchair racers all trace the 12km course. With all these athletes gathered in one spot it's no surprise that there's a big fitness and running trade show held the same weekend. Contact the Bloomsday Lilac Association (☎ 509-838-1579) to register.

Shortly following Bloomsday, the lilacs start blooming and Lilac Festival activities commence with a carnival and big torchlight parade on the third Saturday in May. To see the lilacs, visit Manito Park's Lilac Garden.

The St Patrick's Day parade, held on the Saturday nearest St Patrick's Day (March 17), is also a big deal here.

Places to Stay

Since people from all over the region come here regularly to spend a weekend shopping, Spokane has plenty of inexpensive and moderately priced lodgings. There are three main hotel districts: downtown, north along Division St (US 2) and west of downtown along Sunset Blvd (toward the airport).

Spokane's 'Age of Elegance'

In 1889, a pork-grease fire gutted Spokane's burgeoning downtown business core. Having spent a relatively subdued decade as a booming gold capital and trade center, the city catapulted itself out of the ashes with new architectural aspirations, launching into a building frenzy. Mineral fortunes contributed to the extravagance, and mining tycoons spared no expense in hiring the region's best architect, Kirkland K Cutter, to build their stately mansions. Cutter designed many such houses for Browne's Addition, a now-historic neighborhood of showplace homes.

The explosion of lavish public buildings continued through the 1890s as Spokane sought to establish new institutions of culture and refinement. An economic depression in 1893 took some of the wind out of the reconstruction, but the movement was refueled in the early-1900s with a 'City Beautiful' campaign to construct civic buildings and monuments.

Gothic, Renaissance, Arts & Crafts, Neoclassical and Art Deco are just a few of the styles represented around town. The following are the most prominent examples of Spokane's architectural legacy:

Patrick Clark Mansion Spokane's most famous mansion, at 2208 W 2nd Ave, was built for mining magnate Patrick D. Clark and is now Patsy Clark's, a fancy restaurant. To reach it, head west from downtown on Riverside Ave or W 2nd Ave for about half a mile to the historic Browne's Addition neighborhood. Clark commissioned Kirkland K. Cutter to design the home, and even sent him abroad to gain inspiration from European architecture. Anyone can stop by to admire to Moorish-influenced exterior. However, you'll need a dinner reservation to get a glimpse of the onyx fireplaces inside.

Across the street is **Coeur d'Alene Park**, a pleasant park that was once the destination of many Sunday outings. Today there's a wading pool and plenty of swings for kids.

Campbell House This Tudor-style estate of mining tycoon Amasa Campbell was also built in Browne's Addition during Spokane's 'Age of Elegance.' Admission to the 1898 Campbell House, 2316 W First Ave, is included in the price of a ticket to the adjacent Cheney Cowles Museum.

Spokane County Court House North of downtown, at W Broadway and N Madison St, the Spokane County Court House is almost an apparition. Built in the 1890s by a self-trained architect, the French Renaissance structure was inspired by the chateaus at Chambord and Azay-le-Rideau in France's Loire Valley.

St John's Cathedral The stunning and ornate St John's Cathedral (☎ 509-838-4277), 127 E 12th Ave, built in 1927, is a classic example of English Gothic architecture. Free cathedral tours are given from noon to 3 pm daily except Wednesday and Friday. Follow Stevens St south of downtown to get there. ■

Camping *Riverside State Park* (☎ 509-456-3964), 6 miles northwest of Spokane off Hwy 291, has 101 sites (no hookups) and hot showers for $12 a night. This is a pleasant place to stay and remarkably convenient to downtown Spokane.

Spokane's premier RV park, *Yogi Bear's Camping Resort* (☎ 509-747-9415, 800-494-7275), 7520 S Thomas Mallen Rd, at I-90 exit 272 has pleasant wooded sites for

$23, and is adjacent to a golf course and hiking trails. Sites are the same price at the *KOA of Spokane* (☎ 509-924-4722), 3025 N Barker Rd, located 13 miles east of Spokane off I-90 exit 293.

B&Bs In Browne's Addition, *Fotheringham House Victorian B&B* (☎ 509-838-1891), 2128 W 2nd Ave, dates from 1891 and retains many period touches. Rooms

WASHINGTON

David Thompson – Early Explorer

Meriwether Lewis and William Clark, who began their much-heralded two-year expedition of the Columbia River in 1804, have received most of the glory for exploring the Pacific Northwest. But even before Lewis and Clark came to the Northwest, there was the Canadian explorer and fur trader David Thompson, who is something of a cult hero to Northwest and Canadian historians and 'buckskinners.' The first explorer to paddle the Columbia River in its entirety (and the first white person that many Inland Northwest Native Americans had ever met), Thompson traversed the wilderness for 27 years, and never killed anybody nor lost anyone in his party to accident or attack. Employed by the North West Company as a fur trader, Thompson was an intellectual man who treated the Native Americans he met and the land itself with respect and dignity.

Thompson first crossed the Rockies in the early 1800s, setting up a trading post, the Kootenae House, at the Columbia's headwaters in Canada. In 1810, along with Jaco Findley and Finan McDonald, he established the Spokane House on the Spokane River, the first trading post in present-day Washington. It was preceded in the Northwest only by the Pacific Fur Company in Astoria, OR. Every year Thompson made an incredible 3000-mile journey by canoe, horseback and foot from Kootenae House to Lake Superior with the six tons or so of furs he had collected.

But few people would even know or care much about Thompson if he hadn't been such a good writer, map-maker and surveyor. He made sense of an extremely confusing and difficult terrain, paving the way for other trappers, and he was the first person to document certain plants and animals. Thompson also took the time to meet and get to know the native tribes, recording some of their rituals and practices in detail. Other trappers and explorers traversed this region, but none did so with as much skill and attention.

Eventually, the Hudson's Bay Company took control of the Northwest, and the Spokane House was mothballed because of its distance from the Columbia River. It was replaced by Fort Colvile just to the north. Thompson retired to Montreal in 1812, where he died in 1857. (To read further, pick up a copy of *Sources of the River* by Jack Nisbet.) ■

---

with a shared bathroom cost $75; the room with a private bathroom goes for $85. Close to downtown, the *Cobblestone Inn* (☎ 509-624-9735), 620 S Washington St, has two guest rooms from $69 to $89. The Cobblestone also runs a bakery, which means good breakfast breads for guests, but anyone can stop by – there's a place to sit and eat pastries and lunch.

The Victorian-styled *Marianna Stoltz House* (☎ 509-483-4316), at 427 E Indiana Ave, near Gonzaga University, caters mostly to business travelers, and has rooms for $59 to $89.

Hotels – budget Budget travelers will find incredible deals at one of the clean, quiet motels along Sunset Blvd. The *Boulevard Motel* (☎ 509-747-1060), 2905 W Sunset Blvd, has single/double rooms for $29/35. For slightly more you can enjoy a pool at the park-like *Shangri-La Motel* (☎ 509-747-2066), 2922 W Government Way, where rooms are $42/45. *Cedar Village Motel* (☎ 509-838-8558, (800-700-8558), 5415 W Sunset Blvd, is closer to the airport and has rooms for $28/36. On the northern approach to town the *Liberty Motel* (☎ 509-467-6000), 6801 N Division St, and the *Royal Scot Motel* (☎ 509-467-6672), 20 W Houston Ave both have rooms for about $45.

By all means avoid downtown, where all of the inexpensive motels are located beneath a noisy railroad overpass. If you must stay downtown, try the *Suntree 8 Inn* (☎ 509-838-8504, 800-888-6630), 123 S Post St, with rooms for $40/44, or the *Tradewinds Motel* (☎ 509-838-2091), 907 W 3rd Ave, with rooms for $35/40.

Hotels – middle There are plenty of mid-priced chain motels on the north end of town along Division St near the malls. The *Best Western Tradewinds North* (☎ 509-326-5500), 3033 N Division St near Euclid Ave, has an indoor pool and rooms for $60/62. On the way to the airport, the *Sierra Hotel* (☎ 509-747-2021), 4212 W Sunset Blvd, off I-90 exit 277, has an outdoor pool and rooms for $52.

Downtown, the *WestCoast Ridpath Hotel* (☎ 509-838-2711, 800-426-0670), 515 W Sprague Ave, is a huge old hotel with an outdoor pool open year-round and rooms starting anywhere from $69 to $95. The *Spokane by Courtyard* (☎ 509-456-7600, 800-321-2211), 401 N Riverpoint Blvd, has an indoor pool, hot tub and exercise room; rooms start at $79. East of downtown at the I-90 Hamilton St exit, the *Shilo Inn* (☎ 509-535-9000, 800-222-2244), 923 E 3rd Ave, has an indoor pool and rooms with a buffet breakfast start at $75.

Hotels – top end For some of the nicest digs in town, try *Cavanaugh's Inn at the Park* (☎ 509-326-8000, 800-843-4667), 303 W North River Rd, located on the north bank of the Spokane River near Riverfront Park. There are indoor and outdoor pools, kitchen units and an airport shuttle. Rooms begin at $99/109. In the park at the convention center is the *Double-Tree Hotel* (☎ 509-455-9600, 800-733-5466), 322 N Spokane Falls Court, which offers a full range of amenities and rooms starting at $138.

Places to Eat

Spokane has a number of good, inexpensive restaurants. Enjoy the range of ethnic cuisines while you're here – Spokane is as cosmopolitan as it gets in this part of the Northwest.

Budget West of the downtown area, *The Elk* (☎ 509-456-0454), 1931 W Pacific Ave, is an old drugstore turned cafe, convenient to the Cheney Cowles Museum. It's a sunny, friendly spot and has particularly good breakfasts. Nearby, the *Fitzbillies*

Bagel Bakery (☎ 509-747-1834), 1325 W 1st Ave at Carnegie Square, is a 'New York-style' deli with good bagels and dense 'billie bars' (a Northwest twist on the bagel, they are differently shaped and loaded with whole wheat, raisins and nuts). Lunches are about $5.

Great Harvest Bread Company (☎ 509-624-9370), at 816 W Sprague Ave, is a whole-wheat bakery with lunchtime soup, salads and sandwiches. At *McGowan's Cafe* (☎ 509-624-1870), 404 W Main, in Auntie's Bookstore, pick up pasta salads and sandwiches for a picnic.

Thai Cafe (☎ 509-838-4783), 410 W Sprague Ave, has pad thai for under $10. The other Thai restaurant of note, *Riverview Thai* (☎ 509-325-8370), in the Flour Mill at W 621 Mallon Ave, has well-seasoned entrées and a better, quieter atmosphere than most budget eateries.

There's nothing special about the burgers, chili and salads at *The Onion* (☎ 509-747-3852), 302 W Riverside Ave, but the place is a Spokane institution, and kids enjoy the rollicking waiters. New-wave Italian crops up at *Rock City Grill* (☎ 509-455-4400), 505 W Riverside Ave, where a one person artichoke heart and shiitake mushroom pizza goes for $9.50.

Middle You can eat cheaply at *Espresso Delizioso Cafe* (☎ 509 326 5958), 706 N Monroe St, if you stick to soup and salad, but it's tempting to delve deeper into the eclectic menu. This casually elegant, brick-walled restaurant is low-key and unstuffy; the wait staff model Spokane's version of sophisticated grunge dressing. There's often live folk music. There's a similar atmosphere at *Europa Pizzaria & Bakery* (☎ 509-455-4051), 125 S Wall St, which serves pizzas, calzones, and pastas in an old brick building filled with tapestried furniture. Both these places are open until at least midnight.

Across from Espresso Delizioso Cafe, *Milford's* (☎ 509-326-7251), at N 719 Monroe St, is Spokane's best seafood restaurant. Dinners here cost around $15, and it's easy to spend a lot more. On Monday nights, you can get 2lb of steamer clams for $11.

Vegetarians should head for the *Cafe Mizuna* (☎ 509-747-2004), 214 N Howard St, where there are baba ghanouj pitas ($6) for lunch, and portabello mushroom fajitas ($12) for dinner. On weekends there's live music, usually of the folk variety. More trendy lunch and dinner food (seafood tostadas with black beans and mango salsa) can be had at *Fugazzi* (☎ 509-624-1133), 1 N Post St, one of the best restaurants in Spokane.

Top End *Patsy Clark's* (☎ 509-838-8300), in a huge historic house at 2208 W 2nd Ave, is as formal a place as you'll find in Spokane. People throng to the Sunday brunch, and it's the most popular special-occasion restaurant in town. Dinner entrées run from $13 to $19. For dining with views over the Spokane River head to *Clinker-dagger's* (☎ 509-328-5965), 621 W Mallon Ave, in the Flour Mill, where northwest specialties like stuffed forest mushrooms with grilled salmon cost $18.

One of Spokane's most exclusive restaurants, upscale *Paprika* (☎ 509-455-7545), 1228 S Grand Blvd, near St John's Cathedral forgoes views and architecture in favor of impressing its diners with fine cuisine. You'll spend about $25 for a full dinner with rack of lamb.

Entertainment

For a full listing of what's happening in Spokane and Coeur d'Alene, pick up a free copy of the *Inlander*. Big-name music stars perform at the *Spokane Arena* (☎ 509-324-7000), 720 W Mallon Ave, on the north bank of the river next to Riverfront Park

Brewpubs *Fort Spokane Brewery* (☎ 509-838-3809), 401 W Spokane Falls Blvd, brews several ales. It's well situated just across the street from Riverfront Park, and serves surprisingly good food (sandwiches for about $6). Blues bands play here three or four nights a week (always on Sunday).

The *Birkenbeinder Brewing Company* (☎ 509-458-0854), 35 W Main Ave, brews

10 to 12 of its own beers on the premises, and serves up to 16 different beers on tap.

Cinemas *Magic Lantern Theatre* (☎ 509-838-4919), 123 S Wall St, is the place to go for arty, foreign films. Act III shows first-run films at several places around town: try the theaters at *North Division* (☎ 509-484-6554), 7410 N Division St, or *Newport* (☎ 509-467-4442), N 10404 Newport Hwy. Downtown, the majestic old *Fox Theater* (☎ 509-624-0105), 1005 W Sprague Ave, shows second-run films for only $1.

Performing Arts The *Spokane Opera House* (☎ 509-353-6500), 334 W Spokane Falls Blvd, is part of the Spokane Center convention and trade center next to Riverfront Park. The local opera company doesn't sing here, but various traveling shows do use the opera house. The Spokane Symphony (☎ 509-624-1200) performs here and at *The Met* (☎ 509-455-6500), 901 W Sprague Ave, which also hosts operas, plays and other musical events in a fairly intimate setting.

Live Music *The Pavement*, a free weekly, has extensive music listings though there isn't always much worth listening to.

Near Gonzaga University, the Bayou Brewing Company (☎ 509-484-4818), at 1001 E Trent, typically draws a college crowd for comedy shows, live music and dancing at its two venues, *Fat Tuesday's* and the *Voo Doo Lounge*. The *Espresso Delizioso Cafe* (☎ 509-326-5958), 706 N Monroe St, delivers folk and blues five or six nights a week. *Outback Jack's*, 321 W Sprague, is a divey dance club in a bad part of town.

Spectator Sports

The Spokane Indians (☎ 509-535-2922) play minor league baseball at the fairgrounds, 602 N Havana St (take Sprague Ave east and turn north on Havana St), and the Spokane Chiefs (☎ 509-328-0450) are a minor-league ice hockey team based at the Spokane Arena, 720 W Mallon Ave.

Playfair Race Course (☎ 509-534-0505)

hosts horseracing during the summer and fall, just east of downtown at N Altamont St and E Main Ave.

Getting There & Away

Air Spokane is well-served with flights in all directions. From the Spokane International Airport, Horizon, Southwest, Alaska and United fly to Seattle and Portland. Delta has flights to Los Angeles and Northwest flies to Minneapolis. The airport is on the southeast outskirts of the city, 7 miles from downtown at the junction of I-90 and Hwy 20.

Bus All buses to Spokane arrive and depart from the Spokane Intermodal Transportation Center at 221 W 1st Ave, a combination bus and train station. Greyhound (☎ 509-624-5251) goes to Seattle ($27 one way) and Portland and to points east along I-90; a one-way ticket to Coeur d'Alene, ID, costs $8. Northwestern Trailways (☎ 509-838-5262, 800 366-3830) runs to Seattle via Wenatchee, Leavenworth and Everett, and also makes trips to Pullman and Boise, ID. Borderline Stage has weekday service north to Colville and Kettle Falls; tickets are sold at the Greyhound counter.

Train Amtrak's passenger station (☎ 509-624-5144) is located at the Spokane Intermodal Transportation Center, 221 W 1st Ave. Trains on the *Empire Builder* line pass through town daily in each direction, westbound to Seattle and Portland at 2:40 am, and eastbound to Chicago at 1:35 am; one-way fare to either Seattle or Portland is $56. The ticket counter is open 11:30 am to 5:30 am the following morning on weekdays; on weekends it's open 7:30 pm to 5:30 am.

Car The following car-rental agencies are at the airport: Avis (☎ 509-747-8081), Budget (☎ 509-623-9710), Dollar (☎ 509-747-2191), National (☎ 509-624-8995) and Thrifty (☎ 509-838-8223). Agencies downtown include Enterprise (☎ 509-458-3340), 3 W 3rd Ave, and U-Save (☎ 509-455-8018), 918 W 3rd Ave. AAA (☎ 509-358-6900) is downtown at 1717 W 4th Ave.

Getting Around

To/From the Airport The Spokane Transit bus No 38 runs hourly or half-hourly (depending on the time of day) between the Spokane International Airport and downtown, with stops at The Plaza and the Spokane Intermodal Transportation Center's door No 4. There are no night buses on the weekends. Airport Shuttle Service (☎ 509-535-6979) picks up and drops off door-to-door; the fare from downtown starts at $8.75.

To/From the Bus & Train Station It's easy to catch a transit bus from nearly any street corner near the station, but if you're arriving by train, chances are it's the middle of the night. Since this isn't the best place to hang around outside after hours, you'll probably want to catch a cab.

Bus Spokane Transit (☎ 509-328-7433) buses run along many routes through town. Downtown buses depart from streets bordering The Plaza, a huge indoor transit station at Sprague Ave and Wall St. The information counter is upstairs at the Bus Shop. If you want a route map you'll have to ask for it, as they don't put them out. Bus fare is 75¢.

Visitors can get to all of the sites surrounding Riverfront Park on the Spokane Falls Streetcar. Streetcars pickup from the northwest corner of The Plaza on Wall St and loop clockwise around the park, stopping at the Spokane Arena, Flour Mill and Caterina Winery. Shoppers can avoid downtown parking hassles by catching the streetcar from the Spokane Arena park-and-ride lot on Mallon Ave, where it costs only $1 to park all day.

Taxi For a taxi, call River City Taxi (☎ 509-482-4904), Spokane Cab (☎ 509-535-2535) or Yellow Cab (☎ 509-624-4321).

AROUND SPOKANE
Turnbull National Wildlife Refuge

Pothole lakes dot the 17,000-acre migratory waterfowl refuge, south of Cheney on Badger Lake Rd. Although Turnbull is known for its teeming bird life, especially abundant during the spring and fall, it is also home to threatened water howellia, a pond weed which grows in clay-bottomed ponds. There's a 6-mile auto tour around the refuge ($3 entrance fee) and a couple of hiking trails. Stop by the refuge headquarters (☎ 509-235-4723), 26010 S Smith Rd, for information.

Turnbull is 15 miles southwest of Spokane in nearby Cheney. From Cheney turn south off the main drag (Hwy 904) onto the Cheney-Plaza Rd and head another 4½ miles south to the refuge.

Lake Roosevelt National Recreation Area

A 150-mile-long reservoir held back by the Grand Coulee Dam, Lake Roosevelt is a major recreation area with 38 campgrounds along the 660 miles of Columbia River shoreline. Lake Roosevelt is perhaps most popular with anglers – in addition to prize white sturgeon, which average 100 to 300lb, there are walleye, rainbow trout and Kokanee salmon landlocked by the dam.

Dry, sunny weather prevails near the southern leg of the lake, also drawing people to camp and play on the white sand beaches. As Lake Roosevelt inches its way north to Canada, the desert cliffs and high coulee walls give way to rolling hills and orchards, inevitably turning into dense forests of ponderosa pine around Kettle Falls.

As recreation areas go, Lake Roosevelt remains refreshingly undeveloped, partially because its north and west shores abut the 2300-sq-mile Colville Indian Reservation, but also because the lake offers little shoreline access for motorists. Most roads cut straight across the lake (or dead end) once they've reached it, leading travelers straight back into miles and miles

of desert, farmland, or forest. To explore Lake Roosevelt at any great length is to do so by boat – of the lake's 38 shoreline campgrounds around two-thirds are accessible only to boaters. The enterprising Colville Confederated Tribes operate a luxury houseboat-rental service at Keller Ferry, directly north of Wilbur on Hwy 21.

Orientation

The Grand Coulee Dam is 90 miles from either Spokane or Wenatchee, and 225 miles from Seattle. US 2 runs west from Spokane to the main turnoff points for recreation areas at Fort Spokane, Keller Ferry and the Grand Coulee Dam. Fort Spokane is the closest access point to Spokane, and lies 58 miles northwest via Davenport on Hwy 25.

The free Keller Ferry crosses Lake Roosevelt and provides access to the scenic north-south Hwy 21, which passes through the Colville Indian Reservation along the Sanpoil River to the town of Republic on Hwy 20. Catch the ferry by heading north from Wilbur (or south from Republic) on Hwy 21.

The Colville Indian Reservation is bordered by US 97 on the west, the Columbia River and Lake Roosevelt to the south and east, and the Okanogan National Forest on the north. Most of the reservation's sites and towns are located along Hwy 155, which passes from Omak to the Grand Coulee Dam.

Information

There are 38 park campgrounds on Lake Roosevelt, and with the exception of towns at the Grand Coulee Dam or Kettle Falls there are no hotels or resorts. Management of the lake and the campgrounds is divided among the NPS, the Colville Confederated Tribes and the Spokan tribe. Be sure to obtain a tribal permit when camping on reservation property. Camping fees are $10 in season and free in the off-season. They all have running water and flush toilets, and the larger ones have showers. There are no hookups, and unless you're bringing a large group there are no reservations.

Contact the Lake Roosevelt National Recreation Area headquarters (☎ 509-633-9441), at 1008 Crest Drive, Coulee Dam, WA 99116. Roosevelt Recreation Enterprises (☎ 800-648-5253) also publishes a useful tourist guide to the entire Lake Roosevelt region.

FORT SPOKANE

The army built this post in 1880, at the confluence of the Spokane and Columbia Rivers, east of where the dam now sits, to quell any disturbances that might arise between white settlers and local Native Americans recently confined to reservations. Both sides were supposed to stay clear of each other, and during the fort's tenure, which ended in 1898, there were no hostilities. At its peak in the 1890s, Fort Spokane contained close to 50 buildings.

Colville Confederated Tribes

Eleven different bands make up the Colville Confederated Tribes: the Chelan, Entiat, Lakes, Methow, Moses, Nespelem, Nez Perce, Okanogan, Palouse, Sanpoil and Wenatchee. Up until the mid-1800s, the ancestors of the Colville Confederated Tribes were nomadic, and many tribes fished and traded around the Kettle Falls area. When white fur traders began working the Northwest, it didn't take long before a fur trading post, Fort Colvile, was established at Kettle Falls. Trading was active from 1826 to 1887, and as the years passed, whites began referring to all local Native Americans as 'Colvilles.' In 1872, the Colville Indian Reservation was formed.

Today, the reservation covers 2300 sq miles, about half the size of the original reservation, and there are about 7700 tribal members. The tribal headquarters is near Nespelem, north of Grand Coulee Dam. Tribal industries revolve around timber, and there is a fish hatchery which stocks all of north-central Washington's lakes and streams. ■

Several of the fort's original buildings remain, though many visitors come here just to camp, swim at the beach or boat on Lake Roosevelt. The Fort Spokane Visitors Center is open 1 to 6 pm, Wednesday to Saturday, and from 10 am to 6 pm on Sunday. In the summertime there's a living history program here at 11 am on Sunday mornings.

Orientation & Information

At 58 miles northwest of Spokane, Fort Spokane provides the easiest access to Lake Roosevelt, and is the beginning point for a winding lakeshore drive on Hwy 25. From Spokane head west on US 2 to Davenport and turn north onto Hwy 25, which continues north along the lake another 57 miles from Fort Spokane to Kettle Falls.

The USFS office (☎ 509-725-2715) here is open 8 am to 4:30 pm weekdays, and can answer questions about the Fort Spokane Visitors Center or the campground.

Places to Stay & Eat

Fort Spokane has a large, popular campground with a swimming beach and boat launch just north of Fort Spokane on the mouth of the Spokane River. A hiking trail leads from the campground to a network of interpretive paths at Fort Spokane.

If Fort Spokane is full there are a number of other nice campgrounds north along the highway. There's a family-style restaurant at the *Seven Bays Campground & Marina* (☎ 509-725-1676), 7 miles south of Fort Spokane down Miles-Creston Rd, where you'll also find an RV campground with showers and a marina; full hookups are $15.

KELLER FERRY

The free Keller Ferry across Lake Roosevelt provides access to the scenic north-south Hwy 21, which passes through the Colville Indian Reservation. Catch the ferry by heading north for 14 miles on Hwy 21 from Wilbur, which is 29 miles west of Davenport on US 2. It's 53 miles to Republic. The ferry operates daily from 6 am to 11:30 pm.

Near the ferry landing there's a popular

marina, playground and swimming beach at the Keller Ferry Campground on the south shore. Water-ski equipment and inner tubes can be rented from the Keller Ferry Marina (☎ 509-647-5755), and the Colville Confederated Tribes also rent houseboats.

Places to Stay

Camping *Keller Ferry Campground* is near the ferry on Lake Roosevelt at the Colville Confederated Tribes' marina, and offers showers and campsites on a grassy field. There's a campfire program that discusses Columbia River geology on Saturday evenings.

On the hill to the south above Keller Ferry there's RV camping at the park-like *River Rue Campground* (☎ 509-647-2647), which has full hookups for $18.

Eight miles north of Keller Ferry on the Colville Indian Reservation is *Keller Park Campground*, a small roadside campground with astonishing cliffside views of the Sanpoil River, which suddenly broadens into a wide gorge.

Houseboat Rentals Roosevelt Recreational Enterprises (☎ 509-633-0136, 800-648-5253), run by the Colville Confederated Tribes, rents houseboats at Keller Ferry. Houseboats vary in features and

capacity, but can usually accommodate up to 10 or 13 people. Rates also vary considerably. Weekend stays start at $995 in peak season (late-June to Labor Day), and drop to $795 in the off-season. A week-long stay in peak season costs $1830 to $2060.

GRAND COULEE DAM AREA

The Grand Coulee Dam, with its three powerhouses, is the world's third-largest hydropower producer (after Guri Dam in Venezuela and Itaipu Dam between Paraguay and Brazil), and it also pumps water for irrigation into Banks Lake, a holding reservoir for the Columbia Basin Irrigation Project. Grand Coulee is the only one of the Columbia River's 11 dams operated by the US Bureau of Reclamation, an agency formed in 1902 to help sustain the economy and improve life in western states by providing reliable sources of water and electricity. The Grand Coulee Dam produces about a quarter of the hydropower generated along the Columbia.

Orientation

Three small, rather drab towns cluster around the Grand Coulee Dam, and it's easy to get a little disoriented. Grand Coulee (population 978) and Electric City (population 958) are just above the dam,

JENNIFER SNARSKI

Grand Coulee Dam

RICK GERHARTER

NIK WHEELER

NIK WHEELER

NIK WHEELER

Top Left: Totem poles, Museum of Anthropology, University of British Columbia, Vancouver, BC
Bottom: City skyline, Vancouver, BC

Top Right: A wave of Canadian flags, BC
Middle Right: Chinatown gates, Vancouver, BC

Top Left: Lions Gate Bridge, Vancouver, BC
Bottom Left: Historic Empress Hotel overlooking the
    Inner Harbour, Victoria, BC

Top Right: Butchart Gardens near Victoria, BC
Bottom Right: Morris dancer, Victoria, BC

Building the Grand Coulee Dam

Construction of the Grand Coulee Dam began in 1933, and in 1934 two large towns were hastily constructed below the dam site. On the west bank, Engineers Town housed engineers in rows of small tidy houses. Across the river on the east bank, workmen lived in barracks and small houses in Mason City, one of the first towns built without chimneys, (since all of the buildings used electric heat). Like any frontier town, Mason City was a wild place. Between the dam site and the Canadian border, five camps housed WPA workers, who spent their days clearing brush and buildings from the area set to be flooded by the backwaters of the new dam. WPA workers were paid $40 to $95 a week, and they were charged 50¢ a day for room and board.

It took nine years to complete the dam. A truly massive structure that dwarfs the Great Pyramids of Egypt, the Grand Coulee Dam is big enough to see from space and generates more power than a million locomotives. The dam also changed the landscape in a way that far exceeds the size of the structure itself, putting huge lakes in the middle of the desert and replacing sagebrush with wheat fields.

Grand Coulee Dam was built without fish ladders, a decision that led to the extinction of salmon and other anadromous fish upriver from the dam. But when you're here, it's easy to see why this was done. The 550-foot dam wall is just too big and steep for conventional fish ladders.

The Colville Confederated Tribes lost their best riverfront land when the dam was built. They received no compensation from the government until a 1994 settlement awarded the tribes an initial payment of $59 million and future yearly payments of at least $15.25 million. This is only a small fraction of the income produced by the dam, which pulls in over $400 million a year for its power generation and cheaply irrigates over half a million acres, all on the non-Indian side of the Columbia River. ■

and directly below is Coulee Dam (population 1098), the most interesting of the three. The Colville Indian Reservation has its southern boundary in Coulee Dam and extends northward past Omak. West of the dam there is little other than wheat fields for miles, but be sure to take in the Grand Coulee itself south of the dam which, along with Roosevelt Lake, offers plenty of outdoor recreation.

Hwys 155 and 174 intersect at Coulee Dam, which isn't on the way to anywhere. Davenport is 65 miles east via Wilbur, and Omak is 55 miles north. Coulee City, at the end of Banks Lake in the Grand Coulee, is 30 miles south.

Information

The Grand Coulee Visitor Arrival Center (☎ 509-633-9265), on Hwy 155 at the Grand Coulee Dam has plenty of information on the area around the dam. It's open 9 am to 5 pm daily, and evenings during the summer. Contact the Grand Coulee Dam Chamber of Commerce at ☎ 509-633-3074, 800-268-5332. The Lake Roosevelt National Recreation Area headquarters (☎ 509-633-9441), 1008 Crest Drive in Coulee Dam, can provide details about the numerous Roosevelt Lake campgrounds.

Coulee Community Hospital (☎ 509-633-1753) is just northwest of Grand Coulee on Hwy 174 toward Bridgeport. Wash your clothes in Grand Coulee at King's Court RV Park (☎ 509-633-3655), 212 E Grand.

Grand Coulee Dam

The visitors' center (☎ 509-633-9265) on Hwy 155 near Coulee Dam, has historical exhibits of the dam construction and lots of great WPA-era photos. If you're lucky, someone who worked on the dam will be visiting at the same time and will be regaling people with stories, a not uncommon occurrence. There's also a vaguely propagandistic film about hydropower (featuring lots of Woody Guthrie music) running almost constantly. The visitors' center is open 9 am to 5 pm daily (and evenings during the summer).

Guided **tours** of the dam take in the pump-generator plant, the spillway and two power plants. A simpler, 30-minute self-guided tour involves taking a glass-walled elevator down a 45° incline outside the dam and looking into the hydropower units.

It would be hard to visit Coulee Dam without seeing the dam's nightly **laser show**, which runs from Memorial Day through September and illustrates the history of the Columbia River and its dams. It starts after dark, around 9:30 or 10 pm, switching to 8:30 pm during September. The best views are from the visitors' center or the park below it. Get there early to find parking.

Colville Confederated Tribes Museum

The tribal museum and gift shop (☎ 509-633-0751), 512 Meade Way in Coulee Dam, has dioramas of traditional fishing and village life flanked by collections of baskets, spears and other art and artifacts. A gift shop sells books, beadwork and other crafts. The museum is open 10 am to 9 pm daily, May to September, and 10 am to 6 pm Tuesday to Saturday, October to April.

Colville Indian Reservation

Though the Colville Indian Reservation isn't set up for tourists, respectful visitors are welcome. The tribal headquarters (☎ 509-634-4711) is just south of Nespelem on Hwy 155. Visitors should stick to the roads and not wander off on unauthorized hikes. Some of the reservation's lakes and streams are open to public fishing; get permits at the Tribal Fish & Wildlife Office (☎ 509-634-8845) at tribal headquarters. Amenities on the reservation are limited to a few campgrounds (again, be sure to get a permit), and there are no real restaurants. However, it's easy to make a day trip from Omak or the dam area.

Chief Joseph's Grave Nez Perce leader Chief Joseph and his band were sent to the Colville Reservation several years after their long march across eastern Oregon, Idaho and Montana was halted by the Army in 1878 (see the sidebar on Chief Joseph & the Nez Perce, in the John Day Country section of the Northeastern Oregon chapter). The Nez Perce were assigned first to Oklahoma, but public outcry made the government reconsider these arrangements. In 1884, Chief Joseph and his band were sent to the Colville Reservation. They were prohibited from returning to the main Nez Perce Reservation in Lapwai, ID because they refused to profess Christianity. Joseph died in 1904 and is buried at Nespelem. Find his grave at the northeast edge of town.

Fishing & Boating

Good fishing abounds in the lakes near Grand Coulee Dam. Lake Roosevelt and Banks Lake are most popular, though Lake Rufus Woods, below Grand Coulee Dam, also attracts anglers (launch a boat from the Elmer City launch, a few miles north of Coulee Dam). Spring Canyon, off Hwy 174 about 3 miles east of Grand Coulee, is the nearest boat launch for Lake Roosevelt. Buffalo and McGinnis Lakes, on the Colville Reservation, require a tribal fishing permit, available at businesses on the reservation and in Grand Coulee.

Spring Canyon is also the meeting place on Thursday and Friday evenings for ranger-led **canoe trips** to nearby Crescent Bay Lake; there is no cost and all equipment is provided. Call the Lake Roosevelt National Recreation Area (☎ 509-633-9441) or stop by the dam's visitors' center for a schedule.

Other Activities

The various parks and recreation areas in this area offer plenty to do, though fishing is the biggest draw. **Spring Canyon**, off Hwy 174 about 3 miles east of Grand Coulee, has a boat launch, campground and a nature trail that explores the prairie ecosystem. There's a popular swimming beach here, and the NPS offers interpretive hikes, bike rides, and nature programs nearly every day.

You can go **hiking** near Steamboat Rock, and there is an easy, 6½-mile **biking** trail, the Down River Trail, that follows the Columbia River north from Grand Coulee Dam. Catch the trail at Mason City Park, across from the Coulee Dam Shopping Center. There's also **swimming** at the beaches on Banks Lake in Steamboat Rock State Park.

For a little **horseback riding**, go to Spirit Ridge RV Park (☎ 509-633-1933, 800-548-1408), between Elmer City and Nespelem on Hwy 155. There are nine-hole **golf** courses at Banks Lake Golf & Country Club (☎ 509-633-0163), 3½ miles south of Grand Coulee on Hwy 155.

Special Events
On the Colville Indian Reservation, the Fourth of July Powwow in Nespelem is a 10-day celebration that draws participants from across the Northwest.

Places to Stay
Camping On Lake Roosevelt, the *Spring Canyon Campground*, 3 miles east of Grand Coulee on Hwy 174, is the closest campground to the Grand Coulee Dam. It's popular, and the swimming beach, volley-ball court, and boat launch offer plenty of activities.

Spirit Ridge RV Encampment (☎ 509-633-1933, 800-548-1408) is north of Coulee Dam on Lower River Rd (off Hwy 155) between Elmer City and Nespelem. Besides rather deluxe RV facilities ($18), there are teepee rentals ($15 to $18) and tent sites ($10).

Steamboat Rock State Park (☎ 509-633-1304), 12 miles south of Grand Coulee on Banks Lake, has a handful of $11 tent sites and a bunch of $16 RV sites. On summer weekends, it's wise to reserve a spot. Also on Banks Lake, *Coulee Playland Resort* (☎ 509-633-2671) has RV and tent sites starting at $10. Both of these places are on Hwy 155, southwest of Electric City.

B&Bs In Coulee Dam, the *Four Winds B&B* (☎ 509-633-3146, 800-786-3146), 301 Lincoln Ave, was an old workers' dorm, and displays one of President Roosevelt's wheelchairs as an eerie relic of the WPA era. Rates start at $62 to $74; some rooms can accommodate up to four people.

Hotels Of the three towns near the dam, Coulee Dam is the best bet for a motel room. *Ponderosa Motel* (☎ 509-633-2100, 800-633-6421), 10 Lincoln St, has a pool and a view of the dam, which is essentially right across the street. Rooms start at $72. *Coulee House Motel* (☎ 509-633-1101, 800-715-7767), at the corner of Birch and Roosevelt, also overlooks the dam (with excellent seats for the nightly light show) and has a sauna, spa and huge pool; rooms cost $50.

In Electric City the *Sky Deck Motel* (☎ 509-633-0290, 800-708-3014), on Hwy 155, has a grassy beach and cabins fronting onto Banks Lake for $55 to $65.

Places to Eat
Pickings are slim for food around the Grand Coulee Dam. In Grand Coulee, *Siam Palace* (☎ 509-633-2921), 213 Main St, serves Chinese, Thai and American food. *Melody Restaurant* (☎ 509-633-1151), 110 Roosevelt Way in Coulee Dam, serves American fare at the Coulee House Motel. It's open from early morning till late evening, with a deck looking out on the dam.

Okanogan River Valley

The Okanogan River courses south from the British Columbia Rockies and joins the Columbia near the tiny orchard town of Brewster, a few miles downstream from Chief Joseph Dam. The Okanogan is a slow-moving river, and the surrounding valley is dry and fairly lightly settled, functioning mostly as a transportation corridor. The Colville Indian Reservation lies to the east of the Okanogan River, with its northern border just north of Omak and its southern and eastern borders delineated by the Columbia River. On either side of the valley, hills rise into various scattered parts of the Okanogan National Forest, where grasslands and cultivated orchards give way to ponderosa pine and Douglas fir.

Okanogan is Salish for 'rendezvous.' Native Americans lived here for thousands of years before a succession of white explorers, prospectors, miners, trappers, ranchers, homesteaders, loggers, farmers, missionaries and fruit-growers displaced them. North West Company fur traders, led by David Thompson, traveled through in 1811, and were followed the same summer by Americans from Astor's Pacific Fur Company. The American traders stuck around and built a trading post on the Okanogan River, just up from the Columbia. This 'Fort Okanogan' was soon inherited by the Hudson's Bay Company, who used it to channel furs coming down the Okanogan River from Canada onto boats bound for HBC's Vancouver, WA headquarters.

Prospectors traipsed the 'Cariboo Trail' up the Okanogan Valley to British Columbia's Cariboo gold fields in the 1850s. They were followed by cowboys driving cattle up from the Yakima Valley to the mining camps. Today, US 97 sticks pretty close to the old trail as it runs up the Okanogan from Brewster to the Canadian border.

For a quick roadside history, stop by the interpretive center at Fort Okanogan State Park (☎ 509-923-2473), at the junction of US 97 and Hwy 17 east of Brewster, which sits on a bluff overlooking the confluence of the Okanogan and Columbia Rivers. The museum tells the story of the Native Americans who originally lived here, and of three fur-trading companies who successively occupied this site at the old Fort Okanogan in the early 19th century. It's open 9 am to 6 pm Wednesday to Sunday, June to August; admission is free. Picnic facilities are available on the grounds.

OKANOGAN & OMAK

Okanogan (population 2410) and Omak (population 4365) have very nearly merged to become one town, but they have very distinct characters. Okanogan is the county seat, and its relatively dignified town center befits this role. Omak is the bustling retail center of the valley, and it's best known for its annual rodeo, the Omak Stampede. To the west, lakes and apple orchards dot the foothills of the Cascade mountains, while to the east the hillsides are generally dry and grassy.

You can find surprisingly interesting exhibits, including frontier photographer Frank Matsura's glass-plate photo collection and a quilt display at the **Okanogan County Museum** (☎ 509-422-4272), 1410 N 2nd St. It's open 10 am to 4 pm daily from late May to early fall; admission to the museum is $2.

Orientation & Information

Two roads, US 97 and Hwy 215 (the commercial strip), connect Omak and Okanogan. Twisp lies 29 miles to the west of Omak on Hwy 20, and Hwy 155 cuts southeast across the Colville Indian Reservation 54 miles to connect Okanogan with Coulee Dam.

The Omak Visitor Information office (☎ 509-826-4218, 800-225-6625) is next to the stampede grounds on Hwy 155 just east of downtown. Information is also dispensed at the rest stop on 2nd St (Hwy 20) at Okanogan's American Legion Park (☎ 509-422-9882). The Okanogan National Forest (☎ 509-826-3275) has its headquarters at 1240 S 2nd St.

Mid-Valley Hospital (☎ 509-826-1760), 810 Valley Way, is at the south end of Omak, which is also where you'll find the Log Cabin Public Coin-Op Laundromat (☎ 509-826-4462), at the Log Cabin Trailer Court, 509 Okoma Drive (Hwy 215). Call Omak Cab (☎ 509-826-4123) should you need a lift.

St Mary's Mission

Near the Colville Indian Reservation's northwest corner, 5 miles southeast of

Omak on Hwy 155, St Mary's (☎ 509-525-3320) has been an active mission since 1896. Most of the missionary work now centers around the boarding school, but there's also a church, built in 1910, which is open to visitors.

Activities
There is some pleasant **hiking** in the national forest to the west, between Okanogan and Twisp. The USFS headquarters in Okanogan dispenses trail information. **Biking** is also popular, as Hwy 20 is a long-distance bike-touring route, and there are plenty of back roads up into the Okanogan hills worth cycling. Rent a bike at The Bike Shop (☎ 509-422-0710, 800-464-0710), 137 2nd Ave in Okanogan.

The Bike Shop also rents snowboards and cross-country skis for **skiing** at nearby Loup Loup Summit. The Loup Loup Ski Bowl (☎ 509-826-2720), just off Hwy 20, 18 miles west of Okanogan, is usually open December to March. It's a small ski area with a 1240-foot vertical drop, two lifts and a rope tow, as well as 18.6 miles of groomed cross-country ski trails.

Omak Stampede
The Omak Stampede (☎ 509-826-1002, 800-933-6625) is one of the West's biggest rodeos, with one of the most dramatic and controversial events, the Suicide Race, where horses and their riders pitch down a steep hillside and across the Okanogan River. Horses sometimes die attempting this feat, which has led to protests from animal-rights activists.

At the adjacent Indian Encampment, Native Americans dance, drum and play stick games. There's also country music, a parade and a barbecue. The Stampede is always held the second weekend of August.

Places to Stay & Eat
American Legion Park (☎ 509-422-3600), on the river in downtown Okanogan, has mostly RV sites and costs $5 a night (no hookups). Also in Okanogan, the *Cariboo Inn* (☎ 509-422-6109), 233 Queen St, is an

older downtown hotel with rooms from $27 and a restaurant. The *U&I River's Edge Motel* (☎ 509-422-2920), 838 2nd St, is also a bit dated, but it has a nice riverside setting and is a bargain at $30 for a clean single room. At the south end of town, *Ponderosa Motor Lodge* (☎ 509-422-0400), 1034 S 2nd St, is a standard small town motel with rooms from $35/39. *Cedars Inn Motel* (☎ 509-422-6431), at the junction of Hwy 20 and US 97, has an outdoor pool and a restaurant and costs $41/48 for single/double rooms. All of the motels except the Cariboo Inn have a few rooms with kitchens.

In Omak, rooms at *Leisure Village Motel* (☎ 509-826-4442), 630 Okoma Drive, run $35/45, plus about $5 extra for a kitchen. *Motel Nicholas* (☎ 509-826-4611), 527 E Grape Ave, has refrigerators and charges $32/36. The freshly-fabricated *Omak Inn* (☎ 509-826-3822, 800-204-4800), 912 Koala Drive, off US 97 on the north end of town offers mini-suites in a modern conference-style motel; there's also an indoor pool, spa and fitness center, and an adjacent restaurant and lounge. Its the only motel of its kind in the region, with rooms starting at $60.

Without a doubt, the best restaurant in the area is Omak's *Breadline Cafe* (☎ 509-

826-5836), 102 S Ash. It's possible to get vegetarian dinners, mostly pasta, for under $10 – and, of course, there are plenty of burgers and steaks. The cafe occasionally hosts some alternative, folksy entertainment; it's open for breakfast, lunch and dinner, and is closed Sunday.

Shopping
De Tro's Triangle L Western Store (☎ 509-826-2200) on Main St in Riverside, 7 miles north of Omak, is a large and authentic source for cowboy hats, boots, jeans and saddles.

AROUND OKANOGAN
Conconully Lake
The lakeside hamlet of Conconully (population 193), in the eastern foothills of the North Cascades 18 miles northwest of Omak, is a good place to go for a respite from scorching summer days in the Okanogan valley. The name Conconully comes from the Salish word *konekol't*, meaning 'money hole.' It was named after a creek full of beaver whose pelts were used as money at the local trading post. Most visitors come for **Conconully State Park**. The resorts around Conconully aren't fancy, but they're generally more pleasant than staying in Omak. From Omak, take Kernel Rd (near the north end of town) to the west and follow signs to Conconully.

A couple of **hiking** trails, the Tiffany Lake Trail and the Clark Ridge Trail, start just past the Salmon Meadows Campground, 8½ miles northwest of Conconully on USFS Rd 38. The trails head into the Tiffany Roadless Area and can be fashioned into a loop to make a nice overnight backpack. Conconully Lake is a popular place in the winter for snowmobiling and **cross-country skiing**.

Up the road from Conconully is the *Salmon Meadows Lodge* (☎ 509-826-2604). The original 26-bed historic lodge burned down a few years ago, and is currently undergoing reconstruction. The lodge is rented out to groups, and although it's pretty rustic it's also very popular;

during the winter it's accessible only by snowmobile or skis.

For a meal, the *Salmon Creek Inn* (☎ 509-826-1037) serves Mexican and standard American fare in an older false-fronted building.

TONASKET
Population 1025
Tonasket, 24 miles north of Omak, doesn't hold much interest in and of itself, but there's great lake-speckled country to both the east and west in and around the Okanogan National Forest.

For general information, the chamber of commerce (☎ 509-486-2931) is at 4th St and Whitcomb Ave. The Tonasket Ranger Station (☎ 509-486-2186), 1 W Winesap, can guide you to camping and recreation in the area. There's laundry and public showers at the Junction Motel & Laundromat (☎ 509-486-4421), at the junction of Hwy 20 and US 97.

Places to Stay & Eat
Tonasket City Park is a roadside RV park with hookups for $5. It's north of town on US 97.

Red Apple Inn (☎ 509-486-2119) is a basic motel on US 97 at 1st St that has kitchenettes; rooms start at $36/43. The new *Junction Motel* (☎ 509-486-4500), at the junction of US 97 and Hwy 20 has similar standard rooms for $39/44.

Hidden Hills Guest Ranch (☎ 509-486-1895, 800-468-1890), 144 Fish Lake Rd, is a bit more expensive, with hotel rooms starting at about $85 to $95. It's an old-fashioned inn, attempting to recreate an 1890s atmosphere with modern amenities. The inn's restaurant also serves satisfying home-cooked meals. It can be reached from Conconully by heading north along the Sinlahekin Rd, or by turning west off US 97 onto Pine Creek Rd (which becomes Fish Lake Rd). Pine Creek Rd is about 5 miles north of the community of Riverside and about 10 miles south of Tonasket.

Tonasket's *Okanogan River Natural Foods Co-Op* (☎ 509-486-4188), 21 W 4th St (one block west of US 97) is a good place for campers to stock up. It's also a de facto community center – stop in to find out about the barter fair that's held around here every summer.

There are a few passable places to eat in Tonasket. *Don's Drive Inn* (☎ 509-486-2122), 101 N US 97, pleases crowds on pleasant summer nights. *Shannon's Old Fashioned Ice Cream Parlor* also serves sandwiches and espresso, and the *Roundup Cafe* (☎ 509-486-2695), 319 S Whitcomb Ave, is a decent downtown place to get breakfast.

MANY LAKES RECREATION AREA

The Many Lakes Recreational Area is dotted with lakes that are excellent for fishing. All of the lakes are on the road to Loomis (take 4th St out of Tonasket), which is about 17 miles west; a number of resorts on this road cater to anglers. **Whitestone Lake**, 5½ miles north of Tonasket, has good warm-water fishing for large mouth bass and crappie. **Spectacle Lake**, just past Whitestone Lake has rainbow trout. Past Loomis is **Palmer Lake**, where bass are a big attraction, along with rainbow and brown trout and Kokanee salmon. **Chopaka Lake**, 6.3 miles north of Loomis, is open to fly-fishing only. Fishing licenses and tackle are available from Loomis Grocery & Sporting Goods in Loomis. Most resorts rent boats. Fishing season lasts from around March through the end of July.

Places to Stay & Eat

Near Loomis in the Many Lakes Recreational Area, most of the resorts listed below have places to park an RV or pitch a tent for $10 to $15. There are primitive public campgrounds at Palmer and Chopaka Lakes, but neither have running water. Be sure to call ahead if you're planning to stay here outside the main fishing season, as some of the businesses close up shop as early as August.

The Many Lakes area has several small resorts. Don't expect anything fancy: rustic kitchenette cabins are the standard. *Rainbow Resort* (☎ 509-223-3700), 761 Loomis Hwy, has cabins starting at $40 and RV hookups; it's closed November through March. *Spectacle Falls Resort* (☎ 509-223-4141), 879 Loomis Hwy, is just up the road and offers lodging in trailer homes from $42; it closes in August. *Chopaka Lodge* (☎ 509-223-3131), 1913 Loomis Hwy on Palmer Lake, is the most scenic, and has cute cabins for around $40.

Sun Cove Resort (☎ 509-476-2223), on Wannacut Lake, has lots of activities, including horseback riding and boating, and a heated pool. Cabins run about $58, and there are special rates for larger groups or extended stays. Reach Wannacut Lake by turning north off Loomis Rd between Whitestone and Spectacle Lakes onto Wannacut Lake Rd.

In Loomis, the *Palmer Mountain Restaurant* (☎ 509-223-3311) is a good place to eat.

MT BONAPARTE & BONAPARTE LAKE

East of Tonasket, the Okanogan National Forest contains Mt Bonaparte and Bonaparte Lake, where there are several campgrounds, a resort, and some beautiful hikes in the scenic Okanogan highlands. Bonaparte Lake has good trout fishing during the summer, and during the winter there are 11 miles of groomed **cross-country skiing** trails near the western base of Mt Bonaparte.

To reach Bonaparte Lake head 24 miles east of Tonasket on Hwy 20 and turn north at the sign for the Bonaparte Lake Recreation Area onto Bonaparte Lake Rd (USFS Rd 32). Skiers should pick up the Tonasket-Havillah Rd from downtown Tonasket and follow it 16 miles northeast to the Highland Sno-Park near Havillah. Call the Tonasket Ranger Station (☎ 509-486-2186) for more information.

Hiking

One easy, mile-long hike starts at the Lost Lake Campground (see Places to Stay, below) and ends up at the **Big Tree Botanical Area**, home to two 600-year-old Western larch trees. Another short trail from the campground goes to **Strawberry**

Mountain, featuring views of the surrounding area and Canada.

For a more challenging, 8-mile roundtrip hike, drive 6 miles west from Lost Lake on USFS Rd 33, then turn south onto USFS Rd 300, which ends in a little over a mile at the trailhead for **Mt Bonaparte**, a far-western outrider of the Rocky Mountains. The trail heads up forested slopes to the 7258-foot summit, where there's a fire lookout with great views. Another trail up Mt Bonaparte starts at the Bonaparte Lake campground.

One of the most popular hikes near Bonaparte Lake is the 3-mile **Virginia Lilly Old-Growth Trail**, flush with birds and old-growth trees which yield in many places to incredible views. To reach it, take USFS Rd 20, which forks off Bonaparte Lake Rd less than a mile past the lake, and turn onto USFS Rd 3240.

Places to Stay & Eat
The Bonaparte Lake area contains three excellent lakeside campgrounds, all with running water, pit toilets and sites for $5 to $7. Six miles up USFS Rd 32, *Bonaparte Campground* has sites on Bonaparte Lake; several walk-in sites are set aside for bicyclists. Just north of it is the *Bonaparte Lake Resort* (☎ 509-486-2828), 695 Bonaparte Lake Rd, which has campsites, cabins from $25 to $45 and a pretty good restaurant with dinners from $7 to $12. The extremely popular cabins are wood-heated, and during the winter have no running water; they're often fully booked a year in advance.

Continue another 4 miles past Bonaparte Lake, then turn northwest onto USFS Rd 33 for about another 4 miles to reach *Lost Lake Campground*. Northeast of Bonaparte Lake is *Beth Lake Campground* on tiny Beth Lake. To reach it, turn northwest off USFS Rd 32 at Beaver Lake, and head less than 2 miles up County Rd 9480.

OROVILLE
Population 1550
Oroville is 4 miles south of the USA/Canada border crossing. The town is on the

south shore of **Osoyoos Lake**, the town's main attraction, which has picnicking, swimming and camping at Osoyoos Lake State Park. The apple orchards here are a legacy of Hiram 'Okanogan' Smith, an early settler who carried apple trees down from Fort Hope, BC in his backpack and planted them here in 1861. He also came to mine for gold.

If you have a little extra time, stop by the tiny town of **Molson**, which is now an open-air museum consisting of a bunch of old buildings, two small museums, and farm implements on a roadside field. No gold was ever found at this turn-of-the-century gold mining boomtown, but homesteaders still came to farm the land. It's located 15 miles east of Oroville, and today is little more than a ghost town.

Orientation & Information
Oroville, 19 miles north of Tonasket, is the last town on US 97 and just a few miles south of the Canadian border. The Washington State information center (☎ 509-476-2739) on US 97 north of Oroville is open daily in summer and on weekends during winter. The border crossing is open 24 hours. For information call the US Customs and Immigration office at 509-476-2955; for the Canadian side, call ☎ 604-495-6531.

Places to Stay & Eat
Lake Osoyoos State Park (☎ 509-476-3321) is open year-round, with $10 campsites. When the weather's nice, it's the best place in town.

Camaray Motel (☎ 509-476-3684), 1320 Main St, has a pool, and singles/doubles are $33/39. For a few dollars more, the *Red Apple Inn* (☎ 509-476-3694) is just north of town on US 97 with rooms for $36/44 and a few kitchenettes.

If you pull into Oroville hungry, head to *Hometown Pizza & Bakery* (☎ 509-476-2410), 806 Central, where they make pizzas from scratch. The rest of the restaurants in Oroville are smoky bordertown gambling dens. On Sunday your best bet is the *Peerless Restaurant* (☎ 509-476-4344),

401 Main St, which serves inexpensive steaks and hot sandwiches.

Colville National Forest

The Colville National Forest spans two mountain ranges, the Kettle River and the Selkirk, in the northeastern corner of Washington, with the Columbia River slowing and widening into Lake Roosevelt between them. Most of the activity in the Kettle River Range, also known as the Okanogan Highlands, centers around Republic and Curlew Lake State Park, with the town of Curlew making an interesting stop to the north on Hwy 21.

The Pend Oreille (pronounced *PON-de-RAY*) River flows north through the Selkirk Mountains into Canada, where it joins the Columbia. Most of the recreation centers around fishing, especially lake fishing. The Salmo-Priest Wilderness Area is some of the state's wildest country; it's crossed by hiking trails but has little in the way of facilities. Colville and Metaline Falls make good bases for exploring the Selkirks and the Pend Oreille River area, while Kettle Falls, on Lake Roosevelt, is replete with Columbia River history.

REPUBLIC
Population 1914

Downtown Republic is largely false-fronted, and even though some of these building facades are fairly recently built, there are enough old ones to keep the effect from being phony. A gold rush started things up in 1896, and mining has continued, in fits and starts, to this day, as two mining companies are still the biggest industries in the county. Several timber companies are also nearby, fueled by trees from the Colville National Forest. Republic is an attractive western town and a comfortable place to spend the night. You can poke around the old-fashioned drug store and load up on bulk groceries and local

news at the food co-op before setting out the next day.

Orientation
The Sanpoil River runs north-south through Republic (followed by Hwy 21) from Curlew Lake to the Keller Ferry crossing at Lake Roosevelt. The Keller Ferry runs daily from 6 am to 11:30 pm. The state's highest paved-road pass, Sherman Pass (5575 feet) is on Hwy 20 between Republic and Kettle Falls. Be sure to carry chains if you're driving this stretch between October and April – snowfall can be heavy here.

Information
Tourist information (☎ 509-775-3387) is available from the Stonerose Interpretive Center at 15 N Kean St. The Republic Ranger Station (☎ 509-775-3305), 180 N Jefferson, has information on hiking trails in the nearby Colville National Forest.

The Ferry County Memorial Hospital (☎ 509-775-3333) is at 470 N Klondike Rd in Republic, and there is a laundromat between 8th and 9th Sts near the Frontier Motel.

Stonerose Fossil Center
The area around Republic contains a good selection of plant fossils from the Eocene Epoch some 50 million years ago, and the Stonerose Interpretive Center (☎ 509-775-2295), 15 N Kean St, offers a good introduction to local fossil finds. It's on the west side of town at 6th and N Kean Sts, across from the town park. The oldest known ancestor of the rose family was found near here, which is why it is now called the Stonerose site. Visitors are welcome to dig their own fossils (up to three) with a permit from the interpretive center. Maps and directions are provided, and hammers can be rented for $3. The center and fossil site are open 10 am to 5 pm Tuesday to Saturday, May to October, and also 10 am to 4 pm on Sundays during the summer.

Curlew Lake State Park
Curlew Lake State Park (☎ 509-775-3592), off Hwy 21 approximately 9 miles north of

Republic, makes for good canoeing and boating; several of the lakeside cabin resorts offer rentals. There's also a nice campground, some pleasant swimming, and good fishing for trout and bass in Curlew Lake. During the winter, you can do a little ice fishing, and cross-country skiers can enjoy the open hills around the lake and to the east along the USFS roads.

Hiking

By far the most interesting hike in the area is the **Kettle Crest Trail**, which crosses Hwy 20 at Sherman Pass (Washington's highest paved-road pass) some 20 miles east of Republic. North of the highway, the trail passes through thick forest, with plenty of spur trails leading through wildflowers in the spring. South of the highway, the trail passes through part of the huge 1988 White Mountain burn, which charred 20,000 acres. For several miles, hikers can witness a dramatic stage of forest succession, while interpretive road signs explain the rejuvenating effects of fire. Well into spring, snow lingers on the high ridges of the Kettle Crest Trail, making it popular with cross-country skiers. There is also a primitive campground here.

Places to Stay

Camping Scenic *Curlew Lake State Park* (☎ 509-775-3592) has tent sites (including a handful of very nice walk-in sites) for $10; RV hookups are $14. Most of the Curlew Lake lodges listed below also have RV and tent sites. Campsites are available at the *Triangle J Ranch* for $6 per person per night, and at *Pine Point Resort* for $15/$16 tents/RVs (see below).

Near Sherman Pass, about 20 miles east of Republic, the *Kettle Range Campground* is a small Forest Service campground that makes a good base for day hikes along the Kettle Ridge Trail; sites are free.

Hostels During the summer, the *Triangle J Ranch* (☎ 509-775-3933), 423 Old Kettle Falls Rd, fills up with bicycle tourists; in the fall, hunters bed down here. Hostel facilities include a four-bed dormitory and

a bunkhouse. Use of a big hot tub and an outdoor swimming pool are included in the $11-a-night fee, and an extra $3 will buy breakfast.

Hotels The *Frontier Inn Motel* (☎ 509-775-3361), 979 S Clark Ave, on Republic's main drag is a nice downtown motel with rooms available by reservation only. Single/double rooms cost $36/43, with one room at $28/30. At the other end of town is the *Klondike Motel* (☎ 509-775-3555), 950 N Clark St, with squeaky clean budget rooms for $35/45.

Resorts Curlew Lake has several small cabin resorts, all of which rent boats. On the east side of the lake, *Pine Point Resort* (☎ 509-775-3643), 1060 Pine Point Rd, is a particularly charming spot with campsites and kitchenette cabins starting at $52 to $57 a night. Cabins for the summer months can be booked five years in advance, so don't plan on showing up without a reservation. The resort is 10 miles north of Republic on Hwy 21, and open from mid-April to October 31.

Fisherman's Cove Resort (☎ 509-775-3641, 888-775-3641), 1157 Fisherman's Cove Rd, just north of Pine Point on Hwy 21 is currently open year-round (but call to check) and has cabins with a shared bathhouse starting at $25. Cabins with private bathrooms and kitchens run $50 to $85.

On the west side of Curlew Lake, *Collins Black Beach Resort* (☎ 509-775-3989), 8 miles north of Republic on W Curlew Lake Rd, has cabins for $40 and a few motel rooms starting at $55; it's open April through October. *Tiffany's Resort* (☎ 509-775-3152) is about 4 miles further north. Cabins here start between $43 and $52.

Places to Eat

Kettle Crust Bakery (☎ 509-775-3754), 34 N Clark St, at the Ferry County Co-op has a light lunch menu of vegetarian salads, soups and healthy baked goods in addition to organically grown staples. The *Wild Rose Cafe* (☎ 509-775-2096), 644 S Clark St, just down the street is a cheery spot for breakfast, lunch or dinner. (Don't plan on eating late – dinner shuts down well before 8 or 9 pm.)

Curlew, however, serves the best meals, and it's worth driving the 20 miles from Republic to eat at the *Riverside Bar & Grill* (see Curlew, below).

Shopping

Right at the western edge of the Colville Forest, between Republic and Kettle Falls on Hwy 20, the Tin-Na-Tit Din-Ne-Ki Indian Art Gallery (☎ 509-775-3077) almost literally screams for you to stop. It's a little over the top, but there is some spectacular jewelry and art for sale here. It's open daily from April to December 24.

CURLEW

The little town of Curlew, 21 miles north of Republic, is worth a visit, even if it's just

for dinner. Besides a good restaurant, local attractions include the **Ansorage Hotel** (☎ 509-779-4955), no longer a working hotel but a museum filled with period furnishings. Built in 1903, this impressive building housed travelers and prospective homesteaders fresh off the Great Northern Railroad. It's open 1 to 5 pm on summer weekends. Six miles south of town on Hwy 21, the homespun **Car & Truck Museum** features the world's smallest street-legal car, the 'Peel,' some rare autos and several cars owned by celebrities. It's open in the summer noon to 6 pm daily, and 2 to 6 pm May 1 to Memorial Day.

There are two USA/Canada border crossings in this area: Danville, north of Curlew on Hwy 21, is open 8 am to midnight. Northwest of Curlew, the Midway/Port of Ferry crossing is open 9 am to 5 pm.

Ranald McDonald's Grave

The next time you see a barge ushering a load of wheat down the Columbia, or a train driving freight west to Pacific Rim markets, you can thank a man named Ranald McDonald. Although he was little known, McDonald helped establish the USA's first trade relations with Japan, despite facing huge obstacles of racial prejudice due to his Chinookan heritage.

McDonald was born in 1824 to a Scottish Hudson's Bay Company factor and a Chinook Indian, the daughter of Chief Comcomly (who did business with Lewis and Clark and the Astorians). As a youngster, McDonald met several Japanese sailors whose ship had drifted off course and landed near Cape Flattery. He became fascinated with Japan, which at that time was closed to Westerners, and learned the language from shipwrecked sailors then living at Fort Vancouver.

McDonald's desire to travel abroad intensified after racial discrimination put an end to his short-lived banking career. He became a sailor himself, and on one voyage deliberately shipwrecked in Japan, taking with him books on history and English grammar. His plan worked; curiosity about Western goods and technology won over Japan's impulse to immediately export the unwelcome visitor. McDonald was granted a temporary stay, and he traveled throughout the country as an English teacher and de facto diplomat.

When he finally returned to the US in 1853, he was employed by the US Navy to teach Japanese to interpreters who would be traveling to Japan under the very first US trade treaty.

After traveling all over the world, McDonald retired to northeastern Washington, where he died in 1894. He's buried about 10 miles from Curlew. To reach the cemetery from Curlew, turn west off Hwy 21 onto W Kettle River Rd; follow it 9.5 miles, turn east and cross the river. Then, turn north just after the bridge and go a little over 1 mile to the cemetery on the bluff over the Kettle River. The cabin where McDonald died (he was visiting his niece here) is on private land across the river. ∎

WASHINGTON

Places to Stay & Eat
The *Blue Cougar Motel & Cafe* (☎ 509-779-4817), 2141 Hwy 21 N, has two rooms for $35 each.

The *Riverside Bar & Grill* (☎ 509-779-4813), 813 River St, turns out remarkably good dinners, with specials like grilled halibut and pineapple salsa for about $10. The regular menu features Mexican and American fare. Dinner is served Wednesday to Sunday only. Call for reservations before making the drive.

KETTLE FALLS
Population 1689

Kettle Falls is set in an attractive valley, but there isn't much to keep a traveler here besides an interest in Columbia River history, of which there are several noteworthy examples. The Kettle Falls Campground has a popular swimming beach and marina on Lake Roosevelt.

For at least 9000 years, Kettle Falls was one of the Columbia River's richest fisheries. Native Americans from several different tribes came here each summer to fish and eat salmon, taking as many as 3000 fish a day. The Hudson's Bay Company took note of all the Native Americans gathering at the falls and reckoned it would be a good spot for a fur-trading post. Fort Colvile started operations in 1825, and itself became a hub of activity until it closed in 1871. Catholic missionaries opened St Paul's Mission just up the hill from the trading post in 1848.

Many historic sites – including the original town of Kettle Falls and Fort Colvile – were flooded by Lake Roosevelt when the Columbia River was stopped up by the Grand Coulee Dam in 1939. The town's present site was called Myers Falls until all the transplants from Kettle Falls inundated it.

There are lots of fruit orchards and fruit stands around Kettle Falls, primarily south of town on Peachcrest Rd. Stop by for a bag of peaches, cherries, raspberries, pears or apples.

Orientation
Kettle Falls is 80 miles north of Spokane on US 395, and 31 miles south of the Canadian border. The Columbia River's Lake Roosevelt is just west of town, and Hwy 20 and US 395 meet at the river's west bank.

The nearest border crossing, Laurier/Cascade on US 395, is open 8 am to midnight. On Hwy 25, the Paterson crossing is west of the Columbia River and is open 8 am to midnight. The Boundary/Waneta crossing is on the river's east bank and is open 9 am to 5 pm.

The free Inchelium-Gifford ferry crosses Lake Roosevelt 23 miles south of Kettle Falls. It runs from 6 am to 9:30 pm daily. This is also a good place to spot bald eagles, which winter around Lake Roosevelt.

Information
Contact the Lake Roosevelt National Recreation Area office (☎ 509-738-6266) at 1230 Kettle Park Rd, from 11 am to 5 pm. The Kettle Falls Ranger Station (☎ 509-738-6111), 255 W 11th Ave, can provide information on recreation in the Colville National Forest. If you just need information on the water level in Lake Roosevelt, call ☎ 800-824-4916. The Kettle Falls Area Chamber of Commerce (☎ 509-738-2300), 265 W 3rd Ave (US 395), dispenses general tourist information.

Kettle Falls Historical Center
Drop by the Kettle Falls Historical Center (☎ 509-738-6964), just north of US 395 on the east side of the Columbia River, to see a giant photo mural showing the pre-dam Columbia as it crashed through Kettle Falls. It's a bit disconcerting to look at the riffling, churning water in the photo and then to look out onto the flat lake that is now the river. It's open 11 am to 5 pm Wednesday to Saturday during the summer.

A going concern until 1869, **St Paul's Mission** has been totally restored and is an example of tidy French-Canadian-style log architecture. It's behind the interpretive center, down a dirt road that was once the trail used to portage around the actual falls.

Log Flume Heritage Site
The Log Flume Heritage Site is in the middle of ponderosa pine forests 7 miles

west of the Columbia River on Hwy 20 (at Sherman Creek, milepost 335). It's a nice drive, and the site provides a little snapshot of logging history. In the 1920s, as Washington timber was being shipped worldwide, one traditional logging technique, the low-tech waterpower-and-horse method, was being challenged by a new technique using steam locomotives and trucks. There are several interpretive displays along a winding, wheelchair-accessible trail.

Camp Growden
At another stop on Hwy 20, 11 miles west of Kettle Falls (milepost 331), an old CCC work camp, Camp Growden, recalls the years between 1934 and 1941. It's a peaceful place for a picnic and a short walk on the trail. It's also a good place to look for wildlife, including the occasional moose.

Places to Stay
In town, the NPS *Kettle Falls Campground* on Boise Rd is 2 miles south of the bridge near the mill; it's open year-round and charges $10 in the summer only. It has flush toilets, running water and a boat launch. There are boat rentals and a small store at the adjacent *Kettle Falls Resort & Marina* (☎ 509-738-6121, 800-635-7585), which also rents houseboats. The *Canyon Creek Campground*, 12 miles west of Kettle Falls on Hwy 20, is a small USFS campground with pit toilets, running water and no fee.

My Parents' Estate B&B (☎ 509-738-6220), 719 US 395, is about a mile east of Kettle Falls. Prior to its incarnation as a B&B, this was a Catholic mission and convent, and a boys' school. The grounds cover 47 acres, and there's a gymnasium. Rates run $75 to $100.

Barney's Motel (☎ 509-738-6546), just west of the river where US 395 hits Hwy 20, operates alongside its large cafe on the west bank of Lake Roosevelt. Barney's complex is so well-established that its location is known as 'Barney's Junction.' The motel is neither fancy nor expensive, with rooms starting at $25. Across the

bridge, the *Grandview Inn Motel & RV Park* (☎ 509-738-6733), 978 US 395 at the junction with Hwy 25, has a nice grassy lawn overlooking Lake Roosevelt and single/double rooms from $36/38. Downtown the *Kettle Falls Inn* (☎ 509-738-6514), 203 E 3rd St (US 395), has rooms with microwave ovens and refrigerators for $39/44.

Places to Eat
Barney's Restaurant & Lounge (☎ 509-738-6546), at US 395 and Hwy 20, is the place everybody eats in Kettle Falls. The *Hudson Bay Steak & Seafood Co* (☎ 509-738-6164), near Barney's at 3986 Hwy 20, is the spot for a fancier dinner. The prompt and friendly *Little Gallea Restaurant* (☎ 509-738-6776), downtown on US 395 has hearty breakfasts, sandwiches and burgers for under $5. They also have a reputation for good cheesecake.

Getting There & Away
Borderline Stage buses make the trip between Kettle Falls and Spokane once daily on weekdays. The bus from Colville bypasses Kettle Falls if there aren't any passengers, so be sure to call the office in Spokane (☎ 509-624-7192) for more information.

COLVILLE
Population 6205

Colville is a town of some substance – there's even a McDonald's sign beckoning along the highway. Indeed, it is northeastern Washington's largest town after Spokane and the seat of Stevens County. It's an attractive timber town, with many gracious older homes and gardens around downtown. Colville dates from 1883, when locals appropriated the buildings from nearby Fort Colvile (which was closed), carting everything a few miles away to a townsite along the Colville River. However, today most travelers will probably only stop here as a base before exploring the Colville National Forest; the USFS headquarters are here and can provide information on hiking and camping.

Orientation & Information

The Okanogan Highlands rise to the west of town, and the Kalispell Mountains are to the northeast. Downtown Colville is built on a bench just east of the Colville River. Hwy 20 runs east-west through town, a two-block strip of boutiques centered around Astor St making up the downtown. US 395 heads south out of Colville toward Spokane, 71 miles away. Colville is just 8 miles east of Kettle Falls.

The Colville Chamber of Commerce (☎ 509-684-3973) is at 121 E Astor St. The Colville National Forest Ranger Station (☎ 509-684-4557) is at 695 S Main St.

Coin-Op Laundry (☎ 509-684-2137), 156 E Dominion St is on the main drag at Main St. Mt Carmel Hospital (☎ 509-684-2651), 982 E Columbia Ave, has 24-hour emergency care.

Keller House Interpretive Center

The only real tourist attraction in Colville itself is the Keller House (☎ 509-684-5968), 700 N Wynne St, a rather large bungalow with nice Craftsman details, built in 1910. A lookout, carriage house, log house and some farm machinery have been imported from around the county and flank the house. It's open 1 to 4 pm daily in May; and 10 am to 4 pm Monday to Saturday, and 1 to 4 pm on Sunday, from June to September.

Little Pend Oreille Wildlife Refuge

Bird watchers should swing down to the Little Pend Oreille Wildlife Refuge, where McDowell Lake attracts waterfowl and it's possible to see black bears, especially in the spring or fall. To reach the refuge headquarters (☎ 509-684-8384), take Hwy 20 for about 8 miles east of Colville, then turn south on Narcisse Creek Rd. There are several rudimentary campsites around the 63-sq-mile wildlife area; a stop at the headquarters will set you up with seasonally appropriate camping, hiking and wildlife viewing information.

Skiing

Eastern Washington's **downhill** skiers head to 49 Degrees North (☎ 509-935-6649, or 509-880-9208 for a snow report), 42 miles south of Colville near Chewelah. It's a small ski area with four chair lifts and an 1844-foot vertical drop. Prime-time lift tickets are $28, but they're much cheaper on weekdays. There are also 9.3 miles of cross-country trails. The ski area is closed Wednesday and Thursday, except during holidays.

The snowmobile's reign may be nearing an end in the Colville National Forest, which is gaining a reputation for good **cross-country skiing**. Skiers can find miles of informal trails in the national forest and the Little Pend Oreille Wildlife Refuge. Contact the Colville National Forest ranger station (☎ 509-684-4557) for an update on groomed trails.

Special Events

The Colville Artwalk (☎ 509-685-9243), is an annual arts celebration involving more than 70 regional artists. It's held for 10 days in mid-June, and centers on two Saturdays of downtown demonstrations and exhibitions.

The Colville Rendezvous, held the first weekend of August at the city park, is a fun weekend festival with crafts booths, a wide variety of bands (from bagpipes to country to Dixieland), games and a beer hall.

Places to Stay

Camp for free alongside Mill Creek at the *Douglas Falls Campground* (☎ 509-684-7474), 7 miles north of town on Colville-Aladdin Rd, which is off Hwy 20 just east of town. It's only open in the summer, with pit toilets and a water pump. Campsites at the Pend Oreille Wildlife Refuge (☎ 509-684-8384) are also free and decidedly primitive, with pit toilets and no water; they are open late spring to the first snows.

Carefree Guest Ranch B&B (☎ 509-684-4739), 786 B Arden Butte Rd, is 7 miles south of town. It's an attractive place with horseback riding and a hot tub; double rooms cost about $100. *Benny's Colville Inn* (☎ 509-684-2517), 915 S Main St, a large place at the south end of town, has an indoor pool and hot tub. Rooms start at $46. The smaller *Downtown Motel* (☎ 509-

684-2565), 369 S Main St, is slightly less expensive with rooms at $32/35.

About 25 miles east of Colville on Lake Gillette, the *Beaver Lodge Resort* (☎ 509-684-5657), 2430 Hwy 20 E, has cabins for $40 and campsites near the Pend Oreille Recreational Area. A small restaurant and boat rentals round out the resort.

Places to Eat
It's no culinary mecca, but Colville is not a bad place to stop for a meal. For morning espresso and pastries drop by *Talk 'n Coffee* (☎ 509-684-2373), 119 E Astor St. *Cookie's Cafe* (☎ 509-684-8660), at Oak St at 2nd St in the Pinkney City Mall, is a good breakfast or lunch spot if you're willing to bore through a load of Americana to get into it. Campers can stock up at the *North County Co-op* (☎ 509-684-6132), 282 W Astor St, a good food co-op open to non-members.

Colville's most happening place is *Cafe al Mundo* (☎ 509-684-8092) 117 W Astor St, a youthful eatery and brewpub done up in psychedelic southwest decor. Inexpensive tamales, curries and burritos form the backbone of the eclectic menu; panini sandwiches with soup and salad ($7) make a filling dinner, Brazilian black-bean burritos ($4.25) a quick snack. Espresso, microbrews and live music (typically reggae) are the main draws in the evening.

Cafe Italiano (☎ 509-684-5957), 153 W 2nd St, offers more formal dining; it's a classy new Italian joint with pasta dishes in the $8 to $10 range.

Getting There & Away
Borderline Stage buses (☎ 509-624-7192) make the trip to Spokane once daily on weekdays. Pickup is from the local ticket office at 127 E Astor St.

METALINE FALLS
Metaline (population 301) and Metaline Falls (population 262), small towns separated by the Pend Oreille River, are in the very northeast corner of the state. This is remote, lovely country, with access to the Salmo-Priest Wilderness Area, which is home to a few grizzly bears and rare woodland caribou. Metaline Falls is an exceptionally pretty town that used to house a cement factory, which for years covered pretty much everything in a thin layer of dust.

Like so many falls in the area, Metaline Falls itself was flooded by a dam – this one the Boundary Dam, up near the Canadian border, which was built in the 1960s. The dam itself is worth a visit, even if you normally eschew dam tours. Keep your eyes peeled for mountain goats, bighorn sheep and moose on the road to the Boundary Dam. There's a viewing site at Flume Creek about 3 miles up Boundary Dam Rd from Metaline.

Orientation & Information
Metaline Falls is 97 miles north of Spokane and 10 miles south of the Canadian border. From Hwy 20, take Hwy 31 north, which reaches Metaline first and then, across the river, Metaline Falls.

A visitors' center has been set up in an old railroad car in the town park, across from Katie's Oven Bakery. Contact the Metaline Chamber of Commerce at ☎ 509-446-3683. The Sullivan Lake Ranger Station (☎ 509-446-7300) at Sullivan Lake has information about all of the hiking and campsites in this part of the Colville National Forest.

Boundary Dam
The 340-foot-high Boundary Dam (☎ 509-446-3073), just south of the USA/Canada border, spans two huge rocky cliffs. Its inner workings are pocketed in caverns and connected by tunnels hewn from the limestone. Those who aren't easily spooked should take the dam tour, offered during the summer from 10 am to 5:30 pm. Turn off Hwy 31 just north of Metaline, before the road crosses the river to Metaline Falls, and follow Boundary Rd (also known as County Rd 62) 11½ miles to the dam's access road.

Near the dam on this side of the river is **Crawford State Park** (☎ 509-446-4065). The highlight of this park is **Gardner Cave**, a 1055-foot-long limestone cave. Guided tours of the cave's stalactites and stalagmites leave four times daily from Wednesday to Saturday. The park and cave close down roughly from September 15 to May 1.

On the river's east bank, the **Boundary Vista House** is perched on the canyon wall 500 feet above the water. It's the best place around for a panoramic view, and not a bad place to camp for the night. To get there, you must drive north on Hwy 31 from Metaline Falls to Crescent Lake, turn west onto the access road, and drive 2 miles to the Vista House.

Sullivan Lake

Southeast of Metaline Falls, Sullivan Lake can also be reached by crossing the Pend Oreille River at Ione and heading northeast. Campgrounds at both the north and south ends of the lake are connected by a 3-mile hiking trail that runs along the lake's east shore. Anglers know Sullivan Lake for its brown trout – the 22-pound state-record brown trout came from here. Continue east along USFS Rd 22, at the lake's north end, to reach more hiking trails.

Hiking

The 22-mile-long **Shedroof Divide National Recreation Trail** goes through the Salmo-Priest Wilderness Area; it starts east of Sullivan Lake on USFS Rd 22, just past Pass Creek Pass. From here, it's a fairly rugged trail north with lots of good views and wildlife. Several other trails in the area offer the opportunity to make a loop hike, lasting either a day or overnight. Otherwise, most backpackers hike the trail one way. To reach the northern end of the Shedroof Divide Trail, cut north from USFS Rd 22 onto USFS Rd 2220 about 6 miles east of Sullivan Lake. Follow USFS Rd 2220, a good gravel road, some 12 miles to the Shedroof Divide Trailhead (trail No 535).

The trailhead for the **Hall Mountain** hike is also east of Sullivan Lake on USFS Rd 22; turn south on Johns Creek Rd and take this rough road to the end. Bighorn sheep live on Hall Mountain, and the 2½-mile hike to the summit sometimes rewards hikers with good wildlife viewing.

Abercrombie Mountain, at 7308 feet, is the highest peak in the Washington Selkirks. From the top, there are views into both the Pend Oreille and Columbia River drainages. It's a 4-mile hike up the mountain along the Flume Creek drainage, with over 2000 feet in elevation gain. Reach the trailhead by turning off Boundary Rd at Flume Creek north of Metaline; take USFS Rd 350 and continue about 7 miles to the end of the dirt road.

Places to Stay & Eat

There's free camping at *Campbell Park* by Box Canyon Dam, about halfway between Ione and Metaline. The two USFS campgrounds at Sullivan Lake, *Sullivan Lake Campground* at the north end and *Noisy Creek Campground* at the south end, accept some advance reservations (☎ 800-280-2267). Sites are $6 ($9 for lakeside) and they have running water, pit toilets and some flush toilets, but no hookups.

The *Washington Hotel* (☎ 509-446-4415), 225 5th St, above Katie's Oven Bakery in Metaline Falls, is a classic, old small-town hotel. Built in 1910, it has simple rooms, bathrooms down the hall, and an artist's studio at the foot of the steps. Double rooms go for $25.

The *Circle Motel* (☎ 509-446-4343), just north of Metaline Falls on Hwy 31, is a small motel with basic accommodations; rooms cost $30 to $45 depending on size.

In a town not noted for culinary extravagance, *Katie's Oven Bakery* (☎ 509-446-4806) at the Washington Hotel stands out as the place to eat whenever possible (during the summer they're only open Wednesday to Saturday). While it may mean a diet heavy on cinnamon rolls, it'll be worth it. The lunch menu changes daily and usually includes something vegetarian – expect to find a few good soups, Mediterranean salads and sandwiches. There are also a couple of burger stands in the area.

Entertainment

The *Cutter Theatre* (☎ 509-446-4108), housed in an old school built around 1910 by noted Spokane architect Kirtland Cutter, has recently been restored. Shows range from goofy melodramas to oboe and horn duets. As with everything else in Metaline Falls, it's easy on the wallet.

IONE

Several weekends a year, a train runs along the Pend Oreille River between Ione's historic rail depot and Metaline Falls. The two-hour trip is exceptionally scenic and allows passengers the chance to come to grips with their fear of heights *and* of the dark – the tracks cross Box Canyon on a 156-foot-high trestle and pass through an 821-foot-long tunnel. The $5 trips are usually scheduled on Father's Day weekend (mid-June), the last weekend in July, Labor Day weekend (early September), and a couple of 'autumn colors' weekends in late September and early October. Call Lion's Excursion Train (☎ 509-442-3397) for exact scheduling; two weeks' advance reservations are required.

If you miss the train ride, you can still take in the Pend Oreille scenery by boat. Z-Canyon Tours (☎ 509-442-3728, 800-676-8883) runs a 2½-hour **jet boat tour**, which departs weekends from the Box Canyon Resort on Hwy 31 and zooms past waterfalls and cliffs en route to Boundary Dam; cost for adults is $35.

Though less impressive than Boundary Dam to the north, **Box Canyon Dam** (☎ 509-446-3083) does have a visitors' center with tours and a riverside park. People also fish for trout in the reservoir behind the dam.

Places to Stay & Eat

The USFS *Edgewater Campground* is on the east bank of the Pend Oreille, 2 miles north of Ione; it's primitive, no fee. In Ione the *Riverview Inn* (also known as Del's Motel, ☎ 509-442-3418) is right on the river, albeit right across from the mill, and has single/double motel rooms for $40/45. Next door, *Del's Restaurant* is operated by the same folks and is the only place to eat in town.

Five miles north of Ione is the new *Box Canyon Resort* (☎ 509-442-3728), 8612 Hwy 31, a small roadside motel with the Pend Oreille River running right at its doorstep; the riverside rooms here are a remarkable value at $40/45.

USK

People come to Usk, 49 miles north of Spokane, to hunt and fish. **Brown's Lake** is a fly-fishing-only lake with cutthroat trout, where no motorized boats are allowed. Cross the Pend Oreille River at Usk and head 5 miles north, then 6 miles northeast to the USFS campground on lake's south shore.

Davis Lake, 5½ miles south of Usk on Hwy 211, is popular with anglers early and late in the season, when they haul in largemouth bass, Kokanee salmon, rainbow trout and Eastern brook trout.

The *Inn at Usk* (☎ 509-445-1526), 410 River Rd, is an old country guesthouse with rooms for $25 to $35 and a few tent sites ($6); they also rent canoes. Because it's oriented toward adventure travelers, it's a popular stop for cross-country cyclists making their way across the state on Hwy 20. It rivals the Washington Hotel, up in Metaline Falls, as the best place to stay in Pend Oreille country. Since there's nowhere else to eat around here you'll definitely want to stick around for breakfast ($5) before heading out.

WASHINGTON

Southeastern Washington

Southeastern Washington is the state's loneliest corner. It's filled with the big wheat farms of the Palouse around Pullman, the stark Channeled Scablands of the desert and the asparagus and onion fields around Walla Walla. There isn't a lot to see or do – Fort Walla Walla and Palouse Falls being the main tourist attractions – and many of the small towns consist of little more than a grain elevator and (if you're lucky) a gas station/cafe. The nicest place to stay for a day or two is Walla Walla. Though people aren't much geared toward the tourist trade, they're generally rather pleased and surprised when someone makes a point of visiting.

The Cascade rain shadow looms over this part of Washington: less than 10 inches of rain falls annually in this barren desert landscape. Most of the land in southeastern Washington is underlain by enormous foundations of lava that flooded here over the millennia from volcanic ruptures near the Wallowa Mountains in Oregon. Under Pasco, the lava fills a basin a mile-and-a-half deep. The thin soils that managed to form on this volcanic plateau were swept away during the Spokane Floods, when ice dams in Montana gave way at the end of the last ice age and swept across the Columbia Plateau. It's still easy to see the path of the floods in the area north and south of Ritzville, where the denuded lava flows and gouged-out ponds form a curious geologic area called the Channeled Scablands. Floodwaters diverted the Palouse River's course and created the dramatic Palouse Falls.

However, on the eastern edge of Washington is the Palouse region, an extremely fertile area defined by rolling hills planted in wheat and legumes. Sometime before the last ice age, prevailing southwesterly winds blew across the lava-covered Columbia Plateau, blowing dust for thousands of years north onto its eastern edge.

Dunes gradually accumulated into steep-sided rolling hills, and the resulting soil, called loess, is very fertile.

History

The Yakima, Columbia, Snake and Walla Walla River valleys were each important to prehistoric Native Americans, and the area of their confluence was an ancient crossroads of culture, transport and trade. Originally, Palouse Indians lived along the lower Snake River, where they fished for salmon. They also traveled to collect roots and berries and developed the appaloosa horse.

Lewis and Clark were the first white explorers to make their way through this region in 1805, when they floated down the Snake River to join the Columbia River near Pasco. French-Canadian trappers began working the area soon after, and the Hudson's Bay Company built the first Fort Walla Walla near Wallula Gap in 1818, at the mouth of the Walla Walla River. The area around Walla Walla was first settled with the establishment of the Whitman Mission in 1836, which lead to a bloody confrontation that sparked the Cayuse War.

In the early 1850s Walla Walla was closed to settlement until treaties with the Cayuse Indians were signed. Up north, the Palouse around Pullman did not easily submit to treaties with the whites, and after they defeated army troops at Steptoe Butte in 1858, the US Army went after them with a vengeance. Most Palouse refused to go to reservations, and as whites moved in, they lived under increasingly marginal circumstances.

In 1862, gold was discovered in Idaho and Montana, and the tiny outpost of Walla Walla found itself along the main transportation line between Portland and the gold fields. It was the steamboat terminus of the upper Columbia, bringing goods from Portland up to Walla Walla and the Idaho gold camps. The town boomed more

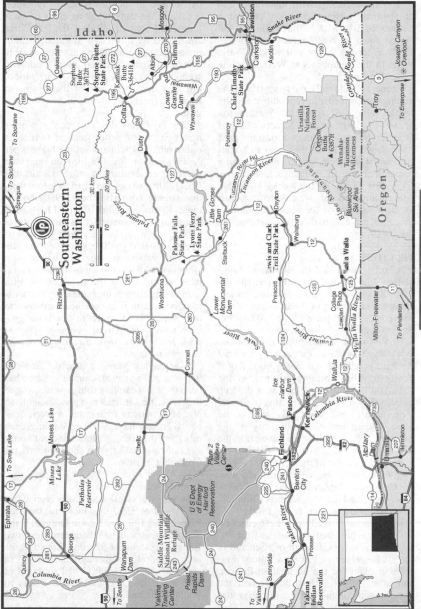

or less immediately, with merchants and provisioners setting up highly profitable businesses. By 1870, Walla Walla was the largest town in Washington Territory. In 1875, a narrow-gauge rail linked Walla Walla to the steamboats at Wallula on the Columbia River.

Farmers also found a ready market in the mining camps for fresh vegetables, and the fertile valleys of southeast Washington began to fall to the plow. Miners who had swarmed through Pullman during the gold rush around the 1860s gave way to homesteaders, who began farming and ranching in the area around Pullman and Moscow, ID, by the 1870s. As the Rocky Mountain gold rush played out, agriculture took over as the mainstay of the local economies. Irrigation projects in the 1900s established the Tri-Cities.

TRI-CITIES
Pasco (population 22,370), Kennewick (population 48,010) and Richland (population 35,090), known as the Tri-Cities, sprawl along the arid banks of the Columbia River between the confluence of the Yakima and Snake rivers, and they constitute Washington's fourth-largest population center. While the Tri-Cities aren't exactly a tourist destination, chances are pretty good that if you're traveling through this part of the state, you'll end up stopping to eat or sleep here, as they're at the intersection of several long, usually hot roads. Richland is the most modern and accessible city of the three and offers the most for travelers in the way of amenities.

Early settlement of the Tri-Cities region awaited the railroads, which pushed across the Columbia Plateau in 1880. Kennewick grew up around the region's first Columbia River irrigation projects in the 1900s.

However, what really put these cities on the map was the Hanford Nuclear Reservation, which was built north of Richland in the 1940s. Hanford was a plutonium-refining plant for the Manhattan Project, and after WWII it also researched the development of nuclear energy. Hanford

was closed in the 1980s due to radiation leaks and the bank-breaking costs of environmental cleanup. Today, the Tri-Cities are the center of a large irrigated farming region, and even in town the summer air is heavy with the peculiar humid odor of sprinkler irrigation. Previous to irrigation, this was the driest part of the desert, as Richland receives only six inches of rain a year.

The Tri-Cities don't particularly offer much charm or sophistication (which is rather odd, as Richland has the highest per capita income in Washington and the greatest concentration of PhDs in the USA). Turn off of the strip developments that largely comprise these 1950s boomtowns to glimpse what life must have been like in these 'Atomic Cities' when things nuclear were in the vanguard. Keep your eyes peeled and you'll begin to see the little whirling nuclear symbol everywhere – on churches (a Richland church has a mural with angels flying through heaven with atomic whirligigs alongside), high schools (the local team is called the Bombers and their mascot is a mushroom cloud) and grocery stores (ie, Atomic Foods). Nuclear pride isn't so dominant any longer, but the vestiges remain.

'Kennewick Man,' a nearly complete, 9300- to 9600-year-old human skeleton has been the most exciting thing to come out of the Tri-Cities in recent years. Scientists, Native American tribes, and esoteric religious groups have all been battling each other for the rights to these ancient bones since their discovery on the banks of the Columbia in 1996.

Orientation
Several major Northwest routes intersect at the Tri-Cities. US 395, which runs between Ritzville on I-90 and I-84 in Oregon, is the main north-south link between these two freeway systems. I-82 runs from Ellensburg and Yakima through the Tri-Cities area and down to I-84; US 12 splits off of I-82 at the Tri-Cities and continues east to Walla Walla and Idaho.

Hanford: Of Atomic Bombs & Nuclear Waste

In 1942, the US government established the Hanford Engineering Works as part of the Manhattan Project, the top-secret, WWII program designed to develop the first atomic bomb. This remote site was considered ideal because of its distance from population centers and its proximity to the Columbia River's water and hydroelectric power. Richland was founded at the same time as an 'Atomic City.' The plutonium reactors built at Hanford were the world's first and they produced the payload for the atomic bomb that fell on Nagasaki in 1945.

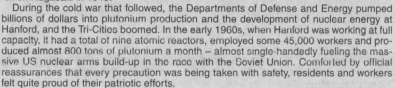

During the cold war that followed, the Departments of Defense and Energy pumped billions of dollars into plutonium production and the development of nuclear energy at Hanford, and the Tri-Cities boomed. In the early 1960s, when Hanford was working at full capacity, it had a total of nine atomic reactors, employed some 45,000 workers and produced almost 800 tons of plutonium a month – almost single-handedly fueling the massive US nuclear arms build-up in the race with the Soviet Union. Comforted by official reassurances that every precaution was being taken with safety, residents and workers felt quite proud of their patriotic efforts.

However, despite the government's zealous commitment, safety oversights and poor planning eventually doomed their efforts. Billions of gallons of radioactive waste were simply buried in underground storage tanks, many of which are now leaking. Until Hanford was closed as a reactor site in the 1980s, the Columbia River was considered the most radioactive river in the world. In 1986 the Department of Energy revealed that, in addition to over a hundred accidental radiation releases over the years, in 1949 there was one deliberate release, called the Green Run, which was done to test radiation monitoring equipment.

As might be expected, severe health problems are rampant in the area, and though many lawsuits have been filed against the plant, few expect to win their cases. The deactivation and environmental cleanup has been extremely difficult and costly, attracting billions of dollars in federal tax money, but officials admit that almost nothing has been cleaned up so far. Some now feel the best plan is to let the buildings sit for another half century until the radioactive isotopes decay enough so that workers will not be endangered as they dismantle the buildings. Ironically, the cleanup now employs more people than Hanford ever did as an active nuclear facility.

Another odd twist in the Hanford saga is that the reservation also contains some of the most pristine wilderness in Washington, a result of the secrecy and security surrounding the plant. Since Hanford's operations use only 6% of the land, the government is now divesting itself of some of the rest, and the western side has been included in the Arid Lands Ecology Reserve: 120 sq miles of native sagebrush grasslands, a rarity in intensely irrigated central Washington. Plant life here includes bluebunch wheat grass, lupine and balsamroot, and the reserve is home to Swainson's and ferruginous hawks, golden eagles, sage sparrows, sagebrush voles and a large and unusual population of desert elk. Though currently a de facto national park, the land's ultimate fate will be decided by contentious debates between environmentalists, the Yakama Nation, land developers and the federal government. ■

From Yakima to Richland on I-82 is 76 miles; from Pasco to Spokane on US 395 is 136 miles; and from Pasco to Walla Walla on US 12 is 47 miles. From Kennewick south to Oregon, at Umatilla, is 30 miles.

It's easy to get misdirected in the Tri-Cities; road signs seem designed to be as confusing as possible, and appear without warning within feet of critical exits. The octopus-like intersections at the south end of the US 395 bridge over the Columbia River are especially confusing.

Only Richland has a gathering of buildings (along George Washington Way and Jadwin Ave) that could be considered a town center. Otherwise, Pasco and Kennewick are amorphous and centerless; they are best thought of as a series of commercial strips and suburbs. Pasco is largely a Hispanic community, home to most of the

area's agricultural workers. The airport, bus and rail stations are all located in Pasco.

The main arterial between Richland and Kennewick is Hwy 240, also called Columbia Drive. The freeway spur I-182 runs east to west between Pasco and Richland.

Information
The Tri-Cities Visitor & Convention Bureau (☎ 509-735-8486, 800-254-5824), is at 6951 Grandridge Blvd, Kennewick, or write PO Box 2241, Tri-Cities, WA 99302.

WASHINGTON

Kennewick Man
Southeastern Washington's most controversial public figure is an anonymous dead guy believed to be over 9300 years old.

It all started in the summer of 1996, when two college students found a nearly complete skeleton on the banks of the Columbia River near Kennewick. The county coroner examined the skeleton, and then called in a forensic anthropologist to help determine if this was a murder victim or the remains of an ancient Indian, in which case the bones would be turned over to local tribes for 'repatriation,' or burial on tribal lands.

However, when anthropologist James Chatters examined the skeleton, he made some astonishing discoveries. The skeleton was that of a Caucasian male, between 40 and 45 years of age, who stood about 5 feet 9 inches. Most startling, when Chatters was cleaning the pelvis structure, he noticed a gray object embedded in the bone. Further examination revealed the object to be a stone projectile point, of a sort usually associated with the Archaic Indian period about 9000 years ago. If the man whose skeleton was found along the Columbia River was Caucasian, what was he doing in western North American at a time when, according to most historical sources, the American Indians had just arrived via the Bering land bridge from Asia? Subsequent radio carbon dating fixed the skeleton's age at between 9300 and 9600 years.

Just who was the Kennewick Man?

Almost immediately, the story of an ancient European skeleton wounded by a prehistoric spear point found its way into the press. As the skeleton was discovered on federal land supervised by the US Army Corps of Engineers, this government agency immediately ordered Chatters to stop his investigation, and sent a representative to collect the bones; the Corps then declared that the skeleton would be returned to local tribes. Under the terms of the federal Native American Graves Protection and Repatriation Act (NAGPRA, 1990), any Native American remains found on public land had to be returned to local tribes. The Umatilla Indians, leading a coalition of Columbia Basin tribes, formally claimed the bones under the act, vowing that they would re-bury the skeleton.

Upset at the prospect of losing a chance to study this rare discovery – which wasn't, they objected, covered by NAGPRA because the remains were not of an American Indian – eight anthropologists initiated a lawsuit against the Army Corps of Engineers in hopes of stalling the re-burial and of preserving the skeleton for further study. Eight other groups, including the Asatru Folk Assembly, a northern California-based religious group

The post office in Richland at 815 Jadwin Ave is convenient.

Columbia River Exhibition of History, Science & Technology

A new and long-awaited science and history museum in Richland's Howard Amon Park, CREHST (☎ 509-943-9000) combines exhibits salvaged from the old Hanford Science Center with new displays on the area's natural and human histories. Impressive local finds, such as a woolly mammoth tusk, chronicle the region's rich prehistoric past, making the museum a worthwhile visit.

Unsurprisingly, the museum's technology section gives over to a preoccupation with the history and continuing debacle of Hanford. Even if nuclear energy and bomb production give you the creeps, there's a lot to learn here about all things atomic; it's also eye-opening to learn about the US Government's policy presumptions during the Cold War years. Other exhibits discuss nuclear energy, energy conservation and radioactivity, and

with beliefs in ancient Norse gods, came forward a few months later to stake their own claims to the skeleton.

The federal court issued a restraining order against the Army Corps of Engineers and Kennewick Man was safely locked in a wooden box inside a vault, away from public view – or so it was thought. Miffed by news that Native Americans had been allowed to perform religious rituals over the skeleton, Asatru leaders threatened a discrimination lawsuit if they weren't allowed to perform their own ceremonies. The Army Corps of Engineers politely relented, and 10 members of the group, clad in Viking garb, traveled to the Tri-Cities to venerate the skeleton with prayer and a ceremonial toast (Asatru members had to drink fruit juice out of their cow horn cups, as the traditional toast of mead was prohibited by the Corps' anti-alcohol rules.)

The Kennewick Man skeleton is of vast interest to scientists, Native Americans and the general public for many reasons. If the skeleton proves to be Caucasian, the presence of Europeans in North American nearly 10,000 years ago utterly upsets the standard theory of human migration to North America. Perhaps when the ancestors of today's Native Americans arrived via the Bering land bridge, they encountered a pre-existing Stone-Age culture made up of Europeans. Other scientists speculate that the skeleton is related to neither the ancestors of Native American tribes nor early Europeans, but rather to an unrelated Caucasoid race from Southeast Asia. This explanation raises as many questions as it does answers. The discovery of the Kennewick Man also brings up the interesting, but thorny, question of just who or what is a 'Native American.'

Who will get to do what with the skeleton? Its identity will first need to be established. In early 1998, the Department of the Interior ruled in favor of further scientific study to determine whether the remains are of an American Indian. However, the bones currently remain locked up in Richland, where they await the action of the courts. ■

demonstrate the methods being used to clean up the site. There are a number of child-oriented displays, like operating the robot pincers that are used to pick up radioactive materials.

CREHST is open 10 am to 5 pm Monday to Saturday, and noon to 5 pm on Sunday; adults/seniors $3.50/2.95, students $2.50.

Washington Public Power Supply System Visitor Center

While the mothballed bomb-making facilities at the Hanford Nuclear Reservation proper are closed to the public, visitors are permitted to drive onto the site for a close-up view of a nuclear power plant still in use for commercial purposes. From Richland follow George Washington Way or Stevens Drive 12 miles north to the Washington Public Power Supply System (or Plant 2) Visitor Center (☎ 509-372-5860), beside an evil-looking containment tank and cooling towers. More fun than the center itself is the science fiction-like drive across the desolate landscape – an ominous, unknown nuclear facility appearing on the horizon every few miles. The visitors' center explains the difference between fusion and fission and the virtues of nuclear energy. It's open 11 am to 4 pm Thursday and Friday, and noon to 5 pm on weekends.

Wineries

The hot, dry summers of the eastern Yakima Valley near Richland give a soft finish to hearty grapes like cabernet and merlot. Who would expect that the grapes for some of Washington's finest wines are grown within sight of the plutonium reactors at Hanford?

Eleven miles west of the Tri-Cities in Benton City, **Kiona Vineyards Winery** (☎ 509-588-6716), 44612 N Sunset Rd, is open noon to 5 pm daily. Try the lemberger, often described as the zinfandel of Washington. **Oakwood Cellars** (☎ 509-588-5332), 40504 DeMoss Rd, is open noon to 6 pm on weekends. Big round cabernets and merlots are the attraction here, as well as a pretty good chardonnay.

Activities

Much of the land between US 240 and the Columbia is interspersed with parks, marinas and golf courses. **Columbia Park** in Kennewick is a vast greenway complete with a golf course, play fields, campground, boat moorage, as well as picnic and swimming areas. Richland's newest park, **Howard Amon Park** on George Washington Way has a riverfront walkway, a children's museum and a grassy beach. It's also home to CREHST, the Tri-Cities' new science and history museum.

Kids of all ages can cool off at **Oasis Waterworks** (☎ 509-735-8442), 6321 W Canal Dr, a waterpark in Kennewick.

Places to Stay

Most lodgings in the Tri-Cities are national motel chains along the major arterials. The cheapest places to stay are along the US 395 strip in Kennewick; the *Tapadera Budget Inn* (☎ 509-783-6191, 800-722-8277), 300-A N Ely, at the corner of US 395 and Clearwater, is a good value with a pool and newly remodeled single/double rooms for $40/47. One of the nicer places to stay in Kennewick is the *Ramada Inn* (☎ 509-586-0541), 435 Clover Island Rd; rooms start at $65/70. This motel complex is on an island in the Columbia, which is linked to the shore by a short bridge.

All the following Richland motels offer pools, a necessity here in summer. For a nice, inexpensive stay, check out the tiki-themed *Bali Hi Motel* (☎ 509-943-3101), 1201 George Washington Way, with rates around $37/41. *Nendel's* (☎ 509-943-4611, 800-547-0106), 615 Jadwin Ave, offers a complimentary continental breakfast and some kitchenettes; rooms start from $42/48. At the *Best Western Tower Inn* (☎ 509-946-4121, 800-635-3980), 1515 George Washington Way, there's an indoor pool, sauna, children's playground and rooms from $69.

The choicest lodgings in Richland, and in the Tri-Cities, are along the Columbia River near Columbia Park; both the following are large convention-style hotels that have better-than-average restaurants. The *DoubleTree Hotel* (☎ 509-946-7611, 800-547-8010), 802 George Washington Way, offers access to the paths along the river, with rooms from $72. The *Shilo Inn Rivershore* (☎ 509-946-4661, 800-222-2244), 50 Comstock St, is next to the golf course and tennis courts; rates are $69.

Places to Eat

Travelers along US 395 swear by the breakfasts at the *Country Gentleman* (☎ 509-783-0128), 300 N Ely in Kennewick; otherwise, you'll have no trouble spotting some tolerable fast food along this ugly 5-mile-long commercial strip.

As with lodging, the nicer places to eat in the Tri-Cities are in Richland. You know this isn't just any eastern Washington town when you can head to *Some Bagels* (☎ 509-946-3185), 1317 George Washington Way; you can also fill up on lattes here. *Jennifer's Bread & Dakery* (☎ 509-946-5514), 701 George Washington Way, serves up breads, pastries and light lunch fare in a building at the corner of Lee St that looks abandoned but really isn't.

Emerald of Siam (☎ 509-946-9328), 1314 Jadwin Ave, serves great Thai food from its unassuming slot in an aging strip mall. *Atomic Ale Brewpub & Eatery* (☎ 509-946-5465), 1015 Lee Blvd, has wood-fired specialty pizzas – an odd thing to find in the middle of a desert, but then again, maybe that atomic thing isn't really a gimmick after all; wash one down with some of their Half-Life Hefeweizen. Behind the Mexican restaurant across the street, *Vannini's* (☎ 509-946-4525), 1026 Lee Blvd, serves Italian sandwiches and pasta in a cheerfully refurbished Pullman dining car. The food is straightforward and relatively inexpensive (dinners start under $10), but it's one of the better restaurants in Richland.

Don't overlook Pasco if you like Mexican food; there are taco stands and cantinas at nearly every parking lot and street corner. If you're intimidated by the Spanish language barrier, cross back over the river to *Casa Chapala* (☎ 509-586-4224), 107 E Columbia Dr, in Kennewick.

For fine dining head to the Shilo Inn or DoubleTree Hotel dining rooms, listed above.

Getting There & Away

Air Horizon, United Express and Delta have flights from the Tri-Cities to Seattle, Portland and Spokane. The Tri-Cities Airport (☎ 509-547-6352) is just north of Pasco off I-182.

Bus Greyhound passes through Pasco on its run between Portland and Spokane. Northwestern Trailways buses go to Walla Walla. The bus depot (☎ 509-547-3151) is at 115 N 2nd St at W Clark St, near the train station.

Train Amtrak's *Empire Builder* passes through Pasco daily en route to Seattle. The depot (☎ 509-545-1554) is at W Clark and N Tacoma Sts.

Getting Around

Ben Franklin Transit (☎ 509-735-5100) buses run daylight hours Monday to Saturday. In Pasco, the Sterl Adams-22nd Ave Transit Center is at 22nd and Sylvester Sts. From here you can catch a bus to Kennewick, Richland or the airport. Call Trans Plus Night Service (☎ 509-582-5555) for share-taxi pick-up from 7 pm to 11 pm; fare is an unbeatable 75¢.

For a cab, call A+ Taxi (☎ 509-586-9149).

WALLA WALLA
Population 29,189

Perhaps it's the awkward, unlikely redundancy of the name itself, or the fact that the state penitentiary is located here (inmates crank out more than 2.5 million license plates a year), but Walla Walla undeservedly suffers a reputation as Washington's town on the backside of beyond. For Puget Sound urbanites, Walla Walla is shorthand for all that's rural and out-of-the-way in eastern Washington.

However, the reality is quite different. Walla Walla possesses a lovely downtown, with one of the most significant enclaves of historic architecture in eastern Washington (it's one of the oldest towns in the state). For its size, Walla Walla has plenty of sophistication, good restaurants, pleasant parks and an academic character, lent by two small but noted colleges. It's also the financial center for this part of the state; you'll be surprised by the number of banks, stockbrokers, furniture stores, art galleries and tuxedo-rental businesses that line the main streets.

Located in a rich agricultural area, Walla Walla is world-famous for its sweet onions, but you'll also find peas, asparagus, grapes and apple orchards. Nearby is Pendleton, OR, the Blue Mountains, the Palouse, and the Wenaha-Tucannon Wilderness, making Walla Walla an easy and pleasant place to spend a day or two.

Orientation

Walla Walla is in a fertile basin where several smaller streams meet the Walla Walla River. Rising behind the town are the Blue Mountains; only 6 miles south is the Oregon border, with Pendleton, OR, 33 miles farther south on Hwy 11. The main road through the area is US 12, which leaves the Columbia River near Wallula. From Walla Walla to Pasco is 47 miles; to Lewiston, ID, is 87 miles.

The principal streets in town are Rose and Main Sts; Main St follows the course of the ancient Nez Perce Trail. Isaacs Ave is the main drag east between downtown and Walla Walla Community College. To the west, separated from Walla Walla by parks and suburbs is College Place. Technically a separate town, College Place is the home of Walla Walla College, a four-year, Seventh-Day Adventist liberal arts institution founded in 1892.

Information

Weekend travelers need to be aware that Walla Walla almost totally closes down on Sunday. You'll find it difficult even to find a place to eat on the Sabbath.

The Walla Walla Area Chamber of Commerce (☎ 509-525-0850) is at 29 E Sumach St, Walla Walla, WA 98362. If you want

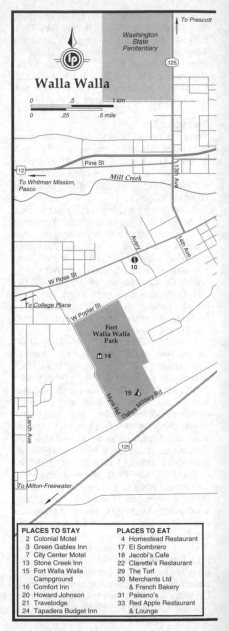

Walla Walla

PLACES TO STAY
2 Colonial Motel
3 Green Gables Inn
7 City Center Motel
13 Stone Creek Inn
15 Fort Walla Walla
    Campground
16 Comfort Inn
20 Howard Johnson
21 Travelodge
24 Tapadera Budget Inn

PLACES TO EAT
4 Homestead Restaurant
17 El Sombrero
18 Jacobi's Cafe
22 Clarette's Restaurant
29 The Turf
30 Merchants Ltd
    & French Bakery
31 Paisano's
33 Red Apple Restaurant
    & Lounge

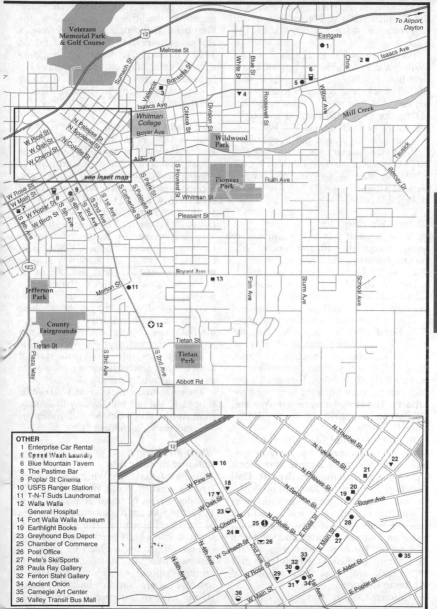

WASHINGTON

OTHER
1 Enterprise Car Rental
6 Speed Wash Laundry
6 Blue Mountain Tavern
8 The Pastime Bar
9 Poplar St Cinema
10 USFS Ranger Station
11 T-N-T Suds Laundromat
12 Walla Walla
    General Hospital
14 Fort Walla Walla Museum
19 Earthlight Books
23 Greyhound Bus Depot
25 Chamber of Commerce
26 Post Office
27 Pete's Ski/Sports
28 Paula Ray Gallery
32 Fenton Stahl Gallery
34 Ancient Onion
35 Carnegie Art Center
36 Valley Transit Bus Mall

information on the Walla Walla district of the Umatilla National Forest, drop by the ranger station (☎ 509-522-6290) at 1415 W Rose St.

The post office is at 128 N 2nd Ave, Walla Walla, WA 98362. Downtown, Earth-light Books (☎ 509-525-4983), 321 E Main St, sells books and tickets to local performances. The free weekly *What's Up?* has listings for local entertainment and night-life. Public radio is heard at 97.9 FM.

Wash your clothes at the Speed Wash Self Service Laundry (☎ 509-525-9856), 2023 Isaacs Ave, or T-N-T Suds (☎ 509-525-9810), 929 S 2nd Ave. Walla Walla General Hospital (☎ 509-525-0408) is at 1025 S 2nd Ave.

Historic Walking Tour

Park the car and take a few minutes to acquaint yourself with the lovely 19th-century buildings and tree-lined streets of Walla Walla. The center of the old town is at 2nd Ave and Main St. In each direction are several blocks of 1890s-era commercial buildings; many still house prominent downtown businesses. Check out the grand **Ellis Hotel**, at the corner of 2nd Ave and Main St, and the window display of antique cameras at Tomlin's Cameras, Drugs & Cosmetics. Head east on Main St past the **Barrett Building**, between 1st and 2nd Aves on Main St. In the next block the **Liberty Theatre**, between 1st Ave and Colville St, is a monument to early Holly-wood Orientalism.

To explore the fine old homes of Walla Walla, continue south on 1st Ave one block, past the 1880s **Baumeister Block** and the art moderne **Northwest Bell Building**, to Poplar St. Turn east on Poplar St and continue through a residential neighborhood with large and sometimes fanciful homes. After two blocks turn south on Palouse St; after another block turn east on Birch St, which ends at Park St. Go north on Park St, which leads over Mill Creek and to the shady campus of **Whitman College**.

Whitman College was established in 1859 as a seminary, and it became a four-year accredited college in 1882. The oldest remaining building on campus is the **Memorial Building**, 345 Boyer Ave, a Romanesque-revival landmark built in 1899. Behind the Memorial Building stretch a series of quads, reminiscent of Ivy League colleges. Walking west along Boyer Ave will bring you back to Main St and downtown.

Fort Walla Walla Park

Built in 1856 as an army fort, the site of Fort Walla Walla is now a large park and nature preserve with an assortment of playing fields, recreation and picnic areas, a campground and the **Fort Walla Walla Museum** (☎ 509-525-7703), on Myra Rd south of W Poplar St. There are two por-tions to the museum. The pioneer village is a collection of 14 historic buildings, including a blacksmith shop, schoolhouse (1867), log cabins and a railway station, arranged around a central meadow. In the fort's old cavalry stables is the museum proper, with collections of farm imple-ments, horse-drawn conveyances, ranching tools and a building filled with old furni-ture, clothing, Native American artifacts and other mementos of old Walla Walla. (Check out the display relating the story of a once-lowly Corsican onion.) It's a good museum, definitely worth a stop.

The museum complex at Fort Walla Walla is open 10 am to 5 pm Tuesday to Sunday, from April through October; adults/seniors and students $4/3, children $1.

Whitman Mission National Historic Site

The site of the 1836 Whitman Mission, 7 miles west of Walla Walla off US 12, was declared a National Historic Site in 1897, the 50th anniversary of the slayings of the 14 missionaries. The monument is situated atop a bluff overlooking the orig-inal mission grounds, which are preserved in a park-like grove of trees. None of the original buildings remain; foundations indicate where various buildings once stood, and an interpretive trail leads through the site. Just off the trail leading

The Whitman Massacre

Walla Walla is the site of one of the seminal confrontations between early white settlers and Native Americans. In 1836, Marcus and Narcissa Whitman, missionaries from the American Board, established a church mission and a farm at Waiilatpu (just west of present-day Walla Walla) in order to minister to local Indians. Relations between the two groups were initially friendly; however, Oregon Trail emigrants often made a detour north to Waiilatpu after the difficult Blue Mountain crossing in order to replenish stores and to rest livestock. As increasing numbers of white settlers began to move across traditional Native American hunting grounds, tensions began to build.

In 1847, an outbreak of measles ran through a Cayuse Indian village, killing many children. Although Whitman was a doctor, he was unable to halt the advance of the disease, which seemed to kill only the local Native Americans because they had no natural immunities to it. The Cayuse blamed Whitman for spreading the disease, and in late fall, Cayuse braves attacked the mission, killing Whitman, his wife and 12 others. Fifty-three settlers, mostly women and children resting at the mission from the rigors of the Oregon Trail, were taken captive.

The Whitman Massacre, as the killings were known, set in motion the Cayuse War, the first of many conflicts between Native Americans and US settlers in the Oregon Territory. The killings also hastened the approval of territorial status for Oregon. By 1848, Oregon had become an official US territory, enabling federal troops to be dispatched in order to apprehend the killers and to protect the settlers from further violence. After two years of skirmishes, four Cayuse braves surrendered and were tried and hanged for the killings.

The Whitman Mission was abandoned and the region was soon closed to settlement by Washington's governor, Isaac Stevens. Treaties between the US Government and the eastern Washington tribes were signed in 1855, and in 1856 the US Army built Fort Walla Walla in order to enforce their terms. ■

to the monument are the graves of the Whitmans and the others who were killed in 1847.

In the visitors' center (☎ 509-529-2761), thoughtful exhibits and a short film detail the story of the Whitmans, the local Native Americans, the Oregon Trail pioneers and the events that led up to the deaths of the missionaries. Maps of the grounds can be picked up at the visitors' center, which is open 8 am to 4:30 pm daily year-round, except major holidays; adults/families $2/4.

Wineries

While hardly the center of the Northwest wine industry, the fertile valley of the Walla Walla River produces some of Washington's most respected red wines. Unfortunately for wine tasters, **Leonetti Cellars**, the most renowned of local vint-

ners, doesn't offer a wine-tasting room; pick up a bottle or try the Cabernet sauvignon in a local restaurant.

The toast of the local wineries are found around Lowden, roughly 13 miles west of Walla Walla on US 12. **L'Ecole No 41** (☎ 509-525-0940), is at 41 Lowden School Rd, in an old schoolhouse. It's are open 11 am to 4 pm Wednesday to Sunday; try the Semillon and merlot.

Waterbrook (☎ 509-522-1918), on McDonald Rd, is open 10:30 am to 4:30 pm daily. Just south of Lowden off Frog Hollow Rd, their specialties are merlot and chardonnay. **Woodward Canyon Winery** (☎ 509-525-4129), on US 12 in Lowden, is open 10 am to 5 pm daily from Memorial Day to Labor Day, and 10 am to 4 pm the rest of the year. They have one of the best chardonnays – and Cabernet sauvignons – in Washington.

WASHINGTON

Activities

Veteran's Memorial Golf Course (☎ 509-527-4507), 201 E Rees Ave, is right off US 12, east of Walla Walla; it's consistently ranked in *Golf Digest's* list of the nation's top 100 courses. Head to Pioneer Park, at Alder and Division Sts, to find an outdoor swimming pool (☎ 509-527-4527).

During the winter, Walla Walla's college crowd takes to the slopes at **Bluewood Ski Area**, 22 miles southeast of Dayton. For rental skis, go to Pete's Ski/Sports (☎ 509-529-9804), 124 E Main St.

Special Events

The Walla Walla Sweet Onion Harvest Festival, held in July at Fort Walla Walla, celebrates the onion that has done so much to bring the name Walla Walla to everyone's lips. Besides the food booths and recipe contests, there are other fun things to do with onions, like use them in a 'shot put' contest. Live music is provided by local old-time fiddle bands.

One of Walla Walla's biggest events is the Balloon Stampede, held in mid-May at Howard Park. Besides the hot-air balloon gathering, attended by over 40 balloonists, there's also a rodeo, carnival, pari-mutuel racing, and sheep dog trials.

The Walla Walla Mountain Man Rendezvous, held in July at Fort Walla Walla, is a summer festival of pioneer skill and daring-do. Competitive events include black-powder musket shooting and tomahawk throwing. Expect to see lots of buckskin and firearms.

Places to Stay

Camping *Fort Walla Walla Campground* (☎ 509-527-3770), 1530 Dalles Military Rd, is in the park near the museum. Facilities include full hookups for RVs, tent sites, flush toilets and showers; it costs $10 to $15 a night.

B&Bs *Green Gables Inn* (☎ 509-525-5501), 922 Bonsella St, is a handsome, 1909 Craftsman home with nice gardens on two lots in a quiet neighborhood. Rooms start at $85. *Stone Creek Inn* (☎ 509-529-

Walla Walla Sweet Onions

The Walla Walla Valley is noted for many crops, including lentils, asparagus and peas, but none are more closely linked with the area than onions. Walla Walla Sweets are renowned throughout the West as the sweetest and most succulent of all yellow onions. In the summer, roadside stands spring up, and many families buy the fresh onions by the bushel from local farmers. Tradition holds that Walla Walla Sweets are so mild that they can be eaten like apples.

Walla Walla onions are in fact a strain of Armenian onions that reached the Walla Walla Valley in 1916 via a Corsican immigrant. The rich volcanic soils of this valley produced onions that were remarkably low in sulfur, the agent that normally makes onions hot and pungent. Local farmers carefully selected the sweetest of individual plants, and by 1925, the Walla Walla Sweet was on its way to becoming the standard onion of the Northwest. ■

8120), 720 Bryant Ave, is a fantastic old mansion once owned by a Washington territorial governor. The 1883 home sits on several acres of manicured lawns beside a creek. Rooms cost $95 to $125.

Hotels You don't have to spend much money to stay in a nice motel in Walla Walla; your pet is welcome at most of the following, and pools are available, too.

One of the best deals is the *Tapadera Budget Inn* (☎ 509-529-2580, 800-722-8277), 211 N 2nd Ave, right downtown. Rooms cost $33/38 and include a continental breakfast; avoid rooms fronting onto noisy 2nd Ave. Out toward Fort Walla Walla is the well-maintained (but not quite aptly named) *City Center Motel* (☎ 509-529-2660, 800-453-3160), 627 W Main St, with rooms for $39/41. Just a block from Whitman College, the *Travelodge* (☎ 509-529-4940, 800-255-3050), 421 E Main St, costs $46/52 a night. On the eastern edge of town, the *Colonial Motel* (☎ 509-529-1220), 2279 E Isaacs Ave, will run you $32/41.

For a little more comfort, go downtown to the *Howard Johnson* (☎ 509-529-4360), 325 E Main St, which offers spa and exercise facilities, a pool and a guest laundry from $72 a night. The *Comfort Inn* (☎ 509-525-2522), 520 N 2nd Ave, with rooms for $56/62, offers the same facilities near the freeway and close to downtown.

Places to Eat

Walla Walla is an unlikely but delightful haven for vegetarians. In part because of Walla Walla College, many of whose students don't eat meat, most restaurants in Walla Walla offer plenty of vegetarian selections.

For breakfast head to *Merchants Ltd & French Bakery* (☎ 509-525-0900), 21 E Main St, a great deli, coffeehouse and bakery. Enjoy a morning pastry and latte from a sidewalk table. With its selection of cheeses and salads, this is also a good place for picnic provisions. For a more traditional breakfast, go to *Clarette's Restaurant* (☎ 509-529-3430), 15 S Touchet St, next to Whitman College. This is one of the very few places open on Sundays, and it is usually very busy. If you stay up late or get up early, go to *Red Apple Restaurant & Lounge* (☎ 509-525-5113), 57 E Main St. It's a little rundown, but the food is good and it's open 24 hours a day.

For Mexican food, go to *El Sombrero* (☎ 509-522-4984), 4 W Oak St at 2nd Ave.

The popular *Jacobi's Cafe* (☎ 509-525-2677), 416 N 2nd Ave, is in the converted old train depot, a nice setting whether you dine inside or out. The dinner menu is extensive, and includes a lot of vegetarian and inexpensive options (most under $10) such as Mexican food, filling appetizers, salads and pizza. There are also a number of regional microbrews on tap. Unfortunately, the youthful wait staff at this college hangout seem to wait on customers by accident, hanging out instead with their friends in the bar.

One of the friendliest and most pleasant

places to eat and have a microbrewed beer or glass of local wine is *The Turf* (☎ 509-522-9807), 10 N 2nd Ave, a little hole-in-the-wall with sandwiches (a gardenburger or hot pastrami sandwich is $5). Expect a friendly welcome.

Classy but casual *Paisano's* (☎ 509-527-3511), 26 E Main St, has a broad menu of contemporary Italian and Mediterranean-influenced cuisine; for lunch, polenta with seasonal vegetables and baby shrimp costs $7, a smoked duck cappellini dinner is $15. It's the sort of place students go to impress a date.

For a hearty dinner with some refinement, go to the woodsy *Homestead Restaurant* (☎ 509-522-0345), 1528 E Isaacs Ave, where there's steak, local grilled lamb chops with coarse-ground mustard ($15), Pacific coast seafood like pan-fried Quilcene oysters ($14) or one of a number of vegetarian dishes like stuffed peppers ($9). It's also open Sunday morning for brunch.

Entertainment

Students from Whitman College hang out drinking at *Jacobi's Cafe*, 416 N 2nd Ave, where microbrewed ales are served up in yard-long tankards. For live music, go to the *Blue Mountain Tavern* (☎ 509-525-9941), 2025 E Isaacs Ave, a pleasant old bar that offers blues and other live music. The arty *Ancient Onion* (☎ 509-525-2107), upstairs at 1st Ave and Main St, is the sort of funkified coffeehouse typical of *real* cities like Portland or Seattle. Acoustic music concerts and poetry readings are held several evenings each month.

If you hanker for something a little more subversive, head to the *Pastime Bar* (☎ 509-525-0873), 215 W Main St. This old bar hasn't changed much since it was established in 1927; not a normal tourist attraction or a student hangout, it's populated with ranchers, scruffy day laborers and the rest of the local population that doesn't quite fit in with the new, smart and sanitized Walla Walla.

For art or foreign films, check what's playing at *Poplar St Cinema* (☎ 509-522-3333), 116 S 3rd Ave.

The Little Theater (☎ 509-529-3683), 1130 E Sumach St, is a well-established community theater group that stages four productions a year. At Whitman College, student productions are presented in the *Harper Joy Theatre* (☎ 509-527-5180).

Shopping
For proof of Walla Walla's tasteful prosperity, you need go no further than the downtown art galleries: these aren't quite what you'd expect in a farm town. Check out the latest show of regional artists at the Paula Ray Gallery (☎ 509-525-3371), 230 E Main St, which was designed to imitate a classical ruin – except with wildlife and blue-chip western art hanging on its jagged walls. The Fenton-Stahl Gallery (☎ 509-522-8470), 31 E Main St, has a selection of raku pottery, stained glass, and oil painting.

If you're looking for a gift or a souvenir, go to the Carnegie Art Center (☎ 509-525-4270), 109 S Palouse St, the regional arts and crafts center in the old community library.

Getting There & Away
Air Horizon Air has frequent flights to Seattle and Portland from the Walla Walla Regional Airport (☎ 509-525-2070), which is northeast of town off US 12.

Bus There's one Greyhound bus daily between Walla Walla and Pasco for connections to Spokane, Seattle and Portland, OR. Two daily buses make the trip between Walla Walla and Pendleton, OR for connections to Portland, OR and Boise, ID. The station (☎ 509-525-9313) is at 315 N 2nd Ave.

Car Budget (☎ 509-525-9043) and Sears Rent-A-Car (☎ 509-525-8811) are both at the airport. Rental agencies in town include Enterprise (☎ 509-529-1988), 491 N Wilbur Ave, and Lightfoot's U-Save Auto Rentals (☎ 509-525-1680), 2933 E Isaacs Ave.

Getting Around
The local bus service is operated by Valley Transit (☎ 509-524-9140), whose main transit center is at N 4th Ave and W Main St. They also run buses to Milton-Freewater, OR; fare $1. Schedules and maps are available at the transit center (the information kiosk has weird hours but schedules and routes are all posted) or from the main office at 1401 W Rose St. There is no service on Sunday.

Call ABC Taxi (☎ 509-529-7726) or A-1 Taxi (☎ 509-529-2525) for a lift.

DAYTON
Population 2563
Dayton is an attractive older town on the southern edge of the Palouse region. Streams flowing out the Blue Mountains cut deep canyons in the lava flows, and though the sun bakes the farmland on the plateaus, down in the shady, well-watered valley things are garden-like and hospitable. The little-known and remote Wehana-Tucannon Wilderness Area is contained within the Umatilla National Forest here, along the Oregon/Washington state line.

The main businesses in Dayton are asparagus processing and raising peas for seed. The very handsome old Dayton train depot, a gingerbread structure built in 1881, now serves as the local community arts building. Stop by to pick up a walking tour map and check out the other historic buildings in town. Of particular note is the old courthouse, built in 1886 and still in use. The chamber of commerce (☎ 509-382-4825) has an office at 166 E Main St.

US 12 between Walla Walla and Clarkston is the exact return route of Lewis and Clark. From Dayton, Walla Walla is 31 miles southeast, and Clarkston 66 miles northeast. As you drive in on US 12, note the human figure etched in the hillside, which is meant to resemble an English chalk man. As a high school project, it sure beats a big 'D' on the side hill.

Wehana-Tucannon Wilderness Area
Part of the Umatilla National Forest, this wilderness area is home to elk, black bear, bighorn sheep, cougar and bobcat. (Expect to meet hunters in the fall.) Rivers and streams here have cut deep canyons into

the basalt lava flow, forming broad table-lands with narrow-valleyed bottomlands.

To reach the wilderness area, follow US 12 northeast from Dayton for 10 miles and turn east onto the Tucannon River Rd. Keep on this road until its end (bear left at the junction 2 miles past Camp Wooten State Park). From here, there's a hiking trail along the Tucannon River, another up Panjab Creek, and many opportunities for days-long backpacking trips or shorter loop hikes. Contact the ranger stations in Pomeroy (☎ 509-843-1891) or Walla Walla (☎ 509-522-6290) for details on trails.

Skiing
Heavily-forested Bluewood Ski Area (☎ 509-382-4725) in the Blue Mountains is 22 miles southeast of Dayton (turn down 4th St, also known as N Touchet Rd). Though not a big resort, Bluewood has the state's second-highest base elevation (4545 feet) and remains uncrowded despite its reputation for good weather and powdery snow. It has 22 runs and a vertical drop of 1125 feet, equipment rentals, a cafeteria, and a ski school. Full-day lift tickets cost $25. Call ☎ 509-382-2877 to hear current snow conditions.

Places to Stay & Eat
Lewis & Clark Trail State Park (☎ 509-337-6457), 5 miles southwest of town on US 12 has 25 campsites for $10, with showers and flush toilets but no hookups.

Purple House B&B (☎ 509-382-3159, 800-486-2574), 415 E Clay St, is a lovely old home with a swimming pool. Expect to pay $85 to $125.

Blue Mountain Motel (☎ 509-382-3040), 414 Main St, is a no-frills but perfectly adequate place with single/double rooms for $36/43. Rooms at the *Weinhard Hotel* (☎ 509-382-4032), 235 E Main St, built by brewer Henry Weinhard's nephew, start at $55. The *Weinhard Espresso Cafe* on the main floor is a great place to fuel up for breakfast or lunch.

Patit Creek Restaurant (☎ 509-382-2625), 725 E Dayton Ave, an unassuming place just northeast of town, turns out some

of eastern Washington's best French cuisine. It's open limited hours for lunch (weekdays only) and dinner; closed Monday. Set aside $20 per person for dinner, and call ahead for a reservation.

If you'd rather eat cheap, join the lite-beer and baseball cap crowd at *Panhandlers Pizza & Pasta* (☎ 509-382-4160), 404 Main St. And, if you're just passing through Dayton, do stop by the *Elk Drug Store* (☎ 509-382-2536), 270 Main St, and have a shake at the soda fountain.

PULLMAN & THE PALOUSE REGION
The Palouse Hills are an extremely fertile region, and it is said that for every 10 miles you travel east, an additional inch of rain falls. Acre after acre, the soft, sensuous Palouse Hills are planted with wheat and legumes. While the richness of the loess soil and the climate are great for agriculture and it's fascinating country to pass through, there's not much to *do* here. Pullman (population 23,641) is the largest and most interesting town, and it's pretty much defined by Washington State University (WSU), Washington's major agricultural school. With over 22,000 students and faculty, the college pretty much sets the pace when it's in session.

The Palouse is worth a drive or bicycle tour in the spring, when the fields are amazing shades of green, or at harvest time, when wheat is shipped down the Snake River on barges. Farming methods now aim at conserving the rich loess soil, and the rolling, seemingly endless green hills are girdled by swaths of stubble wheat that keep the soil from blowing away.

Orientation
Pullman, 7 miles west of the Idaho state line and 76 miles south of Spokane, spreads out from the south fork of the Palouse River. Hwy 27, known in town as Grand Ave, cuts through Pullman on its north-south route; Hwy 270, the east-west road, follows Davis Way at the west end of town, Main St to the east. The large WSU campus, bisected by Stadium Way, takes up a big chunk of town. Downtown proper

is just west of the campus, near the intersection of Main St and Grand Ave.

Southwest of Pullman, the Palouse plateau drops off fairly dramatically to the Snake and Clearwater Rivers. The Snake River cuts its channel about 10 miles southwest of town.

To the south, it's a nice drive between Pullman and Lewiston, ID, and the Snake River, along the Old Lewiston Grade Hwy.

Information
Pullman Chamber of Commerce (☎ 509-334-3565, 800-365-6948), 415 N Grand Ave, suite A, is happy to dispense information and discount coupons.

The WSU Visitors Center (☎ 509-335-8633), 225 N Grand Ave at Hwy 270, provides information and directions to visitors from its off-campus site. Stop here to pick up a campus map and parking permit, buy tickets to WSU games and events, or meet friends and colleagues. It's open 7 am to 4 pm weekdays.

The main post office is on S Grand Ave just south of Crestview St. The area's best bookstore, Book People of Moscow (☎ 208-882-7957), is a few miles east in Moscow, ID at 512 S Main St. In Pullman, there's the university bookstore, Students Book Corporation (☎ 509-332-2537), in the student union building at 700 NE Thatuna St. The *Daily News* publishes in both Moscow and Pullman. Read the *Evergreen Daily* for campus news. Public radio comes in at 1250 AM or 91.7 FM.

Drag your dirty clothes over to Sunshine Center Coin-Op Wash & Dry Clean at 515 S Grand Ave. Pullman Memorial Hospital (☎ 509-332-2541) is a full-service hospital at 1125 NE Washington Ave.

Washington State University
In the late 1800s, local business leaders took advantage of the area's rich agricultural and ranching background to get this state land-grant university. WSU, originally the Washington Agricultural College, opened in 1892 with 21 students. Still largely known for its agriculture department, WSU has some features not found at every university. For instance, bighorn sheep and a grizzly bear live on campus.

Surprisingly, WSU's **Museum of Art** (☎ 509-335-1910), in the Fine Arts Center on Stadium Way and Wilson Rd, mounts some lively, well-curated shows featuring Northwest artists, traveling exhibits and work by students and faculty. There's a vital, unstodgy feeling here, and for those not interested in college sports, it can be one of the most exciting spots in Pullman. Hours are from 10 am to 4 pm on weekdays, 1 to 5 pm on weekends, and Tuesday evenings from 7 to 10 pm; admission is free. Park for free in the garage beneath the Fine Arts Center on evenings and weekends.

Other WSU museums are much smaller and more narrowly defined. The **Jacklin Collection** (☎ 509-335-3009), in room 124 of the Physical Sciences Building, has a huge collection of petrified wood, some dinosaur bones, and fluorescent minerals; it's open 8 am to 5 pm weekdays. Fossils documenting stages of human evolution occasionally share space with a rotating Bigfoot display at the **Museum of Anthropology** (☎ 509-335-3936) in College Hall; call ahead to see if it's out. The museum is open 9 am to 4 pm weekdays, and is closed June 15 to the first week in September.

If you want the structure of an organized campus tour, you can join the hour-long walking tours (☎ 509-335-3581) that leave weekdays at 1 pm from room 442 of the Administration Building.

If you want to park on campus, be sure to pick up a parking permit ($1.50) from either the WSU Visitor Center (see Information above), or the Public Safety Building on campus at the corner of Troy Lane and Wilson Rd (next to the Fine Arts Center). You don't need a permit for a quick trip to places like the bookstore, which has short-term metered parking.

Kamiak Butte
Hike the 3½-mile Pine Ridge Trail through a mixed-conifer forest (the most trees you'll see in the Palouse) to the top of 3641-foot-high Kamiak Butte. From the top of the butte, there are grand views of

the Palouse and south to Oregon's Wallowa Mountains. Thanks to all the trees, this is a good spot for bird watching. Warblers, nuthatches, and pygmy and great-horned owls thrive in these dense woods.

The geology of Kamiak Butte is virtually identical to Steptoe Butte (see Around Pullman, below), and the county park toward the butte's base has camping (and even some shade). It's 10 miles north of Pullman on Hwy 27.

Three Forks Pioneer Museum
A local farmer has salvaged old buildings and antiques and pieced together an old western town on a corner of his spread. To reach the museum, also known as Rossebo's Farm (☎ 509-332-3889), head 2 miles north on Hwy 27, turn west onto the Pullman-Albion Rd. After 2 miles turn north on Anderson Rd and go 2.8 miles to Rossebo Farm. The museum is open 9 am to dusk Sunday, May to September; admission is $2.

Activities
WSU's two indoor **swimming** pools are open to the public. Call ☎ 509-335-9666 for schedule information. Reaney Park, at Reaney Way and Gray Lane, has two outdoor pools.

Hearty cyclists will enjoy the 80-mile loop **biking** tour through the Palouse along the Snake River to Lewiston, ID and back. From Pullman, take the Wawawai-Pullman Rd southwest to the Wawawai River Rd (Hwy 193), which follows the Snake River to Lewiston; it's an uphill haul on US 195 back to Pullman. You'll need to bring your own bike; go to B & L Bicycles (☎ 509-332-1703), E 219 Main St, for information and repair.

National Lentil Festival
The third weekend of September brings Pullman's National Lentil Festival (☎ 509-334-3565), with a parade, entertainment, crafts, a quilt show and a myriad of legume-oriented food booths. Stop by Reaney Park for lentil pancakes, lentil lasagna or lentil ice cream.

Places to Stay
Camping *Pullman RV Park* (☎ 509-334-4555) has sites for $10 in the city park, right where South St runs into the south fork of the Palouse River. Tent campers should head 10 miles north of town to *Kamiak Butte County Park* (☎ 509-397-6238) on Hwy 27; campsites cost $5 and have running water and flush toilets. *Boyer Park & Marina* (☎ 509-397-3791), west of town on the Snake River, is a resort-ish type park just downstream from Lower Granite Dam; it has a swimming beach, boat launch, showers, laundry facilities and a restaurant. Standard tent sites start at $8, hookups at $10; it's $4 more on Friday and Saturday.

Hotels Though there are accommodations on the WSU campus, it's not the cheapest place in town: the *Compton Union Building* (☎ 509-335-9444) rents a single/double room with private bathroom for $45/60. Pullman's least expensive place, the *Cougar Land Motel* (☎ 509-334-3535, 800-334-3574), W 120 Main, has cheap rooms at rock bottom for $32/37. The *Manor Lodge Motel* (☎ 509-334-2511), on 455 SE Paradise St near Main St, is a little nicer, with rooms starting at $39/44. *Nendel's Motor Inn* (☎ 509-332-2646), 915 SE Main St, is just on the edge of campus and has airport transportation and an outdoor pool. Rooms run $39/49 and up.

A couple of fancier motels are near the river on SE Bishop Blvd. *Holiday Inn Express* (☎ 509-334-4437, 800-465-4329), 1190 SE Bishop Blvd, has an indoor pool and rooms for $64. *Quality Inn Paradise Creek* (☎ 509-332-0500, 800-669-3212), 1050 SE Bishop Blvd, is the nicest place to stay in Pullman. The pool is outdoors, but there's an indoor sauna and hot tub. Rooms start at $58/65, which includes continental breakfast in the lobby.

Places to Eat
Benefit from all those dairy students at *Ferdinand's* (☎ 509-335-4014), the on-campus WSU creamery. Besides Cougar Gold cheese (good sharp cheddar) and tasty milkshakes, they serve decent espresso

weekdays from 9:30 am to 4:30 pm from the Food Quality Building on S Fairway Lane. This is one place that Pullman's famous for; don't miss it.

A number of places in town have caught on to the fact that you can sell students a lot of espresso. For a quick latte, try *Grand Ave Espresso*, at the corner of Main St and Grand Ave. Supplement the java with some food at the *Combine Mall Bakery* (☎ 509-332-1774), 215 E Main St, a pleasant place to hang out with a roll and coffee; it's one of the only lunch spots open on Sunday. For more of a meal, try *Swilly's* (☎ 509-334-3395), 200 NE Kamiaken St. It's an easygoing spot with good food and a passably trendy atmosphere.

For a standard student hangout, go for pizza and beer at *Rathaus Pizza & Ale Shoppe* (☎ 509-334-5400), 630 E Main St.

Hilltop Restaurant (☎ 509-334-2555), off Davis Way, is a fairly sedate steak-and-seafood house with a good view of town. It's one of Pullman's two well-established nice dinner places. The other place, *Seasons* (☎ 509-334-1410), 215 SE Paradise St, is a fancy cliffside restaurant in an old house up a flight of stairs. The setting is comfortably elegant, dinner entrées run from $9 to $17 and the food is Pullman's best.

Entertainment

The *Beasley Performing Arts Coliseum* (☎ 509-335-3525), on campus, brings in some biggish names, including rock shows to appease the student population. But the real entertainment here is college sports, especially football. The Cougars play in the PAC-10 football league and usually field strong teams.

The *Palouse Performance Project* (☎ 509-334-9184), 414 E Main, spotlights student-produced performance art and experimental theater. On weekends there's live swing and jazz at *Rico's Smokehouse Tavern* (☎ 509-332-6566), 200 E Main at the corner of Davis St.

Pullman has two movie theaters, the *Old Post Office Theatre* (☎ 509-334-3456), 245 SE Paradise St, and the *Cordova Theatre* (☎ 509-334-1405), 135 N Grand Ave.

Getting There & Away

Air The Pullman-Moscow Regional Airport (☎ 509-334-4555) is east off Farm Way toward the Idaho state line. Horizon flies in from various Northwest cities. There are more frequent flights from the Spokane International Airport, 76 miles north.

Bus Northwestern Trailways (☎ 509-334-1412) picks up passengers bound for Spokane, Lewiston or Boise twice daily from the bus station at 1002 N Grand (sorry, no bus to Walla Walla); a one-way fare to Spokane is $13.

Getting Around

To/From the Airport Link Transportation (☎ 208-882-1223, 800-359-4541) has shuttle service to Spokane and the Spokane International Airport, and if you're staying in town they'll pick you up or drop you off at your motel. One-way fare costs an exorbitant $37.

Bus Pullman Transit (☎ 509-332-6535) runs buses around town and campus; adult fare is 35¢. The Wheatland Express (☎ 509-334-2200) has service between Pullman and Moscow, ID.

AROUND PULLMAN
Colfax
Population 2784

Fifteen miles northwest of Pullman on US 195 is Colfax, in a deep ravine along the Palouse River amid rolling wheat fields. A fair number of antique stores have taken over storefronts in the handsome brick and stone downtown. The **Perkins House** (☎ 509-397-3259), 623 N Perkins Ave, a Victorian house built in 1884 by the town's first permanent resident, has been restored and is open as a museum. The log cabin Perkins built in 1877 is still standing out behind the main house. The house is open 1 to 4 pm on Thursday and Sunday, April 15 to October 15; admission is free.

Steptoe Butte State Park

Steptoe Butte is just about the only public land in the Palouse, and it's a good place to get a bird's-eye view of the country. It's located 15 miles north of Colfax off US 195. Hume Rd leads to the top of the 3612-foot-high butte, where hawks hover and the Rockies are visible off to the east and the Blue Mountains to the south. To the west, the Columbia Plateau appears to extend forever.

Steptoe Butte is an outcropping of Pre-cambrian rock, once an island just off the western edge of the North American conti-nent. Lava flows covered all the lower ground around the butte 10 to 30 million years ago. Loess then blanketed the land, creating the Palouse Hills, none of which comes close to the height of the rocky butte. In more recent history, Palouse Indi-ans defeated Lieutenant Colonel Edward Steptoe and his troops here in 1858.

Although Steptoe Butte is a state park, no camping is permitted. For a scenic stay try the *Hanford Castle B&B* (☎ 509-285-4120), a huge brick Victorian house perched on a Palouse hilltop, surrounded by wheat. It's less than 10 miles north of Steptoe Butte in Oakesdale, off Hwy 271, and offers double rooms for $54.

CLARKSTON & LEWISTON

The twin cities of Clarkston, WA (popula-tion 7000), and Lewiston, ID (population 32,000), sprawl across the flood plains where the mighty Snake and Clearwater Rivers meet. These bustling towns are cen-ters of a vast agricultural area whose prod-ucts include peas, lentils, wheat and livestock. Lewiston is often referred to as the 'Inland Port,' as the Columbia and Snake Rivers' dam-and-lock systems have created hundreds of miles of slack-water reservoirs that allow barges to travel all the way from Lewiston to Portland, OR.

While Clarkston and Lewiston are hardly tourist towns, there is a good reason for the Northwest tourist to make the detour here: about 30 miles upriver be-tween Oregon and Idaho on the Snake River is the white water and wilderness of Hells Canyon, reached by a number of Clarkston- and Lewiston-based jet boat tours and rafting trips.

History

The towns' namesakes, Meriwether Lewis and William Clark, passed through here on both legs of their early 1800s expedition, though there was no settlement in the area until 1860, at the beginning of the Idaho gold rush. The confluence of the Snake and Clearwater Rivers was the head of steam-boat navigation from Portland, and the area boomed as a transport and trade center.

Lewiston and Clarkston continued to grow as trade and transport hubs, espe-cially as federal irrigation projects brought orchards to flower along the protected and temperate canyon bottoms. However, the biggest advance for the area came in 1955, when the Army Corps of Engineers began to build the four Snake River dams that, in 1975, brought slack water to the port of Lewiston. Lewiston is the USA's most inland port: vessels drawing less than 14 feet and weighing less than 12,000 tons can journey all the way from the mouth of the Columbia River to the grain-loading docks at Lewiston, 470 miles from the Pacific Ocean.

Information

The Clarkston Chamber of Commerce (☎ 509-758-7712, 800-933-2128) is at 502 Bridge St, Clarkston, WA 99403, and the Lewiston Chamber of Commerce (☎ 208-743-3531, 800-473-3543) is at 111 Main St, Lewiston, ID 83501.

The USFS headquarters for the Hells Canyon National Recreation Area (☎ 509-758-0616) is at 2535 Riverside Drive in Clarkston. For river permit reservations and information, call ☎ 509-758-1957.

Lewiston's post office is at 1613 Idaho St, Kling's Book Store (☎ 208-743-8501) is at 704 Main St, and St Joseph Regional Med-ical Center (☎ 208-743-2511) is at 415 6th St. Do laundry at Express Mart (☎ 509-758-6927) at 5th and Bridge Sts in Clarkston.

Asotin County Museum

This museum (☎ 509-243-4659) is south of Clarkston in the town of Asotin, at 3rd and Filmore Sts. The main museum building is a 1922, concrete-block building that served

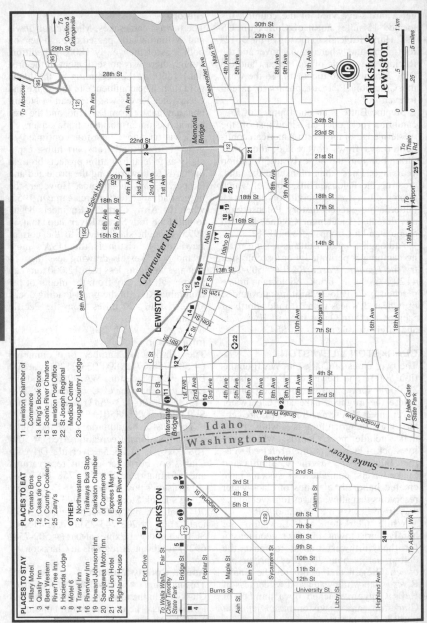

PLACES TO STAY
1 Hillary Motel
3 Quality Inn
4 Best Western
RiverTree Inn
5 Hacienda Lodge
8 Motel 6
14 Travel Inn
16 Riverview Inn
19 Howard Johnsons Inn
20 Sacajawea Motor Inn
21 Red Lion Hotel
24 Highland House

PLACES TO EAT
9 Tomato Bros
12 Casa de Oro
17 Country Cookery
25 Zany's

OTHER
2 Northwestern
Trailways Bus Stop
6 Clarkston Chamber
of Commerce
7 Express Mart
10 Snake River Adventures

11 Lewiston Chamber of
Commerce
13 Kling's Book Store
15 Scenic River Charters
18 Lewiston Post Office
22 St Joseph Regional
Medical Center
23 Cougar Country Lodge

Clarkston & Lewiston

as a funeral home for 50 years. Outside, the grounds are littered with the Asotin County Historical Society's healthy accumulation of historic buildings, including a one-room school, a log cabin, a pioneer home and a blacksmith shop. Old carriages and one of the largest known collections of branding irons are housed in the old pole barn. It's open 1 to 5 pm, Tuesday to Saturday; admission is free.

Hells Gate State Park
This popular state park (☎ 208-799-5015), 4 miles south of downtown Lewiston on Snake River Ave in Idaho, is the antidote to the often scorching-hot days at the bottom of the Snake River canyon. The 960-acre park offers a **swimming** beach, full-service marina, campground, picnic area and ample room to relax along the Snake River. Hells Gate also has a series of short **hiking** trails, and it's the southern access point for the Levee Park way trail.

Horseback riding is another popular pastime; 5 miles of bridle paths wind through the park and up to an overlook. During the summer, horses are available for rent from the corral between the marina and the campgrounds; call Hells Gates Stables (☎ 208-743-3142) for information.

At the center of the park, the **Williams Memorial Visitors Center** is worth a visit. Colorful and well-designed displays explain the geology and history of the Snake River system and touch on the plant and wildlife of central Idaho. There's a staff ranger on duty to answer questions.

The marina at the park is the departure point for most **jet boat tours** up the Snake River; many **charter fishing** trips leave from here as well. The park has a day-use fee of $2 per vehicle.

Buffalo Eddy Pictographs
Twelve miles south of Asotin on Snake River Rd, is a jumble of rocks that constricts the Snake River into a fast-moving channel. On the rocks are number of well-preserved petroglyphs of warriors brandishing weapons; it's easy to imagine that these images once warned of a prehistoric territorial boundary.

There's no sign for the petroglyphs, but they're easy to find. From Asotin, continue on 1st St until it becomes graveled Snake River Rd. The road winds through an increasingly sheer canyon until it passes through a narrow crevice between two rock faces. Pull off the road and explore the rocks near the river for the petroglyphs.

If you want to have more of a look at the Hells Canyon country, but don't fancy a jet boat excursion, continue on Snake River Rd, which follows the river to the mouth of the Grande Ronde River. The canyon walls get higher and higher, and increasingly striated by basalt lava flows; the landscape is stark and otherworldly. The road eventually joins Hwy 3 in Oregon, a fairly bumpy 31 miles from Buffalo Eddy.

Chief Timothy State Park
Located 8 miles west of Clarkston on US 12, this state park and interpretive center (☎ 509-758-9580) serves a recreational and an educational function. The park is mostly located on a landscaped island in Lower Granite Lake on the Snake River, with over 11,000 feet of freshwater shoreline to draw swimmers, picnickers and sunbathers to the swimming beaches. Campers are invited to use the boat ramps and moorage docks, making this a popular place for water-skiing weekends.

The island was once a hill that overlooked a short-lived pioneer community called Silcott, and before that, the valley here was the site of the first farm of Nez Perce Chief Timothy, who at the urging of US Government Indian Agents decided to pursue an agrarian life. The completion of the Lower Granite Dam transformed this location into an island in 1975.

The **Alpowai Interpretive Center**, just before the short bridge to the island, is located on the site of a Nez Perce Indian village from the turn of the 19th century. The center tells the story of the geologic and human history of the area and includes an audiovisual program. It's open 1 to 5 pm Wednesday through Sunday, Memorial

Day weekend to Labor Day, other times by appointment; admission is free.

Rafting & Dories

Purists who scorn noisy jet boats can ride the Snake River in a dory, a small, wooden craft resembling a drift boat. Contact Northwest Dories (☎ 800-877-3679), PO Box 216, Altaville, CA 95221 (or locally at ☎ 208-743-4201, 1127-B Airway Ave, Lewiston, ID 83501), for information on multiple-day Snake River tours ($630 to $935). Raft the Snake with Northwest Voyageurs (☎ 208-628-3022, 800-727-9977), who offer multi-day trips starting at $595 for three days on the river.

Jet Boat Tours

Although the Hells Canyon of the Snake River begins 50 miles south of Lewiston, the city is the center for upstream jet boat tours of the deepest river gorge in North America. Operators offer a wide variety of single-day ($45 to $215), multiple-day trips ($200 and up) and dinner cruises ($40 to $60); most offer fishing expeditions on the side. Trips depart from either the Hells Gate State Park marina in Lewiston or the Swallows Crest Park boat launch in Clarkston.

Expect a day trip to cover anywhere from 90 to over 200 miles. Lunch and beverages are provided, though you'll want to bring a small cooler of your own on some of the longer summertime trips. Buffalo Eddy Pictographs, the Kirkland Historical Ranch, swimming holes and mountain goat herds are typical destinations.

Beamer's Hells Canyon Tours (☎ 509 758-4800 in Clarkston, 208-743-4800 in Lewiston, or 800-522-6966), 1451 Bridge St in Clarkston, is famous for its overnight mail trip to outlying ranches ($215); they have day trips from $90. Snake Dancer Excursions (☎ 208-743-0890, 800-234-1941), 614 Lapwai Rd, Lewiston, and River Quest Excursions (☎ 208-746-8060, 800-589-1129), both have day trips for around $90.

The only two companies that go all the way to Hells Canyon Dam (about 120 miles upriver in Idaho) are based in Lewiston: Snake River Adventures (☎ 208-746-6276, 800-262-8876), 227 Snake River Ave ($150), and Cougar Country Lodge (☎ 208-746-3546, 800-727-6190), 805 Snake River Ave ($250).

Places to Stay

Camping Campers should head to *Hells Gate State Park* (☎ 208-799-5015), 4 miles south of Lewiston on Snake River Ave. Standard sites cost $12, hookups $16. Reservations are accepted for an additional $6. On an island in the Snake River is *Chief Timothy State Park* (☎ 509-758-9580), 8 miles west of Clarkston on US 12 in Washington. Tent/RV sites cost is $11/16. Facilities at both parks include showers, a boat basin and a swimming beach.

B&Bs *Highland House* (☎ 509-758-3126), 707 Highland Ave in Clarkston, is an 1890s Victorian home done up English-style. The five guest rooms (three with private facilities) cost from $45 to $85. The contemporary *Cliff House B&B* (☎ 509-758-1267), 2000 Westlake Dr, 8 miles west of Clarkston, hangs over the Snake River just above Chief Timothy State Park. Rooms cost $60 to $75; two-day minimums on weekends and holidays.

Hotels All of Clarkston's motels are right along the US 12 strip. *Hacienda Lodge* (☎ 509-758-5583, 888-567-2287), 812 Bridge St, is a nice, older motel, with single/double rooms for $32/38; pets are OK. *Motel 6* (☎ 509-758-1631), 222 Bridge St, has a pool, and rooms are $36/42. *Best Western RiverTree Inn* (☎ 509-758-9551, 800-597-3621), 1257 Bridge St, has a pool, exercise room and sauna, and some kitchenettes; rates start at $59. *Quality Inn* (☎ 509-758-9500), 700 Port Drive, also has a pool, and children under 18 are free with parents; rates are $63/68.

In Lewiston, there are three hotels in the $35/45 range: the *Travel Inn* (☎ 208-743-4501), 1021 Main St, is closest to the old town; *Riverview Inn* (☎ 208-746-3311), 1325 Main St, takes pets and has a free

The Snake River Dams: A Salmon's Perspective

Lower Granite, Little Goose, Lower Monumental and Ice Harbor Dams control the Snake River between Lewiston, ID, and the Tri-Cities, where the Snake flows into the Columbia River. These dams, built in the late 1960s and '70s and operated by the Army Corps of Engineers, were the last to enter the Columbia River system. Rather than generating energy or irrigation water, they were designed to control river levels, enabling ships to make it upriver. Because of these dams, Lewiston, ID, is now a seaport.

The tradeoff for this shipping channel has been salmon. Even with all the Columbia River dams, salmon stocks were in pretty good shape before the Snake River dams went in. Now their numbers have dropped sevenfold, despite fish ladders on all the dams between Lewiston and the ocean.

At Lower Granite Dam, 16 miles southwest of Pullman, smolt (juvenile salmon on their way to the ocean) are loaded onto barges that will ferry them around the dams, dropping them back into the river below the Bonneville Dam, the last dam on the Columbia. This keeps the fish from being diced by dam turbines, but there are indications that it also disrupts the instinct that allows the fish to return to their home streams to spawn.

There's serious talk among environmentalists about removing these dams. Good highway and rail systems access Lewiston, and to many, the loss of shipping is minor compared to the loss of native fish.

There are visitors' centers with fish ladders and viewing windows at each of the dams. Stop by and look for spring Chinook from April through the summer, and fall Chinook and steelhead starting in September throughout the fall. ∎

continental breakfast; and the *Sacajawea Motor Inn* (☎ 208-746-1393, 800-333-1393), 1824 Main St, is a large complex with all the usual extras. *Howard Johnsons Inn* (☎ 208-743-9526), 1716 Main St, goes after the business trade with large rooms (starting at $62), a pool and in-room modems. The *Red Lion Hotel* (☎ 208-799-1000, 800 232 6730), 621 21st St, has standard to deluxe room rates; rooms with views over the strip and the Clearwater River cost $96/106.

If you want cheap, head across the Clearwater River from Lewiston where the *Hillary Motel* (☎ 208-743-8514), 2030 North-South Hwy, has rooms ranging from $26 to $45.

Places to Eat

If you're staying along motel row in Lewiston, then the *Country Cookery* (☎ 208-743-4552), 1516 Main St, will be right down the street and is a good place for breakfast. For burgers in a '50's theme restaurant, go to *Zany's* (☎ 208-746-8131), 2006 19th

Ave at 21st St. High-quality Mexican food is found at *Casa de Oro* (☎ 208-798-8681), 504 Main St.

At *Tomato Bros* (☎ 509-758-7902), 200 Bridge St in Clarkston, the wood-fired pizzas are quite good, as are the salads and pasta. For dinner with a view, head to *Three Mile Inn* (☎ 509-243-4158), about 3 miles south of Asotin on Snake River Rd in Washington. The dining room overlooks the rugged canyon and the river; the menu offers steak, seafood and pasta from $10 to $17.

Getting There & Around

Air Horizon Airlines (☎ 208-743-9293) provides service from the Lewiston-Nez Perce County Regional Airport (☎ 208-746-7962) to Spokane, Seattle, Boise, Pullman and Portland. United Express (208-746-9516) also offers a similar service. The airport is located south of Lewiston, off of 17th St (which turns into 5th St).

Bus Northwestern Trailways (☎ 208-746-8108, 800-366-3830 in Idaho) operates three buses a day to Spokane ($20), and one bus a day to Boise ($33). The bus stops at Don's Chevron, 226 22nd St N across the Clearwater River from Lewiston.

Car Hertz (☎ 208-746-0411), Budget (☎ 208-746-0488) and National Car Rental (☎ 208-743-0176) are all at the Lewiston-Nez Perce Regional Airport. Rent-A-Wreck (☎ 208-746-9585) is at 102 Thain Rd in Lewiston.

SNAKE RIVER COUNTRY
Somewhere between Dusty and Washtucna (population 267) the Palouse leaves off and the Channeled Scablands begin; just west of Washtucna, Hwy 26 climbs up on top of the Columbia Plateau. This is pretty desolate country, and since it's not on the way to anything, it's easy to miss one of eastern Washington's geological highlights, Palouse Falls. If you have a boat, Lyons Ferry State Park is a popular place to put in and cruise the Snake River.

Palouse Falls State Park
These dramatic falls drop a spectacular 198 feet from arid Channeled Scablands punctuated with basalt spires into a rock gorge. The native Palouse referred to the local falls as 'the hole in the ground,' and that's indeed what it looks like, albeit an incredibly beautiful hole. It's especially impressive in the spring and early summer, when stream flow is high.

From the foot of the falls, the Palouse River cuts a channel to its confluence with the Snake River, some 5 miles to the south.

A trail starts in the parking lot and leads to an upper pool up above the falls. A number of other trails wind around the plateau and down to the river gorge. It's a fun place to hike, but watch out for rattlesnakes. Scan the canyon below the falls for prairie falcons, golden eagles, Swainson's hawks and other raptors who nest here.

To get to the state park (☎ 509-549-3551) from US 395 and points north, follow Hwy 26 or Hwy 261 to Washtucna,

then turn southwest on Hwy 260 and, after about 6 miles, southeast on Hwy 261; from Colfax, Washtucna is 52 miles west.

If you're approaching from the south, turn off US 12 onto Hwy 261 toward Starbuck and follow that road across the Snake River to the falls, 21 miles northwest.

Lyons Ferry State Park
Five miles south of Palouse Falls the Palouse River joins the Snake beneath the dramatic, tresseled span of the Lyons Ferry Bridge. Lewis and Clark, David Thompson and a plethora of missionaries passed by this river junction, but they were hardly the first. Palouse Indians, whose fish-drying scaffolds Lewis and Clark noted, were also relative latecomers.

The Marmes Rock Shelter, a small, now-flooded cave about a mile up the Palouse River from its confluence with the Snake, has yielded evidence of the earliest-known North American settlement. Pieces of charred human bone (from a cremation hearth), tools and jewelry date back 10,000 years, almost to the last ice age. Get a glimpse of the site either from the river or from the paved road behind the park caretakers' houses.

Construction of Lower Monumental Dam flooded the Marmes site and a sacred Palouse Indian site, but it created a recreational hot spot. There's a boat launch at the state park (☎ 509-646-3252), and plenty of people take their speedboats out here. The old Lyons Ferry, used for years to cross the Snake, is now a fishing pier.

Places to Stay & Eat
The 10 campsites at *Palouse Falls State Park* (☎ 509-646-3252) are one of Washington's best-kept secrets; sites cost $7 and are perfect for tent campers. At *Lyons Ferry State Park* (☎ 509-646-3252) the campground attracts mostly boaters with RVs; sites run $7, and there's a little marina across the river with a grocery and boat rentals.

At Washtucna, *McKenzie's 7-C Drive In* (☎ 509-646-3245) is worth a stop for a milkshake. It's near the Hwy 261 turnoff for Palouse Falls. Other than that, plan on cooking your own food over a camp stove or driving through.

RITZVILLE
Population 2031

Ritzville is mostly an agricultural hub (they call it 'the heart of the wheat belt') and transportation junction. It's where I-90 meets US 395, which cuts south to the Tri Cities and Oregon. It's also where Hwy 261 begins its long route south to the Channeled Scablands near Washtucna. Ritzville is basically a pit stop – take advantage of it, freshen up a bit and admire the scenic rolling fields of wheat, barley and canola, and the rich Palouse soil covering much of the land. It's fairly photogenic for an old farm town.

If you want to take a quick break from driving, browsing the three-block historic area downtown, just north of I-90 exit 220, is pleasant enough. Summertime visitors can stop by the **Burroughs Wheatland Museum** (☎ 509-659-1656), 408 W Main St, housed in a physician's home and exhibiting his medical paraphernalia, and the Ritzville **Railroad Depot Museum** (☎ 509-659-1936), 201 W Railroad Ave, which is also home to a small visitors' center. If you're in town overnight check out the art deco-style **Ritz Theatre** (☎ 509-659-1950), 107 E Main St, which shows second-run movies on weekends.

Places to Stay & Eat

Since it's at a big crossroads, Ritzville has a fair crop of motels and one B&B. The *Portico B&B* (☎ 509-659-0800), 502 S Adams, is in a lovely Victorian mansion, with rooms for $59 or $74.

Best Western Heritage Inn (☎ 509-659-1007, 800-528-1234), 1405 S Smitty's Blvd (near I-90 exit 221), is a good bet for a freeway-side motel with single/double rooms from $53/61. There's an outdoor pool, hot tub, and a coin-op laundry.

Downtown, the *IMA Colwell Motor Inn* (☎ 509-659-1620, 800-341-8000), 501 W 1st St, is also a reasonably nice motel with a pool and a laundry and rooms starting at $42/46. Nearby are the *Top Hat Motel* (☎ 509-659-1100), 210 E 1st St, with rooms for $32/35, and the *Westside Motor Inn* (☎ 509-659-1164), 407 W 1st St, costing $30/36.

There are no hidden culinary gems in Ritzville, but you can get a meal here at almost any time of day. *Perkins Restaurant* (☎ 509-659-0192), 1406 S Smitty Blvd, is right off I-90 exit 221 by the Best Western. Barbecue is the specialty at *Texas John's* (☎ 509-659-1402), 1455 W 1st (at I-90 exit 220), and orders can be made to go. Downtown there's the *Circle T Restaurant & Lounge* (☎ 509-659-0922), 214 W Main St; right next door is the *Ritzville Hotel Cafe & Pub* (☎ 509-659-0712), 220 W Main St, with Widmer beer and meaty pub fare ($5) served in the lower level of a renovated hotel.

WASHINGTON

Vancouver & Vancouver Island

RICK GERHARTER

Vancouver

Population 1.9 million

Easily one of the most spectacularly scenic cities in Canada – if not the world – Vancouver lies nestled between the sea and mountains in the extreme southwestern corner of British Columbia (BC). The natural world intrudes on the city's busy urban life at every turn: Vancouver's impressive high-rise center is dwarfed only by the snow-clad mountains rising immediately north of the city; inlets of the Pacific reach far inland, isolating parts of the city on thumb-like peninsulas; sandy beaches dot the shoreline. Parks are numerous and large. One, Stanley Park, an extension of downtown, equals the size of the downtown business area.

But Vancouver has a lot more to offer than its postcard good looks. Certainly one of the most cosmopolitan cities in North America, Vancouver is still a city of new immigrants: wander the streets and you'll hear the languages of a dozen nations (the city is now the most Asian in all of North America). The recent influx of young people from other parts of Canada also adds spice to the cultural mix. Vancouver, and BC in general, has one of the most dynamic economies in Canada, and the city attracts young professionals and artists from the eastern provinces who come here to enjoy the city's recreation and easygoing sophistication. Yet for all the bustle of these newcomers, the city also offers an old-fashioned cultural refinement which

reflects Vancouver's British heritage. With almost 2 million people in the metropolitan area, Vancouver is Canada's third-largest city (Toronto and Montreal are larger). It also has the lowest median age of any large Canadian city.

Vancouver shares much of its cultural outlook, social attitudes and high spirits with the other cities of the Pacific Northwest. Yet there's more a sense of destiny and savoir-faire here than in Portland or Seattle. Vancouver is Canada's second-largest English-speaking city, making this a national center for the arts, business, fashion, sports and politics. The city is one of Canada's filmmaking centers; there's more New Age awareness, progressive politics and recognition of alternative lifestyles (including a large gay and lesbian population) here than anywhere else in Canada. If this list of attributes reminds you of somewhere else, you're right. Easterners often refer to Vancouver as the California of Canada.

The port, which is the busiest on North America's west coast, operates year-round in the beautiful natural harbor of Burrard Inlet, and it handles nearly all of Canada's trade with Japan and Asia.

HISTORY

The Vancouver area was originally inhabited by the Salish Indians. The first European to see the region was the Spanish explorer Don José Maria Narváez in 1791. For detailed information on Vancouver's early history, see the Early Exploration section in the Facts about Pacific Northwest chapter.

As a condition of confederation with the rest of Canada, Ottawa (on Canada's east coast) promised BC in 1870 that it would build a transcontinental railroad. However, if the Canadian Pacific Railway (CPR) was to link east and west, then BC would need a mainland coastal terminus

BRITISH COLUMBIA
Entered Confederation: July 20, 1871
Area: 948,596 sq km
Population: 3,282,065
Capital: Victoria

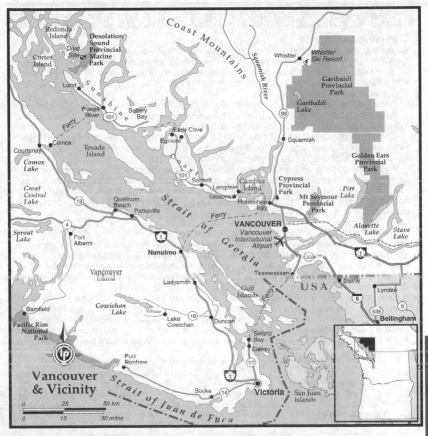

Vancouver & Vicinity

0   25   50 km
0   15   30 miles

since the new province's population center and capital, Victoria, was on an island. Railroad engineers set their sites on the sheltered Burrard Inlet, then a sparse ragtag of saloons, forests, lumber mills and farms. The first train arrived from Montreal in 1886, stopping at a thrown-together, brand-new settlement barely more than a siding, called Vancouver. A year later, the first ship docked from China, and Vancouver began its boom as a trading center and transportation hub. In 1890, just four years after it was founded, Vancouver had already outpaced Victoria in population.

On June 13, 1886, a fire almost completely destroyed the city in less than an hour, killing 21 people. Reconstruction began immediately, and by 1889 the town was rebuilt in brick.

The building of the Panama Canal, which was completed in 1914, meant easier access to markets in Europe and along North America's east coast. This brought about a boom for the BC economy and for its main trade center, Vancouver. As big business grew, so did big unions. In the 1910s, workers in great numbers organized into labor unions, protesting working conditions and pay rates. A

Traveling to Canada

Crossing the Border How thoroughly customs will check you out upon arrival at a Canadian entry point depends on a number of things: firstly, point of departure, nationality and appearance. Arriving from countries known as drug sources or from countries with a history of illegal immigration or refugees will add to the scrutiny. Always make sure your necessary papers are in order.

Don't get caught bringing drugs into Canada: this includes marijuana and hashish. They are termed narcotics in Canada. The sentence is seven years minimum and the judge has little choice by law, no matter who you are.

The border between Canada and the USA has tightened up, even for citizens of these two countries. By law, you are now required to carry a passport. However, you may be asked to produce only a driver's license or nothing at all.

If you are starting and ending your trip in Canada, check that your entry permit to Canada includes multiple entry. For people holding passports from Western countries, multiple entry is generally given. But check, because if not, you may find that your afternoon side trip across the border to the USA is involuntarily extended when Canadian officials won't let you back into Canada.

Documents Visitors to Canada from nearly all Western countries do not need visas but there are exceptions. Visa requirements change frequently, and since visas must be obtained before arrival in Canada, check before you leave – Europeans included. Visitor visas, which are free, are granted for a period of six months and are extendible for a fee. Extensions must be applied for at a Canadian Immigration Centre. A separate visa is required for visitors intending to work or to go to school in Canada.

Visitors from nearly all countries need a passport (exceptions include residents of Greenland). However, a passport and/or visa does not guarantee entry. Admission and duration of permitted stay is at the discretion of the immigration officer at the border. If you are refused entry but have a visa you have the right to appeal at the Immigration Appeal Board at the port of entry. Those under 18 years of age should have a letter from a parent or guardian.

Visitors from countries other than the USA (arriving by air or sea) may be required to have either a return or onward ticket in their possession. These tickets may be 'open,' or undated.

If you've rented a car, trailer or any other vehicle in the USA and you are driving it into Canada, bring a copy of the rental agreement to save any possible aggravation by border officials. The rental agreement should stipulate that taking the vehicle into Canada is permitted.

number of strikes targeted key industries like lumber mills and shipping, and in several instances Vancouver saw armed confrontations between union members and soldiers.

However, one issue where the unions, the government and business were in accord was with non-white workers: the growing Chinese and Japanese population was a problem that only punitive legislation and violence could solve.

Large numbers of Chinese had moved to the province, and were instrumental in building the CPR; they later established their own community just east of downtown, Chinatown. Japanese settlers came slightly later, establishing truck farms and becoming the area's principal commercial fishermen. That these were hard working people seeking opportunity, like the Europeans who were also flooding the province, seemingly didn't matter to whites. On sev-

Money US currency is accepted in Canada for most purchases, so it may not be necessary to exchange money if you're only making a short side trip from the US. You won't get US$ back in change though – transactions are converted to US$ at the current exchange rate (at press time around US$1:C$1.52) and the purchaser receives the change in equivalent Canadian currency. Also keep in mind that banks in the States won't accept Canadian coins for exchange to US$ – it's a good idea to use them up or exchange coins back to US$ before you return.

At many banks in Oregon and Washington, you can exchange US$ and C$ at teller windows; you don't have to use foreign exchange bureaus.

ATM machines, which are omnipresent in British Columbia, link to the major international banking networks (ie, Cirrus, Plus and The Exchange). This is by far the easiest way to exchange money into C$.

Canadian currency is issued in the same denominations as US currency. However, note that there is no dollar bill: this has been replaced by a gold-colored coin popularly known as a 'loonie.' There is also a C$2 coin.

Note that prices quoted in this chapter and in the Vancouver Island chapter are in Canadian dollars.

Customs Canadian Customs allows each adult (age varies by province, but an adult is generally 19 years and older) to bring in 1.1 liters (40 oz) of liquor or a case of beer (24 beers) as well as 200 cigarettes, 50 cigars and 400g of tobacco (all cheaper in the USA). You can bring in gifts up to C$60 in value.

Sporting goods, including 200 rounds of ammunition, cameras and film, can also be brought in without trouble. Registering these items upon arrival might save you some hassle when you leave, especially if you'll be crossing the Canadian/US border a number of times. Pistols, fully automatic weapons and any firearms less than 66cm (26 inches) in length are not permitted into the country. Most rifles and shotguns will be admitted without a permit.

If you have a dog or cat you will need proof that it has had a rabies shot in the past 36 months. The customs officer may confiscate fruit or other agricultural products at the border.

For boaters, pleasure craft may enter Canada either on the trailer or in the water and stay for up to one year. An entry permit is required and is obtainable from the customs office at or near the point of entry. All boats powered by motors over 10hp must be licensed.

For details on US Customs, see Customs in the Facts for the Visitor chapter. ■

eral occasions in the city's early history, Vancouver's Chinatown and Little Tokyo were the scene of white mob violence, and in the 1920s BC passed legislation effectively closing its borders to non-white immigration.

WWI and the Wall Street crash of 1929 brought severe economic depression and hardship to Canada. Vancouver, with its comparatively mild climate – at least for Canada – became a kind of magnet for young Canadian men who were hungry, desperate and out of work. But Vancouver had no work to offer, and held no easy answers for the problems of mass unemployment, and soon the streets were filled with street demonstrations, occupation of public buildings and rioting.

The war years were also hard times for non-white immigrants. During WWI, anti-German riots took hold of the streets of Vancouver, and businesses owned by Germans were burned. In 1941 Japanese Canadians were removed from their land and their fishing boats, and were interned by the government on farms and work camps in inland BC and the Prairie Provinces (Alberta, Saskatchewan and Manitoba).

Prosperity only returned with the advent of WWII, when shipbuilding and armaments manufacturing bolstered the region's traditional economic base of resource exploitation.

WWII catapulted the city into the modern era, and from then on it changed rapidly. The western end became the highrise apartment center it now is. In 1974 Granville Street became a mall. Redevelopment included housing as well as office buildings and this set the basis for the modern, livable city Vancouver is today.

In 1986 the city hosted Expo '86, a very successful world's fair. A few prominent structures remain, while the rest of the area where it took place is now being redeveloped. In April 1993 the city's international reputation was enhanced when it hosted the summit meeting between Russian President Boris Yeltsin and US President Bill Clinton.

During the mid-1990s Vancouver saw a wave of immigration that has had a significant economic and social impact. In advance of China's takeover of Hong Kong in 1997, tens of thousands of wealthy Hong Kong Chinese emigrated to the Vancouver area. Unlike previous waves of emigrants, the Chinese that came to Vancouver were from the Hong Kong business classes. As a result Vancouver real estate prices shot through the roof, with cost of living figures suddenly rivaling those of Paris, London and Tokyo. New suburbs shot up, particularly around Richmond, which are now essentially single-race enclaves of ethnic Chinese.

CLIMATE
Vancouver's mild climate, at least in Canadian terms, further extends the comparison with California, and attracts many eastern Canadians. The average January temperature is 2°C (35°F), the July average is 17°C

(63°F). It rarely snows in Vancouver and it's not often oppressively hot. The only drawback is the rain, particularly in winter when it rarely stops and the cloud cover obliterates the view of the surrounding mountains. Even in summer a rainy spell can last for weeks. But when the sun shines and the mountains reappear, most people here seem to forget all the soakings they've endured.

ORIENTATION
Greater Vancouver is built on a series of peninsulas bounded on the north by Burrard Inlet and on the south by Fraser River and Boundary Bay. The Coast Mountains rise directly behind the city to the north, while to the west the Georgia Strait is cluttered with islands. The many bays, inlets and river branches, as well as the Pacific coastline, are major features of the city. Much of the city's recent growth has pushed suburbs far up the Fraser River to the east.

Hwy 99, the continuation of I-5 from Washington State, enters the city on Oak St, which unfortunately doesn't have a bridge to downtown. If you're heading to downtown, you'll need to detour west to Granville St or east to Cambie St, which have bridges. Hwy 1, the Trans Canada Hwy, bypasses Vancouver proper to the east; from it, Hastings St leads to downtown.

Downtown
Vancouver's city center is itself on a peninsula, cut off from the southern portion of the city by False Creek and from the northern mainland by Burrard Inlet. The tip of this peninsula is preserved as Stanley Park, one of Vancouver's greatest treasures. Three bridges – Burrard, Granville and Cambie – link the southern part of the city, known confusingly as the West Side, with downtown. Only one bridge, the highflying Lions Gate Bridge, links downtown to the northern suburbs, resulting in traffic nightmares.

Pacific Centre, a three-block complex of offices, restaurants, shops and theaters, beginning at the corner of Robson and

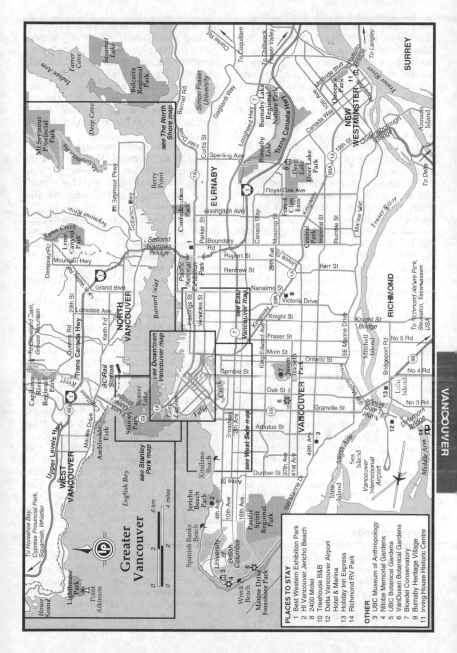

Greater Vancouver

0   3   6 km
0   2   4 miles

PLACES TO STAY
1 Best Western Exhibition Park
2 HI Vancouver Jericho Beach
8 2400 Motel
10 Treehouse B&B
12 Delta Vancouver Airport Hotel & Marina
13 Holiday Inn Express
14 Richmond RV Park

OTHER
3 UBC Museum of Anthropology
4 Nitobe Memorial Gardens
5 UBC Botanical Gardens
6 VanDusen Botanical Gardens
7 Bloedel Conservatory
9 Burnaby Heritage Village
11 Irving House Historic Centre

VANCOUVER

Howe Sts, is pretty much the center of downtown. Robson St and Georgia St, two blocks north, are the two main northwest-southeast streets. Robson St, or Robson-strasse as it is sometimes called, is lined with boutiques and restaurants. Davie St, between Burrard St and Stanley Park, is a secondary commercial and shopping street. Only Georgia St continues through Stanley Park to Lions Gate Bridge.

The main northeast to southwest streets are, from west to east: Burrard, Howe, Granville and Seymour. North of Georgia St, bordered by Howe and Burrard Sts, is the main office, banking and financial district. At the water's edge, at the foot of Howe St, is the impressive Canada Place, the convention center, with its jagged white 'sails.' Much of Granville St, from Nelson St north to West Hastings St, is closed to cars. It's not a true mall as trucks and buses are still permitted and it has never worked very well as a central showcase.

The high-density area to the west of downtown's shopping area is known as the West End – *not* to be confused with West Vancouver on the North Shore, or the West Side, south of downtown.

There are three downtown districts worth noting. Yaletown, on Hamilton and Mainland Sts between Davie and Nelson Sts, is currently the 'hot' part of town with old warehouses being converted into hip bars, restaurants and loft apartments. Gastown, along Water St, north of West Hastings St between Richards and Columbia Sts, is the historic center of old Vancouver, with many restored Victorian buildings. Just to the southeast is bustling Chinatown, in the area around Pender St between Carrall St and Gore Ave.

Neighborhoods

To the south of the West End and downtown, over False Creek, lies most of Vancouver – this vast area is primarily residential. Heading west after crossing Burrard Bridge or Granville Bridge is Kitsilano, filled with students, young professionals and now-successful ex-hippies. Between Kitsilano and Sea Island – where

the Vancouver International Airport is located – are some of the city's most exclusive areas, such as Shaughnessy Heights. Farther south is the rapidly growing largely Asian municipality of Richmond, built on a portion of the Fraser River Delta. Still farther south is the port of Tsawwassen, where you can catch a ferry to Vancouver Island, the Gulf Islands or Seattle.

East of downtown running south from Powell St, Commercial Drive was once the center of the Italian community in Vancouver. It's now the focal point for a developing alternative and student-oriented neighborhood.

Another residential area is Burnaby, east of Vancouver, containing Simon Fraser University. Southeast of Burnaby is the city of New Westminster, once the capital of BC and now an industrial area along the Fraser River. Across the river from New Westminster on the southern side is Surrey.

Over the Lions Gate Bridge and the Second Narrows Bridge lie West Vancouver and North Vancouver (which comprise the North Shore), both essentially upper-middle-class residential areas. The shore of Burrard Inlet in North Vancouver is lined with commercial docks. To the north are two provincial parks, Lynn Canyon Park and Mt Seymour Provincial Park. To the northeast, along Capilano Rd, are Capilano Canyon, the Lions Peaks (from which Lions Gate Bridge takes its name), Grouse Mountain and the Coast Mountains. Farther west and north lie Cypress Provincial Park, Horseshoe Bay (from where you can take a ferry to Vancouver Island) and the Sunshine Coast (which is also reached by ferry from Horseshoe Bay).

Street Savvy

Generally, the avenues in Greater Vancouver run east to west while the streets run north to south. Some of the streets in the downtown area – as well as many of the avenues in the Greater Vancouver area – are given east or west directionals. So Hastings St, for example, is divided into

West Hastings St and East Hastings St. As a general rule the dividing cross street is Main St. However, for address numbering purposes, the downtown east-west streets begin numbering at Carrall St near Chinatown (and with Ontario St on Vancouver's West Side). North-south streets begin numbering at Waterfront Rd, along Burrard Inlet. As a reference in downtown addresses, Robson St begins the 800 block. Don't be confused on the West Side, in Kitsilano, when numbered avenues don't predict the street addresses. For instance, West 1st Ave is, for numbering purposes, is the 1600 block.

Vancouver doesn't really have a freeway system to carry trunk traffic through the city, and congestion on the surface streets can be extreme. The Lions Gate Bridge, which connects Stanley Park with West Vancouver, should especially be avoided during rush hour. Only three lanes wide, the bridge's center lane changes direction during the day to accommodate traffic flow.

INFORMATION
Tourist Offices
The Travel InfoCentre, Plaza Level, Waterfront Centre, 200 Burrard St, is open in the summer 8 am to 6 pm daily, and the rest of the year 8:30 am to 5 pm weekdays, 9 am to 5 pm Saturday. Though usually busy, the staff is friendly and helpful but don't forget to take a number!

The staff will help you with bookings for accommodations, tours, transport and activities. Call ☎ 604-683-2000, 800-663-6000 for information, 604-683-2772 for bookings. At the InfoCentre get a free copy of *The Vancouver Book*, the official visitors' guide, which has information on shopping, accommodations, entertainment, local transport, etc. Also useful is the monthly booklet *Where Vancouver* and *Visitor's Choice*, both available around town, often at hotels.

On the corner of Georgia and Granville Sts (at Eatons department store) is an information kiosk open 10 am to 6 pm Tuesday to Friday in the summer.

Money
All prices quoted in this chapter and the Vancouver Island chapter are in Canadian dollars, unless stated otherwise.

The major national banks, including Toronto Dominion, Bank of Montreal, Canada Trust and CBIC, have branches throughout the city; some branches are open on Saturday. ATM machines are liberally sprinkled throughout all the shopping and business districts.

Thomas Cook Exchange has a number of offices in Vancouver, including one (☎ 604-687-6111) at 1016 W Georgia St, between Thurlow and Burrard Sts, and another at suite 130, 999 Canada Place. American Express (☎ 604-669-2813) is close by at 1040 W Georgia St. Both are open on Saturday. A stroll along Robson St reveals a number of exchange bureaus open until very late at night.

The Vancouver International Airport provides banking as well as money-changing facilities.

Post & Communications
The main post office (☎ 604-662-5725), 349 W Georgia St, between Homer and Hamilton Sts, is open 8 am to 5:30 pm weekdays. It has no separate poste-restante (general delivery) counter: you just join the queue, show some identification and the person behind the counter will look for your mail. The post office also has a good philatelic desk and a photocopier. The American Express office will keep a card holder's mail for one month.

The area code for metro Vancouver, east to Hope, north to Whistler and northeast along the Sunshine Coast is 604. The rest of the province is 250.

Travel Agencies
Travel CUTS, the student travel organization, has four offices in Vancouver: one (☎ 604-681-9136) at suite 501, 602 W Hastings St, between Richards and Homer Sts; another (☎ 604-687-6033) at 1516 Duranleau St, Granville Island; and one each at the University of British Columbia (UBC) and Simon Fraser University.

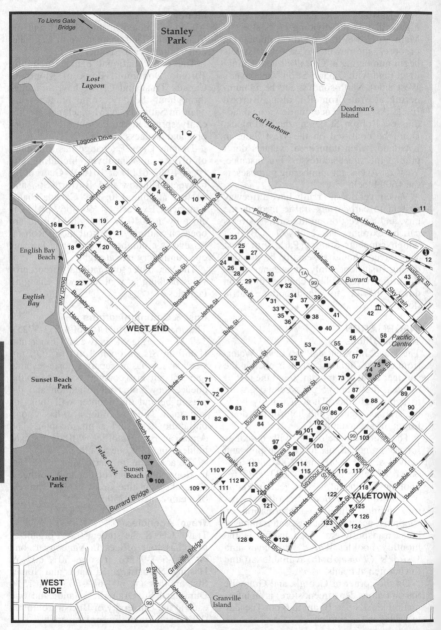

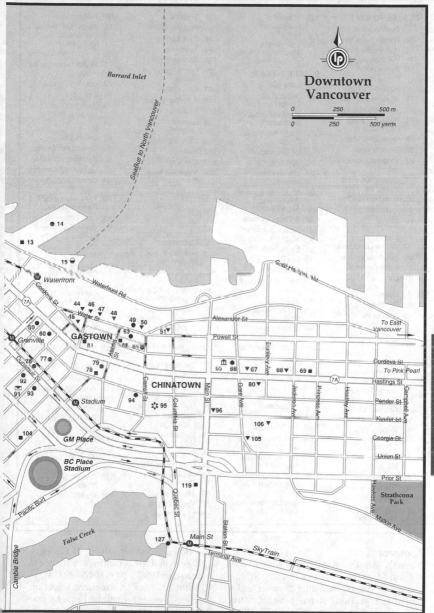

Downtown Vancouver

Burrard Inlet

SeaBus to North Vancouver

● 14

■ 13

15 ◓

Waterfront

Cordova St

Waterfront Rd

(7A)

44 46 47
45   48 Water St
        49 50
59   63   51▼
60 ●   Alexander St
M
Granville
        GASTOWN   81
77 ●
Dunsmuir St
79
78
92
91 93

M Stadium

104

GM Place

BC Place
Stadium

Pacific Blvd

Cambie Bridge

False Creek

Abbott St
Carrall St

CHINATOWN
94
✳ 95
Columbia St

119 ■

Quebec St

127 ● M

Main St

Powell St

🏛 ●
65 66   ▼67   68▼   69 ■

80▼

▼96

106 ▼
▼105

Station St

Main St

Terminal Ave

SkyTrain

Goat He Am... Mt...

Funley Ave

Gore Ave

Jackson Ave

Princess Ave

Heatley Ave

Campbell St S

(7A)

To East
Vancouver

Cordova St
To Pink Pearl
Hastings St
Pender St
Keefer St

Georgia St

Union St

Prior St

Strathcona
Park

Hawkes Ave

Malkin Ave

VANCOUVER

VANCOUVER

PLACES TO STAY
2   Buchan Hotel
7   Westin Bayshore
13 Pan Pacific Hotel Vancouver
16 Sylvia Hotel
17 Oceanside Apartment Hotel
19 Shato Inn Hotel
23 Riviera Motor Inn
24 Robsonstrasse City Motor Inn
25 Greenbriar Hotel
26 Barclay Hotel
27 Tropicana Motor Inn
28 Listel O'Doul's Hotel Best Western
30 Blue Horizon Hotel
43 Days Inn Vancouver Downtown
52 YMCA
54 Wedgewood Hotel
56 Hotel Vancouver
58 Hotel Georgia
61 Cambie International Hostel
62 Dominion Hotel
69 Budget Inn – Patricia Hotel
75 Four Seasons Hotel
78 New Backpackers Hostel
81 HI Vancouver Downtown
84 Burrard Motor Inn
85 Sheraton Wall Centre Hotel
89 Kingston Hotel
98 Holiday Inn Vancouver Downtown
99 Bosman's Motor Hotel
100 Royal Hotel
103 Dufferin Hotel
104 YWCA
112 Quality Hotel/Inn at False Creek

119 Vincent's Backpackers Hostel
120 Travelodge Vancouver Centre

PLACES TO EAT
3   Cafe Slavia
5   Great Wall Mongolian BBQ
6   Musashi Japanese Restaurant
8   Bud's Halibut & Chips
10 Le Gavroche
20 Pepita's
22 Lilliget Feast House
26 Mirabella Spanish Restaurant & Tapas Bar
29 A Taste of India
31 Bread Garden
32 Royal Thai Seafood
33 Cin Cin
34 Milestones
35 Cactus Club Cafe
36 Pezzo
37 Joe Forte's Oysterhouse & Grill
44 Steamworks Brewing Company
45 Water Street Café
46 Umberto Al Porto
47 Old Spaghetti Factory
48 Cottage Deli
50 Brother's Restaurant
51 Incendio
53 Le Crocodile
64 Irish Heather Bistro & Irish House
67 Bodai Vegetarian Restaurant
68 Miu Jay Garden Vegetarian Restaurant
70 Stepho's Souvlaki Greek Taverna

71 Tigãlo's
80 Pho Pasteur
96 Park Lock
101 Templeton
105 Phnom Penh
106 Hon's Wun Tun House
107 Chili Club
109 A Kettle of Fish
110 Etoile
111 Umberto II Giardino
118 Deniro's Bistro
122 Farrago
123 Century Grill
125 Yaletown Brewing Co
126 Mangiamo

OTHER
1   Harbour Ferries
4   Denman Station Cabaret
9   Robson Public Market
11 Harbour Air Seaplanes
12 Waterfront Centre, Travel InfoCentre
14 Canada Place
15 Waterfront Station, Pacific Central Station
18 Carepoint Medical Centre
21 Denman Place Discount Cinema
38 Manhattan Books
39 American Express
40 Robson Galleria
41 Thomas Cook Exchange
42 Canadian Craft Museum
49 Purple Onion
55 Duthie's Books
57 Vancouver Art Gallery
59 The Lookout!
60 Travel CUTS
63 Town Pump

64 Talking Stick
65 Vancouver Police Centennial Museum
66 Firehall Arts Centre
72 Stone Table Coffee House
73 Robson Square
74 Eatons
76 Railway Club
77 Picadilly Pub
79 Lotus
82 Celebrities
83 Davie Laundromat
86 Paradise (cinema)
87 Granville 7 Cinema
88 Commodore Ballroom
90 Ford Centre for the Performing Arts
91 Post Office
92 Vancouver Public Library
93 Queen Elizabeth Theatre
94 World's Thinnest Office Building
95 Dr Sun Yat-Sen Classical Chinese Garden
97 Pacifc Cinémathèque
102 Fred's Uptown Tavern
108 Vancouver Aquatic Centre
113 Odyssey
114 The Gate
115 Arts Club Theatre
116 Richard's on Richards
117 Starfish Room
121 Yale
124 DV8
127 Science World & Alcan OMNIMAX Theatre
128 The Rage, Yuk Yuks
129 MaRS

Bookstores

Duthie's Books (☎ 604-684-4496), 919 Robson St, at the corner of Hornby St, has a range of books, including a travel and a Canadiana section. It has several other branches, including one (☎ 604-689-1802) just down the street at 650 W Georgia St, and one at UBC. Duthie's also operates Manhattan Books (☎ 604-681-9074), 1089 Robson St, with an excellent selection of foreign-language (mainly French) books, magazines and newspapers.

Book Warehouse (☎ 604-872-5711), 632 W Broadway, with branches throughout the city, has good quality books, many at bargain prices. It's open from 10 am to 10 pm daily and they have free coffee. The Granville Book Company (☎ 604-687-2213), at 850 Granville St, is particularly strong in fiction, sci-fi and computer books.

Another bookstore to check out is Blackberry Books (☎ 604-685-6188/4113), 1663 Duranleau St, Granville Island. It's open 9 am to 6 pm daily; till 9 pm on Thursday, Friday and Saturday in the summer.

In Kitsilano, the Travel Bug (☎ 604-737-1122), at 2667 W Broadway, has travel guides and maps, plus language tapes and travel accessories; as does Wanderlust (☎ 604-739-2182) at 1929 W Fourth Ave. Banyen Books (☎ 604-732-7912), 2671 W Broadway, is a well-established and pretty amazing New Age bookstore. Vancouver Kidsbooks (☎ 604-738-5335), at 3083 W Broadway, is a huge store carrying a vast selection of children's books, plus great puppets, games and plush stuffed animals.

At press time, Chapter, Canada's answer to Barnes & Noble, was in the process of opening stores in the downtown area.

Library

The huge, new, architecturally controversial Vancouver Public Library (☎ 604-331-4000) is at the corner of W Georgia and Hamilton Sts. Looking somewhat like the Roman Coliseum, the airy, striking building is open 10 am to 9 pm Monday to Wednesday, and 10 am to 6 pm Thursday to Saturday. In winter (October to March) it's open 1 to 5 pm on Sunday as well.

Newspapers

The two daily newspapers are the *Province* and the *Vancouver Sun*.

The best source for arts and entertainment is *Georgia Straight*, a newsweekly that's available free in coffee shops, music stores and many other locations. Another entertainment-oriented weekly paper is the *WestEnder*. The local gay newspapers are *Xtra West* and *Angles*, both free at many locations.

Laundry

Downtown, do your laundry at Davie Laundromat (☎ 604-682-2717), 1061 Davie St. On the West Side, try the Silver Coin Laundromat (☎ 604-298-7117) at 2822 W 4th Ave.

Medical Services

Vancouver General Hospital (☎ 604-875-4995) is at 855 W 12th Ave. For a walk-in clinic downtown, go to Carepoint Medical Centre (☎ 604-681-5338), 1175 Denman St, which is open daily. On the West Side, go to Khatsahlano Medical Clinic (☎ 604-731-9187), 2689 W Broadway.

Emergency

For police, fire or a medical emergency, call ☎ 911. Or, call ☎ 0 and ask the operator for assistance.

DOWNTOWN

Downtown Vancouver is bordered on two sides by water, and on a third by the enormous Stanley Park. This constriction has forced the city upward: while none of the business towers are startlingly high, the cumulative effect of so many skyscrapers makes Vancouver seem very modern and somewhat forbidding. Another anomaly of downtown Vancouver is that the vast majority of the high-rises in the West End, the area near Stanley Park, are residential towers erected after WWII. A *lot* of people live right downtown, and this has kept small markets and other neighborhood facilities in operation. Downtown has a real lived-in quality unusual in a city of this size.

For travelers, the center of downtown is **Robson St**, especially if you like shopping. A collage of tourist shops, fashion boutiques, coffee shops and restaurants, Robson St is undoubtedly the best place in the city for people watching. Locals, international tourists and recent immigrants all throng here, giving Robson St the cosmopolitan feel of a mini United Nations. Shops and restaurants stay open very late at night, often as late as midnight in the summer months.

VANCOUVER

Walking Tour
Start a walking tour of the downtown area at Robson and Howe Sts, at a small plaza called **Robson Square**. The Vancouver Art Gallery, a handsome turn-of-the-century stone building that was once a courthouse, is to the north; across the street is an artificial waterfall that forms the wall of the new provincial courthouse. To the east is the department store, Eatons, which serves as anchor for the three-block-long underground shopping arcade, Pacific Centre.

Stroll west on Robson St. Part of the fun of browsing here is that the shops are really eclectic: you can find everything here from Giorgio Armani suits to hologram portraits of Elvis to fancy condoms. At Burrard St you can detour north to the tourist office, and have a glimpse of Canada Place – the convention center with its famous white sails – reaching far out into the bay. Farther west on Robson St is the Robson Public Market, 1610 Robson St at Cardero St, a lively food market that's also a good place to buy ethnic takeout food.

At Denman St you can either continue on to Stanley Park, just to the west, or you can turn south and follow Denman St past numerous neighborhood-oriented cafes, shops and inexpensive restaurants. Denman St ends at aptly-named Beach Ave. Here, you get a view over English Bay to the West Side, which is the residential and commercial area flanking the University of British Columbia. A seawall and sandy beachfront extend in both directions. Follow Beach Ave east until Burrard or Hornby Sts. At the base of both streets you can catch a water taxi – actually a mini passenger ferry – across False Creek to the Granville Island Public Market, or to the museums, beaches and green spaces at Vanier Park. Return to Robson St along either Howe or Granville Sts, the latter partly a pedestrian mall with colorful, if rather seedy, street life.

To really put downtown Vancouver in perspective, take the elevator up 553 feet to **The Lookout!** for a 360° view of the city. The Lookout! is atop Harbour Centre at W Hastings and Seymour Sts. Tickets to the top cost C$8/7 adults/seniors and C$5 students, and they're good all day; open 9 am to 9 pm.

Vancouver Art Gallery
The city's art gallery (☎ 604-682-5621), at 750 Hornby St, is right at the center of things, kittycorner to Robson Square. It has a large collection of work by Emily Carr, who was born in Victoria in 1917; as one of the most prominent of Canadian painters who dominated Canadian art from the 1940s to 1960s, she was also among the first to portray BC and its landscapes. Group of Seven artists are well represented in the permanent collection. The museum also hosts various traveling shows, and has an especially good gift shop with local crafts. The Gallery Cafe, which overlooks the Sculpture Garden, is a great place for coffee and a snack.

The gallery is open 10 am to 6 pm Monday to Friday, Thursdays till 9 pm; 10 am to 5 pm Saturday, and noon to 5 pm Sunday. It's closed Monday and Tuesday from mid-October to Easter weekend. Admission costs C$7.50/5 adults/seniors, C$3.50 students and children get in free; it's pay what you want between 5 and 9 pm Thursday.

Canada Place & Waterfront Station
Canada Place, which was built to coincide with Expo '86, juts into the harbor at the foot of Howe St. The building's stridently modern design invites comparisons. Does it resemble an ocean liner with tent-like sails, the white exoskeleton of a very large and spiny insect, or just the Sydney Opera House? In any case, Canada Place has become a major city landmark. The complex contains the World Trade Centre, the Vancouver Trade and Convention Centre and the Pan Pacific Hotel, and is also a terminal for cruise ships. Also here is the CN IMAX Theatre (☎ 604-682-4629) with a five-story-high screen showing films made exclusively for such theaters. At the northern end are the promenade shops and a food court, plus good views across Burrard Inlet.

Just a block away from Canada Place is Waterfront Station, the grand old CPR station. The deteriorating building was restored and now serves as the terminus for an entirely different kind of transportation – the SeaBus. Catch the SeaBus, an aquatic bus, across to North Vancouver (with excellent views of the city and the busy Port of Vancouver). Also at Waterfront Station, you can hop the SkyTrain, a computerized commuter train that runs on an elevated track to the eastern suburbs, with stops at the sports stadiums and Science World on its way.

Canadian Craft Museum

This pleasant museum (☎ 604-687-8266), at 639 Hornby St, is dedicated to the role of crafts in human culture. Dominating the permanent collection are both contemporary and historical works from Canada; touring shows and special collections frequently have a more international focus. As you might expect, the gift shop here is wonderful, and a great place to find a truly unique handmade gift. The museum is open 10 am to 5 pm Monday to Saturday (Thursday till 9 pm), and noon to 5 pm Sunday; closed Tuesday in winter. Admission is C$4/2 adults/seniors and students.

BC Place Stadium & GM Place

These two large sports arenas shore up the eastern edge of downtown. Both are unmistakable. BC Place Stadium (☎ 604-669-2300 for general information, ☎ 604-661-7373 for events), 777 Pacific Blvd S, is covered by a translucent dome-shaped roof. The roof is 'air-supported,' which means it is inflated by huge fans (no, not sports fans), and kept in place by crisscrossed steel wires, hence its quilted appearance. Concerts, trade shows, sports events and other large-scale gatherings are held during the year in this 60,000-capacity stadium, which is also the home ground of the BC Lions football team.

Adjacent, GM Place, built in 1995 with a major financial commitment from General Motors, makes the area the major focus for the city's professional sports. It is home to

the Vancouver Canucks of the National Hockey League (NHL) as well as the Vancouver Grizzlies of the National Basketball Association (NBA).

To get to the stadium, catch either bus No 15 or No 17, or take the SkyTrain to Stadium Station.

Science World & Alcan OMNIMAX Theatre

Another vestige from Expo '86 is the geodesic dome at 1455 Quebec St near Main St Station, on the fringe of downtown, just south of Chinatown. The gleaming dome now houses Science World (☎ 604 268 6363), a science, technology and natural history center with interactive exhibits. Aimed primarily at children, hands-on experiments help explain scientific and physical phenomena; kids also love the laser theater. Also in the dome is the Alcan OMNIMAX Theatre, with one of the world's largest domed screens.

Science World is open 10 am to 5 pm weekdays and 10 am to 6 pm weekends and holidays. Admission to the museum is C$10.50/7 adults/seniors, students and children. Admission is C$9 for the OMNIMAX Theatre. Combination tickets cost C$13.50/9.50.

Stanley Park

Vancouver's largest and much-beloved green space, Stanley Park is a 1000-acre forest of cedar flanked by beaches that extend north and west of downtown. Hiking, biking and jogging trails meander through the woods, and a seawall boardwalk winds more than 9.5km (6 miles) along the park's shoreline. The three park beaches – Second Beach, Third Beach and English Bay Beach – are popular spots in summer for sunbathers and swimmers; additionally, there are several swimming pools. From various points there are nice views of downtown Vancouver, the North Shore and out to sea toward the islands.

Near **Brockton Point**, on the east side of the park, there is a good collection of totem poles. Off the southern side near the yacht club is **Deadman's Island**, once

VANCOUVER

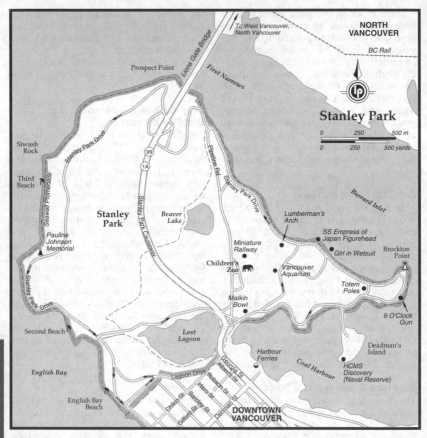

NORTH VANCOUVER

BC Rail

Stanley Park

| 0 | 250 | 500 m |
| 0 | 250 | 500 yards |

To West Vancouver, North Vancouver

Prospect Point

Lions Gate Bridge

First Narrows

Siwash Rock

Stanley Park Drive

Third Beach

99

1A

Seawall Promenade

Stanley Park

Beaver Lake

Stanley Park Causeway

Pipeline Rd

Stanley Park Drive

Burrard Inlet

Lumberman's Arch

SS Empress of Japan Figurehead

Girl in Wetsuit

Brockton Point

Pauline Johnson Memorial

Miniature Railway

Children's Zoo

Vancouver Aquarium

Totem Poles

Stanley Park Drive

Malkin Bowl

9 O'Clock Gun

Second Beach

Lost Lagoon

English Bay

Deadman's Island

Harbour Ferries

Coal Harbour

HCMS Discovery (Naval Reserve)

Lagoon Drive

George St

Alberni St

Robson St

Haro St

Barclay St

Chilco St

Gilford St

Denman St

English Bay Beach

DOWNTOWN VANCOUVER

VANCOUVER

used, it's said, by a northern Native Indian tribe as a camp for women captured in raids. Later it became a burial ground for Chinese people and Native Indians. For children, there's a free petting zoo and a miniature railway.

Lions Gate Bridge extends from the northern tip, and the road – Stanley Park Causeway (also known as Lions Gate Bridge Rd) – through the park to the bridge is usually busy. Just to the west of Lions Gate Bridge is **Prospect Point**, a popular point for views of the Narrows and passing ships.

Vancouver Aquarium One of the city's premier destinations is the Vancouver Aquarium (☎ 604-268-9900), Canada's largest, with 8000 sea creatures. The most popular attraction here is watching the dolphins and killer whales (orcas) engage in 'natural' activities; due to pressure from animal-rights activists, the dolphins and whales no longer 'perform.' There is also a special, albeit controversial, tank for beluga whales. Other exhibits include octopuses, crocodiles, eels, piranhas and a wide variety of local sea life and freshwater fish. The Asian Tropical Seas exhibit is also a standout, as is the Amazon Gallery, a recreation of a tropical rain forest, complete with crocodiles, toucans, piranhas and tree frogs. The aquarium is Canada's largest marine-mammal rescue and rehabilitation center as well.

Vancouver Aquarium is open 9:30 am to 8 pm daily July to early September, and 10 am to 5:30 pm the rest of the year. Admission is C$10 adults; C$8.75 seniors, students and youths (13 to 17); and C$6.75 children. The aquarium is located on the eastern edge of Stanley Park; from downtown follow Georgia St into the park; you'll need to pay for parking if you drive.

Gastown

Vancouver's Victorian-era business district is called Gastown, the name taken from 'Gassy' Jack Deighton, an English sailor who forsook the sea to open a bar servicing the developing timber mills in 1867. When a village sprang up around his establishment it was called Gassy's Town. (A statue of Gassy Jack has been erected in Maple St Square, where Cordova and Water Sts meet.)

Gassy Jack

In the mid-19th century the men working in the sawmills along the shores of Burrard Inlet weren't allowed to drink alcohol on mill property. They had to travel a long way into town, New Westminster, to find somewhere to imbibe. An enterprising former riverboat captain, John Deighton, saw this as his opportunity and landed in his canoe close to the mill area with his wife, a few animals and a small barrel of whiskey. He began selling the whiskey almost immediately and soon became a huge success. He was called 'Gassy Jack' because he talked so much; the community that developed around his saloon, became known as Gassy's Town then Gastown. ∎

After the center of Vancouver moved elsewhere, the whole Gastown area gradually became a skid row, but in the 1970s it was restored and renovated, simply pushing Vancouver's seedier characters a little farther south to Hastings St. The old Victorian buildings now house restaurants, bars, boutiques and galleries; some of the city's best nightlife is here. The brick streets have been lined with old lamps. Street vendors and buskers, or entertainers, add to the holiday feel of the area. The historic flavor is only a little marred by the parking structure several stories high on Water St.

At the western end of Water St is the world's first clock run by steam. The clock stands on a steam tap that vents steam lines that were formerly used to heat local businesses. Although the clock looks old, it was built in 1977. You can see the steam works through the side glass panels and will hear it toot every 15 minutes.

The Gastown area today is bounded by Columbia and Richards Sts, with Water St the main thoroughfare.

Chinatown

About 35,000 people of Chinese descent live in the area around W Pender St, roughly bordered by Abbott St and Gore Ave; thousands of others come here to shop, making this one of one of the largest Chinatowns in North America.

For the most part, this is a real Chinese market and business district; nearly all signs are in Chinese; the menu in McDonalds is written in Chinese characters, and English is rarely spoken. The colors, smells, signs and occasional old Chinese-style balcony can make you believe for a second that you're in Hong Kong. Throughout the day the streets are full of people going in and out of stores that have hanging ducks, bales of strange dried fish, exotic fruits and Asian remedies. There are restaurants and bakeries as well; this is obviously a good place to come for dim sum.

VANCOUVER

For years the area has contended with the rundown blights of Hastings and Main Sts and this is finally taking a toll. Now that the Hong Kong Chinese have colonized Richmond, a suburb of Vancouver, the center of Chinese Canadian business and culture has at least in part relocated there. But there's still plenty of vitality here, and Vancouver's Chinatown is a lot less touristy than San Francisco's.

World's Thinnest Office Building Called the Sam Kee, this building, at 8 W Pender St near the corner of Carrall St, has made it into Ripley's *Believe It or Not!* and *The Guinness Book of World Records*. It's easy to miss not only due to its narrowness but because it looks like the front of the larger building behind, to which it is attached.

Dr Sun Yat-Sen Classical Chinese Garden This is the only full-scale classical Chinese garden (☎ 604-689-7133) found outside of China. Its design is subtle but exquisite in execution and effect. Modeled after the Ming Dynasty gardens, best represented in the city of Suzhou, it makes a real sanctuary in the center of the city. The Taoist principles of yin and yang are incorporated in numerous ways throughout the garden.

The guided tours are included in the admission and are well worthwhile. If possible, go during the week when it won't be too busy. It's open 10 am to 6 pm daily; admission is C$5.25/4.50 adults/seniors and students, and C$12 families. In the summer, the park is open from 10 am to 7:30 pm; the rest of the year, the park closes at dusk. It's at 578 Carrall St behind the Chinese Cultural Centre in Chinatown. The adjacent park, built by local artisans using Chinese materials, is similar in design and has free entry.

Vancouver Police Centennial Museum You don't need to be a local to enjoy this unusual museum (☎ 604-665-3346), 240 E Cordova St. Housed in the city's former morgue and coroner's court, the atmosphere is suitably macabre to tell the story of Vancouver's most famous crimes and criminals. Weapons, counterfeit money, forensic autopsy tools and a century's worth of drug paraphernalia help illustrate the story of law enforcement in BC.

Yaletown
Once the city's downtown warehouse district, Yaletown has been 'loft-icized'; this former eyesore is now home to some of Vancouver's trendiest addresses. Beside some of the city's best restaurants and watering holes, this is also the place to come for art galleries and interior decorating and furniture shopping. On a nice day, this is a great place to wander and window-shop. The center of Yaletown is at Hamilton and Mainland Sts, between Nelson and Davie Sts.

WEST SIDE
Don't let the name confuse you: Vancouver's West Side is in fact the long-established residential neighborhoods and bustling commercial centers south of the downtown across False Creek. Both the Granville and Burrard Bridges lead to the West Side; the main arterials are 4th Ave and Broadway, both of which lead west to the University of British Columbia (UBC) at the tip of the peninsula. Note that the easiest form of transport from downtown to some of the following sites is by water taxi from the base of Burrard and Hornby Sts.

Granville Island
On the southern side of False Creek, under the Granville Bridge, this little, formerly industrial island has been redeveloped into a busy blend of businesses, restaurants, galleries and theaters. The center of activity is the **Granville Island Public Market**, a food lover's dream made manifest. Dozens of greengrocers, fishmongers, butchers, bakers, cheese shops and other food merchants squeeze into the bustling market, making this a great place to experience the natural bounty of BC. There are also coffee shops and counters with takeout food. The

market fronts onto False Creek, and – in all but antediluvian downpours – the waterfront plaza behind the public market is filled with harried shoppers, frolicking children, buskers and swarms of pigeons and gulls.

Granville Island is also a mecca for artisans: a number of craftspeople have studios and shops, there are several commercial art galleries and Emily Carr College of Art & Design (☎ 604-844-3800), 1299 Johnston St, has frequent exhibits in its galleries. A number of ship chandlers and recreational equipment shops are also on Granville Island. At night, the focus shifts from shopping to the performing arts. A number of theater companies and live music clubs open their doors; there are no shortages of places to eat and drink.

The Granville Island Information Centre (☎ 604-666-5784), at 1592 Johnston St, across from the Arts Club Theatre, is open 9 am to 6 pm daily.

Parking can be very tight on Granville Island. Unless you must drive, consider taking bus No 50 from downtown, or take the water taxi. Much of the island's activity is shut down on Monday, although the market remains open Monday in summer.

Vanier Park

Vanier Park, on English Bay south of False Creek and below the Burrard Bridge, is home to a number of museums, a fine beach and a stand of lovely old maple trees. Also in the park are a swimming pool, tennis courts, and other sporting grounds. The park is a popular area and when the weather's fine you'll see people strolling, jogging, cycling, walking their dogs or simply sitting and watching the ships moving between English Bay and False Creek.

In addition to the sights listed below, Vanier Park is also home to the Vancouver Archives, Academy of Music, Canadian Coast Guard and Burrard Civic Marina. To reach Vanier Park from downtown, take the No 22 bus, or take the water taxi from downtown or Granville Island.

Vancouver Museum At 1100 Chestnut St, this museum (☎ 604-736-4431) specializes in the history of Vancouver and southwestern BC. On display are historic photos and artifacts, including an exhibit on the archaeology and ethnology of the area, concentrating on the Salish Indians. There are several examples of most Native Indian crafts (check out the totem pole in front of the museum). The basketry is impressive, especially those made of cedar and pine roots. The part of the museum documenting the European exploration and settlement of Vancouver is also good.

The museum is open 10 am to 7 pm daily from May to September, and 10 am to 5 pm Tuesday to Sunday from October to April. Admission costs C$6/3 adults/students and seniors.

HR MacMillan Planetarium & Pacific Space Centre The planetarium (☎ 604-738-7827), part of the Vancouver Museum complex, has regularly changing, entertaining and educational shows which are projected onto a dome 19m (62 feet) across. Make reservations for these popular shows.

Admission for adults is C$5.50. There are also music-laser shows for C$7.50 at 8:30 pm Sunday to Thursday and at 9:30 pm Friday and Saturday. The planetarium is closed on Monday during the winter, but open daily in the summer months. On Friday, Saturday and Sunday afternoons when the sky is clear, the Gordon Southam Observatory (☎ 604-738-2855) is also open to the public and is free.

Vancouver Maritime Museum This museum (☎ 604-257-8300), 1905 Ogden Ave at the foot of Cypress St, is a five-minute walk from the Vancouver Museum. There are two parts to the museum: the museum itself which is strictly for boat buffs – with lots of wooden models and some old rowboats on display – and the *St Roch*. This 1928 Royal Canadian Mounted Police (RCMP) Arctic patrol sailing ship was the first vessel to navigate the legendary Northwest Passage in

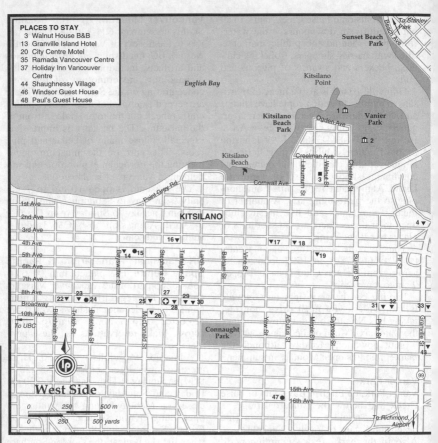

PLACES TO STAY
 3 Walnut House B&B
13 Granville Island Hotel
20 City Centre Motel
35 Ramada Vancouver Centre
37 Holiday Inn Vancouver
   Centre
44 Shaughnessy Village
46 Windsor Guest House
48 Paul's Guest House

VANCOUVER

both directions. There are interesting guided tours on the ship every half-hour or so. The site is open 10 am to 5 pm daily; closed Monday in winter. Admission is C$6/3 adults/seniors and children.

Kitsilano

On the southern shore of English Bay, roughly from Burrard St to UBC, is the neighborhood of Kitsilano. During the 1960s and 1970s, Kitsilano was considered a hippie enclave and a center of counter-cultural sympathies and lifestyles. However, everyone and everything grows up,

and the hippies are now lawyers and the neighborhood has gone genteel. The old single-family homes are now unaffordable to the students who once gave the area its élan, and many old homes are now broken up into flats; new apartment buildings straggle and rise upwards, hoping for glimpses of downtown across the bay.

Kitsilano – usually referred to locally simply as Kits – is still a fun area to explore, particularly along W 4th Ave and W Broadway, the primary commercial streets, which are lined with unusual shops, book-stores and ethnic restaurants. The old coun-

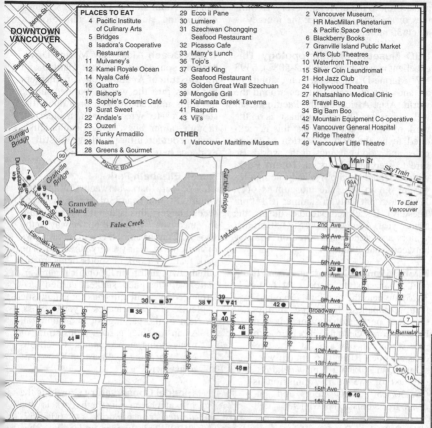

PLACES TO EAT
4 Pacific Institute
     of Culinary Arts
5 Bridges
8 Isadora's Cooperative
     Restaurant
11 Mulvaney's
12 Kamei Royale Ocean
14 Nyala Café
16 Quattro
17 Bishop's
18 Sophie's Cosmic Café
19 Surat Sweet
22 Andale's
23 Ouzeri
25 Funky Armadillo
26 Naam
28 Greens & Gourmet

29 Ecco il Pane
30 Lumiere
31 Szechwan Chongqing
     Seafood Restaurant
32 Picasso Cafe
33 Many's Lunch
36 Tojo's
37 Grand King
     Seafood Restaurant
38 Golden Great Wall Szechuan
39 Mongolie Grill
40 Kalamata Greek Taverna
41 Rasputin
43 Vij's

OTHER
1 Vancouver Maritime Museum

2 Vancouver Museum,
     HR MacMillan Planetarium
     & Pacific Space Centre
6 Blackberry Books
7 Granville Island Public Market
9 Arts Club Theatres
10 Waterfront Theatre
15 Silver Coin Laundromat
21 Hot Jazz Club
24 Hollywood Theatre
27 Khatsahlano Medical Clinic
28 Travel Bug
34 Big Bam Boo
42 Mountain Equipment Co-operative
45 Vancouver General Hospital
47 Ridge Theatre
49 Vancouver Little Theatre

DOWNTOWN VANCOUVER

terculture atmosphere is still here; you'll still find organic food stores and vegetarian restaurants, but chances are good that they are now next door to European clothing boutiques and spendy Italian trattorias.

One thing that hasn't changed in Kitsilano: the beaches. Kits faces onto English Bay, and the sandy strands that flank the water are very popular gathering spots in summer. **Kitsilano Beach**, near Vanier Park, and **Jericho Beach**, farther west on W 4th Ave at Jericho Beach Park, are two of the most popular places to gather and sun-worship.

University of British Columbia
Often just called UBC, the University of British Columbia (☎ 604-822-2211) is at the most westerly point of Vancouver, on the spit jutting out into Georgia Strait. The huge campus serving 32,000 students is spread over 1000 acres, much of which is still forest. Besides the pleasant grounds and the bustle of students, UBC offers a number of excellent gardens and a world-class museum of anthropology. The UBC Aquatic Centre (☎ 604-822-4521), off University Blvd, has pools, saunas and exercise areas open to the public. Bus Nos 4, 10

VANCOUVER

and 14 run to the university every 10 minutes or so from downtown; the journey is about 30 minutes.

UBC Museum of Anthropology This excellent museum (☎ 604-822-5087), 6393 NW Marine Drive, focuses on exhibits of art and artifacts from cultures around the world. Asia, Africa and the Pacific are all well represented but the emphasis is on the work of BC's coastal Indians: this is reckoned to be the best collection of totem poles and wood carvings in the world. Be sure to step outside to see **Totem Park**, with recreated longhouses and totem poles gazing out to sea. The museum is open 11 am to 5 pm daily in summer (till 9 pm Tuesday). It's closed Monday during the school year. Admission is C$6/3.50 adults/seniors and students; it's free on Tuesday between 5 and 9 pm.

Nitobe Memorial Gardens These beautiful Japanese-style gardens (☎ 604-822-3825) are near the museum. Designed by a leading Japanese landscape architect, they're a perfect display of this symbolic art form. Get a free brochure at the gate when you buy a ticket. The gardens are open 10 am to 6 pm daily in summer, and 11 am to 3 pm weekdays the rest of the year. Admission is C$2.50/1.50 adults/seniors and students; free admission in winter.

UBC Botanical Gardens A real gem, these gardens cover 70 acres near the corner of W 16th Ave and SW Marine Drive. There are several thematic plantings, including gardens with plants specific to regions of the world and to particular environments (for instance, the Asian and Alpine gardens); Canada's largest collection of rhododendrons, and a 16th-century apothecary garden. Even off-season, these gardens will please: the aptly-named Winter Garden features plants that bloom in the wintertime. It's open 10 am to 6 pm daily (till 2:30 pm in the

winter). Admission is C$4.50/2.25 adults/seniors and students; free admission in winter.

Wreck Beach Along NW Marine Drive, heading south past the Rose Garden and the Museum of Anthropology, are markers for trails into the woods. Follow one of the trails marked No 4, 5 or 6 down the steep steps to Wreck Beach, a pleasant, though rather busy, nude beach. Kitsilano's counterculture heritage is still in evidence here.

Queen Elizabeth Park
This 53-acre park, between Cambie and Ontario Sts and near 33rd Ave, is the city's second largest; this is also the highest point in Vancouver. Up the hill on the way to the Bloedel Conservatory there are great views of the city in nearly every direction. The park features a mix of sports fields, manicured lawns and formal botanical gardens. The well-designed sunken garden surrounded by small cliffs has some fantastic plants, one with leaves a yard across. Next to the parking lot is an unusual, Asian-looking garden consisting of many pools and fountains. Catch bus No 15 heading southeast on Robson St to get there.

Bloedel Conservatory Crowning the hill at Queen Elizabeth Park is this domed conservatory (☎ 604-257-8570). This 'garden under glass' has three climate zones, including desert and rain forest; in addition to the 500 species of plants, 50 species of free-flying tropical birds live in the conservatory. It's open 9 am to 8 pm weekdays, 10 am to 9 pm weekends. Admission is C$3/1.50 adults/seniors and students.

VanDusen Botanical Gardens
This 55-acre park (☎ 604-299-9000 ext 7194), at Oak St between 33rd and 37th Aves, is not far from Queen Elizabeth Park. The

gardens contain a small lake and a large collection of ornamental plants from around the world. Be sure to find your way through the Elizabethan Hedge Maze. The gardens are open 10 am to 9 pm daily in the summer. The admission price is C$5/2.50 adults/students. Take bus No 17 south on Burrard St from downtown.

RICHMOND

South of the North Arm Fraser River and the Vancouver Airport is Richmond, a suburb that has become closely identified with the recent influx of Hong Kong Chinese; in fact, the area is often referred to as Asia West. But don't expect to find the bustling, slightly seedy and peculiar charm of a Chinatown: everything here is very upscale, very sanitized and very suburban. It's what modern BC would be like if the Chinese, and not the British, had colonized the area. Which is why a detour to Richmond is more interesting than you might expect.

For the real Richmond experience, drive along No 3rd Rd, and stop at one of the many large shopping malls; there are four of them right in a row. Yaohan Centre or Parker Place are both good destinations. Here you'll find brand-new gleaming shopping centers filled almost exclusively with Chinese stores, Chinese products and Chinese shoppers. Needless to say, you will find excellent Chinese food here at very reasonable prices. As you drive through the neighborhoods, you'll also notice the vast new homes favored by the Hong Kong immigrants.

To reach No 3rd Rd in Richmond, take bus No 401, 403, 406 or 407 from Howe St in downtown Vancouver.

The **Richmond Nature Park**, a 200-acre park (☎ 604-273-7015), 11851 Westminster Hwy, is dedicated to environmental education. The park features boardwalks through various ecosystems (a marsh, forest and a pond), with interpretive displays and signage. The Nature House Centre continues the theme with interactive exhibits designed with kids in mind. Free admission; open dawn to dusk.

STEVESTON

Directly south of Richmond is the old fishing village of Steveston, Canada's largest commercial fishing port. Steveston was settled largely by Japanese immigrants early this century; however during WWII nearly all the Japanese Canadians were sent to internment camps far inland, and their boats and homes were sold at auctions.

The old part of town that fronts onto to Fraser River is quite charming, and has a number of good restaurants and pubs. There's lots of activity in the harbor, and the sights and smells of the fishing fleets make for a good escape from the rush of downtown Vancouver. Walk along Government Wharf where fisherfolk hawk their fresh catch directly from the boat.

If you're interested in the history of Steveston, stop by the **Steveston Museum** (☎ 604-271-6868), 3811 Moncton Rd, which tells the story of the town's fishing past and the internment of the Japanese; free admission. There's more history at the **Gulf of Georgia Cannery National Historic Site** (☎ 604-272-5045), at Bayview St and 4th Ave, a museum of the region's maritime past housed in an old fish cannery.

To reach Steveston via public transport, take bus No 401, 406 or 407 south from Howe St.

EAST VANCOUVER

East of Main Street was traditionally the working-class and non-British section of Vancouver; Commercial Drive was once known as 'Little Italy.' The close-in east side is still where most non-Chinese immigrants make their homes. Farther east are the suburbs of Burnaby, Coquitlam and New Westminster. While these mostly residential communities aren't tourist destinations, there are a few interesting sites.

Commercial Drive

Early this century, this street was the center of Vancouver's Italian community, and soon developed a reputation for good food and street life. Nowadays, Commercial

Drive is still about cultural diversity, but of a broader sort. Portuguese, Latin American and Southeast Asian restaurants and markets abound between 1st and 12th Aves. This is also a countercultural area as well, with rainbow flags hanging in shop windows, and earnest political conversations echoing in vegetarian cafes and third-world-solidarity coffee shops. The **Vancouver East Side Cultural Centre** (☎ 604-254-9578), 1895 Venables St, just off Commercial Drive, is a church converted into an avant-garde performance space which captures perfectly the area's left-of-center politics and artistic tastes.

Simon Fraser University

Simon Fraser, established in 1965, sits atop Burnaby Mountain in Burnaby, about 20km (12 miles) east of downtown. A showcase of modern architecture, the university was designed by noted Canadian architect Arthur Erickson; the design, which incorporates unusual use of space and perspective, was – and remains – controversial. There are enormous courtyard-like quadrants and many fountains, including one on a roof. Some areas of the complex are reminiscent of Mayan ruin sites in Mexico. The university's **Museum of Archaeology & Ethnology** (☎ 604-291-

3325) features a collection of coastal Indian artifacts and has a cheap cafeteria. The museum is open 10 am to 4 pm weekdays, and admission is by donation.

For information on tours around the university, call ☎ 604-291-3111. To get there, catch bus No 10 or 14 on E Hastings St then change near Boundary Rd to bus No 135, which will take you to the university.

Burnaby Heritage Village

This museum (☎ 604-293-6501), located at 6501 Deer Lake Ave beside Deer Lake, is in Burnaby's Century Park, near Deer Lake Park and close to the Trans Canada Hwy. It's a replica village that attempts to preserve both the artifacts and atmosphere of a southwestern BC town in the years 1890 to 1925. There's an old schoolhouse, printing shop, drugstore and other establishments; a large, working steam-train model is next to the village. The restored carousel with 36 wooden horses is a highlight. Friendly, informed workers are in period dress. It's open 10 am to 4:30 pm daily during the summer, shorter hours during the rest of the year. Admission is C$6.20/4.35 adults/students and seniors. Catch bus No 120 on E Hastings St.

NEW WESTMINSTER

The oldest town in western Canada, New Westminster was established in 1859, and briefly served as BC's capital city; nowadays New Westminster has been absorbed into greater Vancouver. This was once the area's primary seaport, and the districts along the Fraser River have retained their period charm. The waterfront esplanade has been overhauled and, together with the Westminster Quay Public Market, has become a casual people-watching kind of place with restaurants and bars as well as shops. The small downtown area is here, too, just north of the New Westminster SkyTrain stop.

Irving House Historic Centre

Built in 1865, this 14-room home (☎ 604-521-7656), 302 Royal Ave, is one of the oldest structures in BC, and now func-

tions as a museum of frontier life and furnishings. The original owner was a riverboat captain on the Fraser River. The **New Westminster Museum**, which tells the story of this historic township, is adjacent. It's open 11 am to 5 pm Tuesday to Sunday in summer; 1 to 5 pm weekends only in winter. Admission is by donation.

THE NORTH SHORE

North and West Vancouver, roughly divided by the Capilano River, together make up the North Shore. There are three principal ways to experience this side of the inlet. You can take the SeaBus for city views, stroll Lonsdale Quay and spend a few hours eating and sightseeing around lower North Vancouver. Or, with a vehicle, tour along Marine Drive through West Vancouver, possibly all the way to Horseshoe Bay stopping at parks and enjoying the harbor alongside some of the city's wealthy neighborhoods. Lastly, you can visit one of the provincial parks for some fine vistas and real hiking.

North Vancouver

Lonsdale Quay Market This market is the center of the North Shore SeaBus terminal complex, which includes a water's edge park, offices and apartments. The 1st floor is devoted to fresh and cooked food; the 2nd floor is mainly specialty shops but has a restaurant with good views. As you leave the ferry, there's an information booth to offer guidance on the North Shore's attractions. The local bus terminal is here as well.

The market is open 9:30 am to 6:30 pm daily (till 9 pm Friday). For information, call ☎ 604-985-6261. To get there catch the SeaBus from the downtown terminal at Waterfront Station.

North Vancouver Museum & Archives

The small museum (☎ 604-987-5618), at 333 Chesterfield Ave, offers rather good changing exhibits on a wide range of subjects such as transport, antiques and Native Indian crafts. It's open noon to 5 pm Wednesday to Sunday (till 9 pm Thursday). Admission is by donation.

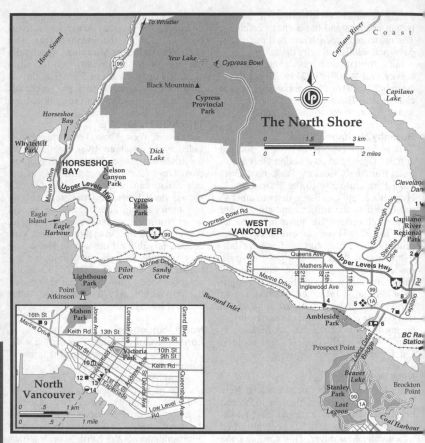

Capilano Suspension Bridge This suspension bridge (☎ 604-985-7474), 3735 Capilano Rd, in Capilano River Regional Park spans the Capilano River for almost 140m (460 feet) at a height of 70m (230 feet). It's pretty impressive; however, the suspension bridge is *very* popular, and the crowds can be oppressive. You decide if you want to pay the steep admission just to walk across a bridge. Open 8 am till 9 pm daily in summer. Admission is C$8.95/7.50/6 adults/seniors/students, and C$2.75 children (six to 12).

To get to the park, from downtown take bus No 246, marked 'Highlands,' going west on W Georgia St or bus No 236 from Lonsdale Quay to Edgemont Village; you then change to bus No 232. (This bus also goes to the Capilano Salmon Hatchery and the Cleveland Dam; in summer, bus No 236 goes all the way to Grouse Mountain.) If you're driving, head north over Lions Gate Bridge to Marine Drive in North Vancouver, then turn left (north) onto Capilano Rd.

Capilano Salmon Hatchery This salmon hatchery is a fish farm (☎ 604-666-1790) run by the government to help stop the depletion of valuable salmon stocks.

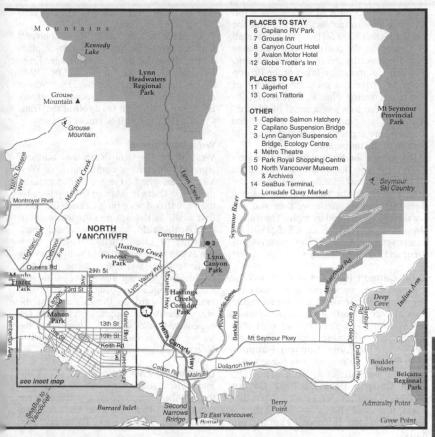

PLACES TO STAY
6 Capilano RV Park
7 Grouse Inn
8 Canyon Court Hotel
9 Avalon Motor Hotel
12 Globe Trotter's Inn

PLACES TO EAT
11 Jägerhof
13 Corsi Trattoria

OTHER
1 Capilano Salmon Hatchery
2 Capilano Suspension Bridge
3 Lynn Canyon Suspension
   Bridge, Ecology Centre
4 Metro Theatre
5 Park Royal Shopping Centre
10 North Vancouver Museum
   & Archives
14 SeaBus Terminal,
   Lonsdale Quay Market

VANCOUVER

Although you can't see the holding pools, there are exhibits with good explanations of the whole process. Salmon in various stages of growth are on display in tanks, and you can see how they are channeled from the river into the hatchery when they head upstream to spawn. Admission is free. It's in Capilano River Regional Park, off Capilano Rd not far north of the suspension bridge.

Cleveland Dam The dam (☎ 604-224-5739) blocks Capilano Lake, which supplies much of Vancouver's drinking water. You'll get good views of the Lions, two peaks of the Coast Mountains. There are picnic areas and trails and it's free. The dam is slightly farther north of the salmon hatchery up Capilano Rd, which becomes Nancy Greene Way.

Grouse Mountain Just out Vancouver's backdoor, Grouse Mountain (☎ 604-984-0661), at 6400 Nancy Greene Way (the northern extension of Capilano Rd), is the city's most convenient ski area; several runs are lit for night skiing. Grouse Mountain is famous for its Swiss-built **Super-skyride** cable car which operates daily from 9 am to 10 pm. The lift remains open all year, and Grouse Mountain has a full schedule of summer activities. From the top – 1100m (3600 feet) – you can see all of Vancouver, the coast, part of Vancouver Island and northward over the mountains. You can rent mountain bikes at the lift-top lodge or strike out on a hiking trail. If you're not feeling athletic, there is a chain-saw sculpture tour and a small movie theater with a complimentary film at the lodge. There are restaurants at the top and bottom of the mountain.

If you take the Superskyride, make sure it's a clear day. If it's raining, foggy or at all hazy with low clouds, forget it: by the time you reach the top you won't see a thing. Go in late afternoon; then you can see the city by day and by night. The Super-skyride is expensive at C$15.95/13.95 adults/seniors; C$9.95/5.95 youths/children; and C$39.95 families.

Lynn Canyon Park Set in thick woods, this park gives a good glimpse of the temperate rain-forest vegetation found in the coastal Pacific Northwest. There are many hiking trails, and you can find your own picnic and swimming spots. Over Lynn Canyon is the **Lynn Canyon Suspension Bridge**; although not as big as Capilano, it's much the same but it's free. The **Lynn Canyon Park Ecology Centre** (☎ 604-987-5922), 3663 Park Rd, has displays, films and slide shows about the biology of the area. It's open 10 am to 5 pm daily.

To get to the park take bus No 228 or 229 from Lonsdale Quay. If you're driving go over Second Narrows Bridge, take Lynn Valley Rd then go right (east) on Peters Rd, where you'll see signs that lead you into the park.

Mt Seymour Provincial Park This park, 13km (8 miles) northeast of downtown, is a quick escape from the city. There is a road most of the way up and a chair lift goes to the peak. The park has several hiking trails and the views of Vancouver's surroundings are beautiful. Some areas are very rugged, so visitors going on overnight trips should

register with park rangers. There's also skiing here in winter.

There are parking lots for RVs but no real tent campgrounds. You can, however, pitch a tent along the many alpine trails. From Lonsdale Quay take bus No 229 or 239 to Phibbs Exchange then bus No 215. If you're driving, head over the Second Narrows Bridge and turn right (east) off of the Trans Canada Hwy onto Mt Seymour Parkway.

West Vancouver
West of the Capilano River and north of Burrard Inlet are the communities of West Vancouver, one of the wealthiest municipalities in Canada. Marine Drive passes by the Park Royal Shopping Centre (Canada's first mall, and still a good place to shop) into **Ambleside** with its water-side park on Burrard Inlet. Farther west is **Dundarave**, a commercial strip with a number of restaurants and cafes, some with balconies overlooking the water, amid the shops. Antique shopping is good in this area. Northward up the hill and on the other side of the Upper Levels Hwy are expensive houses with good views over the harbor. Marine Drive follows the coast to Horseshoe Bay.

Lighthouse Park Here in a stand of original coastal forest are some of the largest trees in the Vancouver area; you'll also see the unusual arbutus, a wide-leaf evergreen with orange peeling bark. There are 13km

---

The Arbutus Tree
Gnarled and peeling, the distinctive arbutus is Canada's only broad-leafed evergreen. It's found only along the shores of the Georgia Strait, rarely more than 8km (13 miles) from the sea. It's a small, generally twisted and bent tree which sheds its bark rather than its leaves. Coastal residents often grow this quirky attractive specimen ornamentally. ■

(8 miles) of hiking trails; the most popular one leads to the **Point Atkinson Lighthouse**, which commands the inlet from its rocky perch. The park is about 9.5km (6 miles) to the left (west) on Marine Drive after crossing Lions Gate Bridge. Catch bus No 250 going west on West Georgia St.

Horseshoe Bay North of Vancouver, the small coastal community of Horseshoe Bay marks the end of Marine Drive and West Vancouver. It's a pretty spot, with great views across the bay and up the fjord to distant glaciered peaks. There are a number of good places to eat and shop here.

Horseshoe Bay is one of BC's busiest ferry terminals; ferries leave here for Nanaimo on Vancouver Island, and for Langdale on the Sunshine Coast. Horseshoe Bay is also about the last convenient stop on the way to the ski slopes at Whistler.

Just beyond Horseshoe Bay, on Marine Drive, is **Whytecliff Park**, a great little park right on the water. Trails lead to vistas and a gazebo, from where you can watch the boat traffic wend its way in and out of Burrard Inlet. This is a favorite spot for scuba diving.

ACTIVITIES
Hiking
There are tons of hiking opportunities in the many provincial mountain parks just north of Vancouver (see the North Shore, above, for more options).

Cypress Provincial Park is the closest, just 8km (5 miles) north of West Vancouver off Hwy 99. It has eight hiking trails, including the Baden-Powell, Yew Lake and Howe Sound Crest trails. Mt Seymour Provincial Park, 13km (8 miles) northeast of downtown, has 10 trails varying in difficulty and length. At both parks you should be prepared for continually changing mountain weather conditions. On clear days both parks offer magnificent views.

There's hiking in **Garibaldi Provincial Park**, north of Vancouver (for details see the North of Vancouver section, later in this chapter). About 48km (30 miles)

northeast of Vancouver is **Golden Ears Provincial Park**. Take Hwy 7 as far as Haney, then turn left (north) and follow the 13km (9-mile) road to Alouette Lake. The park has 11 hiking trails, plus campsites and picnic areas.

Guided Hikes If you want to explore the wilderness parks near Vancouver but want the assurance of having a trained guide on hand, call Hike BC (☎ 604-684-9722) or Active Lifestyles Fitness Services (☎ 604-984-6032). A day of hiking costs around C$60, and will include hotel pickup and delivery and a picnic lunch.

Skiing
Vancouver has some great downhill and cross-country skiing just minutes from the city center; each of the following ski areas allows snowboarding. **Grouse Mountain** (☎ 604-984-0661), off Capilano Rd in North Vancouver, is the nearest to the city and is notable for its night skiing, when most of the downhill runs are illuminated and open till 10 pm. The day pass for an adult is C$30.

Other nearby ski resorts include Cypress Bowl (also with night skiing) and Hollyburn (☎ 604-926-5612 for either resort) both in **Cypress Provincial Park** on Vancouver's North Shore. Cypress Bowl has downhill but is best known for its cross-country trails. Also in the North Shore, **Mt Seymour** (☎ 604-986-2261), in North Vancouver, is a semi-wilderness provincial park only 13km (8 miles) from downtown. The park contains downhill runs, groomed cross-country trails and a tobogganing slope. It also has night skiing.

See the North of Vancouver section, later in this chapter, for information on downhill skiing at Whistler and Blackcomb, and cross-country skiing at Garibaldi Provincial Park.

Biking
A good way to get around Vancouver and its numerous parks and beach areas is by bicycle. Areas with designated bicycle paths include the 9.5km (6-mile) seawall

promenade in Stanley Park; the route from Granville Island, through Vanier Park to Kitsilano Beach; and if you want to keep going west you could take Point Grey Rd to Jericho Beach Park then follow the shoreline to Spanish Banks Beach. See the Getting Around section at the end of this chapter for details on bicycle rental.

Swimming

You can swim at a number of city beaches: Second and Third Beaches in Stanley Park; English Bay and Sunset Beaches downtown; or at Kitsilano and Jericho Beaches on the southern side of English Bay. Kitsilano Beach is the largest and most popular and where the beach-culture scene is at its peak: on a hot summer day as many as 10,000 people hit the sands. The prime spot to see and be seen is around the lifeguard section; other areas attract those who prefer a little more material used in the construction of their bathing suits.

At one portion of the beach you might catch one of the professional or semiprofessional volleyball tournaments which occur pretty regularly throughout the summer months. Wreck Beach (see the University of British Columbia section, earlier in this chapter) is Vancouver's nude beach.

The Vancouver Aquatic Centre (☎ 604-665-3424), 1050 Beach Ave near Sunset Beach, has an indoor heated swimming pool, whirlpool, diving tank, gym and sauna. There's another aquatic center at UBC (see the UBC section) and one (☎ 604-926-8585) in West Vancouver at 776 22nd St. Kitsilano Beach has an outdoor heated saltwater pool (☎ 604-731-0011). Admission to these heated pools is usually C$4.

Canoeing, Kayaking & Windsurfing

If you've got the energy for canoeing or kayaking, the Fraser River and the Chilliwack River (east of Vancouver) offer plenty of opportunities for the beginner to the experienced. On Granville Island you can hire canoes. Ecomarine Ocean Kayak Centre (☎ 604-689-7575), 1668 Duranleau St, hires out solo kayaks for C$19 for two

hours or C$39 a day. It has another outlet at the Jericho Sailing Centre at Jericho Beach in Kitsilano near the HI Vancouver Jericho Beach hostel. Ecomarine also offers educational tours of the islands in Georgia Strait and in Clayoquot Sound on the west coast of Vancouver Island.

In North Vancouver, on Indian Arm, Deep Cove Canoe & Kayak (☎ 604-929-2268), 2156 Banbury Rd, has rentals and will teach you how to use a canoe. At Deer Lake, east of town in Burnaby, you can rent solo canoes for C$12 an hour from Deer Lake Boat Rentals (☎ 604-255-0081).

Windsure Windsurfing School (☎ 604-224-0615), 1300 Discovery St at the Jericho Sailing Centre, gives windsurfing lessons and also rents boards.

Scuba Diving

Scuba diving is popular northwest of the city off Lighthouse Park and at Porteau Cove 26km (16 miles) north of Horseshoe Bay, both in Howe Sound; and on Indian Arm at the eastern end of Burrard Inlet. A number of dive outfitters offer equipment, training and trips, including AB Divers World (☎ 604-732-1344), 1817 W 4th Ave, and Diving Locker (☎ 604-736-2681), 2745 W 4th Ave, both in Kitsilano.

ORGANIZED TOURS

The Gray Line Bus Company (☎ 604-879-3363) offers a wide selection of sightseeing tours ranging from city tours to 10-day tours of the Canadian Rockies. Most begin at the Hotel Vancouver, but all major hotels sell tickets and offer bus pickup. The Deluxe Grand City Tour is a 3½-hour tour taking in most of Vancouver's tourist sites, and costs C$38/36 adults/seniors, and C$27 for children; the tour is available in five different languages.

A less-structured tour is the Decker and Trolley Tour. For a C$22 ticket, you can hop on and off buses at over 20 designated stops, and the ticket is good for two consecutive days. For C$96 you can go on a day trip to Victoria and Butchart Gardens.

Town Tours (☎ 604-451-1777) offers a cheaper 3½-hour tour of the city, with adult tickets at C$23.36. Their Victoria day tour costs C$78.50. Another bus tour option is operated by the Vancouver Trolley Co (☎ 604-451-5581). The ticket costs C$20 and allows you a full day of transport between 16 different stops.

The major long-distance tour operator in western Canada is Brewster Tours (☎ 800-661-1152), which run a great many trips from Vancouver, including circle tours of Vancouver Island and multi-day tours to the Canadian Rockies. Pacific Coach Lines (☎ 604-662-7575), at the Pacific Central Station, operates a number of one-day excursions for about the same price as a normal bus ticket. Destinations include Vancouver Island and the Sunshine Coast.

Harbour Ferries (☎ 604-688-7246) has 1½-hour cruises for C$16, as well as longer more costly evening dinner sailings around False Creek, English Bay and Burrard Inlet. Boats leave from their office at the north foot of Denman St by Stanley Park.

Harbour Air Seaplanes (☎ 604-688-1277) offers air tours aboard float planes from their water terminal at the base of Burrard St (one block north of Canada Place). Their least expensive flight (C$72) tours the Vancouver area for 20 minutes; longer mail-run flights up the Sunshine Coast are available.

SPECIAL EVENTS
Following is a list of some of the major events in Vancouver during the year. *The Vancouver Book*, available from the Travel InfoCentre, has an up-to-date list of current events.

January
  Polar Bear Swim – Since 1819, this popular, chilly affair has been taking place at English Bay Beach annually on January 1. If you can't handle the water, watching is allowed.
February
  Chinese New Year – Chinatown provides the setting for one of Vancouver's most colorful events, with dancers, music, fireworks and food. Based on the Chinese calendar, the celebration begins in early February or at the end of January and lasts for two weeks.

June
  Canadian International Dragon Boat Festival – This annual event takes place in False Creek over three days in late June. It attracts nearly 2000 competitors from around the world and about 150,000 spectators. As well as the boat races, there's music, theater and international cuisine.
July
  Vancouver Folk Music Festival – Held in mid-July, the Folk Music Festival is three days of music, including concerts and workshops, from some of the best North American folk musicians. It attracts about 30,000 visitors and most of the action takes place at Jericho Beach Park. For information about tickets call ☎ 604-879-2931.
August
  Abbotsford International Air Show – Known as Canada's National Air Show, this three-day event, held in early August, has everything that flies, from fighters to the Concorde. It's held 65km (40 miles) southeast of Vancouver in Abbotsford near the US border.
  Gay Pride Day – Also in early August, watch for its festive parade drawing 15,000 people along Denman St.
  Pacific National Exhibition – Known as the PNE (☎ 604-253-2311), this big fair, the second largest in Canada, features a little bit of everything – sports, competitions, international exhibits, concerts and shows, as well as amusement park rides. It starts off each year with a two-hour parade. The exhibition lasts about two weeks, from late August to Labour Day. The PNE takes place in Exhibition Park on E Hastings St near the Second Narrows Bridge. Catch bus No 14 or 16 from downtown.
September
  Vancouver Fringe Festival – This popular theater event presents drama, musical theater, comedy and dance from around the world. It takes place over two weeks from early to mid-September in various theaters around Main St, between E 6th and E 17th Aves in the Mt Pleasant area (just east of False Creek). Call ☎ 604-873-3646 for information.

PLACES TO STAY
Vancouver is unusual in that a great many inexpensive and moderately priced hotels and motels remain in the otherwise high-rent downtown area; these in addition to the landmark luxury and business hotels commonly associated with city centers. Unless you

prefer staying on a motel strip some distance from the city center, there's no reason not to stay right in the center of things.

Summer is very busy in Vancouver, and you should make reservations weeks – even months – in advance if you have your heart set on a specific hotel. The Vancouver Travel InfoCentre(☎ 800-663-6000) offers a free accommodations reservation service, which can be indispensable if you are trying to find a room at the last minute.

Camping
There are no public campgrounds in the Vancouver area and, except for one, the RV parks right in Vancouver do not allow tenting. In North Vancouver, the *Capilano RV Park* (☎ 604-987-4722), 295 Tomahawk Ave, has everything, including a Jacuzzi and tent sites from C$22. Exit onto Capilano Rd South off Hwy 1.

Other campgrounds are south of the city, on or near Hwy 99, which runs to the US border. South of the Middle Arm of the Fraser River, *Richmond RV Park* (☎ 604-270-7878), 6200 River Rd, Richmond, near Hollybridge Way is one of the closest to town. It's open from April to October and has sites from C$16 for two people. *Park-Canada RV Inns* (☎ 604-943-5811), 4799 Hwy 17, Delta, is northeast of the Tsawwassen ferry terminal. It has free showers and sites from C$14.

Hostels
Travelers have an ever-increasing array of hostel choices, including some real dodgy old hotels trying to cash in on the increase in traffic; these didn't make it into this guide. Most of the good hostels are pretty much full throughout the summer and quite busy the rest of the year.

The new *HI Vancouver Downtown* hostel (☎ 604-684-4565), 1114 Burnaby St, at the corner of Thurlow St, is in a former nunnery and health-care center. There are 212 beds with no more than four in any one room. Family rooms are available. Prices are C$19 members, C$23 nonmembers. Facilities include a patio, games room and library. This very convenient hostel is walkable from anywhere in the downtown area and is open 24 hours.

Popular *Vincent's Backpackers Hostel* (☎ 604-682-2441), 927 Main St, is not in the best of areas but is within walking distance of downtown and not too far from the Main St SkyTrain Station, Science World or Pacific Central Station. Take bus No 3, 8 or 19 from downtown along Main St. The office is open 9 am to 11 pm, there's no curfew and the rates are low at C$10/20/25 dormitory/single/double. It can take up to 75 people and offers weekly rates.

Vincent has a new place – the *New Backpackers Hostel* (☎ 604-688-0112), centrally located in the big hotel building at 347 W Pender St. This is generally a more spacious place and the little outdoor courtyard – good for reading – is pleasant. However, the C$10 dorm beds go quickly and you may have to wait for a shower. Single/ double rooms are C$25/35.

The *YMCA* (☎ 604-681-0221) is right downtown at 955 Burrard St at Barclay St. Depending on whether you'd like a TV, singles are C$36 or C$39, doubles are C$44 or C$46 (tax included). Women and couples are allowed and quite a few travelers stay here. The only drawback is the constant unlocking of doors. There are gym and pool facilities and a small inexpensive restaurant serving good-value breakfasts and sandwiches.

The new *YWCA* (☎ 604-895-5830, 800-663-1424 in Canada) at 733 Beatty St between Georgia and Robson Sts near the BC Place Stadium, is really like a hotel and accommodates men, women, couples or families. There are 155 rooms in various configurations ranging from singles with bathrooms down the hall (C$51) to family rooms ($94) and one with five single beds ($141). Doubles start at C$62 and go to C$98 with a private bathroom. Each room comes with a fridge but there are also communal kitchens as well as TV lounges and a laundry. Fitness facilities are offered but are off the premises. The stadium SkyTrain stop is a five-minute walk.

The centrally located *Cambie International Hostel* (☎ 604-684-6466), at 300 Cambie St at Cordova St, has dorm beds in two- or four-bunk rooms costing C$20 for students or AYH/IYH members, and C$27 to anyone else. Bedding is provided, and bathrooms are down the hall; there's also bicycle storage and laundry facilities. A bakery, cafe and saloon on the ground floor make it a convenient and potentially noisy place to spend the night.

Although the *HI Vancouver Jericho Beach* (☎ 604-224-3208, fax 604-224-4852), 1515 Discovery St, Kitsilano, is away from the center of town, its location is great. The hostel is close to the beach in Jericho Beach Park on English Bay, about 20 minutes from downtown by bus. It's open 24 hours, although there is a 'quiet time' between 11 pm and 7 am. With 288 beds, it's the largest hostel in Canada and has complete facilities. The rates are C$16 for members, C$20 for nonmembers. From downtown take bus No 4 south on Granville St.

The *University of British Columbia* rents rooms from about the first week in May to the end of August. Singles/doubles with shared bathroom are C$22/44 or you can get self-contained apartments for C$84 to C$95. Contact the Conference Centre (☎ 604-822-1010), Gage Towers, 5961 Student Union Blvd, UBC Campus, Vancouver, BC V6T 2C9. The pleasant campus has a cafeteria, some cafes, laundromat, pub and sports facilities.

Simon Fraser University, in East Vancouver, rents out rooms from May to August. They're all fully furnished and bathrooms are shared; singles without bedding (bring your own sleeping bag) cost C$19, with bedding C$31, doubles with bedding C$51. The university also has four-bedroom townhouse units for C$115. Contact Housing & Conference Services (☎ 604-291-4503), Room 212, McTaggart-Cowan Hall, Burnaby, BC V5A 1S6.

Up in North Vancouver, the *Globe Trotter's Inn* (☎ 604-988-2082), at 170 W Esplanade, is small and quiet; it's only a five-minute walk to the SeaBus at Lonsdale

Quay and close to all amenities. They have a kitchen and laundry and a range of rooms. Rates are C$17.50 for dorm and C$30/40 to 45 single/double.

B&Bs

As elsewhere in the Pacific Northwest, B&Bs are usually not cheap, averaging C$75 to C$105 double with shared bathroom. Because B&Bs come and go rather quickly, it's good to use a reservation service to book a room. Each of the following have rooms in all price ranges. *Old English B&B Registry* (☎ 604-986-5069), can be contacted at 1226 Silverwood Crescent, North Vancouver, BC V7L 1L3. *Town & Country B&B* (☎ 604-731-5942), is at PO Box 74542, Vancouver, BC V6K 1K2.

Although not a booking agency, you can contact the Western Canada B&B Innkeepers Association (☎ 604-255-9199), PO Box 74534, Vancouver, BC V6K 4P4, for a brochure with member listings in Vancouver and across the province.

The historic neighborhoods of Kitsilano, Kerrisdale and Shaughnessy are where you'd expect to find nice B&Bs. Contact the booking agencies listed above, or if you want to call and reserve on your own, try one of the following. *Windsor Guest House* (☎ 604-872-3060), 325 W 11th Ave, is an 1895 home in Kitsilano with two rooms, one with private bathroom (C$75); C$65 without private bath. *Walnut House B&B* (☎ 604-739-6941), 1350 Walnut St, is another heritage home in Kitsilano's best location. Near the beach and Vanier Park, it has three rooms with private bathrooms; C$100/110 single/double. For a more modern alternative, try *Treehouse B&B* (☎ 604-266-2962), 2490 W 49th Ave, with contemporary decor, Jacuzzi tubs, private baths and three guest rooms at C$110.

An inexpensive and popular place on the West Side is *Paul's Guest House* (☎ 604-872-4753), at 345 W 14th Ave, two blocks east of Cambie St between Alberta and Yukon Sts in a quiet residential area. Paul speaks 11 languages – that should cover most guests! Breakfast includes all the eggs

VANCOUVER

you can eat. It's very clean and friendly and there's a laundry service, TV room and free coffee or tea during the day. Singles are C$50 and doubles C$60 to C$80 from May to September dropping to C$40 to 50 the rest of the year. If this place is full, Paul has another guesthouse just down the street.

Hotels – downtown

Budget Be aware that Vancouver has a great many inexpensive hotels right downtown, especially along Granville, Pender and Hastings Sts. While some are well kept and offer good value, many serve the downtrodden and those on very low incomes or government assistance, whose numbers are greater here than in any other Canadian city.

The best low-cost hotel in town is the *Kingston Hotel* (☎ 604-684-9024), 757 Richards St. It was the city's first B&B hotel and still offers the morning meal (although it's just enough to get the eyes open). Singles range from C$45 to C$65, doubles from C$50 to C$80. Extras offered include a sauna, laundry and an overnight parking subsidy. The *Dufferin Hotel* (☎ 604-683-4251), 900 Seymour St, with prices beginning at C$65/70 single/double, is a good choice and gets the Kingston's overflow. There's a dining room and free parking.

In Gastown, the old but renovated *Dominion Hotel* (☎ 604-681-6666), 210 Abbot St, dates from 1899. The rooms go for C$65 with shared bathroom or C$75 with private bathroom.

Hastings St on either side of Main St is a less-than-wholesome part of town (especially at night), but the *Budget Inn – Patricia Hotel* (☎ 604-255-4301), 403 E Hastings St, breaks ranks. It's large, clean, well kept and a very good value with rooms from C$39/59 single/double. Some rooms have fine views of the harbor.

Middle One of the city's best deals is the *Bosman's Motor Hotel* (☎ 604-684-4010, 800-267-6267) at 1060 Howe St. It is extremely central, has free parking and is everything most people will ever need in a moderately priced lodging with rooms from C$99 to C$109 (each room has two queen-size beds).

A moderately priced motel, the *Burrard Motor Inn* (☎ 604-681-2331, 800-663-0366), 1100 Burrard St, is convenient and a favorite of families and budget travelers with rooms at C$85/95 single/double. The well-loved, slightly faded *Sylvia Hotel* (☎ 604-681-9321), 1154 Gilford St, has a marvelous location on English Bay. The old ivy-covered hotel is where the politically alternative stay when they come to town; don't resist, it is a nice place; C$75/105; kitchen suites from C$110. For good-value suites in a former apartment building, you can't beat the *Oceanside Apartment Hotel* (☎ 604-682-5641), 1847 Pendrell St, with single rooms starting at C$90.

You can't get much closer to Stanley Park than *The Buchan Hotel* (☎ 604-685-5354, 800-668-6654), 1906 Haro St, a nicely appointed older hotel with rooms at C$90/100 single/double; forego a private toilet, and rooms drop to C$65/75. The *Shato Inn Hotel* (☎ 604-681-8920), at 1825 Comox St off Denman St, a couple of blocks from Stanley Park and English Bay Beach, also has some rooms with cooking facilities. Rooms are C$85/90; C$20 extra for the kitchen.

Robson St, west of the busy shopping district, has some good lodging deals in a prime area. The *Barclay Hotel* (☎ 604-688-8850), 1348 Robson St, has air-con, TV and a licensed lounge; C$75/95. *Riviera Motor Inn* (☎ 604-685-1301), 1431 Robson St, has apartments with fully equipped kitchens, beginning at C$78. From some of the apartments you get a good view of the North Shore.

Along Robson St, you get more amenities for a little more money. *Blue Horizon Hotel* (☎ 604-688-4461, 800-663-1333), 1225 Robson St, with rooms at C$145, has great views, balconies and an indoor pool. The *Greenbriar Hotel* (☎ 604-683-4558), 1393 Robson St, is a former apartment building that's been transformed into a suite hotel. It's nicer than it looks from the outside, as each room (C$149 to C$169) has a full kitchen and sitting area in addition to the bedroom. At the *Robsonstrasse City Motor Inn* (☎ 604-687-1674, 888-667-8877), 1394 Robson St, you get kitchenettes, free parking and a guest laundry for C$120/130. The *Tropicana Motor Inn* (☎ 604-687-5724), 1361 Robson St, is another high-rise option in this area with similar amenities, and a pool and sauna; double rooms start at C$139.

Near the Granville Bridge, the *Travelodge Vancouver Centre* (☎ 604-682-2767, 800-665-2080), 1304 Howe St, has basic but fine rooms, and there's a heated outdoor pool; C$95/105. The *Quality Hotel/Inn at False Creek* (☎ 604-682-0229, 800-663-8474), 1335 Howe St, has spacious rooms from C$140 to C$150 for a double. A couple blocks in from the waterfront is the *Holiday Inn Vancouver Downtown* (☎ 604-684-2151, 800-663-9151), 1110 Howe St, a class act for a chain hotel, with large rooms, pool, health club and some kitchens; double rooms cost C$169 to C$189.

The *Days Inn Vancouver Downtown* (☎ 604-681-4335, 800-329-7466), 921 W Pender St, has a great location near the harbor, free parking and small but nicely furnished rooms starting at C$125/135 single/double.

One of the older, more elegant hotels with wooden paneling and chandeliers is the *Hotel Georgia* (☎ 604-682-5566, 800-663-1111), 801 W Georgia St. For this class of hotel, rooms are a good value at C$145 to C$180 for a single and C$175 to C$210 for a double.

Top End Downtown Vancouver has a number of elegant older hotels, as well as brand-new hotel towers with luxury-class accommodations.

Despite the rising skyline, the *Hotel Vancouver* (☎ 604-684-3131, 800-441-1414), 900 W Georgia St, remains a city landmark recognizable by its green copper roof. This Canadian Pacific hotel is one of the largest and most famous in Vancouver, offering all the comforts known to the modern hospitality industry. A recent complete remodel brought this vintage doyenne even more up

to date. Rooms begin at C$220/245 single/double. If you want a more personalized experience, head to the *Wedgewood Hotel* (☎ 604-689-7777, 800-663-0666), 845 Hornby St, another fantastic vintage boutique hotel with luxury-class rooms beginning at C$200 for a double.

There are a couple opulent choices along Robson St, the best of which is *Listel O'Doul's Hotel Best Western* (☎ 604-684-8461, 800-663-8326) at 1300 Robson St. Rooms are modern, large and very well appointed (C$180/200 single/double), and the hotel restaurant is very good. On the shores of Burrard Inlet, by the harbor, are two other notable hotels. *The Pan Pacific Hotel Vancouver* (☎ 604-662-8111, 800-663-1515 in Canada, 800-937-1515 in US), is across from white-winged Canada Place. You pay a lot for the location, with rooms at C$210, but the views are superb and the service extraordinary. *The Westin Bayshore* (☎ 604-682-3377, 800-228-3000), 1601 W Georgia St, offers the same superlatives from a location right on the waterfront and closer to Stanley Park; rooms cost C$260 to C$285 for a double.

An even more stylish alternative is the *Sheraton Wall Centre Hotel* (☎ 604-331-1000, 800-663-9255), 1088 Burrard St, a modern high-rise in the center of the city with a distinctly arty and modernistic atmosphere. Rooms begin at C$190/210.

Vancouver's highest-rated hotel, the *Four Seasons Hotel* (☎ 604 689 9333, 800-268-6282), 791 W Georgia St, is above the Pacific Centre shopping complex. To get to the reception area, take the escalator to the left of the Buddha statue. Room prices vary widely, and start at C$320.

Hotels – West Side
Shaughnessy Village (☎ 604-736-5511), 1125 W 12th Ave, is a high-rise complex incorporating a B&B, hotel, resort, apartment building and fun center all rolled into one. The least expensive rooms, tiny ship-like studio cabins cost C$78/87 single/double with breakfast and come packed with every amenity. In the dead of winter the price plummets to C$40/50. Ask for

one of the limited parking spots when you book the room.

There aren't many mid-range hotel choices in Kitsilano. The *Holiday Inn Vancouver Centre* (☎ 604-879-0511), 711 W Broadway, with rooms at C$159/179, is a large complex with a pool and two restaurants. The *Ramada Vancouver Centre* (☎ 604-872-8661, 800-663-5403), 898 W Broadway, has rooms with balconies for C$155.

In one of the city's top locations, the *Granville Island Hotel* (☎ 604-683-7373), 1253 Johnston St, Granville Island, is a modernistic structure right on the waterfront with great downtown views. The hotel is near the island's famed market, arts and crafts galleries, and theaters; you'll be just seconds away from the water taxis to downtown. Suite-style rooms are C$199/209 for a single/double.

Hotels – East Vancouver

The closest motel strip to downtown is along E Hastings St around Exhibition Park and east into Burnaby. This is a convenient area, close to Second Narrows Bridge leading over Burrard Inlet to North Vancouver. The *Best Western Exhibition Park* (☎ 604-294-4751), 3475 E Hastings St on the corner of Cassiar St, has rooms from C$80.

The second motel area is along Kingsway, a major road which branches off Main St south of 7th Ave. One of the closest motels to town is the *Biltmore Motor Hotel* (☎ 604-872-5252) at 395 Kingsway. It has air-con, TV, licensed restaurant and coffee shop. Rooms start at C$89. A bit farther out, the *2400 Motel* (☎ 604-434-2464, 888-833-2400), 2400 Kingsway, is a great deal with rooms starting at C$65.

One of the more central motels is *City Centre Motel* (☎ 604-876-7166, 800-707-2489), 2111 Main St, a 10-minute walk south of Main St Station, with rooms for C$65.

Hotels – North Shore

Another motel area is on the North Shore, over Lions Gate Bridge. Look along Marine Drive and north up Capilano Rd. There are also a couple of spots on the Esplanade, which runs east-west along the North Shore, past the SeaBus terminal. *Avalon Motor Hotel* (☎ 604-985-4181) is at 1025 Marine Drive, North Vancouver, about a five-minute drive east of the Lions Gate Bridge. Rooms are C$70/75 single/double. The *Canyon Court Motel* (☎ 604-988-3181) is at 1748 Capilano Rd, North Vancouver, close to Lions Gate Bridge; rooms cost around C$100 for single or double. There's a laundry, free coffee and a swimming pool. Kitchens are available for an additional cost.

One of the nicer places to stay is the *Grouse Inn* (☎ 604-988-7101, 800-779-7888), 1633 Capilano Rd, with kitchen suites and a guest laundry, rooms start at C$98 double.

Hotels – near the airport

There are a number of hotels near Richmond that service the Vancouver International Airport. One of the least expensive places to stay out here is *Holiday Inn Express* (☎ 604-223-9971), 9351 Bridgeport Rd, with basic clean rooms at C$69/79. For a bit more luxury, try the *Delta Vancouver Airport Hotel & Marina* (☎ 604-278-1241), 3500 Cessna Drive, with business-class rooms from C$145 to C$205.

PLACES TO EAT

Vancouver is one of the most cosmopolitan cities in North America, and that's good news for food lovers. You can journey gastronomically from country to country and continent to continent just by wandering down the street. Add to this the natural Northwest bounty of farm, garden and sea, and you've got the makings of a real capital of cuisine.

Restaurant food will initially seem more expensive in Vancouver than in other cities of the Pacific Northwest. Budget meals can still be a good deal, with many excellent ethnic restaurants offering dinner entrées around the C$10 mark. However, you'll find that mid-priced restaurants will offer evening main dishes in the C$20 range, with high-end splurges soaring into the C$35 to C$40 stratosphere. If you hail from outside of Canada, at least there's solace that these prices are in Canadian dollars, but there's no denying that after taxes and tips food costs can add up fast.

Be sure to pick up a copy of *The Georgia Straight* when you start making dining choices. Its restaurant section is very thorough and up-to-date, and what's better, there are dozens of discount coupons to clip. Most offer two-for-one entrées, often from new ethnic restaurants. It's a great deal for travelers.

Downtown

Budget If you're looking for inexpensive food, then there are several downtown streets where you can wander and shop the menus. Davie St has a great many good and inexpensive ethnic restaurants. For something different, try *Tigälos* (☎ 604-331-0051), 1157 Davie St, for Portuguese cooking; the rotisseried chicken is a specialty. *Stepho's Souvlaki Greek Taverna* (☎ 604-683-2555), 1124 Davie St, is the local favorite for Greek cooking.

Denman St, near Stanley Park, is another lively, pleasant street to visit around evening mealtime. There's a good selection of eateries, particularly toward the Georgia St end, and lots of people strolling and menu-reading. The *Great Wall Mongolian BBQ* (☎ 604-688-2121), 717 Denman St, creates giant stir-fries, while you watch, with ingredients you select from a buffet. The lunch (C$6) and dinner (C$10), both all-you-can-eat deals, are hard to beat for the fresh and spicy blends. *Musashi Japanese Restaurant* (☎ 604-687-0634), at 780 Denman St between Robson and Alberni Sts, is cozy, casual and cheap. It's closed on Monday. *Cafe Slavia* (☎ 604-687-7440), 815 Denman St, is a small, friendly, inexpensive place with a Slavic slant; it serves food like goulash and perogies (dumplings) for around C$7. *Bud's Halibut & Chips* (☎ 604-683-0661), 1007 Denman St, is a good place for fish and chips.

Open every day until midnight, *Pepita's* (☎ 604-669-4736), at the corner of Denman and Davie Sts, is one of the city's most established Mexican restaurants.

Some restaurants along Robson St are affordable. *Pezzo* (☎ 604-669-9300), 1100 Robson St, is a lively place for gourmet pizza by the slice. *Bread Garden* (☎ 604-688-3213), 812 Bute St, is a bakery and cafe, with fresh sandwiches and soup. There's even a takeout window designed for skateboarders. One of Vancouver's first Indian restaurants, *A Taste of India* (☎ 604-682-3894), 1282 Robson St, is still one of its best. Farther up the street is the *Robson Public Market*, 1610 Robson St, with fresh fruit and vegetables, cheese, bread and other picnic elements. The market also has inexpensive takeout food.

There are plenty of cheap greasy-spoon cafes along Granville St. A great exception is *Templeton* (☎ 604-685-4612), at 1087 Granville St, a hip retro diner that serves up-to-the-minute exciting variations on classic North American cooking.

White Spot, a Vancouver institution famous for its hamburgers, is a chain of family restaurants that began in 1928. With over 30 locations in greater Vancouver, White Spot serves standard food at reasonable prices every day.

Middle Robson St has a great many mid-range restaurants and offers a lively scene and great people watching. *Cactus Club Cafe* (☎ 604-687-3278), 1136 Robson St, is a fun brewpub kind of establishment that serves Tex-Mex dishes, burgers and BBQ ribs. *Milestones* (☎ 604-734-8616), 1145 Robson St, is a modern, high-tech, trend-conscious bar and restaurant with ingredient du jour pizza, pasta and other late '90s kinds of food.

Mirabella Spanish Restaurant & Tapas Bar (☎ 604-681-1175), 1368 Robson St, has an impressive list of tapas as well as full Spanish-style dinners. *Royal Thai Seafood* (☎ 604-602-0603), 770 Bute St, has excellent Thai curries and spice-infused seafood dishes.

The *Chili Club* (☎ 604-681-6000), 1018 Beach Ave, is an upscale Thai restaurant with authentic spice and heat. More or less beneath the Granville Bridge is *A Kettle of Fish* (☎ 604-682-6661), 900 Pacific St, an attractive, well-established restaurant specializing in fresh seafood.

Top End If you have money to blow, then you will be welcome in some wonderful restaurants in downtown Vancouver. Only moderately extravagant in price, *Cin Cin* (☎ 604-688-7338), 1154 Robson St, is a top downtown Italian restaurant with a sophisticated ambiance; entrées range from C$18 to C$28. For steaks, oysters, grilled fish and other stalwarts of traditional Northwest cooking, go to *Joe Forte's Oysterhouse and Grill* (☎ 604-669-1940), 777 Thurlow St. It has an old-fashioned atmosphere, but the crowds are very up-to-date. For a different kind of Northwest tradition, try *Lilliget Feast House* (☎ 604-681-7044), 1724 Davie St, which serves updated versions of salmon and game dishes prepared by Native Indians. Order a multiple-course feast for C$40, or order à la carte (C$16 to C$20 for entrées).

The Umberto's chain of Italian restaurants has done a lot to put Vancouver on the cuisine map. The original restaurant, *Umberto Il Giardino* (☎ 604-669-2422), at 1382 Hornby St, is still one of the city's best for Tuscan cooking.

French-style cuisine is still highly regarded in Vancouver. *Etoile* (☎ 604-681-4444), 1355 Hornby St, updates French classics and introduces sauces to Northwest meat and seafood. There are two prix-fixe menus at C$28 and C$38. A real favorite, *Le Crocodile* (☎ 604-669-4298), 909 Burrard St, specializes in satisfying dishes from Alsace, set in a sumptuous dining room. *Le Gavroche* (☎ 604-685-3924), 1616 Alberni St, bridges the Northwest larder with French haute cuisine; an excellent choice for a romantic dinner.

Gastown

The old Victorian-era city center of Vancouver is rapidly regentrifying and among the first to place roots here were enterprising restaurants. A stroll along Water St reveals dozens of choices, none of which will bend your wallet.

Budget Check into the breeding ground of new and inventive pizza at *Incendio* (☎ 604-688-8694), 103 Columbia St. They also offer inexpensive and excellent pasta.

For soup-and-sandwich lunches, try the *Cottage Deli* (☎ 604-688-0844), 131 Water St, which has views of Burrard Inlet. *The Old Spaghetti Factory* (☎ 604-684-1288), 53 Water St, is part of a large chain offering good values for pasta-based dinners; kids are welcome. The eye-catching decor includes some old machinery, stained-glass Tiffany lamps and even a 1910 Vancouver streetcar. Entrées range from C$8 to C$13.

Middle Both a brewpub and a serious restaurant, *Steamworks Brewing Company* (☎ 604-689-2739), 375 Water St, offers inexpensive Northwest-style food with ales and beers brewed on site. At the absolute heart of Gastown, *Irish Heather Bistro and Irish House* (☎ 604-688-9779), 217 Carrall St, is an interesting mix of Finian bar, Irish restaurant and performance space. *Water Street Café* (☎ 604-689-2832), 300 Water St, is housed in one of the few buildings to escape the Great Fire of 1886. However, the food in this airy and open space is very up-to-date, with designer pizza and Northwest cuisine.

At *Brother's Restaurant* (☎ 604-683-9124), 1 Water St, the decor has a monastic theme and the wait staff is dressed in monks' habits. The 'Brothers' serve seafood, pasta and poultry and items such as the 'Monastery burger.' Meant to be a low-ticket version of the cucina at other Umberto's restaurants, *Umberto Al Porto* (☎ 604-683-8376), 321 Water St, is where to go for a small-scale Italian splurge without threatening the limit of your credit card.

Chinatown

You'll have no problem finding an inexpensive place to eat in Chinatown; most

VANCOUVER

restaurants are friendly and the staff will speak some English. One of the largest restaurants in Chinatown, the *Pink Pearl* (☎ 604-253-4316), at 1132 E Hastings St (see the East Vancouver map), is a good place for dim sum. The long-established *Hon's Won Tun House* (☎ 604-688-0871), 268 Keefer St, is usually choked with local crowds; the jostling and noise will remind you of Hong Kong. Cambodian cooking is similar to Vietnamese, but spicier; give it a try at *Phnom Penh* (☎ 604-253-8899), 244 E Georgia St. Another local favorite, *Park Lock* (☎ 604-688-1581), 544 Main St, specializes in great seafood dishes and especially good dim sum; don't let the modest street-level entry put you off. *Pho Pasteur* (☎ 604-689-8258), 290 E Hastings St, is Chinatown's top Vietnamese restaurant.

The seemingly out-of-place *Bodai Vegetarian Restaurant* (☎ 604-682-2666), 337 E Hastings St, and the *Miu Jay Garden Vegetarian Restaurant* (☎ 604-687-5231), 363 E Hastings St, serve lots of appetizing dishes, some of which include simulated meat. Lunchtime dim sum specials go for around C$5.50.

Yaletown

Middle This warehouse and loft district is also home to some of Vancouver's trendiest restaurants. A real find here is *Deniro's Bistro* (☎ 604-684-2777), 1040 Mainland St, where you'll be served cosmopolitan cuisine in retro-diner ambiance. Look at the changing art displays – they can be exciting and somewhat mind-boggling. The quizzically named *Farrago* (☎ 604-684-4044), 1138 Homer St, in fact serves Mediterranean-style cuisine in an elegant dining room. Although a brewpub, the *Yaletown Brewing Co* (☎ 604-681-2719), 1111 Mainland St, isn't exactly a casual, come-as-you-are kind of place. The crowd is chic, single and loud, and the food upscale and very good.

Top End For some, the center of Yaletown fine dining is *Century Grill* (☎ 604-688-8088), 1095 Hamilton St, where steaks and Northwest cooking meet at this dining room facing onto a loading dock patio. *Mangiamo* (☎ 604-687-1116), 1116 Mainland St, is a stylish Italian restaurant specializing in fresh fish.

Granville Island

With the public market so close at hand, you would rightly expect Granville Island to feature fresh and tempting food. The restaurants recommended here are all moderately priced.

Isadora's Cooperative Restaurant (☎ 604-681-8816), 1540 Old Bridge St, has a healthy cooking bent, with many delicious vegetarian entrées; there's a C$17 prix-fixe menu as well as à la carte specials. And yes, diners can become part owners; the restaurant is a member-owned cooperative. Both a jazz club and a Creole restaurant, *Mulvaney's* (☎ 604-685-6571), 9-1535 Johnston St, brings New Orleans to BC; fresh fish is a specialty. If you like your fish on the rare side, *Kamei Royale Ocean* (☎ 604-602-0005), 1333 Johnston St, is one of the city's best sushi bars and Japanese restaurants.

For something different, try the *Pacific Institute of Culinary Arts* (☎ 604-734-4488), 1505 W 2nd Ave, where cooking students prepare the dishes and serve the public. On a warm summer evening, there's no place like *Bridges* (☎ 604-687-4400), 1696 Duranleau St, with its large outdoor deck and great views. The food's not bad either, mostly pub fare on the patio, or else more serious Northwest cuisine in the upstairs dining room.

West Side

Kitsilano is a diner's dream. Rents are cheaper than downtown, and many ethnic and alternative restaurants thrive in the attention they get from the lively mix of students, young professionals and ex-hippies. More recently, upscale restaurants have also moved into the neighborhood; two of Vancouver's most popular special-occasion restaurants – the Lumiere and Bishops – are located here. The main focus of dining is along W 4th Ave and Broadway.

VANCOUVER

Budget Broadway, roughly between Cambie and Granville Sts, is a small Chinatown; you'll have no trouble finding an inexpensive place to eat. *Golden Great Wall Szechuan* (☎ 604-872-0328), 525 W Broadway, has a good local reputation, specializing in spicy Shanghai cooking. *Mongolie Grill* (☎ 604-874-6121), 467 W Broadway, specializes in choose-your-raw-ingredients brazier cooking. Despite its name, *Many's Lunch* (☎ 604-736-3312), 1453 W Broadway, is open for dinner as well, serving excellent Indian curries. *Surat Sweet* (☎ 604-733-7363), 1938 W 4th Ave, serves vegetarian-only Gujarati Indian cooking. *Vij's* (☎ 604-736-6664), 1480 W 11th Ave, takes homey Indian cooking and refines standard dishes into cosmopolitan cuisine.

Sophie's Cosmic Café (☎ 604-732-6810), 2095 W 4th Ave, is a happening place with queues sometimes out on the street. The walls are covered in all sorts of memorabilia, including an old billiard-table top. The cafe sells an impressive range of burgers, including vegetarian falafel burgers, as well as salads and enchiladas.

Good for lunch and snacks, *Greens & Gourmet* (☎ 604-737-7373), at 2681 W Broadway, is a vegetarian and health-food restaurant charging by weight.

Middle Worth making a detour for, *Grand King Seafood Restaurant* (☎ 604-876-7855), 705 W Broadway, has perhaps the city's best dim sum; dinner entrées are uniformly excellent and innovative. *Szechwan Chongqing Seafood Restaurant* (☎ 604-734-2668), 1668 W Broadway, was recently voted by readers of *Vancouver Sun* as Vancouver's favorite Chinese restaurant. Not only does the staff serve up searingly hot delicacies at this upscale dining room, they also deliver.

For real family-style Greek cooking, go to *Kalamata Greek Taverna* (☎ 604-872-7050), 478 W Broadway, open for dinner only. *Rasputin* (☎ 604-879-6675), 457 W Broadway, brings Russian fine dining to Vancouver. *Tojo's* (☎ 604-872-8050), 202-

777 W Broadway, has topnotch sushi and inventive, unusual Japanese entrées; great views from the dining room.

A relic of Kitsilano's hippie past, *Naam* (☎ 604-738-7151), 2724 W Broadway, is a vegetarian health-food restaurant with aspirations to cuisine. Funky doesn't quite capture the atmosphere; it's more like traveling back in time to the Summer of Love. Go when you aren't in a hurry, or just stay late: Naam is open 24 hours.

In fact, *Funky Armadillo* (☎ 604-739-8131), at 2741 W Broadway, isn't funky at all; it serves excellent Southwest-style cooking out of a friendly, neighborhood-oriented storefront.

Nyala Café (☎ 604-731-7899), 2930 W 4th Ave, serves Ethiopian food to be eaten without the use of cutlery: you use bread instead. On Saturday night there's African or Caribbean music and dancing.

Over on W Broadway, the 3000 block area is sometimes known as Little Greece. Among several popular places is the very good Greek *Ouzeri* (☎ 604-739-9378), at 3189 W Broadway on the corner of Trutch St. It's open till the early hours serving casual tapas-style snacks. The ethnic mix also includes *Andale's* (☎ 604-738-9782), 3211 W Broadway, serving a variety of tasty Mexican and Spanish dishes.

Words you don't often see together are 'health-conscious' and 'French,' but the *Picasso Cafe* (☎ 604-732-3290), 1626 W Broadway, manages to pull it off. Food is uniformly good and prepared with a light hand on the sauces and butter. That's not the only thing unusual about the cafe: the staff is part of a restaurant training program for homeless kids trying to make a change.

While not exactly a bargain, the Italian-by-Northwest cuisine at *Ecco il Pane* (☎ 604-739-1314), 2563 W Broadway, is a good value when compared to its peers. The bakery here is one of the best in town; dinner entrées run less than C$20 but are prepared with skill and finesse; the dining room is stylish yet informal.

Also at the upper end of moderate, *Quattro* (☎ 604-734-4444), 2611 W 4th

Ave, is another popular Italian restaurant with good pastas and grilled meats, and a jungle-like dining room.

Top End If you're looking to splurge, then here are a couple of good suggestions. *Lumiere* (☎ 604-739-8185), at 2551 W Broadway, prepares a kind of French fusion cooking that brings in the best of world cuisine and then drapes it in wonderful sauces. There are two prix-fixe menus, four courses for C$65 and a vegetarian option at C$40. Truly excellent food but try to look your best, as this is a very high-toned place.

There's a lot of internationalism at *Bishop's* (☎ 604-738-2025), 2183 W 4th Ave, the other top-flight restaurant in Kitsilano. In fact, chef John Bishop cooked for a private get-together with presidents Bill Clinton and Boris Yeltsin, as well as a host of celebrities. The entrées are too eclectic to categorize easily – mingling Thai, Chinese, French and Italian – but absolutely fresh ingredients, strong but complementary flavors, and ingenious presentation are the hallmarks that make this a very memorable restaurant.

Commercial Drive

Budget Along a portion of Commercial Drive, between E 6th Ave and Parker St, there are several interesting neighborhood restaurants and cafes popular with the mix of artists, professionals and various alternative types who live in the area.

There are a number of organic groceries and casual cafes here, and you'll have no trouble finding inexpensive food. One place to remember: *Café du Soleil* (☎ 604-254-1145), 1393 Commercial Drive, is a friendly New Agey kind of place with good vegetarian food.

Middle This traditionally Italian district has some fine upmarket Italian food to offer. *Spumante's* (☎ 604-253-8899), 1736 Commercial Drive, serves excellent hearty fare in a tasteful setting; the menu selection is astonishingly broad. For classic

Greek cooking, try *Le Grec* (☎ 604-253-1253), 1447 Commercial Drive. *El Cocal* (☎ 604-255-4580), at 1037 Commercial Drive, specializes in Salvadoran food, with more familiar Mexican dishes thrown in for good measure. Then there's *Havana* (☎ 604-253-9119), at 1212 Commercial Drive, a Spanish/Caribbean tapas bar with a clientele that gets more and more interesting as the evening progresses.

North Vancouver

Lonsdale Quay Market has lots of places to munch at and to buy takeout food. The British-style *Cheshire Cheese Inn* (☎ 604-987-3322), on level 2, sells traditional British food like steak and kidney pudding and shepherd's pie. Nearby, *Sailor Hagar's* (☎ 604-984-3087), 235 W 1st St, is a brewpub with an excellent menu of pub grub.

Several moderately priced restaurants are concentrated near the corner of Lonsdale Ave and Esplanade. *Corsi Trattoria* (☎ 604-987-9910), 1 Lonsdale Ave, is a very homey Italian trattoria where everything is made on the premises, including the pasta and bread.

At 69 Lonsdale Ave, the *Jägerhof* (☎ 604-980-4316), specializes in schnitzels and also serves venison and moose meat. On the walls it has old framed photographs and prints, and mounted animals' heads.

ENTERTAINMENT

Vancouver has a lot going on at night; remember that this is the largest and just about the only city on the entire Canadian west coast. And, in terms of Canadian arts, this is Seattle, San Francisco and LA all rolled into one.

The best source of information on entertainment in Vancouver is *The Georgia Straight*, which comes out every Thursday. The weekly *WestEnder* and the monthly *Playboard* give reviews and dates of events in the visual and performing arts. *Xtra West* has listings for the gay scene. All are free and you can pick them up around town. The daily newspapers, *Vancouver Sun* and *Province* also have complete entertainment

VANCOUVER

listings, which include theater, dance and
concerts.

Tickets for most events are available
from TicketMaster (☎ 604-280-3311).

Coffeehouses

Vancouver is, like other cities in the Northwest, awash in good coffee. If you're just
looking for a cup of joe and a muffin, then
try the following: Seattle latte magnates
Starbucks, Canadian giants Grabbajabba
and Second Cup, and local roasters-made-
good, Blenz, all have multiple outlets
throughout the city.

However, if you're looking for a little
poetry, folk music or performance art with
your coffee, or if you are looking for an
alcohol-free place to meet people, check
out the following. *Talking Stick* (☎ 604-
683-3979), 221 Carrall St in Gastown, has
live music, discussion groups and artsy-
intellectual performances.

Stone Table Coffee House (☎ 604-255-
3538), 1155 Thurlow St, has live music on
weekends. *Café Deux Soleils* (☎ 604-254-
1195), 2096 Commercial Drive, is a New
Age cafe with an interesting clientele and
some live music. *Myles of Beans* (☎ 604-
524-3799), 7010 Kingsway, east of the city,
has live music nightly.

For more literary events, like poetry
readings or performance art, check the listings at *Old Times Cafe* (☎ 604-876-0845),
at Pender and Homer Sts, or *Tygres' Tales*
(☎ 604-731-7273), 2133 Granville St.

Performing Arts

Ballet British Columbia (☎ 604-732-5003),
is Vancouver's top dance troupe; it performs at the Queen Elizabeth Theatre (see
Theater, below). The ballet season runs
from September to June. *Vancouver Opera*
(☎ 604-682-2871) also stages its five productions at the Queen Elizabeth Theatre.
Vancouver Symphony Orchestra (☎ 604-
876-3434) performs at the Orpheum
Theatre, on Granville St at Smithe St.

Theater For same-day, half-price theater
tickets, check the little booth on the ground

level in Robson Galleria, 1025 Robson St.
It's open noon to 1 pm and 4:30 to 6 pm
Monday to Saturday. Otherwise you can
call TicketMaster (☎ 604-280-3311, 604-
873-3311) for normal-priced tickets to almost all theatrical events in the city.

Theater, from mainstream to fringe, is
flourishing in Vancouver. Across the street
from the main post office, on Hamilton St,
the *Queen Elizabeth Theatre* (☎ 604-280-
4444) puts on major international productions; the *Vancouver Playhouse* is part of
the same complex. The new *Ford Centre
for the Performing Arts* (☎ 604-602-0616),
777 Homer St, specializes in grand Broadway musicals.

The *Metro Theatre* (☎ 604-266-7191),
1370 SW Marine Drive, and *Firehall Arts
Centre* (☎ 604-689-0926), 280 E Cordova
St, put on plays by Canadian and foreign
playwrights. The *Arts Theatre* (☎ 604-687-
1644) has more experimental productions
with three locations in town – two on Johnston St on Granville Island, and the other at
1181 Seymour St on the corner of Smithe
St. Also on Granville Island, the *Waterfront
Theatre* (☎ 604-685-6217), 1410 Cartwright
St, is the venue for a number of local theater
companies.

Several fringe theaters worth checking
out are the *Vancouver East Side Cultural
Centre* (☎ 604-254-9578), at 1895 Venables St near Commercial Drive, and the
Vancouver Little Theatre (☎ 604-876-
4165), 3102 Main St at 15th Ave. Vancouver's *TheatreSports League* (☎ 604-687-
1644), the famed improv troupe, now plays
at the Arts Club Theatre on Johnston St,
Granville Island.

Live Music

Downtown around Richards and Seymour
Sts, and in Yaletown around Davie and
Hamilton Sts, it's bustling at night. The
Railway Club (☎ 604-681-1625), 579 Dunsmuir St, is a pub-like place with live music
seven nights a week and good-quality, original jazz on Saturday afternoon. *Richard's
on Richards* (☎ 604-687-6794), at 1036
Richards St, is a popular, dressy singles bar

with a hefty but varying entry charge. The *Starfish Room* (☎ 604-682-4171), 1005 Homer St, is one of the city's top venues for live local and international bands.

Nearby, Granville St is interesting after dark with lots of street activity. The *Commodore Ballroom* (☎ 604-681-7838), 870 Granville St, can accommodate over 1000 people and plays everything from punk to lambada. The *Yale* (☎ 604-681-9253), at 1300 Granville St, is one of the best blues bars in the country. One of the best clubs in town, *The Gate* (☎ 604-608-4283), 1176 Granville St, both looks and sounds great; bands are the best of the locals and sometimes they get touring big names.

There is a fair bit of nightlife in the Gastown area. The *Town Pump* (☎ 604-683-6695), 66 Water St, is a well-known blues venue. The *Purple Onion* (☎ 604-602-9442), 15 Water St, offers live jazz in the lounge, and in the cabaret there's salsa, Latin and funk.

The *Picadilly Pub*, (☎ 604-682-3221), 620 W Pender St, has live R&B on Friday night. There's live, mostly traditional jazz at the *Hot Jazz Club* (☎ 604-873-4131), 2120 Main St. The *Glass Slipper* (☎ 604-877-0066), at 2714 Prince Edward St behind the Biltmore Hotel, has more contemporary jazz plus world music nightly.

Call the *Jazz Hotline* (☎ 604-682-0706) for information on what's going on in the jazz clubs.

Dance Clubs

As elsewhere in the Northwest, if you want to dance – whatever your sexual orientation – head to the gay clubs. If that doesn't suit you, The *Big Bam Boo* (☎ 604-733-2220), 1236 W Broadway, is one of the best nightclubs on the West Side, with pool and sushi on the main floor, and disco downstairs. *MaRS* (☎ 604-663-7707), 1320 Richards St, is the hottest, high-tech place to dance downtown, with amazing light effects and a huge fiber-optic screen above the dance floor. Cutting-edge music and a deafening

sound system make *The Rage* (☎ 604-685-5585), 750 Pacific Blvd S, the favorite for the musically progressive.

Every city's gay scene is different, and much of Vancouver's is drag-oriented. The place to dance and dish is the *Dufferin Hotel* (☎ 604-683-4251), 900 Seymour St, and the *Royal Hotel* (☎ 604-685-5335), 1025 Granville St; the latter the city's only gay bar with live music. The biggest gay bar in Vancouver is *Celebrities* (☎ 604-689-3180), 1022 Davie St, with DJ dancing and crowds every night of the week. *Denman Station Cabaret* (☎ 604-669-3448), 860 Denman St, is a lot of fun, with dancing, darts, drag acts and other entertainers, and theme parties; catch the Electrolush Lounge on Thursday. *The Lotus* (☎ 604-685-7777), downstairs at 455 Abbot St, is Vancouver's only dance club for women and their friends; women only on Fridays. *Odyssey* (☎ 604-689-5256), 1251 Howe St, is the wildest gay dance club; with go-go boys, shower room viewing and theme nights, you are guaranteed to be entertained.

Bars & Brewpubs

Until Expo '86, BC had very strict liquor laws that basically restricted bars to private clubs, restaurants and hotels. Needless to say, that wasn't the kind of atmosphere that would produce a great bar culture. Thus, the classic 'great old bar' really doesn't exist in Vancouver. Most of the fun or hip places to drink are dance clubs or spinoffs of restaurants.

However, there are a few nice places to recommend in Vancouver. *Fred's Uptown Tavern* (☎ 604-331-7979), 1006 Granville St, is a comfortable, pub-like place to meet friends. *DV8* (☎ 604-682-4388), 515 Davie St, is a hip lounge that's open late.

The craze for locally brewed beer is sweeping Vancouver like other Pacific Northwest cities. However, there aren't as many brewpubs as you might expect in a city this size. One of the best here is *Steamworks Brewing Company* (☎ 604-689-2739), 375 Water St, in Gastown, with pool tables, great views over the North Shore, and two levels of seating. *Yaletown Brewing Co* (☎ 604-681-2719), 1111 Mainland St, is upscale and attracts a singles-bar crowd.

Cinemas

Downtown's major first-run multiplex theaters are the *Granville 7 Cinema* (☎ 604-684-4000), 855 Granville St, and *Fifth Avenue Cinemas* (☎ 604-734-7469), 2110 Burrard St. At 919 Granville St, the *Paradise* cinema (☎ 604-681-1732) shows commercial films at half-price every day and the *Denman Place Discount Cinema* (☎ 604-663-2201), 1737 Comox St, shows three films for C$3 on Tuesday.

Vancouver also has a number of low-cost repertory theaters which show a mix of independent, vintage and foreign films. You may need to buy a cheap membership. *Hollywood Theatre* (☎ 604-738-3211) is at 3123 W Broadway; *Ridge Theatre* (☎ 604-738-6311), 3131 Arbutus St, is in the shopping center on the corner of 16th Ave. The schedule at *Pacific Cinémathèque* (☎ 604-688-3456), 1131 Howe St, is so varied that it's best to think of it as an ongoing film festival.

Comedy Clubs

Yuk Yuks (☎ 604-687-5233), 750 Pacific Blvd S, is the city's primary spot for stand-up comedy. For laughs and competitive improvisational acting, you can't beat *TheatreSports League* (☎ 604-687-1644). They perform late-night shows at the Arts Club Theatre, 1585 Johnston St, Granville Island.

SPECTATOR SPORTS

The BC Lions (☎ 604-589-7627) play Canadian-style professional football from July to September in BC Place Stadium. The Vancouver Canadians (☎ 604-872-5232), the local baseball team, play their home games at Nat Bailey Stadium, 4601 Ontario St, next to Queen Elizabeth Park. The new Grizzlies (☎ 604-589-7627) of the National Basketball Association play at GM Place. If you're here during the ice-

hockey season, October to April, try to see a home game of the Vancouver Canucks (☎ 604-254-5141) at GM Place.

SHOPPING
Downtown

Downtown Vancouver has some of the city's most dynamic shopping areas. More than just the busiest shopping street in Vancouver, Robson St is also a major hangout and people-watching area. You can buy everything from couture to condoms, from Italian newspapers to fresh crab; there are lots of tourist shops here as well. If you don't find what you were shopping for, you'll certainly not be bored. The other major focus for downtown shopping is Pacific Centre, which runs from Robson to Pender Sts between Granville and Howe Sts. Most of the stores are national and international chains; the major department-store anchor is Eatons, and the Hudson's Bay Company – The Bay – is just a block south.

Hill's Indian Crafts (☎ 604-685-4294), 165 Water St, has a good selection of carvings, prints, masks and excellent Cowichan sweaters. The Inuit Gallery (☎ 604-688-7323), 345 Water St, sells Inuit sculptures, drawings and tapestries and Northwest coastal Indian masks, carvings and jewelry. Images for a Canadian Heritage (☎ 604-685-7046), 164 Water St, and the Marion Scott Gallery (☎ 604-685-7046), at 671 Howe St, also feature Native Indian art.

If you like furniture, home furnishings and interior decorating, Yaletown is a district definitely worth checking out. The old warehouse-district-gone-lofts is loaded with stylish design shops.

West Side

Next to Robson St, there is no other place in Vancouver more fun to shop than Granville Island. The famed public market – a warehouse-like structure loaded with fresh fish, vegetables, butcher shops, cheese stands, bakeries and everything else you might need to put together a meal – is an amazing place to visit, even if you aren't in the market for a whole salmon or a head of Savoy cabbage. Merchants also sell fancy jams, syrups and other preserved foods that make good gifts; the fishmongers can pack fish for air shipment. In addition to the market, Granville Island has a number of arts and crafts galleries, a good bookstore and chandlers devoted to sailing and kayaking.

Both Broadway and W 4th Ave are lined with shops, many reflecting both the area's old hippie past and its *très* hip and upscale present. However, for a concentrated shot of shopping, head over to South Granville, across the Granville Street Bridge from downtown, between W 4th Ave to W 16th Ave. In many ways a microcosm of Vancouver, you'll find high-end boutiques, Asian groceries, art galleries and antique stores.

There are a number of good places selling camping and outdoor equipment, guidebooks and maps, mainly in the Kitsilano area. At Mountain Equipment Co-operative (☎ 604-872-7859), 130 W Broadway, you can find all kinds of outdoor equipment at reasonable rates.

GETTING THERE & AWAY
See the Traveling to Canada sidebar at the beginning of this chapter for information on arriving in Vancouver, including details on customs and border crossing.

Air
Vancouver International Airport (the international code is YVR, and it's sometimes called this by locals) is about 10km (6 miles) south of the city on Sea Island – between Vancouver and the municipality of Richmond. Vancouver is the largest airport on the Canadian west coast, and is the hub for local commuter flights. Flights to Portland (C$140 return), Seattle (C$120 return) and Victoria (C$80 return) depart regularly. If you're flying on to destinations in the US, you may go through immigrations before boarding at the Vancouver airport.

If you fly into Vancouver on an international flight, upon exiting customs you'll enter the arrivals area. Very conveniently located, a Travel InfoCentre is immediately to the left. The friendly folks here can book you hotel rooms and offer advice and information on Vancouver and BC. There are also a number of ATMs which will ease the transition from your local currency to Canadian dollars.

Both major Canadian airlines – Air Canada and Canadian Airlines – fly to Vancouver, as do many US and Asian airlines. Air BC is a local airline run by Air Canada, serving Seattle, Portland, Vancouver Island and some points in interior BC. North Vancouver Air (☎ 604-278-1608, 800-228-6608) is a commuter service with flights along the Sunshine Coast and Whistler. Some Canadian and foreign airlines with offices in downtown Vancouver are:

Air Canada/Air BC, 1040 W Georgia St
　　(☎ 604-688-5515)
Air China, 1040 W Georgia St
　　(☎ 604-685-0921)
Air India, suite 6, 601 W Broadway
　　(☎ 604-879-0271)
Canadian Airlines International,
　　1030 W Georgia St
　　(☎ 604-279-6611)
Cathay Pacific, 605 W Georgia St
　　(☎ 604-682-9747, 604-661-2907)
Garuda Indonesia, suite 500, 1155 Robson St
　　(☎ 604-681-7034)
Hawaiian Airlines,
　　157-10551 Shellbridge Way, Richmond
　　(☎ 604-231-8100, 800-367-5320)
Korean Air, suite 1010, 1030 W Georgia St
　　(☎ 604-689-2000, 800-438-5000)
Lufthansa Airlines, suite 1401,
　　1030 West Georgia St
　　(☎ 604-683-1313, 800-563-5954)
Singapore Airlines, suite 1111,
　　1030 W Georgia St
　　(☎ 604-689-1233)

Canada 3000 (☎ 604-273-0930), one of the first discount airlines to operate in Canada, offers flights to Vancouver from other major cities Canadian cities; if you choose to fly standby, you can get to Calgary for C$65, or all the way to Toronto for C$155. A US discounter, Reno Air, flies to Vancouver from California and the US Southwest.

Bus

The bus station is part of the train station, Pacific Central Station at 1150 Station St (see the Train section, below). Greyhound (☎ 604-662-3222), Pacific Coach Lines (☎ 604-662-8074) and Maverick Coach Lines (☎ 604-662-8051, 604-255-1171) stop here.

Greyhound buses link Vancouver with Seattle and other cities in the USA, as well as cities in eastern Canada. Greyhound does not have service to Victoria.

Pacific Coach Lines has eight buses daily to Victoria, leaving the bus station every hour at 10 minutes to the hour from 5:50 am to 8:45 pm. The one-way fare is C$25 including ferry; the journey takes about three hours.

Maverick Coach Lines operates eight buses daily to Nanaimo on Vancouver Island for C$18 one way (including ferry); the trip takes 3½ hours. It also has buses to Powell River, Squamish, Whistler and Pemberton.

If you're heading for the USA, Quick Coach Lines (☎ 604-940-4428, 800-665-2122 in Canada) operates a daily bus shuttle to downtown Seattle for C$43 one way; the bus also makes stops at Seattle's Sea-Tac Airport and Bellingham Airport. Buses leave from most major hotels in downtown Vancouver.

See the Train section, below, for details on bus service offered by VIA Rail and Amtrak.

Train

VIA Rail Vancouver is the western terminus for Canada's VIA Rail. The magnificent Pacific Central Station is off Main St, at 1150 Station St, between National and Terminal Aves. The station is marked 'Canadian National' and has a small park in front. For 24-hour information on fares and reservations call ☎ 800-561-8630. The ticket office is open 8 am to 8 pm Monday and Thursday; 8 am to 3:30 pm Tuesday, Wednesday and Friday; 12:30 to 8 pm Sat-

urday; 8 am to 1:30 pm Sunday. Left luggage is open from 8 am to 10 pm (closed between 3:30 and 4 pm).

The route east goes through Kamloops, BC, and Jasper and Edmonton in Alberta. Trains leave Monday, Thursday and Saturday at 8 pm. Stopovers are permitted but you must re-reserve.

VIA Rail also provides a bus service (which allows you to connect to towns no longer part of the rail system) between the towns of Kamloops and Penticton, Edmonton and Calgary, and Saskatoon and Regina.

Amtrak Amtrak's *Mt Baker International* line connects Vancouver to Bellingham and Seattle with one train daily. In addition, Amtrak (☎ 800-872-7245) runs three buses a day from Vancouver to Seattle to connect with other main-line departures; C$26 one way.

Rocky Mountaineer The privately owned *Rocky Mountaineer* train travels through some of the country's most scenic landscapes from BC to Banff and Calgary (VIA Rail no longer provides service along this route). This isn't really a service for people just trying to get from place to place, unless you have a lot of money to spend. Ticket price includes accommodations (there's an obligatory overnight stay in Kamloops) and meals, with more extensive packages available on both the Vancouver and Alberta ends. The cheapest off-season fare from Vancouver to Banff or Jasper is C$475. A basic four-day package will cost C$975.

The service runs between the middle of May and early October. There are seven trips a month in summer. For information, contact a travel agent or Rocky Mountaineer Railtours (☎ 604-606-7200; 800-665-7245 for reservations), suite 130, 1150 Station St, Vancouver, in the main train station.

BC Rail BC has its own railway system, BC Rail (☎ 604-984-5246, 604-631-3500), which operates the *Cariboo Prospector* with service from North Vancouver to Squamish, Whistler, Lillooet, 100 Mile House, Williams Lake, Quesnel and Prince George, where it connects with VIA Rail. One train leaves daily with service as far as Whistler and Lillooet; one-way fare to Whistler is C$29. Three days a week – Sunday, Wednesday and Friday – the train continues on to Prince George. Reservations are advised.

Trains leave from North Vancouver at the BC Rail Station, 1311 W 1st St, at the southern end of Pemberton Ave. To get to the station take bus No 239 west from the SeaBus terminal at Lonsdale Quay.

Car

If you're coming from the US (Washington State), you'll be on I-5 until the border town of Blaine. At the border is the Peace Arch Provincial and State Park. The first town in BC is White Rock. Hwy 99 veers west, then north to Vancouver. Close to the city, it passes over two arms of the Fraser River and eventually turns into Granville St, one of the main thoroughfares of downtown Vancouver.

If you're coming from the eastern part of the province, you'll almost certainly be on the Trans Canada Hwy (Hwy 1), which takes the Port Mann Bridge over the Fraser River and snakes through the eastern end of the city, eventually meeting with Hastings St before going over the Second Narrows Bridge to North Vancouver.

If you're coming from Horseshoe Bay in the north, the Trans Canada Hwy heads through West Vancouver and North Vancouver before going over the Second Narrows Bridge; from there Hwy 99 takes you over Lions Gate Bridge into Stanley Park.

Rental There are many car-rental companies in Vancouver; the larger ones have several offices around town and some also have offices at the international airport. Some have discount coupons which are available at various outlets, including the Travel InfoCentres. For a thorough listing of car-rental companies, check the yellow pages. Following is a small selection with

their downtown addresses; all have service at YVR as well.

Budget, 450 W Georgia St
  (☎ 604-668-7000)
Hertz, 1128 Seymour St
  (☎ 604-688-2411)
Lo-Cost, 1105 Granville St
  (☎ 604-689-9664,
  800-886-1266 in Canada)
National Tilden, 1130 W Georgia St
  (☎ 604-685-6111, 800-387-4747)
Rent-A-Wreck, Sheraton Wall Center,
  1083 Hornby St
  (☎ 604-688-0001, 800-327-0116))
Thrifty, Landmark Hotel, 1400 Robson St
  (☎ 604-688-2207)

Ferry

BC Ferries (☎ 604-277-0277) operates the ferry routes between the mainland and Vancouver Island. The main route is from Tsawwassen to Swartz Bay, just north of Sidney. There are between 8 and 15 ferries in each direction depending on the day and season. Sunday afternoon, Friday evening and holidays are the busiest times and if you have a car there is often a one- or two-ferry wait. To avoid long delays it's worth planning to cross at other times if you can.

Ferries also operate to Nanaimo from Tsawwassen and Horseshoe Bay. The one-way fare on all routes is C$7.50 per adult, C$2.50 for a bicycle and C$24 per car (driver not included). Call ☎ 604-277-0277 for information.

To get to Tsawwassen from downtown Vancouver by city bus, catch the south-bound bus No 601 from the corner of Granville St and W 4th Ave to the Ladner Exchange. From the exchange take bus No 640 to the ferry terminal. A quicker way is to catch the SkyTrain to Scotts Rd Station and there catch the No 640. The fare either way is C$1.50, or C$3 if you travel in peak traffic time. From Swartz Bay you can take bus No 70 into Victoria. To get to Horseshoe Bay from Vancouver take bus No 250 or 257 northbound on Georgia St.

GETTING AROUND

For BC Transit information, call ☎ 604-521-0400 or obtain at least one of the two publications they produce on getting around the city. One is the *Transit Guide*, a map of Greater Vancouver showing bus, train and ferry routes. It costs C$1.25 and can be bought at newsstands and bookstores. *Discover Vancouver on Transit* lists many of the city's attractions and how to get there (and includes Victoria). It's free and is available at the Travel InfoCentre.

To/From the Airport
There are two ways of getting between the airport and downtown by bus – a city bus or the Vancouver Airporter. But the quickest is to take one of the Vancouver Airporter (☎ 604-244-9888) buses, which run from the Pacific Central Station and all major central hotels for C$9 (C$15 return with no time limit). Tickets can be purchased from the driver. Buses leave the airport every 30 minutes starting at 6:15 am and take about 30 minutes. Buses going to downtown hotels leave the airport from level 2, with the last one departing about 12:15 am; for the bus station, buses leave from bay 9 on level 1.

To get to the airport by city bus, take No 20 south on Granville St to 70th Ave. From there transfer to bus No 100 which will take you to the airport. From the airport, do the reverse. The total travel time is one hour and the fare is C$1.50 (C$3 during peak traffic time). You need to have exact change.

A taxi between downtown Vancouver and the airport takes about 25 minutes and costs around C$30.

Bus, SkyTrain & SeaBus
BC Transit (☎ 604-521-0400) offers three modes of public transportation: regular buses, the SkyTrain elevated light-rail system and the SeaBus ferries to North Vancouver.

The transport system is divided into three zones: the inner zone covers central Vancouver; the next zone includes the suburbs of Richmond, Burnaby, New Westminster, North Vancouver, West Vancouver and Sea Island; the outer zone covers Ladner, Tsaw-

wassen, Delta, Surrey, White Rock, Langley, Port Moody and Coquitlam.

During off-peak times (between 9:30 am and 3 pm and after 6:30 pm Monday to Friday, plus weekends and public holidays) you pay a flat C$1.50 for a single journey good for the bus, SkyTrain or SeaBus. In peak times it depends on how many zones you travel across: C$1.50 for one zone, C$2.25 for two, C$3 for three. All-day transit passes are C$4.50 (good for unlimited rides on the bus, SkyTrain and SeaBus after 9:30 am weekdays and all day weekends). Purchase passes at the SkyTrain or SeaBus stations or from shops displaying the 'FareDealer' sign.

SkyTrain The wheelchair-accessible SkyTrain connects downtown Vancouver with Burnaby, New Westminster and Whalley in Surrey. The trains are fully computerized (ie, there's no driver!) and travel mostly above ground along a specially designed track. The trains are scheduled to connect with buses. They leave from Waterfront Station downtown; other handy downtown stops are at Granville St and the Stadium stop, near GM Place.

SeaBus These super-modern catamarans zip back and forth across Burrard Inlet between Waterfront Station downtown and Lonsdale Quay in North Vancouver. They leave every 15 minutes on weekdays, every half-hour at other times. The trip lasts only 12 minutes but gives good views of the harbor and city skyline. Try to avoid rush hours when many commuters are crowding aboard.

Car
If you're driving, you'll notice the city doesn't have any expressways: everyone must travel through the city. Congestion is a big problem, especially along the Lions Gate Bridge (probably best avoided altogether), and Second Narrows Bridge. Hardly any downtown streets have left-hand turn signals, and traffic can back up for blocks during rush hours, especially

with people trying to get onto Georgia St from the south. On a wet or snowy day it's worse: try to avoid rush hours. It's also costly to park and/or very difficult to find a parking spot in the inner city. You're better off parking the car out a bit and catching a bus or SkyTrain into the center; it'll probably be quicker and better for your blood pressure, too.

Taxi
Unless you're staying at a big hotel, your best bet is to phone for a cab; trying to hail one in the streets is likely to prove unsuccessful. Three of the companies are Black Top (☎ 604-683-4567), MacLure's (☎ 604-731-9211, 604-683-6666) and Yellow Cab (☎ 604-681-3311/1111).

Bicycle
Cycling is a good way to get around town, though riding on the sidewalk is illegal and bikes are not allowed on the SeaBus. Get a copy of the Bicycling Association of BC's cycling map of the city, which you can get at the Travel InfoCentres or bike shops. To rent a bike, contact:

Action Rentals, 1793 Robson St
    (☎ 604-683-7044)
Bayshore Bicycles, 745 Denman St
    (☎ 604-688-2453)
Kitzco Beachwear & Rentals, 1168 Denman St
    (☎ 604-684-6269)
Spokes Bicycle Rental & Espresso Bar,
    1798 W Georgia St (☎ 604-688-5141)

There are others so check the yellow pages. Rates start at C$6 an hour, C$15 for four hours or C$20 a day.

Ferry
Two companies operate mini passenger ferry shuttles across False Creek. From 10 am to 8 pm daily Granville Island Ferries (☎ 604-684-7781) runs between the Vancouver Aquatic Centre near Sunset Beach, Granville Island, the Vancouver Maritime Museum at Kitsilano Point and Stamp's Landing near the Cambie Bridge. The Aquabus (☎ 604-689-5858) travels be-

tween the Arts Club Theatre, located on Granville Island, and Hornby St (downtown) via Stamp's Landing and the Concord-Yaletown dock near BC Place. Basic fares are C$1.75.

Water Taxi
If your destination is directly accessible by water, you might want to consider making an entrance on a water taxi. Burrard Water Taxi (☎ 604-293-1160) offers 24-hour water-taxi service to the greater Vancouver maritime region.

North of Vancouver

WHISTLER & AROUND
Whistler is one of the top ski resorts in North America, and has plenty of recreation options even if you are visiting in summer. Don't assume you can't ski if it's high summer in Vancouver: Whistler has runs that remain open nearly year-round. In summer, you can also go hiking, cycling, canoeing, take the cable car up the mountain or visit an aquatic park.

Scenic Drive to Whistler
If you feel like getting out of the city, there are few more scenic routes than this 120km (75-mile) drive from Vancouver: the mountain scenery here rivals the Canadian Rockies. If you're driving, allow plenty of time – the road is narrow, hilly and winding; besides you'll be enjoying the views. Better yet, take one of the train tours that allow you to gawk and photograph all you want.

After leaving Horseshoe Bay, Hwy 99 edges along Howe Sound to **Squamish**, noted for its rock climbing. The granite cliffs here are some of the world's longest unbroken rock faces; pull over and watch for climbers hanging from the rock like colorful spiders. Another good stop is **Shannon Falls**, a very impressive waterfall which cascades 330m (1100 feet) from the granite cliff.

Just northeast of Squamish is **Garibaldi Provincial Park**, a 195-sq-km (76-sq-mile) mountain wilderness. Most of the park is undeveloped and is well known mostly for its hiking areas – Diamond Head, Garibaldi Lake, Cheakamus Lake, Singing Pass and Wedgemount Lake – covered by more than 67km (42 miles) of developed trails. The trails become cross-country ski runs in winter.

Whistler Village

Built almost entirely from scratch, starting in the 1980s, the resorts, hotels and shopping precincts of Whistler were designed to look and feel much older: the massive hotels look like castles and even shopping centers are built of venerable-looking quarried stone. The commercial center of Whistler is a European-like pedestrian village with winding streets, brightly lit shops, fine restaurants and boisterous après-ski brewpubs. Whistler Village has a sort of contrived feel about it – it is very new – but the skiers, shoppers and hikers who gather are having fun and they lend the place a light, relaxing atmosphere.

Skiing

Whistler ski district has three centers: Whistler Village itself, **Blackcomb** (at the base of one of the two lifts) and **Whistler Creek**. The latter is the least expensive, while the village has the most action and socializing – with the larger hotels it is also more costly. Together the three areas make up Canada's largest ski resort.

Blackcomb Mountain has the largest downhill ski area in North America, offering 8500m (5280 feet) of continuous skiing. Whistler Mountain is a close second with 8060m (5006 feet). The usually reliable snow, the vertical drop and mild Pacific air combine to provide some of the most pleasant skiing to be found anywhere, from novice slopes to glacier skiing. The latter is available pretty much all year, providing the country's only summer skiing. Heli-skiing companies based in Whistler Village offer services to more than a 100 other runs on glaciers

near the resort. Snowboarders consider Whistler Mountain, with banked runs and rocky bluffs, to be a boarder's dream come true. There are cross-country trails as well.

For information about either ski slope, or for any of the facilities (including lodgings) in Whistler, contact the central reservation desk (☎ 604-932-4222, 604-664-5625 in Vancouver, 800-944-7853). For a snow report, call ☎ 604-932-4191; in Vancouver call ☎ 604-687-6761.

A one-day lift ticket costs C$55, though there are several ways to reduce the price (including buying your ticket in advance at a 7-11 or a Save-On Food store in Vancouver, for C$48). There are also reduced prices for using particular credit cards.

Places to Stay

By far the easiest way to make reservations is to use the central reservation service (☎ 604-932-3141, 604-687-1032 in Vancouver, 800-944-7853). They can book you rooms at nearly any of the area's two dozen inns and lodges. In winter, expect rooms to begin at C$100 a night, and to go up quickly from there. There are some off-season discounts, though not as many as you might expect: Whistler also does a brisk trade in conventions.

VANCOUVER

Most rooms in Whistler are rather spendy, though there are some budget options. HI *Whistler Hostel* (☎ 604-932-5492) is in a beautiful setting on Alta Lake (on West Rd) about 4km (2½ miles) by foot from Whistler Village. Dorm-style accommodations are C$17.50 for members and C$22.50 nonmembers. With room for just 35 people, it's a good idea to book ahead especially during ski season. The *Whistler Backpackers Guest House* (☎ 604-932-1177), 2124 Lake Placid Rd, in Whistler, is close to the center of things. Private and shared rooms start from C$18 a day in winter, C$15 in summer. The *Shoestring Lodge* (☎ 604-932-3338), at 7124 Nancy Greene Drive, has dorm beds from C$24; private rooms start at C$99. Nesters Rd, about 1.5km (1 mile) north of the village, has several moderately priced pension-style B&Bs.

Places to Eat

There are over 90 restaurants in Whistler, most of them concentrated in the large pedestrian district in Whistler Village. You'll have no trouble finding something good to eat. Like everything else in Whistler, dining is quite expensive, though there are a number of inexpensive options. For Thai food, go to *Thai One On* (☎ 604-932-4822), 4557 Blackcomb Way. *Amami Restaurant* (☎ 604-932-6431), in the Westbrook Whistler Hotel in Whistler Village, is the resort's best Chinese restaurant. For family dining, try *Blacks* (☎ 604-932-6408), 4270 Mountain Square, or the dependable *Spaghetti Factory* (☎ 604-939-1081), in the Crystal Lodge, Whistler Village. Another less expensive dining option is to eat in one of the resort's many bars and pubs.

If you want to splurge, then Whistler has some excellent restaurants. Well-loved, the *Rim Rock Cafe* (☎ 604-932-5565), 2101 Whistler Rd, is one of the top dining rooms, though without undue pretension. Fresh seafood is the specialty. Of the droves of Italian-Northwest cuisine-style restaurants here, probably the best is *Araxi* (☎ 604-932-4540), in the Village Square, Whistler Village. Another standout is *La Rua* (☎ 604-932-5011), in Le Chamois Hotel, Blackcomb, with a number of game dishes and inventive Northwest cooking.

Getting There & Away

Maverick Coach Lines (☎ 604-255-1171) has six buses daily to Whistler from Pacific Central Station in Vancouver. The fare is C$17/32 one way/return. There's one train daily from Vancouver to Whistler on BC Rail (☎ 604-984-5246); the one-way fare is C$29. You can also fly into Whistler from Vancouver on North Vancouver Air (☎ 800-228-6608).

SUNSHINE COAST

The name refers to the coastal area north of Horseshoe Bay to Lund, 24km (15 miles) north of Powell River. It's a narrow strip of land separated from the mainland by the Coast Mountains. The scenery is excellent: hills, mountains, forests, inlets, harbors and beaches. Slow and winding Hwy 101, edging along the coast, is broken at two separate points where you'll need to take a ferry – from Horseshoe Bay to Langdale and from Earls Cove to Saltery Bay. The highway ends completely at Lund. At Powell River there is a ferry over to Comox on Vancouver Island. For information about the ferries, call BC Ferries (☎ 604-277-0277) or pick up a copy of their schedules from one of the Travel InfoCentres.

The region remains quiet but is increasingly busy with both commuters and visitors. For the latter, it can be part of an interesting circuit from Vancouver, around Vancouver Island and back. BC Ferries offers a circular ferry ticket known as the Sunshine Coast Circlepac which includes all four ferries around the loop – to Vancouver Island via Horseshoe Bay or Tsawwassen, then across to Powell River, and then down by Sunshine Coast with ferries at Egmont and Gibbons – at a good reduction from full fare. Economical bus service is available between Vancouver and Powell River, with the two ferries included.

Sechelt and Powell River are the commercial and activity centers of the coast. Aside from the good hiking, camping and fishing in the area, these towns are bases for some of the world's best diving, although it's not for novices and local guides should be used.

In **Powell River**, the Travel InfoCentre (☎ 604-485-4701) is at 4690 Marine Ave. The Beach Gardens Resort Hotel (☎ 604-485-6267), 7074 Westminster Ave, rents boats and diving equipment and runs charters out to dive spots such as the submarine cave formations in Okeover Inlet near Lund. From Powell River there is a 65km (40-mile) canoeing circuit which takes five to seven days.

North of Lund, **Desolation Sound Provincial Marine Park** has abundant wildlife, diving, canoeing and wilderness camping.

Places to Stay & Eat

Accommodations around Powell River include hotels, motels and campgrounds. The *Beach Gardens Resort Hotel* (☎ 604-485-6267), 7074 Westminster St, is one of the more upscale places to stay along the Sunshine Coast, with an indoor pool, fitness center, a good restaurant and easy access to recreation. Rooms begin at C$90/99 single/double. Central and less expensive is *Westview Centre Motel* (☎ 604-485-4023), 4534 Marine Ave, with basic rooms at C$44/56. If you're heading north to Desolation Sound Marine Park, try the European-style pension lodging at *Cedar Lodge B&B Resort* (☎ 604-483-4414), 27km (17 miles) north of Powell River off Hwy 99. There are six units, starting at C$45/50.

Vancouver Island

The attractions of Vancouver Island, the largest island off the west coast of the Americas, range from its rugged wilderness to the grand rooms of its provincial legislature. The island is 450km (279 miles) long and has a population of more than 500,000 people, most of whom live along the southeastern coast.

The geography is scenically varied. A mountain range runs down the center of the island, with its snow-capped peaks setting off the woods and many lakes and streams. The coast can be either rocky and tempestuous or sandy and calm.

Vancouver Island is a popular destination for tourists and Victoria especially can get crowded during mid-summer. For those seeking quieter spots, a little effort will be rewarded, particularly for those who make their way up to northern Vancouver Island.

Victoria

Population 300,000

Victoria, the second largest city in British Columbia and the provincial capital, lies at the southeastern end of Vancouver Island, 90km (56 miles) southwest of Vancouver. Although bounded on three sides by water, Victoria is sheltered from the Pacific Ocean by the Olympic Peninsula across the Strait of Juan de Fuca in Washington State.

With the mildest climate in Canada, architecturally compelling buildings, an interesting history and its famed gardens and parks, it's not surprising that 2 million tourists visit Victoria annually. This quiet, traditional seat of civilization was once described by Rudyard Kipling as 'Brighton Pavilion with the Himalayas for a backdrop.'

Many people come here expecting to find a kind of Olde English theme park; certainly that is the city's reputation and the point of much of the hype generated by the tourist industry. However, anyone who thinks that Victoria is 'English' hasn't been to England recently, and as for this being a city where the Victorian era still prevails, well, go read your British history.

The truth is that Victoria was settled by the same amalgam of trappers, merchants and explorers that settled the rest of the Pacific Northwest some 150 years ago. However, when the line was drawn between Oregon Country and Canada, the first pioneers chose to settle in Victoria in order to keep their British passports. From the time that the US took over Oregon and Washington, up until very recently, an undue emphasis and value has been placed on a British birthright (as opposed to the birthright of neighbors in the US, Native Canadians or settlers from places other than the Scepter'd Isle). Victoria gained its reputation for being more English than England as presumed 'Englishness' became the coin that bought prestige and cachet in the young city.

Nowadays, it's not clear any longer what's authentic and what's laid on for the tourists, but Victoria remains a charming city on a lovely bay. If the crowds thronging the narrow streets get to you, take a whale-watching cruise, or spend a couple hours in the city's excellent museums.

Although it is the provincial capital and home to an important university and naval base, Victoria is not an industrial city. About 30% of its 300,000 or so residents work in tourist and service-oriented businesses, while another 20% work in the public sector. The island is also a major retirement center, with retirees making up around 20% of the population. Along with Vancouver, it is one of the faster-growing cities in Canada.

HISTORY

Victoria's first residents were the Salish Indians, who fished and hunted on the protected bay. Although Nootka Sound, on Vancouver Island's northwest coast, was the site of trade between natives and English Captain James Cook in 1778, and had seen a Spanish settlement in 1792, the felicitous site of future Victoria was not colonized until 1843, when James Douglas, acting for the Hudson's Bay Company

Captain James Cook

(HBC), founded Fort Victoria as a fur-trading post.

The history of BC departs from that of Washington and Oregon when the British and US governments in 1846 resolved their border dispute by fixing the US-Canadian border at the 49th parallel. The HBC, which heretofore had controlled the entire Pacific Northwest from its headquarters at Fort Vancouver, near present day Portland, re-established its head of operations at Fort Victoria. Many of the region's British citizens also moved north from the new US Oregon Territory. In order to better protect its interests and citizens, the British government, in 1849, established Vancouver Island as a crown colony, just in case the Americans got more expansionist-minded. However, the white population in the Victoria area – then the only settled area of what would become British Columbia – was still small: in 1854 the population counted only 250 white people.

Then, in 1858, gold-rush fever struck this remote area of the British empire. The discovery of gold along the Fraser River brought in a flood of people seeking their fortune. By far the vast majority of the estimated 30,000 gold seekers who streamed into the area were Americans who came north from the by-now-spent California gold fields. Fearing domination of mainland Canada by the US, in 1858 Britain named the mainland as a new colony, called British Columbia. In 1866 the two colonies – Vancouver Island and the mainland – merged as the new British colony of British Columbia.

A State or a Province?
As population and trade increased, the need for greater political organization grew. As a colony, BC had little local control, and was largely governed by edict from Whitehall. If BC and its population were to have greater freedom and self-determination, the growing colony had two choices: join the prosperous United States to the south, with which it shared much history and many commercial ties, or join the new Dominion of Canada far to the east

(Britain allowed its former colonies of Upper and Lower Canada to merge as a quasi-independent entity – a dominion – in 1867).

Joining the US made a lot of sense to many in BC, as there were already strong regional ties, and Washington, DC, sent dispatches promising accommodations if BC were to join the States. In many ways, joining Canada made little sense: settlement in eastern Canada was centered in Ontario and Quebec, and between BC and these population and trade centers lay thousands of miles of trackless wilderness. The political debate raged in the colony's drawing rooms and in Victoria's pugnacious newspapers. After Ottawa promised to build a railroad to link eastern and western Canada in 1870, delegates from BC voted to join Canada in 1871 as the province of British Columbia. Victoria was named capital.

The 20th Century
For Victoria, without a rail link to the rest of Canada or the US, industrial growth was not an issue and the city didn't experience the same boom-and-bust cycles that many of the manufacturing and mercantile cities of the West did. The city's beautiful location was an early draw: the fabulous Empress Hotel opened in 1908, and the tourist trade began in earnest. As the seat of emerging political power and with an increasing reputation as a graceful social center, Victoria blossomed in its own way.

Since the war years, Victoria and BC have generally prospered economically, especially under the leadership of the Social Credit Party, supposedly the party of small business. Father and son premiers, WAC and Bill Bennett, effectively ruled the province and the Social Credit Party from 1952 until 1986. With close ties between government ministers and the resources they oversaw, business – especially manufacturing, mining and logging – certainly boomed, but along with prosperity came significant governmental scandals, opportunistic financial shenanigans and major resource mismanagement. Social Credit

Premier Bill Vander Zalm was forced to resign in 1991; reform-minded governments have been in place in Victoria since.

Today, there are still more British-born residents in Victoria than anywhere else in Canada, and they have entrenched their style rather than forgotten it. Rising numbers of immigrants and visitors from around the world are imparting an increasingly cosmopolitan air.

ORIENTATION

The city lies at the southeastern tip of Vancouver Island, actually closer to the USA than to the Canadian mainland. The downtown area is simply laid out and really not very large. Bounded on two sides by water, the central area of the city has very few high-rise buildings, and is easy and pleasant to explore on foot; you'll have little trouble getting your bearings.

The focal point is the Inner Harbour, a section of Victoria Harbour surrounded by several of the city's most important structures. The Empress Hotel faces out over its lawns to the waterfront. Across the way are the enormous provincial Parliament Buildings. In between the two is the Royal BC Museum. To the east of the museum is Thunderbird Park, with its totem poles, and south of this is Beacon Hill Park, the city's largest park. Surrounding the park and extending down to the ocean are well-kept residential houses, many with attractive lawns and gardens.

Along Wharf St, north of the Empress Hotel, is the central Travel InfoCentre, overlooking of the Inner Harbour. Following Wharf St north along the water will take you through Old Town, the restored original area of Victoria, to Bastion Square, the city's old central square and the site of old Fort Victoria. Parallel to Wharf St and a couple of blocks east is Government St, a principal shopping street and tourist hub, also lined with historic buildings. One block east is Douglas St, downtown's main thoroughfare and busy commercial center.

The northern boundary of the downtown area is marked by Fisgard St, between Government and Store Sts, which has a small Chinatown with Oriental-style street lamps and buildings, Chinese characters on the street signs and, of course, restaurants. The area is remarkably neat and clean and very colorful, due mainly to the brightly painted facades of the buildings. Fan Tan Alley, in the middle of Chinatown, has a few small shops and connects Fisgard St with Pandora Ave. In the 1860s when this alley – Canada's first Chinatown – was in its heyday and much bigger, it was lined with opium dens and gambling houses. It's a lot quieter now with no evidence of those early vice-filled days. To keep it that way, the alley is locked at night.

Beyond Downtown

Following Fort St east up the hill and then along Oak Bay Ave will lead you through the 'tweed curtain' to the wealthier, very British area of Oak Bay. The InfoCentre has information on walks to take in this attractive and traditional district.

Both Douglas and Blanshard Sts lead north out of the city: the former to the Trans Canada Hwy (Hwy 1) and Nanaimo, the latter to Hwy 17 (Patricia Bay Hwy), Sidney and the Swartz Bay ferry terminal. To the northwest of downtown is Gorge Rd, an area of heavy motel concentration. It forms part of Hwy 1A, which cuts across Douglas St, runs along the northern side of the gorge and meets up farther west with Craigflower Rd and the Trans Canada Hwy.

Victoria International Airport is in Sidney, about 19km (12 miles) north of Victoria on Hwy 17. The bus station is at 700 Douglas St, on the corner of Belleville St and opposite Crystal Garden.

INFORMATION
Tourist Offices

The Travel InfoCentre (☎ 250-382-2127), 812 Wharf St, is by the water at the Inner Harbour, kitty-corner from the Empress Hotel. It has dozens of pamphlets, maps and information on shopping, sightseeing, transportation, where to stay and where to eat. Ask about the free walking tours at the Travel InfoCentre. The InfoCentre also operates a room reservation service. It's open 9 am to 9 pm daily (Sunday till 7 pm). There is also an office 2km (1 mile) south of the Swartz Bay ferry terminal on Patricia Bay Hwy, and another in Sidney.

If you'd like to find out more about Victoria before you arrive, contact Tourism Victoria (☎ 250-382-2127), 710-1175 Douglas St, Victoria, BC V8W 2E1.

Money

The major banks have branches along Douglas St. The Toronto Dominion Bank, 1070-1080 Douglas St, has regular banking hours, plus it's open on Saturday from 9:30 am to 4:30 pm. You can change money at Money Mart, 1720 Douglas St, opposite the Bay department store, and at Currency Exchange, 724 Douglas St, opposite the Budget car-rental office; its hours are 7 am to 9:30 pm daily. You can also change money at American Express (☎ 250-385-8731), 1203 Douglas St. US currency is accepted in many establishments but usually at a poorer exchange rate than found at money exchange offices or banks.

Post & Communications

The main post office (☎ 250-935-1351) is at 714 Yates St. It's closed on Sunday. The area code for Vancouver is 250.

Travel Agencies

Travel CUTS (☎ 250-721-6916, 800-663-6000) is located in the University of Victoria Student Union Building.

Bookstores

The city's best bookstore is Munro's Books (☎ 250-382-2464), 1108 Government St. Munro's is in a beautiful old building originally built for the Royal Bank and restored in 1984. It is now classified as a heritage building; the atmosphere inside is almost ecclesiastical and is worth a look even if you aren't in the market for a book. Munro's sells a whole range of books and has a good Canadiana section.

Chapters (☎ 250-380-9009), at 1212 Douglas St, has writers and literary speakers almost nightly. Crown Publica-

tions (☎ 250-386-4636), 546 Yates St, sells maps, federal and provincial publications on Canadiana, as well as books on Native Indian culture, nature and travel guides. Maps BC (☎ 250-387-1441), 3rd floor, 1802 Douglas St, is a government office with maps and atlases of the province.

Bolen Books, at 1644 Hillside Ave, in the Hillside Shopping Centre, is the largest independent bookstore in Victoria and has a particularly good selection of computer books.

There are also a number of secondhand bookstores along Fort St, including Renaissance Books next to Da Tandoor restaurant. Consider buying a copy of the booklet *Victoria on Foot* (Terrapin, Victoria, 1989), by Barrie Lee, which gives details of walking tours around the Old Town.

Newspapers & Magazines

The daily paper is the *Times Colonist*. Arts and entertainment news is featured in the weekly *Monday Magazine*.

Laundry

If your hotel doesn't have a laundry, then head over to Maytag Homestyle Laundry (☎ 250-386-1799), 1309 Cook St, with self-service machines, drop-off service and dry cleaning.

Medical Services

If your medical needs aren't grave, then avoid the emergency room and head to the Mayfair Medical Treatment Centre (☎ 250-360-2282), 3147 Douglas St, in the Mayfair Shopping Mall. It's open daily and you don't need an appointment. The Royal Jubilee Hospital (☎ 250-595-9200, 250-595-9212 in an emergency) is at 1900 Fort St.

Useful Organizations

Greenpeace (☎ 250-388-4325), 202-620 View St, has details of environmental issues and helps to organize information nights. Friendly by Nature (☎ 250-388-9292) in Bastion Square, has information on environmental issues in BC and sells T-shirts, etc.

VANCOUVER ISLAND

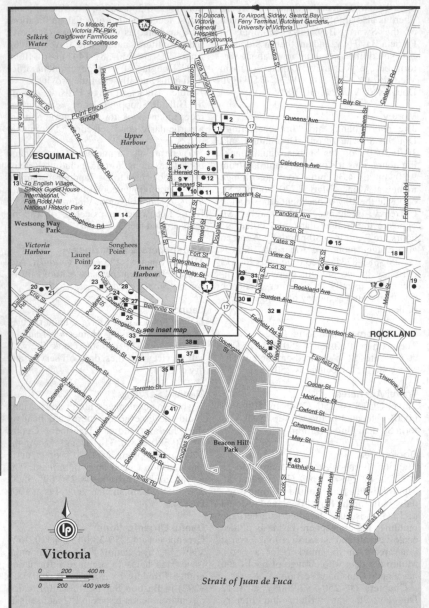

To Motels, Fort
Victoria RV Park,
Craigflower Farmhouse
& Schoolhouse

To Duncan,
Victoria
General
Hospital

To Airport, Sidney, Swartz Bay
Ferry Terminal, Butchart Gardens,
University of Victoria

Selkirk
Water

ESQUIMALT

Esquimalt Rd

To English Village,
Selkirk Guest House
International,
Fort Rodd Hill
National Historic Park

Westsong Way
Park

Victoria
Harbour

Laurel
Point

Upper
Harbour

Point Ellice
Bridge

Songhees
Point

Inner
Harbour

see inset map

VANCOUVER ISLAND

ROCKLAND

Beacon Hill
Park

Victoria

0   200   400 m
0   200   400 yards

Strait of Juan de Fuca

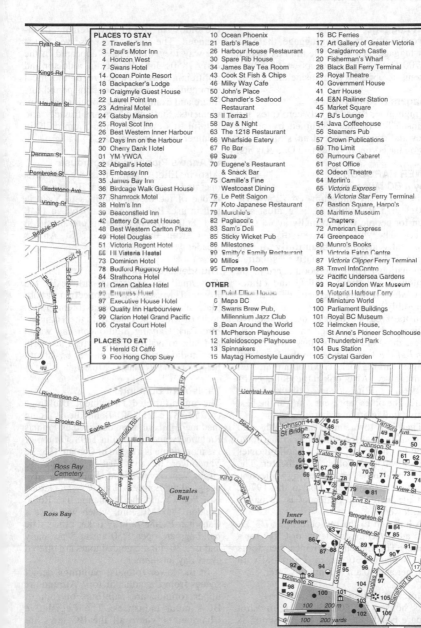

PLACES TO STAY

2 Traveller's Inn
3 Paul's Motor Inn
4 Horizon West
7 Swans Hotel
14 Ocean Pointe Resort
18 Backpacker's Lodge
19 Craigmyle Guest House
22 Laurel Point Inn
23 Admiral Motel
24 Gatsby Mansion
25 Royal Scot Inn
26 Best Western Inner Harbour
27 Days Inn on the Harbour
30 Cherry Bank Hotel
31 YM YWCA
32 Abigail's Hotel
33 Embassy Inn
35 James Bay Inn
36 Birdcage Walk Guest House
37 Shamrock Motel
38 Helm's Inn
39 Beaconsfield Inn
42 Battery St Guest House
48 Best Western Carlton Plaza
49 Hotel Douglas
51 Victoria Regent Hotel
55 HI Victoria Hostel
73 Dominion Hotel
78 Bedford Regency Hotel
84 Strathcona Hotel
91 Green Gables Hotel
96 Empress Hotel
97 Executive House Hotel
98 Quality Inn Harbourview
99 Clarion Hotel Grand Pacific
106 Crystal Court Hotel

PLACES TO EAT

5 Herald St Caffé
9 Foo Hong Chop Suey
10 Ocean Phoenix
21 Barb's Place
26 Harbour House Restaurant
30 Spare Rib House
34 James Bay Tea Room
43 Cook St Fish & Chips
46 Milky Way Cafe
50 John's Place
52 Chandler's Seafood
   Restaurant
53 Il Terrazi
58 Day & Night
63 The 1218 Restaurant
66 Wharfside Eatery
67 Re Bar
69 Suze
70 Eugene's Restaurant
   & Snack Bar
75 Camille's Fine
   Westcoast Dining
76 Le Petit Saigon
77 Koto Japanese Restaurant
79 Murchie's
82 Pagliacci's
83 Sam's Deli
85 Sticky Wicket Pub
86 Milestones
89 Smitty's Family Restaurant
90 Millos
95 Empress Room

OTHER

1 Point Ellice House
6 Maps BC
7 Swans Brew Pub,
   Millennium Jazz Club
8 Bean Around the World
11 McPherson Playhouse
12 Kaleidoscope Playhouse
13 Spinnakers
15 Maytag Homestyle Laundry
16 BC Ferries
17 Art Gallery of Greater Victoria
19 Craigdarroch Castle
20 Fisherman's Wharf
28 Black Ball Ferry Terminal
29 Royal Theatre
40 Government House
41 Carr House
44 E&N Railiner Station
45 Market Square
47 BJ's Lounge
54 Java Coffeehouse
56 Steamers Pub
57 Crown Publications
59 The Limit
60 Rumours Cabaret
61 Post Office
62 Odeon Theatre
64 Merlin's
65 Victoria Express
   & Victoria Star Ferry Terminal
67 Bastion Square, Harpo's
68 Maritime Museum
71 Chapters
72 American Express
74 Greenpeace
80 Munro's Books
81 Victoria Eaton Centre
87 Victoria Clipper Ferry Terminal
88 Travel InfoCentre
92 Pacific Undersea Gardens
93 Royal London Wax Museum
94 Victoria Harbour Ferry
96 Miniature World
100 Parliament Buildings
101 Royal BC Museum
102 Helmcken House,
   St Anne's Pioneer Schoolhouse
103 Thunderbird Park
104 Bus Station
105 Crystal Garden

VANCOUVER ISLAND

Left Luggage

If you want to store your luggage, there are left-luggage lockers beside the bus station at 700 Douglas St. Lockers cost C$2.50; tokens are obtained from inside the station.

Dangers & Annoyances

At nighttime, Broad St between Yates and Johnson Sts is often occupied by prostitutes and drunks. Some drunks also hang out on the corner of Yates and Douglas Sts.

INNER HARBOUR

Royal BC Museum

This excellent museum (☎ 250-387-3701), 675 Belleville St, is a must-see, even for people who normally avoid such places. The wide variety of displays is artistically arranged, beautifully lit and accompanied by informative, succinct explanations. There are good sections on geology, vegetation, wildlife and ethnology. Many of the models and exhibits are incredibly realistic.

In the areas devoted to the BC Native Indians, see the detailed models of villages, the 1914 documentary film *In the Land of the War Canoes* on the Kwakiutl people, and the rock on which a man 'fell from the sky.' Also look at the Haida craftwork in argillite, a dense black carbon shale. The pipes represent some of the best Native Indian art anywhere.

There's a town made up of 19th- and early-20th-century buildings and goods, including a Model T Ford. Chaplin movies are shown in the old movie theater. The museum also has an interesting collection of artifacts from the 1920s to the 1970s. Outside there is a garden of BC's native wildflowers.

Admission to the museum is C$7/3.25/ 2.15 adults/seniors/students, or C$14 for a family. The museum provides free tours and is open 9:30 am to 7 pm daily in summer and 10 am to 5 pm in winter.

Helmcken House

This house (☎ 250-387-4697), in Eliot Square beside the Royal BC Museum, is the oldest in BC to have remained unchanged. The rooms are preserved much the way they would have appeared in the early 1850s. John Helmcken, a doctor and politician, was very active in the local community. The house contains period furniture and examples of decorations and implements. Staff members are friendly and helpful. It's open 11 am to 5 pm daily in summer and admission is C$4.

St Anne's Pioneer Schoolhouse

Also in Eliot Square, this schoolhouse, operated as part of the Royal BC Museum, is one of the oldest buildings in Victoria still in use. Built sometime between 1840 and 1860, it was moved to its present site in 1974 from the grounds of St Anne's Academy.

Thunderbird Park

This small but interesting park beside the Royal BC Museum has a collection of both plain and painted wooden totem poles, some of which are labeled. In the Thunderbird Park Carving Studio you can watch and talk to Native Indian artists at work. The studio is run on a volunteer basis with help from the Royal BC Museum.

Parliament Buildings

The multi-turreted Parliament Buildings (☎ 250-387-6121), 501 Belleville St facing the Inner Harbour, were designed by Francis Rattenbury and finished in 1898. On top of the main dome is a figure of Captain George Vancouver, the first British navigator to circle Vancouver Island. Rattenbury also designed the Empress Hotel, Crystal Garden (see below) and the Parthenon-like Royal London Wax Museum, which was once a Canadian Pacific railway ticket office. The buildings are open 8:30 am to 5 pm daily and free 30-minute guided tours are offered every day in summer.

In the lower rotunda, paintings depict scenes from Canadian history. Around the upper rotunda are paintings of four of BC's main industries. The Legislative Chamber is where all the BC laws are

Captain George Vancouver

made (there is no Senate in the provincial parliament). You can view the debates from the public gallery when the session is in. In the Legislative Library is the dagger used to kill Captain Cook in Hawaii, while on the lawn are a statue of Queen Victoria and a sequoia tree from California planted in the 1860s. The buildings are lit spectacularly at night, by more than 3000 lightbulbs.

Pacific Undersea Gardens
A sort of natural aquarium, the gardens (☎ 250-382-5717), are found on the Inner Harbour at 490 Belleville St. Visitors descend beneath the water's surface to view a range of corralled sea creatures such as octopuses, eels, crabs, etc. Children especially find it intriguing. Admission is C$7/6.25 adults/seniors, C$5 students (12 to 17) and C$3.50 children.

Royal London Wax Museum
This museum (☎ 250-388-4461), 470 Belleville St, in front of the Parliament Buildings, contains more than 200 wax models of historical and contemporary fig-

ures. It's open 9 am to 9 pm daily and costs C$7/6.50/3 adults/seniors/students.

Miniature World
At Miniature World (☎ 250-385-9731), 649 Humboldt St, beside the Empress Hotel, you'll find numerous layouts depicting (in exact detail) various themes, such as the world of Dickens. The highlight is a large model train representing the development of the Canadian Pacific railway from 1885 to 1915. Miniature World is open 9 am to 8 pm daily and admission is C$7/6/5 adults/ students/children.

Crystal Garden
This site (☎ 250-381-1277), 713 Douglas St, is one of the more popular commercial attractions. The principal draw is the colorful tropical-like garden complete with 65 varieties of international endangered animals and birds as well as free-flying butterflies. Designed by Francis Rattenbury, it was fashioned after London's Crystal Palace and built in 1925. Once a focal point for the social elite, it was restored in 1977 as a visitor attraction, but remains a venue for splashy events. It's open 10 am to 9 pm daily in July and August; the rest of the year it closes at 5:30 pm. Admission is C$7/6/4 adults/seniors/children.

OLD TOWN & GOVERNMENT ST
The original Victoria was centered along Wharf St and Bastion Square. This was where the first fur-trading ships moored. Wharf St was once busy with miners, merchants and all those fortune seekers heading for the Klondike.

Bastion Square, along Wharf St between Yates and Fort Sts, was where Fort Victoria was situated and held the courthouse, jail, gallows and brothel. The whole area has been restored and redeveloped. The square is pleasant for strolling around and people watching. Many of the old buildings are now restaurants, boutiques, galleries or offices.

Farther north along Wharf St you'll come to **Market Square**, a former warehouse on

VANCOUVER ISLAND

the corner of Johnson St, dating from the 1890s. Renovated in 1975, this compact, attractive area now has two floors of over 40 shops and restaurants, built around a courtyard shaded by trees. Take a look at the **holograms** in the store which bills itself as an art gallery. They're pretty amazing, easily superior to those generally seen.

Busy Government St is an especially attractive street, with many fine shops and handsome Victorian buildings. It's especially lovely at night, when the structures are lit.

Maritime Museum
This collection of artifacts, models, photographs and naval memorabilia is for nautical buffs only, although everybody will find the elevator inside the front door worth a look. The museum (☎ 250-385-4222), 28 Bastion Square near Government St, is open 9:30 am to 4:30 pm daily and admission is C$5/4/3/2 adults/seniors/students/children.

Victoria Eaton Centre
Although this is a shopping center, it's worth a wandering around. The complex incorporates the facades of the original buildings. As well as shops and eateries, it has fountains, pools and a rooftop garden. It occupies two blocks between Government and Douglas Sts, and between View and Broughton Sts.

FISHERMAN'S WHARF
Just west of the Inner Harbour, around Laurel Point, is Fisherman's Wharf. It's a busy spot, with fishing boats and pleasure craft coming and going. You can sometimes buy fresh seafood from the boats or the little shed, and nearby is Barb's Place, selling fish and chips (see Places to Eat, later in this chapter). Take a look at the mix of houseboats moored at one end of the dock.

SOUTH OF DOWNTOWN
Scenic Marine Drive
Starting either from Fisherman's Wharf or Beacon Hill Park, the Scenic Marine Drive,

with great views out over the sea, skirts the coast along Dallas Rd and Beach Drive. The road heads north past some of Victoria's wealthiest neighborhoods, and the retirement community of Oak Bay where you could stop for afternoon tea at Blethering Place (see the High Tea sidebar, later in this chapter).

You'll see several parks and beaches along the way, though access to the shore for much of the way is restricted because of private housing right on the coastline. The Gray Line double-decker buses include Marine Drive in their tours (see Organized Tours).

Beacon Hill Park
Just southeast of the downtown area, along Douglas St, this 153-acre park is Victoria's largest. The park is an oasis of trees, flowers, ponds and pathways. (You don't see trees of this size anywhere but on the west coast). Also in the park is the 'world's tallest totem' and a cricket pitch. The southern edge overlooks the ocean and offers good views of the coastline. At the lookout above Dallas Rd is a marker indicating the direction of places such as Seattle, and noting the elevations of mountains. At the southwestern corner of the park, the path along the water meets the 'Mile 0' marker, the Pacific terminus of the Trans Canada Hwy. To reach the park, take bus No 5 from downtown.

Carr House
South of the Inner Harbour, a short walk leads to the birthplace of Emily Carr, one of Canada's best-known painters. The Carr House (☎ 250-383-5843), at 207 Government St, shows something of her upbringing and background and also displays some of her work, both in painting and literature. Many of her paintings incorporated subject matter drawn from the culture of the west coast Native Indians, particularly the totem poles. There is also a video about her life and career. It's open 10 am to 5 pm daily and admission is C$5/3 adults/children. Note that the Victoria Art Gallery usually has an Emily Carr exhibit.

Emily Carr

Emily Carr was born in Victoria in 1871 to prosperous parents. Her parents died when she was young and by 16 she was 'waging war' with the family to permit her to attend art school in San Francisco. As her dedication to painting was deemed unladylike, she was forced to make a living from teaching.

Her career as an artist took a pivotal turn when, in 1898, she accompanied a churchman to his mission at Ucluelet on Vancouver Island. The life and arts of the Native Indian village had a profound effect on Carr. Inspired by what she saw, she began using both the landscape and the Native Indians as her subject matters. She soon realized, however, that she needed to learn technique so she headed to London to study landscape painting.

When Carr returned to Canada, she felt that something was still missing from her painting. Working virtually alone, she left at age 39 for Paris to absorb some of the more modern painting techniques and styles. She found what she was looking for and her work took on her unique use of color, brush stroke and subject matter.

Her new paintings, however, were not taken seriously in Canada and were even found to be offensive. Students were removed from her art classes and her income steadily declined. At the age of 42, after a disastrous exhibition of paintings depicting the forests of Vancouver Island, she became a social outcast. To make ends meet she became a landlady in central Victoria.

It wasn't until the late 1920s that her scorned 1912 paintings were shown in eastern Canada and, in a sense, discovered. She then met the members of the increasingly well-known and influential school of painters called the Group of Seven, and with new energy and confidence continued her development as an artist. Through the late 1930s she revisited many of her cherished Indian locales and painted some of her best-known works.

As her health failed and she became bedridden, she began to write. Her book *Klee Wyck* is a collection of stories recalling her life among the Native Indians. The title means 'laughing one,' the name given to her by the Kwakiutl people. *The Book of Small* chronicles her childhood in Victoria, and *The House of All Sorts* describes her years as a landlady.

Her house in Victoria, the Carr House, is open to the public, and some of her paintings can be viewed at the Vancouver Art Gallery as well as at all of the major galleries across the country. Carr produced a rich body of work unlike that of any other Canadian artist and is regarded as Canada's first major woman artist. ■

ROCKLAND AREA

Just east of downtown Victoria, Rockland, which lies between Fort St and Fairfield Rd, and extends east to Moss St, is a wealthy neighborhood filled with handsome old homes and a number of civic buildings.

Art Gallery of Greater Victoria

The gallery (☎ 250-384-4101), in a Victorian mansion at 1040 Moss St, 1.5km (1 mile) east of the downtown area, just off Fort St, is best known for its excellent Asian art, including the Japanese and Chinese collections. It also has artworks from other parts of the world and from widely varying periods of history, including pre-Columbian Latin American objects to contemporary Canadian paintings. Emily Carr's work is usually displayed and there are some good Inuit pieces. Take bus No 10, 11 or 14 from the downtown area. It's open 10 am to 5 pm Monday to Saturday, 10 am to 9 pm Thursday and 1 to 5 pm Sunday. Admission is C$5/3 adults/students and seniors, and children are free.

Government House

This house is the official residence (☎ 250-387-2080) of the province's lieutenant-governor. The impressive grounds are open to the public except when British royalty is in residence. The building is not far from the Art Gallery of Greater Victoria, away from the downtown area, at 1401 Rockland Ave. Take bus No 1 from downtown.

Craigdarroch Castle

Near Government House, but off Fort St, this rather impressive home (☎ 250-592-5323), 1050 Joan Crescent, was built in the mid-1880s by Robert Dunsmuir, a coal millionaire, for himself and his wife. The castle-like house has been completely restored and is now a museum. It's open 9 am to 7 pm daily in summer and 10 am to 4:30 pm the rest of the year. Admission is C$7.50/5 adults/students. To get there take bus No 11 or 14.

NORTHWEST OF DOWNTOWN & ESQUIMALT
Point Ellice House

This beautifully kept house (☎ 250-387-4697), built in 1861, was sold in 1868 to Peter O'Reilly, a member of government and a very successful businessman. Many of the house's immaculate furnishings now on display belonged to him and his wife. It's open 11 am to 5 pm Thursday to Monday mid-June to the end of September, and admission is C$5. It's northwest of the downtown area at 2616 Pleasant St, off Bay St, at Point Ellice Bridge. Take bus No 14 from downtown.

English Village

This gimmicky but effective recreation of some English Tudor-style buildings is on Lampson St, across Victoria Harbour from downtown Victoria. The highlights are the replicas of Shakespeare's birthplace and the thatched cottage of his wife, Anne Hathaway. The cottage (☎ 250-388-4353), at 429 Lampson St, and the rest of the 'village' are furnished with authentic 16th-century antiques. It is open 9 am to 10 pm daily in the summer and 9 am to 5 pm in the winter. Admission is C$7/4.75 adults/children. Take bus No 24 from the downtown area.

Craigflower Farmhouse & Schoolhouse

The farmhouse (☎ 250-387-4697) was built by Kenneth McKenzie in 1856. It was the central home in the first farming community on Vancouver Island and its construction heralded Victoria's change from a fur-trading settlement to a permanent one. Built to remind McKenzie of Scotland, the house was decorated with the many furnishings he had brought from his homeland. Because the family entertained frequently, the house became a social center for Fort Victoria and the Esquimalt Naval Base. Admission also includes a visit to the historic schoolhouse.

The farmhouse is open from noon to 4 pm daily and admission is C$5. It's northwest of town, on the corner of Craigflower and Admirals Rds, near Gorge Rd (Hwy 1A). To get there catch bus No 14 from downtown.

Fort Rodd Hill National Historic Park

This scenic 45-acre park (☎ 250-363-4662) overlooking Esquimalt Harbour contains some historical points of interest. Late-19th-century gun batteries and other artillery installations were originally built to protect the naval base in the bay and, until 1956, when such a defense system was deemed obsolete, were regularly upgraded. There are information signs around the park, as well as guides. The park is open 10 am to 5:30 pm daily (Wednesday till 8:30 pm). Admission is C\$4; ask about the candlelight tours.

Also in the park is the **Fisgard Lighthouse**, western Canada's first, which still works and has been in continuous use since 1860.

The park is at 603 Fort Rodd Hill Rd, off Ocean Blvd, about 12km (7 miles) northwest of downtown, on the western side of Esquimalt Harbour. To get there catch bus No 50 which takes you to within 1km (half mile) of the park.

BUTCHART GARDENS

These gardens, 21km (13 miles) northwest of Victoria, are probably the most publicized of all Victoria's sights. Located on the site of a former limestone quarry, these 50-acre gardens were created by the family of a local cement manufacturer, beginning in 1904. The Butchart Gardens is comprised of smaller individual gardens, including a rose garden, Italian garden and a sunken garden with water features. No doubt the gardens are beautiful and extensive, but admission is costly at C\$13 (students C\$6.50). Whether it's worth it depends on you and your budget. (Budget-oriented flower fans should consider the little-known Horticultural Centre of the Pacific (☎ 250-479-6162), 505 Quayle Rd, as an alternative.)

You can walk through in about 1½ hours, but plant lovers will want to linger much longer. In the evenings from June to September the gardens are illuminated. There are also concerts and puppet shows around dusk. On Saturday nights in July and August there is a spectacular fireworks display set to music at no extra charge.

The gardens (☎ 250-652-4422), at 800 Benvenuto Ave, in Brentwood Bay, are open 9 am till dusk daily year-round. If you're driving, follow Hwy 17 north toward Sidney. City bus Nos 74 and 75 go within 1km (half a mile) during the week and 3km (2 miles) on Sunday.

On the way to the Butchart Gardens you could visit the **Dominion Astrophysical Observatory** (☎ 250-363-0012), where you can peer out to space through a 183cm telescope. There's a museum and the observatory has equipment used to record earthquakes. The observatory is open from 9:15 am to 4:30 pm weekdays, and from 7 to 11 pm Saturday night; admission is free. It's northwest of Victoria, at 5071 W Saanich Rd, on Little Saanich Mountain.

WESTERN SHORE

West of Victoria, Hwy 14 takes you from the city's manicured parks and gardens to the pristine wilderness of Vancouver Island's west coast. The highway runs through Sooke then along the coast overlooking the Strait of Juan de Fuca to Port Renfrew, at the southern end of the West Coast Trail (see the Pacific Rim National Park section, later in this chapter). There are parks and beaches along the way for walking, beachcombing and picnicking.

Before you reach Sooke follow the signs from Milnes Landing to the **Sooke Potholes** where you can go swimming, picnicking and hiking. Sooke's Travel InfoCentre (☎ 250-642-6351) and local museum are housed in the same building at 2070 Phillip's Rd. Victoria's bus network extends to Sooke: take bus No 50 to the Western Exchange then change to No 61.

Farther along Hwy 14, the windswept **French Beach** and **China Beach** provincial parks have swimming, camping and walking trails.

At **Port Renfrew**, often the destination for a day trip from town, the main attraction is **Botanical Beach**, a sandstone shelf, which at low tide is dotted with tidal pools containing all manner of small marine life: starfish, anemones, etc. To return to Victoria without retracing your tracks, take the logging road across the island to Lake Cowichan, from where better roads connect to Duncan and Hwy 1. For those without transportation, the West Coast Trail Connector (☎ 250-475-3010), 767 Audley St (also listed under PBM Transport in the phone book), runs buses from Victoria to Port Renfrew twice a day. Use it for an interesting day trip to the west coast beaches along the Strait of Juan de

Fuca or to begin the hiking trail to Bamfield (for details, see the West Coast Trail under the Pacific Rim National Park section, later in this chapter).

ACTIVITIES
Whale Watching
A number of excursion operators offer trips out into the Georgia Strait to watch orcas, or killer whales. Other wildlife you may see on these trips are bald eagles, seals and sea lions, and many kinds of sea birds.

Going on a whale-watching trip is as easy as walking down to the waterfront and signing up for the next excursion. As there are several operators, you shouldn't have any trouble getting on a boat pretty much when you want, though in high season or if you're part of a large party, you may want to call ahead and reserve a place. Whale-watching trips cost between C$75 and C$80 adults, C$50 to C$55 children, for a three-hour excursion. For information or reservations, contact Ocean Explorations (☎ 250-383-6722, 888-422-6722), at 146 Kingston St, at the Coast Victoria Harbourside Hotel near Fisherman's Wharf; Prince of Whales (☎ 250-383-4884), 812 Wharf St (just below the Travel InfoCentre office); or Cuda Marine (☎ 250-812-6003), on the Wharf St pier.

Swimming
One of the best swimming places is the **Sooke Potholes**, about an hour's drive west of Victoria on Hwy 14, by the town of Sooke, on the southern shore. Watch for signs at Milnes Landing. You can find your own swimming hole but the water ain't balmy. There's good picnicking and some walking trails too. Don't get caught drinking alcohol because the fines are heavy for drinking in a public area.

Also popular is **Thetis Lake Park**, not too far northwest of town (about 20 minutes driving), off the Trans Canada Hwy. It's very busy at the main beach but if you hike around the lake you'll find a quiet spot.

The Crystal Pool & Fitness Centre (☎ 250-380-4636), 2275 Quadra St, on the corner of Wark St – an easy walk from the downtown area – has a pool, a sauna, a whirlpool and locker rooms.

Scuba Diving
The Georgia Strait provides opportunities for world-class diving. The undersea life is tremendously varied and has been featured in *National Geographic*. Several excellent shore dive sites are found near Victoria, including Saanich Inlet, Saxe Point Park, the Ogden Point Breakwater, 10-Mile Point and Willis Point for deep diving. Race Rocks, 18km (11 miles) southwest of Victoria Harbour, offers superb scenery both above and below the water. Diving charters and dive shops in Victoria provide equipment sales, service, rentals and instruction.

Fishing
The waters around Victoria are renowned for deep-sea fishing with salmon being the top prize. The Travel InfoCentre can supply information and you should also check the yellow pages. There are freshwater lakes and streams within an hour or two of Victoria as well as up-island that are good for trout and/or salmon fishing. Saanich Inlet has one of the highest concentrations of salmon in the world.

Scores of charter companies offer deepsea fishing trips of varying lengths. Most supply all equipment, bait and even coffee. For a complete list of outfitters, contact the InfoCentre. Duffy's Salmon Charters (☎ 250-727-2375), for example, has four-hour minimum trips for C$225, but four adults can go for that price.

Other Activities
A popular sport is **windsurfing**, especially in Cadboro Bay near the university, and at Willows Beach in Oak Bay. Rentals are available at both for around C$17; some places offer lessons, too. Oak Bay is also a popular canoeing spot. Ocean River Sports (☎ 250-381-4233), 1437 Store St, rents canoes and kayaks, sells equipment and runs courses. Sports Rent (☎ 250-385-7368), 611 Discovery St, hires canoes and kayaks from C$30 per day.

A few people offer **horseback-riding**

trips in the nearby highlands and lake areas. Some include overnight camping. Inquire at the Travel InfoCentre. Lakeshore Trailrides (☎ 250-479-6853), 482 Sparton Rd, has one-hour rides for C$25.

ORGANIZED TOURS
Most companies offer a variety of options, from bus tours of downtown Victoria to quick trips around the island. Other companies only do one kind of tour, such as day and evening Inner Harbour boat trips or rides by horse-drawn carriage. There are also tours up-island to view wildlife, hiking trips and self-drive tours using recorded tapes. The Travel InfoCentre has details on many of the options.

Gray Line Bus Company (☎ 250-388-5248), 700 Douglas St, offers a variety of tours here, as they do in so many North American cities. Its city bus tour costs C$16 for 1½ hours and takes in some of the major historical and scenic sights. Many of its bus tours include admission to attractions like the Butchart Gardens. You can buy tickets in front of the Empress Hotel, the same place from where buses depart. Heritage Tours (☎ 250-474-4332), 713 Bexhill St, offers more personalized city tours in limousines seating six people for C$75 for 1¼ hours, or C$90 for two hours. The rate is per car, not per person.

Tallyho Sightseeing (☎ 250-479-1113) gives 45-minute city tours in a horse-drawn

The Endangered BC Salmon
As does the rest of the Pacific Northwest, BC confronts the issue of wild salmon depopulation in its rivers. The problems that have put the salmon in danger in BC are much the same as in Oregon and Washington: decades of over-fishing, pollution of streams and rivers, the practice of clear-cutting forests and hydroelectric dams that stop migrating fish. However, BC salmon – and the governmental bodies and environmentalists who work to protect the salmon population spawned in BC rivers – face one unique adversary: Alaska.

While the states of Oregon and Washington, the province of BC, and most of the region's Indian tribes (who often have treaty rights to fish for salmon) have largely worked together to preserve the salmon population by restricting catches and improving watersheds, the government and fishing industry in Alaska has been almost totally uncooperative. Alaska has refused to adopt the fishing restrictions advocated by the other governments in the region, continuing to fish the waters of the Gulf of Alaska with what seems like environmental abandon.

This is a particular problem for BC. Adult salmon – who will later enter Canadian waters to spawn – spend most of their lives in the waters of the Northern Pacific, where Alaskan trawler boats harvest fish in great numbers. Alaskan fishers take a huge bite out of the BC fish population before the fish enter Canadian jurisdiction and protection. The animosity between Canadian and Alaskan fishers is often very intense, highlighted by the 1996 standoff at Prince Rupert, when BC fishers blockaded an Alaska ferry in the Prince Rupert harbor for over a week.

Salmon numbers continue to dwindle in BC. In 1998 the federal government completely banned fishing for coho salmon, in response to evidence pointing to the species' imminent extinction. For instance, in the Skeena and Thompson Rivers, coho stocks are down to 1% of what they were just a few decades ago. (Other species of salmon are still harvested in BC, though in greatly restricted numbers.)

Most Canadian anglers, charter and commercial fishers and Native groups grudgingly accept the government-enforced ban. However, their anger is reserved for the Alaskans, who continue to harvest coho and other salmon by the thousands as those fish swim through US waters on their way toward Canadian rivers. ■

carriage. The standard tour costs C$30 for two people, and leaves from the corner of Belleville and Menzies Sts.

SPECIAL EVENTS
May
Victoria Day Festival – Held during the fourth week of May to celebrate Queen Victoria's birthday, it features a parade, performances by the town's ethnic groups, stage shows and many sporting events. Many people dress in 19th-century-style clothes, and some shopkeepers dress their windows in period manner. Call ☎ 250-382-3111 for information. The Swiftsure Lightship Classic, a sailing race, ends the event. Call ☎ 250-592-2441 for information. The last weekend can get pretty wild – a real street party.

June
Jazz Festival – In late June the Victoria Jazz Society (☎ 250-388-4423) puts on its annual jazz festival at various locations around town.

June/July
Folkfest – Held at the end of June and the beginning of July, this celebrates Canada's cultural diversity. Dance and musical performances take place at Centennial Square.

June/August
Victoria International Festival – This festival, offering classical music performed by Canadian and foreign musicians, lasts through the summer till mid-August. For information contact the McPherson Playhouse (☎ 250-386-6121).

August
First Peoples' Festival – This takes place in mid-August beside the Royal BC Museum and along the Inner Harbour. It lasts three days and includes traditional craftwork, dancing, a potlatch and war-canoe rides. For information call ☎ 250-383-2663.

August/September
Fringe Theatre Festival – Featuring more than 50 performances in various locations around town, the festival includes drama, comedy, acrobatics, jugglers and street performers. It takes place in late August and early September. For details call ☎ 250-383-2663.

September
Classic Boat Festival – During this festival, held on the first weekend in September each year, vintage wooden boats powered by sail or engine compete in various categories. The competition is held on the Inner Harbour. Free entertainment is provided on the quayside for the spectators. For information call ☎ 250-385-7766.

October
Salmon Run – Observe the fish and take part in events and educational displays marking the annual salmon migration at Goldstream Provincial Park (☎ 250-391-2300), north of town.

PLACES TO STAY
Lodging in Victoria can be very expensive, and in summer, hard to find. Reserve as soon as you know your travel plans. In the downtown area there are several older hotels that have been renovated and that are a good value; to stay in the prime locations on the Inner Harbour will take a bite out of your budget. If you're looking for inexpensive lodgings, you'll need to stay at one of the hostels, or else head out of the downtown area to one of the motel strips in the suburbs. Prices for accommodations are very seasonal; if you travel outside of the main summer season, you'll save considerably on rooms.

If you're having trouble finding a room, the InfoCentre's reservation service (☎ 250-382-2127) can help you find a room.

Camping
Closest to town is *Fort Victoria RV Park* (☎ 250-479-8112), 340 Island Hwy, off Island Hwy 1A, 6.5km (4 miles) northwest from the city center. Take bus No 14 or 15 from the downtown area; there's a bus stop at the gate. The park caters mainly to RVs. It does have a few tent sites but there are no trees, and open fires are not allowed. It has full facilities including free showers and charges C$26 per site.

A little farther out, *Thetis Lake Campground* (☎ 250-478-3845), 1938 Trans Canada Hwy, on Rural Route 6, is about a 15-minute drive northwest of the city center. All facilities are available, including a laundry and shower. There's a store, and you can swim in the nearby lake. A site for two people is C$15 including tax; electricity is C$2 extra. The campground is open all year.

The best campground is *Goldstream Provincial Park* (☎ 250-391-2300), on the Trans Canada Hwy, about 20km (12 miles) northwest of Victoria. A tent site costs C$15.50 for one to four people and you can go swimming, fishing or hiking. Take bus No 50 from Douglas St. South of Goldstream Provincial Park, 3.5km (2 miles) off the Trans Canada Hwy, at 2960 Irwin Rd, on Rural Route 6, is *Paradise Campground* (☎ 250-478-6960). It's part of a nature sanctuary and is open from early June to the end of September. It has full facilities, canoe and kayak rentals and charges C$18 for two people.

The Travel InfoCentre can tell you of other campgrounds not too far from town.

Hostels

The *HI Victoria Hostel* (☎ 250-385-4511), 516 Yates St, is in the old part of town just up from Wharf St. It has room for over 100 people, with family rooms, a large common area, kitchen, laundry and a good notice board. Memberships are available. A bed costs C$15 for members and C$19 for nonmembers. In peak season it's advisable to check in before 4 pm.

The *Selkirk Guest House International* (☎ 250-389-1213), 934 Selkirk Ave in Esquimalt over the Johnson St Bridge, is affiliated with Hostelling International. A dorm bed costs C$15 for members, C$19 for nonmembers and the private rooms start at C$35. Travelers with kids can be accommodated economically and should feel right at home in this family-operated hostelry. Features include a garden complete with hot tub on the shore of The Gorge. The No 14 bus from Douglas St gets you within two blocks.

The *Backpacker's Lodge* (☎ 250-386-4471), 1418 Fernwood Rd, has dormitory beds for C$12, and private singles/doubles for C$40/45. The former manager has put together an excellent guide of things to do around town. The hostel has no curfew and is close to the shops and restaurants of Fernwood Village. Buses east along Fort St will take you there; the No 10 Haultain bus goes right past the door.

Also in this neighborhood is *Renouf House* (☎ 250-595-4774), at 2010 Stanley Ave, which has beds in a coed dorm room

for C$20 (bunk and breakfast) in addition to several private B&B rooms (see B&Bs, below).

The *Beverley Lodge* (☎ 250-598-7323), 1729 Oak Bay Ave, offers two- to six-bed bunk rooms in a four-story renovated heritage home for C$18 to C$20. Amenities include a self-service kitchen and an outdoor deck and BBQ. The Beverley Lodge is wheelchair-accessible. Take bus No 1 or 2 from downtown.

The *YM-YWCA* (☎ 250-386-7511) are both in the same building at 880 Courtney St, but the residence is only for women. A dorm bunk with bedding costs C$19. Private single rooms, when available, cost C$37, though they're often fully booked with long-term boarders. There's also a cafeteria and a heated swimming pool.

The *University of Victoria* rents rooms from the start of May to the end of August. Singles/doubles are C$38/50, including breakfast and free parking. You can make use of the university's facilities and there are several licensed cafeterias on campus. Contact Housing & Conference Services (☎ 250-721-8396), at the University of Victoria, PO Box 1700, Victoria, BC V8W 2Y2. Catch bus No 14 on Douglas St to the campus; it takes about 20 minutes.

B&Bs

There are several B&B associations in Victoria that approve members, list them and make reservations at one central office. Prices are between C$45 and C$75 for singles and between C$55 and C$120 for most doubles, though some go up to as much as C$190.

A couple of associations to try are *All Seasons B&B Agency* (☎ 250-655-7173), PO Box 5511, Station B, Victoria, BC V8R 6S4; and *Victoria Vacationer B&B* (☎ 250-382-9469), 1143 Leonard St, Victoria, BC V8V 2S3. Many B&Bs advertise independently and have pamphlets at the Travel InfoCentre. A few of them are listed here.

Northeast of the center, *Renouf House* (☎ 250-595-4774) is a 1912 heritage home at 2010 Stanley Ave. It can cater to people with special diets and has homebaked bread. Private rooms with a shared bathroom start at C\$35/55 single/double, rooms with a private bathroom start at C\$50/70. It is a friendly, casual and comfortable place which also offers kayaking (one of the owners makes kayaks) or sailing tours through Intertidal Explorations. *Marion's B&B* (☎ 250-592-3070), 1730 Taylor St, about a 10-minute bus ride from downtown, is recommended. Rooms are C\$35/55, the good breakfasts are enormous and the owners are friendly and helpful. *Battery St Guest House* (☎ 250-385-4632) is south of the city center, near Beacon Hill Park, at 670 Battery St. It's in an old home dating from 1898. Rooms are C\$50/85. *Craigmyle Guest House* (☎ 250-595-5411), at 1037 Craigdarroch Rd, about 1.5km (1 mile) east of the downtown area, is next to Craigdarroch Castle. Rooms are C\$65/70.

Convenient to sights on the Inner Harbour, *Birdcage Walk Guest House* (☎ 250-389-0804), 505 Government St, offers five guest rooms with private bathrooms in a historic home; rooms cost C\$89/99.

Perhaps the most upscale B&B in Victoria, and surely the one with the best view, is the *Gatsby Mansion* (☎ 250-388-9191, 800-563-9656), 309 Belleville St, right on the Inner Harbour. This Queen Anne showpiece offers rooms for upwards of C\$200 per night; call to inquire about weekend packages.

Hotels – Inner Harbour

The most appealing and most expensive hotels are those along the Inner Harbour, with views of the bay and downtown. From here, it's a short walk to downtown and the shopping precincts.

Middle While these prices certainly press the upper limits of the middle range, they're about the best you'll find in this much-sought-after area. The best deal here is the *Admiral Motel* (☎ 250-388-6267), 257 Belleville St. With singles/doubles at C\$115/135, this attractive motel with larger-than-average rooms is a great choice. Hidden in a grove of trees, the *Best Western Inner Harbour* (☎ 250-384-5122, 800-528-

1234), 412 Quebec St, has balconies and nicely decorated rooms starting at C\$119 single or double. You can't argue with the location of the *Days Inn on the Harbour* (☎ 250-386-3451, 800-325-2525), at 427 Belleville St, located right across from the ferry terminal. Rooms aren't large, but are comfortable, and, depending on the view, go for C\$120 to C\$179 a single, C\$130 to C\$189 double.

A block off the harbor, *Embassy Inn* (☎ 250-382-8161, 800-268-8161), at 520 Menzies St, has both an older and a newer wing. All rooms have balconies, some in the older wing have views; rooms cost C\$99 to C\$135. Also just a block in from the harbor and a block from the Parliament Buildings, the *Royal Scot Inn* (☎ 250-388-5463, 800-663-7515), 425 Quebec St, offers studio, one- and two-bedroom suites starting at C\$119; if you need a little extra room, this is a good choice. There's more of a feeling of a chain hotel to *Quality Inn Harbourview* (☎ 250-386-2421, 800-228-5151), 455 Belleville St, though some rooms have a good view; rooms cost C\$139 to C\$179 single or double.

Top End The *Empress Hotel* (☎ 250-348-8111, 800-441-1414), 721 Government St, is practically synonymous with Victoria. Staying here on honeymoon is a tradition throughout the Pacific Northwest; many well-heeled travelers wouldn't think of staying anywhere else. This grand doyenne is nearly a century old, but she's never looked better. The hotel looks out over the Inner Harbour and, along with the Parliament Buildings, is the focal point of Victoria. Even if you are not staying here, the Empress Hotel is worth a visit; many visitors come here for the famous afternoon tea service. Singles/doubles are priced from C\$225/255.

On the same scale of luxury, but brand-new is *Laurel Point Inn* (☎ 250-386-8721, 800-663-7667), 680 Montreal St. With saunas, an indoor pool, balconies and incredible views, this high-rise motel guards the entrance to the Inner Harbour. Rooms begin at C\$180 single or double. The

Clarion Hotel Grand Pacific (☎ 250-386-0450, 800-458-6262), 450 Quebec St, is another modern luxury hotel above the ferry terminal, with balconies, great views, exercise and health facilities (including a racquetball court), and a pool. Rooms start at C$199 single or double.

Hotels – downtown & Old Town

Budget There are a few reasonable places right in the downtown area. *Hotel Douglas* (☎ 250-383-4157, 800-332-9981), which is centrally located at 1450 Douglas St, on the corner of Pandora Ave, has rooms starting at C$65/70 single/double. It shares its lobby with an art gallery and has a restaurant and bar downstairs. At the *Strathcona Hotel* (☎ 250-383-7137, 800-663-7476), 919 Douglas St, a couple of blocks east of the Inner Harbour, rooms start at C$74/84 single/double. All the rooms have private bathroom, telephone and TV. The hotel has free parking, several bars and a restaurant.

Crystal Court Motel (☎ 250-384-0551) is at 701 Belleville St, on the corner of Douglas St, across the road from the Greyhound Bus Depot and Crystal Garden. Rooms are C$70/73 single/double, and a kitchen costs just C$2 more. It's clean and the rooms have a TV, radio and telephone.

Middle The totally renovated *Dominion Hotel* (☎ 250-384-4136, 800-663-6101), 759 Yates St, has rooms starting at C$99 single or double, free parking and a restaurant. Attractive *Green Gables Hotel* (☎ 250-385-6787, 800-661-4115), 850 Blanshard St, is close to the Inner Harbour and has an indoor pool, as well as a sauna and restaurant; single rooms cost C$105 to C$120, double rooms cost C$159.

Executive House Hotel (☎ 250-388-5111, 800-663-7001), 777 Douglas St, is a high-rise tower a couple of blocks from the waterfront. With good views and high-quality furnishings, these rooms are a good deal, starting at C$99 single/double. The *Best Western Carlton Plaza* (☎ 250-388-5513, 800-663-7241), 642 Johnson St, is an older hotel that's been totally refur-

bished; there's free continental breakfast and free valet parking. Rooms start at C$119 single or double. One of the nicest of the refurbished hotels is *Swans Hotel* (☎ 250-361-3310, 800-668-7926), 506 Pandora Ave, a gem of a building in the Old Town area, right on the waterfront. All rooms are suites, with great contemporary art and luxury touches; single rooms cost C$135 to C$165, double rooms start at C$165.

Top End The *Bedford Regency Hotel* (☎ 250-384-6835, 800-665-6500), 1140 Government St, is right at the center of things in the city's prime shopping and dining area. This totally renovated vintage hotel is a real find: the rooms are exquisitely furnished and the service topnotch. Rooms start at C$165 single or double.

Victoria Regent Hotel (☎ 250-386-2211, 800-663-7472), 1234 Wharf St, near the corner of Yates St, is an all-suites hotel with some of the best views in the city. Rates start at C$159 single/double; you'll pay more if you want a view.

Hotels – around downtown

Victoria is a very compact city, and the following hotels and motels are just a few minutes from the downtown sights.

Budget Opened in 1897, *Cherry Bank Hotel* (☎ 250-385-5380, 800-998-6688), 825 Burdett Ave, is east of the downtown area, up the hill a few blocks, opposite the law courts. It's simple but a reasonable value at C$50/58 single/double with a shared bathroom, or C$66/73 with a private bathroom. Prices include breakfast but rooms do not come with TV or telephone. There's a popular restaurant and a bar on the premises.

Just north of downtown along Douglas St is an area of inexpensive motels. *Traveller's Inn* (☎ 250-370-1000, 888-753-3774), 710 Queens Ave at Douglas St, is one of the best, with clean, large and simple rooms for C$59/69. The *Doric Motel* (☎ 250-386-2481), at 3025 Douglas St, is a five-minute drive north of the downtown area. It has TV, laundry and free coffee. Rooms cost C$64/69 single/double.

Another good area for motels – not far northwest of the downtown area – is along Gorge Rd, which forms a section of Island Hwy 1A. From Gorge Rd it's about a five-minute drive to town. At the *Capri Motel* (☎ 250-384-0521), 21 Gorge Rd E, rooms cost C$60/70 single/double. *Traveller's Inn on Gorge* (☎ 250-388-9901), 120 Gorge Rd E, has a sauna, heated pool and laundromat. Single/double rooms cost C$50/52; kitchenettes are C$10 extra.

Middle Back on the Douglas St motel strip, *Paul's Motor Inn* (☎ 250-382-9231), 1900 Douglas St, has a 24-hour restaurant; single/double rooms start at C$88/93. *Helm's Inn* (☎ 250-385-5767, 800-665-4356), 600 Douglas St, has one-bedroom and studio suites with kitchen starting at C$90/100. Opposite is the *Shamrock Motel* (☎ 250-385-8768), 675 Superior St, where rooms cost C$89/99. *Horizon West* (☎ 250-382-2111, 800-830-2111), 1961 Douglas St, has rooms at C$73/83; farther out, the *Blue Ridge Inn* (☎ 250-388-4345), 3110 Douglas St, has rooms at C$75/85.

Close to downtown is the *James Bay Inn* (☎ 250-384-7151, 800-836-2649). It's the big old hotel with bay windows at 270 Government St, a few blocks south of the downtown area, in a residential area of small, attractive houses. Rooms start at C$95/115.

Top End One of the classiest places to stay in Victoria is *Abigail's Hotel* (☎ 250-388-5363, 800-561-6565), 906 McClure St, a small boutique hotel just east of downtown. This Tudor mansion has sixteen exquisitely furnished rooms, with fresh flowers, goosedown duvets and other niceties. Rooms start at C$139 single or double.

Across the Inner Harbour from downtown and the Parliament Buildings, and with tremendous views of both, the *Ocean Pointe Resort* (☎ 250-360-2999, 800-667-4677), 45 Songees Rd, combines luxury-class rooms with the facilities of a spa. On-site amenities include an indoor pool,

hydrotherapy services, racquetball and squash courts, tennis courts and sauna; rooms are topnotch and start at C$169 for a single or double.

Beaconsfield Inn (☎ 250-384-4044), 998 Humboldt St, is a few blocks east of the downtown area and a couple blocks north of Beacon Hill Park. It's in an Edwardian mansion and the rates include breakfast. Rooms have one bed and start at C$200.

Oak Bay Beach Hotel (☎ 250-598-4556), 1175 Beach Drive, is a seaside hotel east of the downtown area, overlooking Oak Bay. It provides a shuttle service into the city center and offers lunchtime cruises. Rooms start at C$169.

PLACES TO EAT

Though a small city, Victoria has a varied array of restaurants, due in part to its many visitors, and prices are generally good. As befits a tourist town, especially one with British roots, there are numerous cafes and teashops. Some dining rooms offer good lunch specials but are fairly pricey in the evenings. The pubs in town are also good for reasonably priced meals.

Budget

Restaurant food can be expensive in Victoria. A good place to shop around for a decent, inexpensive meal is in Chinatown (Fisgard St between Douglas St and the harbor), or in the Market Square shopping center, at Johnson and Wharf Sts, where there are a number of casual eateries and food booths. One of the best places for breakfast in this area is the *Milky Way Cafe* (☎ 250-360-1113), 126-160 Johnson St. *Foo Hong Chop Suey* (☎ 250-386-9553), 564 Fisgard St, is small and basic yet has good, simple Cantonese food. The *Ocean Phoenix* (☎ 250-360-2818), at 509 Fisgard St, closed Monday, offers a small, neat dining room, an extensive menu and good food. Try the Cantonese lunch specials.

The modest and casual *Day & Night* (☎ 250-382-5553), 622 Yates St, is good for any meal, with good-value plain food, including one of the cheapest breakfasts in town. Sandwiches and pasta dishes start at

High Tea

English-style high tea at the *Empress Hotel* (☎ 250-348-8111, 800-441-1414), 721 Government St, is so mandatory an experience for most visitors as to be almost a cliché. While high tea isn't usually considered a meal in itself, this extravagance of clotted cream, berries, scones and biscuits will surely ruin your appetite for an evening meal. The tearooms at the Empress are lovely, and you should dress up a bit for the experience (in fact, a dress code is in force). High tea isn't cheap, however: you will spend C$29 a person for the honor. Reservations are a good idea in all but the dead of winter.

Another favorite place for afternoon tea is the *James Bay Tea Room* (☎ 250-382-8282), 332 Menzies St. This very English restaurant is also a good place for lunch and dinner with standards like steak-and-kidney pie or roast beef and Yorkshire pudding.

A popular teashop with the locals is the *Blethering Place* (☎ 250-598-1413), 2250 Oak Bay Ave, away from the center of town in Oak Bay Village. It has Devonshire teas for around C$10 and is open 8 am to 10 pm daily. *Murchio's* (☎ 250-383-3112), at 1110 Government St, between View and Fort Sts, is a quality west-coast tea and coffee merchant which also serves a decadent assortment of pastries and chocolates. ∎

C$4. *Smitty's Family Restaurant* (☎ 250-383-5612), 850 Douglas St, is an old standby and best for cheap pancake breakfasts for around C$7 including coffee. It's open 6 am to midnight daily.

Sam's Deli (☎ 250-382-8424), under the maroon awnings at 805 Government St, on the corner of Wharf St and diagonally opposite the main Travel InfoCentre, is a perfect spot to have an espresso and write a postcard. There are a dozen tables outside on the sidewalk and more inside, where the walls are covered in 1920s and 1930s posters. This is a popular place with a European flavor. It serves good-value soups, salads and sandwiches for less than C$5.

It's worth joining the crowds at colorful *John's Place* (☎ 250-389-0799), 723 Pandora Ave, for the large portions at breakfast or lunch. In Bastion Square, opposite Harpo's nightclub, is *C'est Bon* (☎ 250-381-1461), a small French-style bakery with croissants, coffee and lunchtime soups. It's closed Sunday and Monday.

The fish and chips are excellent in Victoria and there are several outlets for them. *Barb's Place* (☎ 250-384-6515), at 310 St Lawrence St, at Fisherman's Wharf, is a wooden shack on the dock serving fish and chips in newspaper. Fresh crabs can be bought from the boats nearby. *Cook St Fish & Chips* (☎ 250-384-1856), at 252 Cook St near Beacon Hill Park, and *Brady's* (☎ 250-382-3695) at 20 W Burnside Rd by the corner of Harriet Rd, are also good spots for fish and chips.

The *Sticky Wicket Pub* (☎ 250-383-7137), on the corner of Douglas and Courtney Sts, has nachos and pizza and a variety of Canadian, US and UK beers. Another cheap but good place is the busy *Eugene's Restaurant & Snack Bar* (☎ 250-381-5456), 1280 Broad St. Simple, basic Greek foods (C$4 to C$8) are served cafeteria-style.

The *Mount Royal Bagel Factory* (☎ 250-380-3588), 1115 N Park St (but with the door on Grant St) in the Fernwood Village area, has fresh Montreal-style bagels.

Middle

An excellent and popular place for good light meals, drinks and a friendly welcome is *Suze* (☎ 250-383-2829), 515 Yates St. The menu involves Pacific Northwest takes on pizza, pasta and fresh seafood dishes; the lounge, with exposed brick and a vintage 25-foot-long mahogany bar, is one of the coziest yet hippest places in Victoria.

Perhaps the most happening place in town is the *Re-Bar* (☎ 250-360-2401), 50 Bastion Square, with an eclectic contemporary international menu and funky decor to match. It's busy all day long for breakfast, coffee, dessert, salads and main dishes, which are mostly vegetarian and all well prepared.

If the weather's good and dining on a outdoor deck is appealing, then *The Wharfside Eatery* (☎ 250-360-1808), 1208 Wharf St, is your best bet. While fresh seafood is the specialty, the menu also offers wood-fired pizzas. Bustling and popular, *Il Terrazi* (☎ 250-361-0028), 555 Johnson St, is the best place in Victoria for Italian pastas, grilled meats and tempting pizzas. The atmosphere is nice, and they have courtyard dining in good weather. Victoria has a number of good Greek restaurants, but *Millos* (☎ 250-382-5544), 716 Burdett St, has the reputation for the best roast lamb; stay late for the belly dancers.

Both a brewpub and a great place for lunch or light dinner, *Swans Brew Pub* (☎ 250-361-3310), 506 Pandora Ave, has good burgers and sandwiches, and one of the most appealing, art-filled barrooms in the city.

The *Spare Rib House* (☎ 250-385-5380), in the Cherry Bank Hotel, 825 Burdett Ave, is good for rib dinners, steaks and seafood. There's a children's menu and live honky-tonk piano entertainment.

Pagliacci's (☎ 250-386-1662), at 1011 Broad St, between Fort and Broughton Sts, is a moderately priced Italian restaurant, with pasta and pizza. At night it is busy, partly for the food, partly for the live music.

Herald St Caffé (☎ 250-381-1441), 546 Herald St, is a small Italian restaurant serving delicious pastas for around C$12 to C$15. It also has vegetarian dishes, great desserts and a wine bar that gets a little crowded after 10 pm.

Le Petit Saigon (☎ 250-386-1412), at 1010 Langely St, is recommended for Vietnamese meals. The menu includes meat, fish and vegetarian dishes.

Milestones (☎ 250-381-2244), at 812 Wharf St, right on the Inner Harbour and below the Travel InfoCentre, has an incredible view of the Parliament Buildings and overlooks the harbor. While Milestones doesn't have a regular bar license (you must order food in order to have a drink), many people do come here for a cocktail and a snack.

Top End

The *Empress Hotel* (☎ 250-384-8111), 721 Government St, has its own array of eating options. The formal dining room, the *Empress Room* is excellent, with top-quality Northwest cuisine and high prices; entrées start around C$30. The *Bengal Lounge* is a real treat. It serves seafood and poultry and a daily curry special for C$16. At lunch there's a C$12 buffet. There is a tiger skin on the wall and it's right out of the days of the British Empire. Downstairs, the *Garden Café* lunch is cheaper.

Chandler's Seafood Restaurant (☎ 250-385-3474), near the Victoria Regent Hotel and the corner of Yates and Wharf Sts, is an established dining room specializing in ocean fare. At 607 Oswego St overlooking the Inner Harbour, the *Harbour House Restaurant* (☎ 250-386-1244), is a formal, elegant seafood and steak house.

Koto Japanese Restaurant (☎ 250-382-1514), 510 Fort St, just up from Wharf St, serves mainly seafood and has a sushi and salad bar; main courses cost C$16 to C$26. There's a detailed, colorful display in the window of the various kinds of dishes available in the restaurant. *The 1218 Restaurant* (☎ 250-386-1218), 1218 Wharf St, offers nouveau Northwest cuisine in a very high-ceilinged and attractive dining room, with some views onto the harbor.

Camille's Fine Westcoast Dining (☎ 250-381-3433), 45 Bastion Square, has the reputation of being Victoria's most inventive restaurant, with fusion cooking bringing the best of Northwest ingredients into contact with eclectic, international cuisine.

ENTERTAINMENT

Monday Magazine, the weekly entertainment paper available free around town, has extensive coverage of what's going on.

Performing Arts

The *Victoria Symphony Orchestra* (☎ 250-846-9771) performs from August through May at the Royal Theatre, 805 Broughton St. The *Pacific Opera Victoria* (☎ 250-385-0222) offer three performances a year at McPherson Playhouse.

Theater Victoria has a number of live theaters that provide venues for plays, concerts, comedies, ballets and operas. The *McPherson Playhouse* (☎ 250-386-6121), 3 Centennial Square, on the corner of Pandora Ave and Government St, regularly puts on plays and comedies. The box office is open 9:30 am to 5:30 pm Monday to Saturday. The elegant *Royal Theatre* (☎ 250-386-6121), 805 Broughton St, between Blanshard and Quadra Sts, hosts a range of performances, including the ballet, symphony, dance and concerts.

Other theaters worth checking out are the *Belfry* (☎ 250-385-6815), 1291 Gladstone Ave, northeast of the downtown area, and the *Phoenix Theatre* (☎ 250-721-8000), on the University of Victoria campus. More experimental theater is staged by Dark Horse Theatre at the *Kaleidoscope Playhouse* (☎ 250-475-4444), 520 Herald St.

Victoria's Fringe Theatre Festival is held in late August and early September (see Special Events, earlier in this chapter, for details).

Live Music

Victoria's best live-jazz venue is *Millennium Jazz Club* (☎ 250-360-9098), 1601 Store St, beneath Swan's Pub. *Pagliacci's* is popular not only for its food but also for the entertainment it provides. It's one of the centers for jazz in Victoria but varies jazz with comedy sessions. For information about jazz around town, call the Jazz Hotline at ☎ 250-658-5255.

One of the most popular nightclubs is *Harpo's* (☎ 250-385-5333), at 15 Bastion Square on the corner of Wharf St, above Rebecca's restaurant. It has live bands playing a variety of music, including rock, Celtic rock, ska, reggae and blues.

In the same building as the Strathcona Hotel, 919 Douglas St, there are several clubs that feature live music including the *Legends* (☎ 250-383-7137), a longstanding rock and blues nightclub and *Big Bad John's*, more for country & western fans. *Steamers Pub* (☎ 250-381-4340), at 570 Yates St just below Government St, is

a good blues bar and has Sunday afternoon sessions.

The Limit (☎ 250-384-3557), at 1318 Broad St, has regional live bands on weekends, and dancing to canned progressive music during the week.

Brewpubs

Spinnakers Brewery Pub (☎ 250-386-2739), 308 Catherine St, often heralded as Canada's first brewpub, is a very jolly place, with a nice mix of locals and visitors. In good weather there's deck seating with views over the Inner Harbour. *Swan's Brew Pub* (☎ 250-361-3310), 1601 Store St, is half the main floor of a popular refurbished hotel. Besides the good beers and ales, the other reason to gather here is to admire the owner's extensive modern art collection, which graces this pub. Two other brewpubs are the *Garrick's Head*, 69 Bastion Square, and the *Sticky Wicket Pub* in the Strathcona Hotel, 919 Douglas St.

Coffeehouses

Besides a good cup of coffee, at *Bean Around the World* (☎ 250-386-7115), 533 Fisgard St, you can also get into one of the discussion groups, 'What Is Reality?' was the topic at one of their philosophy nights. *Java Coffeehouse* (☎ 250-381-2326), 537 Johnson St, is a classic coffeehouse, with more standard entertainment, like live music and poetry readings.

Dance Clubs

The hottest dance club is *Rumours Cabaret* (☎ 250-385-0566), 1325 Government St, a friendly gay-oriented disco with a lively clientele. *BJ's Lounge* (☎ 250-388-0505), downstairs at 642 Johnson St, is a more traditional gay men's dance club. *Merlin's* (☎ 250-381-2331), 1208 Wharf St, is the main straight dance club, with a young crowd and regular theme nights such as Chippendale-style dancers, etc.

Cinema

Admission at commercial cinemas such as the *Odeon Theatre* (☎ 250-383-0513), 780 Yates St, are reduced to nearly half price on

VANCOUVER ISLAND

Tuesday. Another downtown cinema is the *Capital 6* (☎ 250-384-6811), 805 Yates St.

SHOPPING

There are a number of craft shops along Douglas and Government Sts selling Native Indian art and craftwork such as sweaters, moccasins, carvings and prints. Be prepared: the good stuff is expensive.

At 811 Government St, Canadian Impressions (☎ 250-383-2641), has some quality items and Native Indian crafts. The small Indian print greeting cards make good, cheap little presents and some are even signed by the artist. Canadian Impressions has another shop at the airport.

Sasquatch Trading Company (☎ 250-386-9033), at 1233 Government St, has a good selection of Cowichan sweaters. These hand-spun, hand-knitted sweaters average between C$140 and C$200 but are warm and should last a decade or more. No dyes are used. Other stores selling quality sweaters are Hills Indian Crafts (☎ 250-385-3911), at 1008 Government St, Cowichan Trading (☎ 250-383-0321), 1328 Government St, and Indian Craft Shoppe (☎ 250-382-3643), 905 Government St.

On Fort St, between Cook and Quadra Sts, there are a number of antique and bric-a-brac shops.

For chocolate lovers, there's Roger's Chocolates, at 913 Government St, which first opened in 1885. Roger's offers a treat to both nose and tongue. Try one (or more) of the Victoria creams – chocolate-covered discs in more than 20 flavors. Everything on sale here is made on the premises.

GETTING THERE & AWAY
Air

If you're flying to Victoria, you'll arrive at Victoria International Airport in Sidney, about 19km (12 miles) north of Victoria on Hwy 17.

Two airlines with offices in Victoria are: Air Canada (☎ 250-360-9074), 20 Centennial Square, and Canadian Airlines (☎ 250-382-6111), 901 Gordon St. Air Canada and Canadian Airlines connect the airports of Vancouver and Victoria. The normal, one-way, pre-tax economy fare is C$214 return, but weekend return specials can lower this to around C$120 return. A number of smaller regional airlines offer service between Victoria and Vancouver; consult a travel agent for information.

If you are flying to Vancouver and beyond, the cost of a ticket from Victoria is just a few dollars more than one from Vancouver itself, so it's not worth paying the ferry price to catch a flight directly from Vancouver.

You can also catch a seaplane to Victoria harbor from Vancouver harbor with Harbour Air (☎ 250-384-2215, 800-665-0212). The 35-minute flight costs C$79 one way.

Horizon Air (☎ 206-762-3646 in Seattle; 800-547-9308), has service between Vicoria and Seattle, Port Angeles, and Bellingham. North Vancouver Air (☎ 800-228-6608) links Vancouver, Victoria and Tofino.

Bus

Although Greyhound has no service on the island or to the mainland it does have an office (☎ 250-385-5248) in the bus station, at 700 Douglas St, where you can get information and purchase tickets.

Pacific Coach Lines (PCL) (☎ 250-385-4411) operates out of the same station as does Island Coach Lines (☎ 250-385-4411). PCL runs buses to Victoria from Vancouver, some of the southern BC mainland and to Seattle. A bus leaves for Vancouver every hour between 6 am and 9 pm; the one-way fare, which includes the cost of the ferry, is C$25 one way. It's the same price to the Vancouver Airport; it connects with the airport shuttle bus at Delta Pacific Resort. The bus to Seattle, via Sidney and Anacortes, leaves at 10 am and gets there at 5 pm.

Island Coach Lines, sometimes referred to as Laidlaw Lines, covers Vancouver Island. There are eight buses a day to Nanaimo and northern Vancouver Island.

Train

The Esquimalt & Nanaimo Railiner (or E&N Railiner), which is operated by VIA Rail (☎ 250-383-4324, 800-561-8630), connects Victoria with Nanaimo, Parksville and Courtenay. There is one train in each direction per day – northbound from Victoria at 8:15 am, southbound from Courtenay at 1:15 pm. The journey, through some beautiful scenery, takes about 3½ hours. The *Malahat*, as the train is known, is very popular so book ahead. Some one-way fares from Victoria are to Nanaimo C$19, Parksville C$24 and Courtenay C$36. Seven day advance purchases are much cheaper.

For the full schedule, get a copy of the E&N Railiner pamphlet from the station, a travel agency or the Travel InfoCentre. The station, 405 Pandora Ave, is close to town, right at Johnson St Bridge, near the corner of Johnson and Wharf Sts. It's open 7:30 am to noon and 1 to 3 pm.

Car

If you want to rent a car, it's a good idea to shop around as prices can vary. A couple of the cheapest places are ADA Rent A Used Car (☎ 250-474-3455), 892 Goldstream Ave, and Rent-A-Wreck (☎ 250-384-5343), 2634 Douglas St.

All major rental companies are represented in and around the downtown area (as well as at the airport). Three on Douglas St are Avis (☎ 250-386-8468) 843 Douglas St, Budget (☎ 250-388-5525), 757 Douglas St, and Tilden (☎ 250-381-1115), 767 Douglas St.

Ferry

BC Ferries (☎ 250-656-0757, 24 hours), 1112 Fort St, on the corner of Cook St, runs frequent trips from Swartz Bay to Tsawwassen, on the mainland. The 24-mile crossing takes about 1¾ hours. There are between 10 and 15 sailings per day: the schedule varies according to the season. The high-season passenger fare is C$8, while a car costs C$28 or C$30 weekends and holidays. Bus No 70 from the downtown area to the ferry terminal costs C$2.25.

BC Ferries also operates between Swartz Bay and five of the southern Gulf Islands: Galiano, Mayne, Saturna, Salt Spring and Pender. There are about three or four services a day.

The passenger-only *Victoria Clipper* and *Victoria Clipper II*, run by Clipper Navigation (☎ 250-382-8100), 1000 Wharf St, sail between Seattle and Victoria. The journey lasts about 2¾ hours and the fare one way is C$75; it's a little cheaper the rest of the year. For those with cars, the *Princess Marguerite III* operates between and Ogden Point, Victoria, and Seattle. A car and driver costs C$64.

The ferry MV *Coho*, operated by Black Ball Transport (☎ 250-386-2202), 430 Belleville St, is much cheaper. It sails between the Inner Harbour and Port Angeles just across the Strait of Juan de Fuca. It costs US$6.75 per person or US$27.25 with a car. It's a 1½-hour trip, and there are four a day in each direction during the summer months. From Victoria the ferry leaves at 6:20 and 10:30 am and 3 and 7:30 pm.

The passenger-only, summer-only *Victoria Express* (☎ 250-361-9144), at 430 Belleville St, also goes to Port Angeles. The journey time is one hour and the return fare is US$25. The *Victoria Star*, operated by Victoria Cruises (☎ 800-443-4552), which is based in Bellingham, WA, goes back and forth once a day. The passenger-only ferry leaves from Wharf St down from Bastion Square.

Lastly, there's Washington State Ferries (☎ 250-656-1531; 250-381-1551 in Victoria), 2499 Ocean Ave in Sidney. It has a ferry service from Swartz Bay through the San Juan Islands to Anacortes on the Washington mainland. It's a very scenic trip and you can make stopovers on the islands; vehicle fare one way is US$30 in high season.

GETTING AROUND
To/From the Airport

PBM Transport (☎ 250-475-2010), operates the airport bus to the Victoria International Airport from any of 60 downtown area hotels. It leaves every half-hour from downtown and the airport for the 25km (16-mile) trip and costs C$15.

VANCOUVER ISLAND

City bus No 70 passes within 1.5km (1 mile) of the airport, while a taxi to the airport from the downtown area costs about C$35 to C$40.

Bus

For local transit information call BC Transit (☎ 250-382-6161) or get a copy of BC Transit's guide from the Travel Info-Centre listing bus routes and fares. The city buses cover a wide area and run quite frequently. The normal one-way fare is C$1.50; it's C$2.25 if you wish to travel out to the suburbs such as Callwood or Sidney. Have the exact change ready. You can get an all-day pass for C$5 for as many rides as you want, starting as early as you like. These all-day passes are not sold on buses but are available from various outlets around town such as convenience stores.

Bus No 70 goes to the ferry terminal in Swartz Bay; bus No 2 goes to Oak Bay. The Oak Bay Explorer double-decker bus costs just C$1 and takes a 90-minute run between the Empress Hotel and Oak Bay. You can stay on or get off along the way.

Taxi

Two of several cab companies are Victoria Taxi (☎ 250-383-7111) and Blue Bird Cabs (☎ 250-384-1155). You can also hire three-wheeled bicycle taxis called pedicabs – a more leisurely way of getting around.

Bicycle

Downtown you can rent bikes from Harbour Scooters (☎ 250-384-2133), at 843 Douglas St, adjacent to the Avis car-rental office. Bikes are also available at Sports Rent, (☎ 250-385-7368), 611 Discovery St, and at the HI Hostel.

Ferry

Victoria Harbour Ferry runs an enjoyable, albeit short, ferry trip of about half an hour return from the Inner Harbour to Songhees Park (in front of the Ocean Pointe Resort), Fisherman's Wharf and Westbay Marina. The boat takes just a dozen people per trip and costs C$3 one way.

Southern Gulf Islands

Lying north of Victoria, and off Tsawwassen on the mainland, this string of nearly 200 islands in the Georgia Strait is the continuation of Washington State's San Juan Islands.

With a few important exceptions, most of the islands are small and nearly all of them virtually uninhabited, but this island-littered channel is a boater's dream. Vessels of all descriptions cruise in and out of bays, harbors and marinas much of the year. The fishing is varied and excellent: several species of prized salmon can be caught in season. BC Ferries connects with some of the larger islands, so you don't need your own boat to visit them. Lodging is tight, so reservations are mandatory, especially in high season. Pick up a copy of the free newspaper *The Gulf Islander* which details island happenings and lodging options.

Most of the restaurants on the Gulf Islands are associated with lodges, resorts and B&Bs. Campers may want to make sure they have cooking supplies, as casual restaurants can be hard to find.

Due to the mild climate, abundant flora and fauna, relative isolation and natural beauty, the islands are one of Canada's escapist-dream destinations. Indeed, many of the inhabitants are retired people, artists or counterculture types of one sort or another. In fact, some of the 'farmers' are taking their new product to Amsterdam where they compete in contests, much the same way brewers compete for international medals.

Cycling the quiet island roads is a very popular pastime.

Getting There & Away

Ferry service to the islands is good, though potentially very confusing. Pick up one of the ferry schedules (available at most Info-Centres) and give yourself a few minutes to figure out the system. In general, there are more ferries in the morning than in the afternoon, so make sure you know when

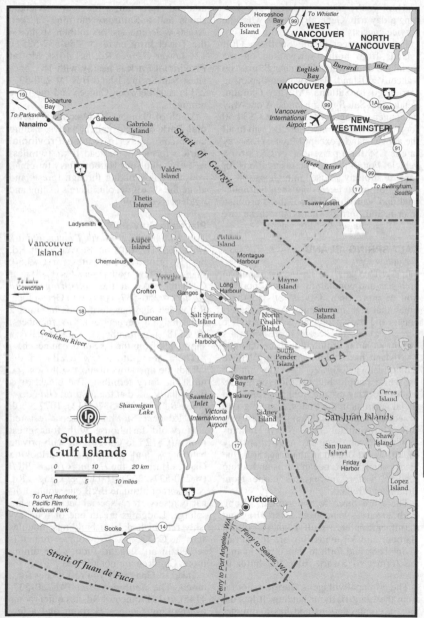

and how you're getting back if you're planning a day trip. Generally, here's what the service consists of.

Ferries connect to the Southern Gulf Islands from both Tsawwassen on the mainland and Swartz Bay near Sidney on Vancouver Island. Tsawwassen-departing ferries go to Saturna, Mayne, Galiano, Pender and Salt Spring Islands. A one-way passenger passage is C$8.50, or C$34.50 for a car. Ferries from Swartz Bay go to all the above islands, except Mayne. One-way fare is C$5 for a passenger, or C$18 for a vehicle. For all these runs, reservations for cars are strongly advised in high season.

In addition to ferries between the mainland and Vancouver Island, there are also inter-island ferries. Fares on these are C$2.50 passenger, C$6 for a car.

SALT SPRING ISLAND
Population 8500

Salt Spring Island is the largest island in both size and population; its usual population of more than 8500 swells to three times that size in summer. Artists, entertainers and craftspeople have chosen to live here. As a consequence, there are craft fairs and art galleries with national reputations. The island has a long, interesting Native Indian history, followed by settlement not by white people but by pioneering US blacks. Seeking escape from prejudice and social tensions in the States, a small group of settlers formed a community at Vesuvius Bay. Unfortunately, the Native Indians didn't care for them any more than they cared for the British in the area. Still, the blacks stuck it out, began farms and set up schools. Later, immigrants came from Britain and Ireland.

There are three ferry terminals: Long Harbour serves Vancouver, Swartz Bay and the other Southern Gulf Islands; Fulford Harbour and Vesuvius Bay are for ferries plying back and forth to Vancouver Island: the former to Swartz Bay, the latter to Crofton.

The principal village is **Ganges**, not far from the Long Harbour landing. It has the most accommodations and has a summer arts and crafts fair, a few tourist-oriented shops and a Saturday morning market. Artists welcome visitors to their studios – the Travel InfoCentre (☎ 250-537-5252), 121 Lower Ganges Rd, has a list. **Mouat Provincial Park** is nearby with 15 campsites. Salt Spring Island Bus (☎ 250-537-2311) runs between Ganges and the ferry terminals.

South of Ganges, **Mt Maxwell Provincial Park** offers excellent views, fishing and picnic areas. In **Ruckle Provincial Park**, a former homestead 10km (6 miles) east of the Fulford Harbour ferry terminal, you can enjoy hiking through forests and along the shoreline, plus there's fishing and wilderness camping.

Places to Stay

The campground at *Ruckle Provincial Park* (☎ 250-391-2300), on Beaver Point Rd, has 70 primitive campsites for C$9.50. There are a few more campsites (C$8) near Cusheon Lake at the *Saltspring Island Hostel* (☎ 250-537-4149), 640 Ocean Lake Rd, which also has dorm beds in either a cedar lodge or teepee for C$14 (members) or C$18 (nonmembers). The hostel is a short walk from the lake or ocean beach.

There are quite a few B&Bs on the island; the operators of most will pick you up at the ferry terminal. The breakfast is particularly good at the pastoral *Old Farmhouse B&B* (☎ 250-537-4113), 1077 North End Rd near St Mary Lake, a restored century-old farmhouse with four guest rooms (C$125 to C$150), all with private bathrooms and balconies. Overlooking Ganges Harbour, the *Hastings House B&B* (☎ 250-537-2362), 160 Upper Ganges Rd, is the sort of ultimate B&B one would ordinarily reserve for a special occasion or big splurge. Lodgings are in one of four lavishly refurbished farm buildings; doubles start at C$375. A five-course dinner is served in an elegant Tudor-style dining room. Children are not allowed.

Head to Ganges if you're looking for a motel. The *Seabreeze Inn* (☎ 250-537-4145), 101 Bittancourt Rd, has quiet rooms overlooking Ganges Harbour and a few kitchenettes; rooms cost C$74/94 single/ double. A number of cottages along St Mary Lake go for roughly the same price as a motel room. The *Cottage Resort* (☎ 250-537-2214), at 175 Suffolk Rd, features a sandy swimming beach, free canoes and rowboats, and small lakefront cottages with a few kitchenettes; cottages rent for C$75 to C$105, depending on the size.

The health-oriented *Salty Springs Spa & Seaside Resort* (☎ 250-537-4111), 1460 North Beach Rd, in Vesuvius Bay, features upscale seaside chalets (some with kitchens) with fireplaces for C$159/189 single/ double. Rooms don't have TV or phone, as guests are expected to be busily rejuvenating themselves with massage and mud baths.

NORTH & SOUTH PENDER ISLANDS
Population 1600

These two islands are joined by a small bridge. There are arts-and-crafts studios to visit and a golf course. For beaches, try Hamilton in Browning Harbour on North Pender and Mortimer Spit on South Pender (just after crossing the bridge). You might see some of the more-or-less tame deer around the islands. You can hike and camp at Prior Centennial Provincial Park on North Pender, close to Medicine Beach at Bedwell Harbour. On South Pender there are good views from the summit of the 255m (850-foot) high Mt Norman.

Places to Stay
Accommodations are mainly in B&Bs and cottages. *Corbett House B&B* (☎ 250-629-6305), 4309 Corbett Rd, 1.5km (1 mile) from the ferry terminal, is a cozy heritage farmhouse with congenial hosts; rooms go for C$70/85 single/double. *Inn on Pender Island* (☎ 250-629-3353, 800-550-0172), 4709 Canal Rd, a small inn in the woods, is popular with cyclists. This is one of the least expensive places to stay on the islands, with an on-site restaurant, and rooms with private entrances and coffeemakers for C$60/70. *Cliffside Inn On-the-Sea* (☎ 250-629-6691), 4230 Armadale Rd, is an oceanfront B&B with great views

(especially from the cliff-side hot tub over the bay). All rooms have private bathrooms; this is very popular as a honeymoon destination.

SATURNA ISLAND
At Saturna Point, by the ferry terminal in Lyall Harbour, there's a store and pub. **Winter Cove Marine Park** has a pleasant sandy beach from where you can go swimming, fishing, boating and hiking. At the top of **Mt Warburton Pike** is a wildlife reserve with feral goats and fine views. There are also good views of the Washington Cascades from the road on the island's leeward side. Just north of Saturna Island is **Cabbage Island Marine Park**, with swimming, fishing and wilderness camping.

Accommodations on Saturna Island are limited to only a few B&Bs, so be sure to book in advance. *Breezy Bay B&B* (☎ 250-539-2937), 131 Payne Rd, on a farm less than 1.5km (1 mile) from the ferry terminal, has singles/doubles for C$55/65. All four rooms at the English-styled *Stone House Farm B&B* (☎ 250-539-2683), 207 Narvaez Bay Rd, feature private bathrooms and balconies, and have views of the waterfront and Mt Baker; rooms cost C$95/100.

MAYNE ISLAND
The ferry between Tsawwassen and Swartz Bay squeezes through Active Pass, which separates Mayne and Galiano Islands. Village Bay, on the southern side of Mayne Island, is the ferry terminal, although there are docking facilities for boaters at other points. There are some late-19th-century buildings at **Miners Bay**, including the museum, which was formerly the jail.

Places to Stay
Mayne Inn Hotel (☎ 250-539-3122), 494 Arbutus Drive, is a small waterfront hotel; all rooms have a view. This is a pleasant and inexpensive place to stay, with rooms starting at C$50/60 single/double.

Fernhill Lodge (☎ 250-539-2544), 610 Fernhill Rd, is a secluded hilltop B&B about 5km (3 miles) from the ferry dock.

The inn is loaded with character, with seven rooms in period theme, a herb garden and a sauna; prices for rooms start at C$75/90. *Oceanwood Country Inn* (☎ 250-539-5074), 630 Dinner Bay Rd, is both pastoral and upscale. All rooms have private bathrooms and views of Navy Channel, some rooms have whirlpool tubs and private balconies. Rooms start at C$120/130, tea service and breakfast included. The restaurant at the Oceanwood is one of the best restaurants in the Gulf Islands, with four-course Northwest cuisine dinners.

GALIANO ISLAND
Population 900

Despite its relatively large size, Galiano Island has fewer than 1000 residents on its long, narrow landmass. About 75% of the island is forest and bush. There's a Travel InfoCentre (☎ 250-539-2233) at the ferry terminal in Sturdies Bay. Again, local artists and artisans invite visitors to their studios.

You can hike almost the length of the east coast and climb either **Mt Sutil** at 323m (1600 feet) or **Mt Galiano** at 342m (1120 feet), from both of which you can see the Olympic Mountains about 90km (56 miles) away. If you're willing to tackle the hills, you can go cycling, while Porlia Pass and Active Pass are popular places for diving and fishing. The coast is lined with cliffs and small bays, and canoeing along the western shoreline is possible in the calmer waters. On the northeastern tip of the island is the rugged **Dionisio Point Provincial Park** with swimming, fishing, hiking and wilderness camping.

Places to Stay

If you want to camp, you can at *Montague Harbour Marine Park* (☎ 250-391-2300), about 9.5km (6 miles) from the Sturdies Bay ferry terminal for C$12; sites are primitive and reservations are available. Around the island there are B&Bs and several places with cottage rentals. *Sutil Lodge* (☎ 250-539-2930) dates from the 1920s and is on the beach at Montague Harbour.

It has singles/doubles from C$60/75 and offers free use of canoes.

Bodega Resort (☎ 250-539-2677), 120 Monasty Rd, is a favorite family destination for its horseback-riding trails and trout-fishing pond. The two-story log cottages have three bedrooms and kitchens and start at C$40/60. *Woodstone Country Inn* (☎ 250-539-2022), on Georgeson Bay Rd, about 3km (2 miles) from the ferry, is more formal and upscale (children are not allowed). There are 12 spacious rooms, all with private bathrooms, some with Jacuzzis, most with fireplaces. Tea and dinner are included in the room rate, which starts at C$95/99 single/double. The inn's restaurant is noted for its fine food, and is open to non-guests.

Southeastern Vancouver Island

DUNCAN & COWICHAN VALLEY

About 60km (37 miles) north of Victoria along the Trans Canada Hwy is the small town of Duncan. It marks the beginning of the Cowichan Valley which runs westward and contains large Cowichan Lake. This is the land of the Cowichan people, who comprise BC's largest Native Indian group. Despite some problems they still maintain aspects of their unique culture.

A good day trip from Victoria, for those with wheels, is to head up to Chemainus, back to Duncan, then over to Lake Cowichan, across to Port Renfrew and down the west coast back to town. It's a lot of driving but if you're in no hurry and can stop a lot it makes an interesting, full day. For information, ask at the Travel InfoCentres. The well-used logging road from Lake Cowichan to Port Renfrew is graveled and in pretty good shape; with a basic map, you shouldn't have any difficulty.

The Travel InfoCentre (☎ 250-746-4636) in Duncan, on the corner of the

Trans Canada Hwy and Coronation St, is open 9 am to 5 pm daily. In Lake Cowichan the Travel InfoCentre (☎ 250-749-4324) is open 9 am to 5 pm Sunday to Thursday, and 8:30 am to 8 pm Friday and Saturday.

There really isn't much to see in Duncan (although the old part of town is worth a look around) or the township of Lake Cowichan, but the valley and lake are good for camping, hiking, swimming, fishing and canoeing. The turnoff for Lake Cowichan is about 4km (2 miles) north of Duncan, left (east) of the Trans Canada Hwy; from the turnoff the lake is another 22km (14 miles).

Since 1985, Duncan, the 'City of Totems,' has developed a project with the Cowichans to have totem poles carved and displayed in the town area. There are now more than 20 examples of this west-coast art form.

Native Heritage Centre

If coming to Duncan from the south on Hwy 1, take the first left turn after crossing the bridge, onto Cowichan Way. The center (☎ 250-746-8119), 200 Cowichan Way, has exhibits of Cowichan craftwork and carvings; you can often watch the carvers and weavers at work. There's a gift shop and restaurant serving Native Indian food. It's open 9:30 am to 5:30 pm daily in summer, and 10 am to 4 pm the rest of the year. The admission price is C$7.25/6/3.25 adults/seniors and students/children, and includes a 20-minute movie about the center and Cowichan people.

BC Forest Museum

This museum (☎ 250-748-9389) is about 3km (1½ miles) north of Duncan, offering both indoor and outdoor features on its 99 acres. There's a stand of original forest of 54m (180-foot) tall Douglas firs that were present before Captain Cook arrived in 1778. Included in the price is a ride around the site in a small steam train. You can visit a bird sanctuary or view a replica of an old logging camp and logging equipment. There are also indoor displays and movies of old logging operations. It's open from

9:30 am to 6 pm daily in the summer and admission is C$7/6/4 adults/seniors and students/children.

Activities

There are many **hiking** trails around Cowichan River and Cowichan Lake. One is the Cowichan River Footpath. It's about 18km (11 miles) long with a good variety of scenery along the way. You can either do it in a day or camp en route. The path goes to Skutz Falls; from there you can head back to Duncan or keep going up the river. Maps of the trail are available at sporting stores. The lake gets warm enough to swim in. You can also go fishing and canoeing in the lake and river.

Places to Stay

Lakeview Park Municipal Campground (☎ 250-749-3350) is on the southern shore of Cowichan Lake about 3km (1½ miles) west of town on South Shore Rd. It has showers, toilets and free firewood. They charge C$15 a car, less without one. Farther west along the lake there is a campground at *Gordon Bay Provincial Park*, about 13km (8 miles) from Hwy 18 on South Shore Rd, with 130 sites for trailers and tents, showers and flush toilets. The fee for a site is C$14.50, and reservations are accepted.

Hotels and motels pop up along the Trans Canada Hwy in Duncan and in the small townships along the river and lake. Two of the cheapest are the *Duncan Motel* (☎ 250-748-2177), 2552 Alexander St, which has some kitchenettes and singles/doubles for C$34/39; and the *Falcon Nest Motel* (☎ 250-748-8188), which has a heated outdoor pool and rooms for C$44/50. The park-like *Best Western Cowichan Valley Inn* (☎ 250-748-2722), 6474 Trans Canada Hwy, is convenient to the BC Forest Museum and Native Heritage Centre, and has a pool, restaurant and pub; rooms cost C$79/85.

Places to Eat

In Duncan most of the eating places are along the Trans Canada Hwy but there are a few small places in the old part of town. *Good Rock Café* (☎ 250-748-4252), is a 1950s-style diner on the corner of Government and Jubilee Sts, complete with jukebox (and old 45s hanging from the ceiling). It's good for breakfasts and has Friday-night East Indian buffets. Also, nearby at 195 Kenneth St, is the *Arbutus Café* (☎ 250-746-5443).

The best restaurant in the area is *Quamichan Inn* (☎ 250-746-7028), 1478 Maple Bay Rd, near the harbor. The inn is in an old home and offers Continental-style cooking in a flower-bedecked dining room. The gardens are lovely; if you like the atmosphere, you can opt to stay in one of the three guest rooms.

Getting There & Away

Island Coach Line buses travel between Duncan and Victoria for C$9 including tax, one way. The 70-minute train trip between Duncan and Victoria on the E&N Railiner costs C$11 including tax; there is one a day in each direction.

CARMANAH PACIFIC PROVINCIAL PARK

Take logging roads from Lake Cowichan to reach this majestic wilderness park adjacent to the West Coast Trail, which was created after years of bitter fighting over logging rights. The park protects a rich rain forest containing some of the world's tallest trees including a giant Sitka spruce 94.5m (315 feet) high. There are some basic tent sites, drinking water, about 5km (3 miles) of marked trails and an information office. Trails extend beyond the park north into the Carmanah Valley with wilderness camping. The rough trails can often be very muddy. The road from Lake Cowichan takes 2½ hours and watch for trucks! Along the way is Nitinaht Lake, the 'confused sea,' renowned for windsurfing, and another road leading to the Ditidaht First Nation visitors' center. It offers tours around the region. The InfoCentre in Duncan has some information on the park (see the Organized Tours section under Victoria for trips to Carmanah).

DUNCAN TO NANAIMO

Crofton

About 16km (10 miles) north of Duncan on Hwy 1A is the small town of Crofton, from where you can catch ferries to Vesuvius Bay in the north of Salt Spring Island (see the Southern Gulf Islands section, earlier in this chapter).

Chemainus

Chemainus, 10km (6 miles) north of Crofton, had a novel and interesting way of putting itself on the tourist map. In 1983 the town sawmill shut down, and to counter the inevitable slow death, an artist was commissioned to paint a large outdoor mural relating to the town's history. People took notice, more murals were painted and now there are over 30 of them. A bustling and prosperous community developed and the sawmill reopened.

The brightly painted Chemainus Theatre has been restored and is the most striking building in town. There are now lots of craft shops and restaurants, all making a short visit a worthwhile proposition. The Travel InfoCentre (☎ 250-246-3944) is in an old railway carriage on Mill St.

Off the coast of Chemainus are **Thetis Island** and **Kuper Island**. Kuper Island is a Native Indian reserve for which you need permission from the chief to visit.

The ferries for these islands leave from Oak St and the ticket office is opposite the Harbourside Café; the fare is C$4 and C$10.75 for a car. The ferry to each island takes about 30 minutes from Chemainus. Thetis Island is primarily geared to boaters and has two marinas. There is a pub, however, at Quinn's Marina: turn left when you get off the ferry then left again into Harbour Drive where you see the anchor sign. There's one restaurant, the Pump House, which you can see to the left as the ferry pulls in. At Pilkey Point there are sandstone formations along the beach.

Places to Stay Once an old mill-workers' dorm, the *Chemainus Hostel* (☎ 250-246-2809), 9694 Chemainus Rd, features separate sleeping areas for men and women, a laundry room and secure bike storage; beds go for C$15. The *Fuller Lake Chemainus Motel* (☎ 250-246-3282), at 9300 Trans Canada Hwy, has a few pleasant rooms and some with kitchenettes for C$45/55 single/double.

Chemainus is largely a land of B&Bs. The *Hummingbird House B&B* (☎ 250-245-8412), 11120 Chemainus Rd, has two rooms in a modern oceanfront home, both with private bathrooms, for C$45/60. Rooms are more nostalgic at the Victorian *Bird Song Cottage* (☎ 250-246-9910), 9909 Maple St, and cost C$70/85.

Ladysmith

Ladysmith, a small town 26km (16 miles) north of Duncan on the Trans Canada Hwy, sits on the 49th parallel, which on the mainland divides Canada from the USA. Originally built as a coal-shipping port by the industrialist James Dunsmuir, the town was named after the South African town of the same name.

The Travel InfoCentre (☎ 250-245-8544) and the Black Nugget Museum, on Gatacre Ave, are in the same building, constructed in 1896 as a hotel. Many of the turn-of-the-century buildings have been restored. The warmest seawaters north of San Francisco are said to flow at **Transfer Beach Park**; it's right in town and you can camp there. About 13km (8 miles) north of town, a 15-minute drive off the highway, on Yellow Point Rd (follow the signs), pub aficionados will find the *Crow & Gate* (☎ 250-722-3731), the oldest British-style pub in the province. The atmosphere is very authentic, though the food is much better than you'd expect at a real English pub: the steak-and-kidney pie and the Cornish pasties are really good, and worth the detour.

Petroglyph Provincial Park

About 3km (1½ miles) south of Nanaimo on the Trans Canada Hwy, this small green park features some ancient Native Indian carvings in sandstone. Most of them are now barely visible having been overgrown with moss and plants. As well as the original petroglyphs there are castings from which you can make rubbings.

NANAIMO & AROUND

Nanaimo is Vancouver Island's second major city, with a rapidly increasing population of over 72,000. Long considered drab and still bad-mouthed by residents of Victoria, Nanaimo gets an unfair rap. It has a diverse cross section of people, a busy little downtown and a major people-oriented waterfront redevelopment.

A number of Native Indian bands once shared the area, which was called *Sne-Ny-Mos*, a Salish word meaning 'meeting place.' Coal was discovered in 1852 and for the next 100 years coal mining was the main industry in the town. Coal has declined in importance, but the city is now the center of a forest-products industry as well as being a major deep-sea fishing port and a terminal for BC Ferries. Tourism continues to gain importance and the city of Nanaimo has become a retirement center as well.

Orientation & Information

Nanaimo, about 110km (68 miles) north of Victoria, is a convenient stopover and a departure point to Vancouver, the islands just off Nanaimo Harbour and places up-island.

The entire waterfront area off Front St along the harbor has been redone with a seaside walkway, docks, shops, restaurants, coffee bars and pubs. Behind the harbor lies the central core. Most of the restaurants and shops are on Commercial and Chapel Sts and Terminal Ave, which run more or less parallel to the harbor. To the south, Nicol St, the southern extension of Terminal Ave, leads to the Trans Canada Hwy. To the north, Terminal Ave forks: the right fork becomes Stewart Ave and leads to the BC Ferries terminal in Departure Bay; the left fork becomes Hwy 19, which heads north up-island to Courtney, Campbell River and Port Hardy. Sealand Market at the Departure Bay ferry terminal has a couple of restaurants, a pub, tourist-oriented shops and the Oceanarium, a

VANCOUVER ISLAND

commercial attraction featuring underwater viewing of sea creatures.

In and around Nanaimo there are quite a few parks. The waterfront promenade, which takes in a number of the downtown ones, begins at the seaplane terminal and heads north to **Georgia Park**, where there are a few totem poles, a display of Native Indian canoes, including a large war canoe and a fine view of Nanaimo Harbour. It then continues to Swy-A-Lana Lagoon (good for children to splash in) and **Mafeo-Sutton Park**, from where ferries leave to Newcastle Island.

There's a Travel InfoCentre (☎ 250-754-8474), 266 Bryden St, just north of the downtown area at the corner of the Island Hwy. Pick up a walking guide of the town's historic area around the harbor. Many of the original buildings have been destroyed and are now marked only by plaques. If you're interested in seeing the ones that are left, get a copy of *Step Into History*, a booklet giving a walking tour of Nanaimo's historic buildings. Throughout the summer there is an information office open daily located in the Bastion historical site on the waterfront.

The Old City Quarter, a small section of downtown around Bastion, Fitzwilliam, Selby and Wesley Sts, is being rejuvenated. The main post office is located near the Harbour Park Shopping Centre which is at the corner of Front St and Terminal Ave. There's a funky and eccentric bookstore, *The Bookstore* (☎ 250-753-3011), at 76 Bastion St. It has everything a real reader could want, including a second floor devoted mainly to children's books. The Nanaimo Regional General Hospital (☎ 250-754-2121) is at 1200 Dufferin Crescent, northwest of the downtown area. The bus station is north of the town center behind the Tally-Ho Hotel at 1 Terminal Ave, while the train station is west at 321 Selby Rd.

Nanaimo Centennial Museum
The small museum (☎ 250-753-1821), at 100 Cameron Rd, displays items of significance in the growth of Nanaimo. Included

are Native Indian, Hudson's Bay Company and coal-mining artifacts. It's open 9 am to 6 pm weekdays, and 10 am to 6 pm weekends. Admission is C$2.

The Bastion
The Bastion, on Front St, on the corner of Bastion St, is the highlight of Nanaimo's old buildings. Built by the Hudson's Bay Company in 1853 for protection from Native Indians, it was never used but for the odd firing of a cannon to quell a disturbance. It's now a museum and tourist office and is open 9 to 11:30 am and noon to 5 pm daily. Admission is free. The cannons are fired over the water at noon Wednesday to Sunday.

Newcastle Island Provincial Marine Park
Just offshore of the downtown area is Newcastle Island, which offers cycling, hiking and beaches. It's also a good place for a picnic or overnight camping. Cars are not allowed. The island was once dotted with mineshafts and sandstone quarries but later became a quiet resort. In summer a small ferry travels between the island and the mainland every hour.

Gabriola Island
Farther out into the strait is Gabriola Island, the most northerly of the Southern Gulf Islands. A fine day can be had exploring, but you'll need a bicycle or car. It has several beaches and three provincial parks offering swimming, shoreline walking and tidal pool examination. At the **Malaspina Galleries** are some unusual sandstone caves carved out by the wind and tides. There is a ferry from Nanaimo (see the Getting There & Away section, later, for details) and a pub at the terminal.

Activities
In 1990, Nanaimo became the first place in North America to feature **bungee jumping**. If you fancy diving 42m (138 feet) off a bridge into the Nanaimo River secured only by a rubber band then call ☎ 250-753-5867 for details. The specially designed

Saunders Bridge is 13km (8 miles) south of Nanaimo and a jump costs C$100.

Off the coast, **scuba diving** is possible among the Northern Gulf Islands in excellent dive sites like Dodd Narrows, Gabriola Passage, Porlier Pass and Northumberland Channel. Three nearby spots where you can go **hiking** or **canoeing** are Nanaimo Lakes, Nanaimo River and Green Mountain. Hikes from Colliery Dam Park lead to Harewood and Overton Lakes. Kayaks can be rented at the Kayak Shack beside the Sealand Market.

Nanaimo also has three good spots for **bird watching**: Buttertubs Marsh Sanctuary, Morrell Sanctuary (take Comox Rd west off Terminal Ave to both) and Piper's Lagoon Park off Hammond Bay north of the city.

Special Events

The top annual event is the Nanaimo Bathtub Race to Vancouver, held each mid-July as part of Nanaimo's Marine Festival. Hundreds of fiberglass tubs start out, about 100 sinking in the first five minutes. Winners complete the 48km (30-mile) passage of the Georgia Strait's wild waters to reach the beaches at Vancouver. For details call ☎ 250-753-7223.

Through June and July the Nanaimo Festival presents both classic and modern plays at Malaspina College south of town. For information call ☎ 250-754-7587.

Places to Stay

Camping The best place for camping is just off the coast at *Newcastle Island Provincial Marine Park* with 18 tent sites at C$9.50; no reservations. See the Getting There & Away section, later, for ferry details. Farther out is the much larger Gabriola Island where there are private campgrounds. Convenient to the ferry, *Gabriola Campground* (☎ 250-247-2079) has 28 beachside campsites at C$14.

North of town are several campgrounds. *Jingle Pot Campsite & RV Park* (☎ 250-758-1614), 4012 Jingle Pot Rd, is 8km (5 miles) north of Nanaimo off Hwy 19. It has showers, laundry and tent sites for

C$12. The closest to town is *Beban Park Campground* (☎ 250-756-5200), at 2300 Bowen Rd, about 1.5km (1 mile) west of Hwy 19, which has sites for C$12. *Brannen Lake Campsites* (☎ 250-756-0404), 4228 Briggs Rd, is on a working farm; sites are C$14.

Hostels Nanaimo has two independent hostels, part of the Pacific Rim Network. The closest to town is the *Nicol St Hostel* (☎ 250-753-1188), 65 Nicol St, several kilometers south of the downtown area. Beds are C$15. Check in between 4 and 11 pm. *Thomson Hostel* (☎ 250-722-2251), 1660 Cedar Hwy, is about 10km (6 miles) south of town, and open for international travelers only. Bus No 11 stops right outside. It offers use of the kitchen and canoes and charges C$13 per night, or you can camp on the lawn. The congenial owner will pick up travelers at the bus station in the evening and drop them off the next morning.

Hotels Many of the motels are on the highway north and south of the city. On the south end of town the *Diplomat Motel* (☎ 250-753-3261), 333 Nicol St, has single/double rooms for C$42. On the north end of town close to the Departure Bay ferry terminal, is the *Colonial Motel* (☎ 250-754-4415), 950 North Terminal Ave, with rooms (some with kitchenettes) starting at C$39/45.

South of town overlooking the harbor, the *Days Inn Harbourview* (☎ 250-754-8171, 800-329-7466), 809 Island Hwy S, has an indoor swimming pool, kitchenettes and rooms starting at C$69/79 single/double. The *Tally-Ho Hotel* (☎ 250-753-2241, 800-663-7322), 1 Terminal Ave, near the ferry terminal, has an outdoor pool and rooms starting at C$65 single or double.

Downtown the *Best Western Dorchester Hotel*, (☎ 250-754-6835, 800-661-2449), is a refurbished historic hotel featuring rooms and suites with harbor views starting at C$85. The *Coast Bastion Inn* (☎ 250-753-6601, 800-663-1144), at 11 Bastion St, is another pleasant downtown waterfront hotel; rooms have views of the harbor and go for C$89/99.

About 5km (3 miles) north of town, the *Long Lake Inn Resort* (☎ 250-758-1144, 800-565-1144), 4700 N Island Hwy, is a large vacation resort featuring a swimming beach, marina and canoe rentals. The balconied rooms all front onto Long Lake and cost C$109 to C$168 single or double.

Places to Eat

A stroll along Commercial St from the corner of Terminal Ave will turn up a number of places. The *Scotch Bakery & Coffee Bar* (☎ 753-3521), 87 Commercial St, has great baked goods, including Nanaimo Bars, a classic Canadian sweet known across the country. On the same side and up the hill is *Charlie's Seafood Bar* (☎ 250-753-7044), 123 Commercial St, a large spacious restaurant with sandwiches and burgers.

For lunch or dinner, *Gina's Café* (☎ 250-753-5411), perched at 47 Skinner St, is recommended for its inexpensive Mexican food, atmosphere and view.

Another fine place for an evening meal is the pleasantly casual *Dinghy Dock Marine Pub* (☎ 250-753-2373), at the waterfront over on Protection Island, an eight-minute trip from downtown on a small ferryboat. Seafood and various barbecue meals are offered for about C$10. The outdoor patio has views across the harbor to Nanaimo and after dinner you can stroll the small, quiet residential island. Get the ferry from the docks at the south end of Government Wharf across from the museum.

Getting There & Away

Bus & Train Island Coach Lines (☎ 250-753-4371) connects Nanaimo with points north and south; the one-way fare to Victoria is C$17. The station is at 1 Terminal Ave north of the center near Comox Rd.

The Ultimate Nanaimo Bar

Nanaimo is rich in history – and the Nanaimo Bar is no exception. An extraordinarily sweet, incredibly delicious dessert, the ever popular Nanaimo Bar is a Canadian classic. Although there are many variations, here's one recipe sure to please your taste buds. Enjoy!

Crust
½ cup butter
½ cup sugar
5 tablespoons powdered cocoa
1 teaspoon vanilla extract
1 egg, lightly beaten
1½ cup graham cracker crumbs
1 cup chopped walnuts

Icing
2 cups powdered sugar
½ cup butter, softened
3 tablespoons English Dessert mix
    or egg custard mix
2 tablespoons milk
4 oz (125g) semisweet chocolate

For the crust, place the butter, sugar, cocoa and vanilla in a saucepan. Cook, stirring, until sugar is dissolved, then add egg and mix well. Remove from heat and stir in graham cracker crumbs and nuts. Pack into an 8-by-12-inch pan and refrigerate until cooled.

To make the icing, combine the powdered sugar, butter, dessert or custard mix, and milk, beating well. Spread over crust and refrigerate for 30 minutes. Melt chocolate in the top of a double boiler over simmering water and pour evenly over icing. Refrigerate once more until chilled. To serve, cut into squares. Makes 24 to 30 squares

Reprinted with permission of the Junior League of San Francisco, from *San Francisco à la Carte: A Cookbook* (New York: Bantam Doubleday Dell, 1991), by Joyce L. Vedral. ■

VANCOUVER ISLAND

The E&N Railiner passes through once a day in each direction; the one-way fare to Victoria is C$19. There's no ticket office at the station, 321 Selby St; call ☎ 800-561-8630 for information. Tickets can be purchased from the conductor.

Ferry The 39km (24-mile) ferry trip to Horseshoe Bay takes about 1½ hours. There are about 12 to 15 services in each direction daily, depending on the season. Tickets are C$8 per person, and C$28 for a vehicle on weekdays, C$2 more on weekends. The terminal is in Departure Bay, at the northern end of Stewart Ave. The ferry between Nanaimo and Tsawwassen, the *Mid-Island Express*, goes four times a day in each direction and takes two hours and is the same price. This ferry terminal is at Duke Point. For more information, call BC Ferries at ☎ 250-381-3431.

Getting Around

Bus For information about local buses call ☎ 250-390-4531 or get a transit guide at the tourist office. All buses pass through the Gordon Exchange at the corner of Front and Gordon Sts. Bus No 2 goes to the Stewart Ave ferry terminal.

Ferry Ferries to Newcastle Island leave from Mafeo-Sutton Park and cost C$4 return. It's the same price to Protection Island. The ferry to Gabriola Island leaves from near the Harbour Park Shopping Centre and takes cars for C$10.75, but only charges C$4 if you're walking and bikes are free. After 2 pm you're stuck on the island until the next morning when the ferry returns. The ferry trip takes about 20 minutes.

PARKSVILLE & QUALICUM BEACH

These towns and the coast towards Comox are known for their long stretches of beach. Though still not fabulous, the beach at Parksville is busier, wider and sandier than at other places – stop by the road, tone up the tan and have a quick swim in the nippy water.

Just south of Parksville is Hwy 4, the road to Port Alberni and the west coast. You can also connect with Hwy 4 from Qualicum Beach via Hwy 4A. At Coombs check out the goats grazing on the roof of the general store! From Parksville to Port Alberni is some very fine scenery, with several provincial parks where you can stop awhile.

Places to Stay

Beaches at Parksville and Rathtrevor (just south of Parksville) are developed with a large number of oceanfront resorts. Facilities vary in style and character from modern condos to funky beach cottages, so it's worth shopping around if you'll be here for awhile. There's slightly less development at Qualicum Beach, though a big luxury resort currently under construction will soon change that.

Camping The popular *Rathtrevor Beach Provincial Park*, 3km (2 miles) southeast of Parksville, has a large campground with 175 forested sites, flush toilets, free hot showers, playground and an RV dump station. Sites cost C$9.50 to C$15.50, and reservations are accepted.

B&Bs A few miles south of Parksville, the Tudor-styled *MacLure House B&B* (☎ 250-248-3470), 1015 E Island Hwy, Unit 11, has four rooms on Rathtrevor Beach, all with private bathrooms for C$72/80 single/double; guests have use of a pool, hot tub and tennis court. The cliffside *Bahari B&B* (☎ 250-752-9278), 5101 Island Hwy in Qualicum Beach, has four guestrooms with private bathrooms, fireplaces and beach access; rooms start at C$75 single or double (no children).

Hotels In Parksville, the *Sandcastle Inn* (☎ 250-248-2334, 800-335-7263), at 374 Island Hwy W, features clean, well-kept motel rooms with ocean views and some kitchenettes starting at C$59 single or double. The *Ocean Crest Motel* (☎ 250-752-5518, 888-234-5661), 3292 W Island Hwy, in Qualicum, has similar amenities and rooms starting at C$55/60 for single/double. The *Old Dutch Inn* (☎ 250-752-6914, 800-661-0199), 2690 W Island Hwy, is nicer, with an indoor pool, hot tub and rooms for C$80/85.

Beach Resorts Rooms at the *Best Western Bayside Inn Resort* (☎ 250-248-8333, 800-663-4232 in Canada), 240 Dogwood St, on Parksville Beach, have both ocean and mountain views and start at C$79, and there's an indoor pool and hot tub, fitness center, volleyball net and scuba shop. Another oceanfront resort, the *Tigh Na Mara Resort Hotel* (☎ 250-248-2072, 800-663-7373), 1095 E Island Hwy, 1.5km (1 mile) south of town, has forested log cabins and condos with kitchens and fireplaces starting at C$94 single or double, plus a fitness room, indoor pool, watercraft rentals and restaurant.

Pacific Shores Nature Resort (☎ 250-468-7121, 800-500-7212), 1655 Stroughler Rd, 3km (2 miles) south of Parksville on Rathrover Beach, is a compound of one- and two-bedroom luxury beachfront condominiums (C$80 to C$180) adjacent to a nature preserve; there's also a few hotel rooms. It offers a bit more seclusion than the resorts in Parksville, but is just as developed as any other beach resort and features an indoor pool and hot tubs.

Around Parksville & Qualicum Beach
About 13km (7 miles) southwest of Parksville at the end of Errington Rd is **Englishman River Falls Provincial Park**, a pleasant side trip with a 30-minute walking trail through the woods past waterfalls and emerald pools. There is also swimming and camping. **Little Qualicum Falls Provincial Park**, 13km (7 miles) southwest of Parksville on Hwy 4, is another good park with hiking, fishing and camping. Both areas are heavily forested and scenic. About 32km (20 miles) southwest of here, Mt Arrowsmith has skiing in winter, hiking trails in summer.

Horne Lake Provincial Park North of Qualicum Beach and 16km (10 miles) off Hwy 19, spelunking (caving) enthusiasts can explore the limestone caves here. There are three undeveloped but explorable

caves, and tours of varying lengths and difficulty occur daily in July and August, on weekends in June and September. They range from inexpensive half-hour introductions to challenging five-hour C$60 trips with full equipment and training in Riverbend Cave, the most spectacular, with a total of 383m (417 yards) of mapped passages. Don't drink much at breakfast because there is no toilet until you're back in daylight. Alternatively, equipment can be rented to explore the lesser two caves, Main and Lower Main, independently. Bring some very warm clothing and a good pair of shoes. For reservations call ☎ 250-248-7829. The park also has a good campground on the lake. The road to the park is an active logging road, so be careful of the trucks.

PORT ALBERNI & AROUND
Population 19,000
Halfway across the island is this town built on forestry and fishing. Over 300 commercial fishing boats work out of the area, most catching salmon. At Harbour Quay, at the bottom of Argyle St, there's an observation tower, the Forestry Visitor Centre (☎ 250-724-7890), open 10 am to 8 pm daily, and some restaurants. Visitors can tour both the paper mill and the sawmill; inquire at the forestry center.

Perhaps the most noteworthy features of Port Alberni are the MVs *Lady Rose* and *Frances Barkley*, which sail out of Harbour Quay to the west coast of the island. They're operated by Alberni Marine Transportation (☎ 250-723-8313). Those planning to canoe or kayak around the Broken Group Islands can take their boats onboard, though the trip is more popular as a scenic cruise. The ferry company is one place that rents canoes and kayaks (see the Getting There & Away section, below, for more information).

In MacMillan Provincial Park, **Cathedral Grove**, right by the road at the western end of Cameron Lake is a must half-hour stop. Regarded by Native Indians as a sacred place, it is a grove of virgin forest with huge Douglas firs and red cedars, some dating back 800 years. A series of trails lead through the delicate, ancient ecosystem of towering trees. It is very popular, so please respect the sign asking you not to touch the trees or plants.

At **Stamp Falls Provincial Park**, 14.5km (9 miles) north of Port Alberni, salmon can sometimes be seen jumping on their way up the river and there are petroglyphs at nearby **Sproat Lake**.

Hikers also come to Port Alberni to reach Della Falls, North America's highest waterfall (see the Strathcona Provincial Park section later in this chapter) by an alternative route: canoeing the length of Great Central Lake from Port Alberni and taking the trail up from there.

Places to Stay

You can camp at *Stamp Falls Provincial Park*, 14.5km (9 miles) west of Port Alberni on Beaver Creek Rd, a small wooded campground near a waterfall, with primitive sites for C$9.50.

The modest *Esta Villa Motel* (☎ 250-724-1261, 800-724-0844), 4014 Johnston Rd, is one of the cheapest places to stay in Port Alberni, with single/double rooms at C$55/59. The *Alberni Inn* (☎ 250-723-9403, 800-815-8007), 3805 Redford St, is a bit nicer, and has a few rooms with full-size kitchens; rooms cost C$61/65. While not incredibly fancy, the conference-styled *Coast Hospitality Inn* (☎ 250-723-8111, 800-663-1144), 3835 Redford St, is the best place to stay. It features an on-site restaurant and pub; rooms cost C$114/120.

Getting There & Away

Bus Island Coach Lines (☎ 250-723-6924), 4541 Margaret St, runs twice daily to Tofino and Ucluelet from Port Alberni. Western Bus Lines (☎ 250-723-3341), at 4521 10th Ave, has one bus Monday and Friday to Bamfield for C$17. It also picks passengers up at the main Island Coach Lines bus station.

Boat Freighters operated by Alberni Marine Transportation (☎ 250-723-8313), take mail and cargo as well as passengers between Kildonan on Alberni Inlet, Bamfield at the end of the West Coast Trail, the Broken Group Islands and Ucluelet. Fares to Bamfield are C$18 one way, to Ucluelet C$20. One-day return trips allow passengers some free time at Bamfield and Ucluelet for exploring. On Sunday during the summer a longer stay in Bamfield is possible.

The freighters depart Port Alberni for Bamfield on Tuesday, Thursday and Saturday all year, and for Ucluelet and the Broken Group Islands on Monday, Wednesday and Friday from 1 June to 30 September. In midsummer there are Sunday cruises to Bamfield only. Regardless of the weather, take a sweater and/or raincoat.

DENMAN & HORNBY ISLANDS

Farther up the east coast are two lesser known Gulf Islands – Denman and Hornby. There's good bird watching on Hornby Island. The ferry for Denman Island leaves from Buckley Bay, about 20km (13 miles) south of Courtenay, and takes 10 minutes. For Hornby Island you take another ferry from Gravely Bay on Denman Island. The fare for each is C$3.50 per person, or C$9.25 with a car.

Each island features provincial parks, hiking, swimming, fishing, scuba diving and beaches, but only *Fillongley Provincial Park* on Denman Island allows camping; there are 10 primitive sites fronting Lambert Channel for C$9.50.

On Hornby Island there is private camping for tents and RVs near the beach at the small, family-oriented *Bradsdadland Country Camp Resort* (☎ 250-335-0757), 1980 Shingle Split Rd; sites cost C$16 to C$19, plus C$1 for each utility hookup. Also near the beach, *Outer Island B&B* (☎ 250-335-2379, 800-364-1331), 4785 DePape Rd, has four rooms in an old farmhouse with both shared and private bathrooms, a small cabin and an outdoor pool; rooms start at C$99/109 single/double. The *Sea Breeze Lodge* (☎ 250-335-2321), at Tralee Point, has 12 modest cottages overlooking the ocean for C$635 to C$700 a week, meals included. It's one of the few places to eat on Hornby Island, and it's

VANCOUVER ISLAND

open to non-guests with advance notice. The two other dinner options are *Thatch* (near the ferry) and *Pizza Galore*.

COURTENAY & COMOX
Population 25,000

Basically commercial centers for the local farming, logging and fishing industries, these two towns are also important supply hubs for Mt Washington, 32km (20 miles) west of Courtenay, and Forbidden Plateau just outside Strathcona Provincial Park, two major summer and winter recreation areas. Courtenay is the larger of these two essentially joined towns. The Travel Info-Centre (☎ 250-334-3234), 2040 Cliffe Ave, in Courtenay, serves both towns and is open 8 am to 8 pm daily.

In Courtenay there is a small museum (☎ 250-334-3234), 360 Cliffe Ave, and not far out is the Puntledge River Fish Hatchery which farms salmon. At the Canadian Air Force base in Comox an international air show takes place each August in even-numbered years.

There is good hiking in the area, from afternoon walks to some overnight climbs. **Miracle Beach Provincial Park** (☎ 250-755-2483), 22km (14 miles) north of Courtenay, has hiking trails, a campground and a long, sandy beach. **Comox Glacier** is a good two-day hike, as is **Mt Albert Edward** in the Forbidden Plateau area, which offers excellent views. Ask at the Travel InfoCentre for more information. You must register if you're going on an overnighter.

Places to Stay

About 6km (4 miles) outside of Courtenay is the *North Comox Lake Mini-Hostel* (☎ 250-338-1914), at 4787 Lake Trail Rd, which charges C$12. Meals are available; call to arrange a pickup at the bus or train station. It's open all year and in summer there is extra sleeping space in a teepee. Near Comox are several places renting cottages by the beach.

Also outside of Courtenay, elaborate English-style gardens and waterfront views

make the *Greystone Manor B&B* (☎ 250-338-1422), 4014 Haas Rd, a pleasant place to stay. Room have private bathrooms and start at C$55/60 for single/double.

In town the *Sleepy Hollow Inn* (☎ 250-334-4476, 800-811-5955), at 1190 Cliffe Ave, has one- and two-bedroom motel units with kitchenettes, an indoor pool and exercise room starting at C$45/50. There's also the recently renovated *Travelodge Courtenay* (☎ 250-334-4491, 800-795-9486), 2605 Island Hwy, with rooms for C$59/65. At the top end, the *Coast Westerly* (☎ 250-338-7741, 800-668-7797), 1590 Cliffe Ave, has the full amenities of a convention-style hotel; balconied rooms overlooking the Courtenay River start at C$93/98.

Pacific Rim National Park

A rough, rugged, inhospitable yet beautiful coastal area, the park is a long, thin strip of land divided into three distinct units – Long Beach, Broken Group Islands and the West Coast Trail. Each is separated by land and water and is reached by a different route.

Whale-watching trips can be a highlight of a visit to the west coast. From mid-February to June, Pacific gray whales migrate up the coast from Mexico to the Arctic Ocean; the peak time to catch them heading north is mid-April. In late fall they head back south. Other attractions are the rain forest and undeveloped beach. With the forests of huge cedar and fir meeting the edge of the beach, and the huge waves rolling in off the Pacific, it really does feel like you are standing at the far edge of the continent.

Hundreds of thousands of geese and ducks fly overhead in spring and fall. Also, the pools left behind by the tides are often filled with interesting life forms: starfish, anemones, sponges, fish, snails and many other small creatures.

For general information about the park, contact Pacific Rim National Park, PO Box 280, Ucluelet, BC V0R 3A0, or call ☎ 250-726-7721 or 250-726-4212.

Getting There & Away

Specific information regarding transportation to and from the various park units is included in the appropriate sections. However, getting there and away is by no means straightforward, so an overview of the logistics involved is helpful.

Easiest to reach is the Long Beach Unit, accessed by Hwy 4 from Port Alberni. Port Alberni is also the terminus for the only public transportation to the northerly park units (see Port Alberni's Getting There & Away section, above), with buses to Ucluelet, Tofino and Bamfield.

Ucluelet, at the southern end of Long Beach, is served by passenger carrying cargo ships from Port Alberni. Freighters from Port Alberni also carry passengers (and their canoes or kayaks) to the Broken Island Unit, and to Bamfield, at the northern end of the redoubtable West Coast Trail. You can also drive a long gravel road from Port Alberni to Bamfield. Port Renfrew, located at the southern edge of the West Coast Trail, is accessed by gravel road from Lake Cowichan, or by Hwy 14 from Victoria. In summer, both Port Renfrew and Bamfield are served by hiker-oriented minibuses.

LONG BEACH

The most northerly third of the park, Long Beach is exactly that – about 20km (12 miles) of wide, log-strewn surf and wind-swept, sandy beach. At other parts, the waves pound into a craggy, rocky shoreline. At each end of Long Beach is a small fishing and tourist village – Tofino in the north, Ucluelet in the south. This area is the easiest to get to in the park, and the closest to all services. Hwy 4 leads from Port Alberni through the magnificent scenery (some heavily logged areas notwithstanding) of the Mackenzie Ranges at the southern edge of Clayoquot (pronounced clak-wot) Sound into this section of the park.

In summer there are interpretive programs and guided walks run by the Wickaninnish Centre next to the beach.

Visitors will find plenty of campgrounds, motels and resorts in either Tofino or Ucluelet but budget accommodations are rather scarce in either place. Ucluelet has the greatest selection of modest mid-priced motels while Tofino is home to BC's most extravagant beach resorts. Travelers should be sure to make reservations well in advance of their visit regardless of how much they plan to pay.

Hiking

There are eight short hiking trails in the park in the Long Beach Unit; the Park Information Office (☎ 250-726-4212) will have a description of them. The **South Beach Trail** leads to an area good for watching, and hearing, the huge waves. **Half Moon Bay Trail** leads to a calm, sandy bay. Radar Hill is good for views and has trails leading down to some small, secluded beaches. The Rainforest and Schooner Cove trails are good, accessible forest walks.

Surfing

Long Beach reputedly has the best surfing in BC. Note that the weather is generally poor here. Most days are cold, windy and rainy. A warm, sunny day about 1km (half a mile) or so from the coast can disappear into mist and fog at Long Beach. A sweater or raincoat is protection not only against the weather but also against the mosquitoes. The water, too, is cold – those doing any water sports should use wetsuits or drysuits. Surfboards can be rented but ask about etiquette as there have been run ins between locals and visitors over which waves are whose.

Other Activities

Another activity is looking for and maybe watching some of the local marine life. Seals, sea lions and porpoises are common, killer and Pacific gray whales a possibility depending on the time of the year. Good viewing spots are Schooner Cove, Quistis Point, Radar Hill with its telescope and Combers Beach near Sea Lion Rocks. Note that you must pay for parking everywhere.

TOFINO
Population 1200

At the northern end of Long Beach, just outside the park boundary, is the village of Tofino, the center of the coast's tourism and one of the major destinations on Vancouver Island. Once a simple fishing village, the winter population of about 1200 swells to at least twice that through the summer. It's a busy, resort-like place with a bit of an undercurrent of tension resulting from the friction between environmentalists and those involved in the resource industries. All in all it makes an interesting town for a few days of activities. The Travel InfoCentre (☎ 250-725-3414), 380 Campbell St, is open 9 am to 7:30 pm daily. The Friends of Clayoquot Sound (☎ 250-725-4218) have an office at 331 Neill St. The Forest Information Centre (☎ 250-725-3295), 316 Main St, is open 10 am to 6 pm daily.

Things to See & Do

The **Whale Centre** (☎ 250-725-2132), at 411 Campbell St, has a small museum and whale exhibit; it's open 9 am to 6 pm daily in summer. The **Eagle Aerie Gallery** (☎ 250-725-3120), on Campbell St, houses the paintings and carvings of Roy Henry Vickers, an internationally established Native Indian artist based in Tofino.

Whale-watching, fishing and rain-forest trips can be arranged in town. For around C$40 several companies offer boat trips to see Pacific gray whales. Best time is March to May when they migrate through the area, but many linger through the summer. Clayoquot Whaler will take you out and also fill you in on the history and Native Indian culture of the area. For information and tickets call Clayoquot Sound Charters (☎ 250-725-2888, 800-665-9425), 320 Main St. The Whale Centre (see above) will also take you to see gray whales and

other wildlife. Remote Passages (☎ 250-725-3330), 585 Campbell St, uses rubber Zodiacs, a good way to get close to the whales.

A good trip is to **Hot Springs Cove** where a 20-minute hike will lead you to the hot springs (which are the only ones on Vancouver Island) overlooking the ocean. There are several pools, which become progressively cooler down the hillside to the sea. You can hire a boat or seaplane to the cove; contact Remote Passages or the Whale Centre. Overnight camping is possible.

Highly recommended is a trip to **Meares Island**, a 15-minute cruise past the Harbour Islands. This is a magical place of virgin rain forest with trees of mind-boggling age and stature: one is over 1000 years old and nearly 19m (63 feet) in diameter. Species include cedar, yew and varieties of spruce.

To organize a trip to Meares Island, call Dutch before 10 am or in the evenings at ☎ 250-725-3793. His small boat, *Salty Dog*, makes the trip several times a day for C$15 return, departing from the dock at the foot of Fourth St. Make arrangements with him for how long you want to stay. Weigh West Marine Resort (☎ 250-725-3277), 634 Campbell St, also offers the same deal but they can't match Dutch for character.

There are several rugged but well-marked trails on the island; the basic loop takes about 2½ hours. Before going on to the island find out about the condition of the trails; except for the boardwalked area at the beginning, mud can be a problem.

Tofino Sea Kayaking Co (☎ 250-725-4222), also at 320 Main St, offers paddling tours to the nearby islands; tours start at C$50 for four hours. Try Springtime Charters (☎ 250-725-2351), 586 Campbell St, for fishing.

Tofino Airlines (☎ 250-725-4454) has scenic flights of the islands that includes whale-watching for C$140 for 20 minutes for three people. The seaplanes leave from the wharf at the bottom of 1st St.

Places to Stay

Tofino is very often booked up in summer, so don't get caught looking after dark or you'll be on the park bench – if it's not taken. Expensive resort hotels and ocean-front housekeeping cottages represent the bulk of the market here, and you can count on spending at least C$100 a night. There are only a few hostels and cheap hotels here, so budget travelers should make reservations for these places far in advance.

Camping There is one place to camp in the park itself, *Green Point Campground* (☎ 250-726-4245, 800-689-9025), near Tofino. It has bathrooms with hot water and flush toilets and costs C$18. Arrive early in the morning to get a place or have reserva tions made by calling the above number. They have a few walk-in sites that are often vacant even at the end of the day when the 'No Vacancy' sign is up.

About 3km (2 miles) south on Mac-kenzie Beach there are several private campgrounds with both tent and RV sites, and some beachfront cottages. *Bella Pacif ica Resort & Campground* (☎ 250-725-3400) has full facilities and good beach sites starting at C$21. The much-smaller *Mackenzie Beach Resort* (☎ 250-725-3439), 1101 Pacific Rim Hwy, charges C$28 and has one and two bedroom beach cottages starting at C$119. *Crystal Cove Beach Resort* (☎ 250-725-4213), 1165 Cedarwood Place, has sites starting at C$22 and log cottages begin at C$160. There is cheaper tent camping on Indian Island off Grice Bay, south of Tofino.

Hostels In town, the *Backpackers' Hostel* (☎ 250-725-2288), 241 Campbell St, has room for 18 people in dorm beds for C$15 and double rooms for C$30, with lower off-season rates. It is pretty basic and cramped but it fills a need. There are two other hostel-style places located on nearby islands. The closest, within view of town, is *L'Auberge on the Island* with rooms in the house for C$19 or camping for C$15. You must use the marine telephone oper-ator to contact them. Call ☎ 0, ask the marine operator for channel 24 Tofino, and then ask for Sea Slip N111658. A call costs about C$3.

Alternatively, try the comfortable, quiet *Vargas Island Inn & Hostel* (☎ 250-725-3309). Here lodge rooms begin at C$60 including meals but hostel accommoda-tions are offered at C$40 per person. Both also include transportation, which is a 20-minute boat ride from town. Cabins and camping are offered at another island re-treat, *Dream Isle*. Call ☎ 0, channel 24 Tofino, Dream Isle 2, Sea Slip N11483.

Hotels Cheapest of the motels is *Dolphin Motel* (☎ 250-725-3377), 1190 Pacific Rim Hwy, about 3km (2 miles) south of town with singles/doubles beginning at C$45/49. Downtown overlooking the bay, *Schooner Motel* (☎ 250-725-3478), 311-312 Camp-bell St, has a few moderately priced rooms (some with kitchens) starting at C$65/69.

The *Best Western Tin Wis Resort* (☎ 250-725-4445, 800-661-9995), 1119 Pacific Rim Hwy, on Templar Channel, has beach access and convention facilities, rooms cost C$125 to C$180 single or double.

Resorts South of Tofino, *Middle Beach Lodge* (☎ 250-725-2900), Pacific Rim Hwy, has rustic oceanfront lodge rooms, suites and cabins (some with fireplaces and kitchens) on a wilderness headland near a sandy beach. There are two lodges – one for families and the other for adults only – and a restaurant; doubles cost C$100 to C$200.

The exclusive *Himwitsa Lodge* (☎ 250-725-3319, 800-899-1947), 300 Main St, at the end of the Trans Canada Hwy, sports a spectacular view of Clayoquot Sound, and has been long-favored by celebrities like Charlton Heston for its spacious guest suites and superb restaurant. All rooms have kitchenettes, VCRs and hot tubs and start at C$140/185 single/double.

About 5km (3 miles) south of Tofino at Chesterman Beach, a multi-million dollar reconstruction of the *Wickaninnish Inn* (☎ 250-725-3100, 800-333-4604), Osprey Lane, is perched on a rugged promontory above the sea. This completely new mega-resort and restaurant is a reincarnation of the landmark lodge put out of commission by the creation of Pacific Rim National Park in 1977. The inn's grand rooms feature views of the pounding surf, while guest rooms have push-button gas fireplaces, two-person hot tubs and private balconies; rooms start at C$200/220 single/double.

Places to Eat

Most restaurants are associated with the lodges and resorts in the area, and are open to non-guests; it's a good idea to call ahead for reservations in high season.

There are also some good places to eat in the town. The *Common Loaf Bake Shop* (☎ 725-3915), at 180 1st St, is recommended. It has just a few tables but a large selection of excellent, delicious home-made muffins, cookies, breads and cakes. In the morning try the still-warm cinnamon buns. The *Alley Way Café* (☎ 250-725-3105), tucked in the yard behind the corner of 1st St and Campbell St, has a range of all-day breakfasts, Mexican-style dishes and various vegetarian meals all under C$8.

Pointe Restaurant at the Wickaninnish Inn, surrounded on all sides with churning surf, is the fine dining option in the Tofino area.

Entertainment

The pub downstairs in Maquinna Lodge (☎ 250-725-3261), 120 First St, is the only place in town for a beer and is a real happening place on Friday and Saturday nights with a DJ and lots of dancing.

UCLUELET
Population 1700

Ucluelet (a Nootka word meaning 'people with a safe landing place') is not as attractive as Tofino and is not exactly a visitor mecca. It's more a town for the locals working in fishing and logging. The Travel InfoCentre (☎ 250-726-4641), 227 Main St, is open 9 am to 6 pm daily in summer.

You might like to walk to the lighthouse at **Amphitrite Point**, at the foot of Peninsula Rd, or take one of the trails at **Terrace Beach** north of town. To the south of town, **Big Beach** is a quiet, rocky bit of shore-

line with tidal pools. Subtidal Adventures (☎ 250-726-7336), on the right as you head into town just after Ucluelet Campground, is an outfitter which offers trips to see Pacific gray whales in March and April only; trips start at C$40 for two hours. It also runs tours around the Broken Group Islands, will drop off people wishing to camp on an island and has scuba-diving cruises. Majestic West Coast Wilderness Adventures (☎ 250-726-2868) offers one- and four-day kayaking trips starting at C$45 for 2½ hours.

Places to Stay

Ucluelet Campground (☎ 250-726-4355), 260 Seaplane Base Rd overlooking the harbor, with hot showers and flush toilets, has sites starting at C$16. Ucluelet has quite a stable of reasonably priced motels, mostly on Peninsula Rd, and a couple of simple cheap ones. *Ucluelet Hotel* (☎ 250-726-4324), 250 Main St, has doubles without bath at C$25. Accommodations can also be cheap at the *Canadian Princess Resort* (☎ 250-726-7771, 800-663-7090), a survey ship moored in Ucluelet Harbour. A berth in a stateroom with a shared bathroom starts at C$45/55 single/double. Fancier rooms are available at the resort's main lodge on shore; rooms cost up to C$155 double. Its popularity with charter anglers means that breakfast is served especially early.

Just around the harbor from Long Beach, the *Pacific Rim Motel* (☎ 250-726-7728), 1755 Peninsula Rd, has rooms for C$60/65. The *West Coast Motel* (☎ 250-726-7732), 247 Hemlock St, has rooms and suites (some equipped with kitchenettes) overlooking the harbor, plus an indoor pool and gym; rooms start at C$69 single or double.

Places to Eat

Most restaurants are located in hotels and lodges; the West Coast Motel, the Canadian Princess Resort and the Ucluelet Hotel (see above) each have dining rooms. A good choice for a light meal is *Blueberries Café & Cappuccino Bar* (☎ 250-726-7707), 1627D Peninsula Rd, with sandwiches and pasta under C$10. For something meaty, try *Mountain Boy Chicken & Ribs* (☎ 250-726-2221), 1627C Peninsula Rd, with barbecued beef ribs for C$12. For fine dining, drive north to the *Wickaninnish Inn* (☎ 250-726-7706), 10km (6 miles) north of Ucluelet, midway between Tofino and Ucluelet.

BROKEN GROUP ISLANDS

The middle section of Pacific Rim National Park, called the Broken Group Islands, is made up of about 100 islands at the entrance to Barkley Sound, famous for its variety of rockfish.

This area is popular with canoeists, is good for wildlife and offers some of the best scuba diving in Canada. You can view wrecks in the shallow waters and observe the abundant marine life found around all the islands. The waters can be dangerous and you should prepare for a trip using *Marine Chart 3670*, which is available from the Canadian Hydrographic Service, Chart Sales, Institute of Ocean Sciences, 9860 Saanich Rd, PO Box 6000, Sidney, BC V8L 4B2.

The only way to reach this section is by boat from Bamfield, Ucluelet or Port Alberni. There are some primitive campgrounds on the islands.

WEST COAST TRAIL

The third and most southerly section of the park is called the West Coast Trail, one of Canada's best-known and toughest hiking paths. The 77km (48-mile) trail runs between Port Renfrew and Bamfield. Either end can be reached by road, but to reach one from the other you've got to walk – and that's a challenge along this rugged, often rain-soaked trail. It is *not* for novices although some people walk for just a day or two at the north end.

Bamfield, the village at the northern head of the West Coast Trail, has a Marine Biological Station, a lifesaving station and not much else. The West Coast Trail Information Centre (☎ 250-728-3234) is 5km (3 miles) southeast of Bamfield on Pachena Bay. **Port Renfrew**, at the southern end of

the trail can be reached by dirt road from Lake Cowichan or by the mostly paved Hwy 14 along the coast from Victoria. There is a seasonal trail information center (☎ 250-647-5434) in the village. To reach the start of the trail from Port Renfrew you must charter a boat to take you across the narrow San Juan River. Because of the difficult terrain, getting out of the bay here is, well, let's say, one of the less enjoyable segments of the trail northbound.

To protect the environment and to keep hiker traffic to manageable limits, a quota system restricts the number of hikers using the trail. Only 52 people are permitted to begin the trail each day, 26 in each direction. Of those, six in each direction are on a first-come, first-served basis, the others have all been prebooked. Prebooking costs C$85, the trail fee without the reservation is C$60. You may well not get a place by turning up at the trailhead and so should put your name on the waiting list; however, you may have to wait several days.

For an information package and reservation registration call ☎ 800-663-6000 from Canada or the USA, or write to Pacific Rim National Park Reserve, Box 280, Ucluelet, BC V0R 3A0. Reservations are taken after March 1 for the upcoming summer, and, on the first day of reservations, July is pretty much booked up. The main season is May to September. You can go two weeks earlier or later at half-price but these times are not recommended as the weather can be even more brutal. July and August are the driest and best months.

The trail is clogged with trees, and the camping areas are wherever you can find them. Passing cliffs, beaches and rain forests, the trail takes between five and eight days to travel. You've got to take all your food. The southernmost part is the roughest and most difficult, but you get to see some spectacular scenery and have a chance to test your stamina. Some people prefer to do this last when the pack is lighter and the legs stronger, others want to get it out of the way and then 'cruise' to the other end. Near the center of the trail you pass close to the old-growth forest of Carmanah Valley. There are wo small ferries to take along the way, totaling C$15, which are operated by Native Indians. The trail was historically used as a lifesaving route for shipwreck survivors and you should carry tide charts.

Places to Stay
Bamfield There are only a few places to stay in and around Bamfield, including two campgrounds. The nearest is 8km (5 miles) east of Bamfield and is run by the Ohiaht people. The other one, *Sea Beam Fishing Resort & Campground* (☎ 250-728-3286), is about 19km (12 miles) north of Bamfield. Campsites cost C$15, rooms cost C$15/30 single/double.

One of the cheapest places to stay is the *Bamfield Lodge* (☎ 250-728-3419), Cape Beale Trail, a no-frills retreat house and marine-education center with a few rustic cottages and lodge rooms with optional meals starting at C$35/60 single/double. They also lead fishing, whale-watching and diving excursions.

There's also a number of waterfront lodges. Good ones to try are the *McKay Bay Lodge* (☎ 250-728-3323), with a hot tub and nine rooms for C$85 to C$95, and the secluded *Woods End Landing Cottages* (☎ 250-728-3383), 168 Wild Duck Rd, which has six private cottages with log beds; cabins rent for C$95 to C$185.

Port Renfrew Accommodations are rather limited in this remote town. You can camp along the beach and there are also a couple of B&Bs. There is also a small store, but supplies are limited. The *Arbutus Beach Lodge* (☎ 250-647-5458), 5 Queesto Drive, has four rooms on the beach with private bathrooms for C$59/74. If Port Renfrew happens to be all booked up, you'll find no shortage of B&Bs in the tiny burg of Sooke (see Western Shore, earlier in this chapter), 68km (42 miles) south.

Getting There & Away
Bamfield can be reached by boat from Ucluelet and Port Alberni; the one-way fare on the MVs *Lady Rose* or *Frances Barkley* from Port Alberni is C$18. There is also a 100km (62-mile) gravel road from Port Alberni to Bamfield. Western Bus Lines (☎ 250-728-3491, 250-723-3341 in Port Alberni) operates the Pachena Bay Express, which connects Pachena Bay and Bamfield with Port Alberni on Monday and Friday. From Victoria, West Coast Trail Express (☎ 250-380-0580) runs a daily 11-person shuttle van to Bamfield and Pachena Bay for C$48. PBM Transport (☎ 250-475-2010) runs buses between Victoria and Port Renfrew.

To save hikers a lot of logistical hassles there is a boat service, West Coast Express Charters (☎ 250-647-5409) which links Bamfield to Port Renfrew three times a week. The Pacheenaht Indian Band (☎ 250-647-5521) runs a similar service but by road.

Northern Vancouver Island

Traveling north of Campbell River, Hwy 19 heads inland and much of the urbanization that characterizes the eastern coastline to the south disappears. It is a less-populated, less-visited, rugged area with lots of good opportunities for outdoor activities. Aside from Strathcona and Cape Scott Provincial Parks, the Telegraph Cove-Port McNeil area is of most interest with its whale watching and Native Indian sites. Many of the travelers you meet will be heading north to Port Hardy to catch the ferry to Prince Rupert (see Port Hardy, later, for details).

CAMPBELL RIVER
Population 27,000
Campbell River is a major center for salmon fishing, and marks the beginning of the northern part of Vancouver Island. It is also the main departure point for Strathcona Provincial Park. The Travel InfoCentre (☎ 250-287-4636), 1235 Shoppers Row, is open 10 am to 8 pm daily. In the same building is the Campbell River Museum, open 10 am to 4 pm daily.

There isn't much to see or do in town itself. Most visitors come here to fish for one or more of the five salmon species – coho, Chinook, sockeye, humpback (or pink) and chum. But there is now another option. Campbell River Snorkel Tours offers fascinating guided river trips to watch the migrating salmon. Get details at the tourist office. Off the coast in **Discovery Passage**, scuba diving is excellent at such dive sites as Row & Be Damned, Whisky Point, Copper Cliffs and Steep Island. On **Quadra Island**, just offshore, you can see marine and bird life or the ancient petroglyphs of the Kwakiutl people at Cape Mudge in the south. Some petroglyphs are in the Kwakiutl Museum along with tribal costumes, ceremonial masks and potlatch artifacts. The island also has hiking trails including one up Chinese Mountain. **Cortes Island**, east of Quadra Island, has plenty of deserted beaches and lots of wildlife. It's about an hour and two ferries from Campbell River.

Places to Stay
About 10km (6 miles) west of Campbell River on Hwy 28 there's a huge riverside campground at *Elk Falls Provincial Park*, with 122 sites and flush toilets for C$9.50. *Loveland Bay Provincial Park*, 19km (12 miles) northeast at Campbell Lake, and *Morton Lake Provincial Park*, 12 miles north off of Hwy 19, are both small and secluded and have primitive sites for C$6.

Numerous motels line the highway south of the downtown area. The *Rustic Motel* (☎ 250-286-6295, 800-567-2007), 2140 N Island Hwy, is a good value for quiet rooms with kitchenettes, suites and cabins starting at C$50/60 singles/doubles. The newly renovated *Best Western Austrian Chalet* (☎ 250-923-4231, 800-667-7207), 462 S Island Hwy, right on the waterfront, has an indoor pool and features loft chalets with some kitchenettes for C$84/94. Campbell River's premier vacation resort is the bayside *Painter's Lodge Holiday & Fishing Resort* (☎ 250-286-1102, 800-663-7090), 1625 MacDonald Rd, a conference-style hotel with a marina, outdoor pool and

tennis courts. Lodge rooms start at C$99 for a double, cabins and suites at C$199.

On Quadra Island there is a backpacker's hostel, *Travellers Rural Retreat* (☎ 250-287-9232) at Quathiaski Cove. Call ahead. Quiet Cortes Island has the *Amigo's Hostel* (☎ 250-935-6403), on Manzanita Rd, about a 20-minute drive from the ferry; rides can be arranged. Cost is C$15. The hosts can tell you how to spend some time around the laid-back, off-the-track island.

Quadra Island features several small waterfront resorts with rooms ranging from C$60 to C$80. If you're looking for a secluded fishing lodge, look no further than the *April Point Lodge & Fishing Resort* (☎ 250-285-2222), on April Point Rd, where there's a number of oceanfront guest houses and lodge rooms with great views, hot tubs and fireplaces for C$99 to C$395. While it's more upscale than your typical fishing lodge, it's earnest enough to offer fishing charters and guides (including seaplane service) and serves sushi in the restaurant.

The *Tsa-Kwa-Luten Lodge* (☎ 250-285-2042, 800-665-7745), on Lighthouse Rd, close to the beach, is a theme lodge run by Native Indians. Don't expect to be put up in traditional tribal homes – Native Indian art, architecture and food prevail as a theme, and the rooms in the 'longhouse' feature modern waterfront hotel units, the cabins have kitchens, and there's a fitness room and sauna; rates are C$80/90 single/double.

Getting There & Around
Island Coach Lines (☎ 250-287-7151), on the corner of 13th Ave and Cedar St, runs one bus north daily to Port Hardy (C$41 one way) and four buses south to Victoria. For information about local buses call ☎ 250-287-7433.

Ferries leave regularly from Discovery Crescent, which is across from Tyee Plaza, for Quathiaski Cove on Quadra Island; the return fare is C$3.50. Another ferry departs Heriot Bay on Quadra Island for Whaletown on Cortes Island; the return fare is C$4.50. Ask about the van service to Cortes four times a week from the Island Coach Lines depot.

VANCOUVER ISLAND

Totem Poles

Totem poles are found along the North Pacific coast, roughly between southern British Columbia and Alaska. Carved on logs of western red cedar by the Haida, Tlingit, Tsimshian and Kwakiutl tribes, totem poles show various animal and human forms stacked on each other, depicting different animal spirits as well as revered and respected supernatural beings. Although Captain Cook noted totem poles as early as 1778, they didn't become abundant until the native peoples decided to display the wealth they acquired from involvement in the fur trade, around the mid-19th century. Traditional totem poles varied greatly in height, though rarely exceeded 18m (60 feet). Modern poles can be much taller – the tallest totem pole in the world, at Alert Bay, BC, is 52m (170 feet).

Totem poles identify a household's particular lineage in the same way a family crest might identify an Englishman with a particular lineage, although the totem pole is more of a historical pictograph depicting the entire ancestral history. Like a family crest, totem poles also carry a sense of prestige and prosperity. There are many different types: free-standing welcome poles would be found at a waterfront or near a village; memorial poles were erected outside the home of a deceased chief; and mortuary poles were implanted with a box of the honored individual's decomposed remains. Incorporated into the design of a house, totem poles also appear as house posts and front doors. Shame poles, carved with upside-down figures, were temporary fixtures and are found only in museums today.

If it were possible to 'read' a totem pole, it would be from top to bottom – from present to past. Despite its position, the top figure, which represents the pole's owner, is actually the least important figure on the pole. The largest figure, usually the one on the bottom, is the most important. Loosely associated with individuals and events, the figures have

STRATHCONA PROVINCIAL PARK

This is the largest park (☎ 250-755-2483) on the island and is basically a wilderness area. To simplify, the three main areas of interest each have different access points. Campbell River acts as the main access point, with Hwy 28 between Campbell River and Gold River cutting across the most developed portion of this park, providing access to campgrounds and some well-marked trails. The Mt Washington area, just out of the park, and Forbidden Plateau are reached by different roads out of Courtenay.

At **Forbidden Plateau**, to the east of the park, are a series of high-altitude hiking trails, as well as trout fishing in the lakes on the plateau. In winter it's a major ski area, the island's original. In summer the chair lift runs 11 am to 6 pm Wednesday to Sunday to give hikers a head start into the alpine areas. A ticket is C$10 return. At **Mt Washington Ski Resort** (☎ 250-338-1515), it's much the same thing. Here the lift operates summer weekends only and is C$12. The Paradise Meadows hike leading to the plateau is popular. This major ski resort has five lifts and 41 major marked runs, plus 35km (22 miles) of cross-country ski trails.

In the Buttle Lake district, two well-known hikes are the **Elk River Trail** and the **Flower Ridge Trail**. Both lead to very fine alpine scenery. Like other developed trails, these two are suitable for all age groups. This area also has a number of short trails and nature walks. Other less-developed trails demand more preparation and lead to remote areas.

In the south part of the park the **Della Falls Trail**, for example, is a tough two- or three-day walk but is great for scenery and ends at the highest falls – 440m (1443 feet) – in North America. You need a good map. Other fine walks are those in the **Beauty Lake** area and one crossing the

VANCOUVER ISLAND

no fixed meanings. A figure might be used to represent a particular person, or it may mark a memorable or adventurous event attributed to a particular creature or spirit. It could also represent a legend. It's up to the community to remember the context in order to make sense of a totem pole.

Because birds, fish and mammals figure so prominently on totem poles, it's possible to identify them without really knowing what they mean. A beak is a dead giveaway for a bird – raven has a straight, mid-sized beak and hawk has a short down-turned beak that also curves inward. Eagle also has a short down-turned beak, and looks a lot like the mythical thunderbird, which has curled horns on its head. Hokw-hokw is a mythical beast with a very long, slender beak used to bust skulls. Beaver looks a lot like bear, except for a pair of large incisors and a cross-hatched tail.

A few animals appear as if viewed from overhead. Killer whale is a good example of this – its fin protrudes from the pole as its head faces downward. Long-snouted wolf also faces downward, as does frog. Pointy-headed shark (or dogfish), with a grimacing mouth full of sharp teeth, and the humpback whale both face upward.

The culture of totem poles was largely squashed after the Canadian government outlawed the potlatch ceremony in 1884. Few totem poles remain today as most cedar logs begin to decay within 60 to 80 years, though totem poles at Ninstints and Skedans in the Queen Charlotte Islands are over 100 years old. New totem poles are rarely constructed for tribal purposes, and instead are more frequently carved for nontraditional use as public art. Modern totem poles commissioned for college campuses, museums and public buildings no longer recount the lineage of any one household, but instead stand to honor the First Nations and their outstanding artistry. ■

Big Interior Massif up to Nine Peaks. From the highest peaks – such as Golden Hinde, at 2200m (7210 feet) the highest on the island, Colonel Foster and others in the 650m (2100-foot) range – you'll be able to see the ocean to the west and Georgia Strait to the east. One thing you won't have to look at is a grizzly bear: there aren't any on Vancouver Island.

Places to Stay

The park has two serviced campgrounds with running water and pit toilets. *Buttle Lake* near the northern entrance to the park is the nicer, the other is at *Ralph River*, at the southern end of the lake on its eastern shore. Campsites are C$12 and C$9.50, respectively. Wilderness camping is free.

Strathcona Park Lodge (☎ 250-286-8206), a resort outside the park on Hwy 28 on Upper Campbell Lake, has a range of accommodations. There are lakefront cottages and apartments priced from C$40 to C$125. You can camp near the beach for C$16 with the use of facilities. Camping equipment can also be rented. Alternatively, you can bed down in hostel-style rooms for C$16 with use of a communal kitchen. Van transportation from Campbell River can be arranged by the lodge.

You can rent canoes, kayaks and bicycles, or go rock climbing, windsurfing, hiking, sailing and swimming. Or you can take organized day trips if you wish. The lodge has an education center which offers courses in various outdoor activities.

GOLD RIVER

In the center of the island, west of Strathcona Provincial Park, Gold River, accessed by Hwy 28, is the last stop on surfaced roads. The little town is a caving capital and is the headquarters of BC's Speleological Association. Visitors can join spelunking trips to **Upana Caves** and also to **Quatsino Cave**, the deepest

VANCOUVER ISLAND

vertical cave in North America. Kayakers can try their luck on the white-water section of the river known as the **Big Drop**. For more information, ask at the Travel InfoCentre (☎ 250-283-2418) in Village Square Plaza.

Summer cruises go to **Friendly Cove**, where Captain Cook first met the west coast Native Indians in 1778. The working freighter, *Uchuk III* (☎ 250-283-2325), a converted WWII mine-sweeper, makes year-round trips to some of the remote villages and settlements in **Nootka Sound** and **Kyuquot Sound**. Passengers can go on a choice of two one-day trips or on an overnight trip.

The *Ridgeview Motel* (☎ 250-283-2277, 800-989-3393), at 395 Donner Court, is pretty much the only motel around here, though it's a sizable one, with single/double rooms for C$75/85.

VALLEY OF 1000 FACES

Worth a visit is the Valley of 1000 Faces west off Hwy 19 at Sayward Junction, north of Campbell River. Along this woodland trail are over 1400 figures painted on slabs of cedar, the work of a Dutch-born artist, Hetty Frederickson. The natural wood grain is used as a base for the image and the slabs are then nailed to trees. Facial portraits, with their wide variety, are best. The trail and gallery (located at the ticket office) are open 10 am to 5 pm daily May 15 to September 1, and admission is C$3 for both.

Nearby, **Sayward** is a logging port, and there are whale-watching tours from the terminal.

PORT McNEILL & AROUND

Here you can go scuba diving, book fishing charters or go on killer-whale tours. Port McNeill is also the departure point for Cormorant and Malcolm Islands. The regional offices of three major logging companies help sustain this town of over 2700. The Travel InfoCentre (☎ 250-956-3131) is next to the ferry terminal. There are several campgrounds, including one near the terminal, and hotels.

Telegraph Cove

East off Hwy 19, about 8km (5 miles) south of Port McNeill and about a five-hour drive to Nanaimo, this small community is one of the best of the west coast's so-called boardwalk villages – villages in which most of the buildings are built over the water on wooden pilings. Formerly a sawmill village, it has good fishing, but the **killer whales** are its main attraction. Johnston Straight, between Sayward and Alert Bay, is one of the very best places in Canada to see them and this is the closest departure point to where the whales are generally found. The boat tour to Robson Bight, an ecological reserve south of Telegraph Cove, is recommended. The tour, run by Stubbs Island Charters (☎ 250-928-3185/17, 800-665-3066 in BC), might seem a bit pricey at C$65, but you are out for five hours and it includes lunch. It's a good idea to book ahead and take warm clothing. Trips run from June through October. Other good trips operate from Port McNeill. All use hydrophones so the whales can be heard as well as seen.

Sea Orca Expeditions (☎ 800-668-6722) offers three-hour whale trips in Zodiacs (recommended) or longer, more expensive sailing trips. Either way, dress warmly.

Alert Bay

Alert Bay, on 5km (3-mile) long Cormorant Island, blends an old fishing settlement with Native Indian culture. The Nimpkish Reserve is here. The **U'Mista Cultural Centre** shows examples of Kwakiutl art, mainly masks, and there is a ceremonial bighouse. Like some other places in BC, Alert Bay claims to have the world's tallest totem pole; here it measures in at 52m (170 feet). There are also a few minor historical sites including the Alert Bay Museum. Gator Gardens Ecological Park, with its giant cedars, mosses and wildlife, is also worth a look. Ferries from Port McNeill take 45 minutes and cost C$4.50 return.

Places to Stay

Port McNeill has a few private campgrounds and modest motels. Don't head up this way without a reservation. *Pacific Hostelry* (☎ 250-974-2026), in Alert Bay, is an associate-HI hostel, open year-round and has room for only 12 people, so call ahead. It costs C$14 for members, C$16 for non-members. The *Dalewood Inn* (☎ 250-956-3304), 1703 Broughton Blvd, is a basic place with rooms for C$56/60 single/double. The *Haida-Way Motor Inn* (☎ 250-956-3373), at 1817 Campbell Way, downtown is another place to try, with rooms for C$63/78.

PORT HARDY

This small town at the northern end of Vancouver Island is best known as the departure point for the ferry trip aboard the *Queen of the North* through the famed Inside Passage to Prince Rupert. The terminal is 3km (2 miles) south of town across Hardy Bay at Bear Cove, which is one of two sites where evidence of the earliest human occupation of the central and northern coastal areas of BC – around 8000 to 10,000 years ago – was found. (The other site is Namanu, now a canning town on the eastern shore of Fitzhugh Sound.)

There's a Travel InfoCentre (☎ 250-949-7622), at 7250 Market St, which is open 9 am to 8 pm daily in the summer. There's a laundromat up the hill on the same side.

There's little in the town itself except a small museum at 1110 Market St, open 10 am to 5 pm Monday to Saturday, but the area around Port Hardy has good salmon fishing and scuba diving. North Island Diving & Water Sports (☎ 250-949-2664), on the corner of Market and Hastings Sts, rents and sells equipment and runs courses. You can also rent canoes and kayaks at the end of the jetty.

Places to Stay

In and around town there are campgrounds, hotels, motels and about 20 B&Bs. Several of the campgrounds are near the ferry terminal. One of the closest campgrounds is *Wildwoods Campsite* (☎ 250-949-6753), on the ferry terminal road, with sites for C$15. Others are *Sunny Sanctuary Campground* (☎ 250-949-8111), 8080 Good-

---

The Inside Passage to Prince Rupert

BC Ferries run the 15-hour, 440km (272-mile) trip along the BC coast, around islands and past some of the province's best scenery. The *Queen of the North* ferry leaves every other day at 7:30 am (check in by 6:30 am, if you have already booked a place) and arrives in Prince Rupert at 10:30 pm. (In winter the ferry leaves just once a week.)

There's a short stop at Bella Bella, about a third of the way up, which is mostly for the locals but also to drop off kayakers. The one-way fare per person is C$102, C$210 for a car and C$350 for RVs up to 6m (20 feet) long. Outside the summer peak period (late May to the end of September) the fares are less.

If you're taking a vehicle in summer you should reserve well in advance. Call the BC Ferries office in Vancouver or Victoria. Both are open daily. However, it's possible to go standby and to do so put your name on the waiting list as early as possible and be at the ferry terminal by 5:30 am at the latest on the day of departure. Binoculars are useful as you're often close to land and the wildlife viewing is good: the possibilities include bald eagles, porpoises, sea lions and humpback and killer whales.

Once in Prince Rupert you can continue on Alaska State Ferries farther north to Juneau and Skagway; catch BC Ferries to the Queen Charlotte Islands; or go by land into the BC interior and up to the Yukon and Alaska. ∎

---

speed Rd, and *Quatse River Campground* (☎ 250-949-2395), 5050 Hardy Bay Rd.

Kay's B&B (☎ 250-949-6776), at 7605 Camarvon Rd, is close to town and costs C$42/57. One of the cheaper hotel options is the *North Shore Inn* (☎ 250-949-8500), 7370 Market St, across Hardy Bay from the ferry terminal, with rooms starting at C$70/79 single/double. Another nice hotel is the *Glen Lyon Inn* (☎ 250-949-7115),

6435 Hardy Bay Rd, with river-view rooms that overlook the marina.

Remember that the town fills up the night before a ferry is due to depart so it's worth booking ahead.

Getting There & Around

Island Coach Lines (☎ 250-949-7532), on the corner of Market and Hastings Sts, has one bus a day to Victoria for C$78. North Island Transportation, operating out of the same office, runs a shuttle bus to/from the ferry terminal for C$5 one way. The bus will pick you up and drop you off wherever you're staying.

CAPE SCOTT PROVINCIAL PARK

About 60km (37 miles) west of Port Hardy over an active logging gravel road, this remote park offers challenging hiking, wilderness camping and exploring along pristine beaches for those wishing to get away from it all. Most accessible is the undisturbed expanse of sandy beach at San Josef Bay under an hour's walk along a well-maintained trail.

Beyond this, things get serious. The eight-hour, 24km (15-mile) slog to wild Cape Scott, an old Danish settlement at the park's far end, weeds out the Sunday strollers. Just submit totally to the 'goddess of mud' and rewards will come to you. Nels Bight Beach, at six hours and with camping, is one of them. Wildlife is abundant.

Note that the west coast of this northern tip of the island is known for strong winds, high tides and heavy rain. You'll need to take all supplies and equipment if you're camping. Also, it's suggested water be purified. Be careful of trucks on the drive in and stay well to the right.

Glossary

alkali – soluble mineral salts found in desert soils and lakes

anadromous – a term used to describe fish that migrate up rivers from salt water to spawn in fresh water

APEC – Asia-Pacific Economic Cooperation; formed in 1989 to hold annual meetings between the major and developing economies of the Asia-Pacific region in an effort to promote open trade, economic cooperation and sustainable growth

ATV – all-terrain vehicle

basalt – a hard, dense volcanic rock often having a glassy appearance

batholith – a large mass of molten igneous rock (usually granite) that has intruded surrounding strata and cooled

DLM – Bureau of Land Management; an agency of the Department of the Interior which controls substantial portions of public lands in the West

boomtown – a town that has experienced quick economic and population growth

brewpub – a pub that brews and sells its own beer

caldera – a very large crater that has resulted from a volcanic explosion or the collapse of a volcanic cone; Crater Lake in Oregon is an example of the latter

CCC – Civilian Conservation Corps, a *New Deal* program established in 1933 to employ single unskilled young men, initially through the conservation of the wild lands of the USA (by 1940, however, most CCC jobs were oriented toward national defense work); Congress disbanded the CCC in 1942

clapboard – a narrow board that is thicker on one edge; the boards are overlapped over a wooden building frame to form an outer wall

clear-cut – a hated sight for environmentalists, this is an area where loggers have cut every tree, large and small, leaving nothing standing

Coast Guard – the branch of the US armed forces that is responsible for guarding the coast, maintaining the safe operation of maritime traffic and enforcing navigation laws

coulee – a deep ravine with sloping sides that is usually dry during the summer

Craftsman – a style of architecture developed during the Arts and Crafts Movement, which was a reaction to the perceived shoddiness of machine-made goods in the late-19th and early-20th centuries; the style is typified by simple, functional designs hand-crafted in traditional mediums

First Nations – a term used to denote Canada's aboriginal peoples; it can be used instead of Native Indians

FDR – Franklin Delano Roosevelt, 32nd president of the USA (1933-45); he introduced the *New Deal*, a series of measures to increase employment and productivity during the Great Depression and WWII; two New Deal programs were the *CCC* and the *WPA*

fry – a small juvenile fish

grist mill – a mill for grinding grain

grunge – the ubiquitous 'Seattle' sound that became immensely popular in the early '90s with the rise of such bands as Nirvana, Pearl Jam, the Melvins, Soundgarden and a host of imitators

HI/AYH – Hostelling International/American Youth Hostels; term given to hostels affiliated with Hostelling International, which is managed by IYHF (International Youth Hostel Federation)

hoodoos – fantastically shaped rock formations produced by weathering, as in the Pinnacles in southern Oregon

Hudson's Bay Company (HBC) – an English trading company begun in 1670 that traded in all areas that had rivers draining into Hudson Bay; in the 18th century the HBC and its main rival, the Northwest Company, both set up forts and trading posts throughout the Northwest and what would become Canada (the two companies amalgamated in 1821)

KOA – Kampgrounds of America; a private RV-oriented organization that provides campgrounds with substantial amenities
kokanee – a small landlocked sockeye salmon

longhouse – Native American communal dwelling that is characterized by a long, central corridor and outlying family compartments

national monument – a place of historic, scenic or scientific interest set aside for preservation, usually by presidential proclamation
National Register of Historic Places or **National Historic District** – a listing of historic buildings that is determined by the *NPS* and based on nominations from property owners and local authorities; in order to qualify for registration, buildings and districts must have played a signficant role in the development of a community
Nature Conservancy – nonprofit organization that purchases land to protect habitats and create natural sanctuaries
New Deal – President *FDR*'s series of programs designed to promote economic recovery and social reform during the 1930s
normal school – a two-year school designed chiefly for the training of elementary teachers
Northwest Passage – the water route across North America from the Atlantic to the Pacific Ocean; explorers from around the world searched for this route for almost 300 years before Norwegian Roald Amundsen successfully navigated the passage in 1906
NPS – National Park Service; a division of the Department of the Interior which administers US national parks and monuments
NRA – National Recreation Area; a term used to describe *NPS* units in areas of con-

siderable scenic or ecological importance which have been modified by human activity, mostly major dam projects

ORV – off-road vehicle

petroglyph – an ancient carving or inscription on a rock
pictograph – a picture or symbol representing a word rather than a sound, usually drawn or painted on a rock
playa – a dry desert lakebed
portage – to carry a ship or boat over land to avoid an impassable stretch of river or from one body of water to another; sometimes refers to the footpath or trail used for those purposes
potlatch – a competitive ceremonial activity that takes place among some Native Indians, usually those found along the coast of BC; it traditionally involves a lavish distribution of gifts and destruction of property to emphasize the wealth and status of the chief or clan
powwow – a Native American social ceremony conducted by a shaman; the gathering or fair usually includes competitive dancing

REI – Recreational Equipment Incorporated; known almost exclusively by its acronym, it is one of the primary retailers of outdoor equipment in the USA
rift – a thin fissure in a rock
RV – recreational vehicle, motorhome

salal – a small, evergreen shrub *(Gaultheria shallon)* found in the Pacific Northwest; the shrub has pink flowers and edible berries
sea stack – hard volcanic coastal rock formations originally covered with softer sedimentary rock that has since eroded away
slag – glassy residue left as the result of the smelting of iron ore

USFS – United States Forest Service; a division of the Department of Agriculture which implements policies on federal forest lands on the principles of 'multiple use'; multiple use includes timber cutting, watershed management, wildlife management and camping and' recreation

USFWS – United States Fish & Wildlife Service; an agency of the federal Department of the Interior with responsibility for fish and wildlife habitat and related matters

USGS – United States Geological Survey; an agency of the federal Department of the Interior responsible for detailed topographic maps of the entire country; USGS maps arc widely available at outdoor-oriented businesses and are particularly popular with hikers and backpackers

WPA – Work Projects Administration; a *New Deal* program set up by President *FDR* in 1935 to increase employment through a series of public works projects, including road building and construction, beautification of public structures (especially post offices), and a well-respected series of state and regional guidebooks

Index

888

SIDEBARS

THANKS

Many thanks to the travelers who used the last edition and wrote to us with helpful hints, useful advice and interesting anecdotes. Your names follow.

Eve C. Alpern
Aaron Bolgatz & Becky
    Anderson
Paula Blomenberg
Alfred J Burke Jr
Rosie Capper
Thor & Sally Chellstorp
Audrey & Brian Clay
Paul D'Souza
Kyril Dambuleff
Robert J Davis
Sarah Egli
Sharon Etleiker

Chris & Jenny Howard
Tysa Jayne
Eddy & Arrie Jessuleen
P Michael Jung
Akino Kameyama
Alan Kendall
Birthe Sørensen &
    Anders Kjølsen
Mr & Mrs Alfred W Lee
Paul Littlefair
Edgar Locke
Kerrick Mainrender
Carole Merritt

Bill & Laura O'Connor
Suzanne O'Keefe
Ian Paul
Ivan Popkowski
Peter Ratcliffe
Marc Rothmeyer
Mrs Phyl Shimeld
Alan Wheatley
Judy Wilcox
William Woodman
Ken Wuschke

LONELY PLANET

Lonely Planet Journeys

JOURNEYS is a unique collection of travel writing – published by the company that understands travel better than anyone else. It is a series for anyone who has ever experienced – or dreamed of – the magical moment when they encountered a strange culture or saw a place for the first time. They are tales to read while you're planning a trip, while you're on the road or while you're in an armchair in front of a fire.

These outstanding titles explore our planet through the eyes of a diverse group of international writers. JOURNEYS books catch the spirit of a place, illuminate a culture, recount a crazy adventure or introduce a fascinating way of life. They always entertain, and always enrich the experience of travel.

ISLANDS IN THE CLOUDS
Travels in the Highlands of New Guinea
Isabella Tree

This is the fascinating account of a journey to the remote and beautiful Highlands of Papua New Guinea and Irian Jaya: one of the most extraordinary and dangerous regions on the planet. Tree travels with a PNG Highlander who introduces her to his intriguing and complex world, changing rapidly as it collides with twentieth-century technology. *Islands in the Clouds* is a thoughtful, moving book.

SEAN & DAVID'S LONG DRIVE
Sean Condon

Sean and David are young townies who have rarely strayed beyond city limits. One day, for no good reason, they set out to discover their homeland, and what follows is a wildly entertaining adventure that covers half of Australia.

'a hilariously detailed log of two burned out friends' – *Rolling Stone*

DRIVE THRU AMERICA
Sean Condon

If you've ever wanted to drive across the USA but couldn't find the time (or afford the gas), *Drive Thru America* is perfect for you. In his search for American myths and realities – along with comfort, cable TV and good, reasonably priced coffee – Sean Condon paints a hilarious road-portrait of the USA.

'entertaining and laugh-out-loud funny' – *Alex Wilber, Travel editor, Amazon.com*

BRIEF ENCOUNTERS
Stories of Love, Sex & Travel
edited by Michelle de Kretser

Love affairs on the road, passionate holiday flings, disastrous pick-ups, erotic encounters . . . In this seductive collection of stories, 22 authors from around the world write about travel romances. Combining fiction and reportage, *Brief Encounters* is must-have reading – for everyone who has dreamt of escape with that perfect stranger.

Includes stories by Pico Iyer, Mary Morris, Emily Perkins, Mona Simpson, Lisa St Aubin de Terán, Paul Theroux and Sara Wheeler.

LONELY PLANET

Lonely Planet Travel Atlases

Lonely Planet has long been famous for the number and quality of its guidebook maps. Now we've gone one step further and produced a handy companion series: Lonely Planet travel atlases – maps of a country produced in book form.

Unlike other maps, which look good but lead travellers astray, our travel atlases have been researched on the road by Lonely Planet's experienced team of writers. All details are carefully checked to ensure the atlas corresponds with the equivalent Lonely Planet guidebook.

- full-colour throughout
- maps researched and checked by Lonely Planet authors
- place names correspond with Lonely Planet guidebooks
- no confusing spelling differences
- legend and travelling information in English, French, German, Japanese and Spanish
- size: 230 x 160 mm

Available now: Chile & Easter Island ● Egypt ● India & Bangladesh ● Israel & the Palestinian Territories ● Jordan, Syria & Lebanon ● Kenya ● Laos ● Portugal ● South Africa, Lesotho & Swaziland ● Thailand ● Turkey ● Vietnam ● Zimbabwe, Botswana & Namibia

---

Lonely Planet TV Series & Videos

Lonely Planet travel guides have been brought to life on television screens around the world. Like our guides, the programs are based on the joy of independent travel, and look honestly at some of the most exciting, picturesque and frustrating places in the world. Each show is presented by one of three travellers from Australia, England or the USA and combines an innovative mixture of video, Super-8 film, atmospheric soundscapes and original music.

Videos of each episode – containing additional footage not shown on television – are available from good book and video shops, but the availability of individual videos varies with regional screening schedules.

Video destinations include: Alaska ● American Rockies ● Australia – The South-East ● Baja California & the Copper Canyon ● Brazil ● Central Asia ● Chile & Easter Island ● Corsica, Sicily & Sardinia – The Mediterranean Islands ● East Africa (Tanzania & Zanzibar) ● Ecuador & the Galapagos Islands ● Greenland & Iceland ● Indonesia ● Israel & the Sinai Desert ● Jamaica ● Japan ● La Ruta Maya ● Morocco ● New York ● North India ● Pacific Islands (Fiji, Solomon Islands & Vanuatu) ● South India ● South West China ● Turkey ● Vietnam ● West Africa ● Zimbabwe, Botswana & Namibia

The Lonely Planet TV series is produced by: Pilot Productions
The Old Studio
18 Middle Row
London W10 5AT, UK

LONELY PLANET

Phrasebooks

L onely Planet phrasebooks are packed with essential words and phrases to help travellers communicate with the locals. With colour tabs for quick reference, an extensive vocabulary and use of script, these handy pocket-sized language guides cover day-to-day travel situations.

- handy pocket-sized books
- easy to understand Pronunciation chapter
- clear & comprehensive Grammar chapter
- romanisation alongside script to allow ease of pronunciation
- script throughout so users can point to phrases for every situation
- full of cultural information and tips for the traveller

'...vital for a real DIY spirit and attitude in language learning'
– Backpacker

'the phrasebooks have good cultural backgrounders and offer solid advice for challenging situations in remote locations'
– San Francisco Examiner

Arabic (Egyptian) • Arabic (Moroccan) • Australian *(Australian English, Aboriginal and Torres Strait languages)* • Baltic States *(Estonian, Latvian, Lithuanian)* • Bengali • Brazilian • British • Burmese • Cantonese • Central Asia • Central Europe *(Czech, French, German, Hungarian, Italian, Slovak)* • Eastern Europe *(Bulgarian, Czech, Hungarian, Polish, Romanian, Slovak)* • Ethiopian (Amharic) • Fijian • French • German • Greek • Hebrew phrasebook • Hill Tribes • Hindi/Urdu • Indonesian • Italian • Japanese • Korean • Lao • Latin American Spanish • Malay • Mandarin • Mediterranean Europe *(Albanian, Croatian, Greek, Italian, Macedonian, Maltese, Serbian, Slovene)* • Mongolian • Nepali • Papua New Guinea • Pilipino (Tagalog) • Quechua • Russian • Scandinavian Europe *(Danish, Finnish, Icelandic, Norwegian, Swedish)* • South-East Asia *(Burmese, Indonesian, Khmer, Lao, Malay, Tagalog Pilipino, Thai, Vietnamese)* • South Pacific Languages • Spanish (Castilian) *(also includes Catalan, Galician and Basque)* • Sri Lanka • Swahili • Thai • Tibetan • Turkish • Ukrainian • USA *(US English, Vernacular, Native American languages, Hawaiian)* • Vietnamese • Western Europe *(Basque, Catalan, Dutch, French, German, Greek, Irish)*

LONELY PLANET

FREE Lonely Planet Newsletters

We love hearing from you and think you'd like to hear from us.

Planet Talk

Our FREE quarterly printed newsletter is full of tips from travellers and anecdotes from Lonely Planet guidebook authors. Every issue is packed with up-to-date travel news and advice, and includes:

- a postcard from Lonely Planet co-founder Tony Wheeler
- a swag of mail from travellers
- a look at life on the road through the eyes of a Lonely Planet author
- topical health advice
- prizes for the best travel yarn
- news about forthcoming Lonely Planet events
- a complete list of Lonely Planet books and other titles

To join our mailing list, residents of the UK, Europe and Africa can email us at go@lonelyplanet.co.uk; residents of North and South America can email us at info@lonelyplanet.com; the rest of the world can email us at talk2us@lonelyplanet.com.au, or contact any Lonely Planet office.

Comet

Our FREE monthly email newsletter brings you all the latest travel news, features, interviews, competitions, destination ideas, travellers' tips & tales, Q&As, raging debates and related links. Find out what's new on the Lonely Planet Web site and which books are about to hit the shelves.

Subscribe from your desktop: www.lonelyplanet.com/comet

LONELY PLANET

Guides by Region

Lonely Planet is known worldwide for publishing practical, reliable and no-nonsense travel information in our guides and on our Web site. The Lonely Planet list covers just about every accessible part of the world. Currently there are 16 series: Travel guides, Shoestring guides, Condensed guides, Phrasebooks, Read This First, Healthy Travel, Walking guides, Cycling guides, Watching Wildlife guides, Pisces Diving & Snorkeling guides, City Maps, Road Atlases, Out to Eat, World Food, Journeys travel literature and Pictorials.

AFRICA Africa on a shoestring • Cairo • Cairo City Map • Cape Town • Cape Town City Map • East Africa • Egypt • Egyptian Arabic phrasebook • Ethiopia, Eritrea & Djibouti • Ethiopian (Amharic) phrasebook • The Gambia & Senegal • Healthy Travel Africa • Kenya • Malawi • Morocco • Moroccan Arabic phrasebook • Mozambique • Read This First: Africa • South Africa, Lesotho & Swaziland • Southern Africa • Southern Africa Road Atlas • Swahili phrasebook • Tanzania, Zanzibar & Pemba • Trekking in East Africa • Tunisia • Watching Wildlife East Africa •   Watching Wildlife Southern Africa • West Africa • World Food Morocco • Zimbabwe, Botswana & Namibia
Travel Literature: Mali Blues: Traveling to an African Beat • The Rainbird: A Central African Journey • Songs to an African Sunset: A Zimbabwean Story

AUSTRALIA & THE PACIFIC Auckland • Australia • Australian phrasebook • Australia Road Atlas • Bushwalking in Australia •Cycling New Zealand • Fiji • Fijian phrasebook • Healthy Travel Australia, NZ and the Pacific • Islands of Australia's Great Barrier Reef • Melbourne • Melbourne City Map • Micronesia • New Caledonia • New South Wales & the ACT • New Zealand • Northern Territory • Outback Australia • Out to Eat – Melbourne • Out to Eat – Sydney • Papua New Guinea • Pidgin phrasebook • Queensland • Rarotonga & the Cook Islands • Samoa • Solomon Islands • South Australia • South Pacific • South Pacific phrasebook • Sydney • Sydney City Map • Sydney Condensed • Tahiti & French Polynesia • Tasmania • Tonga • Tramping in New Zealand • Vanuatu • Victoria • Walking in Australia • Watching Wildlife Australia • Western Australia
Travel Literature: Islands in the Clouds: Travels in the Highlands of New Guinea • Kiwi Tracks: A New Zealand Journey • Sean & David's Long Drive

CENTRAL AMERICA & THE CARIBBEAN Bahamas, Turks & Caicos • Baja California • Bermuda • Central America on a shoestring • Costa Rica • Costa Rica Spanish phrasebook • Cuba • Dominican Republic & Haiti • Eastern Caribbean • Guatemala • Guatemala, Belize & Yucatán: La Ruta Maya • Healthy Travel Central & South America • Jamaica • Mexico • Mexico City • Panama • Puerto Rico • Read This First: Central & South America • World Food Mexico • Yucatán
Travel Literature: Green Dreams: Travels in Central America

EUROPE Amsterdam • Amsterdam City Map • Amsterdam Condensed • Andalucía • Austria • Baltic States phrasebook • Barcelona • Barcelona City Map • Berlin • Berlin City Map • Britain • British phrasebook • Brussels, Bruges & Antwerp • Brussels City Map • Budapest • Budapest City Map • Canary Islands • Central Europe • Central Europe phrasebook • Corfu & the Ionians • Corsica • Crete • Crete Condensed • Croatia • Cycling Britain • Cycling France • Cyprus • Czech & Slovak Republics • Denmark • Dublin • Dublin City Map • Eastern Europe • Eastern Europe phrasebook • Edinburgh • Estonia, Latvia & Lithuania • Europe on a shoestring • Finland • Florence • France • Frankfurt Condensed • French phrasebook • Georgia, Armenia & Azerbaijan • Germany • German phrasebook • Greece • Greek Islands • Greek phrasebook • Hungary • Iceland, Greenland & the Faroe Islands • Ireland • Istanbul • Italian phrasebook • Italy • Krakow • Lisbon • The Loire • London • London City Map • London Condensed • Madrid • Malta • Mediterranean Europe • Mediterranean Europe phrasebook • Moscow • Mozambique • Munich • the Netherlands • Norway • Out to Eat – London • Paris • Paris City Map • Paris Condensed • Poland • Portugal • Portuguese phrasebook • Prague • Prague City Map • Provence & the Côte d'Azur • Read This First: Europe • Romania & Moldova • Rome • Rome City Map • Russia, Ukraine & Belarus • Russian phrasebook • Scandinavia & Baltic Europe • Scandinavian Europe phrasebook • Scotland • Sicily • Slovenia • South-West France • Spain • Spanish phrasebook • St Petersburg • St Petersburg City Map • Sweden • Switzerland • Trekking in Spain • Tuscany • Ukrainian phrasebook • Venice • Vienna • Walking in Britain • Walking in France • Walking in Ireland • Walking in Italy • Walking in Spain • Walking in Switzerland • Western Europe • Western Europe phrasebook • World Food France • World Food Italy • World Food Spain
Travel Literature: Love and War in the Apennines • The Olive Grove: Travels in Greece • On the Shores of the Mediterranean • Round Ireland in Low Gear • A Small Place in Italy • After Yugoslavia

LONELY PLANET

Mail Order

L onely Planet products are distributed worldwide.They are also available by mail order from Lonely Planet, so if you have difficulty finding a title please write to us. North and South American residents should write to 150 Linden St, Oakland, CA 94607, USA; European and African residents should write to 10a Spring Place, London NW5 3BH, UK; and residents of other countries to Locked Bag 1, Footscray, Victoria 3011, Australia.

INDIAN SUBCONTINENT Bangladesh • Bengali phrasebook • Bhutan • Delhi • Goa • Healthy Travel Asia & India • Hindi & Urdu phrasebook • India • Indian Himalaya • Karakoram Highway • Kerala • Mumbai (Bombay) • Nepal • Nepali phrasebook • Pakistan • Rajasthan • Read This First: Asia & India • South India • Sri Lanka • Sri Lanka phrasebook • Tibet • Tibetan phrasebook • Trekking in the Indian Himalaya • Trekking in the Karakoram & Hindukush • Trekking in the Nepal Himalaya
Travel Literature: The Age of Kali: Indian Travels and Encounters • Hello Goodnight: A Life of Goa • In Rajasthan • A Season in Heaven: True Tales from the Road to Kathmandu • Shopping for Buddhas • A Short Walk in the Hindu Kush • Slowly Down the Ganges

ISLANDS OF THE INDIAN OCEAN Madagascar & Comoros • Maldives • Mauritius, Réunion & Seychelles

MIDDLE EAST & CENTRAL ASIA Bahrain, Kuwait & Qatar • Central Asia • Central Asia phrasebook • Dubai • Hebrew phrasebook • Iran • Israel & the Palestinian Territories • Istanbul • Istanbul City Map • Istanbul to Cairo on a shoestring • Jerusalem • Jerusalem City Map • Jordan • Lebanon • Middle East • Oman & the United Arab Emirates • Syria • Turkey • Turkish phrasebook • World Food Turkey • Yemen
Travel Literature: Black on Black: Iran Revisited • The Gates of Damascus • Kingdom of the Film Stars: Journey into Jordan

NORTH AMERICA Alaska • Boston • Boston City Map • California & Nevada • California Condensed • Canada • Chicago • Chicago City Map • Deep South • Florida • Great Lakes • Hawaii • Hiking in Alaska • Hiking in the USA • Honolulu • Las Vegas • Los Angeles • Los Angeles City Map • Louisiana & The Deep South • Miami • Miami City Map • New England • New Orleans • New York City • New York City City Map • New York City Condensed • New York, New Jersey & Pennsylvania • Oahu • Out to Eat – San Francisco • Pacific Northwest • Puerto Rico • Rocky Mountains • San Francisco • San Francisco City Map • Seattle • Southwest • Texas • USA • USA phrasebook • Vancouver • Virginia & the Capital Region • Washington DC • Washington, DC City Map • World Food Deep South, USA • World Food New Orleans
Travel Literature: Caught Inside: A Surfer's Year on the California Coast • Drive Thru America

NORTH-EAST ASIA Beijing • Beijing City Map • Cantonese phrasebook • China • Hiking in Japan • Hong Kong • Hong Kong City Map • Hong Kong Condensed • Hong Kong, Macau & Guangzhou • Japan • Japanese phrasebook • Korea • Korean phrasebook • Kyoto • Mandarin phrasebook • Mongolia • Mongolian phrasebook • Seoul • Shanghai • South-West China • Taiwan • Tokyo
Travel Literature: In Xanadu: A Quest • Lost Japan

SOUTH AMERICA Argentina, Uruguay & Paraguay • Bolivia • Brazil • Brazilian phrasebook • Buenos Aires • Chile & Easter Island • Colombia • Ecuador & the Galapagos Islands • Healthy Travel Central & South America • Latin American Spanish phrasebook • Peru • Quechua phrasebook • Read This First: Central & South America • Rio de Janeiro • Rio de Janeiro City Map • Santiago • South America on a shoestring • Santiago • Trekking in the Patagonian Andes • Venezuela
Travel Literature: Full Circle: A South American Journey

SOUTH-EAST ASIA Bali & Lombok • Bangkok • Bangkok City Map • Burmese phrasebook • Cambodia • Hanoi • Healthy Travel Asia & India • Hill Tribes phrasebook • Ho Chi Minh City • Indonesia • Indonesian phrasebook • Indonesia's Eastern Islands • Jakarta • Java • Lao phrasebook • Laos • Malay phrasebook • Malaysia, Singapore & Brunei • Myanmar (Burma) • Philippines • Pilipino (Tagalog) phrasebook • Read This First: Asia & India • Singapore • Singapore City Map • South-East Asia on a shoestring • South-East Asia phrasebook • Thailand • Thailand's Islands & Beaches • Thailand, Vietnam, Laos & Cambodia Road Atlas • Thai phrasebook • Vietnam • Vietnamese phrasebook • World Food Thailand • World Food Vietnam

ALSO AVAILABLE: Antarctica • The Arctic • The Blue Man: Tales of Travel, Love and Coffee • Brief Encounters: Stories of Love, Sex & Travel • Chasing Rickshaws • The Last Grain Race • Lonely Planet Unpacked • Not the Only Planet: Science Fiction Travel Stories • Lonely Planet On the Edge • Sacred India • Travel with Children • Travel Photography: A Guide to Taking Better Pictures

The Lonely Planet Story

Lonely Planet published its first book in 1973 in response to the numerous 'How did you do it?' questions Maureen and Tony Wheeler were asked after driving, bussing, hitching, sailing and railing their way from England to Australia.

Written at a kitchen table and hand collated, trimmed and stapled, *Across Asia on the Cheap* became an instant local bestseller, inspiring thoughts of another book.

Eighteen months in South-East Asia resulted in their second guide, *South-East Asia on a shoestring*, which they put together in a backstreet Chinese hotel in Singapore in 1975. The 'yellow bible', as it quickly became known to backpackers around the world, soon became *the* guide to the region. It has sold well over half a million copies and is now in its 9th edition, still retaining its familiar yellow cover.

Today there are over 350 titles, including travel guides, walking guides, language kits & phrasebooks, travel atlases, diving guides and travel literature. The company is the largest independent travel publisher in the world. Although Lonely Planet initially specialised in guides to Asia, today there are few corners of the globe that have not been covered.

The emphasis continues to be on travel for independent travellers. Tony and Maureen still travel for several months of each year and play an active part in the writing, updating and quality control of Lonely Planet's guides.

They have been joined by over 120 authors and 280 staff at our offices in Melbourne (Australia), Oakland (USA), London (UK) and Paris (France). Travellers themselves also make a valuable contribution to the guides through the feedback we receive in thousands of letters each year and on our web site.

The people at Lonely Planet strongly believe that travellers can make a positive contribution to the countries they visit, both through their appreciation of the countries' culture, wildlife and natural features, and through the money they spend. In addition, the company makes a direct contribution to the countries and regions it covers. Since 1986 a percentage of the income from each book has been donated to ventures such as famine relief in Africa; aid projects in India; agricultural projects in Central America; Greenpeace's efforts to halt French nuclear testing in the Pacific; and Amnesty International.

LONELY PLANET OFFICES

Australia
PO Box 617, Hawthorn, Victoria 3122
☎ 03 9819 1877 fax 03 9819 6459
email: talk2us@lonelyplanet.com.au

USA
150 Linden St, Oakland, CA 94607
☎ 510 893 8555 TOLL FREE: 800 275 8555
fax 510 893 8572
email: info@lonelyplanet.com

UK
10a Spring Place, London NW5 3BH
☎ 020 7428 4800 fax 020 7428 4828
email: go@lonelyplanet.co.uk

France
1 rue du Dahomey, 75011 Paris
☎ 01 55 25 33 00 fax 01 55 25 33 01
email: bip@lonelyplanet.fr
www.lonelyplanet.fr

World Wide Web: www.lonelyplanet.com *or* AOL keyword: lp
Lonely Planet Images: lpi@lonelyplanet.com.au